RACIAL
AND ETHNIC
DIVERSITY

4th EDITION

RACIAL
AND ETHNIC
DIVERSITY

Asians, Blacks, Hispanics, Native Americans, and Whites

BY CHERYL RUSSELL

New Strategist Publications, Inc.
Ithaca, New York

New Strategist Publications, Inc.
P.O. Box 242, Ithaca, New York 14851
800-848-0842
www.newstrategist.com

ISBN 1-885070-45-4

Printed in the United States of America

Table of Contents

List of Tables

Chapter 2. Asians

Business

Education

Health

Housing

Income

Labor Force

Living Arrangements

Population

Chapter 3. Blacks

Population

Spending

Wealth

Chapter 5. Native Hawaiians and Other Pacific Islanders

Living Arrangements

Population

Chapter 6. Whites

Education

Health

Labor Force

Living Arrangements

Population

Spending

Wealth

Chapter 7. Total Population

Business

Education

Living Arrangements

Population

Wealth

Chapter 8. Attitudes and Behavior

Perceptions of Diversity

Black Progress

Group Stereotypes

Immigration

Language

Personal Outlook and Behavior

Introduction

The 2000 census revealed the diversity of the American population like none before. For the first time in modern history, Americans could identify themselves as multiracial. As 7 million people did so, a rigid racial classification system gave way to the more elastic reality. The new racial concepts make comparisons with the past difficult, but they open the door to a much richer understanding of America's growing diversity.

The fourth edition of *Racial and Ethnic Diversity* is a profile of America at the millennium. It presents the all-important 2000 census numbers on race, numbers that will become the benchmark for understanding diversity in the 21st century. It reveals the social and economic well-being of the many racial and ethnic groups that make up our society. It explores the attitudes of racial and ethnic groups toward themselves and one another.

In addition to 2000 census population numbers on race and ethnicity, the fourth edition of *Racial and Ethnic Diversity* also includes chapters profiling minority-owned businesses based on recently released data from the 1997 economic censuses. It provides much more detail on the Asian population, which the Census Bureau's Current Population Survey has recently begun to provide. And it includes a once-a-decade look not only at American Indians, but also at Native Hawaiians and other Pacific Islanders who, in the past, have been lumped in with Asians.

Understanding the demographics, lifestyles, and attitudes of racial and ethnic groups is of vital importance to researchers and policy makers. *Racial and Ethnic Diversity* provides the key to understanding both the similarities and differences between whites and blacks, Hispanics and non-Hispanics, Asians and American Indians. Whenever possible, the tables in *Racial and Ethnic Diversity* include data that allow researchers to compare characteristics across racial groups.

There's no doubt Americans are more alike than different, and *Racial and Ethnic Diversity* documents our many similarities. But there are also important differences among racial and ethnic groups that, if not taken into account, can derail public policy efforts and business strategies. The living arrangements of Hispanics differ from those of whites or blacks, for example, and those differences affect not only political attitudes but also consumer behavior. The educational level of Asians distinguishes them from other minorities. The substantial educational, employment, and economic gains made by blacks and documented in these pages are contrary to popular perception, but they are of utmost importance to policy makers and business leaders.

Racial and Ethnic Diversity is as complete and up-to-date as possible given the constraints of the data. In a perfect world, the tabulations for each racial and ethnic group would be identical, but this is not possible because the government does not collect some types of information for smaller racial and ethnic groups. The Consumer Expenditure Survey, for example, lacks data on the spending of Asians and American Indians. The Survey of Consumer Finances has limited data on wealth by race and ethnicity. Despite these limitations, the scope of data provided in the fourth edition of *Racial and Ethnic Diversity* is greater than in any previous edition, providing a comprehensive portrait of the races and Hispanics.

New Racial Classifications

The 2000 census transformed racial classification in the U.S. The census allowed Americans, for the first time in modern history, to identify themselves as belonging to more than one racial group. This makes the analysis of racial and ethnic diversity more complex—and more rewarding—than ever before.

On the 2000 census form, respondents were asked to identify themselves as belonging to one or more of six racial groups: American Indians and Alaska Natives, Asians, blacks, Native Hawaiians and other Pacific Islanders, whites, and other race. The multiracial option resulted in 63 combinations of the six racial categories. Respondents were also asked to identify themselves as Hispanic or non-Hispanic, since the government considers Hispanic to be an ethnicity rather than a race.

The new methodology resulted in a multitude of racial and ethnic combinations. In publishing the results, the Census Bureau created three new terms to distinguish one group from another. The "race alone" population consists of people who identified themselves as being of only one race. The "race in combination" population contains people who identified themselves as being of more than one race, such as white and black. The "race, alone or in combination" population includes both those who identified themselves as being of one race and those who identified themselves as being of more than one race (see Table 1). For example, the "black, alone or in combination" population includes those who said they were black alone and those who said they were black and white and those who said they were black, white, and Asian, and so on.

In the new classification system, the numbers no longer add up. This may frustrate some, but it provides a more accurate picture of each racial group than did the previous methodology, which required the multiracial to align themselves with only one race. On 2000 census tables showing the "race alone" population, the 6 million people who identified

Table 1. Total Population by Race Alone and Race in Combination, 2000 Census

(number and percent distribution of people by race alone, race in combination, and race alone or in combination, by race, 2000)

	race, alone or in combination		race alone		race in combination	
	number	percent	number	percent	number	percent
Total population	**281,421,906**	**100.0%**	**281,421,906**	**100.0%**	**281,421,906**	**100.0%**
American Indian	4,119,301	1.5	2,475,956	0.9	1,643,345	0.6
Asian	11,898,828	4.2	10,242,998	3.6	1,655,830	0.6
Black	36,419,434	12.9	34,658,190	12.3	1,761,244	0.6
Native Hawaiian and other Pacific Islanders	874,414	0.3	398,835	0.1	475,579	0.2
White	216,930,975	77.1	211,460,626	75.1	5,470,349	1.9
Other race	18,521,486	6.6	15,359,073	5.5	3,162,413	1.1

Note: Race alone numbers will not add to total because they do not include the multiracial population. Race alone or in combination numbers will not add to total because they count the multiracial population more than once. American Indians include Alaska Natives.
Source: Bureau of the Census, Census 2000 Redistricting Data, P.L. 94-171

themselves as multiracial will be missing. In tables showing the "race in combination" population, some people will be counted more than once depending on the number of races they checked on their census form. People who identified themselves as black and white, for example, will be counted in the "black in combination" population and in the "white in combination" population.

Other government data collection efforts will offer the multiracial option by 2003, but they did not do so in 2000. Consequently, the many tables in *Racial and Ethnic Diversity* that are based on government surveys—such as the Current Population Survey—show different counts for racial groups than does the census. In general, census counts of the "race alone" population will be smaller than survey estimates because they exclude the multiracial. Census counts of the "race, alone or in combination" population will be larger than survey estimates because they include people who would have aligned themselves with another race if forced to make a choice. Census figures also differ from survey estimates because of methodological differences and because the census found millions more people in the U.S. than demographers had estimated.

Racial and Ethnic Diversity shows the 2000 census counts for the six racial groups and their combinations. It also presents 2000 census numbers for Hispanics and non-Hispanic whites. Below is a description of each racial category and its definition in *Racial and Ethnic Diversity*.

American Indian and Alaska Native American Indians and Alaska Natives (Eskimos and Aleuts) are people who reported their race as American Indian and/or entered the name of an American Indian tribe on the 2000 census form. The tribal data shown are based on written entries on the 2000 census questionnaire. American Indians could name more than one tribal group, just as they could name more than one race. In 2000 census data, the term "American Indian" includes those who identified themselves as American Indian and no other race (called "American Indian alone") and those who identified themselves as American Indian and some other race (called "American Indian in combination"). The combination of the two groups is termed "American Indian, alone or in combination." Each table of American Indian census data in *Racial and Ethnic Diversity* notes which definition is used.

In noncensus surveys and data collections, such as the economic census, birth and death records, and so on, the multiracial option was not available in 2000. Consequently, American Indian totals in noncensus data are different from the 2000 census count.

Asian The term "Asian" is defined differently depending on whether census or survey data are shown. In 2000 census data, Asians do not include Pacific Islanders. The term "Asian" includes those who identified themselves as Asian and no other race (called "Asian alone") and those who identified themselves as Asian and some other race (called "Asian in combination"). The combination of the two groups is termed "Asian, alone or in combination." Each table of Asian census data in *Racial and Ethnic Diversity* notes which definition is used. Census data further break down the Asian population by ethnic origin, such as Chinese and Vietnamese.

In the Current Population Survey and other data collections, Asians include Pacific Islanders. In addition, because the multiracial option was not yet included in surveys and other data collection efforts in 2000, the Asian totals in survey data are different from 2000 census counts. In the immigration tables in the Asian and Total Population chapters, people from the Middle East—such as Israel, Egypt, Jordan, Iran, and so on—are identified by the Immigration and Naturalization Service as immigrants from the Asian world region. The Census Bureau considers them white.

Black The black racial category includes those who identified themselves as "black or African American." The term "black" is defined differently depending on whether census or survey data are shown. In 2000 census data, the term "black" includes those who identified themselves as black and no other race (called "black alone") and those who identified themselves as black and some other race (called "black in combination"). The combination of the two groups is termed "black, alone or in combination." Each table of black census data in *Racial and Ethnic Diversity* notes which definition is used.

Because the multiracial option was not yet included in surveys and other data collection efforts in 2000, the black totals in survey data are different from 2000 census counts.

Native Hawaiian and other Pacific Islander The 2000 census, for the first time, identified this group as a racial category separate from Asians. The term "Native Hawaiian and other Pacific Islander" includes those who identified themselves as Native Hawaiian and other Pacific Islander and no other race (called "Native Hawaiian and other Pacific Islander alone") and those who identified themselves as Native Hawaiian and other Pacific Islander and some other race (called "Native Hawaiian and other Pacific Islander in combination"). The combination of the two groups is termed "Native Hawaiian and other Pacific Islander, alone or in combination." Each table of Native Hawaiian and other Pacific Islander census data in *Racial and Ethnic Diversity* notes which definition is used. Native Hawaiians and other Pacific Islanders are further broken down in census data by their ethnic origin, such as Tongan, Fijian, and the individual ethnic category of Native Hawaiian. Native Hawaiians and other Pacific Islanders could identify themselves as belonging to more than one Pacific Islander ethnic group, just as they could identify themselves as being of more than one race. Because Native Hawaiians and other Pacific Islanders are such a small minority, 2000 census counts are the only data available for the group.

White The term "white" is defined differently depending on whether census or survey data are shown. In 2000 census data, the term "white" includes those who identified themselves as white and no other race (called "white alone") and those who identified themselves as white and some other race (called "white in combination"). The combination of the two groups is termed "white, alone or in combination." Each table of white census data in *Racial and Ethnic Diversity* notes which definition is used.

Because the multiracial option was not yet included in surveys and other data collection efforts in 2000, the white totals in survey data are different from 2000 census counts. In the immigration tables in the Total Population chapter, people from the Middle East—such as Israel, Egypt, Jordan, Iran, and so on—are identified by the Immigration and Naturalization Service as immigrants from the Asian world region, although the Census Bureau classifies them as white.

Other Race The 2000 census included "other race" as a sixth racial category. The category was meant to capture the few Americans, such as Creoles, who may not consider themselves as belonging to any of the other five racial groups. In fact, more than 18 million Americans identified themselves as being of other race, including 42 percent of the nation's Hispanics.

Among the 18 million people who claim to be of other race, 90 percent also identified themselves as Hispanic. The government considers Hispanic to be an ethnic identification rather than a race since there are white, black, American Indian, and Asian Hispanics. But many Hispanics consider their ethnicity to be a separate race, and they checked "other race" when they could not find Hispanic listed as a racial category. Because most people of other race are also Hispanic, tables showing the other race population are included in the Hispanic population chapter.

In 2000 census tables, the term "Other race" includes those who identified themselves as "other alone" and those who identified themselves as "other in combination" with white, black, or another of the racial categories. The combination of the two groups is termed "other, alone or in combination." Each table of census data in *Racial and Ethnic Diversity* notes which definition is used.

Hispanic The government classifies people as Hispanic through self-identification in a question separate from race. Because Hispanic is an ethnic origin rather than a race, Hispanics may be of any race. While most Hispanics are white, there are black, Asian, American Indian, and even Native Hawaiian Hispanics (see Table 2). The Hispanic statistics in *Racial and Ethnic Diversity* include people who identified themselves as Hispanic on the 2000 census or on the government's surveys. Hispanics are broken down into individual

Table 2. Hispanics and Non-Hispanics by Race, 2000 Census

(number and percent distribution of Hispanics and non-Hispanics by race, 2000)

	Hispanics		non-Hispanics	
	number	percent distribution	number	percent distribution
Total people	**35,306,818**	**100.0%**	**246,116,088**	**100.0%**
One race	33,081,736	93.7	241,513,942	98.1
White	16,907,852	47.9	194,552,774	79.0
Black	710,353	2.0	33,947,837	13.8
American Indian	407,073	1.2	2,068,883	0.8
Asian	119,829	0.3	10,123,169	4.1
Native Hawaiian and other Pacific Islander	45,326	0.1	353,509	0.1
Other	14,891,303	42.2	467,770	0.2
Two or more races	2,224,082	6.3	4,602,146	1.9

Note: American Indians include Alaska natives.
Source: Bureau of the Census, Overview of Race and Hispanic Origin, *Census 2000 Brief, CENBR/01-1, 2001*

ethnic groups, principally Mexican, Puerto Rican, Cuban, and other Spanish/Hispanic origin. "Other" Hispanic origin includes people from Spain, Central and South America, and the Dominican Republic.

Many Hispanics identified their race as "other" rather than white, black, and so on. In fact, 90 percent of those who identified themselves as "other race" also identified themselves as Hispanic. Because of this, tables showing the "other race" population are included in the Hispanic population chapter.

The 2000 census count of Hispanics differs from numbers based on the Current Population and other surveys. The numbers are not the same in part because of methodological differences and because the 2000 census found more people in the U.S. than demographers had estimated. Numbers from the 2000 census are more accurate than survey data.

Non-Hispanic White The 2000 census classified people as non-Hispanic white if they identified their race as "white alone" and did not indicate their ethnicity as Hispanic. This definition is similar to the one used in the Current Population Survey and other government data collection efforts. Tables on the non-Hispanic white population appear in the White chapters, usually accompanying a similar table for the white population as a whole.

How to Use This Book

Racial and Ethnic Diversity is designed for easy use. It is divided into eight sections: American Indians, Asians, Blacks, Hispanics, Native Hawaiians and other Pacific Islanders, Whites, Total Population, and Attitudes and Behavior.

In all but the Attitudes and Behavior section, ten chapters are arranged alphabetically: Business, Education, Health, Housing, Income, Labor Force, Living Arrangements, Population, Spending, and Wealth. Each chapter includes introductory text describing the most important trends for the particular racial or ethnic group. For some racial groups, particularly Native Hawaiians and other Pacific Islanders, chapters may be missing because the data are unavailable. Within chapters, identical tables appear for each racial group. When tables are not the same, it is because data for the group are not available.

The Total Population section allows readers to compare a racial group's statistics with those for the nation as a whole. If total population statistics appear within an individual racial or ethnic table, however, a table of the same statistics usually is not included in the Total Population chapter.

Underlying most of the tables in *Racial and Ethnic Diversity* are data collected by the federal government, in particular the Census Bureau, the Bureau of Labor Statistics, the National Center for Education Statistics, and the National Center for Health Statistics. The federal government continues to be the best source of up-to-date, reliable information on the changing characteristics of Americans.

Whenever possible, *Racial and Ethnic Diversity* presents 2000 census statistics that benchmark the characteristics of racial and ethnic groups. Many 2000 census statistics have not yet been released, however. Income, labor force, education, and other socioeconomic statistics from the census will become available over the next few years. In addition, the census does not collect some types of data, such as data on health, spending, and wealth. These numbers must be obtained from other government surveys and sources of data collection. One survey of particular importance is the Census Bureau's Current Population Survey. The CPS is a nationally representative survey of the civilian noninstitutional population aged 15 or older. The Census Bureau takes it monthly, collecting information from 50,000 households on employment and unemployment. Each year, the March survey includes a demographic supplement that is the source of most national data on the characteristics of Americans, such as their educational attainment, living arrangements, and incomes. CPS data appear in many tables of this book.

The Attitudes and Behavior section examines the thoughts of blacks, whites, and Hispanics about their lives and a range of diversity issues. Most of the data stem from the 2000 General Social Survey. The GSS is a biennial attitudinal survey taken by the University of Chicago's National Opinion Research Center. NORC is the oldest nonprofit, university-affiliated national survey research facility in the nation. It conducts the GSS through face-to-face interviews with an independently drawn, representative sample of 1,500 to 3,000 noninstitutionalized English-speaking people aged 18 or older living in the United States. The GSS divides respondents into three racial groups—white, black, and other. The "other" racial category includes Asians, American Indians, and Hispanics who did not identify themselves as white or black. The GSS also collects attitudinal data by Hispanic origin, which are tabulated in these pages. When examining the attitudes of Hispanics, it is important to remember that only Hispanics who speak English were included in the GSS sample.

The spending data for blacks, Hispanics, whites, and the total population are from the 2000 Consumer Expenditure Survey, or CEX. The CEX is an ongoing study of the day-to-day spending of American households administered by the Bureau of Labor Statistics. The survey is used to update prices for the Consumer Price Index.

The CEX includes an interview survey and a diary survey administered to two separate, nationally representative samples. The average spending figures shown in the Spending section of this book are the integrated data from both the diary and interview components of the survey. For the interview survey, about 7,500 consumer units are interviewed on a rotating panel basis each quarter for five consecutive quarters. For the diary survey, another 7,500 consumer units keep weekly diaries of spending for two consecutive weeks. Spending data for Asians, American Indians, or Native Hawaiians and other Pacific Islanders are unavailable.

The data in the Wealth section stem from the Survey of Consumer Finances, a triennial survey taken by the Federal Reserve Board. It collects data on the assets, debt, and net worth of American households. The latest data available are from the 1998 survey, for which the Federal Reserve Board interviewed a random sample of 2,813 households and a supplemental sample of 1,496 wealthy households based on tax-return data. Wealth data for Asians, American Indians, or Native Hawaiians and other Pacific Islanders are unavailable.

As we publish *Racial and Ethnic Diversity*, a growing volume of data from the 2000 census is becoming available online. Not only does online access make the data readily available, it allows people to manipulate numbers more easily. But the sheer abundance of census data, their many iterations, and the new complexities of defining racial groups creates a daunting task for those who want to keep up with America's changing diversity. The government's web sites are of great value to researchers with the time and skills to extract the needed nuggets of information. The shift from printed reports to web sites over the past decade—while convenient for number crunchers—has made demographic analysis a bigger chore.

With this volume, extraction and analysis have been done for you. While the government collected most of the data in *Racial and Ethnic Diversity*, the tables published here are not simple reprints of government spreadsheets—as is the case in many reference books. Instead, each table was individually compiled and created, with calculations performed by the author to reveal the trends. Each table tells a story about American Indians, Asians, blacks, Hispanics, Native Hawaiians and other Pacific Islanders, or whites. If you need more information, you can explore the original data using the source listed at the bottom of each table.

Racial and Ethnic Diversity also contains a list of tables to help you locate the information you need. For a more detailed search, use the index at the back of the book. Also at the back of the book you will find a bibliography of data sources, a glossary defining the terms used in the tables and text, and a list of government specialists and web sites.

Racial and Ethnic Diversity gives you the opportunity to discover the many ways Americans are the same—and different. With such knowledge, you will be closer to understanding where the future will take us.

1

American Indians and Alaska Natives

■ Numbering 4.1 million, American Indians are one of the smallest minorities in the U.S., accounting for just 1.5 percent of the population. The largest tribe is the Cherokee, which accounts for 18 percent of all American Indians.

■ On many measures, the health of American Indians is better than that of the average American. They are less likely to die from lung cancer, breast cancer, and cardiovascular diseases, and AIDS is relatively rare in this population segment.

■ Forty-six percent of American Indian householders own their home. Homeownership surpasses 50 percent among American Indians in the South.

■ The median income of American Indian households stood at $31,799 in 1998–2000, well below the national median. Twenty-six percent of American Indians are poor, more than double the 11 percent poverty rate among all Americans.

■ American Indian households are less likely than average to be headed by married couples, but more likely to include children. One in eight American Indian households is a single-parent family headed by a woman.

Note: There are no spending or wealth data available for American Indians.

American Indians account for 1.5 percent of the U.S. population

(percent distribution of people by race and Hispanic origin, 2000 census)

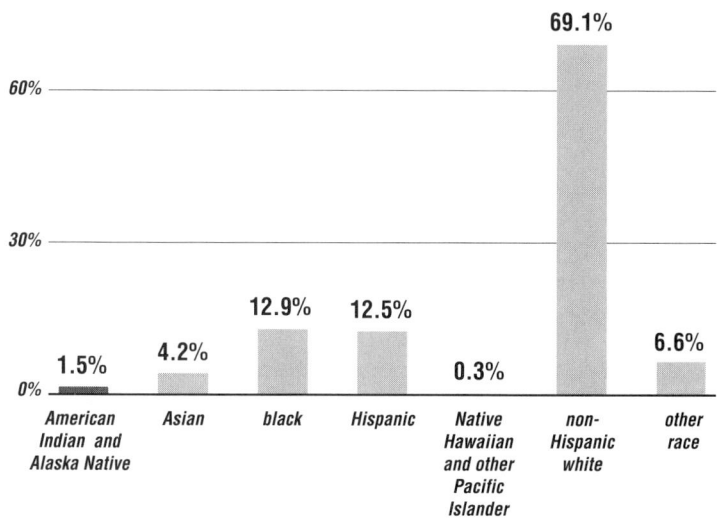

American Indian Firms Are Mostly Sole Proprietorships

American Indians and Alaska Natives own slightly fewer than 200,000 of the nation's 21 million businesses, according to the Survey of Minority-Owned Business Enterprises, a part of the 1997 Economic Censuses. The survey counts as minority-owned any firm in which the majority of owners is black, Alaska Native, American Indian, Asian, Native Hawaiian, Pacific Islander, or Hispanic. Minority ownership is determined for firms in their entirety rather than for individual locations.

American Indians owned slightly fewer than 1 percent of all businesses. In the fishing, hunting, and trapping industry, however, they owned 6 percent of firms. The largest share of American Indian firms are in the service industries—17 percent. Eighty-eight percent of American Indian-owned firms are individual proprietorships, a greater share than the 73 percent of all firms that are owned by one individual.

Fifty-four percent of American Indian-owned businesses are in just 10 states, California having the most. But American Indians own the largest share of businesses in Alaska—11 percent in 1997.

Most American Indian firms have receipts below $25,000

(percent distribution of receipts for firms owned by American Indians, 1997)

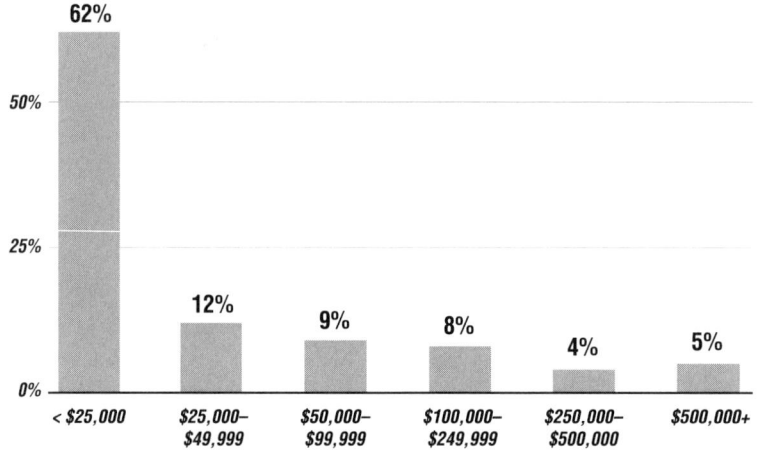

Number and Percent Distribution of Businesses Owned by American Indians, 1997

(total number of firms, number and percent distribution of firms owned by American Indians, and American Indian share of total, by industry, 1997)

SIC code		total firms	firms owned by American Indians		
			number	percent distribution	share of total
	All industries	**20,821,935**	**197,300**	**100.0%**	**0.9%**
	Agricultural services, forestry, fishing	**496,164**	**8,942**	**4.5**	**1.8**
07	Agricultural services	412,852	4,637	2.4	1.1
08	Forestry	14,051	209	0.1	1.5
09	Fishing, hunting, and trapping	69,271	4,096	2.1	5.9
	Mineral industries	**126,809**	**947**	**0.5**	**0.7**
10	Metal mining	1,819	28	0.0	1.5
12	Coal mining	2,242	–	–	–
13	Oil and gas extraction	115,953	862	0.4	0.7
14	Nonmetallic minerals, except fuels	6,862	37	0.0	0.5
	Construction industries, subdividers, and developers	**2,333,424**	**27,435**	**13.9**	**1.2**
15	Building construction, general contractors and operative builders	472,111	3,129	1.6	0.7
16	Heavy construction contractors other than buildings	64,314	1,095	0.6	1.7
17	Special trade contractors	1,739,060	23,100	11.7	1.3
6552	Subdividers and developers not elsewhere classified (excl. cemeteries)	58,362	115	0.1	0.2
	Manufacturing	**688,782**	**6,717**	**3.4**	**1.0**
20	Food and kindred products	30,256	216	0.1	0.7
21	Tobacco products	133	1	0.0	0.8
22	Textile mill products	8,213	71	0.0	0.9
23	Apparel and other textile products	54,889	474	0.2	0.9
24	Lumber and wood products	106,569	1,640	0.8	1.5
25	Furniture and fixtures	28,712	242	0.1	0.8
26	Paper and allied products	7,186	49	0.0	0.7
27	Printing and publishing	119,936	598	0.3	0.5
28	Chemicals and allied products	10,941	41	0.0	0.4
29	Petroleum and coal products	1,434	–	–	–
30	Rubber and miscellaneous plastics	16,296	25	0.0	0.2

(continued)

(continued from previous page)

SIC code		total firms	firms owned by American Indians		
			number	percent distribution	share of total
31	Leather and leather products	5,251	88	0.0%	1.7%
32	Stone, clay, and glass products	29,262	339	0.2	1.2
33	Primary metal industries	7,703	53	0.0	0.7
34	Fabricated metal products	63,141	851	0.4	1.3
35	Industrial machinery and equipment	85,401	675	0.3	0.8
36	Electronic and other electric equipment	28,324	165	0.1	0.6
37	Transportation equipment	13,673	63	0.0	0.5
38	Instruments and related products	12,423	21	0.0	0.2
39	Miscellaneous manufacturing industries	65,185	1,112	0.6	1.7
	Transportation, communication, and utilities	**919,570**	**6,291**	**3.2**	**0.7**
41	Local and interurban passenger transportation	116,993	736	0.4	0.6
42	Motor freight transportation and warehousing	544,523	3,644	1.8	0.7
44	Water transportation	15,788	102	0.1	0.6
45	Transportation by air	20,706	142	0.1	0.7
46	Pipelines, except natural gas	136	4	0.0	2.9
47	Transportation services	129,652	848	0.4	0.7
48	Communications	61,180	411	0.2	0.7
49	Electric, gas, and sanitary services	31,345	419	0.2	1.3
	Wholesale trade	**797,856**	**4,365**	**2.2**	**0.5**
50	Durable goods	489,308	2,980	1.5	0.6
51	Nondurable goods	309,731	1,385	0.7	0.4
	Retail trade	**2,889,041**	**14,768**	**7.5**	**0.5**
52	Building materials, hardware, garden supply, and mobile home dealers	85,060	564	0.3	0.7
53	General merchandise stores	35,027	459	0.2	1.3
54	Food stores	216,067	1,403	0.7	0.6
55	Automotive dealers and gasoline service stations	255,259	1,853	0.9	0.7
56	Apparel and accessory stores	127,848	788	0.4	0.6
57	Home furniture, furnishings, and equipment stores	153,248	1,104	0.6	0.7
58	Eating and drinking places	493,313	1,724	0.9	0.3
59	Miscellaneous retail	1,528,857	6,885	3.5	0.5

(continued)

(continued from previous page)

SIC code		total firms	firms owned by American Indians		
			number	percent distribution	share of total
	Finance, insurance, and real estate (excl. subdividers and developers)	**2,237,675**	**4,616**	**2.3%**	**0.2%**
60	Depository institutions	24,616	39	0.0	0.2
61	Nondepository credit institutions	45,905	202	0.1	0.4
62	Security and commodity brokers, dealers, exchanges, and services	91,446	438	0.2	0.5
63	Insurance carriers	9,108	29	0.0	0.3
64	Insurance agents, brokers, and services	411,902	1,016	0.5	0.2
65pt	Real estate (excl. subdividers and developers)	1,503,438	2,573	1.3	0.2
67	Holding and other investment offices, except trusts	157,652	323	0.2	0.2
	Service industries (excl. membership organizations, private household)	**8,891,024**	**34,144**	**17.3**	**0.4**
70	Hotels, rooming houses, camps, and other lodging places	93,380	589	0.3	0.6
72	Personal services	1,348,554	5,534	2.8	0.4
73	Business services	2,221,047	8,267	4.2	0.4
75	Automotive repair, services, parking	448,584	2,575	1.3	0.6
76	Miscellaneous repair services	231,371	1,500	0.8	0.6
78	Motion pictures	87,700	503	0.3	0.6
79	Amusement and recreation services	603,896	2,180	1.1	0.4
80	Health services	1,004,672	2,167	1.1	0.2
81	Legal services	353,147	815	0.4	0.2
82	Educational services	270,648	817	0.4	0.3
83	Social services	665,067	3,427	1.7	0.5
84	Museums, art galleries, botanical and zoological gardens	5,205	1	0.0	0.0
87	Engineering, accounting, research, management and related services	1,446,195	5,076	2.6	0.4
89	Services not elsewhere classified	119,931	745	0.4	0.6
	Industries not classified	**1,480,003**	**89,243**	**45.2**	**6.0**

Note: American Indians include Alaska Natives; (–) means data not available or suppressed for purposes of confidentiality.
Source: Bureau of the Census, Minority- and Women-Owned Businesses, *1997 Economic Census, Internet site <www.census.gov/csd/mwb/>; calculations by New Strategist*

Characteristics of Businesses Owned by American Indians, 1997

(number of firms owned by American Indians by industry and selected characteristics of firm, 1997)

SIC code		total firms		firms with paid employees			
		number	sales and receipts (in 000s)	number	sales and receipts (in 000s)	employees	payroll (in 000s)
	Total firms owned by Amer. Indians	**197,300**	**$34,343,907**	**33,277**	**$29,226,260**	**298,661**	**$6,624,235**
	Agricultural services, forestry, fishing	**8,942**	**360,484**	**797**	**174,841**	**2,760**	**50,041**
07	Agricultural services	4,637	224,595	712	139,771	2,285	36,212
08	Forestry	209	25,513	40	21,128	441	11,513
09	Fishing, hunting, and trapping	4,096	110,376	45	13,942	34	2,316
	Mineral industries	**947**	**543,908**	**199**	**465,764**	**2,124**	**64,737**
10	Metal mining	28	2,236	7	–	0–19	–
12	Coal mining	–	–	–	–	–	–
13	Oil and gas extraction	862	531,229	152	453,771	1,962	61,182
14	Nonmetallic minerals, except fuels	37	6,882	20	–	20–99	–
	Construction industries, subdividers, and developers	**27,435**	**5,384,815**	**6,012**	**4,648,924**	**38,419**	**1,021,524**
15	Building construction, general contractors and operative builders	3,129	1,732,017	1,244	1,616,766	7,509	224,658
16	Heavy construction contractors other than buildings	1,095	1,071,263	535	1,037,237	8,608	250,141
17	Special trade contractors	23,100	2,564,381	4,226	1,986,557	22,260	545,357
6552	Subdividers and developers not elsewhere classified (excl. cemeteries)	115	17,154	11	8,364	42	1,368
	Manufacturing	**6,717**	**2,503,417**	**1,612**	**2,334,452**	**21,206**	**563,454**
20	Food and kindred products	216	218,438	87	215,052	791	17,396
21	Tobacco products	1	–	1	–	0–19	–
22	Textile mill products	71	40,404	16	40,152	612	9,943
23	Apparel and other textile products	474	34,751	37	29,336	433	5,889
24	Lumber and wood products	1,640	330,250	302	257,857	2,558	59,919
25	Furniture and fixtures	242	34,927	52	30,252	365	8,554
26	Paper and allied products	49	55,348	18	55,102	318	9,642
27	Printing and publishing	598	202,453	219	194,483	2,510	60,807
28	Chemicals and allied products	41	31,695	25	–	100–249	–
29	Petroleum and coal products	–	–	–	–	–	–

(continued)

(continued from previous page)

SIC code		total firms		firms with paid employees			
		number	sales and receipts (in 000s)	number	sales and receipts (in 000s)	employees	payroll (in 000s)
30	Rubber and miscellaneous plastics	25	$113,288	20		–1,000–2,499	–
31	Leather and leather products	88	–	10	$4,175	55	$1,060
32	Stone, clay, and glass products	339	60,718	43	55,163	395	9,095
33	Primary metal industries	53	74,872	14	57,869	373	8,229
34	Fabricated metal products	851	411,421	155	398,586	3,589	112,631
35	Industrial machinery and equipment	675	387,089	317	372,721	3,675	115,918
36	Electronic, other electric equipment	165	132,515	78	125,419	1,639	35,094
37	Transportation equipment	63	297,326	56	296,106	1,944	62,448
38	Instruments and related products	21	15,714	20	–	100–249	–
39	Misc. manufacturing industries	1,112	55,933	150	43,734	542	10,433
	Transportation, communication, and utilities	**6,291**	**1,620,515**	**1,118**	**1,347,949**	**10,584**	**276,381**
41	Local and interurban passenger transportation	736	93,834	140	78,781	1,869	34,178
42	Motor freight transportation and warehousing	3,644	692,977	688	523,442	5,435	138,831
44	Water transportation	102	–	30	–	100–249	–
45	Transportation by air	142	107,270	43	–	500–999	–
46	Pipelines, except natural gas	4	–	4	–	20–99	–
47	Transportation services	848	92,586	99	66,195	621	19,970
48	Communications	411	149,251	74	140,255	1,154	31,777
49	Electric, gas, and sanitary services	419	458,558	55	432,017	533	23,830
	Wholesale trade	**4,365**	**3,155,143**	**1,145**	**3,036,534**	**9,801**	**260,713**
50	Durable goods	2,980	1,825,534	670	1,764,258	5,790	167,124
51	Nondurable goods	1,385	1,329,609	476	1,272,275	4,011	93,589
	Retail trade	**14,768**	**4,618,484**	**4,645**	**4,245,552**	**31,451**	**441,783**
52	Building materials, hardware, garden supply, and mobile home dealers	564	271,102	295	253,909	1,716	35,510
53	General merchandise stores	459	88,796	120	75,496	770	10,610
54	Food stores	1,403	607,958	729	570,732	5,076	47,089
55	Automotive dealers and gasoline service stations	1,853	2,136,531	865	2,043,281	6,936	157,133
56	Apparel and accessory stores	788	119,350	209	99,155	1,576	13,213
57	Home furniture, furnishings, and equipment stores	1,104	276,787	456	240,424	1,590	29,105

(continued)

(continued from previous page)

SIC code		total firms		firms with paid employees			
		number	sales and receipts (in 000s)	number	sales and receipts (in 000s)	employees	payroll (in 000s)
58	Eating and drinking places	1,724	$310,058	1,039	$291,172	8,881	$75,128
59	Miscellaneous retail	6,885	807,901	944	671,383	4,906	73,995
	Finance, insurance, and real estate (excl. subdividers and developers)	**4,616**	**1,190,741**	**1,004**	**1,025,527**	**4,585**	**133,050**
60	Depository institutions	39	38,444	32	–	250–499	–
61	Nondepository credit institutions	202	71,672	99	65,336	488	12,089
62	Security and commodity brokers, dealers, exchanges, and services	438	65,761	91	32,632	311	8,345
63	Insurance carriers	29	13,711	10	–	20–99	–
64	Insurance agents, brokers, services	1,016	192,801	317	166,254	1,422	41,462
65pt	Real estate (excl. subdividers and developers)	2,573	295,048	401	210,691	1,765	46,658
67	Holding and other investment offices, except trusts	323	513,304	58	498,968	202	10,564
	Service industries (excl. membership organizations, private household)	**34,144**	**5,202,704**	**4,826**	**4,497,918**	**66,627**	**1,541,895**
70	Hotels, rooming houses, camps, and other lodging places	589	327,019	249	312,450	5,875	81,117
72	Personal services	5,534	174,764	470	93,833	2,404	34,193
73	Business services	8,267	1,185,081	907	1,027,653	17,173	379,126
75	Automotive repair, services, parking	2,575	315,902	700	263,075	2,600	57,261
76	Miscellaneous repair services	1,500	156,186	291	125,655	1,477	40,408
78	Motion pictures	503	–	125	–	500–999	–
79	Amusement and recreation services	2,180	1,196,140	195	1,133,921	12,464	289,125
80	Health services	2,167	347,959	557	313,569	6,449	144,267
81	Legal services	815	120,717	263	95,736	872	24,458
82	Educational services	817	71,620	53	44,630	1,004	23,627
83	Social services	3,427	206,817	186	174,079	4,563	68,643
84	Museums, art galleries, botanical and zoological gardens	1	–	1	–	0–19	–
87	Engineering, accounting, research, management and related services	5,076	1,003,920	822	833,751	10,339	372,603
89	Services not elsewhere classified	745	56,533	60	50,469	679	19,063
	Industries not classified	**89,243**	**9,763,696**	**12,086**	**7,448,800**	**111,103**	**2,270,656**

Note: American Indians include Alaska natives; (–) means data not available or suppressed for purposes of confidentiality.
Source: Bureau of the Census, Minority- and Women-Owned Businesses, *1997 Economic Census, Internet site <www.census.gov/csd/mwb/>*

American Indian-Owned Businesses by Legal Form of Organization, Receipt Size, and Employees, 1997

(number and percent distribution of American Indian-owned firms by legal form of organization, size of receipts, and number of employees, 1997)

	total	percent distribution
Total firms owned by American Indians	**197,300**	**100.0%**
Legal form of organization		
C corporations	9,379	4.8
Subchapter S corporations	9,618	4.9
Individual proprietorships	173,385	87.9
Partnerships	4,626	2.3
Other	293	0.1
Size of receipts		
Under $5,000	50,433	25.6
$5,000 to $9,999	30,387	15.4
$10,000 to $24,999	41,515	21.0
$25,000 to $49,999	23,541	11.9
$50,000 to $99,999	18,483	9.4
$100,000 to $249,999	15,815	8.0
$250,000 to $499,999	7,979	4.0
$500,000 to $999,999	4,255	2.2
$1,000,000 or more	4,892	2.5
Number of employees		
Firms with employees	33,277	100.0
No employees*	3,705	11.1
1 to 3 employees	18,262	54.9
5 to 9 employees	5,666	17.0
10 to 19 employees	2,932	8.8
20 to 49 employees	2,079	6.2
50 to 99 employees	278	0.8
100 to 499 employees	333	1.0
500 employees or more	22	0.1

Note: American Indians include Alaska Natives.
* Firms that reported annual payroll but no employees on the payroll during the specified period in 1997.
Source: Bureau of the Census, American Indians and Alaska Natives, *1997 Economic Census, Survey of Minority-Owned Business Enterprises, Company Statistics Series, EC97CS-6, 2001; calculations by New Strategist*

American Indian-Owned Businesses by State, 1997

(number of total firms and receipts and number and percent distribution of American Indian firms and receipts in the ten states with the largest number of American Indian-owned firms, and American Indian share of total firms and receipts, 1997)

| | total firms | American Indian firms | | | total sales and receipts (millions) | American Indian sales and receipts | | |
		number	percent distribution	percent of total		amount (millions)	percent distribution	percent of total
Total firms	20,821,934	197,300	100.0%	0.9%	$18,553,243	$34,344	100.0%	0.2%
Total in top ten states	8,956,984	106,444	54.0	1.2	7,681,420	19,412	56.5	0.3
California	2,565,734	26,603	13.5	1.0	2,178,292	5,836	17.0	0.3
Texas	1,525,972	15,668	7.9	1.0	1,415,536	3,320	9.7	0.2
Oklahoma	280,722	15,066	7.6	5.4	172,370	2,646	7.7	1.5
Florida	1,301,920	10,546	5.3	0.8	828,429	1,519	4.4	0.2
North Carolina	570,484	7,148	3.6	1.3	518,649	912	2.7	0.2
New Mexico	131,685	6,838	3.5	5.2	79,752	580	1.7	0.7
Alaska	64,134	6,820	3.5	10.6	36,912	1,709	5.0	4.6
New York	1,509,829	6,443	3.3	0.4	1,488,913	1,417	4.1	0.1
Michigan	677,473	5,802	2.9	0.9	715,376	720	2.1	0.1
Arizona	329,031	5,510	2.8	1.7	247,191	753	2.2	0.3

Note: American Indians include Alaska Natives.
Source: Bureau of the Census, American Indians and Alaska Natives, *1997 Economic Census, Survey of Minority-Owned Business Enterprises, Company Statistics Series, EC97CS-6, 2001; calculations by New Strategist*

American Indian-Owned Businesses by Metropolitan Area, 1997

(number and percent distribution of American Indian firms and receipts in the ten metropolitan areas with the largest number of American Indian-owned firms, and metropolitan area's share of total American Indian firms and receipts in state, 1997)

	firms			sales and receipts		
	number	percent distribution	percent of Amer. Ind. firms in state	amount (in millions)	percent distribution	percent of Amer. Ind. receipts in state
Total American Indian firms/receipts	197,300	100.0%	–	$34,344	100.0%	–
Total in top metropolitan areas	32,905	16.7	–	7,551	22.0	–
Los Angeles–Long Beach, CA PMSA	8,541	4.3	32.1%	2,890	8.4	49.5%
Tulsa, OK MSA	3,822	1.9	25.4	933	2.7	35.3
Oklahoma City, OK MSA	3,295	1.7	21.9	668	1.9	25.2
Houston, TX PMSA	3,128	1.6	20.0	477	1.4	14.4
New York, NY PMSA	2,801	1.4	43.5	891	2.6	62.9
Dallas, TX PMSA	2,510	1.3	16.0	729	2.1	22.0
Orange County, CA PMSA	2,287	1.2	8.6	193	0.6	3.3
Atlanta, GA MSA	2,227	1.1	49.8	245	0.7	49.5
Chicago, IL PMSA	2,161	1.1	54.8	371	1.1	55.9
Sacramento, CA PMSA	2,133	1.1	8.0	154	0.4	2.6

Note: American Indians include Alaska natives; for definitions of PMSA and MSA, see glossary; (–) means data not available or not applicable.
Source: Bureau of the Census, American Indians and Alaska Natives, *1997 Economic Census, Survey of Minority-Owned Business Enterprises, Company Statistics Series, EC97CS-6, 2001; calculations by New Strategist*

Most American Indian College Students Attend Public Institutions

More than 145,000 American Indians were enrolled in college in 1999, accounting for 1 percent of total college enrollment. Among American Indians in college, the 60 percent majority are women. Most American Indian college students are enrolled in public institutions, with about half attending two-year schools and half going to four-year schools. The 57 percent majority are full-time students. More than 90 percent are undergraduates.

American Indians earned 8,711 bachelor's degrees in 1999–2000, just 0.7 percent of the total. Twenty-one percent—the largest share—of the 259 associate's degrees awarded in area, ethnic, and cultural studies went to American Indians in 1999–2000.

■ Because American Indians have relatively low incomes, it is difficult for them to pay for a college education.

Most American Indian college students are women

(percent distribution of American Indians enrolled in college, by sex, 1999)

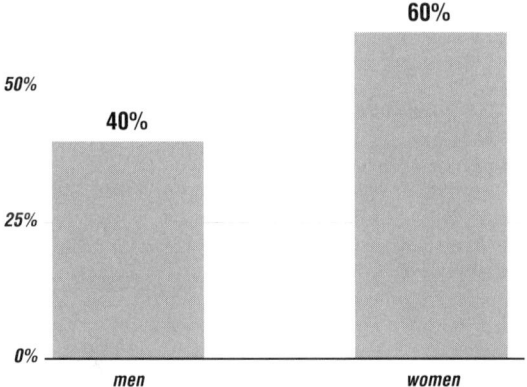

College Enrollment of American Indians, 1999

(number and percent distribution of American Indians enrolled in degree-granting institutions by sex, type of institution, and level of study, 1999)

	number	percent distribution
Total American Indians enrolled	**145,300**	**100.0%**
Men	58,500	40.3
Women	86,800	59.7
Public	124,100	85.4
Private	21,200	14.6
Two-year institution	72,100	49.6
Four-year institution	73,200	50.4
Full-time students	83,100	57.2
Part-time students	62,200	42.8
Undergraduate	133,300	91.7
Graduate	9,900	6.8
First-professional	2,100	1.4

Source: National Center for Education Statistics, Digest of Education Statistics 2001, *Internet site <http://nces.ed.gov/pubsearch/pubsinfo.asp?pubid=2002130>; calculations by New Strategist*

Associate's Degrees Earned by American Indians by Field of Study, 1999–2000

(total number of associate's degrees conferred and number and percent earned by American Indians, by field of study, 1999–2000)

	total	earned by American Indians	
		number	percent
Total associate's degrees	**564,933**	**6,494**	**1.1%**
Agriculture and natural resources	6,667	103	1.5
Architecture and related programs	392	–	–
Area, ethnic, and cultural studies	259	54	20.8
Biological, life sciences	1,434	40	2.8
Business	92,274	1,191	1.3
Communications	2,754	26	0.9
Communications technologies	1,709	6	0.4
Computer and information sciences	20,450	248	1.2
Construction trades	2,337	46	2.0
Education	8,226	208	2.5
Engineering	1,752	17	1.0
Engineering-related technologies	35,395	359	1.0
English language and literature, letters	947	12	1.3
Foreign languages and literatures	501	1	0.2
Health professions and related sciences	84,081	922	1.1
Home economics	8,381	104	1.2
Law and legal studies	7,265	88	1.2
Liberal arts and sciences, general studies, and humanities	187,454	1,982	1.1
Library science	98	2	2.0
Mathematics	675	7	1.0
Mechanics and repairers	11,614	128	1.1
Multi/interdisciplinary studies	11,784	95	0.8
Parks, recreation, leisure and fitness	855	8	0.9
Philosophy and religion	63	–	–
Physical sciences	2,460	21	0.9
Precision production trades	11,814	141	1.2
Protective services	16,298	222	1.4
Psychology	1,455	39	2.7
Public administration and services	3,656	120	3.3
R.O.T.C. and military technoloiges	65	–	–
Social sciences and history	5,136	127	2.5
Theological studies, religious vocations	636	2	0.3
Transportation and material moving	1,021	11	1.1
Visual and performing arts	17,100	144	0.8
Not classified	2,798	20	0.7

Note: (–) means no degrees were awarded; American Indians include Alaska Natives.
Source: National Center for Education Statistics, Digest of Education Statistics 2001, *Internet site <http://nces.ed.gov/pubsearch/pubsinfo.asp?pubid=2002130>; calculations by New Strategist*

Bachelor's Degrees Earned by American Indians by Field of Study, 1999–2000

(total number of bachelor's degrees conferred and number and percent earned by American Indians, by field of study, 1999–2000)

	total	earned by American Indians number	earned by American Indians percent
Total bachelor's degrees	**1,237,875**	**8,711**	**0.7%**
Agriculture and natural resources	24,247	233	1.0
Architecture and related programs	8,462	61	0.7
Area, ethnic, and cultural studies	6,381	93	1.5
Biological, life sciences	63,532	391	0.6
Business	257,709	1,486	0.6
Communications	55,760	297	0.5
Communications technologies	1,150	8	0.7
Computer and information sciences	36,195	174	0.5
Construction trades	186	2	1.1
Education	108,168	948	0.9
Engineering	58,427	335	0.6
Engineering-related technologies	13,872	104	0.7
English language and literature, letters	50,920	320	0.6
Foreign languages and literatures	14,968	67	0.4
Health professions and related sciences	78,458	571	0.7
Home economics	17,779	113	0.6
Law and legal studies	1,925	12	0.6
Liberal arts and sciences, general studies, and humanities	36,104	377	1.0
Library science	154	2	1.3
Mathematics	12,070	72	0.6
Mechanics and repairers	70	–	–
Multi/interdisciplinary studies	27,460	220	0.8
Parks, recreation, leisure and fitness	19,111	156	0.8
Philosophy and religion	8,366	49	0.6
Physical sciences	18,385	115	0.6
Precision production trades	393	5	1.3
Protective services	24,877	280	1.1
Psychology	74,060	537	0.7
Public administration and services	20,185	221	1.1
R.O.T.C. and military technoloiges	7	–	–
Social sciences and history	127,101	970	0.8
Theological studies, religious vocations	6,809	35	0.5
Transportation and material moving	3,395	33	1.0
Visual and performing arts	58,791	418	0.7
Not classified	2,398	6	0.3

Note: (–) means no degrees were awarded. American Indians include Alaska Natives.
Source: National Center for Education Statistics, Digest of Education Statistics 2001, Internet site <http://nces.ed.gov/pubsearch/pubsinfo.asp?pubid=2002130>; calculations by New Strategist

Master's Degrees Earned by American Indians by Field of Study, 1999–2000

(total number of master's degrees conferred and number and percent earned by American Indians, by field of study, 1999–2000)

	total	earned by American Indians	
		number	percent
Total master's degrees	**457,056**	**2,232**	**0.5%**
Agriculture and natural resources	4,375	26	0.6
Architecture and related programs	4,268	11	0.3
Area, ethnic, and cultural studies	1,591	18	1.1
Biological, life sciences	6,198	27	0.4
Business	112,258	414	0.4
Communications	5,169	19	0.4
Communications technologies	436	1	0.2
Computer and information sciences	14,264	27	0.2
Construction trades	12	–	–
Education	124,240	740	0.6
Engineering	25,596	67	0.3
Engineering-related technologies	914	2	0.2
English language and literature, letters	7,230	46	0.6
Foreign languages and literatures	2,780	6	0.2
Health professions and related sciences	42,456	242	0.6
Home economics	2,830	13	0.5
Law and legal studies	3,750	6	0.2
Liberal arts and sciences, general studies, and humanities	3,256	21	0.6
Library science	4,577	17	0.4
Mathematics	3,412	10	0.3
Multi/interdisciplinary studies	3,064	23	0.8
Parks, recreation, leisure and fitness	2,478	11	0.4
Philosophy and religion	1,329	4	0.3
Physical sciences	4,841	19	0.4
Precision production trades	5	–	–
Protective services	2,609	23	0.9
Psychology	14,465	79	0.5
Public administration and services	25,594	204	0.8
Social sciences and history	14,066	88	0.6
Theological studies, religious vocations	5,576	13	0.2
Transportation and material moving	697	8	1.1
Visual and performing arts	10,918	45	0.4
Not classified	1,802	2	0.1

Note: (–) means no degrees were awarded; American Indians include Alaska Natives.
Source: National Center for Education Statistics, Digest of Education Statistics 2001, *Internet site <http://nces.ed.gov/pubsearch/pubsinfo.asp?pubid=2002130>; calculations by New Strategist*

Doctoral Degrees Earned by American Indians by Field of Study, 1999–2000

(total number of doctoral degrees conferred and number and percent earned by American Indians, by field of study, 1999–2000)

	total	earned by American Indians number	earned by American Indians percent
Total doctoral degrees	**44,808**	**159**	**0.4%**
Agriculture and natural resources	1,181	2	0.2
Architecture and related programs	129	–	–
Area, ethnic, and cultural studies	217	2	0.9
Biological, life sciences	4,867	8	0.2
Business	1,196	5	0.4
Communications	347	1	0.3
Communications technologies	10	–	–
Computer and information sciences	777	–	–
Education	6,830	44	0.6
Engineering	5,384	5	0.1
Engineering-related technologies	6	–	–
English language and literature, letters	1,628	6	0.4
Foreign languages and literatures	915	1	0.1
Health professions and related sciences	2,676	8	0.3
Home economics	357	1	0.3
Law and legal studies	74	–	–
Liberal arts and sciences, general studies, and humanities	83	1	1.2
Library science	68	1	1.5
Mathematics	1,106	2	0.2
Multi/interdisciplinary studies	384	3	0.8
Parks, recreation, leisure and fitness	134	1	0.7
Philosophy and religion	586	1	0.2
Physical sciences	4,018	15	0.4
Protective services	52	–	–
Psychology	4,310	31	0.7
Public administration and services	537	2	0.4
Social sciences and history	4,095	17	0.4
Theological studies, religious vocations	1,643	1	0.1
Visual and performing arts	1,127	1	0.1
Not classified	71	–	–

Note: (–) means no degrees were awarded; American Indians include Alaska Natives.
Source: National Center for Education Statistics, Digest of Education Statistics 2001, *Internet site <http://nces.ed.gov/pubsearch/pubsinfo.asp?pubid=2002130>; calculations by New Strategist*

First-Professional Degrees Earned by American Indians by Field of Study, 1999–2000

(total number of first-professional degrees conferred and number and percent earned by American Indians, by field of study, 1999–2000)

	total	earned by American Indians	
		number	percent
Total first-professional degrees	**80,259**	**564**	**0.7%**
Dentistry (D.D.S. or D.M.D.)	4,250	14	0.3
Medicine (M.D.)	15,286	124	0.8
Optometry (O.D.)	1,293	9	0.7
Osteopathic medicine (D.O.)	2,236	14	0.6
Pharmacy (Pharm.D.)	5,669	30	0.5
Podiatry (Pod.D., D.P., or D.P.M.)	569	2	0.4
Veterinary medicine (D.V.M.)	2,251	14	0.6
Chiropractic (D.C. or D.C.M.)	3,809	15	0.4
Naturopathic medicine	202	1	0.5
Law (LL.B. or J.D.)	38,152	324	0.8
Theology (M.Div., M.H.L., B.D., or Ord. and M.H.L./Rav.)	6,129	17	0.3
Other	413	–	–

Note: (–) means no degrees were awarded. American Indians include Alaska Natives.
Source: National Center for Education Statistics, Digest of Education Statistics 2001, *Internet site <http://nces.ed.gov/pubsearch/pubsinfo.asp?pubid=2002130>; calculations by New Strategist*

American Indians: Health

On Many Measures, the Health of American Indians
Is Better than Average

American Indians are less likely to die from lung cancer, breast cancer, or cardiovascular disease than is the average American, and AIDS is relatively rare in this segment of the population. But American Indians are twice as likely to die in motor vehicle accidents. Teen births are common among American Indians, with 8 percent of births occurring to girls under age 18—83 percent higher than among the total population. Because many American Indians are nonmetropolitan residents, only 19 percent live in counties with polluted air.

The 41,668 births to American Indian women in 2000 accounted for only 1 percent of all U.S. births. But American Indians, including Aleuts and Eskimos, accounted for 25 percent of births in Alaska, 16 percent in South Dakota, 13 percent in New Mexico, and 12 percent in Montana.

Among American Indians, heart disease and cancer are the two leading causes of death, but they account for only 37 percent of all deaths versus the 53 percent majority of deaths among all Americans. Accidents and diabetes are much more likely causes of death among American Indians than among the U.S. population as a whole.

■ Many of the health problems of American Indians are common in populations where poverty is widespread, including tuberculosis and homicide.

Many American Indian babies are born to teenagers

(percent distribution of births to American Indian women by age, 2000)

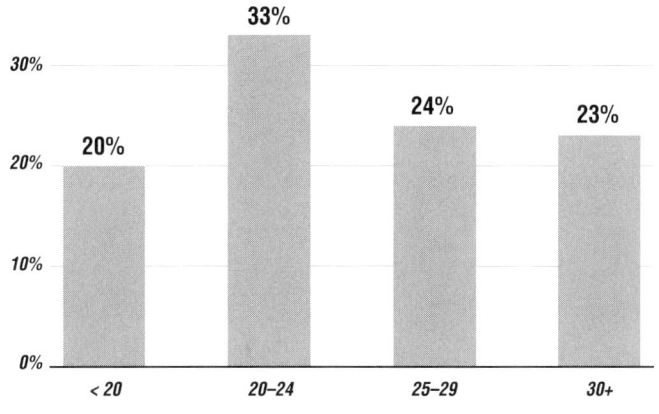

Health Indicators for American Indians, 1998

(selected indicators of total and American Indian health status, and index of American Indian health indicators to total, 1998)

	total population indicator	American Indian indicator	index of American Indian to total
Infant mortality rate (deaths before age 1 per 1,000 live births)	7.2	9.3	129
Total deaths per 100,000 population	471.7	458.1	97
Motor vehicle crash deaths per 100,000 population	15.7	31.8	203
Work-related injury deaths per 100,000 people aged 16 or older	2.9	1.7	59
Suicides per 100,000 population	10.4	13.4	129
Homicides per 100,000 population	7.3	9.9	136
Lung cancer deaths per 100,000 population	37.0	25.1	68
Female breast cancer deaths per 100,000 population	18.8	10.3	55
Cardiovascular disease deaths per 100,000 population	161.2	123.8	77
Heart disease deaths per 100,000 population	126.7	97.1	77
Stroke deaths per 100,000 population	25.1	19.6	78
Reported incidence of AIDS per 100,000 population	19.5	9.4	48
Reported incidence of tuberculosis per 100,000 population	6.8	12.6	185
Reported incidence of syphilis per 100,000 population	2.6	2.8	108
Prevalence of low birth weight, as percent of total live births	7.6	6.8	89
Births to girls aged 10 to 17, as percent of total live births	4.6	8.4	183
Percent of mothers without care, first trimester of pregnancy	17.2	31.2	181
Percent under age 18 living in poverty	18.9	–	–
Percent living in counties exceeding U.S. air quality standards	23.5	18.9	80

Note: American Indians include Aleuts and Eskimos. (–) means data are not available. The index for each indicator is calculated by dividing the American Indian figure by the total population figure and multiplying by 100. For example, the index of 97 in the second row indicates that the American Indian death rate is 3 percent below the rate for the total population.
Source: National Center for Health Statistics, Healthy People 2000 Final Review, 2001; *calculations by New Strategist*

Births to American Indian Women by Age, 2000

(total number of births, number and percent distribution of births to American Indian women, and American Indian share of total, by age, 2000)

| | total | American Indian | | |
		number	percent distribution	share of total
Total births	**4,058,814**	**41,668**	**100.0%**	**1.0%**
Under age 15	8,519	160	0.4	1.9
Aged 15 to 19	468,990	8,055	19.3	1.7
Aged 20 to 24	1,017,806	13,633	32.7	1.3
Aged 25 to 29	1,087,547	10,053	24.1	0.9
Aged 30 to 34	929,278	6,097	14.6	0.7
Aged 35 to 39	452,057	2,983	7.2	0.7
Aged 40 to 44	90,013	658	1.6	0.7
Aged 45 or older	4,604	29	0.1	0.6

Note: American Indians include Aleuts and Eskimos.
Source: National Center for Health Statistics, Births: Final Data for 2000, National Vital Statistics Report, Vol. 50, No. 5, 2002; calculations by New Strategist

Births to American Indian Women by Birth Order, 2000

(number and percent distribution of births to American Indian women, by birth order, 2000)

	number	percent distribution
Births to American Indians	**41,668**	**100.0%**
First child	14,551	34.9
Second child	11,660	28.0
Third child	7,370	17.7
Fourth or later child	7,928	19.0

Note: American Indians include Aleuts and Eskimos. Numbers will not add to total because not stated is not shown.
Source: National Center for Health Statistics, Births: Final Data for 2000, *National Vital Statistics Report, Vol. 50, No. 5, 2002; calculations by New Strategist*

Births to American Indian Teenagers and Unmarried Women, 2000

(percent of births to American Indian women under age 20 and to unmarried American Indian women, 2000)

	percent to women	
	under age 20	unmarried
American Indian births	19.7%	58.4%

Note: American Indians include Aleuts and Eskimos.
Source: National Center for Health Statistics, Births: Final Data for 2000, *National Vital Statistics Report, Vol. 50, No. 5, 2002; calculations by New Strategist*

Births to American Indian Women by State, 2000

(total number of births, number and percent distribution of births to American Indian women, and American Indian share of total births by state, 2000)

| | total | American Indian births | | |
		number	percent distribtution	share of total
Total births	**4,058,814**	**41,668**	**100.0%**	**1.0%**
Alabama	63,299	182	0.4	0.3
Alaska	9,974	2,509	6.0	25.2
Arizona	85,273	5,675	13.6	6.7
Arkansas	37,783	242	0.6	0.6
California	531,959	3,032	7.3	0.6
Colorado	65,438	644	1.5	1.0
Connecticut	43,026	129	0.3	0.3
Delaware	11,051	39	0.1	0.4
District of Columbia	7,666	9	0.0	0.1
Florida	204,125	1,129	2.7	0.6
Georgia	132,644	303	0.7	0.2
Hawaii	17,551	189	0.5	1.1
Idaho	20,366	288	0.7	1.4
Illinois	185,036	277	0.7	0.1
Indiana	87,699	142	0.3	0.2
Iowa	38,266	226	0.5	0.6
Kansas	39,666	432	1.0	1.1
Kentucky	56,029	75	0.2	0.1
Louisiana	67,898	390	0.9	0.6
Maine	13,603	118	0.3	0.9
Maryland	74,316	237	0.6	0.3
Massachusetts	81,614	163	0.4	0.2
Michigan	136,171	680	1.6	0.5
Minnesota	67,604	1,232	3.0	1.8
Mississippi	44,075	248	0.6	0.6
Missouri	76,463	344	0.8	0.4
Montana	10,957	1,328	3.2	12.1
Nebraska	24,646	431	1.0	1.7
Nevada	30,829	433	1.0	1.4
New Hampshire	14,609	28	0.1	0.2
New Jersey	115,632	184	0.4	0.2

(continued)

(continued from previous page)

| | total | American Indian births | | |
		number	percent distribtution	share of total
New Mexico	27,223	3,433	8.2%	12.6%
New York	258,737	713	1.7	0.3
North Carolina	120,311	1,740	4.2	1.4
North Dakota	7,676	788	1.9	10.3
Ohio	155,472	324	0.8	0.2
Oklahoma	49,782	5,214	12.5	10.5
Oregon	45,804	729	1.7	1.6
Pennsylvania	146,281	384	0.9	0.3
Rhode Island	12,505	153	0.4	1.2
South Carolina	56,114	188	0.5	0.3
South Dakota	10,345	1,684	4.0	16.3
Tennessee	79,611	154	0.4	0.2
Texas	363,414	818	2.0	0.2
Utah	47,353	693	1.7	1.5
Vermont	6,500	19	0.0	0.3
Virginia	98,938	109	0.3	0.1
Washington	81,036	1,972	4.7	2.4
West Virginia	20,865	12	0.0	0.1
Wisconsin	69,326	936	2.2	1.4
Wyoming	6,253	267	0.6	4.3

Note: American Indians include Aleuts and Eskimos.
Source: National Center for Health Statistics, Births: Final Data for 2000, *National Vital Statistics Report, Vol. 50, No. 5, 2002; calculations by New Strategist*

AIDS Cases among American Indians, through June 2000

(total number of AIDS cases diagnosed, number diagnosed among American Indians, and American Indian share of total, by sex and age at diagnosis, through June 2000)

	total	American Indian	
		number	share of total
Total AIDS cases	**729,326**	**2,234**	**0.3%**
Males aged 13 or older	601,471	1,804	0.3
Females aged 13 or older	119,454	399	0.3
Children under age 13	8,401	31	0.4

Source: National Center for Health Statistics, Health United States, 2001*; calculations by New Strategist*

Leading Causes of Death among American Indians, 1999

(total number of deaths among American Indians, and number and percent of deaths accounted for by the ten leading causes of death for American Indians, 1999)

		number	percent
Total American Indian deaths		**11,312**	**100.0%**
1.	Diseases of heart	2,404	21.3
2.	Malignant neoplasms	1,836	16.2
3.	Accidents	1,324	11.7
4.	Diabetes mellitus	726	6.4
5.	Cerebrovascular diseases	545	4.8
6.	Chronic liver disease and cirrhosis	513	4.5
7.	Chronic lower respiratory diseases	406	3.6
8.	Influenza and pneumonia	315	2.8
9.	Suicide	290	2.6
10.	Homicide	252	2.2
	All other causes	2,701	23.9

Note: American Indians include Aleuts and Eskimos.
Source: National Center for Health Statistics, Health United States, 2001*; calculations by New Strategist*

American Indians: Housing

Most American Indians Living in the South Are Homeowners

Only 46 percent of households headed by American Indians owned their home in 1999, much lower than the 67 percent homeownership rate among all Americans. By region, the homeownership rate is highest for American Indians in the South, at 53 percent.

The homeownership rate reaches 57 percent for American Indian households in the suburbs of metropolitan areas. In contrast, it is only 32 percent for those in the central cities.

■ The low incomes of American Indian households makes it difficult for many to afford a home.

American Indian homeownership is highest in the South

(percent of American Indian households that own their home, by region, 1999)

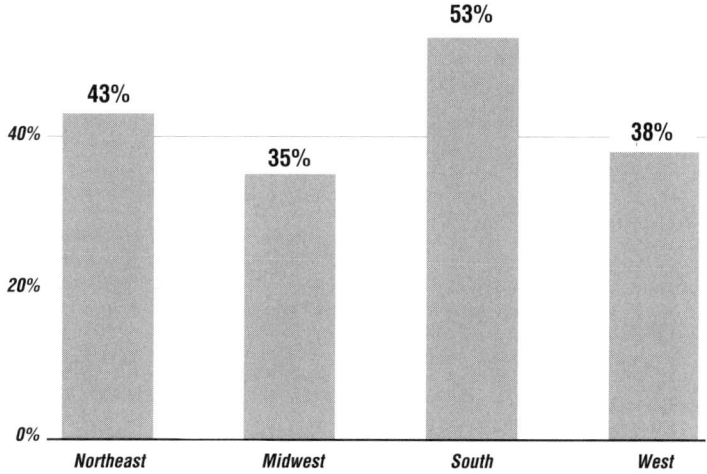

Region of Residence and Metropolitan Status of Housing Units Occupied by American Indians, 1999

(number, percent distribution, and percent of housing units occupied by American Indians, by regional, metropolitan, and homeownership status, 1999; numbers in thousands)

	total		owner			renter		
	number	percent distribution	number	percent distribution	share of total	number	percent distribution	share of total
Housing units occupied by American Indians	**666**	**100.0%**	**306**	**100.0%**	**45.9%**	**360**	**100.0%**	**54.1%**
Northeast	60	9.0	26	8.5	43.3	34	9.4	56.7
Midwest	139	20.9	49	16.0	35.3	90	25.0	64.7
South	160	24.0	85	27.8	53.1	75	20.8	46.9
West	307	46.1	146	47.7	47.6	161	44.7	52.4
In metropolitan areas	356	53.5	157	51.3	44.1	199	55.3	55.9
In central cities	188	28.2	61	19.9	32.4	127	35.3	67.6
In suburbs	168	25.2	96	31.4	57.1	72	20.0	42.9
Outside metropolitan areas	310	46.5	149	48.7	48.1	161	44.7	51.9

Source: Bureau of the Census, American Housing Survey for the United States: 1999, *Current Housing Reports, H150/99, 2000; calculations by New Strategist*

American Indians Have Below-Average Incomes

The median annual income of the nation's 872,000 American Indian households stood at $31,799 in the 1998–2000 period, much less than the $41,789 median income of all households during those years. The median income of American Indian households was greater than the $28,679 median of black households and about the same as the $31,703 median of Hispanic households.

American Indians are more likely to be poor than any other race or Hispanic origin group. Twenty-six percent of American Indians lived below the poverty level in the 1998–2000 period, much higher than the 12 percent poverty rate of all Americans. During those years, a slightly smaller 24 percent of blacks and 23 percent of Hispanics were poor.

■ American Indian households have below-average incomes because few are headed by married couples, the most affluent household type.

American Indians are more likely to be poor

(percent of people below poverty level by race and Hispanic origin, 1998–2000 three-year average)

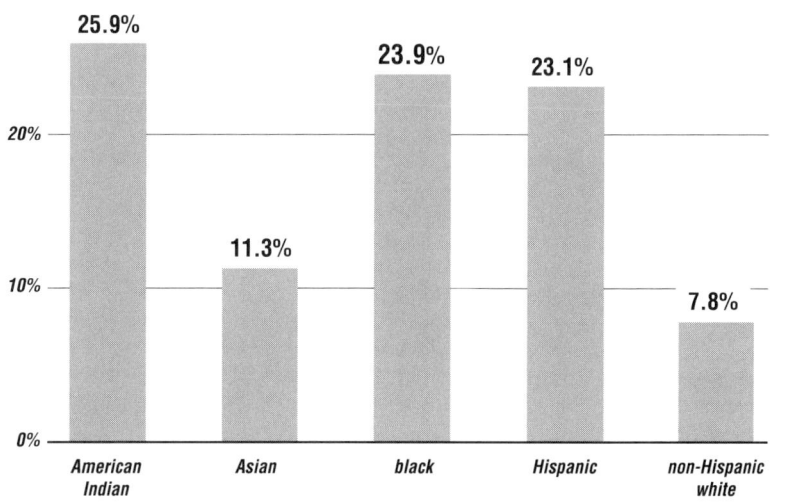

Household Income and Poverty of American Indians, 1998–2000

(number of households headed by American Indians, median household income, and number and percent of American Indians below poverty level, 1998–2000 three year average)

American Indian households	**872,000**
Median household income	$31,799
Number of poor	**701,000**
Poverty rate	25.9%

Note: American Indians include Alaska Natives.
Source: Bureau of the Census, Money Income in the United States: 2000, *Current Population Reports, P60-213, 2001; and* Poverty in the United States: 2000, *Current Population Reports, P60-214, 2001*

American Indians: Living Arrangements

Married Couples Head Fewer than Half of American Indian Households

Married couples account for only 44 percent of households headed by American Indians. Among households nationally, married couples account for a larger 52 percent share. Among American Indian couples, those with children under age 18 at home outnumber those without. Among all married couples, those without children outnumber those with children at home.

Female-headed families account for a substantial 19 percent of American Indian households, much larger than their 12 percent share of all households. Single-person households account for a smaller share of American Indian households (23 percent) than nationally (26 percent).

Twenty-eight percent of American Indians are children under age 18 living with their parents. Only 23 percent of all Americans are children living at home.

■ The large share of families headed by women without a spouse contributes to the high poverty rate among American Indians.

Women head many American Indian households

(percent distribution of American Indian households by household type, 2000 census)

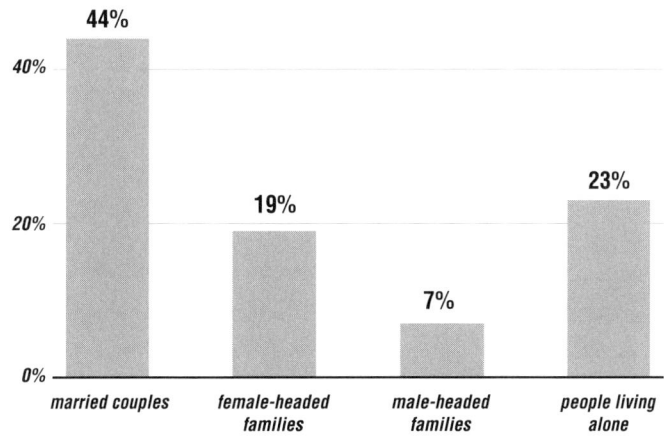

American Indian Households by Household Type, 2000 Census

(number of total households, number and percent distribution of American Indian households, and American Indian share of total, by type, 2000)

	total	American Indian households number	American Indian households percent distribution	American Indian households share of total
Total households	**105,480,101**	**1,342,217**	**100.0%**	**1.3%**
Family households	**71,787,347**	**935,579**	**69.7**	**1.3**
Married couples	54,493,232	585,062	43.6	1.1
With children under age 18	24,835,505	310,428	23.1	1.2
Without children under age 18	29,657,727	274,634	20.5	0.9
Female householder, no spouse present	12,900,103	259,164	19.3	2.0
With children under age 18	7,561,874	163,597	12.2	2.2
Without children under age 18	5,338,229	95,567	7.1	1.8
Male householder, no spouse present	4,394,012	91,353	6.8	2.1
With children under age 18	2,190,989	51,717	3.9	2.4
Without children under age 18	2,203,023	39,636	3.0	1.8
Nonfamily households	**33,692,754**	**406,638**	**30.3**	**1.2**
Living alone	27,230,075	313,915	23.4	1.2
Living with nonrelatives	6,462,679	92,723	6.9	1.4

Note: Number of American Indian households includes householders who identified themselves as American Indian alone and in combination with other races; American Indian numbers include Alaska natives.
Source: Bureau of the Census, Census 2000 PHC-T-15, Table 3, General Demographic Characteristics for the American Indian and Alaska Native Population*; calculations by New Strategist*

American Indian Living Arrangements, 2000 Census

(number and percent distribution of American Indians by living arrangement, 2000)

	number	percent
Total American Indians	**4,119,301**	**100.0%**
In households	**4,010,141**	**97.4**
Householder	1,342,217	32.6
Spouse	565,453	13.7
Child	1,486,645	36.1
Own child under age 18	1,153,943	28.0
Other relative	349,949	8.5
Under age 18	180,014	4.4
Nonrelatives	265,877	6.5
Unmarried partner	112,930	2.7
In group quarters	**109,160**	**2.6**
Institutionalized population	54,035	1.3
Noninstitutionalized population	55,125	1.3

Note: Number of American Indians includes those who identified themselves as American Indian alone and in combination with other races; American Indian numbers include Alaska natives.
Source: Bureau of the Census, Census 2000 PHC-T-15, Table 3, General Demographic Characteristics for the American Indian and Alaska Native Population; calculations by New Strategist

More than 4 Million People Are American Indian

Many American Indians are of mixed race. While 2.5 million people identify their race as only American Indian, another 1.6 million say they are American Indian and some other race—in most cases, white.

The American Indian population grew 26 percent between 1990 and 2000, based on the number of people identifying themselves as American Indian alone. The figure more than doubled during the decade when those who identify themselves as American Indian and some other race are included in the total.

The largest American Indian tribe is the Cherokee, accounting for 18 percent of the total. Only 39 percent of Cherokees say they are Cherokee alone. The Navajo are the second largest American Indian tribe, followed by Latin American Indians. One in four American Indians did not specify a tribe on the 2000 census.

Forty-three percent of American Indians live in the West, and another 31 percent in the South. California is home to 15 percent of American Indians. American Indians account for 19 percent of Alaska's population, the largest Indian share among the 50 states. In New Mexico and Oklahoma, American Indians are a substantial 11 percent of the population.

■ Much of the growth of the American Indian population during the past decade is a result of people for the first time having the opportunity to identify themselves as multiracial on the 2000 census.

More people identify themselves as American Indian

(number of people identifying themselves as American Indian or Alaska Native, 1990 and 2000; numbers in millions)

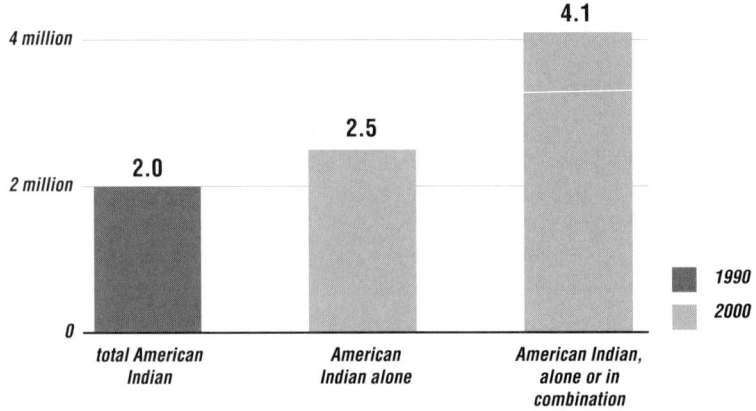

American Indians, 1990 and 2000 Censuses

(number of American Indians, 1990 and 2000; percent change in number, 1990–2000)

	1990	2000		percent change 1990–2000	
		American Indian alone	Amer. Indian, alone or in combination	American Indian alone	Amer. Indian, alone or in combination
Total American Indians	1,959,234	2,475,956	4,119,301	26.4%	110.3%

Note: American Indians include Alaska Natives.
Source: Bureau of the Census, The American Indian and Alaska Native Population: 2000, *Census 2000 Brief, C2KBR/01-15, 2002; calculations by New Strategist*

American Indians by Racial Combination, 2000 Census

(number of total people, number of American Indians by racial identification, and American Indian share of total; number and percent distribution of American Indians by racial combination, 2000)

	number	percent
Total people	**281,421,906**	**100.0%**
American Indian, alone or in combination		
with one or more other races	**4,119,301**	**1.5**
American Indian alone	2,475,956	0.9
American Indian in combination	1,643,345	0.6
American Indian, alone or in combination		
with one or more other races	**4,119,301**	**100.0**
American Indian alone	2,475,956	60.1
American Indian in combination	1,643,345	39.9
American Indian and white	1,082,683	26.3
American Indian and black	182,494	4.4
American Indian, black, and white	112,207	2.7
American Indian and Asian	52,429	1.3
All other combinations	213,532	5.2

Note: American Indians include Alaska Natives.
Source: Bureau of the Census, Overview of Race and Hispanic Origin, *Census 2000 Brief, CENBR/01-1, 2001*

American Indians by Hispanic Origin, 2000 Census

(number and percent distribution of American Indians by Hispanic origin and racial combination, 2000)

	American Indian, alone or in combination		American Indian alone		American Indian in combination	
	number	percent distribution	number	percent distribution	number	percent distribution
Total American Indians	**4,119,301**	**100.0%**	**2,475,956**	**100.0%**	**1,643,345**	**100.0%**
Hispanic	674,601	16.4	407,073	16.4	267,528	16.3
Mexican	395,074	9.6	258,119	10.4	136,955	8.3
Puerto Rican	45,891	1.1	21,643	0.9	24,248	1.5
Cuban	5,210	0.1	1,658	0.1	3,552	0.2
Other Hispanic	228,426	5.5	125,653	5.1	102,773	6.3
Non-Hispanic	3,444,700	83.6	2,068,883	83.6	1,375,817	83.7

Note: American Indians include Alaska Natives.
Source: Bureau of the Census, Census 2000 PHC-T-15, Table 3, General Demographic Characteristics for the American Indian and Alaska Native Population; *calculations by New Strategist*

American Indians and Alaska Natives by Tribe and Racial Combination, 2000 Census

(number of people identifying themselves as American Indian/Alaska Native alone, American Indian/Alaska Native in combination, and American Indian/Alaska Native and tribal grouping alone or in combination, by tribal grouping, 2000)

	American Indian/Alaska Native alone		American Indian/Alaska Native in combination		Amer. Indian/Alaska Native and tribal grouping alone or in combination
	one tribal grouping	more than one tribal grouping	one tribal grouping	more than one tribal grouping	
Total American Indians and Alaska Natives	**2,423,531**	**52,425**	**1,585,396**	**57,949**	**4,119,301**
Apache	57,060	7,917	24,947	6,909	96,833
Blackfeet	27,104	4,358	41,389	12,899	85,750
Cherokee	281,069	18,793	390,902	38,769	729,533
Cheyenne	11,191	1,365	4,655	993	18,204
Chickasaw	20,887	3,014	12,025	2,425	38,351
Chippewa	105,907	2,730	38,635	2,397	149,669
Choctaw	87,349	9,552	50,123	11,750	158,774
Colville	7,833	193	1,308	59	9,393
Comanche	10,120	1,568	6,120	1,568	19,376
Cree	2,488	724	3,577	945	7,734
Creek	40,223	5,495	21,652	3,940	71,310
Crow	9,117	574	2,812	891	13,394
Delaware	8,304	602	6,866	569	16,341
Houma	6,798	79	1,794	42	8,713
Iroquois	45,212	2,318	29,763	3,529	80,822
Kiowa	8,559	1,130	2,119	434	12,242
Latin American Indian	104,354	1,850	73,042	1,694	180,940
Lumbee	51,913	642	4,934	379	57,868
Menominee	7,883	258	1,551	148	9,840
Navajo	269,202	6,789	19,491	2,715	298,197
Osage	7,658	1,354	5,491	1,394	15,897
Ottawa	6,432	623	3,174	448	10,677
Paiute	9,705	1,163	2,315	349	13,532
Pima	8,519	999	1,741	234	11,493
Potawatomi	15,817	592	8,602	584	25,595
Pueblo	59,533	3,527	9,943	1,082	74,085
Puget Sound Salish	11,034	226	3,212	159	14,631
Seminole	12,431	2,982	9,505	2,513	27,431
Shoshone	7,739	714	3,039	534	12,026

(continued)

(continued from previous page)

	American Indian/ Alaska Native alone		American Indian/Alaska Native in combination		Amer. Indian/ Alaska Native and tribal grouping alone or in combination
	one tribal grouping	more than one tribal grouping	one tribal grouping	more than one tribal grouping	
Sioux	108,272	4,794	35,179	5,115	153,360
Tohono O'odham	17,466	714	1,748	159	20,087
Ute	7,309	715	1,944	417	10,385
Yakama	8,481	561	1,619	190	10,851
Yaqui	15,224	1,245	5,184	759	22,412
Yuman	7,295	526	1,051	104	8,976
Other specified American Indian tribes	240,521	9,468	100,346	7,323	357,658
American Indian tribe not specified	109,644	57	86,173	28	195,902
Alaska Athabascan	14,520	815	3,218	285	18,838
Aleut	11,941	832	3,850	355	16,978
Eskimo	45,919	1,418	6,919	505	54,761
Tlingit-Haida	14,825	1,059	6,047	434	22,365
Other specified Alaska Native tribes	2,552	435	841	145	3,973
Alaska Native tribe not specified	6,161	370	2,053	118	8,702
Amer. Indian/Alaska Native tribes, not specified	511,960	–	544,497	–	1,056,457

Note: Numbers may not add to total because people could identify themselves with more than one tribe; (–) means not applicable.
Source: Bureau of the Census, The American Indian and Alaska Native Population: 2000, *Census 2000 Brief, C2KBR/01-15, 2002; calculations by New Strategist*

American Indians and Alaska Natives Ranked by Tribe, 2000 Census

(number and percent distribution of people identifying themselves as American Indian/Alaska Native alone or in combination and tribal grouping alone or in combination, by tribal grouping, 2000; ranked by size)

	American Indian/Alaska Native alone or in combination	
	number	percent distribution
Total American Indians and Alaska Natives	**4,119,301**	**100.0%**
Cherokee	729,533	17.7
Navajo	298,197	7.2
Latin American Indian	180,940	4.4
Choctaw	158,774	3.9
Sioux	153,360	3.7
Chippewa	149,669	3.6
Apache	96,833	2.4
Blackfeet	85,750	2.1
Iroquois	80,822	2.0
Pueblo	74,085	1.8
Creek	71,310	1.7
Lumbee	57,868	1.4
Eskimo	54,761	1.3
Chickasaw	38,351	0.9
Seminole	27,431	0.7
Potawatomi	25,595	0.6
Yaqui	22,412	0.5
Tlingit-Haida	22,365	0.5
Tohono O'odham	20,087	0.5
Comanche	19,376	0.5
Alaska Athabascan	18,838	0.5
Cheyenne	18,204	0.4
Aleut	16,978	0.4
Delaware	16,341	0.4
Osage	15,897	0.4
Puget Sound Salish	14,631	0.4
Paiute	13,532	0.3
Crow	13,394	0.3
Kiowa	12,242	0.3
Shoshone	12,026	0.3

(continued)

(continued from previous page)

	American Indian/Alaska Native alone or in combination	
	number	percent distribution
Pima	11,493	0.3%
Yakama	10,851	0.3
Ottawa	10,677	0.3
Ute	10,385	0.3
Menominee	9,840	0.2
Colville	9,393	0.2
Yuman	8,976	0.2
Houma	8,713	0.2
Cree	7,734	0.2

Note: Numbers will not add to total because people could identify themselves with more than one tribe and tribe not specified is not shown.
Source: Bureau of the Census, The American Indian and Alaska Native Population: 2000, *Census 2000 Brief, C2KBR/01-15, 2002; calculations by New Strategist*

American Indians by Age, 2000 Census

(number of people identifying themselves as American Indian alone or in combination, American Indian alone, and American Indian in combination, and percent of American Indian alone or in combination identifying themselves as American Indian in combination, by age, 2000)

	American Indian, alone or in combination	American Indian alone	American Indian in combination	
			number	percent of American Indian alone or in combination
Total American Indians	**4,119,301**	**2,475,956**	**1,643,345**	**39.9%**
Under age 5	358,816	213,052	145,764	40.6
Aged 5 to 9	389,906	239,007	150,899	38.7
Aged 10 to 14	400,989	245,677	155,312	38.7
Aged 15 to 19	381,024	232,351	148,673	39.0
Aged 20 to 24	315,568	198,010	117,558	37.3
Aged 25 to 29	292,807	186,689	106,118	36.2
Aged 30 to 34	294,716	186,072	108,644	36.9
Aged 35 to 39	326,794	202,013	124,781	38.2
Aged 40 to 44	317,193	189,201	127,992	40.4
Aged 45 to 49	273,977	159,422	114,555	41.8
Aged 50 to 54	227,045	128,303	98,742	43.5
Aged 55 to 59	162,057	90,531	71,526	44.1
Aged 60 to 64	118,746	67,189	51,557	43.4
Aged 65 to 69	88,510	49,463	39,047	44.1
Aged 70 to 74	68,110	36,434	31,676	46.5
Aged 75 to 79	49,271	25,608	23,663	48.0
Aged 80 to 84	29,374	14,646	14,728	50.1
Aged 85 or older	24,398	12,288	12,110	49.6
Aged 18 to 24	462,801	287,785	175,016	37.8
Aged 18 or older	2,735,799	1,635,644	1,100,155	40.2
Aged 65 or older	259,663	138,439	121,224	46.7

Note: American Indians include Alaska Natives.
Source: U.S. Census Bureau, Census 2000 Summary File 1; calculations by New Strategist

American Indian Share of Total Population by Age, 2000 Census

(number of total people, number and percent distribution of those identifying themselves as American Indian alone or in combination, and American Indian alone or in combination share of total, by age, 2000)

	total	American Indian, alone or in combination		
		number	percent distribution	share of total
Total people	**281,421,906**	**4,119,301**	**100.0%**	**1.5%**
Under age 5	19,175,798	358,816	8.7	1.9
Aged 5 to 9	20,549,505	389,906	9.5	1.9
Aged 10 to 14	20,528,072	400,989	9.7	2.0
Aged 15 to 19	20,219,890	381,024	9.2	1.9
Aged 20 to 24	18,964,001	315,568	7.7	1.7
Aged 25 to 29	19,381,336	292,807	7.1	1.5
Aged 30 to 34	20,510,388	294,716	7.2	1.4
Aged 35 to 39	22,706,664	326,794	7.9	1.4
Aged 40 to 44	22,441,863	317,193	7.7	1.4
Aged 45 to 49	20,092,404	273,977	6.7	1.4
Aged 50 to 54	17,585,548	227,045	5.5	1.3
Aged 55 to 59	13,469,237	162,057	3.9	1.2
Aged 60 to 64	10,805,447	118,746	2.9	1.1
Aged 65 to 69	9,533,545	88,510	2.1	0.9
Aged 70 to 74	8,857,441	68,110	1.7	0.8
Aged 75 to 79	7,415,813	49,271	1.2	0.7
Aged 80 to 84	4,945,367	29,374	0.7	0.6
Aged 85 or older	4,239,587	24,398	0.6	0.6
Aged 18 to 24	27,143,454	462,801	11.2	1.7
Aged 18 or older	209,128,094	2,735,799	66.4	1.3
Aged 65 or older	34,991,753	259,663	6.3	0.7

Note: American Indians include Alaska Natives.
Source: U.S. Census Bureau, Census 2000 Summary File 1; calculations by New Strategist

American Indians by Age and Sex, 2000 Census

(number of American Indians by age and sex, and sex ratio by age, 2000)

	total	females	males	sex ratio
Total American Indians	**4,119,301**	**2,086,059**	**2,033,242**	**97**
Under age 5	358,816	175,987	182,829	104
Aged 5 to 9	389,906	192,862	197,044	102
Aged 10 to 14	400,989	197,575	203,414	103
Aged 15 to 19	381,024	186,801	194,223	104
Aged 20 to 24	315,568	154,003	161,565	105
Aged 25 to 29	292,807	143,966	148,841	103
Aged 30 to 34	294,716	146,840	147,876	101
Aged 35 to 39	326,794	166,455	160,339	96
Aged 40 to 44	317,193	164,338	152,855	93
Aged 45 to 49	273,977	142,422	131,555	92
Aged 50 to 54	227,045	117,951	109,094	92
Aged 55 to 59	162,057	84,433	77,624	92
Aged 60 to 64	118,746	61,987	56,759	92
Aged 65 to 69	88,510	47,688	40,822	86
Aged 70 to 74	68,110	38,091	30,019	79
Aged 75 to 79	49,271	29,191	20,080	69
Aged 80 to 84	29,374	18,732	10,642	57
Aged 85 or older	24,398	16,737	7,661	46
Aged 18 to 24	462,801	225,877	236,924	105
Aged 18 or older	2,735,799	1,404,708	1,331,091	95
Aged 65 or older	259,663	150,439	109,224	73

Note: American Indians include those who identified themselves as American Indian alone and those who identified themselves as American Indian in combination with one or more other races; American Indians include Alaska natives; the sex ratio is the number of males per 100 females.
Source: U.S. Census Bureau, Census 2000 Summary File 1; calculations by New Strategist

American Indians by Region, 1990 and 2000 Censuses

(number of American Indians by region, 1990 and 2000; percent change in number identifying themselves as American Indian alone and as American Indian alone or in combination, 1990–2000)

		2000		percent change 1990–2000	
	1990	American Indian alone	Amer. Indian, alone or in combination	American Indian alone	Amer. Indian, alone or in combination
Total Amer. Indians	**1,959,234**	**2,475,956**	**4,119,301**	**26.4%**	**110.3%**
Northeast	125,148	162,558	374,035	29.9	198.9
Midwest	337,899	399,490	714,792	18.2	111.5
South	562,731	725,919	1,259,230	29.0	123.8
West	933,456	1,187,989	1,771,244	27.3	89.8

Note: American Indians include Alaska Natives.
Source: Bureau of the Census, The American Indian and Alaska Native Population: 2000, *Census 2000 Brief, C2KBR/01-15, 2002; calculations by New Strategist*

American Indians by Region and Division, 2000 Census

(number of total people, number and percent distribution of American Indians, and American Indian share of total, by region and division, 2000)

	total	American Indians number	percent distribution	share of total
Total population	**281,421,906**	**4,119,301**	**100.0%**	**1.5%**
Northeast	**53,594,378**	**374,035**	**9.1**	**0.7**
New England	13,922,517	100,700	2.4	0.7
Middle Atlantic	39,671,861	273,335	6.6	0.7
Midwest	**64,392,776**	**714,792**	**17.4**	**1.1**
East North Central	45,155,037	382,297	9.3	0.8
West North Central	19,237,739	332,495	8.1	1.7
South	**100,236,820**	**1,259,230**	**30.6**	**1.3**
South Atlantic	51,769,160	444,058	10.8	0.9
East South Central	17,022,810	127,744	3.1	0.8
West South Central	31,444,850	687,428	16.7	2.2
West	**63,197,932**	**1,771,244**	**43.0**	**2.8**
Mountain	18,172,295	754,952	18.3	4.2
Pacific	45,025,637	1,016,292	24.7	2.3

Note: American Indians include those who identified themselves as American Indian alone and those who identified themselves as American Indian in combination with one or more other races; American Indians include Alaska Natives.
Source: Bureau of the Census, Profiles of General Demographic Characteristics, *2000 Census of Population and Housing, 2001; calculations by New Strategist*

American Indians by State, 1990 and 2000 Censuses

(number of American Indians by state, 1990 and 2000; percent change in number identifying themselves as American Indian alone and as American Indian alone or in combination, 1990–2000)

	1990	2000 American Indian alone	2000 Amer. Indian, alone or in combination	percent change 1990–2000 American Indian alone	percent change 1990–2000 Amer. Indian, alone or in combination
Total Amer. Indians	**1,959,234**	**2,475,956**	**4,119,301**	**26.4%**	**110.3%**
Alabama	16,506	22,430	44,449	35.9	169.3
Alaska	85,698	98,043	119,241	14.4	39.1
Arizona	203,527	255,879	292,552	25.7	43.7
Arkansas	12,773	17,808	37,002	39.4	189.7
California	242,164	333,346	627,562	37.7	159.1
Colorado	27,776	44,241	79,689	59.3	186.9
Connecticut	6,654	9,639	24,488	44.9	268.0
Delaware	2,019	2,731	6,069	35.3	200.6
District of Columbia	1,466	1,713	4,775	16.8	225.7
Florida	36,335	53,541	117,880	47.4	224.4
Georgia	13,348	21,737	53,197	62.8	298.5
Hawaii	5,099	3,535	24,882	−30.7	388.0
Idaho	13,780	17,645	27,237	28.0	97.7
Illinois	21,836	31,006	73,161	42.0	235.0
Indiana	12,720	15,815	39,263	24.3	208.7
Iowa	7,349	8,989	18,246	22.3	148.3
Kansas	21,965	24,936	47,363	13.5	115.6
Kentucky	5,769	8,616	24,552	49.3	325.6
Louisiana	18,541	25,477	42,878	37.4	131.3
Maine	5,998	7,098	13,156	18.3	119.3
Maryland	12,972	15,423	39,437	18.9	204.0
Massachusetts	12,241	15,015	38,050	22.7	210.8
Michigan	55,638	58,479	124,412	5.1	123.6
Minnesota	49,909	54,967	81,074	10.1	62.4
Mississippi	8,525	11,652	19,555	36.7	129.4
Missouri	19,835	25,076	60,099	26.4	203.0
Montana	47,679	56,068	66,320	17.6	39.1
Nebraska	12,410	14,896	22,204	20.0	78.9
Nevada	19,637	26,420	42,222	34.5	115.0
New Hampshire	2,134	2,964	7,885	38.9	269.5

(continued)

(continued from previous page)

	1990	2000 American Indian alone	2000 Amer. Indian, alone or in combination	percent change 1990–2000 American Indian alone	percent change 1990–2000 Amer. Indian, alone or in combination
New Jersey	14,970	19,492	49,104	30.2%	228.0%
New Mexico	134,355	173,483	191,475	29.1	42.5
New York	62,651	82,461	171,581	31.6	173.9
North Carolina	80,155	99,551	131,736	24.2	64.4
North Dakota	25,917	31,329	35,228	20.9	35.9
Ohio	20,358	24,486	76,075	20.3	273.7
Oklahoma	252,420	273,230	391,949	8.2	55.3
Oregon	38,496	45,211	85,667	17.4	122.5
Pennsylvania	14,733	18,348	52,650	24.5	257.4
Rhode Island	4,071	5,121	10,725	25.8	163.4
South Carolina	8,246	13,718	27,456	66.4	233.0
South Dakota	50,575	62,283	68,281	23.1	35.0
Tennessee	10,039	15,152	39,188	50.9	290.4
Texas	65,877	118,362	215,599	79.7	227.3
Utah	24,283	29,684	40,445	22.2	66.6
Vermont	1,696	2,420	6,396	42.7	277.1
Virginia	15,282	21,172	52,864	38.5	245.9
Washington	81,483	93,301	158,940	14.5	95.1
West Virginia	2,458	3,606	10,644	46.7	333.0
Wisconsin	39,387	47,228	69,386	19.9	76.2
Wyoming	9,479	11,133	15,012	17.4	58.4

Note: American Indians include Alaska Natives.
Source: Bureau of the Census, The American Indian American Population: 2000, *Census 2000 Brief, C2KBR/ 01-15, 2002; calculations by New Strategist*

American Indian Share of Total Population by State, 2000 Census

(number of total people, number and percent distribution of American Indians, and American Indian share of total, by state, 2000)

	total	American Indians number	American Indians percent distribution	American Indians share of total
Total population	**281,421,906**	**4,119,301**	**100.0%**	**1.5%**
Alabama	4,447,100	44,449	1.1	1.0
Alaska	626,932	119,241	2.9	19.0
Arizona	5,130,632	292,552	7.1	5.7
Arkansas	2,673,400	37,002	0.9	1.4
California	33,871,648	627,562	15.2	1.9
Colorado	4,301,261	79,689	1.9	1.9
Connecticut	3,405,565	24,488	0.6	0.7
Delaware	783,600	6,069	0.1	0.8
District of Columbia	572,059	4,775	0.1	0.8
Florida	15,982,378	117,880	2.9	0.7
Georgia	8,186,453	53,197	1.3	0.6
Hawaii	1,211,537	24,882	0.6	2.1
Idaho	1,293,953	27,237	0.7	2.1
Illinois	12,419,293	73,161	1.8	0.6
Indiana	6,080,485	39,263	1.0	0.6
Iowa	2,926,324	18,246	0.4	0.6
Kansas	2,688,418	47,363	1.1	1.8
Kentucky	4,041,769	24,552	0.6	0.6
Louisiana	4,468,976	42,878	1.0	1.0
Maine	1,274,923	13,156	0.3	1.0
Maryland	5,296,486	39,437	1.0	0.7
Massachusetts	6,349,097	38,050	0.9	0.6
Michigan	9,938,444	124,412	3.0	1.3
Minnesota	4,919,479	81,074	2.0	1.6
Mississippi	2,844,658	19,555	0.5	0.7
Missouri	5,595,211	60,099	1.5	1.1
Montana	902,195	66,320	1.6	7.4
Nebraska	1,711,263	22,204	0.5	1.3
Nevada	1,998,257	42,222	1.0	2.1
New Hampshire	1,235,786	7,885	0.2	0.6
New Jersey	8,414,350	49,104	1.2	0.6

(continued)

(continued from previous page)

| | total | American Indians | | |
		number	percent distribution	share of total
New Mexico	1,819,046	191,475	4.6%	10.5%
New York	18,976,457	171,581	4.2	0.9
North Carolina	8,049,313	131,736	3.2	1.6
North Dakota	642,200	35,228	0.9	5.5
Ohio	11,353,140	76,075	1.8	0.7
Oklahoma	3,450,654	391,949	9.5	11.4
Oregon	3,421,399	85,667	2.1	2.5
Pennsylvania	12,281,054	52,650	1.3	0.4
Rhode Island	1,048,319	10,725	0.3	1.0
South Carolina	4,012,012	27,456	0.7	0.7
South Dakota	754,844	68,281	1.7	9.0
Tennessee	5,689,283	39,188	1.0	0.7
Texas	20,851,820	215,599	5.2	1.0
Utah	2,233,169	40,445	1.0	1.8
Vermont	608,827	6,396	0.2	1.1
Virginia	7,078,515	52,864	1.3	0.7
Washington	5,894,121	158,940	3.9	2.7
West Virginia	1,808,344	10,644	0.3	0.6
Wisconsin	5,363,675	69,386	1.7	1.3
Wyoming	493,782	15,012	0.4	3.0

Note: American Indians include those who identified themselves as American Indian alone and those who identified themselves as American Indian in combination with one or more other races; American Indians include Alaska Natives.
Source: Bureau of the Census, Census 2000 Redistricting Data, *P.L. 94-171; calculations by New Strategist*

American Indians in Combination by State, 2000 Census

(number of American Indians identifying themselves as American Indian alone or in combination, number identifying themselves as American Indian in combination, and American Indian in combination share of American Indian alone or in combination, by state, 2000)

	American Indian, alone or in combination	American Indian in combination	
		number	percent of American Indian, alone or in combination
Total American Indians	**4,119,301**	**1,643,345**	**39.9%**
Alabama	44,449	22,019	49.5
Alaska	119,241	21,198	17.8
Arizona	292,552	36,673	12.5
Arkansas	37,002	19,194	51.9
California	627,562	294,216	46.9
Colorado	79,689	35,448	44.5
Connecticut	24,488	14,849	60.6
Delaware	6,069	3,338	55.0
District of Columbia	4,775	3,062	64.1
Florida	117,880	64,339	54.6
Georgia	53,197	31,460	59.1
Hawaii	24,882	21,347	85.8
Idaho	27,237	9,592	35.2
Illinois	73,161	42,155	57.6
Indiana	39,263	23,448	59.7
Iowa	18,246	9,257	50.7
Kansas	47,363	22,427	47.4
Kentucky	24,552	15,936	64.9
Louisiana	42,878	17,401	40.6
Maine	13,156	6,058	46.0
Maryland	39,437	24,014	60.9
Massachusetts	38,050	23,035	60.5
Michigan	124,412	65,933	53.0
Minnesota	81,074	26,107	32.2
Mississippi	19,555	7,903	40.4
Missouri	60,099	35,023	58.3
Montana	66,320	10,252	15.5
Nebraska	22,204	7,308	32.9
Nevada	42,222	15,802	37.4

(continued)

(continued from previous page)

	American Indian, alone or in combination	American Indian in combination	
		number	percent of American Indian, alone or in combination
New Hampshire	7,885	4,921	62.4%
New Jersey	49,104	29,612	60.3
New Mexico	191,475	17,992	9.4
New York	171,581	89,120	51.9
North Carolina	131,736	32,185	24.4
North Dakota	35,228	3,899	11.1
Ohio	76,075	51,589	67.8
Oklahoma	391,949	118,719	30.3
Oregon	85,667	40,456	47.2
Pennsylvania	52,650	34,302	65.2
Rhode Island	10,725	5,604	52.3
South Carolina	27,456	13,738	50.0
South Dakota	68,281	5,998	8.8
Tennessee	39,188	24,036	61.3
Texas	215,599	97,237	45.1
Utah	40,445	10,761	26.6
Vermont	6,396	3,976	62.2
Virginia	52,864	31,692	60.0
Washington	158,940	65,639	41.3
West Virginia	10,644	7,038	66.1
Wisconsin	69,386	22,158	31.9
Wyoming	15,012	3,879	25.8

Note: American Indians include Alaska Natives.
Source: Bureau of the Census, The American Indian Population: 2000, *Census 2000 Brief, C2KBR/01-15, 2002; calculations by New Strategist*

American Indians by Metropolitan Area, 2000 Census

(number of total people, number of American Indians, and American Indian share of total in the 100 largest metropolitan areas, 2000)

	total population	American Indian number	American Indian share of total
1. New York–Northern New Jersey–Long Island, NY–NJ–CT–PA CMSA	21,199,865	161,724	0.8%
• Bergen–Passaic, NJ PMSA	1,373,167	7,506	0.5
• Bridgeport, CT PMSA	459,479	2,667	0.6
• Danbury, CT PMSA	217,980	1,031	0.5
• Dutchess County, NY PMSA	280,150	1,850	0.7
• Jersey City, NJ PMSA	608,975	5,140	0.8
• Middlesex–Somerset–Hunterdon, NJ PMSA	1,169,641	5,845	0.5
• Monmouth–Ocean, NJ PMSA	1,126,217	5,016	0.4
• Nassau–Suffolk, NY PMSA	2,753,913	14,832	0.5
• New Haven–Meriden, CT PMSA	542,149	3,860	0.7
• New York, NY PMSA	9,314,235	95,093	1.0
• Newark, NJ PMSA	2,032,989	10,695	0.5
• Newburgh, NY–PA PMSA	387,669	3,245	0.8
• Stamford–Norwalk, CT PMSA	353,556	1,418	0.4
• Trenton, NJ PMSA	350,761	1,895	0.5
• Waterbury, CT PMSA	228,984	1,631	0.7
2. Los Angeles–Riverside–Orange County, CA CMSA	16,373,645	258,989	1.6
• Los Angeles–Long Beach, CA PMSA	9,519,338	138,696	1.5
• Orange County, CA PMSA	2,846,289	37,584	1.3
• Riverside–San Bernardino, CA PMSA	3,254,821	69,439	2.1
• Ventura, CA PMSA	753,197	13,270	1.8
3. Chicago–Gary–Kenosha, IL–IN–WI CMSA	9,157,540	55,705	0.6
• Chicago, IL PMSA	8,272,768	49,473	0.6
• Gary, IN PMSA	631,362	4,332	0.7
• Kankakee, IL PMSA	103,833	586	0.6
• Kenosha, WI PMSA	149,577	1,314	0.9
4. Washington–Baltimore, DC–MD–VA–WV CMSA	7,608,070	58,385	0.8
• Baltimore, MD PMSA	2,552,994	17,441	0.7
• Hagerstown, MD PMSA	131,923	633	0.5
• Washington, DC–MD–VA–WV PMSA	4,923,153	40,311	0.8
5. San Francisco–Oakland–San Jose, CA CMSA	7,039,362	106,413	1.5
• Oakland, CA PMSA	2,392,557	38,103	1.6

(continued)

	population	American Indian total number	share of total
• San Francisco, CA PMSA	1,731,183	19,159	1.1%
• San Jose, CA PMSA	1,682,585	22,648	1.3
• Santa Cruz–Watsonville, CA PMSA	255,602	5,296	2.1
• Santa Rosa, CA PMSA	458,614	11,038	2.4
• Vallejo–Fairfield–Napa, CA PMSA	518,821	10,169	2.0
6. Philadelphia–Wilmington–Atlantic City, PA–NJ–DE–MD CMSA	6,188,463	36,306	0.6
• Atlantic–Cape May, NJ PMSA	354,878	2,437	0.7
• Philadelphia, PA–NJ PMSA	5,100,931	27,760	0.5
• Vineland–Millville–Bridgeton, NJ PMSA	146,438	2,546	1.7
• Wilmington–Newark, DE–MD PMSA	586,216	3,563	0.6
7. Boston–Worcester–Lawrence, MA– NH–ME–CT CMSA	5,819,100	32,729	0.6
• Boston, MA–NH PMSA	3,406,829	17,945	0.5
• Brockton, MA PMSA	255,459	1,624	0.6
• Fitchburg–Leominster, MA PMSA	142,284	918	0.6
• Lawrence, MA–NH PMSA	396,230	2,269	0.6
• Lowell, MA–NH PMSA	301,686	1,395	0.5
• Manchester, NH PMSA	198,378	1,206	0.6
• Nashua, NH PMSA	190,949	988	0.5
• New Bedford, MA PMSA	175,198	1,670	1.0
• Portsmouth–Rochester, NH–ME PMSA	240,698	1,333	0.6
• Worcester, MA–CT PMSA	511,389	3,381	0.7
8. Detroit–Ann Arbor–Flint, MI CMSA	5,456,428	52,426	1.0
• Ann Arbor, MI PMSA	578,736	5,727	1.0
• Detroit, MI PMSA	4,441,551	39,829	0.9
• Flint, MI PMSA	436,141	6,870	1.6
9. Dallas–Fort Worth, TX CMSA	5,221,801	57,020	1.1
• Dallas, TX PMSA	3,519,176	37,122	1.1
• Fort Worth–Arlington, TX PMSA	1,702,625	19,898	1.2
10. Houston–Galveston–Brazoria, TX CMSA	4,669,571	39,631	0.8
• Brazoria, TX PMSA	241,767	2,530	1.0
• Galveston–Texas City, TX PMSA	250,158	2,246	0.9
• Houston, TX PMSA	4,177,646	34,855	0.8
11. Atlanta, GA MSA	4,112,198	26,810	0.7
12. Miami–Fort Lauderdale, FL CMSA	3,876,380	17,675	0.5
• Fort Lauderdale, FL PMSA	1,623,018	8,140	0.5
• Miami, FL PMSA	2,253,362	9,535	0.4
13. Seattle–Tacoma–Bremerton, WA CMSA	3,554,760	81,958	2.3

(continued)

(continued from previous page)

	population	American Indian total number	American Indian share of total
• Bremerton, WA PMSA	231,969	7,348	3.2%
• Olympia, WA PMSA	207,355	5,817	2.8
• Seattle–Bellevue–Everett, WA PMSA	2,414,616	48,874	2.0
• Tacoma, WA PMSA	700,820	19,919	2.8
14. Phoenix–Mesa, AZ MSA	3,251,876	91,520	2.8
15. Minneapolis–St. Paul, MN–WI MSA	2,968,806	37,986	1.3
16. Cleveland–Akron, OH CMSA	2,945,831	18,146	0.6
• Akron, OH PMSA	694,960	4,594	0.7
• Cleveland–Lorain–Elyria, OH PMSA	2,250,871	13,552	0.6
17. San Diego, CA MSA	2,813,833	46,177	1.6
18. St. Louis, MO–IL MSA	2,603,607	16,341	0.6
19. Denver–Boulder–Greeley, CO CMSA	2,581,506	42,423	1.6
• Boulder–Longmont, CO PMSA	291,288	3,451	1.2
• Denver, CO PMSA	2,109,282	36,061	1.7
• Greeley, CO PMSA	180,936	2,911	1.6
20. Tampa–St. Petersburg–Clearwater, FL MSA	2,395,997	19,265	0.8
21. Pittsburgh, PA MSA	2,358,695	8,855	0.4
22. Portland–Salem, OR–WA CMSA	2,265,223	45,246	2.0
• Portland–Vancouver, OR–WA PMSA	1,918,009	35,789	1.9
• Salem, OR PMSA	347,214	9,457	2.7
23. Cincinnati–Hamilton, OH–KY– IN CMSA	1,979,202	11,236	0.6
• Cincinnati, OH–KY–IN PMSA	1,646,395	9,240	0.6
• Hamilton–Middletown, OH PMSA	332,807	1,996	0.6
24. Sacramento–Yolo, CA CMSA	1,796,857	42,520	2.4
• Sacramento, CA PMSA	1,628,197	38,768	2.4
• Yolo, CA PMSA	168,660	3,752	2.2
25. Kansas City, MO–KS MSA	1,776,062	20,635	1.2
26. Milwaukee–Racine, WI CMSA	1,689,572	16,010	0.9
• Milwaukee–Waukesha, WI PMSA	1,500,741	14,562	1.0
• Racine, WI PMSA	188,831	1,448	0.8
27. Orlando, FL MSA	1,644,561	12,811	0.8
28. Indianapolis, IN MSA	1,607,486	9,659	0.6
29. San Antonio, TX MSA	1,592,383	20,404	1.3
30. Norfolk–Virginia Beach–Newport News, VA–NC MSA	1,569,541	15,769	1.0
31. Las Vegas, NV–AZ MSA	1,563,282	26,909	1.7

(continued)

(continued from previous page)

	population	American Indian	
		total number	share of total
32. Columbus, OH MSA	1,540,157	12,356	0.8%
33. Charlotte–Gastonia–Rock Hill, NC–SC MSA	1,499,293	10,861	0.7
34. New Orleans, LA MSA	1,337,726	10,195	0.8
35. Salt Lake City–Ogden, UT MSA	1,333,914	16,809	1.3
36. Greensboro–Winston-Salem–High Point, NC MSA	1,251,509	9,091	0.7
37. Austin–San Marcos, TX MSA	1,249,763	13,831	1.1
38. Nashville, TN MSA	1,231,311	8,455	0.7
39. Providence–Fall River–Warwick, RI–MA MSA	1,188,613	10,894	0.9
40. Raleigh–Durham–Chapel Hill, NC MSA	1,187,941	9,040	0.8
41. Hartford, CT MSA	1,183,110	7,643	0.6
42. Buffalo–Niagara Falls, NY MSA	1,170,111	12,017	1.0
43. Memphis, TN–AR–MS MSA	1,135,614	5,906	0.5
44. West Palm Beach–Boca Raton, FL MSA	1,131,184	5,627	0.5
45. Jacksonville, FL MSA	1,100,491	8,754	0.8
46. Rochester, NY MSA	1,098,201	8,001	0.7
47. Grand Rapids–Muskegon–Holland, MI MSA	1,088,514	12,234	1.1
48. Oklahoma City, OK MSA	1,083,346	71,926	6.6
49. Louisville, KY–IN MSA	1,025,598	6,550	0.6
50. Richmond–Petersburg, VA MSA	996,512	7,681	0.8
51. Greenville–Spartanburg–Anderson, SC MSA	962,441	5,017	0.5
52. Dayton–Springfield, OH MSA	950,558	7,118	0.7
53. Fresno, CA MSA	922,516	25,418	2.8
54. Birmingham, AL MSA	921,106	5,610	0.6
55. Honolulu, HI MSA	876,156	15,921	1.8
56. Albany–Schenectady–Troy, NY MSA	875,583	5,323	0.6
57. Tucson, AZ MSA	843,746	33,910	4.0
58. Tulsa, OK MSA	803,235	86,118	10.7
59. Syracuse, NY MSA	732,117	9,142	1.2
60. Omaha, NE–IA MSA	716,998	7,116	1.0
61. Albuquerque, NM MSA	712,738	47,280	6.6
62. Knoxville, TN MSA	687,249	5,368	0.8
63. El Paso, TX MSA	679,622	7,684	1.1
64. Bakersfield, CA MSA	661,645	17,399	2.6
65. Allentown–Bethlehem–Easton, PA MSA	637,958	2,696	0.4
66. Harrisburg–Lebanon–Carlisle, PA MSA	629,401	2,647	0.4
67. Scranton–Wilkes-Barre–Hazleton, PA MSA	624,776	1,689	0.3
68. Toledo, OH MSA	618,203	4,632	0.7

(continued)

(continued from previous page)

	population	American Indian total number	American Indian share of total
69. Baton Rouge, LA MSA	602,894	3,185	0.5%
70. Youngstown–Warren, OH MSA	594,746	3,343	0.6
71. Springfield, MA MSA	591,932	3,988	0.7
72. Sarasota–Bradenton, FL MSA	589,959	3,272	0.6
73. Little Rock–North Little Rock, AR MSA	583,845	5,665	1.0
74. McAllen–Edinburg–Mission, TX MSA	569,463	3,251	0.6
75. Stockton–Lodi, CA MSA	563,598	13,070	2.3
76. Charleston–North Charleston, SC MSA	549,033	4,555	0.8
77. Wichita, KS MSA	545,220	11,458	2.1
78. Mobile, AL MSA	540,258	6,187	1.1
79. Columbia, SC MSA	536,691	3,427	0.6
80. Colorado Springs, CO MSA	516,929	10,493	2.0
81. Fort Wayne, IN MSA	502,141	3,620	0.7
82. Daytona Beach, FL MSA	493,175	3,716	0.8
83. Lakeland–Winter Haven, FL MSA	483,924	3,988	0.8
84. Johnson City–Kingsport–Bristol, TN–VA MSA	480,091	2,698	0.6
85. Lexington, KY MSA	479,198	2,843	0.6
86. Augusta–Aiken, GA–SC MSA	477,441	3,644	0.8
87. Melbourne–Titusville–Palm Bay, FL MSA	476,230	4,102	0.9
88. Lancaster, PA MSA	470,658	1,881	0.4
89. Chattanooga, TN–GA MSA	465,161	3,388	0.7
90. Des Moines, IA MSA	456,022	2,729	0.6
91. Kalamazoo–Battle Creek, MI MSA	452,851	6,264	1.4
92. Lansing–East Lansing, MI MSA	447,728	5,525	1.2
93. Modesto, CA MSA	446,997	11,241	2.5
94. Fort Myers–Cape Coral, FL MSA	440,888	2,700	0.6
95. Jackson, MS MSA	440,801	1,474	0.3
96. Boise City, ID MSA	432,345	6,319	1.5
97. Madison, WI MSA	426,526	3,331	0.8
98. Spokane, WA MSA	417,939	10,212	2.4
99. Pensacola, FL MSA	412,153	7,449	1.8
100. Canton–Massillon, OH MSA	406,934	3,008	0.7

Note: American Indians include those who identified themselves as American Indian alone and those who identified themselves as American Indian in combination with one or more other races. American Indians include Alaska Natives. For definitions of CMSA, PMSA, and MSA, see glossary.
Source: Bureau of the Census, Profiles of General Demographic Characteristics, *2000 Census of Population and Housing, May 2001; calculations by New Strategist*

2

Asians

■ The Asian population in the United States numbered 12 million in 2000, up 72 percent since 1990. Despite rapid growth, only 4 percent of Americans are Asian.

■ Asians own 4 percent of all U.S. firms, including 16 percent of hotels, motels, and other lodging places.

■ Asians are much better educated than the population as a whole. Forty-four percent are college graduates compared with 26 percent of the total population.

■ Asians are relatively healthy, with lower mortality rates from heart disease and cancer than the average American. Tuberculosis is the only ailment that afflicts Asians at an above-average rate.

■ The median income of Asian households, at $55,525 in 2000, was fully 32 percent above the national average. Among full-time workers, Asian men earn 10 percent more than the average man. Asian women earn 14 percent more than the average woman.

■ Asian households are more likely to be headed by married couples than is the average household—59 versus 52 percent. Fifty-eight percent of Asian couples are dual-earners.

Note: There are no spending or wealth data available for Asians.

Asians account for 4.2 percent of the U.S. population

(percent distribution of people by race and Hispanic origin, 2000 census)

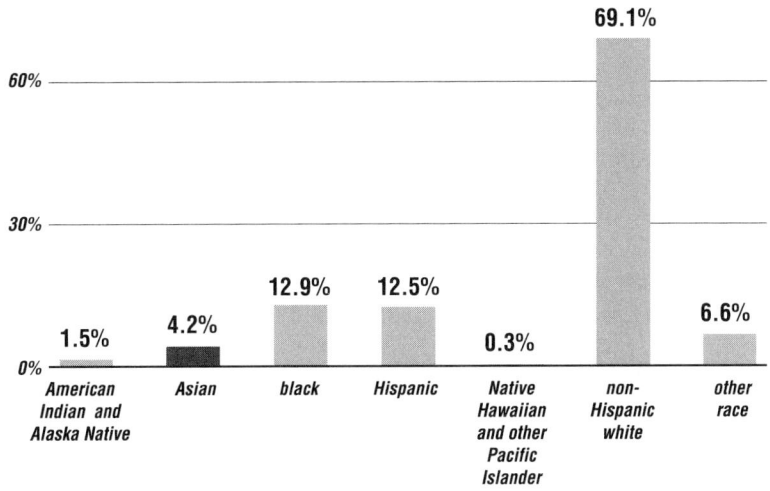

Asian Firms Are Mostly Sole Proprietorships

Asians own slightly more than 900,000 of the nation's 21 million businesses, according to the Survey of Minority-Owned Business Enterprises, a part of the 1997 Economic Censuses. The survey counts as minority-owned any firm in which the majority of owners is black, Alaska Native, American Indian, Asian, Native Hawaiian, Pacific Islander, or Hispanic. Minority ownership is determined for firms in their entirety rather than for individual locations.

Asians own 4 percent of all businesses in the nation. In the food store industry, however, they own nearly 17 percent of firms. Chinese Americans own 28 percent of all Asian-owned firms, followed by Asian Indians, who own 18 percent. The largest share of Asian firms are in the service industries—fully 44 percent. Another 21 percent are in retail trade. Seventy-one percent of Asian-owned firms are individual proprietorships, a slightly lower share than the 73 percent of all firms that are owned by one individual.

Eighty percent of Asian-owned businesses are in just 10 states, California being home to 35 percent. But Asians own the largest share of businesses in Hawaii—54 percent in 1997.

Most Asian firms have receipts below $50,000

(percent distribution of receipts for firms owned by Asians, 1997)

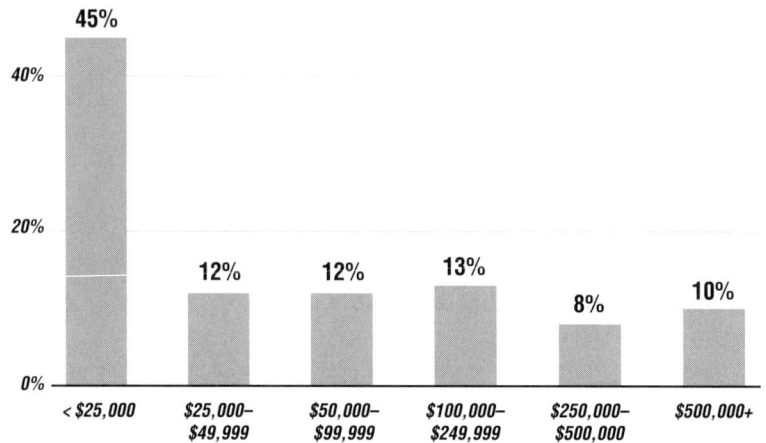

Number and Percent Distribution of Businesses Owned by Asians, 1997

(total number of firms, number and percent distribution of firms owned by Asians, and Asian share of total, by industry, 1997)

SIC code		total firms	firms owned by Asians		
			number	percent distribution	percent of total
	All industries	**20,821,935**	**912,960**	**100.0%**	**4.4%**
	Agricultural services, forestry, fishing	**496,164**	**12,988**	**1.4**	**2.6**
07	Agricultural services	412,852	7,965	0.9	1.9
08	Forestry	14,051	62	0.0	0.4
09	Fishing, hunting, and trapping	69,271	4,961	0.5	7.2
	Mineral industries	**126,809**	**660**	**0.1**	**0.5**
10	Metal mining	1,819	16	0.0	0.9
12	Coal mining	2,242	5	0.0	0.2
13	Oil and gas extraction	115,953	620	0.1	0.5
14	Nonmetallic minerals, except fuels	6,862	18	0.0	0.3
	Construction industries, subdividers, and developers	**2,333,424**	**27,711**	**3.0**	**1.2**
15	Building construction, general contractors and operative builders	472,111	5,707	0.6	1.2
16	Heavy construction contractors other than buildings	64,314	415	0.0	0.6
17	Special trade contractors	1,739,060	20,621	2.3	1.2
6552	Subdividers and developers not elsewhere classified (excl. cemeteries)	58,362	970	0.1	1.7
	Manufacturing	**688,782**	**23,242**	**2.5**	**3.4**
20	Food and kindred products	30,256	1,732	0.2	5.7
21	Tobacco products	133	0	0.0	0.0
22	Textile mill products	8,213	522	0.1	6.4
23	Apparel and other textile products	54,889	8,406	0.9	15.3
24	Lumber and wood products	106,569	384	0.0	0.4
25	Furniture and fixtures	28,712	429	0.0	1.5
26	Paper and allied products	7,186	204	0.0	2.8
27	Printing and publishing	119,936	3,409	0.4	2.8
28	Chemicals and allied products	10,941	383	0.0	3.5
29	Petroleum and coal products	1,434	23	0.0	1.6
30	Rubber and miscellaneous plastics	16,296	359	0.0	2.2

(continued)

SIC code		total firms	firms owned by Asians		
			number	percent distribution	percent of total
31	Leather and leather products	5,251	437	0.0%	8.3%
32	Stone, clay, and glass products	29,262	436	0.0	1.5
33	Primary metal industries	7,703	127	0.0	1.6
34	Fabricated metal products	63,141	897	0.1	1.4
35	Industrial machinery and equipment	85,401	1,381	0.2	1.6
36	Electronic and other electric equipment	28,324	1,676	0.2	5.9
37	Transportation equipment	13,673	191	0.0	1.4
38	Instruments and related products	12,423	397	0.0	3.2
39	Miscellaneous manufacturing industries	65,185	1,885	0.2	2.9
	Transportation, communications, and utilities	**919,570**	**37,501**	**4.1**	**4.1**
41	Local and interurban passenger transportation	116,993	17,544	1.9	15.0
42	Motor freight transportation and warehousing	544,523	9,170	1.0	1.7
44	Water transportation	15,788	146	0.0	0.9
45	Transportation by air	20,706	303	0.0	1.5
46	Pipelines, except natural gas	136	0	0.0	0.0
47	Transportation services	129,652	8,280	0.9	6.4
48	Communications	61,180	1,887	0.2	3.1
49	Electric, gas, and sanitary services	31,345	176	0.0	0.6
	Wholesale trade	**797,856**	**50,400**	**5.5**	**6.3**
50	Durable goods	489,308	28,444	3.1	5.8
51	Nondurable goods	309,731	21,962	2.4	7.1
	Retail trade	**2,889,041**	**195,691**	**21.4**	**6.8**
52	Building materials, hardware, garden supply, and mobile home dealers	85,060	1,221	0.1	1.4
53	General merchandise stores	35,027	3,274	0.4	9.3
54	Food stores	216,067	35,796	3.9	16.6
55	Automotive dealers and gasoline service stations	255,259	7,314	0.8	2.9
56	Apparel and accessory stores	127,848	12,777	1.4	10.0
57	Home furniture, furnishings, and equipment stores	153,248	5,061	0.6	3.3
58	Eating and drinking places	493,313	69,903	7.7	14.2
59	Miscellaneous retail	1,528,857	60,444	6.6	4.0

(continued)

(continued from previous page)

SIC code		total firms	firms owned by Asians		
			number	percent distribution	percent of total
	Finance, insurance, and real estate (excl. subdividers and developers)	**2,237,675**	**68,765**	**7.5%**	**3.1%**
60	Depository institutions	24,616	269	0.0	1.1
61	Nondepository credit institutions	45,905	1,307	0.1	2.8
62	Security and commodity brokers, dealers, exchanges, and services	91,446	2,821	0.3	3.1
63	Insurance carriers	9,108	81	0.0	0.9
64	Insurance agents, brokers, and services	411,902	9,985	1.1	2.4
65pt	Real estate (excl. subdividers and developers)	1,503,438	50,783	5.6	3.4
67	Holding and other investment offices, except trusts	157,652	3,549	0.4	2.3
	Service industries (excl. membership organizations, private household)	**8,891,024**	**406,010**	**44.5**	**4.6**
70	Hotels, rooming houses, camps, and other lodging places	93,380	15,153	1.7	16.2
72	Personal services	1,348,554	99,829	10.9	7.4
73	Business services	2,221,047	92,061	10.1	4.1
75	Automotive repair, services, parking	448,584	10,744	1.2	2.4
76	Miscellaneous repair services	231,371	4,935	0.5	2.1
78	Motion pictures	87,700	4,338	0.5	4.9
79	Amusement and recreation services	603,896	11,920	1.3	2.0
80	Health services	1,004,672	74,471	8.2	7.4
81	Legal services	353,147	5,634	0.6	1.6
82	Educational services	270,648	9,026	1.0	3.3
83	Social services	665,067	13,158	1.4	2.0
84	Museums, art galleries, botanical and zoological gardens	5,205	11	0.0	0.2
87	Engineering, accounting, research, management and related services	1,446,195	61,767	6.8	4.3
89	Services not elsewhere classified	119,931	3,024	0.3	2.5
	Industries not classified	**1,480,003**	**90,509**	**9.9**	**6.1**

Note: Asians include Native Hawaiian and other Pacific Islanders.
Source: Bureau of the Census, Minority- and Women-Owned Businesses, *1997 Economic Census, Internet site <www.census.gov/csd/mwb/>; calculations by New Strategist*

Characteristics of Businesses Owned by Asians, 1997

(number of firms owned by Asians by industry and selected characteristics of firm, 1997)

SIC code		total firms		firms with paid employees			
		number	sales and receipts (in 000s)	number	sales and receipts (in 000s)	employees	payroll (in 000s)
	Firms owned by Asians	912,960	$306,932,982	289,999	$278,294,345	2,203,079	$46,179,519
	Agricultural services, forestry, fishing	**12,988**	**1,140,670**	**1,927**	**791,843**	**11,359**	**226,707**
07	Agricultural services	7,965	916,667	1,816	741,182	11,105	219,098
08	Forestry	62	6,561	5	4,196	25	386
09	Fishing, hunting, and trapping	4,961	217,442	105	46,465	229	7,223
	Mineral industries	**660**	**253,329**	**87**	**229,059**	**1,007**	**33,447**
10	Metal mining	16	–	11	–	0–19	–
12	Coal mining	5	–	0	0	0	0
13	Oil and gas extraction	620	238,431	61	215,792	932	31,048
14	Nonmetallic minerals, except fuels	18	12,230	15	–	20–99	–
	Construction industries, subdividers, developers	**27,711**	**7,485,505**	**6,398**	**6,522,807**	**42,533**	**1,386,303**
15	Building construction, general contractors and operative builders	5,707	2,924,283	2,253	2,686,060	12,381	404,081
16	Heavy construction contractors other than buildings	415	865,325	240	857,267	5,035	214,592
17	Special trade contractors	20,621	3,360,043	3,752	2,821,556	24,752	757,605
6552	Subdividers and developers not elsewhere classified (excl. cemeteries)	970	335,854	155	157,924	366	10,025

(continued)

(continued from previous page)

SIC code		total firms		firms with paid employees			
		number	sales and receipts (in 000s)	number	sales and receipts (in 000s)	employees	payroll (in 000s)
	Manufacturing	**23,242**	**$28,952,417**	**10,553**	**$28,271,707**	**238,167**	**$5,513,875**
20	Food and kindred products	1,732	2,095,819	811	2,064,094	12,635	278,562
21	Tobacco products	0	0	0	0	0	0
22	Textile mill products	522	914,183	327	901,956	9,188	195,235
23	Apparel and other textile products	8,406	3,199,207	3,437	2,994,463	78,268	869,829
24	Lumber and wood products	384	301,337	159	285,968	3,081	63,841
25	Furniture and fixtures	429	380,475	217	372,424	4,471	91,983
26	Paper and allied products	204	686,333	133	684,107	4,140	96,369
27	Printing and publishing	3,409	1,446,100	1,442	1,298,549	13,882	399,100
28	Chemicals and allied products	383	1,919,757	317	1,908,496	7,132	255,334
29	Petroleum and coal products	23	29,458	11	–	100–249	–
30	Rubber and miscellaneous plastics	359	1,567,358	335	1,560,050	12,274	300,928
31	Leather and leather products	437	179,041	55	174,857	1,558	31,790
32	Stone, clay, and glass products	436	267,121	124	256,648	2,384	55,165
33	Primary metal industries	127	1,164,408	78	1,160,456	7,699	223,636
34	Fabricated metal products	897	1,797,054	542	1,780,370	13,657	422,401
35	Industrial machinery and equipment	1,381	1,801,424	744	1,756,172	13,259	457,290
36	Electronic and other electric equipment	1,676	7,891,450	976	7,798,533	33,616	1,186,593
37	Transportation equipment	191	2,109,471	185	–	10,000–24,999	–
38	Instruments and related products	397	826,264	315	805,426	6,093	201,150
39	Miscellaneous manufacturing industries	1,885	376,157	379	335,785	3,787	71,017

(continued)

(continued from previous page)

SIC code		total firms		firms with paid employees			
		number	sales and receipts (in 000s)	number	sales and receipts (in 000s)	employees	payroll (in 000s)
	Transportation, communications, utilities	**37,501**	**$5,625,483**	**5,916**	**$4,427,646**	**52,441**	**$1,220,240**
41	Local and interurban passenger transportation	17,544	942,113	509	439,747	9,934	202,935
42	Motor freight transportation and warehousing	9,170	1,210,276	1,167	922,294	12,517	285,079
44	Water transportation	146	94,044	52	92,551	496	12,191
45	Transportation by air	303	255,729	83	203,773	2,172	40,746
46	Pipelines, except natural gas	0	0	0	0	0	0
47	Transportation services	8,280	2,099,840	3,617	1,824,718	22,453	524,273
48	Communications	1,887	930,866	442	857,455	4,295	141,688
49	Electric, gas, and sanitary services	176	92,614	53	87,108	574	13,327
	Wholesale trade	**50,400**	**105,466,223**	**30,095**	**102,902,082**	**211,510**	**6,128,070**
50	Durable goods	28,444	64,884,426	17,384	63,187,577	112,795	3,411,960
51	Nondurable goods	21,962	40,581,797	12,718	39,714,505	98,714	2,716,110
	Retail trade	**195,691**	**67,895,241**	**106,264**	**62,467,158**	**644,644**	**7,497,710**
52	Building materials, hardware, garden supply, and mobile home dealers	1,221	594,682	695	566,187	4,595	82,124
53	General merchandise stores	3,274	588,143	964	426,138	3,307	38,059
54	Food stores	35,796	17,246,789	20,954	15,703,430	97,646	1,310,196
55	Automotive dealers and gasoline service stations	7,314	14,213,487	5,233	14,005,949	40,021	792,374
56	Apparel and accessory stores	12,777	3,679,256	4,707	3,059,978	25,443	301,484
57	Home furniture, furnishings, and equipment stores	5,061	3,171,866	2,807	3,016,847	14,012	293,268
58	Eating and drinking places	69,903	15,803,629	53,839	15,047,576	393,391	3,684,572
59	Miscellaneous retail	60,444	12,597,390	17,161	10,641,052	66,229	995,633

(continued)

(continued from previous page)

SIC code		total firms		firms with paid employees			
		number	sales and receipts (in 000s)	number	sales and receipts (in 000s)	employees	payroll (in 000s)
	Finance, insurance, and real estate (excl. subdividers and developers)	**68,765**	**$11,398,069**	**9,429**	**$7,585,054**	**42,243**	**$1,185,688**
60	Depository institutions	269	1,171,533	242	1,169,650	4,289	154,864
61	Nondepository credit institutions	1,307	406,317	591	–	2,500-4,999	–
62	Security and commodity brokers, dealers, exchanges, and services	2,821	1,341,497	569	948,338	4,046	289,136
63	Insurance carriers	81	776,563	68	–	1,000-2,499	–
64	Insurance agents, brokers, and services	9,985	879,685	1,132	535,541	4,244	137,691
65pt	Real estate (excluding subdividers and developers)	50,783	5,908,986	6,505	3,131,977	21,208	350,553
67	Holding and other investment offices, except trusts	3,549	913,488	353	679,036	2,955	73,777
	Service industries (excl. membership organizations and private household)	**406,010**	**67,762,462**	**107,910**	**57,153,191**	**896,731**	**21,719,605**
70	Hotels, rooming houses, camps, and other lodging places	15,153	7,232,831	10,331	6,780,236	131,251	1,672,367
72	Personal services	99,829	6,421,431	18,287	4,573,774	100,620	1,271,210
73	Business services	92,061	14,731,722	16,392	11,908,831	247,582	4,916,478
75	Automotive repair, services, and parking	10,744	1,825,814	4,887	1,493,446	22,665	359,669
76	Miscellaneous repair services	4,935	506,665	1,195	369,831	4,746	112,958
78	Motion pictures	4,338	849,533	1,622	712,091	8,326	169,552
79	Amusement and recreation services	11,920	903,134	1,499	679,624	14,931	250,734
80	Health services	74,471	22,358,437	37,461	20,031,966	238,549	8,688,455

(continued)

(continued from previous page)

SIC code		total firms		firms with paid employees			
		number	sales and receipts (in 000s)	number	sales and receipts (in 000s)	employees	payroll (in 000s)
81	Legal services	5,634	$747,644	1,605	$615,187	5,423	$251,458
82	Educational services	9,026	435,262	910	259,805	6,528	104,160
83	Social services	13,158	625,020	1,761	438,929	14,303	161,956
84	Museums, art galleries, botanical and zoological gardens	11	–	11	–	100–249	–
87	Engineering, accounting, research, management and related services	61,767	10,876,133	11,685	9,103,055	99,437	3,691,228
89	Services not elsewhere classified	3,024	–	324	–	1,000–2,499	–
	Industries not classified	**90,509**	**10,953,582**	**11,937**	**7,943,797**	**62,443**	**1,267,874**

Note: Asians include Native Hawaiian and other Pacific Islanders; (–) means data not available or suppressed for purposes of confidentiality.
Source: Bureau of the Census, Minority- and Women-Owned Businesses, 1997 Economic Census, Internet site <www.census.gov/csd/mwb/>

Distribution of Asian-Owned Businesses by Asian Origin, 1997

(percent distribution of firms owned by Asians by industry and Asian origin, 1997)

SIC code		total Asian-owned firms	Asian Indian	Chinese	Filipino	Japanese	Korean	Vietnamese	other
	All industries	**100.0%**	**18.3%**	**27.7%**	**9.3%**	**9.4%**	**14.8%**	**10.7%**	**7.8%**
	Agricultural services, forestry, fishing	**100.0**	**4.5**	**8.3**	**6.4**	**31.2**	**5.1**	**31.4**	**5.7**
07	Agricultural services	100.0	6.9	10.9	9.6	43.2	7.7	10.4	5.9
08	Forestry	100.0	1.6	0.0	9.7	4.8	8.1	6.5	54.8
09	Fishing, hunting, and trapping	100.0	0.6	4.4	1.1	12.2	1.0	65.3	4.8
	Mineral industries	**100.0**	**24.5**	**19.2**	**1.7**	**24.8**	**10.6**	**0.0**	**14.1**
10	Metal mining	100.0	–	50.0	0.0	0.0	6.3	0.0	0.0
12	Coal mining	100.0	0.0	–	–	0.0	20.0	0.0	0.0
13	Oil and gas extraction	100.0	24.8	18.9	1.1	23.9	11.0	0.0	15.0
14	Nonmetallic minerals, except fuels	100.0	0.0	0.0	–	88.9	0.0	0.0	0.0
	Construction industries, subdividers, developers	**100.0**	**10.8**	**24.2**	**10.8**	**10.5**	**19.8**	**8.5**	**9.4**
15	Building construction, general contractors and operative builders	100.0	15.2	35.0	10.4	12.7	9.6	6.2	8.8
16	Heavy construction contractors other than buildings	100.0	19.5	15.2	13.5	15.7	4.1	1.4	13.7
17	Special trade contractors	100.0	9.4	21.0	11.3	9.8	22.2	9.7	9.6
6552	Subdividers and developers not elsewhere classified (excl. cemeteries)	100.0	10.4	31.6	1.8	10.1	35.4	0.7	6.8

(continued)

(continued from previous page)

SIC code	Manufacturing	total Asian-owned firms	Asian Indian	Chinese	Filipino	Japanese	Korean	Vietnamese	other
		100.0%	11.5%	28.8%	6.9%	10.0%	15.6%	17.3%	7.7%
20	Food and kindred products	100.0	11.7	39.6	7.0	12.4	11.6	4.9	10.7
21	Tobacco products								
22	Textile mill products	100.0	2.5	19.3	2.5	8.2	43.3	16.1	7.9
23	Apparel and other textile products	100.0	2.8	34.0	6.4	4.3	22.4	22.3	7.1
24	Lumber and wood products	100.0	6.0	21.6	3.1	27.1	5.5	14.6	10.4
25	Furniture and fixtures	100.0	7.9	20.5	1.6	9.3	7.9	25.6	17.0
26	Paper and allied products	100.0	–	34.8	2.9	10.3	14.7	14.7	9.8
27	Printing and publishing	100.0	18.5	26.8	13.2	9.5	11.9	11.0	6.7
28	Chemicals and allied products	100.0	49.3	24.0	4.4	7.3	5.2	2.1	7.8
29	Petroleum and coal products	100.0	–	13.0	0.0	0.0	17.4	0.0	13.0
30	Rubber and miscellaneous plastics	100.0	29.2	25.3	5.8	11.7	7.0	6.7	–
31	Leather and leather products	100.0	2.1	24.9	5.5	–	12.4	45.5	5.5
32	Stone, clay, and glass products	100.0	7.3	20.4	6.2	31.9	7.8	6.9	6.0
33	Primary metal industries	100.0	37.8	11.0	4.7	16.5	14.2	14.2	0.8
34	Fabricated metal products	100.0	25.9	21.2	7.6	17.7	9.5	10.5	6.4
35	Industrial machinery and equipment	100.0	17.2	23.7	2.7	11.2	11.2	24.3	7.2
36	Electronic and other electric equipment	100.0	23.2	22.7	5.3	11.0	9.4	19.6	7.7
37	Transportation equipment	100.0	9.4	13.1	–	32.5	4.2	24.1	11.0
38	Instruments and related products	100.0	13.4	28.7	2.8	13.4	16.1	13.4	8.6
39	Miscellaneous manufacturing industries	100.0	10.9	24.8	8.4	18.8	10.5	14.7	7.6

(continued)

(continued from previous page)

SIC code		total Asian-owned firms	Asian Indian	Chinese	Filipino	Japanese	Korean	Vietnamese	other
	Transportation, communications, utilities	**100.0%**	**28.0%**	**19.7%**	**9.7%**	**6.4%**	**9.9%**	**6.2%**	**17.7%**
41	Local and interurban passenger transportation	100.0	34.5	17.2	5.1	1.0	9.1	3.9	28.1
42	Motor freight transportation and warehousing	100.0	30.2	17.8	14.7	3.7	7.3	11.4	10.7
44	Water transportation	100.0	8.9	10.3	4.8	32.2	6.2	26.7	5.5
45	Transportation by air	100.0	26.1	15.2	6.6	17.2	10.9	0.0	12.2
46	Pipelines, except natural gas								
47	Transportation services	100.0	15.6	27.5	11.9	18.7	13.6	4.8	5.8
48	Communications	100.0	15.4	20.0	18.7	11.4	14.2	7.4	9.7
49	Electric, gas, and sanitary services	100.0	10.8	23.3	7.4	15.3	3.4	8.0	25.6
	Wholesale trade	**100.0**	**13.3**	**46.3**	**5.3**	**10.8**	**13.7**	**2.0**	**7.0**
50	Durable goods	100.0	14.8	45.7	6.6	10.9	11.2	2.0	7.2
51	Nondurable goods	100.0	11.5	47.1	3.6	10.7	17.0	2.0	6.7
	Retail trade	**100.0**	**17.1**	**30.9**	**4.8**	**7.0**	**21.9**	**8.2**	**9.1**
52	Building materials, hardware, garden supply, and mobile home dealers	100.0	13.6	29.1	3.6	29.8	12.0	4.8	5.0
53	General merchandise stores	100.0	22.8	11.9	6.7	4.8	38.8	6.3	8.1
54	Food stores	100.0	24.9	17.7	2.6	1.4	28.9	8.8	15.3
55	Automotive dealers and gasoline service stations	100.0	33.2	11.1	3.3	6.7	16.4	8.8	18.5
56	Apparel and accessory stores	100.0	10.2	15.0	2.6	4.8	49.4	11.0	6.4
57	Home furniture, furnishings, and equipment stores	100.0	9.9	32.4	7.4	10.2	12.4	19.3	7.3
58	Eating and drinking places	100.0	7.1	53.8	1.6	6.0	14.6	8.2	8.5
59	Miscellaneous retail	100.0	23.8	19.0	10.0	11.3	21.2	6.2	6.0

(continued)

(continued from previous page)

SIC code	Finance, insurance, real estate	total Asian-owned firms	Asian Indian	Chinese	Filipino	Japanese	Korean	Vietnamese	other
	(excl. subdividers and developers)	**100.0%**	**19.4%**	**40.1%**	**12.2%**	**11.8%**	**6.0%**	**4.7%**	**4.5%**
60	Depository institutions	100.0	3.0	29.0	18.2	7.4	17.8	1.9	17.8
61	Nondepository credit institutions	100.0	16.3	28.8	16.4	10.2	7.7	9.7	8.1
62	Security and commodity brokers, dealers, exchanges, services	100.0	17.4	38.3	13.5	10.1	9.6	4.2	5.1
63	Insurance carriers	100.0	7.4	25.9	9.9	32.1	8.6	6.2	8.6
64	Insurance agents, brokers, and services	100.0	15.1	32.0	20.8	13.5	8.6	5.3	4.2
65pt	Real estate (excluding subdividers and developers)	100.0	20.2	42.2	10.6	11.1	5.3	4.8	4.2
67	Holding and other investment offices, except trusts	100.0	23.2	40.1	6.9	18.9	3.3	0.9	6.1
	Service industries (excl. membership organizations and private household)	**100.0**	**19.5**	**22.2**	**11.5**	**10.1**	**14.3**	**14.0**	**6.4**
70	Hotels, rooming houses, camps, and other lodging places	100.0	75.2	8.6	3.6	1.7	4.5	0.3	5.6
72	Personal services	100.0	6.8	17.0	6.3	5.1	22.7	36.8	4.6
73	Business services	100.0	16.4	23.8	11.5	13.0	16.9	9.6	6.0
75	Automotive repair, services, and parking	100.0	13.6	15.2	8.2	10.7	20.5	19.8	9.5
76	Miscellaneous repair services	100.0	9.6	24.8	12.8	8.3	22.2	12.7	6.2
78	Motion pictures	100.0	13.1	21.6	7.2	10.4	18.6	15.2	11.7
79	Amusement and recreation services	100.0	4.8	23.8	14.1	20.0	16.0	2.4	10.3
80	Health services	100.0	32.9	19.0	20.3	7.8	7.2	5.3	6.6

(continued)

(continued from previous page)

SIC code		total Asian-owned firms	Asian Indian	Chinese	Filipino	Japanese	Korean	Vietnamese	other
81	Legal services	100.0%	9.8%	30.8%	10.2%	24.1%	9.4%	8.1%	3.5%
82	Educational services	100.0	9.6	35.5	8.6	17.2	19.9	1.8	4.7
83	Social services	100.0	16.9	22.0	18.4	–	4.9	6.4	19.0
84	Museums, art galleries, botanical and zoological gardens	100.0	81.8	9.1	0.0	0.0	9.1	0.0	0.0
87	Engineering, accounting, research, management and related services	100.0	23.3	33.3	10.6	13.9	7.4	3.4	5.6
89	Services not elsewhere classified	100.0	8.7	27.9	7.8	30.6	7.7	3.1	9.2
	Industries not classified	**100.0**	**19.2**	**32.1**	**9.4**	**6.1**	**11.2**	**8.7**	**9.6**

Note: Asians include Native Hawaiians and other Pacific Islanders; (–) means data not available or suppressed for purposes of confidentiality.
Source: Bureau of the Census, Minority- and Women-Owned Businesses, 1997 Economic Census, Internet site <www.census.gov/csd/mwb/>; calculations by New Strategist

Asian-Owned Businesses by Legal Form of Organization, Receipt Size, and Employees, 1997

(number and percent distribution of Asian-owned firms by legal form of organization, size of receipts, and number of employees, 1997)

	total	percent distribution
Total Asian-owned firms	**912,960**	**100.0%**
Legal form of organization		
C corporations	127,480	14.0
Subchapter S corporations	92,877	10.2
Individual proprietorships	648,337	71.0
Partnerships	40,854	4.5
Other	3,412	0.4
Size of receipts		
Under $5,000	151,751	16.6
$5,000 to $9,999	107,890	11.8
$10,000 to $24,999	147,311	16.1
$25,000 to $49,999	111,734	12.2
$50,000 to $99,999	110,215	12.1
$100,000 to $249,999	121,016	13.3
$250,000 to $499,999	71,182	7.8
$500,000 to $999,999	46,608	5.1
$1,000,000 or more	45,252	5.0
Number of employees		
Firms with employees	**289,999**	**100.0**
No employees*	43,658	15.1
1 to 3 employees	145,331	50.1
5 to 9 employees	53,786	18.5
10 to 19 employees	25,820	8.9
20 to 49 employees	15,344	5.3
50 to 99 employees	3,975	1.4
100 to 499 employees	1,953	0.7
500 employees or more	131	0.0

Note: Asians include Native Hawaiians and other Pacific Islanders.
* Firms that reported annual payroll but no employees on the payroll during the specified period in 1997.
Source: Bureau of the Census, Asians and Pacific Islanders, 1997 Economic Census, Survey of Minority-Owned Business Enterprises, Company Statistics Series, EC97CS-5, 2001; calculations by New Strategist

Asian-Owned Businesses by State, 1997

(number of total firms and receipts and number and percent distribution of Asian firms and receipts in the ten states with the largest number of Asian-owned firms, and Asian share of total firms and receipts, 1997)

	total firms	Asian firms			total sales and receipts (in millions)	Asian sales and receipts		
		number	percent distribution	percent of total		amount (in millions)	percent distribution	percent of total
Total firms	**20,821,934**	**912,960**	**100.0%**	**4.4%**	**$18,553,243**	**$306,933**	**100.0%**	**1.7%**
Total in top ten states	**9,861,474**	**730,138**	**80.0**	**7.4**	**8,707,996**	**246,719**	**80.4**	**2.8**
California	2,565,734	316,048	34.6	12.3	2,178,292	121,566	39.6	5.6
New York	1,509,829	123,258	13.5	8.2	1,488,913	31,611	10.3	2.1
Texas	1,525,972	60,226	6.6	3.9	1,415,536	18,849	6.1	1.3
Hawaii	93,981	50,634	5.5	53.9	55,361	14,523	4.7	26.2
New Jersey	654,227	41,432	4.5	6.3	690,008	16,734	5.5	2.4
Illinois	882,053	36,857	4.0	4.2	993,117	14,728	4.8	1.5
Florida	1,301,920	33,769	3.7	2.6	828,429	10,467	3.4	1.3
Washington	447,433	23,309	2.6	5.2	357,323	8,008	2.6	2.2
Virginia	480,122	22,441	2.5	4.7	415,093	4,439	1.4	1.1
Maryland	400,203	22,164	2.4	5.5	285,924	5,794	1.9	2.0

Note: Asians include Native Hawaiians and other Pacific Islanders.
Source: Bureau of the Census, Asians and Pacific Islanders, 1997 Economic Census, Survey of Minority-Owned Business Enterprises, Company Statistics Series, EC97CS-5, 2001; calculations by New Strategist

Asian-Owned Businesses by Metropolitan Area, 1997

(number and percent distribution of Asian-owned firms and receipts in the ten metropolitan areas with the largest number of Asian-owned firms, and metropolitan area's share of total Asian firms and receipts in state, 1997)

	total	percent distribution	percent of Asian firms in state	amount (in millions)	percent distribution	percent of Asian receipts in state
Total Asian firms/receipts	**912,960**	**100.0%**	–	**$306,933**	**100.0%**	–
Total in top metropolitan areas	**478,709**	**52.4**	–	**173,432**	**56.5**	–
Los Angeles–Long Beach, CA PMSA	114,462	12.5	36.2%	55,113	18.0%	45.3%
New York, NY PMSA	101,814	11.2	82.6	25,500	8.3	80.7
Orange County, CA PMSA	44,840	4.9	14.2	14,889	4.9	12.2
Honolulu, HI MSA	39,252	4.3	77.5	11,865	3.9	81.7
San Francisco, CA PMSA	35,247	3.9	11.2	12,456	4.1	10.2
Chicago, IL PMSA	32,733	3.6	88.8	13,244	4.3	89.9
Washington, DC–MD–VA–WV PMSA	30,784	3.4	–	7,346	2.4	–
Oakland, CA PMSA	27,524	3.0	8.7	12,720	4.1	10.5
San Jose, CA PMSA	26,477	2.9	8.4	11,485	3.7	9.4
Houston, TX PMSA	25,576	2.8	42.5	8,814	2.9	46.8

Note: Asians include Native Hawaiians and other Pacific Islanders. (–) means data not available or not applicable. For definitions of PMSA and MSA, see glossary.
Source: Bureau of the Census, Asians and Pacific Islanders, *1997 Economic Census, Survey of Minority-Owned Business Enterprises, Company Statistics Series, EC97CS-5, 2001; calculations by New Strategist*

Asians Are Far Better Educated than the Average American

Asians are much more likely to be college graduates than the population as a whole. In 2000, 44 percent of Asians aged 25 or older were college graduates versus 26 percent of the total population. Fifteen percent of Asians had an advanced degree compared with a smaller 9 percent of the total population.

Not only are Asians better educated than the average person, they are more likely to be enrolled in school. Only 44 percent of all Americans aged 20 or 21 are students, for example, versus 66 percent of Asians in the age group. Forty-five percent of Asians aged 22 to 24 are in school versus 25 percent of all Americans in the age group. Slightly more than 1 million Asians were enrolled in college in 2000.

Asians earned more than 77,000 bachelor's degrees in 1999–2000, accounting for 6 percent of all bachelor's degrees awarded that year. Asians earned more than 20 percent of first-professional degrees awarded in the fields of dentistry, optometry, and pharmacy in 1999-00.

■ The educational level of Asians is much higher than that of the average American because many are highly educated immigrants with professional jobs.

Many Asians have a college degree

(percent of total people and Asians aged 25 or older with a college degree)

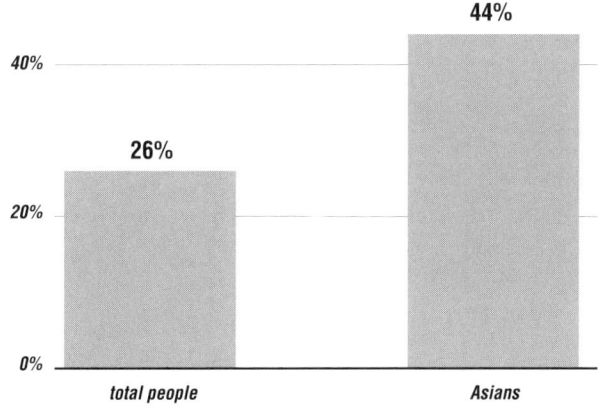

Educational Attainment of Asians by Sex, 2000

(number and percent distribution of Asians aged 25 or older by educational attainment and sex, 2000; numbers in thousands)

	total		men		women	
	number	*percent*	*number*	*percent*	*number*	*percent*
Total Asians	**6,667**	**100.0%**	**3,140**	**100.0%**	**3,527**	**100.0%**
Not a high school graduate	956	14.4	370	11.8	586	16.6
High school graduate or more	5,709	85.6	2,770	88.2	2,940	83.4
High school graduate only	1,474	22.1	641	20.4	832	23.6
Some college or associate's degree	1,306	19.6	636	20.3	671	19.0
Bachelor's degree or more	2,929	43.9	1,493	47.5	1,437	40.7
Bachelor's degree only	1,912	28.7	873	27.8	1,040	29.5
Master's degree	628	9.4	373	11.9	255	7.2
Professional degree	182	2.7	99	3.2	83	2.4
Doctoral degree	207	3.1	148	4.7	59	1.7

Source: Bureau of the Census, Educational Attainment in the United States: March 2000 (Update), *detailed tables for Current Population Report P20-536, 2000; Internet site <www.census.gov/population/socdemo/education/p20-536/tab01.txt>; calculations by New Strategist*

Educational Attainment of Asian Men by Age, 2000

(number and percent distribution of Asian men aged 25 or older by age and educational attainment, 2000; numbers in thousands)

	total	not a high school graduate	high school graduate or more	high school graduate only	some college	associate's degree	bachelor's degree or more	bachelor's degree only	master's degree	professional degree	doctoral degree
			total				total				
Total Asian men	**3,140**	**370**	**2,770**	**641**	**402**	**234**	**1,493**	**873**	**373**	**99**	**148**
Aged 25 to 29	475	38	437	61	89	25	262	181	54	17	10
Aged 30 to 34	457	31	426	96	81	40	209	108	67	18	16
Aged 35 to 39	434	45	390	83	57	32	218	127	43	11	37
Aged 40 to 44	394	42	351	65	50	22	214	120	61	12	21
Aged 45 to 49	339	34	305	83	44	23	155	102	38	3	12
Aged 50 to 54	339	32	307	70	28	39	170	99	39	12	20
Aged 55 to 59	177	15	164	44	21	13	86	41	23	16	6
Aged 60 to 64	146	23	123	47	5	14	57	29	15	7	6
Aged 65 or older	379	112	267	93	27	25	122	68	31	3	20
Aged 65 to 69	147	40	107	28	16	17	46	13	20	3	10
Aged 70 to 74	93	20	73	37	3	3	30	15	8	–	7
Aged 75 or older	139	52	88	28	8	7	45	40	2	–	3

(continued)

(continued from previous page)

	total	not a high school graduate	high school graduate or more				bachelor's degree or more				
			total	high school graduate only	some college	associate's degree	total	bachelor's degree only	master's degree	professional degree	doctoral degree
Total Asian men	**100.0%**	**11.8%**	**88.2%**	**20.4%**	**12.8%**	**7.5%**	**47.5%**	**27.8%**	**11.9%**	**3.2%**	**4.7%**
Aged 25 to 29	100.0	8.0	92.0	12.8	18.7	5.3	55.2	38.1	11.4	3.6	2.1
Aged 30 to 34	100.0	6.8	93.2	21.0	17.7	8.8	45.7	23.6	14.7	3.9	3.5
Aged 35 to 39	100.0	10.4	89.9	19.1	13.1	7.4	50.2	29.3	9.9	2.5	8.5
Aged 40 to 44	100.0	10.7	89.1	16.5	12.7	5.6	54.3	30.5	15.5	3.0	5.3
Aged 45 to 49	100.0	10.0	90.0	24.5	13.0	6.8	45.7	30.1	11.2	0.9	3.5
Aged 50 to 54	100.0	9.4	90.6	20.6	8.3	11.5	50.1	29.2	11.5	3.5	5.9
Aged 55 to 59	100.0	8.5	92.7	24.9	11.9	7.3	48.6	23.2	13.0	9.0	3.4
Aged 60 to 64	100.0	15.8	84.2	32.2	3.4	9.6	39.0	19.9	10.3	4.8	4.1
Aged 65 or older	100.0	29.6	70.4	24.5	7.1	6.6	32.2	17.9	8.2	0.8	5.3
Aged 65 to 69	100.0	27.2	72.8	19.0	10.9	11.6	31.3	8.8	13.6	2.0	6.8
Aged 70 to 74	100.0	21.5	78.5	39.8	3.2	3.2	32.3	16.1	8.6	–	7.5
Aged 75 or older	100.0	37.4	63.3	20.1	5.8	5.0	32.4	28.8	1.4	–	2.2

Note: (–) means sample is too small to make a reliable estimate.
Source: Bureau of the Census, Educational Attainment in the United States: March 2000 (Update), detailed tables for Current Population Report P20-536, 2000; Internet site <www.census.gov/population/socdemo/education/p20-536/tab01.txt>; calculations by New Strategist

Educational Attainment of Asian Women by Age, 2000

(number and percent distribution of Asian women aged 25 or older by age and educational attainment, 2000; numbers in thousands)

	total	not a high school graduate	high school graduate or more				bachelor's degree or more				
			total	high school graduate only	some college	associate's degree	total	bachelor's degree only	master's degree	professional degree	doctoral degree
Total Asian women	3,527	586	2,940	832	437	234	1,437	1,040	255	83	59
Aged 25 to 29	513	25	487	92	85	39	271	199	52	13	7
Aged 30 to 34	451	35	417	80	84	29	224	129	55	25	15
Aged 35 to 39	502	52	450	118	62	42	228	166	35	14	13
Aged 40 to 44	503	71	431	136	40	42	213	171	26	6	10
Aged 45 to 49	431	44	387	111	57	30	189	150	31	2	6
Aged 50 to 54	323	60	262	86	31	24	121	92	20	9	–
Aged 55 to 59	201	57	145	46	15	5	79	54	16	6	3
Aged 60 to 64	183	62	119	38	25	9	47	38	7	2	–
Aged 65 or older	421	181	240	126	37	13	64	41	13	7	3
Aged 65 to 69	165	55	110	66	11	0	33	24	4	3	2
Aged 70 to 74	110	53	57	26	10	10	11	9	2	–	–
Aged 75 or older	146	73	74	34	15	4	21	8	7	5	1

(continued)

(continued from previous page)

	total	not a high school graduate	high school graduate or more				bachelor's degree or more				
			total	high school graduate only	some college	associate's degree	total	bachelor's degree only	master's degree	professional degree	doctoral degree
Total Asian women	**100.0%**	**16.6%**	**83.4%**	**23.6%**	**12.4%**	**6.6%**	**40.7%**	**29.5%**	**7.2%**	**2.4%**	**1.7%**
Aged 25 to 29	100.0	4.9	94.9	17.9	16.6	7.6	52.8	38.8	10.1	2.5	1.4
Aged 30 to 34	100.0	7.8	92.5	17.7	18.6	6.4	49.7	28.6	12.2	5.5	3.3
Aged 35 to 39	100.0	10.4	89.6	23.5	12.4	8.4	45.4	33.1	7.0	2.8	2.6
Aged 40 to 44	100.0	14.1	85.7	27.0	8.0	8.3	42.3	34.0	5.2	1.2	2.0
Aged 45 to 49	100.0	10.2	89.8	25.8	13.2	7.0	43.9	34.8	7.2	0.5	1.4
Aged 50 to 54	100.0	18.6	81.1	26.6	9.6	7.4	37.5	28.5	6.2	2.8	–
Aged 55 to 59	100.0	28.4	72.1	22.9	7.5	2.5	39.3	26.9	8.0	3.0	1.5
Aged 60 to 64	100.0	33.9	65.0	20.8	13.7	4.9	25.7	20.8	3.8	1.1	–
Aged 65 or older	100.0	43.0	57.0	29.9	8.8	3.1	15.2	9.7	3.1	1.7	0.7
Aged 65 to 69	100.0	33.3	66.7	40.0	6.7	0.0	20.0	14.5	2.4	1.8	1.2
Aged 70 to 74	100.0	48.2	51.8	23.6	9.1	9.1	10.0	8.2	1.8	–	–
Aged 75 or older	100.0	50.0	50.7	23.3	10.3	2.7	14.4	5.5	4.8	3.4	0.7

Note: (–) means sample is too small to make a reliable estimate.
Source: Bureau of the Census, Educational Attainment in the United States: March 2000 (Update), detailed tables for Current Population Report P20-536, 2000: Internet site <www.census.gov/population/socdemo/education/p20-536/tab01.txt>; calculations by New Strategist

Asian High School and College Graduates by Age and Sex, 2000

(percent of Asians aged 25 or older who are high school or college graduates, by age and sex, 2000)

	total	men	women
High school graduates			
Total Asians	**85.6%**	**88.2%**	**83.4%**
Aged 25 to 29	93.5	91.9	95.0
Aged 30 to 34	92.8	93.4	92.3
Aged 35 to 39	89.7	89.7	89.7
Aged 40 to 44	87.3	89.4	85.7
Aged 45 to 49	89.9	89.7	90.0
Aged 50 to 54	86.2	90.8	81.5
Aged 55 to 59	81.3	92.1	71.8
Aged 60 to 64	74.1	84.4	66.0
Aged 65 or older	63.4	70.5	57.0
Aged 65 to 69	69.5	72.6	66.8
Aged 70 to 74	63.7	79.1	50.7
Aged 75 or older	56.5	62.6	50.8
College graduates			
Total Asians	**43.9**	**47.6**	**40.7**
Aged 25 to 29	53.9	55.3	52.7
Aged 30 to 34	47.6	45.7	49.7
Aged 35 to 39	47.6	50.2	45.4
Aged 40 to 44	47.7	54.4	42.4
Aged 45 to 49	44.7	45.6	43.9
Aged 50 to 54	44.0	50.2	37.5
Aged 55 to 59	43.5	48.5	39.1
Aged 60 to 64	31.8	39.1	26.0
Aged 65 or older	23.3	32.2	15.3
Aged 65 to 69	25.4	31.5	20.0
Aged 70 to 74	20.2	32.9	9.6
Aged 75 or older	23.2	32.4	14.4

Source: Bureau of the Census, Educational Attainment in the United States: March 2000 (Update), *detailed tables for Current Population Report P20-536, 2000; Internet site <www.census.gov/population/socdemo/education/p20-536/tab01a.txt>*

Asian High School and College Graduates by Age and Region, 2000

(percent of Asians aged 25 or older who are high school or college graduates, by age and region, 2000)

	Northeast	Midwest	South	West
High school graduates				
Total Asians	**83.4%**	**84.3%**	**84.9%**	**86.9%**
Aged 25 to 34	89.9	92.6	88.5	96.7
Aged 35 to 44	84.8	92.8	85.8	90.1
Aged 45 to 54	82.2	85.2	88.9	90.5
Aged 55 to 64	88.9	56.5	77.9	79.1
Aged 65 or older	62.8	53.0	66.7	64.1
College graduates				
Total Asians	**49.9**	**52.2**	**41.6**	**41.1**
Aged 25 to 34	55.6	55.0	48.9	48.9
Aged 35 to 44	48.9	63.1	41.3	46.2
Aged 45 to 54	48.7	45.2	36.9	45.5
Aged 55 to 64	63.3	44.9	47.8	29.2
Aged 65 or older	31.0	28.8	21.9	20.8

Source: Bureau of the Census, Educational Attainment in the United States: March 2000 (Update), *Detailed tables for Current Population Reports, P20-536, 2000; Internet site <www.census.gov/population/socdemo/education/p20-536/tab12.txt>; calculations by New Strategist*

Asian High School and College Graduates by State, 2000

(percent of Asians aged 25 or older who are high school or college graduates, for the 25 largest states, 2000)

	high school graduate or more	college graduate
Total Asians	**85.6%**	**43.9%**
Alabama	–	–
Arizona	–	–
California	86.8	44.2
Colorado	–	–
Florida	92.4	39.3
Georgia	–	–
Illinois	88.0	63.9
Indiana	–	–
Kentucky	–	–
Louisiana	–	–
Maryland	92.9	52.5
Massachusetts	76.8	50.7
Michigan	89.4	63.3
Minnesota	80.4	45.0
Missouri	–	–
New Jersey	84.1	50.7
New York	84.2	48.6
North Carolina	–	–
Ohio	78.7	37.8
Pennsylvania	89.2	54.3
Tennessee	–	–
Texas	70.1	33.7
Virginia	96.5	57.9
Washington	86.8	45.8
Wisconsin	–	–

Note: (–) means sample is too small to make a reliable estimate.
Source: Bureau of the Census, Educational Attainment in the United States: March 2000 (Update), *Detailed tables for Current Population Reports, P20-536, 2000; Internet site <www.census.gov/population/socdemo/ education/p20-536/tab14.txt>*

School Enrollment of Asians by Age and Sex, 2000

(number and percent of Asians aged 3 or older enrolled in school, by age and sex, October 2000; numbers in thousands)

	total		men		women	
	number	*percent*	*number*	*percent*	*number*	*percent*
Total Asians	**3,442**	**32.6%**	**1,774**	**35.0%**	**1,668**	**30.4%**
Aged 3 to 4	224	56.0	110	56.0	114	55.9
Aged 5 to 6	366	97.6	211	96.8	155	98.6
Aged 7 to 9	484	97.8	242	99.5	241	96.2
Aged 10 to 13	638	97.6	324	97.0	314	98.2
Aged 14 to 15	335	99.6	204	99.3	131	100.0
Aged 16 to 17	292	98.4	153	97.8	139	99.1
Aged 18 to 19	257	78.8	122	75.5	135	82.0
Aged 20 to 21	206	66.2	111	67.2	95	65.1
Aged 22 to 24	229	45.3	120	49.1	109	41.7
Aged 25 to 29	188	18.7	66	16.0	122	20.6
Aged 30 to 34	86	8.9	51	10.2	36	7.5
Aged 35 to 44	98	5.1	49	5.4	49	4.9
Aged 45 to 54	29	2.1	11	1.7	18	2.4
Aged 55 or older	8	0.5	–	–	8	0.9

Note: (–) means sample is too small to make a reliable estimate.
Source: Bureau of the Census, Current Population Survey, Internet site <www.census.gov/population/socdemo/school/ppl-148/tab01.txt>

Asian Families with Children in College, 2000

(total number of Asian families, number with children aged 18 to 24, and number and percent with children aged 18 to 24 attending college full-time as of October 2000, by household income in 1999; numbers in thousands)

	total	with children aged 18–24	with one or more children attending college full-time		
			number	percent of total families	percent of families with children 18–24
Total Asian families	**2,604**	**479**	**297**	**11.4%**	**62.0 %**
Under $20,000	325	73	44	13.5	60.3
$20,000 to $29,999	298	51	28	9.4	54.9
$30,000 to $39,999	284	62	43	15.1	69.4
$40,000 to $49,999	202	49	30	14.9	61.2
$50,000 to $74,999	382	46	23	6.0	50.0
$75,000 or more	714	138	88	12.3	63.8

Note: Numbers will not add to total because not reported is not shown.
Source: Bureau of the Census, Current Population Survey, Internet site <www.census.gov/population/socdemo/school/ppl-148/tab15.txt>

College Enrollment of Asians by Age, 2000

(number and percent distribution of Asians aged 15 or older enrolled in college by age and type of school, October 2000; numbers in thousands)

	total	undergraduate total	two-year	four-year	graduate
Total Asians enrolled	**1,048**	**787**	**214**	**573**	**261**
Aged 15 to 17	12	12	–	12	–
Aged 18 to 19	212	212	64	148	–
Aged 20 to 21	201	194	40	154	7
Aged 22 to 24	227	168	45	123	59
Aged 25 to 29	188	110	16	94	78
Aged 30 to 34	81	32	14	18	49
Aged 35 to 39	54	20	12	8	34
Aged 40 to 44	43	28	18	10	15
Aged 45 to 49	11	7	1	6	4
Aged 50 to 54	14	4	4	–	10
Aged 55 or older	8	1	–	1	7
Percent distribution by age					
Total Asians enrolled	**100.0%**	**100.0%**	**100.0%**	**100.0%**	**100.0%**
Aged 15 to 17	1.1	1.5	–	2.1	–
Aged 18 to 19	20.2	26.9	29.9	25.8	–
Aged 20 to 21	19.2	24.7	18.7	26.9	2.7
Aged 22 to 24	21.7	21.3	21.0	21.5	22.6
Aged 25 to 29	17.9	14.0	7.5	16.4	29.9
Aged 30 to 34	7.7	4.1	6.5	3.1	18.8
Aged 35 to 39	5.2	2.5	5.6	1.4	13.0
Aged 40 to 44	4.1	3.6	8.4	1.7	5.7
Aged 45 to 49	1.0	0.9	0.5	1.0	1.5
Aged 50 to 54	1.3	0.5	1.9	–	3.8
Aged 55 or older	0.8	0.1	–	0.2	2.7

(continued)

(continued from previous page)

Percent distribution by type of school	total	undergraduate			graduate
		total	two-year	four-year	
Total Asians enrolled	**100.0%**	**75.1%**	**20.4%**	**54.7%**	**24.9%**
Aged 15 to 17	100.0	100.0	–	100.0	–
Aged 18 to 19	100.0	100.0	30.2	69.8	–
Aged 20 to 21	100.0	96.5	19.9	76.6	3.5
Aged 22 to 24	100.0	74.0	19.8	54.2	26.0
Aged 25 to 29	100.0	58.5	8.5	50.0	41.5
Aged 30 to 34	100.0	39.5	17.3	22.2	60.5
Aged 35 to 39	100.0	37.0	22.2	14.8	63.0
Aged 40 to 44	100.0	65.1	41.9	23.3	34.9
Aged 45 to 49	100.0	63.6	9.1	54.5	36.4
Aged 50 to 54	100.0	28.6	28.6	–	71.4
Aged 55 or older	100.0	12.5	–	12.5	87.5

Note: (–) means sample is too small to make a reliable estimate.
Source: Bureau of the Census, Current Population, Survey, Internet site <www.census.gov/population/socdemo/school/ppl-148/tab09.txt>; calculations by New Strategist

Associate's Degrees Earned by Asians by Field of Study, 1999–2000

(total number of associate's degrees conferred and number and percent earned by Asians, by field of study, 1999–2000)

	total	earned by Asians	
		number	percent
Total associate's degrees	**564,933**	**27,764**	**4.9%**
Agriculture and natural resources	6,667	46	0.7
Architecture and related programs	392	28	7.1
Area, ethnic, and cultural studies	259	5	1.9
Biological, life sciences	1,434	112	7.8
Business	92,274	5,179	5.6
Communications	2,754	114	4.1
Communications technologies	1,709	48	2.8
Computer and information sciences	20,450	1,563	7.6
Construction trades	2,337	55	2.4
Education	8,226	115	1.4
Engineering	1,752	163	9.3
Engineering-related technologies	35,395	2,106	5.9
English language and literature, letters	947	47	5.0
Foreign languages and literatures	501	32	6.4
Health professions and related sciences	84,081	3,050	3.6
Home economics	8,381	525	6.3
Law and legal studies	7,265	144	2.0
Liberal arts and sciences, general studies, and humanities	187,454	10,070	5.4
Library science	98	6	6.1
Mathematics	675	93	13.8
Mechanics and repairers	11,614	735	6.3
Multi/interdisciplinary studies	11,784	690	5.9
Parks, recreation, leisure, and fitness	855	21	2.5
Philosophy and religion	63	2	3.2
Physical sciences	2,460	197	8.0
Precision production trades	11,814	567	4.8
Protective services	16,298	317	1.9
Psychology	1,455	53	3.6
Public administration and services	3,656	105	2.9
R.O.T.C. and military technologies	65	2	3.1
Social sciences and history	5,136	371	7.2
Theological studies, religious vocations	636	4	0.6
Transportation and material moving	1,021	30	2.9
Visual and performing arts	17,100	954	5.6
Not classified	2,798	215	7.7

Note: Asians include Pacific Islanders.
Source: National Center for Education Statistics, Digest of Education Statistics 2001, *Internet site <http:// nces.ed.gov/pubsearch/pubsinfo.asp?pubid=2002130>; calculations by New Strategist*

Bachelor's Degrees Earned by Asians by Field of Study, 1999–2000

(total number of bachelor's degrees conferred and number and percent earned by Asians, by field of study, 1999–2000)

	total	earned by Asians number	earned by Asians percent
Total bachelor's degrees	**1,237,875**	**77,793**	**6.3%**
Agriculture and natural resources	24,247	717	3.0
Architecture and related programs	8,462	772	9.1
Area, ethnic, and cultural studies	6,381	832	13.0
Biological, life sciences	63,532	8,279	13.0
Business	257,709	17,575	6.8
Communications	55,760	1,921	3.4
Communications technologies	1,150	52	4.5
Computer and information sciences	36,195	5,499	15.2
Construction trades	186	4	2.2
Education	108,168	1,899	1.8
Engineering	58,427	7,043	12.1
Engineering-related technologies	13,872	749	5.4
English language and literature, letters	50,920	1,985	3.9
Foreign languages and literatures	14,968	761	5.1
Health professions and related sciences	78,458	4,533	5.8
Home economics	17,779	697	3.9
Law and legal studies	1,925	85	4.4
Liberal arts and sciences, general studies, and humanities	36,104	1,401	3.9
Library science	154	3	1.9
Mathematics	12,070	982	8.1
Mechanics and repairers	70	1	1.4
Multi/interdisciplinary studies	27,460	2,067	7.5
Parks, recreation, leisure, and fitness	19,111	367	1.9
Philosophy and religion	8,366	449	5.4
Physical sciences	18,385	1,630	8.9
Precision production trades	393	11	2.8
Protective services	24,877	640	2.6
Psychology	74,060	4,330	5.8
Public administration and services	20,185	606	3.0
R.O.T.C. and military technologies	7	0	0.0
Social sciences and history	127,101	8,243	6.5
Theological studies, religious vocations	6,809	146	2.1
Transportation and material moving	3,395	81	2.4
Visual and performing arts	58,791	3,357	5.7
Not classified	2,398	76	3.2

Note: Asians include Pacific Islanders.
Source: National Center for Education Statistics, Digest of Education Statistics 2001, *Internet site <http:// nces.ed.gov/pubsearch/pubsinfo.asp?pubid=2002130>; calculations by New Strategist*

Master's Degrees Earned by Asians by Field of Study, 1999–2000

(total number of master's degrees conferred and number and percent earned by Asians, by field of study, 1999–2000)

	total	earned by Asians number	earned by Asians percent
Total master's degrees	**457,056**	**22,899**	**5.0%**
Agriculture and natural resources	4,375	110	2.5
Architecture and related programs	4,268	284	6.7
Area, ethnic, and cultural studies	1,591	85	5.3
Biological, life sciences	6,198	611	9.9
Business	112,258	7,371	6.6
Communications	5,169	204	3.9
Communications technologies	436	25	5.7
Computer and information sciences	14,264	2,086	14.6
Construction trades	12	–	–
Education	124,240	2,538	2.0
Engineering	25,596	2,471	9.7
Engineering-related technologies	914	32	3.5
English language and literature, letters	7,230	231	3.2
Foreign languages and literatures	2,780	118	4.2
Health professions and related sciences	42,456	2,724	6.4
Home economics	2,830	105	3.7
Law and legal studies	3,750	136	3.6
Liberal arts and sciences, general studies, and humanities	3,256	67	2.1
Library science	4,577	100	2.2
Mathematics	3,412	212	6.2
Multi/interdisciplinary studies	3,064	120	3.9
Parks, recreation, leisure, and fitness	2,478	47	1.9
Philosophy and religion	1,329	57	4.3
Physical sciences	4,841	272	5.6
Precision production trades	5	0	0.0
Protective services	2,609	31	1.2
Psychology	14,465	518	3.6
Public administration and services	25,594	834	3.3
Social sciences and history	14,066	596	4.2
Theological studies, religious vocations	5,576	257	4.6
Transportation and material moving	697	13	1.9
Visual and performing arts	10,918	580	5.3
Not classified	1,802	64	3.6

Note: Asians include Pacific Islanders.
Source: National Center for Education Statistics, Digest of Education Statistics 2001, *Internet site <http:// nces.ed.gov/pubsearch/pubsinfo.asp?pubid=2002130>; calculations by New Strategist*

Doctoral Degrees Earned by Asians by Field of Study, 1999–2000

(total number of doctoral degrees conferred and number and percent earned by Asians, by field of study, 1999–2000)

	total	*earned by Asians*	
		number	*percent*
Total doctoral degrees	**44,808**	**2,380**	**5.3%**
Agriculture and natural resources	1,181	33	2.8
Architecture and related programs	129	1	0.8
Area, ethnic, and cultural studies	217	9	4.1
Biological, life sciences	4,867	434	8.9
Business	1,196	64	5.4
Communications	347	3	0.9
Communications technologies	10	0	0.0
Computer and information sciences	777	58	7.5
Education	6,830	176	2.6
Engineering	5,384	391	7.3
Engineering-related technologies	6	0	0.0
English language and literature, letters	1,628	59	3.6
Foreign languages and literatures	915	43	4.7
Health professions and related sciences	2,676	242	9.0
Home economics	357	13	3.6
Law and legal studies	74	2	2.7
Liberal arts and sciences, general studies, and humanities	83	2	2.4
Library science	68	2	2.9
Mathematics	1,106	72	6.5
Multi/interdisciplinary studies	384	19	4.9
Parks, recreation, leisure, and fitness	134	3	2.2
Philosophy and religion	586	16	2.7
Physical sciences	4,018	210	5.2
Protective services	52	0	0.0
Psychology	4,310	189	4.4
Public administration and services	537	24	4.5
Social sciences and history	4,095	165	4.0
Theological studies, religious vocations	1,643	99	6.0
Visual and performing arts	1,127	50	4.4
Not classified	71	1	1.4

Note: Asians include Pacific Islanders.
Source: National Center for Education Statistics, Digest of Education Statistics 2001, *Internet site <http://nces.ed.gov/pubsearch/pubsinfo.asp?pubid=2002130>; calculations by New Strategist*

First-Professional Degrees Earned by Asians by Field of Study, 1999–2000

(total number of first-professional degrees conferred and number and percent earned by Asians, by field of study, 1999–2000)

	total	earned by Asians	
		number	percent
Total first-professional degrees	**80,259**	**8,576**	**10.7%**
Dentistry (D.D.S. or D.M.D.)	4,250	948	22.3
Medicine (M.D.)	15,286	2,639	17.3
Optometry (O.D.)	1,293	269	20.8
Osteopathic medicine (D.O.)	2,236	279	12.5
Pharmacy (Pharm.D.)	5,669	1,139	20.1
Podiatry (Pod.D., D.P., or D.P.M.)	569	93	16.3
Veterinary medicine (D.V.M.)	2,251	38	1.7
Chiropractic (D.C. or D.C.M.)	3,809	355	9.3
Naturopathic medicine	202	11	5.4
Law (LL.B. or J.D.)	38,152	2,467	6.5
Theology (M.Div., M.H.L., B.D., or Ord. and M.H.L./Rav.)	6,129	320	5.2
Other	413	18	4.4

Note: Asians include Pacific Islanders.
Source: National Center for Education Statistics, Digest of Education Statistics 2001, *Internet site <http://nces.ed.gov/pubsearch/pubsinfo.asp?pubid=2002130>; calculations by New Strategist*

Asians: Health

Asians Are Healthier than the Average Person

For all but a few health conditions, Asians fare much better than the average American. Infant mortality and death rates from motor vehicle accidents, heart disease, and cancer are all far lower among Asians than among the population as a whole. The incidence of tuberculosis among Asians is well above average, however. Many Asians are immigrants living in cramped quarters where tuberculosis spreads easily. Because Asians are more metropolitan than other racial or ethnic groups in the U.S., they are more likely to live in counties with poor air quality.

More than 200,000 babies were born to Asian women in 2000, or nearly 5 percent of all babies born that year. Asians account for 73 percent of all births in Hawaii and for 12 percent of those in California.

Eighty-two percent of Asians are covered by health insurance, most of them with employment-based coverage. Thirteen percent of Asians are disabled, far below the 20 percent average. The leading causes of death among Asians are heart disease and cancer, which accounted for 53 percent of Asian deaths in 1999.

■ The Asian health advantage could diminish if poorly educated immigrants become a larger share of the Asian population.

Most Asians have health insurance

(percent distribution of Asians by health insurance coverage status, 2000)

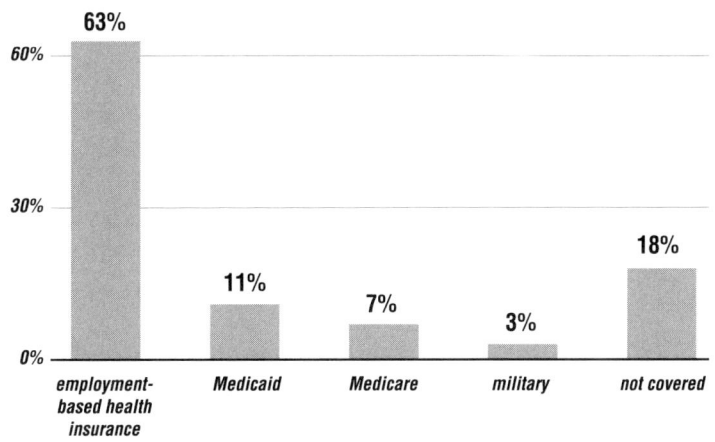

Health Indicators for Asians, 1998

(selected indicators of total and Asian health status, and index of Asian health indicators to total, 1998)

	total population indicator	Asian indicator	index of Asian to total
Infant mortality rate (deaths before age 1 per 1,000 live births)	7.2	5.5	76
Total deaths per 100,000 population	471.7	264.6	56
Motor vehicle crash deaths per 100,000 population	15.7	8.6	55
Work-related injury deaths per 100,000 people aged 16 or older	2.9	1.9	66
Suicides per 100,000 population	10.4	5.9	57
Homicides per 100,000 population	7.3	3.7	51
Lung cancer deaths per 100,000 population	37.0	17.2	46
Female breast cancer deaths per 100,000 population	18.8	9.9	53
Cardiovascular disease deaths per 100,000 population	161.2	95.6	59
Heart disease deaths per 100,000 population	126.7	67.5	53
Stroke deaths per 100,000 population	25.1	22.7	90
Reported incidence of AIDS per 100,000 population	19.5	4.3	22
Reported incidence of tuberculosis per 100,000 population	6.8	36.6	538
Reported incidence of syphilis per 100,000 population	2.6	0.4	15
Prevalence of low birth weight, as percent of total live births	7.6	7.4	97
Births to girls aged 10 to 17, as percent of total live births	4.6	2.0	43
Percent of mothers without care, first trimester of pregnancy	17.2	16.9	98
Percent under age 18 living in poverty	18.9	–	–
Percent living in counties exceeding U.S. air quality standards	23.5	44.9	191

Note: Asians include Pacific Islanders; (–) means data are not available. The index for each indicator is calculated by dividing the Asian figure by the total population figure and multiplying by 100. For example, the index of 56 in the second row indicates that the Asian death rate is 44 percent below the rate for the total population.
Source: National Center for Health Statistics, Healthy People 2000 Final Review, 2001; *calculations by New Strategist*

Births to Asian Women by Age, 2000

(total number of births, number and percent distribution of births to Asian women, and Asian share of total, by age, 2000)

| | | Asian | | |
	total	number	percent distribution	share of total
Total births	**4,058,814**	**200,543**	**100.0%**	**4.9%**
Under age 15	8,519	112	0.1	1.3
Aged 15 to 19	468,990	8,968	4.5	1.9
Aged 20 to 24	1,017,806	28,766	14.3	2.8
Aged 25 to 29	1,087,547	61,346	30.6	5.6
Aged 30 to 34	929,278	63,665	31.7	6.9
Aged 35 to 39	452,057	31,068	15.5	6.9
Aged 40 to 44	90,013	6,242	3.1	6.9
Aged 45 or older	4,604	376	0.2	8.2

Note: Asians include Pacific Islanders.
Source: National Center for Health Statistics, Births: Final Data for 2000, *National Vital Statistics Report, Vol. 50, No. 5, 2002; calculations by New Strategist*

Births to Asian Women by Birth Order, 2000

(number and percent distribution of births to Asian women, by birth order, 2000)

	number	percent distribution
Births to Asians	**200,543**	**100.0%**
First child	93,007	46.4
Second child	68,069	33.9
Third child	24,740	12.3
Fourth or later child	13,821	6.9

Note: Asians include Pacific Islanders. Numbers will not add to total because not stated is not shown.
Source: National Center for Health Statistics, Births: Final Data for 2000, *National Vital Statistics Report, Vol. 50, No. 5, 2002; calculations by New Strategist*

Births to Asian Teenagers and Unmarried Women by Ethnicity, 2000

(percent of births to Asian women under age 20 and to unmarried Asian women, by ethnicity, 2000)

	percent to women	
	under age 20	unmarried
Asian births	**4.5%**	**14.8%**
Chinese	0.9	7.6
Japanese	1.9	9.5
Hawaiian	17.4	50.0
Filipino	5.3	20.3
Other Asian	4.8	13.8

Note: Asians include Pacific Islanders.
Source: National Center for Health Statistics, Births: Final Data for 2000, *National Vital Statistics Report, Vol. 50, No. 5, 2002; calculations by New Strategist*

Births to Asian Women by State, 2000

(total number of births, number and percent distribution of births to Asian women, and Asian share of total births by state, 2000)

| | | Asian births | | |
	total	number	percent distribtution	share of total
Total births	**4,058,814**	**200,543**	**100.0%**	**4.9%**
Alabama	63,299	544	0.3	0.9
Alaska	9,974	639	0.3	6.4
Arizona	85,273	2,051	1.0	2.4
Arkansas	37,783	501	0.2	1.3
California	531,959	64,243	32.0	12.1
Colorado	65,438	2,079	1.0	3.2
Connecticut	43,026	1,805	0.9	4.2
Delaware	11,051	369	0.2	3.3
District of Columbia	7,666	177	0.1	2.3
Florida	204,125	5,021	2.5	2.5
Georgia	132,644	3,534	1.8	2.7
Hawaii	17,551	12,868	6.4	73.3
Idaho	20,366	298	0.1	1.5
Illinois	185,036	8,052	4.0	4.4
Indiana	87,699	1,191	0.6	1.4
Iowa	38,266	919	0.5	2.4
Kansas	39,666	1,067	0.5	2.7
Kentucky	56,029	611	0.3	1.1
Louisiana	67,898	1,032	0.5	1.5
Maine	13,603	188	0.1	1.4
Maryland	74,316	3,615	1.8	4.9
Massachusetts	81,614	4,812	2.4	5.9
Michigan	136,171	3,815	1.9	2.8
Minnesota	67,604	3,491	1.7	5.2
Mississippi	44,075	394	0.2	0.9
Missouri	76,463	1,477	0.7	1.9
Montana	10,957	114	0.1	1.0
Nebraska	24,646	577	0.3	2.3
Nevada	30,829	1,994	1.0	6.5
New Hampshire	14,609	329	0.2	2.3
New Jersey	115,632	9,473	4.7	8.2

(continued)

(continued from previous page)

| | total | Asian births | | |
		number	percent distribtution	share of total
New Mexico	27,223	402	0.2%	1.5%
New York	258,737	19,534	9.7	7.5
North Carolina	120,311	2,774	1.4	2.3
North Dakota	7,676	97	0.0	1.3
Ohio	155,472	2,895	1.4	1.9
Oklahoma	49,782	994	0.5	2.0
Oregon	45,804	2,345	1.2	5.1
Pennsylvania	146,281	3,957	2.0	2.7
Rhode Island	12,505	436	0.2	3.5
South Carolina	56,114	851	0.4	1.5
South Dakota	10,345	131	0.1	1.3
Tennessee	79,611	1,324	0.7	1.7
Texas	363,414	11,736	5.9	3.2
Utah	47,353	1,436	0.7	3.0
Vermont	6,500	82	0.0	1.3
Virginia	98,938	5,113	2.5	5.2
Washington	81,036	6,891	3.4	8.5
West Virginia	20,865	108	0.1	0.5
Wisconsin	69,326	2,098	1.0	3.0
Wyoming	6,253	59	0.0	0.9

Note: Asians include Pacific Islanders.
Source: National Center for Health Statistics, Births: Final Data for 2000, *National Vital Statistics Report, Vol. 50, No. 5, 2002; calculations by New Strategist*

Health Insurance Coverage of Asians by Age, 2000

(number and percent distribution of Asians by age and health insurance coverage status, 2000; numbers in thousands)

| | | covered by private or government health insurance | | | | | | | |
| | | private health insurance | | | government health insurance | | | | |
	total	total	total	employ-ment based	total	Medicaid	Medicare	Military	not covered
Total Asians	**11,332**	**9,295**	**7,909**	**7,114**	**2,093**	**1,301**	**856**	**290**	**2,037**
Under 18	3,129	2,690	2,175	2,027	708	602	38	94	439
Aged 18–24	1,136	784	707	554	117	79	0	38	352
Aged 25–34	2,078	1,602	1,545	1,424	108	73	7	31	476
Aged 35–44	1,895	1,589	1,479	1,381	168	102	27	54	307
Aged 45–54	1,492	1,244	1,157	1,055	125	85	21	33	248
Aged 55–64	768	591	493	412	138	86	32	24	177
Aged 65+	833	795	353	262	731	274	731	16	38
Total Asians	**100.0%**	**82.0%**	**69.8%**	**62.8%**	**18.5%**	**11.5%**	**7.6%**	**2.6%**	**18.0%**
Under 18	100.0	86.0	69.5	64.8	22.6	19.2	1.2	3.0	14.0
Aged 18–24	100.0	69.0	62.2	48.8	10.3	7.0	0.0	3.3	31.0
Aged 25–34	100.0	77.1	74.4	68.5	5.2	3.5	0.3	1.5	22.9
Aged 35–44	100.0	83.9	78.0	72.9	8.9	5.4	1.4	2.8	16.2
Aged 45–54	100.0	83.4	77.5	70.7	8.4	5.7	1.4	2.2	16.6
Aged 55–64	100.0	77.0	64.2	53.6	18.0	11.2	4.2	3.1	23.0
Aged 65+	100.0	95.4	42.4	31.5	87.8	32.9	87.8	1.9	4.6

Note: Numbers will not add to total because some people have more than one type of health insurance.
Source: Bureau of the Census, Internet site <http://ferret.bls.census.gov/macro/032001/health/h01_008.htm>

Asians with Disabilities by Sex and Age, 1997

(total number of Asians and number and percent with disabilities, by sex, age, and severity of disability, 1997; numbers in thousands)

| | | with a disability | | | | | |
| | | total | | severe | | needs assistance | |
	total	number	percent	number	percent	number	percent
Total Asians	**9,159**	**1,192**	**13.0%**	**776**	**8.5%**	**223**	**2.4%**
Under age 15	2,089	63	3.0	34	1.6	5	0.3
Aged 15 to 24	1,454	77	5.3	33	2.3	5	0.4
Aged 25 to 64	4,971	647	13.0	390	7.9	87	1.7
Aged 65 or older	645	404	62.6	317	49.2	125	19.4
Asian females	**4,713**	**655**	**13.9**	**439**	**9.3**	**136**	**2.9**
Under age 15	973	6	0.6	6	0.6	–	–
Aged 15 to 24	720	25	3.5	15	2.1	–	–
Aged 25 to 64	2,664	391	14.7	232	8.7	60	2.3
Aged 65 or older	357	233	65.3	186	52.0	75	21.1
Asian males	**4,445**	**537**	**12.1**	**337**	**7.6**	**87**	**2.0**
Under age 15	1,117	58	5.2	29	2.6	5	0.5
Aged 15 to 24	733	52	7.1	18	2.5	5	0.7
Aged 25 to 64	2,307	257	11.1	158	6.8	26	1.1
Aged 65 or older	288	171	59.4	132	45.7	50	17.3

Note: (–) means sample is too small to make a reliable estimate. For the definition of disability, see glossary.
Source: Bureau of the Census, Americans with Disabilities: 1997, detailed tables from Current Population Reports P70-73, 2001

AIDS Cases among Asians, through June 2000

(total number of AIDS cases diagnosed, number diagnosed among Asians, and Asian share of total, by sex and age at diagnosis, through June 2000)

		Asian	
	total	number	share of total
Total AIDS cases	**729,326**	**5,504**	**0.8%**
Males aged 13 or older	601,471	4,792	0.8
Females aged 13 or older	119,454	663	0.6
Children under age 13	8,401	49	0.6

Source: National Center for Health Statistics, Health United States, 2001*; calculations by New Strategist*

Leading Causes of Death among Asians, 1999

(total number of deaths among Asians, and number and percent of deaths accounted for by the ten leading causes of death for Asians, 1999)

		number	percent
Total Asian deaths		**33,694**	**100.0%**
1.	Diseases of heart	9,102	27.0
2.	Malignant neoplasms	8,814	26.2
3.	Cerebrovascular diseases	3,111	9.2
4.	Accidents	1,566	4.6
5.	Diabetes mellitus	1,148	3.4
6.	Chronic lower respiratory diseases	1,121	3.3
7.	Influenza and pneumonia	843	2.5
8.	Suicide	659	2.0
9.	Nephritis, nephrotic syndrome, and nephrosis	577	1.7
10.	Septicemia	397	1.2
	All other causes	6,356	18.9

Source: National Center for Health Statistics, Health United States, 2001*; calculations by New Strategist*

More than Half of Asian Householders Own Their Home

Asians are less likely than the average American to own a home. Just 51 percent of Asian householders owned their home in 1999. This compares with a homeownership rate of 67 percent for all households. Although Asians are less likely than average to own a home, they are more likely to be homeowners than blacks, Hispanics, or American Indians.

Among Asian married couples, the 63 percent majority are homeowners. Homeownership among the couples surpasses 50 percent in the 30-to-34 age group and peaks at 74 percent among those aged 45 to 54.

Twenty percent of Asians moved between March 1999 and March 2000, a higher rate of mobility than for the population as a whole. Three percent of Asians aged 1 or older moved to the U.S. from abroad during those 12 months.

■ Asian homeownership could decline in the years ahead if immigrants from poor countries become a larger share of the Asian population.

Asian homeownership is about the same in every region

(percent of Asian households that own their home, by region, 1999)

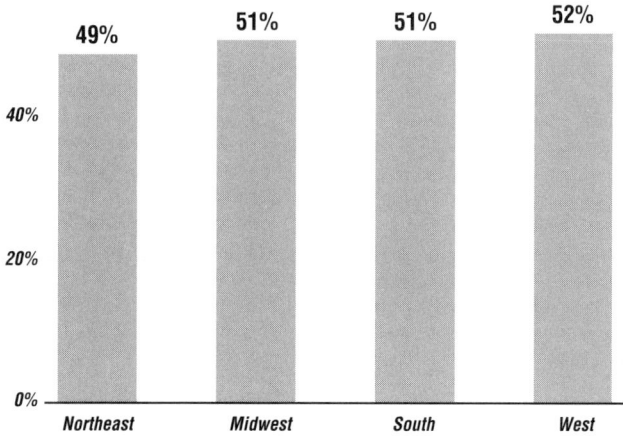

Region of Residence and Metropolitan Status of Housing Units Occupied by Asians, 1999

(number, percent distribution, and percent of housing units occupied by Asians, by regional, metropolitan, and homeownership status, 1999; numbers in thousands)

	total		owner			renter		
	number	percent distribution	number	percent distribution	share of total	number	percent distribution	share of total
Housing units occupied by Asians	**3,049**	**100.0%**	**1,566**	**100.0%**	**51.4%**	**1,483**	**100.0%**	**48.6%**
Northeast	536	17.6	264	16.9	49.3	272	18.3	50.7
Midwest	331	10.9	170	10.9	51.4	161	10.9	48.6
South	504	16.5	259	16.5	51.4	245	16.5	48.6
West	1,677	55.0	873	55.7	52.1	805	54.3	48.0
In metropolitan areas	2,963	97.2	1,509	96.4	50.9	1,454	98.0	49.1
In central cities	1,374	45.1	560	35.8	40.8	814	54.9	59.2
In suburbs	1,589	52.1	949	60.6	59.7	640	43.2	40.3
Outside metropolitan areas	86	2.8	56	3.6	65.1	30	2.0	34.9

Source: Bureau of the Census, American Housing Survey for the United States: 1999, *Current Housing Reports, H150/99, 2000; calculations by New Strategist*

Asian Homeowners by Family Type and Age of Householder, 2000

(number of families headed by Asians, and number and percent of families owning their home, by family type and by age of householder for married couples, 2000; numbers in thousands)

	total	*homeowners*	
		number	*percent*
Asian married couples	**1,996**	**1,252**	**62.7%**
Under age 25	42	6	14.3
Aged 25 to 29	149	42	28.2
Aged 30 to 34	267	140	52.4
Aged 35 to 39	250	134	53.6
Aged 40 to 44	285	204	71.6
Aged 45 to 54	544	402	73.9
Aged 55 to 64	247	173	70.0
Aged 65 to 74	161	118	73.3
Aged 75 or older	51	34	66.7
Asian female-headed families	**331**	**147**	**44.4**
Asian male-headed families	**179**	**99**	**55.3**

Source: Bureau of the Census, America's Families and Living Arrangements: March 2000, *detailed tables from Current Population Report P20–537, Internet site <www.census.gov/population/www/socdemo/hh-fam/p20-537_00.html>; calculations by New Strategist*

Geographical Mobility of Asians by Age, 1999–2000

(total number of Asians aged 1 or older, and number and percent who moved between March 1999 and March 2000, by age of person and type of move; numbers in thousands)

	total	same house (non-movers)	total movers in U.S.	same county	different county, same state	different state, same division	different division, same region	different region	moved from abroad
Asians aged 1 or older	**10,779**	**8,577**	**2,202**	**1,126**	**368**	**233**	**38**	**113**	**323**
Aged 1–4	708	522	186	96	29	13	–	13	35
Aged 5–9	798	628	170	104	20	15	–	10	20
Aged 10–14	857	719	138	71	17	13	4	9	24
Aged 15–17	556	482	74	37	20	–	6	5	4
Aged 18–19	382	291	91	54	19	9	2	–	7
Aged 20–24	810	526	284	145	42	28	4	15	49
Aged 25–29	987	617	370	146	75	63	2	13	71
Aged 30–34	908	677	231	115	21	36	7	11	41
Aged 35–39	937	726	211	115	22	12	–	20	41
Aged 40–44	897	774	123	71	23	13	–	6	10
Aged 45–49	770	663	107	41	40	8	7	3	9
Aged 50–54	662	580	82	42	16	12	4	6	2
Aged 55–59	378	336	42	26	6	8	2	–	–
Aged 60–61	140	134	6	4	–	–	–	–	1
Aged 62–64	189	169	20	11	4	1	–	2	1
Aged 65–69	312	282	30	21	7	–	–	–	2
Aged 70–74	203	184	19	17	–	–	–	–	2
Aged 75–79	160	150	10	6	2	–	–	–	2
Aged 80–84	64	60	4	4	–	–	–	–	–
Aged 85+	62	57	5	–	5	1	–	–	–

(continued)

(continued from previous page)

Asians aged 1 or older	total	same house (non-movers)	total movers in U.S.	same county	different county, same state	different state, same division	different division, same region	different region	moved from abroad
	100.0%	79.6%	20.4%	10.4%	3.4%	2.2%	0.4%	1.0%	3.0%
Aged 1–4	100.0	73.7	26.3	13.6	4.1	1.8	–	1.8	4.9
Aged 5–9	100.0	78.7	21.3	13.0	2.5	1.9	–	1.3	2.5
Aged 10–14	100.0	83.9	16.1	8.3	2.0	1.5	0.5	1.1	2.8
Aged 15–17	100.0	86.7	13.3	6.7	3.6	–	1.1	0.9	0.7
Aged 18–19	100.0	76.2	23.8	14.1	5.0	2.4	0.5	–	1.8
Aged 20–24	100.0	64.9	35.1	17.9	5.2	3.5	0.5	1.9	6.0
Aged 25–29	100.0	62.5	37.5	14.8	7.6	6.4	0.2	1.3	7.2
Aged 30–34	100.0	74.6	25.4	12.7	2.3	4.0	0.8	1.2	4.5
Aged 35–39	100.0	77.5	22.5	12.3	2.3	1.3	–	2.1	4.4
Aged 40–44	100.0	86.3	13.7	7.9	2.6	1.4	–	0.7	1.1
Aged 45–49	100.0	86.1	13.9	5.3	5.2	1.0	0.9	0.4	1.2
Aged 50–54	100.0	87.6	12.4	6.3	2.4	1.8	0.6	0.9	0.3
Aged 55–59	100.0	88.9	11.1	6.9	1.6	2.1	0.5	–	–
Aged 60–61	100.0	95.7	4.3	2.9	–	–	–	–	0.7
Aged 62–64	100.0	89.4	10.6	5.8	2.1	0.5	–	1.1	0.5
Aged 65–69	100.0	90.4	9.6	6.7	2.2	–	–	–	0.6
Aged 70–74	100.0	90.6	9.4	8.4	–	–	–	–	1.0
Aged 75–79	100.0	93.8	6.3	3.8	1.3	–	–	–	1.3
Aged 80–84	100.0	93.8	6.3	6.3	–	–	–	–	–
Aged 85+	100.0	91.9	8.1	–	8.1	1.6	–	–	–

Note: (–) means sample is too small to make a reliable estimate.
Source: Bureau of the Census, Geographical Mobility: March 1999 to March 2000, *Current Population Reports, P20-538, 2001; Internet site <www.census.gov/population/www/socdemo/migrate/p20-538.html>; calculations by New Strategist*

Asians: Income

Asians Have the Highest Incomes

The median income of Asian households rose 12 percent between 1990 and 2000, after adjusting for inflation, as the booming economy of the mid-to-late 1990s boosted earnings. The median household income of Asians is significantly higher than that of any other racial or ethnic group, reaching $55,525 in 2000.

Thirty-three percent of Asian households had incomes of $75,000 or more in 1999. Asian couples had the highest incomes, with a median of more than $64,000. More than 40 percent of Asian couples had incomes of $75,000 or more.

Asian men who worked full-time earned a median of $40,950 in 2000, up 19 percent since 1990 after adjusting for inflation. Asian women earned a median of $31,161 up 14 percent since 1990. Asian men and women who work full-time earn more than the average full-time worker. Asian women earn 76 percent as much as Asian men.

Asians are much less likely to be poor than blacks and Hispanics. Because many Asians are recent immigrants, poverty is higher among Asians than among non-Hispanic whites. Eleven percent of Asians are poor versus 8 percent of non-Hispanic whites.

■ Because Asians are better educated than any other racial or ethnic group, their incomes are likely to remain well above average.

Asian households have the highest incomes

(median income of households by race and Hispanic origin of householder, 2000)

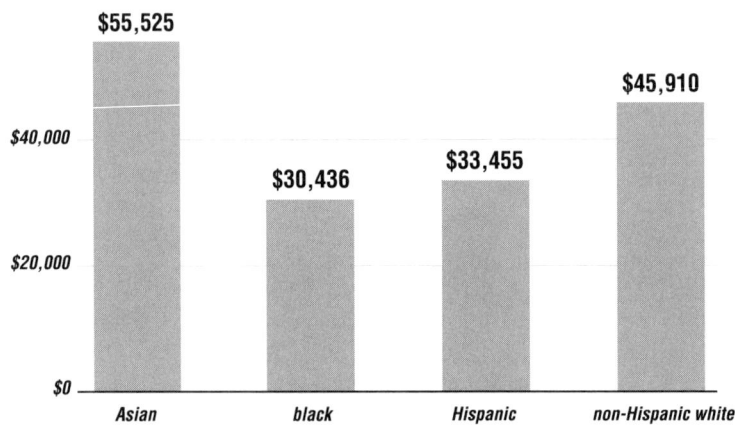

Median Income of Asian Households, 1990 to 2000

(median income of Asian households, and index of Asian to total household median income, 1990 to 2000; percent change in incomes and indexes, 1990–2000; in 2000 dollars)

	median income	index Asian/total
2000	$55,525	132
1999	52,925	125
1998	49,212	120
1997	48,415	122
1996	47,307	122
1995	45,603	119
1994	46,595	125
1993	45,105	123
1992	45,611	123
1991	45,145	121
1990	49,369	128
Percent change		
1990–2000	12.5%	2.6%

Note: Indexes are calculated by dividing the median income of Asian households by the median of total households and multiplying by 100.
Source: Bureau of the Census, Current Population Survey, Internet site <www.census.gov/hhes/income/histinc/h05.html>; calculations by New Strategist

Income Distribution of Asian Households by Household Type, 1999

(number and percent distribution of Asian households by income and household type, 1999; households in thousands as of 2000)

	total	married couples	female family hh, no spouse present	male family hh, no spouse present	nonfamily households
Total households	**3,337**	**1,996**	**331**	**179**	**831**
Under $10,000	286	94	56	14	128
$10,000 to $19,999	321	143	59	18	112
$20,000 to $34,999	530	236	73	45	181
$35,000 to $49,999	505	299	61	12	128
$50,000 to $74,999	606	389	41	35	143
$75,000 or more	1,090	835	41	55	139
Median income	$51,093	$64,524	$30,377	$50,357	$34,544
Total households	**100.0%**	**100.0%**	**100.0%**	**100.0%**	**100.0%**
Under $10,000	8.6	4.7	16.9	7.8	15.4
$10,000 to $19,999	9.6	7.2	17.8	10.1	13.5
$20,000 to $34,999	15.9	11.8	22.1	25.1	21.8
$35,000 to $49,999	15.1	15.0	18.4	6.7	15.4
$50,000 to $74,999	18.2	19.5	12.4	19.6	17.2
$75,000 or more	32.7	41.8	12.4	30.7	16.7

Source: Bureau of the Census, The Asian and Pacific Islander Population in the United States: March 2000 (Update), *detailed tables for Current Population Report PPL-146, 2001; calculations by New Strategist*

Median Earnings of Asians Working Full-Time by Sex, 1990 to 2000

(median earnings of Asians working full-time, year-round by sex; index of Asian to total population median earnings, and Asian women's earnings as a percent of Asian men's earnings, 1990 to 2000; percent change in earnings and indexes, 1990–2000; in 2000 dollars)

	Asian men		Asian women		Asian women's earnings as a percent of Asian men's earnings
	median earnings	index Asian/total	median earnings	index Asian/total	
2000	$40,950	110	$31,161	114	76.1%
1999	38,055	102	29,633	109	77.9
1998	36,751	98	28,563	105	77.7
1997	37,109	100	29,725	111	80.1
1996	37,661	107	27,936	108	74.2
1995	35,452	100	27,933	111	78.8
1994	36,902	103	28,144	110	76.3
1993	36,349	101	28,635	112	78.8
1992	36,828	100	27,512	107	74.7
1991	37,355	103	26,226	103	70.2
1990	34,365	94	27,379	108	79.7
Percent change					
1990–2000	19.2%	16.4%	13.8%	5.9%	−4.5%

Note: The Asian/total indexes are calculated by dividing the median earnings of Asian men and women by the median earnings of total men and women and multiplying by 100.
Source: Bureau of the Census, Current Population Survey, Internet site <www.census.gov/hhes/income/histinc/ p38c.html>; calculations by New Strategist

Earnings Distribution of Asians by Sex, 1999

(number and percent distribution of Asians aged 15 or older working full-time, year-round by earnings and sex, 1999; people in thousands as of 2000)

	men	women
Total Asians	**2,297**	**1,670**
Under $10,000	61	80
$10,000 to $19,999	353	379
$20,000 to $34,999	639	560
$35,000 to $49,999	434	330
$50,000 to $74,999	427	226
$75,000 or more	382	96
Median earnings	$38,301	$30,071
Total Asians	**100.0%**	**100.0%**
Under $10,000	2.7	4.8
$10,000 to $19,999	15.4	22.7
$20,000 to $34,999	27.8	33.5
$35,000 to $49,999	18.9	19.8
$50,000 to $74,999	18.6	13.5
$75,000 or more	16.6	5.7

Source: Bureau of the Census, The Asian and Pacific Islander Population in the United States: March 2000 (Update), *detailed tables for Current Population Report PPL-146, 2001; calculations by New Strategist*

Poverty Status of Asian Families, 1999

(total number of Asian families with a householder aged 15 or older, and number and percent below poverty level by type of family, 1999; families in thousands as of 2000)

	total	in poverty	
		number	percent
Total families	**2,506**	**258**	**10.3%**
Married couples	1,996	162	8.1
Female householder, no spouse present	331	76	23.1
Male householder, no spouse present	179	20	11.3

Source: Bureau of the Census, The Asian and Pacific Islander Population in the United States: March 2000; *PPL-146, Internet site <www.census.gov/population/www/socdemo/race/ppl-146.html>*

Poverty Status of Asians by Sex and Age, 1999

(total number of Asians, and number and percent below poverty level by sex and age, 1999; people in thousands as of 2000)

	total	in poverty number	in poverty percent
Total Asians	**10,916**	**1,163**	**10.7%**
Under age 18	3,057	361	11.8
Aged 18 to 64	7,059	717	10.2
Aged 65 or older	800	85	10.6
Asian females	**5,603**	**618**	**11.0**
Under age 18	1,498	168	11.2
Aged 18 to 64	3,684	408	11.1
Aged 65 or older	421	42	10.0
Asian males	**5,312**	**545**	**10.3**
Under age 18	1,559	193	12.4
Aged 18 to 64	3,374	309	9.1
Aged 65 or older	379	43	11.4

Source: Bureau of the Census, The Asian and Pacific Islander Population in the United States: March 2000; *PPL-146, Internet site <www.census.gov/population/www/socdemo/race/ppl-146.html>*

Asians: Labor Force

More Than One-Third of Asian Workers
Are Managers or Professionals

More than 5 million Asians were in the civilian labor force in 2000, or 66 percent of those aged 16 or older. Seventy-four percent of Asian men and 59 percent of Asian women are in the labor force.

Both husband and wife work in the 58 percent majority of Asian married couples, a slightly higher share than among all Americans. Among Asian couples with a householder aged 45 to 54, fully 70 percent are dual-earners.

The number of workers classified as Asian or "other" race (primarily American Indians) will grow 44 percent between 2000 and 2010, according to projections by the Bureau of Labor Statistics. The Asian and "other" share of the labor force will reach 6.1 percent in 2010.

■ Asian household income is well above average because so many Asian households are headed by two-earner couples.

Asians are more likely to be managers or professionals

*(percent of total and Asian workers aged 16 or older employed
in managerial or professional specialty occupation, 2000)*

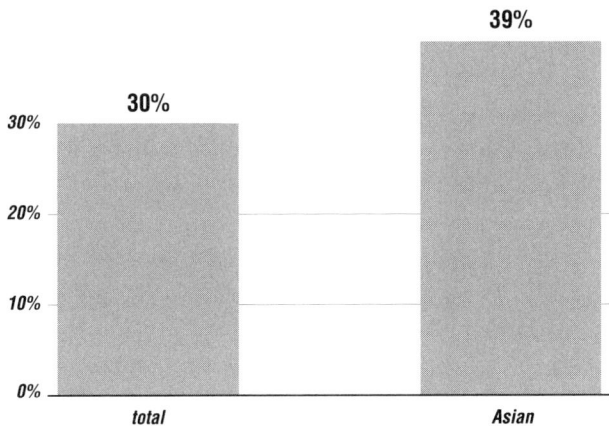

Employment Status of Asians by Sex, 2000

(employment status of the civilian noninstitutionalized Asian population aged 16 or older, by sex, 2000; numbers in thousands)

	total	*men*	*women*
Total Asians aged 16 or older	**8,225**	**3,941**	**4,284**
In labor force	**5,458**	**2,917**	**2,541**
Employed	5,246	2,796	2,450
Unemployed	212	121	91
Not in labor force	**2,767**	**1,024**	**1,743**
Percent in labor force	**66.4%**	**74.0%**	**59.3%**
Percent unemployed	3.9	4.1	3.6
Percent not in labor force	**33.6**	**26.0**	**40.7**

Note: The civilian labor force equals the number of employed plus the number of unemployed. The civilian population equals the number in the labor force plus the number not in the labor force.
Source: Bureau of the Census, The Asian and Pacific Islander Population in the United States: March 2000 (Update), *detailed tables for Current Population Report PPL-146, 2001; calculations by New Strategist*

Asian Workers by Occupation, 2000

(total number of employed people aged 16 or older in the civilian labor force; number and percent distribution of employed Asians, and Asian share of total, by occupation, 2000; numbers in thousands)

	total	Asians		
		number	percent distribution	Asian of total
Total employed	**134,338**	**5,246**	**100.0%**	**3.9%**
Managerial and professional specialty	40,493	2,064	39.3	5.1
Executive, administrative, and managerial	19,764	915	17.4	4.6
Professional specialty	20,729	1,149	21.9	5.5
Technical, sales, and administrative support	39,541	1,476	28.1	3.7
Technical and related support	4,384	251	4.8	5.7
Sales	16,138	620	11.8	3.8
Administrative support, including clerical	19,020	605	11.5	3.2
Service occupations	18,671	780	14.9	4.2
Service workers, private household	884	45	0.9	5.1
Service workers, except private household	17,787	735	14.0	4.1
Precision production, craft, and repair	14,386	299	5.7	2.1
Operators, fabricators, and laborers	18,002	595	11.3	3.3
Machine operators, assemblers, and inspectors	7,352	353	6.7	4.8
Transportation and material moving	5,340	94	1.8	1.8
Handlers, equipment cleaners, helpers, and laborers	4,310	147	2.8	3.4
Farming, forestry, and fishing	3,245	33	0.6	1.0

Note: The total labor force figures shown here are slightly different from those shown in other chapters because they are based on a different source of data.
Source: Bureau of the Census, The Asian and Pacific Islander Population in the United States: March 2000 (Update), *detailed tables for Current Population Report PPL-146, 2001; calculations by New Strategist*

Labor Force Status of Asian Married Couples, 2000

(number and percent distribution of Asian married couples by age of householder and labor force status of husband and wife, 2000; numbers in thousands)

| | total | husband and/or wife in labor force | | | neither husband nor wife in labor force |
		husband and wife	husband only	wife only	
Total Asian couples	**1,996**	**1,151**	**530**	**98**	**217**
Under age 20	10	7	3	–	–
Aged 20 to 24	32	12	17	–	2
Aged 25 to 29	149	84	53	7	5
Aged 30 to 34	267	169	85	10	3
Aged 35 to 39	250	158	83	4	5
Aged 40 to 44	285	190	85	2	7
Aged 45 to 54	544	383	112	25	25
Aged 55 to 64	247	116	72	35	24
Aged 65 or older	212	33	18	15	147
Total Asian couples	**100.0%**	**57.7%**	**26.6%**	**4.9%**	**10.9%**
Under age 20	100.0	70.0	30.0	–	–
Aged 20 to 24	100.0	37.5	53.1	–	6.3
Aged 25 to 29	100.0	56.4	35.6	4.7	3.4
Aged 30 to 34	100.0	63.3	31.8	3.7	1.1
Aged 35 to 39	100.0	63.2	33.2	1.6	2.0
Aged 40 to 44	100.0	66.7	29.8	0.7	2.5
Aged 45 to 54	100.0	70.4	20.6	4.6	4.6
Aged 55 to 64	100.0	47.0	29.1	14.2	9.7
Aged 65 or older	100.0	15.6	8.5	7.1	69.3

Note: (–) means sample is too small to make a reliable estimate.
Source: Bureau of the Census, Household and Family Characteristics: March 2000 (Update), *detailed tables for Current Population Report P20-537, Internet site <www.census.gov/population/socdemo/hh-fam/p20-537/ 2000/tabFG1.txt>; calculations by New Strategist*

Projections of the Asian Labor Force by Sex, 2000 and 2010

(number of Asians in the civilian labor force, labor force participation rate of Asians, and Asian share of total labor force, by sex, 2000 and 2010; percent change in number and percentage point change in rate and share, 2000–2010; numbers in thousands)

| | Asians in labor force | | |
	2000	2010	percent change 2000–2010
Total	6,687	9,636	44.1%
Men	3,570	5,070	42.0
Women	3,116	4,566	46.5

| | Asian labor force participation rate | | |
	2000	2010	percentage point change 2000–2010
Total	66.5%	67.5%	1.0
Men	74.9	74.8	–0.1
Women	58.9	60.9	2.0

| | Asian share of total labor force | | |
	2000	2010	percentage point change 2000–2010
Total	4.7%	6.1%	1.4
Men	2.5	3.2	0.7
Women	2.2	2.9	0.7

Note: Projections are for Asians and "others," some of whom are American Indians.
Source: Bureau of Labor Statistics, Monthly Labor Review, *November 2001*

Asian Households Are More Likely to Be Headed by Married Couples

Because many of the Asians immigrating to the U.S. are young adults, Asian householders are much younger than average. Only 11 percent were aged 65 or older in 2000, compared with 21 percent of households nationally.

Partly because of their younger age, Asian households are more likely to be headed by married couples than is the average household—59 versus 52 percent, according to the 2000 census. Asian householders are less likely to live alone, single-person households accounting for only 19 percent of the Asian total versus 26 percent of households nationally. Because married couples are more common among Asians, Asian children are more likely to live with both parents than is the average American child, 81 versus 69 percent.

Many Asians are immigrants trying to establish themselves in the United States, which explains why more than one in ten Asian men and women are living in the households of relatives. Among all men and women, the proportion is just 5 percent. The fact also explains why Asian households are larger than average.

■ Because many Asians are immigrants from traditional countries, nuclear families (husband, wife, and children) are more common among Asian households than households nationally.

Asian households are more traditional

(percent distribution of Asian households by household type, 2000 census)

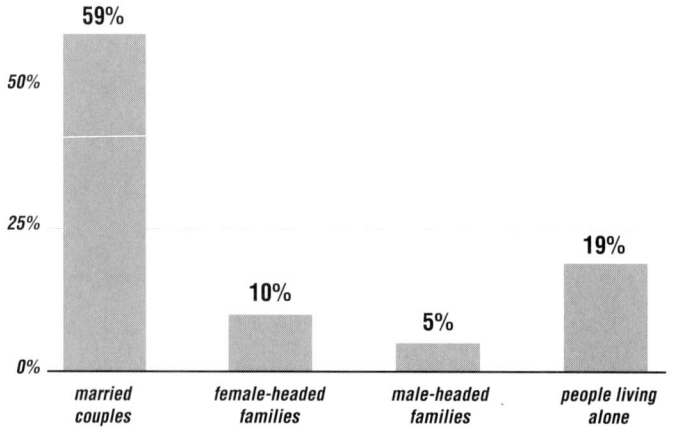

Asian Households by Age of Householder, 2000

(number of total households, number and percent distribution of Asian households, and Asian share of total, by age of householder, 2000; numbers in thousands)

	total	Asian households number	percent distribution	share of total
Total households	**104,705**	**3,337**	**100.0%**	**3.2%**
Under age 20	914	51	1.5	5.6
Aged 20 to 24	4,946	187	5.6	3.8
Aged 25 to 29	8,520	401	12.0	4.7
Aged 30 to 34	10,107	440	13.2	4.4
Aged 35 to 39	11,728	397	11.9	3.4
Aged 40 to 44	12,227	426	12.8	3.5
Aged 45 to 54	20,927	728	21.8	3.5
Aged 55 to 64	13,592	346	10.4	2.5
Aged 65 or older	21,744	363	10.9	1.7
Aged 65 to 74	11,325	247	7.4	2.2
Aged 75 or older	10,419	116	3.5	1.1

Source: Bureau of the Census, America's Families and Living Arrangements: March 2000, *detailed tables from Current Population Report P20-537, Internet site <www.census.gov/population/www/socdemo/hh-fam/p20-537_00.html>; calculations by New Strategist*

Asian Households by Household Type, 2000

(number of total households, number and percent distribution of Asian households, and Asian share of total, by type, 2000; numbers in thousands)

	total	Asian households number	percent distribution	share of total
Total households	**104,705**	**3,337**	**100.0%**	**3.2%**
Family households	**72,025**	**2,506**	**75.1**	**3.5**
Married couples	55,311	1,996	59.8	3.6
With children under age 18	25,248	1,145	34.3	4.5
Without children under age 18	30,062	852	25.5	2.8
Female householder, no spouse present	12,687	331	9.9	2.6
With children under age 18	7,571	170	5.1	2.2
Without children under age 18	5,116	162	4.9	3.2
Male householder, no spouse present	4,028	179	5.4	4.4
With children under age 18	1,786	40	1.2	2.2
Without children under age 18	2,242	138	4.1	6.2
Nonfamily households	**32,680**	**831**	**24.9**	**2.5**
Female householder	18,039	399	12.0	2.2
Living alone	15,543	311	9.3	2.0
Male householder	14,641	432	12.9	3.0
Living alone	11,181	313	9.4	2.8

Source: Bureau of the Census, America's Families and Living Arrangements: March 2000, *detailed tables from Current Population Report P20-537, Internet site <www.census.gov/population/www/socdemo/hh-fam/p20-537_00.html>; calculations by New Strategist*

Asian Households by Household Type, 2000 Census

(number of total households, number and percent distribution of Asian households, and Asian share of total, by type, 2000)

		Asian households		
	total	*number*	*percent distribution*	*share of total*
Total households	**105,480,101**	**3,510,868**	**100.0%**	**3.3%**
Family households	**71,787,347**	**2,592,267**	**73.8**	**3.6**
Married couples	54,493,232	2,082,057	59.3	3.8
With children under age 18	24,835,505	1,191,733	33.9	4.8
Without children under age 18	29,657,727	890,324	25.4	3.0
Female householder, no spouse present	12,900,103	336,750	9.6	2.6
With children under age 18	7,561,874	163,804	4.7	2.2
Without children under age 18	5,338,229	172,946	4.9	3.2
Male householder, no spouse present	4,394,012	173,460	4.9	3.9
With children under age 18	2,190,989	53,896	1.5	2.5
Without children under age 18	2,203,023	119,564	3.4	5.4
Nonfamily households	**33,692,754**	**918,601**	**26.2**	**2.7**
Living alone	27,230,075	664,347	18.9	2.4
Living with nonrelatives	6,462,679	254,254	7.2	3.9

Note: Number of Asian households includes householders who identified themselves as Asian alone and in combination with other races.
Source: Bureau of the Census, Census 2000 PHC-T-15, Table 4, General Demographic Characteristics for the Asian Population; calculations by New Strategist

Asian Households by Size, 2000

(number of total households, number and percent distribution of Asian households, and Asian share of total, by size, 2000; numbers in thousands)

	total	Asian households		
		number	percent distribution	share of total
Total households	**104,705**	**3,337**	**100.0%**	**3.2%**
One person	26,724	625	18.7	2.3
Two people	34,666	870	26.1	2.5
Three people	17,152	639	19.1	3.7
Four people	15,309	645	19.3	4.2
Five people	6,981	287	8.6	4.1
Six people	2,445	166	5.0	6.8
Seven or more people	1,428	105	3.1	7.4

Source: Bureau of the Census, America's Families and Living Arrangements: March 2000, *detailed tables from Current Population Report P20-537, Internet site <www.census.gov/population/www/socdemo/hh-fam/p20-537_00.html>; calculations by New Strategist*

Asian Households by Age of Householder and Household Type, 2000

(number and percent distribution of Asian households by age of householder and household type, 2000; numbers in thousands)

| | total | family households | | | | nonfamily households | |
		total	married couples	female hh, no spouse present	male hh, no spouse present	female house-holder	male house-holder
Asian households	**3,337**	**2,506**	**1,996**	**331**	**179**	**399**	**432**
Under age 20	51	35	10	15	9	10	6
Aged 20 to 24	187	85	32	29	25	35	67
Aged 25 to 29	401	220	149	42	29	73	109
Aged 30 to 34	440	319	267	15	37	52	69
Aged 35 to 39	397	313	250	42	20	28	57
Aged 40 to 44	426	349	285	52	12	36	40
Aged 45 to 54	728	633	544	70	19	54	40
Aged 55 to 64	346	294	247	35	11	34	18
Aged 65 or older	363	259	212	32	15	76	27
Aged 65 to 74	247	190	161	22	7	46	10
Aged 75 to 84	116	69	51	10	8	30	17
Asian households	**100.0%**	**75.1%**	**59.8%**	**9.9%**	**5.4%**	**12.0%**	**12.9%**
Under age 20	100.0	68.6	19.6	29.4	17.6	19.6	11.8
Aged 20 to 24	100.0	45.5	17.1	15.5	13.4	18.7	35.8
Aged 25 to 29	100.0	54.9	37.2	10.5	7.2	18.2	27.2
Aged 30 to 34	100.0	72.5	60.7	3.4	8.4	11.8	15.7
Aged 35 to 39	100.0	78.8	63.0	10.6	5.0	7.1	14.4
Aged 40 to 44	100.0	81.9	66.9	12.2	2.8	8.5	9.4
Aged 45 to 54	100.0	87.0	74.7	9.6	2.6	7.4	5.5
Aged 55 to 64	100.0	85.0	71.4	10.1	3.2	9.8	5.2
Aged 65 or older	100.0	71.3	58.4	8.8	4.1	20.9	7.4
Aged 65 to 74	100.0	76.9	65.2	8.9	2.8	18.6	4.0
Aged 75 to 84	100.0	59.5	44.0	8.6	6.9	25.9	14.7

Source: Bureau of the Census, America's Families and Living Arrangements: March 2000, *detailed tables from Current Population Report P20-537, Internet site <www.census.gov/population/www/socdemo/hh-fam/p20-537_00.html>; calculations by New Strategist*

Asian Married Couples by Age of Children and Age of Householder, 2000

(number and percent distribution of Asian married couples by presence and age of own children at home and age of householder, 2000; numbers in thousands)

	total					age of householder					
		< age 20	20–24	25–29	30–34	35–39	40–44	45–54	55–64	65–74	75+
Asian married couples	1,996	10	32	149	267	250	285	544	247	161	51
With children of any age	1,403	3	9	60	192	207	268	459	131	52	20
With children under age 18	1,145	3	9	60	192	207	261	355	45	10	2
Aged 12 to 17	533	–	–	3	21	49	130	281	41	9	–
Aged 6 to 11	550	–	–	23	73	112	175	146	17	1	2
Under age 6	500	3	9	58	158	134	94	37	5	–	2
Under age 1	91	–	–	14	33	26	15	2	–	–	–
Asian married couples	100.0%	100.0%	100.0%	100.0%	100.0%	100.0%	100.0%	100.0%	100.0%	100.0%	100.0%
With children of any age	70.3	30.0	28.1	40.3	71.9	82.8	94.0	84.4	53.0	32.3	39.2
With children under age 18	57.4	30.0	28.1	40.3	71.9	82.8	91.6	65.3	18.2	6.2	3.9
Aged 12 to 17	26.7	–	–	2.0	7.9	19.6	45.6	51.7	16.6	5.6	–
Aged 6 to 11	27.6	–	–	15.4	27.3	44.8	61.4	26.8	6.9	0.6	3.9
Under age 6	25.1	30.0	28.1	38.9	59.2	53.6	33.0	6.8	2.0	–	3.9
Under age 1	4.6	–	–	9.4	12.4	10.4	5.3	0.4	–	–	–

Note: Numbers will not add to total because households may have children in more than one age group; (–) means sample is too small to make a reliable estimate.
Source: Bureau of the Census, America's Families and Living Arrangements: March 2000, detailed tables from Current Population Report P20-537, Internet site <www.census.gov/population/www/socdemo/hh-fam/p20-537_00.html>; calculations by New Strategist

Asian Female-Headed Families by Age of Children and Age of Householder, 2000

(number and percent distribution of Asian female-headed families by presence and age of own children at home and age of householder, 2000; numbers in thousands)

	total						age of householder				
		< age 20	20–24	25–29	30–34	35–39	40–44	45–54	55–64	65–74	75+
Asian female-headed families	331	15	29	42	15	42	52	70	35	22	10
With children of any age	241	6	15	19	14	42	44	50	27	17	6
With children under age 18	170	1	15	19	14	42	39	31	8	–	–
Aged 12 to 17	94	–	–	–	3	30	28	26	6	–	–
Aged 6 to 11	89	–	2	18	10	28	15	14	1	–	–
Under age 6	40	1	14	10	6	7	2	–	–	–	–
Under age 1	1	–	–	–	1	–	–	–	–	–	–
Asian female-headed families	100.0%	100.0%	100.0%	100.0%	100.0%	100.0%	100.0%	100.0%	100.0%	100.0%	100.0%
With children of any age	72.8	40.0	51.7	45.2	93.3	100.0	84.6	71.4	77.1	77.3	60.0
With children under age 18	51.4	6.7	51.7	45.2	93.3	100.0	75.0	44.3	22.9	–	–
Aged 12 to 17	28.4	–	–	–	20.0	71.4	53.8	37.1	17.1	–	–
Aged 6 to 11	26.9	–	6.9	42.9	66.7	66.7	28.8	20.0	2.9	–	–
Under age 6	12.1	6.7	48.3	23.8	40.0	16.7	3.8	–	–	–	–
Under age 1	0.3	–	–	–	6.7	–	–	–	–	–	–

Note: Numbers will not add to total because households may have children in more than one age group; (–) means sample is too small to make a reliable estimate.
Source: Bureau of the Census, America's Families and Living Arrangements: March 2000, detailed tables from Current Population Report P20-537, Internet site <www.census.gov/population/www/socdemo/hh-fam/p20-537_00.html>; calculations by New Strategist

Asian Single-Person Households by Age of Householder, 2000

(total number of Asian households, number and percent distribution of Asian single-person households, and single-person share of total, by age of householder, 2000; numbers in thousands)

| | total | single-person households | | |
		number	percent distribution	share of total
Asian households	**3,337**	**625**	**100.0%**	**18.7%**
Under age 20	51	10	1.6	19.6
Under age 25	187	59	9.4	31.6
Aged 25 to 29	401	136	21.8	33.9
Aged 30 to 34	440	87	13.9	19.8
Aged 35 to 39	397	72	11.5	18.1
Aged 40 to 44	426	49	7.8	11.5
Aged 45 to 54	728	73	11.7	10.0
Aged 55 to 64	346	45	7.2	13.0
Aged 65 to 74	247	50	8.0	20.2
Aged 75 or older	116	43	6.9	37.1

Source: Bureau of the Census, America's Families and Living Arrangements: March 2000, *detailed tables from Current Population Report P20-537, Internet site <www.census.gov/population/www/socdemo/hh-fam/p20-537_00.html>; calculations by New Strategist*

Asian Children by Living Arrangement, 2000

(number and percent distribution of Asian children under age 18 by living arrangement, 2000; numbers in thousands)

	number	percent distribution
Total Asian children	**3,047**	**100.0%**
Living with both parents	2,454	80.5
Living with mother only	428	14.0
Living with father only	76	2.5
Living with neither parent	88	2.9
Living with both parents	**2,454**	**100.0**
Child of householder	2,395	97.6
Grandchild of householder	33	1.3
Other relative of householder	26	1.1
Living with mother only	**428**	**100.0**
Child of householder	335	78.3
Grandchild of householder	62	14.5
Other relative of householder	20	4.7
Nonrelative of householder	11	2.6
Living with father only	**76**	**100.0**
Child of householder	59	77.6
Grandchild of householder	9	11.8
Other relative of householder	7	9.2
Living with neither parent	**88**	**100.0**
Grandchild of householder	29	33.0
Other relative of householder	45	51.1
Foster child	1	1.1
Other nonrelative of householder	12	13.6

Source: Bureau of the Census, America's Families and Living Arrangements: March 2000, *detailed tables from Current Population Report P20-537, Internet site <www.census.gov/population/www/socdemo/hh-fam/p20-537_00.html>; calculations by New Strategist*

Asian Men by Living Arrangement and Age, 2000

(number and percent distribution of Asian men aged 15 or older by living arrangement and age, 2000; numbers in thousands)

	total	15–19	20–24	25–29	30–34	35–39	40–44	45–54	55–64	65–74	75+
Asian men	**4,041**	**481**	**419**	**475**	**457**	**435**	**393**	**677**	**322**	**240**	**141**
Householder	**2,565**	**15**	**122**	**259**	**348**	**327**	**325**	**617**	**270**	**190**	**93**
Married couple hh or spouse	1,954	–	30	121	243	250	273	558	241	173	67
Male family householder	179	9	25	29	37	20	12	19	11	7	8
Living alone	313	3	32	83	54	50	28	27	14	8	14
Living with nonrelatives	119	3	35	26	14	7	12	13	4	2	4
Not a householder	**1,476**	**466**	**297**	**216**	**109**	**108**	**68**	**60**	**52**	**50**	**48**
Child of householder	837	434	185	100	56	30	24	7	–	–	–
In family, other relative of hh	408	28	66	47	31	36	20	40	45	50	45
Not in family	231	4	46	69	22	42	24	13	7	–	3
Asian men	**100.0%**	**100.0%**	**100.0%**	**100.0%**	**100.0%**	**100.0%**	**100.0%**	**100.0%**	**100.0%**	**100.0%**	**100.0%**
Householder	**63.5**	**3.1**	**29.1**	**54.5**	**76.1**	**75.2**	**82.7**	**91.1**	**83.9**	**79.2**	**66.0**
Married couple hh or spouse	48.4	–	7.2	25.5	53.2	57.5	69.5	82.4	74.8	72.1	47.5
Male family householder	4.4	1.9	6.0	6.1	8.1	4.6	3.1	2.8	3.4	2.9	5.7
Living alone	7.7	0.6	7.6	17.5	11.8	11.5	7.1	4.0	4.3	3.3	9.9
Living with nonrelatives	2.9	0.6	8.4	5.5	3.1	1.6	3.1	1.9	1.2	0.8	2.8
Not a householder	**36.5**	**96.9**	**70.9**	**45.5**	**23.9**	**24.8**	**17.3**	**8.9**	**16.1**	**20.8**	**34.0**
Child of householder	20.7	90.2	44.2	21.1	12.3	6.9	6.1	1.0	–	–	–
In family, other relative of hh	10.1	5.8	15.8	9.9	6.8	8.3	5.1	5.9	14.0	20.8	31.9
Not in family	5.7	0.8	11.0	14.5	4.8	9.7	6.1	1.9	2.2	–	2.1

Note: (–) means sample is too small to make a reliable estimate.
Source: Bureau of the Census, America's Families and Living Arrangements: March 2000, detailed tables from Current Population Report P20-537, Internet site <www.census.gov/population/www/socdemo/hh-fam/p20-537_00.html>; calculations by New Strategist

Asian Women by Living Arrangement and Age, 2000

(number and percent distribution of Asian women aged 15 or older by living arrangement and age, 2000; numbers in thousands)

Asian women	total	15–19	20–24	25–29	30–34	35–39	40–44	45–54	55–64	65–74	75+
Asian women	4,373	456	393	514	451	504	503	753	384	275	147
Householder	2,955	39	127	353	357	423	445	632	317	191	75
Married couple hh or spouse	2,225	14	62	238	290	353	356	508	247	123	35
Female family householder	331	15	29	42	15	42	52	70	35	22	10
Living alone	311	6	27	54	33	23	21	46	31	42	30
Living with nonrelatives	88	4	9	19	19	5	16	8	4	4	–
Not a householder	1,418	417	266	161	94	81	58	121	67	84	72
Child of householder	697	356	174	73	31	35	13	12	5	–	–
In family, other relative of hh	492	33	30	59	37	22	34	78	55	78	66
Not in family	229	28	62	29	26	24	11	31	7	6	6
Asian women	100.0%	100.0%	100.0%	100.0%	100.0%	100.0%	100.0%	100.0%	100.0%	100.0%	100.0%
Householder	67.6	8.6	32.3	68.7	79.2	83.9	88.5	83.9	82.6	69.5	51.0
Married couple hh or spouse	50.9	3.1	15.8	46.3	64.3	70.0	70.8	67.5	64.3	44.7	23.8
Female family householder	7.6	3.3	7.4	8.2	3.3	8.3	10.3	9.3	9.1	8.0	6.8
Living alone	7.1	1.3	6.9	10.5	7.3	4.6	4.2	6.1	8.1	15.3	20.4
Living with nonrelatives	2.0	0.9	2.3	3.7	4.2	1.0	3.2	1.1	1.0	1.5	–
Not a householder	32.4	91.4	67.7	31.3	20.8	16.1	11.5	16.1	17.4	30.5	49.0
Child of householder	15.9	78.1	44.3	14.2	6.9	6.9	2.6	1.6	1.3	–	–
In family, other relative of hh	11.3	7.2	7.6	11.5	8.2	4.4	6.8	10.4	14.3	28.4	44.9
Not in family	5.2	6.1	15.8	5.6	5.8	4.8	2.2	4.1	1.8	2.2	4.1

Note: (–) means sample is too small to make a reliable estimate.

Source: Bureau of the Census, America's Families and Living Arrangements: March 2000, detailed tables from Current Population Report P20-537, Internet site <www.census.gov/population/www/socdemo/hh-fam/p20-537_00.html>; calculations by New Strategist

Asian Men by Marital Status and Age, 2000

(number and percent distribution of Asian men aged 15 or older by age and marital status, 2000; numbers in thousands)

	total	never married	married	divorced	widowed
Asian men	**4,041**	**1,528**	**2,281**	**183**	**49**
Under age 20	483	483	–	–	–
Aged 20 to 24	419	372	47	–	–
Aged 25 to 29	475	315	146	14	–
Aged 30 to 34	457	135	302	19	2
Aged 35 to 39	434	100	292	40	3
Aged 40 to 44	394	58	304	31	–
Aged 45 to 49	339	29	297	13	–
Aged 50 to 54	339	11	305	22	–
Aged 55 to 59	177	3	164	11	–
Aged 60 to 64	146	9	110	17	9
Aged 65 or older	379	14	313	16	36
Aged 65 to 69	147	2	133	7	5
Aged 70 to 74	93	4	83	0	6
Aged 75 or older	139	8	97	9	25
Asian men	**100.0%**	**37.8%**	**56.4%**	**4.5%**	**1.2%**
Under age 20	100.0	100.0	–	–	–
Aged 20 to 24	100.0	88.8	11.2	–	–
Aged 25 to 29	100.0	66.3	30.7	2.9	–
Aged 30 to 34	100.0	29.5	66.1	4.2	0.4
Aged 35 to 39	100.0	23.0	67.3	9.2	0.7
Aged 40 to 44	100.0	14.7	77.2	7.9	–
Aged 45 to 49	100.0	8.6	87.6	3.8	–
Aged 50 to 54	100.0	3.2	90.0	6.5	–
Aged 55 to 59	100.0	1.7	92.7	6.2	–
Aged 60 to 64	100.0	6.2	75.3	11.6	6.2
Aged 65 or older	100.0	3.7	82.6	4.2	9.5
Aged 65 to 69	100.0	1.4	90.5	4.8	3.4
Aged 70 to 74	100.0	4.3	89.2	0.0	6.5
Aged 75 or older	100.0	5.8	69.8	6.5	18.0

Note: (–) means sample is too small to make a reliable estimate.
Source: Bureau of the Census, Marital Status and Living Arrangements: March 2000 (Update), detailed tables for Current Population Report P20-537, 2001; Internet site <www.census.gov/population/socdemo/hh-fam/p20-537/2000/tabA1.txt>

Asian Women by Marital Status and Age, 2000

(number and percent distribution of Asian women aged 15 or older by age and marital status, 2000; numbers in thousands)

	total	never married	married	divorced	widowed
Asian women	**4,374**	**1,259**	**2,513**	**314**	**287**
Under age 20	456	432	13	6	4
Aged 20 to 24	391	318	70	3	–
Aged 25 to 29	513	214	283	16	–
Aged 30 to 34	451	102	323	25	1
Aged 35 to 39	502	72	370	51	9
Aged 40 to 44	503	43	396	59	5
Aged 45 to 49	431	47	311	59	13
Aged 50 to 54	323	14	244	44	20
Aged 55 to 59	201	7	167	7	19
Aged 60 to 64	183	4	126	29	24
Aged 65 or older	421	7	210	14	191
Aged 65 to 69	165	2	108	7	48
Aged 70 to 74	110	2	57	5	46
Aged 75 or older	146	3	45	2	97
Asian women	**100.0%**	**28.8%**	**57.5%**	**7.2%**	**6.6%**
Under age 20	100.0	94.7	2.9	1.3	0.9
Aged 20 to 24	100.0	81.3	17.9	0.8	–
Aged 25 to 29	100.0	41.7	55.2	3.1	–
Aged 30 to 34	100.0	22.6	71.6	5.5	0.2
Aged 35 to 39	100.0	14.3	73.7	10.2	1.8
Aged 40 to 44	100.0	8.5	78.7	11.7	1.0
Aged 45 to 49	100.0	10.9	72.2	13.7	3.0
Aged 50 to 54	100.0	4.3	75.5	13.6	6.2
Aged 55 to 59	100.0	3.5	83.1	3.5	9.5
Aged 60 to 64	100.0	2.2	68.9	15.8	13.1
Aged 65 or older	100.0	1.7	49.9	3.3	45.4
Aged 65 to 69	100.0	1.2	65.5	4.2	29.1
Aged 70 to 74	100.0	1.8	51.8	4.5	41.8
Aged 75 or older	100.0	2.1	30.8	1.4	66.4

Note: (–) means sample is too small to make a reliable estimate.
Source: Bureau of the Census, Marital Status and Living Arrangements: March 2000 (Update), *detailed tables for Current Population Report P20-537, 2001; Internet site <www.census.gov/population/socdemo/hh-fam/p20-537/2000/tabA1.txt>*

The Asian Population Numbers nearly 12 Million

Between 1990 and 2000, the Asian population rose substantially, growing from 48 to 72 percent depending on whether the comparison is with those who identify their race as Asian alone or those who describe themselves as Asian in combination with one or more other races. Despite the rapid growth of Asians, they account for just 4 percent of the total U.S. population and are greatly outnumbered by blacks and Hispanics.

Behind the growth of the Asian population is immigration. Asian immigrants accounted for 31 percent of all immigrants to the U.S. in 2000, the largest numbers coming from China, the Philippines, and India. One-fourth of the nation's foreign-born are from Asian countries.

Forty-nine percent of Asians live in the West, where they account for 12 percent of the population of the Pacific division. California is home to 35 percent of the nation's Asian population, including 50 percent of Filipinos and 40 percent of Chinese and Vietnamese. Los Angeles has more Asians (1.9 million) than any other metropolitan area, but Asians account for a larger share of the San Francisco metropolitan area population—20 percent in San Francisco versus 12 percent in Los Angeles.

■ The Asian population is much larger in some areas than others, but the Asian influence on American culture can be felt everywhere.

The Asian population grew rapidly during the 1990s

(number of people identifying themselves as Asian, 1990 and 2000; numbers in millions)

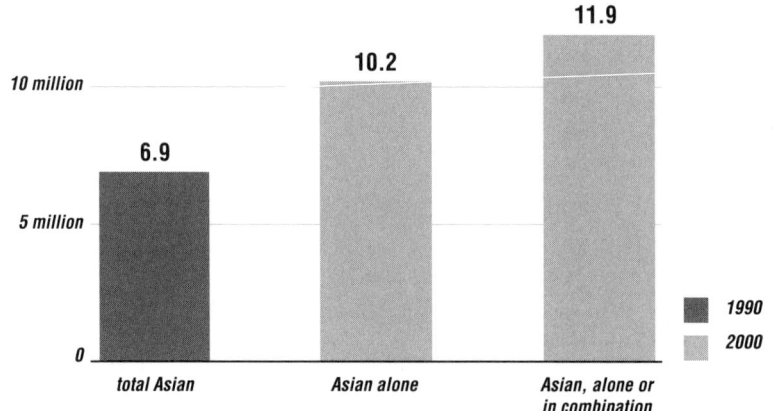

Asians, 1990 and 2000 Censuses

(number of Asians, 1990 and 2000; percent change in number, 1990–2000)

	1990	2000		percent change 1990–2000	
		Asian alone	Asian, alone or in combination	Asian alone	Asian, alone or in combination
Total Asians	6,908,638	10,242,998	11,898,828	48.3%	72.2%

Source: Bureau of the Census, The Asian Population: 2000, *Census 2000 Brief, C2KBR/01-16, 2002; calculations by New Strategist*

Asians by Racial Combination, 2000 Census

(number of total people, number of Asians by racial identification, and Asian share of total; number and percent distribution of Asians by racial combination, 2000)

	number	percent
Total people	**281,421,906**	**100.0%**
Asian, alone or in combination with one or more other races	**11,898,828**	**4.2**
Asian alone	10,242,998	3.6
Asian in combination	1,655,830	0.6
Asian, alone or in combination with one or more other races	**11,898,828**	**100.0**
Asian alone	10,242,998	86.1
Asian in combination	1,655,830	13.9
Asian and white	868,395	7.3
Asian and Native Hawaiian	138,802	1.2
Asian and black	106,782	0.9
Asian, Native Hawaiian, and white	89,611	0.8
All other combinations	452,240	3.8

Note: Native Hawaiians include other Pacific Islanders.
Source: Bureau of the Census, Overview of Race and Hispanic Origin, *Census 2000 Brief, CENBR/01-1, 2001*

Asians by Hispanic Origin, 2000 Census

(number and percent distribution of Asians by Hispanic origin and racial combination, 2000)

	Asian, alone or in combination		Asian alone		Asian in combination	
	number	percent distribution	number	percent distribution	number	percent distribution
Total Asians	**11,898,828**	**100.0%**	**10,242,998**	**100.0%**	**1,655,830**	**100.0%**
Hispanic	319,334	2.7	119,829	1.2	199,505	12.0
Mexican	134,382	1.1	52,023	0.5	82,359	5.0
Puerto Rican	43,137	0.4	16,269	0.2	26,868	1.6
Cuban	8,587	0.1	4,263	0.0	4,324	0.3
Other Hispanic	113,228	1.0	47,274	0.5	65,954	4.0
Non-Hispanic	11,579,494	97.3	10,123,169	98.8	1,456,325	88.0

Source: Bureau of the Census, Census 2000 PHC-T-15, Table 4, General Demographic Characteristics for the Asian Population; *calculations by New Strategist*

Asians by Ethnicity and Racial Combination, 2000 Census

(number of people identifying themselves as Asian alone, Asian in combination, and Asian and ethnic group alone or in combination, by ethnic group, 2000)

	Asian alone		Asian in combination		Asian and ethnic group alone or in combination
	one Asian ethnic group	more than one Asian ethnic group	one Asian ethnic group	more than one Asian ethnic group	
Total Asians	**10,019,405**	**223,593**	**1,516,841**	**138,989**	**11,898,828**
Asian Indian	1,678,765	40,013	165,437	15,384	1,899,599
Bangladeshi	41,280	5,625	9,655	852	57,412
Bhutanese	183	9	17	3	212
Burmese	13,159	1,461	1,837	263	16,270
Cambodian	171,937	11,832	20,830	1,453	206,052
Chinese	2,314,537	130,826	201,688	87,790	2,734,841
Filipino	1,850,314	57,811	385,236	71,454	2,364,815
Hmong	169,428	5,284	11,153	445	186,310
Indo Chinese	113	55	23	8	199
Indonesian	39,757	4,429	17,256	1,631	63,073
Iwo Jiman	15	3	60	0	78
Japanese	796,700	55,537	241,209	55,486	1,148,932
Korean	1,076,872	22,550	114,211	14,794	1,228,427
Laotian	168,707	10,396	17,914	1,186	198,203
Malaysian	10,690	4,339	2,837	700	18,566
Maldivian	27	2	22	0	51
Nepalese	7,858	351	1,128	62	9,399
Okinawan	3,513	2,625	2,816	1,645	10,599
Pakistani	153,533	11,095	37,587	2,094	204,309
Singaporean	1,437	580	307	70	2,394
Sri Lankan	20,145	1,219	2,966	257	24,587
Taiwanese	118,048	14,096	11,394	1,257	144,795
Thai	112,989	7,929	27,170	2,195	150,283
Vietnamese	1,122,528	47,144	48,639	5,425	1,223,736
Other Asian	146,870	19,576	195,449	7,535	369,430

Note: Numbers may not add to total because people could identify themselves with more than one ethnic group.
Source: Bureau of the Census, The Asian Population: 2000, *Census 2000 Brief, C2KBR/01-16, 2002*

Asians Ranked by Ethnic Group, 2000 Census

(number and percent distribution of people identifying themselves as Asian alone or in combination and ethnic group alone or in combination, by ethnic group, 2000; ranked by size)

	number	percent
Total Asians	**11,898,828**	**100.0%**
Chinese	2,734,841	23.0
Filipino	2,364,815	19.9
Asian Indian	1,899,599	16.0
Korean	1,228,427	10.3
Vietnamese	1,223,736	10.3
Japanese	1,148,932	9.7
Cambodian	206,052	1.7
Pakistani	204,309	1.7
Laotian	198,203	1.7
Hmong	186,310	1.6
Thai	150,283	1.3
Taiwanese	144,795	1.2
Indonesian	63,073	0.5
Bangladeshi	57,412	0.5
Sri Lankan	24,587	0.2
Malaysian	18,566	0.2
Burmese	16,270	0.1
Okinawan	10,599	0.1
Nepalese	9,399	0.1
Singaporean	2,394	0.0
Bhutanese	212	0.0
Indo Chinese	199	0.0
Iwo Jiman	78	0.0
Maldivian	51	0.0
Other Asian	369,430	3.1

Note: Numbers will not add to total because people could identify themselves with more than one ethnic group.
Source: Bureau of the Census, The Asian Population: 2000, *Census 2000 Brief, C2KBR/01-16, 2002*

Asians by Age, 2000 Census

(number of people identifying themselves as Asian alone or in combination, Asian alone, and Asian in combination, and percent of Asian alone or in combination identifying themselves as Asian in combination, by age, 2000)

	Asian, alone or in combination	Asian alone	Asian in combination	
			number	percent of Asian, alone or in combination
Total Asians	**11,898,828**	**10,242,998**	**1,655,830**	**13.9%**
Under age 5	919,078	670,406	248,672	27.1
Aged 5 to 9	897,412	680,536	216,876	24.2
Aged 10 to 14	873,617	684,525	189,092	21.6
Aged 15 to 19	916,676	746,511	170,165	18.6
Aged 20 to 24	961,389	816,452	144,937	15.1
Aged 25 to 29	1,116,520	986,222	130,298	11.7
Aged 30 to 34	1,062,354	949,418	112,936	10.6
Aged 35 to 39	1,014,467	909,439	105,028	10.4
Aged 40 to 44	938,398	846,118	92,280	9.8
Aged 45 to 49	820,538	749,777	70,761	8.6
Aged 50 to 54	678,180	626,255	51,925	7.7
Aged 55 to 59	468,743	433,749	34,994	7.5
Aged 60 to 64	369,731	342,795	26,936	7.3
Aged 65 to 69	295,106	274,085	21,021	7.1
Aged 70 to 74	236,587	220,066	16,521	7.0
Aged 75 to 79	167,596	155,965	11,631	6.9
Aged 80 to 84	94,760	88,183	6,577	6.9
Aged 85 or older	67,676	62,496	5,180	7.7
Aged 18 to 24	1,346,262	1,133,431	212,831	15.8
Aged 18 or older	8,676,918	7,777,999	898,919	10.4
Aged 65 or older	861,725	800,795	60,930	7.1

Source: U.S. Census Bureau, Census 2000 Summary File 1; calculations by New Strategist

Asian Share of Total Population by Age, 2000 Census

(number of total people, number and percent distribution of those identifying themselves as Asian alone or in combination, and Asian alone or in combination share of total, by age, 2000)

	total	Asian, alone or in combination		
		number	percent distribution	share of total
Total people	**281,421,906**	**11,898,828**	**100.0%**	**4.2%**
Under age 5	19,175,798	919,078	7.7	4.8
Aged 5 to 9	20,549,505	897,412	7.5	4.4
Aged 10 to 14	20,528,072	873,617	7.3	4.3
Aged 15 to 19	20,219,890	916,676	7.7	4.5
Aged 20 to 24	18,964,001	961,389	8.1	5.1
Aged 25 to 29	19,381,336	1,116,520	9.4	5.8
Aged 30 to 34	20,510,388	1,062,354	8.9	5.2
Aged 35 to 39	22,706,664	1,014,467	8.5	4.5
Aged 40 to 44	22,441,863	938,398	7.9	4.2
Aged 45 to 49	20,092,404	820,538	6.9	4.1
Aged 50 to 54	17,585,548	678,180	5.7	3.9
Aged 55 to 59	13,469,237	468,743	3.9	3.5
Aged 60 to 64	10,805,447	369,731	3.1	3.4
Aged 65 to 69	9,533,545	295,106	2.5	3.1
Aged 70 to 74	8,857,441	236,587	2.0	2.7
Aged 75 to 79	7,415,813	167,596	1.4	2.3
Aged 80 to 84	4,945,367	94,760	0.8	1.9
Aged 85 or older	4,239,587	67,676	0.6	1.6
Aged 18 to 24	27,143,454	1,346,262	11.3	5.0
Aged 18 or older	209,128,094	8,676,918	72.9	4.1
Aged 65 or older	34,991,753	861,725	7.2	2.5

Source: U.S. Census Bureau, Census 2000 Summary File 1; calculations by New Strategist

Asians by Age and Sex, 2000 Census

(number of Asians by age and sex, and sex ratio by age, 2000)

	total	females	males	sex ratio
Total Asians	**11,898,828**	**6,119,790**	**5,779,038**	**94**
Under age 5	919,078	455,110	463,968	102
Aged 5 to 9	897,412	437,671	459,741	105
Aged 10 to 14	873,617	425,044	448,573	106
Aged 15 to 19	916,676	450,293	466,383	104
Aged 20 to 24	961,389	481,776	479,613	100
Aged 25 to 29	1,116,520	567,665	548,855	97
Aged 30 to 34	1,062,354	544,359	517,995	95
Aged 35 to 39	1,014,467	522,649	491,818	94
Aged 40 to 44	938,398	493,107	445,291	90
Aged 45 to 49	820,538	439,051	381,487	87
Aged 50 to 54	678,180	363,918	314,262	86
Aged 55 to 59	468,743	248,253	220,490	89
Aged 60 to 64	369,731	196,557	173,174	88
Aged 65 to 69	295,106	165,921	129,185	78
Aged 70 to 74	236,587	136,608	99,979	73
Aged 75 to 79	167,596	95,367	72,229	76
Aged 80 to 84	94,760	55,681	39,079	70
Aged 85 or older	67,676	40,760	26,916	66
Aged 18 to 24	1,346,262	671,887	674,375	100
Aged 18 or older	8,676,918	4,541,783	4,135,135	91
Aged 65 or older	861,725	494,337	367,388	74

Note: Asians include those who identified themselves as Asian alone and those who identified themselves as Asian in combination with one or more other races; the sex ratio is the number of males per 100 females.
Source: U.S. Census Bureau, Census 2000 Summary File 1; calculations by New Strategist

Asian Immigrants by Country of Birth, 2000

(total number of immigrants, number of Asian immigrants, Asian share of total, and Asian immigrants by country of birth, 2000)

	number	share of total immigrants	share of Asian immigrants
Total immigrants	**849,807**	**100.0%**	–
Total Asian immigrants	**265,400**	**31.2**	**100.0%**
China, People's Republic	45,652	5.4	17.2
Philippines	42,474	5.0	16.0
India	42,046	4.9	15.8
Vietnam	26,747	3.1	10.1
Korea	15,830	1.9	6.0
Pakistan	14,535	1.7	5.5
Taiwan	9,040	1.1	3.4
Iran	8,519	1.0	3.2
Bangladesh	7,215	0.8	2.7
Japan	7,094	0.8	2.7
Hong Kong	5,419	0.6	2.0
Iraq	5,134	0.6	1.9
Jordan	3,909	0.5	1.5
Thailand	3,785	0.4	1.4
Lebanon	3,674	0.4	1.4
Israel	2,806	0.3	1.1
Turkey	2,613	0.3	1.0
Syria	2,374	0.3	0.9
Cambodia	2,142	0.3	0.8
Yemen	1,789	0.2	0.7
Indonesia	1,774	0.2	0.7
Malaysia	1,556	0.2	0.6
Laos	1,380	0.2	0.5
Burma	1,201	0.1	0.5
Sri Lanka	1,123	0.1	0.4
Saudi Arabia	1,063	0.1	0.4
Kuwait	1,018	0.1	0.4
Afghanistan	1,012	0.1	0.4
Singapore	671	0.1	0.3
Nepal	617	0.1	0.2
United Arab Emirates	436	0.1	0.2
Macau	270	0.0	0.1
Cyprus	162	0.0	0.1
Bahrain	106	0.0	0.0
Qatar	97	0.0	0.0
Oman	51	0.0	0.0
Mongolia	46	0.0	0.0
Brunei	16	0.0	0.0
Bhutan	3	0.0	0.0
Maldives	1	0.0	0.0

Source: U.S. Immigration and Naturalization Service, 2000 Statistical Yearbook of the Immigration and Naturalization Service, Internet site <www.ins.usdoj.gov/graphics/aboutins/statistics/IMM00yrbk/IMM2000list.htm>; calculations by New Strategist

Asian Foreign-Born by Country of Birth, 2000

(total number of foreign-born, number of Asian foreign-born, Asian share of total, and Asian foreign-born by country of birth, 2000; numbers in thousands)

	number	share of total foreign-born	share of Asian foreign-born
Total foreign-born	28,379	100.0%	–
Total Asian foreign-born	7,246	25.5	100.0%
China	1,391	4.9	19.2
Philippines	1,222	4.3	16.9
India	1,007	3.5	13.9
Vietnam	863	3.0	11.9
South Korea	701	2.5	9.7
Iran	306	1.1	4.2
Japan	274	1.0	3.8
Pakistan	197	0.7	2.7
Thailand	147	0.5	2.0
Other Asian	146	0.5	2.0
Lebanon	127	0.4	1.8
Cambodia	122	0.4	1.7
Turkey	97	0.3	1.3
Bangladesh	85	0.3	1.2
Israel	82	0.3	1.1
Iraq	81	0.3	1.1
Laos	74	0.3	1.0
Indonesia	53	0.2	0.7
Syria	45	0.2	0.6
Malaysia	43	0.2	0.6
Jordan	39	0.1	0.5
Burma	35	0.1	0.5
Palestine	33	0.1	0.5
Singapore	29	0.1	0.4
Afghanistan	27	0.1	0.4
Saudi Arabia	20	0.1	0.3

Source: Bureau of the Census, detailed tables for The Foreign Born Population in the United States: March 2000, *Current Population Report P20-534; Internet site <www.census.gov/population/www/socdemo/foreign/ p20-534.html>; calculations by New Strategist*

Asian Foreign-Born by Selected Characteristics, 2000

(number and percent distribution of the Asian foreign-born population by selected characteristics, 2000; numbers in thousands)

	number	percent
Total Asian foreign-born	**7,246**	**100.0%**
Age		
Under age 18	657	9.1
Aged 18 to 24	761	10.5
Aged 25 to 34	1,546	21.3
Aged 35 to 44	1,593	22.0
Aged 45 to 54	1,304	18.0
Aged 55 to 64	695	9.6
Aged 65 or older	690	9.5
Sex		
Male	3,466	47.8
Female	3,780	52.2
Race		
White	1,096	15.1
Black	49	0.7
American Indian	39	0.5
Asian	6,063	83.7
Hispanic origin		
Hispanic	74	1.0
Non-Hispanic white	1,050	14.5
Citizenship status		
Naturalized citizen	3,415	47.1
Not a U.S. citizen	3,831	52.9
Year of arrival		
Arrived 1990 or later	2,852	39.4
Arrived before 1990	4,394	60.6

(continued)

(continued from previous page)

	number	percent
Household income in 1999		
Total households	**2,811**	**100.0%**
Under $5,000	152	5.4
$5,000 to $9,999	136	4.8
$10,000 to $14,999	165	5.9
$15,000 to $24,999	242	8.6
$25,000 to $34,999	295	10.5
$35,000 to $49,999	389	13.8
$50,000 to $74,999	495	17.6
$75,000 to $99,999	337	12.0
$100,000 and over	599	21.3
Median income	$51,363	–
Poverty rate	–	12.8
Median earnings of full-time year-round workers aged 16+		
Men	$36,911	–
Women	29,662	–
Education		
Total aged 25 or older	**5,827**	**100.0**
Not a high school graduate	943	16.2
High school graduate or more	4,884	83.8
Bachelors degree or more	2,618	44.9
Graduate/professional degree	985	16.9

Note: (–) means not applicable.
Source: Bureau of the Census, detailed tables for The Foreign Born Population in the United States: March 2000, *Current Population Report P20-534; Internet site <www.census.gov/population/www/socdemo/foreign/p20-534.html>; calculations by New Strategist*

Asians by Region, 1990 and 2000 Censuses

(number of Asians by region, 1990 and 2000; percent change in number identifying themselves as Asian alone and as Asian alone or in combination, 1990–2000)

| | | 2000 | | percent change 1990–2000 | |
	1990	Asian alone	Asian, alone or in combination	Asian alone	Asian, alone or in combination
Total Asians	**6,908,638**	**10,242,998**	**11,898,828**	**48.3%**	**72.2%**
Northeast	1,324,865	2,119,426	2,368,297	60.0	78.8
Midwest	755,403	1,197,554	1,392,938	58.5	84.4
South	1,094,179	1,922,407	2,267,094	75.7	107.2
West	3,734,191	5,003,611	5,870,499	34.0	57.2

Source: Bureau of the Census, The Asian Population: 2000, *Census 2000 Brief, C2KBR/01-16, 2002; calculations by New Strategist*

Asians by Region and Division, 2000 Census

(number of total people, number and percent distribution of Asians, and Asian share of total, by region and division, 2000, numbers in thousands)

	total	Asian number	Asian percent distribution	Asian share of total
Total population	**281,421,906**	**11,898,828**	**100.0%**	**4.2%**
Northeast	**53,594,378**	**2,368,297**	**19.9**	**4.4**
New England	13,922,517	426,140	3.6	3.1
Middle Atlantic	39,671,861	1,942,157	16.3	4.9
Midwest	**64,392,776**	**1,392,938**	**11.7**	**2.2**
East North Central	45,155,037	1,017,361	8.6	2.3
West North Central	19,237,739	375,577	3.2	2.0
South	**100,236,820**	**2,267,094**	**19.1**	**2.3**
South Atlantic	51,769,160	1,305,708	11.0	2.5
East South Central	17,022,810	168,719	1.4	1.0
West South Central	31,444,850	792,667	6.7	2.5
West	**63,197,932**	**5,870,499**	**49.3**	**9.3**
Mountain	18,172,295	455,816	3.8	2.5
Pacific	45,025,637	5,414,683	45.5	12.0

Note: Asians include those who identified themselves as Asian alone and those who identified themselves as Asian in combination with one or more other races.
Source: Bureau of the Census, Profiles of General Demographic Characteristics, *2000 Census of Population and Housing, 2001; calculations by New Strategist*

Asians by Region, Division, and Ethnicity, 2000 Census

(number and percent distribution of Asians by region, division, and ethnicity, 2000)

	total	Asian Indian	Chinese	Filipino	Japanese	Korean	Vietnamese	other
Total Asians	10,242,998	1,678,765	2,432,585	1,850,314	796,700	1,076,872	1,122,528	1,285,234
Northeast	2,119,426	554,302	691,755	202,100	76,350	246,144	115,487	233,288
New England	374,361	76,157	115,976	20,668	17,415	29,337	46,452	68,356
Middle Atlantic	1,745,065	478,145	575,779	181,432	58,935	216,807	69,035	164,932
Midwest	1,197,554	293,012	212,081	151,057	63,012	132,378	106,938	239,076
East North Central	880,635	245,456	164,054	127,900	50,332	100,017	51,320	141,556
West North Central	316,919	47,556	48,027	23,157	12,680	32,361	55,618	97,520
South	1,922,407	440,714	342,523	244,547	77,468	224,260	335,679	257,216
South Atlantic	1,101,965	261,130	194,871	161,319	44,569	152,526	139,202	148,348
East South Central	136,378	30,333	24,259	13,867	10,719	16,663	20,618	19,919
West South Central	684,064	149,251	123,393	69,361	22,180	55,017	175,859	88,949
West	5,003,611	390,737	1,186,226	1,252,610	579,870	474,090	564,424	555,654
Mountain	353,429	40,187	66,676	74,585	39,722	40,831	43,672	47,756
Pacific	4,650,182	350,550	1,119,550	1,178,025	540,148	433,259	520,752	507,898

Percent distribution by Asian ethnicity

	total	Asian Indian	Chinese	Filipino	Japanese	Korean	Vietnamese	other
Total Asians	100.0%	16.4%	23.7%	18.1%	7.8%	10.5%	11.0%	12.5%
Northeast	100.0	26.2	32.6	9.5	3.6	11.6	5.4	11.0
New England	100.0	20.3	31.0	5.5	4.7	7.8	12.4	18.3
Middle Atlantic	100.0	27.4	33.0	10.4	3.4	12.4	4.0	9.5
Midwest	100.0	24.5	17.7	12.6	5.3	11.1	8.9	20.0
East North Central	100.0	27.9	18.6	14.5	5.7	11.4	5.8	16.1
West North Central	100.0	15.0	15.2	7.3	4.0	10.2	17.5	30.8
South	100.0	22.9	17.8	12.7	4.0	11.7	17.5	13.4
South Atlantic	100.0	23.7	17.7	14.6	4.0	13.8	12.6	13.5
East South Central	100.0	22.2	17.8	10.2	7.9	12.2	15.1	14.6
West South Central	100.0	21.8	18.0	10.1	3.2	8.0	25.7	13.0
West	100.0	7.8	23.7	25.0	11.6	9.5	11.3	11.1
Mountain	100.0	11.4	18.9	21.1	11.2	11.6	12.4	13.5
Pacific	100.0	7.5	24.1	25.3	11.6	9.3	11.2	10.9

(continued)

(continued from previous page)

Percent distribution by region and division	total	Asian Indian	Chinese	Filipino	Japanese	Korean	Vietnamese	other
Total Asians	**100.0%**	**100.0%**	**100.0%**	**100.0%**	**100.0%**	**100.0%**	**100.0%**	**100.0%**
Northeast	**20.7**	**33.0**	**28.4**	**10.9**	**9.6**	**22.9**	**10.3**	**18.2**
New England	3.7	4.5	4.8	1.1	2.2	2.7	4.1	5.3
Middle Atlantic	17.0	28.5	23.7	9.8	7.4	20.1	6.1	12.8
Midwest	**11.7**	**17.5**	**8.7**	**8.2**	**7.9**	**12.3**	**9.5**	**18.6**
East North Central	8.6	14.6	6.7	6.9	6.3	9.3	4.6	11.0
West North Central	3.1	2.8	2.0	1.3	1.6	3.0	5.0	7.6
South	**18.8**	**26.3**	**14.1**	**13.2**	**9.7**	**20.8**	**29.9**	**20.0**
South Atlantic	10.8	15.6	8.0	8.7	5.6	14.2	12.4	11.5
East South Central	1.3	1.8	1.0	0.7	1.3	1.5	1.8	1.5
West South Central	6.7	8.9	5.1	3.7	2.8	5.1	15.7	6.9
West	**48.8**	**23.3**	**48.8**	**67.7**	**72.8**	**44.0**	**50.3**	**43.2**
Mountain	3.5	2.4	2.7	4.0	5.0	3.8	3.9	3.7
Pacific	45.4	20.9	46.0	63.7	67.8	40.2	46.4	39.5

Note: Asians include only those who identified themselves as Asian alone. Other Asian includes other Asian alone or two or more Asian ethnic categories.
Source: Bureau of the Census, Profiles of General Demographic Characteristics, *2000 Census of Population and Housing, 2001; calculations by New Strategist*

Asians by State, 1990 and 2000 Censuses

(number of Asians by state, 1990 and 2000; percent change in number identifying themselves as Asian alone and as Asian alone or in combination, 1990–2000)

	1990	2000 Asian alone	2000 Asian, alone or in combination	percent change 1990–2000 Asian alone	percent change 1990–2000 Asian, alone or in combination
Total Asians	**6,908,638**	**10,242,998**	**11,898,828**	**48.3%**	**72.2%**
Alabama	21,088	31,346	39,458	48.6	87.1
Alaska	17,814	25,116	32,686	41.0	83.5
Arizona	51,699	92,236	118,672	78.4	129.5
Arkansas	12,125	20,220	25,401	66.8	109.5
California	2,735,060	3,697,513	4,155,685	35.2	51.9
Colorado	57,122	95,213	120,779	66.7	111.4
Connecticut	50,078	82,313	95,368	64.4	90.4
Delaware	8,888	16,259	18,944	82.9	113.1
District of Columbia	10,923	15,189	17,956	39.1	64.4
Florida	149,856	266,256	333,013	77.7	122.2
Georgia	73,764	173,170	199,812	134.8	170.9
Hawaii	522,967	503,868	703,232	-3.7	34.5
Idaho	8,492	11,889	17,390	40.0	104.8
Illinois	282,569	423,603	473,649	49.9	67.6
Indiana	36,660	59,126	72,839	61.3	98.7
Iowa	25,037	36,635	43,119	46.3	72.2
Kansas	30,708	46,806	56,049	52.4	82.5
Kentucky	16,983	29,744	37,062	75.1	118.2
Louisiana	40,173	54,758	64,350	36.3	60.2
Maine	6,450	9,111	11,827	41.3	83.4
Maryland	138,148	210,929	238,408	52.7	72.6
Massachusetts	142,137	238,124	264,814	67.5	86.3
Michigan	103,501	176,510	208,329	70.5	101.3
Minnesota	76,952	141,968	162,414	84.5	111.1
Mississippi	12,679	18,626	23,281	46.9	83.6
Missouri	39,271	61,595	76,210	56.8	94.1
Montana	3,958	4,691	7,101	18.5	79.4
Nebraska	11,945	21,931	26,809	83.6	124.4
Nevada	35,232	90,266	112,456	156.2	219.2
New Hampshire	9,121	15,931	19,219	74.7	110.7

(continued)

(continued from previous page)

	1990	2000 Asian alone	2000 Asian, alone or in combination	percent change 1990–2000 Asian alone	percent change 1990–2000 Asian, alone or in combination
New Jersey	270,839	480,276	524,356	77.3%	93.6%
New Mexico	13,363	19,255	26,619	44.1	99.2
New York	689,303	1,044,976	1,169,200	51.6	69.6
North Carolina	49,970	113,689	136,212	127.5	172.6
North Dakota	3,317	3,606	4,967	8.7	49.7
Ohio	89,723	132,633	159,776	47.8	78.1
Oklahoma	32,002	46,767	58,723	46.1	83.5
Oregon	64,232	101,350	127,339	57.8	98.2
Pennsylvania	135,784	219,813	248,601	61.9	83.1
Rhode Island	18,019	23,665	28,290	31.3	57.0
South Carolina	21,399	36,014	44,931	68.3	110.0
South Dakota	2,938	4,378	6,009	49.0	104.5
Tennessee	30,944	56,662	68,918	83.1	122.7
Texas	311,918	562,319	644,193	80.3	106.5
Utah	25,696	37,108	48,692	44.4	89.5
Vermont	3,134	5,217	6,622	66.5	111.3
Virginia	156,036	261,025	304,559	67.3	95.2
Washington	195,918	322,335	395,741	64.5	102.0
West Virginia	7,283	9,434	11,873	29.5	63.0
Wisconsin	52,782	88,763	102,768	68.2	94.7
Wyoming	2,638	2,771	4,107	5.0	55.7

Source: Bureau of the Census, The Asian American Population: 2000, *Census 2000 Brief, C2KBR/01-16, 2002; calculations by New Strategist*

Asian Share of Total Population by State, 2000 Census

(number of total people, number and percent distribution of Asians, and Asian share of total, by state, 2000)

	total	Asian number	Asian percent distribution	Asian share of total
Total population	**281,421,906**	**11,898,828**	**100.0%**	**4.2%**
Alabama	4,447,100	39,458	0.3	0.9
Alaska	626,932	32,686	0.3	5.2
Arizona	5,130,632	118,672	1.0	2.3
Arkansas	2,673,400	25,401	0.2	1.0
California	33,871,648	4,155,685	34.9	12.3
Colorado	4,301,261	120,779	1.0	2.8
Connecticut	3,405,565	95,368	0.8	2.8
Delaware	783,600	18,944	0.2	2.4
District of Columbia	572,059	17,956	0.2	3.1
Florida	15,982,378	333,013	2.8	2.1
Georgia	8,186,453	199,812	1.7	2.4
Hawaii	1,211,537	703,232	5.9	58.0
Idaho	1,293,953	17,390	0.1	1.3
Illinois	12,419,293	473,649	4.0	3.8
Indiana	6,080,485	72,839	0.6	1.2
Iowa	2,926,324	43,119	0.4	1.5
Kansas	2,688,418	56,049	0.5	2.1
Kentucky	4,041,769	37,062	0.3	0.9
Louisiana	4,468,976	64,350	0.5	1.4
Maine	1,274,923	11,827	0.1	0.9
Maryland	5,296,486	238,408	2.0	4.5
Massachusetts	6,349,097	264,814	2.2	4.2
Michigan	9,938,444	208,329	1.8	2.1
Minnesota	4,919,479	162,414	1.4	3.3
Mississippi	2,844,658	23,281	0.2	0.8
Missouri	5,595,211	76,210	0.6	1.4
Montana	902,195	7,101	0.1	0.8
Nebraska	1,711,263	26,809	0.2	1.6
Nevada	1,998,257	112,456	0.9	5.6
New Hampshire	1,235,786	19,219	0.2	1.6
New Jersey	8,414,350	524,356	4.4	6.2

(continued)

(continued from previous page)

| | total | Asian | | |
		number	percent distribution	share of total
New Mexico	1,819,046	26,619	0.2%	1.5%
New York	18,976,457	1,169,200	9.8	6.2
North Carolina	8,049,313	136,212	1.1	1.7
North Dakota	642,200	4,967	0.0	0.8
Ohio	11,353,140	159,776	1.3	1.4
Oklahoma	3,450,654	58,723	0.5	1.7
Oregon	3,421,399	127,339	1.1	3.7
Pennsylvania	12,281,054	248,601	2.1	2.0
Rhode Island	1,048,319	28,290	0.2	2.7
South Carolina	4,012,012	44,931	0.4	1.1
South Dakota	754,844	6,009	0.1	0.8
Tennessee	5,689,283	68,918	0.6	1.2
Texas	20,851,820	644,193	5.4	3.1
Utah	2,233,169	48,692	0.4	2.2
Vermont	608,827	6,622	0.1	1.1
Virginia	7,078,515	304,559	2.6	4.3
Washington	5,894,121	395,741	3.3	6.7
West Virginia	1,808,344	11,873	0.1	0.7
Wisconsin	5,363,675	102,768	0.9	1.9
Wyoming	493,782	4,107	0.0	0.8

Note: Asians include those who identified themselves as Asian alone and those who identified themselves as Asian in combination with one or more other races.
Source: Bureau of the Census, Profiles of General Demographic Characteristics, *2000 Census of Population and Housing, 2001; calculations by New Strategist*

Asians in Combination by State, 2000 Census

(number of Asians identifying themselves as Asian alone or in combination, number identifying themselves as Asian in combination, and Asian in combination share of Asian alone or in combination, by state, 2000)

	Asian, alone or in combination	Asian in combination	
		number	percent of Asian, alone or in combination
Total Asians	**11,898,828**	**1,655,830**	**13.9%**
Alabama	39,458	8,112	20.6
Alaska	32,686	7,570	23.2
Arizona	118,672	26,436	22.3
Arkansas	25,401	5,181	20.4
California	4,155,685	458,172	11.0
Colorado	120,779	25,566	21.2
Connecticut	95,368	13,055	13.7
Delaware	18,944	2,685	14.2
District of Columbia	17,956	2,767	15.4
Florida	333,013	66,757	20.0
Georgia	199,812	26,642	13.3
Hawaii	703,232	199,364	28.3
Idaho	17,390	5,501	31.6
Illinois	473,649	50,046	10.6
Indiana	72,839	13,713	18.8
Iowa	43,119	6,484	15.0
Kansas	56,049	9,243	16.5
Kentucky	37,062	7,318	19.7
Louisiana	64,350	9,592	14.9
Maine	11,827	2,716	23.0
Maryland	238,408	27,479	11.5
Massachusetts	264,814	26,690	10.1
Michigan	208,329	31,819	15.3
Minnesota	162,414	20,446	12.6
Mississippi	23,281	4,655	20.0
Missouri	76,210	14,615	19.2
Montana	7,101	2,410	33.9
Nebraska	26,809	4,878	18.2
Nevada	112,456	22,190	19.7
New Hampshire	19,219	3,288	17.1

(continued)

(continued from previous page)

| | Asian, alone or in combination | Asian in combination | |
		number	percent of Asian, alone or in combination
New Jersey	524,356	44,080	8.4%
New Mexico	26,619	7,364	27.7
New York	1,169,200	124,224	10.6
North Carolina	136,212	22,523	16.5
North Dakota	4,967	1,361	27.4
Ohio	159,776	27,143	17.0
Oklahoma	58,723	11,956	20.4
Oregon	127,339	25,989	20.4
Pennsylvania	248,601	28,788	11.6
Rhode Island	28,290	4,625	16.3
South Carolina	44,931	8,917	19.8
South Dakota	6,009	1,631	27.1
Tennessee	68,918	12,256	17.8
Texas	644,193	81,874	12.7
Utah	48,692	11,584	23.8
Vermont	6,622	1,405	21.2
Virginia	304,559	43,534	14.3
Washington	395,741	73,406	18.5
West Virginia	11,873	2,439	20.5
Wisconsin	102,768	14,005	13.6
Wyoming	4,107	1,336	32.5

Source: Bureau of the Census, The Asian American Population: 2000, *Census 2000 Brief, C2KBR/01-X, 2001; calculations by New Strategist*

Asians by State and Ethnicity, 2000 Census

(number of Asians by state and ethnicity, 2000)

	total	Asian Indian	Chinese	Filipino	Japanese	Korean	Vietnamese	other Asian
Total Asians	**10,242,998**	**1,678,765**	**2,432,585**	**1,850,314**	**796,700**	**1,076,872**	**1,122,528**	**1,285,234**
Alabama	31,346	6,900	6,337	2,727	1,966	4,116	4,628	4,672
Alaska	25,116	723	1,464	12,712	1,414	4,573	814	3,416
Arizona	92,236	14,741	21,221	16,176	7,712	9,123	12,931	10,332
Arkansas	20,220	3,104	3,126	2,489	1,036	1,550	3,974	4,941
California	3,697,513	314,819	980,642	918,678	288,854	345,882	447,032	401,606
Colorado	95,213	11,720	15,658	8,941	11,571	16,395	15,457	15,471
Connecticut	82,313	23,662	19,172	7,643	4,196	7,064	7,538	13,038
Delaware	16,259	5,280	4,128	2,018	614	1,991	817	1,411
District of Columbia	15,189	2,845	3,734	2,228	1,117	1,095	1,903	2,267
Florida	266,256	70,740	46,368	54,310	10,897	19,139	33,190	31,612
Georgia	173,170	46,132	27,446	11,036	7,242	28,745	29,016	23,553
Hawaii	503,868	1,441	56,600	170,635	201,764	23,537	7,867	42,024
Idaho	11,889	1,289	2,224	1,614	2,642	1,250	1,323	1,547
Illinois	423,603	124,723	76,725	86,298	20,379	51,453	19,101	44,924
Indiana	59,126	14,685	12,531	6,674	5,065	7,502	4,843	7,826
Iowa	36,635	5,641	6,161	2,272	1,474	5,063	7,129	8,895
Kansas	46,806	8,153	7,624	3,509	1,935	4,529	11,623	9,433
Kentucky	29,744	6,771	5,397	3,106	3,683	3,818	3,596	3,373
Louisiana	54,758	8,280	7,474	4,504	1,519	2,876	24,358	5,747
Maine	9,111	1,021	2,034	1,159	616	875	1,323	2,083
Maryland	210,929	49,909	49,400	26,608	6,620	39,155	16,744	22,493
Massachusetts	238,124	43,801	84,392	8,273	10,539	17,369	33,962	39,788
Michigan	176,510	54,631	33,189	17,377	11,288	20,886	13,673	25,466
Minnesota	141,968	16,887	16,060	6,284	3,816	12,584	18,824	67,513
Mississippi	18,626	3,827	3,099	2,608	766	1,334	5,387	1,605
Missouri	61,595	12,169	13,667	7,735	3,337	6,767	10,626	7,294
Montana	4,691	379	827	859	885	833	199	709
Nebraska	21,931	3,273	3,093	2,101	1,582	2,423	6,364	3,095
Nevada	90,266	5,535	14,113	40,529	8,277	7,554	4,420	9,838
New Hampshire	15,931	3,873	4,074	1,203	877	1,800	1,697	2,407
New Jersey	480,276	169,180	100,355	85,245	14,672	65,349	15,180	30,295
New Mexico	19,255	3,104	3,979	2,888	1,964	1,791	3,274	2,255
New York	1,044,976	251,724	424,774	81,681	37,279	119,846	23,818	105,854

(continued)

(continued from previous page)

	total	Asian Indian	Chinese	Filipino	Japanese	Korean	Vietnamese	other Asian
North Carolina	113,689	26,197	18,984	9,592	5,664	12,600	15,596	25,056
North Dakota	3,606	822	606	643	186	411	478	460
Ohio	132,633	38,752	30,425	12,393	10,732	13,376	9,812	17,143
Oklahoma	46,767	8,502	6,964	4,028	2,505	5,074	12,566	7,128
Oregon	101,350	9,575	20,930	10,627	12,131	12,387	18,890	16,810
Pennsylvania	219,813	57,241	50,650	14,506	6,984	31,612	30,037	28,783
Rhode Island	23,665	2,942	4,974	2,062	784	1,560	952	10,391
South Carolina	36,014	8,356	5,967	6,423	2,448	3,665	4,248	4,907
South Dakota	4,378	611	816	613	350	584	574	830
Tennessee	56,662	12,835	9,426	5,426	4,304	7,395	7,007	10,269
Texas	562,319	129,365	105,829	58,340	17,120	45,571	134,961	71,133
Utah	37,108	3,065	8,045	3,106	6,186	3,473	5,968	7,265
Vermont	5,217	858	1,330	328	403	669	980	649
Virginia	261,025	48,815	36,966	47,609	9,080	45,279	37,309	35,967
Washington	322,335	23,992	59,914	65,373	35,985	46,880	46,149	44,042
West Virginia	9,434	2,856	1,878	1,495	887	857	379	1,082
Wisconsin	88,763	12,665	11,184	5,158	2,868	6,800	3,891	46,197
Wyoming	2,771	354	609	472	485	412	100	339

Note: Asians include only those who identified themselves as Asian alone. Other Asian includes other Asian alone or two or more Asian ethnic categories.
Source: Bureau of the Census, Profiles of General Demographic Characteristics, *2000 Census of Population and Housing, 2001*

Distribution of Asians by Ethnicity for States, 2000 Census

(percent distribution of Asians by state and ethnicity, 2000)

	total	Asian Indian	Chinese	Filipino	Japanese	Korean	Vietnamese	other Asian
Total Asians	**100.0%**	**16.4%**	**23.7%**	**18.1%**	**7.8%**	**10.5%**	**11.0%**	**12.5%**
Alabama	100.0	22.0	20.2	8.7	6.3	13.1	14.8	14.9
Alaska	100.0	2.9	5.8	50.6	5.6	18.2	3.2	13.6
Arizona	100.0	16.0	23.0	17.5	8.4	9.9	14.0	11.2
Arkansas	100.0	15.4	15.5	12.3	5.1	7.7	19.7	24.4
California	100.0	8.5	26.5	24.8	7.8	9.4	12.1	10.9
Colorado	100.0	12.3	16.4	9.4	12.2	17.2	16.2	16.2
Connecticut	100.0	28.7	23.3	9.3	5.1	8.6	9.2	15.8
Delaware	100.0	32.5	25.4	12.4	3.8	12.2	5.0	8.7
District of Columbia	100.0	18.7	24.6	14.7	7.4	7.2	12.5	14.9
Florida	100.0	26.6	17.4	20.4	4.1	7.2	12.5	11.9
Georgia	100.0	26.6	15.8	6.4	4.2	16.6	16.8	13.6
Hawaii	100.0	0.3	11.2	33.9	40.0	4.7	1.6	8.3
Idaho	100.0	10.8	18.7	13.6	22.2	10.5	11.1	13.0
Illinois	100.0	29.4	18.1	20.4	4.8	12.1	4.5	10.6
Indiana	100.0	24.8	21.2	11.3	8.6	12.7	8.2	13.2
Iowa	100.0	15.4	16.8	6.2	4.0	13.8	19.5	24.3
Kansas	100.0	17.4	16.3	7.5	4.1	9.7	24.8	20.2
Kentucky	100.0	22.8	18.1	10.4	12.4	12.8	12.1	11.3
Louisiana	100.0	15.1	13.6	8.2	2.8	5.3	44.5	10.5
Maine	100.0	11.2	22.3	12.7	6.8	9.6	14.5	22.9
Maryland	100.0	23.7	23.4	12.6	3.1	18.6	7.9	10.7
Massachusetts	100.0	18.4	35.4	3.5	4.4	7.3	14.3	16.7
Michigan	100.0	31.0	18.8	9.8	6.4	11.8	7.7	14.4
Minnesota	100.0	11.9	11.3	4.4	2.7	8.9	13.3	47.6
Mississippi	100.0	20.5	16.6	14.0	4.1	7.2	28.9	8.6
Missouri	100.0	19.8	22.2	12.6	5.4	11.0	17.3	11.8
Montana	100.0	8.1	17.6	18.3	18.9	17.8	4.2	15.1
Nebraska	100.0	14.9	14.1	9.6	7.2	11.0	29.0	14.1
Nevada	100.0	6.1	15.6	44.9	9.2	8.4	4.9	10.9
New Hampshire	100.0	24.3	25.6	7.6	5.5	11.3	10.7	15.1
New Jersey	100.0	35.2	20.9	17.7	3.1	13.6	3.2	6.3
New Mexico	100.0	16.1	20.7	15.0	10.2	9.3	17.0	11.7
New York	100.0	24.1	40.6	7.8	3.6	11.5	2.3	10.1

(continued)

(continued from previous page)

	total	Asian Indian	Chinese	Filipino	Japanese	Korean	Vietnamese	other Asian
North Carolina	100.0%	23.0%	16.7%	8.4%	5.0%	11.1%	13.7%	22.0%
North Dakota	100.0	22.8	16.8	17.8	5.2	11.4	13.3	12.8
Ohio	100.0	29.2	22.9	9.3	8.1	10.1	7.4	12.9
Oklahoma	100.0	18.2	14.9	8.6	5.4	10.8	26.9	15.2
Oregon	100.0	9.4	20.7	10.5	12.0	12.2	18.6	16.6
Pennsylvania	100.0	26.0	23.0	6.6	3.2	14.4	13.7	13.1
Rhode Island	100.0	12.4	21.0	8.7	3.3	6.6	4.0	43.9
South Carolina	100.0	23.2	16.6	17.8	6.8	10.2	11.8	13.6
South Dakota	100.0	14.0	18.6	14.0	8.0	13.3	13.1	19.0
Tennessee	100.0	22.7	16.6	9.6	7.6	13.1	12.4	18.1
Texas	100.0	23.0	18.8	10.4	3.0	8.1	24.0	12.6
Utah	100.0	8.3	21.7	8.4	16.7	9.4	16.1	19.6
Vermont	100.0	16.4	25.5	6.3	7.7	12.8	18.8	12.4
Virginia	100.0	18.7	14.2	18.2	3.5	17.3	14.3	13.8
Washington	100.0	7.4	18.6	20.3	11.2	14.5	14.3	13.7
West Virginia	100.0	30.3	19.9	15.8	9.4	9.1	4.0	11.5
Wisconsin	100.0	14.3	12.6	5.8	3.2	7.7	4.4	52.0
Wyoming	100.0	12.8	22.0	17.0	17.5	14.9	3.6	12.2

Note: Asians include only those who identified themselves as Asian alone. Other Asian includes other Asian alone or two or more Asian ethnic categories.
Source: Bureau of the Census, Profiles of General Demographic Characteristics, *2000 Census of Population and Housing, 2001; calculations by New Strategist*

Distribution of Asian Ethnic Groups by State, 2000 Census

(percent distribution of Asian ethnic groups by state, 2000)

	total	Asian Indian	Chinese	Filipino	Japanese	Korean	Vietnamese	other Asian
Total Asians	**100.0%**	**100.0%**	**100.0%**	**100.0%**	**100.0%**	**100.0%**	**100.0%**	**100.0%**
Alabama	0.3	0.4	0.3	0.1	0.2	0.4	0.4	0.4
Alaska	0.2	0.0	0.1	0.7	0.2	0.4	0.1	0.3
Arizona	0.9	0.9	0.9	0.9	1.0	0.8	1.2	0.8
Arkansas	0.2	0.2	0.1	0.1	0.1	0.1	0.4	0.4
California	36.1	18.8	40.3	49.6	36.3	32.1	39.8	31.2
Colorado	0.9	0.7	0.6	0.5	1.5	1.5	1.4	1.2
Connecticut	0.8	1.4	0.8	0.4	0.5	0.7	0.7	1.0
Delaware	0.2	0.3	0.2	0.1	0.1	0.2	0.1	0.1
District of Columbia	0.1	0.2	0.2	0.1	0.1	0.1	0.2	0.2
Florida	2.6	4.2	1.9	2.9	1.4	1.8	3.0	2.5
Georgia	1.7	2.7	1.1	0.6	0.9	2.7	2.6	1.8
Hawaii	4.9	0.1	2.3	9.2	25.3	2.2	0.7	3.3
Idaho	0.1	0.1	0.1	0.1	0.3	0.1	0.1	0.1
Illinois	4.1	7.4	3.2	4.7	2.6	4.8	1.7	3.5
Indiana	0.6	0.9	0.5	0.4	0.6	0.7	0.4	0.6
Iowa	0.4	0.3	0.3	0.1	0.2	0.5	0.6	0.7
Kansas	0.5	0.5	0.3	0.2	0.2	0.4	1.0	0.7
Kentucky	0.3	0.4	0.2	0.2	0.5	0.4	0.3	0.3
Louisiana	0.5	0.5	0.3	0.2	0.2	0.3	2.2	0.4
Maine	0.1	0.1	0.1	0.1	0.1	0.1	0.1	0.2
Maryland	2.1	3.0	2.0	1.4	0.8	3.6	1.5	1.8
Massachusetts	2.3	2.6	3.5	0.4	1.3	1.6	3.0	3.1
Michigan	1.7	3.3	1.4	0.9	1.4	1.9	1.2	2.0
Minnesota	1.4	1.0	0.7	0.3	0.5	1.2	1.7	5.3
Mississippi	0.2	0.2	0.1	0.1	0.1	0.1	0.5	0.1
Missouri	0.6	0.7	0.6	0.4	0.4	0.6	0.9	0.6
Montana	0.0	0.0	0.0	0.0	0.1	0.1	0.0	0.1
Nebraska	0.2	0.2	0.1	0.1	0.2	0.2	0.6	0.2
Nevada	0.9	0.3	0.6	2.2	1.0	0.7	0.4	0.8
New Hampshire	0.2	0.2	0.2	0.1	0.1	0.2	0.2	0.2
New Jersey	4.7	10.1	4.1	4.6	1.8	6.1	1.4	2.4
New Mexico	0.2	0.2	0.2	0.2	0.2	0.2	0.3	0.2
New York	10.2	15.0	17.5	4.4	4.7	11.1	2.1	8.2

(continued)

(continued from previous page)

	total	Asian Indian	Chinese	Filipino	Japanese	Korean	Vietnamese	other Asian
North Carolina	1.1%	1.6%	0.8%	0.5%	0.7%	1.2%	1.4%	1.9%
North Dakota	0.0	0.0	0.0	0.0	0.0	0.0	0.0	0.0
Ohio	1.3	2.3	1.3	0.7	1.3	1.2	0.9	1.3
Oklahoma	0.5	0.5	0.3	0.2	0.3	0.5	1.1	0.6
Oregon	1.0	0.6	0.9	0.6	1.5	1.2	1.7	1.3
Pennsylvania	2.1	3.4	2.1	0.8	0.9	2.9	2.7	2.2
Rhode Island	0.2	0.2	0.2	0.1	0.1	0.1	0.1	0.8
South Carolina	0.4	0.5	0.2	0.3	0.3	0.3	0.4	0.4
South Dakota	0.0	0.0	0.0	0.0	0.0	0.1	0.1	0.1
Tennessee	0.6	0.8	0.4	0.3	0.5	0.7	0.6	0.8
Texas	5.5	7.7	4.4	3.2	2.1	4.2	12.0	5.5
Utah	0.4	0.2	0.3	0.2	0.8	0.3	0.5	0.6
Vermont	0.1	0.1	0.1	0.0	0.1	0.1	0.1	0.1
Virginia	2.5	2.9	1.5	2.6	1.1	4.2	3.3	2.8
Washington	3.1	1.4	2.5	3.5	4.5	4.4	4.1	3.4
West Virginia	0.1	0.2	0.1	0.1	0.1	0.1	0.0	0.1
Wisconsin	0.9	0.8	0.5	0.3	0.4	0.6	0.3	3.6
Wyoming	0.0	0.0	0.0	0.0	0.1	0.0	0.0	0.0

Note: Asians include only those who identified themselves as Asian alone. Other Asian includes other Asian alone or two or more Asian ethnic categories.
Source: Bureau of the Census, Profiles of General Demographic Characteristics, *2000 Census of Population and Housing, 2001; calculations by New Strategist*

Asians by Metropolitan Area, 2000 Census

(number of total people, number of Asians, and Asian share of total in the 100 largest metropolitan areas, 2000)

			Asian	
		total population	number	share of total
1.	New York–Northern New Jersey–Long Island, NY–NJ–CT–PA CMSA	21,199,865	1,587,782	7.5%
	• Bergen–Passaic, NJ PMSA	1,373,167	120,819	8.8
	• Bridgeport, CT PMSA	459,479	12,237	2.7
	• Danbury, CT PMSA	217,980	7,892	3.6
	• Dutchess County, NY PMSA	280,150	8,086	2.9
	• Jersey City, NJ PMSA	608,975	62,549	10.3
	• Middlesex–Somerset–Hunterdon, NJ PMSA	1,169,641	139,236	11.9
	• Monmouth–Ocean, NJ PMSA	1,126,217	34,871	3.1
	• Nassau–Suffolk, NY PMSA	2,753,913	111,093	4.0
	• New Haven–Meriden, CT PMSA	542,149	16,642	3.1
	• New York, NY PMSA	9,314,235	938,235	10.1
	• Newark, NJ PMSA	2,032,989	90,903	4.5
	• Newburgh, NY–PA PMSA	387,669	6,747	1.7
	• Stamford–Norwalk, CT PMSA	353,556	15,670	4.4
	• Trenton, NJ PMSA	350,761	19,128	5.5
	• Waterbury, CT PMSA	228,984	3,674	1.6
2.	Los Angeles–Riverside–Orange County, CA CMSA	16,373,645	1,886,481	11.5
	• Los Angeles–Long Beach, CA PMSA	9,519,338	1,245,019	13.1
	• Orange County, CA PMSA	2,846,289	423,911	14.9
	• Riverside–San Bernardino, CA PMSA	3,254,821	168,695	5.2
	• Ventura, CA PMSA	753,197	48,856	6.5
3.	Chicago–Gary–Kenosha, IL–IN–WI CMSA	9,157,540	432,175	4.7
	• Chicago, IL PMSA	8,272,768	422,572	5.1
	• Gary, IN PMSA	631,362	6,852	1.1
	• Kankakee, IL PMSA	103,833	949	0.9
	• Kenosha, WI PMSA	149,577	1,802	1.2
4.	Washington–Baltimore, DC–MD–VA–WV CMSA	7,608,070	453,616	6.0
	• Baltimore, MD PMSA	2,552,994	79,477	3.1
	• Hagerstown, MD PMSA	131,923	1,301	1.0
	• Washington, DC–MD–VA–WV PMSA	4,923,153	372,838	7.6
5.	San Francisco–Oakland–San Jose, CA CMSA	7,039,362	1,432,025	20.3
	• Oakland, CA PMSA	2,392,557	448,918	18.8
	• San Francisco, CA PMSA	1,731,183	424,345	24.5
	• San Jose, CA PMSA	1,682,585	462,261	27.5
	• Santa Cruz–Watsonville, CA PMSA	255,602	11,916	4.7
	• Santa Rosa, CA PMSA	458,614	19,030	4.1
	• Vallejo–Fairfield–Napa, CA PMSA	518,821	65,555	12.6

(continued)

(continued from previous page)

	total population	Asian number	Asian share of total
6. Philadelphia–Wilmington–Atlantic City, PA–NJ–DE–MD CMSA	6,188,463	224,401	3.6%
• Atlantic City–Cape May, NJ PMSA	354,878	15,038	4.2
• Philadelphia, PA–NJ PMSA	5,100,931	192,095	3.8
• Vineland–Millville–Bridgeton, NJ PMSA	146,438	1,815	1.2
• Wilmington–Newark, DE–MD PMSA	586,216	15,453	2.6
7. Boston–Worcester–Lawrence, MA–NH–ME–CT CMSA	5,819,100	256,660	4.4
• Boston, MA–NH PMSA	3,406,829	183,349	5.4
• Brockton, MA PMSA	255,459	3,999	1.6
• Fitchburg–Leominster, MA PMSA	142,284	3,830	2.7
• Lawrence, MA–NH PMSA	396,230	9,492	2.4
• Lowell, MA–NH PMSA	301,686	24,810	8.2
• Manchester, NH PMSA	198,378	3,921	2.0
• Nashua, NH PMSA	190,949	5,125	2.7
• New Bedford, MA PMSA	175,198	1,565	0.9
• Portsmouth–Rochester, NH–ME PMSA	240,698	3,792	1.6
• Worcester, MA–CT PMSA	511,389	16,777	3.3
8. Detroit–Ann Arbor–Flint, MI CMSA	5,456,428	149,538	2.7
• Ann Arbor, MI PMSA	578,736	24,520	4.2
• Detroit, MI PMSA	4,441,551	120,425	2.7
• Flint, MI PMSA	436,141	4,593	1.1
9. Dallas–Fort Worth, TX CMSA	5,221,801	219,260	4.2
• Dallas, TX PMSA	3,519,176	158,004	4.5
• Fort Worth–Arlington, TX PMSA	1,702,625	61,256	3.6
10. Houston–Galveston–Brazoria, TX CMSA	4,669,571	252,137	5.4
• Brazoria, TX PMSA	241,767	5,574	2.3
• Galveston–Texas City, TX PMSA	250,158	6,129	2.5
• Houston, TX PMSA	4,177,646	240,434	5.8
11. Atlanta, GA MSA	4,112,198	152,247	3.7
12. Miami–Fort Lauderdale, FL CMSA	3,876,380	86,428	2.2
• Fort Lauderdale, FL PMSA	1,623,018	45,601	2.8
• Miami, FL PMSA	2,253,362	40,827	1.8
13. Seattle–Tacoma–Bremerton, WA CMSA	3,554,760	339,371	9.5
• Bremerton, WA PMSA	231,969	14,585	6.3
• Olympia, WA PMSA	207,355	12,036	5.8
• Seattle–Bellevue–Everett, WA PMSA	2,414,616	263,947	10.9
• Tacoma, WA PMSA	700,820	48,803	7.0
14. Phoenix–Mesa, AZ MSA	3,251,876	85,231	2.6
15. Minneapolis–St. Paul, MN–WI MSA	2,968,806	139,076	4.7
16. Cleveland–Akron, OH CMSA	2,945,831	47,290	1.6
• Akron, OH PMSA	694,960	10,556	1.5
• Cleveland–Lorain–Elyria, OH PMSA	2,250,871	36,734	1.6

(continued)

(continued from previous page)

	total population	Asian number	share of total
17. San Diego, CA MSA	2,813,833	295,346	10.5%
18. St. Louis, MO–IL MSA	2,603,607	44,900	1.7
19. Denver–Boulder–Greeley, CO CMSA	2,581,506	89,844	3.5
• Boulder–Longmont, CO PMSA	291,288	10,887	3.7
• Denver, CO PMSA	2,109,282	76,711	3.6
• Greeley, CO PMSA	180,936	2,246	1.2
20. Tampa–St. Petersburg–Clearwater, FL MSA	2,395,997	54,754	2.3
21. Pittsburgh, PA MSA	2,358,695	30,328	1.3
22. Portland–Salem, OR–WA CMSA	2,265,223	114,978	5.1
• Portland–Vancouver, OR–WA PMSA	1,918,009	107,277	5.6
• Salem, OR PMSA	347,214	7,701	2.2
23. Cincinnati–Hamilton, OH–KY–IN CMSA	1,979,202	29,134	1.5
• Cincinnati, OH–KY–IN PMSA	1,646,395	23,173	1.4
• Hamilton–Middletown, OH PMSA	332,807	5,961	1.8
24. Sacramento–Yolo, CA CMSA	1,796,857	193,395	10.8
• Sacramento, CA PMSA	1,628,197	173,658	10.7
• Yolo, CA PMSA	168,660	19,737	11.7
25. Kansas City, MO–KS MSA	1,776,062	34,900	2.0
26. Milwaukee–Racine, WI CMSA	1,689,572	37,850	2.2
• Milwaukee–Waukesha, WI PMSA	1,500,741	36,112	2.4
• Racine, WI PMSA	188,831	1,738	0.9
27. Orlando, FL MSA	1,644,561	53,885	3.3
28. Indianapolis, IN MSA	1,607,486	24,145	1.5
29. San Antonio, TX MSA	1,592,383	32,076	2.0
30. Norfolk–Virginia Beach–Newport News, VA–NC MSA	1,569,541	54,165	3.5
31. Las Vegas, NV–AZ MSA	1,563,282	92,343	5.9
32. Columbus, OH MSA	1,540,157	42,350	2.7
33. Charlotte–Gastonia–Rock Hill, NC–SC MSA	1,499,293	32,311	2.2
34. New Orleans, LA MSA	1,337,726	32,699	2.4
35. Salt Lake City–Ogden, UT MSA	1,333,914	37,302	2.8
36. Greensboro–Winston-Salem–High Point, NC MSA	1,251,509	20,126	1.6
37. Austin–San Marcos, TX MSA	1,249,763	50,829	4.1
38. Nashville, TN MSA	1,231,311	24,088	2.0
39. Providence–Fall River–Warwick, RI–MA MSA	1,188,613	31,378	2.6
40. Raleigh–Durham–Chapel Hill, NC MSA	1,187,941	38,974	3.3
41. Hartford, CT MSA	1,183,110	30,752	2.6
42. Buffalo–Niagara Falls, NY MSA	1,170,111	17,549	1.5
43. Memphis, TN–AR–MS MSA	1,135,614	18,535	1.6
44. West Palm Beach–Boca Raton, FL MSA	1,131,184	21,261	1.9
45. Jacksonville, FL MSA	1,100,491	31,410	2.9
46. Rochester, NY MSA	1,098,201	23,327	2.1
47. Grand Rapids–Muskegon–Holland, MI MSA	1,088,514	20,134	1.8

(continued)

(continued from previous page)

	total population	Asian number	share of total
48. Oklahoma City, OK MSA	1,083,346	32,283	3.0%
49. Louisville, KY–IN MSA	1,025,598	13,520	1.3
50. Richmond–Petersburg, VA MSA	996,512	23,813	2.4
51. Greenville–Spartanburg–Anderson, SC MSA	962,441	13,055	1.4
52. Dayton–Springfield, OH MSA	950,558	14,906	1.6
53. Fresno, CA MSA	922,516	75,764	8.2
54. Birmingham, AL MSA	921,106	9,220	1.0
55. Honolulu, HI MSA	876,156	539,384	61.6
56. Albany–Schenectady–Troy, NY MSA	875,583	18,780	2.1
57. Tucson, AZ MSA	843,746	22,373	2.7
58. Tulsa, OK MSA	803,235	12,589	1.6
59. Syracuse, NY MSA	732,117	12,715	1.7
60. Omaha, NE–IA MSA	716,998	13,708	1.9
61. Albuquerque, NM MSA	712,738	15,864	2.2
62. Knoxville, TN MSA	687,249	8,092	1.2
63. El Paso, TX MSA	679,622	9,043	1.3
64. Bakersfield, CA MSA	661,645	27,500	4.2
65. Allentown–Bethlehem–Easton, PA MSA	637,958	11,883	1.9
66. Harrisburg–Lebanon–Carlisle, PA MSA	629,401	11,200	1.8
67. Scranton–Wilkes-Barre–Hazleton, PA MSA	624,776	4,662	0.7
68. Toledo, OH MSA	618,203	8,662	1.4
69. Baton Rouge, LA MSA	602,894	10,176	1.7
70. Youngstown–Warren, OH MSA	594,746	3,336	0.6
71. Springfield, MA MSA	591,932	13,317	2.2
72. Sarasota–Bradenton, FL MSA	589,959	6,224	1.1
73. Little Rock–North Little Rock, AR MSA	583,845	7,410	1.3
74. McAllen–Edinburg–Mission, TX MSA	569,463	3,946	0.7
75. Stockton–Lodi, CA MSA	563,598	76,656	13.6
76. Charleston–North Charleston, SC MSA	549,033	9,321	1.7
77. Wichita, KS MSA	545,220	18,049	3.3
78. Mobile, AL MSA	540,258	7,276	1.3
79. Columbia, SC MSA	536,691	9,413	1.8
80. Colorado Springs, CO MSA	516,929	18,559	3.6
81. Fort Wayne, IN MSA	502,141	6,273	1.2
82. Daytona Beach, FL MSA	493,175	6,311	1.3
83. Lakeland–Winter Haven, FL MSA	483,924	5,681	1.2
84. Johnson City–Kingsport–Bristol, TN–VA MSA	480,091	2,486	0.5
85. Lexington, KY MSA	479,198	8,701	1.8
86. Augusta–Aiken, GA–SC MSA	477,441	9,031	1.9
87. Melbourne–Titusville–Palm Bay, FL MSA	476,230	9,503	2.0
88. Lancaster, PA MSA	470,658	7,751	1.6
89. Chattanooga, TN–GA MSA	465,161	5,438	1.2

(continued)

(continued from previous page)

	total population	Asian	
		number	share of total
90. Des Moines, IA MSA	456,022	11,836	2.6%
91. Kalamazoo–Battle Creek, MI MSA	452,851	7,432	1.6
92. Lansing–East Lansing, MI MSA	447,728	13,468	3.0
93. Modesto, CA MSA	446,997	24,464	5.5
94. Fort Myers–Cape Coral, FL MSA	440,888	4,519	1.0
95. Jackson, MS MSA	440,801	3,891	0.9
96. Boise City, ID MSA	432,345	8,871	2.1
97. Madison, WI MSA	426,526	16,723	3.9
98. Spokane, WA MSA	417,939	10,987	2.6
99. Pensacola, FL MSA	412,153	10,800	2.6
100. Canton–Massillon, OH MSA	406,934	2,760	0.7

Note: Asians include those who identified themselves as Asian alone and those who identified themselves as Asian in combination with one or more other races. For definitions of CMSA, PMSA, and MSA, see glossary.
Source: Bureau of the Census, Profiles of General Demographic Characteristics, *2000 Census of Population and Housing, May 2001; calculations by New Strategist*

3

Blacks

■ The black population stood at 36 million in 2000, accounting for 13 percent of the U.S. population.

■ Blacks own 823,000 of the nation's businesses, or 4 percent of the total. They own a much larger 21 percent of local and interurban passenger transportation businesses.

■ Seventy-eight percent of blacks aged 25 or older are high school graduates. While this figure is lower than the share among the total population, it is much higher than it once was. As recently as 1980, barely half of blacks had graduated from high school.

■ Seventy-one percent of blacks say they are in excellent or good health. Eighty-two percent are covered by health insurance, most through an employer.

■ A 46 percent minority of black householders own their home. In the South, however, most are homeowners.

■ Black median household income, at $30,436 in 2000, was just 72 percent of the median for all households. Behind the lower income of blacks is the fact that married couples—typically the most affluent household type—account for only 31 percent of black households.

■ Married couples with children account for only 16 percent of black households. Just 38 percent of black children live with both parents.

■ The average black household spent $28,152 in 2000, 74 percent as much as the average household. Blacks spend 12 percent more than average on telephone services and 17 percent more on infants' furniture.

Blacks account for 12.9 percent of the U.S. population

(percent distribution of people by race and Hispanic origin, 2000 census)

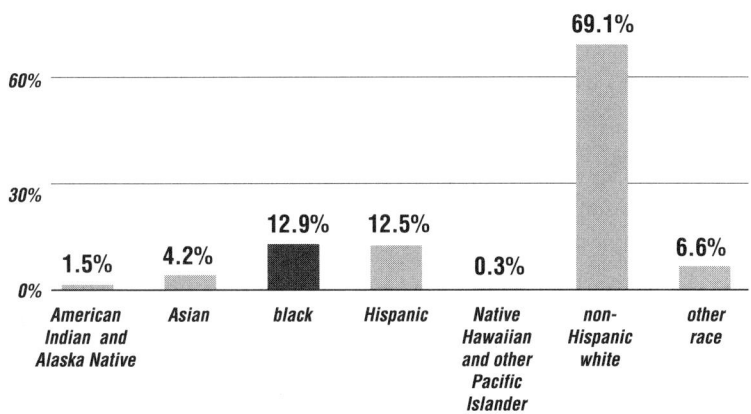

Most Black-Owned Firms Are in the Service Industries

Blacks own 823,499 of the nation's 21 million businesses, according to the Survey of Minority-Owned Business Enterprises, a part of the 1997 Economic Censuses. The survey counts as minority-owned any firm in which the majority of owners is black, Alaska Native, American Indian, Asian, Native Hawaiian, Pacific Islander, or Hispanic. Minority ownership is determined for firms in their entirety rather than for individual locations.

Blacks own 4 percent of the nation's businesses. In the local and interurban passenger transportation industry, however, they own 21 percent of firms. The largest share of black firms are in the service industries—fully 53 percent. Ninety percent of black-owned firms are individual proprietorships, larger than the 73 percent of all firms that are owned by one individual.

Sixty-four percent of black-owned businesses are in just 10 states, with New York home to the largest share at 11 percent. Blacks own the largest percentage of businesses in Maryland—12 percent in 1997.

Most black-owned firms have receipts below $25,000

(percent distribution of receipts for firms owned by blacks, 1997)

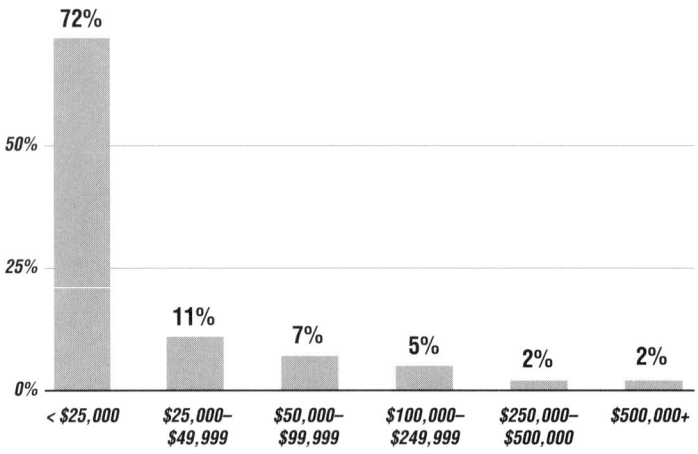

Number and Percent Distribution of Businesses Owned by Blacks, 1997

(total number of firms, number and percent distribution of firms owned by blacks, and black share of total, by industry, 1997)

SIC code		total firms	firms owned by blacks		
			number	percent distribution	percent of total
	All industries	**20,821,935**	**823,499**	**100.0%**	**4.0%**
	Agricultural services, forestry, fishing	**496,164**	**12,464**	**1.5**	**2.5**
07	Agricultural services	412,852	11,742	1.4	2.8
08	Forestry	14,051	223	0.0	1.6
09	Fishing, hunting, and trapping	69,271	500	0.1	0.7
	Mineral industries	**126,809**	**231**	**0.0**	**0.2**
10	Metal mining	1,819	13	0.0	0.7
12	Coal mining	2,242	6	0.0	0.3
13	Oil and gas extraction	115,953	202	0.0	0.2
14	Nonmetallic minerals, except fuels	6,862	9	0.0	0.1
	Construction industries, subdividers, developers	**2,333,424**	**56,508**	**6.9**	**2.4**
15	Building construction, general contractors and operative builders	472,111	8,159	1.0	1.7
16	Heavy construction contractors other than buildings	64,314	1,305	0.2	2.0
17	Special trade contractors	1,739,060	46,819	5.7	2.7
6552	Subdividers and developers not elsewhere classified (excl. cemeteries)	58,362	225	0.0	0.4
	Manufacturing	**688,782**	**10,447**	**1.3**	**1.5**
20	Food and kindred products	30,256	783	0.1	2.6
21	Tobacco products	133	1	0.0	0.8
22	Textile mill products	8,213	57	0.0	0.7
23	Apparel and other textile products	54,889	1,115	0.1	2.0
24	Lumber and wood products	106,569	2,498	0.3	2.3
25	Furniture and fixtures	28,712	337	0.0	1.2
26	Paper and allied products	7,186	202	0.0	2.8
27	Printing and publishing	119,936	2,763	0.3	2.3
28	Chemicals and allied products	10,941	112	0.0	1.0
29	Petroleum and coal products	1,434	5	0.0	0.3
30	Rubber and miscellaneous plastics	16,296	51	0.0	0.3
31	Leather and leather products	5,251	58	0.0	1.1

(continued)

(continued from previous page)

SIC code		total firms	firms owned by blacks		
			number	percent distribution	percent of total
32	Stone, clay, and glass products	29,262	268	0.0%	0.9%
33	Primary metal industries	7,703	94	0.0	1.2
34	Fabricated metal products	63,141	464	0.1	0.7
35	Industrial machinery and equipment	85,401	497	0.1	0.6
36	Electronic and other electric equipment	28,324	388	0.0	1.4
37	Transportation equipment	13,673	60	0.0	0.4
38	Instruments and related products	12,423	38	0.0	0.3
39	Miscellaneous manufacturing industries	65,185	662	0.1	1.0
	Transportation, communications, utilities	**919,570**	**71,586**	**8.7**	**7.8**
41	Local and interurban passenger transportation	116,993	24,086	2.9	20.6
42	Motor freight transportation and warehousing	544,523	37,429	4.5	6.9
44	Water transportation	15,788	124	0.0	0.8
45	Transportation by air	20,706	210	0.0	1.0
46	Pipelines, except natural gas	136	1	0.0	0.7
47	Transportation services	129,652	5,720	0.7	4.4
48	Communications	61,180	3,307	0.4	5.4
49	Electric, gas, and sanitary services	31,345	711	0.1	2.3
	Wholesale trade	**797,856**	**8,120**	**1.0**	**1.0**
50	Durable goods	489,308	4,013	0.5	0.8
51	Nondurable goods	309,731	4,107	0.5	1.3
	Retail trade	**2,889,041**	**87,568**	**10.6**	**3.0**
52	Building materials, hardware, garden supply, and mobile home dealers	85,060	944	0.1	1.1
53	General merchandise stores	35,027	993	0.1	2.8
54	Food stores	216,067	8,255	1.0	3.8
55	Automotive dealers and gasoline service stations	255,259	4,073	0.5	1.6
56	Apparel and accessory stores	127,848	6,646	0.8	5.2
57	Home furniture, furnishings, and equipment stores	153,248	2,823	0.3	1.8
58	Eating and drinking places	493,313	13,111	1.6	2.7
59	Miscellaneous retail	1,528,857	50,754	6.2	3.3

(continued)

(continued from previous page)

SIC code		total firms	firms owned by blacks		
			number	percent distribution	percent of total
	Finance, insurance, real estate (excl. subdividers and developers)	**2,237,675**	**37,934**	**4.6%**	**1.7%**
60	Depository institutions	24,616	347	0.0	1.4
61	Nondepository credit institutions	45,905	982	0.1	2.1
62	Security and commodity brokers, dealers, exchanges, and services	91,446	1,749	0.2	1.9
63	Insurance carriers	9,108	111	0.0	1.2
64	Insurance agents, brokers, services	411,902	11,373	1.4	2.8
65pt	Real estate (excl. subdividers and developers)	1,503,438	22,118	2.7	1.5
67	Holding and other investment offices, except trusts	157,652	1,263	0.2	0.8
	Service industries (excl. membership organizations, private household)	**8,891,024**	**437,646**	**53.1**	**4.9**
70	Hotels, rooming houses, camps, and other lodging places	93,380	1,222	0.1	1.3
72	Personal services	1,348,554	103,865	12.6	7.7
73	Business services	2,221,047	104,939	12.7	4.7
75	Automotive repair, services, parking	448,584	15,922	1.9	3.5
76	Miscellaneous repair services	231,371	5,049	0.6	2.2
78	Motion pictures	87,700	2,297	0.3	2.6
79	Amusement and recreation services	603,896	29,343	3.6	4.9
80	Health services	1,004,672	51,732	6.3	5.1
81	Legal services	353,147	8,799	1.1	2.5
82	Educational services	270,648	8,249	1.0	3.0
83	Social services	665,067	66,530	8.1	10.0
84	Museums, art galleries, botanical and zoological gardens	5,205	6	0.0	0.1
87	Engineering, accounting, research, management and related services	1,446,195	37,505	4.6	2.6
89	Services not elsewhere classified	119,931	2,279	0.3	1.9
	Industries not classified	**1,480,003**	**101,128**	**12.3**	**6.8**

Source: Bureau of the Census, Minority- and Women-Owned Businesses, *1997 Economic Census, Internet site <www.census.gov/csd/mwb/>; calculations by New Strategist*

Characteristics of Businesses Owned by Blacks, 1997

(number of firms owned by blacks by industry and selected characteristics of firm, 1997)

SIC code		total firms		firms with paid employees			
		number	sales and receipts (in 000s)	number	sales and receipts (in 000s)	employees	payroll (in 000s)
	Firms owned by blacks	823,499	$71,214,662	93,235	$56,377,860	718,341	$14,322,312
	Agricultural services, forestry, fishing	**12,464**	**417,169**	**1,356**	**259,649**	**5,457**	**77,198**
07	Agricultural services	11,742	398,558	1,331	255,006	5,427	76,768
08	Forestry	223	6,306	8	2,200	24	364
09	Fishing, hunting, and trapping	500	12,305	17	2,443	6	67
	Mineral industries	**231**	**21,551**	**16**	**12,867**	**186**	**5,319**
10	Metal mining	13	–	0	0	0	0
12	Coal mining	6	93	1	–	0–19	–
13	Oil and gas extraction	202	13,409	12	–	100–249	–
14	Nonmetallic minerals, except fuels	9	–	3	–	20–99	–
	Construction industries, subdividers, developers	**56,508**	**7,712,059**	**12,973**	**6,587,348**	**70,928**	**1,510,252**
15	Building construction, general contractors and operative builders	8,159	2,748,172	2,204	2,516,447	15,045	395,251
16	Heavy construction contractors other than buildings	1,305	992,073	470	969,098	6,346	203,920
17	Special trade contractors	46,819	3,948,663	10,253	3,089,266	49,463	908,956
6552	Subdividers and developers not elsewhere classified (excl. cemeteries)	225	23,152	46	12,537	75	2,125
	Manufacturing	**10,447**	**3,682,510**	**1,931**	**3,463,861**	**26,624**	**652,787**
20	Food and kindred products	783	494,090	110	481,438	947	24,468
21	Tobacco products	1	–	0	0	0	0
22	Textile mill products	57	–	14	–	20–99	–
23	Apparel and other textile products	1,115	226,104	228	210,877	3,939	52,645
24	Lumber and wood products	2,498	196,190	232	117,601	1,162	19,368
25	Furniture and fixtures	337	54,973	65	49,985	472	10,435
26	Paper and allied products	202	174,054	46	172,407	1,198	30,845
27	Printing and publishing	2,763	510,036	557	473,456	4,961	128,870
28	Chemicals and allied products	112	333,212	92	331,629	1,967	56,545
29	Petroleum and coal products	5	–	2	–	20–99	–
30	Rubber and miscellaneous plastics	51	260,191	37	–	1,000–2,499	–
31	Leather and leather products	58	586	1	–	0–19	–

(continued)

(continued from previous page)

SIC code		total firms		firms with paid employees			
		number	sales and receipts (in 000s)	number	sales and receipts (in 000s)	employees	payroll (in 000s)
32	Stone, clay, and glass products	268	$72,163	59	$69,372	494	$14,551
33	Primary metal industries	94	91,158	25	89,171	608	14,616
34	Fabricated metal products	464	574,576	119	551,702	3,829	122,004
35	Industrial machinery and equipment	497	159,237	164	150,968	1,831	49,063
36	Electronic, other electric equipment	388	125,211	62	109,899	973	22,703
37	Transportation equipment	60	201,563	34	200,596	1,183	32,637
38	Instruments and related products	38	45,176	23	44,687	561	12,484
39	Misc. manufacturing industries	662	113,604	65	100,735	695	18,043
	Transportation, communications, and utilities	**71,586**	**6,376,645**	**6,184**	**4,252,240**	**47,289**	**909,470**
41	Local and interurban passenger transportation	24,086	1,196,335	1,160	698,152	20,258	292,182
42	Motor freight transportation and warehousing	37,429	3,367,978	3,614	1,946,733	14,872	365,357
44	Water transportation	124	45,624	36	42,428	832	16,183
45	Transportation by air	210	–	41	35,015	1,764	18,790
46	Pipelines, except natural gas	1	–	0	0	0	0
47	Transportation services	5,720	293,082	720	153,394	2,566	47,310
48	Communications	3,307	623,471	477	578,164	5,557	128,216
49	Electric, gas, and sanitary services	711	809,905	139	798,356	1,440	41,432
	Wholesale trade	**8,120**	**5,818,734**	**2,139**	**5,573,907**	**13,746**	**471,320**
50	Durable goods	4,013	3,570,685	1,293	3,462,236	8,706	342,277
51	Nondurable goods	4,107	2,248,048	846	2,111,671	5,039	129,044
	Retail trade	**87,568**	**13,803,266**	**14,074**	**12,244,399**	**125,480**	**1,497,111**
52	Building materials, hardware, garden supply, mobile home dealers	944	108,309	242	84,661	837	13,342
53	General merchandise stores	993	41,205	87	21,014	223	2,253
54	Food stores	8,255	1,513,741	2,470	1,187,313	10,030	108,257
55	Automotive dealers and gasoline service stations	4,073	6,856,574	1,271	6,674,494	16,867	447,786
56	Apparel and accessory stores	6,646	378,475	1,080	266,699	3,653	38,219
57	Home furniture, furnishings, and equipment stores	2,823	283,125	750	233,568	2,275	32,762
58	Eating and drinking places	13,111	2,807,246	5,108	2,647,045	80,696	705,769
59	Miscellaneous retail	50,754	1,814,590	3,098	1,129,605	10,899	148,723

(continued)

(continued from previous page)

SIC code		total firms		firms with paid employees			
		number	sales and receipts (in 000s)	number	sales and receipts (in 000s)	employees	payroll (in 000s)
	Finance, insurance, real estate (excl. subdividers, developers)	**37,934**	**$3,088,582**	**4,820**	**$2,189,556**	**18,379**	**$498,318**
60	Depository institutions	347	183,765	341	–	1,000–2,499	–
61	Nondepository credit institutions	982	178,135	349	160,814	1,510	47,826
62	Security and commodity brokers, dealers, exchanges, and services	1,749	417,869	234	378,530	2,048	132,092
63	Insurance carriers	111	489,588	67	487,951	2,289	57,060
64	Insurance agents, brokers, services	11,373	645,551	1,865	401,264	4,668	102,153
65pt	Real estate (excluding subdividers and developers)	22,118	1,088,428	1,904	508,011	5,664	98,042
67	Holding and other investment offices, except trusts	1,263	85,246	68	–	500–999	–
	Service industries (excl. membership organizations, private hh)	**437,646**	**25,925,092**	**43,529**	**19,503,488**	**388,398**	**8,212,775**
70	Hotels, rooming houses, camps, and other lodging places	1,222	58,503	236	–	500–999	–
72	Personal services	103,865	2,716,514	5,481	1,121,385	23,882	339,687
73	Business services	104,939	7,300,408	9,123	5,930,953	156,974	2,769,477
75	Automotive repair, services, and parking	15,922	834,119	2,795	565,902	8,922	132,872
76	Miscellaneous repair services	5,049	380,573	582	296,202	2,784	71,016
78	Motion pictures	2,297	361,641	398	316,305	1,344	153,492
79	Amusement, recreation services	29,343	1,152,652	997	584,878	3,307	212,423
80	Health services	51,732	6,375,807	11,752	5,452,737	100,450	2,433,532
81	Legal services	8,799	1,120,994	2,164	897,660	7,954	261,718
82	Educational services	8,249	240,830	455	175,903	4,262	77,865
83	Social services	66,530	1,730,719	5,924	1,122,763	42,428	470,612
84	Museums, art galleries, botanical and zoological gardens	6	1,412	5	–	0–19	–
87	Engineering, accounting, research, management and related services	37,505	3,490,799	3,529	2,875,307	34,463	1,252,117
89	Services not elsewhere classified	2,279	160,121	179	124,174	775	28,744
	Industries not classified	**101,128**	**4,369,056**	**6,347**	**2,290,545**	**21,853**	**487,761**

Note: (–) means data not available or suppressed for purposes of confidentiality.
Source: Bureau of the Census, Minority- and Women-Owned Businesses, *1997 Economic Census, Internet site <www.census.gov/csd/mwb/>*

Black-Owned Businesses by Legal Form of Organization, Receipt Size, and Employees, 1997

(number and percent distribution of black-owned firms by legal form of organization, size of receipts, and number of employees, 1997)

	total	percent distribution
Total black-owned firms	**823,499**	**100.0%**
Legal form of organization		
C corporations	42,729	5.2
Subchapter S corporations	29,410	3.6
Individual proprietorships	737,076	89.5
Partnerships	13,595	1.7
Other	688	0.1
Size of receipts		
Under $5,000	247,536	30.1
$5,000 to $9,999	156,255	19.0
$10,000 to $24,999	188,811	22.9
$25,000 to $49,999	92,756	11.3
$50,000 to $99,999	59,391	7.2
$100,000 to $249,999	42,466	5.2
$250,000 to $499,999	19,099	2.3
$500,000 to $999,999	8,500	1.0
$1,000,000 or more	8,682	1.1
Number of employees		
Firms with employees	93,235	100.0
No employees*	15,217	16.3
1 to 3 employees	49,262	52.8
5 to 9 employees	14,734	15.8
10 to 19 employees	7,171	7.7
20 to 49 employees	4,477	4.8
50 to 99 employees	1,484	1.6
100 to 499 employees	836	0.9
500 employees or more	53	0.1

*Firms that reported annual payroll but no employees on the payroll during the specified period in 1997.
Source: Bureau of the Census, Blacks, 1997 Economic Census, Survey of Minority-Owned Business Enterprises, Company Statistics Series, EC97CS-3, 2001; calculations by New Strategist*

Black-Owned Businesses by State, 1997

(number of total firms and receipts and number and percent distribution of black-owned firms and receipts in the ten states with the largest number of black-owned firms, and black share of total firms and receipts, 1997)

	total firms	black firms			total sales and receipts (in millions)	black sales and receipts		
		number	percent distribution	percent of total		amount (in millions)	percent distribution	percent of total
Total firms	20,821,934	823,499	100.0%	4.0%	$18,553,243	$71,215	100.0%	0.4%
Total in top ten states	10,586,153	530,772	64.5	5.0	9,500,804	44,054	61.9	0.5
New York	1,509,829	86,469	10.5	5.7	1,488,913	5,067	7.1	0.3
California	2,565,734	79,110	9.6	3.1	2,178,292	6,395	9.0	0.3
Texas	1,525,972	60,427	7.3	4.0	1,415,536	6,857	9.6	0.5
Florida	1,301,920	59,732	7.3	4.6	828,429	4,092	5.7	0.5
Georgia	568,552	55,766	6.8	9.8	580,345	4,111	5.8	0.7
Maryland	400,203	47,614	5.8	11.9	285,924	3,965	5.6	1.4
Illinois	882,053	41,244	5.0	4.7	993,117	3,913	5.5	0.4
North Carolina	570,484	39,901	4.8	7.0	518,649	2,299	3.2	0.4
Virginia	480,122	33,539	4.1	7.0	415,093	3,408	4.8	0.8
Ohio	781,284	26,970	3.3	3.5	796,506	3,947	5.5	0.5

Source: Bureau of the Census, Blacks, 1997 Economic Census, Survey of Minority-Owned Business Enterprises, Company Statistics Series, EC97CS-3, 2001; calculations by New Strategist

Black-Owned Businesses by Metropolitan Area, 1997

(number and percent distribution of black-owned firms and receipts in the ten metropolitan areas with the largest number of black-owned firms, and metropolitan area's share of total black firms and receipts in state, 1997)

	firms			sales and receipts			
	number	percent distribution	percent of black firms in state	amount (in millions)	percent distribution	percent of black receipt in state
Total black firms/receipts	**823,499**	**100.0%**	–	**$71,215**	**100.0%**	–
Total in top metropolitan areas	**320,028**	**38.9**	–	**28,512**	**40.0**	–
New York, NY PMSA	69,410	8.4	80.3%	4,003	5.6	79.0%
Washington, DC–MD–VA–WV PMSA	48,709	5.9	–	5,410	7.6	–
Los Angeles–Long Beach, CA PMSA	38,277	4.6	48.4	3,322	4.7	51.9
Chicago, IL PMSA	35,569	4.3	86.2	3,375	4.7	86.3
Atlanta, GA MSA	34,592	4.2	62.0	2,959	4.2	72.0
Houston, TX PMSA	24,286	2.9	40.2	1,846	2.6	26.9
Philadelphia, PA–NJ PMSA	17,863	2.2	–	1,660	2.3	–
Detroit, MI PMSA	17,692	2.1	70.9	3,507	4.9	75.9
Miami, FL PMSA	16,918	2.1	28.3	1,070	1.5	26.1
Baltimore, MD PMSA	16,712	2.0	35.1	1,360	1.9	34.3

Note: (–) means data not available or not applicable. For definitions of PMSA and MSA, see glossary.
Source: Bureau of the Census, Blacks, 1997 Economic Census, Survey of Minority-Owned Business Enterprises, Company Statistics Series, EC97CS-3, 2001; calculations by New Strategist

Blacks Are Gaining on Whites in Educational Attainment

Seventy-eight percent of blacks aged 25 or older are high school graduates. While this figure is almost 6 percentage points lower than the share among the total population, blacks are rapidly gaining on whites. As recently as 1980, barely half of blacks had graduated from high school. The surge in attainment is due to the much greater educational level of younger blacks. Among blacks aged 25 to 44, from 86 to 89 percent are high school graduates.

Sixteen percent of blacks aged 25 or older had a bachelor's degree in 2000, compared with 26 percent of the total population. Among black families with children aged 18 to 24, fully 40 percent have a child in college full-time. The proportion rises to more than 60 percent among black families with incomes of $50,000 or more. More than 2 million blacks were in college in 2000, with 57 percent in four-year undergraduate programs and another 15 percent in graduate school.

Blacks earned 9 percent of bachelor's degrees, 8 percent of master's degrees, and 5 percent of doctorates awarded in 1999-00. They earned 12 percent of first-professional degrees in theology and 8 percent of degrees in pharmacy.

■ The proportion of blacks with a college education will continue to climb as the growing black middle class encourages its children to get the educational credentials necessary for a middle-class lifestyle.

The educational attainment of blacks is rising

(percent of blacks aged 25 or older who are high school or college graduates, 1980 and 2000)

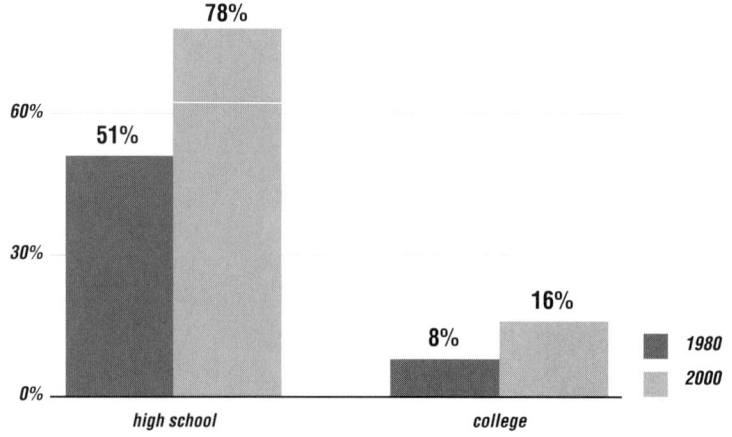

Educational Attainment of Blacks by Sex, 2000

(number and percent distribution of blacks aged 25 or older by educational attainment and sex, 2000; numbers in thousands)

	total		men		women	
	number	percent	number	percent	number	percent
Total blacks	**20,036**	**100.0%**	**8,879**	**100.0%**	**11,157**	**100.0%**
Not a high school graduate	4,316	21.5	1,895	21.3	2,421	21.7
High school graduate or more	15,720	78.5	6,984	78.7	8,736	78.3
High school graduate only	7,050	35.2	3,259	36.7	3,791	34.0
Some college or associate's degree	5,366	26.8	2,280	25.7	3,086	27.7
Bachelor's degree or more	3,304	16.5	1,445	16.3	1,859	16.7
Bachelor's degree only	2,278	11.4	1,016	11.4	1,263	11.3
Master's degree	839	4.2	337	3.8	502	4.5
Professional degree	115	0.6	56	0.6	59	0.5
Doctoral degree	72	0.4	36	0.4	35	0.3

Source: Bureau of the Census, Educational Attainment in the United States: March 2000 (Update), *detailed tables for Current Population Report P20-536, 2000; Internet site <www.census.gov/population/socdemo/ education/p20-536/tab01.txt>; calculations by New Strategist*

Educational Attainment of Black Men by Age, 2000

(number and percent distribution of black men aged 25 or older by age and educational attainment, 2000; numbers in thousands)

	total	not a high school graduate	high school graduate or more				bachelor's degree or more				
			total	high school graduate only	some college	associate's degree	total	bachelor's degree only	master's degree	professional degree	doctoral degree
Total black men	**8,879**	**1,895**	**6,984**	**3,259**	**1,766**	**514**	**1,445**	**1,016**	**337**	**56**	**36**
Aged 25 to 29	1,102	147	954	405	287	62	200	175	20	5	–
Aged 30 to 34	1,203	131	1,072	554	232	72	214	169	39	2	4
Aged 35 to 39	1,337	140	1,197	533	315	95	254	198	47	6	3
Aged 40 to 44	1,290	160	1,131	553	295	87	196	131	57	5	3
Aged 45 to 49	1,065	174	890	390	239	63	198	121	56	15	6
Aged 50 to 54	806	179	628	236	169	53	170	106	51	5	8
Aged 55 to 59	556	167	389	187	92	25	85	55	21	7	2
Aged 60 to 64	424	188	235	116	49	22	48	21	20	5	2
Aged 65 or older	1,095	605	490	285	87	36	82	41	27	5	9
Aged 65 to 69	376	171	205	112	47	8	38	16	15	–	7
Aged 70 to 74	285	153	132	75	21	15	21	9	9	3	–
Aged 75 or older	434	282	152	98	18	13	23	16	3	2	2

(continued)

(continued from previous page)

	total	not a high school graduate	high school graduate or more					bachelor's degree or more			
			total	high school graduate only	some college	associate's degree	total	bachelor's degree only	master's degree	professional degree	doctoral degree
Total black men	**100.0%**	**21.3%**	**78.7%**	**36.7%**	**19.9%**	**5.8%**	**16.3%**	**11.4%**	**3.8%**	**0.6%**	**0.4%**
Aged 25 to 29	100.0	13.3	86.6	36.8	26.0	5.6	18.1	15.9	1.8	0.5	–
Aged 30 to 34	100.0	10.9	89.1	46.1	19.3	6.0	17.8	14.0	3.2	0.2	0.3
Aged 35 to 39	100.0	10.5	89.5	39.9	23.6	7.1	19.0	14.8	3.5	0.4	0.2
Aged 40 to 44	100.0	12.4	87.7	42.9	22.9	6.7	15.2	10.2	4.4	0.4	0.2
Aged 45 to 49	100.0	16.3	83.6	36.6	22.4	5.9	18.6	11.4	5.3	1.4	0.6
Aged 50 to 54	100.0	22.2	77.9	29.3	21.0	6.6	21.1	13.2	6.3	0.6	1.0
Aged 55 to 59	100.0	30.0	70.0	33.6	16.5	4.5	15.3	9.9	3.8	1.3	0.4
Aged 60 to 64	100.0	44.3	55.4	27.4	11.6	5.2	11.3	5.0	4.7	1.2	0.5
Aged 65 or older	100.0	55.3	44.7	26.0	7.9	3.3	7.5	3.7	2.5	0.5	0.8
Aged 65 to 69	100.0	45.5	54.5	29.8	12.5	2.1	10.1	4.3	4.0	–	1.9
Aged 70 to 74	100.0	53.7	46.3	26.3	7.4	5.3	7.4	3.2	3.2	1.1	–
Aged 75 or older	100.0	65.0	35.0	22.6	4.1	3.0	5.3	3.7	0.7	0.5	0.5

Note: (–) means sample is too small to make a reliable estimate.
Source: Bureau of the Census, Educational Attainment in the United States: March 2000 (Update), detailed tables for Current Population Report P20-536, 2000; Internet site <www.census.gov/population/socdemo/education/p20-536/tab01.txt>; calculations by New Strategist

Educational Attainment of Black Women by Age, 2000

(number and percent distribution of black women aged 25 or older by age and educational attainment, 2000; numbers in thousands)

| | total | not a high school graduate | high school graduate or more | | | | bachelor's degree or more | | | | |
			total	high school graduate only	some college	associate's degree	total	bachelor's degree only	master's degree	professional degree	doctoral degree
Total black women	**11,157**	**2,421**	**8,736**	**3,791**	**2,238**	**848**	**1,859**	**1,263**	**502**	**59**	**35**
Aged 25 to 29	1,418	208	1,212	450	383	138	241	175	48	14	4
Aged 30 to 34	1,439	167	1,272	511	350	157	254	176	67	8	3
Aged 35 to 39	1,565	202	1,363	534	381	136	312	252	45	4	11
Aged 40 to 44	1,508	213	1,295	513	367	134	281	199	65	15	2
Aged 45 to 49	1,271	209	1,063	446	254	110	253	177	63	5	8
Aged 50 to 54	961	165	795	355	158	81	201	107	86	6	2
Aged 55 to 59	732	209	523	300	94	30	99	52	43	1	3
Aged 60 to 64	603	179	424	217	111	20	76	43	30	3	–
Aged 65 or older	1,659	870	789	465	141	44	139	81	54	2	2
Aged 65 to 69	493	227	265	157	39	10	59	27	28	2	2
Aged 70 to 74	469	225	245	130	37	18	60	41	19	0	–
Aged 75 or older	697	417	280	177	65	16	22	14	8	–	–

(continued)

(continued from previous page)

	total	not a high school graduate	high school graduate or more				bachelor's degree or more				
			total	high school graduate only	some college	associate's degree	total	bachelor's degree only	master's degree	professional degree	doctoral degree
Total black women	**100.0%**	**21.7%**	**78.3%**	**34.0%**	**20.1%**	**7.6%**	**16.7%**	**11.3%**	**4.5%**	**0.5%**	**0.3%**
Aged 25 to 29	100.0	14.7	85.5	31.7	27.0	9.7	17.0	12.3	3.4	1.0	0.3
Aged 30 to 34	100.0	11.6	88.4	35.5	24.3	10.9	17.7	12.2	4.7	0.6	0.2
Aged 35 to 39	100.0	12.9	87.1	34.1	24.3	8.7	19.9	16.1	2.9	0.3	0.7
Aged 40 to 44	100.0	14.1	85.9	34.0	24.3	8.9	18.6	13.2	4.3	1.0	0.1
Aged 45 to 49	100.0	16.4	83.6	35.1	20.0	8.7	19.9	13.9	5.0	0.4	0.6
Aged 50 to 54	100.0	17.2	82.7	36.9	16.4	8.4	20.9	11.1	8.9	0.6	0.2
Aged 55 to 59	100.0	28.6	71.4	41.0	12.8	4.1	13.5	7.1	5.9	0.1	0.4
Aged 60 to 64	100.0	29.7	70.3	36.0	18.4	3.3	12.6	7.1	5.0	0.5	–
Aged 65 or older	100.0	52.4	47.6	28.0	8.5	2.7	8.4	4.9	3.3	0.1	0.1
Aged 65 to 69	100.0	46.0	53.8	31.8	7.9	2.0	12.0	5.5	5.7	0.4	0.4
Aged 70 to 74	100.0	48.0	52.2	27.7	7.9	3.8	12.8	8.7	4.1	0.0	–
Aged 75 or older	100.0	59.8	40.2	25.4	9.3	2.3	3.2	2.0	1.1	–	–

Note: (–) means sample is too small to make a reliable estimate.
Source: Bureau of the Census, Educational Attainment in the United States: March 2000 (Update), detailed tables for Current Population Report P20-536, 2000; Internet site <www.census.gov/population/socdemo/education/p20-536/tab01.txt>; calculations by New Strategist

Black High School and College Graduates by Age and Sex, 2000

(percent of blacks aged 25 or older who are high school or college graduates by age and sex, 2000)

	total	men	women
High school graduates			
Total blacks	**78.5%**	**78.7%**	**78.3%**
Aged 25 to 29	85.9	86.6	85.3
Aged 30 to 34	88.7	89.1	88.4
Aged 35 to 39	88.3	89.6	87.1
Aged 40 to 44	86.6	87.6	85.9
Aged 45 to 49	83.6	83.5	83.6
Aged 50 to 54	80.5	77.8	82.8
Aged 55 to 59	70.7	69.8	71.4
Aged 60 to 64	64.2	55.6	70.2
Aged 65 or older	46.5	44.7	47.6
Aged 65 to 69	54.1	54.5	53.8
Aged 70 to 74	50.0	46.5	52.2
Aged 75 or older	38.2	35.1	40.1
College graduates			
Total blacks	**16.5**	**16.3**	**16.7**
Aged 25 to 29	17.5	18.1	17.0
Aged 30 to 34	17.7	17.9	17.6
Aged 35 to 39	19.6	19.0	20.0
Aged 40 to 44	17.0	15.1	18.6
Aged 45 to 49	19.3	18.5	19.9
Aged 50 to 54	21.0	21.0	21.0
Aged 55 to 59	14.3	15.3	13.5
Aged 60 to 64	12.1	11.4	12.5
Aged 65 or older	8.1	7.4	8.5
Aged 65 to 69	11.1	9.9	12.1
Aged 70 to 74	10.7	7.4	12.7
Aged 75 or older	3.9	5.3	3.1

Source: Bureau of the Census, Educational Attainment in the United States: March 2000 (Update), *detailed tables for Current Population Report P20-536, 2000; Internet site <www.census.gov/population/socdemo/education/p20-536/tab01a.txt>*

Black High School and College Graduates by Age and Region, 2000

(percent of blacks aged 25 or older who are high school or college graduates, by age and region, 2000)

	Northeast	Midwest	South	West
High school graduates				
Total blacks	**77.4%**	**79.5%**	**76.9%**	**88.9%**
Aged 25 to 34	84.4	84.8	89.0	89.3
Aged 35 to 44	86.1	86.8	86.5	96.5
Aged 45 to 54	79.2	86.6	80.1	92.0
Aged 55 to 64	67.8	73.4	63.7	84.2
Aged 65 or older	52.5	48.3	42.2	62.6
College graduates				
Total blacks	**18.4**	**17.5**	**14.6**	**22.6**
Aged 25 to 34	22.9	18.1	15.6	18.5
Aged 35 to 44	20.7	20.0	15.5	26.4
Aged 45 to 54	18.9	22.1	18.7	26.3
Aged 55 to 64	15.3	12.3	10.9	27.3
Aged 65 or older	7.5	8.3	8.1	8.8

Source: Bureau of the Census, Educational Attainment in the United States: March 2000 (Update), *Detailed tables for Current Population Reports, P20-536, 2000; Internet site <www.census.gov/population/socdemo/education/p20-536/tab12.txt>; calculations by New Strategist*

Black High School and College Graduates by State, 2000

(percent of blacks aged 25 or older who are high school or college graduates, for the 25 largest states, 2000)

	high school graduate or more	college graduate
Total blacks	**78.5%**	**16.5%**
Alabama	73.2	17.8
Arizona	97.0	31.1
California	87.8	21.8
Colorado	90.9	23.8
Florida	74.7	15.3
Georgia	77.2	12.3
Illinois	79.3	21.0
Indiana	84.1	15.6
Kentucky	77.2	5.7
Louisiana	71.7	10.3
Maryland	84.3	17.5
Massachusetts	72.3	12.3
Michigan	78.7	14.7
Minnesota	–	–
Missouri	77.7	25.7
New Jersey	81.1	22.5
New York	74.8	19.3
North Carolina	72.1	14.7
Ohio	80.2	12.5
Pennsylvania	80.8	15.0
Tennessee	76.8	17.4
Texas	84.6	14.3
Virginia	76.1	18.1
Washington	93.0	23.7
Wisconsin	73.3	9.1

Note: (–) means sample is too small to make a reliable estimate.
Source: Bureau of the Census, Educational Attainment in the United States: March 2000 (Update), *Detailed tables for Current Population Reports, P20-536, 2000; Internet site <www.census.gov/population/socdemo/ education/p20-536/tab14.txt>*

School Enrollment of Blacks by Age and Sex, 2000

(number and percent of blacks aged 3 or older enrolled in school, by age and sex, October 2000; numbers in thousands)

	total		men		women	
	number	*percent*	*number*	*percent*	*number*	*percent*
Total blacks	**11,503**	**34.0%**	**5,536**	**35.3%**	**5,967**	**32.9%**
Aged 3 to 4	725	59.9	353	57.6	372	62.3
Aged 5 to 6	1,219	96.3	606	95.8	613	96.8
Aged 7 to 9	1,975	97.5	1,017	98.3	959	96.8
Aged 10 to 13	2,700	98.4	1,380	98.7	1,320	98.2
Aged 14 to 15	1,260	99.6	628	99.6	631	99.6
Aged 16 to 17	1,106	91.4	550	89.1	556	93.8
Aged 18 to 19	716	57.2	311	52.4	405	61.5
Aged 20 to 21	416	36.6	154	30.5	262	41.3
Aged 22 to 24	393	24.2	172	21.8	221	26.4
Aged 25 to 29	353	14.3	120	11.3	232	16.5
Aged 30 to 34	252	9.6	98	8.3	154	10.7
Aged 35 to 44	249	4.4	112	4.3	137	4.5
Aged 45 to 54	97	2.3	25	1.3	72	3.1
Aged 55 or older	41	0.8	9	0.4	32	1.1

Source: Bureau of the Census, Current Population Survey, Internet site <www.census.gov/population/socdemo/school/ppl-148/tab01.txt>

Black Families with Children in College, 2000

(total number of black families, number with children aged 18 to 24, and number and percent with children aged 18 to 24 attending college full-time as of October 2000, by household income in 1999; numbers in thousands)

	total	with children aged 18–24	with one or more children attending college full-time		
			number	percent of total families	percent of families with children 18–24
Total black families	**8,887**	**1,641**	**650**	**7.3%**	**39.6%**
Under $20,000	2,816	502	122	4.3	24.3
$20,000 to $29,999	1,266	204	73	5.8	35.8
$30,000 to $39,999	930	182	78	8.4	42.9
$40,000 to $49,999	630	95	50	7.9	52.6
$50,000 to $74,999	1,101	251	156	14.2	62.2
$75,000 or more	785	158	97	12.4	61.4

Note: Numbers will not add to total because not reported is not shown.
Source: Bureau of the Census, Current Population Survey, Internet site <www.census.gov/population/socdemo/school/ppl-148/tab15.txt>

College Enrollment of Blacks by Age, 2000

(number and percent distribution of blacks aged 15 or older enrolled in college by age and type of school, October 2000; numbers in thousands)

	total	undergraduate total	two-year	four-year	graduate
Total blacks enrolled	**2,165**	**1,841**	**603**	**1,238**	**324**
Aged 15 to 17	19	19	5	14	–
Aged 18 to 19	455	445	166	279	10
Aged 20 to 21	375	358	94	264	17
Aged 22 to 24	386	331	80	251	55
Aged 25 to 29	325	248	80	168	77
Aged 30 to 34	242	177	52	125	65
Aged 35 to 39	134	106	56	50	28
Aged 40 to 44	109	74	29	45	35
Aged 45 to 49	58	42	25	17	16
Aged 50 to 54	33	22	12	10	11
Aged 55 or older	27	20	5	15	7

Percent distribution by age

	total	undergraduate total	two-year	four-year	graduate
Total blacks enrolled	**100.0%**	**100.0%**	**100.0%**	**100.0%**	**100.0%**
Aged 15 to 17	0.9	1.0	0.8	1.1	–
Aged 18 to 19	21.0	24.2	27.5	22.5	3.1
Aged 20 to 21	17.3	19.4	15.6	21.3	5.2
Aged 22 to 24	17.8	18.0	13.3	20.3	17.0
Aged 25 to 29	15.0	13.5	13.3	13.6	23.8
Aged 30 to 34	11.2	9.6	8.6	10.1	20.1
Aged 35 to 39	6.2	5.8	9.3	4.0	8.6
Aged 40 to 44	5.0	4.0	4.8	3.6	10.8
Aged 45 to 49	2.7	2.3	4.1	1.4	4.9
Aged 50 to 54	1.5	1.2	2.0	0.8	3.4
Aged 55 or older	1.2	1.1	0.8	1.2	2.2

(continued)

(continued from previous page)

	total	undergraduate			graduate
		total	two-year	four-year	
Percent distribution by type of school					
Total blacks enrolled	**100.0%**	**85.0%**	**27.9%**	**57.2%**	**15.0%**
Aged 15 to 17	100.0	100.0	26.3	73.7	–
Aged 18 to 19	100.0	97.8	36.5	61.3	2.2
Aged 20 to 21	100.0	95.5	25.1	70.4	4.5
Aged 22 to 24	100.0	85.8	20.7	65.0	14.2
Aged 25 to 29	100.0	76.3	24.6	51.7	23.7
Aged 30 to 34	100.0	73.1	21.5	51.7	26.9
Aged 35 to 39	100.0	79.1	41.8	37.3	20.9
Aged 40 to 44	100.0	67.9	26.6	41.3	32.1
Aged 45 to 49	100.0	72.4	43.1	29.3	27.6
Aged 50 to 54	100.0	66.7	36.4	30.3	33.3
Aged 55 or older	100.0	74.1	18.5	55.6	25.9

Note: (–) means sample is too small to make a reliable estimate.
Source: Bureau of the Census, Current Population Survey, Internet site <www.census.gov/population/socdemo/school/ppl-148/tab09.txt>; calculations by New Strategist

Associate's Degrees Earned by Non-Hispanic Blacks by Field of Study, 1999–2000

(total number of associate's degrees conferred and number and percent earned by non-Hispanic blacks, by field of study, 1999–2000)

	total	earned by non-Hispanic blacks	
		number	percent
Total associate's degrees	**564,933**	**60,181**	**10.7%**
Agriculture and natural resources	6,667	53	0.8
Architecture and related programs	392	11	2.8
Area, ethnic, and cultural studies	259	26	10.0
Biological, life sciences	1,434	144	10.0
Business	92,274	14,656	15.9
Communications	2,754	263	9.5
Communications technologies	1,709	188	11.0
Computer and information sciences	20,450	3,005	14.7
Construction trades	2,337	141	6.0
Education	8,226	1,136	13.8
Engineering	1,752	136	7.8
Engineering-related technologies	35,395	3,823	10.8
English language and literature, letters	947	66	7.0
Foreign languages and literatures	501	20	4.0
Health professions and related sciences	84,081	8,562	10.2
Home economics	8,381	1,253	15.0
Law and legal studies	7,265	1,149	15.8
Liberal arts and sciences, general studies, and humanities	187,454	17,539	9.4
Library science	98	1	1.0
Mathematics	675	40	5.9
Mechanics and repairers	11,614	783	6.7
Multi/interdisciplinary studies	11,784	1,228	10.4
Parks, recreation, leisure, and fitness	855	105	12.3
Philosophy and religion	63	3	4.8
Physical sciences	2,460	240	9.8
Precision production trades	11,814	637	5.4
Protective services	16,298	1,689	10.4
Psychology	1,455	142	9.8
Public administration and services	3,656	890	24.3
R.O.T.C. and military technologies	65	27	41.5
Social sciences and history	5,136	617	12.0
Theological studies, religious vocations	636	125	19.7
Transportation and material moving	1,021	32	3.1
Visual and performing arts	17,100	1,090	6.4
Not classified	2,798	361	12.9

Source: National Center for Education Statistics, Digest of Education Statistics 2001, *Internet site <http:// nces.ed.gov/pubsearch/pubsinfo.asp?pubid=2002130>; calculations by New Strategist*

Bachelor's Degrees Earned by Non-Hispanic Blacks by Field of Study, 1999–2000

(total number of bachelor's degrees conferred and number and percent earned by non-Hispanic blacks, by field of study, 1999–2000)

	total	earned by non-Hispanic blacks number	earned by non-Hispanic blacks percent
Total bachelor's degrees	**1,237,875**	**107,891**	**8.7%**
Agriculture and natural resources	24,247	668	2.8
Architecture and related programs	8,462	324	3.8
Area, ethnic, and cultural studies	6,381	824	12.9
Biological, life sciences	63,532	4,874	7.7
Business	257,709	23,645	9.2
Communications	55,760	4,968	8.9
Communications technologies	1,150	118	10.3
Computer and information sciences	36,195	3,527	9.7
Construction trades	186	1	0.5
Education	108,168	7,723	7.1
Engineering	58,427	3,153	5.4
Engineering-related technologies	13,872	1,404	10.1
English language and literature, letters	50,920	3,884	7.6
Foreign languages and literatures	14,968	573	3.8
Health professions and related sciences	78,458	7,817	10.0
Home economics	17,779	1,508	8.5
Law and legal studies	1,925	299	15.5
Liberal arts and sciences, general studies, and humanities	36,104	4,280	11.9
Library science	154	21	13.6
Mathematics	12,070	999	8.3
Mechanics and repairers	70	3	4.3
Multi/interdisciplinary studies	27,460	2,488	9.1
Parks, recreation, leisure, and fitness	19,111	1,565	8.2
Philosophy and religion	8,366	417	5.0
Physical sciences	18,385	1,187	6.5
Precision production trades	393	36	9.2
Protective services	24,877	4,141	16.6
Psychology	74,060	7,838	10.6
Public administration and services	20,185	4,194	20.8
R.O.T.C. and military technologies	7	0	0.0
Social sciences and history	127,101	11,878	9.3
Theological studies, religious vocations	6,809	320	4.7
Transportation and material moving	3,395	188	5.5
Visual and performing arts	58,791	2,879	4.9
Not classified	2,398	147	6.1

Source: National Center for Education Statistics, Digest of Education Statistics 2001, *Internet site <http:// nces.ed.gov/pubsearch/pubsinfo.asp?pubid=2002130>; calculations by New Strategist*

Master's Degrees Earned by Non-Hispanic Blacks by Field of Study, 1999–2000

(total number of master's degrees conferred and number and percent earned by non-Hispanic blacks, by field of study, 1999–2000)

		earned by non-Hispanic blacks	
	total	*number*	*percent*
Total master's degrees	**457,056**	**35,625**	**7.8%**
Agriculture and natural resources	4,375	108	2.5
Architecture and related programs	4,268	153	3.6
Area, ethnic, and cultural studies	1,591	99	6.2
Biological, life sciences	6,198	230	3.7
Business	112,258	8,630	7.7
Communications	5,169	433	8.4
Communications technologies	436	28	6.4
Computer and information sciences	14,264	567	4.0
Construction trades	12	1	8.3
Education	124,240	12,100	9.7
Engineering	25,596	683	2.7
Engineering-related technologies	914	97	10.6
English language and literature, letters	7,230	331	4.6
Foreign languages and literatures	2,780	39	1.4
Health professions and related sciences	42,456	2,684	6.3
Home economics	2,830	252	8.9
Law and legal studies	3,750	156	4.2
Liberal arts and sciences, general studies, and humanities	3,256	214	6.6
Library science	4,577	234	5.1
Mathematics	3,412	107	3.1
Multi/interdisciplinary studies	3,064	230	7.5
Parks, recreation, leisure, and fitness	2,478	182	7.3
Philosophy and religion	1,329	51	3.8
Physical sciences	4,841	130	2.7
Precision production trades	5	0	0.0
Protective services	2,609	328	12.6
Psychology	14,465	1,489	10.3
Public administration and services	25,594	4,075	15.9
Social sciences and history	14,066	1,021	7.3
Theological studies, religious vocations	5,576	394	7.1
Transportation and material moving	697	26	3.7
Visual and performing arts	10,918	441	4.0
Not classified	1,802	112	6.2

Source: National Center for Education Statistics, Digest of Education Statistics 2001, *Internet site <http:// nces.ed.gov/pubsearch/pubsinfo.asp?pubid=2002130>; calculations by New Strategist*

Doctoral Degrees Earned by Non-Hispanic Blacks by Field of Study, 1999–2000

(total number of doctoral degrees conferred and number and percent earned by non-Hispanic blacks, by field of study, 1999–2000)

	total	earned by non-Hispanic blacks	
		number	percent
Total doctoral degrees	**44,808**	**2,220**	**5.0%**
Agriculture and natural resources	1,181	25	2.1
Architecture and related programs	129	5	3.9
Area, ethnic, and cultural studies	217	21	9.7
Biological, life sciences	4,867	107	2.2
Business	1,196	56	4.7
Communications	347	20	5.8
Communications technologies	10	2	20.0
Computer and information sciences	777	15	1.9
Education	6,830	803	11.8
Engineering	5,384	94	1.7
Engineering-related technologies	6	0	0.0
English language and literature, letters	1,628	71	4.4
Foreign languages and literatures	915	8	0.9
Health professions and related sciences	2,676	112	4.2
Home economics	357	21	5.9
Law and legal studies	74	1	1.4
Liberal arts and sciences, general studies, and humanities	83	6	7.2
Library science	68	5	7.4
Mathematics	1,106	16	1.4
Multi/interdisciplinary studies	384	20	5.2
Parks, recreation, leisure, and fitness	134	3	2.2
Philosophy and religion	586	20	3.4
Physical sciences	4,018	71	1.8
Protective services	52	5	9.6
Psychology	4,310	229	5.3
Public administration and services	537	58	10.8
Social sciences and history	4,095	203	5.0
Theological studies, religious vocations	1,643	186	11.3
Visual and performing arts	1,127	31	2.8
Not classified	71	6	8.5

Source: National Center for Education Statistics, Digest of Education Statistics 2001, *Internet site <http://nces.ed.gov/pubsearch/pubsinfo.asp?pubid=2002130>; calculations by New Strategist*

First-Professional Degrees Earned by Non-Hispanic Blacks by Field of Study, 1999–2000

(total number of first-professional degrees conferred and number and percent earned by non-Hispanic blacks, by field of study, 1999–2000)

	total	earned by non-Hispanic blacks	
		number	percent
Total first-professional degrees	**80,259**	**5,552**	**6.9%**
Dentistry (D.D.S. or D.M.D.)	4,250	197	4.6
Medicine (M.D.)	15,286	1,106	7.2
Optometry (O.D.)	1,293	30	2.3
Osteopathic medicine (D.O.)	2,236	77	3.4
Pharmacy (Pharm.D.)	5,669	465	8.2
Podiatry (Pod.D., D.P., or D.P.M.)	569	41	7.2
Veterinary medicine (D.V.M.)	2,251	49	2.2
Chiropractic (D.C. or D.C.M.)	3,809	82	2.2
Naturopathic medicine	202	2	1.0
Law (LL.B. or J.D.)	38,152	2,771	7.3
Theology (M.Div., M.H.L., B.D., or Ord. and M.H.L./Rav.)	6,129	721	11.8
Other	413	11	2.7

Source: National Center for Education Statistics, Digest of Education Statistics 2001, *Internet site <http://nces.ed.gov/pubsearch/pubsinfo.asp?pubid=2002130>; calculations by New Strategist*

Most Blacks Say Their Health Is Good or Excellent

While blacks fare poorly on many health indicators, the 71 percent majority say they are in excellent or good health. This compares with a larger 80 percent of the total population who rate their health positively. Only 29 percent of blacks say they are in fair or poor health, somewhat greater than the 21 percent of the total population who feel that way.

More than 622,000 babies were born to black women in 2000, accounting for 15 percent of all babies born that year. Sixty-nine percent of black babies are born to unmarried women, the highest proportion among all racial and ethnic groups. Blacks accounted for 45 percent of all births in Mississippi and more than one-third of births in Georgia, Louisiana, Maryland, and South Carolina.

Only 54 percent of blacks are covered by employment-based health insurance, much lower than the 64 percent share among the total population. Twenty percent of blacks have Medicaid coverage. Blacks visit a doctor an average of 2.1 times a year, less than the 2.8 times the average American goes to the doctor. Disability rates among blacks are about average, with 21 percent of blacks disabled.

Heart disease, cancer, and cerebrovascular disease are the three leading causes of death among blacks, just as they are for the population as a whole. But AIDS ranks seventh as a cause of death among blacks, while it is not among the top ten for the total population. Blacks account for 39 percent of all AIDS cases diagnosed, and for an even larger 60 percent of cases diagnosed among women and 61 percent among children under age 13.

■ While blacks have made substantial gains in income and education over the past few decades, their health status is lagging.

Most blacks are in good health

(percent of total people and blacks aged 18 or older who say their health is excellent or good, 2000)

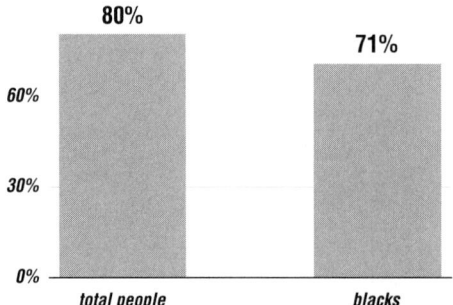

Black Health Status, 2000

"Would you say your own health, in general, is excellent, good, fair, or poor?"

(percent of total people and blacks aged 18 or older responding, 2000)

	excellent	good	fair	poor
Total	31%	49%	16%	5%
Black	24	47	21	8

Source: 2000 General Social Survey, National Opinion Research Center, University of Chicago; calculations by New Strategist

Health Indicators for Blacks, 1998

(selected indicators of total and black health status, and index of black health indicators to total, 1998)

	total population indicator	black indicator	index of black to total
Infant mortality rate (deaths before age 1 per 1,000 live births)	7.2	14.3	199
Total deaths per 100,000 population	471.7	690.9	146
Motor vehicle crash deaths per 100,000 population	15.7	16.6	106
Work-related injury deaths per 100,000 people aged 16 or older	2.9	2.4	83
Suicides per 100,000 population	10.4	5.9	57
Homicides per 100,000 population	7.3	25.2	345
Lung cancer deaths per 100,000 population	37.0	44.6	121
Female breast cancer deaths per 100,000 population	18.8	25.3	135
Cardiovascular disease deaths per 100,000 population	161.2	240.2	149
Heart disease deaths per 100,000 population	126.7	183.3	145
Stroke deaths per 100,000 population	25.1	41.4	165
Reported incidence of AIDS per 100,000 population	19.5	82.9	425
Reported incidence of tuberculosis per 100,000 population	6.8	17.8	262
Reported incidence of syphilis per 100,000 population	2.6	17.1	658
Prevalence of low birth weight, as percent of total live births	7.6	13.0	171
Births to girls aged 10 to 17, as percent of total live births	4.6	7.6	165
Percent of mothers without care, first trimester of pregnancy	17.2	26.7	155
Percent under age 18 living in poverty	18.9	36.7	194
Percent living in counties exceeding U.S. air quality standards	23.5	24.9	106

Note: The index for each indicator is calculated by dividing the black figure by the total population figure and multiplying by 100. For example, the index of 146 in the second row indicates that the black death rate is 46 percent above the rate for the total population.
Source: National Center for Health Statistics, Healthy People 2000 Final Review, 2001; *calculations by New Strategist*

Births to Black Women by Age, 2000

(total number of births, number and percent distribution of births to black women, and black share of total, by age, 2000)

	total	black number	percent distribution	share of total
Total births	**4,058,814**	**622,598**	**100.0%**	**15.3%**
Under age 15	8,519	3,808	0.6	44.7
Aged 15 to 19	468,990	118,954	19.1	25.4
Aged 20 to 24	1,017,806	202,596	32.5	19.9
Aged 25 to 29	1,087,547	141,968	22.8	13.1
Aged 30 to 34	929,278	94,808	15.2	10.2
Aged 35 to 39	452,057	49,295	7.9	10.9
Aged 40 to 44	90,013	10,699	1.7	11.9
Aged 45 or older	4,604	470	0.1	10.2

Source: National Center for Health Statistics, Births: Final Data for 2000, *National Vital Statistics Report, Vol. 50, No. 5, 2002; calculations by New Strategist*

Births to Black Women by Birth Order, 2000

(number and percent distribution of births to black women, by birth order, 2000)

	number	percent distribution
Births to blacks	**622,598**	**100.0%**
First child	232,353	37.3
Second child	184,064	29.6
Third child	110,858	17.8
Fourth or later child	93,017	14.9

Note: Numbers will not add to total because not stated is not shown.
Source: National Center for Health Statistics, Births: Final Data for 2000, *National Vital Statistics Report, Vol. 50, No. 5, 2002; calculations by New Strategist*

Births to Unmarried Black Women by Age, 2000

(total number of births to blacks, number of births to unmarried black women, and unmarried share of total, by age, 2000)

	total	unmarried blacks number	unmarried blacks share of total
Births to blacks	**622,598**	**426,649**	**68.5%**
Under age 15	3,808	3,785	99.4
Aged 15 to 19	118,954	113,671	95.6
Aged 20 to 24	202,596	163,259	80.6
Aged 25 to 29	141,968	80,916	57.0
Aged 30 to 34	94,808	40,501	42.7
Aged 35 to 39	49,295	19,907	40.4
Aged 40 or older	11,169	4,610	41.3

Source: National Center for Health Statistics, Births: Final Data for 2000, *National Vital Statistics Report, Vol. 50, No. 5, 2002*

Births to Black Women by State, 2000

(total number of births, number and percent distribution of births to black women, and black share of total, by state, 2000)

	total	black births number	percent distribtution	share of total
Total births	**4,058,814**	**622,598**	**100.0%**	**15.3%**
Alabama	63,299	20,512	3.3	32.4
Alaska	9,974	462	0.1	4.6
Arizona	85,273	2,787	0.4	3.3
Arkansas	37,783	7,969	1.3	21.1
California	531,959	35,046	5.6	6.6
Colorado	65,438	3,031	0.5	4.6
Connecticut	43,026	5,273	0.8	12.3
Delaware	11,051	2,634	0.4	23.8
District of Columbia	7,666	5,157	0.8	67.3
Florida	204,125	47,367	7.6	23.2
Georgia	132,644	44,161	7.1	33.3
Hawaii	17,551	472	0.1	2.7
Idaho	20,366	75	0.0	0.4
Illinois	185,036	34,317	5.5	18.5
Indiana	87,699	9,521	1.5	10.9
Iowa	38,266	1,234	0.2	3.2
Kansas	39,666	2,870	0.5	7.2
Kentucky	56,029	5,127	0.8	9.2
Louisiana	67,898	28,351	4.6	41.8
Maine	13,603	112	0.0	0.8
Maryland	74,316	24,910	4.0	33.5
Massachusetts	81,614	8,086	1.3	9.9
Michigan	136,171	24,314	3.9	17.9
Minnesota	67,604	4,450	0.7	6.6
Mississippi	44,075	19,893	3.2	45.1
Missouri	76,463	11,474	1.8	15.0
Montana	10,957	45	0.0	0.4
Nebraska	24,646	1,377	0.2	5.6
Nevada	30,829	2,369	0.4	7.7
New Hampshire	14,609	182	0.0	1.2
New Jersey	115,632	21,131	3.4	18.3

(continued)

(continued from previous page)

	total	black births number	black births percent distribtution	black births share of total
New Mexico	27,223	498	0.1%	1.8%
New York	258,737	54,822	8.8	21.2
North Carolina	120,311	29,369	4.7	24.4
North Dakota	7,676	82	0.0	1.1
Ohio	155,472	23,726	3.8	15.3
Oklahoma	49,782	4,787	0.8	9.6
Oregon	45,804	1,020	0.2	2.2
Pennsylvania	146,281	20,684	3.3	14.1
Rhode Island	12,505	1,121	0.2	9.0
South Carolina	56,114	19,734	3.2	35.2
South Dakota	10,345	106	0.0	1.0
Tennessee	79,611	16,909	2.7	21.2
Texas	363,414	41,308	6.6	11.4
Utah	47,353	328	0.1	0.7
Vermont	6,500	32	0.0	0.5
Virginia	98,938	22,529	3.6	22.8
Washington	81,036	3,497	0.6	4.3
West Virginia	20,865	778	0.1	3.7
Wisconsin	69,326	6,502	1.0	9.4
Wyoming	6,253	57	0.0	0.9

Source: National Center for Health Statistics, Births: Final Data for 2000, *National Vital Statistics Report, Vol. 50, No. 5, 2002; calculations by New Strategist*

Health Insurance Coverage of Blacks by Age, 2000

(number and percent distribution of blacks by age and health insurance coverage status, 2000; numbers in thousands)

	total	covered by private or government health insurance							not covered
		private health insurance			government health insurance				
		total	total	employ- ment based	total	Medicaid	Medicare	Military	
Total blacks	**35,919**	**29,295**	**21,182**	**19,562**	**11,116**	**7,250**	**3,808**	**1,380**	**6,623**
Under 18	11,574	10,013	6,316	5,956	4,597	4,103	158	459	1,561
Aged 18–24	3,995	2,640	2,053	1,740	795	628	73	128	1,355
Aged 25–34	5,146	3,828	3,275	3,110	742	580	107	123	1,318
Aged 35–44	5,739	4,519	3,884	3,695	870	572	161	250	1,219
Aged 45–54	4,277	3,563	2,991	2,837	785	465	294	179	713
Aged 55–64	2,399	1,975	1,489	1,386	660	345	360	99	425
Aged 65+	2,789	2,758	1,172	838	2,667	556	2,654	140	32
Total blacks	**100.0%**	**81.6%**	**59.0%**	**54.5%**	**30.9%**	**20.2%**	**10.6%**	**3.8%**	**18.4%**
Under 18	100.0	86.5	54.6	51.5	39.7	35.5	1.4	4.0	13.5
Aged 18–24	100.0	66.1	51.4	43.6	19.9	15.7	1.8	3.2	33.9
Aged 25–34	100.0	74.4	63.6	60.4	14.4	11.3	2.1	2.4	25.6
Aged 35–44	100.0	78.7	67.7	64.4	15.2	10.0	2.8	4.4	21.2
Aged 45–54	100.0	83.3	69.9	66.3	18.4	10.9	6.9	4.2	16.7
Aged 55–64	100.0	82.3	62.1	57.8	27.5	14.4	15.0	4.1	17.7
Aged 65+	100.0	98.9	42.0	30.0	95.6	19.9	95.2	5.0	1.1

Note: Numbers will not add to total because some people have more than one type of health insurance.
Source: Bureau of the Census, Internet site <http://ferret.bls.census.gov/macro/032001/health/h01_005.htm>

Acute Health Conditions among Blacks, 1996

(number of acute conditions among total people and blacks and black share of total, rate of acute conditions per 100 total people and blacks and index of black rate to total, by type of acute condition, 1996; numbers in thousands)

	number of conditions			rate per 100 population		
		black			black	
	total people	number	share of total	total people	rate	index of black rate to total
Total acute conditions	**432,001**	**47,500**	**11.0%**	**163.5**	**143.1**	**88**
Infective and parasitic diseases	**54,192**	**6,300**	**11.6**	**20.5**	**19.0**	**93**
Common childhood diseases	3,118	579	18.6	1.2	1.7	142
Intestinal virus	15,980	1,811	11.3	6.0	5.5	92
Viral infections	15,067	2,373	15.7	5.7	7.2	126
Other	20,027	1,536	7.7	7.6	4.6	61
Respiratory conditions	**208,623**	**22,097**	**10.6**	**78.9**	**66.6**	**84**
Common cold	62,251	8,644	13.9	23.6	26.0	110
Other acute upper respiratory infections	29,866	2,770	9.3	11.3	8.3	73
Influenza	95,049	9,313	9.8	36.0	28.1	78
Acute bronchitis	12,116	631	5.2	4.6	1.9	41
Pneumonia	4,791	249	5.2	1.8	0.8	44
Other respiratory conditions	4,550	489	10.7	1.7	1.5	88
Digestive system conditions	**17,646**	**2,279**	**12.9**	**6.7**	**6.9**	**103**
Dental conditions	2,970	712	24.0	1.1	2.1	191
Indigestion, nausea, and vomiting	7,963	1,053	13.2	3.0	3.2	107
Other digestive conditions	6,713	514	7.7	2.5	1.5	60
Injuries	**57,279**	**6,898**	**12.0**	**21.7**	**20.8**	**96**
Fractures and dislocations	8,465	612	7.2	3.2	1.8	56
Sprains and strains	12,977	2,111	16.3	4.9	6.4	131
Open wounds and lacerations	9,027	1,069	11.8	3.4	3.2	94
Contusions and superficial injuries	9,979	1,433	14.4	3.8	4.3	113
Other current injuries	16,832	1,673	9.9	6.4	5.0	78
Selected other acute conditions	**63,090**	**6,558**	**10.4**	**23.9**	**19.8**	**83**
Eye conditions	3,478	442	12.7	1.3	1.3	100
Acute ear infections	21,766	1,649	7.6	8.2	5.0	61
Other ear conditions	3,833	293	7.6	1.5	0.9	60
Acute urinary conditions	8,405	923	11.0	3.2	2.8	88
Disorders of menstruation	839	–	–	0.3	–	–
Other disorders of female genital tract	1,597	123	7.7	0.6	0.4	67
Delivery and other conditions of pregnancy	3,279	399	12.2	1.2	1.2	100

(continued)

(continued from previous page)

	number of conditions			rate per 100 population		
		black			black	
	total people	number	share of total	total people	rate	index of black rate to total
Skin conditions	4,986	723	14.5%	1.9	2.2	116
Acute musculoskeletal conditions	8,461	989	11.7	3.2	3.0	94
Headache, excluding migraine	1,738	498	28.7	0.7	1.5	214
Fever, unspecified	4,708	519	11.0	1.8	1.6	89
All other acute conditions	**31,170**	**3,369**	**10.8**	**11.8**	**10.2**	**86**

Note: The acute conditions shown here are those that caused people to restrict their activity for at least half a day or to contact a physician about the illness or injury. (–) means not applicable or sample is too small to make a reliable estimate. The index is calculated by dividing the black rate by the rate for the total population and multiplying by 100.
Source: National Center for Health Statistics, Current Estimates from the National Health Interview Survey, 1996, *Series 10, No. 200, 1999; calculations by New Strategist*

Chronic Health Conditions among Blacks, 1996

(number of chronic conditions among total people and blacks and black share of total, rate of chronic conditions per 1,000 total people and blacks and index of black rate to total, by type of chronic condition, 1996; numbers in thousands)

	number of conditions			rate per 1,000 population		
		black			black	
	total people	number	share of total	total people	rate	index of black rate to total
Selected skin and musculoskeletal conditions						
Arthritis	33,638	3,734	11.1%	127.3	112.5	88
Gout, including gouty arthritis	2,487	302	12.1	9.4	9.1	97
Intervertebral disc disorders	6,700	546	8.1	25.4	16.5	65
Bone spur or tendinitis, unspecified	2,934	149	5.1	11.1	4.5	40
Disorders of bone or cartilage	1,730	101	5.8	6.5	3.0	47
Trouble with bunions	2,360	184	7.8	8.9	5.5	62
Bursitis, unclassified	5,006	371	7.4	18.9	11.2	59
Sebaceous skin cyst	1,190	81	6.8	4.5	2.4	54
Trouble with acne	4,952	474	9.6	18.7	14.3	76
Psoriasis	2,940	74	2.5	11.1	2.2	20
Dermatitis	8,249	982	11.9	31.2	29.6	95
Trouble with dry skin, unclassified	6,627	619	9.3	25.1	18.7	74
Trouble with ingrown nails	5,807	612	10.5	22.0	18.4	84
Trouble with corns and calluses	3,778	752	19.9	14.3	22.7	158
Impairments						
Visual impairment	8,280	1,061	12.8	31.3	32.0	102
Color blindness	2,811	89	3.2	10.6	2.7	25
Cataracts	7,022	594	8.5	26.6	17.9	67
Glaucoma	2,595	409	15.8	9.8	12.3	126
Hearing impairment	22,044	1,301	5.9	83.4	39.2	47
Tinnitus	7,866	500	6.4	29.8	15.1	51
Speech impairment	2,720	624	22.9	10.3	18.8	183
Absence of extremities	1,285	99	7.7	4.9	3.0	61
Paralysis of extremities, complete or partial	2,138	507	23.7	8.1	15.3	189
Deformity/orthopedic impairment	29,499	3,214	10.9	111.6	96.9	87
Back	16,905	1,665	9.8	64.0	50.2	78
Upper extremities	4,170	463	11.1	15.8	14.0	88
Lower extremitites	12,696	1,642	12.9	48.0	49.5	103

(continued)

(continued from previous page)

	number of conditions			rate per 1,000 population		
		black			black	
	total people	number	share of total	total people	rate	index of black rate to total
Selected digestive conditions						
Ulcer	3,709	623	16.8%	14.0	18.8	134
Hernia of abdominal cavity	4,470	176	3.9	16.9	5.3	31
Gastritis or duodenitis	3,729	514	13.8	14.1	15.5	110
Frequent indigestion	6,420	617	9.6	24.3	18.6	77
Enteritis or colitis	1,686	59	3.5	6.4	1.8	28
Spastic colon	2,083	68	3.3	7.9	2.0	26
Diverticula of intestines	2,529	67	2.6	9.6	2.0	21
Frequent constipation	3,149	420	13.3	11.9	12.7	106
Selected conditions of the genitourinary, nervous, endocrine, metabolic, and blood and blood-forming systems						
Goiter or other disorders of thyroid	4,598	410	8.9	17.4	12.4	71
Diabetes	7,627	1,541	20.2	28.9	46.4	161
Anemias	3,457	734	21.2	13.1	22.1	169
Epilepsy	1,335	198	14.8	5.1	6.0	117
Migraine headache	11,546	1,413	12.2	43.7	42.6	97
Neuralgia or neuritis, unspecified	353	35	9.9	1.3	1.1	81
Kidney trouble	2,553	180	7.1	9.7	5.4	56
Bladder trouble	3,139	258	8.2	11.9	7.8	65
Diseases of prostate	2,803	163	5.8	10.6	4.9	46
Diseases of female genital organs	4,420	651	14.7	16.7	19.6	117
Selected circulatory conditions						
Rheumatic fever with or without heart disease	1,759	127	7.2	6.7	3.8	57
Heart disease	20,653	1,975	9.6	78.2	59.5	76
Ischemic heart disease	7,672	422	5.5	29.0	12.7	44
Heart rhythm disorders	8,716	977	11.2	33.0	29.4	89
Tachycardia or rapid heart	2,310	180	7.8	8.7	5.4	62
Heart murmurs	4,783	632	13.2	18.1	19.0	105
Other and unspecified heart rhythm disorders	1,624	164	10.1	6.1	4.9	81
Other selected diseases of heart, excluding hypertension	4,265	576	13.5	16.1	17.4	108
High blood pressure (hypertension)	28,314	4,502	15.9	107.1	135.7	127
Cerebrovascular disease	2,999	368	12.3	11.3	11.1	98
Hardening of the arteries	1,556	89	5.7	5.9	2.7	45
Varicose veins of lower extremities	7,399	657	8.9	28.0	19.8	71
Hemorrhoids	8,531	630	7.4	32.3	19.0	59

(continued)

(continued from previous page)

	number of conditions			rate per 1,000 population		
		black			black	
	total people	number	share of total	total people	rate	index of black rate to total
Selected respiratory conditions						
Chronic bronchitis	14,150	1,672	11.8%	53.5	50.4	94
Asthma	14,596	2,311	15.8	55.2	69.6	126
Hay fever or allergic rhinitis without asthma	23,721	2,137	9.0	89.8	64.4	72
Chronic sinusitis	33,161	4,353	13.1	125.5	131.2	105
Deviated nasal septum	1,985	20	1.0	7.5	0.6	8
Chronic disease of tonsils or adenoids	2,513	221	8.8	9.5	6.7	70
Emphysema	1,821	105	5.8	6.9	3.2	46

Note: Chronic conditions are those that last longer than three months or belong to a group of conditions considered chronic regardless of when they began. The index is calculated by dividing the black rate by the rate for the total population and multiplying by 100.
Source: National Center for Health Statistics, Current Estimates from the National Health Interview Survey, 1996, Series 10, No. 200, 1999; calculations by New Strategist

Physician Office Visits by Blacks, 1999

(number and percent distribution of physician office visits by blacks and number of visits per person per year, by age, 1999)

	number of visits (in 000s)	percent distribution	per person per year
Total visits by blacks	**73,792**	**100.0%**	**2.1**
Under age 15	14,645	19.8	1.5
Aged 15 to 24	6,780	9.2	1.2
Aged 25 to 44	17,817	24.1	1.6
Aged 45 to 64	20,133	27.3	3.2
Aged 65 to 74	7,906	10.7	4.8
Aged 75 or older	6,692	9.1	6.1

Source: National Center for Health Statistics, National Ambulatory Medical Care Survey: 1999 Summary, Advance Data, *No. 322, 2001; calculations by New Strategist*

Blacks with Disabilities by Sex and Age, 1997

(total number of blacks and number and percent with disabilities, by sex, age, and severity of disability, 1997; numbers in thousands)

		with a disability					
		total		severe		needs assistance	
	total	*number*	*percent*	*number*	*percent*	*number*	*percent*
Total blacks	**34,369**	**7,338**	**21.3%**	**5,382**	**15.7%**	**1,495**	**4.3%**
Under age 15	9,584	800	8.4	397	4.1	32	0.3
Aged 15 to 24	5,589	672	12.0	421	7.5	27	0.5
Aged 25 to 64	16,538	4,136	25.0	3,187	19.3	776	4.7
Aged 65 or older	2,659	1,729	65.0	1,376	51.8	660	24.8
Black females	**18,322**	**3,957**	**21.6**	**2,871**	**15.7**	**873**	**4.8**
Under age 15	4,726	284	6.0	112	2.4	7	0.1
Aged 15 to 24	2,904	330	11.4	197	6.8	15	0.5
Aged 25 to 64	9,081	2,257	24.9	1,695	18.7	405	4.5
Aged 65 or older	1,611	1,086	67.4	867	53.8	446	27.7
Black males	**16,048**	**3,380**	**21.1**	**2,511**	**15.6**	**621**	**3.9**
Under age 15	4,858	517	10.6	285	5.9	25	0.5
Aged 15 to 24	2,685	342	12.7	224	8.3	12	0.4
Aged 25 to 64	7,457	1,879	25.2	1,493	20.0	371	5.0
Aged 65 or older	1,048	643	61.4	509	48.6	214	20.4

Note: For the definition of disability, see glossary.
Source: Bureau of the Census, Americans with Disabilities: 1997, *detailed tables from Current Population Reports P70-73, 2001*

Blacks with Disabilities by Employment Status and Earnings, 1997

(total number of blacks aged 21 to 64, number and percent employed, median earnings, and index of earnings to total, by disability status, 1997)

	total (in 000s)	employed number (in 000s)	employed percent	median earnings	index of earnings by disability status to total black earnings
Total blacks	**18,489**	**13,157**	**71.2%**	**$19,237**	**100**
Not disabled	**14,124**	**11,622**	**82.3**	**19,746**	**103**
Disabled	**4,365**	**1,535**	**35.2**	**14,842**	**77**
Not severely	1,047	839	80.2	17,371	90
Severely	3,317	696	21.0	10,337	54

Note: For the definition of disability, see glossary.
Source: Bureau of the Census, Americans with Disabilities: 1997, *detailed tables from Current Population Reports P70-73, 2001; calculations by New Strategist*

AIDS Cases among Blacks, through June 2000

(total number of AIDS cases diagnosed, number diagnosed among blacks, and black share of total, by sex and age at diagnosis, through June 2000)

	total	black number	black share of total
Total AIDS cases	**729,326**	**282,434**	**38.7%**
Males aged 13 or older	601,471	205,630	34.2
Females aged 13 or older	119,454	71,656	60.0
Children under age 13	8,401	5,148	61.3

Source: National Center for Health Statistics, Health United States, 2001; *calculations by New Strategist*

Leading Causes of Death among Blacks, 1999

(total number of deaths among blacks, and number and percent accounted for by the ten leading causes of death for blacks, 1999)

	number	percent
Total black deaths	**285,064**	**100.0%**
1. Diseases of heart	78,574	27.6
2. Malignant neoplasms	61,951	21.7
3. Cerebrovascular diseases	18,884	6.6
4. Accidents	12,728	4.5
5. Diabetes mellitus	11,927	4.2
6. Chronic lower respiratory diseases	7,915	2.8
7. Human immunodeficiency virus infection	7,893	2.8
8. Homicide and legal intervention	7,648	2.7
9. Nephritis, nephrotic syndrome, and nephrosis	6,711	2.4
10. Influenza and pneumonia	5,876	2.1
All other causes	64,957	22.8

Source: National Center for Health Statistics, Deaths: Final Data for 1999, *National Vital Statistics Reports, Vol. 49, No. 8, 2001; calculations by New Strategist*

Life Expectancy of Blacks at Birth and Age 65 by Sex, 1990 and 2000

(number of years of life remaining for blacks at birth and age 65, by sex, 1990 and 2000; change in years, 1990–2000)

	total	female	male
Birth			
2000	71.8	75.0	68.3
1990	69.1	73.6	64.5
Change, 1990–2000	2.7	1.4	3.8
Age 65			
2000	16.2	17.5	14.6
1990	15.4	17.2	13.2
Change, 1990–2000	0.8	0.3	1.4

Source: National Center for Health Statistics, Health United States, 2001; *and* Deaths: Preliminary Data for 2000, *National Vital Statistics Report, Vol. 49, No. 12, 2001; calculations by New Strategist*

Most Black Householders in the South Are Homeowners

Forty-six percent of the nation's 13 million black householders own their home. This compares with a much higher homeownership rate of 67 percent for all households. Among black married couples, the homeownership rate is fully 71 percent. But among black female-headed families—which are almost as numerous as black couples—only 33 percent own a home.

Black homeowners paid a median of $44,447 for their home, and most used savings for the down payment. Their homes are now worth a median of $80,302.

Most black householders are satisfied with their homes. On a scale of one to ten, 61 percent of black homeowners rate their home an eight or higher. Among black renters, however, barely more than half rate their home at least an eight. Twenty-four percent of black householders think their neighborhood has a crime problem, with 8 percent so bothered by crime they want to move.

Nineteen percent of blacks moved between 1999 and 2000, a higher mobility rate than for the population as a whole. The main reason black householders move is to establish their own household, followed by the need for a larger house or apartment.

■ Because so many black households are female-headed families—one of the household types least likely to own a home—black homeownership is well below average.

Black homeownership is lowest in the Northeast

(percent of black households that own their home, by region, 1999)

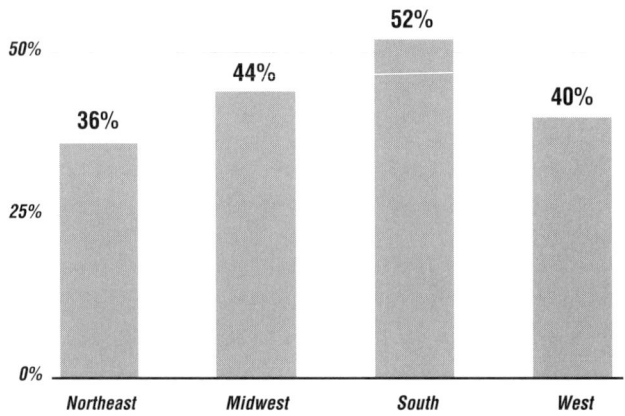

Region of Residence and Metropolitan Status of
Housing Units Occupied by Blacks, 1999

(number, percent distribution, and percent of housing units occupied by blacks, by regional, metropolitan, and homeownership status, 1999; numbers in thousands)

	total		owner			renter		
	number	percent distribution	number	percent distribution	share of total	number	percent distribution	share of total
Housing units occupied by blacks	**12,936**	**100.0%**	**6,013**	**100.0%**	**46.5%**	**6,923**	**100.0%**	**53.5%**
Northeast	2,334	18.0	844	14.0	36.2	1,491	21.5	63.9
Midwest	2,453	19.0	1,090	18.1	44.4	1,363	19.7	55.6
South	6,927	53.5	3,592	59.7	51.9	3,335	48.2	48.1
West	1,222	9.4	487	8.1	39.9	735	10.6	60.1
In metropolitan areas	11,137	86.1	4,933	82.0	44.3	6,204	89.6	55.7
In central cities	7,117	55.0	2,706	45.0	38.0	4,411	63.7	62.0
In suburbs	4,020	31.1	2,228	37.1	55.4	1,793	25.9	44.6
Outside metro. areas	1,799	13.9	1,080	18.0	60.0	719	10.4	40.0

Source: Bureau of the Census, American Housing Survey for the United States: 1999, *Current Housing Reports, H150/99, 2000; calculations by New Strategist*

Black Homeowners by Family Type and Age of Householder, 2000

(number of families headed by blacks, and number and percent of families owning their home, by family type and by age of householder for married couples and female-headed families, 2000; numbers in thousands)

	total	homeowners	
		number	percent
Black married couples	**4,144**	**2,954**	**71.3%**
Under age 25	93	32	34.4
Aged 25 to 29	312	140	44.9
Aged 30 to 34	471	258	54.8
Aged 35 to 39	572	372	65.0
Aged 40 to 44	622	443	71.2
Aged 45 to 54	984	785	79.8
Aged 55 to 64	554	453	81.8
Aged 65 to 74	360	321	89.2
Aged 75 or older	175	151	86.3
Black female-headed families	**3,814**	**1,267**	**33.2**
Under age 25	502	31	6.2
Aged 25 to 29	494	76	15.4
Aged 30 to 34	545	129	23.7
Aged 35 to 39	443	145	32.7
Aged 40 to 44	475	148	31.2
Aged 45 to 54	658	277	42.1
Aged 55 to 64	323	199	61.6
Aged 65 to 74	229	150	65.5
Aged 75 or older	146	113	77.4
Black male-headed families	**706**	**336**	**47.6**

Source: Bureau of the Census, America's Families and Living Arrangements: March 2000, *detailed tables from Current Population Report P20–537, Internet site <www.census.gov/population/www/socdemo/hh-fam/p20-537_00.html>; calculations by New Strategist*

Characteristics of Housing Units Occupied by Blacks, 1999

(number and percent distribution of housing units occupied by blacks, by selected housing characteristics and homeownership status, 1999; numbers in thousands)

	total		owner-occupied		renter-occupied	
	number	*percent distribution*	*number*	*percent distribution*	*number*	*percent distribution*
Housing units occupied by blacks	**12,936**	**100.0%**	**6,013**	**100.0%**	**6,923**	**100.0%**
Units in structure						
One, detached	6,076	47.0	4,650	77.3	1,425	20.6
One, attached	1,411	10.9	551	9.2	861	12.4
Two to four	1,728	13.4	202	3.4	1,526	22.0
Five to nine	1,022	7.9	28	0.5	994	14.4
10 to 19	804	6.2	24	0.4	780	11.3
20 to 49	593	4.6	20	0.3	572	8.3
50 or more	716	5.5	44	0.7	672	9.7
Mobile home or trailer	586	4.5	493	8.2	93	1.3
Median square footage of unit	1,518	–	1,621	–	1,254	–
Number of rooms in unit						
One room	66	0.5	–	–	66	1.0
Two rooms	148	1.1	–	–	148	2.1
Three rooms	1,695	13.1	78	1.3	1,527	22.1
Four rooms	2,953	22.8	516	8.6	2,437	35.2
Five rooms	3,212	24.8	1,539	25.6	1,673	24.2
Six rooms	2,613	20.2	1,867	31.0	746	10.8
Seven rooms	1,283	9.9	1,029	17.1	254	3.7
Eight rooms	609	4.7	563	9.4	46	0.7
Nine rooms	241	1.9	230	3.8	11	0.2
Ten or more rooms	205	1.6	192	3.2	14	0.2
Complete bathrooms						
None	146	1.1	36	0.6	110	1.6
One	7,160	55.3	1,953	32.5	5,207	75.2
One and one-half	2,010	15.5	1,309	21.8	701	10.1
Two or more	3,620	28.0	2,715	45.2	906	13.1

(continued)

(continued from previous page)

	total		owner-occupied		renter-occupied	
	number	percent distribution	number	percent distribution	number	percent distribution
Heating fuel						
Housing units with heating fuel	12,891	100.0%	6,013	100.0%	6,878	100.0%
Electricity	4,324	33.5	1,649	27.4	2,675	38.9
Piped gas	6,718	52.1	3,415	56.8	3,303	48.0
Bottled gas	509	3.9	386	6.4	124	1.8
Fuel oil	1,065	8.3	405	6.7	659	9.6
Kerosene or other liquid fuel	145	1.1	84	1.4	61	0.9
Coal or coke	2	0.0	2	0.0	–	–
Wood	107	0.8	65	1.1	42	0.6
Solar energy	3	0.0	3	0.0	–	–
Other	18	0.1	4	0.1	14	0.2
Selected equipment						
Dishwasher	4,256	32.9	2,422	40.3	1,834	26.5
Washing machine	8,182	63.2	5,388	89.6	2,794	40.4
Clothes dryer	6,895	53.3	4,785	79.6	2,109	30.5
Disposal in kitchen sink	3,910	30.2	1,748	29.1	2,163	31.2
Central air conditioning	6,065	46.9	3,300	54.9	2,764	39.9
Porch, deck, balcony, or patio	9,231	71.4	5,072	84.4	4,158	60.1
Telephone	12,084	93.4	5,756	95.7	6,328	91.4
Usable fireplace	2,335	18.1	1,772	29.5	563	8.1
Garage or carport	4,612	35.7	3,254	54.1	1,357	19.6
No cars, trucks, or vans	2,923	22.6	554	9.2	2,369	34.2
Overall opinion of housing unit						
1 (worst)	192	1.5	39	0.6	153	2.2
2	98	0.8	19	0.3	79	1.1
3	157	1.2	25	0.4	133	1.9
4	230	1.8	38	0.6	192	2.8
5	1,077	8.3	270	4.5	807	11.7
6	895	6.9	281	4.7	614	8.9
7	1,797	13.9	681	11.3	1,115	16.1
8	3,202	24.8	1,619	26.9	1,583	22.9
9	1,470	11.4	792	13.2	679	9.8
10 (best)	3,178	24.6	1,942	32.3	1,236	17.9

Note: Numbers may not add to total because not reported is not shown and more than one category may apply; (–) means not applicable or sample is too small to make a reliable estimate.
Source: Bureau of the Census, American Housing Survey for the United States: 1999, *Current Housing Reports, H150/99, 2000; calculations by New Strategist*

Neighborhood Characteristics of Housing Units Occupied by Blacks, 1999

(number and percent distribution of housing units occupied by blacks, by selected neighborhood characteristics and homeownership status, 1999; numbers in thousands)

	total number	total percent distribution	owner-occupied number	owner-occupied percent distribution	renter-occupied number	renter-occupied percent distribution
Housing units occupied by blacks	**12,936**	**100.0%**	**6,013**	**100.0%**	**6,923**	**100.0%**
Overall opinion of neighborhood						
1 (worst)	284	2.2	68	1.1	216	3.1
2	136	1.1	24	0.4	112	1.6
3	253	2.0	60	1.0	193	2.8
4	350	2.7	93	1.5	257	3.7
5	1,264	9.8	426	7.1	838	12.1
6	923	7.1	326	5.4	597	8.6
7	1,832	14.2	852	14.2	980	14.2
8	2,990	23.1	1,474	24.5	1,516	21.9
9	1,561	12.1	890	14.8	670	9.7
10 (best)	2,651	20.5	1,459	24.3	1,192	17.2
Neighborhood problems						
Street noise or traffic present	4,480	34.6	1,722	28.6	2,759	39.9
Condition not bothersome	2,625	20.3	1,033	17.2	1,592	23.0
Condition bothersome	1,842	14.2	686	11.4	1,156	16.7
So bothered they want to move	908	7.0	248	4.1	660	9.5
Neighborhood crime present	3,098	23.9	1,145	19.0	1,953	28.2
Condition not bothersome	1,282	9.9	443	7.4	839	12.1
Condition bothersome	1,804	13.9	697	11.6	1,107	16.0
So bothered they want to move	973	7.5	267	4.4	706	10.2
Odors present	1,108	8.6	390	6.5	718	10.4
Condition not bothersome	373	2.9	148	2.5	225	3.3
Condition bothersome	735	5.7	242	4.0	492	7.1
So bothered they want to move	383	3.0	86	1.4	297	4.3
No other problems	10,497	81.1	4,892	81.4	5,605	81.0
With other problems	2,190	16.9	1,019	16.9	1,171	16.9
Noise	353	2.7	138	2.3	215	3.1
Litter or housing deterioration	396	3.1	195	3.2	201	2.9
Poor city or county services	208	1.6	106	1.8	102	1.5
Undesirable commercial, institutional, industrial	85	0.7	39	0.6	45	0.7
People	615	4.8	230	3.8	385	5.6
Other	1,126	8.7	516	8.6	611	8.8

(continued)

(continued from previous page)

	total		owner-occupied		renter-occupied	
	number	percent distribution	number	percent distribution	number	percent distribution
Neighborhood conditions						
With public transportation	9,057	70.0%	3,587	59.7%	5,470	79.0%
Satisfactory public elementary school*	3,580	73.5	1,601	74.7	1,980	72.6
Satisfactory neighborhood shopping	10,242	79.2	4,514	75.1	5,729	82.8
Satisfactory police protection	10,938	84.6	5,147	85.6	5,790	83.6
Description of area within 300 feet						
Single-family detached homes	9,544	73.8	5,087	84.6	4,457	64.4
Single-family attached homes	2,366	18.3	815	13.6	1,551	22.4
Apartment buildings	6,365	49.2	1,151	19.1	5,213	75.3
Mobile homes	1,249	9.7	867	14.4	382	5.5
Commercial, institutional	4,899	37.9	1,447	24.1	3,452	49.9
Industrial	770	6.0	250	4.2	520	7.5
Body of water	1,158	9.0	532	8.8	625	9.0
Open space, park, woods, farm, or ranch	3,880	30.0	1,849	30.8	2,031	29.3
Four-or-more lane highway, railroad, airport	2,345	18.1	758	12.6	1,587	22.9

* Percentage based only on households with children aged 0 to 13.
Note: Numbers may not add to total because more than one problem could be cited and not reported is not shown;
Source: Bureau of the Census, American Housing Survey for the United States: 1999, *Current Housing Reports, H150/99, 2000; calculations by New Strategist*

Housing Value and Purchase Price for Black Homeowners, 1999

(number and percent distribution of black homeowners, by value of home, purchase price, and major source of down payment, 1999; numbers in thousands)

	number	percent distribution
Total black homeowners	6,013	100.0%
Value of home		
Under $50,000	1,468	24.4
$50,000 to $79,999	1,526	25.4
$80,000 to $99,999	943	15.7
$100,000 to $149,999	1,080	18.0
$150,000 to $199,999	514	8.5
$200,000 to $299,999	327	5.4
$300,000 or more	157	2.6
Median value	$80,302	–
Purchase price*		
Home purchased or built	5,570	92.6
Under $50,000	2,657	44.2
$50,000 to $79,999	1,037	17.2
$80,000 to $99,999	425	7.1
$100,000 to $149,999	433	7.2
$150,000 to $199,999	193	3.2
$200,000 to $299,999	117	1.9
$300,000 or more	33	0.5
Received as inheritance or gift	673	11.2
Median purchase price	$44,447	–
Major source of down payment		
Home purchased or built	5,570	92.6
Sale of previous home	696	11.6
Savings or cash on hand	3,536	58.8
Sale of other investment	43	0.7
Borrowing, other than mortgage on this property	224	3.7
Inheritance or gift	91	1.5
Land where built used for financing	57	0.9
Other	217	3.6
No down payment	523	8.7

Note: Numbers may not add to total because not reported is not shown; (–) means not applicable.
Source: Bureau of the Census, American Housing Survey for the United States: 1999, *Current Housing Reports, H150/99, 2000; calculations by New Strategist*

Geographical Mobility of Blacks by Age, 1999–2000

(total number of blacks aged 1 or older, and number and percent who moved between March 1999 and March 2000, by age of person and type of move; numbers in thousands)

	total	same house (non-movers)	total movers in U.S.	same county	different county, same state	different state, same division	different division, same region	different region	moved from abroad
Blacks aged 1 or older	**34,948**	**28,226**	**6,722**	**4,078**	**1,208**	**807**	**111**	**346**	**172**
Aged 1–4	2,457	1,779	678	454	118	59	9	24	14
Aged 5–9	3,308	2,512	796	530	111	100	6	37	12
Aged 10–14	3,328	2,726	602	323	153	86	6	18	16
Aged 15–17	1,839	1,556	283	179	35	39	9	19	1
Aged 18–19	1,218	923	295	184	47	45	–	9	10
Aged 20–24	2,762	1,912	850	523	160	71	14	47	35
Aged 25–29	2,521	1,731	790	459	153	96	15	48	19
Aged 30–34	2,642	1,974	668	370	160	72	11	31	25
Aged 35–39	2,901	2,390	511	320	79	64	7	31	10
Aged 40–44	2,798	2,283	515	306	87	82	6	27	8
Aged 45–49	2,336	2,051	285	170	59	31	10	13	–
Aged 50–54	1,767	1,605	162	102	17	24	7	10	3
Aged 55–59	1,288	1,200	88	51	15	11	–	9	2
Aged 60–61	426	391	35	10	9	11	–	3	2
Aged 62–64	601	570	31	18	–	8	2	–	3
Aged 65–69	869	827	42	29	1	2	4	4	2
Aged 70–74	755	714	41	19	2	3	–	8	9
Aged 75–79	534	513	21	10	–	4	4	4	–
Aged 80–84	330	314	16	13	–	–	–	3	–
Aged 85+	267	254	13	8	2	–	–	–	2

(continued)

(continued from previous page)

	total	same house (non-movers)	total movers in U.S.	same county	different county, same state	different state, same division	different division, same region	different region	moved from abroad
Blacks aged 1 or older	**100.0%**	**80.8%**	**19.2%**	**11.7%**	**3.5%**	**2.3%**	**0.3%**	**1.0%**	**0.5%**
Aged 1–4	100.0	72.4	27.6	18.5	4.8	2.4	0.4	1.0	0.6
Aged 5–9	100.0	75.9	24.1	16.0	3.4	3.0	0.2	1.1	0.4
Aged 10–14	100.0	81.9	18.1	9.7	4.6	2.6	0.2	0.5	0.5
Aged 15–17	100.0	84.6	15.4	9.7	1.9	2.1	0.5	1.0	0.1
Aged 18–19	100.0	75.8	24.2	15.1	3.9	3.7	–	0.7	0.8
Aged 20–24	100.0	69.2	30.8	18.9	5.8	2.6	0.5	1.7	1.3
Aged 25–29	100.0	68.7	31.3	18.2	6.1	3.8	0.6	1.9	0.8
Aged 30–34	100.0	74.7	25.3	14.0	6.1	2.7	0.4	1.2	0.9
Aged 35–39	100.0	82.4	17.6	11.0	2.7	2.2	0.2	1.1	0.3
Aged 40–44	100.0	81.6	18.4	10.9	3.1	2.9	0.2	1.0	0.3
Aged 45–49	100.0	87.8	12.2	7.3	2.5	1.3	0.4	0.6	–
Aged 50–54	100.0	90.8	9.2	5.8	1.0	1.4	0.4	0.6	0.2
Aged 55–59	100.0	93.2	6.8	4.0	1.2	0.9	–	0.7	0.2
Aged 60–61	100.0	91.8	8.2	2.3	2.1	2.6	–	0.7	0.5
Aged 62–64	100.0	94.8	5.2	3.0	–	1.3	0.3	–	0.5
Aged 65–69	100.0	95.2	4.8	3.3	0.1	0.2	0.5	0.5	0.2
Aged 70–74	100.0	94.6	5.4	2.5	0.3	0.4	—	1.1	1.2
Aged 75–79	100.0	96.1	3.9	1.9	–	0.7	0.7	0.7	–
Aged 80–84	100.0	95.2	4.8	3.9	–	–	–	0.9	–
Aged 85+	100.0	95.1	4.9	3.0	0.7	–	–	–	0.7

Note: (–) means sample is too small to make a reliable estimate.
Source: Bureau of the Census, Geographical Mobility: March 1999 to March 2000, *Current Population Reports, P20-538, 2001; Internet site <www.census.gov/population/www/socdemo/migrate/p20-538.html>; calculations by New Strategist*

Reasons for Moving among Black Households by Homeownership Status, 1999

(number and percent distribution of black households moving in the past 12 months by main reason for move and for choosing new neighborhood and house, and by comparison with previous home and neighborhood, by homeownership status, 1999; numbers in thousands)

	total		owner-occupied		renter-occupied	
	number	percent distribution	number	percent distribution	number	percent distribution
Total black movers	**2,700**	**100.0%**	**471**	**100.0%**	**2,230**	**100.0%**
Main reason for leaving previous housing unit						
Private displacement	43	1.6	–	–	43	1.9
Government displacement	19	0.7	–	–	19	1.9
Disaster loss (fire, flood, etc.)	36	1.3	6	1.3	30	0.9
New job or job transfer	181	6.7	25	5.3	157	1.3
To be closer to work/school/other	187	6.9	12	2.5	175	7.0
Other financial/employment	106	3.9	12	2.5	94	7.8
To establish own household	443	16.4	75	15.9	368	16.5
Needed larger house or apartment	310	11.5	73	15.5	237	10.6
Married, widowed, divorced, separated	100	3.7	18	3.8	82	3.7
Other family/personal	193	7.1	43	9.1	149	6.7
Wanted better home	258	9.6	40	8.5	218	9.8
Change from owner to renter/ renter to owner	90	3.3	69	14.6	21	0.9
Wanted lower rent or maintenance	125	4.6	9	–	116	5.2
Other housing related reasons	132	4.9	9	1.9	123	5.5
Other	273	10.1	36	7.6	237	10.6
All reported reasons equal	57	2.1	8	1.7	48	2.2
Main reason for choosing present neighborhood						
Convenient to job	456	16.9	46	9.8	410	18.4
Convenient to friends or relatives	362	13.4	60	12.7	303	13.6
Convenient to leisure activities	23	0.9	3	0.6	19	0.9
Convenient to public transportation	60	2.2	3	0.6	57	2.6
Good schools	148	5.5	14	3.0	134	6.0
Other public services	36	1.3	1	0.2	35	1.6
Looks/design of neighborhood	358	13.3	98	20.8	260	11.7
House most important consideration	389	14.4	98	20.8	291	13.0
Other	431	16.0	55	11.7	376	16.9
All reported reasons equal	80	3.0	23	4.9	57	2.6

(continued)

(continued from previous page)

	total		owner-occupied		renter-occupied	
	number	percent distribution	number	percent distribution	number	percent distribution
Neighborhood search						
Looked at just this neighborhood	1,182	43.8%	192	40.8%	990	44.4%
Looked at other neighborhood(s)	1,389	51.4	240	51.0	1,150	51.6
Main reason for choosing present home						
Financial reasons	793	29.4	107	22.7	685	30.7
Room layout/design	393	14.6	87	18.5	305	13.7
Kitchen	3	0.1	–	–	3	0.1
Size	368	13.6	79	16.8	289	13.0
Exterior appearance	96	3.6	15	3.2	81	3.6
Yard/trees/view	57	2.1	21	4.5	36	1.6
Quality of construction	72	2.7	39	8.3	33	1.5
Only one available	251	9.3	5	1.1	246	11.0
Other	258	9.6	26	5.5	232	10.4
All reported reasons equal	117	4.3	30	6.4	87	3.9
Comparison to previous home						
Better home	1,394	51.6	332	70.5	1,061	47.6
Worse home	426	15.8	31	6.6	396	17.8
About the same	746	27.6	71	15.1	674	30.2
Comparison to previous neighborhood						
Better neighborhood	1,079	40.0	249	52.9	831	37.3
Worse neighborhood	393	14.6	31	6.6	362	16.2
About the same	976	36.1	134	28.5	842	37.8
Same neighborhood	111	4.1	15	3.2	96	4.3

Note: Numbers may not add to total because more than one category may apply and unreported reasons are not shown; (–) means sample is too small to make a reliable estimate.
Source: Bureau of the Census, American Housing Survey for the United States: 1999, *Current Housing Reports, H150/99, 2000; calculations by New Strategist*

Blacks: Income

Black Incomes Are Growing as Blacks Make Gains in Education and Jobs

The median income of black households rose 27 percent between 1990 and 2000, to $30,436, after adjusting for inflation. Black household income grew much faster than Asian, Hispanic, and non-Hispanic white household income during those years.

Despite these gains, median household income for blacks stood at just 72 percent of the median for all households in 2000. Incomes of blacks are lower because just 31 percent of all black households are married couples—typically the most affluent household type. Black couples had a median income of $50,749 in 2000, while female-headed families had a median income of just $21,698.

For black men and women, incomes peak in the 45-to-54 age group. Black men who work full-time had a median income of $30,886 in 2000, while their female counterparts had a median income of $25,736. The earnings of blacks rise steadily with education. Black men with at least a bachelor's degree who work full-time earned a median of $47,162 in 2000, while similarly educated black women earned $40,485.

Black families are more likely to be poor than the average American family, but the percentage of black families in poverty fell from 31 percent in the early 1990s to 19 percent in 2000.

■ Black household income will remain below average as long as female-headed families account for such a large share of black households.

Black household income grew the fastest

(percent change in median household income by race and Hispanic origin of householder, 1990 to 2000; in 2000 dollars)

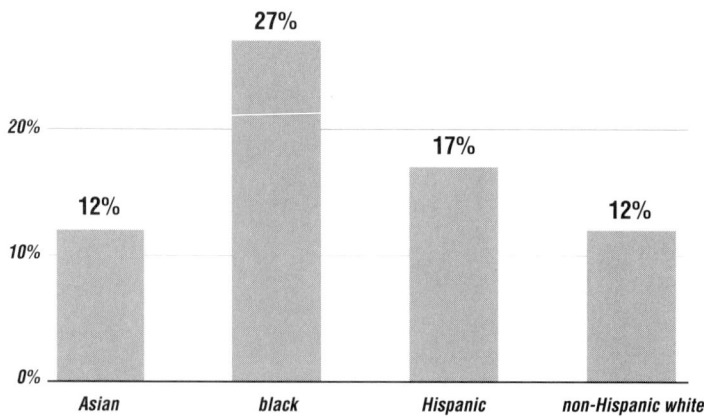

Median Income of Black Households, 1990 to 2000

(median income of black households, and index of black to total household median income, 1990 to 2000; percent change in incomes and indexes, 1990–2000; in 2000 dollars)

	median income	index black/total
2000	$30,436	72
1999	28,848	68
1998	26,751	65
1997	26,803	68
1996	25,669	66
1995	25,144	66
1994	24,202	65
1993	22,975	63
1992	22,630	61
1991	23,294	62
1990	23,979	62
Percent change		
1990–2000	26.9%	15.8%

Note: Indexes are calculated by dividing the median income of black households by the median of total households and multiplying by 100.
Source: Bureau of the Census, Current Population Survey, Internet site <www.census.gov/hhes/income/histinc/h05.html>; calculations by New Strategist

High-Income Black Households, 2000

(number, percent distribution, and average income of black households with incomes of $100,000 or more, 2000; households in thousands as of 2001)

	total	percent	average income
Total black households	**13,355**	**100.0%**	**$40,068**
$100,000 to $149,999	623	4.7	117,058
$150,000 to $199,999	116	0.9	170,105
$200,000 to $249,999	34	0.3	220,791
$250,000 or more	43	0.3	555,712

Source: Bureau of the Census, Current Population Survey, Internet site <http://ferret.bls.census.gov/macro/032001/hhinc/new07_000 .htm>; calculations by New Strategist

Income Distribution of Black Households by Age of Householder, 2000

(number and percent distribution of black households by income and age of householder, 2000; households in thousands as of 2001)

	total	< 25	25–34	35–44	45–54	55–64	65+
Black households	**13,355**	**1,087**	**2,796**	**3,273**	**2,707**	**1,553**	**1,939**
Under $10,000	2,209	283	368	342	341	327	549
$10,000 to $19,999	2,428	243	480	455	413	275	562
$20,000 to $29,999	1,954	220	483	467	318	196	270
$30,000 to $39,999	1,701	117	422	501	327	174	162
$40,000 to $49,999	1,349	80	311	392	296	152	119
$50,000 to $59,999	1,021	62	212	323	225	118	82
$60,000 to $69,999	746	42	199	214	170	64	56
$70,000 to $79,999	530	14	91	160	149	72	44
$80,000 to $89,999	342	10	66	104	91	47	23
$90,000 to $99,999	257	2	48	62	97	21	25
$100,000 or more	815	12	113	253	281	108	48
Median income	$30,436	$20,486	$31,347	$37,546	$38,450	$28,446	$16,481
Black households	**100.0%**	**100.0%**	**100.0%**	**100.0%**	**100.0%**	**100.0%**	**100.0%**
Under $10,000	16.5	26.0	13.2	10.4	12.6	21.1	28.3
$10,000 to $19,999	18.2	22.4	17.2	13.9	15.3	17.7	29.0
$20,000 to $29,999	14.6	20.2	17.3	14.3	11.7	12.6	13.9
$30,000 to $39,999	12.7	10.8	15.1	15.3	12.1	11.2	8.4
$40,000 to $49,999	10.1	7.4	11.1	12.0	10.9	9.8	6.1
$50,000 to $59,999	7.6	5.7	7.6	9.9	8.3	7.6	4.2
$60,000 to $69,999	5.6	3.9	7.1	6.5	6.3	4.1	2.9
$70,000 to $79,999	4.0	1.3	3.3	4.9	5.5	4.6	2.3
$80,000 to $89,999	2.6	0.9	2.4	3.2	3.4	3.0	1.2
$90,000 to $99,999	1.9	0.2	1.7	1.9	3.6	1.4	1.3
$100,000 or more	6.1	1.1	4.0	7.7	10.4	7.0	2.5

Source: Bureau of the Census, Current Population Survey, Internet site <http://ferret.bls.census.gov/macro/032001/hhinc/new02_003 .htm>; calculations by New Strategist

Income Distribution of Black Households by Household Type, 2000

(number and percent distribution of black households by income and household type, 2000; households in thousands as of 2001)

| | | family households | | | | nonfamily households | | | | |
	total	total	married couples	female hh, no spouse present	male hh, no spouse present	total	female householder total	female householder living alone	male householder total	male householder living alone
Black households	**13,355**	**8,814**	**4,290**	**3,762**	**762**	**4,541**	**2,534**	**2,209**	**2,007**	**1,603**
Under $10,000	2,209	951	142	729	79	1,258	836	806	422	378
$10,000 to $19,999	2,428	1,468	371	995	103	960	550	500	410	376
$20,000 to $29,999	1,954	1,299	478	707	115	655	362	330	293	248
$30,000 to $39,999	1,701	1,132	545	467	121	570	305	261	264	223
$40,000 to $49,999	1,349	982	555	318	109	367	180	128	186	134
$50,000 to $59,999	1,021	760	491	185	82	262	94	54	168	118
$60,000 to $69,999	746	555	386	125	44	191	83	57	107	61
$70,000 to $79,999	530	440	319	76	43	91	33	28	59	35
$80,000 to $89,999	342	293	239	35	19	46	24	12	23	5
$90,000 to $99,999	257	204	157	30	17	54	21	21	33	17
$100,000 or more	815	729	605	91	33	86	44	13	42	7
Median income	$30,436	$36,063	$50,729	$21,698	$37,015	$20,551	$16,807	$14,825	$24,811	$21,286

(continued)

(continued from previous page)

Black households	total	family households				nonfamily households					
		total	married couples	female hh, no spouse present	male hh, no spouse present	total	female householder		male householder		
							total	living alone	total	living alone	
	100.0%	100.0%	100.0%	100.0%	100.0%	100.0%	100.0%	100.0%	100.0%	100.0%	
Under $10,000	16.5	10.8	3.3	19.4	10.4	27.7	33.0	36.5	21.0	23.6	
$10,000 to $19,999	18.2	16.7	8.6	26.4	13.5	21.1	21.7	22.6	20.4	23.5	
$20,000 to $29,999	14.6	14.7	11.1	18.8	15.1	14.4	14.3	14.9	14.6	15.5	
$30,000 to $39,999	12.7	12.8	12.7	12.4	15.9	12.6	12.0	11.8	13.2	13.9	
$40,000 to $49,999	10.1	11.1	12.9	8.5	14.3	8.1	7.1	5.8	9.3	8.4	
$50,000 to $59,999	7.6	8.6	11.4	4.9	10.8	5.8	3.7	2.4	8.4	7.4	
$60,000 to $69,999	5.6	6.3	9.0	3.3	5.8	4.2	3.3	2.6	5.3	3.8	
$70,000 to $79,999	4.0	5.0	7.4	2.0	5.6	2.0	1.3	1.3	2.9	2.2	
$80,000 to $89,999	2.6	3.3	5.6	0.9	2.5	1.0	0.9	0.5	1.1	0.3	
$90,000 to $99,999	1.9	2.3	3.7	0.8	2.2	1.2	0.8	1.0	1.6	1.1	
$100,000 or more	6.1	8.3	14.1	2.4	4.3	1.9	1.7	0.6	2.1	0.4	

Source: Bureau of the Census, Current Population Survey, Internet site <http://ferret.bls.census.gov/macro/032001/hhinc/new01_003.htm>; calculations by New Strategist

Income Distribution of Black Men by Age, 2000

(number and percent distribution of black men aged 15 or older by income and age, median income of men with income, percent working full-time, and median income of full-time workers, 2000; men in thousands as of 2001)

	total	< 25	25–34	35–44	45–54	55–64	65+
Black men	**11,841**	**2,798**	**2,317**	**2,649**	**1,935**	**1,032**	**1,110**
Without income	1,717	1,148	231	148	101	56	34
With income	10,124	1,650	2,086	2,501	1,834	976	1,076
Under $10,000	2,381	984	256	361	271	178	331
$10,000 to $19,999	2,267	369	484	423	362	220	408
$20,000 to $29,999	1,883	190	494	613	264	187	136
$30,000 to $39,999	1,426	69	405	404	334	109	104
$40,000 to $49,999	758	10	197	238	189	92	33
$50,000 to $74,999	980	18	172	322	314	117	39
$75,000 to $99,999	256	11	42	89	64	42	11
$100,000 or more	173	–	38	53	33	35	14
Median income of men with income	$21,659	$7,085	$25,996	$27,031	$30,313	$23,943	$14,020
Percent working full-time	49.0%	18.4%	67.6%	69.5%	64.9%	52.1%	8.0%
Median income of men working full-time	$30,886	$18,244	$29,893	$31,604	$35,906	$35,701	$36,431
Black men	**100.0%**	**100.0%**	**100.0%**	**100.0%**	**100.0%**	**100.0%**	**100.0%**
Without income	14.5	41.0	10.0	5.6	5.2	5.4	3.1
With income	85.5	59.0	90.0	94.4	94.8	94.6	96.9
Under $10,000	20.1	35.2	11.0	13.6	14.0	17.2	29.8
$10,000 to $19,999	19.1	13.2	20.9	16.0	18.7	21.3	36.8
$20,000 to $29,999	15.9	6.8	21.3	23.1	13.6	18.1	12.3
$30,000 to $39,999	12.0	2.5	17.5	15.3	17.3	10.6	9.4
$40,000 to $49,999	6.4	0.4	8.5	9.0	9.8	8.9	3.0
$50,000 to $74,999	8.3	0.6	7.4	12.2	16.2	11.3	3.5
$75,000 to $99,999	2.2	0.4	1.8	3.4	3.3	4.1	1.0
$100,000 or more	1.5	–	1.6	2.0	1.7	3.4	1.3

Note: (–) means sample is too small to make a reliable estimate.
Source: Bureau of the Census, Current Population Survey, Internet sites <http://ferret.bls.census.gov/macro/032001/perinc/new01_008 .htm> and <http://ferret.bls.census.gov/macro/032001/perinc/new01_023.htm>; calculations by New Strategist

Income Distribution of Black Women by Age, 2000

(number and percent distribution of black women aged 15 or older by income and age, median income of women with income, percent working full-time, and median income of full-time workers, 2000; women in thousands as of 2001)

	total	< age 25	25–34	35–44	45–54	55–64	65+
Black women	**14,364**	**3,057**	**2,829**	**3,090**	**2,342**	**1,367**	**1,680**
Without income	1,840	1,046	187	200	180	160	68
With income	12,524	2,011	2,642	2,890	2,162	1,207	1,612
Under $10,000	4,152	1,180	559	596	408	458	952
$10,000 to $19,999	3,196	479	741	692	530	315	439
$20,000 to $29,999	2,332	255	675	682	460	142	119
$30,000 to $39,999	1,349	76	402	431	286	111	45
$40,000 to $49,999	642	8	128	195	202	91	19
$50,000 to $74,999	648	12	85	242	206	74	29
$75,000 to $99,999	138	–	47	45	37	5	8
$100,000 or more	63	–	7	10	34	11	2
Median income of women with income	$16,084	$7,226	$20,232	$21,901	$22,783	$14,297	$8,678
Percent working full-time	44.5%	21.6%	61.4%	64.6%	60.7%	37.6%	3.9%
Median income of women working full-time	$25,736	$18,014	$25,124	$26,760	$28,745	$26,620	$27,843
Black women	**100.0%**	**100.0%**	**100.0%**	**100.0%**	**100.0%**	**100.0%**	**100.0%**
Without income	12.8	34.2	6.6	6.5	7.7	11.7	4.0
With income	87.2	65.8	93.4	93.5	92.3	88.3	96.0
Under $10,000	28.9	38.6	19.8	19.3	17.4	33.5	56.7
$10,000 to $19,999	22.3	15.7	26.2	22.4	22.6	23.0	26.1
$20,000 to $29,999	16.2	8.3	23.9	22.1	19.6	10.4	7.1
$30,000 to $39,999	9.4	2.5	14.2	13.9	12.2	8.1	2.7
$40,000 to $49,999	4.5	0.3	4.5	6.3	8.6	6.7	1.1
$50,000 to $74,999	4.5	0.4	3.0	7.8	8.8	5.4	1.7
$75,000 to $99,999	1.0	–	1.7	1.5	1.6	0.4	0.5
$100,000 or more	0.4	–	0.2	0.3	1.5	0.8	0.1

Note: (–) means sample is too small to make a reliable estimate.
Source: Bureau of the Census, Current Population Survey, Internet sites <http://ferret.bls.census.gov/macro/032001/perinc/new01_013.htm> and <http://ferret.bls.census.gov/macro/032001/perinc/new01_028.htm>; calculations by New Strategist

Median Earnings of Blacks Working Full-Time by Sex, 1990 to 2000

(median earnings of blacks working full-time, year-round by sex; index of black to total population median earnings, and black women's earnings as a percent of black men's earnings, 1990 to 2000; percent change in earnings and indexes, 1990–2000; in 2000 dollars)

	black men		black women		black women's earnings as a percent of black men's earnings
	median earnings	index black/total	median earnings	index black/total	
2000	$30,409	81	$25,117	92	82.6%
1999	31,035	82	25,043	92	80.7
1998	28,543	77	23,898	88	83.7
1997	28,282	78	23,577	88	83.4
1996	28,864	82	23,473	91	81.3
1995	27,429	78	23,203	92	84.6
1994	27,327	77	22,916	90	83.9
1993	27,075	76	23,308	91	86.1
1992	27,024	74	23,847	92	88.2
1991	27,342	75	23,186	91	84.8
1990	27,110	76	23,163	91	85.4
Percent change					
1990–2000	12.2%	6.8%	8.4%	0.9%	–3.3%

Note: The black/total indexes are calculated by dividing the median earnings of black men and women by the median earnings of total men and women and multiplying by 100.
Source: Bureau of the Census, Current Population Survey, Internet site <www.census.gov/hhes/income/histinc/p38b.html>; calculations by New Strategist

Median Earnings of Blacks Working Full-Time by Education and Sex, 2000

(median earnings of blacks aged 25 or older working full-time, year-round by educational attainment and sex, and black women's earnings as a percent of black men's earnings, 2000)

	men	*women*	*black women's earnings as a percent of black men's earnings*
Total blacks	**$31,422**	**$25,937**	**82.5%**
Less than 9th grade	25,693	17,367	67.6
9th to 12th grade, no diploma	21,527	17,849	82.9
High school graduate	27,454	21,081	76.8
Some college, no degree	35,512	26,293	74.0
Associate's degree	31,512	27,131	86.1
Bachelor's degree or more	47,162	40,485	85.8
Bachelor's degree	45,068	38,017	84.4
Master's degree	50,630	45,076	89.0
Professional degree	62,462	67,088	107.4
Doctoral degree	73,614	54,289	73.7

Source: Bureau of the Census, Current Population Survey, Internet sites <http://ferret.bls.census.gov/macro/032001/perinc/new03_078 .htm> and <http://ferret.bls.census.gov/macro/032001/perinc/new03_148.htm>; calculations by New Strategist

Poverty Status of Black Families, 1990 to 2000

(total number of black families, and number and percent below poverty level by type of family and presence of children under age 18 at home, 1990 to 2000; percent change in numbers and rates, 1990–2000; families in thousands as of March the following year)

	total families			married couples			female hh, no spouse present		
		in poverty			in poverty			in poverty	
	total	number	percent	total	number	percent	total	number	percent
With and without children under age 18									
2000	8,814	1,685	19.1%	4,290	260	6.1%	3,762	1,301	34.6%
1999	8,664	1,898	21.9	4,144	294	7.1	3,814	1,499	39.3
1998	8,452	1,981	23.4	3,979	290	7.3	3,813	1,557	40.8
1997	8,408	1,985	23.6	3,921	312	8.0	3,926	1,563	39.8
1996	8,455	2,206	26.1	3,851	352	9.1	3,947	1,724	43.7
1995	8,055	2,127	26.4	3,713	314	8.5	3,769	1,701	45.1
1994	8,093	2,212	27.3	3,842	336	8.7	3,716	1,715	46.2
1993	7,993	2,499	31.3	3,715	458	12.3	3,828	1,906	49.9
1992	7,982	2,484	31.1	3,777	490	13.0	3,738	1,878	50.2
1991	7,716	2,343	30.4	3,631	399	11.0	3,582	1,834	51.2
1990	7,471	2,193	29.3	3,569	448	12.6	3,430	1,648	48.1
Percent change									
1990–2000	18.0%	−23.2%	−34.8%	20.2%	−42.0%	−51.6%	9.7%	−21.1%	−28.1%
With children under age 18									
2000	5,601	1,395	24.9%	2,386	150	6.3%	2,833	1,162	41.0%
1999	5,585	1,615	28.9	2,307	199	8.6	2,892	1,333	46.1
1998	5,491	1,673	30.5	2,198	189	8.6	2,940	1,397	47.5
1997	5,647	1,721	30.5	2,275	205	9.0	3,060	1,436	46.9
1996	5,695	1,941	34.1	2,174	239	11.0	3,120	1,593	51.1
1995	5,340	1,821	34.1	2,119	209	9.9	2,884	1,533	53.2
1994	5,439	1,954	35.9	2,147	245	11.4	2,951	1,591	53.9
1993	5,525	2,171	39.3	2,147	298	13.9	3,084	1,780	57.7
1992	5,448	2,132	39.1	2,229	343	15.4	2,971	1,706	57.4
1991	5,143	2,016	39.2	2,129	263	12.4	2,771	1,676	60.5
1990	5,069	1,887	37.2	2,104	301	14.3	2,698	1,513	56.1
Percent change									
1990–2000	10.5%	−26.1%	−33.1%	13.4%	−50.2%	−55.9%	5.0%	−23.2%	−26.9%

Source: Bureau of the Census, Current Population Survey, Internet sites <www.census.gov/hhes/poverty/histpov/hstpov4.html> and <http://ferret.bls.census.gov/macro/032001/pov/new16a_000.htm>; calculations by New Strategist

Poverty Status of Blacks by Sex and Age, 2000

(total number of blacks, and number and percent below poverty level by sex and age, 2000; people in thousands as of 2001)

		in poverty	
	total	*number*	*percent*
Total blacks	**35,752**	**7,862**	**22.0%**
Under age 18	11,407	3,487	30.6
Aged 18 to 24	3,995	941	23.6
Aged 25 to 34	5,146	882	17.1
Aged 35 to 44	5,739	896	15.6
Aged 45 to 54	4,277	582	13.6
Aged 55 to 59	1,339	253	18.9
Aged 60 to 64	1,060	197	18.6
Aged 65 or older	2,789	623	22.4
Aged 65 to 74	1,630	317	19.4
Aged 75 or older	1,159	306	26.4
Black females	**19,072**	**4,595**	**24.1**
Under age 18	5,637	1,728	30.7
Aged 18 to 24	2,127	595	28.0
Aged 25 to 34	2,829	609	21.5
Aged 35 to 44	3,090	566	18.3
Aged 45 to 54	2,342	348	14.9
Aged 55 to 59	749	163	21.7
Aged 60 to 64	618	153	24.7
Aged 65 or older	1,680	434	25.8
Aged 65 to 74	978	230	23.5
Aged 75 or older	701	204	29.1
Black males	**16,680**	**3,267**	**19.6**
Under age 18	5,770	1,758	30.5
Aged 18 to 24	1,868	346	18.5
Aged 25 to 34	2,317	272	11.8
Aged 35 to 44	2,649	330	12.5
Aged 45 to 54	1,935	234	12.1
Aged 55 to 59	590	90	15.3
Aged 60 to 64	442	45	10.1
Aged 65 or older	1,110	190	17.1
Aged 65 to 74	652	87	13.3
Aged 75 or older	458	103	22.4

Source: Bureau of the Census, Current Population Survey, Internet site <http://ferret.bls.census.gov/macro/032001/pov/new01_001.htm>; calculations by New Strategist

Twenty-Two Percent of Black Workers Are Managers, Administrators, or Professionals

Blacks working as managers or professionals account for 8 percent of Americans employed in those occupations. The largest share of blacks (29 percent) work in technical, sales, or administrative support jobs. Blacks account for 11 percent of all workers, but for 20 percent of licensed practical nurses, 23 percent of social workers, and 32 percent of postal clerks.

Overall, 69 percent of black men were in the labor force in 2000, below the 75 percent level for all men. Sixty percent of black women were in the labor force, a slightly higher rate than that for all women. Among black couples, fully 60 percent have both husband and wife in the labor force. Nevertheless, only 37 percent of black households have two or more earners, well below the overall rate of 45 percent because married couples head so few black households.

Black workers spent a median of 23 minutes getting to work in 2000, traveling a median distance of 10 miles. Seventy percent of black workers get to work by car, driving alone.

Between 2000 and 2010, the number of black workers will grow 21 percent. The black share of the labor force will rise from 12 to 13 percent during the decade.

■ Black incomes are rising as younger, better-educated blacks enter high-paying white-collar occupations.

Blacks are more likely than Hispanics to be managers or professionals

(percent of employed blacks and Hispanics aged 16 or older in managerial or professional specialty occupations, 2000)

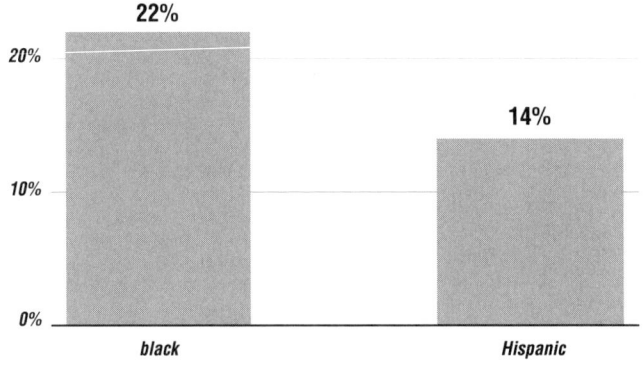

Labor Force Participation Rate of Blacks by Age and Sex, 2000

(percent of blacks aged 16 or older in the civilian labor force, by age and sex, 2000)

	men	*women*
Total blacks	**69.0%**	**63.2%**
Aged 16 to 19	39.0	39.4
Aged 20 to 24	73.4	70.5
Aged 25 to 29	85.0	81.4
Aged 30 to 34	90.3	81.0
Aged 35 to 39	86.9	80.3
Aged 40 to 44	83.6	79.3
Aged 45 to 49	80.0	77.6
Aged 50 to 54	77.8	71.4
Aged 55 to 59	67.3	59.7
Aged 60 to 64	44.2	34.6
Aged 65 or older	14.2	9.9
Aged 65 to 69	21.4	19.1
Aged 70 to 74	14.2	7.6
Aged 75 or older	6.8	4.2

Note: The civilian labor force equals the number of employed plus the number of unemployed.
Source: Bureau of Labor Statistics, Employment and Earnings, *January 2001*

Employment Status of Blacks by Sex and Age, 2000

(employment status of the civilian noninstitutionalized black population aged 16 or older, by sex and age, 2000; numbers in thousands)

| | civilian labor force | | | | | not in labor force | |
	total	percent of population	employed	unemployed	percent unemployed	total	percent of population
Total blacks	**16,603**	**65.8%**	**15,334**	**1,269**	**7.6%**	**8,615**	**34.2%**
Aged 16 to 19	967	39.2	729	239	24.7	1,500	60.8
Aged 20 to 24	1,932	71.8	1,642	290	15.0	758	28.2
Aged 25 to 34	4,328	84.1	4,036	292	6.8	816	15.9
Aged 35 to 44	4,665	82.3	4,404	261	5.6	1,004	17.7
Aged 45 to 54	3,161	76.8	3,031	130	4.1	957	23.2
Aged 55 to 64	1,227	52.2	1,190	37	3.0	1,124	47.8
Aged 65 or older	322	11.6	302	20	6.1	2,456	88.4
Black men	**7,816**	**69.0**	**7,180**	**636**	**8.1**	**3,504**	**31.0**
Aged 16 to 19	473	39.0	348	125	26.4	740	61.0
Aged 20 to 24	906	73.4	755	151	16.7	329	26.6
Aged 25 to 34	2,019	87.7	1,882	136	6.8	282	12.3
Aged 35 to 44	2,214	85.3	2,087	127	5.7	383	14.7
Aged 45 to 54	1,467	79.1	1,396	71	4.8	389	21.0
Aged 55 to 64	580	57.1	564	16	2.7	435	42.9
Aged 65 or older	157	14.2	147	10	2.5	947	85.8
Black women	**8,787**	**63.2**	**8,154**	**633**	**7.2**	**5,111**	**36.8**
Aged 16 to 19	494	39.4	380	114	23.0	761	60.6
Aged 20 to 24	1,026	70.5	887	139	13.5	430	29.5
Aged 25 to 34	2,310	81.2	2,154	156	6.8	535	18.8
Aged 35 to 44	2,451	79.8	2,317	134	5.5	621	20.2
Aged 45 to 54	1,694	74.9	1,635	59	3.5	568	25.1
Aged 55 to 64	647	48.4	626	21	3.3	689	51.6
Aged 65 or older	165	9.9	155	10	6.0	1,508	90.1

Note: The civilian labor force equals the number of employed plus the number of unemployed. The civilian population equals the number in the labor force plus the number not in the labor force.
Source: Bureau of Labor Statistics, Employment and Earnings, *January 2001; calculations by New Strategist*

Black Workers by Occupation, 2000

(total number of employed people aged 16 or older in the civilian labor force; number and percent distribution of employed blacks, and black share of total, by occupation, 2000; numbers in thousands)

	total	black number	black percent distribution	black share of total
Total employed	**135,208**	**15,334**	**100.0%**	**11.3%**
Managerial and professional specialty	40,887	3,349	21.8	8.2
Executive, administrative, and managerial	19,774	1,512	9.9	7.6
Professional specialty	21,113	1,836	12.0	8.7
Technical, sales, and administrative support	39,442	4,497	29.3	11.4
Technicians and related support	4,385	492	3.2	11.2
Sales occupations	16,340	1,436	9.4	8.8
Administrative support, including clerical	18,717	2,570	16.8	13.7
Service occupations	18,278	3,301	21.5	18.1
Private household	792	118	0.8	14.9
Protective service	2,399	471	3.1	19.6
Service, except private household and protective	15,087	2,712	17.7	18.0
Precision production, craft, and repair	14,882	1,191	7.8	8.0
Mechanics and repairers	4,875	399	2.6	8.2
Construction trades	6,120	431	2.8	7.0
Other precision production, craft, and repair	3,887	360	2.3	9.3
Operators, fabricators, and laborers	18,319	2,830	18.5	15.4
Machine operators, assemblers, and inspectors	7,319	1,080	7.0	14.8
Transportation and material moving occupations	5,557	915	6.0	16.5
Handlers, equipment cleaners, helpers, and laborers	5,443	835	5.4	15.3
Construction laborers	1,015	113	0.7	11.1
Other handlers, equipment cleaners, helpers, and laborers	4,428	722	4.7	16.3
Farming, forestry, and fishing	3,399	166	1.1	4.9

Source: Bureau of Labor Statistics, Employment and Earnings, *January 2001; calculations by New Strategist*

Black Worker Share by Detailed Occupation, 2000

(total number of employed people aged 16 or older in the civilian labor force and black share of total employed, by occupation, 2000; numbers in thousands)

	total	percent black
Total employed	**135,208**	**11.3%**
Managerial and professional specialty	**40,887**	**8.2**
Executive, administrative, and managerial	19,774	7.6
Officials and administrators, public administration	651	13.1
Administrators, protective services	62	16.1
Financial managers	784	6.1
Personnel and labor relations managers	226	7.9
Purchasing managers	123	7.0
Managers, marketing, advertising, and public relations	755	4.2
Administrators, education and related fields	848	13.5
Managers, medicine and health	752	9.7
Postmasters and mail superintendents	55	5.4
Managers, food serving and lodging establishments	1,446	9.9
Managers, properties and real estate	552	8.2
Funeral directors	58	10.9
Management-related occupations	4,932	9.5
Accountants and auditors	1,592	8.9
Underwriters	104	7.7
Other financial officers	837	9.4
Management analysts	426	7.2
Personnel, training, and labor relations specialists	628	11.6
Buyers, wholesale and retail trade, except farm products	224	5.9
Construction inspectors	72	4.7
Inspectors and compliance officers, except construction	255	13.9
Professional specialty	21,113	8.7
Engineers, architects, and surveyors	2,326	5.3
Architects	215	1.6
Engineers	2,093	5.7
Aerospace engineers	78	5.4
Chemical engineers	85	5.1
Civil engineers	288	6.1
Electrical and electronic engineers	725	6.3
Industrial engineers	244	6.4
Mechanical engineers	342	4.7
Mathematical and computer scientists	2,074	8.1
Computer systems analysts and scientists	1,797	8.0
Operations and systems researchers and analysts	227	10.9

(continued)

(continued from previous page)

	total	percent black
Natural scientists	566	5.4%
Chemists, except biochemists	153	11.0
Agricultural and food scientists	53	6.1
Biological and life scientists	114	4.0
Medical scientists	84	4.6
Health diagnosing occupations	1,038	5.2
Physicians	719	6.3
Dentists	168	3.4
Veterinarians	55	3.4
Health assessment and treating occupations	2,966	9.0
Registered nurses	2,111	9.5
Pharmacists	208	3.3
Dietitians	97	18.4
Therapists	478	8.1
Respiratory therapists	78	10.8
Occupational therapists	55	3.5
Physical therapists	144	6.5
Speech therapists	102	4.5
Physicians' assistants	72	5.6
Teachers, except college and university	5,353	10.4
Prekindergarten and kindergarten	626	13.3
Elementary school	2,177	11.3
Secondary school	1,319	8.9
Special education	362	9.2
Counselors, educational and vocational	258	17.1
Librarians, archivists, and curators	263	6.0
Librarians	232	6.7
Social scientists and urban planners	450	7.8
Economists	139	6.3
Psychologists	265	8.1
Social, recreation, and religious workers	1,492	17.4
Social workers	828	22.7
Recreation workers	126	9.5
Clergy	369	14.1
Lawyers and judges	926	5.7
Lawyers	881	5.4
Writers, artists, entertainers, and athletes	2,439	6.9
Authors	138	7.7
Technical writers	70	2.1
Designers	738	4.0
Musicians and composers	161	13.5
Actors and directors	139	12.8

(continued)

(continued from previous page)

	total	*percent black*
Painters, sculptors, craft artists, and artist printmakers	238	6.8%
Photographers	148	5.7
Editors and reporters	288	5.0
Public relations specialists	205	10.8
Announcers	54	10.5
Athletes	90	10.9
Technical, sales, and administrative support	**39,442**	**11.4**
Technicians and related support	4,385	11.2
Health technologists and technicians	1,724	15.0
Clinical laboratory technologists and technicians	342	18.0
Dental hygienists	112	2.4
Radiologic technicians	161	10.8
Licensed practical nurses	374	20.0
Engineering and related technologists and technicians	1,002	10.0
Electrical and electronic technicians	468	11.0
Drafting occupations	219	6.2
Surveying and mapping technicians	79	6.5
Science technicians	270	8.7
Biological technicians	108	7.1
Chemical technicians	71	7.2
Technicians, except health, engineering, and science	1,389	7.9
Airplane pilots and navigators	129	1.9
Computer programmers	699	8.1
Legal assistants	387	8.4
Sales occupations	16,340	8.8
Supervisors and proprietors	4,937	6.6
Sales representatives, finance and business services	2,934	7.6
Insurance sales	577	6.5
Real estate sales	787	5.3
Securities and financial services sales	600	8.2
Advertising and related sales	165	9.2
Sales occupations, other business services	805	9.9
Sales representatives, commodities, except retail	1,581	2.8
Sales representatives, mining, manufacturing, and wholesale	1,549	2.8
Sales workers, retail and personal services	6,782	12.3
Sales workers, motor vehicles and boats	329	9.1
Sales workers, apparel	411	14.2
Sales workers, shoes	114	16.1
Sales workers, furniture and home furnishings	185	6.6
Sales workers, radio, television, hi-fi, and appliances	258	7.6
Sales workers, hardware and building supplies	328	4.0
Sales workers, parts	186	5.8

(continued)

(continued from previous page)

	total	percent black
Sales workers, other commodities	1,428	9.6%
Sales counter clerks	185	9.2
Cashiers	2,939	16.5
Street and door-to-door sales workers	311	7.7
News vendors	110	6.8
Sales-related occupations	107	9.3
Demonstrators, promoters, and models	71	8.3
Administrative support occupations, including clerical	18,717	13.7
Supervisors, administrative support	710	17.0
Supervisors, general office	404	17.4
Supervisors, financial records processing	73	8.7
Supervisors, distribution, scheduling, and adjusting clerks	217	17.4
Computer equipment operators	323	16.6
Computer operators	321	16.6
Secretaries, stenographers, and typists	3,328	9.9
Secretaries	2,623	8.5
Stenographers	154	4.7
Typists	551	17.8
Information clerks	2,071	11.3
Interviewers	212	16.1
Hotel clerks	130	15.9
Transportation ticket and reservation agents	287	11.7
Receptionists	1,017	9.7
Records processing, except financial	1,119	16.9
Order clerks	305	24.4
Personnel clerks, except payroll and timekeeping	84	18.7
Library clerks	152	10.8
File clerks	338	15.3
Records clerks	227	13.4
Financial records processing	2,269	9.2
Bookkeepers, accounting and auditing clerks	1,719	7.8
Payroll and timekeeping clerks	174	8.7
Billing clerks	198	16.3
Billing, posting, and calculating machine operators	134	16.8
Duplicating, mail and other office machine operators	55	16.8
Communications equipment operators	167	21.8
Telephone operators	156	22.9
Mail and message distributing	978	21.9
Postal clerks, except mail carriers	304	32.4
Mail carriers, postal service	340	14.7
Mail clerks, except postal service	178	22.6
Messengers	157	16.7

(continued)

(continued from previous page)

	total	percent black
Material recording, scheduling, and distributing clerks	2,052	15.3%
Dispatchers	269	15.1
Production coordinators	227	12.0
Traffic, shipping, and receiving clerks	661	16.1
Stock and inventory clerks	460	15.1
Weighers, measurers, checkers, and samplers	64	19.3
Expediters	310	13.4
Adjusters and investigators	1,818	17.5
Insurance adjusters, examiners, and investigators	451	14.6
Investigators and adjusters, except insurance	1,097	17.0
Eligibility clerks, social welfare	94	16.1
Bill and account collectors	176	28.2
Miscellaneous administrative support	3,826	14.3
General office clerks	864	12.9
Bank tellers	431	13.7
Data-entry keyers	749	18.8
Statistical clerks	104	15.8
Teachers' aides	710	12.8
Service occupations	**18,278**	**18.1**
Private household	792	14.9
Child care workers	275	11.6
Cleaners and servants	500	16.9
Protective service	2,399	19.6
Supervisors	201	13.9
Police and detectives	116	10.5
Guards	53	28.4
Firefighting and fire prevention	248	8.7
Firefighting	233	9.0
Police and detectives	1,060	18.3
Police and detectives, public service	560	13.0
Sheriffs, bailiffs, and other law enforcement officers	156	20.2
Correctional institution officers	344	25.9
Guards	889	25.7
Guards and police, except public services	745	27.5
Service occupations, except private household and protective service	15,087	18.0
Food preparation and service occupations	6,327	11.9
Supervisors, food preparation and service	434	11.8
Bartenders	365	2.0
Waiters and waitresses	1,440	4.4
Cooks	2,076	17.6
Food counter, fountain and related occupations	357	12.6
Kitchen workers, food preparation	317	13.0

(continued)

(continued from previous page)

	total	percent black
Waiters' and waitresses' assistants	670	10.5%
Miscellaneous food preparation	668	16.9
Health service occupations	2,557	31.4
Dental assistants	218	5.1
Health aides, except nursing	356	26.4
Nursing aides, orderlies, and attendants	1,983	35.2
Cleaning and building service occupations	3,127	22.2
Supervisors	166	21.9
Maids and housemen	650	27.7
Janitors and cleaners	2,233	20.9
Pest control occupations	71	15.0
Personal service occupations	3,077	14.8
Supervisors	119	17.8
Barbers	108	27.8
Hairdressers and cosmetologists	820	10.9
Attendants, amusement and recreation facilities	246	9.9
Public transportation attendants	127	12.3
Welfare service aides	99	30.3
Family child care providers	457	14.8
Early childhood teachers' assistants	480	17.4
Precision production, craft, and repair	**14,882**	**8.0**
Mechanics and repairers	4,875	8.2
Supervisors	223	5.4
Mechanics and repairers, except supervisors	4,652	8.3
Vehicle and mobile equipment mechanics and repairers	1,787	7.1
Automobile mechanics	860	7.3
Bus, truck, and stationary engine mechanics	345	6.6
Aircraft engine mechanics	126	8.3
Small engine repairers	60	8.8
Automobile body and related repairers	186	8.7
Heavy equipment mechanics	162	3.8
Industrial machinery repairers	524	9.3
Electrical and electronic equipment repairers	999	10.7
Electronic repairers, communications and industrial equipment	192	13.8
Data processing equipment repairers	342	9.8
Telephone line installers and repairers	53	3.8
Telephone installers and repairers	295	11.6
Heating, air conditioning, and refrigeration mechanics	371	6.3
Miscellaneous mechanics and repairers	949	8.2
Office machine repairers	53	6.2
Millwrights	78	9.0

(continued)

(continued from previous page)

	total	*percent black*
Construction trades	6,120	7.0%
Supervisors	967	6.3
Construction trades, except supervisors	5,153	7.2
Brickmasons and stonemasons	242	13.0
Tile setters, hard and soft	94	2.0
Carpet installers	125	7.4
Carpenters	1,467	6.0
Drywall installers	206	6.1
Electricians	860	7.7
Electrical power installers and repairers	132	8.0
Painters, construction and maintenance	624	7.4
Plumbers, pipefitters, and steamfitters	540	6.1
Concrete and terrazzo finishers	99	11.0
Insulation workers	58	12.3
Roofers	215	7.3
Structural metalworkers	79	11.8
Extractive occupations	128	3.6
Precision production occupations	3,759	9.5
Supervisors	1,129	9.0
Precision metalworking	865	6.3
Tool and die makers	121	3.8
Machinists	488	7.3
Sheet-metal workers	121	5.6
Precision woodworking occupations	127	8.3
Cabinet makers and bench carpenters	89	6.6
Precision textile, apparel, and furnishings machine workers	192	7.8
Dressmakers	77	8.6
Upholsterers	64	6.9
Precision workers, assorted materials	554	12.2
Optical goods workers	77	7.7
Electrical and electronic equipment assemblers	336	15.2
Precision food production occupations	481	13.1
Butchers and meat cutters	265	14.5
Bakers	154	12.6
Food batchmakers	62	8.1
Precision inspectors, testers, and related workers	148	11.3
Inspectors, testers, and graders	136	11.6
Plant and system operators	264	10.2
Water and sewage treatment plant operators	69	7.1
Stationary engineers	118	12.0
Operators, fabricators, and laborers	**18,319**	**15.4**
Machine operators, assemblers, and inspectors	7,319	14.7

(continued)

(continued from previous page)

	total	percent black
Machine operators and tenders, except precision	4,546	14.9%
Metalworking and plastic working machine operators	349	10.7
Punching and stamping press machine operators	94	11.8
Grinding, abrading, buffing, and polishing machine operators	98	10.2
Metal and plastic processing machine operators	150	15.1
Molding and casting machine operators	84	10.6
Woodworking machine operators	137	8.9
Sawing machine operators	78	9.0
Printing machine operators	369	7.4
Printing press operators	292	7.9
Textile, apparel, and furnishings machine operators	854	18.3
Textile sewing machine operators	425	16.3
Pressing machine operators	81	13.9
Laundering and dry cleaning machine operators	214	18.0
Machine operators, assorted materials	2,665	15.8
Packaging and filling machine operators	345	17.3
Mixing and blending machine operators	112	17.9
Separating, filtering, and clarifying machine operators	62	10.1
Painting and paint spraying machine operators	187	9.0
Furnace, kiln, and oven operators, except food	53	8.9
Slicing and cutting machine operators	149	14.6
Photographic process machine operators	103	9.8
Fabricators, assemblers, and hand working occupations	2,070	13.9
Welders and cutters	594	10.2
Assemblers	1,299	16.4
Production inspectors, testers, samplers, and weighers	703	16.3
Production inspectors, checkers, and examiners	497	14.9
Production testers	64	9.8
Graders and sorters, except agricultural	134	25.3
Transportation and material moving occupations	5,557	16.5
Motor vehicle operators	4,222	16.7
Supervisors	77	15.0
Truck drivers	3,088	14.4
Drivers, sales workers	167	11.2
Bus drivers	539	26.1
Taxicab drivers and chauffeurs	280	26.0
Parking lot attendants	60	27.8
Transportation occupations, except motor vehicles	183	13.7
Rail transportation	127	15.8
Locomotive operating occupations	63	15.6
Water transportation	56	9.1
Material moving equipment operators	1,152	16.0

(continued)

(continued from previous page)

	total	percent black
Operating engineers	253	12.8%
Crane and tower operators	70	7.6
Excavating and loading machine operators	98	4.6
Grader, dozer, and scraper operators	52	4.8
Industrial truck and tractor equipment operators	569	22.1
Handlers, equipment cleaners, helpers, and laborers	5,443	15.3
Helpers, construction and extractive occupations	120	7.8
Helpers, construction trades	111	8.4
Construction laborers	1,015	11.2
Production helpers	75	18.5
Freight, stock, and material handlers	2,015	17.7
Garbage collectors	54	44.0
Stock handlers and baggers	1,125	12.8
Machine feeders and offbearers	82	15.4
Freight, stock, and material handlers, not elsewhere classified	739	23.3
Garage and service station related occupations	184	8.0
Vehicle washers and equipment cleaners	313	17.6
Hand packers and packagers	366	15.9
Laborers, except construction	1,307	15.5
Farming, forestry, and fishing	**3,399**	**4.9**
Farm operators and managers	1,125	0.9
Farmers, except horticultural	879	0.6
Horticultural specialty farmers	69	4.5
Managers, farms, except horticultural	149	0.7
Other agricultural and related occupations	2,115	7.1
Farm occupations, except managerial	847	4.7
Farm workers	768	4.7
Related agricultural occupations	1,268	8.7
Supervisors	174	2.4
Groundskeepers and gardeners, except farm	870	10.9
Animal caretakers, except farm	148	3.7
Graders and sorters, agricultural products	68	8.6
Forestry and logging occupations	109	4.4
Timber cutting and logging occupations	66	6.3
Fishers, hunters, and trappers	51	3.6

Source: Bureau of Labor Statistics, Employment and Earnings, *January 2001*

Black Workers by Industry, 2000

(total number of employed people aged 16 or older in the civilian labor force; number and percent distribution of employed blacks, and black share of total, by industry, 2000; numbers in thousands)

	total	black number	black percent distribution	black share of total
Total employed	**135,208**	**15,334**	**100.0%**	**11.3%**
Agriculture	3,305	138	0.9	4.2
Mining	521	27	0.2	5.2
Construction	9,433	634	4.1	6.7
Manufacturing	19,940	2,059	13.4	10.3
Durable goods	12,168	1,145	7.5	9.4
Nondurable goods	7,772	914	6.0	11.8
Transportation, communications, and other public utilities	9,740	1,527	10.0	15.7
Wholesale and retail trade	27,832	2,664	17.4	9.6
Wholesale trade	5,421	411	2.7	7.6
Retail trade	22,411	2,254	14.7	10.1
Finance, insurance, and real estate	8,727	915	6.0	10.5
Services	49,695	6,370	41.5	12.8
Private households	894	141	0.9	15.8
Other service industries	48,801	6,230	40.6	12.8
Professional and related services	32,784	4,330	28.2	13.2
Public administration	6,015	1,000	6.5	16.6

Source: Bureau of Labor Statistics, Employment and Earnings, *January 2001; calculations by New Strategist*

Black Households by Number of Earners, 2000

(number and percent distribution of black households by number of earners, 2000; numbers in thousands)

	number	percent distribution
Black households	**12,849**	**100.0%**
No earners	2,492	19.4
One earner	5,593	43.5
Two or more earners	4,764	37.1
Two earners	3,770	29.3
Three earners	780	6.1
Four or more earners	214	1.7

Source: Bureau of the Census, Current Population Survey, Internet site <http://ferret.bls.census.gov/macro/032000/hhinc/new01_003 .htm>; calculations by New Strategist

Labor Force Status of Black Married Couples, 2000

(number and percent distribution of black married couples by age of householder and labor force status of husband and wife, 2000; numbers in thousands)

	total	husband and/or wife in labor force			neither husband nor wife in labor force
		husband and wife	husband only	wife only	
Total black couples	**4,144**	**2,505**	**614**	**453**	**571**
Under age 20	9	3	6	–	–
Aged 20 to 24	84	57	17	10	–
Aged 25 to 29	312	223	76	9	5
Aged 30 to 34	471	379	67	23	2
Aged 35 to 39	572	465	82	21	4
Aged 40 to 44	622	455	89	51	28
Aged 45 to 54	984	690	130	116	49
Aged 55 to 64	554	214	96	130	113
Aged 65 or older	535	21	51	93	370
Total black couples	**100.0%**	**60.4%**	**14.8%**	**10.9%**	**13.8%**
Under age 20	100.0	33.3	66.7	–	–
Aged 20 to 24	100.0	67.9	20.2	11.9	–
Aged 25 to 29	100.0	71.5	24.4	2.9	1.6
Aged 30 to 34	100.0	80.5	14.2	4.9	0.4
Aged 35 to 39	100.0	81.3	14.3	3.7	0.7
Aged 40 to 44	100.0	73.2	14.3	8.2	4.5
Aged 45 to 54	100.0	70.1	13.2	11.8	5.0
Aged 55 to 64	100.0	38.6	17.3	23.5	20.4
Aged 65 or older	100.0	3.9	9.5	17.4	69.2

Note: (–) means sample is too small to make a reliable estimate.
Source: Bureau of the Census, Household and Family Characteristics: March 2000 (Update), *detailed tables for Current Population Reports P20-537, Internet site <www.census.gov/population/socdemo/hh-fam/p20-537/2000/tabFG1.txt>; calculations by New Strategist*

Union Membership of Blacks, 2000

(number of employed black wage and salary workers aged 16 or older, number and percent represented by unions or who are union members, and median weekly earnings by union membership status; by sex, 2000; numbers in thousands)

	total	men	women
Total employed blacks	**14,544**	**6,701**	**7,843**
Represented by unions	2,744	1,388	1,356
Percent of employed	18.9%	20.7%	17.3%
Members of unions	2,489	1,282	1,208
Percent of employed	17.1%	19.1%	15.4%
Median weekly earnings, total	**$468**	**$503**	**$429**
Represented by unions	590	614	555
Members of unions	596	619	564
Non-union	436	479	408

Note: Workers represented by unions are either members of a labor union or similar employee association or workers who report no union affiliation but whose jobs are covered by a union or an employee association contract. Members of unions are union members as well as members of employee associations similar to unions.
Source: Bureau of Labor Statistics, Employment and Earnings, *January 2001*

Journey to Work for Black Workers, 1999

(number and percent distribution of black workers aged 16 or older by principal means of transportation to work, travel time from home to work, distance from home to work, and departure time to work, 1999; numbers in thousands)

	number	percent
Black workers	**13,125**	**100.0%**
Principal means of transportation to work		
Drives self	9,138	69.6
Car pool	1,424	10.8
Mass transportation	1,748	13.3
Taxicab	53	0.4
Bicycle or motorcycle	63	0.5
Walks only	443	3.4
Other means	102	0.8
Works at home	153	1.2
Travel time from home to work		
Less than 15 minutes	3,639	27.7
15 to 29 minutes	4,777	36.4
30 to 44 minutes	2,076	15.8
45 to 59 minutes	853	6.5
1 hour or more	823	6.3
Works at home	153	1.2
No fixed place of work	804	6.1
Median travel time (minutes)	23	–
Distance from home to work		
Less than 1 mile	462	3.5
1 to 4 miles	2,979	22.7
5 to 9 miles	2,785	21.2
10 to 19 miles	3,695	28.2
20 to 29 miles	1,309	10.0
30 miles or more	938	7.1
Works at home	153	1.2
No fixed place of work	804	6.1
Median distance (miles)	10	–
Departure time to work		
12:00 a.m. to 2:59 a.m.	122	0.9I
3:00 a.m. to 5:59 a.m.	1,339	10.2
6:00 a.m. to 6:59 a.m.	2,232	17.0
7:00 a.m. to 7:29 a.m.	1,711	13.0
7:30 a.m. to 7:59 a.m.	1,499	11.4
8:00 a.m. to 8:29 a.m.	1,275	9.7
8:30 a.m. to 8:59 a.m.	500	3.8
9:00 a.m. to 9:59 a.m.	611	4.7
10:00 a.m. to 3:59 p.m.	1,609	12.3
4:00 p.m. to 11:59 p.m.	1,033	7.9

Note: Numbers may not add to total because not reported is not shown; (–) means not applicable.
Source: Bureau of the Census, American Housing Survey for the United States: 1999, *Current Housing Reports, H150/99, 2000; calculations by New Strategist*

Projections of the Black Labor Force by Sex, 2000 and 2010

(number of blacks in the civilian labor force, labor force participation rate of blacks, and black share of total labor force, by sex, 2000 and 2010; percent change in number and percentage point change in rate and share, 2000–2010; numbers in thousands)

	blacks in labor force		
	2000	*2010*	*percent change 2000–2010*
Total	**16,603**	**20,041**	**20.7%**
Men	7,816	8,991	15.0
Women	8,787	11,050	25.8

	black labor force participation rate		
	2000	*2010*	*percentage point change 2000–2010*
Total	**65.8%**	**67.1%**	**1.3**
Men	69.0	68.2	–0.8
Women	63.2	66.2	3.0

	black share of total labor force		
	2000	*2010*	*percentage point change 2000–2010*
Total	**11.8%**	**12.7%**	**0.9**
Men	5.5	5.7	0.2
Women	6.2	7.0	0.8

Source: Bureau of Labor Statistics, Monthly Labor Review, *November 2001*

Black Households Are Diverse, Married Couples Only Slightly Outnumbering Female-Headed Families

Black householders are younger than average. Consequently, blacks account for a larger share of young adults than older householders. More than 15 percent of householders under age 30 are black compared with only 9 percent of householders aged 65 or older.

Female-headed single-parent families are almost as common as married couples among black households. According to the 2000 census, female-headed families accounted for 30.7 percent of black households while married couples accounted for a slightly larger 31.4 percent. Only 16 percent of black households are married couples with children under age 18. Just 38 percent of black children live with both parents, while a larger 49 percent live with their mother only.

Only 30 percent of black women are currently married, versus 52 percent of women in the nation as a whole. The proportion of black women who are married peaks at just 44 percent among women aged 55 to 59. Among all women in the age group, a much larger 67 to 68 percent are currently married.

■ Because so many black households are female-headed families, the poorest household type, the income of black households is well below average.

Black households are diverse

(percent distribution of black households by household type, 2000 census)

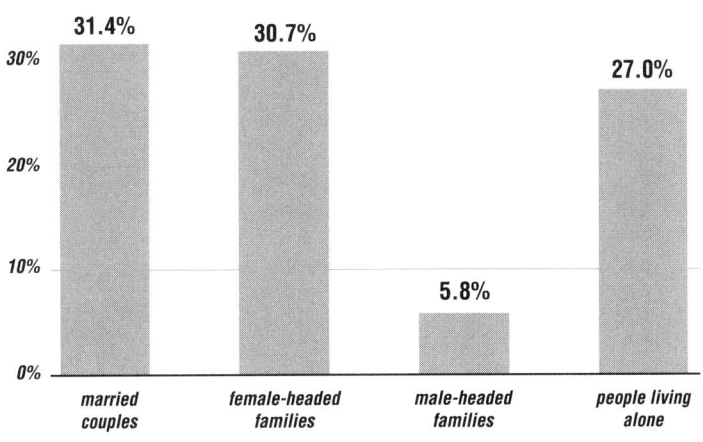

Black Households by Age of Householder, 2000

(number of total households, number and percent distribution of black households, and black share of total, by age of householder, 2000, numbers in thousands)

		black households		
	total	*number*	*percent distribution*	*share of total*
Total households	**104,705**	**12,849**	**100.0%**	**12.3%**
Under age 20	914	188	1.5	20.6
Aged 20 to 24	4,946	815	6.3	16.5
Aged 25 to 29	8,520	1,291	10.0	15.2
Aged 30 to 34	10,107	1,433	11.2	14.2
Aged 35 to 39	11,728	1,515	11.8	12.9
Aged 40 to 44	12,227	1,634	12.7	13.4
Aged 45 to 54	20,927	2,566	20.0	12.3
Aged 55 to 64	13,592	1,522	11.8	11.2
Aged 65 or older	21,744	1,886	14.7	8.7
Aged 65 to 74	11,325	1,110	8.6	9.8
Aged 75 or older	10,419	776	6.0	7.4

Source: Bureau of the Census, America's Families and Living Arrangements: March 2000, *detailed tables from Current Population Report P20-537, Internet site <www.census.gov/population/www/socdemo/hh-fam/p20-537_00.html>; calculations by New Strategist*

Black Households by Household Type, 2000

(number of total households, number and percent distribution of black households, and black share of total, by type, 2000; numbers in thousands)

	total	black households number	percent distribution	share of total
Total households	**104,705**	**12,849**	**100.0%**	**12.3%**
Family households	**72,025**	**8,664**	**67.4**	**12.0**
Married couples	55,311	4,144	32.3	7.5
With children under age 18	25,248	2,093	16.3	8.3
Without children under age 18	30,062	2,050	16.0	6.8
Female householder, no spouse present	12,687	3,814	29.7	30.1
With children under age 18	7,571	2,409	18.7	31.8
Without children under age 18	5,116	1,405	10.9	27.5
Male householder, no spouse present	4,028	706	5.5	17.5
With children under age 18	1,786	280	2.2	15.7
Without children under age 18	2,242	427	3.3	19.0
Nonfamily households	**32,680**	**4,185**	**32.6**	**12.8**
Female householder	18,039	2,309	18.0	12.8
Living alone	15,543	2,025	15.8	13.0
Male householder	14,641	1,876	14.6	12.8
Living alone	11,181	1,580	12.3	14.1

Source: Bureau of the Census, America's Families and Living Arrangements: March 2000, *detailed tables from Current Population Report P20-537, Internet site <www.census.gov/population/www/socdemo/hh-fam/p20-537_00.html>; calculations by New Strategist*

Black Households by Household Type, 2000 Census

(number of total households, number and percent distribution of black households, and black share of total, by type, 2000)

	total	black households number	percent distribution	share of total
Total households	105,480,101	12,437,890	100.0%	11.8%
Family households	71,787,347	8,444,000	67.9	11.8
Married couples	54,493,232	3,903,128	31.4	7.2
With children under age 18	24,835,505	2,005,033	16.1	8.1
Without children under age 18	29,657,727	1,898,095	15.3	6.4
Female householder, no spouse present	12,900,103	3,816,288	30.7	29.6
With children under age 18	7,561,874	2,395,221	19.3	31.7
Without children under age 18	5,338,229	1,421,067	11.4	26.6
Male householder, no spouse present	4,394,012	724,584	5.8	16.5
With children under age 18	2,190,989	358,634	2.9	16.4
Without children under age 18	2,203,023	365,950	2.9	16.6
Nonfamily households	33,692,754	3,993,890	32.1	11.9
Living alone	27,230,075	3,356,094	27.0	12.3
Living with nonrelatives	6,462,679	637,796	5.1	9.9

Note: Number of black households includes householders who identified themselves as black alone and in combination with other races.
Source: Bureau of the Census, Census 2000 PHC-T-15, Table 2, General Demographic Characteristics for the Black or African American Population; calculations by New Strategist

Black Households by Size, 2000

(number of total households, number and percent distribution of black households, and black share of total, by size, 2000; numbers in thousands)

| | total | black households | | |
		number	percent distribution	share of total
Total households	**104,705**	**12,849**	**100.0%**	**12.3%**
One person	26,724	3,605	28.1	13.5
Two people	34,666	3,436	26.7	9.9
Three people	17,152	2,525	19.7	14.7
Four people	15,309	1,739	13.5	11.4
Five people	6,981	898	7.0	12.9
Six people	2,445	418	3.3	17.1
Seven or more people	1,428	229	1.8	16.0

Source: Bureau of the Census, America's Families and Living Arrangements: March 2000, *detailed tables from Current Population Report P20-537, Internet site <www.census.gov/population/www/socdemo/hh-fam/p20-537_00.html>; calculations by New Strategist*

Black Households by Age of Householder and Household Type, 2000

(number and percent distribution of black households by age of householder and household type, 2000; numbers in thousands)

	total	family households				nonfamily households	
		total	married couples	female hh, no spouse present	male hh, no spouse present	female house-holder	male house-holder
Black households	**12,849**	**8,664**	**4,144**	**3,814**	**706**	**2,309**	**1,876**
Under age 20	188	141	9	96	36	36	10
Aged 20 to 24	815	569	84	406	78	153	93
Aged 25 to 29	1,291	871	312	494	65	188	232
Aged 30 to 34	1,433	1,089	471	545	74	135	209
Aged 35 to 39	1,515	1,122	572	443	108	170	223
Aged 40 to 44	1,634	1,204	622	475	106	192	238
Aged 45 to 54	2,566	1,759	984	658	117	416	391
Aged 55 to 64	1,522	938	554	323	61	371	212
Aged 65 or older	1,886	972	535	375	62	647	268
Aged 65 to 74	1,110	623	360	229	34	340	148
Aged 75 to 84	776	349	175	146	28	307	120
Black households	**100.0%**	**67.4%**	**32.3%**	**29.7%**	**5.5%**	**18.0%**	**14.6%**
Under age 20	100.0	75.0	4.8	51.1	19.1	19.1	5.3
Aged 20 to 24	100.0	69.8	10.3	49.8	9.6	18.8	11.4
Aged 25 to 29	100.0	67.5	24.2	38.3	5.0	14.6	18.0
Aged 30 to 34	100.0	76.0	32.9	38.0	5.2	9.4	14.6
Aged 35 to 39	100.0	74.1	37.8	29.2	7.1	11.2	14.7
Aged 40 to 44	100.0	73.7	38.1	29.1	6.5	11.8	14.6
Aged 45 to 54	100.0	68.6	38.3	25.6	4.6	16.2	15.2
Aged 55 to 64	100.0	61.6	36.4	21.2	4.0	24.4	13.9
Aged 65 or older	100.0	51.5	28.4	19.9	3.3	34.3	14.2
Aged 65 to 74	100.0	56.1	32.4	20.6	3.1	30.6	13.3
Aged 75 to 84	100.0	45.0	22.6	18.8	3.6	39.6	15.5

Source: Bureau of the Census, America's Families and Living Arrangements: March 2000, detailed tables from Current Population Report P20-537, Internet site <www.census.gov/population/www/socdemo/hh-fam/p20-537_00.html>; calculations by New Strategist

Black Married Couples by Age of Children and Age of Householder, 2000

(number and percent distribution of black married couples by presence and age of own children at home and age of householder, 2000; numbers in thousands)

	total	age of householder									
		< age 20	20–24	25–29	30–34	35–39	40–44	45–54	55–64	65–74	75+
Black married couples	**4,144**	**9**	**84**	**312**	**471**	**572**	**622**	**984**	**554**	**360**	**175**
With children of any age	**2,620**	**6**	**52**	**218**	**398**	**491**	**510**	**634**	**206**	**79**	**26**
With children under age 18	2,093	3	52	218	398	484	430	432	68	9	–
Aged 12 to 17	1,069	3	–	18	103	259	295	329	55	6	–
Aged 6 to 11	1,116	–	14	110	236	300	245	184	25	2	–
Under age 6	865	–	42	181	279	197	100	56	11	–	–
Under age 1	153	–	10	59	47	18	14	5	–	–	–
Black married couples	**100.0%**	**100.0%**	**100.0%**	**100.0%**	**100.0%**	**100.0%**	**100.0%**	**100.0%**	**100.0%**	**100.0%**	**100.0%**
With children of any age	**63.2**	**66.7**	**61.9**	**69.9**	**84.5**	**85.8**	**82.0**	**64.4**	**37.2**	**21.9**	**14.9**
With children under age 18	50.5	33.3	61.9	69.9	84.5	84.6	69.1	43.9	12.3	2.5	–
Aged 12 to 17	25.8	33.3	–	5.8	21.9	45.3	47.4	33.4	9.9	1.7	–
Aged 6 to 11	26.9	–	16.7	35.3	50.1	52.4	39.4	18.7	4.5	0.6	–
Under age 6	20.9	–	50.0	58.0	59.2	34.4	16.1	5.7	2.0	–	–
Under age 1	3.7	–	11.9	18.9	10.0	3.1	2.3	0.5	–	–	–

Note: Numbers will not add to total because households may have children in more than one age group; (–) means sample is too small to make a reliable estimate.
Source: Bureau of the Census, America's Families and Living Arrangements: March 2000, detailed tables from Current Population Report P20-537, Internet site <www.census.gov/population/www/socdemo/hh-fam/p20-537_00.html>; calculations by New Strategist

Black Female-Headed Families by Age of Children and Age of Householder, 2000

(number and percent distribution of black female-headed families by presence and age of own children at home and age of householder, 2000; numbers in thousands)

	total	age of householder									
		< age 20	20–24	25–29	30–34	35–39	40–44	45–54	55–64	65–74	75+
Black female-headed families	3,814	96	406	494	545	443	475	658	323	229	146
With children of any age	3,337	73	370	461	531	420	430	561	236	148	105
With children under age 18	2,409	71	370	461	531	391	325	221	31	2	4
Aged 12 to 17	1,002	5	3	34	247	282	230	168	30	2	2
Aged 6 to 11	1,325	7	85	354	407	231	169	65	7	–	–
Under age 6	1,062	63	343	295	200	81	63	14	–	–	2
Under age 1	195	24	92	48	21	3	6	–	–	–	–
Black female-headed families	100.0%	100.0%	100.0%	100.0%	100.0%	100.0%	100.0%	100.0%	100.0%	100.0%	100.0%
With children of any age	87.5	76.0	91.1	93.3	97.4	94.8	90.5	85.3	73.1	64.6	71.9
With children under age 18	63.2	74.0	91.1	93.3	97.4	88.3	68.4	33.6	9.6	0.9	2.7
Aged 12 to 17	26.3	5.2	0.7	6.9	45.3	63.7	48.4	25.5	9.3	0.9	1.4
Aged 6 to 11	34.7	7.3	20.9	71.7	74.7	52.1	35.6	9.9	2.2	–	–
Under age 6	27.8	65.6	84.5	59.7	36.7	18.3	13.3	2.1	–	–	1.4
Under age 1	5.1	25.0	22.7	9.7	3.9	0.7	1.3	–	–	–	–

Note: Numbers will not add to total because households may have children in more than one age group; (–) means sample is too small to make a reliable estimate. Source: Bureau of the Census, America's Families and Living Arrangements: March 2000, detailed tables from Current Population Report P20-537, Internet site <www.census.gov/population/www/socdemo/hh-fam/p20-537_00.html>; calculations by New Strategist

Black Single-Person Households by Age of Householder, 2000

(total number of black households, number and percent distribution of black single-person households, and single-person household share of total, by age of householder, 2000; numbers in thousands)

| | total | single-person households | | |
		number	percent distribution	share of total
Black households	**12,849**	**3,605**	**100.0%**	**28.1%**
Under age 20	188	25	0.7	13.3
Under age 25	815	176	4.9	21.6
Aged 25 to 29	1,291	328	9.1	25.4
Aged 30 to 34	1,433	300	8.3	20.9
Aged 35 to 39	1,515	310	8.6	20.5
Aged 40 to 44	1,634	370	10.3	22.6
Aged 45 to 54	2,566	691	19.2	26.9
Aged 55 to 64	1,522	526	14.6	34.6
Aged 65 to 74	1,110	461	12.8	41.5
Aged 75 or older	776	418	11.6	53.9

Source: Bureau of the Census, America's Families and Living Arrangements: March 2000, *detailed tables from Current Population Report P20-537, Internet site <www.census.gov/population/www/socdemo/hh-fam/p20-537_00.html>; calculations by New Strategist*

Black Children by Living Arrangement, 2000

(number and percent distribution of black children under age 18 by living arrangement, 2000; numbers in thousands)

	number	percent distribution
Total black children	**11,412**	**100.0%**
Living with both parents	4,286	37.6
Living with mother only	5,596	49.0
Living with father only	484	4.2
Living with neither parent	1,046	9.2
In group quarters	1	0.0
Living with both parents	**4,286**	**100.0**
Child of householder	4,192	97.8
Grandchild of householder	77	1.8
Other relative of householder	16	0.4
Living with mother only	**5,596**	**100.0**
Child of householder	4,690	83.8
Grandchild of householder	643	11.5
Other relative of householder	114	2.0
Nonrelative of householder	148	2.6
Living with father only	**484**	**100.0**
Child of householder	403	83.3
Grandchild of householder	46	9.5
Other relative of householder	23	4.8
Living with neither parent	**1,046**	**100.0**
Grandchild of householder	599	57.3
Other relative of householder	281	26.9
Foster child	73	7.0
Other nonrelative of householder	93	8.9
In group quarters	1	0.1

Source: Bureau of the Census, America's Families and Living Arrangements: March 2000, *detailed tables from Current Population Report P20-537, Internet site <www.census.gov/population/www/socdemo/hh-fam/p20-537_00.html>; calculations by New Strategist*

Black Men by Living Arrangement and Age, 2000

(number and percent distribution of black men aged 15 or older by living arrangement and age, 2000; numbers in thousands)

	total	15–19	20–24	25–29	30–34	35–39	40–44	45–54	55–64	65–74	75+
Black men	**11,689**	**1,533**	**1,274**	**1,102**	**1,201**	**1,337**	**1,290**	**1,872**	**979**	**661**	**434**
Householder	**6,802**	**47**	**246**	**583**	**714**	**948**	**966**	**1,504**	**878**	**547**	**367**
Married couple hh or spouse	4,219	1	76	286	432	616	622	996	605	365	219
Male family householder	706	36	78	65	74	108	106	117	61	34	28
Living alone	1,580	8	67	175	178	172	211	338	189	126	114
Living with nonrelatives	297	2	25	57	30	52	27	53	23	22	6
Not a householder	**4,887**	**1,486**	**1,028**	**519**	**487**	**389**	**324**	**368**	**101**	**114**	**67**
Child of householder	2,953	1,235	670	286	240	222	117	130	28	22	–
In family, other relative of hh	995	219	176	90	94	72	107	97	41	38	60
Not in family	939	32	182	143	153	95	100	141	32	54	7
Black men	**100.0%**	**100.0%**	**100.0%**	**100.0%**	**100.0%**	**100.0%**	**100.0%**	**100.0%**	**100.0%**	**100.0%**	**100.0%**
Householder	**58.2**	**3.1**	**19.3**	**52.9**	**59.5**	**70.9**	**74.9**	**80.3**	**89.7**	**82.8**	**84.6**
Married couple hh or spouse	36.1	0.1	6.0	26.0	36.0	46.1	48.2	53.2	61.8	55.2	50.5
Male family householder	6.0	2.3	6.1	5.9	6.2	8.1	8.2	6.3	6.2	5.1	6.5
Living alone	13.5	0.5	5.3	15.9	14.8	12.9	16.4	18.1	19.3	19.1	26.3
Living with nonrelatives	2.5	0.1	2.0	5.2	2.5	3.9	2.1	2.8	2.3	3.3	1.4
Not a householder	**41.8**	**96.9**	**80.7**	**47.1**	**40.5**	**29.1**	**25.1**	**19.7**	**10.3**	**17.2**	**15.4**
Child of householder	25.3	80.6	52.6	26.0	20.0	16.6	9.1	6.9	2.9	3.3	–
In family, other relative of hh	8.5	14.3	13.8	8.2	7.8	5.4	8.3	5.2	4.2	5.7	13.8
Not in family	8.0	2.1	14.3	13.0	12.7	7.1	7.8	7.5	3.3	8.2	1.6

Note: (–) means sample is too small to make a reliable estimate.
Source: Bureau of the Census, America's Families and Living Arrangements: March 2000, detailed tables from Current Population Report P20-537, Internet site <www.census.gov/population/www/socdemo/hh-fam/p20-537_00.html>; calculations by New Strategist

Black Women by Living Arrangement and Age, 2000

(number and percent distribution of black women aged 15 or older by living arrangement and age, 2000; numbers in thousands)

	total	15–19	20–24	25–29	30–34	35–39	40–44	45–54	55–64	65–74	75+
Black women	**14,168**	**1,523**	**1,489**	**1,418**	**1,440**	**1,565**	**1,509**	**2,231**	**1,335**	**963**	**696**
Householder	**10,146**	**145**	**690**	**1,028**	**1,180**	**1,245**	**1,263**	**1,950**	**1,216**	**869**	**559**
Married couple hh or spouse	4,023	13	130	347	500	632	595	876	521	300	107
Female family householder	3,814	96	406	494	545	443	475	658	323	229	146
Living alone	2,025	17	109	152	121	138	159	354	337	335	304
Living with nonrelatives	284	19	45	35	14	32	34	62	35	5	2
Not a householder	**4,022**	**1,378**	**799**	**390**	**260**	**320**	**246**	**281**	**119**	**94**	**137**
Child of householder	2,380	1,104	593	211	128	125	103	92	17	5	2
In family, other relative of hh	1,031	222	109	84	56	74	70	126	82	79	130
Not in family	611	52	97	95	76	121	73	63	20	10	5
Black women	**100.0%**	**100.0%**	**100.0%**	**100.0%**	**100.0%**	**100.0%**	**100.0%**	**100.0%**	**100.0%**	**100.0%**	**100.0%**
Householder	**71.6**	**9.5**	**46.3**	**72.5**	**81.9**	**79.6**	**83.7**	**87.4**	**91.1**	**90.2**	**80.3**
Married couple hh or spouse	28.4	0.9	8.7	24.5	34.7	40.4	39.4	39.3	39.0	31.2	15.4
Female family householder	26.9	6.3	27.3	34.8	37.8	28.3	31.5	29.5	24.2	23.8	21.0
Living alone	14.3	1.1	7.3	10.7	8.4	8.8	10.5	15.9	25.2	34.8	43.7
Living with nonrelatives	2.0	1.2	3.0	2.5	1.0	2.0	2.3	2.8	2.6	0.5	0.3
Not a householder	**28.4**	**90.5**	**53.7**	**27.5**	**18.1**	**20.4**	**16.3**	**12.6**	**8.9**	**9.8**	**19.7**
Child of householder	16.8	72.5	39.8	14.9	8.9	8.0	6.8	4.1	1.3	0.5	0.3
In family, other relative of hh	7.3	14.6	7.3	5.9	3.9	4.7	4.6	5.6	6.1	8.2	18.7
Not in family	4.3	3.4	6.5	6.7	5.3	7.7	4.8	2.8	1.5	1.0	0.7

Note: (–) means sample is too small to make a reliable estimate.
Source: Bureau of the Census, America's Families and Living Arrangements: March 2000, detailed tables from Current Population Report P20-537, Internet site <www.census.gov/population/www/socdemo/hh-fam/p20-537_00.html>; calculations by New Strategist

Black Men by Marital Status and Age, 2000

(number and percent distribution of black men aged 15 or older by age and marital status, 2000; numbers in thousands)

	total	never married	married	divorced	widowed
Black men	**11,687**	**5,246**	**4,501**	**1,612**	**328**
Under age 20	1,534	1,511	1	22	–
Aged 20 to 24	1,274	1,158	90	27	–
Aged 25 to 29	1,102	698	323	82	–
Aged 30 to 34	1,203	554	469	180	–
Aged 35 to 39	1,337	416	672	239	9
Aged 40 to 44	1,290	338	667	274	10
Aged 45 to 49	1,065	253	515	284	13
Aged 50 to 54	806	123	515	151	18
Aged 55 to 59	556	53	350	126	28
Aged 60 to 64	424	42	282	80	21
Aged 65 or older	1,095	99	616	148	230
Aged 65 to 69	376	49	213	82	30
Aged 70 to 74	285	17	172	42	54
Aged 75 or older	434	33	231	24	146
Black men	**100.0%**	**44.9%**	**38.5%**	**13.8%**	**2.8%**
Under age 20	100.0	98.5	0.1	1.4	–
Aged 20 to 24	100.0	90.9	7.1	2.1	–
Aged 25 to 29	100.0	63.3	29.3	7.4	–
Aged 30 to 34	100.0	46.1	39.0	15.0	–
Aged 35 to 39	100.0	31.1	50.3	17.9	0.7
Aged 40 to 44	100.0	26.2	51.7	21.2	0.8
Aged 45 to 49	100.0	23.8	48.4	26.7	1.2
Aged 50 to 54	100.0	15.3	63.9	18.7	2.2
Aged 55 to 59	100.0	9.5	62.9	22.7	5.0
Aged 60 to 64	100.0	9.9	66.5	18.9	5.0
Aged 65 or older	100.0	9.0	56.3	13.5	21.0
Aged 65 to 69	100.0	13.0	56.6	21.8	8.0
Aged 70 to 74	100.0	6.0	60.4	14.7	18.9
Aged 75 or older	100.0	7.6	53.2	5.5	33.6

Note: (–) means sample is too small to make a reliable estimate.
Source: Bureau of the Census, Marital Status and Living Arrangements: March 2000 (Update), *detailed tables for Current Population Report P20-537, 2001; Internet site <www.census.gov/population/socdemo/hh-fam/p20-537/ 2000/tabA1.txt>*

Black Women by Marital Status and Age, 2000

(number and percent distribution of black women aged 15 or older by age and marital status, 2000; numbers in thousands)

	total	never married	married	divorced	widowed
Black women	**14,167**	**6,008**	**4,320**	**2,473**	**1,367**
Under age 20	1,522	1,489	17	14	3
Aged 20 to 24	1,488	1,318	140	27	2
Aged 25 to 29	1,418	892	389	128	9
Aged 30 to 34	1,439	627	543	254	14
Aged 35 to 39	1,565	500	677	372	16
Aged 40 to 44	1,508	459	634	389	27
Aged 45 to 49	1,271	314	524	361	71
Aged 50 to 54	961	153	408	326	74
Aged 55 to 59	732	98	320	219	94
Aged 60 to 64	603	58	224	171	150
Aged 65 or older	1,659	99	445	209	906
Aged 65 to 69	493	43	171	96	184
Aged 70 to 74	469	31	148	54	236
Aged 75 or older	697	25	126	59	486
Black women	**100.0%**	**42.4%**	**30.5%**	**17.5%**	**9.6%**
Under age 20	100.0	97.8	1.1	0.9	0.2
Aged 20 to 24	100.0	88.6	9.4	1.8	0.1
Aged 25 to 29	100.0	62.9	27.4	9.0	0.6
Aged 30 to 34	100.0	43.6	37.7	17.7	1.0
Aged 35 to 39	100.0	31.9	43.3	23.8	1.0
Aged 40 to 44	100.0	30.4	42.0	25.8	1.8
Aged 45 to 49	100.0	24.7	41.2	28.4	5.6
Aged 50 to 54	100.0	15.9	42.5	33.9	7.7
Aged 55 to 59	100.0	13.4	43.7	29.9	12.8
Aged 60 to 64	100.0	9.6	37.1	28.4	24.9
Aged 65 or older	100.0	6.0	26.8	12.6	54.6
Aged 65 to 69	100.0	8.7	34.7	19.5	37.3
Aged 70 to 74	100.0	6.6	31.6	11.5	50.3
Aged 75 or older	100.0	3.6	18.1	8.5	69.7

Source: Bureau of the Census, Marital Status and Living Arrangements: March 2000 (Update), *detailed tables for Current Population Report P20-537, 2001; Internet site <www.census.gov/population/socdemo/hh-fam/p20-537/ 2000/tabA1.txt>*

Blacks: Population

Blacks Are Still the Largest Minority, but Hispanics Are Not Far Behind

The black population grew from 30 million in 1990 to 36 million in 2000, using the "black, alone or in combination" population from the 2000 census. Blacks account for 12.9 percent of the U.S. population, slightly larger than the 12.5 percent share held by Hispanics. Hispanics will soon outnumber blacks because the Hispanic population is growing faster.

More than half of blacks live in the South, where they account for 19 percent of the population. In Mississippi, 37 percent of the population is black, as is 33 percent of the population in Louisiana and 30 percent in South Carolina. No single state is home to more than 10 percent of the black population.

Among metropolitan areas, New York has the largest number of blacks, more than 3.8 million in 2000. Blacks account for 18 percent of the population of the greater New York metropolitan area. Among the 100 largest metropolitan areas, the black share of the population is highest in Jackson, Mississippi (46 percent) and Memphis, Tennessee-Arkansas-Mississippi (44 percent).

■ Unlike Hispanics or Asians, most of whom live in only a few states, blacks are an important segment of the population throughout the country. This distribution adds to their cultural influence and political power.

The black population tops 36 million

(number of people identifying themselves as black, 1990 and 2000; numbers in millions)

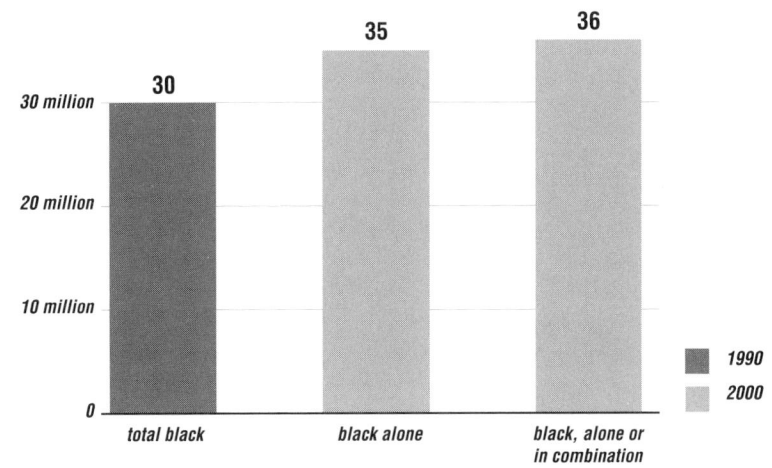

Blacks, 1990 and 2000 Censuses

(number of blacks, 1990 and 2000; percent change in number, 1990–2000)

		2000		percent change, 1990–2000	
	1990	*black alone*	*black, alone or in combination*	*black alone*	*black, alone or in combination*
Total blacks	29,986,060	34,658,190	36,419,434	15.6%	21.5%

Source: Bureau of the Census, The Black Population: 2000, *Census 2000 Brief, C2KBR/01-5, 2001; calculations by New Strategist*

Blacks by Racial Combination, 2000 Census

(number of total people, number of blacks by racial identification, and black share of total; number and percent distribution of blacks by racial combination, 2000)

	number	percent
Total people	**281,421,906**	**100.0%**
Black, alone or in combination with one or more other races	**36,419,434**	**12.9**
Black alone	34,658,190	12.3
Black in combination	1,761,244	0.6
Black, alone or in combination with one or more other races	**36,419,434**	**100.0**
Black alone	34,658,190	95.2
Black in combination	1,761,244	4.8
Black and white	784,764	2.2
Black and other race	417,249	1.1
Black and American Indian	182,494	0.5
Black, white, and American Indian	112,207	0.3
Black and Asian	106,782	0.3
Black, white, and other race	43,172	0.1
Black and all other combinations	114,576	0.3

Note: American Indians include Alaska Natives.
Source: Bureau of the Census, The Black Population: 2000, *Census 2000 Brief, C2KBR/01-5, 2001*

Blacks by Hispanic Origin, 2000 Census

(number and percent distribution of blacks by Hispanic origin and racial combination, 2000)

	black, alone or in combination		black alone		black in combination	
	number	percent distribution	number	percent distribution	number	percent distribution
Total blacks	**36,419,434**	**100.0%**	**34,658,190**	**100.0%**	**1,761,244**	**100.0%**
Hispanic	1,035,683	2.8	710,353	2.0	325,330	18.5
Mexican	245,899	0.7	160,218	0.5	85,681	4.9
Puerto Rican	308,786	0.8	222,148	0.6	86,638	4.9
Cuban	60,821	0.2	47,671	0.1	13,150	0.7
Other Hispanic	420,177	1.2	280,316	0.8	139,861	7.9
Non-Hispanic	35,383,751	97.2	33,947,837	98.0	1,435,914	81.5

Source: Bureau of the Census, Census 2000 PHC-T-15, Table 2, General Demographic Characteristics for the Black or African American Population; *calculations by New Strategist*

Blacks by Age, 2000 Census

(number of people identifying themselves as black alone or in combination, black alone, and black in combination, and percent of black alone or in combination identifying themselves as black in combination, by age, 2000)

	black, alone or in combination	black alone	black in combination number	percent of black alone or in combination
Total blacks	**36,419,434**	**34,658,190**	**1,761,244**	**4.8%**
Under age 5	3,166,859	2,804,786	362,073	11.4
Aged 5 to 9	3,490,717	3,205,512	285,205	8.2
Aged 10 to 14	3,332,324	3,121,530	210,794	6.3
Aged 15 to 19	3,093,824	2,929,553	164,271	5.3
Aged 20 to 24	2,759,272	2,628,752	130,520	4.7
Aged 25 to 29	2,658,466	2,548,968	109,498	4.1
Aged 30 to 34	2,715,440	2,618,602	96,838	3.6
Aged 35 to 39	2,917,159	2,826,361	90,798	3.1
Aged 40 to 44	2,781,722	2,700,418	81,304	2.9
Aged 45 to 49	2,339,345	2,275,191	64,154	2.7
Aged 50 to 54	1,855,083	1,805,457	49,626	2.7
Aged 55 to 59	1,340,069	1,306,641	33,428	2.5
Aged 60 to 64	1,088,474	1,063,469	25,005	2.3
Aged 65 to 69	900,785	881,786	18,999	2.1
Aged 70 to 74	746,514	731,386	15,128	2.0
Aged 75 to 79	560,952	550,024	10,928	1.9
Aged 80 to 84	353,135	346,465	6,670	1.9
Aged 85 or older	319,294	313,289	6,005	1.9
Aged 18 to 24	3,997,739	3,804,437	193,302	4.8
Aged 18 or older	24,574,177	23,772,494	801,683	3.3
Aged 65 or older	2,880,680	2,822,950	57,730	2.0

Source: U.S. Census Bureau, Census 2000 Summary File 1; calculations by New Strategist

Black Share of Total Population by Age, 2000 Census

(number of total people, number and percent distribution of those identifying themselves as black alone or in combination, and black alone or in combination share of total, by age, 2000)

		black, alone or in combination		
	total	number	percent distribution	share of total
Total people	**281,421,906**	**36,419,434**	**100.0%**	**12.9%**
Under age 5	19,175,798	3,166,859	8.7	16.5
Aged 5 to 9	20,549,505	3,490,717	9.6	17.0
Aged 10 to 14	20,528,072	3,332,324	9.1	16.2
Aged 15 to 19	20,219,890	3,093,824	8.5	15.3
Aged 20 to 24	18,964,001	2,759,272	7.6	14.6
Aged 25 to 29	19,381,336	2,658,466	7.3	13.7
Aged 30 to 34	20,510,388	2,715,440	7.5	13.2
Aged 35 to 39	22,706,664	2,917,159	8.0	12.8
Aged 40 to 44	22,441,863	2,781,722	7.6	12.4
Aged 45 to 49	20,092,404	2,339,345	6.4	11.6
Aged 50 to 54	17,585,548	1,855,083	5.1	10.5
Aged 55 to 59	13,469,237	1,340,069	3.7	9.9
Aged 60 to 64	10,805,447	1,088,474	3.0	10.1
Aged 65 to 69	9,533,545	900,785	2.5	9.4
Aged 70 to 74	8,857,441	746,514	2.0	8.4
Aged 75 to 79	7,415,813	560,952	1.5	7.6
Aged 80 to 84	4,945,367	353,135	1.0	7.1
Aged 85 or older	4,239,587	319,294	0.9	7.5
Aged 18 to 24	27,143,454	3,997,739	11.0	14.7
Aged 18 or older	209,128,094	24,574,177	67.5	11.8
Aged 65 or older	34,991,753	2,880,680	7.9	8.2

Source: U.S. Census Bureau, Census 2000 Summary File 1; calculations by New Strategist

Blacks by Age and Sex, 2000 Census

(number of blacks by age and sex, and sex ratio by age, 2000)

	total	females	males	sex ratio
Total blacks	**36,419,434**	**19,104,101**	**17,315,333**	**91**
Under age 5	3,166,859	1,559,803	1,607,056	103
Aged 5 to 9	3,490,717	1,720,081	1,770,636	103
Aged 10 to 14	3,332,324	1,642,923	1,689,401	103
Aged 15 to 19	3,093,824	1,531,337	1,562,487	102
Aged 20 to 24	2,759,272	1,417,226	1,342,046	95
Aged 25 to 29	2,658,466	1,395,554	1,262,912	90
Aged 30 to 34	2,715,440	1,430,263	1,285,177	90
Aged 35 to 39	2,917,159	1,546,322	1,370,837	89
Aged 40 to 44	2,781,722	1,476,603	1,305,119	88
Aged 45 to 49	2,339,345	1,253,183	1,086,162	87
Aged 50 to 54	1,855,083	1,001,540	853,543	85
Aged 55 to 59	1,340,069	736,586	603,483	82
Aged 60 to 64	1,088,474	608,322	480,152	79
Aged 65 to 69	900,785	518,210	382,575	74
Aged 70 to 74	746,514	448,580	297,934	66
Aged 75 to 79	560,952	349,972	210,980	60
Aged 80 to 84	353,135	234,874	118,261	50
Aged 85 or older	319,294	232,722	86,572	37
Aged 18 to 24	3,997,739	2,039,037	1,958,702	96
Aged 18 or older	24,574,177	13,271,768	11,302,409	85
Aged 65 or older	2,880,680	1,784,358	1,096,322	61

Note: Blacks include those who identified themselves as black alone and those who identified themselves as black in combination with one or more other races; the sex ratio is the number of males per 100 females.
Source: U.S. Census Bureau, Census 2000 Summary File 1; calculations by New Strategist

Blacks by Region, 1990 and 2000 Censuses

(number of blacks by region, 1990 and 2000; percent change in number identifying themselves as black alone and as black alone or in combination, 1990–2000)

		2000		percent change, 1990–2000	
	1990	*black alone*	*black, alone or in combination*	*black alone*	*black, alone or in combination*
Total blacks	**29,986,060**	**34,658,190**	**36,419,434**	**15.6%**	**21.5%**
Northeast	5,613,222	6,099,881	6,556,909	8.7	16.8
Midwest	5,715,940	6,499,733	6,838,669	13.7	19.6
South	15,828,888	18,981,692	19,528,231	19.9	23.4
West	2,828,010	3,076,884	3,495,625	8.8	23.6

Source: Bureau of the Census, The Black Population: 2000, *Census 2000 Brief, C2KBR/01-5, 2001; calculations by New Strategist*

Blacks by Region and Division, 2000 Census

(number of total people, number and percent distribution of blacks, and black share of total, by region and division, 2000)

	total	black number	black percent distribution	black share of total
Total population	**281,421,906**	**36,419,434**	**100.0%**	**12.9%**
Northeast	**53,594,378**	**6,556,909**	**18.0**	**12.2**
New England	13,922,517	821,871	2.3	5.9
Middle Atlantic	39,671,861	5,735,038	15.7	14.5
Midwest	**64,392,776**	**6,838,669**	**18.8**	**10.6**
East North Central	45,155,037	5,649,306	15.5	12.5
West North Central	19,237,739	1,189,363	3.3	6.2
South	**100,236,820**	**19,528,231**	**53.6**	**19.5**
South Atlantic	51,769,160	11,379,006	31.2	22.0
East South Central	17,022,810	3,475,933	9.5	20.4
West South Central	31,444,850	4,673,292	12.8	14.9
West	**63,197,932**	**3,495,625**	**9.6**	**5.5**
Mountain	18,172,295	611,049	1.7	3.4
Pacific	45,025,637	2,884,576	7.9	6.4

Note: Blacks include those who identified themselves as black alone and those who identified themselves as black in combination with one or more other races.
Source: Bureau of the Census, Profiles of General Demographic Characteristics, 2000 Census of Population and Housing, May 2001; calculations by New Strategist

Blacks by State, 1990 and 2000 Censuses

(number of blacks by state, 1990 and 2000; percent change in number identifying themselves as black alone and as black alone or in combination, 1990–2000)

		2000		percent change 1990–2000	
	1990	*black alone*	*black, alone or in combination*	*black alone*	*black, alone or in combination*
Total blacks	**29,986,060**	**34,658,190**	**36,419,434**	**15.6%**	**21.5%**
Alabama	1,020,705	1,155,930	1,168,998	13.2	14.5
Alaska	22,451	21,787	27,147	-3.0	20.9
Arizona	110,524	158,873	185,599	43.7	67.9
Arkansas	373,912	418,950	427,152	12.0	14.2
California	2,208,801	2,263,882	2,513,041	2.5	13.8
Colorado	133,146	165,063	190,717	24.0	43.2
Connecticut	274,269	309,843	339,078	13.0	23.6
Delaware	112,460	150,666	157,152	34.0	39.7
District of Columbia	399,604	343,312	350,455	-14.1	-12.3
Florida	1,759,534	2,335,505	2,471,730	32.7	40.5
Georgia	1,746,565	2,349,542	2,393,425	34.5	37.0
Hawaii	27,195	22,003	33,343	-19.1	22.6
Idaho	3,370	5,456	8,127	61.9	141.2
Illinois	1,694,273	1,876,875	1,937,671	10.8	14.4
Indiana	432,092	510,034	538,015	18.0	24.5
Iowa	48,090	61,853	72,512	28.6	50.8
Kansas	143,076	154,198	170,610	7.8	19.2
Kentucky	262,907	295,994	311,878	12.6	18.6
Louisiana	1,299,281	1,451,944	1,468,317	11.7	13.0
Maine	5,138	6,760	9,553	31.6	85.9
Maryland	1,189,899	1,477,411	1,525,036	24.2	28.2
Massachusetts	300,130	343,454	398,479	14.4	32.8
Michigan	1,291,706	1,412,742	1,474,613	9.4	14.2
Minnesota	94,944	171,731	202,972	80.9	113.8
Mississippi	915,057	1,033,809	1,041,708	13.0	13.8
Missouri	548,208	629,391	655,377	14.8	19.5
Montana	2,381	2,692	4,441	13.1	86.5
Nebraska	57,404	68,541	75,833	19.4	32.1
Nevada	78,771	135,477	150,508	72.0	91.1
New Hampshire	7,198	9,035	12,218	25.5	69.7
New Jersey	1,036,825	1,141,821	1,211,750	10.1	16.9

(continued)

(continued from previous page)

	1990	2000 black alone	2000 black, alone or in combination	percent change 1990–2000 black alone	percent change 1990–2000 black, alone or in combination
New Mexico	30,210	34,343	42,412	13.7%	40.4%
New York	2,859,055	3,014,385	3,234,165	5.4	13.1
North Carolina	1,456,323	1,737,545	1,776,283	19.3	22.0
North Dakota	3,524	3,916	5,372	11.1	52.4
Ohio	1,154,826	1,301,307	1,372,501	12.7	18.8
Oklahoma	233,801	260,968	284,766	11.6	21.8
Oregon	46,178	55,662	72,647	20.5	57.3
Pennsylvania	1,089,795	1,224,612	1,289,123	12.4	18.3
Rhode Island	38,861	46,908	58,051	20.7	49.4
South Carolina	1,039,884	1,185,216	1,200,901	14.0	15.5
South Dakota	3,258	4,685	6,687	43.8	105.2
Tennessee	778,035	932,809	953,349	19.9	22.5
Texas	2,021,632	2,404,566	2,493,057	18.9	23.3
Utah	11,576	17,657	24,382	52.5	110.6
Vermont	1,951	3,063	4,492	57.0	130.2
Virginia	1,162,994	1,390,293	1,441,207	19.5	23.9
Washington	149,801	190,267	238,398	27.0	59.1
West Virginia	56,295	57,232	62,817	1.7	11.6
Wisconsin	244,539	304,460	326,506	24.5	33.5
Wyoming	3,606	3,722	4,863	3.2	34.9

Source: Bureau of the Census, The Black Population: 2000, *Census 2000 Brief, C2KBR/01-5, 2001; calculations by New Strategist*

Black Share of Total Population by State, 2000 Census

(number of total people, number and percent distribution of blacks, and black share of total, by state, 2000)

	total	blacks number	blacks percent distribution	blacks share of total
Total population	**281,421,906**	**36,419,434**	**100.0%**	**12.9%**
Alabama	4,447,100	1,168,998	3.2	26.3
Alaska	626,932	27,147	0.1	4.3
Arizona	5,130,632	185,599	0.5	3.6
Arkansas	2,673,400	427,152	1.2	16.0
California	33,871,648	2,513,041	6.9	7.4
Colorado	4,301,261	190,717	0.5	4.4
Connecticut	3,405,565	339,078	0.9	10.0
Delaware	783,600	157,152	0.4	20.1
District of Columbia	572,059	350,455	1.0	61.3
Florida	15,982,378	2,471,730	6.8	15.5
Georgia	8,186,453	2,393,425	6.6	29.2
Hawaii	1,211,537	33,343	0.1	2.8
Idaho	1,293,953	8,127	0.0	0.6
Illinois	12,419,293	1,937,671	5.3	15.6
Indiana	6,080,485	538,015	1.5	8.8
Iowa	2,926,324	72,512	0.2	2.5
Kansas	2,688,418	170,610	0.5	6.3
Kentucky	4,041,769	311,878	0.9	7.7
Louisiana	4,468,976	1,468,317	4.0	32.9
Maine	1,274,923	9,553	0.0	0.7
Maryland	5,296,486	1,525,036	4.2	28.8
Massachusetts	6,349,097	398,479	1.1	6.3
Michigan	9,938,444	1,474,613	4.0	14.8
Minnesota	4,919,479	202,972	0.6	4.1
Mississippi	2,844,658	1,041,708	2.9	36.6
Missouri	5,595,211	655,377	1.8	11.7
Montana	902,195	4,441	0.0	0.5
Nebraska	1,711,263	75,833	0.2	4.4
Nevada	1,998,257	150,508	0.4	7.5
New Hampshire	1,235,786	12,218	0.0	1.0
New Jersey	8,414,350	1,211,750	3.3	14.4

(continued)

(continued from previous page)

	total	blacks		
		number	*percent distribution*	*share of total*
New Mexico	1,819,046	42,412	0.1%	2.3%
New York	18,976,457	3,234,165	8.9	17.0
North Carolina	8,049,313	1,776,283	4.9	22.1
North Dakota	642,200	5,372	0.0	0.8
Ohio	11,353,140	1,372,501	3.8	12.1
Oklahoma	3,450,654	284,766	0.8	8.3
Oregon	3,421,399	72,647	0.2	2.1
Pennsylvania	12,281,054	1,289,123	3.5	10.5
Rhode Island	1,048,319	58,051	0.2	5.5
South Carolina	4,012,012	1,200,901	3.3	29.9
South Dakota	754,844	6,687	0.0	0.9
Tennessee	5,689,283	953,349	2.6	16.8
Texas	20,851,820	2,493,057	6.8	12.0
Utah	2,233,169	24,382	0.1	1.1
Vermont	608,827	4,492	0.0	0.7
Virginia	7,078,515	1,441,207	4.0	20.4
Washington	5,894,121	238,398	0.7	4.0
West Virginia	1,808,344	62,817	0.2	3.5
Wisconsin	5,363,675	326,506	0.9	6.1
Wyoming	493,782	4,863	0.0	1.0

Note: Blacks include those who identified themselves as black alone and those who identified themselves as black in combination with one or more other races.
Source: Bureau of the Census, Profiles of General Demographic Characteristics, *2000 Census of Population and Housing, May 2001; calculations by New Strategist*

Blacks in Combination by State, 2000 Census

(number of blacks identifying themselves as black alone or in combination, number identifying themselves as black in combination, and black in combination share of black alone or in combination, by state, 2000)

	black, alone or in combination	black in combination number	black in combination percent of black, alone or in combination
Total blacks	**36,419,434**	**1,761,244**	**4.8%**
Alabama	1,168,998	13,068	1.1
Alaska	27,147	5,360	19.7
Arizona	185,599	26,726	14.4
Arkansas	427,152	8,202	1.9
California	2,513,041	249,159	9.9
Colorado	190,717	25,654	13.5
Connecticut	339,078	29,235	8.6
Delaware	157,152	6,486	4.1
District of Columbia	350,455	7,143	2.0
Florida	2,471,730	136,225	5.5
Georgia	2,393,425	43,883	1.8
Hawaii	33,343	11,340	34.0
Idaho	8,127	2,671	32.9
Illinois	1,937,671	60,796	3.1
Indiana	538,015	27,981	5.2
Iowa	72,512	10,659	14.7
Kansas	170,610	16,412	9.6
Kentucky	311,878	15,884	5.1
Louisiana	1,468,317	16,373	1.1
Maine	9,553	2,793	29.2
Maryland	1,525,036	47,625	3.1
Massachusetts	398,479	55,025	13.8
Michigan	1,474,613	61,871	4.2
Minnesota	202,972	31,241	15.4
Mississippi	1,041,708	7,899	0.8
Missouri	655,377	25,986	4.0
Montana	4,441	1,749	39.4
Nebraska	75,833	7,292	9.6
Nevada	150,508	15,031	10.0
New Hampshire	12,218	3,183	26.1

(continued)

(continued from previous page)

| | black, alone or in combination | black in combination | |
		number	percent of black, alone or in combination
New Jersey	1,211,750	69,929	5.8%
New Mexico	42,412	8,069	19.0
New York	3,234,165	219,780	6.8
North Carolina	1,776,283	38,738	2.2
North Dakota	5,372	1,456	27.1
Ohio	1,372,501	71,194	5.2
Oklahoma	284,766	23,798	8.4
Oregon	72,647	16,985	23.4
Pennsylvania	1,289,123	64,511	5.0
Rhode Island	58,051	11,143	19.2
South Carolina	1,200,901	15,685	1.3
South Dakota	6,687	2,002	29.9
Tennessee	953,349	20,540	2.2
Texas	2,493,057	88,491	3.5
Utah	24,382	6,725	27.6
Vermont	4,492	1,429	31.8
Virginia	1,441,207	50,914	3.5
Washington	238,398	48,131	20.2
West Virginia	62,817	5,585	8.9
Wisconsin	326,506	22,046	6.8
Wyoming	4,863	1,141	23.5

Source: Bureau of the Census, The Black Population: 2000, *Census 2000 Brief, C2KBR/01-5, 2001; calculations by New Strategist*

Blacks by Metropolitan Area, 2000 Census

(number of total people, number of blacks, and black share of total in the 100 largest metropolitan areas, 2000)

	total population	black number	black share of total
1. New York–Northern New Jersey–Long Island, NY–NJ–CT–PA CMSA	21,199,865	3,890,464	18.4%
• Bergen–Passaic, NJ PMSA	1,373,167	120,649	8.8
• Bridgeport, CT PMSA	459,479	57,594	12.5
• Danbury, CT PMSA	217,980	7,558	3.5
• Dutchess County, NY PMSA	280,150	28,463	10.2
• Jersey City, NJ PMSA	608,975	89,768	14.7
• Middlesex–Somerset–Hunterdon, NJ PMSA	1,169,641	100,625	8.6
• Monmouth–Ocean, NJ PMSA	1,126,217	70,481	6.3
• Nassau–Suffolk, NY PMSA	2,753,913	252,581	9.2
• New Haven–Meriden, CT PMSA	542,149	76,206	14.1
• New York, NY PMSA	9,314,235	2,451,277	26.3
• Newark, NJ PMSA	2,032,989	473,829	23.3
• Newburgh, NY–PA PMSA	387,669	32,659	8.4
• Stamford–Norwalk, CT PMSA	353,556	34,971	9.9
• Trenton, NJ PMSA	350,761	72,561	20.7
• Waterbury, CT PMSA	228,984	21,242	9.3
2. Los Angeles–Riverside–Orange County, CA CMSA	16,373,645	1,357,494	8.3
• Los Angeles–Long Beach, CA PMSA	9,519,338	999,747	10.5
• Orange County, CA PMSA	2,846,289	59,426	2.1
• Riverside–San Bernardino, CA PMSA	3,254,821	280,081	8.6
• Ventura, CA PMSA	753,197	18,240	2.4
3. Chicago–Gary–Kenosha, IL–IN–WI CMSA	9,157,540	1,754,708	19.2
• Chicago, IL PMSA	8,272,768	1,602,248	19.4
• Gary, IN PMSA	631,362	127,180	20.1
• Kankakee, IL PMSA	103,833	16,651	16.0
• Kenosha, WI PMSA	149,577	8,629	5.8
4. Washington–Baltimore, DC–MD–VA–WV CMSA	7,608,070	2,064,180	27.1
• Baltimore, MD PMSA	2,552,994	718,236	28.1
• Hagerstown, MD PMSA	131,923	10,879	8.2
• Washington, DC–MD–VA–WV PMSA	4,923,153	1,335,065	27.1
5. San Francisco–Oakland–San Jose, CA CMSA	7,039,362	573,036	8.1
• Oakland, CA PMSA	2,392,557	331,363	13.8
• San Francisco, CA PMSA	1,731,183	104,572	6.0
• San Jose, CA PMSA	1,682,585	56,596	3.4
• Santa Cruz–Watsonville, CA PMSA	255,602	3,771	1.5
• Santa Rosa, CA PMSA	458,614	9,282	2.0
• Vallejo–Fairfield–Napa, CA PMSA	518,821	67,452	13.0

(continued)

(continued from previous page)

		total population	black number	share of total
6.	Philadelphia–Wilmington–Atlantic City, PA–NJ–DE–MD CMSA	6,188,463	1,258,667	20.3%
	• Atlantic City–Cape May, NJ PMSA	354,878	52,768	14.9
	• Philadelphia, PA–NJ PMSA	5,100,931	1,065,713	20.9
	• Vineland–Millville–Bridgeton, NJ PMSA	146,438	31,470	21.5
	• Wilmington–Newark, DE–MD PMSA	586,216	108,716	18.5
7.	Boston–Worcester–Lawrence, MA–NH–ME–CT CMSA	5,819,100	347,644	6.0
	• Boston, MA–NH PMSA	3,406,829	267,507	7.9
	• Brockton, MA PMSA	255,459	25,014	9.8
	• Fitchburg–Leominster, MA PMSA	142,284	4,534	3.2
	• Lawrence, MA–NH PMSA	396,230	9,561	2.4
	• Lowell, MA–NH PMSA	301,686	6,986	2.3
	• Manchester, NH PMSA	198,378	3,359	1.7
	• Nashua, NH PMSA	190,949	3,027	1.6
	• New Bedford, MA PMSA	175,198	7,405	4.2
	• Portsmouth–Rochester, NH–ME PMSA	240,698	2,341	1.0
	• Worcester, MA–CT PMSA	511,389	17,910	3.5
8.	Detroit–Ann Arbor–Flint, MI CMSA	5,456,428	1,185,075	21.7
	• Ann Arbor, MI PMSA	578,736	46,500	8.0
	• Detroit, MI PMSA	4,441,551	1,045,652	23.5
	• Flint, MI PMSA	436,141	92,923	21.3
9.	Dallas–Fort Worth, TX CMSA	5,221,801	744,894	14.3
	• Dallas, TX PMSA	3,519,176	546,907	15.5
	• Fort Worth–Arlington, TX PMSA	1,702,625	197,987	11.6
10.	Houston–Galveston–Brazoria, TX CMSA	4,669,571	810,881	17.4
	• Brazoria, TX PMSA	241,767	21,374	8.8
	• Galveston–Texas City, TX PMSA	250,158	39,643	15.8
	• Houston, TX PMSA	4,177,646	749,864	17.9
11.	Atlanta, GA MSA	4,112,198	1,216,230	29.6
12.	Miami–Fort Lauderdale, FL CMSA	3,876,380	847,626	21.9
	• Fort Lauderdale, FL PMSA	1,623,018	360,611	22.2
	• Miami, FL PMSA	2,253,362	487,015	21.6
13.	Seattle–Tacoma–Bremerton, WA CMSA	3,554,760	204,186	5.7
	• Bremerton, WA PMSA	231,969	8,722	3.8
	• Olympia, WA PMSA	207,355	6,509	3.1
	• Seattle–Bellevue–Everett, WA PMSA	2,414,616	129,007	5.3
	• Tacoma, WA PMSA	700,820	59,948	8.6
14.	Phoenix–Mesa, AZ MSA	3,251,876	137,766	4.2
15.	Minneapolis–St. Paul, MN–WI MSA	2,968,806	184,688	6.2
16.	Cleveland–Akron, OH CMSA	2,945,831	512,708	17.4
	• Akron, OH PMSA	694,960	80,816	11.6
	• Cleveland–Lorain–Elyria, OH PMSA	2,250,871	431,892	19.2

(continued)

(continued from previous page)

	total population	black number	black share of total
17. San Diego, CA MSA	2,813,833	186,679	6.6%
18. St. Louis, MO–IL MSA	2,603,607	489,448	18.8
19. Denver–Boulder–Greeley, CO CMSA	2,581,506	136,253	5.3
• Boulder–Longmont, CO PMSA	291,288	3,484	1.2
• Denver, CO PMSA	2,109,282	131,312	6.2
• Greeley, CO PMSA	180,936	1,457	0.8
20. Tampa–St. Petersburg–Clearwater, FL MSA	2,395,997	258,091	10.8
21. Pittsburgh, PA MSA	2,358,695	202,160	8.6
22. Portland–Salem, OR–WA CMSA	2,265,223	68,663	3.0
• Portland–Vancouver, OR–WA PMSA	1,918,009	64,483	3.4
• Salem, OR PMSA	347,214	4,180	1.2
23. Cincinnati–Hamilton, OH–KY–IN CMSA	1,979,202	240,428	12.1
• Cincinnati, OH–KY–IN PMSA	1,646,395	221,456	13.5
• Hamilton–Middletown, OH PMSA	332,807	18,972	5.7
24. Sacramento–Yolo, CA CMSA	1,796,857	147,978	8.2
• Sacramento, CA PMSA	1,628,197	143,600	8.8
• Yolo, CA PMSA	168,660	4,378	2.6
25. Kansas City, MO–KS MSA	1,776,062	238,440	13.4
26. Milwaukee–Racine, WI CMSA	1,689,572	266,251	15.8
• Milwaukee–Waukesha, WI PMSA	1,500,741	245,151	16.3
• Racine, WI PMSA	188,831	21,100	11.2
27. Orlando, FL MSA	1,644,561	245,054	14.9
28. Indianapolis, IN MSA	1,607,486	232,887	14.5
29. San Antonio, TX MSA	1,592,383	114,041	7.2
30. Norfolk–Virginia Beach–Newport News, VA–NC MSA	1,569,541	501,284	31.9
31. Las Vegas, NV–AZ MSA	1,563,282	139,068	8.9
32. Columbus, OH MSA	1,540,157	221,098	14.4
33. Charlotte–Gastonia–Rock Hill, NC–SC MSA	1,499,293	314,252	21.0
34. New Orleans, LA MSA	1,337,726	508,464	38.0
35. Salt Lake City–Ogden, UT MSA	1,333,914	19,878	1.5
36. Greensboro–Winston-Salem–High Point, NC MSA	1,251,509	258,896	20.7
37. Austin–San Marcos, TX MSA	1,249,763	105,909	8.5
38. Nashville, TN MSA	1,231,311	197,581	16.0
39. Providence–Fall River–Warwick, RI–MA MSA	1,188,613	58,370	4.9
40. Raleigh–Durham–Chapel Hill, NC MSA	1,187,941	276,761	23.3
41. Hartford, CT MSA	1,183,110	122,242	10.3
42. Buffalo–Niagara Falls, NY MSA	1,170,111	143,805	12.3
43. Memphis, TN–AR–MS MSA	1,135,614	496,864	43.8
44. West Palm Beach–Boca Raton, FL MSA	1,131,184	168,585	14.9
45. Jacksonville, FL MSA	1,100,491	244,672	22.2
46. Rochester, NY MSA	1,098,201	121,207	11.0
47. Grand Rapids–Muskegon–Holland, MI MSA	1,088,514	86,910	8.0

(continued)

(continued from previous page)

	total population	black number	share of total
48. Oklahoma City, OK MSA	1,083,346	123,478	11.4%
49. Louisville, KY–IN MSA	1,025,598	148,513	14.5
50. Richmond–Petersburg, VA MSA	996,512	306,673	30.8
51. Greenville–Spartanburg–Anderson, SC MSA	962,441	171,363	17.8
52. Dayton–Springfield, OH MSA	950,558	142,143	15.0
53. Fresno, CA MSA	922,516	52,881	5.7
54. Birmingham, AL MSA	921,106	279,452	30.3
55. Honolulu, HI MSA	876,156	29,764	3.4
56. Albany–Schenectady–Troy, NY MSA	875,583	59,188	6.8
57. Tucson, AZ MSA	843,746	30,893	3.7
58. Tulsa, OK MSA	803,235	76,558	9.5
59. Syracuse, NY MSA	732,117	53,046	7.2
60. Omaha, NE–IA MSA	716,998	64,110	8.9
61. Albuquerque, NM MSA	712,738	22,004	3.1
62. Knoxville, TN MSA	687,249	41,951	6.1
63. El Paso, TX MSA	679,622	23,482	3.5
64. Bakersfield, CA MSA	661,645	43,735	6.6
65. Allentown–Bethlehem–Easton, PA MSA	637,958	22,384	3.5
66. Harrisburg–Lebanon–Carlisle, PA MSA	629,401	53,399	8.5
67. Scranton–Wilkes-Barre–Hazleton, PA MSA	624,776	10,372	1.7
68. Toledo, OH MSA	618,203	83,716	13.5
69. Baton Rouge, LA MSA	602,894	194,378	32.2
70. Youngstown–Warren, OH MSA	594,746	64,384	10.8
71. Springfield, MA MSA	591,932	44,926	7.6
72. Sarasota–Bradenton, FL MSA	589,959	37,387	6.3
73. Little Rock–North Little Rock, AR MSA	583,845	130,309	22.3
74. McAllen–Edinburg–Mission, TX MSA	569,463	3,327	0.6
75. Stockton–Lodi, CA MSA	563,598	42,459	7.5
76. Charleston–North Charleston, SC MSA	549,033	171,817	31.3
77. Wichita, KS MSA	545,220	49,975	9.2
78. Mobile, AL MSA	540,258	149,583	27.7
79. Columbia, SC MSA	536,691	174,929	32.6
80. Colorado Springs, CO MSA	516,929	39,993	7.7
81. Fort Wayne, IN MSA	502,141	40,735	8.1
82. Daytona Beach, FL MSA	493,175	47,678	9.7
83. Lakeland–Winter Haven, FL MSA	483,924	68,439	14.1
84. Johnson City–Kingsport–Bristol, TN–VA MSA	480,091	11,240	2.3
85. Lexington, KY MSA	479,198	48,102	10.0
86. Augusta–Aiken, GA–SC MSA	477,441	167,107	35.0
87. Melbourne–Titusville–Palm Bay, FL MSA	476,230	42,635	9.0
88. Lancaster, PA MSA	470,658	15,651	3.3
89. Chattanooga, TN–GA MSA	465,161	67,818	14.6

(continued)

(continued from previous page)

	total population	black number	black share of total
90. Des Moines, IA MSA	456,022	20,863	4.6%
91. Kalamazoo–Battle Creek, MI MSA	452,851	46,597	10.3
92. Lansing–East Lansing, MI MSA	447,728	40,800	9.1
93. Modesto, CA MSA	446,997	14,187	3.2
94. Fort Myers–Cape Coral, FL MSA	440,888	31,155	7.1
95. Jackson, MS MSA	440,801	202,392	45.9
96. Boise City, ID MSA	432,345	3,594	0.8
97. Madison, WI MSA	426,526	20,241	4.7
98. Spokane, WA MSA	417,939	9,366	2.2
99. Pensacola, FL MSA	412,153	70,156	17.0
100. Canton–Massillon, OH MSA	406,934	30,270	7.4

Note: Blacks include those who identified themselves as black alone and those who identified themselves as black in combination with one or more other races. For definitions of CMSA, PMSA, and MSA, see glossary.
Source: Bureau of the Census, Profiles of General Demographic Characteristics, *2000 Census of Population and Housing, May 2001; calculations by New Strategist*

Black Spending Is Rising as Blacks Earn Higher Incomes

The nation's 13 million black households spent an average of $28,152 in 2000, according to the Bureau of Labor Statistics' Consumer Expenditure Survey. Black households (called consumer units by the Bureau of Labor Statistics) spend 74 percent as much as the average consumer unit.

While black spending is below average in many categories, it is above average on a wide variety of items—despite blacks' lower incomes. Blacks spend more than average on such items as rice, pork, poultry, fish, telephone service, infants' furniture, children's clothes, intracity mass transit fares, taxi fares, wigs and hairpieces, and personal care services (e.g., manicures and hair styling).

■ Because the incomes of blacks are rising faster than those of other racial or ethnic groups, black spending should approach or exceed the average for more items in the years ahead.

Black households spend 26 percent less than the average household

(average annual spending of total and black consumer units, 2000)

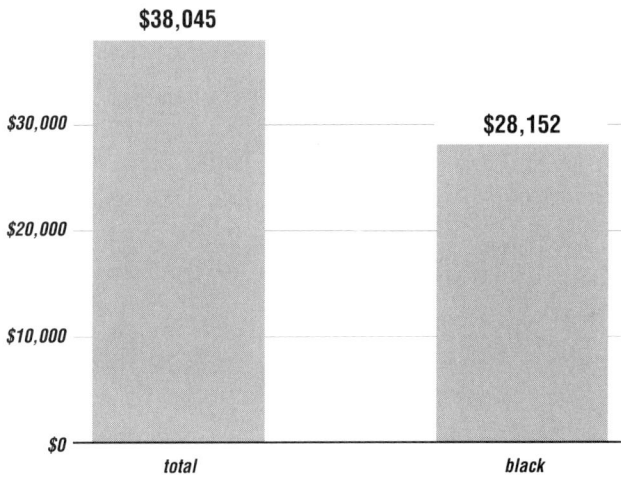

Average and Indexed Spending of Black Households, 2000

(average annual expenditures of total and black consumer units, and indexed expenditures of black consumer units, 2000)

	average spending of total consumer units	black consumer units average spending	indexed spending*
Number of consumer units (in 000s)	109,367	13,230	–
Average before-tax income of consumer unit	$44,649.00	$32,657.00	73
Average spending of consumer unit, total	38,044.67	28,152.24	74
FOOD	**$5,157.88**	**$4,094.85**	**79**
FOOD AT HOME	3,021.00	2,690.58	89
Cereals and bakery products	453.33	392.97	87
Cereals and cereal products	156.40	158.71	101
Flour	7.98	9.75	122
Prepared flour mixes	13.35	11.76	88
Ready-to-eat and cooked cereals	86.88	85.11	98
Rice	19.55	27.36	140
Pasta, cornmeal, and other cereal products	28.64	24.72	86
Bakery products	296.93	234.26	79
Bread	84.04	71.88	86
White bread	36.62	34.63	95
Bread, other than white	47.42	37.25	79
Crackers and cookies	71.03	53.86	76
Cookies	47.71	37.47	79
Crackers	23.32	16.39	70
Frozen and refrigerated bakery products	24.53	20.87	85
Other bakery products	117.33	87.66	75
Biscuits and rolls	38.53	24.28	63
Cakes and cupcakes	38.42	34.23	89
Bread and cracker products	4.41	2.30	52
Sweetrolls, coffee cakes, doughnuts	22.68	14.68	65
Pies, tarts, turnovers	13.28	12.16	92
Meats, poultry, fish, and eggs	**795.43**	**908.64**	**114**
Beef	238.19	235.66	99
Ground beef	87.76	91.65	104
Roast	39.84	31.01	78
Chuck roast	13.33	11.53	86
Round roast	11.46	7.56	66
Other roast	15.05	11.92	79
Steak	94.52	93.84	99
Round steak	15.31	14.54	95
Sirloin steak	29.86	26.84	90
Other steak	49.35	52.46	106
Other beef	16.08	19.16	119

(continued)

(continued from previous page)

	average spending of total consumer units	black consumer units	
		average spending	indexed spending
Pork	$166.94	$199.18	119
Bacon	26.05	32.80	126
Pork chops	40.57	53.95	133
Ham	36.26	35.24	97
Ham, not canned	34.52	34.04	99
Canned ham	1.74	1.20	69
Sausage	25.24	33.54	133
Other pork	38.82	43.65	112
Other meats	100.54	106.34	106
Frankfurters	20.68	21.47	104
Lunch meats (cold cuts)	67.99	61.20	90
Bologna, liverwurst, salami	23.73	27.42	116
Other lunch meats	44.26	33.78	76
Lamb, organ meats, and others	11.87	23.67	199
Lamb and organ meats	9.71	13.14	135
Mutton, goat, and game	2.16	10.53	488
Poultry	145.16	185.19	128
Fresh and frozen chicken	114.43	142.12	124
Fresh and frozen whole chicken	31.25	42.23	135
Fresh and frozen chicken parts	83.18	99.89	120
Other poultry	30.73	43.07	140
Fish and seafood	110.14	138.86	126
Canned fish and seafood	15.67	14.20	91
Fresh fish and shellfish	66.82	97.86	146
Frozen fish and shellfish	27.65	26.81	97
Eggs	34.46	43.41	126
Dairy products	**324.63**	**244.58**	**75**
Fresh milk and cream	131.22	101.69	77
Fresh milk, all types	119.61	95.98	80
Cream	11.61	5.71	49
Other dairy products	193.41	142.89	74
Butter	17.00	15.99	94
Cheese	95.96	63.69	66
Ice cream and related products	56.56	45.63	81
Miscellaneous dairy products	23.89	17.57	74
Fruits and vegetables	**520.83**	**453.78**	**87**
Fresh fruits	163.17	131.48	81
Apples	29.49	25.83	88
Bananas	31.70	30.15	95
Oranges	18.93	18.60	98
Citrus fruits, excl. oranges	14.31	10.80	75
Other fresh fruits	68.74	46.10	67

(continued)

(continued from previous page)

	average spending of total consumer units	black consumer units	
		average spending	indexed spending
Fresh vegetables	$158.72	$128.67	81
Potatoes	28.07	25.06	89
Lettuce	20.75	18.24	88
Tomatoes	29.53	25.67	87
Other fresh vegetables	80.38	59.70	74
Processed fruits	115.01	117.59	102
Frozen fruits and fruit juices	14.37	11.26	78
Frozen orange juice	6.90	5.57	81
Frozen fruits	3.62	2.31	64
Frozen fruit juices	3.84	3.38	88
Canned fruits	15.48	12.33	80
Dried fruits	5.50	3.63	66
Fresh fruit juice	23.44	24.62	105
Canned and bottled fruit juice	56.21	65.73	117
Processed vegetables	83.94	76.04	91
Frozen vegetables	26.42	24.70	93
Canned and dried vegetables and juices	57.52	51.35	89
Canned beans	12.67	12.11	96
Canned corn	6.80	7.95	117
Canned miscellaneous vegetables	17.95	12.70	71
Dried peas	0.34	0.50	147
Dried beans	2.53	2.42	96
Dried miscellaneous vegetables	7.22	8.04	111
Dried processed vegetables	0.41	0.25	61
Frozen vegetable juices	0.29	0.46	159
Fresh and canned vegetable juices	9.30	6.93	75
Other food at home	**926.77**	**690.61**	**75**
Sugar and other sweets	117.14	88.95	76
Candy and chewing gum	76.30	44.00	58
Sugar	16.80	21.47	128
Artificial sweeteners	4.19	5.80	138
Jams, preserves, other sweets	19.86	17.67	89
Fats and oils	83.09	83.29	100
Margarine	11.61	11.92	103
Fats and oils	23.35	29.90	128
Salad dressings	27.18	24.17	89
Nondairy cream and imitation milk	9.15	6.09	67
Peanut butter	11.81	11.20	95
Miscellaneous foods	437.02	315.79	72
Frozen prepared foods	90.20	65.97	73
Frozen meals	28.50	27.81	98
Other frozen prepared foods	61.70	38.16	62
Canned and packaged soups	35.54	29.08	82

(continued)

(continued from previous page)

	average spending of total consumer units	black consumer units	
		average spending	indexed spending
Potato chips, nuts, and other snacks	$92.50	$56.85	61
Potato chips and other snacks	71.67	42.68	60
Nuts	20.83	14.17	68
Condiments and seasonings	84.61	66.09	78
Salt, spices, and other seasonings	20.65	22.70	110
Olives, pickles, relishes	9.77	6.44	66
Sauces and gravies	37.23	26.08	70
Baking needs and misc. products	16.96	10.87	64
Other canned/packaged prepared foods	134.17	97.81	73
Prepared salads	18.55	13.34	72
Prepared desserts	9.31	7.17	77
Baby food	32.26	27.62	86
Miscellaneous prepared foods	73.91	49.65	67
Vitamin supplements	0.14	0.03	21
Nonalcoholic beverages	249.58	185.72	74
Cola	86.99	61.79	71
Other carbonated drinks	47.39	32.32	68
Coffee	41.85	24.31	58
Roasted coffee	27.50	16.66	61
Instant and freeze-dried coffee	14.35	7.64	53
Noncarbonated fruit-flavored drinks, incl. nonfrozen lemonade	19.42	20.85	107
Tea	15.68	13.56	86
Nonalcoholic beer	0.27	0.29	107
Other nonalcoholic beverages and ice	37.99	32.61	86
Food prepared by CU on out-of-town trips	39.94	16.86	42
FOOD AWAY FROM HOME	**2,136.88**	**1,404.28**	**66**
Meals at restaurants, carry-outs, other	**1,750.33**	**1,212.70**	**69**
Lunch	662.90	535.03	81
At fast food, take-out, delivery, concession stands, buffet, cafeteria (other than employer, school cafeteria)	368.00	330.93	90
At full-service restaurants	208.12	101.26	49
At vending machines, mobile vendors	6.52	7.38	113
At employer and school cafeterias	80.26	95.47	119
Dinner	697.99	383.84	55
At fast food, take-out, delivery, concession stands, buffet, cafeteria (other than employer and school cafeteria)	206.92	158.87	77
At full-service restaurants	487.70	219.94	45
At vending machines, mobile vendors	1.02	2.45	240
At employer and school cafeterias	2.35	2.59	110
Snacks and nonalcoholic beverages	227.71	175.76	77
At fast food, take-out, delivery, concession stands, buffet, cafeteria (other than employer and school cafeteria)	158.55	111.96	71

(continued)

(continued from previous page)

	average spending of total consumer units	black consumer units	
		average spending	indexed spending
At full-service restaurants	$20.15	$14.49	72
At vending machines, mobile vendors	38.52	37.58	98
At employer and school cafeterias	10.49	11.74	112
Breakfast and brunch	161.73	118.06	73
At fast food, take-out, delivery, concession stands, buffet, cafeteria (other than employer and school cafeteria)	77.12	70.35	91
At full-service restaurants	79.64	41.84	53
At vending machines, mobile vendors	1.35	1.19	88
At employer and school cafeterias	3.62	4.68	129
Board (including at school)	**39.03**	**25.80**	**66**
Catered affairs	**54.02**	**19.89**	**37**
Food on trips	**216.06**	**81.12**	**38**
School lunches	**58.46**	**48.33**	**83**
Meals as pay	**18.97**	**16.44**	**87**
ALCOHOLIC BEVERAGES	**$371.81**	**$211.14**	**57**
At home	**226.64**	**122.43**	**54**
Beer and ale	112.01	74.07	66
Whiskey	13.49	11.24	83
Wine	80.04	22.71	28
Other alcoholic beverages	21.10	14.42	68
Away from home	**145.17**	**88.71**	**61**
Beer and ale	62.46	48.49	78
At fast food, take-out, delivery, concession stands, buffet, and cafeteria	13.37	6.24	47
At full-service restaurants	45.05	16.69	37
At vending machines, mobile vendors	0.40	0.54	135
At catered affairs	3.64	25.02	687
Wine	17.79	8.51	48
At fast food, take-out, delivery, concession stands, buffet and cafeteria	1.23	0.33	27
At full-service restaurants	16.16	5.53	34
At catered affairs	0.39	2.65	679
Other alcoholic beverages	64.92	31.70	49
At fast food, take-out, delivery, concession stands, buffet, and cafeteria	3.04	1.02	34
At full-service restaurants	25.74	8.02	31
At machines and mobile vendors	0.29	0.56	193
At catered affairs	1.60	11.02	689
Alcoholic beverages purchased on trips	34.24	11.08	32
HOUSING	**$12,318.51**	**$9,905.54**	**80**
SHELTER	**7,114.26**	**5,677.51**	**80**
Owned dwellings**	**4,602.32**	**2,607.38**	**57**

(continued)

(continued from previous page)

	average spending of total consumer units	black consumer units	
		average spending	indexed spending
Mortgage interest and charges	$2,638.81	$1,574.25	60
Mortgage interest	2,460.48	1,476.34	60
Interest paid, home equity loan	98.22	78.84	80
Interest paid, home equity line of credit	79.76	19.06	24
Prepayment penalty charges	0.34	–	–
Property taxes	1,138.55	639.98	56
Maintenance, repairs, insurance, other expenses	824.96	393.15	48
Homeowner's and related insurance	234.84	152.84	65
Homeowner's insurance	234.84	152.84	65
Ground rent	38.67	10.46	27
Maintenance and repair services	438.92	180.70	41
Painting and papering	49.93	22.44	45
Plumbing and water heating	41.62	30.14	72
Heat, air conditioning, electrical work	79.19	29.63	37
Roofing and gutters	75.27	20.58	27
Other repair and maintenance services	157.99	66.33	42
Repair, replacement of hard-surface flooring	33.61	10.97	33
Repair of built-in appliances	1.31	0.62	47
Maintenance and repair materials	78.08	21.29	27
Paints, wallpaper, and supplies	16.03	4.86	30
Tools, equipment for painting, wallpapering	1.72	0.52	30
Plumbing supplies and equipment	6.13	4.74	77
Electrical supplies, heating and cooling equipment	4.35	0.54	12
Hard-surface flooring, repair and replacement	6.98	2.33	33
Roofing and gutters	6.41	1.83	29
Plaster, paneling, siding, windows, doors, screens, awnings	12.14	3.21	26
Patio, walk, fence, driveway, masonry, brick, and stucco materials	0.60	0.32	53
Landscape maintenance	2.92	0.13	4
Miscellaneous supplies and equipment	20.80	2.80	13
Insulation, other maintenance, repair	13.45	1.37	10
Finish basement, remodel rooms, build patios, walks, etc.	7.35	1.43	19
Property management and security	30.99	25.26	82
Property management	21.49	19.90	93
Management and upkeep services for security	9.50	5.36	56
Parking	3.45	2.59	75
Rented dwellings	**2,034.11**	**2,843.04**	**140**
Rent	1,977.33	2,750.44	139
Rent as pay	29.24	76.46	261
Maintenance, insurance, and other expenses	27.54	16.15	59
Tenant's insurance	8.86	5.12	58

(continued)

(continued from previous page)

	average spending of total consumer units	black consumer units	
		average spending	indexed spending
Maintenance and repair services	$11.13	$8.06	72
Repair and maintenance services	9.98	7.91	79
Repair and replacement of hard-surface flooring	1.08	0.10	9
Repair of built-in appliances	0.07	0.06	86
Maintenance and repair materials	7.55	2.97	39
Paint, wallpaper, and supplies	1.54	1.02	66
Painting and wallpapering tools	0.17	0.11	65
Plastering, paneling, roofing, gutters, etc.	0.48	0.38	79
Patio, walk, fence, driveway, masonry, brick, and stucco materials	0.03	–	–
Plumbing supplies and equipment	0.39	0.28	72
Electrical supplies, heating and cooling equipment	0.25	–	–
Miscellaneous supplies and equipment	3.60	0.24	7
Insulation, other maintenance and repair	0.92	0.24	26
Materials for additions, finishing basements, remodeling rooms	2.67	–	–
Construction materials for jobs not started	0.01	–	–
Hard-surface flooring	0.49	0.94	192
Landscape maintenance	0.60	–	–
Other lodging	**477.84**	**227.09**	**48**
Owned vacation homes	147.91	84.99	57
Mortgage interest and charges	63.65	47.97	75
Mortgage interest	61.19	47.97	78
Interest paid, home equity loan	1.35	–	–
Interest paid, home equity line of credit	1.11	–	–
Property taxes	51.97	25.24	49
Maintenance, insurance, and other expenses	32.29	11.78	36
Homeowner's and related insurance	10.74	8.66	81
Homeowner's insurance	10.74	8.66	81
Fire and extended coverage	'(3)	–	–
Ground rent	2.97	0.26	9
Maintenance and repair services	13.56	0.65	5
Maintenance and repair materials	0.48	0.22	46
Property management and security	3.89	1.78	46
Property management	2.56	0.83	32
Management and upkeep services for security	1.33	0.95	71
Parking	0.65	0.21	32
Housing while attending school	78.31	37.54	48
Lodging on out-of-town trips	251.62	104.56	42
UTILITIES, FUELS, PUBLIC SERVICES	**2,488.90**	**2,570.54**	**103**
Natural gas	**307.35**	**342.08**	**111**
Natural gas (renter)	60.47	114.80	190

(continued)

(continued from previous page)

	average spending of total consumer units	black consumer units	
		average spending	indexed spending
Natural gas (owner)	$244.63	$226.44	93
Natural gas (vacation)	2.25	0.84	37
Electricity	**911.44**	**938.17**	**103**
Electricity (renter)	213.85	410.39	192
Electricity (owner)	690.09	524.92	76
Electricity (vacation)	7.50	2.85	38
Fuel oil and other fuels	**96.94**	**42.94**	**44**
Fuel oil	55.08	27.95	51
Fuel oil (renter)	6.54	4.95	76
Fuel oil (owner)	47.74	21.79	46
Fuel oil (vacation)	0.81	1.21	149
Coal	0.58	–	–
Coal (renter)	0.14	–	–
Coal (owner)	0.44	–	–
Bottled/tank gas	35.26	12.46	35
Gas (renter)	4.76	1.83	38
Gas (owner)	28.79	10.41	36
Gas (vacation)	1.71	0.22	13
Wood and other fuels	6.02	2.54	42
Wood and other fuels (renter)	1.09	0.28	26
Wood and other fuels (owner)	4.88	2.11	43
Wood and other fuels (vacation)	0.05	0.14	280
Telephone services	**876.75**	**986.30**	**112**
Telephone services in home city, excl. mobile phones	757.26	891.17	118
Telephone services for mobile phones	119.49	95.13	80
Water and other public services	**296.42**	**261.06**	**88**
Water and sewerage maintenance	212.72	201.81	95
Water and sewerage maintenance (renter)	29.99	55.64	186
Water and sewerage maintenance (owner)	181.10	145.07	80
Water and sewerage maintenance (vacation)	1.63	1.09	67
Trash and garbage collection	81.74	58.66	72
Trash and garbage collection (renter)	8.30	14.45	174
Trash and garbage collection (owner)	71.34	43.21	61
Trash and garbage collection (vacation)	2.10	1.00	48
Septic tank cleaning	1.96	0.59	30
Septic tank cleaning (renter)	0.04	0.10	250
Septic tank cleaning (owner)	1.92	0.50	26
HOUSEHOLD SERVICES	**684.38**	**468.22**	**68**
Personal services	**326.20**	**292.10**	**90**
Babysitting and child care in own home	32.21	11.17	35
Babysitting and child care in someone else's home	32.59	36.35	112
Care for elderly, invalids, handicapped, etc.	50.38	14.13	28

(continued)

(continued from previous page)

	average spending of total consumer units	black consumer units	
		average spending	indexed spending
Adult day care centers	$2.60	$0.88	34
Day care centers, nurseries, and preschools	208.42	229.57	110
Other household services	**358.18**	**176.12**	**49**
Housekeeping services	88.15	20.02	23
Gardening, lawn care service	78.26	40.82	52
Water softening service	3.11	0.82	26
Nonclothing laundry and dry cleaning, sent out	1.48	2.04	138
Nonclothing laundry and dry cleaning, coin-operated	4.64	7.57	163
Termite/pest control services	9.57	4.94	52
Home security system service fee	18.67	25.59	137
Other home services	14.28	5.74	40
Termite/pest control products	0.49	0.45	92
Moving, storage, and freight express	32.43	13.26	41
Appliance repair, including service center	12.58	8.99	71
Reupholstering and furniture repair	9.26	2.35	25
Repairs/rentals of lawn/garden equipment, hand/power tools, etc.	4.96	2.56	52
Appliance rental	3.77	4.15	110
Rental of office equipment for nonbusiness use	0.53	0.36	68
Repair of misc. household equipment and furnishings	11.73	–	–
Repair of computer systems for nonbusiness use	2.75	3.49	127
Computer information services	61.36	32.97	54
Rental, installation of dishwashers, range hoods, and garbage disposals	0.15	–	–
HOUSEKEEPING SUPPLIES	**482.32**	**302.65**	**63**
Laundry and cleaning supplies	**130.76**	**125.75**	**96**
Soaps and detergents	69.27	69.58	100
Other laundry cleaning products	61.49	56.17	91
Other household products	**225.90**	**125.66**	**56**
Cleansing and toilet tissue, paper towels, and napkins	68.45	60.95	89
Miscellaneous household products	90.48	40.57	45
Lawn and garden supplies	66.97	24.15	36
Postage and stationery	**125.66**	**51.23**	**41**
Stationery, stationery supplies, giftwrap	63.65	22.27	35
Postage	60.60	27.40	45
Delivery services	1.41	1.56	111
HOUSEHOLD FURNISHINGS, EQUIPMENT	**1,548.63**	**886.62**	**57**
Household textiles	**106.49**	**57.00**	**54**
Bathroom linens	17.55	9.30	53
Bedroom linens	44.52	28.21	63
Kitchen and dining room linens	9.31	4.14	44
Curtains and draperies	21.06	11.99	57

(continued)

(continued from previous page)

	average spending of total consumer units	black consumer units	
		average spending	indexed spending
Slipcovers and decorative pillows	$2.75	$0.12	4
Sewing materials for household items	9.75	2.44	25
Other linens	1.53	0.80	52
Furniture	**390.63**	**283.26**	**73**
Mattresses and springs	52.89	48.20	91
Other bedroom furniture	69.11	72.64	105
Sofas	89.15	63.36	71
Living room chairs	43.84	14.78	34
Living room tables	17.19	10.76	63
Kitchen and dining room furniture	46.46	33.32	72
Infants' furniture	6.22	7.29	117
Outdoor furniture	15.16	5.69	38
Wall units, cabinets, and other furniture	50.61	27.23	54
Floor coverings	**44.38**	**24.88**	**56**
Wall-to-wall carpet (renter)	1.38	1.98	143
Wall-to-wall carpet (replacement) (owner)	27.78	14.84	53
Room-size rugs and other floor coverings, nonpermanent	15.22	8.05	53
Major appliances	**188.96**	**108.41**	**57**
Dishwashers (built-in), garbage disposals, range hoods (renter)	0.87	0.74	85
Dishwashers (built-in), garbage disposals, range hoods (owner)	14.10	2.42	17
Refrigerators and freezers (renter)	7.35	11.30	154
Refrigerators and freezers (owner)	44.34	17.96	41
Washing machines (renter)	4.79	11.39	238
Washing machines (owner)	18.53	10.69	58
Clothes dryers (renter)	3.36	5.51	164
Clothes dryers (owner)	12.02	7.40	62
Cooking stoves, ovens (renter)	2.80	5.04	180
Cooking stoves, ovens (owner)	23.95	9.99	42
Microwave ovens (renter)	2.38	3.99	168
Microwave ovens (owner)	7.36	3.10	42
Portable dishwashers (renter)	0.16	–	–
Portable dishwashers (owner)	0.76	0.28	37
Window air conditioners (renter)	1.85	3.51	190
Window air conditioners (owner)	4.82	5.09	106
Electric floor-cleaning equipment	25.98	3.89	15
Sewing machines	4.78	1.74	36
Miscellaneous household appliances	8.77	4.36	50
Small appliances and miscellaneous housewares	**87.37**	**35.91**	**41**
Housewares	64.87	22.26	34
Plastic dinnerware	1.45	0.67	46
China and other dinnerware	11.43	1.54	13

(continued)

(continued from previous page)

	average spending of total consumer units	black consumer units average spending	indexed spending
Flatware	$3.61	$1.59	44
Glassware	8.02	3.08	38
Silver serving pieces	2.35	1.24	53
Other serving pieces	1.43	1.20	84
Nonelectric cookware	16.67	6.82	41
Tableware, nonelectric kitchenware	19.90	6.11	31
Small appliances	22.51	13.65	61
Small electric kitchen appliances	17.04	10.35	61
Portable heating and cooling equipment	5.47	3.30	60
Miscellaneous household equipment	**730.81**	**377.16**	**52**
Window coverings	13.02	8.94	69
Infants' equipment	8.01	3.49	44
Laundry and cleaning equipment	10.08	6.54	65
Outdoor equipment	18.39	5.49	30
Clocks	13.91	3.36	24
Lamps and lighting fixtures	10.80	7.32	68
Other household decorative items	177.30	102.29	58
Telephones and accessories	29.19	13.02	45
Lawn and garden equipment	46.82	13.57	29
Power tools	21.32	3.74	18
Office furniture for home use	13.67	8.20	60
Hand tools	7.26	2.05	28
Indoor plants and fresh flowers	57.01	27.15	48
Closet and storage items	8.03	2.56	32
Rental of furniture	3.12	4.40	141
Luggage	8.32	4.28	51
Computers and computer hardware, nonbusiness use	187.83	124.32	66
Computer software and accessories, nonbusiness use	17.49	8.06	46
Telephone answering devices	1.97	1.56	79
Calculators	1.64	1.58	96
Business equipment for home use	1.83	1.69	92
Other hardware	24.09	1.30	5
Smoke alarms (owner)	0.56	0.80	143
Smoke alarms (renter)	0.16	0.16	100
Other household appliances (owner)	7.59	3.66	48
Other household appliances (renter)	1.22	1.60	131
Miscellaneous household equipment and parts	40.18	16.04	40
APPAREL AND SERVICES	**$1,856.16**	**$1,695.20**	**91**
Men, aged 16 or older	**344.29**	**245.29**	**71**
Suits	33.23	36.72	111
Sport coats and tailored jackets	11.31	6.71	59
Coats and jackets	34.76	31.53	91

(continued)

(continued from previous page)

	average spending of total consumer units	black consumer units	
		average spending	indexed spending
Underwear	$17.45	$10.44	60
Hosiery	11.50	7.67	67
Nightwear	3.34	2.73	82
Accessories	23.29	11.81	51
Sweaters and vests	15.96	10.92	68
Active sportswear	16.11	9.76	61
Shirts	85.47	46.48	54
Pants	68.65	55.86	81
Shorts and shorts sets	13.64	5.74	42
Uniforms	5.52	5.59	101
Costumes	4.06	3.33	82
Boys, aged 2 to 15	**95.76**	**144.64**	**151**
Coats and jackets	7.84	14.86	190
Sweaters	3.56	4.08	115
Shirts	20.84	40.84	196
Underwear	5.09	10.33	203
Nightwear	2.95	3.97	135
Hosiery	4.30	6.31	147
Accessories	4.40	2.50	57
Suits, sport coats, and vests	3.64	4.43	122
Pants	23.39	33.23	142
Shorts and shorts sets	8.95	12.36	138
Uniforms	3.66	3.41	93
Active sportswear	3.81	5.66	149
Costumes	3.33	2.66	80
Women, aged 16 or older	**607.11**	**473.20**	**78**
Coats and jackets	43.26	36.67	85
Dresses	86.74	80.24	93
Sport coats and tailored jackets	8.33	4.01	48
Sweaters and vests	49.27	24.63	50
Shirts, blouses, and tops	99.26	67.04	68
Skirts	12.76	7.86	62
Pants	85.55	63.44	74
Shorts and shorts sets	20.40	7.55	37
Active sportswear	27.78	19.49	70
Nightwear	32.21	23.48	73
Undergarments	32.20	40.93	127
Hosiery	20.95	23.27	111
Suits	33.80	41.78	124
Accessories	39.29	20.71	53
Uniforms	8.69	9.41	108
Costumes	6.63	2.69	41

(continued)

(continued from previous page)

	average spending of total consumer units	black consumer units	
		average spending	indexed spending
Girls, aged 2 to 15	**$118.09**	**$131.07**	**111**
Coats and jackets	6.95	13.53	195
Dresses and suits	18.19	16.46	90
Shirts, blouses, and sweaters	28.79	25.75	89
Skirts and pants	21.75	32.48	149
Shorts and shorts sets	8.35	12.13	145
Active sportswear	8.97	3.42	38
Underwear and nightwear	7.40	9.28	125
Hosiery	4.92	5.85	119
Accessories	4.98	1.71	34
Uniforms	3.90	8.13	208
Costumes	3.87	2.33	60
Children under age 2	**81.92**	**89.04**	**109**
Coats, jackets, and snowsuits	2.70	3.45	128
Outerwear including dresses	22.97	28.26	123
Underwear	44.65	39.50	88
Nightwear and loungewear	3.99	4.60	115
Accessories	7.61	13.25	174
Footwear	**343.09**	**351.99**	**103**
Men's	117.55	91.42	78
Boys'	37.26	58.51	157
Women's	155.95	157.76	101
Girls'	32.33	44.30	137
Other apparel products and services	**265.90**	**259.96**	**98**
Material for making clothes	4.75	0.88	19
Sewing patterns and notions	4.69	1.82	39
Watches	22.63	24.15	107
Jewelry	107.32	63.13	59
Shoe repair and other shoe services	1.83	0.95	52
Coin-operated apparel laundry and dry cleaning	37.93	66.76	176
Apparel alteration, repair, and tailoring services	5.70	3.54	62
Clothing rental	3.37	3.10	92
Watch and jewelry repair	4.74	1.81	38
Professional laundry, dry cleaning	72.40	93.62	129
Clothing storage	0.55	0.20	36
TRANSPORTATION	**$7,417.36**	**$5,214.38**	**70**
VEHICLE PURCHASES	**3,418.27**	**2,284.95**	**67**
Cars and trucks, new	**1,604.95**	**869.07**	**54**
New cars	917.02	567.27	62
New trucks	687.94	301.80	44
Cars and trucks, used	**1,769.85**	**1,413.57**	**80**
Used cars	1,011.25	1,013.36	100
Used trucks	758.60	400.21	53

(continued)

(continued from previous page)

	average spending of total consumer units	black consumer units	
		average spending	indexed spending
Other vehicles	**$43.46**	**$2.31**	**5**
New motorcycles	18.45	–	–
Used motorcycles	17.38	2.31	13
GASOLINE AND MOTOR OIL	**1,291.25**	**955.84**	**74**
Gasoline	1,175.50	897.82	76
Diesel fuel	12.98	13.28	102
Gasoline on trips	91.79	38.04	41
Motor oil	10.05	6.31	63
Motor oil on trips	0.93	0.38	41
OTHER VEHICLE EXPENSES	**2,281.28**	**1,705.16**	**75**
Vehicle finance charges	**328.24**	**289.52**	**88**
Automobile finance charges	169.25	189.95	112
Truck finance charges	138.62	98.59	71
Motorcycle and plane finance charges	1.58	0.12	8
Other vehicle finance charges	18.79	0.86	5
Maintenance and repairs	**623.76**	**451.66**	**72**
Coolant, additives, brake and transmission fluids	4.47	3.96	89
Tires	87.23	63.23	72
Parts, equipment, and accessories	48.46	24.93	51
Vehicle audio equipment	2.41	–	–
Vehicle products	4.10	3.22	79
Miscellaneous auto repair, servicing	26.74	15.22	57
Body work and painting	26.35	13.79	52
Clutch, transmission repair	42.61	38.62	91
Drive shaft and rear-end repair	3.66	2.00	55
Brake work	54.04	47.13	87
Repair to steering or front-end	18.02	11.61	64
Repair to engine cooling system	20.55	16.53	80
Motor tune-up	44.41	35.34	80
Lube, oil change, and oil filters	58.75	37.90	65
Front-end alignment, wheel balance, rotation	10.79	8.50	79
Shock absorber replacement	4.25	2.84	67
Gas tank repair, replacement	3.55	5.24	148
Tire repair and other repair work	29.75	23.06	78
Vehicle air conditioning repair	19.80	12.02	61
Exhaust system repair	13.34	6.98	52
Electrical system repair	30.31	20.42	67
Motor repair, replacement	64.46	57.50	89
Auto repair service policy	5.71	1.62	28
Vehicle insurance	**778.13**	**633.75**	**81**
Vehicle rental, leases, licenses, other charges	**551.15**	**330.23**	**60**
Leased and rented vehicles	392.88	244.12	62

(continued)

(continued from previous page)

	average spending of total consumer units	black consumer units	
		average spending	indexed spending
Rented vehicles	$44.95	$26.45	59
Auto rental	7.21	8.67	120
Auto rental, out-of-town trips	29.62	13.91	47
Truck rental	3.21	1.98	62
Truck rental, out-of-town trips	4.71	1.90	40
Leased vehicles	347.93	217.66	63
Car lease payments	174.84	100.42	57
Cash down payment (car lease)	13.99	7.22	52
Termination fee (car lease)	1.81	10.34	571
Truck lease payments	148.45	97.15	65
Cash down payment (truck lease)	7.72	2.53	33
Termination fee (truck lease)	1.11	–	–
State and local registration	85.19	42.78	50
Driver's license	6.85	4.19	61
Vehicle inspection	9.41	6.39	68
Parking fees	29.38	18.37	63
Parking fees in home city, excluding residence	25.33	16.95	67
Parking fees, out-of-town trips	4.05	1.42	35
Tolls	10.90	3.83	35
Tolls on out-of-town trips	3.51	2.07	59
Towing charges	4.68	4.39	94
Automobile service clubs	8.35	4.09	49
PUBLIC TRANSPORTATION	**426.56**	**268.43**	**63**
Airline fares	274.02	108.47	40
Intercity bus fares	16.10	12.75	79
Intracity mass transit fares	47.41	97.18	205
Local transportation on out-of-town trips	10.66	4.89	46
Taxi fares and limousine service on trips	6.26	2.87	46
Taxi fares and limousine service	12.15	19.52	161
Intercity train fares	21.12	8.79	42
Ship fares	36.58	11.12	30
School bus	2.26	2.84	126
HEALTH CARE	**$2,065.67**	**$1,106.60**	**54**
HEALTH INSURANCE	**982.65**	**639.29**	**65**
Commercial health insurance	**194.39**	**81.59**	**42**
Traditional fee-for-service health plan (not BCBS)	77.07	33.69	44
Preferred-provider health plan (not BCBS)	117.32	47.90	41
Blue Cross, Blue Shield	**232.50**	**127.91**	**55**
Traditional fee-for-service health plan	49.89	34.02	68
Preferred-provider health plan	60.94	31.51	52
Health maintenance organization	73.18	48.25	66

(continued)

(continued from previous page)

	average spending of total consumer units	black consumer units	
		average spending	indexed spending
Commercial Medicare supplement	$43.77	$10.56	24
Other BCBS health insurance	4.71	3.58	76
Health maintenance plans (HMOs)	**254.81**	**234.96**	**92**
Medicare payments	**164.04**	**125.94**	**77**
Commercial Medicare supplements/ other health insurance	**136.91**	**68.89**	**50**
Commercial Medicare supplement (not BCBS)	88.22	51.21	58
Other health insurance (not BCBS)	48.69	17.68	36
MEDICAL SERVICES	**567.85**	**190.67**	**34**
Physician's services	134.41	51.60	38
Dental services	220.79	67.47	31
Eye care services	35.05	12.32	35
Service by professionals other than physician	36.87	9.87	27
Lab tests, X-rays	20.12	7.55	38
Hospital room	35.95	10.60	29
Hospital services other than room	41.13	20.85	51
Care in convalescent or nursing home	32.35	4.28	13
Repair of medical equipment	0.61	–	–
Other medical services	10.56	6.12	58
DRUGS	**416.45**	**235.30**	**57**
Nonprescription drugs	65.09	33.45	51
Nonprescription vitamins	46.19	15.08	33
Prescription drugs	305.17	186.77	61
MEDICAL SUPPLIES	**98.73**	**41.34**	**42**
Eyeglasses and contact lenses	58.43	27.39	47
Hearing aids	11.78	0.48	4
Topicals and dressings	20.99	11.38	54
Medical equipment for general use	2.04	0.77	38
Supportive, convalescent medical equipment	3.18	0.67	21
Rental of medical equipment	0.85	0.32	38
Rental of supportive, convalescent medical equipment	1.46	0.34	23
ENTERTAINMENT	**$1,863.50**	**$1,014.12**	**54**
FEES AND ADMISSIONS	**514.85**	**180.63**	**35**
Recreation expenses on trips	25.49	10.58	42
Social, recreation, civic club membership	98.18	26.31	27
Fees for participant sports	71.49	22.17	31
Participant sports on trips	35.05	8.11	23
Movie, theater, opera, ballet	89.16	46.35	52
Movie, other admissions on trips	44.94	17.24	38
Admission to sports events	35.33	11.60	33
Admission to sports events on trips	14.98	5.74	38

(continued)

(continued from previous page)

	average spending of total consumer units	black consumer units	
		average spending	indexed spending
Fees for recreational lessons	$74.74	$21.95	29
Other entertainment services on trips	25.49	10.58	42
TELEVISION, RADIO, SOUND EQUIPMENT	**621.82**	**567.33**	**91**
Television	**453.53**	**461.11**	**102**
Community antenna and cable service	321.18	342.52	107
Black-and-white TV sets	0.77	1.24	161
Color TV, console	30.19	29.28	97
Color TV, portable, table model	34.35	33.38	97
VCRs and video disc players	23.80	18.81	79
Video cassettes, tapes, and discs	20.80	15.72	76
Video game hardware and software	18.72	16.72	89
Repair of TV, radio, and sound equipment	3.23	2.02	63
Rental of television sets	0.49	1.43	292
Radio and sound equipment	**168.29**	**106.22**	**63**
Radios	10.44	4.48	43
Tape recorders and players	4.39	9.96	227
Sound components and component systems	23.16	19.17	83
Miscellaneous sound equipment	0.42	–	–
Sound equipment accessories	4.04	0.45	11
Satellite dishes	2.70	1.02	38
Compact disc, tape, record, video mail order clubs	8.52	5.14	60
Records, CDs, audio tapes, needles	39.46	30.19	77
Rental of VCR, radio, sound equipment	0.54	0.52	96
Musical instruments and accessories	31.70	4.33	14
Rental and repair of musical instruments	1.34	0.30	22
Rental of video cassettes, tapes, discs, films	41.56	30.67	74
PETS, TOYS, PLAYGROUND EQUIPMENT	**333.71**	**159.24**	**48**
Pets	**209.43**	**69.16**	**33**
Pet food	85.97	30.05	35
Pet purchase, supplies, and medicines	38.10	21.49	56
Pet services	19.36	5.04	26
Veterinarian services	66.00	12.58	19
Toys, games, hobbies, and tricycles	**120.96**	**88.43**	**73**
Playground equipment	**3.32**	**1.64**	**49**
OTHER ENTERTAINMENT SUPPLIES, EQUIPMENT, SERVICES	**393.12**	**106.92**	**27**
Unmotored recreational vehicles	**48.06**	**6.82**	**14**
Boat without motor and boat trailers	15.87	–	–
Trailer and other attachable campers	32.19	6.82	21
Motorized recreational vehicles	**81.96**	**17.18**	**21**
Motorized camper	21.35	13.78	65
Other vehicle	21.74	0.08	0

(continued)

(continued from previous page)

	average spending of total consumer units	black consumer units	
		average spending	indexed spending
Motorboats	$38.87	$3.32	9
Rental of recreational vehicles	**2.79**	**0.98**	**35**
Boat and trailer rental on trips	0.59	–	–
Rental of campers on trips	0.61	–	–
Rental of other vehicles on trips	1.40	0.93	66
Rental of other RVs	0.03	–	–
Outboard motors	**3.58**	**–**	**–**
Docking and landing fees	**8.17**	**0.40**	**5**
Sports, recreation, exercise equipment	**143.58**	**41.49**	**29**
Athletic gear, game tables, exercise equipment	58.64	23.62	40
Bicycles	11.73	6.77	58
Camping equipment	17.02	5.24	31
Hunting and fishing equipment	25.85	2.18	8
Winter sports equipment	5.84	0.37	6
Water sports equipment	8.24	0.09	1
Other sports equipment	14.25	2.39	17
Rental and repair of miscellaneous sports equipment	2.02	0.83	41
Photographic equipment and supplies	**94.91**	**37.52**	**40**
Film	21.40	9.55	45
Other photographic supplies	1.44	1.90	132
Film processing	31.43	10.75	34
Repair and rental of photographic equipment	0.27	0.11	41
Photographic equipment	20.21	7.03	35
Photographer fees	20.17	8.17	41
Fireworks	**1.18**	**–**	**–**
Souvenirs	**2.00**	**0.19**	**10**
Visual goods	**1.09**	**–**	**–**
Pinball, electronic video games	**5.80**	**2.34**	**40**
PERSONAL CARE PRODUCTS AND SERVICES	**$563.62**	**$627.43**	**111**
Personal care products	**256.30**	**221.29**	**86**
Hair care products	51.46	42.61	83
Hair accessories	6.59	5.01	76
Wigs and hairpieces	1.17	6.02	515
Oral hygiene products	25.78	21.05	82
Shaving products	13.19	7.74	59
Cosmetics, perfume, and bath products	119.91	107.46	90
Deodorants, feminine hygiene, miscellaneous products	29.21	28.61	98
Electric personal care appliances	8.99	2.79	31
Personal care services	**307.31**	**406.14**	**132**
READING	**$146.47**	**$71.98**	**49**
Newspaper subscriptions	47.43	21.65	46

(continued)

(continued from previous page)

	average spending of total consumer units	black consumer units	
		average spending	indexed spending
Newspapers, nonsubscriptions	$12.26	$12.86	105
Magazine subscriptions	19.10	8.66	45
Magazines, nonsubscriptions	9.50	5.47	58
Books purchased through book clubs	8.03	3.56	44
Books not purchased through book clubs	49.52	19.69	40
Encyclopedia and other reference book sets	0.51	0.08	16
EDUCATION	**$631.93**	**$382.90**	**61**
College tuition	363.29	205.88	57
Elementary and high school tuition	101.42	51.25	51
Other school tuition	24.42	12.23	50
Other school expenses including rentals	24.00	18.27	76
Books, supplies for college	52.66	37.04	70
Books, supplies for elementary, high school	13.92	13.09	94
Books, supplies for day care, nursery school	3.09	2.71	88
Miscellaneous school expenses and supplies	49.13	42.42	86
TOBACCO PRODUCTS AND SMOKING SUPPLIES	**$318.62**	**$243.41**	**76**
Cigarettes	293.90	234.49	80
Other tobacco products	22.52	7.94	35
Smoking accessories	2.03	0.99	49
FINANCIAL PRODUCTS AND SERVICES	**$775.78**	**$571.65**	**74**
Miscellaneous fees, gambling losses	41.60	18.42	44
Legal fees	103.96	34.08	33
Funeral expenses	70.69	91.67	130
Safe deposit box rental	4.58	1.58	34
Checking accounts, other bank service charges	19.89	17.15	86
Cemetery lots, vaults, and maintenance fees	13.47	10.43	77
Accounting fees	55.18	20.26	37
Miscellaneous personal services	31.39	34.34	109
Finance charges, except mortgage and vehicles	253.37	241.46	95
Occupational expenses	96.24	52.94	55
Expenses for other properties	79.73	46.22	58
Interest paid, home equity line of credit (other property)	0.98	–	–
Credit card memberships	4.71	3.09	66
CASH CONTRIBUTIONS	**$1,192.44**	**$699.69**	**59**
Cash contributions to non-household members, including students, alimony, child support	296.07	184.15	62
Gifts of cash, stocks, bonds to non-household members	267.48	43.40	16
Contributions to charities	139.87	32.82	23
Contributions to religious organizations	445.63	427.82	96

(continued)

(continued from previous page)

	average spending of total consumer units	black consumer units average spending	black consumer units indexed spending
Contributions to educational organizations	$19.96	$7.66	38
Political contributions	6.65	0.80	12
Other contributions	16.80	3.05	18
PERSONAL INSURANCE, PENSIONS	**$3,364.92**	**$2,313.36**	**69**
Life and other personal insurance	**398.61**	**358.18**	**90**
Life, endowment, annuity, other personal insurance	387.97	351.21	91
Other nonhealth insurance	10.64	6.97	66
Pensions and Social Security	**2,966.31**	**1,955.17**	**66**
Deductions for government retirement	70.32	72.64	103
Deductions for railroad retirement	3.29	6.69	203
Deductions for private pensions	362.64	168.77	47
Nonpayroll deposit to retirement plans	389.65	119.78	31
Deductions for Social Security	2,140.41	1,587.30	74
PERSONAL TAXES	**$3,117.45**	**$1,626.16**	**52**
Federal income taxes	2,409.33	1,240.16	51
State and local income taxes	561.80	337.80	60
Other taxes	146.32	48.20	33
GIFTS*	**$1,083.14**	**$571.18**	**53**
FOOD	**70.09**	**26.12**	**37**
Fresh fruits	4.58	1.19	26
Candy and chewing gum	12.50	2.26	18
Board (including at school)	20.21	14.96	74
Catered affairs	15.59	1.71	11
ALCOHOLIC BEVERAGES	**14.49**	**9.76**	**67**
Beer and ale	3.64	3.82	105
Wine	6.76	3.88	57
Whiskey and other alcoholic beverages	3.73	1.75	47
HOUSING	**291.10**	**132.93**	**46**
Housekeeping supplies	**39.10**	**13.63**	**35**
Miscellaneous household products	7.32	1.04	14
Lawn and garden supplies	3.08	1.62	53
Postage and stationery	24.95	9.09	36
Stationery, stationery supplies, giftwraps	20.28	6.60	33
Postage	4.57	2.49	54
Household textiles	**13.20**	**2.55**	**19**
Bathroom linens	2.79	1.29	46
Bedroom linens	6.85	–	–
Appliances and miscellaneous housewares	**28.14**	**5.52**	**20**
Major appliances	7.61	2.45	32
Electric floor-cleaning equipment	3.01	–	–

(continued)

(continued from previous page)

	average spending of total consumer units	black consumer units	
		average spending	indexed spending
Small appliances and miscellaneous housewares	$20.53	$3.07	15
Glassware	3.60	0.61	17
Nonelectric cookware	3.66	0.09	2
Tableware, nonelectric kitchenware	4.34	0.58	13
Small electric kitchen appliances	2.68	1.36	51
Miscellaneous household equipment	70.31	19.43	28
Infants' equipment	2.72	1.13	42
Outdoor equipment	2.86	–	–
Household decorative items	27.33	10.47	38
Indoor plants, fresh flowers	16.04	5.32	33
Computers and computer hardware, nonbusiness use	8.97	0.89	10
Miscellaneous household equipment and parts	2.53	0.25	10
Other housing	**140.36**	**91.80**	**65**
Repair or maintenance services	3.74	1.09	29
Housing while attending school	42.32	16.22	38
Natural gas (renter)	3.11	4.00	129
Electricity (renter)	13.28	12.67	95
Telephone services in home city, excl. mobile phones	13.64	16.71	123
Water, sewerage maintenance (renter)	2.67	2.69	101
Care for elderly, invalids, handicapped	2.10	2.14	102
Day-care centers, nurseries, and preschools	21.46	19.06	89
Housekeeping services	3.44	0.62	18
Gardening, lawn care service	3.14	1.71	54
Repair of misc. household equipment and furnishings	7.78	–	–
Bedroom furniture except mattress and springs	2.06	0.94	46
APPAREL AND SERVICES	**244.25**	**193.59**	**79**
Men and boys, aged 2 or older	**67.55**	**38.23**	**57**
Men's coats and jackets	3.30	7.09	215
Men's underwear	2.10	1.94	92
Men's accessories	3.40	0.56	16
Men's sweaters and vests	2.72	2.30	85
Men's active sportswear	4.35	1.00	23
Men's shirts	20.77	6.97	34
Men's pants	7.11	0.70	10
Boys' shirts	5.56	4.63	83
Boys' pants	2.84	2.41	85
Women and girls, aged 2 or older	**85.28**	**87.04**	**102**
Women's coats and jackets	3.57	4.39	123
Women's dresses	10.62	14.25	134
Women's vests and sweaters	8.86	6.43	73
Women's shirts, tops, blouses	10.59	10.12	96
Women's pants	5.94	6.38	107

(continued)

(continued from previous page)

	average spending of total consumer units	black consumer units	
		average spending	indexed spending
Women's active sportswear	$3.47	$3.00	86
Women's sleepwear	6.15	11.40	185
Women's undergarments	2.69	6.37	237
Women's accessories	4.17	1.51	36
Girls' dresses and suits	4.03	3.42	85
Girls' shirts, blouses, sweaters	6.18	4.00	65
Girls' skirts and pants	2.78	2.47	89
Girls' active sportswear	2.10	2.04	97
Girls' accessories	2.18	0.42	19
Children under age 2	**40.71**	**33.59**	**83**
Infant dresses, outerwear	14.51	13.27	91
Infant underwear	18.27	13.39	73
Infant nightwear, loungewear	2.46	2.10	85
Infant accessories	4.02	3.59	89
Other apparel products and services	**50.71**	**34.73**	**68**
Watches	3.43	1.42	41
Jewelry	16.85	6.78	40
Men's footwear	8.66	2.51	29
Boys' footwear	4.70	3.43	73
Women's footwear	10.06	13.13	131
Girls' footwear	5.21	4.81	92
TRANSPORTATION	**70.27**	**23.41**	**33**
New cars	6.08	–	–
New trucks	14.04	–	–
Used cars	12.52	–	–
Used trucks	2.82	3.58	127
Gasoline on trips	12.55	4.46	36
Airline fares	8.51	6.86	81
Local transportation on trips	2.13	0.67	31
Intercity train fares	2.23	1.82	82
Ship fares	2.98	1.95	65
HEALTH CARE	**38.08**	**5.60**	**15**
Physician's services	2.66	0.89	33
Dental services	3.49	0.85	24
Hospital room	2.73	–	–
Care in convalescent or nursing home	18.42	–	–
Nonprescription drugs	2.15	0.96	45
ENTERTAINMENT	**93.76**	**42.99**	**46**
Toys, games, hobbies, and tricycles	29.58	16.59	56
Movie, other admissions on trips	9.17	3.20	35
Admission to sports events on trips	3.06	1.07	35
Fees for recreational lessons	6.30	1.39	22

(continued)

(continued from previous page)

	average spending of total consumer units	black consumer units	
		average spending	indexed spending
Cable service and community antenna	$4.65	$6.35	137
Color TV, portable, table model	2.10	0.51	24
Musical instruments and accessories	2.32	0.19	8
Athletic gear, game tables, and exercise equipment	9.47	6.94	73
PERSONAL CARE PRODUCTS AND SERVICES	**19.20**	**10.47**	**55**
Hair care products	2.14	1.13	53
Cosmetics, perfume, bath preparation	13.00	6.00	46
Deodorants, feminine hygiene, misc. personal care	2.00	2.00	100
READING	**2.00**	–	–
EDUCATION	**151.00**	**39.00**	**26**
College tuition	114.00	30.00	26
Elementary and high school tuition	11.00	1.00	9
Other school tuition	3.00	–	–
Other school expenses including rentals	5.00	1.00	20
College books and supplies	10.00	3.00	30
Miscellaneous school supplies	5.00	2.00	40
ALL OTHER GIFTS	**89.00**	**87.00**	**98**
Gifts of trip expenses	49.00	14.00	29
Miscellaneous fees, gambling losses	2.00	–	–
Legal fees	4.00	5.00	125
Funeral expenses	28.00	63.00	225
Cemetery lots, vaults, maintenance fees	3.00	3.00	100
Accounting fees	2.00	–	–

* The index compares the spending of the average black consumer unit with the spending of the average consumer unit by dividing black spending by average spending in each category and multiplying by 100. An index of 100 means black spending in the category equals average spending. An index of 125 means black spending is 25 percent above average, while an index of 75 means black spending is 25 percent below average.
** This figure does not include the amount paid for mortgage principal, which is considered an asset.
*** Expenditures on gifts are also included in the preceding product and service categories. Food spending, for example, includes the amount spent on gifts of food. Only gift expenditures exceeding $2.00 for the average consumer unit are shown.
Note: The Bureau of Labor Statistics uses consumer unit rather than household as the sampling unit in the Consumer Expenditure Survey. For the definition of consumer unit, see glossary. Expenditures for gifts may not add to category totals because listings are incomplete. (–) means not applicable or sample is too small to make a reliable estimate.
Source: Bureau of Labor Statistics, unpublished data from the 2000 Consumer Expenditure Survey; calculations by New Strategist

Nonwhite and Hispanic Households Have Little Net Worth

The median net worth (assets minus debts) of nonwhite and Hispanic households amounted to just $16,400 in 1998, far below the $71,600 net worth of the average American household. On every measure of wealth, nonwhites and Hispanics have less than the average household. Their financial assets are just 29 percent as high as the average, and their nonfinancial assets are only 53 percent of the average. The debts of nonwhite and Hispanic households are also below average. (Note: The Federal Reserve collects wealth data for only two racial and ethnic categories: non-Hispanic whites, and nonwhites and Hispanics. The nonwhite-and-Hispanic category includes primarily blacks and Hispanics, but also some Asians and American Indians.)

The net worth of nonwhite and Hispanic households is below average in large part because blacks and Hispanics are less likely to own a home than is the average householder. Home equity accounts for the largest share of Americans' net worth. In 1998, 47 percent of nonwhite and Hispanic householders owned a home.

Nonwhite and Hispanic householders have a median of only $6,400 in financial assets. The median debt of nonwhite and Hispanic householders stood at $15,300 in 1998, much lower than average in part because fewer have mortgage debt.

The employers of the majority of working blacks offer a pension plan at work, but only 42 percent of black men and women are covered by their employer's plan. Those most likely to have pension coverage are older black professionals working for large corporations.

■ The net worth of blacks will rise as homeownership increases and as black homeowners age and gain more equity in their homes.

The net worth of nonwhite and Hispanic households is far below average

(median net worth of total and nonwhite/Hispanic households, 1998)

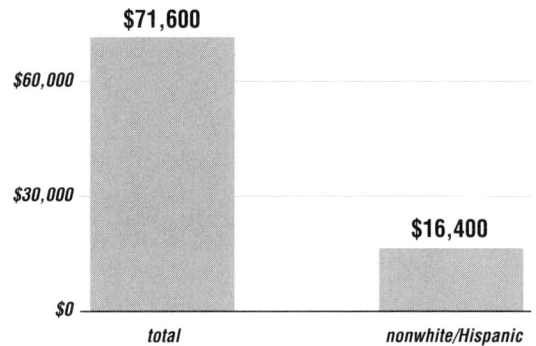

Net Worth, Assets, and Debt of Nonwhite and Hispanic Households, 1998

(median net worth, median value of assets for owners, and median amount of debt for debtors, for total and nonwhite/Hispanic households, and index of nonwhite/Hispanic to total, 1998)

	total	nonwhite and Hispanic	index of nonwhite/Hispanic to total
Median net worth	**$71,600**	**$16,400**	**23**
Median value of financial assets	22,400	6,400	29
Median value of nonfinancial assets	97,800	52,000	53
Median amount of debt	33,300	15,300	46

Note: The index is calculated by dividing the nonwhite/Hispanic figure by the total figure and multiplying by 100.
Source: Federal Reserve Board, Family Finances in the U.S.: Recent Evidence from the 1998 Survey of Consumer Finances, *Federal Reserve Bulletin, January 2000; calculations by New Strategist*

Financial Assets of Nonwhite and Hispanic Households, 1998

(percent of nonwhite/Hispanic households owning financial assets, and median value of assets for owners, 1998)

	percent owning asset	median value
Any financial asset	**81.2%**	**$6,400**
Transaction accounts	75.8	1,300
Certificates of deposit	6.4	6,300
Savings bonds	9.2	700
Bonds	0.4	14,200
Stocks	9.1	9,000
Mutual funds	8.4	10,000
Retirement accounts	32.0	13,000
Life insurance	20.8	5,000
Other managed assets	1.7	23,000
Other financial assets	8.3	1,000

Source: Federal Reserve Board, Family Finances in the U.S.: Recent Evidence from the 1998 Survey of Consumer Finances, *Federal Reserve Bulletin, January 2000; calculations by New Strategist*

Nonfinancial Assets of Nonwhite and Hispanic Households, 1998

(percent of nonwhite/Hispanic households owning nonfinancial assets, and median value of assets for owners, 1998)

	percent owning asset	median value
Any nonfinancial asset	**76.4%**	**$52,000**
Vehicles	67.2	8,000
Primary residence	46.8	85,000
Other residential property	8.4	59,000
Nonresidential property	5.8	24,000
Business	8.4	30,000
Other nonfinancial asset	3.1	5,000

Source: Federal Reserve Board, Family Finances in the U.S.: Recent Evidence from the 1998 Survey of Consumer Finances, *Federal Reserve Bulletin, January 2000; calculations by New Strategist*

Debt of Nonwhite and Hispanic Households, 1998

(percent of nonwhite/Hispanic households with debt, and median amount of debt for those with debts, 1998)

	percent with debt	median amount
Any debt	**71.1%**	**$15,300**
Home-secured	30.7	62,000
Other residential property	4.0	30,000
Installment loans	41.6	7,200
Other lines of credit	1.9	700
Credit card	43.3	1,100
Other debt	8.8	1,700

Source: Federal Reserve Board, Family Finances in the U.S.: Recent Evidence from the 1998 Survey of Consumer Finances, *Federal Reserve Bulletin, January 2000; calculations by New Strategist*

Pension Coverage of Black Men, 2000

(total number of employed black men aged 15 or older, number and percent with an employer-offered pension plan, and number and percent included in pension plan by selected characteristics, 2000; numbers in thousands)

| | | with employer-offered pension plan at work | | | |
| | | | | included in plan | |
Employed black men	total	number	percent	number	percent
Employed black men	**8,138**	**4,437**	**54.5%**	**3,408**	**41.9%**
Age					
Under age 65	7,928	4,338	54.7	3,345	42.2
Aged 15 to 24	1,418	522	36.8	211	14.9
Aged 25 to 44	4,273	2,494	58.4	1,913	44.8
Aged 45 to 64	2,237	1,322	59.1	1,221	54.6
Aged 65 or older	210	100	47.3	63	30.0
Worked					
Full-time	7,135	4,124	57.8	3,290	46.1
50 weeks or more	5,805	3,552	61.2	3,028	52.2
27 to 49 weeks	735	326	44.3	178	24.2
26 weeks or less	595	246	41.4	84	14.2
Part-time	1,003	314	31.3	118	11.8
50 weeks or more	373	146	39.1	74	19.9
27 to 49 weeks	160	57	35.8	23	14.6
26 weeks or less	470	111	23.5	20	4.3
Size of employer					
Under 25 employees	1,675	309	18.5	239	14.3
25 to 99 employees	941	400	42.5	269	28.6
100 to 499 employees	1,115	625	56.0	465	41.7
500 to 999 employees	531	339	63.9	271	51.1
1,000 or more employees	3,876	2,764	71.3	2,164	55.8

(continued)

(continued from previous page)

		with employer-offered pension plan at work			
				included in plan	
	total	number	percent	number	percent
Occupation					
Executive, administrative, and managerial	728	426	58.5%	368	50.5%
Professional specialty	670	430	64.2	351	52.4
Technical, related support	175	125	71.7	98	55.7
Sales workers	661	333	50.3	224	33.8
Administrative support, including clerical	641	403	62.9	327	51.1
Precision production, craft, and repair	1,129	573	50.8	461	40.8
Machine operators, assemblers, inspectors	622	394	63.3	338	54.3
Transportation, material moving occupations	874	502	57.5	408	46.6
Handlers, equip. cleaners, helpers, and laborers	872	404	46.3	221	25.3
Service workers	1,468	708	48.3	499	34.0
Private household	10	–	–	–	–
Service workers except private household	1,458	708	48.6	499	34.3
Farming, forestry, fishing	188	61	32.5	52	27.7
Armed forces	110	78	70.4	62	56.4
Earnings					
Under $15,000	2,348	813	34.6	336	14.3
$15,000 to $24,999	1,686	852	50.5	625	37.1
$25,000 to $49,999	2,872	1,831	63.8	1,579	55.0
$50,000 to $74,999	844	662	78.4	622	73.7
$75,000 to $99,999	230	164	71.3	153	66.5
$100,000 or more	155	111	71.6	94	60.6

Note: (–) means sample is too small to make a reliable estimate.
Source: Bureau of the Census, Current Population Survey, Internet site <http://ferret.bls.census.gov/macro/032001/noncash/nc8_008 .htm>; calculations by New Strategist

Pension Coverage of Black Women, 2000

(total number of employed black women aged 15 or older, number and percent with an employer-offered pension plan, and number and percent included in pension plan by selected characteristics, 2000; numbers in thousands)

		with employer-offered pension plan at work			
				included in plan	
	total	number	percent	number	percent
Employed black women	**9,332**	**5,400**	**57.9%**	**3,956**	**42.4%**
Age					
Under age 65	9,117	5,309	58.2	3,905	42.8
Aged 15 to 24	1,652	660	40.0	248	15.0
Aged 25 to 44	4,958	3,060	61.7	2,276	45.9
Aged 45 to 64	2,507	1,588	63.4	1,381	55.1
Aged 65 or older	215	91	42.2	51	23.9
Worked					
Full-time	7,707	4,816	62.5	3,726	48.3
50 weeks or more	6,392	4,177	65.3	3,368	52.7
27 to 49 weeks	714	429	60.1	281	39.4
26 weeks or less	601	211	35.0	77	12.9
Part-time	1,625	583	35.9	230	14.2
50 weeks or more	669	267	39.8	122	18.3
27 to 49 weeks	350	163	46.5	71	20.4
26 weeks or less	606	154	25.5	37	6.0
Size of employer					
Under 25 employees	1,491	302	20.3	200	13.4
25 to 99 employees	1,071	455	42.5	286	26.7
100 to 499 employees	1,230	653	53.1	447	36.3
500 to 999 employees	654	423	64.6	310	47.4
1,000 or more employees	4,886	3,567	73.0	2,713	55.5

(continued)

(continued from previous page)

		with employer-offered pension plan at work			
				included in plan	
	total	number	percent	number	percent
Occupation					
Executive, administrative, and managerial	1,071	747	69.7%	637	59.5%
Professional specialty	1,214	853	70.2	709	58.4
Technical related support	370	242	65.5	206	55.8
Sales workers	1,043	524	50.2	258	24.8
Administrative support, including clerical	2,151	1,478	68.7	1,124	52.2
Precision production, craft, and repair	188	100	53.4	71	38.0
Machine operators, assemblers, inspectors	543	312	57.4	203	37.3
Transportation, material moving occupations	123	76	61.4	66	53.4
Handlers, equip. cleaners, helpers, and laborers	203	90	44.2	46	22.7
Service workers	2,386	951	39.9	615	25.8
Private household	153	4	2.4	4	2.6
Service workers except private household	2,233	948	42.4	611	27.4
Farming, forestry, fishing	23	11	46.7	5	21.5
Armed forces	16	16	100.0	16	100.0
Earnings					
Under $15,000	3,433	1,275	37.1	532	15.5
$15,000 to $24,999	2,346	1,483	63.2	1,124	47.9
$25,000 to $49,999	2,845	2,098	73.7	1,805	63.4
$50,000 to $74,999	564	425	75.4	387	68.6
$75,000 to $99,999	105	89	84.8	78	74.3
$100,000 or more	38	29	76.3	29	76.3

Source: Bureau of the Census, Current Population Survey, Internet site <http://ferret.bls.census.gov/macro/ 032001/noncash/nc8_009 .htm>; calculations by New Strategist

CHAPTER

4

Hispanics

■ Hispanics numbered 35 million in 2000, accounting for nearly 13 percent of the total U.S. population. The Hispanic population grew 58 percent between 1990 and 2000.

■ Hispanics own more than 1 million businesses, or 6 percent of the nation's total. They own 8 percent of agricultural service firms.

■ Only 57 percent of Hispanics are high school graduates. Hispanics lag in educational attainment because many are immigrants who came to the United States as adults with few years of schooling.

■ Thirty-two percent of Hispanics did not have health insurance coverage in 2000, more than double the 14 percent of all Americans who lack coverage.

■ Only 45 percent of Hispanic households own their home, far below the homeownership rate of 67 percent for all households.

■ The median income of Hispanic households stood at $33,455 in 2000, up 17 percent since 1990 after adjusting for inflation.

■ Hispanic women are less likely to be in the labor force than Asian, black, or non-Hispanic white women. Fifty-one percent of Hispanic married couples are dual earners.

■ Married couples head more than half of Hispanic households. Sixty-seven percent of Hispanic couples have children under age 18 at home compared with 46 percent of all couples.

■ Hispanic households spent an average of $32,735 in 2000, 86 percent as much as the average household. Hispanic households spent 12 percent more than the average household on clothes and 16 percent more on groceries.

Hispanics account for 12.5 percent of the U.S. population

(percent distribution of people by race and Hispanic origin, 2000 census)

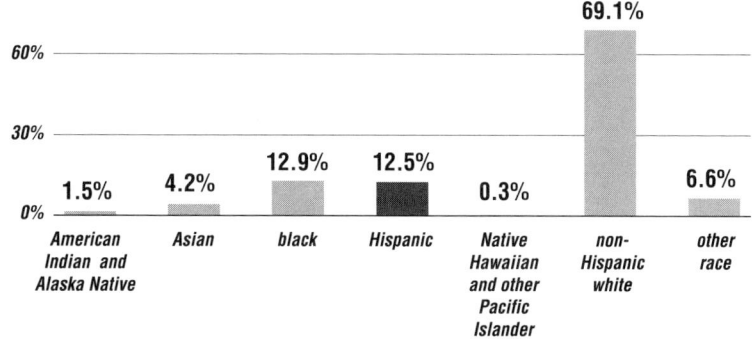

RACIAL AND ETHNIC DIVERSITY **337**

Hispanics Own More Than 1 Million Firms in the U.S.

Hispanics own nearly 1.2 million of the nation's 21 million businesses, according to the Survey of Minority-Owned Business Enterprises, a part of the 1997 Economic Censuses. The survey counts as minority-owned any firm in which the majority of owners is black, Alaska Native, American Indian, Asian, Native Hawaiian, Pacific Islander, or Hispanic. Minority ownership is determined for firms in their entirety rather than for individual locations.

Hispanics own 6 percent of all businesses in the nation. In the tobacco products industry, however, they own 17 percent of firms. The largest share of Hispanic firms are in the service industries—42 percent. Mexican Americans own the largest share—39 percent—of all Hispanic-owned firms. Eighty-six percent of Hispanic-owned firms are individual proprietorships, a much greater share than the 73 percent of all firms that are owned by one individual.

Eighty-six percent of Hispanic-owned businesses are in just 10 states. California is home to the largest share, 28 percent, followed by Texas with 20 percent. Hispanics own the largest share of businesses in New Mexico—21 percent in 1997.

Most Hispanic-owned firms have receipts below $25,000

(percent distribution of receipts for firms owned by Hispanics, 1997)

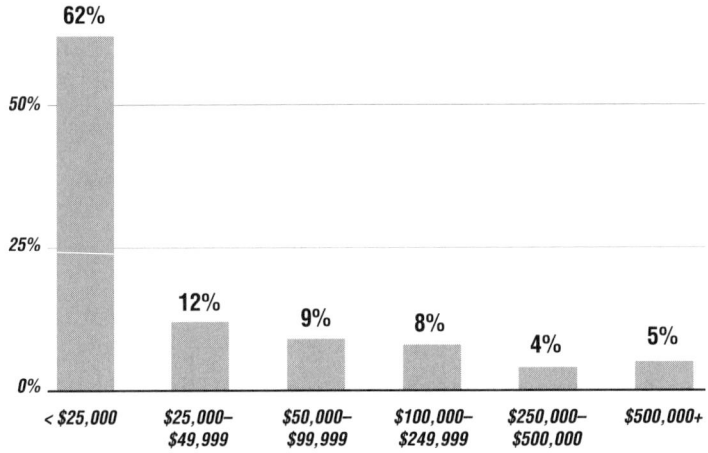

Number and Percent Distribution of Businesses Owned by Hispanics, 1997

(total number of firms, number and percent distribution of firms owned by Hispanics, and Hispanic share of total, by industry, 1997)

SIC code		total firms	firms owned by Hispanics		
			number	percent distribution	percent of total
	All industries	**20,821,935**	**1,199,896**	**100.0%**	**5.8%**
	Agricultural services, forestry, fishing	**496,164**	**40,040**	**3.3**	**8.1**
07	Agricultural services	412,852	36,872	3.1	8.9
08	Forestry	14,051	334	0.0	2.4
09	Fishing, hunting, and trapping	69,271	2,835	0.2	4.1
	Mineral industries	**126,809**	**1,909**	**0.2**	**1.5**
10	Metal mining	1,819	45	0.0	2.5
12	Coal mining	2,242	9	0.0	0.4
13	Oil and gas extraction	115,953	1,801	0.2	1.6
14	Nonmetallic minerals, except fuels	6,862	55	0.0	0.8
	Construction industries, subdividers, developers	**2,333,424**	**152,573**	**12.7**	**6.5**
15	Building construction, general contractors and operative builders	472,111	16,345	1.4	3.5
16	Heavy construction contractors other than buildings	64,314	2,643	0.2	4.1
17	Special trade contractors	1,739,060	132,656	11.1	7.6
6552	Subdividers and developers not elsewhere classified (excl. cemeteries)	58,362	930	0.1	1.6
	Manufacturing	**688,782**	**25,552**	**2.1**	**3.7**
20	Food and kindred products	30,256	2,207	0.2	7.3
21	Tobacco products	133	23	0.0	17.3
22	Textile mill products	8,213	409	0.0	5.0
23	Apparel and other textile products	54,889	4,157	0.3	7.6
24	Lumber and wood products	106,569	1,715	0.1	1.6
25	Furniture and fixtures	28,712	1,503	0.1	5.2
26	Paper and allied products	7,186	206	0.0	2.9
27	Printing and publishing	119,936	3,736	0.3	3.1
28	Chemicals and allied products	10,941	160	0.0	1.5
29	Petroleum and coal products	1,434	12	0.0	0.8
30	Rubber and miscellaneous plastics	16,296	372	0.0	2.3
31	Leather and leather products	5,251	397	0.0	7.6

(continued)

(continued from previous page)

SIC code		total firms	firms owned by Hispanics		
			number	percent distribution	percent of total
32	Stone, clay, and glass products	29,262	746	0.1%	2.5%
33	Primary metal industries	7,703	276	0.0	3.6
34	Fabricated metal products	63,141	2,504	0.2	4.0
35	Industrial machinery and equipment	85,401	2,830	0.2	3.3
36	Electronic and other electric equipment	28,324	977	0.1	3.4
37	Transportation equipment	13,673	289	0.0	2.1
38	Instruments and related products	12,423	183	0.0	1.5
39	Miscellaneous manufacturing industries	65,185	2,858	0.2	4.4
	Transportation, communications, utilities	**919,570**	**84,554**	**7.0**	**9.2**
41	Local and interurban passenger transportation	116,993	14,063	1.2	12.0
42	Motor freight transportation and warehousing	544,523	54,981	4.6	10.1
44	Water transportation	15,788	308	0.0	2.0
45	Transportation by air	20,706	856	0.1	4.1
46	Pipelines, except natural gas	136	–	–	–
47	Transportation services	129,652	10,649	0.9	8.2
48	Communications	61,180	2,935	0.2	4.8
49	Electric, gas, and sanitary services	31,345	766	0.1	2.4
	Wholesale trade	**797,856**	**31,480**	**2.6**	**3.9**
50	Durable goods	489,308	18,231	1.5	3.7
51	Nondurable goods	309,731	13,251	1.1	4.3
	Retail trade	**2,889,041**	**155,061**	**12.9**	**5.4**
52	Building materials, hardware, garden supply, and mobile home dealers	85,060	2,793	0.2	3.3
53	General merchandise stores	35,027	1,867	0.2	5.3
54	Food stores	216,067	18,063	1.5	8.4
55	Automotive dealers and gasoline service stations	255,259	10,950	0.9	4.3
56	Apparel and accessory stores	127,848	9,585	0.8	7.5
57	Home furniture, furnishings, and equipment stores	153,248	6,577	0.5	4.3
58	Eating and drinking places	493,313	34,862	2.9	7.1
59	Miscellaneous retail	1,528,857	70,413	5.9	4.6

(continued)

(continued from previous page)

SIC code		total firms	firms owned by Hispanics		
			number	percent distribution	percent of total
	Finance, insurance, real estate (excl. subdividers and developers)	**2,237,675**	**56,629**	**4.7%**	**2.5%**
60	Depository institutions	24,616	252	0.0	1.0
61	Nondepository credit institutions	45,905	1,960	0.2	4.3
62	Security and commodity brokers, dealers, exchanges, and services	91,446	2,057	0.2	2.2
63	Insurance carriers	9,108	97	0.0	1.1
64	Insurance agents, brokers, services	411,902	11,915	1.0	2.9
65pt	Real estate (excluding subdividers and developers)	1,503,438	39,060	3.3	2.6
67	Holding and other investment offices, except trusts	157,652	1,304	0.1	0.8
	Service industries (excl. membership organizations, private hh)	**8,891,024**	**500,449**	**41.7**	**5.6**
70	Hotels, rooming houses, camps, and other lodging places	93,380	1,795	0.1	1.9
72	Personal services	1,348,554	99,389	8.3	7.4
73	Business services	2,221,047	157,907	13.2	7.1
75	Automotive repair, services, parking	448,584	37,357	3.1	8.3
76	Miscellaneous repair services	231,371	12,655	1.1	5.5
78	Motion pictures	87,700	3,958	0.3	4.5
79	Amusement and recreation services	603,896	24,622	2.1	4.1
80	Health services	1,004,672	44,806	3.7	4.5
81	Legal services	353,147	9,903	0.8	2.8
82	Educational services	270,648	8,170	0.7	3.0
83	Social services	665,067	44,993	3.7	6.8
84	Museums, art galleries, botanical and zoological gardens	5,205	3	0.0	0.1
87	Engineering, accounting, research, management and related services	1,446,195	51,740	4.3	3.6
89	Services not elsewhere classified	119,931	3,203	0.3	2.7
	Industries not classified	**1,480,003**	**151,931**	**12.7**	**10.3**

Note: (–) means data not available or suppressed for purposes of confidentiality.
Source: Bureau of the Census, Minority- and Women-Owned Businesses, *1997 Economic Census, Internet site <www.census.gov/csd/mwb/>; calculations by New Strategist*

Characteristics of Businesses Owned by Hispanics, 1997

(number of firms owned by Hispanics by industry and selected characteristics of firm, 1997)

SIC code		total firms		firms with paid employees			
		number	sales and receipts (in 000s)	number	sales and receipts (in 000s)	employees	payroll (in 000s)
	Firms owned by Hispanics	1,199,896	$186,274,582	211,884	$158,674,537	1,388,746	$29,830,028
	Agricultural services, forestry, fishing	**40,040**	**2,279,397**	**5,925**	**1,309,733**	**25,955**	**416,702**
07	Agricultural services	36,872	2,109,344	5,568	1,220,041	24,716	396,342
08	Forestry	334	52,400	98	41,485	1,141	17,476
09	Fishing, hunting, and trapping	2,835	117,652	259	48,207	98	2,885
	Mineral industries	**1,909**	**429,446**	**325**	**367,442**	**3,569**	**97,854**
10	Metal mining	45	3,982	20	2,657	67	2,572
12	Coal mining	9	239	0	0	0	0
13	Oil and gas extraction	1,801	390,240	278	330,216	3,126	84,994
14	Nonmetallic minerals, except fuels	55	34,985	27	34,570	375	10,288
	Construction industries, subdividers, developers	**152,573**	**21,923,384**	**31,478**	**19,146,212**	**168,873**	**4,218,419**
15	Building construction, general contractors and operative builders	16,345	5,248,828	4,984	4,754,034	27,108	731,864
16	Heavy construction contractors other than buildings	2,643	2,827,244	1,308	2,790,331	20,804	677,687
17	Special trade contractors	132,656	13,602,223	25,110	11,545,488	120,791	2,803,472
6552	Subdividers and developers not elsewhere classified (excl. cemeteries)	930	245,090	78	56,359	169	5,396

(continued)

(continued from previous page)

SIC code	Manufacturing	total firms		firms with paid employees			
		number	sales and receipts (in 000s)	number	sales and receipts (in 000s)	employees	payroll (in 000s)
	Manufacturing	**25,552**	**$28,684,759**	**10,173**	**$27,719,404**	**171,738**	**$4,549,598**
20	Food and kindred products	2,207	1,986,260	994	1,961,448	15,254	299,155
21	Tobacco products	23	–	5	–	100–249	–
22	Textile mill products	409	366,051	213	362,739	5,068	84,835
23	Apparel and other textile products	4,157	1,176,700	1,443	1,098,786	22,994	328,548
24	Lumber and wood products	1,715	676,874	589	637,757	6,930	146,262
25	Furniture and fixtures	1,503	548,908	596	518,846	6,476	125,710
26	Paper and allied products	206	265,340	81	262,620	1,842	48,373
27	Printing and publishing	3,736	865,824	1,413	803,169	9,031	244,232
28	Chemicals and allied products	160	418,559	115	410,705	1,239	45,269
29	Petroleum and coal products	12	56,225	12	56,225	132	3,986
30	Rubber and miscellaneous plastics	372	725,071	305	722,346	6,869	168,219
31	Leather and leather products	397	–	91	–	500–999	–
32	Stone, clay, and glass products	746	270,132	291	260,802	2,754	62,182
33	Primary metal industries	276	659,807	94	650,191	3,220	104,124
34	Fabricated metal products	2,504	1,889,844	1,131	1,848,967	20,124	517,960
35	Industrial machinery and equipment	2,830	2,264,904	1,401	2,214,201	17,393	559,907
36	Electronic and other electric equipment	977	15,265,009	351	14,769,489	40,546	1,508,553
37	Transportation equipment	289	461,852	252	459,593	4,291	117,298
38	Instruments and related products	183	186,814	142	183,634	1,810	56,631
39	Miscellaneous manufacturing industries	2,858	539,890	664	451,969	5,117	118,470

(continued)

(continued from previous page)

SIC code		total firms		firms with paid employees			
		number	sales and receipts (in 000s)	number	sales and receipts (in 000s)	employees	payroll (in 000s)
	Transportation, communications, utilities	**84,554**	**$8,293,935**	**12,735**	**$5,605,332**	**79,682**	**$1,587,106**
41	Local and interurban passenger transportation	14,063	659,007	623	342,789	12,595	201,158
42	Motor freight transportation and warehousing	54,981	4,686,480	7,541	2,697,455	36,786	736,393
44	Water transportation	308	241,589	101	232,683	3,157	37,427
45	Transportation by air	856	378,866	249	348,320	2,603	66,002
46	Pipelines, except natural gas	—	—	—	—	—	—
47	Transportation services	10,649	1,349,374	3,538	1,132,772	18,439	384,254
48	Communications	2,935	817,011	525	722,013	5,077	137,547
49	Electric, gas, and sanitary services	766	—	165	129,300	1,025	24,325
	Wholesale trade	**31,480**	**40,386,625**	**14,125**	**38,746,137**	**94,281**	**2,388,988**
50	Durable goods	18,231	18,939,767	8,657	17,833,390	46,803	1,250,623
51	Nondurable goods	13,251	21,446,858	5,469	20,912,747	47,479	1,138,366
	Retail trade	**155,061**	**32,280,310**	**48,713**	**28,599,447**	**324,474**	**3,892,182**
52	Building materials, hardware, garden supply, and mobile home dealers	2,793	638,260	1,069	579,469	5,191	91,260
53	General merchandise stores	1,867	191,064	224	127,883	1,125	17,827
54	Food stores	18,063	5,483,604	7,806	4,655,236	37,354	473,075
55	Automotive dealers and gasoline service stations	10,950	10,904,860	4,692	10,362,590	25,827	609,416
56	Apparel and accessory stores	9,585	963,116	2,464	753,733	8,289	96,681
57	Home furniture, furnishings, and equipment stores	6,577	1,536,536	2,966	1,391,817	12,032	195,093
58	Eating and drinking places	34,862	7,945,774	21,430	7,411,978	205,446	1,953,014
59	Miscellaneous retail	70,413	4,617,096	8,112	3,316,741	29,209	455,816

(continued)

(continued from previous page)

SIC code	total firms		firms with paid employees			
	number	sales and receipts (in 000s)	number	sales and receipts (in 000s)	employees	payroll (in 000s)
Finance, insurance, real estate (excl. subdividers and developers)	**56,629**	**$6,644,826**	**9,944**	**$4,728,312**	**34,783**	**$949,006**
60 Depository institutions	252	880,287	246	–	5,000–9,999	–
61 Nondepository credit institutions	1,960	355,485	901	325,313	2,866	83,173
62 Security and commodity brokers, dealers, exchanges, and services	2,057	856,081	436	703,154	2,516	236,645
63 Insurance carriers	97	117,044	51	–	500–999	–
64 Insurance agents, brokers, and services	11,915	1,149,109	3,034	792,373	7,793	173,458
65pt Real estate (excluding subdividers and developers)	39,060	3,089,228	5,132	1,777,451	14,495	258,393
67 Holding and other investment offices, except trusts	1,304	197,591	161	134,411	879	33,997
Service industries (excl. membership organizations and private household)	**500,449**	**39,177,767**	**70,838**	**30,406,573**	**463,889**	**11,297,362**
70 Hotels, rooming houses, camps, and other lodging places	1,795	323,505	571	276,971	6,458	77,746
72 Personal services	99,389	2,296,098	9,596	932,445	22,829	258,808
73 Business services	157,907	11,996,181	11,436	9,181,439	170,618	3,982,245
75 Automotive repair, services, and parking	37,357	3,703,521	11,662	3,060,863	43,534	782,424
76 Miscellaneous repair services	12,655	924,818	2,430	682,769	8,219	189,644
78 Motion pictures	3,958	441,936	786	347,484	2,939	91,007
79 Amusement and recreation services	24,622	1,222,398	1,827	745,357	15,308	205,330
80 Health services	44,806	8,068,091	16,900	7,130,702	96,349	2,837,150

(continued)

(continued from previous page)

SIC code		total firms		firms with paid employees			
		number	sales and receipts (in 000s)	number	sales and receipts (in 000s)	employees	payroll (in 000s)
81	Legal services	9,903	$1,917,684	3,638	$1,660,250	13,672	$531,700
82	Educational services	8,170	–	674	–	5,000–9,999	–
83	Social services	44,993	993,072	3,297	582,531	16,976	202,437
84	Museums, art galleries, botanical and zoological gardens	3	–	3	–	0–19	–
87	Engineering, accounting, research, management and related services	51,740	6,587,455	7,712	5,267,832	54,312	1,911,571
89	Services not elsewhere classified	3,203	366,733	357	317,934	2,916	102,975
	Industries not classified	**151,931**	**6,174,133**	**7,909**	**2,045,945**	**21,502**	**432,812**

Note: (–) means data not available or suppressed for purposes of confidentiality.
Source: Bureau of the Census, Minority- and Women-Owned Businesses, *1997 Economic Census, Internet site <www.census.gov/csd/mwb/>*

Distribution of Hispanic-Owned Businesses by Industry and Hispanic Origin, 1997

(percent distribution of firms owned by Hispanics by Hispanic origin, by industry, 1997)

SIC code		Hispanic-owned firms	Cuban	Mexican	Puerto Rican	Spaniard	Latin American	other
	All industries	**100.0%**	**10.4%**	**39.3%**	**5.8%**	**4.8%**	**23.9%**	**15.7%**
	Agricultural services, forestry, fishing	**100.0**	**5.1**	**60.9**	**3.5**	**4.6**	**13.1**	**12.7**
07	Agricultural services	100.0	4.3	62.5	3.7	4.5	13.3	11.7
08	Forestry	100.0	–	58.4	0.0	1.2	6.0	29.9
09	Fishing, hunting, and trapping	100.0	15.8	40.5	2.2	6.6	11.7	23.2
	Mineral industries	**100.0**	**2.1**	**35.3**	**2.9**	**5.5**	**8.4**	**45.8**
10	Metal mining	100.0	0.0	53.3	0.0	0.0	35.6	11.1
12	Coal mining	100.0	11.1	–	0.0	0.0	44.4	–
13	Oil and gas extraction	100.0	1.7	35.2	2.8	5.7	7.7	46.8
14	Nonmetallic minerals, except fuels	100.0	16.4	25.5	7.3	3.6	–	45.5
	Construction industries, subdividers, developers	**100.0**	**8.1**	**49.7**	**4.2**	**4.6**	**18.5**	**14.9**
15	Building construction, general contractors and operative builders	100.0	8.9	50.9	6.3	6.8	12.3	14.9
16	Heavy construction contractors other than buildings	100.0	7.2	49.8	1.1	7.1	12.8	21.9
17	Special trade contractors	100.0	8.0	49.6	4.1	4.3	19.4	14.7
6552	Subdividers and developers not elsewhere classified (excl. cemeteries)	100.0	–	40.9	2.0	7.2	–	18.9

(continued)

(continued from previous page)

SIC code	Manufacturing	Hispanic-owned firms 100.0%	Cuban 10.6%	Mexican 44.3%	Puerto Rican 4.6%	Spaniard 5.3%	Latin American 22.5%	other 12.8%
20	Food and kindred products	100.0	7.6	48.7	5.1	3.8	25.0	9.8
21	Tobacco products	100.0	95.7	0.0	0.0	0.0	0.0	4.3
22	Textile mill products	100.0	19.6	28.6	0.0	0.0	25.9	25.9
23	Apparel and other textile products	100.0	12.9	44.8	2.4	2.7	28.6	8.6
24	Lumber and wood products	100.0	6.9	41.4	4.3	4.3	15.6	27.5
25	Furniture and fixtures	100.0	15.8	43.3	3.6	8.3	20.3	8.9
26	Paper and allied products	100.0	10.7	42.7	7.3	4.9	22.3	11.7
27	Printing and publishing	100.0	13.5	37.6	6.9	7.6	22.8	11.6
28	Chemicals and allied products	100.0	26.9	18.8	1.3	–	31.9	6.9
29	Petroleum and coal products	100.0	0.0	66.7	0.0	8.3	–	8.3
30	Rubber and miscellaneous plastics	100.0	11.6	43.3	9.4	4.3	16.9	14.8
31	Leather and leather products	100.0	4.8	41.3	4.5	16.6	27.2	5.8
32	Stone, clay, and glass products	100.0	5.8	47.7	3.6	6.2	22.4	14.3
33	Primary metal industries	100.0	8.7	59.8	4.3	2.9	13.0	11.2
34	Fabricated metal products	100.0	7.7	51.9	3.6	5.5	18.2	13.2
35	Industrial machinery and equipment	100.0	5.6	51.0	5.0	5.9	22.5	10.0
36	Electronic and other electric equipment	100.0	7.8	45.8	6.0	8.9	17.2	14.2
37	Transportation equipment	100.0	20.1	47.8	4.5	4.5	20.1	3.5
38	Instruments and related products	100.0	15.8	23.0	9.3	5.5	24.0	21.9
39	Miscellaneous manufacturing industries	100.0	11.3	40.7	5.3	3.1	22.1	17.4

(continued)

(continued from previous page)

SIC code		Hispanic-owned firms	Cuban	Mexican	Puerto Rican	Spaniard	Latin American	other
	Transportation, communications, utilities	**100.0%**	**10.6%**	**34.3%**	**5.0%**	**3.2%**	**31.8%**	**15.0%**
41	Local and interurban passenger transportation	100.0	5.8	13.3	5.6	–	58.5	12.7
42	Motor freight transportation and warehousing	100.0	11.5	40.6	4.7	2.3	25.5	15.4
44	Water transportation	100.0	23.4	15.6	5.2	11.7	19.5	25.0
45	Transportation by air	100.0	13.8	19.3	3.7	8.3	43.0	11.9
46	Pipelines, except natural gas	–	–	–	–	–	–	–
47	Transportation services	100.0	12.1	31.7	5.5	4.0	32.2	14.5
48	Communications	100.0	11.4	31.7	8.2	8.9	22.5	17.3
49	Electric, gas, and sanitary services	100.0	6.5	44.4	5.9	5.5	13.2	24.5
	Wholesale trade	**100.0**	**14.9**	**35.0**	**4.8**	**5.6**	**24.6**	**15.1**
50	Durable goods	100.0	14.8	34.9	4.7	5.9	24.4	15.3
51	Nondurable goods	100.0	14.9	35.2	4.9	5.2	24.9	14.8
	Retail trade	**100.0**	**9.0**	**45.7**	**5.8**	**4.3**	**20.3**	**14.8**
52	Building materials, hardware, garden supply, and mobile home dealers	100.0	11.1	44.1	5.4	9.2	14.2	16.1
53	General merchandise stores	100.0	8.3	44.4	6.5	5.6	19.4	15.7
54	Food stores	100.0	8.2	41.6	6.9	2.6	30.2	10.5
55	Automotive dealers and gasoline service stations	100.0	12.2	47.9	4.2	3.5	16.8	15.4
56	Apparel and accessory stores	100.0	12.9	43.5	5.1	2.6	24.0	12.0
57	Home furniture, furnishings, and equipment stores	100.0	10.5	46.0	5.9	5.5	18.3	13.8
58	Eating and drinking places	100.0	5.7	55.4	3.8	3.1	18.8	13.2
59	Miscellaneous retail	100.0	9.7	42.0	6.9	5.4	19.0	16.9

(continued)

(continued from previous page)

SIC code		Hispanic-owned firms	Cuban	Mexican	Puerto Rican	Spaniard	Latin American	other
	Finance, insurance, real estate (excl. subdividers and developers)	**100.0%**	**16.3%**	**34.5%**	**6.3%**	**9.1%**	**19.6%**	**14.3%**
60	Depository institutions	100.0	12.7	43.3	17.1	3.2	9.9	13.9
61	Nondepository credit institutions	100.0	27.2	35.2	4.9	4.6	14.9	13.0
62	Security and commodity brokers, dealers, exchanges, and services	100.0	10.1	33.3	7.1	7.9	17.7	23.9
63	Insurance carriers	100.0	15.5	42.3	7.2	7.2	15.5	13.4
64	Insurance agents, brokers, and services	100.0	15.7	35.1	5.8	9.6	17.7	16.1
65pt	Real estate (excluding subdividers and developers)	100.0	16.1	34.2	6.5	9.2	20.5	13.5
67	Holding and other investment offices, except trusts	100.0	21.2	33.9	4.7	9.8	22.1	8.4
	Service industries (excl. membership organizations and private household)	**100.0**	**11.0**	**36.6**	**6.7**	**4.8**	**25.2**	**15.7**
70	Hotels, rooming houses, camps, and other lodging places	100.0	9.6	31.2	5.4	8.1	21.5	24.3
72	Personal services	100.0	8.2	43.0	6.5	4.3	23.0	15.0
73	Business services	100.0	10.9	32.4	5.8	4.3	30.2	16.4
75	Automotive repair, services, and parking	100.0	9.9	44.8	4.3	4.0	23.6	13.4
76	Miscellaneous repair services	100.0	11.4	41.4	6.0	5.3	22.1	13.8
78	Motion pictures	100.0	8.0	38.0	7.7	7.1	21.9	17.4
79	Amusement and recreation services	100.0	8.8	37.7	6.5	8.3	18.5	20.1
80	Health services	100.0	19.6	26.3	9.9	5.0	26.3	13.0

(continued)

(continued from previous page)

SIC code		Hispanic-owned firms	Cuban	Mexican	Puerto Rican	Spaniard	Latin American	other
81	Legal services	100.0%	14.4%	38.8%	8.7%	7.2%	14.2%	16.7%
82	Educational services	100.0	9.3	31.3	10.8	6.5	25.2	17.0
83	Social services	100.0	4.2	43.9	8.6	2.6	23.5	17.2
84	Museums, art galleries, botanical and zoological gardens	100.0	–	0.0	0.0	0.0	33.3	0.0
87	Engineering, accounting, research, management and related services	100.0	16.9	32.1	6.8	6.5	22.3	15.4
89	Services not elsewhere classified	100.0	12.4	35.6	7.7	10.2	22.0	12.0
	Industries not classified	**100.0**	**10.5**	**30.6**	**5.6**	**4.3**	**29.5**	**19.5**

Note: (–) means data not available or suppressed for purposes of confidentiality.
Source: Bureau of the Census, Minority- and Women-Owned Businesses, 1997 Economic Census, Internet site <www.census.gov/csd/mwb/>; calculations by New Strategist

Hispanic-Owned Businesses by Legal Form of Organization, Receipt Size, and Employees, 1997

(number and percent distribution of Hispanic-owned firms by legal form of organization, size of receipts, and number of employees, 1997)

	total	percent distribution
Total Hispanic-owned firms	**1,199,896**	**100.0%**
Legal form of organization		
C corporations	78,463	6.5
Subchapter S corporations	65,244	5.4
Individual proprietorships	1,027,411	85.6
Partnerships	27,998	2.3
Other	781	0.1
Size of receipts		
Under $5,000	263,071	21.9
$5,000 to $9,999	212,214	17.7
$10,000 to $24,999	273,321	22.8
$25,000 to $49,999	144,941	12.1
$50,000 to $99,999	107,489	9.0
$100,000 to $249,999	96,789	8.1
$250,000 to $499,999	47,816	4.0
$500,000 to $999,999	27,590	2.3
$1,000,000 or more	26,666	2.2
Number of employees		
Firms with employees	211,884	100.0
No employees*	29,118	13.7
1 to 3 employees	111,727	52.7
5 to 9 employees	37,727	17.8
10 to 19 employees	19,860	9.4
20 to 49 employees	9,260	4.4
50 to 99 employees	3,070	1.4
100 to 499 employees	1,006	0.5
500 employees or more	115	0.1

* Firms that reported annual payroll but no employees on the payroll during the specified period in 1997.
Source: Bureau of the Census, Hispanics, 1997 Economic Census, Survey of Minority-Owned Business Enterprises, Company Statistics Series, EC97CS-4, 2001; calculations by New Strategist

Hispanic-Owned Businesses by State, 1997

(number of total firms and receipts and number and percent distribution of Hispanic-owned firms and receipts in the ten states with the largest number of Hispanic-owned firms, and Hispanic share of total firms and receipts, 1997)

	total firms	Hispanic firms			total sales and receipts (in millions)	Hispanic sales and receipts		
		number	percent distribution	percent of total		amount (in millions)	percent distribution	percent of total
Total firms	**20,821,934**	**1,199,896**	**100.0%**	**5.8%**	**$18,553,243**	**$186,275**	**100.0%**	**1.0%**
Total in top ten states	**9,790,822**	**1,033,759**	**86.2**	**10.6**	**8,613,961**	**159,520**	**85.6**	**1.9**
California	2,565,734	336,405	28.0	13.1	2,178,292	51,682	27.7	2.4
Texas	1,525,972	240,396	20.0	15.8	1,415,536	39,482	21.2	2.8
Florida	1,301,920	193,902	16.2	14.9	828,429	35,351	19.0	4.3
New York	1,509,829	104,189	8.7	6.9	1,488,913	10,311	5.5	0.7
New Jersey	654,227	36,116	3.0	5.5	690,008	5,107	2.7	0.7
Illinois	882,053	31,010	2.6	3.5	993,117	4,815	2.6	0.5
Arizona	329,031	28,894	2.4	8.8	247,191	4,227	2.3	1.7
New Mexico	131,685	28,285	2.4	21.5	79,752	3,668	2.0	4.6
Colorado	410,249	20,859	1.7	5.1	277,630	3,068	1.6	1.1
Virginia	480,122	13,703	1.1	2.9	415,093	1,809	1.0	0.4

Source: Bureau of the Census, Hispanics, 1997 Economic Census, Survey of Minority-Owned Business Enterprises, Company Statistics Series, EC97CS-4, 2001; calculations by New Strategist

Hispanic-Owned Businesses by Metropolitan Area, 1997

(number and percent distribution of Hispanic-owned firms and receipts in the ten metropolitan areas with the largest number of Hispanic-owned firms, and metropolitan area's share of total Hispanic firms and receipts in state, 1997)

	firms			sales and receipts		
	number	percent distribution	percent of Hispanic firms in state	amount (in millions)	percent distribution	percent of Hispanic receipts in state
Total Hispanic firms/receipts	**1,199,896**	**100.0%**	–	**$186,275**	**100.0%**	–
Total in top metropolitan areas	**555,290**	**46.3**	–	**97,734**	**52.5**	–
Los Angeles–Long Beach, CA PMSA	136,678	11.4	40.6%	16,246	8.7%	31.4%
Miami, FL PMSA	120,605	10.1	62.2	26,730	14.3	75.6
New York, NY PMSA	84,880	7.1	81.5	8,054	4.3	78.1
Houston, TX PMSA	41,769	3.5	17.4	12,415	6.7	31.4
San Antonio, TX MSA	34,834	2.9	14.5	7,697	4.1	19.5
Riverside–San Bernardino, CA PMSA	32,198	2.7	9.6	5,405	2.9	10.5
San Diego, CA MSA	28,087	2.3	8.3	5,217	2.8	10.1
Chicago, IL PMSA	27,482	2.3	88.6	4,554	2.4	94.6
Dallas, TX PMSA	24,573	2.0	10.2	2,753	1.5	7.0
Orange County, CA PMSA	24,184	2.0	7.2	8,663	4.7	16.8

Note: For definitions of PMSA and MSA, see glossary. (–) means not applicable.
Source: Bureau of the Census, Hispanics, 1997 Economic Census, Survey of Minority-Owned Business Enterprises, Company Statistics Series, EC97CS-4, 2001; calculations by New Strategist

Hispanics: Education

Hispanic Educational Attainment Lags behind That of Whites, Blacks, and Asians

Hispanics are much less educated than the average American because many are immigrants who came to the United States as adults with few years of schooling. Only 57 percent of Hispanics had a high school diploma in 2000, versus 84 percent of the total population. The proportion of Hispanics with a high school diploma ranges from 51 percent among Mexican Americans to 73 percent of Cuban Americans.

Only 11 percent of Hispanics have a college degree, versus 26 percent of the total population. More than 1.4 million Hispanics were enrolled in college in 2000, 51 percent of them in four-year undergraduate degree programs.

Hispanics earned nearly 75,000 bachelor's degrees in 1999–2000, or 6 percent of all such degrees awarded that year. Hispanics earned 17 percent of bachelor's degrees in foreign languages and literature. At the first-professional degree level, Hispanics earned 6 percent of law degrees.

■ Because so many Hispanics are from countries such as Mexico where adults have little schooling, the educational attainment of the Hispanic population as a whole will remain well below average.

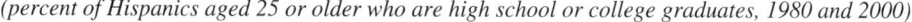

Hispanic educational attainment is growing slowly

(percent of Hispanics aged 25 or older who are high school or college graduates, 1980 and 2000)

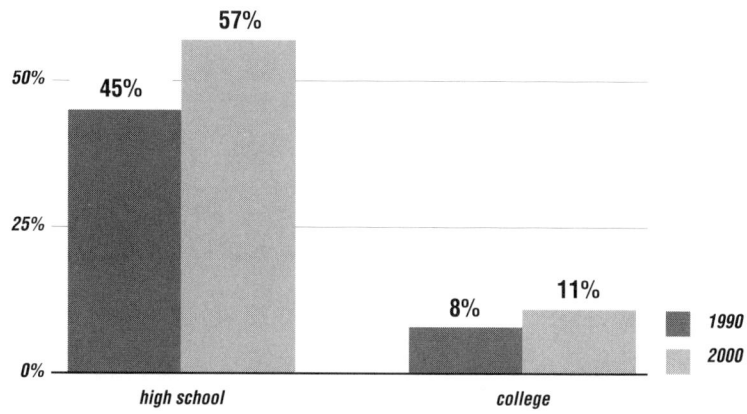

Educational Attainment of Hispanics by Sex, 2000

(number and percent distribution of Hispanics aged 25 or older by educational attainment and sex, 2000; numbers in thousands)

	total		men		women	
	number	*percent*	*number*	*percent*	*number*	*percent*
Total Hispanics	**17,150**	**100.0%**	**8,365**	**100.0%**	**8,785**	**100.0%**
Not a high school graduate	7,367	43.0	3,632	43.4	3,735	42.5
High school graduate or more	9,784	57.0	4,734	56.6	5,051	57.5
High school graduate only	4,791	27.9	2,370	28.3	2,421	27.6
Some college or associate's degree	3,171	18.5	1,469	17.6	1,703	19.4
Bachelor's degree or more	1,822	10.6	895	10.7	927	10.6
Bachelor's degree only	1,249	7.3	611	7.3	638	7.3
Master's degree	372	2.2	175	2.1	197	2.2
Professional degree	117	0.7	58	0.7	59	0.7
Doctoral degree	84	0.5	51	0.6	33	0.4

Source: Bureau of the Census, Educational Attainment in the United States: March 2000 (Update), *detailed tables for Current Population Report P20-536, 2000; Internet site <www.census.gov/population/socdemo/education/p20-536/tab01.txt>; calculations by New Strategist*

Educational Attainment of Hispanic Men by Age, 2000

(number and percent distribution of Hispanic men aged 25 or older by age and educational attainment, 2000; numbers in thousands)

| | total | not a high school graduate | high school graduate or more | | | | | bachelor's degree or more | | | | |
			total	high school graduate only	some college	associate's degree	total	bachelor's degree only	master's degree	professional degree	doctoral degree
Total Hispanic men	**8,365**	**3,632**	**4,734**	**2,370**	**1,091**	**378**	**895**	**611**	**175**	**58**	**51**
Aged 25 to 29	1,416	578	840	428	226	68	118	97	12	9	–
Aged 30 to 34	1,439	595	843	442	188	85	128	100	18	4	6
Aged 35 to 39	1,422	573	850	474	178	52	146	109	18	10	9
Aged 40 to 44	1,058	423	635	291	163	48	133	89	28	12	4
Aged 45 to 49	810	330	479	231	113	38	97	55	32	3	7
Aged 50 to 54	679	289	390	156	89	31	114	70	28	7	9
Aged 55 to 59	461	212	248	125	48	18	57	28	20	4	5
Aged 60 to 64	359	207	152	76	34	8	34	24	7	2	1
Aged 65 or older	720	425	294	147	51	29	67	40	11	7	9
Aged 65 to 69	273	140	131	56	25	21	29	18	6	3	2
Aged 70 to 74	196	114	83	45	12	8	18	12	4	0	2
Aged 75 or older	251	170	83	47	15	0	21	11	1	4	5

(continued)

(continued from previous page)

	total	not a high school graduate	high school graduate or more				bachelor's degree or more				
			total	high school graduate only	some college	associate's degree	total	bachelor's degree only	master's degree	professional degree	doctoral degree
Total Hispanic men	**100.0%**	**43.4%**	**56.6%**	**28.3%**	**13.0%**	**4.5%**	**10.7%**	**7.3%**	**2.1%**	**0.7%**	**0.6%**
Aged 25 to 29	100.0	40.8	59.3	30.2	16.0	4.8	8.3	6.9	0.8	0.6	–
Aged 30 to 34	100.0	41.3	58.6	30.7	13.1	5.9	8.9	6.9	1.3	0.3	0.4
Aged 35 to 39	100.0	40.3	59.8	33.3	12.5	3.7	10.3	7.7	1.3	0.7	0.6
Aged 40 to 44	100.0	40.0	60.0	27.5	15.4	4.5	12.6	8.4	2.6	1.1	0.4
Aged 45 to 49	100.0	40.7	59.1	28.5	14.0	4.7	12.0	6.8	4.0	0.4	0.9
Aged 50 to 54	100.0	42.6	57.4	23.0	13.1	4.6	16.8	10.3	4.1	1.0	1.3
Aged 55 to 59	100.0	46.0	53.8	27.1	10.4	3.9	12.4	6.1	4.3	0.9	1.1
Aged 60 to 64	100.0	57.7	42.3	21.2	9.5	2.2	9.5	6.7	1.9	0.6	0.3
Aged 65 or older	100.0	59.0	40.8	20.4	7.1	4.0	9.3	5.6	1.5	1.0	1.3
Aged 65 to 69	100.0	51.3	48.0	20.5	9.2	7.7	10.6	6.6	2.2	1.1	0.7
Aged 70 to 74	100.0	58.2	42.3	23.0	6.1	4.1	9.2	6.1	2.0	0.0	1.0
Aged 75 or older	100.0	67.7	33.1	18.7	6.0	0.0	8.4	4.4	0.4	1.6	2.0

Note: (–) means sample is too small to make a reliable estimate.
Source: Bureau of the Census, Educational Attainment in the United States: March 2000 (Update), detailed tables for Current Population Report P20-536, 2000; Internet site <www.census.gov/population/socdemo/education/p20-536/tab01.txt>; calculations by New Strategist

Educational Attainment of Hispanic Women by Age, 2000

(number and percent distribution of Hispanic women aged 25 or older by age and educational attainment, 2000; numbers in thousands)

	total	not a high school graduate	high school graduate or more				bachelor's degree or more					
			total	high school graduate only	some college	associate's degree	total	bachelor's degree only	master's degree	professional degree	doctoral degree
Total Hispanic women	**8,785**	**3,735**	**5,051**	**2,421**	**1,222**	**481**	**927**	**638**	**197**	**59**	**33**
Aged 25 to 29	1,415	476	939	421	268	94	156	118	26	10	2
Aged 30 to 34	1,390	527	863	409	223	86	145	110	19	9	7
Aged 35 to 39	1,388	459	928	406	211	107	204	143	50	11	0
Aged 40 to 44	1,105	432	672	300	171	68	133	89	24	8	12
Aged 45 to 49	771	327	445	203	102	36	104	70	29	5	–
Aged 50 to 54	759	339	420	217	95	32	76	43	22	7	4
Aged 55 to 59	529	292	237	129	53	20	35	19	8	7	1
Aged 60 to 64	396	210	184	126	26	15	17	7	7	1	2
Aged 65 or older	1,032	672	360	212	71	23	54	39	11	–	4
Aged 65 to 69	373	227	143	76	28	16	23	15	7	–	1
Aged 70 to 74	290	189	99	64	27	1	7	6	1	–	–
Aged 75 or older	370	254	117	72	16	5	24	18	3	–	3

(continued)

(continued from previous page)

	total	not a high school graduate	high school graduate or more					bachelor's degree or more			
			total	high school graduate only	some college	associate's degree	total	bachelor's degree only	master's degree	professional degree	doctoral degree
Total Hispanic women	**100.0%**	**42.5%**	**57.5%**	**27.6%**	**13.9%**	**5.5%**	**10.6%**	**7.3%**	**2.2%**	**0.7%**	**0.4%**
Aged 25 to 29	100.0	33.6	66.4	29.8	18.9	6.6	11.0	8.3	1.8	0.7	0.1
Aged 30 to 34	100.0	37.9	62.1	29.4	16.0	6.2	10.4	7.9	1.4	0.6	0.5
Aged 35 to 39	100.0	33.1	66.9	29.3	15.2	7.7	14.7	10.3	3.6	0.8	0.0
Aged 40 to 44	100.0	39.1	60.8	27.1	15.5	6.2	12.0	8.1	2.2	0.7	1.1
Aged 45 to 49	100.0	42.4	57.7	26.3	13.2	4.7	13.5	9.1	3.8	0.6	–
Aged 50 to 54	100.0	44.7	55.3	28.6	12.5	4.2	10.0	5.7	2.9	0.9	0.5
Aged 55 to 59	100.0	55.2	44.8	24.4	10.0	3.8	6.6	3.6	1.5	1.3	0.2
Aged 60 to 64	100.0	53.0	46.5	31.8	6.6	3.8	4.3	1.8	1.8	0.3	0.5
Aged 65 or older	100.0	65.1	34.9	20.5	6.9	2.2	5.2	3.8	1.1	–	0.4
Aged 65 to 69	100.0	60.9	38.3	20.4	7.5	4.3	6.2	4.0	1.9	–	0.3
Aged 70 to 74	100.0	65.2	34.1	22.1	9.3	0.3	2.4	2.1	0.3	–	–
Aged 75 or older	100.0	68.6	31.6	19.5	4.3	1.4	6.5	4.9	0.8	–	0.8

Note: (–) means sample is too small to make a reliable estimate.
Source: Bureau of the Census, Educational Attainment in the United States: March 2000 (Update), detailed tables for Current Population Report P20-536, 2000; Internet site <www.census.gov/population/socdemo/education/p20-536/tab01.txt>; calculations by New Strategist

Educational Attainment of Hispanics by Ethnicity, 2000

(number and percent distribution of Hispanics aged 25 or older by educational attainment and ethnicity, 2000; numbers in thousands)

	total Hispanics	Mexican	Puerto Rican	Cuban	Central and South American	other Hispanic
Total Hispanics	**17,150**	**10,625**	**1,612**	**965**	**2,768**	**1,180**
Not a high school graduate	7,367	5,209	575	260	988	335
High school graduate or more	9,783	5,416	1,037	705	1,781	845
High school graduate only	4,791	2,801	476	318	816	381
Some college or associate's degree	3,171	1,877	352	164	484	293
Bachelor's degree or more	1,821	738	209	222	481	171
Bachelor's degree	1,249	546	138	134	326	105
Advanced degree	572	192	71	88	155	66
Total Hispanics	**100.0%**	**100.0%**	**100.0%**	**100.0%**	**100.0%**	**100.0%**
Not a high school graduate	43.0	49.0	35.7	26.9	35.7	28.4
High school graduate or more	57.0	51.0	64.3	73.1	64.3	71.6
High school graduate only	27.9	26.4	29.5	33.0	29.5	32.3
Some college or associate's degree	18.5	17.7	21.8	17.0	17.5	24.8
Bachelor's degree or more	10.6	6.9	13.0	23.0	17.4	14.5
Bachelor's degree	7.3	5.1	8.6	13.9	11.8	8.9
Advanced degree	3.3	1.8	4.4	9.1	5.6	5.6

Source: Bureau of the Census, Current Population Survey, Internet site <www.census.gov/population/socdemo/ hispanic/p20-535/tab07-1 .txt>; calculations by New Strategist

Hispanic High School and College Graduates by Age and Sex, 2000

(percent of Hispanics aged 25 or older who are high school or college graduates by age and sex, 2000)

	total	men	women
High school graduates			
Total Hispanics	**57.0%**	**56.6%**	**57.5%**
Aged 25 to 29	62.8	59.2	66.4
Aged 30 to 34	60.3	58.6	62.1
Aged 35 to 39	63.3	59.8	66.9
Aged 40 to 44	60.5	60.1	60.8
Aged 45 to 49	58.4	59.2	57.6
Aged 50 to 54	56.3	57.5	55.3
Aged 55 to 59	49.1	53.6	45.1
Aged 60 to 64	44.6	42.2	46.7
Aged 65 or older	37.4	41.0	34.9
Aged 65 to 69	42.7	48.1	38.7
Aged 70 to 74	37.3	41.8	34.3
Aged 75 or older	31.9	32.6	31.4
College graduates			
Total Hispanics	**10.6**	**10.7**	**10.6**
Aged 25 to 29	9.7	8.3	11.0
Aged 30 to 34	9.7	8.9	10.5
Aged 35 to 39	12.5	10.3	14.7
Aged 40 to 44	12.3	12.6	12.1
Aged 45 to 49	12.7	12.0	13.4
Aged 50 to 54	13.2	16.8	10.0
Aged 55 to 59	9.3	12.3	6.7
Aged 60 to 64	6.9	9.4	4.6
Aged 65 or older	6.9	9.3	5.3
Aged 65 to 69	8.2	10.6	6.4
Aged 70 to 74	5.1	9.0	2.4
Aged 75 or older	7.1	8.2	6.4

Source: Bureau of the Census, Educational Attainment in the United States: March 2000 (Update), *detailed tables for Current Population Report P20-536, 2000; Internet site <www.census.gov/population/socdemo/ education/p20-536/tab01a.txt>*

Hispanic High School and College Graduates by Age and Region, 2000

(percent of Hispanics aged 25 or older who are high school or college graduates, by age and region, 2000)

	Northeast	Midwest	South	West
High school graduates				
Total Hispanics	**60.2%**	**58.7%**	**60.0%**	**53.2%**
Aged 25 to 34	66.7	59.0	65.6	57.7
Aged 35 to 44	69.6	64.7	64.7	56.5
Aged 45 to 54	62.1	60.7	61.2	52.1
Aged 55 to 64	41.7	42.2	50.8	46.5
Aged 65 or older	31.0	39.7	40.7	36.2
College graduates				
Total Hispanics	**12.4**	**10.9**	**13.6**	**7.6**
Aged 25 to 34	13.3	11.3	11.5	6.9
Aged 35 to 44	13.7	11.9	16.0	9.0
Aged 45 to 54	15.0	12.9	17.4	8.6
Aged 55 to 64	8.5	5.9	10.3	6.3
Aged 65 or older	5.0	1.5	9.9	5.0

Source: Bureau of the Census, Educational Attainment in the United States: March 2000 (Update), *Detailed tables for Current Population Reports, P20-536, 2000; Internet site <www.census.gov/population/socdemo/education/p20-536/tab12.txt>; calculations by New Strategist*

Hispanic High School and College Graduates by State, 2000

(percent of Hispanics aged 25 or older who are high school or college graduates, for the 25 largest states, 2000)

	high school graduate or more	college graduate
Total Hispanics	**57.0%**	**10.6%**
Alabama	–	–
Arizona	55.4	5.6
California	51.3	7.1
Colorado	63.1	9.8
Florida	70.5	20.4
Georgia	58.0	13.3
Illinois	55.6	9.5
Indiana	67.5	19.1
Kentucky	–	–
Louisiana	–	–
Maryland	55.0	21.7
Massachusetts	55.8	8.8
Michigan	69.6	10.7
Minnesota	–	–
Missouri	–	–
New Jersey	67.8	11.2
New York	57.3	12.5
North Carolina	41.4	11.3
Ohio	65.2	15.9
Pennsylvania	59.8	15.0
Tennessee	–	–
Texas	54.1	8.7
Virginia	72.3	23.7
Washington	52.4	12.3
Wisconsin	–	–

Note: (–) means sample is too small to make a reliable estimate.
Source: Bureau of the Census, Educational Attainment in the United States: March 2000 (Update), Detailed tables for Current Population Reports, P20-536, 2000; Internet site <www.census.gov/population/socdemo/ education/p20-536/tab14.txt>

School Enrollment of Hispanics by Age and Sex, 2000

(number and percent of Hispanics aged 3 or older enrolled in school, by age and sex, October 2000; numbers in thousands)

	total		men		women	
	number	*percent*	*number*	*percent*	*number*	*percent*
Total Hispanics	**10,163**	**32.6%**	**5,037**	**32.5%**	**5,127**	**32.8%**
Aged 3 to 4	518	35.9	233	31.9	285	40.0
Aged 5 to 6	1,390	94.3	733	95.4	657	93.1
Aged 7 to 9	1,936	97.5	926	96.6	1,011	98.4
Aged 10 to 13	2,437	97.4	1,285	98.4	1,152	96.4
Aged 14 to 15	1,093	96.2	558	96.9	535	95.4
Aged 16 to 17	959	87.0	474	85.7	485	88.3
Aged 18 to 19	617	49.5	315	48.0	302	51.1
Aged 20 to 21	311	26.1	148	24.2	162	28.1
Aged 22 to 24	309	18.2	137	15.2	172	21.6
Aged 25 to 29	198	7.4	67	5.1	131	9.5
Aged 30 to 34	160	5.6	82	5.7	78	5.5
Aged 35 to 44	173	3.4	60	2.3	113	4.4
Aged 45 to 54	48	1.6	18	1.2	30	2.0
Aged 55 or older	14	0.4	–	–	14	0.7

Note: (–) means sample is too small to make a reliable estimate.
Source: Bureau of the Census, Current Population Survey, Internet site <www.census.gov/population/socdemo/school/ppl-148/tab01.txt>

Hispanic Families with Children in College, 2000

(total number of Hispanic families, number with children aged 18 to 24, and number and percent with children aged 18 to 24 attending college full-time as of October 2000, by household income in 1999; numbers in thousands)

	total	with children aged 18–24	with one or more children attending college full-time		
			number	percent of total families	percent of families with children 18–24
Total Hispanic families	**7,758**	**1,753**	**580**	**7.5%**	**33.1%**
Under $20,000	2,238	436	74	3.3	17.0
$20,000 to $29,999	1,399	341	118	8.4	34.6
$30,000 to $39,999	1,007	203	63	6.3	31.0
$40,000 to $49,999	585	159	79	13.5	49.7
$50,000 to $74,999	903	219	97	10.7	44.3
$75,000 or more	658	140	81	12.3	57.9

Note: Numbers will not add to total because not reported is not shown.
Source: Bureau of the Census, Current Population Survey, Internet site <www.census.gov/population/socdemo/school/ppl-148/tab15.txt>

College Enrollment of Hispanics by Age, 2000

(number and percent distribution of Hispanics aged 15 or older enrolled in college by age and type of school, October 2000; numbers in thousands)

	total	undergraduate			*graduate*
		total	*two-year*	*four-year*	
Total Hispanics enrolled	**1,426**	**1,228**	**506**	**722**	**198**
Aged 15 to 17	24	22	13	9	2
Aged 18 to 19	348	341	167	174	7
Aged 20 to 21	268	263	93	170	5
Aged 22 to 24	281	235	76	159	46
Aged 25 to 29	167	133	47	86	34
Aged 30 to 34	141	101	40	61	40
Aged 35 to 39	99	79	39	40	20
Aged 40 to 44	48	38	18	20	10
Aged 45 to 49	21	8	8	–	13
Aged 50 to 54	21	5	5	–	16
Aged 55 or older	6	1	–	1	5
Percent distribution by age					
Total Hispanics enrolled	**100.0%**	**100.0%**	**100.0%**	**100.0%**	**100.0%**
Aged 15 to 17	1.7	1.8	2.6	1.2	1.0
Aged 18 to 19	24.4	27.8	33.0	24.1	3.5
Aged 20 to 21	18.8	21.4	18.4	23.5	2.5
Aged 22 to 24	19.7	19.1	15.0	22.0	23.2
Aged 25 to 29	11.7	10.8	9.3	11.9	17.2
Aged 30 to 34	9.9	8.2	7.9	8.4	20.2
Aged 35 to 39	6.9	6.4	7.7	5.5	10.1
Aged 40 to 44	3.4	3.1	3.6	2.8	5.1
Aged 45 to 49	1.5	0.7	1.6	–	6.6
Aged 50 to 54	1.5	0.4	1.0	–	8.1
Aged 55 or older	0.4	0.1	–	0.1	2.5

(continued)

(continued from previous page)

	total	undergraduate			graduate
		total	two-year	four-year	
Percent distribution by type of school					
Total Hispanics enrolled	**100.0%**	**86.1%**	**35.5%**	**50.6%**	**13.9%**
Aged 15 to 17	100.0	91.7	54.2	37.5	8.3
Aged 18 to 19	100.0	98.0	48.0	50.0	2.0
Aged 20 to 21	100.0	98.1	34.7	63.4	1.9
Aged 22 to 24	100.0	83.6	27.0	56.6	16.4
Aged 25 to 29	100.0	79.6	28.1	51.5	20.4
Aged 30 to 34	100.0	71.6	28.4	43.3	28.4
Aged 35 to 39	100.0	79.8	39.4	40.4	20.2
Aged 40 to 44	100.0	79.2	37.5	41.7	20.8
Aged 45 to 49	100.0	38.1	38.1	–	61.9
Aged 50 to 54	100.0	23.8	23.8	–	76.2
Aged 55 or older	100.0	16.7	–	16.7	83.3

Note: (–) means sample is too small to make a reliable estimate.
Source: Bureau of the Census, Current Population Survey, Internet site <www.census.gov/population/socdemo/ school/ppl-148/tab09.txt>; calculations by New Strategist

Associate's Degrees Earned by Hispanics by Field of Study, 1999–2000

(total number of associate's degrees conferred and number and percent earned by Hispanics, by field of study, 1999–2000)

	total	earned by Hispanics	
		number	percent
Total associate's degrees	**564,933**	**51,541**	**9.1%**
Agriculture and natural resources	6,667	86	1.3
Architecture and related programs	392	30	7.7
Area, ethnic, and cultural studies	259	30	11.6
Biological, life sciences	1,434	142	9.9
Business	92,274	9,275	10.1
Communications	2,754	228	8.3
Communications technologies	1,709	162	9.5
Computer and information sciences	20,450	1,695	8.3
Construction trades	2,337	112	4.8
Education	8,226	994	12.1
Engineering	1,752	163	9.3
Engineering-related technologies	35,395	3,733	10.5
English language and literature, letters	947	84	8.9
Foreign languages and literatures	501	99	19.8
Health professions and related sciences	84,081	5,406	6.4
Home economics	8,381	1,079	12.9
Law and legal studies	7,265	735	10.1
Liberal arts and sciences, general studies, and humanities	187,454	18,856	10.1
Library science	98	6	6.1
Mathematics	675	101	15.0
Mechanics and repairers	11,614	1,020	8.8
Multi/interdisciplinary studies	11,784	1,058	9.0
Parks, recreation, leisure, and fitness	855	62	7.3
Philosophy and religion	63	7	11.1
Physical sciences	2,460	201	8.2
Precision production trades	11,814	1,052	8.9
Protective services	16,298	1,609	9.9
Psychology	1,455	200	13.7
Public administration and services	3,656	514	14.1
R.O.T.C. and military technologies	65	13	20.0
Social sciences and history	5,136	799	15.6
Theological studies, religious vocations	636	30	4.7
Transportation and material moving	1,021	82	8.0
Visual and performing arts	17,100	1,612	9.4
Not classified	2,798	266	9.5

Source: National Center for Education Statistics, Digest of Education Statistics 2001, *Internet site <http://nces.ed.gov/pubsearch/pubsinfo.asp?pubid=2002130>; calculations by New Strategist*

Bachelor's Degrees Earned by Hispanics by Field of Study, 1999–2000

(total number of bachelor's degrees conferred and number and percent earned by Hispanics, by field of study, 1999–2000)

	total	earned by Hispanics number	earned by Hispanics percent
Total bachelor's degrees	**1,237,875**	**74,963**	**6.1%**
Agriculture and natural resources	24,247	736	3.0
Architecture and related programs	8,462	584	6.9
Area, ethnic, and cultural studies	6,381	736	11.5
Biological, life sciences	63,532	3,326	5.2
Business	257,709	14,869	5.8
Communications	55,760	2,934	5.3
Communications technologies	1,150	111	9.7
Computer and information sciences	36,195	1,828	5.1
Construction trades	186	4	2.2
Education	108,168	4,865	4.5
Engineering	58,427	3,187	5.5
Engineering-related technologies	13,872	776	5.6
English language and literature, letters	50,920	2,757	5.4
Foreign languages and literatures	14,968	2,536	16.9
Health professions and related sciences	78,458	3,506	4.5
Home economics	17,779	672	3.8
Law and legal studies	1,925	155	8.1
Liberal arts and sciences, general studies, and humanities	36,104	3,482	9.6
Library science	154	6	3.9
Mathematics	12,070	632	5.2
Mechanics and repairers	70	1	1.4
Multi/interdisciplinary studies	27,460	2,856	10.4
Parks, recreation, leisure, and fitness	19,111	935	4.9
Philosophy and religion	8,366	406	4.9
Physical sciences	18,385	654	3.6
Precision production trades	393	11	2.8
Protective services	24,877	2,420	9.7
Psychology	74,060	5,755	7.8
Public administration and services	20,185	1,669	8.3
R.O.T.C. and military technologies	7	0	0.0
Social sciences and history	127,101	9,035	7.1
Theological studies, religious vocations	6,809	159	2.3
Transportation and material moving	3,395	160	4.7
Visual and performing arts	58,791	3,047	5.2
Not classified	2,398	153	6.4

Source: National Center for Education Statistics, Digest of Education Statistics 2001, *Internet site <http://nces.ed.gov/pubsearch/pubsinfo.asp?pubid=2002130>; calculations by New Strategist*

Master's Degrees Earned by Hispanics by Field of Study, 1999–2000

(total number of master's degrees conferred and number and percent earned by Hispanics, by field of study, 1999–2000)

		earned by Hispanics	
	total	number	percent
Total master's degrees	**457,056**	**19,093**	**4.2%**
Agriculture and natural resources	4,375	109	2.5
Architecture and related programs	4,268	193	4.5
Area, ethnic, and cultural studies	1,591	106	6.7
Biological, life sciences	6,198	248	4.0
Business	112,258	4,241	3.8
Communications	5,169	187	3.6
Communications technologies	436	14	3.2
Computer and information sciences	14,264	253	1.8
Construction trades	12	0	0.0
Education	124,240	6,303	5.1
Engineering	25,596	751	2.9
Engineering-related technologies	914	30	3.3
English language and literature, letters	7,230	265	3.7
Foreign languages and literatures	2,780	308	11.1
Health professions and related sciences	42,456	1,415	3.3
Home economics	2,830	118	4.2
Law and legal studies	3,750	132	3.5
Liberal arts and sciences, general studies, and humanities	3,256	108	3.3
Library science	4,577	121	2.6
Mathematics	3,412	91	2.7
Multi/interdisciplinary studies	3,064	133	4.3
Parks, recreation, leisure, and fitness	2,478	61	2.5
Philosophy and religion	1,329	55	4.1
Physical sciences	4,841	93	1.9
Precision production trades	5	0	0.0
Protective services	2,609	117	4.5
Psychology	14,465	774	5.4
Public administration and services	25,594	1,647	6.4
Social sciences and history	14,066	584	4.2
Theological studies, religious vocations	5,576	156	2.8
Transportation and material moving	697	26	3.7
Visual and performing arts	10,918	418	3.8
Not classified	1,802	36	2.0

Source: National Center for Education Statistics, Digest of Education Statistics 2001, *Internet site <http:// nces.ed.gov/pubsearch/pubsinfo.asp?pubid=2002130>; calculations by New Strategist*

Doctoral Degrees Earned by Hispanics by Field of Study, 1999–2000

(total number of doctoral degrees conferred and number and percent earned by Hispanics, by field of study, 1999–2000)

	total	earned by Hispanics	
		number	percent
Total doctoral degrees	**44,808**	**1,291**	**2.9%**
Agriculture and natural resources	1,181	16	1.4
Architecture and related programs	129	5	3.9
Area, ethnic, and cultural studies	217	8	3.7
Biological, life sciences	4,867	143	2.9
Business	1,196	18	1.5
Communications	347	10	2.9
Communications technologies	10	0	0.0
Computer and information sciences	777	13	1.7
Education	6,830	262	3.8
Engineering	5,384	89	1.7
Engineering-related technologies	6	0	0.0
English language and literature, letters	1,628	49	3.0
Foreign languages and literatures	915	78	8.5
Health professions and related sciences	2,676	59	2.2
Home economics	357	8	2.2
Law and legal studies	74	0	0.0
Liberal arts and sciences, general studies, and humanities	83	2	2.4
Library science	68	1	1.5
Mathematics	1,106	12	1.1
Multi/interdisciplinary studies	384	7	1.8
Parks, recreation, leisure, and fitness	134	2	1.5
Philosophy and religion	586	16	2.7
Physical sciences	4,018	72	1.8
Protective services	52	2	3.8
Psychology	4,310	225	5.2
Public administration and services	537	16	3.0
Social sciences and history	4,095	130	3.2
Theological studies, religious vocations	1,643	26	1.6
Visual and performing arts	1,127	22	2.0
Not classified	71	0	0.0

Source: National Center for Education Statistics, Digest of Education Statistics 2001, *Internet site <http://nces.ed.gov/pubsearch/pubsinfo.asp?pubid=2002130>; calculations by New Strategist*

First-Professional Degrees Earned by Hispanics by Field of Study, 1999–2000

(total number of first-professional degrees conferred and number and percent earned by Hispanics, by field of study, 1999–2000)

	total	earned by Hispanics	
		number	*percent*
Total first-professional degrees	**80,259**	**3,865**	**4.8%**
Dentistry (D.D.S. or D.M.D.)	4,250	182	4.3
Medicine (M.D.)	15,286	825	5.4
Optometry (O.D.)	1,293	45	3.5
Osteopathic medicine (D.O.)	2,236	82	3.7
Pharmacy (Pharm.D.)	5,669	195	3.4
Podiatry (Pod.D., D.P., or D.P.M.)	569	18	3.2
Veterinary medicine (D.V.M.)	2,251	74	3.3
Chiropractic (D.C. or D.C.M.)	3,809	116	3.0
Naturopathic medicine	202	7	3.5
Law (LL.B. or J.D.)	38,152	2,183	5.7
Theology (M.Div., M.H.L., B.D., or Ord. and M.H.L./Rav.)	6,129	131	2.1
Other	413	7	1.7

Source: National Center for Education Statistics, Digest of Education Statistics 2001, *Internet site <http://nces.ed.gov/pubsearch/pubsinfo.asp?pubid=2002130>; calculations by New Strategist*

Millions of Hispanics Lack Health Insurance

Seventy-eight percent of Hispanics rate their health as excellent or good, slightly less than the 80 percent share among the total population. Hispanics fare better than the total population on some health measures and worse on others. They are less likely to die of cancer or heart disease than the average American, but their homicide rate is 36 percent above average. Infant mortality is relatively low, but the incidence of AIDS and tuberculosis is above average.

More than 815,000 babies were born to Hispanic women in 2000, or 20 percent of all births that year. Mexican Americans account for 71 percent of Hispanic births. In California, 49 percent of births in 2000 were to Hispanics. The figure is 46 percent in Texas and 41 percent in Arizona.

Hispanics are more likely to be without health insurance than any other racial or ethnic group. In 2000, 32 percent did not have health insurance, more than double the 14 percent among the total population. Fourteen percent of Hispanics had a disability in 1997, less than the proportion among Americans as a whole because Hispanics are younger than average.

The leading cause of death among Hispanics is heart disease, which is also true for the population as a whole. But heart disease accounts for only 25 percent of Hispanic deaths versus a larger 30 percent of total deaths.

■ The health status of Hispanics is greatly influenced by immigration. Not only do immigrants boost the Hispanic birth rate, but they are less likely to be covered by health insurance than is the average American.

Hispanics account for a large share of births in the U.S.

(Hispanic share of total births, by age of mother, 2000)

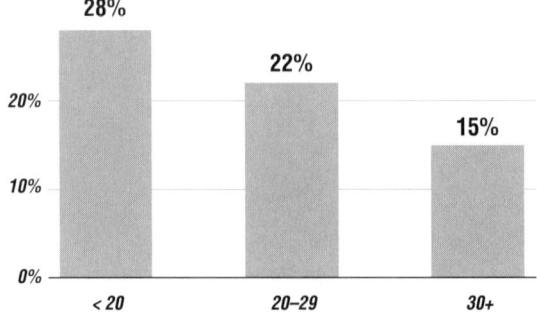

Hispanic Health Status, 2000

"Would you say your own health, in general, is excellent, good, fair, or poor?"

(percent of total people and Hispanics aged 18 or older responding, 2000)

	excellent	good	fair	poor
Total	31%	49%	16%	5%
Hispanic	26	52	18	3

Source: 2000 General Social Survey, National Opinion Research Center, University of Chicago; calculations by New Strategist

Health Indicators for Hispanics, 1998

(selected indicators of total and Hispanic health status, and index of Hispanic health indicators to total, 1998)

	total population indicator	Hispanic indicator	index of Hispanic to total
Infant mortality rate (deaths before age 1 per 1,000 live births)	7.2	5.8	81
Total deaths per 100,000 population	471.7	342.8	73
Motor vehicle crash deaths per 100,000 population	15.7	14.9	95
Work-related injury deaths per 100,000 people aged 16 or older	2.9	3.4	117
Suicides per 100,000 population	10.4	6.0	58
Homicides per 100,000 population	7.3	9.9	136
Lung cancer deaths per 100,000 population	37.0	13.6	37
Female breast cancer deaths per 100,000 population	18.8	12.1	64
Cardiovascular disease deaths per 100,000 population	161.2	109.3	68
Heart disease deaths per 100,000 population	126.7	84.2	66
Stroke deaths per 100,000 population	25.1	19.0	76
Reported incidence of AIDS per 100,000 population	19.5	33.0	169
Reported incidence of tuberculosis per 100,000 population	6.8	13.6	200
Reported incidence of syphilis per 100,000 population	2.6	1.5	58
Prevalence of low birth weight, as percent of total live births	7.6	6.4	84
Births to girls aged 10 to 17, as percent of total live births	4.6	6.9	150
Percent of mothers without care, first trimester of pregnancy	17.2	25.7	149
Percent under age 18 living in poverty	18.9	34.4	182
Percent living in counties exceeding U.S. air quality standards	23.5	43.8	186

Note: The index for each indicator is calculated by dividing the Hispanic figure by the total population figure and multiplying by 100. For example, the index of 73 in the second row indicates that the Hispanic death rate is 27 percent below the rate for the total population.
Source: National Center for Health Statistics, Healthy People 2000 Final Review, *2001; calculations by New Strategist*

Births to Hispanic Women by Age, 2000

(total number of births, number and percent distribution of births to Hispanic women, and Hispanic share of total, by age, 2000)

		Hispanic		
	total	number	percent distribution	share of total
Total births	**4,058,814**	**815,868**	**100.0%**	**20.1%**
Under age 15	8,519	2,638	0.3	31.0
Aged 15 to 19	468,990	129,469	15.9	27.6
Aged 20 to 24	1,017,806	247,552	30.3	24.3
Aged 25 to 29	1,087,547	218,167	26.7	20.1
Aged 30 to 34	929,278	141,493	17.3	15.2
Aged 35 to 39	452,057	62,993	7.7	13.9
Aged 40 to 44	90,013	12,987	1.6	14.4
Aged 45 or older	4,604	569	0.1	12.4

Source: National Center for Health Statistics, Births: Final Data for 2000, *National Vital Statistics Report, Vol. 50, No. 5, 2002; calculations by New Strategist*

Births to Hispanic Women by Age and Ethnicity, 2000

(number and percent distribution of births to Hispanic women by age and ethnicity, 2000)

	total	Mexican	Puerto Rican	Cuban	Central & South American	other Hispanic
Total Hispanic births	**815,868**	**581,915**	**58,124**	**13,429**	**113,344**	**49,056**
Under age 15	2,638	1,974	255	15	202	192
Aged 15 to 19	129,469	97,101	11,356	997	10,965	9,050
Aged 20 to 24	247,552	182,867	19,093	2,318	28,527	14,747
Aged 25 to 29	218,167	157,439	13,499	3,918	31,332	11,979
Aged 30 to 34	141,493	94,699	9,058	3,676	25,768	8,292
Aged 35 to 39	62,993	39,392	4,066	2,141	13,428	3,966
Aged 40 to 44	12,987	8,070	773	353	2,987	804
Aged 45 or older	569	373	24	11	135	26
Percent distribution by ethnicity						
Total Hispanic births	**100.0%**	**71.3%**	**7.1%**	**1.6%**	**13.9%**	**6.0%**
Under age 15	100.0	74.8	9.7	0.6	7.7	7.3
Aged 15 to 19	100.0	75.0	8.8	0.8	8.5	7.0
Aged 20 to 24	100.0	73.9	7.7	0.9	11.5	6.0
Aged 25 to 29	100.0	72.2	6.2	1.8	14.4	5.5
Aged 30 to 34	100.0	66.9	6.4	2.6	18.2	5.9
Aged 35 to 39	100.0	62.5	6.5	3.4	21.3	6.3
Aged 40 to 44	100.0	62.1	6.0	2.7	23.0	6.2
Aged 45 or older	100.0	65.6	4.2	1.9	23.7	4.6
Percent distribution by age						
Total Hispanic births	**100.0%**	**100.0%**	**100.0%**	**100.0%**	**100.0%**	**100.0%**
Under age 15	0.3	0.3	0.4	0.1	0.2	0.4
Aged 15 to 19	15.9	16.7	19.5	7.4	9.7	18.4
Aged 20 to 24	30.3	31.4	32.8	17.3	25.2	30.1
Aged 25 to 29	26.7	27.1	23.2	29.2	27.6	24.4
Aged 30 to 34	17.3	16.3	15.6	27.4	22.7	16.9
Aged 35 to 39	7.7	6.8	7.0	15.9	11.8	8.1
Aged 40 to 44	1.6	1.4	1.3	2.6	2.6	1.6
Aged 45 or older	0.1	0.1	0.0	0.1	0.1	0.1

Source: National Center for Health Statistics, Births: Final Data for 2000, *National Vital Statistics Report, Vol. 50, No. 5, 2002; calculations by New Strategist*

Births to Hispanic Women by Birth Order, 2000

(number and percent distribution of births to Hispanic women, by birth order, 2000)

	number	percent distribution
Total Hispanic births	**815,868**	**100.0%**
First child	302,797	37.1
Second child	247,472	30.3
Third child	152,300	18.7
Fourth or later child	109,074	13.4

Note: Numbers will not add to total because not stated is not shown.
Source: National Center for Health Statistics, Births: Final Data for 2000, *National Vital Statistics Report, Vol. 50, No. 5, 2002; calculations by New Strategist*

Births to Unmarried Hispanic Women by Age, 1999

(total number of births to Hispanics, number of births to unmarried Hispanic women, and unmarried share of total, by age, 1999)

	total	unmarried Hispanics number	share of total
Births to Hispanics	**815,868**	**348,173**	**42.7%**
Under age 15	2,638	2,458	93.2
Aged 15 to 19	129,469	94,028	72.6
Aged 20 to 24	247,552	122,678	49.6
Aged 25 to 29	218,167	72,389	33.2
Aged 30 to 34	141,493	36,510	25.8
Aged 35 to 39	62,993	16,208	25.7
Aged 40 or older	13,556	3,902	28.8

Source: National Center for Health Statistics, Births: Final Data for 2000, *National Vital Statistics Report, Vol. 50, No. 5, 2002*

Births to Unmarried Hispanic Women by Ethnicity, 2000

(percent of births to unmarried Hispanic women, by ethnicity, 2000)

	percent to unmarried women
Births to Hispanics	**42.7%**
Mexican	40.7
Puerto Rican	59.6
Cuban	27.3
Central and South American	44.7
Other Hispanic	46.2

Source: National Center for Health Statistics, Births: Final Data for 2000, *National Vital Statistics Report, Vol. 50, No. 5, 2002; calculations by New Strategist*

Births to Hispanic Women by State, 2000

(total number of births, number and percent distribution of births to Hispanic women, and Hispanic share of total, by state, 2000)

		Hispanic births		
	total	number	percent distribtution	share of total
Total births	**4,058,814**	**815,868**	**100.0%**	**20.1%**
Alabama	63,299	1,901	0.2	3.0
Alaska	9,974	597	0.1	6.0
Arizona	85,273	34,695	4.3	40.7
Arkansas	37,783	2,343	0.3	6.2
California	531,959	258,105	31.6	48.5
Colorado	65,438	18,237	2.2	27.9
Connecticut	43,026	6,472	0.8	15.0
Delaware	11,051	1,022	0.1	9.2
District of Columbia	7,666	876	0.1	11.4
Florida	204,125	45,856	5.6	22.5
Georgia	132,644	13,363	1.6	10.1
Hawaii	17,551	2,302	0.3	13.1
Idaho	20,366	2,599	0.3	12.8
Illinois	185,036	39,313	4.8	21.2
Indiana	87,699	5,456	0.7	6.2
Iowa	38,266	2,135	0.3	5.6
Kansas	39,666	4,761	0.6	12.0
Kentucky	56,029	1,089	0.1	1.9
Louisiana	67,898	1,532	0.2	2.3
Maine	13,603	141	0.0	1.0
Maryland	74,316	4,812	0.6	6.5
Massachusetts	81,614	9,279	1.1	11.4
Michigan	136,171	6,949	0.9	5.1
Minnesota	67,604	3,952	0.5	5.8
Mississippi	44,075	623	0.1	1.4
Missouri	76,463	2,661	0.3	3.5
Montana	10,957	330	0.0	3.0
Nebraska	24,646	2,596	0.3	10.5
Nevada	30,829	10,195	1.2	33.1
New Hampshire	14,609	373	0.0	2.6
New Jersey	115,632	22,457	2.8	19.4

(continued)

(continued from previous page)

| | total | Hispanic births | | |
		number	percent distribtution	share of total
New Mexico	27,223	13,941	1.7%	51.2%
New York	258,737	53,847	6.6	20.8
North Carolina	120,311	12,557	1.5	10.4
North Dakota	7,676	132	0.0	1.7
Ohio	155,472	4,150	0.5	2.7
Oklahoma	49,782	4,357	0.5	8.8
Oregon	45,804	7,401	0.9	16.2
Pennsylvania	146,281	7,549	0.9	5.2
Rhode Island	12,505	2,103	0.3	16.8
South Carolina	56,114	2,261	0.3	4.0
South Dakota	10,345	223	0.0	2.2
Tennessee	79,611	3,220	0.4	4.0
Texas	363,414	166,931	20.5	45.9
Utah	47,353	5,938	0.7	12.5
Vermont	6,500	33	0.0	0.5
Virginia	98,938	7,725	0.9	7.8
Washington	81,036	11,367	1.4	14.0
West Virginia	20,865	50	0.0	0.2
Wisconsin	69,326	4,493	0.6	6.5
Wyoming	6,253	568	0.1	9.1

Source: National Center for Health Statistics, Births: Final Data for 2000, *National Vital Statistics Report, Vol. 50, No. 5, 2002; calculations by New Strategist*

Health Insurance Coverage of Hispanics by Age, 2000

(number and percent distribution of Hispanics by age and health insurance coverage status, 2000; numbers in thousands)

	total	covered by private or government health insurance							not covered
		private health insurance			government health insurance				
		total	total	employ-ment based	total	Medicaid	Medicare	Military	
Total Hispanics	**33,862**	**23,035**	**16,257**	**15,128**	**8,215**	**6,273**	**2,192**	**543**	**10,827**
Under 18	12,029	9,036	5,460	5,174	4,091	3,909	72	170	2,993
Aged 18–24	4,178	2,087	1,662	1,452	548	480	15	65	2,091
Aged 25–34	5,641	3,337	2,865	2,741	573	471	34	92	2,304
Aged 35–44	5,037	3,250	2,864	2,725	500	405	64	70	1,787
Aged 45–54	3,212	2,241	1,942	1,855	385	291	88	48	971
Aged 55–64	1,883	1,290	954	851	388	227	204	35	593
Aged 65+	1,882	1,793	509	329	1,730	491	1,714	63	89
Total Hispanics	**100.0%**	**68.0%**	**48.0%**	**44.7%**	**24.3%**	**18.5%**	**6.5%**	**1.6%**	**32.0%**
Under 18	100.0	75.1	45.4	43.0	34.0	32.5	0.6	1.4	24.9
Aged 18–24	100.0	50.0	39.8	34.8	13.1	11.5	0.4	1.6	50.0
Aged 25–34	100.0	59.2	50.8	48.6	10.2	8.3	0.6	1.6	40.8
Aged 35–44	100.0	64.5	56.9	54.1	9.9	8.0	1.3	1.4	35.5
Aged 45–54	100.0	69.8	60.5	57.8	12.0	9.1	2.7	1.5	30.2
Aged 55–64	100.0	68.5	50.7	45.2	20.6	12.1	10.8	1.9	31.5
Aged 65+	100.0	95.3	27.0	17.5	91.9	26.1	91.1	3.3	4.7

Note: Numbers will not add to total because some people have more than one type of health insurance.
Source: Bureau of the Census, Internet site <http://ferret.bls.census.gov/macro/032001/health/h01_011.htm>

Hispanics with Disabilities by Sex and Age, 1997

(total number of Hispanics and number and percent with disabilities, by sex, age, and severity of disability, 1997; numbers in thousands)

	total	with a disability total number	total percent	severe number	severe percent	needs assistance number	needs assistance percent
Total Hispanics	**30,086**	**4,151**	**13.8%**	**2,906**	**9.7%**	**820**	**2.7%**
Under age 15	9,133	533	5.8	275	3.0	61	0.7
Aged 15 to 24	5,398	414	7.7	251	4.7	39	0.7
Aged 25 to 64	13,966	2,297	16.4	1,632	11.7	391	2.8
Aged 65 or older	1,590	907	57.1	748	47.0	329	20.7
Hispanic females	**14,714**	**2,215**	**15.1**	**1,594**	**10.8**	**433**	**2.9**
Under age 15	4,457	203	4.6	101	2.3	29	0.6
Aged 15 to 24	2,481	185	7.4	113	4.6	10	0.4
Aged 25 to 64	6,872	1,295	18.9	920	13.4	213	3.1
Aged 65 or older	904	531	58.8	460	50.9	181	20.0
Hispanic males	**15,372**	**1,937**	**12.6**	**1,311**	**8.5**	**387**	**2.5**
Under age 15	4,676	329	7.0	174	3.7	32	0.7
Aged 15 to 24	2,917	230	7.9	138	4.7	29	1.0
Aged 25 to 64	7,094	1,002	14.1	712	10.0	178	2.5
Aged 65 or older	686	376	54.9	288	42.0	148	21.6

Note: For the definition of disability, see glossary.
Source: Bureau of the Census, Americans with Disabilities: 1997, *detailed tables from Current Population Reports P70-73, 2001*

Hispanics with Disabilities by Employment Status and Earnings, 1997

(total number of Hispanics aged 21 to 64, number and percent employed, median earnings, and index of earnings to total, by disability status, 1997)

	total (in 000s)	employed number (in 000s)	employed percent	median earnings	index of earnings by disability status to total Hispanic earnings
Total Hispanics	**16,108**	**11,593**	**72.0%**	**$16,869**	**100**
Not disabled	**13,699**	**10,583**	**77.3**	**17,146**	**102**
Disabled	**2,410**	**1,009**	**41.9**	**12,504**	**74**
Not severely	707	557	78.9	13,904	82
Severely	1,703	452	26.5	11,487	68

Note: For the definition of disability, see glossary.
Source: Bureau of the Census, Americans with Disabilities: 1997, *detailed tables from Current Population Reports P70-73, 2001; calculations by New Strategist*

AIDS Cases among Hispanics, through June 2000

(total number of AIDS cases diagnosed, number diagnosed among Hispanics, and Hispanic share of total, by sex and age at diagnosis, through June 2000)

	total	Hispanic number	Hispanic share of total
Total AIDS cases	**729,326**	**113,422**	**15.6%**
Males aged 13 or older	601,471	92,440	15.4
Females aged 13 or older	119,454	19,359	16.2
Children under age 13	8,401	1,623	19.3

Source: National Center for Health Statistics, Health United States, 2001; *calculations by New Strategist*

Leading Causes of Death among Hispanics, 1999

(total number of deaths among Hispanics, and number and percent accounted for by the ten leading causes of death for Hispanics, 1999)

		number	*percent*
Total Hispanic deaths		**103,740**	**100.0%**
1.	Diseases of heart	25,866	24.9
2.	Malignant neoplasms	20,233	19.5
3.	Accidents	8,650	8.3
4.	Cerebrovascular diseases	5,907	5.7
5.	Diabetes mellitus	5,182	5.0
6.	Chronic liver disease and cirrhosis	2,972	2.9
7.	Homicide and legal intervention	2,864	2.8
8.	Chronic lower respiratory disease	2,859	2.8
9.	Influenza and pneumonia	2,246	2.2
10.	Certain conditions originating in the perinatal period	2,153	2.1
	All other causes	24,808	23.9

Source: National Center for Health Statistics, Deaths: Final Data for 1999, *National Vital Statistics Reports, Vol. 49, No. 8, 2001; calculations by New Strategist*

Hispanics: Housing

Hispanics Are Much Less Likely than the Average American to Own a Home

Forty-five percent of the nation's 9 million Hispanic householders own their home. This compares with a homeownership rate of 67 percent for all households. Among Hispanic married couples, the 57 percent majority are homeowners. The percentage peaks at 77 percent among Hispanic couples aged 65 to 74.

Hispanic homeowners valued their home at a median of $98,749 in 1999. Most bought their home using savings as a down payment.

Regardless of their homeownership status, most Hispanics are satisfied with their home. On a scale of one to ten, 65 percent rate their home an eight or higher. Most Hispanics are also satisfied with their neighborhood. But 19 percent say their neighborhood has a crime problem—15 percent of homeowners and 21 percent of renters. Nine percent of Hispanic renters are so bothered by crime in their neighborhood that they want to move.

Twenty-one percent of Hispanics moved between March 1999 and March 2000. This mobility rate is higher than that for the total population because Hispanics are younger than average and because so many are renters. Renters have higher mobility rates than homeowners. The main reason Hispanics moved in 1999 was the need for a larger house or apartment.

■ Hispanic homeownership will continue to lag behind the national average because many Hispanics are immigrants with low incomes.

Hispanic homeownership is lowest in the Northeast

(percent of Hispanic households that own their home, by region, 1999)

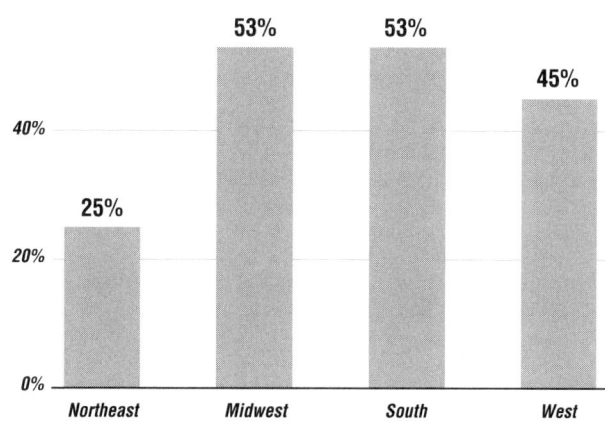

Region of Residence and Metropolitan Status of
Housing Units Occupied by Hispanics, 1999

(number, percent distribution, and percent of housing units occupied by Hispanics, by regional, metropolitan, and homeownership status, 1999; numbers in thousands)

	total		owner			renter		
	number	percent distribution	number	percent distribution	share of total	number	percent distribution	share of total
Housing units occupied by Hispanics	**9,041**	**100.0%**	**4,087**	**100.0%**	**45.2%**	**4,955**	**100.0%**	**54.8%**
Northeast	1,460	16.1	369	9.0	25.3	1,091	22.0	74.7
Midwest	680	7.5	359	8.8	52.8	321	6.5	47.2
South	3,168	35.0	1,691	41.4	53.4	1,477	29.8	46.6
West	3,734	41.3	1,668	40.8	44.7	2,066	41.7	55.3
In metropolitan areas	8,194	90.6	3,597	88.0	43.9	4,597	92.8	56.1
In central cities	4,300	47.6	1,502	36.8	34.9	2,799	56.5	65.1
In suburbs	3,894	43.1	2,096	51.3	53.8	1,798	36.3	46.2
Outside metro areas	847	9.4	489	12.0	57.7	358	7.2	42.3

Source: Bureau of the Census, American Housing Survey for the United States: 1999, *Current Housing Reports, H150/99, 2000; calculations by New Strategist*

Hispanic Homeowners by Family Type and Age of Householder, 2000

(number of families headed by Hispanics, number and percent of families owning their home, by family type and by age of householder for married couples, 2000; numbers in thousands)

		homeowners	
	total	*number*	*percent*
Hispanic married couples	**5,133**	**2,930**	**57.1%**
Under age 25	315	79	25.1
Aged 25 to 29	618	211	34.1
Aged 30 to 34	818	381	46.6
Aged 35 to 39	854	498	58.3
Aged 40 to 44	680	462	67.9
Aged 45 to 54	911	608	66.7
Aged 55 to 64	509	375	73.7
Aged 65 to 74	291	225	77.3
Aged 75 or older	136	92	67.6
Hispanic female-headed families	**1,769**	**557**	**31.5**
Hispanic male-headed families	**658**	**233**	**35.4**

Source: Bureau of the Census, America's Families and Living Arrangements: March 2000, *detailed tables from Current Population Report P20–537, Internet site <www.census.gov/population/www/socdemo/hh-fam/p20-537_00.html>; calculations by New Strategist*

Characteristics of Housing Units Occupied by Hispanics, 1999

(number and percent distribution of housing units occupied by Hispanics, by selected housing characteristics and homeownership status, 1999; numbers in thousands)

	total		owner-occupied		renter-occupied	
	number	*percent distribution*	*number*	*percent distribution*	*number*	*percent distribution*
Housing units occupied by Hispanics	**9,041**	**100.0%**	**4,087**	**100.0%**	**4,955**	**100.0%**
Units in structure						
One, detached	4,372	48.4	3,393	83.0	979	19.8
One, attached	740	8.2	194	4.7	546	11.0
Two to four	1,137	12.6	122	3.0	1,016	20.5
Five to nine	725	8.0	23	0.6	702	14.2
10 to 19	613	6.8	18	0.4	596	12.0
20 to 49	605	6.7	24	0.6	581	11.7
50 or more	447	4.9	44	1.1	402	8.1
Mobile home or trailer	401	4.4	269	6.6	133	2.7
Median square footage of unit	1,432	–	1,522	–	1,102	–
Number of rooms in unit						
One room	53	0.6	2	–	52	1.0
Two rooms	171	1.9	4	–	167	3.4
Three rooms	1,232	13.6	75	1.8	1,157	23.4
Four rooms	2,503	27.7	569	13.9	1,933	39.0
Five rooms	2,230	24.7	1,144	28.0	1,086	21.9
Six rooms	1,595	17.6	1,173	28.7	422	8.5
Seven rooms	671	7.4	583	14.3	88	1.8
Eight rooms	337	3.7	311	7.6	26	0.5
Nine rooms	147	1.6	133	3.3	13	0.3
Ten or more rooms	102	1.1	92	2.3	10	0.2
Complete bathrooms						
None	75	0.8	19	0.5	56	1.1
One	5,122	56.7	1,362	33.3	3,760	75.9
One and one-half	1,013	11.2	612	15.0	400	8.1
Two or more	2,831	31.3	2,093	51.2	738	14.9

(continued)

(continued from previous page)

	total		owner-occupied		renter-occupied	
	number	percent distribution	number	percent distribution	number	percent distribution
Heating fuel						
Housing units with heating fuel	8,847	100.0%	4,049	100.0%	4,798	100.0%
Electricity	3,121	35.3	1,258	31.1	1,863	38.8
Piped gas	4,648	52.5	2,430	60.0	2,218	46.2
Bottled gas	210	2.4	149	3.7	61	1.3
Fuel oil	729	8.2	142	3.5	588	12.3
Kerosene or other liquid fuel	39	0.4	10	0.2	29	0.6
Coal or coke	3	0.0	1	0.0	1.0	–
Wood	72	0.8	54	1.3	18	0.4
Solar energy	–	–	–	–	–	–
Other	25	0.3	5	0.1	20	0.4
Selected equipment						
Dishwasher	3,301	36.5	1,921	47.0	1,380	27.9
Washing machine	5,432	60.1	3,688	90.2	1,744	35.2
Clothes dryer	4,440	49.1	3,214	78.6	1,226	24.7
Disposal in kitchen sink	3,714	41.1	1,801	44.1	1,913	38.6
Central air conditioning	3,852	42.6	2,138	52.3	1,715	34.6
Porch, deck, balcony, or patio	6,353	70.3	3,493	85.5	2,860	57.7
Telephone	8,470	93.7	3,914	95.8	4,556	91.9
Usable fireplace	1,635	18.1	1,218	29.8	416	8.4
Garage or carport	4,430	49.0	2,890	70.7	1,540	31.1
No cars, trucks, or vans	1,369	15.1	157	3.8	1,212	24.5
Overall opinion of housing unit						
1 (worst)	107	1.2	12	0.3	95	1.9
2	52	0.6	6	0.1	45	0.9
3	80	0.9	11	0.3	69	1.4
4	149	1.6	16	0.4	133	2.7
5	802	8.9	176	4.3	626	12.6
6	514	5.7	170	4.2	344	6.9
7	1,152	12.7	465	11.4	686	13.8
8	2,352	26.0	1,143	28.0	1,209	24.4
9	1,201	13.3	644	15.8	557	11.2
10 (best)	2,323	25.7	1,294	31.7	1,030	20.8

Note: Numbers may not add to total because not reported is not shown and more than one category may apply; (–) means not applicable or sample is too small to make a reliable estimate.
Source: Bureau of the Census, American Housing Survey for the United States: 1999, *Current Housing Reports, H150/99, 2000; calculations by New Strategist*

Neighborhood Characteristics of Housing Units Occupied by Hispanics,1999

(number and percent distribution of housing units occupied by Hispanics, by selected neighborhood characteristics and homeownership status, 1999; numbers in thousands)

	total		owner-occupied		renter-occupied	
	number	*percent distribution*	*number*	*percent distribution*	*number*	*percent distribution*
Housing units occupied by Hispanics	**9,041**	**100.0%**	**4,087**	**100.0%**	**4,955**	**100.0%**
Overall opinion of neighborhood						
1 (worst)	160	1.8	45	1.1	115	2.3
2	92	1.0	18	0.4	74	1.5
3	135	1.5	24	0.6	111	2.2
4	185	2.0	39	1.0	146	2.9
5	819	9.1	278	6.8	541	10.9
6	584	6.5	240	5.9	344	6.9
7	1,253	13.9	539	13.2	715	14.4
8	2,106	23.3	1,047	25.6	1,059	21.4
9	1,271	14.1	645	15.8	626	12.6
10 (best)	2,077	23.0	1,028	25.2	1,049	21.2
Neighborhood problems						
Street noise or traffic present	2,566	28.4	965	23.6	1,601	32.3
Condition not bothersome	1,362	15.1	502	12.3	861	17.4
Condition bothersome	1,204	13.3	464	11.4	741	15.0
So bothered they want to move	527	5.8	150	3.7	377	7.6
Neighborhood crime present	1,685	18.6	630	15.4	1,056	21.3
Condition not bothersome	588	6.5	258	6.3	330	6.7
Condition bothersome	1,098	12.1	372	9.1	725	14.6
So bothered they want to move	608	6.7	163	4.0	446	9.0
Odors present	733	8.1	293	7.2	440	8.9
Condition not bothersome	226	2.5	92	2.3	134	2.7
Condition bothersome	508	5.6	202	4.9	306	6.2
So bothered they want to move	259	2.9	82	2.0	177	3.6
No other problems	7,549	83.5	3,373	82.5	4,177	84.3
With other problems	1,394	15.4	667	16.3	727	14.7
Noise	272	3.0	111	2.7	161	3.2
Litter or housing deterioration	212	2.3	88	2.2	124	2.5
Poor city or county services	122	1.3	56	1.4	66	1.3
Undesirable commercial, institutional, industrial	59	0.7	20	0.5	39	0.8
People	457	5.1	195	4.8	262	5.3
Other	648	7.2	325	8.0	323	6.5

(continued)

(continued from previous page)

	total		owner-occupied		renter-occupied	
	number	percent distribution	number	percent distribution	number	percent distribution
Neighborhood conditions						
With public transportation	6,499	71.9%	2,490	60.9%	4,009	80.9%
Satisfactory public elementary school*	3,449	78.2	1,529	79.0	1,919	77.5
Satisfactory neighborhood shopping	7,911	87.5	3,470	84.9	4,441	89.6
Satisfactory police protection	7,821	86.5	3,528	86.3	4,293	86.6
Description of area within 300 feet						
Single-family detached homes	6,783	75.0	3,630	88.8	3,153	63.6
Single-family attached homes	1,230	13.6	375	9.2	855	17.3
Apartment buildings	4,624	51.1	692	16.9	3,932	79.4
Mobile homes	807	8.9	524	12.8	283	5.7
Commercial, institutional	3,338	36.9	880	21.5	2,458	49.6
Industrial	638	7.1	187	4.6	451	9.1
Body of water	855	9.5	410	10.0	445	9.0
Open space, park, woods, farm, or ranch	2,495	27.6	1,083	26.5	1,412	28.5
Four-or-more lane highway, railroad, airport	1,544	17.1	498	12.2	1,046	21.1

* Percentage based only on households with children aged 0 to 13.
Note: Numbers may not add to total because more than one problem could be cited and not reported is not shown;
Source: Bureau of the Census, American Housing Survey for the United States: 1999, *Current Housing Reports, H150/99, 2000; calculations by New Strategist*

Housing Value and Purchase Price for Hispanic Homeowners, 1999

(number and percent distribution of Hispanic homeowners, by value of home, purchase price, and major source of down payment, 1999; numbers in thousands)

	number	percent distribution
Total Hispanic homeowners	**4,087**	**100.0%**
Value of home		
Under $50,000	777	19.0
$50,000 to $79,999	757	18.5
$80,000 to $99,999	543	13.3
$100,000 to $149,999	874	21.4
$150,000 to $199,999	563	13.8
$200,000 to $299,999	362	8.9
$300,000 or more	211	5.2
Median value	98,749	–
Purchase price*		
Home purchased or built	3,925	96.0
Under $50,000	1,471	36.0
$50,000 to $79,999	750	18.4
$80,000 to $99,999	404	9.9
$100,000 to $149,999	510	12.5
$150,000 to $199,999	285	7.0
$200,000 to $299,999	153	3.7
$300,000 or more	70	1.7
Received as inheritance or gift	282	6.9
Median purchase price	$63,773	–
Major source of down payment		
Home purchased or built	3,925	96.0
Sale of previous home	688	16.8
Savings or cash on hand	2,478	60.6
Sale of other investment	33	0.8
Borrowing, other than mortgage on this property	155	3.8
Inheritance or gift	72	1.8
Land where built used for financing	36	0.9
Other	158	3.9
No down payment	216	5.3

Note: Numbers may not add to total because not reported is not shown; (–) means not applicable.
Source: Bureau of the Census, American Housing Survey for the United States: 1999, *Current Housing Reports, H150/99, 2000; calculations by New Strategist*

Geographical Mobility of Hispanics by Age, 1999–2000

(total number of Hispanics aged 1 or older, and number and percent who moved between March 1999 and March 2000, by age of person and type of move; numbers in thousands)

	total	same house (non-movers)	total movers in U.S.	same county	different county, same state	different state, same division	different division, same region	different region	moved from abroad
Hispanics aged 1 or older	**32,103**	**25,347**	**6,756**	**4,254**	**1,006**	**335**	**217**	**318**	**626**
Aged 1–4	2,963	2,184	779	536	90	31	45	34	44
Aged 5–9	3,351	2,672	679	420	118	31	27	32	50
Aged 10–14	2,995	2,452	543	347	80	23	11	37	45
Aged 15–17	1,685	1,375	310	186	37	18	9	17	43
Aged 18–19	1,204	886	318	194	47	16	5	11	45
Aged 20–24	2,755	1,773	982	621	111	50	39	39	122
Aged 25–29	2,831	1,890	941	616	124	46	29	53	73
Aged 30–34	2,829	2,170	659	405	121	31	17	27	58
Aged 35–39	2,810	2,296	514	316	81	26	15	27	51
Aged 40–44	2,164	1,832	332	207	70	14	8	6	26
Aged 45–49	1,580	1,374	206	125	34	18	1	5	23
Aged 50–54	1,438	1,265	173	111	24	4	4	8	22
Aged 55–59	990	872	118	65	23	16	2	9	5
Aged 60–61	335	306	29	20	2	3	–	1	3
Aged 62–64	420	388	32	16	5	2	2	–	7
Aged 65–69	646	590	56	30	11	3	–	7	4
Aged 70–74	486	445	41	22	13	2	–	–	4
Aged 75–79	306	284	22	3	13	–	3	2	–
Aged 80–84	207	193	14	11	1	–	–	–	1
Aged 85+	108	99	9	4	–	1	–	3	–

(continued)

(continued from previous page)

	total	same house (non-movers)	total movers in U.S.	same county	different county, same state	different state, same division	different division, same region	different region	moved from abroad
Hispanics aged									
1 or older	**100.0%**	**79.0%**	**21.0%**	**13.3%**	**3.1%**	**1.0%**	**0.7%**	**1.0%**	**1.9%**
Aged 1–4	100.0	73.7	26.3	18.1	3.0	1.0	1.5	1.1	1.5
Aged 5–9	100.0	79.7	20.3	12.5	3.5	0.9	0.8	1.0	1.5
Aged 10–14	100.0	81.9	18.1	11.6	2.7	0.8	0.4	1.2	1.5
Aged 15–17	100.0	81.6	18.4	11.0	2.2	1.1	0.5	1.0	2.6
Aged 18–19	100.0	73.6	26.4	16.1	3.9	1.3	0.4	0.9	3.7
Aged 20–24	100.0	64.4	35.6	22.5	4.0	1.8	1.4	1.4	4.4
Aged 25–29	100.0	66.8	33.2	21.8	4.4	1.6	1.0	1.9	2.6
Aged 30–34	100.0	76.7	23.3	14.3	4.3	1.1	0.6	1.0	2.1
Aged 35–39	100.0	81.7	18.3	11.2	2.9	0.9	0.5	1.0	1.8
Aged 40–44	100.0	84.7	15.3	9.6	3.2	0.6	0.4	0.3	1.2
Aged 45–49	100.0	87.0	13.0	7.9	2.2	1.1	0.1	0.3	1.5
Aged 50–54	100.0	88.0	12.0	7.7	1.7	0.3	0.3	0.6	1.5
Aged 55–59	100.0	88.1	11.9	6.6	2.3	1.6	0.2	0.9	0.5
Aged 60–61	100.0	91.3	8.7	6.0	0.6	0.9	–	0.3	0.9
Aged 62–64	100.0	92.4	7.6	3.8	1.2	0.5	0.5	–	1.7
Aged 65–69	100.0	91.3	8.7	4.6	1.7	0.5	–	1.1	0.6
Aged 70–74	100.0	91.6	8.4	4.5	2.7	0.4	–	–	0.8
Aged 75–79	100.0	92.8	7.2	1.0	4.2	–	1.0	0.7	–
Aged 80–84	100.0	93.2	6.8	5.3	0.5	–	–	–	0.5
Aged 85+	100.0	91.7	8.3	3.7	–	0.9	–	2.8	–

Note: (–) means sample is too small to make a reliable estimate.
Source: Bureau of the Census, Geographical Mobility: March 1999 to March 2000, *Current Population Reports, P20-538, 2001; Internet site <www.census.gov/population/www/socdemo/migrate/p20-538.html>; calculations by New Strategist*

Reasons for Moving among Hispanic Households by Homeownership Status, 1999

(number and percent distribution of Hispanic households moving in the past 12 months by main reason for move and for choosing new neighborhood and house, and by comparison with previous home and neighborhood, by homeownership status, 1999; numbers in thousands)

	total		owner-occupied		renter-occupied	
	number	*percent distribution*	*number*	*percent distribution*	*number*	*percent distribution*
Total Hispanic movers	**2,182**	**100.0%**	**458**	**100.0%**	**1,724**	**100.0%**
Main reason for leaving previous housing unit						
Private displacement	38	1.7	5	1.1	32	1.9
Government displacement	4	0.2	–	–	4	0.2
Disaster loss (fire, flood, etc.)	13	0.6	5	1.1	8	0.5
New job or job transfer	198	9.1	36	7.9	162	9.4
To be closer to work/school/other	196	9.0	22	4.8	174	10.1
Other financial/employment	80	3.7	7	1.5	73	4.2
To establish own household	253	11.6	57	12.4	196	11.4
Needed larger house or apartment	274	12.6	70	15.3	204	11.8
Married, widowed, divorced, separated	73	3.3	17	3.7	55	3.2
Other family/personal	174	8.0	16	3.5	158	9.2
Wanted better home	175	8.0	42	9.2	133	7.7
Change from owner to renter/ renter to owner	114	5.2	95	20.7	19	1.1
Wanted lower rent or maintenance	114	5.2	11	2.4	103	6.0
Other housing related reasons	114	5.2	10	2.2	104	6.0
Other	190	8.7	30	6.6	161	9.3
All reported reasons equal	78	3.6	21	4.6	57	3.3
Main reason for choosing present neighborhood						
Convenient to job	368	16.9	51	11.1	316	18.3
Convenient to friends or relatives	354	16.2	66	14.4	288	16.7
Convenient to leisure activities	20	0.9	3	0.7	17	1.0
Convenient to public transportation	27	1.2	–	–	27	1.6
Good schools	136	6.2	23	5.0	113	6.6
Other public services	20	0.9	–	–	20	1.2
Looks/design of neighborhood	270	12.4	84	18.3	186	10.8
House most important consideration	297	13.6	110	24.0	187	10.8
Other	323	14.8	40	8.7	282	16.4
All reported reasons equal	114	5.2	33	7.2	81	4.7
Neighborhood search						
Looked at just this neighborhood	1,089	49.9	173	37.8	916	53.1
Looked at other neighborhood(s)	1,040	47.7	274	59.8	766	44.4

(continued)

(continued from previous page)

	total		owner-occupied		renter-occupied	
	number	*percent distribution*	*number*	*percent distribution*	*number*	*percent distribution*
Main reason for choosing present home						
Financial reasons	630	28.9%	122	26.6%	508	29.5%
Room layout/design	298	13.7	76	16.6	222	12.9
Kitchen	10	0.5	–	–	10	0.6
Size	282	12.9	56	12.2	226	13.1
Exterior appearance	53	2.4	18	3.9	35	2.0
Yard/trees/view	49	2.2	23	5.0	26	1.5
Quality of construction	53	2.4	28	6.1	25	1.5
Only one available	218	10.0	18	3.9	201	11.7
Other	245	11.2	45	9.8	199	11.5
All reported reasons equal	124	5.7	40	8.7	84	4.9
Comparison to previous home						
Better home	1,235	56.6	325	71.0	910	52.8
Worse home	309	14.2	32	7.0	278	16.1
About the same	584	26.8	90	19.7	493	28.6
Comparison to previous neighborhood						
Better neighborhood	945	43.3	270	59.0	675	39.2
Worse neighborhood	272	12.5	25	5.5	247	14.3
About the same	790	36.2	133	29.0	658	38.2
Same neighborhood	117	5.4	15	3.3	102	5.9

Note: Numbers may not add to total because more than one category may apply and unreported reasons are not shown; (–) means sample is too small to make a reliable estimate.
Source: Bureau of the Census, American Housing Survey for the United States: 1999, *Current Housing Reports, H150/99, 2000; calculations by New Strategist*

The Incomes of Hispanics Are Rising, but Remain Well Below Average

The median income of Hispanic households rose 17 percent between 1990 and 2000, to $33,455 after adjusting for inflation. While this gain was greater than the 10 percent rise experienced by the average household, the median income of Hispanic households was only 79 percent of the overall median in 2000.

Hispanic household income peaks among householders aged 45 to 54, with a median of $41,107. By household type, median income is greatest for married couples, at $41,116. Hispanic men who work full-time had a median income of $25,042 in 2000, while their female counterparts had an income of $21,025.

Between 1990 and 2000, the median earnings of Hispanic men who work full-time barely changed, rising just 0.3 percent after adjusting for inflation. The median earnings of Hispanic women who work full-time rose 2 percent. Hispanics earn less than the average worker because many are recent immigrants with little education.

Nineteen percent of Hispanic families are poor, including 14 percent of married couples and 34 percent of female-headed families. Between 1990 and 2000, the number of Hispanic families in poverty grew 15 percent, but the poverty rate for Hispanic families fell 26 percent.

■ The economic status of Hispanics will remain below that of the average American as long as immigrants account for a large share of the Hispanic population.

Households headed by Cuban Hispanics are most likely to have high incomes

(percent of Hispanic households with incomes of $75,000 or more, by ethnicity, 2000)

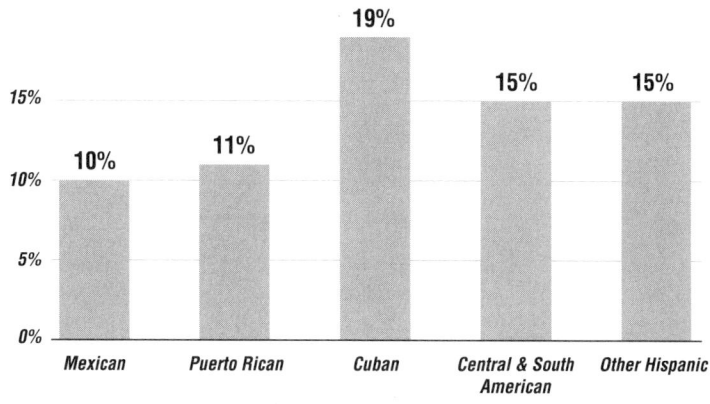

Median Income of Hispanic Households, 1990 to 2000

(median income of Hispanic households, and index of Hispanic to total household median income, 1990 to 2000; percent change in incomes and indexes, 1990–2000; in 2000 dollars)

	median income	index Hispanic/total
2000	$33,455	79
1999	31,767	75
1998	29,894	73
1997	28,491	72
1996	27,226	70
1995	25,668	67
1994	26,958	73
1993	26,919	73
1992	27,266	74
1991	28,105	75
1990	28,671	75
Percent change		
1990–2000	16.7%	6.4%

Note: Indexes are calculated by dividing the median income of Hispanic households by the median of total households and multiplying by 100.
Source: Bureau of the Census, Current Population Survey, Internet site <www.census.gov/hhes/income/histinc/h05.html>; calculations by New Strategist

High-Income Hispanic Households, 2000

(number, percent distribution, and average income of Hispanic households with incomes of $100,000 or more, 2000; households in thousands as of 2001)

	total	percent	average income
Total Hispanic households	**9,663**	**100.0%**	**$42,410**
$100,000 to $149,999	381	3.9	116,853
$150,000 to $199,999	99	1.0	167,541
$200,000 to $249,999	30	0.3	216,646
$250,000 or more	46	0.5	378,042

Source: Bureau of the Census, Current Population Survey, Internet site <http://ferret.bls.census.gov/macro/032001/hhinc/new07_000 .htm>; calculations by New Strategist

Income Distribution of Hispanic Households by Age of Householder, 2000

(number and percent distribution of Hispanic households by income and age of householder, 2000; households in thousands as of 2001)

	total	< 25	25–34	35–44	45–54	55–64	65+
Hispanic households	**9,663**	**970**	**2,500**	**2,479**	**1,636**	**1,006**	**1,072**
Under $10,000	1,022	141	206	155	108	139	274
$10,000 to $19,999	1,707	202	410	376	210	181	326
$20,000 to $29,999	1,602	176	460	419	234	135	179
$30,000 to $39,999	1,352	146	384	350	237	131	103
$40,000 to $49,999	1,032	86	274	299	204	110	59
$50,000 to $59,999	824	81	226	249	150	83	35
$60,000 to $69,999	617	71	184	164	111	56	30
$70,000 to $79,999	449	23	124	143	91	40	28
$80,000 to $89,999	314	11	77	104	70	46	7
$90,000 to $99,999	188	16	50	43	46	21	10
$100,000 or more	556	17	103	178	175	63	20
Median income	$33,455	$27,890	$34,095	$38,060	$41,107	$32,186	$17,258
Hispanic households	**100.0%**	**100.0%**	**100.0%**	**100.0%**	**100.0%**	**100.0%**	**100.0%**
Under $10,000	10.6	14.5	8.2	6.3	6.6	13.8	25.6
$10,000 to $19,999	17.7	20.8	16.4	15.2	12.8	18.0	30.4
$20,000 to $29,999	16.6	18.1	18.4	16.9	14.3	13.4	16.7
$30,000 to $39,999	14.0	15.1	15.4	14.1	14.5	13.0	9.6
$40,000 to $49,999	10.7	8.9	11.0	12.1	12.5	10.9	5.5
$50,000 to $59,999	8.5	8.4	9.0	10.0	9.2	8.3	3.3
$60,000 to $69,999	6.4	7.3	7.4	6.6	6.8	5.6	2.8
$70,000 to $79,999	4.6	2.4	5.0	5.8	5.6	4.0	2.6
$80,000 to $89,999	3.2	1.1	3.1	4.2	4.3	4.6	0.7
$90,000 to $99,999	1.9	1.6	2.0	1.7	2.8	2.1	0.9
$100,000 or more	5.8	1.8	4.1	7.2	10.7	6.3	1.9

Source: Bureau of the Census, Current Population Survey, Internet site <http://ferret.bls.census.gov/macro/032001/hhinc/new02_004 .htm>; calculations by New Strategist

Income Distribution of Hispanic Households by Household Type, 2000

(number and percent distribution of Hispanic households by income and household type, 2000; households in thousands as of 2001)

| | | family households | | | | nonfamily households | | | | |
| | | | | | | | female householder | | male householder | |
	total	total	married couples	female hh, no spouse present	male hh, no spouse present	total	total	living alone	total	living alone
Hispanic households	**9,663**	**7,727**	**5,246**	**1,746**	**736**	**1,936**	**911**	**736**	**1,024**	**667**
Under $10,000	1,022	551	214	306	31	471	290	278	181	149
$10,000 to $19,999	1,707	1,260	743	422	95	446	236	212	209	176
$20,000 to $29,999	1,602	1,272	805	331	137	331	117	91	213	135
$30,000 to $39,999	1,352	1,144	782	246	117	208	86	52	121	78
$40,000 to $49,999	1,032	873	622	162	88	159	64	45	95	48
$50,000 to $59,999	824	715	546	97	72	111	47	22	65	40
$60,000 to $69,999	617	554	406	69	79	61	21	7	40	14
$70,000 to $79,999	449	397	331	34	32	51	19	12	32	7
$80,000 to $89,999	314	281	232	28	22	33	9	7	24	10
$90,000 to $99,999	188	170	133	22	16	18	5	2	13	2
$100,000 or more	556	508	433	29	46	48	16	6	32	8
Median income	$33,455	$36,578	$41,116	$23,671	$39,015	$21,263	$16,074	$13,295	$25,488	$20,597

(continued)

(continued from previous page)

Hispanic households	total	family households				nonfamily households				
		total	married couples	female hh, no spouse present	male hh, no spouse present	total	female householder		male householder	
							total	living alone	total	living alone
	100.0%	100.0%	100.0%	100.0%	100.0%	100.0%	100.0%	100.0%	100.0%	100.0%
Under $10,000	10.6	7.1	4.1	17.5	4.2	24.3	31.8	37.8	17.7	22.3
$10,000 to $19,999	17.7	16.3	14.2	24.2	12.9	23.0	25.9	28.8	20.4	26.4
$20,000 to $29,999	16.6	16.5	15.3	19.0	18.6	17.1	12.8	12.4	20.8	20.2
$30,000 to $39,999	14.0	14.8	14.9	14.1	15.9	10.7	9.4	7.1	11.8	11.7
$40,000 to $49,999	10.7	11.3	11.9	9.3	12.0	8.2	7.0	6.1	9.3	7.2
$50,000 to $59,999	8.5	9.3	10.4	5.6	9.8	5.7	5.2	3.0	6.3	6.0
$60,000 to $69,999	6.4	7.2	7.7	4.0	10.7	3.2	2.3	1.0	3.9	2.1
$70,000 to $79,999	4.6	5.1	6.3	1.9	4.3	2.6	2.1	1.6	3.1	1.0
$80,000 to $89,999	3.2	3.6	4.4	1.6	3.0	1.7	1.0	1.0	2.3	1.5
$90,000 to $99,999	1.9	2.2	2.5	1.3	2.2	0.9	0.5	0.3	1.3	0.3
$100,000 or more	5.8	6.6	8.3	1.7	6.3	2.5	1.8	0.8	3.1	1.2

Source: Bureau of the Census, Current Population Survey, Internet site <http://ferret.bls.census.gov/macro/032001/hhinc/new01_004.htm>; calculations by New Strategist

Income Distribution of Hispanic Households by Ethnicity, 1999

(number and percent distribution of Hispanic households by income and ethnicity, 1999; households in thousands as of 2000)

	total	Mexican	Puerto Rican	Cuban	Central & South American	other Hispanic
Total Hispanic households	**9,319**	**5,733**	**1,004**	**523**	**1,372**	**687**
Under $10,000	1,107	600	191	89	137	91
$10,000 to $19,999	1,813	1181	187	98	225	121
$20,000 to $34,999	2,319	1483	209	104	365	158
$35,000 to $49,999	1,553	957	172	67	251	109
$50,000 to $74,999	1,413	913	136	69	189	106
$75,000 or more	1,114	599	109	100	205	101
Median income	$31,061	$30,703	$28,411	$30,725	$33,340	$32,376
Total Hispanic households	**100.0%**	**100.0%**	**100.0%**	**100.0%**	**100.0%**	**100.0%**
Under $10,000	11.9	10.5	19.0	17.0	10.0	13.2
$10,000 to $19,999	19.5	20.6	18.6	18.7	16.4	17.6
$20,000 to $34,999	24.9	25.9	20.8	19.9	26.6	23.0
$35,000 to $49,999	16.7	16.7	17.1	12.8	18.3	15.9
$50,000 to $74,999	15.2	15.9	13.5	13.2	13.8	15.4
$75,000 or more	12.0	10.4	10.9	19.1	14.9	14.7

Source: Bureau of the Census, Current Population Survey, Internet site <www.census.gov/population/www/socdemo/hispanic/ho00-09 .html>; calculations by New Strategist

Income Distribution of Hispanic Men by Age, 2000

(number and percent distribution of Hispanic men aged 15 or older by income and age, median income of men with income, percent working full-time, and median income of full-time workers, 2000; men in thousands as of 2001)

	total	< 25	25–34	35–44	45–54	55–64	65+
Hispanic men	**11,644**	**3,005**	**2,861**	**2,557**	**1,545**	**899**	**777**
Without income	1,391	985	150	77	73	66	40
With income	10,253	2,020	2,711	2,480	1,472	833	737
Under $10,000	2,008	836	301	231	167	163	310
$10,000 to $19,999	3,161	740	893	651	379	266	231
$20,000 to $29,999	2,107	286	659	614	304	145	99
$30,000 to $39,999	1,240	82	401	386	229	100	43
$40,000 to $49,999	703	53	200	244	147	42	17
$50,000 to $74,999	711	20	197	230	158	80	26
$75,000 to $99,999	167	2	37	63	41	14	6
$100,000 or more	157	1	21	58	48	24	4
Median income of men with income	$19,829	$11,686	$21,661	$25,011	$25,203	$19,374	$11,735
Percent working full-time	58.1%	32.6%	73.6%	78.2%	70.7%	54.6%	12.5%
Median income of men working full-time	$25,042	$17,105	$25,021	$27,364	$30,312	$26,820	$26,637
Hispanic men	**100.0%**	**100.0%**	**100.0%**	**100.0%**	**100.0%**	**100.0%**	**100.0%**
Without income	11.9	32.8	5.2	3.0	4.7	7.3	5.1
With income	88.1	67.2	94.8	97.0	95.3	92.7	94.9
Under $10,000	17.2	27.8	10.5	9.0	10.8	18.1	39.9
$10,000 to $19,999	27.1	24.6	31.2	25.5	24.5	29.6	29.7
$20,000 to $29,999	18.1	9.5	23.0	24.0	19.7	16.1	12.7
$30,000 to $39,999	10.6	2.7	14.0	15.1	14.8	11.1	5.5
$40,000 to $49,999	6.0	1.8	7.0	9.5	9.5	4.7	2.2
$50,000 to $74,999	6.1	0.7	6.9	9.0	10.2	8.9	3.3
$75,000 to $99,999	1.4	0.1	1.3	2.5	2.7	1.6	0.8
$100,000 or more	1.3	0.0	0.7	2.3	3.1	2.7	0.5

Source: Bureau of the Census, Current Population Survey, Internet sites <http://ferret.bls.census.gov/macro/ 032001/perinc/new01_009 .htm> and <http://ferret.bls.census.gov/macro/032001/perinc/new01_024.htm>; calculations by New Strategist

Income Distribution of Hispanic Women by Age, 2000

(number and percent distribution of Hispanic women aged 15 or older by income and age, median income of women with income, percent working full-time, and median income of full-time workers, 2000; women in thousands as of 2001)

	total	< 25	25–34	35–44	45–54	55–64	65+
Hispanic women	**11,878**	**2,862**	**2,780**	**2,481**	**1,667**	**984**	**1,104**
Without income	2,795	1,155	580	430	274	240	115
With income	9,083	1,707	2,200	2,051	1,393	744	989
Under $10,000	3,733	984	694	618	394	325	717
$10,000 to $19,999	2,592	473	672	639	435	191	183
$20,000 to $29,999	1,395	190	408	402	250	97	48
$30,000 to $39,999	683	41	223	191	137	69	22
$40,000 to $49,999	304	11	103	81	75	25	8
$50,000 to $74,999	274	5	76	93	69	27	8
$75,000 to $99,999	63	1	13	20	24	4	2
$100,000 or more	35	1	10	8	10	4	2
Median income of women with income	$12,249	$7,851	$15,264	$15,835	$16,197	$11,924	$7,524
Percent working full-time	34.4%	18.8%	42.9%	45.9%	53.0%	30.2%	2.9%
Median income of women working full-time	$21,025	$16,240	$21,901	$21,774	$21,367	$23,585	$23,462
Hispanic women	**100.0%**	**100.0%**	**100.0%**	**100.0%**	**100.0%**	**100.0%**	**100.0%**
Without income	23.5	40.4	20.9	17.3	16.4	24.4	10.4
With income	76.5	59.6	79.1	82.7	83.6	75.6	89.6
Under $10,000	31.4	34.4	25.0	24.9	23.6	33.0	64.9
$10,000 to $19,999	21.8	16.5	24.2	25.8	26.1	19.4	16.6
$20,000 to $29,999	11.7	6.6	14.7	16.2	15.0	9.9	4.3
$30,000 to $39,999	5.8	1.4	8.0	7.7	8.2	7.0	2.0
$40,000 to $49,999	2.6	0.4	3.7	3.3	4.5	2.5	0.7
$50,000 to $74,999	2.3	0.2	2.7	3.7	4.1	2.7	0.7
$75,000 to $99,999	0.5	0.0	0.5	0.8	1.4	0.4	0.2
$100,000 or more	0.3	0.0	0.4	0.3	0.6	0.4	0.2

Source: Bureau of the Census, Current Population Survey, Internet sites <http://ferret.bls.census.gov/macro/032001/perinc/new01_014 .htm> and <http://ferret.bls.census.gov/macro/032001/perinc/new01_029.htm>; calculations by New Strategist

Median Earnings of Hispanics Working Full-Time by Sex, 1990 to 2000

(median earnings of Hispanics working full-time, year-round by sex; index of Hispanic to total population median earnings, and Hispanic women's earnings as a percent of Hispanic men's earnings, 1990 to 2000; percent change in earnings and indexes, 1990–2000; in 2000 dollars)

	Hispanic men		Hispanic women		Hispanic women's earnings as a percent of Hispanic men's earnings
	median earnings	index Hispanic/total	median earnings	index Hispanic/total	
2000	$24,638	66	$20,527	75	83.3%
1999	23,728	63	20,063	74	84.6
1998	23,515	63	20,282	74	86.3
1997	23,128	64	20,301	76	87.8
1996	23,017	66	20,404	79	88.6
1995	22,882	65	19,288	76	84.3
1994	23,381	66	20,222	79	86.5
1993	23,700	66	19,711	77	83.2
1992	23,578	65	20,616	80	87.4
1991	24,488	67	20,120	79	82.2
1990	24,570	69	20,122	79	81.9

Percent change

1990–2000	0.3%	–4.6%	2.0%	–5.1%	1.7%

Note: The Hispanic/total indexes are calculated by dividing the median earnings of Hispanic men and women by the median earnings of total men and women and multiplying by 100.
Source: Bureau of the Census, Current Population Survey, Internet site <www.census.gov/hhes/income/histinc/p38d.html>; calculations by New Strategist

Earnings Distribution of Hispanic Men Working Full-Time by Ethnicity, 1999

(number and percent distribution of Hispanic men aged 15 or older working full-time, year-round by earnings and ethnicity, 1999; men in thousands as of 2000)

	total	Mexican	Puerto Rican	Cuban	Central & South American	other Hispanic
Total Hispanic men	**6,476**	**4,310**	**505**	**308**	**979**	**373**
Under $10,000	343	242	14	11	59	16
$10,000 to $19,999	2,211	1606	111	94	327	74
$20,000 to $34,999	2,188	1446	197	85	327	134
$35,000 to $49,999	975	606	95	51	143	80
$50,000 to $74,999	547	321	66	31	84	45
$75,000 or more	212	89	22	36	40	26
Median earnings	$23,634	$22,476	$28,850	$28,455	$23,296	$30,536
Total Hispanic men	**100.0%**	**100.0%**	**100.0%**	**100.0%**	**100.0%**	**100.0%**
Under $10,000	5.3	5.6	2.8	3.6	6.0	4.3
$10,000 to $19,999	34.1	37.3	22.0	30.5	33.4	19.8
$20,000 to $34,999	33.8	33.5	39.0	27.6	33.4	35.9
$35,000 to $49,999	15.1	14.1	18.8	16.6	14.6	21.4
$50,000 to $74,999	8.4	7.4	13.1	10.1	8.6	12.1
$75,000 or more	3.3	2.1	4.4	11.7	4.1	7.0

Source: Bureau of the Census, Current Population Survey, Internet site <www.census.gov/population/socdemo/hispanic/p20-535/tab11-2 .txt>; calculations by New Strategist

Earnings Distribution of Hispanic Women Working Full-Time by Ethnicity, 1999

(number and percent distribution of Hispanic women aged 15 or older working full-time, year-round by earnings and ethnicity, 1999; women in thousands as of 2000)

	total	Mexican	Puerto Rican	Cuban	Central & South American	other Hispanic
Total Hispanic women	**3,770**	**2,248**	**396**	**185**	**657**	**284**
Under $10,000	337	226	27	15	50	19
$10,000 to $19,999	1,613	1,028	135	59	288	102
$20,000 to $34,999	1,163	659	150	59	186	109
$35,000 to $49,999	433	241	54	30	76	32
$50,000 to $74,999	169	80	24	16	33	16
$75,000 or more	55	13	6	5	23	7
Median earnings	$19,570	$18,608	$23,000	$24,205	$19,665	$22,019
Total Hispanic women	**100.0%**	**100.0%**	**100.0%**	**100.0%**	**100.0%**	**100.0%**
Under $10,000	8.9	10.1	6.8	8.1	7.6	6.7
$10,000 to $19,999	42.8	45.7	34.1	31.9	43.8	35.9
$20,000 to $34,999	30.8	29.3	37.9	31.9	28.3	38.4
$35,000 to $49,999	11.5	10.7	13.6	16.2	11.6	11.3
$50,000 to $74,999	4.5	3.6	6.1	8.6	5.0	5.6
$75,000 or more	1.5	0.6	1.5	2.7	3.5	2.5

Source: Bureau of the Census, Current Population Survey, Internet site <www.census.gov/population/socdemo/hispanic/p20-535/tab11-3 .txt>; calculations by New Strategist

Median Earnings of Hispanics Working Full-Time by Education and Sex, 2000

(median earnings of Hispanics aged 25 or older working full-time, year-round by educational attainment and sex, and Hispanic women's earnings as a percent of Hispanic men's earnings, 2000)

	men	women	Hispanic women's earnings as a percent of Hispanic men's earnings
Total Hispanics	**$26,418**	**$21,362**	**80.9%**
Less than 9th grade	19,419	14,560	75.0
9th to 12th grade, no diploma	21,605	15,365	71.1
High school graduate	27,359	20,860	76.2
Some college, no degree	33,148	25,308	76.3
Associate's degree	36,073	26,619	73.8
Bachelor's degree or more	46,489	36,365	78.2
Bachelor's degree	42,828	32,097	74.9
Master's degree	51,075	45,773	89.6
Professional degree	100,000	61,000	61.0
Doctoral degree	73,330	41,874	57.1

Source: Bureau of the Census, Current Population Survey, Internet sites <http://ferret.bls.census.gov/macro/032001/perinc/new03_079 .htm> and <http://ferret.bls.census.gov/macro/032001/perinc/new03_149.htm>; calculations by New Strategist

Poverty Status of Hispanic Families, 1990 to 2000

(total number of Hispanic families, and number and percent below poverty level by type of family and presence of children under age 18 at home, 1990 to 2000; percent change in numbers and rates, 1990–2000; families in thousands as of March the following year)

	total families			married couples			female hh, no spouse present		
		in poverty			in poverty			in poverty	
	total	*number*	*percent*	*total*	*number*	*percent*	*total*	*number*	*percent*
With and without children < age 18									
2000	7,728	1,431	18.5%	5,246	741	14.1%	1,746	597	34.2%
1999	7,561	1,525	20.2	5,133	728	14.2	1,769	686	38.8
1998	7,273	1,648	22.7	4,945	775	15.7	1,728	756	43.7
1997	6,961	1,721	24.7	4,804	836	17.4	1,612	767	47.6
1996	6,631	1,748	26.4	4,520	815	18.0	1,617	823	50.9
1995	6,287	1,695	27.0	4,247	803	18.9	1,604	792	49.4
1994	6,202	1,724	27.8	4,236	827	19.5	1,485	773	52.1
1993	5,946	1,625	27.3	4,038	770	19.1	1,498	772	51.6
1992	5,733	1,529	26.7	3,940	743	18.8	1,348	664	49.3
1991	5,177	1,372	26.5	3,532	674	19.1	1,261	627	49.7
1990	4,981	1,244	25.0	3,454	605	17.5	1,186	573	48.3
Percent change									
1990–2000	55.1%	15.0%	−26.0%	51.9%	22.5%	−19.4%	47.2%	4.2%	−29.2%
With children under age 18									
2000	5,363	1,226	22.9%	3,650	616	16.9%	1,309	541	41.4%
1999	5,320	1,330	25.0	3,609	607	16.8	1,353	630	46.6
1998	5,078	1,454	28.6	3,398	656	19.3	1,355	707	52.2
1997	4,910	1,492	30.4	3,293	692	21.0	1,292	701	54.2
1996	4,689	1,549	33.0	3,124	687	22.0	1,274	760	59.7
1995	4,422	1,470	33.2	2,902	657	22.6	1,283	735	57.3
1994	4,377	1,497	34.2	2,923	698	23.9	1,182	700	59.2
1993	4,153	1,424	34.3	2,747	652	23.7	1,167	706	60.5
1992	3,962	1,302	32.9	2,692	615	22.9	1,037	598	57.7
1991	3,621	1,219	33.7	2,445	575	23.5	972	584	60.1
1990	3,497	1,085	31.0	2,405	501	20.8	921	536	58.2
Percent change									
1990–2000	53.4%	15.1%	−26.1%	51.8%	23.0%	−18.8%	42.1%	0.9%	−28.9%

Source: Bureau of the Census, Current Population Survey, Internet sites <www.census.gov/hhes/poverty/ histpov/hstpov4.html> and <http://ferret.bls.census.gov/macro/032001/pov/new16a_000.htm>; calculations by New Strategist

Poverty Status of Hispanics by Sex and Age, 2000

(total number of Hispanics, and number and percent below poverty level by sex and age, 2000; people in thousands as of 2001)

	total	in poverty number	in poverty percent
Total Hispanics	**33,716**	**7,153**	**21.2%**
Under age 18	11,884	3,328	28.0
Aged 18 to 24	4,178	896	21.5
Aged 25 to 34	5,641	1,080	19.1
Aged 35 to 44	5,037	782	15.5
Aged 45 to 54	3,212	395	12.3
Aged 55 to 59	1,052	134	12.8
Aged 60 to 64	831	184	22.1
Aged 65 or older	1,882	353	18.8
Aged 65 to 74	1,153	218	18.9
Aged 75 or older	729	135	18.5
Hispanic females	**16,855**	**3,866**	**22.9**
Under age 18	5,776	1,639	28.4
Aged 18 to 24	2,063	519	25.1
Aged 25 to 34	2,780	622	22.4
Aged 35 to 44	2,481	454	18.3
Aged 45 to 54	1,667	220	13.2
Aged 55 to 59	551	90	16.3
Aged 60 to 64	433	106	24.5
Aged 65 or older	1,104	216	19.6
Aged 65 to 74	653	118	18.0
Aged 75 or older	451	98	21.8
Hispanic males	**16,861**	**3,287**	**19.5**
Under age 18	6,107	1,690	27.7
Aged 18 to 24	2,115	378	17.9
Aged 25 to 34	2,861	458	16.0
Aged 35 to 44	2,557	328	12.8
Aged 45 to 54	1,545	175	11.3
Aged 55 to 59	501	45	9.0
Aged 60 to 64	398	78	19.5
Aged 65 or older	777	137	17.6
Aged 65 to 74	500	100	20.1
Aged 75 or older	278	36	13.1

Source: Bureau of the Census, Current Population Survey, Internet site <http://ferret.bls.census.gov/macro/032001/pov/new01_001.htm>; calculations by New Strategist

Poverty Status of Hispanics by Ethnicity, 1999

(number and percent of Hispanics below poverty level by ethnicity, 1999; people in thousands as of 2000)

	total	Mexican	Puerto Rican	Cuban	Central & South American	other Hispanic
Total Hispanics	**7,439**	**5,214**	**760**	**224**	**789**	**452**
Under age 18	3,506	2,597	370	50	288	201
Aged 18 to 64	3,575	2,448	356	95	461	215
Aged 65 or older	358	169	34	79	40	36
Total Hispanics	**22.8%**	**24.1%**	**25.8%**	**17.3%**	**16.7%**	**21.6%**
Under age 18	30.3	31.5	37.2	20.2	20.9	28.7
Aged 18 to 64	18.5	19.7	20.1	12.2	14.8	17.2
Aged 65 or older	20.4	18.1	18.8	28.9	17.9	25.3

Source: Bureau of the Census, Current Population Survey, Internet site <www.census.gov/population/socdemo/hispanic/p20-535/tab14-1 .txt>; calculations by New Strategist

Hispanic Women Are Less Likely to Work than the Average Woman

The labor force participation rate of Hispanic men, at 81 percent, is significantly higher than the 75 percent rate for all men. In contrast, only 57 percent of Hispanic women are in the labor force compared with 60 percent of all women. Among Hispanic women, those of Cuban origin are least likely to work, with a labor force participation rate of just 52 percent.

Only 14 percent of Hispanic workers are in managerial or professional specialty jobs, accounting for 5 percent of Americans employed in those occupations. The occupational distribution of Hispanics varies by ethnicity, however. Fully 23 percent of Cuban Americans are employed in managerial or professional specialty occupations. In contrast, the figure is just 12 percent among Mexican Americans. Hispanics account for 11 percent of all workers, but for 26 percent of bakers, 32 percent of private household service workers, and 47 percent of farm workers.

Fifty-two percent of Hispanic households have two or more earners, a greater share than the 45 percent of all households with at least two earners. Nevertheless, among Hispanic married couples, only 51 percent are dual earner, a smaller portion than the 56 percent national share. For 34 percent of Hispanic couples, the husband is the only worker, compared with the much lower figure of 21 percent of all couples.

Hispanic workers spend a median of 22 minutes commuting to their job each day and travel a median distance of 9 miles. Sixty-five percent drive their car alone to work.

Between 2000 and 2010, the number of Hispanic workers will grow 36 percent. Hispanics will account for 13 percent of the labor force in 2010.

■ Because a large share of Hispanics are poorly educated immigrants, they are far less likely to be employed in professional or managerial occupations than other Americans.

Hispanics are less likely to be managers or professionals

(percent of total and Hispanic workers aged 16 or older employed in managerial or professional specialty occupations, 2000)

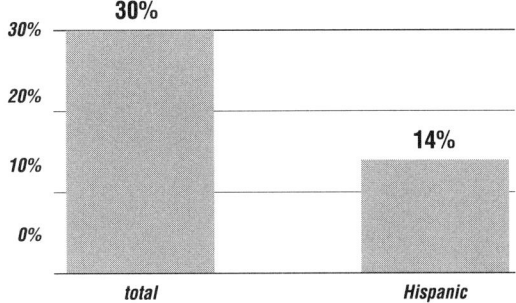

Labor Force Participation Rate of Hispanics by Age and Sex, 2000

(percent of Hispanics aged 16 or older in the civilian labor force, by age and sex, 2000)

	men	women
Total Hispanics	**80.6%**	**56.9%**
Aged 16 to 19	50.9	41.4
Aged 20 to 24	89.2	64.9
Aged 25 to 34	94.0	65.3
Aged 35 to 44	93.3	69.9
Aged 45 to 54	87.5	68.3
Aged 55 to 64	69.4	41.3
Aged 65 or older	18.2	7.7

Note: The civilian labor force equals the number of employed plus the number of unemployed.
Source: Bureau of Labor Statistics, Employment and Earnings, _January 2001_

Employment Status of Hispanics by Sex and Age, 2000

(employment status of the civilian noninstitutionalized Hispanic population aged 16 or older, by sex and age, 2000; numbers in thousands)

	civilian labor force					not in labor force	
	total	percent of population	employed	unemployed	percent unemployed	total	percent of population
Total Hispanics	**15,368**	**68.6%**	**14,492**	**876**	**5.7%**	**7,025**	**31.4%**
Aged 16 to 19	1,083	46.3	902	181	16.7	1,258	53.7
Aged 20 to 24	2,155	77.7	1,994	162	7.5	620	22.3
Aged 25 to 34	4,485	79.7	4,270	215	4.8	1,141	20.3
Aged 35 to 44	4,086	81.6	3,903	183	4.5	921	18.4
Aged 45 to 54	2,357	77.7	2,278	79	3.3	676	22.3
Aged 55 to 64	983	54.1	939	44	4.5	836	46.0
Aged 65 or older	218	12.2	206	12	5.7	1,573	87.8
Hispanic men	**8,919**	**80.6**	**8,478**	**441**	**4.9**	**2,145**	**19.4**
Aged 16 to 19	613	50.9	517	96	15.7	592	49.1
Aged 20 to 24	1,299	89.2	1,214	85	6.5	158	10.8
Aged 25 to 34	2,652	94.0	2,554	98	3.7	168	6.0
Aged 35 to 44	2,338	93.3	2,249	89	3.8	168	6.7
Aged 45 to 54	1,305	87.5	1,264	41	3.1	187	12.5
Aged 55 to 64	573	69.4	550	23	4.1	253	30.6
Aged 65 or older	138	18.2	130	9	6.3	620	81.8
Hispanic women	**6,449**	**56.9**	**6,014**	**435**	**6.7**	**4,880**	**43.1**
Aged 16 to 19	470	41.4	385	85	18.1	666	58.6
Aged 20 to 24	856	64.9	780	77	8.9	463	35.1
Aged 25 to 34	1,833	65.3	1,716	117	6.4	973	34.7
Aged 35 to 44	1,748	69.9	1,654	94	5.4	754	30.1
Aged 45 to 54	1,053	68.3	1,015	38	3.6	489	31.7
Aged 55 to 64	410	41.3	389	21	5.1	583	58.7
Aged 65 or older	80	7.7	152	4	4.8	952	92.2

Note: The civilian labor force equals the number of employed plus the number of unemployed. The civilian population equals the number of people in the labor force plus the number not in the labor force.
Source: Bureau of Labor Statistics, Employment and Earnings, *January 2001; calculations by New Strategist*

Employment Status of Hispanics by Sex and Ethnicity, 2000

(employment status of the civilian noninstitutionalized Hispanic population aged 16 or older, by sex and ethnicity, 2000; numbers in thousands)

	civilian labor force					not in labor force	
	total	percent of population	employed	unemployed	percent unemployed	total	percent of population
Total Hispanics	**15,368**	**68.6%**	**14,492**	**876**	**5.7%**	**7,025**	**31.4%**
Mexican	9,955	69.2	9,364	591	5.9	4,430	30.8
Puerto Rican	1,278	63.1	1,196	82	6.4	747	36.9
Cuban	680	61.6	650	30	4.4	424	38.4
Hispanic men	**8,919**	**80.6**	**8,478**	**441**	**4.9**	**2,145**	**19.4**
Mexican	6,028	82.2	5,718	310	5.1	1,308	17.8
Puerto Rican	637	70.2	601	36	5.7	271	29.8
Cuban	395	71.8	378	16	4.1	155	28.2
Hispanic women	**6,449**	**56.9**	**6,014**	**435**	**6.7**	**4,880**	**43.1**
Mexican	3,927	55.7	3,646	281	7.2	3,123	44.3
Puerto Rican	640	57.4	595	46	7.1	476	42.7
Cuban	286	51.5	272	13	4.7	269	48.5

Note: The civilian labor force equals the number of employed plus the number of unemployed. The civilian population equals the number in the labor force plus the number not in the labor force. Numbers will not add to total because not all ethnicities are shown.
Source: Bureau of Labor Statistics, Employment and Earnings, *January 2001; calculations by New Strategist*

Hispanic Workers by Occupation, 2000

(total number of employed people aged 16 or older in the civilian labor force; number and percent distribution of employed Hispanics, and Hispanic share of total, by occupation, 2000; numbers in thousands)

		Hispanic		
	total	*number*	*percent distribution*	*share of total*
Total employed	**135,208**	**14,492**	**100.0%**	**10.7%**
Managerial and professional specialty	40,887	2,036	14.0	5.0
Executive, administrative, and managerial	19,774	1,072	7.4	5.4
Professional specialty	21,113	964	6.7	4.6
Technical, sales, and administrative support	39,442	3,504	24.2	8.9
Technicians and related support	4,385	303	2.1	6.9
Sales occupations	16,340	1,385	9.6	8.5
Administrative support, including clerical	18,717	1,816	12.5	9.7
Service occupations	18,278	2,867	19.8	15.7
Private household	792	251	1.7	31.7
Protective service	2,399	208	1.4	8.7
Service, except private household and protective	15,087	2,408	16.6	16.0
Precision production, craft, and repair	14,882	2,075	14.3	13.9
Mechanics and repairers	4,875	522	3.6	10.7
Construction trades	6,120	1,004	6.9	16.4
Other precision production, craft, and repair	3,887	550	3.8	14.1
Operators, fabricators, and laborers	18,319	3,202	22.1	17.5
Machine operators, assemblers, and inspectors	7,319	1,416	9.8	19.3
Transportation and material moving occupations	5,557	662	4.6	11.9
Handlers, equipment cleaners, helpers, and laborers	5,443	1,125	7.8	20.7
Construction laborers	1,015	281	1.9	27.7
Other handlers, equipment cleaners, helpers, laborers	4,428	844	5.8	19.1
Farming, forestry, and fishing	3,399	807	5.6	23.7

Source: Bureau of Labor Statistics, Employment and Earnings, *January 2001; calculations by New Strategist*

Hispanic Workers by Occupation and Ethnicity, 2000

(number and percent distribution of employed Hispanics aged 16 or older in the civilian labor force, by ethnicity, 2000; numbers in thousands)

	total	Mexican	Puerto Rican	Cuban
Total employed Hispanics	**14,492**	**9,364**	**1,196**	**650**
Managerial and professional specialty	2,036	1,107	224	151
Executive, administrative, and managerial	1,072	602	111	73
Professional specialty	964	504	113	77
Technical, sales, and administrative support	3,504	2,060	394	216
Technicians and related support	303	171	33	20
Sales occupations	1,385	816	134	96
Administrative support, including clerical	1,816	1,073	227	99
Service occupations	2,867	1,818	224	87
Private household	251	133	5	3
Protective service	208	112	37	12
Service, except private household and protective	2,408	1,573	182	72
Precision production, craft, and repair	2,075	1,456	119	87
Mechanics and repairers	522	323	45	36
Construction trades	1,004	739	45	35
Other precision production, craft, and repair	550	394	29	16
Operators, fabricators, and laborers	3,202	2,202	222	99
Machine operators, assemblers, and inspectors	1,416	976	102	39
Transportation and material moving occupations	662	423	52	28
Handlers, equipment cleaners, helpers, and laborers	1,125	804	68	33
Construction laborers	281	220	8	5
Other handlers, equipment cleaners, helpers, laborers	844	583	59	28
Farming, forestry, and fishing	807	721	12	11

(continued)

(continued from previous page)

	total	Mexican	Puerto Rican	Cuban
Percent distribution by occupation				
Total employed Hispanics	**100.0%**	**100.0%**	**100.0%**	**100.0%**
Managerial and professional specialty	14.0	11.8	18.7	23.2
Executive, administrative, and managerial	7.4	6.4	9.3	11.2
Professional specialty	6.7	5.4	9.4	11.8
Technical, sales, and administrative support	24.2	22.0	32.9	33.2
Technicians and related support	2.1	1.8	2.8	3.1
Sales occupations	9.6	8.7	11.2	14.8
Administrative support, including clerical	12.5	11.5	19.0	15.2
Service occupations	19.8	19.4	18.7	13.4
Private household	1.7	1.4	0.4	0.5
Protective service	1.4	1.2	3.1	1.8
Service, except private household and protective	16.6	16.8	15.2	11.1
Precision production, craft, and repair	14.3	15.5	9.9	13.4
Mechanics and repairers	3.6	3.4	3.8	5.5
Construction trades	6.9	7.9	3.8	5.4
Other precision production, craft, and repair	3.8	4.2	2.4	2.5
Operators, fabricators, and laborers	22.1	23.5	18.6	15.2
Machine operators, assemblers, and inspectors	9.8	10.4	8.5	6.0
Transportation and material moving occupations	4.6	4.5	4.3	4.3
Handlers, equipment cleaners, helpers, and laborers	7.8	8.6	5.7	5.1
Construction laborers	1.9	2.3	0.7	0.8
Other handlers, equipment cleaners, helpers, laborers	5.8	6.2	4.9	4.3
Farming, forestry, and fishing	5.6	7.7	1.0	1.7

Note: Numbers will not add to total because not all ethnicities are shown.
Source: Bureau of Labor Statistics, Employment and Earnings, *January 2001; calculations by New Strategist*

Hispanic Worker Share by Detailed Occupation, 2000

(total number of employed people aged 16 or older in the civilian labor force and Hispanic share of total employed, by occupation, 2000; numbers in thousands)

	total	percent Hispanic
Total employed	**135,208**	**10.7%**
Managerial and professional specialty	**40,887**	**5.0**
Executive, administrative, and managerial	19,774	5.4
Officials and administrators, public administration	651	7.0
Administrators, protective services	62	3.4
Financial managers	784	4.3
Personnel and labor relations managers	226	4.0
Purchasing managers	123	3.2
Managers, marketing, advertising, and public relations	755	4.2
Administrators, education and related fields	848	5.7
Managers, medicine and health	752	5.4
Postmasters and mail superintendents	55	3.8
Managers, food serving and lodging establishments	1,446	9.2
Managers, properties and real estate	552	7.2
Funeral directors	58	7.2
Management-related occupations	4,932	5.4
Accountants and auditors	1,592	5.1
Underwriters	104	3.8
Other financial officers	837	4.9
Management analysts	426	2.9
Personnel, training, and labor relations specialists	628	6.3
Buyers, wholesale and retail trade, except farm products	224	6.5
Construction inspectors	72	4.3
Inspectors and compliance officers, except construction	255	6.8
Professional specialty	21,113	4.6
Engineers, architects, and surveyors	2,326	3.9
Architects	215	5.5
Engineers	2,093	3.7
Aerospace engineers	78	3.6
Chemical engineers	85	1.0
Civil engineers	288	2.7
Electrical and electronic engineers	725	3.6
Industrial engineers	244	4.0
Mechanical engineers	342	3.7
Mathematical and computer scientists	2,074	3.7
Computer systems analysts and scientists	1,797	3.6
Operations and systems researchers and analysts	227	4.4

(continued)

(continued from previous page)

	total	percent Hispanic
Natural scientists	566	3.2%
Chemists, except biochemists	153	2.2
Agricultural and food scientists	53	3.9
Biological and life scientists	114	6.0
Medical scientists	84	4.6
Health diagnosing occupations	1,038	3.4
Physicians	719	3.7
Dentists	168	2.2
Veterinarians	55	1.5
Health assessment and treating occupations	2,966	3.4
Registered nurses	2,111	2.8
Pharmacists	208	3.8
Dietitians	97	4.8
Therapists	478	5.0
Respiratory therapists	78	5.3
Occupational therapists	55	5.8
Physical therapists	144	6.8
Speech therapists	102	2.0
Physicians' assistants	72	7.8
Teachers, except college and university	5,353	5.2
Prekindergarten and kindergarten	626	8.0
Elementary school	2,177	5.6
Secondary school	1,319	4.2
Special education	362	3.2
Counselors, educational and vocational	258	5.3
Librarians, archivists, and curators	263	5.8
Librarians	232	6.6
Social scientists and urban planners	450	4.1
Economists	139	4.4
Psychologists	265	4.0
Social, recreation, and religious workers	1,492	6.4
Social workers	828	8.5
Recreation workers	126	4.9
Clergy	369	4.5
Lawyers and judges	926	4.1
Lawyers	881	3.9
Writers, artists, entertainers, and athletes	2,439	5.6
Authors	138	2.2
Technical writers	70	1.7
Designers	738	6.3
Musicians and composers	161	6.0
Actors and directors	139	6.1

(continued)

(continued from previous page)

	total	percent Hispanic
Painters, sculptors, craft artists, and artist printmakers	238	4.2%
Photographers	148	5.9
Editors and reporters	288	3.0
Public relations specialists	205	5.5
Announcers	54	6.0
Athletes	90	5.5
Technical, sales, and administrative support	**39,442**	**8.9**
Technicians and related support	4,385	6.9
Health technologists and technicians	1,724	8.2
Clinical laboratory technologists and technicians	342	7.5
Dental hygienists	112	1.7
Radiologic technicians	161	7.7
Licensed practical nurses	374	5.0
Engineering and related technologists and technicians	1,002	6.1
Electrical and electronic technicians	468	7.1
Drafting occupations	219	4.7
Surveying and mapping technicians	79	7.8
Science technicians	270	8.4
Biological technicians	108	8.2
Chemical technicians	71	7.6
Technicians, except health, engineering, and science	1,389	5.7
Airplane pilots and navigators	129	4.3
Computer programmers	699	3.5
Legal assistants	387	9.8
Sales occupations	16,340	8.5
Supervisors and proprietors	4,937	7.3
Sales representatives, finance and business services	2,934	4.9
Insurance sales	577	4.4
Real estate sales	787	5.0
Securities and financial services sales	600	3.4
Advertising and related sales	165	5.7
Sales occupations, other business services	805	6.2
Sales representatives, commodities, except retail	1,581	6.4
Sales representatives, mining, manufacturing, and wholesale	1,549	6.4
Sales workers, retail and personal services	6,782	11.4
Sales workers, motor vehicles and boats	329	8.4
Sales workers, apparel	411	13.8
Sales workers, shoes	114	14.6
Sales workers, furniture and home furnishings	185	7.7
Sales workers, radio, television, hi-fi, and appliances	258	6.2
Sales workers, hardware and building supplies	328	7.4
Sales workers, parts	186	15.2

(continued)

(continued from previous page)

	total	percent Hispanic
Sales workers, other commodities	1,428	9.0%
Sales counter clerks	185	8.7
Cashiers	2,939	13.5
Street and door-to-door sales workers	311	13.5
News vendors	110	7.5
Sales-related occupations	107	2.2
Demonstrators, promoters, and models	71	1.8
Administrative support occupations, including clerical	18,717	9.7
Supervisors, administrative support	710	9.4
Supervisors, general office	404	7.0
Supervisors, financial records processing	73	6.2
Supervisors, distribution, scheduling, and adjusting clerks	217	15.2
Computer equipment operators	323	7.4
Computer operators	321	7.4
Secretaries, stenographers, and typists	3,328	8.6
Secretaries	2,623	8.7
Stenographers	154	4.4
Typists	551	9.3
Information clerks	2,071	10.4
Interviewers	212	9.2
Hotel clerks	130	8.2
Transportation ticket and reservation agents	287	9.4
Receptionists	1,017	11.6
Records processing, except financial	1,119	10.6
Order clerks	305	12.4
Personnel clerks, except payroll and timekeeping	84	4.8
Library clerks	152	6.5
File clerks	338	12.0
Records clerks	227	10.7
Financial records processing	2,269	7.3
Bookkeepers, accounting and auditing clerks	1,719	6.1
Payroll and timekeeping clerks	174	8.4
Billing clerks	198	12.4
Billing, posting, and calculating machine operators	134	12.3
Duplicating, mail and other office machine operators	55	9.6
Communications equipment operators	167	10.7
Telephone operators	156	10.4
Mail and message distributing	978	7.7
Postal clerks, except mail carriers	304	6.2
Mail carriers, postal service	340	5.9
Mail clerks, except postal service	178	11.2
Messengers	157	10.4

(continued)

(continued from previous page)

	total	*percent Hispanic*
Material recording, scheduling, and distributing clerks	2,052	12.8%
Dispatchers	269	9.0
Production coordinators	227	6.6
Traffic, shipping, and receiving clerks	661	17.5
Stock and inventory clerks	460	13.1
Weighers, measurers, checkers, and samplers	64	16.7
Expediters	310	10.5
Adjusters and investigators	1,818	10.1
Insurance adjusters, examiners, and investigators	451	7.0
Investigators and adjusters, except insurance	1,097	11.5
Eligibility clerks, social welfare	94	9.5
Bill and account collectors	176	9.5
Miscellaneous administrative support	3,826	10.4
General office clerks	864	10.5
Bank tellers	431	8.2
Data-entry keyers	749	11.2
Statistical clerks	104	8.4
Teachers' aides	710	14.4
Service occupations	**18,278**	**15.7**
Private household	792	31.7
Child care workers	275	19.9
Cleaners and servants	500	37.7
Protective service	2,399	8.7
Supervisors	201	7.8
Police and detectives	116	3.0
Guards	53	18.5
Firefighting and fire prevention	248	5.4
Firefighting	233	5.0
Police and detectives	1,060	8.4
Police and detectives, public service	560	10.1
Sheriffs, bailiffs, and other law enforcement officers	156	5.8
Correctional institution officers	344	6.9
Guards	889	10.0
Guards and police, except public services	745	10.6
Service occupations, except private household and protective service	15,087	16.0
Food preparation and service occupations	6,327	17.2
Supervisors, food preparation and service	434	12.0
Bartenders	365	13.2
Waiters and waitresses	1,440	11.0
Cooks	2,076	21.6
Food counter, fountain and related occupations	357	11.8
Kitchen workers, food preparation	317	12.3

(continued)

(continued from previous page)

	total	percent Hispanic
Waiters' and waitresses' assistants	670	18.8%
Miscellaneous food preparation	668	26.0
Health service occupations	2,557	10.1
Dental assistants	218	10.6
Health aides, except nursing	356	8.7
Nursing aides, orderlies, and attendants	1,983	10.4
Cleaning and building service occupations	3,127	23.4
Supervisors	166	20.2
Maids and housemen	650	28.3
Janitors and cleaners	2,233	22.5
Pest control occupations	71	11.7
Personal service occupations	3,077	10.8
Supervisors	119	8.8
Barbers	108	12.7
Hairdressers and cosmetologists	820	10.7
Attendants, amusement and recreation facilities	246	6.0
Public transportation attendants	127	7.9
Welfare service aides	99	12.7
Family child care providers	457	13.3
Early childhood teachers' assistants	480	10.6
Precision production, craft, and repair	**14,882**	**13.9**
Mechanics and repairers	4,875	10.7
Supervisors	223	8.4
Mechanics and repairers, except supervisors	4,652	10.8
Vehicle and mobile equipment mechanics and repairers	1,787	13.1
Automobile mechanics	860	15.6
Bus, truck, and stationary engine mechanics	345	9.1
Aircraft engine mechanics	126	9.0
Small engine repairers	60	5.1
Automobile body and related repairers	186	16.1
Heavy equipment mechanics	162	10.0
Industrial machinery repairers	524	8.0
Electrical and electronic equipment repairers	999	7.8
Electronic repairers, communications and industrial equipment	192	9.8
Data processing equipment repairers	342	4.8
Telephone line installers and repairers	53	9.9
Telephone installers and repairers	295	9.5
Heating, air conditioning, and refrigeration mechanics	371	11.9
Miscellaneous mechanics and repairers	949	10.7
Office machine repairers	53	5.8
Millwrights	78	3.9

(continued)

(continued from previous page)

	total	percent Hispanic
Construction trades	6,120	16.4%
Supervisors	967	7.5
Construction trades, except supervisors	5,153	18.1
Brickmasons and stonemasons	242	18.6
Tile setters, hard and soft	94	34.4
Carpet installers	125	18.9
Carpenters	1,467	16.3
Drywall installers	206	39.2
Electricians	860	9.1
Electrical power installers and repairers	132	9.9
Painters, construction and maintenance	624	24.4
Plumbers, pipefitters, and steamfitters	540	13.5
Concrete and terrazzo finishers	99	36.1
Insulation workers	58	21.5
Roofers	215	30.1
Structural metalworkers	79	8.9
Extractive occupations	128	7.8
Precision production occupations	3,759	14.4
Supervisors	1,129	10.6
Precision metalworking	865	8.9
Tool and die makers	121	3.9
Machinists	488	8.8
Sheet-metal workers	121	10.0
Precision woodworking occupations	127	10.0
Cabinet makers and bench carpenters	89	9.6
Precision textile, apparel, and furnishings machine workers	192	25.2
Dressmakers	77	20.8
Upholsterers	64	25.1
Precision workers, assorted materials	554	14.8
Optical goods workers	77	9.3
Electrical and electronic equipment assemblers	336	15.7
Precision food production occupations	481	32.9
Butchers and meat cutters	265	38.3
Bakers	154	26.1
Food batchmakers	62	26.5
Precision inspectors, testers, and related workers	148	8.2
Inspectors, testers, and graders	136	7.7
Plant and system operators	264	11.8
Water and sewage treatment plant operators	69	7.6
Stationary engineers	118	11.5
Operators, fabricators, and laborers	**18,319**	**17.5**
Machine operators, assemblers, and inspectors	7,319	19.3

(continued)

(continued from previous page)

	total	percent Hispanic
Machine operators and tenders, except precision	4,546	20.7%
Metalworking and plastic working machine operators	349	10.8
Punching and stamping press machine operators	94	10.4
Grinding, abrading, buffing, and polishing machine operators	98	17.2
Metal and plastic processing machine operators	150	17.4
Molding and casting machine operators	84	14.7
Woodworking machine operators	137	11.1
Sawing machine operators	78	11.8
Printing machine operators	369	12.1
Printing press operators	292	13.4
Textile, apparel, and furnishings machine operators	854	33.0
Textile sewing machine operators	425	40.6
Pressing machine operators	81	49.9
Laundering and dry cleaning machine operators	214	25.6
Machine operators, assorted materials	2,665	19.9
Packaging and filling machine operators	345	34.0
Mixing and blending machine operators	112	11.7
Separating, filtering, and clarifying machine operators	62	15.8
Painting and paint spraying machine operators	187	20.3
Furnace, kiln, and oven operators, except food	53	4.2
Slicing and cutting machine operators	149	25.9
Photographic process machine operators	103	11.4
Fabricators, assemblers, and hand working occupations	2,070	17.1
Welders and cutters	594	15.3
Assemblers	1,299	18.2
Production inspectors, testers, samplers, and weighers	703	17.3
Production inspectors, checkers, and examiners	497	13.2
Production testers	64	10.7
Graders and sorters, except agricultural	134	36.1
Transportation and material moving occupations	5,557	11.9
Motor vehicle operators	4,222	11.8
Supervisors	77	10.8
Truck drivers	3,088	12.5
Drivers, sales workers	167	6.8
Bus drivers	539	8.0
Taxicab drivers and chauffeurs	280	14.0
Parking lot attendants	60	16.6
Transportation occupations, except motor vehicles	183	3.6
Rail transportation	127	5.1
Locomotive operating occupations	63	6.9
Water transportation	56	0.2
Material moving equipment operators	1,152	13.7

(continued)

(continued from previous page)

	total	percent Hispanic
Operating engineers	253	10.4%
Crane and tower operators	70	4.6
Excavating and loading machine operators	98	9.7
Grader, dozer, and scraper operators	52	4.5
Industrial truck and tractor equipment operators	569	18.4
Handlers, equipment cleaners, helpers, and laborers	5,443	20.7
Helpers, construction and extractive occupations	120	29.6
Helpers, construction trades	111	30.4
Construction laborers	1,015	27.7
Production helpers	75	20.7
Freight, stock, and material handlers	2,015	14.6
Garbage collectors	54	11.6
Stock handlers and baggers	1,125	14.1
Machine feeders and offbearers	82	11.6
Freight, stock, and material handlers, not elsewhere classified	739	15.9
Garage and service station related occupations	184	16.1
Vehicle washers and equipment cleaners	313	28.2
Hand packers and packagers	366	34.7
Laborers, except construction	1,307	18.4
Farming, forestry, and fishing	**3,399**	**23.7**
Farm operators and managers	1,125	3.0
Farmers, except horticultural	879	1.7
Horticultural specialty farmers	69	11.9
Managers, farms, except horticultural	149	5.6
Other agricultural and related occupations	2,115	36.1
Farm occupations, except managerial	847	47.6
Farm workers	768	47.4
Related agricultural occupations	1,268	28.4
Supervisors	174	15.9
Groundskeepers and gardeners, except farm	870	30.9
Animal caretakers, except farm	148	9.0
Graders and sorters, agricultural products	68	70.9
Forestry and logging occupations	109	7.8
Timber cutting and logging occupations	66	4.8
Fishers, hunters, and trappers	51	2.0

Source: Bureau of Labor Statistics, Employment and Earnings, *January 2001*

Hispanic Workers by Industry, 2000

(total number of employed people aged 16 or older in the civilian labor force; number and percent distribution of employed Hispanics, and Hispanic share of total, by industry, 2000; numbers in thousands)

| | | Hispanic | | |
	total	*number*	*percent distribution*	*share of total*
Total employed	**135,208**	**14,492**	**100.0%**	**10.7%**
Agriculture	3,305	744	5.1	22.5
Mining	521	43	0.3	8.3
Construction	9,433	1,406	9.7	14.9
Manufacturing	19,940	2,453	16.9	12.3
Durable goods	12,168	1,229	8.5	10.1
Nondurable goods	7,772	1,212	8.4	15.6
Transportation, communications, and other public utilities	9,740	916	6.3	9.4
Wholesale and retail trade	27,832	3,396	23.4	12.2
Wholesale trade	5,421	645	4.5	11.9
Retail trade	22,411	2,757	19.0	12.3
Finance, insurance, and real estate	8,727	602	4.2	6.9
Services	49,695	4,522	31.2	9.1
Private households	894	266	1.8	29.8
Other service industries	48,801	4,246	29.3	8.7
Professional and related services	32,784	2,328	16.1	7.1
Public administration	6,015	439	3.0	7.3

Source: Bureau of Labor Statistics, Employment and Earnings, *January 2001; calculations by New Strategist*

Hispanic Households by Number of Earners, 2000

(number and percent distribution of Hispanic households by number of earners, 2000; numbers in thousands)

	number	percent distribution
Hispanic households	**9,319**	**100.0%**
No earners	1,168	12.5
One earner	3,321	35.6
Two or more earners	4,830	51.8
Two earners	3,354	36.0
Three earners	974	10.5
Four or more earners	502	5.4

Source: Bureau of the Census, Current Population Survey, Internet site <http://ferret.bls.census.gov/macro/ 032000/hhinc/new01_004 .htm>; calculations by New Strategist

Labor Force Status of Hispanic Married Couples, 2000

(number and percent distribution of Hispanic married couples by age of householder and labor force status of husband and wife, 2000; numbers in thousands)

	total	husband and/or wife in labor force			neither husband nor wife in labor force
		husband and wife	husband only	wife only	
Total Hispanic couples	**5,133**	**2,642**	**1,764**	**213**	**514**
Under age 20	28	9	19	–	–
Aged 20 to 24	287	121	154	10	3
Aged 25 to 29	618	329	269	5	15
Aged 30 to 34	818	442	339	19	17
Aged 35 to 39	854	545	291	10	8
Aged 40 to 44	680	441	198	18	24
Aged 45 to 54	911	549	264	55	43
Aged 55 to 64	509	184	179	64	82
Aged 65 or older	427	22	49	34	321
Total Hispanic couples	**100.0%**	**51.5%**	**34.4%**	**4.1%**	**10.0%**
Under age 20	100.0	32.1	67.9	–	–
Aged 20 to 24	100.0	42.2	53.7	3.5	1.0
Aged 25 to 29	100.0	53.2	43.5	0.8	2.4
Aged 30 to 34	100.0	54.0	41.4	2.3	2.1
Aged 35 to 39	100.0	63.8	34.1	1.2	0.9
Aged 40 to 44	100.0	64.9	29.1	2.6	3.5
Aged 45 to 54	100.0	60.3	29.0	6.0	4.7
Aged 55 to 64	100.0	36.1	35.2	12.6	16.1
Aged 65 or older	100.0	5.2	11.5	8.0	75.2

Note: (–) means sample is too small to make a reliable estimate.
Source: Bureau of the Census, Household and Family Characteristics: March 2000 (Update), *detailed tables for Current Population Report P20-537, Internet site <www.census.gov/population/socdemo/hh-fam/p20-537/2000/tabFG1.txt>; calculations by New Strategist*

Union Membership of Hispanics, 2000

(number of employed Hispanic wage and salary workers aged 16 or older, number and percent represented by unions or who are union members, and median weekly earnings by union membership status; by sex, 2000; numbers in thousands)

	total	men	women
Total employed Hispanics	**13,609**	**7,884**	**5,725**
Represented by unions	1,740	1,063	677
Percent of employed	12.8%	13.5%	11.8%
Members of unions	1,554	972	582
Percent of employed	11.4%	12.3%	10.2%
Median weekly earnings, total	**$396**	**$414**	**$364**
Represented by unions	580	620	492
Members of unions	584	631	489
Non-union	377	394	346

Note: Workers represented by unions are either members of a labor union or similar employee association or workers who report no union affiliation but whose jobs are covered by a union or an employee association contract. Members of unions are union members as well as members of employee associations similar to unions.
Source: Bureau of Labor Statistics, Employment and Earnings, *January 2001*

Journey to Work for Hispanic Workers, 1999

(number and percent distribution of Hispanic workers aged 16 or older by principal means of transportation to work, travel time from home to work, distance from home to work, and departure time to work, 1999; numbers in thousands)

	number	percent
Hispanic workers	**12,209**	**100.0%**
Principal means of transportation to work		
Drives self	7,916	64.8
Car pool	2,152	17.6
Mass transportation	1,150	9.4
Taxicab	13	0.1
Bicycle or motorcycle	73	0.6
Walks only	515	4.2
Other means	191	1.6
Works at home	200	1.6
Travel time from home to work		
Less than 15 minutes	3,664	30.0
15 to 29 minutes	3,970	32.5
30 to 44 minutes	1,888	15.5
45 to 59 minutes	676	5.5
1 hour or more	770	6.3
Works at home	200	1.6
No fixed place of work	1,042	8.5
Median travel time (minutes)	22	–
Distance from home to work		
Less than 1 mile	546	4.5
1 to 4 miles	2,755	22.6
5 to 9 miles	2,484	20.3
10 to 19 miles	2,956	24.2
20 to 29 miles	1,239	10.1
30 miles or more	986	8.1
Works at home	200	1.6
No fixed place of work	1,042	8.5
Median distance (miles)	9	–
Departure time to work		
12:00 a.m. to 2:59 a.m.	73	0.6%
3:00 a.m. to 5:59 a.m.	1,557	12.8
6:00 a.m. to 6:59 a.m.	2,433	19.9
7:00 a.m. to 7:29 a.m.	1,695	13.9
7:30 a.m. to 7:59 a.m.	1,338	11.0
8:00 a.m. to 8:29 a.m.	1,277	10.5
8:30 a.m. to 8:59 a.m.	497	4.1
9:00 a.m. to 9:59 a.m.	577	4.7
10:00 a.m. to 3:59 p.m.	1,160	9.5
4:00 p.m. to 11:59 p.m.	687	5.6

Note: Numbers may not add to total because not reported is not shown; (–) means not applicable.
Source: Bureau of the Census, American Housing Survey for the United States: 1999, *Current Housing Reports, H150/99, 2000; calculations by New Strategist*

Projections of the Hispanic Labor Force by Sex, 2000 and 2010

(number of Hispanics in the civilian labor force, labor force participation rate of Hispanics, and Hispanic share of total labor force, by sex, 2000 and 2010; percent change in number and percentage point change in rate and share, 2000–2010; numbers in thousands)

	Hispanics in labor force		
	2000	*2010*	*percent change 2000–10*
Total	15,368	20,947	36.3%
Men	8,919	11,723	31.4
Women	6,449	9,224	43.0

	Hispanic labor force participation rate		
	2000	*2010*	*percentage point change 2000–10*
Total	68.6%	69.0%	0.4
Men	80.6	79.0	−1.6
Women	56.9	59.4	2.5

	Hispanic share of total labor force		
	2000	*2010*	*percentage point change 2000–10*
Total	10.9%	13.3%	2.4
Men	6.3	7.4	1.1
Women	4.6	5.8	1.2

Source: Bureau of Labor Statistics, Monthly Labor Review, *November 2001*

Most Hispanic Couples Have Children under Age 18 at Home

Hispanic householders are much younger than average. Only 11 percent are aged 65 or older, versus 21 percent of all householders. Twenty-two percent are under age 30, versus 14 percent nationally. Consequently, Hispanics account for a relatively large share of households headed by young adults. More than one in eight householders under age 35 is Hispanic.

Married couples account for 55 percent of Hispanic households, slightly greater than married couples' 52 percent share of all households. But 37 percent of Hispanic households are nuclear families (defined as a husband, wife, and children under age 18 at home), much larger than the 24 percent share held by nuclear families nationally. Although Hispanics head only 9 percent of all households, they head 14 percent of the nation's nuclear families. Hispanics and blacks are almost equal in number in the U.S., but Hispanic couples with children outnumber their black counterparts by 1.3 million.

Many Hispanics are immigrants trying to establish themselves in the United States, which explains why 12 percent of Hispanic men and 15 percent of Hispanic women are living in the households of relatives. Among all men and women, the proportion is just 5 percent. This also explains why Hispanic households are larger than average. Among households with seven or more people, Hispanics head 37 percent.

■ Married couples with children account for a larger share of Hispanic households than of black or white households because many Hispanics are immigrants from countries where traditional family life is common.

Many Hispanic households are nuclear families

(percent of Hispanic and total households headed by married couples with children under age 18 at home, 2000)

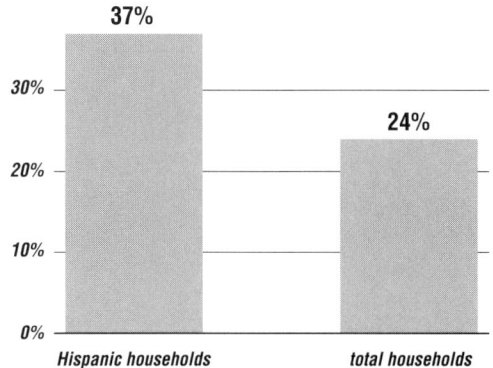

Hispanic Households by Age of Householder, 2000

(number of total households, number and percent distribution of Hispanic households, and Hispanic share of total, by age of householder, 2000; numbers in thousands)

		Hispanic households		
	total	number	percent distribution	share of total
Total households	**104,705**	**9,319**	**100.0%**	**8.9%**
Under age 20	914	156	1.7	17.1
Aged 20 to 24	4,946	715	7.7	14.5
Aged 25 to 29	8,520	1,133	12.2	13.3
Aged 30 to 34	10,107	1,344	14.4	13.3
Aged 35 to 39	11,728	1,371	14.7	11.7
Aged 40 to 44	12,227	1,124	12.1	9.2
Aged 45 to 54	20,927	1,546	16.6	7.4
Aged 55 to 64	13,592	929	10.0	6.8
Aged 65 or older	21,744	1,002	10.8	4.6
Aged 65 to 74	11,325	643	6.9	5.7
Aged 75 or older	10,419	359	3.9	3.4

Source: Bureau of the Census, America's Families and Living Arrangements: March 2000, *detailed tables from Current Population Report P20-537, Internet site <www.census.gov/population/www/socdemo/hh-fam/p20-537_00.html>; calculations by New Strategist*

Hispanic Households by Household Type, 2000

(number of total households, number and percent distribution of Hispanic households, and Hispanic share of total, by type, 2000; numbers in thousands)

	total	Hispanic households number	percent distribution	share of total
Total households	**104,705**	**9,319**	**100.0%**	**8.9%**
Family households	**72,025**	**7,561**	**81.1**	**10.5**
Married couples	55,311	5,133	55.1	9.3
With children under age 18	25,248	3,423	36.7	13.6
Without children under age 18	30,062	1,710	18.3	5.7
Female householder, no spouse present	12,687	1,769	19.0	13.9
With children under age 18	7,571	1,145	12.3	15.1
Without children under age 18	5,116	625	6.7	12.2
Male householder, no spouse present	4,028	658	7.1	16.3
With children under age 18	1,786	246	2.6	13.8
Without children under age 18	2,242	412	4.4	18.4
Nonfamily households	**32,680**	**1,758**	**18.9**	**5.4**
Female householder	18,039	783	8.4	4.3
Living alone	15,543	630	6.8	4.1
Male householder	14,641	974	10.5	6.7
Living alone	11,181	666	7.1	6.0

Source: Bureau of the Census, America's Families and Living Arrangements: March 2000, *detailed tables from Current Population Report P20-537, Internet site <www.census.gov/population/www/socdemo/hh-fam/p20-537_00.html>; calculations by New Strategist*

Hispanic Households by Age of Householder and Household Type, 2000

(number and percent distribution of Hispanic households by age of householder and household type, 2000; numbers in thousands)

	total	family households				nonfamily households	
		total	married couples	female hh, no spouse present	male hh, no spouse present	female house-holder	male house-holder
Hispanic households	**9,319**	**7,561**	**5,133**	**1,769**	**658**	**783**	**974**
Under age 20	156	125	28	64	32	13	18
Aged 20 to 24	715	547	287	149	111	67	101
Aged 25 to 29	1,133	928	618	204	106	64	141
Aged 30 to 34	1,344	1,139	818	229	92	48	157
Aged 35 to 39	1,371	1,202	854	266	82	50	119
Aged 40 to 44	1,124	984	680	246	58	44	95
Aged 45 to 54	1,546	1,288	911	307	71	119	139
Aged 55 to 64	929	724	509	158	57	111	94
Aged 65 or older	1002	623	427	146	50	268	110
Aged 65 to 74	643	421	291	102	28	147	74
Aged 75 to 84	359	202	136	44	22	121	36
Hispanic households	**100.0%**	**81.1%**	**55.1%**	**19.0%**	**7.1%**	**8.4%**	**10.5%**
Under age 20	100.0	80.1	17.9	41.0	20.5	8.3	11.5
Aged 20 to 24	100.0	76.5	40.1	20.8	15.5	9.4	14.1
Aged 25 to 29	100.0	81.9	54.5	18.0	9.4	5.6	12.4
Aged 30 to 34	100.0	84.7	60.9	17.0	6.8	3.6	11.7
Aged 35 to 39	100.0	87.7	62.3	19.4	6.0	3.6	8.7
Aged 40 to 44	100.0	87.5	60.5	21.9	5.2	3.9	8.5
Aged 45 to 54	100.0	83.3	58.9	19.9	4.6	7.7	9.0
Aged 55 to 64	100.0	77.9	54.8	17.0	6.1	11.9	10.1
Aged 65 or older	100.0	62.2	42.6	14.6	5.0	26.7	11.0
Aged 65 to 74	100.0	65.5	45.3	15.9	4.4	22.9	11.5
Aged 75 to 84	100.0	56.3	37.9	12.3	6.1	33.7	10.0

Source: Bureau of the Census, America's Families and Living Arrangements: March 2000, *detailed tables from Current Population Report P20-537, Internet site <www.census.gov/population/www/socdemo/hh-fam/p20-537_00.html>; calculations by New Strategist*

Hispanics Households by Size, 2000

(number of total households, number and percent distribution of Hispanic households, and Hispanic share of total, by size, 2000; numbers in thousands)

| | total | Hispanic households | | |
		number	percent distribution	share of total
Total households	**104,705**	**9,319**	**100.0%**	**8.9%**
One person	26,724	1,296	13.9	4.8
Two people	34,666	1,945	20.9	5.6
Three people	17,152	1,787	19.2	10.4
Four people	15,309	1,939	20.8	12.7
Five people	6,981	1,265	13.6	18.1
Six people	2,445	558	6.0	22.8
Seven or more people	1,428	529	5.7	37.0

Source: Bureau of the Census, America's Families and Living Arrangements: March 2000, *detailed tables from Current Population Report P20-537, Internet site <www.census.gov/population/www/socdemo/hh-fam/p20-537_00.html>; calculations by New Strategist*

Hispanic Married Couples by Age of Children and Age of Householder, 2000

(number and percent distribution of Hispanic married couples by presence and age of own children at home and age of householder, 2000; numbers in thousands)

	total	< age 20	20–24	25–29	30–34	35–39	40–44	45–54	55–64	65–74	75+
Hispanic married couples	**5,133**	**28**	**287**	**618**	**818**	**854**	**680**	**911**	**509**	**291**	**136**
With children of any age	**3,975**	**25**	**227**	**510**	**727**	**775**	**624**	**699**	**269**	**83**	**36**
With children under age 18	3,423	25	226	508	727	760	581	488	92	12	4
Aged 12 to 17	1,464	2	–	32	185	395	395	368	76	7	4
Aged 6 to 11	1,806	1	36	235	461	500	347	190	29	5	1
Under age 6	1,862	24	220	446	521	380	176	81	13	–	–
Under age 1	331	8	65	87	89	55	21	5	1	–	–
Hispanic married couples	**100.0%**	**100.0%**	**100.0%**	**100.0%**	**100.0%**	**100.0%**	**100.0%**	**100.0%**	**100.0%**	**100.0%**	**100.0%**
With children of any age	**77.4**	**89.3**	**79.1**	**82.5**	**88.9**	**90.7**	**91.8**	**76.7**	**52.8**	**28.5**	**26.5**
With children under age 18	66.7	89.3	78.7	82.2	88.9	89.0	85.4	53.6	18.1	4.1	2.9
Aged 12 to 17	28.5	7.1	–	5.2	22.6	46.3	58.1	40.4	14.9	2.4	2.9
Aged 6 to 11	35.2	3.6	12.5	38.0	56.4	58.5	51.0	20.9	5.7	1.7	0.7
Under age 6	36.3	85.7	76.7	72.2	63.7	44.5	25.9	8.9	2.6	–	–
Under age 1	6.4	28.6	22.6	14.1	10.9	6.4	3.1	0.5	0.2	–	–

age of householder

Note: Numbers will not add to total because households may have children in more than one age group; (–) means sample is too small to make a reliable estimate.
Source: Bureau of the Census, America's Families and Living Arrangements: March 2000, detailed tables from Current Population Report P20-537, Internet site <www.census.gov/population/www/socdemo/hh-fam/p20-537_00.html>; calculations by New Strategist

Hispanic Female-Headed Families by Age of Children and Age of Householder, 2000

(number and percent distribution of Hispanic female-headed families by presence and age of own children at home and age of householder, 2000; numbers in thousands)

	total		age of householder								
		< age 20	20–24	25–29	30–34	35–39	40–44	45–54	55–64	65–74	75+
Hispanic female-headed families	**1,769**	**64**	**149**	**204**	**229**	**266**	**246**	**307**	**158**	**102**	**44**
With children of any age	**1,543**	**31**	**123**	**181**	**208**	**249**	**232**	**275**	**126**	**90**	**28**
With children under age 18	1,145	29	119	181	205	235	194	155	28	–	–
Aged 12 to 17	550	–	2	15	92	163	132	128	18	–	–
Aged 6 to 11	577	–	20	117	163	130	98	41	7	–	–
Under age 6	464	29	112	130	92	69	24	4	4	–	–
Under age 1	81	16	29	19	14	4	–	–	–	–	–
Hispanic female-headed families	**100.0%**	**100.0%**	**100.0%**	**100.0%**	**100.0%**	**100.0%**	**100.0%**	**100.0%**	**100.0%**	**100.0%**	**100.0%**
With children of any age	**87.2**	**48.4**	**82.6**	**88.7**	**90.8**	**93.6**	**94.3**	**89.6**	**79.7**	**88.2**	**63.6**
With children under age 18	64.7	45.3	79.9	88.7	89.5	88.3	78.9	50.5	17.7	–	–
Aged 12 to 17	31.1	–	1.3	7.4	40.2	61.3	53.7	41.7	11.4	–	–
Aged 6 to 11	32.6	–	13.4	57.4	71.2	48.9	39.8	13.4	4.4	–	–
Under age 6	26.2	45.3	75.2	63.7	40.2	25.9	9.8	1.3	2.5	–	–
Under age 1	4.6	25.0	19.5	9.3	6.1	1.5	–	–	–	–	–

Note: Numbers will not add to total because households may have children in more than one age group; (–) means sample is too small to make a reliable estimate.
Source: Bureau of the Census, America's Families and Living Arrangements: March 2000, detailed tables from Current Population Report P20-537, Internet site <www.census.gov/population/www/socdemo/hh-fam/p20-537_00.html>; calculations by New Strategist

Hispanic Single-Person Households by Age of Householder, 2000

(total number of Hispanic households, number and percent distribution of Hispanic single-person households, and single-person household share of total, by age of householder, 2000; numbers in thousands)

| | total | single-person households | | |
		number	percent distribution	share of total
Hispanic households	**9,319**	**1,296**	**100.0%**	**13.9%**
Under age 20	156	12	0.9	7.7
Under age 25	715	73	5.6	10.2
Aged 25 to 29	1,133	111	8.6	9.8
Aged 30 to 34	1,344	135	10.4	10.0
Aged 35 to 39	1,371	117	9.0	8.5
Aged 40 to 44	1,124	98	7.6	8.7
Aged 45 to 54	1,546	207	16.0	13.4
Aged 55 to 64	929	184	14.2	19.8
Aged 65 to 74	643	211	16.3	32.8
Aged 75 or older	359	147	11.3	40.9

Source: Bureau of the Census, America's Families and Living Arrangements: March 2000, *detailed tables from Current Population Report P20-537, Internet site <www.census.gov/population/www/socdemo/hh-fam/p20-537_00.html>; calculations by New Strategist*

Hispanic Children by Living Arrangement and Age, 2000

(number and percent distribution of Hispanic children under age 18 by living arrangement, 2000; numbers in thousands)

	number	percent distribution
Total Hispanic children	**11,613**	**100.0%**
Living with both parents	7,561	65.1
Living with mother only	2,919	25.1
Living with father only	506	4.4
Living with neither parent	626	5.4
In group quarters	2	0.0
Living with both parents	**7,561**	**100.0**
Child of householder	7,240	95.8
Grandchild of householder	140	1.9
Other relative of householder	173	2.3
Nonrelative of householder	8	0.1
Living with mother only	**2,919**	**100.0**
Child of householder	2,270	77.8
Grandchild of householder	340	11.6
Other relative of householder	181	6.2
Nonrelative of householder	128	4.4
Living with father only	**506**	**100.0**
Child of householder	402	79.4
Grandchild of householder	45	8.9
Other relative of householder	46	9.1
Nonrelative of householder	12	2.4
Living with neither parent	**626**	**100.0**
Grandchild of householder	181	28.9
Other relative of householder	251	40.1
Foster child	47	7.5
Other nonrelative of householder	147	23.5
In group quarters	2	0.0

Source: Bureau of the Census, America's Families and Living Arrangements: March 2000, *detailed tables from Current Population Report P20-537, Internet site <www.census.gov/population/www/socdemo/hh-fam/p20-537_00.html>; calculations by New Strategist*

Hispanic Men by Living Arrangement and Age, 2000

(number and percent distribution of Hispanic men aged 15 or older by living arrangement and age, 2000; numbers in thousands)

	total	15–19	20–24	25–29	30–34	35–39	40–44	45–54	55–64	65–74	75+
Hispanic men	11,327	1,508	1,454	1,416	1,440	1,423	1,058	1,490	821	469	250
Householder	6,799	62	436	862	1,048	1,085	856	1,177	673	403	211
Married couple hh or spouse	5,167	13	224	615	799	884	703	967	522	300	167
Male family householder	658	32	111	106	92	82	58	71	57	28	8
Living alone	666	6	36	80	95	80	72	112	85	70	30
Living with nonrelatives	308	11	65	61	62	39	23	27	9	5	6
Not a householder	4,528	1,446	1,018	554	392	338	202	313	148	66	39
Child of householder	2,171	1,133	516	183	113	95	49	66	16	–	–
In family, other relative of hh	1,412	203	271	210	149	115	83	168	103	57	39
Not in family	945	110	231	161	130	128	70	79	29	9	–
Hispanic men	100.0%	100.0%	100.0%	100.0%	100.0%	100.0%	100.0%	100.0%	100.0%	100.0%	100.0%
Householder	60.0	4.1	30.0	60.9	72.8	76.2	80.9	79.0	82.0	85.9	84.4
Married couple hh or spouse	45.6	0.9	15.4	43.4	55.5	62.1	66.4	64.9	63.6	64.0	66.8
Male family householder	5.8	2.1	7.6	7.5	6.4	5.8	5.5	4.8	6.9	6.0	3.2
Living alone	5.9	0.4	2.5	5.6	6.6	5.6	6.8	7.5	10.4	14.9	12.0
Living with nonrelatives	2.7	0.7	4.5	4.3	4.3	2.7	2.2	1.8	1.1	1.1	2.4
Not a householder	40.0	95.9	70.0	39.1	27.2	23.8	19.1	21.0	18.0	14.1	15.6
Child of householder	19.2	75.1	35.5	12.9	7.8	6.7	4.6	4.4	1.9	–	–
In family, other relative of hh	12.5	13.5	18.6	14.8	10.3	8.1	7.8	11.3	12.5	12.2	15.6
Not in family	8.3	7.3	15.9	11.4	9.0	9.0	6.6	5.3	3.5	1.9	–

Note: (–) means sample is too small to make a reliable estimate.
Source: Bureau of the Census, America's Families and Living Arrangements: March 2000, detailed tables from Current Population Report P20-537, Internet site <www .census.gov/population/www/socdemo/hh-fam/p20-537_00.html>; calculations by New Strategist

Hispanic Women by Living Arrangement and Age, 2000

Hispanics: Living Arrangements

(number and percent distribution of Hispanic women aged 15 or older by living arrangement and age, 2000; numbers in thousands)

	total	15–19	20–24	25–29	30–34	35–39	40–44	45–54	55–64	65–74	75+
Hispanic women	**11,465**	**1,380**	**1,301**	**1,415**	**1,391**	**1,389**	**1,106**	**1,530**	**924**	**663**	**370**
Householder	**7,854**	**125**	**643**	**990**	**1,163**	**1,198**	**939**	**1,278**	**744**	**511**	**266**
Married couple hh or spouse	5,302	48	427	722	886	882	649	852	475	261	101
Female family householder	1,769	64	149	204	229	266	246	307	158	102	44
Living alone	630	5	37	32	40	38	26	95	99	141	117
Living with nonrelatives	153	8	30	32	8	12	18	24	12	7	4
Not a householder	**3,611**	**1,255**	**658**	**425**	**228**	**191**	**167**	**252**	**180**	**152**	**104**
Child of householder	1,715	978	375	156	71	52	43	30	12	–	–
In family, other relative of hh	1,262	186	144	139	85	64	79	174	151	138	102
Not in family	634	91	139	130	72	75	45	48	17	14	2
Hispanic women	**100.0%**	**100.0%**	**100.0%**	**100.0%**	**100.0%**	**100.0%**	**100.0%**	**100.0%**	**100.0%**	**100.0%**	**100.0%**
Householder	**68.5**	**9.1**	**49.4**	**70.0**	**83.6**	**86.2**	**84.9**	**83.5**	**80.5**	**77.1**	**71.9**
Married couple hh or spouse	46.2	3.5	32.8	51.0	63.7	63.5	58.7	55.7	51.4	39.4	27.3
Female family householder	15.4	4.6	11.5	14.4	16.5	19.2	22.2	20.1	17.1	15.4	11.9
Living alone	5.5	0.4	2.8	2.3	2.9	2.7	2.4	6.2	10.7	21.3	31.6
Living with nonrelatives	1.3	0.6	2.3	2.3	0.6	0.9	1.6	1.6	1.3	1.1	1.1
Not a householder	**31.5**	**90.9**	**50.6**	**30.0**	**16.4**	**13.8**	**15.1**	**16.5**	**19.5**	**22.9**	**28.1**
Child of householder	15.0	70.9	28.8	11.0	5.1	3.7	3.9	2.0	1.3	–	–
In family, other relative of hh	11.0	13.5	11.1	9.8	6.1	4.6	7.1	11.4	16.3	20.8	27.6
Not in family	5.5	6.6	10.7	9.2	5.2	5.4	4.1	3.1	1.8	2.1	0.5

Note: (–) means sample is too small to make a reliable estimate.
Source: Bureau of the Census, America's Families and Living Arrangements: March 2000, detailed tables from Current Population Report P20-537, Internet site <www.census.gov/population/www/socdemo/hh-fam/p20-537_00.html>; calculations by New Strategist

RACIAL AND ETHNIC DIVERSITY **447**

Hispanic Men by Marital Status and Age, 2000

(number and percent distribution of Hispanic men aged 15 or older by age and marital status, 2000; numbers in thousands)

	total	never married	married	divorced	widowed
Hispanic men	**11,327**	**4,249**	**5,952**	**957**	**170**
Under age 20	1,509	1,478	21	10	–
Aged 20 to 24	1,453	1,105	319	30	–
Aged 25 to 29	1,416	594	746	77	–
Aged 30 to 34	1,439	414	920	101	4
Aged 35 to 39	1,422	298	978	139	6
Aged 40 to 44	1,058	134	790	132	3
Aged 45 to 49	810	107	579	119	4
Aged 50 to 54	679	43	510	121	5
Aged 55 to 59	461	27	325	86	23
Aged 60 to 64	359	21	259	62	16
Aged 65 or older	720	27	504	83	107
Aged 65 to 69	273	11	199	43	21
Aged 70 to 74	196	9	134	28	24
Aged 75 or older	251	7	171	12	62
Hispanic men	**100.0%**	**37.5%**	**52.5%**	**8.4%**	**1.5%**
Under age 20	100.0	97.9	1.4	0.7	–
Aged 20 to 24	100.0	76.0	22.0	2.1	–
Aged 25 to 29	100.0	41.9	52.7	5.4	–
Aged 30 to 34	100.0	28.8	63.9	7.0	0.3
Aged 35 to 39	100.0	21.0	68.8	9.8	0.4
Aged 40 to 44	100.0	12.7	74.7	12.5	0.3
Aged 45 to 49	100.0	13.2	71.5	14.7	0.5
Aged 50 to 54	100.0	6.3	75.1	17.8	0.7
Aged 55 to 59	100.0	5.9	70.5	18.7	5.0
Aged 60 to 64	100.0	5.8	72.1	17.3	4.5
Aged 65 or older	100.0	3.8	70.0	11.5	14.9
Aged 65 to 69	100.0	4.0	72.9	15.8	7.7
Aged 70 to 74	100.0	4.6	68.4	14.3	12.2
Aged 75 or older	100.0	2.8	68.1	4.8	24.7

Note: (–) means sample is too small to make a reliable estimate.
Source: Bureau of the Census, Marital Status and Living Arrangements: March 2000 (Update), *detailed tables for Current Population Report P20-537, 2001; Internet site <www.census.gov/population/socdemo/hh-fam/p20-537/2000/tabA1.txt>*

Hispanic Women by Marital Status and Age, 2000

(number and percent distribution of Hispanic women aged 15 or older by age and marital status, 2000; numbers in thousands)

	total	never married	married	divorced	widowed
Hispanic women	**11,466**	**3,309**	**5,935**	**1,511**	**711**
Under age 20	1,379	1,266	92	19	3
Aged 20 to 24	1,302	721	516	60	5
Aged 25 to 29	1,415	473	828	108	6
Aged 30 to 34	1,390	248	954	176	11
Aged 35 to 39	1,388	186	947	233	22
Aged 40 to 44	1,105	129	705	239	32
Aged 45 to 49	771	84	475	170	41
Aged 50 to 54	759	81	468	165	45
Aged 55 to 59	529	43	313	113	60
Aged 60 to 64	396	21	218	80	79
Aged 65 or older	1,033	58	417	151	407
Aged 65 to 69	373	17	176	68	112
Aged 70 to 74	290	25	125	46	94
Aged 75 or older	370	16	116	37	201
Hispanic women	**100.0%**	**28.9%**	**51.8%**	**13.2%**	**6.2%**
Under age 20	100.0	91.8	6.7	1.4	0.2
Aged 20 to 24	100.0	55.4	39.6	4.6	0.4
Aged 25 to 29	100.0	33.4	58.5	7.6	0.4
Aged 30 to 34	100.0	17.8	68.6	12.7	0.8
Aged 35 to 39	100.0	13.4	68.2	16.8	1.6
Aged 40 to 44	100.0	11.7	63.8	21.6	2.9
Aged 45 to 49	100.0	10.9	61.6	22.0	5.3
Aged 50 to 54	100.0	10.7	61.7	21.7	5.9
Aged 55 to 59	100.0	8.1	59.2	21.4	11.3
Aged 60 to 64	100.0	5.3	55.1	20.2	19.9
Aged 65 or older	100.0	5.6	40.4	14.6	39.4
Aged 65 to 69	100.0	4.6	47.2	18.2	30.0
Aged 70 to 74	100.0	8.6	43.1	15.9	32.4
Aged 75 or older	100.0	4.3	31.4	10.0	54.3

Source: Bureau of the Census, Marital Status and Living Arrangements: March 2000 (Update), *detailed tables for Current Population Report P20-537, 2001; Internet site <www.census.gov/population/socdemo/hh-fam/p20-537/ 2000/tabA1.txt>*

Hispanics Are About to Become the Largest Minority Group in the U.S.

The Hispanic population grew from 22 million in 1990 to 35 million in 2000, up fully 58 percent during the decade. Hispanics account for 12.5 percent of the U.S. population, up from 9 percent in 1990. The Hispanic population is growing rapidly because of immigration. Forty-five percent of immigrants to the U.S. in 2000 were from Mexico, Latin America, the Caribbean, or Spain. Twenty percent were from Mexico alone. The 51 percent majority of the nation's foreign-born population is from Latin America.

Hispanics may be of any race. On the 2000 census, 48 percent of Hispanics identified themselves as white alone. Another 42 percent identified themselves as "other" race, considering their Hispanic ethnicity to be a separate race. Hispanics accounted for fully 90 percent of those identifying themselves as "other" race on the 2000 census.

Among Hispanics, the largest ethnic groups are Mexican Americans (58 percent), Puerto Ricans (10 percent), and Cubans (4 percent). A variety of countries account for the ethnic background of a substantial 28 percent of Hispanics, the largest being the Dominican Republic (2 percent), El Salvador (2 percent), and Guatemala (1 percent).

Hispanics are most likely to live in the West (43 percent) and South (33 percent). Thirty-one percent of Hispanics live in California, where they account for 32 percent of the state's population. Another 19 percent of Hispanics live in Texas, where they, too, account for 32 percent of the population. Los Angeles is home to more Hispanics than any other U.S. metropolitan area—6.6 million. Hispanics account for 40 percent of the Los Angeles population.

■ Hispanics are growing rapidly in almost every state. Because many are not citizens, however, their political power is diluted.

The Hispanic population grew rapidly during the 1990s

(number of people identifying themselves as Hispanic, 1990 and 2000; numbers in millions)

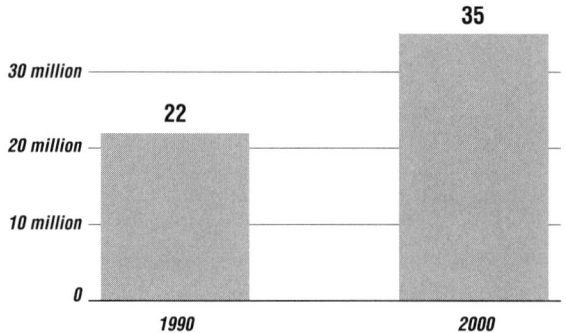

Hispanics, 1990 and 2000 Censuses

(number of total people, number of Hispanics, and Hispanic share of total, 1990 and 2000; percent change in number of Hispanics, 1990–2000)

	1990			2000			percent change in Hipanics 1990–2000
		Hispanic			Hispanic		
	total	number	share of total	total	number	share of total	
Total people	248,709,873	22,354,059	9.0%	281,421,906	35,305,818	12.5%	57.9%

Source: Bureau of the Census, The Hispanic Population: 2000, *Census 2000 Brief, C2KBR/01-3, 2001; calculations by New Strategist*

Hispanics and Non-Hispanics by Race, 2000 Census

(number and percent distribution of Hispanics and non-Hispanics by race, 2000)

	Hispanics		non-Hispanics	
	number	percent distribution	number	percent of distribution
Total people	**35,306,818**	**100.0%**	**246,116,088**	**100.0%**
One race	**33,081,736**	**93.7**	**241,513,942**	**98.1**
American Indian	407,073	1.2	2,068,883	0.8
Asian	119,829	0.3	10,123,169	4.1
Black	710,353	2.0	33,947,837	13.8
Native Hawaiian	45,326	0.1	353,509	0.1
White	16,907,852	47.9	194,552,774	79.0
Other	14,891,303	42.2	467,770	0.2
Two or more races	**2,224,082**	**6.3**	**4,602,146**	**1.9**

Note: American Indians include Alaska Natives. Native Hawaiians include other Pacific Islanders.
Source: Bureau of the Census, Overview of Race and Hispanic Origin, *Census 2000 Brief, CENBR/01-1, 2001*

Hispanic Origin of the Other Race Population, 2000 Census

(number of people of other race alone or in combination, other race alone, and other race in combination, by Hispanic origin, 2000)

	other race, alone or in combination		other race alone		other race in combination	
	number	*percent*	*number*	*percent*	*number*	*percent*
Total people	**18,521,486**	**100.0%**	**15,359,073**	**100.0%**	**3,162,413**	**100.0%**
Hispanic	16,750,841	90.4	14,891,303	97.0	1,859,538	58.8
Non-Hispanic	1,770,645	9.6	467,770	3.0	1,302,875	41.2

Source: Bureau of the Census, Overview of Race and Hispanic Origin, *Census 2000 Brief, CENBR/01-1, 2001*

Hispanics by Ethnic Origin, 2000 Census

(number and percent distribution of Hispanics by ethnic origin, 2000)

	number	percent distribution
Total Hispanics	**35,305,818**	**100.0%**
Mexican	20,640,711	58.5
Puerto Rican	3,406,178	9.6
Cuban	1,241,685	3.5
Other Hispanic	10,017,244	28.4
Dominican (Dominican Republic)	764,945	2.2
Central American (excl. Mexican)	1,686,937	4.8
Costa Rican	68,588	0.2
Guatemalan	372,487	1.1
Honduran	217,569	0.6
Nicaraguan	177,684	0.5
Panamanian	91,723	0.3
Salvadoran	655,165	1.9
Other Central American	103,721	0.3
South American	1,353,562	3.8
Argentinean	100,864	0.3
Bolivian	42,068	0.1
Chilean	68,849	0.2
Colombian	470,684	1.3
Ecuadorian	260,559	0.7
Paraguayan	8,769	0.0
Peruvian	233,926	0.0
Uruguayan	18,804	0.7
Venezuelan	91,507	0.1
Other South American	57,532	0.3
Spaniard	100,135	0.2
All other Hispanic	6,111,665	0.3

Source: Bureau of the Census, The Hispanic Population, *Census 2000 Brief, C2KBR/01-3, 2001*

Hispanics by Age, 2000 Census

(number of total people, number and percent distribution of Hispanics, and Hispanic share of total, by age, 2000)

| | | Hispanics | | |
	total	number	percent distribution	share of total
Total people	**281,421,906**	**35,305,818**	**100.0%**	**12.5%**
Under age 5	19,175,798	3,717,974	10.5	19.4
Aged 5 to 9	20,549,505	3,623,680	10.3	17.6
Aged 10 to 14	20,528,072	3,163,412	9.0	15.4
Aged 15 to 19	20,219,890	3,171,646	9.0	15.7
Aged 20 to 24	18,964,001	3,409,427	9.7	18.0
Aged 25 to 29	19,381,336	3,385,334	9.6	17.5
Aged 30 to 34	20,510,388	3,124,901	8.9	15.2
Aged 35 to 39	22,706,664	2,825,158	8.0	12.4
Aged 40 to 44	22,441,863	2,304,152	6.5	10.3
Aged 45 to 49	20,092,404	1,775,168	5.0	8.8
Aged 50 to 54	17,585,548	1,360,935	3.9	7.7
Aged 55 to 59	13,469,237	960,033	2.7	7.1
Aged 60 to 64	10,805,447	750,407	2.1	6.9
Aged 65 to 69	9,533,545	599,353	1.7	6.3
Aged 70 to 74	8,857,441	477,266	1.4	5.4
Aged 75 to 79	7,415,813	326,726	0.9	4.4
Aged 80 to 84	4,945,367	179,538	0.5	3.6
Aged 85 or older	4,239,587	150,708	0.4	3.6
Aged 18 to 24	27,143,454	4,743,880	13.4	17.5
Aged 18 or older	209,128,094	22,963,559	65.0	11.0
Aged 65 or older	34,991,753	1,733,591	4.9	5.0

Source: U.S. Census Bureau, Census 2000 Summary File 1; calculations by New Strategist

Other Race by Age, 2000 Census

(number of people identifying themselves as other race alone or in combination, other race alone, and other race in combination, and percent of other race alone or in combination identifying themselves as other race in combination, by age, 2000)

| | other race, alone or in combination | other race alone | other race in combination | |
			number	percent of other race, alone or in combination
Total others	**18,521,486**	**15,359,073**	**3,162,413**	**17.1%**
Under age 5	2,016,773	1,646,056	370,717	18.4
Aged 5 to 9	1,948,423	1,613,292	335,131	17.2
Aged 10 to 14	1,699,140	1,414,466	284,674	16.8
Aged 15 to 19	1,748,498	1,485,107	263,391	15.1
Aged 20 to 24	1,941,639	1,665,119	276,520	14.2
Aged 25 to 29	1,887,344	1,610,011	277,333	14.7
Aged 30 to 34	1,691,079	1,420,203	270,876	16.0
Aged 35 to 39	1,487,065	1,233,608	253,457	17.0
Aged 40 to 44	1,205,498	990,684	214,814	17.8
Aged 45 to 49	901,493	735,465	166,028	18.4
Aged 50 to 54	651,338	524,104	127,234	19.5
Aged 55 to 59	416,516	328,970	87,546	21.0
Aged 60 to 64	301,449	232,984	68,465	22.7
Aged 65 to 69	222,380	168,334	54,046	24.3
Aged 70 to 74	169,146	125,235	43,911	26.0
Aged 75 to 79	116,047	83,593	32,454	28.0
Aged 80 to 84	64,082	44,668	19,414	30.3
Aged 85 or older	53,576	37,174	16,402	30.6
Aged 18 to 24	2,688,472	2,303,589	384,883	14.3
Aged 18 or older	11,855,485	9,838,622	2,016,863	17.0
Aged 65 or older	625,231	459,004	166,227	26.6

Source: U.S. Census Bureau, Census 2000 Summary File 1; calculations by New Strategist

Other Race Share of Total Population by Age, 2000 Census

(number of total people, number and percent distribution of people identifying themselves as other race alone or in combination, and other race share of total, 2000)

	total	other race, alone or in combination		
		number	percent distribution	share of total
Total other races	**281,421,906**	**18,521,486**	**100.0%**	**6.6%**
Under age 5	19,175,798	2,016,773	10.9	10.5
Aged 5 to 9	20,549,505	1,948,423	10.5	9.5
Aged 10 to 14	20,528,072	1,699,140	9.2	8.3
Aged 15 to 19	20,219,890	1,748,498	9.4	8.6
Aged 20 to 24	18,964,001	1,941,639	10.5	10.2
Aged 25 to 29	19,381,336	1,887,344	10.2	9.7
Aged 30 to 34	20,510,388	1,691,079	9.1	8.2
Aged 35 to 39	22,706,664	1,487,065	8.0	6.5
Aged 40 to 44	22,441,863	1,205,498	6.5	5.4
Aged 45 to 49	20,092,404	901,493	4.9	4.5
Aged 50 to 54	17,585,548	651,338	3.5	3.7
Aged 55 to 59	13,469,237	416,516	2.2	3.1
Aged 60 to 64	10,805,447	301,449	1.6	2.8
Aged 65 to 69	9,533,545	222,380	1.2	2.3
Aged 70 to 74	8,857,441	169,146	0.9	1.9
Aged 75 to 79	7,415,813	116,047	0.6	1.6
Aged 80 to 84	4,945,367	64,082	0.3	1.3
Aged 85 or older	4,239,587	53,576	0.3	1.3
Aged 18 to 24	27,143,454	2,688,472	14.5	9.9
Aged 18 or older	209,128,094	11,855,485	64.0	5.7
Aged 65 or older	34,991,753	625,231	3.4	1.8

Source: U.S. Census Bureau, Census 2000 Summary File 1; calculations by New Strategist

Hispanics by Age and Sex, 2000 Census

(number of Hispanics by age and sex, and sex ratio by age, 2000)

	total	females	males	sex ratio
Total Hispanics	**35,305,818**	**17,144,023**	**18,161,795**	**106**
Under age 5	3,717,974	1,817,543	1,900,431	105
Aged 5 to 9	3,623,680	1,771,795	1,851,885	105
Aged 10 to 14	3,163,412	1,546,227	1,617,185	105
Aged 15 to 19	3,171,646	1,483,090	1,688,556	114
Aged 20 to 24	3,409,427	1,534,288	1,875,139	122
Aged 25 to 29	3,385,334	1,559,188	1,826,146	117
Aged 30 to 34	3,124,901	1,456,837	1,668,064	114
Aged 35 to 39	2,825,158	1,350,696	1,474,462	109
Aged 40 to 44	2,304,152	1,125,604	1,178,548	105
Aged 45 to 49	1,775,168	888,473	886,695	100
Aged 50 to 54	1,360,935	696,699	664,236	95
Aged 55 to 59	960,033	503,868	456,165	91
Aged 60 to 64	750,407	402,998	347,409	86
Aged 65 to 69	599,353	331,169	268,184	81
Aged 70 to 74	477,266	271,575	205,691	76
Aged 75 to 79	326,726	191,263	135,463	71
Aged 80 to 84	179,538	111,619	67,919	61
Aged 85 or older	150,708	101,091	49,617	49
Aged 18 to 24	4,743,880	2,145,528	2,598,352	121
Aged 18 or older	22,963,559	11,136,608	11,826,951	106
Aged 65 or older	1,733,591	1,006,717	726,874	72

Note: The sex ratio is the number of males per 100 females.
Source: U.S. Census Bureau, Census 2000 Summary File 1; calculations by New Strategist

Hispanics by Age and Ethnicity, 2000

(number and percent distribution of Hispanics by age and ethnicity, 2000; numbers in thousands)

	total	Mexican	Puerto Rican	Cuban	Central and South American	other Hispanic
Total Hispanics	**32,804**	**21,701**	**2,959**	**1,300**	**4,743**	**2,101**
Under age 5	3,665	2,701	278	67	404	215
Aged 5–9	3,351	2,375	287	59	422	207
Aged 10–14	2,995	2,078	284	70	366	197
Aged 15–19	2,888	1,993	278	78	368	171
Aged 20–24	2,755	1,929	220	61	415	130
Aged 25–29	2,831	1,979	223	63	408	159
Aged 30–34	2,829	1,854	263	104	442	166
Aged 35–44	4,974	3,087	430	221	901	335
Aged 45–54	3,019	1,828	307	167	495	222
Aged 55–64	1,745	942	212	137	300	155
Aged 65–74	1,132	615	118	159	150	90
Aged 75–84	513	270	57	93	56	37
Aged 85+	108	51	3	21	16	16
Aged 18–24	3,958	2,746	336	86	581	208
Aged 18+	21,109	13,372	1,949	1,051	3,349	1,388
Aged 65+	1,753	936	178	273	222	143
Percent distribution by ethnicity						
Total Hispanics	**100.0%**	**66.2%**	**9.0%**	**4.0%**	**14.5%**	**6.4%**
Under age 5	100.0	73.7	7.6	1.8	11.0	5.9
Aged 5–9	100.0	70.9	8.6	1.8	12.6	6.2
Aged 10–14	100.0	69.4	9.5	2.3	12.2	6.6
Aged 15–19	100.0	69.0	9.6	2.7	12.7	5.9
Aged 20–24	100.0	70.0	8.0	2.2	15.1	4.7
Aged 25–29	100.0	69.9	7.9	2.2	14.4	5.6
Aged 30–34	100.0	65.5	9.3	3.7	15.6	5.9
Aged 35–44	100.0	62.1	8.6	4.4	18.1	6.7
Aged 45–54	100.0	60.5	10.2	5.5	16.4	7.4
Aged 55–64	100.0	54.0	12.1	7.9	17.2	8.9
Aged 65–74	100.0	54.3	10.4	14.0	13.3	8.0
Aged 75–84	100.0	52.6	11.1	18.1	10.9	7.2
Aged 85+	100.0	47.2	2.8	19.4	14.8	14.8
Aged 18–24	100.0	69.4	8.5	2.2	14.7	5.3
Aged 18+	100.0	63.3	9.2	5.0	15.9	6.6
Aged 65+	100.0	53.4	10.2	15.6	12.7	8.2

Note: The numbers of Hispanics by ethnic origin shown in this table differ from those in other tables because the data here are from the March 2000 Current Population Survey sample rather than the 2000 census count.
Source: U.S. Census Bureau, Current Population Survey, Internet site <www.census.gov/population/socdemo/ hispanic/p20-535/tab01-1.txt>; calculations by New Strategist

Hispanic Immigrants by Country of Birth, 2000

(total number of immigrants admitted for legal permanent residence, number of Hispanic immigrants, Hispanic share of total, and share of Hispanic immigrants by country of birth, 2000)

	number	share of total immigrants	share of Hispanic immigrants
Total immigrants	**849,807**	**100.0%**	–
Total Hispanic immigrants	**385,898**	**45.4**	**100.0%**
Mexico	173,919	20.5	45.1
Caribbean	88,198	10.4	22.9
Haiti	22,364	2.6	5.8
Cuba	20,831	2.5	5.4
Dominican Republic	17,536	2.1	4.5
Jamaica	16,000	1.9	4.1
Trinidad and Tobago	6,660	0.8	1.7
Barbados	783	0.1	0.2
Bahamas, The	768	0.1	0.2
Grenada	655	0.1	0.2
St. Lucia	601	0.1	0.2
St. Kitts-Nevis	504	0.1	0.1
St. Vincent and the Grenadines	500	0.1	0.1
Antigua-Barbuda	431	0.1	0.1
Dominica	96	0.0	0.0
Bermuda	72	0.0	0.0
Montserrat	71	0.0	0.0
British Virgin Islands	67	0.0	0.0
Netherlands Antilles	53	0.0	0.0
Guadeloupe	51	0.0	0.0
Turks and Caicos Islands	46	0.0	0.0
Cayman Islands	31	0.0	0.0
Anguilla	27	0.0	0.0
Aruba	25	0.0	0.0
Martinique	20	0.0	0.0
Puerto Rico	3	0.0	0.0
U.S. Virgin Islands	3	0.0	0.0

(continued)

(continued from previous page)

	number	share of total immigrants	share of Hispanic immigrants
Central America	66,443	7.8%	17.2%
Nicaragua	24,029	2.8	6.2
El Salvador	22,578	2.7	5.9
Guatemala	9,970	1.2	2.6
Honduras	5,939	0.7	1.5
Panama	1,843	0.2	0.5
Costa Rica	1,324	0.2	0.3
Belize	760	0.1	0.2
South America	56,074	6.6	14.5
Colombia	14,498	1.7	3.8
Peru	9,613	1.1	2.5
Ecuador	7,685	0.9	2.0
Brazil	6,959	0.8	1.8
Guyana	5,746	0.7	1.5
Venezuela	4,716	0.6	1.2
Argentina	2,331	0.3	0.6
Bolivia	1,772	0.2	0.5
Chile	1,712	0.2	0.4
Uruguay	430	0.1	0.1
Paraguay	342	0.0	0.1
Suriname	257	0.0	0.1
French Guiana	13	0.0	0.0
Spain	1,264	0.1	0.3

Note: (–) means not applicable.
Source: U.S. Immigration and Naturalization Service, 2000 Statistical Yearbook of the Immigration and Naturalization Service, Internet site <www.ins.usdoj.gov/graphics/aboutins/statistics/IMM00yrbk/ IMM2000list.htm>; calculations by New Strategist

Latin American Foreign-Born by Country of Birth, 2000

(total number of foreign born, number of Latin American foreign born, Latin American share of total, and share of Latin American foreign-born by country of birth, 2000; numbers in thousands)

Latin American and Mexican Foreign-Born by Selected Characteristics, 2000

(number and percent distribution of the Latin American and Mexican foreign-born by selected characteristics, 2000; numbers in thousands)

	total		Mexico	
	number	*percent*	*number*	*percent*
Latin American foreign-born	**14,477**	**100.0%**	**7,841**	**100.0%**
Age				
Under age 18	1,684	11.6	1,019	13.0
Aged 18 to 24	1,898	13.1	1,187	15.1
Aged 25 to 34	3,547	24.5	2,265	28.9
Aged 35 to 44	3,362	23.2	1,682	21.5
Aged 45 to 54	1,914	13.2	896	11.4
Aged 55 to 64	1,097	7.6	432	5.5
Aged 65 or older	976	6.7	360	4.6
Sex				
Male	7,373	50.9	4,246	54.2
Female	7,105	49.1	3,595	45.8
Race				
American Indian	134	0.9	108	1.4
Asian	193	1.3	15	0.2
Black	1,646	11.4	41	0.5
White	12,504	86.4	7,677	97.9
Hispanic origin				
Hispanic	12,476	86.2	7,760	99.0
Non-Hispanic white	611	4.2	67	0.9
Citizenship status				
Naturalized citizen	4,098	28.3	1,592	20.3
Not a U.S. citizen	10,379	71.7	6,249	79.7
Year of arrival				
Arrived 1990 or later	6,039	41.7	3,500	44.6
Arrived before 1990	8,439	58.3	4,341	55.4
Household income in 1999				
Total households	5,591	100.0	2,841	100.0
Under $5,000	246	4.4	114	4.0
$5,000 to $9,999	408	7.3	161	5.7
$10,000 to $14,999	564	10.1	311	10.9
$15,000 to $24,999	1,137	20.3	673	23.7
$25,000 to $34,999	924	16.5	511	18.0
$35,000 to $49,999	924	16.5	477	16.8
$50,000 to $74,999	739	13.2	344	12.1
$75,000 to $99,999	339	6.1	139	4.9
$100,000 and over	310	5.5	92	3.2

(continued)

(continued from previous page)

	total		Mexico	
	number	*percent*	*number*	*percent*
Median income	**$29,388**	–	**$27,345**	–
Poverty rate	**21.9%**	–	**25.8%**	–
Median earnings of full-time year-round workers aged 16+				
Men	$20,974	–	$19,181	–
Women	17,213	–	15,149	–
Education				
Total aged 25 or older	10,896	100.0%	5,634	100.0%
Not a high school graduate	5,493	50.4	3,731	66.2
High school graduate or more	5,403	49.6	1,903	33.8
Bachelors degree or more	1,220	11.2	236	4.2
Graduate/professional degree	384	3.5	58	1.0

Note: (–) means not applicable.
Source: Bureau of the Census, detailed tables for The Foreign-Born Population in the United States: March 2000, *Current Population Report P20-534; Internet site <www.census.gov/population/www/socdemo/foreign/p20-534.html>; calculations by New Strategist*

Hispanics by Region, 1990 and 2000 Censuses

(number of Hispanics by region, 1990 and 2000; percent change, 1990–2000)

	1990	2000	percent change 1990–2000
Total Hispanics	**22,354,059**	**35,305,818**	**57.9%**
Northeast	3,754,389	5,254,087	39.9
Midwest	1,726,509	3,124,532	81.0
South	6,767,021	11,586,696	71.2
West	10,106,140	15,340,503	51.8

Source: Bureau of the Census, The Hispanic Population: 2000, *Census 2000 Brief, C2KBR/01-3, 2001; calculations by New Strategist*

Hispanics by Region and Division, 2000 Census

(number of total people, number and percent distribution of Hispanics, and Hispanic share of total, by region and division, 2000)

	total	Hispanic		
		number	percent distribution	share of total
Total population	**281,421,906**	**35,305,818**	**100.0%**	**12.5%**
Northeast	**53,594,378**	**5,254,087**	**14.9**	**9.8**
New England	13,922,517	875,225	2.5	6.3
Middle Atlantic	39,671,861	4,378,862	12.4	11.0
Midwest	**64,392,776**	**3,124,532**	**8.8**	**4.9**
East North Central	45,155,037	2,478,719	7.0	5.5
West North Central	19,237,739	645,813	1.8	3.4
South	**100,236,820**	**11,586,696**	**32.8**	**11.6**
South Atlantic	51,769,160	4,243,946	12.0	8.2
East South Central	17,022,810	299,176	0.8	1.8
West South Central	31,444,850	7,043,574	20.0	22.4
West	**63,197,932**	**15,340,503**	**43.5**	**24.3**
Mountain	18,172,295	3,543,573	10.0	19.5
Pacific	45,025,637	11,796,930	33.4	26.2

Source: Bureau of the Census, Profiles of General Demographic Characteristics, *2000 Census of Population and Housing, 2001; calculations by New Strategist*

Hispanics by Region, Division, and Ethnicity, 2000 Census

(number and percent distribution of Hispanics by region, division, and ethnicity, 2000)

	total	*Mexican*	*Puerto Rican*	*Cuban*	*other Hispanic*
Total Hispanics	**35,305,818**	**20,640,711**	**3,406,178**	**1,241,685**	**10,017,244**
Northeast	**5,254,087**	**479,169**	**2,074,574**	**168,959**	**2,531,385**
New England	875,225	60,173	428,936	18,669	367,447
Middle Atlantic	4,378,862	418,996	1,645,638	150,290	2,163,938
Midwest	**3,124,532**	**2,200,196**	**325,363**	**45,305**	**553,668**
East North Central	2,478,719	1,735,583	301,006	36,054	406,076
West North Central	645,813	464,613	24,357	9,251	147,592
South	**11,586,696**	**6,548,081**	**759,305**	**921,427**	**3,357,883**
South Atlantic	4,243,946	1,074,939	645,530	873,492	1,649,985
East South Central	299,176	174,895	25,975	11,073	87,233
West South Central	7,043,574	5,298,247	87,800	36,862	1,620,665
West	**15,340,503**	**11,413,265**	**246,936**	**105,994**	**3,574,308**
Mountain	3,543,573	2,379,589	52,480	24,852	1,086,652
Pacific	11,796,930	9,033,676	194,456	81,142	2,487,656

Percent distribution by Hispanic ethnicity

	total	*Mexican*	*Puerto Rican*	*Cuban*	*other Hispanic*
Total Hispanics	**100.0%**	**58.5%**	**9.6%**	**3.5%**	**28.4%**
Northeast	**100.0**	**9.1**	**39.5**	**3.2**	**48.2**
New England	100.0	6.9	49.0	2.1	42.0
Middle Atlantic	100.0	9.6	37.6	3.4	49.4
Midwest	**100.0**	**70.4**	**10.4**	**1.4**	**17.7**
East North Central	100.0	70.0	12.1	1.5	16.4
West North Central	100.0	71.9	3.8	1.4	22.9
South	**100.0**	**56.5**	**6.6**	**8.0**	**29.0**
South Atlantic	100.0	25.3	15.2	20.6	38.9
East South Central	100.0	58.5	8.7	3.7	29.2
West South Central	100.0	75.2	1.2	0.5	23.0
West	**100.0**	**74.4**	**1.6**	**0.7**	**23.3**
Mountain	100.0	67.2	1.5	0.7	30.7
Pacific	100.0	76.6	1.6	0.7	21.1

(continued)

(continued from previous page)

	total	Mexican	Puerto Rican	Cuban	other Hispanic
Percent distribution by region/division					
Total Hispanics	**100.0%**	**100.0%**	**100.0%**	**100.0%**	**100.0%**
Northeast	**14.9**	**2.3**	**60.9**	**13.6**	**25.3**
New England	2.5	0.3	12.6	1.5	3.7
Middle Atlantic	12.4	2.0	48.3	12.1	21.6
Midwest	**8.8**	**10.7**	**9.6**	**3.6**	**5.5**
East North Central	7.0	8.4	8.8	2.9	4.1
West North Central	1.8	2.3	0.7	0.7	1.5
South	**32.8**	**31.7**	**22.3**	**74.2**	**33.5**
South Atlantic	12.0	5.2	19.0	70.3	16.5
East South Central	0.8	0.8	0.8	0.9	0.9
West South Central	20.0	25.7	2.6	3.0	16.2
West	**43.5**	**55.3**	**7.2**	**8.5**	**35.7**
Mountain	10.0	11.5	1.5	2.0	10.8
Pacific	33.4	43.8	5.7	6.5	24.8

Source: Bureau of the Census, Profiles of General Demographic Characteristics, *2000 Census of Population and Housing, 2001; calculations by New Strategist*

Hispanics by State, 1990 and 2000 Censuses

(number of Hispanics by state, 1990 and 2000; percent change, 1990–2000)

	1990	2000	percent change 1990–2000
Total Hispanics	**22,354,059**	**35,305,818**	**57.9%**
Alabama	24,629	75,830	207.9
Alaska	17,803	25,852	45.2
Arizona	688,338	1,295,617	88.2
Arkansas	19,876	86,866	337.0
California	7,687,938	10,966,556	42.6
Colorado	424,302	735,601	73.4
Connecticut	213,116	320,323	50.3
Delaware	15,820	37,277	135.6
District of Columbia	32,710	44,953	37.4
Florida	1,574,143	2,682,715	70.4
Georgia	108,922	435,227	299.6
Hawaii	81,390	87,699	7.8
Idaho	52,927	101,690	92.1
Illinois	904,446	1,530,262	69.2
Indiana	98,788	214,536	117.2
Iowa	32,647	82,473	152.6
Kansas	93,670	188,252	101.0
Kentucky	21,984	59,939	172.6
Louisiana	93,044	107,738	15.8
Maine	6,829	9,360	37.1
Maryland	125,102	227,916	82.2
Massachusetts	287,549	428,729	49.1
Michigan	201,596	323,877	60.7
Minnesota	53,884	143,382	166.1
Mississippi	15,931	39,569	148.4
Missouri	61,702	118,592	92.2
Montana	12,174	18,081	48.5
Nebraska	36,969	94,425	155.4
Nevada	124,419	393,970	216.6
New Hampshire	11,333	20,489	80.8
New Jersey	739,861	1,117,191	51.0
New Mexico	579,224	765,386	32.1
New York	2,214,026	2,867,583	29.5

(continued)

(continued from previous page)

	1990	2000	percent change 1990–2000
North Carolina	76,726	378,963	393.9%
North Dakota	4,665	7,786	66.9
Ohio	139,696	217,123	55.4
Oklahoma	86,160	179,304	108.1
Oregon	112,707	275,314	144.3
Pennsylvania	232,262	394,088	69.7
Rhode Island	45,752	90,820	98.5
South Carolina	30,551	95,076	211.2
South Dakota	5,252	10,903	107.6
Tennessee	32,741	123,838	278.2
Texas	4,339,905	6,669,666	53.7
Utah	84,597	201,559	138.3
Vermont	3,661	5,504	50.3
Virginia	160,288	329,540	105.6
Washington	214,570	441,509	105.8
West Virginia	8,489	12,279	44.6
Wisconsin	93,194	192,921	107.0
Wyoming	25,751	31,669	23.0

Source: Bureau of the Census, The Hispanic Population: 2000, *Census 2000 Brief, C2KBR/01-3, 2001; calculations by New Strategist*

Hispanic Share of Total Population by State, 2000 Census

(number of total people, number and percent distribution of Hispanics, and Hispanic share of total, by state, 2000)

		Hispanics		
	total	*number*	*percent distribution*	*share of total*
Total population	**281,421,906**	**35,305,818**	**100.0%**	**12.5%**
Alabama	4,447,100	75,830	0.2	1.7
Alaska	626,932	25,852	0.1	4.1
Arizona	5,130,632	1,295,617	3.7	25.3
Arkansas	2,673,400	86,866	0.2	3.2
California	33,871,648	10,966,556	31.1	32.4
Colorado	4,301,261	735,601	2.1	17.1
Connecticut	3,405,565	320,323	0.9	9.4
Delaware	783,600	37,277	0.1	4.8
District of Columbia	572,059	44,953	0.1	7.9
Florida	15,982,378	2,682,715	7.6	16.8
Georgia	8,186,453	435,227	1.2	5.3
Hawaii	1,211,537	87,699	0.2	7.2
Idaho	1,293,953	101,690	0.3	7.9
Illinois	12,419,293	1,530,262	4.3	12.3
Indiana	6,080,485	214,536	0.6	3.5
Iowa	2,926,324	82,473	0.2	2.8
Kansas	2,688,418	188,252	0.5	7.0
Kentucky	4,041,769	59,939	0.2	1.5
Louisiana	4,468,976	107,738	0.3	2.4
Maine	1,274,923	9,360	0.0	0.7
Maryland	5,296,486	227,916	0.6	4.3
Massachusetts	6,349,097	428,729	1.2	6.8
Michigan	9,938,444	323,877	0.9	3.3
Minnesota	4,919,479	143,382	0.4	2.9
Mississippi	2,844,658	39,569	0.1	1.4
Missouri	5,595,211	118,592	0.3	2.1
Montana	902,195	18,081	0.1	2.0
Nebraska	1,711,263	94,425	0.3	5.5
Nevada	1,998,257	393,970	1.1	19.7
New Hampshire	1,235,786	20,489	0.1	1.7
New Jersey	8,414,350	1,117,191	3.2	13.3

(continued)

(continued from previous page)

| | total | Hispanics | | |
		number	percent distribution	share of total
New Mexico	1,819,046	765,386	2.2%	42.1%
New York	18,976,457	2,867,583	8.1	15.1
North Carolina	8,049,313	378,963	1.1	4.7
North Dakota	642,200	7,786	0.0	1.2
Ohio	11,353,140	217,123	0.6	1.9
Oklahoma	3,450,654	179,304	0.5	5.2
Oregon	3,421,399	275,314	0.8	8.0
Pennsylvania	12,281,054	394,088	1.1	3.2
Rhode Island	1,048,319	90,820	0.3	8.7
South Carolina	4,012,012	95,076	0.3	2.4
South Dakota	754,844	10,903	0.0	1.4
Tennessee	5,689,283	123,838	0.4	2.2
Texas	20,851,820	6,669,666	18.9	32.0
Utah	2,233,169	201,559	0.6	9.0
Vermont	608,827	5,504	0.0	0.9
Virginia	7,078,515	329,540	0.9	4.7
Washington	5,894,121	441,509	1.3	7.5
West Virginia	1,808,344	12,279	0.0	0.7
Wisconsin	5,363,675	192,921	0.5	3.6
Wyoming	493,782	31,669	0.1	6.4

Source: Bureau of the Census, Profiles of General Demographic Characteristics, *2000 Census of Population and Housing, 2001; calculations by New Strategist*

Hispanics by State and Ethnicity, 2000 Census

(number of Hispanics by state and ethnicity, 2000)

	total	Mexican	Puerto Rican	Cuban	other Hispanic
Total Hispanics	**35,305,818**	**20,640,711**	**3,406,178**	**1,241,685**	**10,017,244**
Alabama	75,830	44,522	6,322	2,354	22,632
Alaska	25,852	13,334	2,649	553	9,316
Arizona	1,295,617	1,065,578	17,587	5,272	207,180
Arkansas	86,866	61,204	2,473	950	22,239
California	10,966,556	8,455,926	140,570	72,286	2,297,774
Colorado	735,601	450,760	12,993	3,701	268,147
Connecticut	320,323	23,484	194,443	7,101	95,295
Delaware	37,277	12,986	14,005	932	9,354
District of Columbia	44,953	5,098	2,328	1,101	36,426
Florida	2,682,715	363,925	482,027	833,120	1,003,643
Georgia	435,227	275,288	35,532	12,536	111,871
Hawaii	87,699	19,820	30,005	711	37,163
Idaho	101,690	79,324	1,509	408	20,449
Illinois	1,530,262	1,144,390	157,851	18,438	209,583
Indiana	214,536	153,042	19,678	2,754	39,062
Iowa	82,473	61,154	2,690	750	17,879
Kansas	188,252	148,270	5,237	1,680	33,065
Kentucky	59,939	31,385	6,469	3,516	18,569
Louisiana	107,738	32,267	7,670	8,448	59,353
Maine	9,360	2,756	2,275	478	3,851
Maryland	227,916	39,900	25,570	6,754	155,692
Massachusetts	428,729	22,288	199,207	8,867	198,367
Michigan	323,877	220,769	26,941	7,219	68,948
Minnesota	143,382	95,613	6,616	2,527	38,626
Mississippi	39,569	21,616	2,881	1,508	13,564
Missouri	118,592	77,887	6,677	3,022	31,006
Montana	18,081	11,735	931	285	5,130
Nebraska	94,425	71,030	1,993	859	20,543
Nevada	393,970	285,764	10,420	11,498	86,288
New Hampshire	20,489	4,590	6,215	785	8,899
New Jersey	1,117,191	102,929	366,788	77,337	570,137
New Mexico	765,386	330,049	4,488	2,588	428,261
New York	2,867,583	260,889	1,050,293	62,590	1,493,811

(continued)

(continued from previous page)

	total	Mexican	Puerto Rican	Cuban	other Hispanic
North Carolina	378,963	246,545	31,117	7,389	93,912
North Dakota	7,786	4,295	507	250	2,734
Ohio	217,123	90,663	66,269	5,152	55,039
Oklahoma	179,304	132,813	8,153	1,759	36,579
Oregon	275,314	214,662	5,092	3,091	52,469
Pennsylvania	394,088	55,178	228,557	10,363	99,990
Rhode Island	90,820	5,881	25,422	1,128	58,389
South Carolina	95,076	52,871	12,211	2,875	27,119
South Dakota	10,903	6,364	637	163	3,739
Tennessee	123,838	77,372	10,303	3,695	32,468
Texas	6,669,666	5,071,963	69,504	25,705	1,502,494
Utah	201,559	136,416	3,977	940	60,226
Vermont	5,504	1,174	1,374	310	2,646
Virginia	329,540	73,979	41,131	8,332	206,098
Washington	441,509	329,934	16,140	4,501	90,934
West Virginia	12,279	4,347	1,609	453	5,870
Wisconsin	192,921	126,719	30,267	2,491	33,444
Wyoming	31,669	19,963	575	160	10,971

Source: Bureau of the Census, Profiles of General Demographic Characteristics, *2000 Census of Population and Housing, 2001*

Distribution of Hispanics by Ethnicity for States, 2000 Census

(percent distribution of Hispanics by state and ethnicity, 2000)

	total	Mexican	Puerto Rican	Cuban	other Hispanic
Total Hispanics	**100.0%**	**58.5%**	**9.6%**	**3.5%**	**28.4%**
Alabama	100.0	58.7	8.3	3.1	29.8
Alaska	100.0	51.6	10.2	2.1	36.0
Arizona	100.0	82.2	1.4	0.4	16.0
Arkansas	100.0	70.5	2.8	1.1	25.6
California	100.0	77.1	1.3	0.7	21.0
Colorado	100.0	61.3	1.8	0.5	36.5
Connecticut	100.0	7.3	60.7	2.2	29.7
Delaware	100.0	34.8	37.6	2.5	25.1
District of Columbia	100.0	11.3	5.2	2.4	81.0
Florida	100.0	13.6	18.0	31.1	37.4
Georgia	100.0	63.3	8.2	2.9	25.7
Hawaii	100.0	22.6	34.2	0.8	42.4
Idaho	100.0	78.0	1.5	0.4	20.1
Illinois	100.0	74.8	10.3	1.2	13.7
Indiana	100.0	71.3	9.2	1.3	18.2
Iowa	100.0	74.2	3.3	0.9	21.7
Kansas	100.0	78.8	2.8	0.9	17.6
Kentucky	100.0	52.4	10.8	5.9	31.0
Louisiana	100.0	29.9	7.1	7.8	55.1
Maine	100.0	29.4	24.3	5.1	41.1
Maryland	100.0	17.5	11.2	3.0	68.3
Massachusetts	100.0	5.2	46.5	2.1	46.3
Michigan	100.0	68.2	8.3	2.2	21.3
Minnesota	100.0	66.7	4.6	1.8	26.9
Mississippi	100.0	54.6	7.3	3.8	34.3
Missouri	100.0	65.7	5.6	2.5	26.1
Montana	100.0	64.9	5.1	1.6	28.4
Nebraska	100.0	75.2	2.1	0.9	21.8
Nevada	100.0	72.5	2.6	2.9	21.9
New Hampshire	100.0	22.4	30.3	3.8	43.4
New Jersey	100.0	9.2	32.8	6.9	51.0
New Mexico	100.0	43.1	0.6	0.3	56.0
New York	100.0	9.1	36.6	2.2	52.1

(continued)

(continued from previous page)

	total	Mexican	Puerto Rican	Cuban	other Hispanic
North Carolina	100.0%	65.1%	8.2%	1.9%	24.8%
North Dakota	100.0	55.2	6.5	3.2	35.1
Ohio	100.0	41.8	30.5	2.4	25.3
Oklahoma	100.0	74.1	4.5	1.0	20.4
Oregon	100.0	78.0	1.8	1.1	19.1
Pennsylvania	100.0	14.0	58.0	2.6	25.4
Rhode Island	100.0	6.5	28.0	1.2	64.3
South Carolina	100.0	55.6	12.8	3.0	28.5
South Dakota	100.0	58.4	5.8	1.5	34.3
Tennessee	100.0	62.5	8.3	3.0	26.2
Texas	100.0	76.0	1.0	0.4	22.5
Utah	100.0	67.7	2.0	0.5	29.9
Vermont	100.0	21.3	25.0	5.6	48.1
Virginia	100.0	22.4	12.5	2.5	62.5
Washington	100.0	74.7	3.7	1.0	20.6
West Virginia	100.0	35.4	13.1	3.7	47.8
Wisconsin	100.0	65.7	15.7	1.3	17.3
Wyoming	100.0	63.0	1.8	0.5	34.6

Source: Bureau of the Census, Profiles of General Demographic Characteristics, *2000 Census of Population and Housing, 2001; calculations by New Strategist*

Distribution of Hispanic Ethnic Groups by State, 2000 Census

(percent distribution of Hispanic ethnic groups by state, 2000)

	total	Mexican	Puerto Rican	Cuban	other Hispanic
Total Hispanics	**100.0%**	**100.0%**	**100.0%**	**100.0%**	**100.0%**
Alabama	0.2	0.2	0.2	0.2	0.2
Alaska	0.1	0.1	0.1	0.0	0.1
Arizona	3.7	5.2	0.5	0.4	2.1
Arkansas	0.2	0.3	0.1	0.1	0.2
California	31.1	41.0	4.1	5.8	22.9
Colorado	2.1	2.2	0.4	0.3	2.7
Connecticut	0.9	0.1	5.7	0.6	1.0
Delaware	0.1	0.1	0.4	0.1	0.1
District of Columbia	0.1	0.0	0.1	0.1	0.4
Florida	7.6	1.8	14.2	67.1	10.0
Georgia	1.2	1.3	1.0	1.0	1.1
Hawaii	0.2	0.1	0.9	0.1	0.4
Idaho	0.3	0.4	0.0	0.0	0.2
Illinois	4.3	5.5	4.6	1.5	2.1
Indiana	0.6	0.7	0.6	0.2	0.4
Iowa	0.2	0.3	0.1	0.1	0.2
Kansas	0.5	0.7	0.2	0.1	0.3
Kentucky	0.2	0.2	0.2	0.3	0.2
Louisiana	0.3	0.2	0.2	0.7	0.6
Maine	0.0	0.0	0.1	0.0	0.0
Maryland	0.6	0.2	0.8	0.5	1.6
Massachusetts	1.2	0.1	5.8	0.7	2.0
Michigan	0.9	1.1	0.8	0.6	0.7
Minnesota	0.4	0.5	0.2	0.2	0.4
Mississippi	0.1	0.1	0.1	0.1	0.1
Missouri	0.3	0.4	0.2	0.2	0.3
Montana	0.1	0.1	0.0	0.0	0.1
Nebraska	0.3	0.3	0.1	0.1	0.2
Nevada	1.1	1.4	0.3	0.9	0.9
New Hampshire	0.1	0.0	0.2	0.1	0.1
New Jersey	3.2	0.5	10.8	6.2	5.7
New Mexico	2.2	1.6	0.1	0.2	4.3
New York	8.1	1.3	30.8	5.0	14.9

(continued)

(continued from previous page)

	total	Mexican	Puerto Rican	Cuban	other Hispanic
North Carolina	1.1%	1.2%	0.9%	0.6%	0.9%
North Dakota	0.0	0.0	0.0	0.0	0.0
Ohio	0.6	0.4	1.9	0.4	0.5
Oklahoma	0.5	0.6	0.2	0.1	0.4
Oregon	0.8	1.0	0.1	0.2	0.5
Pennsylvania	1.1	0.3	6.7	0.8	1.0
Rhode Island	0.3	0.0	0.7	0.1	0.6
South Carolina	0.3	0.3	0.4	0.2	0.3
South Dakota	0.0	0.0	0.0	0.0	0.0
Tennessee	0.4	0.4	0.3	0.3	0.3
Texas	18.9	24.6	2.0	2.1	15.0
Utah	0.6	0.7	0.1	0.1	0.6
Vermont	0.0	0.0	0.0	0.0	0.0
Virginia	0.9	0.4	1.2	0.7	2.1
Washington	1.3	1.6	0.5	0.4	0.9
West Virginia	0.0	0.0	0.0	0.0	0.1
Wisconsin	0.5	0.6	0.9	0.2	0.3
Wyoming	0.1	0.1	0.0	0.0	0.1

Source: Bureau of the Census, Profiles of General Demographic Characteristics, *2000 Census of Population and Housing, 2001; calculations by New Strategist*

Hispanics by Metropolitan Area, 2000 Census

(number of total people, number of Hispanics, and Hispanic share of total in the 100 largest metropolitan areas, 2000)

	total population	Hispanic number	Hispanic share of total
1. New York–Northern New Jersey–Long Island, NY–NJ–CT–PA CMSA	21,199,865	3,852,138	18.2%
• Bergen–Passaic, NJ PMSA	1,373,167	237,869	17.3
• Bridgeport, CT PMSA	459,479	56,914	12.4
• Danbury, CT PMSA	217,980	15,333	7.0
• Dutchess County, NY PMSA	280,150	18,060	6.4
• Jersey City, NJ PMSA	608,975	242,123	39.8
• Middlesex–Somerset–Hunterdon, NJ PMSA	1,169,641	131,122	11.2
• Monmouth–Ocean, NJ PMSA	1,126,217	63,813	5.7
• Nassau–Suffolk, NY PMSA	2,753,913	282,693	10.3
• New Haven–Meriden, CT PMSA	542,149	53,331	9.8
• New York, NY PMSA	9,314,235	2,339,836	25.1
• Newark, NJ PMSA	2,032,989	270,557	13.3
• Newburgh, NY–PA PMSA	387,669	42,053	10.8
• Stamford–Norwalk, CT PMSA	353,556	38,291	10.8
• Trenton, NJ PMSA	350,761	33,898	9.7
• Waterbury, CT PMSA	228,984	26,245	11.5
2. Los Angeles–Riverside–Orange County, CA CMSA	16,373,645	6,598,488	40.3
• Los Angeles–Long Beach, CA PMSA	9,519,338	4,242,213	44.6
• Orange County, CA PMSA	2,846,289	875,579	30.8
• Riverside–San Bernardino, CA PMSA	3,254,821	1,228,962	37.8
• Ventura, CA PMSA	753,197	251,734	33.4
3. Chicago–Gary–Kenosha, IL–IN–WI CMSA	9,157,540	1,498,507	16.4
• Chicago, IL PMSA	8,272,768	1,416,584	17.1
• Gary, IN PMSA	631,362	66,207	10.5
• Kankakee, IL PMSA	103,833	4,959	4.8
• Kenosha, WI PMSA	149,577	10,757	7.2
4. Washington–Baltimore, DC–MD–VA–WV CMSA	7,608,070	484,902	6.4
• Baltimore, MD PMSA	2,552,994	51,329	2.0
• Hagerstown, MD PMSA	131,923	1,570	1.2
• Washington, DC–MD–VA–WV PMSA	4,923,153	432,003	8.8
5. San Francisco–Oakland–San Jose, CA CMSA	7,039,362	1,383,661	19.7
• Oakland, CA PMSA	2,392,557	441,686	18.5
• San Francisco, CA PMSA	1,731,183	291,563	16.8
• San Jose, CA PMSA	1,682,585	403,401	24.0
• Santa Cruz–Watsonville, CA PMSA	255,602	68,486	26.8
• Santa Rosa, CA PMSA	458,614	79,511	17.3
• Vallejo–Fairfield–Napa, CA PMSA	518,821	99,014	19.1

(continued)

(continued from previous page)

	total population	Hispanic number	share of total
6. Philadelphia–Wilmington–Atlantic City, PA–NJ–DE–MD CMSA	6,188,463	348,135	5.6%
• Atlantic City–Cape May, NJ PMSA	354,878	34,107	9.6
• Philadelphia, PA–NJ PMSA	5,100,931	258,606	5.1
• Vineland–Millville–Bridgeton, NJ PMSA	146,438	27,823	19.0
• Wilmington–Newark, DE–MD PMSA	586,216	27,599	4.7
7. Boston–Worcester–Lawrence, MA–NH–ME–CT CMSA	5,819,100	358,231	6.2
• Boston, MA–NH PMSA	3,406,829	202,513	5.9
• Brockton, MA PMSA	255,459	9,524	3.7
• Fitchburg–Leominster, MA PMSA	142,284	11,838	8.3
• Lawrence, MA–NH PMSA	396,230	55,558	14.0
• Lowell, MA–NH PMSA	301,686	17,242	5.7
• Manchester, NH PMSA	198,378	5,965	3.0
• Nashua, NH PMSA	190,949	6,546	3.4
• New Bedford, MA PMSA	175,198	10,395	5.9
• Portsmouth–Rochester, NH–ME PMSA	240,698	2,402	1.0
• Worcester, MA–CT PMSA	511,389	36,248	7.1
8. Detroit–Ann Arbor–Flint, MI CMSA	5,456,428	155,903	2.9
• Ann Arbor, MI PMSA	578,736	17,676	3.1
• Detroit, MI PMSA	4,441,551	128,075	2.9
• Flint, MI PMSA	436,141	10,152	2.3
9. Dallas–Fort Worth, TX CMSA	5,221,801	1,120,350	21.5
• Dallas, TX PMSA	3,519,176	810,499	23.0
• Fort Worth–Arlington, TX PMSA	1,702,625	309,851	18.2
10. Houston–Galveston–Brazoria, TX CMSA	4,669,571	1,348,588	28.9
• Brazoria, TX PMSA	241,767	55,063	22.8
• Galveston–Texas City, TX PMSA	250,158	44,939	18.0
• Houston, TX PMSA	4,177,646	1,248,586	29.9
11. Atlanta, GA MSA	4,112,198	268,851	6.5
12. Miami–Fort Lauderdale, FL CMSA	3,876,380	1,563,389	40.3
• Fort Lauderdale, FL PMSA	1,623,018	271,652	16.7
• Miami, FL PMSA	2,253,362	1,291,737	57.3
13. Seattle–Tacoma–Bremerton, WA CMSA	3,554,760	184,297	5.2
• Bremerton, WA PMSA	231,969	9,609	4.1
• Olympia, WA PMSA	207,355	9,392	4.5
• Seattle–Bellevue–Everett, WA PMSA	2,414,616	126,675	5.2
• Tacoma, WA PMSA	700,820	38,621	5.5
14. Phoenix–Mesa, AZ MSA	3,251,876	817,012	25.1
15. Minneapolis–St. Paul, MN–WI MSA	2,968,806	99,121	3.3
16. Cleveland–Akron, OH CMSA	2,945,831	80,736	2.7
• Akron, OH PMSA	694,960	5,874	0.8
• Cleveland–Lorain–Elyria, OH PMSA	2,250,871	74,862	3.3

(continued)

(continued from previous page)

	total population	Hispanic	
		number	share of total
17. San Diego, CA MSA	2,813,833	750,965	26.7%
18. St. Louis, MO–IL MSA	2,603,607	39,677	1.5
19. Denver–Boulder–Greeley, CO CMSA	2,581,506	476,627	18.5
• Boulder–Longmont, CO PMSA	291,288	30,456	10.5
• Denver, CO PMSA	2,109,282	397,236	18.8
• Greeley, CO PMSA	180,936	48,935	27.0
20. Tampa–St. Petersburg–Clearwater, FL MSA	2,395,997	248,642	10.4
21. Pittsburgh, PA MSA	2,358,695	17,100	0.7
22. Portland–Salem, OR–WA CMSA	2,265,223	196,638	8.7
• Portland–Vancouver, OR–WA PMSA	1,918,009	142,444	7.4
• Salem, OR PMSA	347,214	54,194	15.6
23. Cincinnati–Hamilton, OH–KY–IN CMSA	1,979,202	22,488	1.1
• Cincinnati, OH–KY–IN PMSA	1,646,395	17,717	1.1
• Hamilton–Middletown, OH PMSA	332,807	4,771	1.4
24. Sacramento–Yolo, CA CMSA	1,796,857	278,182	15.5
• Sacramento, CA PMSA	1,628,197	234,475	14.4
• Yolo, CA PMSA	168,660	43,707	25.9
25. Kansas City, MO–KS MSA	1,776,062	92,910	5.2
26. Milwaukee–Racine, WI CMSA	1,689,572	109,501	6.5
• Milwaukee–Waukesha, WI PMSA	1,500,741	94,511	6.3
• Racine, WI PMSA	188,831	14,990	7.9
27. Orlando, FL MSA	1,644,561	271,627	16.5
28. Indianapolis, IN MSA	1,607,486	42,994	2.7
29. San Antonio, TX MSA	1,592,383	816,037	51.2
30. Norfolk–Virginia Beach–Newport News, VA–NC MSA	1,569,541	48,963	3.1
31. Las Vegas, NV–AZ MSA	1,563,282	322,038	20.6
32. Columbus, OH MSA	1,540,157	28,115	1.8
33. Charlotte–Gastonia–Rock Hill, NC–SC MSA	1,499,293	77,092	5.1
34. New Orleans, LA MSA	1,337,726	58,545	4.4
35. Salt Lake City–Ogden, UT MSA	1,333,914	144,600	10.8
36. Greensboro–Winston-Salem–High Point, NC MSA	1,251,509	62,210	5.0
37. Austin–San Marcos, TX MSA	1,249,763	327,760	26.2
38. Nashville, TN MSA	1,231,311	40,139	3.3
39. Providence–Fall River–Warwick, RI–MA MSA	1,188,613	93,868	7.9
40. Raleigh–Durham–Chapel Hill, NC MSA	1,187,941	72,580	6.1
41. Hartford, CT MSA	1,183,110	113,540	9.6
42. Buffalo–Niagara Falls, NY MSA	1,170,111	33,967	2.9
43. Memphis, TN–AR–MS MSA	1,135,614	27,520	2.4
44. West Palm Beach–Boca Raton, FL MSA	1,131,184	140,675	12.4
45. Jacksonville, FL MSA	1,100,491	42,122	3.8
46. Rochester, NY MSA	1,098,201	47,559	4.3
47. Grand Rapids–Muskegon–Holland, MI MSA	1,088,514	68,916	6.3
48. Oklahoma City, OK MSA	1,083,346	72,998	6.7

(continued)

(continued from previous page)

	total population	Hispanic number	share of total
49. Louisville, KY–IN MSA	1,025,598	16,479	1.6%
50. Richmond–Petersburg, VA MSA	996,512	23,283	2.3
51. Greenville–Spartanburg–Anderson, SC MSA	962,441	26,167	2.7
52. Dayton–Springfield, OH MSA	950,558	11,329	1.2
53. Fresno, CA MSA	922,516	406,151	44.0
54. Birmingham, AL MSA	921,106	16,598	1.8
55. Honolulu, HI MSA	876,156	58,729	6.7
56. Albany–Schenectady–Troy, NY MSA	875,583	23,798	2.7
57. Tucson, AZ MSA	843,746	247,578	29.3
58. Tulsa, OK MSA	803,235	38,570	4.8
59. Syracuse, NY MSA	732,117	15,112	2.1
60. Omaha, NE–IA MSA	716,998	39,735	5.5
61. Albuquerque, NM MSA	712,738	296,373	41.6
62. Knoxville, TN MSA	687,249	8,628	1.3
63. El Paso, TX MSA	679,622	531,654	78.2
64. Bakersfield, CA MSA	661,645	254,036	38.4
65. Allentown–Bethlehem–Easton, PA MSA	637,958	50,607	7.9
66. Harrisburg–Lebanon–Carlisle, PA MSA	629,401	19,557	3.1
67. Scranton–Wilkes-Barre–Hazleton, PA MSA	624,776	7,467	1.2
68. Toledo, OH MSA	618,203	27,125	4.4
69. Baton Rouge, LA MSA	602,894	10,576	1.8
70. Youngstown–Warren, OH MSA	594,746	10,743	1.8
71. Springfield, MA MSA	591,932	74,277	12.5
72. Sarasota–Bradenton, FL MSA	589,959	38,682	6.6
73. Little Rock–North Little Rock, AR MSA	583,845	12,337	2.1
74. McAllen–Edinburg–Mission, TX MSA	569,463	503,100	88.3
75. Stockton–Lodi, CA MSA	563,598	172,073	30.5
76. Charleston–North Charleston, SC MSA	549,033	13,091	2.4
77. Wichita, KS MSA	545,220	40,353	7.4
78. Mobile, AL MSA	540,258	7,353	1.4
79. Columbia, SC MSA	536,691	12,859	2.4
80. Colorado Springs, CO MSA	516,929	58,401	11.3
81. Fort Wayne, IN MSA	502,141	16,707	3.3
82. Daytona Beach, FL MSA	493,175	31,648	6.4
83. Lakeland–Winter Haven, FL MSA	483,924	45,933	9.5
84. Johnson City–Kingsport–Bristol, TN–VA MSA	480,091	4,425	0.9
85. Lexington, KY MSA	479,198	11,880	2.5
86. Augusta–Aiken, GA–SC MSA	477,441	11,670	2.4
87. Melbourne–Titusville–Palm Bay, FL MSA	476,230	21,970	4.6
88. Lancaster, PA MSA	470,658	26,742	5.7
89. Chattanooga, TN–GA MSA	465,161	7,006	1.5
90. Des Moines, IA MSA	456,022	19,130	4.2
91. Kalamazoo–Battle Creek, MI MSA	452,851	16,296	3.6

(continued)

(continued from previous page)

	total population	Hispanic	
		number	share of total
92. Lansing–East Lansing, MI MSA	447,728	21,201	4.7%
93. Modesto, CA MSA	446,997	141,871	31.7
94. Fort Myers–Cape Coral, FL MSA	440,888	42,042	9.5
95. Jackson, MS MSA	440,801	4,240	1.0
96. Boise City, ID MSA	432,345	37,922	8.8
97. Madison, WI MSA	426,526	14,387	3.4
98. Spokane, WA MSA	417,939	11,561	2.8
99. Pensacola, FL MSA	412,153	10,903	2.6
100. Canton–Massillon, OH MSA	406,934	3,650	0.9

Note: For definitions of CMSA, PMSA, and MSA, see glossary.
Source: Bureau of the Census, Profiles of General Demographic Characteristics, *2000 Census of Population and Housing, May 2001; calculations by New Strategist*

Hispanic Spending Is Focused on the Home

The nation's 9 million Hispanic households spent an average of $32,735 in 2000, according to the Bureau of Labor Statistics' Consumer Expenditure Survey. Hispanic households (called consumer units by the Bureau of Labor Statistics) spend 86 percent as much as the average household, although their incomes are just 78 percent of the average.

While Hispanic spending is below average in many categories, it is above average on a wide variety of items. Hispanics spend 16 percent more than the average household on food at home. Behind the higher spending are their larger families. Hispanics spend 84 percent more than the average household on rice and more than three times as much on dried beans. They spend 32 percent more on beer consumed at home, 53 percent more on soaps and detergents, 15 percent more on furniture, 67 percent more on infants' clothes, 51 percent more on footwear, and 41 percent more on portable color television sets.

■ Hispanic spending is greatly influenced by immigration. Because many Hispanics come from Mexico and other countries with traditional, family-oriented cultures, their spending on food, cleaning supplies, and other items for the home is much higher than average.

Hispanic households spend 14 percent less than the average household

(average annual spending of total and Hispanic consumer units, 2000)

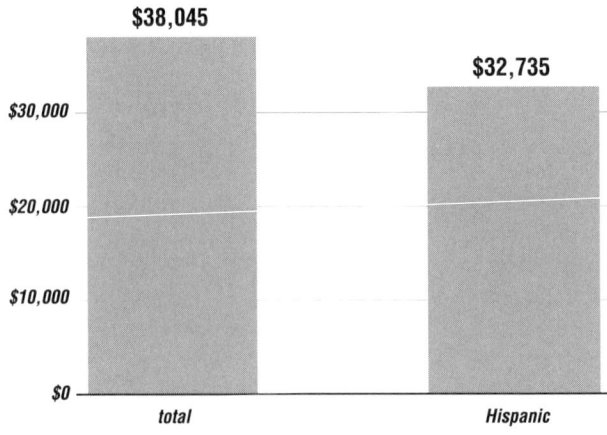

Average and Indexed Spending of Households by Hispanic Origin, 2000

(average annual expenditures of total, Hispanic, and non-Hispanic consumer units (CUs), and indexed expenditures of Hispanic and non-Hispanic consumer units, 2000)

	average spending of total consumer units	Hispanic CUs average spending	Hispanic CUs indexed spending*	non-Hispanic CUs average spending	non-Hispanic CUs indexed spending
Number of consumer units (in 000s)	109,367	9,473	–	99,894	–
Average before-tax income of CU	$44,649.00	$34,891.00	78	$45,669.00	102
Average spending of CU, total	38,044.67	32,734.95	86	38,548.91	101
FOOD	**$5,157.88**	**$5,361.60**	**104**	**$5,139.23**	**100**
FOOD AT HOME	3,021.00	3,496.40	116	2,976.85	99
Cereals and bakery products	453.33	490.56	108	449.87	99
Cereals and cereal products	156.40	200.94	128	152.26	97
Flour	7.98	18.04	226	7.04	88
Prepared flour mixes	13.35	12.15	91	13.47	101
Ready-to-eat and cooked cereals	86.88	93.30	107	86.29	99
Rice	19.55	36.02	184	18.02	92
Pasta, cornmeal, other cereal products	28.64	41.43	145	27.45	96
Bakery products	296.93	289.62	98	297.61	100
Bread	84.04	96.85	115	82.85	99
White bread	36.62	45.71	125	35.77	98
Bread, other than white	47.42	51.14	108	47.08	99
Crackers and cookies	71.03	56.60	80	72.37	102
Cookies	47.71	40.12	84	48.41	101
Crackers	23.32	16.49	71	23.96	103
Frozen and refrigerated bakery products	24.53	16.47	67	25.28	103
Other bakery products	117.33	119.69	102	117.11	100
Biscuits and rolls	38.53	24.79	64	39.80	103
Cakes and cupcakes	38.42	47.66	124	37.56	98
Bread and cracker products	4.41	4.03	91	4.45	101
Sweetrolls, coffee cakes, doughnuts	22.68	29.76	131	22.03	97
Pies, tarts, turnovers	13.28	13.46	101	13.27	100
Meats, poultry, fish, and eggs	**795.43**	**1,035.90**	**130**	**773.09**	**97**
Beef	238.19	325.97	137	230.04	97
Ground beef	87.76	114.93	131	85.24	97
Roast	39.84	52.72	132	38.64	97
Chuck roast	13.33	21.14	159	12.60	95
Round roast	11.46	13.36	117	11.28	98
Other roast	15.05	18.22	121	14.75	98
Steak	94.52	138.29	146	90.45	96
Round steak	15.31	31.49	206	13.81	90
Sirloin steak	29.86	47.32	158	28.24	95
Other steak	49.35	59.48	121	48.40	98
Other beef	16.08	20.02	125	15.71	98

(continued)

(continued from previous page)

	average spending of total consumer units	Hispanic CUs		non-Hispanic CUs	
		average spending	indexed spending	average spending	indexed spending
Pork	$166.94	$212.95	128	$162.67	97
Bacon	26.05	27.88	107	25.88	99
Pork chops	40.57	61.15	151	38.65	95
Ham	36.26	47.56	131	35.21	97
Ham, not canned	34.52	45.65	132	33.49	97
Canned ham	1.74	1.92	110	1.72	99
Sausage	25.24	25.16	100	25.25	100
Other pork	38.82	51.19	132	37.68	97
Other meats	100.54	115.91	115	99.11	99
Frankfurters	20.68	25.57	124	20.22	98
Lunch meats (cold cuts)	67.99	66.73	98	68.11	100
Bologna, liverwurst, salami	23.73	28.13	119	23.32	98
Other lunch meats	44.26	38.60	87	44.79	101
Lamb, organ meats, and others	11.87	23.62	199	10.78	91
Lamb and organ meats	9.71	22.51	232	8.52	88
Mutton, goat, and game	2.16	1.11	51	2.26	105
Poultry	145.16	190.04	131	140.99	97
Fresh and frozen chicken	114.43	165.12	144	109.73	96
Fresh and frozen whole chicken	31.25	62.80	201	28.32	91
Fresh and frozen chicken parts	83.18	102.32	123	81.40	98
Other poultry	30.73	24.92	81	31.27	102
Fish and seafood	110.14	136.46	124	107.69	98
Canned fish and seafood	15.67	16.33	104	15.61	100
Fresh fish and shellfish	66.82	90.26	135	64.64	97
Frozen fish and shellfish	27.65	29.86	108	27.45	99
Eggs	34.46	54.57	158	32.59	95
Dairy products	**324.63**	**359.18**	**111**	**321.43**	**99**
Fresh milk and cream	131.22	170.38	130	127.58	97
Fresh milk, all types	119.61	156.86	131	116.15	97
Cream	11.61	13.52	116	11.44	99
Other dairy products	193.41	188.80	98	193.84	100
Butter	17.00	12.81	75	17.39	102
Cheese	95.96	101.78	106	95.42	99
Ice cream and related products	56.56	51.79	92	57.01	101
Miscellaneous dairy products	23.89	22.42	94	24.03	101
Fruits and vegetables	**520.83**	**670.47**	**129**	**506.93**	**97**
Fresh fruits	163.17	228.24	140	157.12	96
Apples	29.49	37.11	126	28.78	98
Bananas	31.70	50.32	159	29.97	95
Oranges	18.93	27.92	147	18.09	96
Citrus fruits, excl. oranges	14.31	25.52	178	13.27	93
Other fresh fruits	68.74	87.38	127	67.01	97

(continued)

(continued from previous page)

	average spending of total consumer units	Hispanic CUs		non-Hispanic CUs	
		average spending	indexed spending	average spending	indexed spending
Fresh vegetables	$158.72	$227.89	144	$152.30	96
Potatoes	28.07	35.18	125	27.40	98
Lettuce	20.75	26.05	126	20.26	98
Tomatoes	29.53	55.33	187	27.13	92
Other fresh vegetables	80.38	111.33	139	77.50	96
Processed fruits	115.01	125.45	109	114.04	99
Frozen fruits and fruit juices	14.37	11.55	80	14.63	102
Frozen orange juice	6.90	6.25	91	6.96	101
Frozen fruits	3.62	1.67	46	3.80	105
Frozen fruit juices	3.84	3.63	95	3.86	101
Canned fruits	15.48	14.21	92	15.60	101
Dried fruits	5.50	4.28	78	5.62	102
Fresh fruit juice	23.44	25.11	107	23.28	99
Canned and bottled fruit juice	56.21	70.31	125	54.91	98
Processed vegetables	83.94	88.89	106	83.48	99
Frozen vegetables	26.42	17.65	67	27.24	103
Canned and dried vegetables and juices	57.52	71.24	124	56.24	98
Canned beans	12.67	13.59	107	12.59	99
Canned corn	6.80	8.68	128	6.62	97
Canned miscellaneous vegetables	17.95	15.99	89	18.14	101
Dried peas	0.34	0.26	76	0.35	103
Dried beans	2.53	8.98	355	1.93	76
Dried miscellaneous vegetables	7.22	9.52	132	7.00	97
Dried processed vegetables	0.41	1.57	383	0.30	73
Frozen vegetable juices	0.29	0.39	134	0.28	97
Fresh and canned vegetable juices	9.30	12.28	132	9.03	97
Other food at home	**926.77**	**940.30**	**101**	**925.53**	**100**
Sugar and other sweets	117.14	109.73	94	117.83	101
Candy and chewing gum	76.30	58.70	77	77.93	102
Sugar	16.80	29.19	174	15.65	93
Artificial sweeteners	4.19	3.27	78	4.27	102
Jams, preserves, other sweets	19.86	18.58	94	19.98	101
Fats and oils	83.09	99.50	120	81.56	98
Margarine	11.61	10.83	93	11.68	101
Fats and oils	23.35	41.90	179	21.62	93
Salad dressings	27.18	29.53	109	26.96	99
Nondairy cream and imitation milk	9.15	7.38	81	9.31	102
Peanut butter	11.81	9.86	83	11.99	102
Miscellaneous foods	437.02	405.28	93	439.97	101
Frozen prepared foods	90.20	69.69	77	92.10	102
Frozen meals	28.50	16.95	59	29.57	104
Other frozen prepared foods	61.70	52.74	85	62.53	101
Canned and packaged soups	35.54	34.01	96	35.68	100

(continued)

(continued from previous page)

	average spending of total consumer units	Hispanic CUs		non-Hispanic CUs	
		average spending	indexed spending	average spending	indexed spending
Potato chips, nuts, and other snacks	$92.50	$68.26	74	$94.75	102
Potato chips and other snacks	71.67	54.85	77	73.23	102
Nuts	20.83	13.41	64	21.52	103
Condiments and seasonings	84.61	76.51	90	85.36	101
Salt, spices, and other seasonings	20.65	25.64	124	20.19	98
Olives, pickles, relishes	9.77	7.58	78	9.97	102
Sauces and gravies	37.23	32.74	88	37.65	101
Baking needs and misc. products	16.96	10.55	62	17.55	103
Other canned/packaged prepared foods	134.17	156.81	117	132.07	98
Prepared salads	18.55	13.49	73	19.02	103
Prepared desserts	9.31	9.64	104	9.28	100
Baby food	32.26	34.85	108	32.02	99
Miscellaneous prepared foods	73.91	98.70	134	71.60	97
Vitamin supplements	0.14	0.13	93	0.14	100
Nonalcoholic beverages	249.58	291.74	117	245.67	98
Cola	86.99	111.86	129	84.68	97
Other carbonated drinks	47.39	50.99	108	47.06	99
Coffee	41.85	44.73	107	41.58	99
Roasted coffee	27.50	27.86	101	27.46	100
Instant and freeze-dried coffee	14.35	16.86	117	14.12	98
Noncarbonated fruit-flavored drinks, incl. nonfrozen lemonade	19.42	28.16	145	18.61	96
Tea	15.68	14.63	93	15.77	101
Nonalcoholic beer	0.27	–	–	0.30	111
Other nonalcoholic beverages and ice	37.99	41.38	109	37.67	99
Food prepared by CU on out-of-town trips	39.94	34.04	85	40.50	101
FOOD AWAY FROM HOME	**2,136.88**	**1,865.20**	**87**	**2,162.39**	**101**
Meals at restaurants, carry-outs other	**1,750.33**	**1,619.58**	**93**	**1,762.48**	**101**
Lunch	662.90	670.47	101	662.19	100
At fast food, take-out, delivery, concession stands, buffet, and cafeteria (other than employer and school cafeteria)	368.00	423.56	115	362.84	99
At full-service restaurants	208.12	146.56	70	213.84	103
At vending machines, mobile vendors	6.52	18.43	283	5.42	83
At employer and school cafeterias	80.26	81.93	102	80.10	100
Dinner	697.99	545.51	78	712.16	102
At fast food, take-out, delivery, concession stands, buffet, and cafeteria (other than employer and school cafeteria)	206.92	260.83	126	201.91	98
At full-service restaurants	487.70	279.63	57	507.03	104
At vending machines, mobile vendors	1.02	2.51	246	0.89	87
At employer and school cafeterias	2.35	2.54	108	2.34	100

(continued)

(continued from previous page)

	average spending of total consumer units	Hispanic CUs		non-Hispanic CUs	
		average spending	indexed spending	average spending	indexed spending
Snacks and nonalcoholic beverages	$227.71	$224.18	98	$228.04	100
At fast food, take-out, delivery, concession stands, buffet, and cafeteria (other than employer and school cafeteria)	158.55	153.59	97	159.01	100
At full-service restaurants	20.15	19.93	99	20.18	100
At vending machines, mobile vendors	38.52	40.94	106	38.29	99
At employer and school cafeterias	10.49	9.73	93	10.56	101
Breakfast and brunch	161.73	179.42	111	160.08	99
At fast food, take-out, delivery, concession stands, buffet, and cafeteria (other than employer and school cafeteria)	77.12	108.16	140	74.23	96
At full-service restaurants	79.64	60.79	76	81.39	102
At vending machines, mobile vendors	1.35	3.79	281	1.12	83
At employer and school cafeterias	3.62	6.68	185	3.34	92
Board (including at school)	**39.03**	**29.31**	**75**	**39.95**	**102**
Catered affairs	**54.02**	**29.09**	**54**	**56.39**	**104**
Food on trips	**216.06**	**122.31**	**57**	**224.95**	**104**
School lunches	**58.46**	**45.88**	**78**	**59.65**	**102**
Meals as pay	**18.97**	**19.02**	**100**	**18.96**	**100**
ALCOHOLIC BEVERAGES	**$371.81**	**$284.79**	**77**	**$379.92**	**102**
At home	**226.64**	**202.90**	**90**	**228.84**	**101**
Beer and ale	112.01	147.78	132	108.69	97
Whiskey	13.49	8.80	65	13.92	103
Wine	80.04	34.03	43	84.32	105
Other alcoholic beverages	21.10	12.29	58	21.91	104
Away from home	**145.17**	**81.89**	**56**	**151.08**	**104**
Beer and ale	62.46	36.41	58	64.88	104
At fast food, take-out, delivery, concession stands, buffet, and cafeteria	13.37	11.95	89	13.50	101
At full-service restaurants	45.05	24.39	54	46.97	104
At vending machines, mobile vendors	0.40	–	–	0.44	110
At catered affairs	3.64	0.07	2	3.97	109
Wine	17.79	10.88	61	18.43	104
At fast food, take-out, delivery, concession stands, buffet and cafeteria	1.23	1.86	151	1.18	96
At full-service restaurants	16.16	9.01	56	16.83	104
At catered affairs	0.39	0.01	3	0.42	108
Other alcoholic beverages	64.92	34.59	53	67.78	104
At fast food, take-out, delivery, concession stands, buffet, and cafeteria	3.04	3.00	99	3.05	100
At full-service restaurants	25.74	14.40	56	26.80	104
At machines and mobile vendors	0.29	0.38	131	0.29	100
At catered affairs	1.60	0.03	2	1.75	109
Alcoholic beverages purchased on trips	34.24	16.77	49	35.90	105

(continued)

(continued from previous page)

	average spending of total consumer units	Hispanic CUs		non-Hispanic CUs	
		average spending	indexed spending	average spending	indexed spending
HOUSING	**$12,318.51**	**$10,849.81**	**88**	**$12,457.64**	**101**
SHELTER	**7,114.26**	**6,437.15**	**90**	**7,178.47**	**101**
Owned dwellings**	**4,602.32**	**2,948.92**	**64**	**4,759.11**	**103**
Mortgage interest and charges	2,638.81	1,751.04	66	2,722.99	103
Mortgage interest	2,460.48	1,661.11	68	2,536.28	103
Interest paid, home equity loan	98.22	52.84	54	102.52	104
Interest paid, home equity line of credit	79.76	35.61	45	83.95	105
Prepayment penalty charges	0.34	1.48	435	0.24	71
Property taxes	1,138.55	664.62	58	1,183.50	104
Maintenance, repairs, insurance, other expenses	824.96	533.26	65	852.62	103
Homeowner's and related insurance	234.84	130.30	55	244.76	104
Homeowner's insurance	234.84	130.30	55	244.76	104
Ground rent	38.67	33.62	87	39.15	101
Maintenance and repair services	438.92	270.61	62	454.88	104
Painting and papering	49.93	23.06	46	52.48	105
Plumbing and water heating	41.62	19.58	47	43.70	105
Heat, air conditioning, electrical work	79.19	33.68	43	83.51	105
Roofing and gutters	75.27	67.53	90	76.00	101
Other repair and maintenance services	157.99	106.34	67	162.89	103
Repair, replacement of hard-surface flooring	33.61	20.32	60	34.87	104
Repair of built-in appliances	1.31	0.10	8	1.43	109
Maintenance and repair materials	78.08	79.83	102	77.91	100
Paints, wallpaper, and supplies	16.03	15.97	100	16.03	100
Tools, equip. for painting, wallpapering	1.72	1.72	100	1.72	100
Plumbing supplies and equipment	6.13	3.35	55	6.39	104
Electrical supplies, heating/cooling equip.	4.35	4.39	101	4.35	100
Hard-surface flooring, repair, and replacement	6.98	6.52	93	7.03	101
Roofing and gutters	6.41	8.06	126	6.25	98
Plaster, paneling, siding, windows, doors, screens, awnings	12.14	13.81	114	11.98	99
Patio, walk, fence, driveway, masonry, brick, and stucco materials	0.60	0.41	68	0.61	102
Landscape maintenance	2.92	2.27	78	2.98	102
Miscellaneous supplies and equipment	20.80	23.33	112	20.56	99
Insulation, other maintenance, repair	13.45	19.42	144	12.89	96
Finish basement, remodel rooms, build patios, walks, etc.	7.35	3.91	53	7.67	104
Property management and security	30.99	16.79	54	32.33	104
Property management	21.49	13.27	62	22.27	104
Management, upkeep services for security	9.50	3.52	37	10.06	106
Parking	3.45	2.11	61	3.58	104

(continued)

(continued from previous page)

	average spending of total consumer units	Hispanic CUs		non-Hispanic CUs	
		average spending	indexed spending	average spending	indexed spending
Rented dwellings	**$2,034.11**	**$3,307.05**	**163**	**$1,913.39**	**94**
Rent	1,977.33	3,225.26	163	1,858.99	94
Rent as pay	29.24	54.89	188	26.81	92
Maintenance, insurance, other expenses	27.54	26.90	98	27.60	100
Tenant's insurance	8.86	2.52	28	9.46	107
Maintenance and repair services	11.13	3.54	32	11.85	106
Repair and maintenance services	9.98	3.54	35	10.59	106
Repair and replacement of hard-surface flooring	1.08	–	–	1.18	109
Repair of built-in appliances	0.07	–	–	0.07	100
Maintenance and repair materials	7.55	20.83	276	6.29	83
Paint, wallpaper, and supplies	1.54	3.16	205	1.39	90
Painting and wallpapering tools	0.17	0.34	200	0.15	88
Plastering, paneling, roofing, gutters, etc.	0.48	0.33	69	0.49	102
Patio, walk, fence, driveway, masonry, brick, and stucco materials	0.03	0.37	1,233	–	–
Plumbing supplies and equipment	0.39	1.43	367	0.29	74
Electrical supplies, heating and cooling equipment	0.25	0.03	12	0.27	108
Miscellaneous supplies and equipment	3.60	13.40	372	2.67	74
Insulation, other maintenance and repair	0.92	1.16	126	0.90	98
Materials for additions, finishing basements, remodeling rooms	2.67	12.24	458	1.76	66
Construction materials for jobs not started	0.01	–	–	0.02	200
Hard-surface flooring	0.49	1.77	361	0.37	76
Landscape maintenance	0.60	–	–	0.66	110
Other lodging	**477.84**	**181.19**	**38**	**505.97**	**106**
Owned vacation homes	147.91	30.45	21	159.05	108
Mortgage interest and charges	63.65	8.75	14	68.85	108
Mortgage interest	61.19	8.45	14	66.19	108
Interest paid, home equity loan	1.35	0.29	21	1.45	107
Interest paid, home equity line of credit	1.11	–	–	1.21	109
Property taxes	51.97	12.32	24	55.73	107
Maintenance, insurance, other expenses	32.29	9.38	29	34.46	107
Homeowner's and related insurance	10.74	5.00	47	11.29	105
Homeowner's insurance	10.74	5.00	47	11.29	105
Ground rent	2.97	2.23	75	3.04	102
Maintenance and repair services	13.56	0.77	6	14.77	109
Maintenance and repair materials	0.48	–	–	0.52	108
Property management and security	3.89	1.39	36	4.13	106
Property management	2.56	0.76	30	2.73	107
Management and upkeep services for security	1.33	0.63	47	1.40	105

(continued)

(continued from previous page)

	average spending of total consumer units	Hispanic CUs		non-Hispanic CUs	
		average spending	indexed spending	average spending	indexed spending
Parking	$0.65	–	–	$0.71	109
Housing while attending school	78.31	$52.99	68	80.71	103
Lodging on out-of-town trips	251.62	97.75	39	266.21	106
UTILITIES, FUELS, AND PUBLIC SERVICES	**2,488.90**	**2,170.08**	**87**	**2,519.14**	**101**
Natural gas	**307.35**	**242.49**	**79**	**313.50**	**102**
Natural gas (renter)	60.47	99.05	164	56.81	94
Natural gas (owner)	244.63	143.11	59	254.26	104
Natural gas (vacation)	2.25	0.32	14	2.43	108
Electricity	**911.44**	**749.43**	**82**	**926.80**	**102**
Electricity (renter)	213.85	304.07	142	205.29	96
Electricity (owner)	690.09	442.76	64	713.54	103
Electricity (vacation)	7.50	2.59	35	7.96	106
Fuel oil and other fuels	**96.94**	**29.94**	**31**	**103.30**	**107**
Fuel oil	55.08	6.55	12	59.68	108
Fuel oil (renter)	6.54	0.57	9	7.10	109
Fuel oil (owner)	47.74	5.98	13	51.70	108
Fuel oil (vacation)	0.81	–	–	0.89	110
Coal	0.58	–	–	0.63	109
Coal (renter)	0.14	–	–	0.15	107
Coal (owner)	0.44	–	–	0.48	109
Bottled/tank gas	35.26	18.76	53	36.83	104
Gas (renter)	4.76	2.17	46	5.00	105
Gas (owner)	28.79	16.13	56	29.99	104
Gas (vacation)	1.71	0.46	27	1.83	107
Wood and other fuels	6.02	4.63	77	6.15	102
Wood and other fuels (renter)	1.09	0.43	39	1.16	106
Wood and other fuels (owner)	4.88	4.20	86	4.94	101
Wood and other fuels (vacation)	0.05	–	–	0.06	120
Telephone services	**876.75**	**888.85**	**101**	**875.61**	**100**
Telephone services in home city, excl. mobile phones	757.26	788.83	104	754.27	100
Telephone services for mobile phones	119.49	100.01	84	121.34	102
Water and other public services	**296.42**	**259.37**	**88**	**299.94**	**101**
Water and sewerage maintenance	212.72	192.18	90	214.67	101
Water, sewerage maintenance (renter)	29.99	41.95	140	28.86	96
Water, sewerage maintenance (owner)	181.10	149.77	83	184.07	102
Water, sewerage maintenance (vacation)	1.63	0.46	28	1.74	107
Trash and garbage collection	81.74	66.27	81	83.21	102
Trash and garbage collection (renter)	8.30	11.89	143	7.96	96
Trash and garbage collection (owner)	71.34	54.12	76	72.98	102
Trash and garbage collection (vacation)	2.10	0.26	12	2.28	109

(continued)

(continued from previous page)

	average spending of total consumer units	Hispanic CUs		non-Hispanic CUs	
		average spending	indexed spending	average spending	indexed spending
Septic tank cleaning	$1.96	$0.91	46	$2.06	105
Septic tank cleaning (renter)	0.04	0.13	325	0.03	75
Septic tank cleaning (owner)	1.92	0.78	41	2.03	106
HOUSEHOLD SERVICES	**684.38**	**465.48**	**68**	**705.17**	**103**
Personal services	**326.20**	**254.71**	**78**	**332.98**	**102**
Babysitting and child care in own home	32.21	58.49	182	29.72	92
Babysitting and child care in someone else's home	32.59	65.83	202	29.44	90
Care for elderly, invalids, handicapped, etc.	50.38	2.16	4	54.95	109
Adult day care centers	2.60	0.14	5	2.83	109
Day care centers, nurseries, preschools	208.42	128.09	61	216.03	104
Other household services	**358.18**	**210.77**	**59**	**372.18**	**104**
Housekeeping services	88.15	46.36	53	92.11	104
Gardening, lawn care service	78.26	29.22	37	82.91	106
Water softening service	3.11	1.28	41	3.28	105
Nonclothing laundry, dry cleaning, sent out	1.48	0.66	45	1.55	105
Nonclothing laundry and dry cleaning, coin-operated	4.64	12.32	266	3.92	84
Termite/pest control services	9.57	5.37	56	9.97	104
Home security system service fee	18.67	11.34	61	19.37	104
Other home services	14.28	8.94	63	14.78	104
Termite/pest control products	0.49	0.14	29	0.53	108
Moving, storage, and freight express	32.43	22.93	71	33.33	103
Appliance repair, including service center	12.58	5.26	42	13.27	105
Reupholstering and furniture repair	9.26	3.21	35	9.84	106
Repairs/rentals of lawn/garden equipment, hand/power tools, etc.	4.96	1.47	30	5.29	107
Appliance rental	3.77	4.97	132	3.65	97
Rental of office equip. for nonbusiness use	0.53	0.32	60	0.55	104
Repair of miscellaneous household equipment and furnishings	11.73	24.06	205	10.59	90
Repair of computer systems for nonbusiness use	2.75	1.51	55	2.87	104
Computer information services	61.36	31.27	51	64.21	105
Rental, installation of dishwashers, range hoods, and garbage disposals	0.15	0.12	80	0.15	100
HOUSEKEEPING SUPPLIES	**482.32**	**473.77**	**98**	**483.11**	**100**
Laundry and cleaning supplies	**130.76**	**171.68**	**131**	**126.96**	**97**
Soaps and detergents	69.27	105.92	153	65.86	95
Other laundry cleaning products	61.49	65.76	107	61.10	99
Other household products	**225.90**	**226.57**	**100**	**225.84**	**100**
Cleansing and toilet tissue, paper towels, and napkins	68.45	92.02	134	66.26	97

(continued)

(continued from previous page)

	average spending of total consumer units	Hispanic CUs		non-Hispanic CUs	
		average spending	indexed spending	average spending	indexed spending
Miscellaneous household products	$90.48	$85.66	95	$90.93	100
Lawn and garden supplies	66.97	48.89	73	68.65	103
Postage and stationery	**125.66**	**75.51**	**60**	**130.32**	**104**
Stationery, stationery supplies, giftwrap	63.65	33.54	53	66.45	104
Postage	60.60	41.80	69	62.35	103
Delivery services	1.41	0.17	12	1.52	108
HOUSEHOLD FURNISHINGS AND EQUIPMENT	**$1,548.63**	**$1,303.33**	**84**	**$1,571.75**	**101**
Household textiles	**106.49**	**88.70**	**83**	**108.17**	**102**
Bathroom linens	17.55	27.42	156	16.64	95
Bedroom linens	44.52	33.64	76	45.53	102
Kitchen and dining room linens	9.31	9.00	97	9.34	100
Curtains and draperies	21.06	10.84	51	22.03	105
Slipcovers and decorative pillows	2.75	1.71	62	2.85	104
Sewing materials for household items	9.75	4.32	44	10.27	105
Other linens	1.53	1.78	116	1.51	99
Furniture	**390.63**	**447.40**	**115**	**385.25**	**99**
Mattresses and springs	52.89	76.05	144	50.69	96
Other bedroom furniture	69.11	109.57	159	65.28	94
Sofas	89.15	92.64	104	88.82	100
Living room chairs	43.84	35.40	81	44.64	102
Living room tables	17.19	16.98	99	17.21	100
Kitchen and dining room furniture	46.46	58.97	127	45.28	97
Infants' furniture	6.22	7.24	116	6.12	98
Outdoor furniture	15.16	4.04	27	16.21	107
Wall units, cabinets, and other furniture	50.61	46.53	92	51.00	101
Floor coverings	**44.38**	**27.40**	**62**	**45.99**	**104**
Wall-to-wall carpet (renter)	1.38	0.82	59	1.43	104
Wall-to-wall carpet (replacement) (owner)	27.78	21.97	79	28.34	102
Room-size rugs and other floor coverings, nonpermanent	15.22	4.60	30	16.22	107
Major appliances	**188.96**	**166.17**	**88**	**191.14**	**101**
Dishwashers (built-in), garbage disposals, range hoods (renter)	0.87	0.35	40	0.92	106
Dishwashers (built-in), garbage disposals, range hoods (owner)	14.10	4.22	30	15.03	107
Refrigerators and freezers (renter)	7.35	7.74	105	7.31	99
Refrigerators and freezers (owner)	44.34	28.73	65	45.82	103
Washing machines (renter)	4.79	3.15	66	4.94	103
Washing machines (owner)	18.53	18.32	99	18.55	100
Clothes dryers (renter)	3.36	1.69	50	3.52	105
Clothes dryers (owner)	12.02	9.13	76	12.29	102
Cooking stoves, ovens (renter)	2.80	3.04	109	2.78	99
Cooking stoves, ovens (owner)	23.95	21.15	88	24.21	101

(continued)

(continued from previous page)

	average spending of total consumer units	Hispanic CUs		non-Hispanic CUs	
		average spending	indexed spending	average spending	indexed spending
Microwave ovens (renter)	$2.38	$3.45	145	$2.28	96
Microwave ovens (owner)	7.36	4.71	64	7.61	103
Portable dishwashers (renter)	0.16	–	–	0.17	106
Portable dishwashers (owner)	0.76	–	–	0.83	109
Window air conditioners (renter)	1.85	3.09	167	1.73	94
Window air conditioners (owner)	4.82	3.78	78	4.92	102
Electric floor-cleaning equipment	25.98	37.17	143	24.94	96
Sewing machines	4.78	8.81	184	4.40	92
Miscellaneous household appliances	8.77	7.63	87	8.87	101
Small appliances and misc. housewares	**87.37**	**66.09**	**76**	**89.36**	**102**
Housewares	64.87	48.06	74	66.43	102
Plastic dinnerware	1.45	1.72	119	1.43	99
China and other dinnerware	11.43	6.27	55	11.91	104
Flatware	3.61	2.19	61	3.74	104
Glassware	8.02	5.51	69	8.25	103
Silver serving pieces	2.35	1.04	44	2.48	106
Other serving pieces	1.43	0.67	47	1.50	105
Nonelectric cookware	16.67	23.54	141	16.04	96
Tableware, nonelectric kitchenware	19.90	7.11	36	21.09	106
Small appliances	22.51	18.04	80	22.93	102
Small electric kitchen appliances	17.04	13.28	78	17.39	102
Portable heating and cooling equipment	5.47	4.75	87	5.54	101
Miscellaneous household equipment	**730.81**	**507.57**	**69**	**751.84**	**103**
Window coverings	13.02	2.50	19	14.02	108
Infants' equipment	8.01	10.27	128	7.80	97
Laundry and cleaning equipment	10.08	10.57	105	10.04	100
Outdoor equipment	18.39	7.91	43	19.37	105
Clocks	13.91	10.22	73	14.25	102
Lamps and lighting fixtures	10.80	5.98	55	11.26	104
Other household decorative items	177.30	95.77	54	184.88	104
Telephones and accessories	29.19	35.36	121	28.61	98
Lawn and garden equipment	46.82	13.51	29	49.98	107
Power tools	21.32	37.97	178	19.77	93
Office furniture for home use	13.67	8.01	59	14.21	104
Hand tools	7.26	4.88	67	7.48	103
Indoor plants and fresh flowers	57.01	28.99	51	59.67	105
Closet and storage items	8.03	6.78	84	8.14	101
Rental of furniture	3.12	6.07	195	2.84	91
Luggage	8.32	4.74	57	8.66	104
Computers and computer hardware, nonbusiness use	187.83	122.67	65	194.01	103
Computer software and accessories, nonbusiness use	17.49	13.66	78	17.85	102

(continued)

(continued from previous page)

	average spending of total consumer units	Hispanic CUs		non-Hispanic CUs	
		average spending	indexed spending	average spending	indexed spending
Telephone answering devices	$1.97	$0.93	47	$2.07	105
Calculators	1.64	1.20	73	1.68	102
Business equipment for home use	1.83	1.68	92	1.84	101
Other hardware	24.09	16.61	69	24.79	103
Smoke alarms (owner)	0.56	0.05	9	0.61	109
Smoke alarms (renter)	0.16	0.15	94	0.16	100
Other household appliances (owner)	7.59	7.61	100	7.59	100
Other household appliances (renter)	1.22	4.74	389	0.88	72
Misc. household equipment and parts	40.18	48.76	121	39.38	98
APPAREL AND SERVICES	**$1,856.16**	**$2,075.58**	**112**	**$1,835.82**	**99**
Men, aged 16 or older	**344.29**	**359.08**	**104**	**342.97**	**100**
Suits	33.23	21.16	64	34.38	103
Sport coats and tailored jackets	11.31	5.21	46	11.89	105
Coats and jackets	34.76	28.96	83	35.29	102
Underwear	17.45	22.78	131	16.95	97
Hosiery	11.50	16.96	147	10.99	96
Nightwear	3.34	1.79	54	3.49	104
Accessories	23.29	29.83	128	22.68	97
Sweaters and vests	15.96	12.54	79	16.29	102
Active sportswear	16.11	10.05	62	16.67	103
Shirts	85.47	90.44	106	85.00	99
Pants	68.65	96.85	141	66.03	96
Shorts and shorts sets	13.64	13.56	99	13.65	100
Uniforms	5.52	6.12	111	5.47	99
Costumes	4.06	2.83	70	4.18	103
Boys, aged 2 to 15	**95.76**	**123.51**	**129**	**93.15**	**97**
Coats and jackets	7.84	8.49	108	7.78	99
Sweaters	3.56	4.35	122	3.48	98
Shirts	20.84	23.17	111	20.62	99
Underwear	5.09	5.73	113	5.04	99
Nightwear	2.95	3.24	110	2.92	99
Hosiery	4.30	5.43	126	4.20	98
Accessories	4.40	6.29	143	4.23	96
Suits, sport coats, and vests	3.64	5.81	160	3.43	94
Pants	23.39	36.53	156	22.15	95
Shorts and shorts sets	8.95	9.80	109	8.87	99
Uniforms	3.66	3.82	104	3.64	99
Active sportswear	3.81	7.74	203	3.44	90
Costumes	3.33	3.12	94	3.35	101
Women, aged 16 or older	**607.11**	**540.33**	**89**	**613.37**	**101**
Coats and jackets	43.26	39.59	92	43.60	101
Dresses	86.74	95.74	110	85.90	99

(continued)

(continued from previous page)

	average spending of total consumer units	Hispanic CUs		non-Hispanic CUs	
		average spending	indexed spending	average spending	indexed spending
Sport coats and tailored jackets	$8.33	$4.44	53	$8.70	104
Sweaters and vests	49.27	30.31	62	51.03	104
Shirts, blouses, and tops	99.26	98.13	99	99.37	100
Skirts	12.76	10.40	82	12.97	102
Pants	85.55	94.66	111	84.70	99
Shorts and shorts sets	20.40	23.56	115	20.10	99
Active sportswear	27.78	15.54	56	28.92	104
Nightwear	32.21	26.65	83	32.73	102
Undergarments	32.20	36.88	115	31.77	99
Hosiery	20.95	15.90	76	21.42	102
Suits	33.80	16.33	48	35.46	105
Accessories	39.29	21.67	55	40.93	104
Uniforms	8.69	4.94	57	9.04	104
Costumes	6.63	5.59	84	6.73	102
Girls, aged 2 to 15	**118.09**	**150.31**	**127**	**115.07**	**97**
Coats and jackets	6.95	8.26	119	6.83	98
Dresses and suits	18.19	27.18	149	17.36	95
Shirts, blouses, and sweaters	28.79	33.50	116	28.35	98
Skirts and pants	21.75	26.52	122	21.30	98
Shorts and shorts sets	8.35	8.96	107	8.29	99
Active sportswear	8.97	15.34	171	8.38	93
Underwear and nightwear	7.40	8.51	115	7.30	99
Hosiery	4.92	6.33	129	4.79	97
Accessories	4.98	5.95	119	4.89	98
Uniforms	3.90	6.21	159	3.68	94
Costumes	3.87	3.54	91	3.90	101
Children under age 2	**81.92**	**136.90**	**167**	**76.80**	**94**
Coats, jackets, and snowsuits	2.70	3.35	124	2.64	98
Outerwear including dresses	22.97	27.71	121	22.52	98
Underwear	44.65	88.14	197	40.61	91
Nightwear and loungewear	3.99	4.77	120	3.92	98
Accessories	7.61	12.93	170	7.12	94
Footwear	**343.09**	**516.37**	**151**	**326.99**	**95**
Men's	117.55	211.29	180	108.84	93
Boys'	37.26	53.71	144	35.73	96
Women's	155.95	196.46	126	152.19	98
Girls'	32.33	54.92	170	30.24	94
Other apparel products and services	**265.90**	**249.09**	**94**	**267.49**	**101**
Material for making clothes	4.75	0.63	13	5.13	108
Sewing patterns and notions	4.69	2.29	49	4.92	105
Watches	22.63	23.86	105	22.51	99
Jewelry	107.32	58.23	54	111.98	104
Shoe repair and other shoe services	1.83	1.08	59	1.90	104

(continued)

	average spending of total consumer units	Hispanic CUs		non-Hispanic CUs	
		average spending	*indexed spending*	*average spending*	*indexed spending*
Coin-operated apparel laundry and dry cleaning	$37.93	$106.48	281	$31.43	83
Apparel alteration, repair, tailoring services	5.70	2.84	50	5.97	105
Clothing rental	3.37	1.54	46	3.55	105
Watch and jewelry repair	4.74	6.50	137	4.57	96
Professional laundry, dry cleaning	72.40	45.64	63	74.93	103
Clothing storage	0.55	–	–	0.60	109
TRANSPORTATION	**$7,417.36**	**$6,719.21**	**91**	**$7,483.58**	**101**
VEHICLE PURCHASES	**3,418.27**	**3,145.94**	**92**	**3,444.09**	**101**
Cars and trucks, new	**1,604.95**	**1,079.37**	**67**	**1,654.79**	**103**
New cars	917.02	563.93	61	950.50	104
New trucks	687.94	515.44	75	704.29	102
Cars and trucks, used	**1,769.85**	**2,057.51**	**116**	**1,742.57**	**98**
Used cars	1,011.25	1,212.48	120	992.17	98
Used trucks	758.60	845.04	111	750.40	99
Other vehicles	**43.46**	**9.05**	**21**	**46.73**	**108**
New motorcycles	18.45	6.70	36	19.57	106
Used motorcycles	17.38	2.35	14	18.81	108
GASOLINE AND MOTOR OIL	**1,291.25**	**1,243.72**	**96**	**1,295.75**	**100**
Gasoline	1,175.50	1,164.76	99	1,176.52	100
Diesel fuel	12.98	4.91	38	13.74	106
Gasoline on trips	91.79	60.79	66	94.73	103
Motor oil	10.05	12.65	126	9.81	98
Motor oil on trips	0.93	0.61	66	0.96	103
OTHER VEHICLE EXPENSES	**2,281.28**	**1,944.50**	**85**	**2,313.20**	**101**
Vehicle finance charges	**328.24**	**274.20**	**84**	**333.36**	**102**
Automobile finance charges	169.25	146.90	87	171.37	101
Truck finance charges	138.62	125.96	91	139.82	101
Motorcycle and plane finance charges	1.58	0.05	3	1.72	109
Other vehicle finance charges	18.79	1.29	7	20.45	109
Maintenance and repairs	**623.76**	**545.61**	**87**	**631.14**	**101**
Coolant, additives, brake/transmission fluids	4.47	4.31	96	4.48	100
Tires	87.23	73.90	85	88.49	101
Parts, equipment, and accessories	48.46	59.02	122	47.46	98
Vehicle audio equipment	2.41	4.91	204	2.18	90
Vehicle products	4.10	2.00	49	4.29	105
Miscellaneous auto repair, servicing	26.74	14.05	53	27.92	104
Body work and painting	26.35	17.57	67	27.18	103
Clutch, transmission repair	42.61	42.08	99	42.66	100
Drive shaft and rear-end repair	3.66	4.52	123	3.57	98
Brake work	54.04	34.68	64	55.88	103
Repair to steering or front-end	18.02	21.43	119	17.70	98

(continued)

(continued from previous page)

	average spending of total consumer units	Hispanic CUs		non-Hispanic CUs	
		average spending	indexed spending	average spending	indexed spending
Repair to engine cooling system	$20.55	$17.31	84	$20.86	102
Motor tune-up	44.41	43.51	98	44.49	100
Lube, oil change, and oil filters	58.75	50.28	86	59.55	101
Front-end alignment, wheel balance, rotation	10.79	8.38	78	11.01	102
Shock absorber replacement	4.25	4.21	99	4.25	100
Gas tank repair, replacement	3.55	3.58	101	3.55	100
Tire repair and other repair work	29.75	20.77	70	30.60	103
Vehicle air conditioning repair	19.80	15.44	78	20.21	102
Exhaust system repair	13.34	9.53	71	13.70	103
Electrical system repair	30.31	29.05	96	30.43	100
Motor repair, replacement	64.46	62.78	97	64.62	100
Auto repair service policy	5.71	2.29	40	6.03	106
Vehicle insurance	**778.13**	**696.31**	**89**	**785.89**	**101**
Vehicle rental, leases, licenses, other charges	**551.15**	**428.38**	**78**	**562.80**	**102**
Leased and rented vehicles	392.88	297.17	76	401.96	102
Rented vehicles	44.95	36.49	81	45.75	102
Auto rental	7.21	3.04	42	7.60	105
Auto rental, out-of-town trips	29.62	21.36	72	30.40	103
Truck rental	3.21	5.32	166	3.01	94
Truck rental, out-of-town trips	4.71	6.40	136	4.55	97
Leased vehicles	347.93	260.68	75	356.20	102
Car lease payments	174.84	106.77	61	181.29	104
Cash down payment (car lease)	13.99	16.87	121	13.72	98
Termination fee (car lease)	1.81	–	–	1.98	109
Truck lease payments	148.45	124.37	84	150.74	102
Cash down payment (truck lease)	7.72	9.13	118	7.59	98
Termination fee (truck lease)	1.11	3.55	320	0.88	79
State and local registration	85.19	70.98	83	86.54	102
Driver's license	6.85	6.13	89	6.92	101
Vehicle inspection	9.41	11.37	121	9.23	98
Parking fees	29.38	18.37	63	30.42	104
Parking fees in home city, excl. residence	25.33	15.46	61	26.27	104
Parking fees, out-of-town trips	4.05	2.91	72	4.16	103
Tolls	10.90	15.45	142	10.48	96
Tolls on out-of-town trips	3.51	1.62	46	3.69	105
Towing charges	4.68	4.01	86	4.74	101
Automobile service clubs	8.35	3.28	39	8.83	106
PUBLIC TRANSPORTATION	**426.56**	**385.05**	**90**	**430.53**	**101**
Airline fares	274.02	204.02	74	280.66	102
Intercity bus fares	16.10	15.16	94	16.19	101
Intracity mass transit fares	47.41	93.42	197	43.04	91

(continued)

	average spending of total consumer units	Hispanic CUs		non-Hispanic CUs	
		average spending	indexed spending	average spending	indexed spending
Local transportation on out-of-town trips	$10.66	$5.97	56	$11.11	104
Taxi fares and limousine service on trips	6.26	3.50	56	6.52	104
Taxi fares and limousine service	12.15	27.23	224	10.75	88
Intercity train fares	21.12	10.34	49	22.15	105
Ship fares	36.58	18.57	51	38.29	105
School bus	2.26	6.84	303	1.83	81
HEALTH CARE	**$2,065.67**	**$1,243.46**	**60**	**$2,143.61**	**104**
HEALTH INSURANCE	**982.65**	**599.96**	**61**	**1,018.94**	**104**
Commercial health insurance	**194.39**	**92.68**	**48**	**204.03**	**105**
Traditional fee-for-service health plan (not BCBS)	77.07	36.17	47	80.95	105
Preferred-provider health plan (not BCBS)	117.32	56.50	48	123.08	105
Blue Cross, Blue Shield	**232.50**	**113.20**	**49**	**243.81**	**105**
Traditional fee-for-service health plan	49.89	7.54	15	53.91	108
Preferred-provider health plan	60.94	32.85	54	63.60	104
Health maintenance organization	73.18	61.85	85	74.25	101
Commercial Medicare supplement	43.77	8.78	20	47.09	108
Other BCBS health insurance	4.71	2.18	46	4.95	105
Health maintenance plans (HMOs)	**254.81**	**226.54**	**89**	**257.49**	**101**
Medicare payments	**164.04**	**110.72**	**67**	**169.10**	**103**
Commercial Medicare supplements/ other health insurance	**136.91**	**56.82**	**42**	**144.50**	**106**
Commercial Medicare supplement (not BCBS)	88.22	29.37	33	93.80	106
Other health insurance (not BCBS)	48.69	27.46	56	50.70	104
MEDICAL SERVICES	**567.85**	**363.74**	**64**	**587.21**	**103**
Physician's services	134.41	100.85	75	137.59	102
Dental services	220.79	119.81	54	230.37	104
Eye care services	35.05	31.19	89	35.42	101
Service by professionals other than physician	36.87	10.80	29	39.34	107
Lab tests, X-rays	20.12	13.51	67	20.74	103
Hospital room	35.95	32.39	90	36.29	101
Hospital services other than room	41.13	43.13	105	40.94	100
Care in convalescent or nursing home	32.35	0.20	1	35.40	109
Repair of medical equipment	0.61	6.67	1,093	0.04	7
Other medical services	10.56	5.19	49	11.07	105
DRUGS	**416.45**	**211.11**	**51**	**435.88**	**105**
Nonprescription drugs	65.09	63.39	97	65.25	100
Nonprescription vitamins	46.19	25.08	54	48.15	104
Prescription drugs	305.17	122.64	40	322.47	106
MEDICAL SUPPLIES	**98.73**	**68.65**	**70**	**101.59**	**103**
Eyeglasses and contact lenses	58.43	42.69	73	59.92	103

(continued)

(continued from previous page)

	average spending of total consumer units	Hispanic CUs		non-Hispanic CUs	
		average spending	indexed spending	average spending	indexed spending
Hearing aids	$11.78	$1.01	9	$12.80	109
Topicals and dressings	20.99	21.59	103	20.94	100
Medical equipment for general use	2.04	1.29	63	2.11	103
Supportive, convalescent medical equipment	3.18	1.76	55	3.32	104
Rental of medical equipment	0.85	0.06	7	0.92	108
Rental of supportive, convalescent medical equipment	1.46	0.26	18	1.58	108
ENTERTAINMENT	**$1,863.50**	**$1,186.30**	**64**	**$1,927.55**	**103**
FEES AND ADMISSIONS	**514.85**	**262.39**	**51**	**538.79**	**105**
Recreation expenses on trips	25.49	16.90	66	26.30	103
Social, recreation, civic club membership	98.18	33.15	34	104.35	106
Fees for participant sports	71.49	28.23	39	75.59	106
Participant sports on trips	35.05	14.91	43	36.96	105
Movie, theater, opera, ballet	89.16	71.21	80	90.86	102
Movie, other admissions on trips	44.94	26.71	59	46.66	104
Admission to sports events	35.33	11.19	32	37.62	106
Admission to sports events on trips	14.98	8.90	59	15.55	104
Fees for recreational lessons	74.74	34.28	46	78.58	105
Other entertainment services on trips	25.49	16.90	66	26.30	103
TELEVISION, RADIO, SOUND EQUIPMENT	**621.82**	**544.58**	**88**	**629.14**	**101**
Television	**453.53**	**390.02**	**86**	**459.55**	**101**
Community antenna and cable service	321.18	251.74	78	327.76	102
Black-and-white TV sets	0.77	1.05	136	0.74	96
Color TV, console	30.19	29.37	97	30.27	100
Color TV, portable, table model	34.35	48.47	141	33.01	96
VCRs and video disc players	23.80	27.96	117	23.41	98
Video cassettes, tapes, and discs	20.80	14.58	70	21.39	103
Video game hardware and software	18.72	12.25	65	19.33	103
Repair of TV, radio, and sound equipment	3.23	3.16	98	3.24	100
Rental of television sets	0.49	1.45	296	0.40	82
Radio and sound equipment	**168.29**	**154.56**	**92**	**169.59**	**101**
Radios	10.44	10.91	105	10.40	100
Tape recorders and players	4.39	2.81	64	4.54	103
Sound components, component systems	23.16	31.64	137	22.36	97
Miscellaneous sound equipment	0.42	0.09	21	0.45	107
Sound equipment accessories	4.04	5.28	131	3.92	97
Satellite dishes	2.70	6.32	234	2.36	87
Compact disc, tape, record, video mail order clubs	8.52	7.03	83	8.67	102
Records, CDs, audio tapes, needles	39.46	35.87	91	39.80	101
Rental of VCR, radio, sound equipment	0.54	0.35	65	0.55	102
Musical instruments and accessories	31.70	14.57	46	33.33	105

(continued)

(continued from previous page)

	average spending of total consumer units	Hispanic CUs		non-Hispanic CUs	
		average spending	*indexed spending*	*average spending*	*indexed spending*
Rental and repair of musical instruments	$1.34	$1.30	97	$1.35	101
Rental of video cassettes, tapes, discs, films	41.56	38.40	92	41.86	101
PETS, TOYS, PLAYGROUND EQUIPMENT	**333.71**	**217.72**	**65**	**344.64**	**103**
Pets	**209.43**	**123.34**	**59**	**217.52**	**104**
Pet food	85.97	66.58	77	87.77	102
Pet purchase, supplies, and medicines	38.10	22.18	58	39.58	104
Pet services	19.36	5.22	27	20.70	107
Veterinarian services	66.00	29.36	44	69.47	105
Toys, games, hobbies, and tricycles	**120.96**	**91.96**	**76**	**123.71**	**102**
Playground equipment	**3.32**	**2.42**	**73**	**3.41**	**103**
OTHER ENTERTAINMENT SUPPLIES, EQUIPMENT, SERVICES	**393.12**	**161.61**	**41**	**414.98**	**106**
Unmotored recreational vehicles	**48.06**	**2.34**	**5**	**52.39**	**109**
Boat without motor and boat trailers	15.87	2.34	15	17.15	108
Trailer and other attachable campers	32.19	–	–	35.24	109
Motorized recreational vehicles	**81.96**	**–**	**–**	**89.73**	**109**
Motorized camper	21.35	–	–	23.37	109
Other vehicle	21.74	–	–	23.80	109
Motorboats	38.87	–	–	42.56	109
Rental of recreational vehicles	**2.79**	**0.95**	**34**	**2.97**	**106**
Boat and trailer rental on trips	0.59	0.56	95	0.59	100
Rental of campers on trips	0.61	0.34	56	0.64	105
Rental of other vehicles on trips	1.40	–	–	1.54	110
Rental of other RVs	0.03	0.05	167	0.03	100
Outboard motors	**3.58**	**–**	**–**	**3.92**	**109**
Docking and landing fees	**8.17**	**3.44**	**42**	**8.62**	**106**
Sports, recreation, exercise equipment	**143.58**	**89.54**	**62**	**148.62**	**104**
Athletic gear, game tables, exercise equip.	58.64	28.19	48	61.47	105
Bicycles	11.73	15.71	134	11.35	97
Camping equipment	17.02	10.95	64	17.58	103
Hunting and fishing equipment	25.85	17.08	66	26.66	103
Winter sports equipment	5.84	1.41	24	6.26	107
Water sports equipment	8.24	1.88	23	8.84	107
Other sports equipment	14.25	13.66	96	14.30	100
Rental and repair of misc. sports equip.	2.02	0.66	33	2.15	106
Photographic equipment and supplies	**94.91**	**57.98**	**61**	**98.41**	**104**
Film	21.40	15.64	73	21.94	103
Other photographic supplies	1.44	–	–	1.57	109
Film processing	31.43	18.44	59	32.66	104
Repair and rental of photographic equip.	0.27	0.27	100	0.27	100
Photographic equipment	20.21	10.68	53	21.11	104
Photographer fees	20.17	12.94	64	20.86	103

(continued)

(continued from previous page)

	average spending of total consumer units	Hispanic CUs		non-Hispanic CUs	
		average spending	indexed spending	average spending	indexed spending
Fireworks	$1.18	$1.25	106	$1.18	100
Souvenirs	2.00	–	–	2.18	109
Visual goods	1.09	–	–	1.20	110
Pinball, electronic video games	5.80	6.11	105	5.77	99
PERSONAL CARE PRODUCTS AND SERVICES	**$563.62**	**$564.29**	**100**	**$563.64**	**100**
Personal care products	**256.30**	**301.58**	**118**	**252.10**	**98**
Hair care products	51.46	77.18	150	49.07	95
Hair accessories	6.59	7.30	111	6.52	99
Wigs and hairpieces	1.17	0.21	18	1.26	108
Oral hygiene products	25.78	34.88	135	24.93	97
Shaving products	13.19	13.03	99	13.20	100
Cosmetics, perfume, and bath products	119.91	132.47	110	118.75	99
Deodorants, feminine hygiene, miscellaneous products	29.21	27.12	93	29.41	101
Electric personal care appliances	8.99	9.40	105	8.95	100
Personal care services	**307.31**	**262.70**	**85**	**311.54**	**101**
READING	**$146.47**	**$58.60**	**40**	**$154.80**	**106**
Newspaper subscriptions	47.43	15.78	33	50.43	106
Newspapers, nonsubscriptions	12.26	8.63	70	12.61	103
Magazine subscriptions	19.10	6.30	33	20.31	106
Magazines, nonsubscriptions	9.50	4.88	51	9.93	105
Books purchased through book clubs	8.03	4.20	52	8.40	105
Books not purchased through book clubs	49.52	18.48	37	52.46	106
Encyclopedias, other reference book sets	0.51	0.34	67	0.52	102
EDUCATION	**$631.93**	**$362.52**	**57**	**$657.47**	**104**
College tuition	363.29	147.65	41	383.74	106
Elementary and high school tuition	101.42	77.09	76	103.73	102
Other school tuition	24.42	25.35	104	24.33	100
Other school expenses including rentals	24.00	17.17	72	24.65	103
Books, supplies for college	52.66	30.16	57	54.79	104
Books, supplies for elementary, high school	13.92	15.27	110	13.79	99
Books, supplies for day care, nursery school	3.09	2.82	91	3.11	101
Misc. school expenses and supplies	49.13	47.01	96	49.33	100
TOBACCO PRODUCTS AND SMOKING SUPPLIES	**$318.62**	**$173.26**	**54**	**$332.40**	**104**
Cigarettes	293.90	163.11	55	306.30	104
Other tobacco products	22.52	8.57	38	23.85	106
Smoking accessories	2.03	1.59	78	2.07	102

(continued)

(continued from previous page)

	average spending of total consumer units	Hispanic CUs		non-Hispanic CUs	
		average spending	indexed spending	average spending	indexed spending
FINANCIAL PRODUCTS AND SERVICES	**$775.78**	**$601.82**	**78**	**$792.24**	**102**
Miscellaneous fees, gambling losses	41.60	26.70	64	42.98	103
Legal fees	103.96	40.45	39	109.98	106
Funeral expenses	70.69	44.14	62	73.21	104
Safe deposit box rental	4.58	1.00	22	4.92	107
Checking accounts, other bank service charges	19.89	17.63	89	20.11	101
Cemetery lots, vaults, maintenance fees	13.47	12.57	93	13.56	101
Accounting fees	55.18	38.31	69	56.78	103
Miscellaneous personal services	31.39	24.08	77	32.06	102
Finance charges, except mortgage and vehicles	253.37	274.64	108	251.35	99
Occupational expenses	96.24	86.00	89	97.21	101
Expenses for other properties	79.73	31.75	40	84.28	106
Interest paid, home equity line of credit (other property)	0.98	–	–	1.07	109
Credit card memberships	4.71	4.54	96	4.73	100
CASH CONTRIBUTIONS	**$1,192.44**	**$645.36**	**54**	**$1,244.32**	**104**
Cash contributions to non-CU members, incl. students, alimony, child support	296.07	199.87	68	305.19	103
Gifts of cash, stocks, bonds to non-CU members	267.48	102.03	38	283.17	106
Contributions to charities	139.87	42.97	31	149.05	107
Contributions to religious organizations	445.63	285.61	64	460.80	103
Contributions to educational organizations	19.96	6.19	31	21.27	107
Political contributions	6.65	1.16	17	7.17	108
Other contributions	16.80	7.53	45	17.68	105
PERSONAL INSURANCE AND PENSIONS	**$3,364.92**	**$2,608.34**	**78**	**$3,436.67**	**102**
Life and other personal insurance	398.61	188.81	47	418.51	105
Life, endowment, annuity, other personal insurance	387.97	184.70	48	407.25	105
Other nonhealth insurance	10.64	4.11	39	11.26	106
Pensions and Social Security	2,966.31	2,419.53	82	3,018.16	102
Deductions for government retirement	70.32	38.85	55	73.30	104
Deductions for railroad retirement	3.29	–	–	3.60	109
Deductions for private pensions	362.64	243.38	67	373.94	103
Nonpayroll deposit to retirement plans	389.65	162.12	42	411.23	106
Deductions for Social Security	2,140.41	1,975.18	92	2,156.08	101
PERSONAL TAXES	**$3,117.45**	**$1,580.63**	**51**	**$3,277.99**	**105**
Federal income taxes	2,409.33	1,257.52	52	2,529.64	105

(continued)

(continued from previous page)

	average spending of total consumer units	Hispanic CUs		non-Hispanic CUs	
		average spending	indexed spending	average spending	indexed spending
State and local income taxes	$561.80	$271.05	48	$592.18	105
Other taxes	146.32	52.06	36	156.17	107
GIFTS***	**$1,083.14**	**$825.28**	**76**	**$1,107.63**	**102**
FOOD	**70.09**	**43.56**	**62**	**72.58**	**104**
Fresh fruits	4.58	4.65	102	4.58	100
Candy and chewing gum	12.50	4.81	38	13.22	106
Board (including at school)	20.21	21.03	104	20.13	100
Catered affairs	15.59	2.17	14	16.87	108
ALCOHOLIC BEVERAGES	**14.49**	**11.37**	**78**	**14.78**	**102**
Beer and ale	3.64	2.75	76	3.73	102
Wine	6.76	5.75	85	6.85	101
Whiskey and other alcoholic beverages	3.73	2.66	71	3.82	102
HOUSING	**291.10**	**207.50**	**71**	**298.96**	**103**
Housekeeping supplies	**39.10**	**35.74**	**91**	**39.41**	**101**
Miscellaneous household products	7.32	7.52	103	7.30	100
Lawn and garden supplies	3.08	3.46	112	3.04	99
Postage and stationery	24.95	16.97	68	25.69	103
Stationery, stationery supplies, giftwraps	20.28	8.62	43	21.36	105
Postage	4.57	8.35	183	4.21	92
Household textiles	**13.20**	**12.61**	**96**	**13.26**	**100**
Bathroom linens	2.79	2.12	76	2.86	103
Bedroom linens	6.85	9.41	137	6.61	96
Appliances and misc. housewares	**28.14**	**12.41**	**44**	**29.61**	**105**
Major appliances	7.61	8.13	107	7.57	99
Electric floor-cleaning equipment	3.01	6.15	204	2.72	90
Small appliances and misc. housewares	20.53	4.28	21	22.04	107
Glassware	3.60	0.41	11	3.90	108
Nonelectric cookware	3.66	0.68	19	3.94	108
Tableware, nonelectric kitchenware	4.34	0.45	10	4.70	108
Small electric kitchen appliances	2.68	1.57	59	2.79	104
Miscellaneous household equipment	**70.31**	**35.45**	**50**	**73.59**	**105**
Infants' equipment	2.72	3.22	118	2.68	99
Outdoor equipment	2.86	–	–	3.13	109
Household decorative items	27.33	12.92	47	28.67	105
Indoor plants, fresh flowers	16.04	6.32	39	16.96	106
Computers and computer hardware, nonbusiness use	8.97	1.18	13	9.71	108
Misc. household equipment and parts	2.53	0.77	30	2.69	106
Other housing	**140.36**	**111.28**	**79**	**143.10**	**102**
Repair or maintenance services	3.74	1.40	37	3.96	106
Housing while attending school	42.32	33.52	79	43.15	102
Natural gas (renter)	3.11	3.26	105	3.09	99

(continued)

	average spending of total consumer units	Hispanic CUs		non-Hispanic CUs	
		average spending	indexed spending	average spending	indexed spending
Electricity (renter)	$13.28	$14.28	108	$13.18	99
Telephone services in home city, excl. mobile phones	13.64	15.83	116	13.43	98
Water, sewerage maintenance (renter)	2.67	3.13	117	2.62	98
Care for elderly, invalids, handicapped	2.10	0.59	28	2.24	107
Day-care centers, nurseries, preschools	21.46	15.98	74	21.98	102
Housekeeping services	3.44	1.31	38	3.64	106
Gardening, lawn care service	3.14	0.47	15	3.39	108
Repair of misc. household equipment and furnishings	7.78	–	–	8.50	109
Bedroom furniture except mattresses and springs	2.06	0.59	29	2.20	107
APPAREL AND SERVICES	**244.25**	**291.41**	**119**	**239.89**	**98**
Men and boys, aged 2 or older	**67.55**	**64.58**	**96**	**67.82**	**100**
Men's coats and jackets	3.30	11.26	341	2.56	78
Men's underwear	2.10	1.53	73	2.15	102
Men's accessories	3.40	0.89	26	3.63	107
Men's sweaters and vests	2.72	1.04	38	2.88	106
Men's active sportswear	4.35	1.09	25	4.65	107
Men's shirts	20.77	14.83	71	21.33	103
Men's pants	7.11	8.58	121	6.97	98
Boys' shirts	5.56	5.69	102	5.55	100
Boys' pants	2.84	4.88	172	2.64	93
Women and girls, aged 2 or older	**85.28**	**96.18**	**113**	**84.27**	**99**
Women's coats and jackets	3.57	4.48	125	3.48	97
Women's dresses	10.62	11.63	110	10.53	99
Women's vests and sweaters	8.86	3.16	36	9.39	106
Women's shirts, tops, blouses	10.59	13.35	126	10.33	98
Women's pants	5.94	10.18	171	5.55	93
Women's active sportswear	3.47	0.76	22	3.72	107
Women's sleepwear	6.15	9.72	158	5.82	95
Women's undergarments	2.69	0.71	26	2.87	107
Women's accessories	4.17	3.51	84	4.23	101
Girls' dresses and suits	4.03	11.28	280	3.36	83
Girls' shirts, blouses, sweaters	6.18	6.11	99	6.19	100
Girls' skirts and pants	2.78	3.25	117	2.74	99
Girls' active sportswear	2.10	3.86	184	1.94	92
Girls' accessories	2.18	1.55	71	2.23	102
Children under age 2	**40.71**	**61.14**	**150**	**38.82**	**95**
Infant dresses, outerwear	14.51	12.87	89	14.66	101
Infant underwear	18.27	36.28	199	16.60	91
Infant nightwear, loungewear	2.46	2.40	98	2.46	100
Infant accessories	4.02	8.15	203	3.64	91

(continued)

(continued from previous page)

	average spending of total consumer units	Hispanic CUs		non-Hispanic CUs	
		average spending	indexed spending	average spending	indexed spending
Other apparel products and services	**$50.71**	**$69.52**	**137**	**$48.98**	**97**
Watches	3.43	3.45	101	3.43	100
Jewelry	16.85	7.49	44	17.74	105
Men's footwear	8.66	21.89	253	7.44	86
Boys' footwear	4.70	6.66	142	4.52	96
Women's footwear	10.06	18.26	182	9.29	92
Girls' footwear	5.21	11.69	224	4.61	88
TRANSPORTATION	**70.27**	**25.70**	**37**	**74.51**	**106**
New cars	6.08	–	–	6.66	110
New trucks	14.04	–	–	15.37	109
Used cars	12.52	0.42	3	13.67	109
Used trucks	2.82	–	–	3.09	110
Gasoline on trips	12.55	6.42	51	13.13	105
Airline fares	8.51	4.70	55	8.87	104
Local transportation on trips	2.13	1.46	69	2.20	103
Intercity train fares	2.23	1.24	56	2.32	104
Ship fares	2.98	2.94	99	2.98	100
HEALTH CARE	**38.08**	**12.09**	**32**	**40.55**	**106**
Physician's services	2.66	1.65	62	2.76	104
Dental services	3.49	1.41	40	3.68	105
Hospital room	2.73	–	–	2.99	110
Care in convalescent or nursing home	18.42	0.05	0	20.16	109
Nonprescription drugs	2.15	2.86	133	2.08	97
ENTERTAINMENT	**93.76**	**69.09**	**74**	**96.09**	**102**
Toys, games, hobbies, and tricycles	29.58	22.62	76	30.24	102
Movie, other admissions on trips	9.17	7.12	78	9.37	102
Admission to sports events on trips	3.06	2.37	77	3.12	102
Fees for recreational lessons	6.30	5.63	89	6.37	101
Cable service and community antenna	4.65	5.11	110	4.61	99
Color TV, portable, table model	2.10	0.89	42	2.21	105
Musical instruments and accessories	2.32	1.79	77	2.37	102
Athletic gear, game tables, and exercise equipment	9.47	8.25	87	9.59	101
PERSONAL CARE PRODUCTS AND SERVICES	**19.20**	**30.85**	**161**	**18.12**	**94**
Hair care products	2.14	9.52	445	1.45	68
Cosmetics, perfume, bath preparation	13.00	17.00	131	12.00	92
Deodorants, feminine hygiene, miscellaneous personal care	2.00	2.00	100	2.00	100
READING	**2.00**	**1.00**	**50**	**2.00**	**100**
EDUCATION	**151.00**	**71.00**	**47**	**159.00**	**105**
College tuition	114.00	47.00	41	121.00	106

(continued)

(continued from previous page)

	average spending of total consumer units	Hispanic CUs		non-Hispanic CUs	
		average spending	indexed spending	average spending	indexed spending
Elementary and high school tuition	$11.00	$5.00	45	$11.00	100
Other school tuition	3.00	2.00	67	3.00	100
Other school expenses including rentals	5.00	3.00	60	5.00	100
College books and supplies	10.00	5.00	50	11.00	110
Miscellaneous school supplies	5.00	6.00	120	5.00	100
ALL OTHER GIFTS	**89.00**	**62.00**	**70**	**91.00**	**102**
Gifts of trip expenses	49.00	27.00	55	51.00	104
Miscellaneous fees, gambling losses	2.00	–	–	2.00	100
Legal fees	4.00	1.00	25	4.00	100
Funeral expenses	28.00	30.00	107	28.00	100
Cemetery lots, vaults, maintenance fees	3.00	3.00	100	3.00	100
Accounting fees	2.00	1.00	50	2.00	100

* The index compares the spending of the average Hispanic consumer unit with the spending of the average consumer unit by dividing Hispanic spending by average spending in each category and multiplying by 100. An index of 100 means Hispanic spending in the category equals average spending. An index of 125 means Hispanic spending is 25 percent above average, while an index of 75 means Hispanic spending is 25 percent below average.
** This figure does not include the amount paid for mortgage principal, which is considered an asset.
*** Expenditures on gifts are also included in the preceding product and service categories. Food spending, for example, includes the amount spent on gifts of food. Only gift expenditures exceeding $2.00 for the average consumer unit are shown.
Note: The Bureau of Labor Statistics uses consumer unit rather than household as the sampling unit in the Consumer Expenditure Survey. For the definition of consumer unit, see glossary. Expenditures for gifts may not add to category total because listings are incomplete. (–) means not applicable or sample is too small to make a reliable estimate.
Source: Bureau of Labor Statistics, unpublished data from the 2000 Consumer Expenditure Survey; calculations by New Strategist

Hispanics and Nonwhites Have Little Net Worth Because Few Are Homeowners

The median net worth (assets minus debts) of Hispanic and nonwhite households amounted to just $16,400 in 1998, far below the $71,600 net worth of the average American household. On every measure of wealth, Hispanics and nonwhites have less than the average household. Their financial assets are just 29 percent as high as the average, and their nonfinancial assets are only 53 percent of the average. The debts of Hispanic and nonwhite households are also below average. (Note: The Federal Reserve collects wealth data for only two racial and ethnic categories: non-Hispanic whites, and nonwhites and Hispanics. The nonwhite-and-Hispanic category includes primarily blacks and Hispanics, but also some Asians and American Indians.)

The net worth of Hispanic and nonwhite households is below average in large part because Hispanics and blacks are less likely to own a home than is the average householder. Home equity accounts for the largest share of Americans' net worth. In 1998, 47 percent of Hispanic and nonwhite householders owned a home.

Hispanic and nonwhite householders have a median of only $6,400 in financial assets. The median debt of Hispanic and nonwhite householders stood at $15,300 in 1998, much lower than average in part because fewer have mortgage debt.

A minority of Hispanics are covered by a pension plan at work. Only 28 percent of employed Hispanic men and 29 percent of employed Hispanic women are covered by an employer's pension plan. Those most likely to have pension coverage are high-earning professionals and Hispanics in the armed forces.

■ For Hispanic immigrants with little education or earning power, homeownership is often beyond reach. Until immigrants become a smaller share of the Hispanic population, Hispanic wealth is likely to remain well below average.

The net worth of Hispanic and nonwhite households is far below average

(median net worth of total and Hispanic/nonwhite households, 1998)

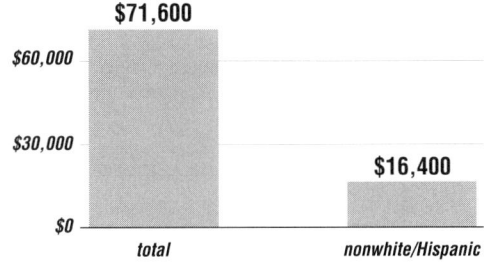

Net Worth, Assets, and Debt of Hispanic and Nonwhite Households, 1998

(median net worth, median value of assets for owners, and median amount of debt for debtors, for total and Hispanic/nonwhite households, and index of Hispanic/nonwhite to total, 1998)

	total	Hispanic and nonwhite	index of Hispanic/nonwhite to total
Median net worth	**$71,600**	**$16,400**	**23**
Median value of financial assets	22,400	6,400	29
Median value of nonfinancial assets	97,800	52,000	53
Median amount of debt	33,300	15,300	46

Note: The index is calculated by dividing the Hispanic/nonwhite figure by the total figure and multiplying by 100.
Source: Federal Reserve Board, Family Finances in the U.S.: Recent Evidence from the 1998 Survey of Consumer Finances, *Federal Reserve Bulletin, January 2000; calculations by New Strategist*

Financial Assets of Hispanic and Nonwhite Households, 1998

(percent of Hispanic/nonwhite households owning financial assets, and median value of assets for owners, 1998)

	percent owning asset	median value
Any financial asset	**81.2%**	**$6,400**
Transaction accounts	75.8	1,300
Certificates of deposit	6.4	6,300
Savings bonds	9.2	700
Bonds	0.4	14,200
Stocks	9.1	9,000
Mutual funds	8.4	10,000
Retirement accounts	32.0	13,000
Life insurance	20.8	5,000
Other managed assets	1.7	23,000
Other financial assets	8.3	1,000

Source: Federal Reserve Board, Family Finances in the U.S.: Recent Evidence from the 1998 Survey of Consumer Finances, *Federal Reserve Bulletin, January 2000; calculations by New Strategist*

Nonfinancial Assets of Hispanic and Nonwhite Households, 1998

(percent of Hispanic/nonwhite households owning nonfinancial assets, and median value of assets for owners, 1998)

	percent owning asset	median value
Any nonfinancial asset	**76.4%**	**$52,000**
Vehicles	67.2	8,000
Primary residence	46.8	85,000
Other residential property	8.4	59,000
Nonresidential property	5.8	24,000
Business	8.4	30,000
Other nonfinancial asset	3.1	5,000

Source: Federal Reserve Board, Family Finances in the U.S.: Recent Evidence from the 1998 Survey of Consumer Finances, *Federal Reserve Bulletin, January 2000; calculations by New Strategist*

Debt of Hispanic and Nonwhite Households, 1998

(percent of Hispanic/nonwhite households with debt, and median amount of debt for those with debts, 1998)

	percent with debt	median amount
Any debt	**71.1%**	**$15,300**
Home-secured	30.7	62,000
Other residential property	4.0	30,000
Installment loans	41.6	7,200
Other lines of credit	1.9	700
Credit card	43.3	1,100
Other debt	8.8	1,700

Source: Federal Reserve Board, Family Finances in the U.S.: Recent Evidence from the 1998 Survey of Consumer Finances, *Federal Reserve Bulletin, January 2000; calculations by New Strategist*

Pension Coverage of Hispanic Men, 2000

(total number of employed Hispanic men aged 15 or older, number and percent with an employer-offered pension plan, and number and percent included in pension plan by selected characteristics, 2000; numbers in thousands)

		with employer-offered pension plan at work			
				included in plan	
	total	number	percent	number	percent
Employed Hispanic men	**9,077**	**3,474**	**38.3%**	**2,528**	**27.9%**
Age					
Under age 65	8,915	3,429	38.5	2,498	28.0
Aged 15 to 24	1,886	492	26.1	188	10.0
Aged 25 to 44	5,062	1,972	38.9	1,496	29.6
Aged 45 to 64	1,967	965	49.0	814	41.4
Aged 65 or older	162	46	28.1	31	18.9
Worked					
Full-time	8,152	3,227	39.6	2,463	30.2
50 weeks or more	6,766	2,811	41.5	2,226	32.9
27 to 49 weeks	838	276	33.0	178	21.2
26 weeks or less	548	139	25.5	59	10.8
Part-time	925	247	26.7	66	7.1
50 weeks or more	445	118	26.6	53	11.8
27 to 49 weeks	152	61	40.3	7	4.8
26 weeks or less	329	68	20.6	6	1.8
Size of employer					
Under 25 employees	3,133	386	12.3	282	9.0
25 to 99 employees	1,619	480	29.7	344	21.2
100 to 499 employees	1,175	552	47.0	391	33.2
500 to 999 employees	394	241	61.0	183	46.4
1,000 or more employees	2,756	1,815	65.9	1,329	48.2

(continued)

(continued from previous page)

		with employer-offered pension plan at work			
				included in plan	
	total	number	percent	number	percent
Occupation					
Executive, administrative, and managerial	538	291	54.0%	246	45.7%
Professional specialty	417	277	66.5	230	55.1
Technical, related support	155	114	73.5	94	60.6
Sales workers	676	265	39.1	158	23.4
Administrative support, including clerical	468	252	53.8	189	40.5
Precision production, craft, and repair	1,963	681	34.7	528	26.9
Machine operators, assemblers, inspectors	928	384	41.3	301	32.4
Transportation, material moving occupations	667	284	42.6	198	29.6
Handlers, equip. cleaners, helpers, and laborers	1,028	330	32.1	187	18.2
Service workers	1,461	468	32.0	315	21.5
Private household	18	–	–	–	–
Service workers except private household	1,443	468	32.4	315	21.8
Farming, forestry, fishing	734	100	13.7	56	7.6
Armed forces	41	29	69.0	27	65.4
Earnings					
Under $15,000	2,838	539	19.0	162	5.7
$15,000 to $24,999	2,606	802	30.8	526	20.2
$25,000 to $49,999	2,659	1,460	54.9	1,227	46.1
$50,000 to $74,999	675	469	69.5	421	62.4
$75,000 to $99,999	149	120	80.5	108	72.5
$100,000 or more	140	86	61.4	84	60.0

Note: (–) means sample is too small to make a reliable estimate.
Source: Bureau of the Census, Current Population Survey, Internet site <http://ferret.bls.census.gov/macro/ 032001/noncash/nc8_011 .htm>; calculations by New Strategist

Pension Coverage of Hispanic Women, 2000

(total number of employed Hispanic women aged 15 or older, number and percent with an employer-offered pension plan, and number and percent included in pension plan by selected characteristics, 2000; numbers in thousands)

	total	with employer-offered pension plan at work		included in plan	
		number	*percent*	*number*	*percent*
Employed Hispanic women	**7,013**	**2,933**	**41.8%**	**2,029**	**28.9%**
Age					
Under age 65	6,922	2,901	41.9	2,008	29.0
Aged 15 to 24	1,521	477	31.3	169	11.1
Aged 25 to 44	3,726	1,643	44.1	1,193	32.0
Aged 45 to 64	1,675	781	46.6	646	38.6
Aged 65 or older	91	32	34.9	21	23.4
Worked					
Full-time	5,403	2,463	45.6	1,850	34.2
50 weeks or more	4,084	2,021	49.5	1,602	39.2
27 to 49 weeks	651	297	45.6	182	27.9
26 weeks or less	668	145	21.8	66	9.8
Part-time	1,610	469	29.2	179	11.1
50 weeks or more	770	243	31.6	110	14.3
27 to 49 weeks	336	114	33.9	38	11.4
26 weeks or less	503	112	22.3	30	6.0
Size of employer					
Under 25 employees	1,949	226	11.6	160	8.2
25 to 99 employees	980	327	33.3	200	20.4
100 to 499 employees	856	391	45.7	278	32.5
500 to 999 employees	372	216	58.0	148	39.8
1,000 or more employees	2,856	1,774	62.1	1,243	43.5

(continued)

(continued from previous page)

	total	with employer-offered pension plan at work		included in plan	
		number	percent	number	percent
Occupation					
Executive, administrative, and managerial	632	371	58.7%	299	47.2%
Professional specialty	600	403	67.2	337	56.2
Technical, related support	190	117	61.4	88	46.2
Sales workers	863	313	36.3	162	18.8
Administrative support, including clerical	1,463	793	54.2	564	38.6
Precision production, craft, and repair	196	92	47.1	60	30.8
Machine operators, assemblers, inspectors	662	232	35.0	149	22.5
Transportation, material moving occupations	62	31	50.7	24	38.2
Handlers, equip. cleaners, helpers, laborers	252	83	32.9	47	18.6
Service workers	1,900	466	24.6	277	14.6
Private household	248	5	1.9	–	–
Service workers except private household	1,652	462	28.0	277	16.8
Farming, forestry, fishing	182	20	11.1	12	6.4
Armed forces	11	10	98.1	10	98.1
Earnings					
Under $15,000	3,547	851	24.0	352	9.9
$15,000 to $24,999	1,727	892	51.7	643	37.2
$25,000 to $49,999	1,410	960	68.1	819	58.1
$50,000 to $74,999	240	181	75.4	171	71.3
$75,000 to $99,999	56	43	76.8	39	69.6
$100,000 or more	27	7	25.9	6	22.2

Note: (–) means sample is too small to make a reliable estimate.
Source: Bureau of the Census, Current Population Survey, Internet site <http://ferret.bls.census.gov/macro/ 032001/noncash/nc8_012 .htm>; calculations by New Strategist

5

Native Hawaiians and Other Pacific Islanders

■ Numbering only 874,000, Native Hawaiians and other Pacific Islanders are the smallest minority in the U.S., accounting for only 0.3 percent of the population.

■ Not surprisingly, Hawaii is home to the largest number of Native Hawaiians and other Pacific Islanders—32 percent of the total. California is home to another 25 percent.

■ Among metropolitan areas, Honolulu is home to the largest number of Native Hawaiians and other Pacific Islanders. Twenty-two percent of Honolulu's population is made up of this racial group.

■ Married couples head slightly more than half of Native Hawaiian and other Pacific Islander households. Sixty-one percent of the couples have children under age 18 at home, a much greater share than the 46 percent among all couples.

Note: There are no spending or wealth data available for Native Hawaiians.

Native Hawaiians account for 0.3 percent of the U.S. population

(percent distribution of people by race and Hispanic origin, 2000 census)

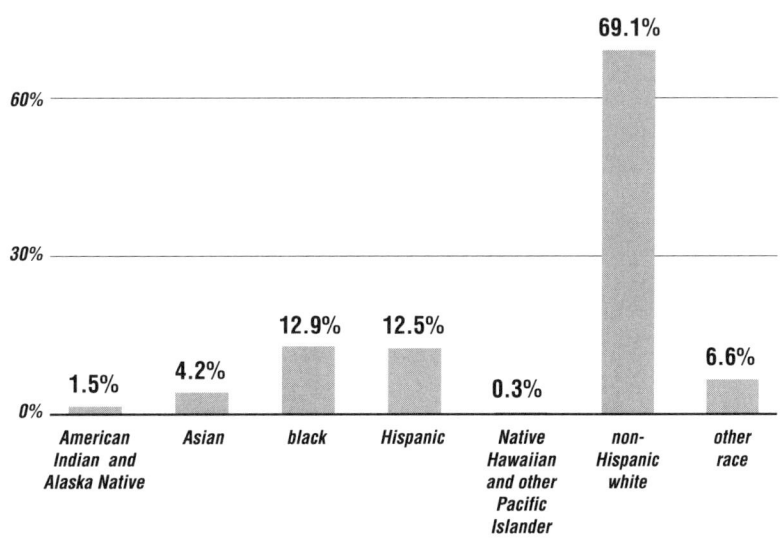

More than 30 Percent of Native Hawaiian Households Are Nuclear Families

Married couples account for 51 percent of households headed by Native Hawaiians, about the same as the 52 percent share among all households. Nuclear families are much more common among Native Hawaiian households, however. Couples with children under age 18 at home accounted for 31 percent of the Native Hawaiian households compared with 24 percent of total households.

Female-headed families account for a substantial 17 percent of Native Hawaiian households, much larger than their 12 percent share of all households. Single-person households account for a much smaller share of Native Hawaiian households (17 percent) than nationally (26 percent).

Twenty-nine percent of Native Hawaiians are children under age 18 living with their parents. Only 23 percent of all Americans are children living at home.

■ Native Hawaiian households account for a tiny share of all households, and most are located in just a few states, especially Hawaii.

Nuclear families are a large share of Native Hawaiian households

(percent of Native Hawaiian and total households headed by married couples with children under age 18 at home, 2000 census)

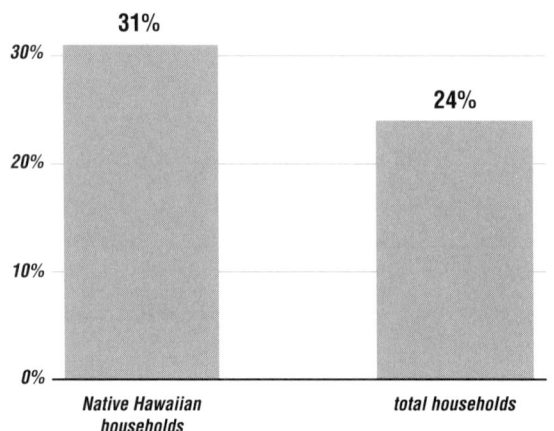

Native Hawaiian Households by Household Type, 2000 Census

(number of total households, number and percent distribution of Native Hawaiian households, and Native Hawaiian share of total, by type, 2000)

	total	Native Hawaiian households		
		number	percent distribution	share of total
Total households	**105,480,101**	**224,670**	**100.0%**	**0.2%**
Family households	**71,787,347**	**168,377**	**74.9**	**0.2**
Married couples	54,493,232	113,554	50.5	0.2
With children under age 18	24,835,505	68,829	30.6	0.3
Without children under age 18	29,657,727	44,725	19.9	0.2
Female householder, no spouse present	12,900,103	38,534	17.2	0.3
With children under age 18	7,561,874	24,020	10.7	0.3
Without children under age 18	5,338,229	14,514	6.5	0.3
Male householder, no spouse present	4,394,012	16,289	7.3	0.4
With children under age 18	2,190,989	8,307	3.7	0.4
Without children under age 18	2,203,023	7,982	3.6	0.4
Nonfamily households	**33,692,754**	**56,293**	**25.1**	**0.2**
Living alone	27,230,075	38,238	17.0	0.1
Living with nonrelatives	6,462,679	18,055	8.0	0.3

Note: Number of Native Hawaiian households includes householders who identified themselves as Native Hawaiian alone and in combination with other races; Native Hawaiians include other Pacific Islanders.
Source: Bureau of the Census, Census 2000 PHC-T-15, Table 5, General Demographic Characteristics for the Native Hawaiian and Other Pacific Islander Population; calculations by New Strategist

Native Hawaiian Living Arrangements, 2000 Census

(number and percent distribution of Native Hawaiians by living arrangement, 2000)

	number	*percent*
Total Native Hawaiians	**874,414**	**100.0%**
In households	**846,690**	**96.8**
Householder	224,670	25.7
Spouse	117,334	13.4
Child	330,925	37.8
Own child under age 18	254,811	29.1
Other relative	107,090	12.2
Under age 18	48,413	5.5
Nonrelatives	66,671	7.6
Unmarried partner	20,610	2.4
In group quarters	**27,724**	**3.2**
Institutionalized population	9,271	1.1
Noninstitutionalized population	18,453	2.1

Note: Number of Native Hawaiians includes those who identified themselves as Native Hawaiian alone and in combination with other races; Native Hawaiians include other Pacific Islanders.
Source: Bureau of the Census, Census 2000 PHC-T-15, Table 5, General Demographic Characteristics for the Native Hawaiian and Other Pacific Islander Population; calculations by New Strategist

Native Hawaiians and Other Pacific Islanders Are a Tiny Minority

Fewer than 1 million Americans identify their race as Native Hawaiian or other Pacific Islander. Among those who do, a larger share (54 percent) say they are Native Hawaiian/other Pacific Islander and some other race than Native Hawaiian/other Pacific Islander alone (46 percent).

The Native Hawaiian/other Pacific Islander population grew only 9 percent between 1990 and 2000, based on the number of people identifying themselves as Native Hawaiian/other Pacific Islander alone. The figure more than doubled during the decade when those who identify themselves as Native Hawaiian/other Pacific Islander and some other race are included in the total.

Native Hawaiians and other Pacific Islanders are a youthful population. Thirty-six percent are under age 18, much higher than the 26 percent share among all Americans.

Not surprisingly, 73 percent of Native Hawaiians and other Pacific Islanders live in the West, with 65 percent in the Pacific division. Hawaii is home to 32 percent, and California to another 25 percent. Native Hawaiians and other Pacific Islanders account for 23 percent of Hawaii's population.

■ Native Hawaiians and other Pacific Islanders are included with Asian Americans in most statistics. The 2000 census offers the unique opportunity to examine the characteristics of this population independently.

Few Americans are Native Hawaiian or other Pacific Islander

(number of people identifying themselves as Native Hawaiian or other Pacific Islander, 1990 and 2000)

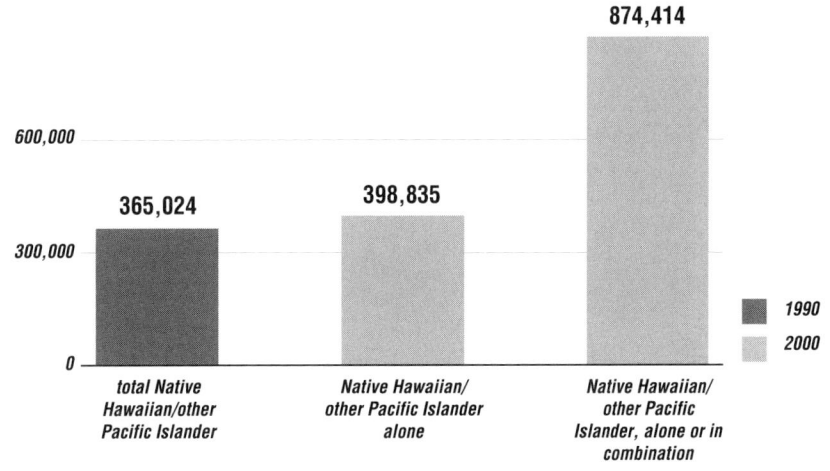

Native Hawaiians, 1990 and 2000 Censuses

(number of Native Hawaiians, 1990 and 2000; percent change in number, 1990–2000)

		2000		percent change 1990–2000	
	1990	Native Hawaiian alone	Native Hawaiian, alone or in combination	Native Hawaiian alone	Native Hawaiian, alone or in combination
Total Native Hawaiians	365,024	398,835	874,414	9.3%	139.5%

Note: Native Hawaiians include other Pacific Islanders.
Source: Bureau of the Census, The Native Hawaiian and Other Pacific Islander Population: 2000, *Census 2000 Brief, C2KBR/01-14, 2001; calculations by New Strategist*

Native Hawaiians by Racial Combination, 2000 Census

(number of total people and Native Hawaiians by racial identification and Native Hawaiian share of total; number and percent distribution of Native Hawaiians by racial combination, 2000)

	number	percent
Total people	**281,421,906**	**100.0%**
Native Hawaiian, alone or in combination		
with one or more other races	**874,414**	**0.3**
Native Hawaiian alone	398,835	0.1
Native Hawaiian in combination	475,579	0.2
Native Hawaiian, alone or in combination		
with one or more other races	**874,414**	**100.0**
Native Hawaiian alone	398,835	45.6
Native Hawaiian in combination	475,579	54.4
Native Hawaiian and Asian	138,802	15.9
Native Hawaiian and white	112,964	12.9
Native Hawaiian, Asian, and white	89,611	10.2
Native Hawaiian and black	29,876	3.4
All other combinations	104,326	11.9

Note: Native Hawaiians include other Pacific Islanders.
Source: Bureau of the Census, Overview of Race and Hispanic Origin, *Census 2000 Brief, CENBR/01-1, 2001*

Native Hawaiians by Hispanic Origin, 2000 Census

(number and percent distribution of Native Hawaiians by Hispanic origin and racial combination, 2000)

	Native Hawaiian, alone or in combination		Native Hawaiian alone		Native Hawaiian in combination	
	number	percent distribution	number	percent distribution	number	percent distribution
Total Native Hawaiians	**874,414**	**100.0%**	**398,835**	**100.0%**	**475,579**	**100.0%**
Hispanic	126,265	14.4	45,326	11.4	80,939	17.0
Mexican	40,801	4.7	17,877	4.5	22,924	4.8
Puerto Rican	28,471	3.3	8,972	2.2	19,499	4.1
Cuban	3,849	0.4	2,529	0.6	1,320	0.3
Other Hispanic	53,144	6.1	15,948	4.0	37,196	7.8
Non-Hispanic	748,149	85.6	353,509	88.6	394,640	83.0

Note: Native Hawaiians include other Pacific Islanders.
Source: Bureau of the Census, Census 2000 PHC-T-15, Table 5, General Demographic Characteristics for the Native Hawaiian and Other Pacific Islander Population; calculations by New Strategist

Native Hawaiians and Other Pacific Islanders by
Pacific Islander Group and Racial Combination, 2000 Census

(number of people identifying themselves as Native Hawaiian/other Pacific Islander alone, Native Hawaiian/other Pacific Islander in combination, and Native Hawaiian/other Pacific Islander alone or in combination and Pacific Islander group alone or in combination, by Pacific Islander group, 2000)

	Native Hawaiian/other Pacific Islander alone		Native Hawaiian/other Pacific Islander in combination		Native Hawaiian and other Pacific Islander, and Pacific Islander group, alone or in combination
	one Pacific Islander group	more than one Pacific Islander group	one Pacific Islander group	more than one Pacific Islander group	
Total Native Hawaiians/ other Pacific Islanders	**389,612**	**9,223**	**447,113**	**28,466**	**874,414**
Polynesian					
Native Hawaiian	140,652	5,157	241,510	13,843	401,162
Samoan	91,029	5,727	28,287	8,238	133,281
Tongan	27,713	2,227	5,675	1,225	36,840
Tahitian	800	199	1,137	1,177	3,313
Tokelauan	129	142	134	169	574
Polynesian, not specified	3,497	1,547	3,005	747	8,796
Micronesian					
Guamanian or Chamorro	58,240	1,247	30,241	2,883	92,611
Mariana Islander	60	11	60	10	141
Saipanese	195	122	120	38	475
Palauan	2,228	102	1,004	135	3,469
Carolinian	91	40	30	12	173
Kosraean	157	11	51	7	226
Pohnpeian	486	77	116	21	700
Chuukese	367	50	220	17	654
Yapese	236	13	111	8	368
Marshallese	5,479	183	849	139	6,650
I-Kiribati	90	17	47	21	175
Micronesian, not specified	7,509	411	1,768	252	9,940
Melanesian					
Fijian	9,796	169	3,461	155	13,581
Papua New Guinean	135	3	83	3	224
Solomon Islander	12	3	10	0	25
Ni-Vanuatu	6	1	7	4	18
Melanesian, not specified	147	15	149	4	315
Other Pacific Islander	40,558	1,309	129,083	4,007	174,912

Note: Numbers may not add to total because people could identify themselves with more than one Pacific Islander group.
Source: Bureau of the Census, The Native Hawaiian and Other Pacific Islander Population: 2000, *Census 2000 Brief, C2KBR/01-14, 2001; calculations by New Strategist*

Native Hawaiians and Other Pacific Islanders
Ranked by Pacific Islander Group, 2000 Census

(number and percent distribution of people identifying themselves as Native Hawaiian/other Pacific Islander alone or in combination and Pacific Islander group alone or in combination, by Pacific Islander group, 2000; ranked by size)

	Native Hawaiian/other Pacific Islander and Pacific Islander group, alone or in combination	
	number	*percent distribution*
Total Native Hawaiians and other Pacific Islanders	**874,414**	**100.0%**
Native Hawaiian	401,162	45.9
Samoan	133,281	15.2
Guamanian or Chamorro	92,611	10.6
Tongan	36,840	4.2
Fijian	13,581	1.6
Marshallese	6,650	0.8
Palauan	3,469	0.4
Tahitian	3,313	0.4
Pohnpeian	700	0.1
Chuukese	654	0.1
Tokelauan	574	0.1
Saipanese	475	0.1
Yapese	368	0.0
Kosraean	226	0.0
Papua New Guinean	224	0.0
I-Kiribati	175	0.0
Carolinian	173	0.0
Mariana Islander	141	0.0
Solomon Islander	25	0.0
Ni-Vanuatu	18	0.0

Note: Numbers will not add to total because people could identify themselves with more than one Pacific Islander group and other Pacific Islander group is not shown.
Source: Bureau of the Census, The Native Hawaiian and Other Pacific Islander Population: 2000, *Census 2000 Brief, C2KBR/01-14, 2001; calculations by New Strategist*

Native Hawaiians by Age, 2000 Census

(number of people identifying themselves as Native Hawaiian alone or in combination, Native Hawaiian alone, and Native Hawaiian in combination, and percent identifying themselves as Native Hawaiian in combination, by age, 2000)

	Native Hawaiian, alone or in combination	*Native Hawaiian alone*	Native Hawaiian in combination	
			number	*percent of Native Hawaiian, alone or in combination*
Total Native Hawaiians	**874,414**	**398,835**	**475,579**	**54.4%**
Under age 5	88,495	33,391	55,104	62.3
Aged 5 to 9	90,039	36,503	53,536	59.5
Aged 10 to 14	85,129	35,772	49,357	58.0
Aged 15 to 19	86,341	37,328	49,013	56.8
Aged 20 to 24	81,872	38,693	43,179	52.7
Aged 25 to 29	71,967	35,224	36,743	51.1
Aged 30 to 34	67,769	33,129	34,640	51.1
Aged 35 to 39	67,419	33,031	34,388	51.0
Aged 40 to 44	58,697	28,760	29,937	51.0
Aged 45 to 49	47,899	23,675	24,224	50.6
Aged 50 to 54	37,994	18,938	19,056	50.2
Aged 55 to 59	27,111	13,428	13,683	50.5
Aged 60 to 64	19,880	10,142	9,738	49.0
Aged 65 to 69	15,429	7,698	7,731	50.1
Aged 70 to 74	11,572	5,529	6,043	52.2
Aged 75 to 79	7,927	3,614	4,313	54.4
Aged 80 to 84	4,793	2,155	2,638	55.0
Aged 85 or older	4,081	1,825	2,256	55.3
Aged 18 to 24	118,405	54,508	63,897	54.0
Aged 18 or older	560,943	271,656	289,287	51.6
Aged 65 or older	43,802	20,821	22,981	52.5

Note: Native Hawaiians include other Pacific Islanders.
Source: U.S. Census Bureau, Census 2000 Summary File 1; calculations by New Strategist

Native Hawaiian Share of Total Population by Age, 2000 Census

(number of total people, number and percent distribution of those identifying themselves as Native Hawaiian alone or in combination, and Native Hawaiian alone or in combination share of total, by age, 2000)

	total	Native Hawaiian, alone or in combination		
		number	percent distribution	share of total
Total people	**281,421,906**	**874,414**	**100.0%**	**0.3%**
Under age 5	19,175,798	88,495	10.1	0.5
Aged 5 to 9	20,549,505	90,039	10.3	0.4
Aged 10 to 14	20,528,072	85,129	9.7	0.4
Aged 15 to 19	20,219,890	86,341	9.9	0.4
Aged 20 to 24	18,964,001	81,872	9.4	0.4
Aged 25 to 29	19,381,336	71,967	8.2	0.4
Aged 30 to 34	20,510,388	67,769	7.8	0.3
Aged 35 to 39	22,706,664	67,419	7.7	0.3
Aged 40 to 44	22,441,863	58,697	6.7	0.3
Aged 45 to 49	20,092,404	47,899	5.5	0.2
Aged 50 to 54	17,585,548	37,994	4.3	0.2
Aged 55 to 59	13,469,237	27,111	3.1	0.2
Aged 60 to 64	10,805,447	19,880	2.3	0.2
Aged 65 to 69	9,533,545	15,429	1.8	0.2
Aged 70 to 74	8,857,441	11,572	1.3	0.1
Aged 75 to 79	7,415,813	7,927	0.9	0.1
Aged 80 to 84	4,945,367	4,793	0.5	0.1
Aged 85 or older	4,239,587	4,081	0.5	0.1
Aged 18 to 24	27,143,454	118,405	13.5	0.4
Aged 18 or older	209,128,094	560,943	64.2	0.3
Aged 65 or older	34,991,753	43,802	5.0	0.1

Note: Native Hawaiians include other Pacific Islanders.
Source: U.S. Census Bureau, Census 2000 Summary File 1; calculations by New Strategist

Native Hawaiians by Age and Sex, 2000 Census

(number of Native Hawaiians by age and sex, and sex ratio by age, 2000)

	total	females	males	sex ratio
Total Native Hawaiians	**874,414**	**434,733**	**439,681**	**101**
Under age 5	88,495	43,106	45,389	105
Aged 5 to 9	90,039	44,257	45,782	103
Aged 10 to 14	85,129	41,414	43,715	106
Aged 15 to 19	86,341	42,038	44,303	105
Aged 20 to 24	81,872	39,701	42,171	106
Aged 25 to 29	71,967	35,019	36,948	106
Aged 30 to 34	67,769	33,687	34,082	101
Aged 35 to 39	67,419	33,788	33,631	100
Aged 40 to 44	58,697	29,365	29,332	100
Aged 45 to 49	47,899	24,300	23,599	97
Aged 50 to 54	37,994	19,145	18,849	98
Aged 55 to 59	27,111	13,833	13,278	96
Aged 60 to 64	19,880	10,385	9,495	91
Aged 65 to 69	15,429	8,130	7,299	90
Aged 70 to 74	11,572	6,520	5,052	77
Aged 75 to 79	7,927	4,608	3,319	72
Aged 80 to 84	4,793	2,897	1,896	65
Aged 85 or older	4,081	2,540	1,541	61
Aged 18 to 24	118,405	57,615	60,790	106
Aged 18 or older	560,943	281,832	279,111	99
Aged 65 or older	43,802	24,695	19,107	77

Note: Native Hawaiians include those who identified themselves as Native Hawaiian alone and those who identified themselves as Native Hawaiian in combination with one or more other races; Native Hawaiians include other Pacific Islanders; the sex ratio is the number of males per 100 females.
Source: U.S. Census Bureau, Census 2000 Summary File 1; calculations by New Strategist

Native Hawaiians by Region, 1990 and 2000 Censuses

(number of Native Hawaiians by region, 1990 and 2000; percent change in number identifying themselves as Native Hawaiian alone and as Native Hawaiian alone or in combination, 1990–2000)

| | | 2000 | | percent change 1990–2000 | |
	1990	*Native Hawaiian alone*	*Native Hawaiian, alone or in combination*	*Native Hawaiian alone*	*Native Hawaiian, alone or in combination*
Total Native Hawaiians	**365,024**	**398,835**	**874,414**	**9.3%**	**139.5%**
Northeast	10,510	20,880	63,907	98.7	508.1
Midwest	12,666	22,492	55,364	77.6	337.1
South	28,069	51,217	117,947	82.5	320.2
West	313,779	304,246	637,196	–3.0	103.1

Note: Native Hawaiians include other Pacific Islanders.
Source: Bureau of the Census, The Native Hawaiian and Other Pacific Islander Population: 2000, *Census 2000 Brief, C2KBR/01-14, 2001; calculations by New Strategist*

Native Hawaiians by Region and Division, 2000 Census

(number of total people, number and percent distribution of Native Hawaiians, and Native Hawaiian share of the total population by region and division, 2000)

	total	Native Hawaiian number	percent distribution	share of total
Total population	**281,421,906**	**874,414**	**100.0%**	**0.3%**
Northeast	**53,594,378**	**63,907**	**7.3**	**0.1**
New England	13,922,517	16,440	1.9	0.1
Middle Atlantic	39,671,861	47,467	5.4	0.1
Midwest	**64,392,776**	**55,364**	**6.3**	**0.1**
East North Central	45,155,037	34,785	4.0	0.1
West North Central	19,237,739	20,579	2.4	0.1
South	**100,236,820**	**117,947**	**13.5**	**0.1**
South Atlantic	51,769,160	64,545	7.4	0.1
East South Central	17,022,810	12,819	1.5	0.1
West South Central	31,444,850	40,583	4.6	0.1
West	**63,197,932**	**637,196**	**72.9**	**1.0**
Mountain	18,172,295	68,776	7.9	0.4
Pacific	45,025,637	568,420	65.0	1.3

Note: Native Hawaiians include those who identified themselves as Native Hawaiian alone and those who identified themselves as Native Hawaiian in combination with one or more other races; Native Hawaiians include other Pacific Islanders.
Source: Bureau of the Census, Profiles of General Demographic Characteristics, 2000 Census of Population and Housing, 2001; calculations by New Strategist

Native Hawaiians by State, 1990 and 2000 Censuses

(number of Native Hawaiians by state, 1990 and 2000; percent change in number identifying themselves as Native Hawaiian alone and identifying themselves as Native Hawaiian alone or in combination, 1990–2000)

	1990	2000		percent change 1990–2000	
		Native Hawaiian alone	Native Hawaiian, alone or in combination	Native Hawaiian alone	Native Hawaiian, alone or in combination
Total Native Hawaiians	**365,024**	**398,835**	**874,414**	**9.3%**	**139.5%**
Alabama	709	1,409	3,169	98.7	347.0
Alaska	1,914	3,309	5,515	72.9	188.1
Arizona	3,507	6,733	13,415	92.0	282.5
Arkansas	405	1,668	3,129	311.9	672.6
California	110,599	116,961	221,458	5.8	100.2
Colorado	2,740	4,621	10,153	68.6	270.5
Connecticut	620	1,366	4,076	120.3	557.4
Delaware	169	283	671	67.5	297.0
District of Columbia	291	348	785	19.6	169.8
Florida	4,446	8,625	23,998	94.0	439.8
Georgia	2,017	4,246	9,689	110.5	380.4
Hawaii	162,269	113,539	282,667	−30.0	74.2
Idaho	873	1,308	2,847	49.8	226.1
Illinois	2,742	4,610	11,848	68.1	332.1
Indiana	957	2,005	4,367	109.5	356.3
Iowa	439	1,009	2,196	129.8	400.2
Kansas	1,042	1,313	3,117	26.0	199.1
Kentucky	829	1,460	3,162	76.1	281.4
Louisiana	926	1,240	3,237	33.9	249.6
Maine	233	382	792	63.9	239.9
Maryland	1,571	2,303	6,179	46.6	293.3
Massachusetts	1,255	2,489	8,704	98.3	593.5
Michigan	1,482	2,692	7,276	81.6	391.0
Minnesota	934	1,979	5,867	111.9	528.2
Mississippi	337	667	1,901	97.9	464.1
Missouri	2,006	3,178	6,635	58.4	230.8
Montana	301	470	1,077	56.1	257.8
Nebraska	477	836	1,733	75.3	263.3
Nevada	2,895	8,426	16,234	191.1	460.8
New Hampshire	222	371	777	67.1	250.0

(continued)

(continued from previous page)

	1990	2000 Native Hawaiian alone	2000 Native Hawaiian, alone or in combination	percent change 1990–2000 Native Hawaiian alone	percent change 1990–2000 Native Hawaiian, alone or in combination
New Jersey	1,682	3,329	10,065	97.9%	498.4%
New Mexico	761	1,503	3,069	97.5	303.3
New York	4,457	8,818	28,612	97.8	542.0
North Carolina	2,196	3,983	8,574	81.4	290.4
North Dakota	145	230	475	58.6	227.6
Ohio	1,456	2,749	6,984	88.8	379.7
Oklahoma	1,561	2,372	5,123	52.0	228.2
Oregon	5,037	7,976	16,019	58.3	218.0
Pennsylvania	1,654	3,417	8,790	106.6	431.4
Rhode Island	306	567	1,783	85.3	482.7
South Carolina	983	1,628	3,778	65.6	284.3
South Dakota	185	261	556	41.1	200.5
Tennessee	895	2,205	4,587	146.4	412.5
Texas	7,541	14,434	29,094	91.4	285.8
Utah	7,675	15,145	21,367	97.3	178.4
Vermont	81	141	308	74.1	280.2
Virginia	3,017	3,946	9,984	30.8	230.9
Washington	15,040	23,953	42,761	59.3	184.3
West Virginia	176	400	887	127.3	404.0
Wisconsin	801	1,630	4,310	103.5	438.1
Wyoming	168	302	614	79.8	265.5

Note: Native Hawaiians include other Pacific Islanders.
Source: Bureau of the Census, The Native Hawaiian and Other Pacific Islander Population: 2000, *Census 2000 Brief, C2KBR/01-14, 2001; calculations by New Strategist*

Native Hawaiian Share of Total Population by State, 2000 Census

(number of total people, number and percent distribution of Native Hawaiians, and Native Hawaiian share of total population by state, 2000)

			Native Hawaiians	
	total	*number*	*percent distribution*	*share of total*
Total population	**281,421,906**	**874,414**	**100.0%**	**0.3%**
Alabama	4,447,100	3,169	0.4	0.1
Alaska	626,932	5,515	0.6	0.9
Arizona	5,130,632	13,415	1.5	0.3
Arkansas	2,673,400	3,129	0.4	0.1
California	33,871,648	221,458	25.3	0.7
Colorado	4,301,261	10,153	1.2	0.2
Connecticut	3,405,565	4,076	0.5	0.1
Delaware	783,600	671	0.1	0.1
District of Columbia	572,059	785	0.1	0.1
Florida	15,982,378	23,998	2.7	0.2
Georgia	8,186,453	9,689	1.1	0.1
Hawaii	1,211,537	282,667	32.3	23.3
Idaho	1,293,953	2,847	0.3	0.2
Illinois	12,419,293	11,848	1.4	0.1
Indiana	6,080,485	4,367	0.5	0.1
Iowa	2,926,324	2,196	0.3	0.1
Kansas	2,688,418	3,117	0.4	0.1
Kentucky	4,041,769	3,162	0.4	0.1
Louisiana	4,468,976	3,237	0.4	0.1
Maine	1,274,923	792	0.1	0.1
Maryland	5,296,486	6,179	0.7	0.1
Massachusetts	6,349,097	8,704	1.0	0.1
Michigan	9,938,444	7,276	0.8	0.1
Minnesota	4,919,479	5,867	0.7	0.1
Mississippi	2,844,658	1,901	0.2	0.1
Missouri	5,595,211	6,635	0.8	0.1
Montana	902,195	1,077	0.1	0.1
Nebraska	1,711,263	1,733	0.2	0.1
Nevada	1,998,257	16,234	1.9	0.8
New Hampshire	1,235,786	777	0.1	0.1
New Jersey	8,414,350	10,065	1.2	0.1

(continued)

(continued from previous page)

| | | Native Hawaiians | | |
	total	number	percent distribution	share of total
New Mexico	1,819,046	3,069	0.4%	0.2%
New York	18,976,457	28,612	3.3	0.2
North Carolina	8,049,313	8,574	1.0	0.1
North Dakota	642,200	475	0.1	0.1
Ohio	11,353,140	6,984	0.8	0.1
Oklahoma	3,450,654	5,123	0.6	0.1
Oregon	3,421,399	16,019	1.8	0.5
Pennsylvania	12,281,054	8,790	1.0	0.1
Rhode Island	1,048,319	1,783	0.2	0.2
South Carolina	4,012,012	3,778	0.4	0.1
South Dakota	754,844	556	0.1	0.1
Tennessee	5,689,283	4,587	0.5	0.1
Texas	20,851,820	29,094	3.3	0.1
Utah	2,233,169	21,367	2.4	1.0
Vermont	608,827	308	0.0	0.1
Virginia	7,078,515	9,984	1.1	0.1
Washington	5,894,121	42,761	4.9	0.7
West Virginia	1,808,344	887	0.1	0.0
Wisconsin	5,363,675	4,310	0.5	0.1
Wyoming	493,782	614	0.1	0.1

Note: The Native Hawaiian numbers include those who identified themselves as Native Hawaiian alone and those who identified themselves as Native Hawaiian in combination with one or more other races; Native Hawaiians include other Pacific Islanders.
Source: Bureau of the Census, Profiles of General Demographic Characteristics, *2000 Census of Population and Housing, 2001; calculations by New Strategist*

Native Hawaiians in Combination by State, 2000 Census

(number of Native Hawaiians identifying themselves as Native Hawaiian alone or in combination, number identifying themselves as Native Hawaiian in combination, and Native Hawaiian in combination share of Native Hawaiian alone or in combination, by state, 2000)

	Native Hawaiian, alone or in combination	Native Hawaiian in combination	
		number	percent of Native Hawaiian, alone or in combination
Total Native Hawaiians	**874,414**	**475,579**	**54.4%**
Alabama	3,169	1,760	55.5
Alaska	5,515	2,206	40.0
Arizona	13,415	6,682	49.8
Arkansas	3,129	1,461	46.7
California	221,458	104,497	47.2
Colorado	10,153	5,532	54.5
Connecticut	4,076	2,710	66.5
Delaware	671	388	57.8
District of Columbia	785	437	55.7
Florida	23,998	15,373	64.1
Georgia	9,689	5,443	56.2
Hawaii	282,667	169,128	59.8
Idaho	2,847	1,539	54.1
Illinois	11,848	7,238	61.1
Indiana	4,367	2,362	54.1
Iowa	2,196	1,187	54.1
Kansas	3,117	1,804	57.9
Kentucky	3,162	1,702	53.8
Louisiana	3,237	1,997	61.7
Maine	792	410	51.8
Maryland	6,179	3,876	62.7
Massachusetts	8,704	6,215	71.4
Michigan	7,276	4,584	63.0
Minnesota	5,867	3,888	66.3
Mississippi	1,901	1,234	64.9
Missouri	6,635	3,457	52.1
Montana	1,077	607	56.4
Nebraska	1,733	897	51.8
Nevada	16,234	7,808	48.1
New Hampshire	777	406	52.3

(continued)

(continued from previous page)

	Native Hawaiian, alone or in combination	Native Hawaiian in combination	
		number	percent of Native Hawaiian, alone or in combination
New Jersey	10,065	6,736	66.9%
New Mexico	3,069	1,566	51.0
New York	28,612	19,794	69.2
North Carolina	8,574	4,591	53.5
North Dakota	475	245	51.6
Ohio	6,984	4,235	60.6
Oklahoma	5,123	2,751	53.7
Oregon	16,019	8,043	50.2
Pennsylvania	8,790	5,373	61.1
Rhode Island	1,783	1,216	68.2
South Carolina	3,778	2,150	56.9
South Dakota	556	295	53.1
Tennessee	4,587	2,382	51.9
Texas	29,094	14,660	50.4
Utah	21,367	6,222	29.1
Vermont	308	167	54.2
Virginia	9,984	6,038	60.5
Washington	42,761	18,808	44.0
West Virginia	887	487	54.9
Wisconsin	4,310	2,680	62.2
Wyoming	614	312	50.8

Source: Bureau of the Census, The Native Hawaiian Population: 2000, *Census 2000 Brief, C2KBR/01-14, 2001; calculations by New Strategist*

Native Hawaiians by Metropolitan Area, 2000 Census

(number of total people, number of Native Hawaiians, and Native Hawaiian share of total in the 100 largest metropolitan areas, 2000)

	total population	Native Hawaiian number	Native Hawaiian share of total
1. New York–Northern New Jersey–Long Island, NY–NJ–CT–PA CMSA	21,199,865	34,386	0.2%
• Bergen–Passaic, NJ PMSA	1,373,167	1,480	0.1
• Bridgeport, CT PMSA	459,479	615	0.1
• Danbury, CT PMSA	217,980	179	0.1
• Dutchess County, NY PMSA	280,150	232	0.1
• Jersey City, NJ PMSA	608,975	1,158	0.2
• Middlesex–Somerset–Hunterdon, NJ PMSA	1,169,641	1,267	0.1
• Monmouth–Ocean, NJ PMSA	1,126,217	819	0.1
• Nassau–Suffolk, NY PMSA	2,753,913	2,507	0.1
• New Haven–Meriden, CT PMSA	542,149	638	0.1
• New York, NY PMSA	9,314,235	21,142	0.2
• Newark, NJ PMSA	2,032,989	2,754	0.1
• Newburgh, NY–PA PMSA	387,669	345	0.1
• Stamford–Norwalk, CT PMSA	353,556	338	0.1
• Trenton, NJ PMSA	350,761	679	0.2
• Waterbury, CT PMSA	228,984	233	0.1
2. Los Angeles–Riverside–Orange County, CA CMSA	16,373,645	86,637	0.5
• Los Angeles–Long Beach, CA PMSA	9,519,338	49,514	0.5
• Orange County, CA PMSA	2,846,289	16,666	0.6
• Riverside–San Bernardino, CA PMSA	3,254,821	16,955	0.5
• Ventura, CA PMSA	753,197	3,502	0.5
3. Chicago–Gary–Kenosha, IL–IN–WI CMSA	9,157,540	9,934	0.1
• Chicago, IL PMSA	8,272,768	9,284	0.1
• Gary, IN PMSA	631,362	470	0.1
• Kankakee, IL PMSA	103,833	52	0.1
• Kenosha, WI PMSA	149,577	128	0.1
4. Washington–Baltimore, DC–MD–VA–WV CMSA	7,608,070	10,820	0.1
• Baltimore, MD PMSA	2,552,994	2,584	0.1
• Hagerstown, MD PMSA	131,923	111	0.1
• Washington, DC–MD–VA–WV PMSA	4,923,153	8,125	0.2
5. San Francisco–Oakland–San Jose, CA CMSA	7,039,362	67,631	1.0
• Oakland, CA PMSA	2,392,557	24,769	1.0
• San Francisco, CA PMSA	1,731,183	21,002	1.2
• San Jose, CA PMSA	1,682,585	11,957	0.7
• Santa Cruz–Watsonville, CA PMSA	255,602	1,054	0.4
• Santa Rosa, CA PMSA	458,614	2,186	0.5
• Vallejo–Fairfield–Napa, CA PMSA	518,821	6,663	1.3

(continued)

(continued from previous page)

			Native Hawaiian	
		total population	number	share of total
6.	Philadelphia–Wilmington–Atlantic City, PA–NJ–DE–MD CMSA	6,188,463	6,208	0.1%
	• Atlantic City–Cape May, NJ PMSA	354,878	402	0.1
	• Philadelphia, PA–NJ PMSA	5,100,931	5,155	0.1
	• Vineland–Millville–Bridgeton, NJ PMSA	146,438	224	0.2
	• Wilmington–Newark, DE–MD PMSA	586,216	427	0.1
7.	Boston–Worcester–Lawrence, MA–NH–ME–CT CMSA	5,819,100	7,184	0.1
	• Boston, MA–NH PMSA	3,406,829	4,447	0.1
	• Brockton, MA PMSA	255,459	308	0.1
	• Fitchburg–Leominster, MA PMSA	142,284	140	0.1
	• Lawrence, MA–NH PMSA	396,230	403	0.1
	• Lowell, MA–NH PMSA	301,686	387	0.1
	• Manchester, NH PMSA	198,378	149	0.1
	• Nashua, NH PMSA	190,949	155	0.1
	• New Bedford, MA PMSA	175,198	375	0.2
	• Portsmouth–Rochester, NH–ME PMSA	240,698	178	0.1
	• Worcester, MA–CT PMSA	511,389	642	0.1
8.	Detroit–Ann Arbor–Flint, MI CMSA	5,456,428	3,953	0.1
	• Ann Arbor, MI PMSA	578,736	520	0.1
	• Detroit, MI PMSA	4,441,551	3,167	0.1
	• Flint, MI PMSA	436,141	266	0.1
9.	Dallas–Fort Worth, TX CMSA	5,221,801	8,259	0.2
	• Dallas, TX PMSA	3,519,176	4,287	0.1
	• Fort Worth–Arlington, TX PMSA	1,702,625	3,972	0.2
10.	Houston–Galveston–Brazoria, TX CMSA	4,669,571	6,082	0.1
	• Brazoria, TX PMSA	241,767	178	0.1
	• Galveston–Texas City, TX PMSA	250,158	277	0.1
	• Houston, TX PMSA	4,177,646	5,627	0.1
11.	Atlanta, GA MSA	4,112,198	4,506	0.1
12.	Miami–Fort Lauderdale, FL CMSA	3,876,380	6,553	0.2
	• Fort Lauderdale, FL PMSA	1,623,018	3,086	0.2
	• Miami, FL PMSA	2,253,362	3,467	0.2
13.	Seattle–Tacoma–Bremerton, WA CMSA	3,554,760	34,441	1.0
	• Bremerton, WA PMSA	231,969	3,100	1.3
	• Olympia, WA PMSA	207,355	1,852	0.9
	• Seattle–Bellevue–Everett, WA PMSA	2,414,616	19,908	0.8
	• Tacoma, WA PMSA	700,820	9,581	1.4
14.	Phoenix–Mesa, AZ MSA	3,251,876	9,092	0.3
15.	Minneapolis–St. Paul, MN–WI MSA	2,968,806	4,338	0.1
16.	Cleveland–Akron, OH CMSA	2,945,831	1,806	0.1
	• Akron, OH PMSA	694,960	350	0.1
	• Cleveland–Lorain–Elyria, OH PMSA	2,250,871	1,456	0.1

(continued)

(continued from previous page)

	total population	Native Hawaiian	
		number	share of total
17. San Diego, CA MSA	2,813,833	24,524	0.9%
18. St. Louis, MO–IL MSA	2,603,607	2,174	0.1
19. Denver–Boulder–Greeley, CO CMSA	2,581,506	5,756	0.2
• Boulder–Longmont, CO PMSA	291,288	459	0.2
• Denver, CO PMSA	2,109,282	4,920	0.2
• Greeley, CO PMSA	180,936	377	0.2
20. Tampa–St. Petersburg–Clearwater, FL MSA	2,395,997	3,074	0.1
21. Pittsburgh, PA MSA	2,358,695	1,197	0.1
22. Portland–Salem, OR–WA CMSA	2,265,223	13,291	0.6
• Portland–Vancouver, OR–WA PMSA	1,918,009	11,385	0.6
• Salem, OR PMSA	347,214	1,906	0.5
23. Cincinnati–Hamilton, OH–KY–IN CMSA	1,979,202	1,296	0.1
• Cincinnati, OH–KY–IN PMSA	1,646,395	1,046	0.1
• Hamilton–Middletown, OH PMSA	332,807	250	0.1
24. Sacramento–Yolo, CA CMSA	1,796,857	16,483	0.9
• Sacramento, CA PMSA	1,628,197	15,414	0.9
• Yolo, CA PMSA	168,660	1,069	0.6
25. Kansas City, MO–KS MSA	1,776,062	3,241	0.2
26. Milwaukee–Racine, WI CMSA	1,689,572	1,531	0.1
• Milwaukee–Waukesha, WI PMSA	1,500,741	1,384	0.1
• Racine, WI PMSA	188,831	147	0.1
27. Orlando, FL MSA	1,644,561	3,296	0.2
28. Indianapolis, IN MSA	1,607,486	1,305	0.1
29. San Antonio, TX MSA	1,592,383	2,973	0.2
30. Norfolk–Virginia Beach–Newport News, VA–NC MSA	1,569,541	3,334	0.2
31. Las Vegas, NV–AZ MSA	1,563,282	13,324	0.9
32. Columbus, OH MSA	1,540,157	1,470	0.1
33. Charlotte–Gastonia–Rock Hill, NC–SC MSA	1,499,293	1,218	0.1
34. New Orleans, LA MSA	1,337,726	967	0.1
35. Salt Lake City–Ogden, UT MSA	1,333,914	16,031	1.2
36. Greensboro–Winston-Salem–High Point, NC MSA	1,251,509	897	0.1
37. Austin–San Marcos, TX MSA	1,249,763	1,908	0.2
38. Nashville, TN MSA	1,231,311	1,207	0.1
39. Providence–Fall River–Warwick, RI–MA MSA	1,188,613	2,053	0.2
40. Raleigh–Durham–Chapel Hill, NC MSA	1,187,941	1,074	0.1
41. Hartford, CT MSA	1,183,110	1,557	0.1
42. Buffalo–Niagara Falls, NY MSA	1,170,111	652	0.1
43. Memphis, TN–AR–MS MSA	1,135,614	946	0.1
44. West Palm Beach–Boca Raton, FL MSA	1,131,184	2,057	0.2
45. Jacksonville, FL MSA	1,100,491	1,744	0.2
46. Rochester, NY MSA	1,098,201	885	0.1
47. Grand Rapids–Muskegon–Holland, MI MSA	1,088,514	987	0.1

(continued)

(continued from previous page)

	total population	Native Hawaiian number	share of total
48. Oklahoma City, OK MSA	1,083,346	1,733	0.2%
49. Louisville, KY–IN MSA	1,025,598	815	0.1
50. Richmond–Petersburg, VA MSA	996,512	1,118	0.1
51. Greenville–Spartanburg–Anderson, SC MSA	962,441	732	0.1
52. Dayton–Springfield, OH MSA	950,558	711	0.1
53. Fresno, CA MSA	922,516	2,996	0.3
54. Birmingham, AL MSA	921,106	519	0.1
55. Honolulu, HI MSA	876,156	189,292	21.6
56. Albany–Schenectady–Troy, NY MSA	875,583	582	0.1
57. Tucson, AZ MSA	843,746	2,097	0.2
58. Tulsa, OK MSA	803,235	837	0.1
59. Syracuse, NY MSA	732,117	518	0.1
60. Omaha, NE–IA MSA	716,998	926	0.1
61. Albuquerque, NM MSA	712,738	1,476	0.2
62. Knoxville, TN MSA	687,249	398	0.1
63. El Paso, TX MSA	679,622	1,211	0.2
64. Bakersfield, CA MSA	661,645	1,878	0.3
65. Allentown–Bethlehem–Easton, PA MSA	637,958	525	0.1
66. Harrisburg–Lebanon–Carlisle, PA MSA	629,401	479	0.1
67. Scranton–Wilkes-Barre–Hazleton, PA MSA	624,776	269	0.0
68. Toledo, OH MSA	618,203	341	0.1
69. Baton Rouge, LA MSA	602,894	357	0.1
70. Youngstown–Warren, OH MSA	594,746	283	0.0
71. Springfield, MA MSA	591,932	1,258	0.2
72. Sarasota–Bradenton, FL MSA	589,959	516	0.1
73. Little Rock–North Little Rock, AR MSA	583,845	534	0.1
74. McAllen–Edinburg–Mission, TX MSA	569,463	242	0.0
75. Stockton–Lodi, CA MSA	563,598	4,588	0.8
76. Charleston–North Charleston, SC MSA	549,033	786	0.1
77. Wichita, KS MSA	545,220	749	0.1
78. Mobile, AL MSA	540,258	365	0.1
79. Columbia, SC MSA	536,691	657	0.1
80. Colorado Springs, CO MSA	516,929	2,546	0.5
81. Fort Wayne, IN MSA	502,141	366	0.1
82. Daytona Beach, FL MSA	493,175	461	0.1
83. Lakeland–Winter Haven, FL MSA	483,924	511	0.1
84. Johnson City–Kingsport–Bristol, TN–VA MSA	480,091	199	0.0
85. Lexington, KY MSA	479,198	291	0.1
86. Augusta–Aiken, GA–SC MSA	477,441	782	0.2
87. Melbourne–Titusville–Palm Bay, FL MSA	476,230	716	0.2
88. Lancaster, PA MSA	470,658	354	0.1
89. Chattanooga, TN–GA MSA	465,161	453	0.1
90. Des Moines, IA MSA	456,022	537	0.1

(continued)

(continued from previous page)

| | | Native Hawaiian | |
	total population	number	share of total
91. Kalamazoo–Battle Creek, MI MSA	452,851	342	0.1%
92. Lansing–East Lansing, MI MSA	447,728	481	0.1
93. Modesto, CA MSA	446,997	3,567	0.8
94. Fort Myers–Cape Coral, FL MSA	440,888	514	0.1
95. Jackson, MS MSA	440,801	222	0.1
96. Boise City, ID MSA	432,345	1,302	0.3
97. Madison, WI MSA	426,526	408	0.1
98. Spokane, WA MSA	417,939	1,459	0.3
99. Pensacola, FL MSA	412,153	958	0.2
100. Canton–Massillon, OH MSA	406,934	153	0.0

Note: Native Hawaiians include those who identified themselves as Native Hawaiian alone and those who identified themselves as Native Hawaiian in combination with one or more other races; Native Hawaiians include other Pacific Islanders. For definitions of CMSA, PMSA, and MSA, see glossary.
Source: Bureau of the Census, Profiles of General Demographic Characteristics, *2000 Census of Population and Housing, May 2001; calculations by New Strategist*

Whites

■ The white population numbered 217 million in 2000, accounting for 77 percent of the total U.S. population. A smaller 69 percent of Americans are non-Hispanic white.

■ Eighty-eight percent of non-Hispanic whites are high school graduates, while 28 percent have a college degree.

■ Eighty-one percent of non-Hispanic whites report being in excellent or good health, while only 4 percent say their health is poor.

■ Seventy-four percent of non-Hispanic white householders own their home, a greater share than the 67 percent of all householders who are homeowners.

■ The median income of non-Hispanic white households stood at $45,910 in 2000, 9 percent greater than the national median. Non-Hispanic white married couples had a median income of $62,109.

■ Among non-Hispanic white households, 56 percent are married couples and 23 percent are nuclear families (husband, wife, and children under age 18). Single-parent families headed by women account for only 5 percent of all non-Hispanic white households.

■ The nation's non-Hispanic white households spent an average of $39,991 in 2000, 5 percent more than the average household.

■ Note: There are no business-ownership data for whites.

Non-Hispanic whites account for 69.1 percent of the U.S. population

(percent distribution of people by race and Hispanic origin, 2000 census)

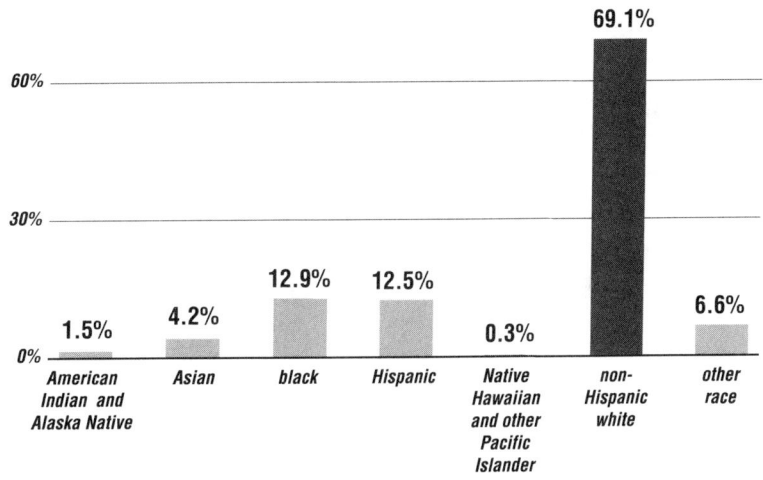

Non-Hispanic Whites Are Better Educated than the White Population as a Whole

The educational attainment of non-Hispanic whites is higher than that of the total white population because most Hispanics, many of whom are poorly educated, are white. While 88 percent of non-Hispanic whites are high school graduates, the share is a smaller 85 percent among all whites. Twenty-eight percent of non-Hispanic whites have a college degree compared with 26 percent of the total white population.

Among white families with children aged 18 to 24, 48 percent have at least one child in college full-time. The figure is a higher 52 percent among non-Hispanic white families.

Non-Hispanic whites earned 75 percent of all bachelor's degrees in 1999-00, as well as 70 percent of master's degrees, and 61 percent of doctorates. Among first-professional degrees awarded in 1999–2000, non-Hispanic whites accounted for 92 percent of degrees in veterinary medicine, but for only 63 percent of degrees in dentistry.

■ The share of college degrees earned by non-Hispanic whites is shrinking as minorities make up a growing proportion of college students.

Non-Hispanic whites are more likely to be high school and college graduates

(percent of whites and non-Hispanic whites aged 25 or older who are high school or college graduates, 2000)

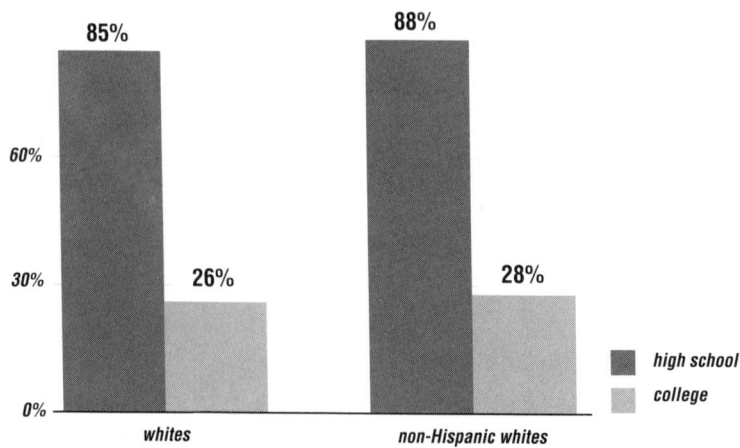

Educational Attainment of Whites by Sex, 2000

(number and percent distribution of whites aged 25 or older by educational attainment and sex, 2000; numbers in thousands)

	total number	total percent	men number	men percent	women number	women percent
Total whites	**147,067**	**100.0%**	**70,900**	**100.0%**	**76,167**	**100.0%**
Not a high school graduate	22,188	15.1	10,745	15.2	11,444	15.0
High school graduate or more	124,879	84.9	60,157	84.8	64,723	85.0
High school graduate only	49,105	33.4	22,557	31.8	26,548	34.9
Some college or associate's degree	37,353	25.4	17,373	24.5	19,980	26.2
Bachelor's degree or more	38,421	26.1	20,227	28.5	18,195	23.9
Bachelor's degree only	25,511	17.3	12,961	18.3	12,550	16.5
Master's degree	8,889	6.0	4,433	6.3	4,456	5.9
Professional degree	2,287	1.6	1,595	2.2	693	0.9
Doctoral degree	1,734	1.2	1,238	1.7	496	0.7

Source: Bureau of the Census, Educational Attainment in the United States: March 2000 (Update), *detailed tables for Current Population Report P20-536, 2000; Internet site <www.census.gov/population/socdemo/education/p20-536/tab01.txt>; calculations by New Strategist*

Educational Attainment of Non-Hispanic Whites by Sex, 2000

(number and percent distribution of non-Hispanic whites aged 25 or older by educational attainment and sex, 2000; numbers in thousands)

	total number	total percent	men number	men percent	women number	women percent
Total non-Hispanic whites	**130,783**	**100.0%**	**62,977**	**100.0%**	**67,807**	**100.0%**
Not a high school graduate	15,133	11.6	7,271	11.5	7,866	11.6
High school graduate or more	115,650	88.4	55,706	88.5	59,941	88.4
High school graduate only	44,554	34.1	20,309	32.2	24,244	35.8
Some college or associate's degree	34,390	26.3	16,011	25.4	18,378	27.1
Bachelor's degree or more	36,706	28.1	19,386	30.8	17,319	25.5
Bachelor's degree only	24,331	18.6	12,381	19.7	11,950	17.6
Master's degree	8,543	6.5	4,274	6.8	4,269	6.3
Professional degree	2,176	1.7	1,540	2.4	636	0.9
Doctoral degree	1,656	1.3	1,191	1.9	464	0.7

Source: Bureau of the Census, Educational Attainment in the United States: March 2000 (Update), *detailed tables for Current Population Report P20-536, 2000; Internet site <www.census.gov/population/socdemo/education/p20-536/tab01.txt>; calculations by New Strategist*

Educational Attainment of White Men by Age, 2000

(number and percent distribution of white men aged 25 or older by age and educational attainment, 2000; numbers in thousands)

	total	not a high school graduate	high school graduate or more					bachelor's degree or more				
			total	high school graduate only	some college	associate's degree	total	bachelor's degree only	master's degree	professional degree	doctoral degree
Total white men	70,900	10,745	60,157	22,557	12,211	5,162	20,227	12,961	4,433	1,595	1,238
Aged 25 to 29	7,274	972	6,301	2,336	1,376	566	2,023	1,713	210	73	27
Aged 30 to 34	7,870	1,015	6,855	2,479	1,380	614	2,382	1,768	404	125	85
Aged 35 to 39	9,189	1,107	8,083	3,225	1,588	739	2,531	1,686	559	168	118
Aged 40 to 44	9,305	1,088	8,218	3,134	1,572	874	2,638	1,705	586	185	162
Aged 45 to 49	8,172	806	7,367	2,508	1,517	739	2,603	1,574	659	219	151
Aged 50 to 54	7,032	741	6,292	1,874	1,371	577	2,470	1,444	648	213	165
Aged 55 to 59	5,309	707	4,605	1,736	893	330	1,646	865	447	172	162
Aged 60 to 64	4,415	846	3,566	1,435	686	274	1,171	638	323	124	86
Aged 65 or older	12,335	3,461	8,874	3,831	1,829	450	2,764	1,568	598	316	282
Aged 65 to 69	3,818	852	2,965	1,258	599	170	938	530	204	91	113
Aged 70 to 74	3,275	911	2,363	985	480	130	768	429	180	79	80
Aged 75 or older	5,242	1,697	3,544	1,588	749	149	1,058	610	214	145	89

(continued)

(continued from previous page)

| | | not a high school graduate | high school graduate or more | | | | | | | | |
| | total | | total | high school graduate only | some college | associate's degree | bachelor's degree or more | | | | |
							total	bachelor's degree only	master's degree	professional degree	doctoral degree
Total white men	**100.0%**	**15.2%**	**84.8%**	**31.8%**	**17.2%**	**7.3%**	**28.5%**	**18.3%**	**6.3%**	**2.2%**	**1.7%**
Aged 25 to 29	100.0	13.4	86.6	32.1	18.9	7.8	27.8	23.5	2.9	1.0	0.4
Aged 30 to 34	100.0	12.9	87.1	31.5	17.5	7.8	30.3	22.5	5.1	1.6	1.1
Aged 35 to 39	100.0	12.0	88.0	35.1	17.3	8.0	27.5	18.3	6.1	1.8	1.3
Aged 40 to 44	100.0	11.7	88.3	33.7	16.9	9.4	28.4	18.3	6.3	2.0	1.7
Aged 45 to 49	100.0	9.9	90.1	30.7	18.6	9.0	31.9	19.3	8.1	2.7	1.8
Aged 50 to 54	100.0	10.5	89.5	26.6	19.5	8.2	35.1	20.5	9.2	3.0	2.3
Aged 55 to 59	100.0	13.3	86.7	32.7	16.8	6.2	31.0	16.3	8.4	3.2	3.1
Aged 60 to 64	100.0	19.2	80.8	32.5	15.5	6.2	26.5	14.5	7.3	2.8	1.9
Aged 65 or older	100.0	28.1	71.9	31.1	14.8	3.6	22.4	12.7	4.8	2.6	2.3
Aged 65 to 69	100.0	22.3	77.7	32.9	15.7	4.5	24.6	13.9	5.3	2.4	3.0
Aged 70 to 74	100.0	27.8	72.2	30.1	14.7	4.0	23.5	13.1	5.5	2.4	2.4
Aged 75 or older	100.0	32.4	67.6	30.3	14.3	2.8	20.2	11.6	4.1	2.8	1.7

Source: Bureau of the Census, Educational Attainment in the United States: March 2000 (Update), detailed tables for Current Population Report P20-536, 2000; Internet site <www.census.gov/population/socdemo/education/p20-536/tab01.txt>; calculations by New Strategist

Educational Attainment of White Women by Age, 2000

(number and percent distribution of white women aged 25 or older by age and educational attainment, 2000; numbers in thousands)

	total	not a high school graduate	high school graduate or more				bachelor's degree or more				
			total	high school graduate only	some college	associate's degree	total	bachelor's degree only	master's degree	professional degree	doctoral degree
Total white women	**76,167**	**11,444**	**64,723**	**26,548**	**13,403**	**6,577**	**18,195**	**12,550**	**4,456**	**693**	**496**
Aged 25 to 29	7,282	732	6,552	2,027	1,509	735	2,281	1,845	346	62	28
Aged 30 to 34	7,894	871	7,024	2,325	1,435	806	2,458	1,886	406	117	49
Aged 35 to 39	9,135	1,003	8,133	2,986	1,659	956	2,532	1,792	584	116	40
Aged 40 to 44	9,286	902	8,383	3,127	1,751	1,063	2,442	1,661	589	95	97
Aged 45 to 49	8,303	782	7,522	2,564	1,533	869	2,556	1,647	743	90	76
Aged 50 to 54	7,282	775	6,507	2,539	1,374	649	1,945	1,192	589	80	84
Aged 55 to 59	5,770	858	4,912	2,199	1,088	409	1,216	682	433	47	54
Aged 60 to 64	4,670	891	3,781	1,935	702	284	860	523	282	28	27
Aged 65 or older	16,545	4,630	11,915	6,846	2,353	806	1,910	1,324	486	59	41
Aged 65 to 69	4,282	925	3,358	1,925	639	184	610	391	194	14	11
Aged 70 to 74	4,153	1,007	3,144	1,810	617	232	485	337	102	30	16
Aged 75 or older	8,109	2,698	5,411	3,110	1,097	390	814	595	190	15	14

(continued)

(continued from previous page)

	total	not a high school graduate	high school graduate or more					bachelor's degree or more				
			total	high school graduate only	some college	associate's degree	total	bachelor's degree only	master's degree	professional degree	doctoral degree
Total white women	**100.0%**	**15.0%**	**85.0%**	**34.9%**	**17.6%**	**8.6%**	**23.9%**	**16.5%**	**5.9%**	**0.9%**	**0.7%**
Aged 25 to 29	100.0	10.1	90.0	27.8	20.7	10.1	31.3	25.3	4.8	0.9	0.4
Aged 30 to 34	100.0	11.0	89.0	29.5	18.2	10.2	31.1	23.9	5.1	1.5	0.6
Aged 35 to 39	100.0	11.0	89.0	32.7	18.2	10.5	27.7	19.6	6.4	1.3	0.4
Aged 40 to 44	100.0	9.7	90.3	33.7	18.9	11.4	26.3	17.9	6.3	1.0	1.0
Aged 45 to 49	100.0	9.4	90.6	30.9	18.5	10.5	30.8	19.8	8.9	1.1	0.9
Aged 50 to 54	100.0	10.6	89.4	34.9	18.9	8.9	26.7	16.4	8.1	1.1	1.2
Aged 55 to 59	100.0	14.9	85.1	38.1	18.9	7.1	21.1	11.8	7.5	0.8	0.9
Aged 60 to 64	100.0	19.1	81.0	41.4	15.0	6.1	18.4	11.2	6.0	0.6	0.6
Aged 65 or older	100.0	28.0	72.0	41.4	14.2	4.9	11.5	8.0	2.9	0.4	0.2
Aged 65 to 69	100.0	21.6	78.4	45.0	14.9	4.3	14.2	9.1	4.5	0.3	0.3
Aged 70 to 74	100.0	24.2	75.7	43.6	14.9	5.6	11.7	8.1	2.5	0.7	0.4
Aged 75 or older	100.0	33.3	66.7	38.4	13.5	4.8	10.0	7.3	2.3	0.2	0.2

Source: Bureau of the Census, Educational Attainment in the United States: March 2000 (Update), detailed tables for Current Population Report P20-536, 2000; Internet site <www.census.gov/population/socdemo/education/p20-536/tab01.txt>; calculations by New Strategist

Educational Attainment of Non-Hispanic White Men by Age, 2000

(number and percent distribution of non-Hispanic white men aged 25 or older by age and educational attainment, 2000; numbers in thousands)

| | total | not a high school graduate | high school graduate or more | | | | | | | | |
| | | | total | high school graduate only | some college | associate's degree | bachelor's degree or more | | | | |
							total	bachelor's degree only	master's degree	professional degree	doctoral degree
Total non-Hispanic white men	62,977	7,269	55,706	20,309	11,209	4,802	19,386	12,381	4,274	1,540	1,191
Aged 25 to 29	5,940	421	5,518	1,927	1,172	501	1,918	1,626	199	66	27
Aged 30 to 34	6,514	444	6,070	2,061	1,208	535	2,266	1,677	388	121	80
Aged 35 to 39	7,847	565	7,283	2,784	1,420	691	2,388	1,579	541	159	109
Aged 40 to 44	8,313	686	7,628	2,851	1,433	826	2,518	1,621	566	173	158
Aged 45 to 49	7,400	487	6,914	2,287	1,414	702	2,511	1,521	630	216	144
Aged 50 to 54	6,384	468	5,918	1,724	1,285	546	2,363	1,378	620	206	159
Aged 55 to 59	4,868	503	4,366	1,616	847	314	1,589	837	427	168	157
Aged 60 to 64	4,069	646	3,423	1,367	653	266	1,137	614	316	122	85
Aged 65 or older	11,643	3,053	8,591	3,693	1,778	423	2,697	1,529	586	309	273
Aged 65 to 69	3,559	717	2,843	1,208	574	151	910	512	198	89	111
Aged 70 to 74	3,086	801	2,286	943	469	122	752	418	176	79	79
Aged 75 or older	4,998	1,535	3,463	1,541	735	149	1,038	599	213	142	84

(continued)

(continued from previous page)

Total non-Hispanic white men	total	not a high school graduate	high school graduate or more				bachelor's degree or more				
			total	high school graduate only	some college	associate's degree	total	bachelor's degree only	master's degree	professional degree	doctoral degree
white men	**100.0%**	**11.5%**	**88.5%**	**32.2%**	**17.8%**	**7.6%**	**30.8%**	**19.7%**	**6.8%**	**2.4%**	**1.9%**
Aged 25 to 29	100.0	7.1	92.9	32.4	19.7	8.4	32.3	27.4	3.4	1.1	0.5
Aged 30 to 34	100.0	6.8	93.2	31.6	18.5	8.2	34.8	25.7	6.0	1.9	1.2
Aged 35 to 39	100.0	7.2	92.8	35.5	18.1	8.8	30.4	20.1	6.9	2.0	1.4
Aged 40 to 44	100.0	8.3	91.8	34.3	17.2	9.9	30.3	19.5	6.8	2.1	1.9
Aged 45 to 49	100.0	6.6	93.4	30.9	19.1	9.5	33.9	20.6	8.5	2.9	1.9
Aged 50 to 54	100.0	7.3	92.7	27.0	20.1	8.6	37.0	21.6	9.7	3.2	2.5
Aged 55 to 59	100.0	10.3	89.7	33.2	17.4	6.5	32.6	17.2	8.8	3.5	3.2
Aged 60 to 64	100.0	15.9	84.1	33.6	16.0	6.5	27.9	15.1	7.8	3.0	2.1
Aged 65 or older	100.0	26.2	73.8	31.7	15.3	3.6	23.2	13.1	5.0	2.7	2.3
Aged 65 to 69	100.0	20.1	79.9	33.9	16.1	4.2	25.6	14.4	5.6	2.5	3.1
Aged 70 to 74	100.0	26.0	74.1	30.6	15.2	4.0	24.4	13.5	5.7	2.6	2.6
Aged 75 or older	100.0	30.7	69.3	30.8	14.7	3.0	20.8	12.0	4.3	2.8	1.7

Source: Bureau of the Census, Educational Attainment in the United States: March 2000 (Update), detailed tables for Current Population Report P20-536, 2000; Internet site <www.census.gov/population/socdemo/education/p20-536/tab01.txt>; calculations by New Strategist

Educational Attainment of Non-Hispanic White Women by Age, 2000

(number and percent distribution of non-Hispanic white women aged 25 or older by age and educational attainment, 2000; numbers in thousands)

	total	not a high school graduate	high school graduate or more				bachelor's degree or more				
			total	high school graduate only	some college	associate's degree	total	bachelor's degree only	master's degree	professional degree	doctoral degree
Total non-Hispanic white women	**67,807**	**7,866**	**59,941**	**24,244**	**12,255**	**6,123**	**17,319**	**11,950**	**4,269**	**636**	**464**
Aged 25 to 29	5,950	288	5,662	1,631	1,259	643	2,129	1,732	319	52	26
Aged 30 to 34	6,576	365	6,211	1,936	1,224	730	2,321	1,783	389	107	42
Aged 35 to 39	7,801	560	7,240	2,592	1,462	851	2,335	1,656	535	104	40
Aged 40 to 44	8,234	486	7,748	2,844	1,588	998	2,318	1,578	566	88	86
Aged 45 to 49	7,579	466	7,114	2,377	1,441	839	2,457	1,579	716	86	76
Aged 50 to 54	6,578	459	6,120	2,335	1,286	621	1,878	1,155	570	73	80
Aged 55 to 59	5,259	580	4,679	2,075	1,036	388	1,180	662	425	40	53
Aged 60 to 64	4,286	687	3,597	1,813	675	268	841	515	275	26	25
Aged 65 or older	15,544	3,976	11,569	6,642	2,283	784	1,860	1,289	475	59	37
Aged 65 to 69	3,922	704	3,219	1,852	611	168	588	378	186	14	10
Aged 70 to 74	3,873	822	3,050	1,748	591	230	481	333	102	30	16
Aged 75 or older	7,748	2,450	5,299	3,042	1,081	385	791	578	187	15	11

(continued)

(continued from previous page)

	total	not a high school graduate	high school graduate or more				bachelor's degree or more				
			total	high school graduate only	some college	associate's degree	total	bachelor's degree only	master's degree	professional degree	doctoral degree
Total non-Hispanic white women	**100.0%**	**11.6%**	**88.4%**	**35.8%**	**18.1%**	**9.0%**	**25.5%**	**17.6%**	**6.3%**	**0.9%**	**0.7%**
Aged 25 to 29	100.0	4.8	95.2	27.4	21.2	10.8	35.8	29.1	5.4	0.9	0.4
Aged 30 to 34	100.0	5.6	94.4	29.4	18.6	11.1	35.3	27.1	5.9	1.6	0.6
Aged 35 to 39	100.0	7.2	92.8	33.2	18.7	10.9	29.9	21.2	6.9	1.3	0.5
Aged 40 to 44	100.0	5.9	94.1	34.5	19.3	12.1	28.2	19.2	6.9	1.1	1.0
Aged 45 to 49	100.0	6.1	93.9	31.4	19.0	11.1	32.4	20.8	9.4	1.1	1.0
Aged 50 to 54	100.0	7.0	93.0	35.5	19.6	9.4	28.5	17.6	8.7	1.1	1.2
Aged 55 to 59	100.0	11.0	89.0	39.5	19.7	7.4	22.4	12.6	8.1	0.8	1.0
Aged 60 to 64	100.0	16.0	83.9	42.3	15.7	6.3	19.6	12.0	6.4	0.6	0.6
Aged 65 or older	100.0	25.6	74.4	42.7	14.7	5.0	12.0	8.3	3.1	0.4	0.2
Aged 65 to 69	100.0	18.0	82.1	47.2	15.6	4.3	15.0	9.6	4.7	0.4	0.3
Aged 70 to 74	100.0	21.2	78.8	45.1	15.3	5.9	12.4	8.6	2.6	0.8	0.4
Aged 75 or older	100.0	31.6	68.4	39.3	14.0	5.0	10.2	7.5	2.4	0.2	0.1

Source: Bureau of the Census, Educational Attainment in the United States: March 2000 (Update), detailed tables for Current Population Report P20-536, 2000; Internet site <www.census.gov/population/socdemo/education/p20-536/tab01.txt>; calculations by New Strategist

White High School and College Graduates by Age and Sex, 2000

(percent of whites aged 25 or older who are high school or college graduates by age and sex, 2000)

	total	men	women
High school graduates			
Total whites	**84.9%**	**84.8%**	**85.0%**
Aged 25 to 29	88.3	86.6	90.0
Aged 30 to 34	88.0	87.1	89.0
Aged 35 to 39	88.5	88.0	89.0
Aged 40 to 44	89.3	88.3	90.3
Aged 45 to 49	90.4	90.1	90.6
Aged 50 to 54	89.4	89.5	89.4
Aged 55 to 59	85.9	86.7	85.1
Aged 60 to 64	80.9	80.8	80.9
Aged 65 or older	72.0	71.9	72.0
Aged 65 to 69	78.1	77.7	78.4
Aged 70 to 74	74.2	72.2	75.7
Aged 75 or older	67.1	67.6	66.7
College graduates			
Total whites	**26.1**	**28.5**	**23.9**
Aged 25 to 29	29.6	27.8	31.3
Aged 30 to 34	30.7	30.3	31.1
Aged 35 to 39	27.6	27.5	27.7
Aged 40 to 44	27.3	28.3	26.3
Aged 45 to 49	31.3	31.9	30.8
Aged 50 to 54	30.8	35.1	26.7
Aged 55 to 59	25.8	31.0	21.1
Aged 60 to 64	22.4	26.5	18.4
Aged 65 or older	16.2	22.4	11.5
Aged 65 to 69	19.1	24.6	14.2
Aged 70 to 74	16.9	23.5	11.7
Aged 75 or older	14.0	20.2	10.0

Source: Bureau of the Census, Educational Attainment in the United States: March 2000 (Update), *detailed tables for Current Population Report P20-536, 2000; Internet site <www.census.gov/population/socdemo/ education/p20-536/tab01a.txt>*

Non-Hispanic White High School and College Graduates by Age and Sex, 2000

(percent of non-Hispanic whites aged 25 or older who are high school or college graduates by age and sex, 2000)

	total	men	women
High school graduates			
Total non-Hispanic whites	**88.4%**	**88.5%**	**88.4%**
Aged 25 to 29	94.0	92.9	95.2
Aged 30 to 34	93.8	93.2	94.4
Aged 35 to 39	92.8	92.8	92.8
Aged 40 to 44	92.9	91.8	94.1
Aged 45 to 49	93.6	93.4	93.8
Aged 50 to 54	92.9	92.7	93.0
Aged 55 to 59	89.3	89.7	89.0
Aged 60 to 64	84.0	84.1	84.0
Aged 65 or older	74.1	73.8	74.4
Aged 65 to 69	81.0	79.9	82.1
Aged 70 to 74	76.7	74.1	78.8
Aged 75 or older	68.7	69.3	68.4
College graduates			
Total non-Hispanic whites	**28.1**	**30.8**	**25.5**
Aged 25 to 29	34.0	32.3	35.8
Aged 30 to 34	35.0	34.8	35.3
Aged 35 to 39	30.2	30.4	29.9
Aged 40 to 44	29.2	30.3	28.2
Aged 45 to 49	33.2	33.9	32.4
Aged 50 to 54	32.7	37.0	28.5
Aged 55 to 59	27.3	32.6	22.4
Aged 60 to 64	23.7	28.0	19.6
Aged 65 or older	16.8	23.2	12.0
Aged 65 to 69	20.0	25.5	15.0
Aged 70 to 74	17.7	24.4	12.4
Aged 75 or older	14.3	20.7	10.2

Source: Bureau of the Census, Educational Attainment in the United States: March 2000 (Update), *detailed tables for Current Population Report P20-536, 2000; Internet site <www.census.gov/population/socdemo/education/p20-536/tab01a.txt>*

White High School and College Graduates by Age and Region, 2000

(percent of whites aged 25 or older who are high school or college graduates, by age and region, 2000)

	Northeast	Midwest	South	West
High school graduates				
Total whites	**86.1%**	**87.8%**	**82.8%**	**84.0%**
Aged 25 to 34	91.5	92.5	87.9	82.1
Aged 35 to 44	92.5	91.1	87.7	85.1
Aged 45 to 54	91.8	93.7	87.4	87.9
Aged 55 to 64	84.6	88.1	78.8	86.0
Aged 65 or older	69.4	71.8	70.0	78.6
College graduates				
Total whites	**28.9**	**25.1**	**25.2**	**26.1**
Aged 25 to 34	36.0	31.7	29.3	25.7
Aged 35 to 44	29.8	26.1	27.4	27.0
Aged 45 to 54	34.7	29.2	30.1	31.4
Aged 55 to 64	28.4	23.4	20.9	26.7
Aged 65 or older	16.2	13.4	16.8	18.5

Source: Bureau of the Census, Educational Attainment in the United States: March 2000 (Update), *Detailed tables for Current Population Report P20-536, 2000; Internet site <www.census.gov/population/socdemo/education/p20-536/tab12.txt>; calculations by New Strategist*

Non-Hispanic White High School and College Graduates by Age and Region, 2000

(percent of non-Hispanic whites aged 25 or older who are high school or college graduates, by age and region, 2000)

	Northeast	Midwest	South	West
High school graduates				
Total non-Hispanic whites	**88.2%**	**88.8%**	**85.8%**	**92.7%**
Aged 25 to 34	94.5	94.8	92.8	94.0
Aged 35 to 44	94.5	92.2	91.4	94.6
Aged 45 to 54	94.0	94.5	90.2	96.0
Aged 55 to 64	87.6	89.1	81.6	93.1
Aged 65 or older	71.0	72.0	72.2	84.7
College graduates				
Total non-Hispanic whites	**30.2**	**25.6**	**26.8**	**31.3**
Aged 25 to 34	39.0	33.1	33.1	34.7
Aged 35 to 44	31.3	26.7	29.2	33.0
Aged 45 to 54	36.1	29.6	31.5	36.6
Aged 55 to 64	29.8	23.8	21.9	30.5
Aged 65 or older	16.7	13.5	17.3	20.4

Source: Bureau of the Census, Educational Attainment in the United States: March 2000 (Update), *Detailed tables for Current Population Report P20-536, 2000; Internet site <www.census.gov/population/socdemo/ education/p20-536/tab12.txt>; calculations by New Strategist*

White High School and College Graduates by State, 2000

(percent of whites aged 25 or older who are high school or college graduates, for the 25 largest states, 2000)

	high school graduate or more	college graduate
Total whites	**84.9%**	**26.1%**
Alabama	78.7	21.2
Arizona	84.6	23.8
California	79.9	25.5
Colorado	89.8	34.9
Florida	85.1	23.6
Georgia	84.9	28.0
Illinois	86.5	26.7
Indiana	84.8	17.2
Kentucky	78.7	21.8
Louisiana	84.4	27.3
Maryland	86.0	37.0
Massachusetts	86.3	33.5
Michigan	87.4	23.4
Minnesota	91.3	30.8
Missouri	87.8	25.9
New Jersey	88.7	30.3
New York	83.9	29.2
North Carolina	81.7	25.5
Ohio	88.0	26.0
Pennsylvania	86.1	24.7
Tennessee	80.3	22.0
Texas	78.8	25.0
Virginia	88.5	34.0
Washington	92.5	28.6
Wisconsin	87.5	24.5

Source: Bureau of the Census, Educational Attainment in the United States: March 2000 (Update), *Detailed tables for Current Population Report P20-536, 2000; Internet site <www.census.gov/population/socdemo/education/p20-536/tab14.txt>*

Non-Hispanic White High School and College Graduates by State, 2000

(percent of non-Hispanic whites aged 25 or older who are high school or college graduates, for the 25 largest states, 2000)

	high school graduate or more	college graduate
Total non-Hispanic whites	**88.4%**	**28.1%**
Alabama	78.9	21.3
Arizona	93.7	29.4
California	92.7	33.7
Colorado	94.3	39.0
Florida	88.5	24.2
Georgia	85.9	28.4
Illinois	89.8	28.6
Indiana	85.2	17.1
Kentucky	79.0	21.8
Louisiana	84.0	27.2
Maryland	87.3	37.4
Massachusetts	87.6	34.4
Michigan	87.8	23.7
Minnesota	91.7	31.1
Missouri	88.1	26.0
New Jersey	91.2	32.8
New York	88.1	31.8
North Carolina	83.3	26.0
Ohio	88.2	26.1
Pennsylvania	86.6	24.9
Tennessee	80.7	22.0
Texas	90.3	32.6
Virginia	89.2	34.4
Washington	93.7	29.0
Wisconsin	88.5	24.9

Source: Bureau of the Census, Educational Attainment in the United States: March 2000 (Update), *Detailed tables for Current Population Report P20-536, 2000; Internet site <www.census.gov/population/socdemo/education/p20-536/tab14.txt>*

School Enrollment of Whites by Age and Sex, 2000

(number and percent of whites aged 3 or older enrolled in school, by age and sex, October 2000; numbers in thousands)

	total		male		female	
	number	*percent*	*number*	*percent*	*number*	*percent*
Total whites	**56,344**	**26.1%**	**28,075**	**26.5%**	**28,269**	**25.7%**
Aged 3 to 4	3,091	50.2	1,549	49.1	1,543	51.4
Aged 5 to 6	5,959	95.3	3,037	94.8	2,922	95.8
Aged 7 to 9	9,441	98.2	4,817	97.8	4,624	98.5
Aged 10 to 13	12,620	98.3	6,463	98.3	6,157	98.4
Aged 14 to 15	6,176	98.4	3,172	98.4	3,004	98.3
Aged 16 to 17	5,845	92.8	3,018	93.1	2,827	92.5
Aged 18 to 19	3,924	61.3	1,901	58.5	2,022	64.2
Aged 20 to 21	2,688	44.9	1,282	41.8	1,406	48.2
Aged 22 to 24	2,101	23.7	1,025	23.2	1,076	24.2
Aged 25 to 29	1,473	10.4	669	9.5	805	11.3
Aged 30 to 34	939	6.0	380	4.9	559	7.1
Aged 35 to 44	1,256	3.4	483	2.6	773	4.2
Aged 45 to 54	670	2.1	209	1.3	461	2.9
Aged 55 or older	161	0.3	70	0.3	91	0.3

Source: Bureau of the Census, Current Population Survey, Internet site <www.census.gov/population/socdemo/school/ppl-148/tab01.txt>

School Enrollment of Non-Hispanic Whites by Age and Sex, 2000

(number and percent of non-Hispanic whites aged 3 or older enrolled in school, by age and sex, October 2000; numbers in thousands)

	total		male		female	
	number	*percent*	*number*	*percent*	*number*	*percent*
Total non-Hispanic whites	**46,660**	**25.0%**	**23,260**	**25.5%**	**23,400**	**24.6%**
Aged 3 to 4	2,607	54.6	1,328	54.1	1,279	55.2
Aged 5 to 6	4,639	95.5	2,332	94.5	2,307	96.4
Aged 7 to 9	7,576	98.4	3,920	98.1	3,656	98.6
Aged 10 to 13	10,305	98.5	5,238	98.2	5,068	98.8
Aged 14 to 15	5,135	98.9	2,638	98.8	2,497	99.0
Aged 16 to 17	4,933	94.0	2,574	94.7	2,359	93.3
Aged 18 to 19	3,337	63.9	1,608	61.2	1,729	66.7
Aged 20 to 21	2,388	49.2	1,135	45.8	1,253	52.7
Aged 22 to 24	1,809	24.9	893	25.0	916	24.8
Aged 25 to 29	1,286	11.1	603	10.5	684	11.8
Aged 30 to 34	785	6.1	302	4.7	483	7.4
Aged 35 to 44	1,092	3.4	428	2.7	663	4.2
Aged 45 to 54	622	2.2	191	1.4	430	3.0
Aged 55 or older	147	0.3	70	0.3	76	0.3

Source: Bureau of the Census, Current Population Survey, Internet site <www.census.gov/population/socdemo/school/ppl-148/tab01.txt>

White Families with Children in College, 2000

(total number of white families, number with children aged 18 to 24, and number and percent with children aged 18 to 24 attending college full-time as of October 2000, by household income in 1999; numbers in thousands)

	total	with children aged 18–24	with one or more children attending college full-time		
			number	percent of total families	percent of families with children 18–24
Total white families	**60,903**	**8,471**	**4,084**	**6.7%**	**48.2%**
Under $20,000	7,613	882	172	2.3	19.5
$20,000 to $29,999	6,901	808	312	4.5	38.6
$30,000 to $39,999	6,774	788	305	4.5	38.7
$40,000 to $49,999	5,362	704	318	5.9	45.2
$50,000 to $74,999	11,105	1,617	877	7.9	54.2
$75,000 or more	13,414	2,443	1,573	11.7	64.4

Note: Numbers will not add to total because not reported is not shown.
Source: Bureau of the Census, Current Population Survey, Internet site <www.census.gov/population/socdemo/school/ppl-148/tab15.txt>

Non-Hispanic White Families with Children in College, 2000

(total number of non-Hispanic white families, number with children aged 18 to 24, and number and percent with children aged 18 to 24 attending college full-time as of October 2000, by household income in 1999; numbers in thousands)

	total	with children aged 18–24	with one or more children attending college full-time		
			number	percent of total families	percent of families with children 18–24
Total non-Hispanic white families	**53,532**	**6,798**	**3,532**	**6.6%**	**52.0%**
Under $20,000	5,499	482	105	1.9	21.8
$20,000 to $29,999	5,552	473	194	3.5	41.0
$30,000 to $39,999	5,824	598	246	4.2	41.1
$40,000 to $49,999	4,812	548	239	5.0	43.6
$50,000 to $74,999	10,251	1,406	784	7.6	55.8
$75,000 or more	12,788	2,310	1,498	11.7	64.8

Note: Numbers will not add to total because not reported is not shown.
Source: Bureau of the Census, Current Population Survey, Internet site <www.census.gov/population/socdemo/school/ppl-148/tab15.txt>

College Enrollment of Whites by Age, 2000

(number and percent distribution of whites aged 15 or older enrolled in college by age and type of school, October 2000; numbers in thousands)

	total	undergraduate total	two-year	four-year	graduate
Total whites enrolled	**12,002**	**9,690**	**3,036**	**6,654**	**2,312**
Aged 15 to 17	117	112	58	54	5
Aged 18 to 19	2,915	2,892	936	1,956	23
Aged 20 to 21	2,590	2,537	574	1,963	53
Aged 22 to 24	2,063	1,605	396	1,209	458
Aged 25 to 29	1,432	874	316	558	558
Aged 30 to 34	908	522	191	331	386
Aged 35 to 39	677	446	215	231	231
Aged 40 to 44	521	321	148	173	200
Aged 45 to 49	399	218	113	105	181
Aged 50 to 54	241	98	51	47	143
Aged 55 or older	89	52	37	21	58
Percent distribution by age					
Total whites enrolled	**100.0%**	**100.0%**	**100.0%**	**100.0%**	**100.0%**
Aged 15 to 17	1.0	1.2	1.9	0.8	0.2
Aged 18 to 19	24.3	29.8	30.8	29.4	1.0
Aged 20 to 21	21.6	26.2	18.9	29.5	2.3
Aged 22 to 24	17.2	16.6	13.0	18.2	19.8
Aged 25 to 29	11.9	9.0	10.4	8.4	24.1
Aged 30 to 34	7.6	5.4	6.3	5.0	16.7
Aged 35 to 39	5.6	4.6	7.1	3.5	10.0
Aged 40 to 44	4.3	3.3	4.9	2.6	8.7
Aged 45 to 49	3.3	2.2	3.7	1.6	7.8
Aged 50 to 54	2.0	1.0	1.7	0.7	6.2
Aged 55 or older	0.7	0.5	1.2	0.3	2.5

(continued)

(continued from previous page)

| | total | undergraduate | | | graduate |
		total	two-year	four-year	
Percent distribution by type of school					
Total whites enrolled	**100.0%**	**80.7%**	**25.3%**	**55.4%**	**19.3%**
Aged 15 to 17	100.0	95.7	49.6	46.2	4.3
Aged 18 to 19	100.0	99.2	32.1	67.1	0.8
Aged 20 to 21	100.0	98.0	22.2	75.8	2.0
Aged 22 to 24	100.0	77.8	19.2	58.6	22.2
Aged 25 to 29	100.0	61.0	22.1	39.0	39.0
Aged 30 to 34	100.0	57.5	21.0	36.5	42.5
Aged 35 to 39	100.0	65.9	31.8	34.1	34.1
Aged 40 to 44	100.0	61.6	28.4	33.2	38.4
Aged 45 to 49	100.0	54.6	28.3	26.3	45.4
Aged 50 to 54	100.0	40.7	21.2	19.5	59.3
Aged 55 or older	100.0	58.4	41.6	23.6	65.2

Source: Bureau of the Census, Current Population Survey, Internet site <www.census.gov/population/socdemo/school/ppl-148/tab09.txt>; calculations by New Strategist

College Enrollment of Non-Hispanic Whites by Age, 2000

(number and percent distribution of non-Hispanic whites aged 15 or older enrolled in college by age and type of school, October 2000; numbers in thousands)

	total	*undergraduate*			*graduate*
		total	*two-year*	*four-year*	
Total non-Hispanic whites enrolled	**10,637**	**8,523**	**2,544**	**5,979**	**2,114**
Aged 15 to 17	91	88	44	44	3
Aged 18 to 19	2,580	2,565	776	1,789	15
Aged 20 to 21	2,333	2,285	480	1,805	48
Aged 22 to 24	1,794	1,384	322	1,062	410
Aged 25 to 29	1,275	750	273	477	525
Aged 30 to 34	770	425	151	274	345
Aged 35 to 39	585	372	179	193	213
Aged 40 to 44	473	283	130	153	190
Aged 45 to 49	378	210	105	105	168
Aged 50 to 54	220	93	46	47	127
Aged 55 or older	133	63	37	26	70
Percent distribution by age					
Total non-Hispanic whites enrolled	**100.0%**	**100.0%**	**100.0%**	**100.0%**	**100.0%**
Aged 15 to 17	0.9	1.0	1.7	0.7	0.1
Aged 18 to 19	24.3	30.1	30.5	29.9	0.7
Aged 20 to 21	21.9	26.8	18.9	30.2	2.3
Aged 22 to 24	16.9	16.2	12.7	17.8	19.4
Aged 25 to 29	12.0	8.8	10.7	8.0	24.8
Aged 30 to 34	7.2	5.0	5.9	4.6	16.3
Aged 35 to 39	5.5	4.4	7.0	3.2	10.1
Aged 40 to 44	4.4	3.3	5.1	2.6	9.0
Aged 45 to 49	3.6	2.5	4.1	1.8	7.9
Aged 50 to 54	2.1	1.1	1.8	0.8	6.0
Aged 55 or older	1.3	0.7	1.5	0.4	3.3

(continued)

(continued from previous page)

| Percent distribution by type of school | total | undergraduate | | | graduate |
		total	two-year	four-year	
Total non-Hispanic whites enrolled	**100.0%**	**80.1%**	**23.9%**	**56.2%**	**19.9%**
Aged 15 to 17	100.0	96.7	48.4	48.4	3.3
Aged 18 to 19	100.0	99.4	30.1	69.3	0.6
Aged 20 to 21	100.0	97.9	20.6	77.4	2.1
Aged 22 to 24	100.0	77.1	17.9	59.2	22.9
Aged 25 to 29	100.0	58.8	21.4	37.4	41.2
Aged 30 to 34	100.0	55.2	19.6	35.6	44.8
Aged 35 to 39	100.0	63.6	30.6	33.0	36.4
Aged 40 to 44	100.0	59.8	27.5	32.3	40.2
Aged 45 to 49	100.0	55.6	27.8	27.8	44.4
Aged 50 to 54	100.0	42.3	20.9	21.4	57.7
Aged 55 or older	100.0	47.4	27.8	19.5	52.6

Source: Bureau of the Census, Current Population Survey, Internet site <www.census.gov/population/socdemo/ school/ppl-148/tab09.txt>; calculations by New Strategist

Associate's Degrees Earned by Non-Hispanic Whites by Field of Study, 1999–2000

(total number of associate's degrees conferred and number and percent earned by non-Hispanic whites, by field of study, 1999–2000)

	total	earned by non-Hispanic whites	
		number	percent
Total associate's degrees	**564,933**	**408,508**	**72.3%**
Agriculture and natural resources	6,667	6,316	94.7
Architecture and related programs	392	312	79.6
Area, ethnic, and cultural studies	259	119	45.9
Biological, life sciences	1,434	968	67.5
Business	92,274	74,627	80.9
Communications	2,754	2,059	74.8
Communications technologies	1,709	1,245	72.8
Computer and information sciences	20,450	13,451	65.8
Construction trades	2,337	1,978	84.6
Education	8,226	5,698	69.3
Engineering	1,752	1,203	68.7
Engineering-related technologies	35,395	25,110	70.9
English language and literature, letters	947	712	75.2
Foreign languages and literatures	501	320	63.9
Health professions and related sciences	84,081	65,616	78.0
Home economics	8,381	5,292	63.1
Law and legal studies	7,265	5,125	70.5
Liberal arts and sciences, general studies, and humanities	187,454	134,558	71.8
Library science	98	82	83.7
Mathematics	675	400	59.3
Mechanics and repairers	11,614	8,793	75.7
Multi/interdisciplinary studies	11,784	8,564	72.7
Parks, recreation, leisure, and fitness	855	634	74.2
Philosophy and religion	63	46	73.0
Physical sciences	2,460	1,735	70.5
Precision production trades	11,814	9,357	79.2
Protective services	16,298	12,426	76.2
Psychology	1,455	998	68.6
Public administration and services	3,656	2,006	54.9
R.O.T.C. and military technologies	65	23	35.4
Social sciences and history	5,136	3,108	60.5
Theological studies, religious vocations	636	447	70.3
Transportation and material moving	1,021	807	79.0
Visual and performing arts	17,100	12,495	73.1
Not classified	2,798	1,878	67.1

Source: National Center for Education Statistics, Digest of Education Statistics 2001, *Internet site <http://nces.ed.gov/pubsearch/pubsinfo.asp?pubid=2002130>; calculations by New Strategist*

Bachelor's Degrees Earned by Non-Hispanic Whites by Field of Study, 1999–2000

(total number of bachelor's degrees conferred and number and percent earned by non-Hispanic whites, by field of study, 1999–2000)

	total	earned by non-Hispanic whites	
		number	percent
Total bachelor's degrees	**1,237,875**	**928,013**	**75.0%**
Agriculture and natural resources	24,247	21,563	88.9
Architecture and related programs	8,462	6,163	72.8
Area, ethnic, and cultural studies	6,381	3,696	57.9
Biological, life sciences	63,532	45,247	71.2
Business	257,709	186,605	72.4
Communications	55,760	44,015	78.9
Communications technologies	1,150	836	72.7
Computer and information sciences	36,195	22,149	61.2
Construction trades	186	171	91.9
Education	108,168	91,816	84.9
Engineering	58,427	40,052	68.6
Engineering-related technologies	13,872	10,404	75.0
English language and literature, letters	50,920	41,424	81.4
Foreign languages and literatures	14,968	10,554	70.5
Health professions and related sciences	78,458	61,168	78.0
Home economics	17,779	14,540	81.8
Law and legal studies	1,925	1,354	70.3
Liberal arts and sciences, general studies, and humanities	36,104	25,899	71.7
Library science	154	121	78.6
Mathematics	12,070	8,896	73.7
Mechanics and repairers	70	55	78.6
Multi/interdisciplinary studies	27,460	19,319	70.4
Parks, recreation, leisure, and fitness	19,111	15,818	82.8
Philosophy and religion	8,366	6,882	82.3
Physical sciences	18,385	14,197	77.2
Precision production trades	393	322	81.9
Protective services	24,877	17,244	69.3
Psychology	74,060	54,295	73.3
Public administration and services	20,185	13,279	65.8
R.O.T.C. and military technologies	7	7	100.0
Social sciences and history	127,101	93,149	73.3
Theological studies, religious vocations	6,809	5,950	87.4
Transportation and material moving	3,395	2,779	81.9
Visual and performing arts	58,791	46,104	78.4
Not classified	2,398	1,940	80.9

Source: National Center for Education Statistics, Digest of Education Statistics 2001, *Internet site <http://nces.ed.gov/pubsearch/pubsinfo.asp?pubid=2002130>; calculations by New Strategist*

Master's Degrees Earned by Non-Hispanic Whites by Field of Study, 1999–2000

(total number of master's degrees conferred and number and percent earned by non-Hispanic whites, by field of study, 1999–2000)

		earned by non-Hispanic whites	
	total	number	percent
Total master's degrees	**457,056**	**317,999**	**69.6%**
Agriculture and natural resources	4,375	3,310	75.7
Architecture and related programs	4,268	2,601	60.9
Area, ethnic, and cultural studies	1,591	1,023	64.3
Biological, life sciences	6,198	4,309	69.5
Business	112,258	73,252	65.3
Communications	5,169	3,227	62.4
Communications technologies	436	290	66.5
Computer and information sciences	14,264	4,472	31.4
Construction trades	12	5	41.7
Education	124,240	99,300	79.9
Engineering	25,596	11,427	44.6
Engineering-related technologies	914	610	66.7
English language and literature, letters	7,230	5,919	81.9
Foreign languages and literatures	2,780	1,645	59.2
Health professions and related sciences	42,456	33,419	78.7
Home economics	2,830	2,112	74.6
Law and legal studies	3,750	1,375	36.7
Liberal arts and sciences, general studies, and humanities	3,256	2,671	82.0
Library science	4,577	3,948	86.3
Mathematics	3,412	1,794	52.6
Multi/interdisciplinary studies	3,064	2,286	74.6
Parks, recreation, leisure, and fitness	2,478	2,055	82.9
Philosophy and religion	1,329	1,028	77.4
Physical sciences	4,841	2,939	60.7
Precision production trades	5	4	80.0
Protective services	2,609	2,037	78.1
Psychology	14,465	11,088	76.7
Public administration and services	25,594	17,613	68.8
Social sciences and history	14,066	8,784	62.4
Theological studies, religious vocations	5,576	4,072	73.0
Transportation and material moving	697	602	86.4
Visual and performing arts	10,918	7,340	67.2
Not classified	1,802	1,442	80.0

Source: National Center for Education Statistics, Digest of Education Statistics 2001, *Internet site <http://nces.ed.gov/pubsearch/pubsinfo.asp?pubid=2002130>; calculations by New Strategist*

Doctoral Degrees Earned by Non-Hispanic Whites by Field of Study, 1999–2000

(total number of doctoral degrees conferred and number and percent earned by non-Hispanic whites, by field of study, 1999–2000)

	total	earned by non-Hispanic whites number	earned by non-Hispanic whites percent
Total doctoral degrees	**44,808**	**27,520**	**61.4%**
Agriculture and natural resources	1,181	559	47.3
Architecture and related programs	129	68	52.7
Area, ethnic, and cultural studies	217	140	64.5
Biological, life sciences	4,867	2,880	59.2
Business	1,196	665	55.6
Communications	347	238	68.6
Communications technologies	10	5	50.0
Computer and information sciences	777	302	38.9
Education	6,830	4,915	72.0
Engineering	5,384	2,001	37.2
Engineering-related technologies	6	2	33.3
English language and literature, letters	1,628	1,284	78.9
Foreign languages and literatures	915	513	56.1
Health professions and related sciences	2,676	1,717	64.2
Home economics	357	238	66.7
Law and legal studies	74	11	14.9
Liberal arts and sciences, general studies, and humanities	83	69	83.1
Library science	68	36	52.9
Mathematics	1,106	482	43.6
Multi/interdisciplinary studies	384	279	72.7
Parks, recreation, leisure, and fitness	134	104	77.6
Philosophy and religion	586	448	76.5
Physical sciences	4,018	2,115	52.6
Protective services	52	40	76.9
Psychology	4,310	3,466	80.4
Public administration and services	537	376	70.0
Social sciences and history	4,095	2,645	64.6
Theological studies, religious vocations	1,643	1,070	65.1
Visual and performing arts	1,127	790	70.1
Not classified	71	62	87.3

Source: National Center for Education Statistics, Digest of Education Statistics 2001, *Internet site <http://nces.ed.gov/pubsearch/pubsinfo.asp?pubid=2002130>; calculations by New Strategist*

First-Professional Degrees Earned by Non-Hispanic Whites by Field of Study, 1999–2000

(total number of first-professional degrees conferred and number and percent earned by non-Hispanic whites, by field of study, 1999–2000)

	total	earned by non-Hispanic whites	
		number	percent
Total first-professional degrees	**80,259**	**59,601**	**74.3%**
Dentistry (D.D.S. or D.M.D.)	4,250	2,658	62.5
Medicine (M.D.)	15,286	10,475	68.5
Optometry (O.D.)	1,293	865	66.9
Osteopathic medicine (D.O.)	2,236	1,770	79.2
Pharmacy (Pharm.D.)	5,669	3,725	65.7
Podiatry (Pod.D., D.P., or D.P.M.)	569	409	71.9
Veterinary medicine (D.V.M.)	2,251	2,064	91.7
Chiropractic (D.C. or D.C.M.)	3,809	2,880	75.6
Naturopathic medicine	202	171	84.7
Law (LL.B. or J.D.)	38,152	29,920	78.4
Theology (M.Div., M.H.L., B.D., or Ord. and M.H.L./Rav.)	6,129	4,493	73.3
Other	413	171	41.4

Source: National Center for Education Statistics, Digest of Education Statistics 2001, *Internet site <http://nces.ed.gov/pubsearch/pubsinfo.asp?pubid=2002130>; calculations by New Strategist*

Most Whites Say Their Health Is Excellent or Good

Eighty-one percent of whites report being in excellent or good health, while just 19 percent say their health is only fair or poor. Because whites comprise the majority of Americans, these proportions closely match those of the total population.

Health indicators for whites are close to the average on most measures, with a few exceptions. The incidence of AIDS, tuberculosis, and syphilis is much lower among whites than among the total population. The suicide rate for whites is slightly higher than average.

Seventy-nine percent of all births in 2000 were to white women, but only 58 percent were to non-Hispanic white women. In six states (Arizona, California, Hawaii, New Mexico, New York, and Texas), non-Hispanic whites account for a minority of births.

Among all racial and ethnic groups, non-Hispanic whites are least likely to be without health insurance. Only 10 percent are uninsured. Twenty percent of non-Hispanic whites are disabled, about the same rate as for the population as a whole.

Among non-Hispanic whites, heart disease and cancer are the two leading causes of death, accounting for 54 percent of the total. Alzheimer's disease is the eighth leading cause of death among non-Hispanic whites.

■ As the white population ages, the percentage of Americans with disabilities will rise.

Non-Hispanic whites account for a minority of births to women under age 20

(non-Hispanic white share of total births, by age of mother, 2000)

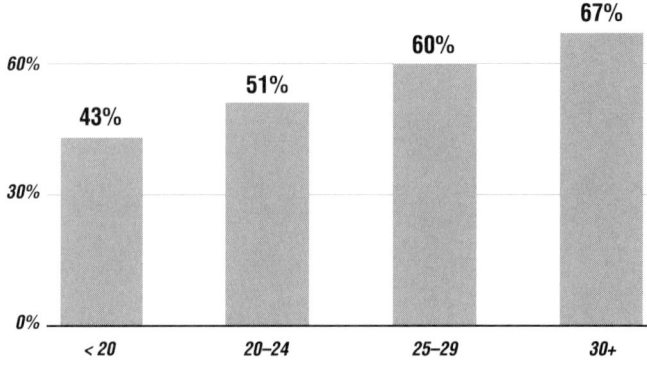

White and Non-Hispanic White Health Status, 2000

"Would you say your own health, in general, is excellent, good, fair, or poor?"

(percent of total people, whites, and non-Hispanic whites aged 18 or older responding, 2000)

	excellent	good	fair	poor
Total	**31%**	**49%**	**16%**	**5%**
White	33	48	15	4
Non-Hispanic white	33	48	14	4

Source: 2000 General Social Survey, National Opinion Research Center, University of Chicago; calculations by New Strategist

Health Indicators for Whites, 1998

(selected indicators of total and white health status, and index of white health indicators to total, 1998)

	total population indicator	white indicator	index of white to total
Infant mortality rate (deaths before age 1 per 1,000 live births)	7.2	6.0	83
Total deaths per 100,000 population	471.7	450.3	95
Motor vehicle crash deaths per 100,000 population	15.7	15.7	100
Work-related injury deaths per 100,000 people aged 16 or older	2.9	2.9	100
Suicides per 100,000 population	10.4	11.2	108
Homicides per 100,000 population	7.3	4.3	59
Lung cancer deaths per 100,000 population	37.0	36.8	99
Female breast cancer deaths per 100,000 population	18.8	18.3	97
Cardiovascular disease deaths per 100,000 population	161.2	154.1	96
Heart disease deaths per 100,000 population	126.7	122.0	96
Stroke deaths per 100,000 population	25.1	23.3	93
Reported incidence of AIDS per 100,000 population	19.5	8.5	44
Reported incidence of tuberculosis per 100,000 population	6.8	2.3	34
Reported incidence of syphilis per 100,000 population	2.6	0.5	19
Prevalence of low birth weight, as percent of total live births	7.6	6.5	86
Births to girls aged 10 to 17, as percent of total live births	4.6	3.5	76
Percent of mothers without care, first trimester of pregnancy	17.2	15.2	88
Percent under age 18 living in poverty	18.9	15.1	80
Percent living in counties exceeding U.S. air quality standards	23.5	22.6	96

Note: The index for each indicator is calculated by dividing the white figure by the total population figure and multiplying by 100. For example, the index of 95 in the second row indicates that the white death rate is 5 percent below the rate for the total population.
Source: National Center for Health Statistics, Healthy People 2000 Final Review, 2001; *calculations by New Strategist*

Births to White Women by Age, 2000

(total number of births, number and percent distribution of births to white women, and white share of total, by age, 2000)

| | | non-Hispanic white | | |
	total	number	percent distribution	share of total
Total births	**4,058,814**	**3,194,005**	**100.0%**	**78.7%**
Under age 15	8,519	4,439	0.1	52.1
Aged 15 to 19	468,990	333,013	10.4	71.0
Aged 20 to 24	1,017,806	772,811	24.2	75.9
Aged 25 to 29	1,087,547	874,180	27.4	80.4
Aged 30 to 34	929,278	764,708	23.9	82.3
Aged 35 to 39	452,057	368,711	11.5	81.6
Aged 40 to 44	90,013	72,414	2.3	80.4
Aged 45 or older	4,604	3,729	0.1	81.0

Source: National Center for Health Statistics, Births: Final Data for 2000, *National Vital Statistics Report, Vol. 50, No. 5, 2002; calculations by New Strategist*

Births to Non-Hispanic White Women by Age, 2000

(total number of births, number and percent distribution of births to non-Hispanic white women, and non-Hispanic white share of total, by age, 2000)

| | | non-Hispanic white | | |
	total	number	percent distribution	share of total
Total births	**4,058,814**	**2,362,968**	**100.0%**	**58.2%**
Under age 15	8,519	1,840	0.1	21.6
Aged 15 to 19	468,990	204,056	8.6	43.5
Aged 20 to 24	1,017,806	523,971	22.2	51.5
Aged 25 to 29	1,087,547	651,445	27.6	59.9
Aged 30 to 34	929,278	617,371	26.1	66.4
Aged 35 to 39	452,057	302,576	12.8	66.9
Aged 40 to 44	90,013	58,631	2.5	65.1
Aged 45 or older	4,604	3,078	0.1	66.9

Source: National Center for Health Statistics, Births: Final Data for 2000, *National Vital Statistics Report, Vol. 50, No. 5, 2002; calculations by New Strategist*

Births to White Women by Birth Order, 2000

(number and percent distribution of births to white women, by birth order, 2000)

	number	percent distribution
Births to whites	**3,194,005**	**100.0%**
First child	1,282,493	40.2
Second child	1,048,894	32.8
Third child	533,629	16.7
Fourth or later child	314,789	9.9

Note: Numbers will not add to total because not stated is not shown.
Source: National Center for Health Statistics, Births: Final Data for 2000, *National Vital Statistics Report, Vol. 50, No. 5, 2002; calculations by New Strategist*

Births to Non-Hispanic White Women by Birth Order, 2000

(number and percent distribution of births to non-Hispanic white women, by birth order, 2000)

	number	percent distribution
Births to non-Hispanic whites	**2,362,968**	**100.0%**
First child	974,641	41.2
Second child	796,440	33.7
Third child	379,234	16.0
Fourth or later child	204,101	8.6

Note: Numbers will not add to total because not stated is not shown.
Source: National Center for Health Statistics, Births: Final Data for 2000, *National Vital Statistics Report, Vol. 50, No. 5, 2002; calculations by New Strategist*

Births to Unmarried White Women by Age, 2000

(total number of births to whites, number of births to unmarried white women, and unmarried share of total, by age, 2000)

		unmarried whites	
	total	number	share of total
Births to whites	**3,194,005**	**866,355**	**27.1%**
Under age 15	4,439	4,173	94.0
Aged 15 to 19	333,013	242,505	72.8
Aged 20 to 24	772,811	322,075	41.7
Aged 25 to 29	874,180	162,667	18.6
Aged 30 to 34	764,708	83,128	10.9
Aged 35 to 39	368,711	41,364	11.2
Aged 40 or older	76,143	10,443	13.7

Source: National Center for Health Statistics, Births: Final Data for 2000, *National Vital Statistics Report, Vol. 50, No. 5, 2002*

Births to Unmarried Non-Hispanic White Women by Age, 2000

(total number of births to non-Hispanic whites, number to unmarried non-Hispanic white women, and unmarried share of total, by age, 2000)

		unmarried non-Hispanic whites	
	total	number	share of total
Births to non-Hispanic whites	**2,362,968**	**521,686**	**22.1%**
Under age 15	1,840	1,754	95.3
Aged 15 to 19	204,056	149,174	73.1
Aged 20 to 24	523,971	200,383	38.2
Aged 25 to 29	651,445	91,142	14.0
Aged 30 to 34	617,371	47,267	7.7
Aged 35 to 39	302,576	25,398	8.4
Aged 40 or older	61,709	6,568	10.6

Source: National Center for Health Statistics, Births: Final Data for 2000, *National Vital Statistics Report, Vol. 50, No. 5, 2002*

Births to White Women by State, 2000

(total number of births, number and percent distribution of births to white women, and white share of total, by state, 2000)

	total	white births		
		number	percent distribtution	share of total
Total births	**4,058,814**	**3,194,005**	**100.0%**	**78.7%**
Alabama	63,299	42,061	1.3	66.4
Alaska	9,974	6,364	0.2	63.8
Arizona	85,273	74,760	2.3	87.7
Arkansas	37,783	29,071	0.9	76.9
California	531,959	429,638	13.5	80.8
Colorado	65,438	59,684	1.9	91.2
Connecticut	43,026	35,819	1.1	83.2
Delaware	11,051	8,009	0.3	72.5
District of Columbia	7,666	2,323	0.1	30.3
Florida	204,125	150,608	4.7	73.8
Georgia	132,644	84,646	2.7	63.8
Hawaii	17,551	4,022	0.1	22.9
Idaho	20,366	19,705	0.6	96.8
Illinois	185,036	142,390	4.5	77.0
Indiana	87,699	76,845	2.4	87.6
Iowa	38,266	35,887	1.1	93.8
Kansas	39,666	35,297	1.1	89.0
Kentucky	56,029	50,216	1.6	89.6
Louisiana	67,898	38,125	1.2	56.2
Maine	13,603	13,185	0.4	96.9
Maryland	74,316	45,554	1.4	61.3
Massachusetts	81,614	68,553	2.1	84.0
Michigan	136,171	107,362	3.4	78.8
Minnesota	67,604	58,431	1.8	86.4
Mississippi	44,075	23,540	0.7	53.4
Missouri	76,463	63,168	2.0	82.6
Montana	10,957	9,470	0.3	86.4
Nebraska	24,646	22,261	0.7	90.3
Nevada	30,829	26,033	0.8	84.4
New Hampshire	14,609	14,070	0.4	96.3
New Jersey	115,632	84,844	2.7	73.4

(continued)

(continued from previous page)

| | total | white births | | |
		number	percent distribtution	share of total
New Mexico	27,223	22,890	0.7%	84.1%
New York	258,737	183,668	5.8	71.0
North Carolina	120,311	86,428	2.7	71.8
North Dakota	7,676	6,709	0.2	87.4
Ohio	155,472	128,527	4.0	82.7
Oklahoma	49,782	38,787	1.2	77.9
Oregon	45,804	41,710	1.3	91.1
Pennsylvania	146,281	121,256	3.8	82.9
Rhode Island	12,505	10,795	0.3	86.3
South Carolina	56,114	35,341	1.1	63.0
South Dakota	10,345	8,424	0.3	81.4
Tennessee	79,611	61,224	1.9	76.9
Texas	363,414	309,552	9.7	85.2
Utah	47,353	44,896	1.4	94.8
Vermont	6,500	6,367	0.2	98.0
Virginia	98,938	71,187	2.2	72.0
Washington	81,036	68,676	2.2	84.7
West Virginia	20,865	19,967	0.6	95.7
Wisconsin	69,326	59,790	1.9	86.2
Wyoming	6,253	5,870	0.2	93.9

Source: National Center for Health Statistics, Births: Final Data for 2000, *National Vital Statistics Report, Vol. 50, No. 5, 2002; calculations by New Strategist*

Births to Non-Hispanic White Women by State, 2000

(total number of births, number and percent distribution of births to non-Hispanic white women, and non-Hispanic white share of total, by state, 2000)

	total	non-Hispanic white births number	non-Hispanic white births percent distribtution	non-Hispanic white births share of total
Total births	**4,058,814**	**2,362,968**	**100.0%**	**58.2%**
Alabama	63,299	40,154	1.7	63.4
Alaska	9,974	5,770	0.2	57.9
Arizona	85,273	39,873	1.7	46.8
Arkansas	37,783	26,657	1.1	70.6
California	531,959	171,552	7.3	32.2
Colorado	65,438	41,822	1.8	63.9
Connecticut	43,026	28,785	1.2	66.9
Delaware	11,051	6,999	0.3	63.3
District of Columbia	7,666	1,463	0.1	19.1
Florida	204,125	106,200	4.5	52.0
Georgia	132,644	70,521	3.0	53.2
Hawaii	17,551	3,285	0.1	18.7
Idaho	20,366	17,021	0.7	83.6
Illinois	185,036	103,267	4.4	55.8
Indiana	87,699	71,214	3.0	81.2
Iowa	38,266	33,608	1.4	87.8
Kansas	39,666	30,181	1.3	76.1
Kentucky	56,029	49,133	2.1	87.7
Louisiana	67,898	36,592	1.5	53.9
Maine	13,603	13,019	0.6	95.7
Maryland	74,316	41,013	1.7	55.2
Massachusetts	81,614	60,419	2.6	74.0
Michigan	136,171	92,551	3.9	68.0
Minnesota	67,604	52,098	2.2	77.1
Mississippi	44,075	22,879	1.0	51.9
Missouri	76,463	60,502	2.6	79.1
Montana	10,957	8,835	0.4	80.6
Nebraska	24,646	19,200	0.8	77.9
Nevada	30,829	15,724	0.7	51.0
New Hampshire	14,609	13,135	0.6	89.9
New Jersey	115,632	64,098	2.7	55.4

(continued)

(continued from previous page)

| | total | non-Hispanic white births | | |
		number	percent distribtution	share of total
New Mexico	27,223	9,055	0.4%	33.3%
New York	258,737	125,365	5.3	48.5
North Carolina	120,311	73,966	3.1	61.5
North Dakota	7,676	6,395	0.3	83.3
Ohio	155,472	124,378	5.3	80.0
Oklahoma	49,782	34,120	1.4	68.5
Oregon	45,804	34,291	1.5	74.9
Pennsylvania	146,281	113,556	4.8	77.6
Rhode Island	12,505	7,825	0.3	62.6
South Carolina	56,114	33,175	1.4	59.1
South Dakota	10,345	8,224	0.3	79.5
Tennessee	79,611	58,028	2.5	72.9
Texas	363,414	142,142	6.0	39.1
Utah	47,353	38,809	1.6	82.0
Vermont	6,500	6,173	0.3	95.0
Virginia	98,938	63,528	2.7	64.2
Washington	81,036	55,774	2.4	68.8
West Virginia	20,865	19,867	0.8	95.2
Wisconsin	69,326	55,418	2.3	79.9
Wyoming	6,253	5,309	0.2	84.9

Source: National Center for Health Statistics, Births: Final Data for 2000, *National Vital Statistics Report, Vol. 50, No. 5, 2002; calculations by New Strategist*

Health Insurance Coverage of Whites by Age, 2000

(number and percent distribution of whites by age and health insurance coverage status, 2000; numbers in thousands)

| | | covered by private or government health insurance | | | | | | | |
| | | private health insurance | | | government health insurance | | | | |
	total	total	total	employ-ment based	total	Medicaid	Medicare	Military	not covered
Total whites	226,401	197,153	169,752	149,313	52,790	19,448	32,048	6,540	29,248
Under 18	56,817	50,653	42,247	39,667	11,201	9,671	296	1,543	6,164
Aged 18–24	21,532	16,021	14,583	12,000	2,224	1,588	88	598	5,511
Aged 25–34	29,867	23,847	22,010	20,795	2,454	1,649	305	658	6,020
Aged 35–44	36,691	31,426	29,591	27,931	2,781	1,684	608	846	5,265
Aged 45–54	31,964	28,429	26,720	24,942	2,808	1,284	984	921	3,534
Aged 55–64	20,409	17,824	15,926	13,978	3,095	1,164	1,641	761	2,586
Aged 65+	29,122	28,953	18,677	9,999	28,227	2,407	28,128	1,212	169
Total whites	100.0%	87.1%	75.0%	66.0%	23.3%	8.6%	14.2%	2.9%	12.9%
Under 18	100.0	89.2	74.4	69.8	19.7	17.0	0.5	2.7	10.8
Aged 18–24	100.0	74.4	67.7	55.7	10.3	7.4	0.4	2.8	25.6
Aged 25–34	100.0	79.8	73.7	69.6	8.2	5.5	1.0	2.2	20.2
Aged 35–44	100.0	85.7	80.6	76.1	7.6	4.6	1.7	2.3	14.3
Aged 45–54	100.0	88.9	83.6	78.0	8.8	4.0	3.1	2.9	11.1
Aged 55–64	100.0	87.3	78.0	68.5	15.2	5.7	8.0	3.7	12.7
Aged 65+	100.0	99.4	64.1	34.3	96.9	8.3	96.6	4.2	0.6

Note: Numbers will not add to total because some people have more than one type of health insurance.
Source: Bureau of the Census, Current Population Survey, Internet site <http://ferret.bls.census.gov/macro/032001/health/h01_002.htm>

Health Insurance Coverage of Non-Hispanic Whites by Age, 2000

(number and percent distribution of non-Hispanic whites by age and health insurance coverage status, 2000; numbers in thousands)

| | | covered by private or government health insurance | | | | | | | |
| | | private health insurance | | | government health insurance | | | | |
	total	total	total	employ- ment based	total	Medicaid	Medicare	Military	not covered
Total non-Hispanic whites	**194,196**	**175,319**	**154,272**	**134,903**	**45,117**	**13,591**	**29,938**	**6,075**	**18,877**
Under 18	45,433	42,134	37,052	34,742	7,421	6,035	228	1,408	3,300
Aged 18–24	17,534	14,039	12,992	10,601	1,714	1,142	74	537	3,494
Aged 25–34	24,501	20,698	19,300	18,203	1,926	1,207	272	584	3,803
Aged 35–44	31,925	28,341	26,855	25,325	2,333	1,313	552	787	3,584
Aged 45–54	28,887	26,295	24,869	23,178	2,440	1,009	897	875	2,592
Aged 55–64	18,608	16,590	15,014	13,165	2,726	949	1,442	729	2,018
Aged 65+	27,308	27,223	18,189	9,689	26,558	1,936	26,474	1,156	85
Total non-Hispanic whites	**100.0%**	**90.3%**	**79.4%**	**69.5%**	**23.2%**	**7.0%**	**15.4%**	**3.1%**	**9.7%**
Under 18	100.0	92.7	81.6	76.5	16.3	13.3	0.5	3.1	7.3
Aged 18–24	100.0	80.1	74.1	60.5	9.8	6.5	0.4	3.1	19.9
Aged 25–34	100.0	84.5	78.8	74.3	7.9	4.9	1.1	2.4	15.5
Aged 35–44	100.0	88.8	84.1	79.3	7.3	4.1	1.7	2.5	11.2
Aged 45–54	100.0	91.0	86.1	80.2	8.4	3.5	3.1	3.0	9.0
Aged 55–64	100.0	89.2	80.7	70.7	14.6	5.1	7.7	3.9	10.8
Aged 65+	100.0	99.7	66.6	35.5	97.3	7.1	96.9	4.2	0.3

Note: Numbers will not add to total because some people have more than one type of health insurance.
Source: Bureau of the Census, Current Population Survey, Internet site <http://ferret.bls.census.gov/macro/032001/health/h01_003.htm>

Acute Health Conditions among Whites, 1996

(number of acute conditions among total people and whites and white share of total, rate of acute conditions per 100 total people and whites and index of white rate to total, by type of acute condition, 1996; numbers in thousands)

	number of conditions			rate per 100 population		
		white			white	
	total people	number	share of total	total people	rate	index of white rate to total
Total acute conditions	**432,001**	**371,304**	**85.9%**	**163.5**	**168.7**	**103**
Infective and parasitic diseases	54,192	46,298	85.4	20.5	21.0	102
Common childhood diseases	3,118	2,428	77.9	1.2	1.1	92
Intestinal virus	15,980	13,801	86.4	6.0	6.3	105
Viral infections	15,067	12,201	81.0	5.7	5.5	96
Other	20,027	17,868	89.2	7.6	8.1	107
Respiratory conditions	**208,623**	**179,091**	**85.8**	**78.9**	**81.4**	**103**
Common cold	62,251	51,261	82.3	23.6	23.3	99
Other acute upper respiratory infections	29,866	26,169	87.6	11.3	11.9	105
Influenza	95,049	82,048	86.3	36.0	37.3	104
Acute bronchitis	12,116	11,485	94.8	4.6	5.2	113
Pneumonia	4,791	4,376	91.3	1.8	2.0	111
Other respiratory conditions	4,550	3,751	82.4	1.7	1.7	100
Digestive system conditions	**17,646**	**14,971**	**84.8**	**6.7**	**6.8**	**101**
Dental conditions	2,970	2,023	68.1	1.1	0.9	82
Indigestion, nausea, and vomiting	7,963	6,748	84.7	3.0	3.1	103
Other digestive conditions	6,713	6,199	92.3	2.5	2.8	112
Injuries	**57,279**	**48,607**	**84.9**	**21.7**	**22.1**	**102**
Fractures and dislocations	8,465	7,853	92.8	3.2	3.6	113
Sprains and strains	12,977	10,428	80.4	4.9	4.7	96
Open wounds and lacerations	9,027	7,674	85.0	3.4	3.5	103
Contusions and superficial injuries	9,979	8,229	82.5	3.8	3.7	97
Other current injuries	16,832	14,422	85.7	6.4	6.6	103
Selected other acute conditions	**63,090**	**55,090**	**87.3**	**23.9**	**25.0**	**105**
Eye conditions	3,478	2,875	82.7	1.3	1.3	100
Acute ear infections	21,766	19,823	91.1	8.2	9.0	110
Other ear conditions	3,833	3,541	92.4	1.5	1.6	107
Acute urinary conditions	8,405	7,267	86.5	3.2	3.3	103
Disorders of menstruation	839	839	100.0	0.3	0.4	133
Other disorders of female genital tract	1,597	1,474	92.3	0.6	0.7	117
Delivery and other conditions of pregnancy	3,279	2,744	83.7	1.2	1.2	100

(continued)

(continued from previous page)

	number of conditions			rate per 100 population		
		white			white	
	total people	number	share of total	total people	rate	index of white rate to total
Skin conditions	4,986	4,263	85.5%	1.9	1.9	100
Acute musculoskeletal conditions	8,461	7,082	83.7	3.2	3.2	100
Headache, excluding migraine	1,738	1,094	62.9	0.7	0.5	71
Fever, unspecified	4,708	4,089	86.9	1.8	1.9	106
All other acute conditions	**31,170**	**27,247**	**87.4**	**11.8**	**12.4**	**105**

Note: The acute conditions shown here are those that caused people to restrict their activity for at least half a day or to contact a physician about the illness or injury. (–) means not applicable or sample is too small to make a reliable estimate. The index is calculated by dividing the white rate by the rate for the total population and multiplying by 100.
Source: National Center for Health Statistics, Current Estimates *from the National Health Interview Survey, 1996, Series 10, No. 200, 1999; calculations by New Strategist*

Chronic Health Conditions among Whites, 1996

(number of chronic conditions among total people and whites and white share of total, rate of chronic conditions per 1,000 total people and whites and index of white rate to total, by type of chronic condition, 1996; numbers in thousands)

	number of conditions			rate per 1,000 population		
		white			white	
	total people	number	share of total	total people	rate	index of white rate to total
Selected skin and musculoskeletal conditions						
Arthritis	33,638	29,309	87.1%	127.3	133.2	105
Gout, including gouty arthritis	2,487	2,122	85.3	9.4	9.6	103
Intervertebral disc disorders	6,700	6,096	91.0	25.4	27.7	109
Bone spur or tendinitis, unspecified	2,934	2,735	93.2	11.1	12.4	112
Disorders of bone or cartilage	1,730	1,596	92.3	6.5	7.3	112
Trouble with bunions	2,360	2,151	91.1	8.9	9.8	110
Bursitis, unclassified	5,006	4,511	90.1	18.9	20.5	108
Sebaceous skin cyst	1,190	1,087	91.3	4.5	4.9	110
Trouble with acne	4,952	4,333	87.5	18.7	19.7	105
Psoriasis	2,940	2,814	95.7	11.1	12.8	115
Dermatitis	8,249	6,932	84.0	31.2	31.5	101
Trouble with dry skin, unclassified	6,627	5,595	84.4	25.1	25.4	101
Trouble with ingrown nails	5,807	5,102	87.9	22.0	23.2	105
Trouble with corns and calluses	3,778	2,899	76.7	14.3	13.2	92
Impairments						
Visual impairment	8,280	7,126	86.1	31.3	32.4	103
Color blindness	2,811	2,656	94.5	10.6	12.1	114
Cataracts	7,022	6,339	90.3	26.6	28.8	108
Glaucoma	2,595	2,186	84.2	9.8	9.9	101
Hearing impairment	22,044	20,332	92.2	83.4	92.4	111
Tinnitus	7,866	7,216	91.7	29.8	32.8	110
Speech impairment	2,720	1,970	72.4	10.3	9.0	87
Absence of extremities	1,285	1,188	92.5	4.9	5.4	110
Paralysis of extremities, complete or partial	2,138	1,603	75.0	8.1	7.3	90
Deformity or orthopedic impairment	29,499	25,577	86.7	111.6	116.2	104
Back	16,905	14,907	88.2	64.0	67.7	106
Upper extremities	4,170	3,639	87.3	15.8	16.5	105
Lower extremitites	12,696	10,630	83.7	48.0	48.3	101

(continued)

(continued from previous page)

| | number of conditions | | | rate per 1,000 population | | |
| | | white | | | white | |
	total people	number	share of total	total people	rate	index of white rate to total
Selected digestive conditions						
Ulcer	3,709	2,934	79.1%	14.0	13.3	95
Hernia of abdominal cavity	4,470	4,254	95.2	16.9	19.3	114
Gastritis or duodenitis	3,729	3,185	85.4	14.1	14.5	103
Frequent indigestion	6,420	5,685	88.6	24.3	25.8	106
Enteritis or colitis	1,686	1,563	92.7	6.4	7.1	111
Spastic colon	2,083	2,015	96.7	7.9	9.2	116
Diverticula of intestines	2,529	2,462	97.4	9.6	11.2	117
Frequent constipation	3,149	2,659	84.4	11.9	12.1	102
Selected conditions of the genitourinary, nervous, endocrine, metabolic, and blood and blood-forming systems						
Goiter or other disorders of the thyroid	4,598	4,140	90.0	17.4	18.8	108
Diabetes	7,627	5,635	73.9	28.9	25.6	89
Anemias	3,457	2,601	75.2	13.1	11.8	90
Epilepsy	1,335	1,084	81.2	5.1	4.9	97
Migraine headache	11,546	9,828	85.1	43.7	44.7	102
Neuralgia or neuritis, unspecified	353	317	89.8	1.3	1.4	111
Kidney trouble	2,553	2,372	92.9	9.7	10.8	111
Bladder trouble	3,139	2,867	91.3	11.9	13.0	109
Diseases of prostate	2,803	2,583	92.2	10.6	11.7	111
Diseases of female genital organs	4,420	3,515	79.5	16.7	16.0	96
Selected circulatory conditions						
Rheumatic fever with or without heart disease	1,759	1,633	92.8	6.7	7.4	111
Heart disease	20,653	18,336	88.8	78.2	83.3	107
Ischemic heart disease	7,672	7,130	92.9	29.0	32.4	112
Heart rhythm disorders	8,716	7,654	87.8	33.0	34.8	105
Tachycardia or rapid heart	2,310	2,129	92.2	8.7	9.7	111
Heart murmurs	4,783	4,066	85.0	18.1	18.5	102
Other and unspecified heart rhythm disorders	1,624	1,459	89.8	6.1	6.6	109
Other selected diseases of heart, excluding hypertension	4,265	3,552	83.3	16.1	16.1	100
High blood pressure (hypertension)	28,314	23,122	81.7	107.1	105.1	98
Cerebrovascular disease	2,999	2,592	86.4	11.3	11.8	104
Hardening of the arteries	1,556	1,467	94.3	5.9	6.7	113
Varicose veins of lower extremities	7,399	6,500	87.8	28.0	29.5	105
Hemorrhoids	8,531	7,798	91.4	32.3	35.4	110

(continued)

(continued from previous page)

	number of conditions			rate per 1,000 population		
	total people	white		total people	white	
		number	share of total		rate	index of white rate to total
Selected respiratory conditions						
Chronic bronchitis	14,150	11,970	84.6%	53.5	54.4	102
Asthma	14,596	11,763	80.6	55.2	53.5	97
Hay fever or allergic rhinitis without asthma	23,721	20,428	86.1	89.8	92.8	103
Chronic sinusitis	33,161	27,817	83.9	125.5	126.4	101
Deviated nasal septum	1,985	1,964	98.9	7.5	8.9	119
Chronic disease of tonsils or adenoids	2,513	2,150	85.6	9.5	9.8	103
Emphysema	1,821	1,684	92.5	6.9	7.7	111

Note: Chronic conditions are those that last longer than three months or belong to a group of conditions considered chronic regardless of when they began. The index is calculated by dividing the white rate by the rate for the total population and multiplying by 100.
Source: National Center for Health Statistics, Current Estimates from the National Health Interview Survey, 1996, *Series 10, No. 200, 1999; calculations by New Strategist*

Physician Office Visits by Whites, 1999

(number and percent distribution of physician office visits by whites and number of visits per person per year, by age, 1999)

	number of visits (in 000s)	percent distribution	per person per year
Total visits by whites	**654,712**	**100.0%**	**2.9**
Under age 15	95,373	14.6	2.0
Aged 15 to 24	49,875	7.6	1.7
Aged 25 to 44	161,500	24.7	2.4
Aged 45 to 64	175,226	26.8	3.5
Aged 65 to 74	82,018	12.5	5.3
Aged 75 or older	90,720	13.9	6.7

Source: National Center for Health Statistics, National Ambulatory Medical Care Survey: 1999 Summary, Advance Data, *No. 322, 2001; calculations by New Strategist*

Non-Hispanic Whites with Disabilities by Sex and Age, 1997

(total number of non-Hispanic whites and number and percent with disabilities, by sex, age, and severity of disability, 1997; numbers in thousands)

| | | with a disability | | | | | |
| | | total | | severe | | needs assistance | |
	total	number	percent	number	percent	number	percent
Total non-Hispanic whites	**193,234**	**39,478**	**20.4%**	**23,627**	**12.2%**	**7,413**	**3.8%**
Under age 15	38,505	3,173	8.2	1,492	3.9	127	0.3
Aged 15 to 24	24,307	2,727	11.2	1,206	5.0	286	1.2
Aged 25 to 64	103,353	19,239	18.6	11,386	11.0	2,823	2.7
Aged 65 or older	27,069	14,338	53.0	9,544	35.3	4,177	15.4
Non-Hispanic white females	**98,570**	**21,212**	**21.5**	**13,167**	**13.4**	**4,425**	**4.5**
Under age 15	18,863	1,119	5.9	512	2.7	56	0.3
aged 15 to 24	12,071	1,225	10.2	595	4.9	129	1.1
aged 25 to 64	51,982	10,079	19.4	5,956	11.5	1,469	2.8
aged 65 or older	15,655	8,787	56.1	6,105	39.0	2,771	17.7
Non-Hispanic white males	**94,664**	**18,266**	**19.3**	**10,460**	**11.0**	**2,988**	**3.2**
Under age 15	19,642	2,054	10.5	980	5.0	71	0.4
aged 15 to 24	12,236	1,502	12.3	611	5.0	157	1.3
aged 25 to 64	51,372	9,160	17.8	5,430	10.6	1,354	2.6
aged 65 or older	11,414	5,550	48.6	3,439	30.1	1,406	12.3

Note: For the definition of disability, see glossary.
Source: Bureau of the Census, Americans with Disabilities: 1997, *detailed tables from Current Population Reports P70-73, 2001*

Whites with Disabilities by Employment Status and Earnings, 1997

(total number of whites aged 21 to 64, number and percent employed, median earnings, and index of earnings to total, by disability status, 1997)

	total (in 000s)	employed number (in 000s)	employed percent	median earnings	index of earnings by disability status to total white earnings
Total whites	**127,263**	**101,111**	**79.5%**	**$23,657**	**100**
Not disabled	**105,026**	**89,286**	**85.0**	**24,382**	**103**
Disabled	**22,236**	**11,825**	**53.2**	**18,396**	**78**
Not severely	8,946	7,367	82.3	20,950	89
Severely	13,290	4,459	33.6	13,780	58

Note: For the definition of disability, see glossary.
Source: Bureau of the Census, Americans with Disabilities: 1997, *detailed tables from Current Population Reports P70-73, 2001; calculations by New Strategist*

Non-Hispanic Whites with Disabilities by Employment Status and Earnings, 1997

(total number of non-Hispanic whites aged 21 to 64, number and percent employed, median earnings, and index of earnings to total, by disability status, 1997)

	total (in 000s)	employed number (in 000s)	employed percent	median earnings	index of earnings by disability status to total non-Hispanic white earnings
Total non-Hispanic whites	**112,457**	**90,387**	**80.4%**	**24,656**	**100**
Not disabled	**92,371**	**79,474**	**86.0**	**25,474**	**103**
Disabled	**20,085**	**10,913**	**54.3**	**18,936**	**77**
Not severely	8,299	6,860	82.7	21,413	89
Severely	11,786	4,052	34.4	14,255	58

Note: For the definition of disability, see the glossary.
Source: Bureau of the Census, Americans with Disabilities: 1997, *detailed tables from Current Population Reports P70-73, 2001; calculations by New Strategist*

AIDS Cases among Non-Hispanic Whites, through June 2000

(total number of AIDS cases diagnosed, number diagnosed among non-Hispanic whites, and non-Hispanic white share of total, by sex and age at diagnosis, through June 2000)

	total	non-Hispanic whites	
		number	share of total
Total AIDS cases	**729,326**	**324,730**	**44.5%**
Males aged 13 or older	601,471	295,990	49.2
Females aged 13 or older	119,454	27,205	22.8
Children under age 13	8,401	1,535	18.3

Source: National Center for Health Statistics, Health United States, 2001; *calculations by New Strategist*

Leading Causes of Death among Whites, 1999

(total number of deaths among whites, and number and percent of deaths accounted for by the ten leading causes of death for whites, 1999)

		number	*percent*
Total white deaths		**2,061,348**	**100.0%**
1.	Diseases of heart	635,118	30.8
2.	Malignant neoplasms	477,238	23.2
3.	Cerebrovascular diseases	144,827	7.0
4.	Chronic lower respiratory diseases	114,735	5.6
5.	Accidents	82,245	4.0
6.	Pneumonia and influenza	56,694	2.8
7.	Diabetes mellitus	54,599	2.6
8.	Alzheimer's disease	41,877	2.0
9.	Nephritis, nephrotic syndrome, nephrosis	28,041	1.4
10.	Suicide	26,300	1.3
	All other causes	399,674	19.4

Source: National Center for Health Statistics, Deaths: Final Data for 1999, *National Vital Statistics Reports, Vol. 49, No. 8, 2001; calculations by New Strategist*

Leading Causes of Death among Non-Hispanic Whites, 1999

(total number of deaths among non-Hispanic whites, and number and percent of deaths accounted for by the ten leading causes of death for non-Hispanic whites, 1999)

		number	*percent*
Total non-Hispanic white deaths		**1,953,197**	**100.0%**
1.	Diseases of heart	607,704	31.1
2.	Malignant neoplasms	456,315	23.4
3.	Cerebrovascular diseases	138,716	7.1
4.	Chronic lower respiratory diseases	111,620	5.7
5.	Influenza and pneumonia	54,280	2.8
6.	Accidents	73,326	3.8
7.	Diabetes mellitus	49,347	2.5
8.	Alzheimer's disease	40,835	2.1
9.	Nephritis, nephrotic syndrome, nephrosis	26,418	1.4
10.	Suicide	24,534	1.3
	All other causes	370,102	18.9

Source: National Center for Health Statistics, Deaths: Final Data for 1999, *National Vital Statistics Reports, Vol. 49, No. 8, 2001; calculations by New Strategist*

Life Expectancy of Whites at Birth and Age 65 by Sex, 1990 and 2000

(number of years of life remaining for whites at birth and age 65, by sex, 1990 and 2000; change in years, 1990–2000)

	total	*female*	*male*
Birth			
2000	77.4	80.0	74.8
1990	76.1	79.4	72.7
Change, 1990–2000	1.3	0.6	2.1
Age 65			
2000	17.9	19.2	16.3
1990	17.3	19.1	15.2
Change, 1990–2000	0.6	0.1	1.1

Source: National Center for Health Statistics, Health United States, 2001*; and* Deaths: Preliminary Data for 2000, *National Vital Statistics Report, Vol. 49, No. 12, 2001; calculations by New Strategist*

Whites: Housing

More than Seven out of Ten White Householders Own Their Home

Seventy percent of the nation's white householders own their home, as do an even greater 74 percent of non-Hispanic whites. Homeownership among non-Hispanic whites ranges from a high of 77 percent in the Midwest to a low of 68 percent in the West.

Among non-Hispanic white married couples, 87 percent are homeowners. Homeownership is above 90 percent for couples aged 45 or older. The majority of non-Hispanic white male- and female-headed families also own a home.

Only 14 percent of non-Hispanic whites moved between 1999 and 2000, a lower mobility rate than for Asians, blacks, or Hispanics. One reason for the lower mobility of non-Hispanic whites is their higher homeownership rate. Homeowners are much less likely to move than renters. Non-Hispanic whites in their twenties are most likely to move, with 36 percent of those aged 20 to 24 moving between 1999 and 2000. People aged 65 or older are least likely to move.

■ The homeownership rate of non-Hispanic whites is likely to climb as the baby-boom generation enters the ages of peak homeownership.

Homeownership among non-Hispanic whites is highest in the Midwest

(percent of non-Hispanic white households that own their home, by region, 1999)

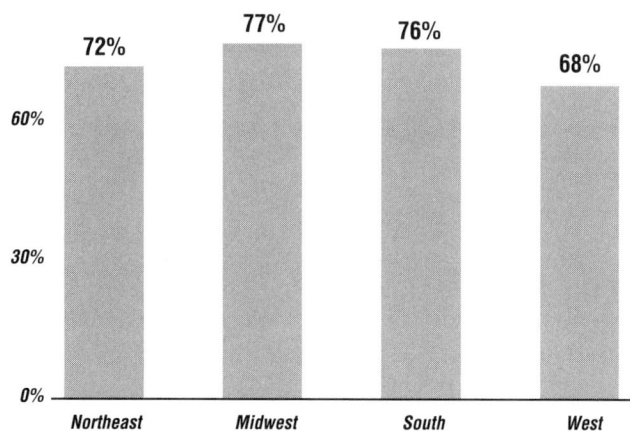

Region of Residence and Metropolitan Status of Housing Units Occupied by Whites, 1999

(number, percent distribution, and percent of housing units occupied by whites, by regional, metropolitan, and homeownership status, 1999; numbers in thousands)

	total		owner			renter		
	number	percent distribution	number	percent distribution	share of total	number	percent distribution	share of total
Housing units occupied by whites	**83,624**	**100.0%**	**60,041**	**100.0%**	**71.8%**	**23,583**	**100.0%**	**28.2%**
Northeast	16,372	19.6	11,388	19.0	69.6	4,985	21.1	30.4
Midwest	21,159	25.3	16,141	26.9	76.3	5,018	21.3	23.7
South	28,209	33.7	20,981	34.9	74.4	7,228	30.6	25.6
West	17,884	21.4	11,531	19.2	64.5	6,352	26.9	35.5
In metropolitan areas	63,108	75.5	44,134	73.5	69.9	18,974	80.5	30.1
In central cities	21,096	25.2	11,845	19.7	56.1	9,251	39.2	43.9
In suburbs	42,012	50.2	32,289	53.8	76.9	9,723	41.2	23.1
Outside metro areas	20,516	24.5	15,907	26.5	77.5	4,608	19.5	22.5

Source: Bureau of the Census, American Housing Survey for the United States: 1999, *Current Housing Reports, H150/99, 2000; calculations by New Strategist*

Region of Residence and Metropolitan Status of Housing Units Occupied by Non-Hispanic Whites, 1999

(number, percent distribution, and percent of housing units occupied by non-Hispanic whites, by regional, metropolitan, and homeownership status, 1999; numbers in thousands)

	total		owner			renter		
	number	percent distribution	number	percent distribution	share of total	number	percent distribution	share of total
Housing units occupied by non-Hispanic whites	**76,891**	**100.0%**	**56,716**	**100.0%**	**73.8%**	**20,175**	**100.0%**	**26.2%**
Northeast	15,508	20.2	11,107	19.6	71.6	4,985	24.7	32.1
Midwest	20,716	26.9	15,880	28.0	76.7	5,018	24.9	24.2
South	25,575	33.3	19,534	34.4	76.4	7,228	35.8	28.3
West	15,091	19.6	10,195	18.0	67.6	6,352	31.5	42.1
In metropolitan areas	57,041	74.2	41,221	72.7	72.3	18,974	94.0	33.3
In central cities	18,114	23.6	10,674	18.8	58.9	9,251	45.9	51.1
In suburbs	38,927	50.6	30,547	53.9	78.5	9,723	48.2	25.0
Outside metro areas	19,850	25.8	15,495	27.3	78.1	4,608	22.8	23.2

Source: Bureau of the Census, American Housing Survey for the United States: 1999, *Current Housing Reports, H150/99, 2000; calculations by New Strategist*

White Homeowners by Family Type and Age of Householder, 2000

(number of families headed by whites, and number and percent of families owning their home, by family type and by age of householder, 2000; numbers in thousands)

	total	homeowners	
		number	percent
White married couples	**48,790**	**40,895**	**83.8%**
Under age 25	1298	496	38.2
Aged 25 to 29	3,293	1,878	57.0
Aged 30 to 34	4,835	3,546	73.3
Aged 35 to 39	6,016	4,837	80.4
Aged 40 to 44	6,255	5,392	86.2
Aged 45 to 54	11,174	10,038	89.8
Aged 55 to 64	7,269	6,646	91.4
Aged 65 to 74	5,380	5,061	94.1
Aged 75 or older	3,270	3,001	91.8
White female-headed families	**8,380**	**4,529**	**54.0**
Under age 25	770	170	22.1
Aged 25 to 29	733	178	24.3
Aged 30 to 34	853	272	31.9
Aged 35 to 39	1,174	560	47.7
Aged 40 to 44	1,281	739	57.7
Aged 45 to 54	1,555	990	63.7
Aged 55 to 64	701	499	71.2
Aged 65 to 74	632	534	84.5
Aged 75 or older	681	588	86.3
White male-headed families	**3,081**	**1,859**	**60.3**
Under age 25	401	164	40.9
Aged 25 to 29	323	110	34.1
Aged 30 to 34	339	177	52.2
Aged 35 to 39	402	210	52.2
Aged 40 to 44	440	297	67.5
Aged 45 to 54	573	415	72.4
Aged 55 to 64	268	197	73.5
Aged 65 to 74	159	135	84.9
Aged 75 or older	177	154	87.0

Source: Bureau of the Census, America's Families and Living Arrangements: March 2000, detailed tables from Current Population Report P20–537, Internet site <www.census.gov/population/www/socdemo/hh-fam/p20-537_00.html>; calculations by New Strategist

Non-Hispanic White Homeowners by Family Type and Age of Householder, 2000

(number of families headed by non-Hispanic whites, and number and percent of families owning their home, by family type and by age of householder, 2000; numbers in thousands)

	total	homeowners	
		number	percent
Non-Hispanic white married couples	**43,865**	**38,064**	**86.8%**
Under age 25	992	421	42.4
Aged 25 to 29	2,708	1,677	61.9
Aged 30 to 34	4,055	3,178	78.4
Aged 35 to 39	5,183	4,351	83.9
Aged 40 to 44	5,609	4,956	88.4
Aged 45 to 54	10,293	9,446	91.8
Aged 55 to 64	6,784	6,279	92.6
Aged 65 to 74	5,104	4,845	94.9
Aged 75 or older	3,138	2,911	92.8
Non-Hispanic white female-headed families	**6,732**	**3,993**	**59.3**
Under age 25	587	125	21.3
Aged 25 to 29	550	155	28.2
Aged 30 to 34	635	238	37.5
Aged 35 to 39	918	484	52.7
Aged 40 to 44	1,050	647	61.6
Aged 45 to 54	1,277	891	69.8
Aged 55 to 64	548	431	78.6
Aged 65 to 74	532	461	86.7
Aged 75 or older	637	561	88.1
Non-Hispanic white male-headed families	**2,468**	**1,639**	**66.4**
Under age 25	264	132	50.0
Aged 25 to 29	223	92	41.3
Aged 30 to 34	253	151	59.7
Aged 35 to 39	333	186	55.9
Aged 40 to 44	386	270	69.9
Aged 45 to 54	508	386	76.0
Aged 55 to 64	213	169	79.3
Aged 65 to 74	133	115	86.5
Aged 75 or older	155	139	89.7

Source: Bureau of the Census, America's Families and Living Arrangements: March 2000, *detailed tables from Current Population Report P20–537, Internet site <www.census.gov/population/www/socdemo/hh-fam/p20-537_00.html>; calculations by New Strategist*

Geographical Mobility of Whites by Age, 1999–2000

(total number of whites aged 1 or older, and number and percent who moved between March 1999 and March 2000, by age of person and type of move; numbers in thousands)

	total	same house (non-movers)	total movers in U.S.	same county	different county, same state	different state, same division	different division, same region	different region	moved from abroad
Whites aged 1 or older	**221,703**	**187,810**	**33,893**	**18,811**	**7,135**	**2,992**	**1,076**	**2,633**	**1,247**
Aged 1–4	12,336	9,588	2,748	1,641	529	191	100	205	82
Aged 5–9	15,979	13,319	2,660	1,542	511	200	94	205	109
Aged 10–14	15,808	13,783	2,025	1,138	359	207	46	191	83
Aged 15–17	9,441	8,282	1,159	633	212	117	36	101	60
Aged 18–19	6,402	4,987	1,415	784	300	150	25	94	61
Aged 20–24	14,671	9,388	5,283	3,026	1,100	439	164	349	205
Aged 25–29	14,556	9,881	4,675	2,617	1,066	281	176	390	144
Aged 30–34	15,764	12,423	3,341	1,881	700	256	114	239	149
Aged 35–39	18,324	15,355	2,969	1,638	653	291	59	228	100
Aged 40–44	18,591	16,338	2,253	1,234	462	264	64	155	75
Aged 45–49	16,476	14,915	1,561	806	363	188	38	95	71
Aged 50–54	14,314	13,123	1,191	624	278	131	39	69	51
Aged 55–59	11,079	10,220	859	428	186	105	30	83	26
Aged 60–61	3,781	3,530	251	109	61	37	14	26	4
Aged 62–64	5,303	5,020	283	119	68	39	10	38	9
Aged 65–69	8,099	7,738	361	197	67	25	22	44	6
Aged 70–74	7,428	7,099	329	159	73	23	22	43	9
Aged 75–79	6,462	6,234	228	99	64	10	19	35	2
Aged 80–84	4,085	3,911	174	70	51	28	1	23	1
Aged 85+	2,805	2,675	130	65	33	8	3	20	–

(continued)

(continued from previous page)

	total	same house (non-movers)	total movers in U.S.	same county	different county, same state	different state, same division	different division, same region	different region	moved from abroad
Whites aged 1 or older	**100.0%**	**84.7%**	**15.3%**	**8.5%**	**3.2%**	**1.3%**	**0.5%**	**1.2%**	**0.6%**
Aged 1–4	100.0	77.7	22.3	13.3	4.3	1.5	0.8	1.7	0.7
Aged 5–9	100.0	83.4	16.6	9.7	3.2	1.3	0.6	1.3	0.7
Aged 10–14	100.0	87.2	12.8	7.2	2.3	1.3	0.3	1.2	0.5
Aged 15–17	100.0	87.7	12.3	6.7	2.2	1.2	0.4	1.1	0.6
Aged 18–19	100.0	77.9	22.1	12.2	4.7	2.3	0.4	1.5	1.0
Aged 20–24	100.0	64.0	36.0	20.6	7.5	3.0	1.1	2.4	1.4
Aged 25–29	100.0	67.9	32.1	18.0	7.3	1.9	1.2	2.7	1.0
Aged 30–34	100.0	78.8	21.2	11.9	4.4	1.6	0.7	1.5	0.9
Aged 35–39	100.0	83.8	16.2	8.9	3.6	1.6	0.3	1.2	0.5
Aged 40–44	100.0	87.9	12.1	6.6	2.5	1.4	0.3	0.8	0.4
Aged 45–49	100.0	90.5	9.5	4.9	2.2	1.1	0.2	0.6	0.4
Aged 50–54	100.0	91.7	8.3	4.4	1.9	0.9	0.3	0.5	0.4
Aged 55–59	100.0	92.2	7.8	3.9	1.7	0.9	0.3	0.7	0.2
Aged 60–61	100.0	93.4	6.6	2.9	1.6	1.0	0.4	0.7	0.1
Aged 62–64	100.0	94.7	5.3	2.2	1.3	0.7	0.2	0.7	0.2
Aged 65–69	100.0	95.5	4.5	2.4	0.8	0.3	0.3	0.5	0.1
Aged 70–74	100.0	95.6	4.4	2.1	1.0	0.3	0.3	0.6	0.1
Aged 75–79	100.0	96.5	3.5	1.5	1.0	0.2	0.3	0.5	0.0
Aged 80–84	100.0	95.7	4.3	1.7	1.2	0.7	0.0	0.6	0.0
Aged 85+	100.0	95.4	4.6	2.3	1.2	0.3	0.1	0.7	–

Note: (–) means sample is too small to make a reliable estimate.
Source: Bureau of the Census, Geographical Mobility: March 1999 to March 2000, *Current Population Reports, P20-538, 2001; Internet site <www.census.gov/population/www/socdemo/migrate/p20-538.html>; calculations by New Strategist*

Geographical Mobility of Non-Hispanic Whites by Age, 1999–2000

(total number of non-Hispanic whites aged 1 or older, and number and percent who moved between March 1999 and March 2000, by age of person and type of move; numbers in thousands)

	total	same house (non-movers)	total movers in U.S.	same county	different county, same state	different state, same division	different division, same region	different region	moved from abroad
Non-Hispanic whites aged 1 or older	191,197	163,595	27,602	14,827	6,205	2,682	882	2,346	660
Aged 1–4	9,542	7,510	2,032	1,146	444	162	68	171	43
Aged 5–9	12,747	10,729	2,018	1,144	400	169	66	175	63
Aged 10–14	12,988	11,453	1,535	817	298	186	35	160	39
Aged 15–17	7,828	6,957	871	463	175	101	27	87	17
Aged 18–19	5,269	4,145	1,124	607	256	137	20	86	18
Aged 20–24	12,039	7,681	4,358	2,441	996	389	133	311	87
Aged 25–29	11,890	8,090	3,800	2,040	953	239	150	341	77
Aged 30–34	13,090	10,361	2,729	1,505	589	226	97	218	94
Aged 35–39	15,647	13,159	2,488	1,338	575	272	44	204	55
Aged 40–44	16,547	14,609	1,938	1,034	398	252	56	149	49
Aged 45–49	14,978	13,609	1,369	690	331	172	37	92	48
Aged 50–54	12,962	11,938	1,024	515	255	127	35	62	32
Aged 55–59	10,127	9,378	749	372	164	90	28	75	21
Aged 60–61	3,451	3,228	223	90	59	33	14	25	2
Aged 62–64	4,904	4,647	257	105	63	38	7	38	5
Aged 65–69	7,482	7,173	309	167	57	22	22	37	4
Aged 70–74	6,959	6,670	289	138	60	22	22	43	5
Aged 75–79	6,162	5,956	206	95	50	10	16	33	2
Aged 80–84	3,881	3,720	161	59	50	28	1	23	–
Aged 85+	2,703	2,582	121	61	33	7	3	17	–

(continued)

(continued from previous page)

Non-Hispanic whites aged 1 or older	total	same house (non-movers)	total movers in U.S.	same county	different county, same state	different state, same division	different division, same region	different region	moved from abroad
	100.0%	85.6%	14.4%	7.8%	3.2%	1.4%	0.5%	1.2%	0.3%
Aged 1–4	100.0	78.7	21.3	12.0	4.7	1.7	0.7	1.8	0.5
Aged 5–9	100.0	84.2	15.8	9.0	3.1	1.3	0.5	1.4	0.5
Aged 10–14	100.0	88.2	11.8	6.3	2.3	1.4	0.3	1.2	0.3
Aged 15–17	100.0	88.9	11.1	5.9	2.2	1.3	0.3	1.1	0.2
Aged 18–19	100.0	78.7	21.3	11.5	4.9	2.6	0.4	1.6	0.3
Aged 20–24	100.0	63.8	36.2	20.3	8.3	3.2	1.1	2.6	0.7
Aged 25–29	100.0	68.0	32.0	17.2	8.0	2.0	1.3	2.9	0.6
Aged 30–34	100.0	79.2	20.8	11.5	4.5	1.7	0.7	1.7	0.7
Aged 35–39	100.0	84.1	15.9	8.6	3.7	1.7	0.3	1.3	0.4
Aged 40–44	100.0	88.3	11.7	6.2	2.4	1.5	0.3	0.9	0.3
Aged 45–49	100.0	90.9	9.1	4.6	2.2	1.1	0.2	0.6	0.3
Aged 50–54	100.0	92.1	7.9	4.0	2.0	1.0	0.3	0.5	0.2
Aged 55–59	100.0	92.6	7.4	3.7	1.6	0.9	0.3	0.7	0.2
Aged 60–61	100.0	93.5	6.5	2.6	1.7	1.0	0.4	0.7	0.1
Aged 62–64	100.0	94.8	5.2	2.1	1.3	0.8	0.1	0.8	0.1
Aged 65–69	100.0	95.9	4.1	2.2	0.8	0.3	0.3	0.5	0.1
Aged 70–74	100.0	95.8	4.2	2.0	0.9	0.3	0.3	0.6	0.1
Aged 75–79	100.0	96.7	3.3	1.5	0.8	0.2	0.3	0.5	0.0
Aged 80–84	100.0	95.9	4.1	1.5	1.3	0.7	0.0	0.6	–
Aged 85+	100.0	95.5	4.5	2.3	1.2	0.3	0.1	0.6	–

Note: (–) means sample is too small to make a reliable estimate.
Source: Bureau of the Census, Geographical Mobility: March 1999 to March 2000, Current Population Reports, P20-538, 2001; Internet site <www.census.gov/population/www/socdemo/migrate/p20-538.html>; calculations by New Strategist

Non-Hispanic Whites Have Higher Incomes than All Whites

The median income of white households rose 10 percent between 1990 and 2000, to $44,232 after adjusting for inflation. The median income of non-Hispanic white households rose a larger 12 percent to $45,910. Non-Hispanic white incomes are higher than those of whites as a whole because most Hispanics—who tend to have low incomes—are white.

Among white households, median income peaks at $61,682 in the 45-to-54 age group. The income peak is an even higher $63,904 among non-Hispanic white householders in the 45-to-54 age group. By household type, non-Hispanic white married couples have the highest median income—$62,109 in 2000.

White men who work full-time earned a median of $38,869 in 2000, just 5 percent more than in 1990, after adjusting for inflation. The median earnings of non-Hispanic white men rose a larger 6 percent during those years. The median earnings of white women who work full-time rose 9 percent between 1990 and 2000, while non-Hispanic white women saw a 13 percent increase. Since 1990, the median income of non-Hispanic white women has grown from 68 to 72 percent of the median income of non-Hispanic white men.

The poverty rate of white families fell from 8 to 7 percent between 1990 and 2000. For non-Hispanic white families, the poverty rate fell from 7 to 5 percent. Overall, 9 percent of whites are poor, including 13 percent of children under age 18.

■ Non-Hispanic white households have much higher incomes than black or Hispanic households. Behind the income gap is the higher educational level of non-Hispanic whites and the larger proportion of households headed by dual-earner married couples.

Household income tops $45,000 for most non-Hispanic whites

(median income of households headed by whites and non-Hispanic whites, 2000)

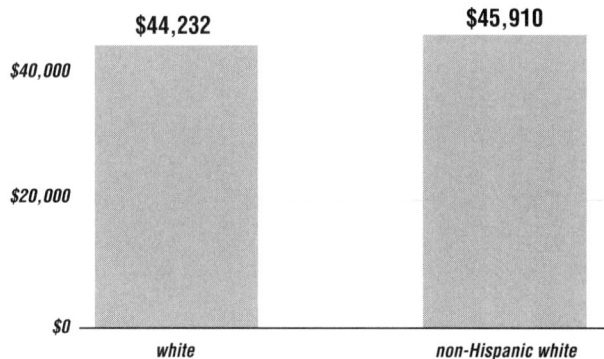

Median Income of White Households, 1990 to 2000

(median income of white households, and index of white to total household median income, 1990 to 2000; percent change in incomes and indexes, 1990–2000; in 2000 dollars)

	median income	index white/total
2000	$44,232	105
1999	43,932	104
1998	43,171	105
1997	41,699	105
1996	40,623	105
1995	40,159	105
1994	39,166	105
1993	38,768	106
1992	38,863	105
1991	39,101	105
1990	40,100	104
Percent change		
1990–2000	10.3%	0.6%

Note: Indexes are calculated by dividing the median income of white households by the median of total households and multiplying by 100.
Source: Bureau of the Census, Current Population Survey, Internet site <www.census.gov/hhes/income/histinc/h05.html>; calculations by New Strategist

Median Income of Non-Hispanic White Households, 1990 to 2000

(median income of non-Hispanic white households, and index of non-Hispanic white to total household median income, 1990 to 2000; percent change in incomes and indexes, 1990–2000; in 2000 dollars)

	median income	index non-Hispanic white/total
2000	$45,910	109
1999	45,856	109
1998	44,782	109
1997	43,416	110
1996	42,400	109
1995	41,745	109
1994	40,430	109
1993	40,195	109
1992	40,168	109
1991	40,035	107
1990	41,016	107
Percent change		
1990–2000	11.9%	2.1%

Note: Indexes are calculated by dividing the median income of non-Hispanic white households by the median of total households and multiplying by 100.
Source: Bureau of the Census, Current Population Survey, Internet site <www.census.gov/hhes/income/histinc/h05.html>; calculations by New Strategist

High-Income White and Non-Hispanic White Households, 2000

(number, percent distribution, and average income of white and non-Hispanic white households with incomes of $100,000 or more, 2000; households in thousands as of 2001)

	total	percent	average income
Total white households	**88,545**	**100.0%**	**$59,277**
$100,000 to $149,999	8,109	9.2	118,833
$150,000 to $199,999	2,338	2.6	169,527
$200,000 to $249,999	941	1.1	219,203
$250,000 or more	1,194	1.3	465,763
Total non-Hispanic white households	**79,376**	**100.0**	**61,237**
$100,000 to $149,999	7,751	9.8	118,897
$150,000 to $199,999	2,242	2.8	169,599
$200,000 to $249,999	912	1.1	219,298
$250,000 or more	1,155	1.5	469,008

Source: Bureau of the Census, Current Population Survey, Internet site <http://ferret.bls.census.gov/macro/ 032001/hhinc/new07_000 .htm>; calculations by New Strategist

Income Distribution of White Households by Age of Householder, 2000

(number and percent distribution of white households by income and age of householder, 2000; households in thousands as of 2001)

	total	< 25	25–34	35–44	45–54	55–64	65+
White households	**88,543**	**4,955**	**14,652**	**19,473**	**18,169**	**11,903**	**19,391**
Under $10,000	6,950	597	764	845	852	1,042	2,851
$10,000 to $19,999	11,536	920	1,336	1,474	1,202	1,261	5,344
$20,000 to $29,999	11,604	1,014	1,969	1,892	1,526	1,451	3,749
$30,000 to $39,999	10,261	776	2,006	2,073	1,742	1,293	2,373
$40,000 to $49,999	8,702	478	1,718	2,101	1,765	1,219	1,423
$50,000 to $59,999	7,668	352	1,736	1,957	1,677	1,022	924
$60,000 to $69,999	6,662	294	1,315	1,872	1,619	880	683
$70,000 to $79,999	5,415	142	1,000	1,644	1,407	771	451
$80,000 to $89,999	4,114	100	662	1,265	1,211	553	322
$90,000 to $99,999	3,045	57	519	910	930	411	216
$100,000 or more	12,583	224	1,625	3,444	4,235	1,998	1,057
Median income	$44,232	$29,414	$47,028	$56,498	$61,682	$47,075	$23,620
White households	**100.0%**	**100.0%**	**100.0%**	**100.0%**	**100.0%**	**100.0%**	**100.0%**
Under $10,000	7.8	12.0	5.2	4.3	4.7	8.8	14.7
$10,000 to $19,999	13.0	18.6	9.1	7.6	6.6	10.6	27.6
$20,000 to $29,999	13.1	20.5	13.4	9.7	8.4	12.2	19.3
$30,000 to $39,999	11.6	15.7	13.7	10.6	9.6	10.9	12.2
$40,000 to $49,999	9.8	9.6	11.7	10.8	9.7	10.2	7.3
$50,000 to $59,999	8.7	7.1	11.8	10.0	9.2	8.6	4.8
$60,000 to $69,999	7.5	5.9	9.0	9.6	8.9	7.4	3.5
$70,000 to $79,999	6.1	2.9	6.8	8.4	7.7	6.5	2.3
$80,000 to $89,999	4.6	2.0	4.5	6.5	6.7	4.6	1.7
$90,000 to $99,999	3.4	1.2	3.5	4.7	5.1	3.5	1.1
$100,000 or more	14.2	4.5	11.1	17.7	23.3	16.8	5.5

Source: Bureau of the Census, Current Population Survey, Internet site <http://ferret.bls.census.gov/macro/032001/hhinc/new02_002 .htm>; calculations by New Strategist

Income Distribution of Non-Hispanic White Households by Age of Householder, 2000

(number and percent distribution of non-Hispanic white households by income and age of house-holder, 2000; households in thousands as of 2001)

	total	< 25	25–34	35–44	45–54	55–64	65+
Non-Hispanic white households	**79,375**	**4,037**	**12,300**	**17,135**	**16,593**	**10,943**	**18,367**
Under $10,000	6,005	464	580	701	752	915	2,592
$10,000 to $19,999	9,911	729	946	1,122	995	1,083	5,037
$20,000 to $29,999	10,060	842	1,535	1,498	1,297	1,317	3,571
$30,000 to $39,999	8,983	635	1,645	1,744	1,516	1,169	2,273
$40,000 to $49,999	7,724	400	1,460	1,815	1,571	1,114	1,363
$50,000 to $59,999	6,888	277	1,520	1,715	1,537	946	891
$60,000 to $69,999	6,077	228	1,142	1,716	1,511	825	655
$70,000 to $79,999	4,988	123	886	1,504	1,317	733	422
$80,000 to $89,999	3,814	89	590	1,164	1,141	510	316
$90,000 to $99,999	2,867	43	469	869	887	393	206
$100,000 or more	12,061	207	1,526	3,284	4,066	1,938	1,040
Median income	$45,910	$29,782	$49,889	$59,785	$63,904	$48,699	$23,966
Non-Hispanic white households	**100.0%**	**100.0%**	**100.0%**	**100.0%**	**100.0%**	**100.0%**	**100.0%**
Under $10,000	7.6	11.5	4.7	4.1	4.5	8.4	14.1
$10,000 to $19,999	12.5	18.1	7.7	6.5	6.0	9.9	27.4
$20,000 to $29,999	12.7	20.9	12.5	8.7	7.8	12.0	19.4
$30,000 to $39,999	11.3	15.7	13.4	10.2	9.1	10.7	12.4
$40,000 to $49,999	9.7	9.9	11.9	10.6	9.5	10.2	7.4
$50,000 to $59,999	8.7	6.9	12.4	10.0	9.3	8.6	4.9
$60,000 to $69,999	7.7	5.6	9.3	10.0	9.1	7.5	3.6
$70,000 to $79,999	6.3	3.0	7.2	8.8	7.9	6.7	2.3
$80,000 to $89,999	4.8	2.2	4.8	6.8	6.9	4.7	1.7
$90,000 to $99,999	3.6	1.1	3.8	5.1	5.3	3.6	1.1
$100,000 or more	15.2	5.1	12.4	19.2	24.5	17.7	5.7

Source: Bureau of the Census, Current Population Survey, Internet site <http://ferret.bls.census.gov/macro/032001/hhinc/new02_005 .htm>; calculations by New Strategist

Income Distribution of White Households by Household Type, 2000

(number and percent distribution of white households by income and household type, 2000; households in thousands as of 2001)

	total	family households				nonfamily households				
		total	married couples	female hh, no spouse present	male hh, no spouse present	total	female householder		male householder	
							total	living alone	total	living alone
White households	88,543	60,214	48,647	8,293	3,274	28,329	15,748	13,681	12,581	9,488
Under $10,000	6,950	2,134	1,085	875	173	4,817	3,254	3,186	1,563	1,450
$10,000 to $19,999	11,536	5,184	3,324	1,532	328	6,352	4,191	4,037	2,161	1,931
$20,000 to $29,999	11,604	6,880	4,801	1,569	510	4,723	2,626	2,342	2,098	1,698
$30,000 to $39,999	10,261	6,826	5,166	1,218	440	3,434	1,726	1,507	1,709	1,333
$40,000 to $49,999	8,702	6,359	5,040	923	395	2,343	1,119	884	1,224	882
$50,000 to $59,999	7,668	5,806	4,859	629	317	1,863	816	563	1,047	676
$60,000 to $69,999	6,662	5,424	4,593	488	344	1,239	534	340	706	434
$70,000 to $79,999	5,415	4,457	3,975	300	183	957	417	264	540	316
$80,000 to $89,999	4,114	3,519	3,154	226	137	596	262	153	335	190
$90,000 to $99,999	3,045	2,640	2,396	148	95	406	141	52	263	132
$100,000 or more	12,583	10,987	10,252	385	350	1,597	663	352	934	443
Median income	$44,232	$54,293	$60,080	$31,230	$44,020	$25,985	$21,287	$18,695	$31,873	$27,326

(continued)

(continued from previous page)

White households	total	family households				nonfamily households				
		total	married couples	female hh, no spouse present	male hh, no spouse present	total	female householder		male householder	
							total	living alone	total	living alone
	100.0%	100.0%	100.0%	100.0%	100.0%	100.0%	100.0%	100.0%	100.0%	100.0%
Under $10,000	7.8	3.5	2.2	10.6	5.3	17.0	20.7	23.3	12.4	15.3
$10,000 to $19,999	13.0	8.6	6.8	18.5	10.0	22.4	26.6	29.5	17.2	20.4
$20,000 to $29,999	13.1	11.4	9.9	18.9	15.6	16.7	16.7	17.1	16.7	17.9
$30,000 to $39,999	11.6	11.3	10.6	14.7	13.4	12.1	11.0	11.0	13.6	14.0
$40,000 to $49,999	9.8	10.6	10.4	11.1	12.1	8.3	7.1	6.5	9.7	9.3
$50,000 to $59,999	8.7	9.6	10.0	7.6	9.7	6.6	5.2	4.1	8.3	7.1
$60,000 to $69,999	7.5	9.0	9.4	5.9	10.5	4.4	3.4	2.5	5.6	4.6
$70,000 to $79,999	6.1	7.4	8.2	3.6	5.6	3.4	2.6	1.9	4.3	3.3
$80,000 to $89,999	4.6	5.8	6.5	2.7	4.2	2.1	1.7	1.1	2.7	2.0
$90,000 to $99,999	3.4	4.4	4.9	1.8	2.9	1.4	0.9	0.4	2.1	1.4
$100,000 or more	14.2	18.2	21.1	4.6	10.7	5.6	4.2	2.6	7.4	4.7

Source: Bureau of the Census, Current Population Survey, Internet site <http://ferret.bls.census.gov/macro/032001/hhinc/new01_002.htm>; calculations by New Strategist

Income Distribution of Non-Hispanic White Households by Household Type, 2000

(number and percent distribution of non-Hispanic white households by income and household type, 2000; households in thousands as of 2001)

		family households				nonfamily households				
							female householder		male householder	
	total	total	married couples	female hh, no spouse present	male hh, no spouse present	total	total	living alone	total	living alone
Non-Hispanic white households	**79,375**	**52,876**	**43,624**	**6,681**	**2,571**	**26,499**	**14,886**	**12,982**	**11,614**	**8,860**
Under $10,000	6,005	1,632	882	606	142	4,374	2,978	2,922	1,393	1,311
$10,000 to $19,999	9,911	3,982	2,603	1,138	241	5,928	3,965	3,833	1,965	1,766
$20,000 to $29,999	10,060	5,655	4,024	1,257	373	4,404	2,510	2,253	1,894	1,570
$30,000 to $39,999	8,983	5,747	4,427	988	331	3,236	1,646	1,459	1,590	1,258
$40,000 to $49,999	7,724	5,530	4,441	780	311	2,193	1,057	838	1,137	839
$50,000 to $59,999	6,888	5,125	4,332	544	250	1,764	776	543	987	639
$60,000 to $69,999	6,077	4,895	4,204	418	272	1,183	514	334	668	420
$70,000 to $79,999	4,988	4,077	3,659	267	151	910	403	257	508	309
$80,000 to $89,999	3,814	3,245	2,934	198	114	566	253	146	315	180
$90,000 to $99,999	2,867	2,478	2,271	127	80	389	137	50	254	131
$100,000 or more	12,061	10,510	9,847	356	306	1,552	648	345	903	436
Median income	$45,910	$57,182	$62,109	$33,163	$45,694	$26,331	$21,567	$19,062	$32,386	$28,019

(continued)

(continued from previous page)

Non-Hispanic white households	total	family households				nonfamily households					
		total	married couples	female hh, no spouse present	male hh, no spouse present	total	female householder		male householder		
							total	living alone	total	living alone
	100.0%	100.0%	100.0%	100.0%	100.0%	100.0%	100.0%	100.0%	100.0%	100.0%	
Under $10,000	7.6	3.1	2.0	9.1	5.5	16.5	20.0	22.5	12.0	14.8	
$10,000 to $19,999	12.5	7.5	6.0	17.0	9.4	22.4	26.6	29.5	16.9	19.9	
$20,000 to $29,999	12.7	10.7	9.2	18.8	14.5	16.6	16.9	17.4	16.3	17.7	
$30,000 to $39,999	11.3	10.9	10.1	14.8	12.9	12.2	11.1	11.2	13.7	14.2	
$40,000 to $49,999	9.7	10.5	10.2	11.7	12.1	8.3	7.1	6.5	9.8	9.5	
$50,000 to $59,999	8.7	9.7	9.9	8.1	9.7	6.7	5.2	4.2	8.5	7.2	
$60,000 to $69,999	7.7	9.3	9.6	6.3	10.6	4.5	3.5	2.6	5.8	4.7	
$70,000 to $79,999	6.3	7.7	8.4	4.0	5.9	3.4	2.7	2.0	4.4	3.5	
$80,000 to $89,999	4.8	6.1	6.7	3.0	4.4	2.1	1.7	1.1	2.7	2.0	
$90,000 to $99,999	3.6	4.7	5.2	1.9	3.1	1.5	0.9	0.4	2.2	1.5	
$100,000 or more	15.2	19.9	22.6	5.3	11.9	5.9	4.4	2.7	7.8	4.9	

Source: Bureau of the Census, Current Population Survey, Internet site <http://ferret.bls.census.gov/macro/032001/hhinc/new01_005.htm>; calculations by New Strategist

Income Distribution of White Men by Age, 2000

(number and percent distribution of white men aged 15 or older by income and age, median income of men with income, percent working full-time, and median income of full-time workers, 2000; men in thousands as of 2001)

	total	< 25	25–34	35–44	45–54	55–64	65+
White men	**87,223**	**15,782**	**14,937**	**18,392**	**15,795**	**9,755**	**12,562**
Without income	5,009	3,631	352	305	294	252	175
With income	82,214	12,151	14,585	18,087	15,501	9,503	12,387
Under $10,000	12,721	6,077	1,124	1,245	1,159	1,030	2,088
$10,000 to $19,999	15,141	3,115	2,589	2,136	1,604	1,548	4,153
$20,000 to $29,999	13,514	1,692	3,085	2,925	1,926	1,343	2,541
$30,000 to $39,999	11,263	724	2,853	2,883	2,305	1,305	1,194
$40,000 to $49,999	8,106	238	1,775	2,293	2,074	972	756
$50,000 to $74,999	11,716	225	2,060	3,723	3,265	1,621	826
$75,000 to $99,999	4,540	59	574	1,379	1,467	713	347
$100,000 or more	5,210	20	528	1,504	1,703	972	482
Median income of men with income	$29,696	$9,995	$31,110	$39,147	$42,227	$35,554	$19,865
Percent working full-time	57.3%	25.4%	78.2%	82.0%	78.8%	56.9%	9.5%
Median income of men working full-time	$40,350	$21,031	$34,994	$42,440	$48,145	$48,027	$49,019
White men	**100.0%**	**100.0%**	**100.0%**	**100.0%**	**100.0%**	**100.0%**	**100.0%**
Without income	5.7	23.0	2.4	1.7	1.9	2.6	1.4
With income	94.3	77.0	97.6	98.3	98.1	97.4	98.6
Under $10,000	14.6	38.5	7.5	6.8	7.3	10.6	16.6
$10,000 to $19,999	17.4	19.7	17.3	11.6	10.2	15.9	33.1
$20,000 to $29,999	15.5	10.7	20.7	15.9	12.2	13.8	20.2
$30,000 to $39,999	12.9	4.6	19.1	15.7	14.6	13.4	9.5
$40,000 to $49,999	9.3	1.5	11.9	12.5	13.1	10.0	6.0
$50,000 to $74,999	13.4	1.4	13.8	20.2	20.7	16.6	6.6
$75,000 to $99,999	5.2	0.4	3.8	7.5	9.3	7.3	2.8
$100,000 or more	6.0	0.1	3.5	8.2	10.8	10.0	3.8

Source: Bureau of the Census, Current Population Survey, Internet sites <http://ferret.bls.census.gov/macro/032001/perinc/new01_007 .htm> and <http://ferret.bls.census.gov/macro/032001/perinc/new01_022.htm>; calculations by New Strategist

Income Distribution of Non-Hispanic White Men by Age, 2000

(number and percent distribution of non-Hispanic white men aged 15 or older by income and age, median income of men with income, percent working full-time, and median income of full-time workers, 2000; men in thousands as of 2001)

	total	< age 25	25–34	35–44	45–54	55–64	65+
Non-Hispanic white men	**76,090**	**12,913**	**12,191**	**15,977**	**14,307**	**8,895**	**11,807**
Without income	3,690	2,687	212	240	227	187	136
With income	72,400	10,226	11,979	15,737	14,080	8,708	11,671
Under $10,000	10,802	5,295	827	1,028	994	878	1,782
$10,000 to $19,999	12,081	2,393	1,724	1,509	1,237	1,287	3,930
$20,000 to $29,999	11,507	1,423	2,455	2,343	1,633	1,207	2,447
$30,000 to $39,999	10,095	646	2,478	2,518	2,084	1,215	1,152
$40,000 to $49,999	7,431	188	1,581	2,059	1,933	931	738
$50,000 to $74,999	11,043	204	1,868	3,507	3,114	1,547	801
$75,000 to $99,999	4,381	57	536	1,319	1,426	700	340
$100,000 or more	5,062	19	510	1,451	1,656	948	478
Median income of men with income	$31,213	$9,397	$33,005	$41,362	$44,959	$37,316	$20,408
Percent working full-time	57.2%	23.8%	79.3%	82.6%	79.7%	57.2%	9.3%
Median income of men working full-time	$42,224	$21,945	$36,567	$45,872	$50,242	$50,362	$51,145
Non-Hispanic white men	**100.0%**	**100.0%**	**100.0%**	**100.0%**	**100.0%**	**100.0%**	**100.0%**
Without income	4.8	20.8	1.7	1.5	1.6	2.1	1.2
With income	95.2	79.2	98.3	98.5	98.4	97.9	98.8
Under $10,000	14.2	41.0	6.8	6.4	6.9	9.9	15.1
$10,000 to $19,999	15.9	18.5	14.1	9.4	8.6	14.5	33.3
$20,000 to $29,999	15.1	11.0	20.1	14.7	11.4	13.6	20.7
$30,000 to $39,999	13.3	5.0	20.3	15.8	14.6	13.7	9.8
$40,000 to $49,999	9.8	1.5	13.0	12.9	13.5	10.5	6.3
$50,000 to $74,999	14.5	1.6	15.3	22.0	21.8	17.4	6.8
$75,000 to $99,999	5.8	0.4	4.4	8.3	10.0	7.9	2.9
$100,000 or more	6.7	0.1	4.2	9.1	11.6	10.7	4.0

Source: Bureau of the Census, Current Population Survey, Internet sites <http://ferret.bls.census.gov/macro/032001/perinc/new01_010 .htm> and <http://ferret.bls.census.gov/macro/032001/perinc/new01_025.htm>; calculations by New Strategist

Income Distribution of White Women by Age, 2000

(number and percent distribution of white women aged 15 or older by income and age, median income of women with income, percent working full-time, and median income of full-time workers, 2000; women in thousands as of 2001)

	total	< age 25	25–34	35–44	45–54	55–64	65+
White women	**91,837**	**15,225**	**14,930**	**18,299**	**16,169**	**10,654**	**16,560**
Without income	8,936	3,874	1,467	1,299	1,054	877	364
With income	82,901	11,351	13,463	17,000	15,115	9,777	16,196
Under $10,000	27,885	6,518	3,340	4,283	3,342	3,325	7,076
$10,000 to $19,999	19,839	2,826	3,049	3,417	2,929	2,079	5,541
$20,000 to $29,999	13,509	1,306	2,799	3,240	2,759	1,607	1,800
$30,000 to $39,999	8,704	411	2,027	2,273	2,170	1,068	755
$40,000 to $49,999	4,946	157	935	1,438	1,440	608	368
$50,000 to $74,999	5,502	85	927	1,563	1,778	742	405
$75,000 to $99,999	1,375	24	219	401	377	223	135
$100,000 or more	1,139	23	168	386	319	124	118
Median income of women with income	$16,216	$7,853	$20,972	$21,889	$24,663	$16,988	$11,221
Percent working full-time	36.1%	19.9%	50.2%	51.4%	54.9%	35.7%	3.4%
Median income of women working full-time	$29,661	$19,103	$28,840	$31,101	$32,494	$30,540	$35,004
White women	**100.0%**	**100.0%**	**100.0%**	**100.0%**	**100.0%**	**100.0%**	**100.0%**
Without income	9.7	25.4	9.8	7.1	6.5	8.2	2.2
With income	90.3	74.6	90.2	92.9	93.5	91.8	97.8
Under $10,000	30.4	42.8	22.4	23.4	20.7	31.2	42.7
$10,000 to $19,999	21.6	18.6	20.4	18.7	18.1	19.5	33.5
$20,000 to $29,999	14.7	8.6	18.7	17.7	17.1	15.1	10.9
$30,000 to $39,999	9.5	2.7	13.6	12.4	13.4	10.0	4.6
$40,000 to $49,999	5.4	1.0	6.3	7.9	8.9	5.7	2.2
$50,000 to $74,999	6.0	0.6	6.2	8.5	11.0	7.0	2.4
$75,000 to $99,999	1.5	0.2	1.5	2.2	2.3	2.1	0.8
$100,000 or more	1.2	0.2	1.1	2.1	2.0	1.2	0.7

Source: Bureau of the Census, Current Population Survey, Internet sites <http://ferret.bls.census.gov/macro/032001/perinc/new01_012 .htm> and <http://ferret.bls.census.gov/macro/032001/perinc/new01_027.htm>; calculations by New Strategist

Income Distribution of Non-Hispanic White Women by Age, 2000

(number and percent distribution of non-Hispanic white women aged 15 or older by income and age, median income of women with income, percent working full-time, and median income of full-time workers, 2000; women in thousands as of 2001)

	total	< 25	25–34	35–44	45–54	55–64	65+
Non-Hispanic white women	**80,544**	**12,492**	**12,310**	**15,948**	**14,580**	**9,712**	**15,501**
Without income	6,250	2,762	911	892	785	644	255
With income	74,294	9,730	11,399	15,056	13,795	9,068	15,246
Under $10,000	24,338	5,591	2,684	3,697	2,960	3,018	6,387
$10,000 to $19,999	17,368	2,371	2,408	2,815	2,517	1,895	5,367
$20,000 to $29,999	12,190	1,126	2,422	2,856	2,526	1,511	1,751
$30,000 to $39,999	8,063	370	1,815	2,091	2,046	1,008	734
$40,000 to $49,999	4,661	146	842	1,361	1,369	581	360
$50,000 to $74,999	5,251	80	860	1,478	1,717	717	400
$75,000 to $99,999	1,317	23	208	381	355	218	133
$100,000 or more	1,106	22	160	378	309	120	116
Median income of women with income	$16,804	$7,828	$22,097	$22,912	$25,638	$17,505	$11,531
Percent working full-time	36.4%	20.1%	51.8%	52.1%	55.1%	36.3%	3.5%
Median income of women working full-time	$30,777	$19,975	$30,151	$32,255	$33,860	$30,969	$35,359
Non-Hispanic white women	**100.0%**	**100.0%**	**100.0%**	**100.0%**	**100.0%**	**100.0%**	**100.0%**
Without income	7.8	22.1	7.4	5.6	5.4	6.6	1.6
With income	92.2	77.9	92.6	94.4	94.6	93.4	98.4
Under $10,000	30.2	44.8	21.8	23.2	20.3	31.1	41.2
$10,000 to $19,999	21.6	19.0	19.6	17.7	17.3	19.5	34.6
$20,000 to $29,999	15.1	9.0	19.7	17.9	17.3	15.6	11.3
$30,000 to $39,999	10.0	3.0	14.7	13.1	14.0	10.4	4.7
$40,000 to $49,999	5.8	1.2	6.8	8.5	9.4	6.0	2.3
$50,000 to $74,999	6.5	0.6	7.0	9.3	11.8	7.4	2.6
$75,000 to $99,999	1.6	0.2	1.7	2.4	2.4	2.2	0.9
$100,000 or more	1.4	0.2	1.3	2.4	2.1	1.2	0.7

Source: Bureau of the Census, Current Population Survey, Internet sites <http://ferret.bls.census.gov/macro/032001/perinc/new01_015 .htm> and <http://ferret.bls.census.gov/macro/032001/perinc/new01_030.htm>; calculations by New Strategist

Median Earnings of Whites Working Full-Time by Sex, 1990 to 2000

(median earnings of whites who work full-time, year-round by sex; index of white to total popula-tion median earnings, and white women's earnings as a percent of white men's earnings,1990 to 2000; percent change in earnings and indexes, 1990–2000; in 2000 dollars)

	white men		white women		white women's earnings as a percent of white men's earnings
	median earnings	index white/total	median earnings	index white/total	
2000	$38,869	104	$28,080	103	72.2%
1999	38,499	102	27,559	101	71.6
1998	38,169	102	27,692	101	72.6
1997	37,656	105	27,104	101	72.0
1996	36,037	103	26,411	102	73.3
1995	36,124	102	25,725	102	71.2
1994	36,369	102	26,039	102	71.6
1993	36,568	102	25,904	101	70.8
1992	37,231	102	26,055	101	70.0
1991	37,487	103	25,755	101	68.7
1990	37,082	104	25,741	101	69.4
Percent change					
1990–2000	4.8%	–0.2%	9.1%	1.5%	4.1%

Note: The white/total indexes are calculated by dividing the median earnings of white men and women by the median earnings of total men and women and multiplying by 100.
Source: Bureau of the Census, Current Population Survey, Internet site <www.census.gov/hhes/income/histinc/ p38a.html>; calculations by New Strategist

Median Earnings of Non-Hispanic Whites Working Full-Time by Sex, 1990 to 2000

(median earnings of non-Hispanic whites who work full-time, year-round by sex; index of non-Hispanic white to total population median earnings, and non-Hispanic white women's earnings as a percent of non-Hispanic white men's earnings, 1990 to 2000; percent change in earnings and indexes, 1990–2000; in 2000 dollars)

	non-Hispanic white men		non-Hispanic white women		non-Hispanic white women's earnings as a percent of non-Hispanic white men's earnings
	median earnings	index non-Hispanic white/total	median earnings	index non-Hispanic white/total	
2000	$41,157	110	$29,604	108	71.9%
1999	41,679	111	28,340	104	68.0
1998	39,818	107	28,363	104	71.2
1997	39,158	109	27,728	104	70.8
1996	38,744	110	27,209	105	70.2
1995	38,628	109	26,568	105	68.8
1994	37,568	106	26,699	104	71.1
1993	37,605	105	26,327	103	70.0
1992	38,275	105	26,417	102	69.0
1991	38,454	106	26,127	103	67.9
1990	38,690	109	26,138	103	67.6
Percent change					
1990–2000	6.4%	1.2%	13.3%	5.4%	6.5%

Note: The non-Hispanic white/total indexes are calculated by dividing the median earnings of non-Hispanic white men and women by the median earnings of total men and women and multiplying by 100.
Source: Bureau of the Census, Current Population Survey, Internet site <www.census.gov/hhes/income/histinc/p38e.html>; calculations by New Strategist

Median Earnings of Whites Working Full-Time by Education and Sex, 2000

(median earnings of whites aged 25 or older working full-time, year-round by educational attainment and sex, and white women's earnings as a percent of white men's earnings, 2000)

	men	women	white women's earnings as a percent of white men's earnings
Total whites	**$40,927**	**$29,794**	**72.8%**
Less than 9th grade	20,184	14,985	74.2
9th to 12th grade, no diploma	25,030	16,957	67.7
High school graduate	34,583	24,579	71.1
Some college, no degree	40,028	27,401	68.5
Associate's degree	41,864	30,567	73.0
Bachelor's degree or more	60,862	41,362	68.0
Bachelor's degree	55,270	38,509	69.7
Master's degree	65,101	47,142	72.4
Professional degree	94,709	56,405	59.6
Doctoral degree	76,312	55,581	72.8

Source: Bureau of the Census, Current Population Survey, Internet sites <http://ferret.bls.census.gov/macro/032001/perinc/new03_077 .htm> and <http://ferret.bls.census.gov/macro/032001/perinc/new03_147.htm>; calculations by New Strategist

Median Earnings of Non-Hispanic Whites Working Full-Time by Education and Sex, 2000

(median earnings of non-Hispanic whites aged 25 or older working full-time, year-round by educational attainment and sex, and non-Hispanic white women's earnings as a percent of non-Hispanic white men's earnings, 2000)

	men	*women*	*non-Hispanic white women's earnings as a percent of non-Hispanic white men's earnings*
Total non-Hispanic whites	**42,365**	**30,658**	**72.4%**
Less than 9th grade	24,277	16,067	66.2
9th to 12th grade, no diploma	26,569	18,002	67.8
High school graduate	35,600	25,127	70.6
Some college, no degree	40,576	27,793	68.5
Associate's degree	42,204	30,816	73.0
Bachelor's degree or more	61,197	41,547	67.9
Bachelor's degree	55,896	39,122	70.0
Master's degree	65,311	47,296	72.4
Professional degree	94,599	56,302	59.5
Doctoral degree	76,502	55,771	72.9

Source: Bureau of the Census, Current Population Survey, Internet sites <http://ferret.bls.census.gov/macro/032001/perinc/new03_080 .htm> and <http://ferret.bls.census.gov/macro/032001/perinc/new03_150.htm>; calculations by New Strategist

Poverty Status of White Families, 1990 to 2000

(total number of white families, and number and percent below poverty level by type of family and presence of children under age 18 at home, 1990 to 2000; percent change in numbers and rates, 1990–2000; families in thousands as of March the following year)

	total families			married couples			female hh, no spouse present		
		in poverty			in poverty			in poverty	
	total	number	percent	total	number	percent	total	number	percent
With and without children < age 18									
2000	60,222	4,151	6.9%	48,655	2,162	4.4%	8,293	1,655	20.0%
1999	60,256	4,377	7.3	48,794	2,161	4.4	8,380	1,883	22.5
1998	60,077	4,829	8.0	48,461	2,400	5.0	8,529	2,123	24.9
1997	59,515	4,990	8.4	48,070	2,312	4.8	8,308	2,305	27.7
1996	58,934	5,059	8.6	47,650	2,416	5.1	8,339	2,276	27.3
1995	58,872	4,994	8.5	47,877	2,443	5.1	8,284	2,200	26.6
1994	58,444	5,312	9.1	47,905	2,629	5.5	8,031	2,329	29.0
1993	57,881	5,452	9.4	47,452	2,757	5.8	8,131	2,376	29.2
1992	57,669	5,255	9.1	47,383	2,677	5.7	7,868	2,245	28.5
1991	57,224	5,022	8.8	47,124	2,573	5.5	7,726	2,192	28.4
1990	56,803	4,622	8.1	47,014	2,386	5.1	7,512	2,010	26.8
Percent change									
1990–2000	6.0%	−10.2%	−14.8%	3.5%	−9.4%	−13.7%	10.4%	−17.7%	−25.4%
With children under age 18									
2000	29,747	3,049	10.3%	22,609	1,316	5.8%	5,356	1,474	27.5%
1999	27,841	3,236	10.8	22,660	1,333	5.9	5,500	1,656	30.1
1998	29,984	3,665	12.2	22,634	1,503	6.6	5,691	1,926	33.8
1997	30,060	3,895	13.0	22,783	1,516	6.7	5,502	2,069	37.6
1996	29,826	3,863	13.0	22,757	1,548	6.8	5,501	2,032	36.9
1995	29,713	3,839	12.9	22,663	1,583	7.0	5,554	1,980	35.6
1994	29,548	4,025	13.6	22,839	1,706	7.5	5,390	2,064	38.3
1993	29,234	4,226	14.5	22,670	1,868	8.2	5,361	2,123	39.6
1992	28,790	4,020	14.0	22,440	1,753	7.8	5,099	2,021	39.6
1991	28,369	3,880	13.7	22,214	1,715	7.7	4,969	1,969	39.6
1990	28,117	3,553	12.6	22,289	1,572	7.1	4,786	1,814	37.9
Percent change									
1990–2000	5.8%	−14.2%	−18.3%	1.4%	−16.3%	−18.3%	11.9%	−18.7%	−27.4%

Source: Bureau of the Census, Current Population Survey, Internet sites <www.census.gov/hhes/poverty/histpov/hstpov4.html> and <http://ferret.bls.census.gov/macro/032001/pov/new16a_000.htm>; calculations by New Strategist

Poverty Status of Non-Hispanic White Families, 1990 to 2000

(total number of non-Hispanic white families, and number and percent below poverty level by type of family and presence of children under age 18 at home, 1990 to 2000; percent change in numbers and rates, 1990–2000; families in thousands as of March the following year)

	total families			married couples			female hh, no spouse present		
		in poverty			in poverty			in poverty	
	total	number	percent	total	number	percent	total	number	percent
With and without children < age 18									
2000	52,883	2,819	5.3%	43,632	1,447	3.3%	6,681	1,126	16.9%
1999	53,071	2,942	5.5	43,870	1,457	3.3	6,733	1,255	18.6
1998	53,107	3,264	6.1	43,669	1,639	3.8	6,909	1,428	20.7
1997	52,875	3,357	6.3	43,427	1,501	3.5	6,826	1,598	23.4
1996	52,625	3,433	6.5	43,276	1,628	3.8	6,875	1,538	22.4
1995	52,861	3,384	6.4	43,771	1,664	3.8	6,792	1,463	21.5
1994	53,029	3,833	7.2	44,178	1,915	4.3	6,764	1,678	24.8
1993	52,470	3,988	7.6	43,745	2,042	4.7	6,798	1,699	25.0
1992	52,302	3,840	7.3	43,661	1,978	4.5	6,629	1,637	24.7
1991	52,288	3,719	7.1	43,724	1,918	4.4	6,553	1,610	24.6
1990	52,038	3,442	6.6	43,682	1,799	4.1	6,408	1,480	23.1
Percent change									
1990–2000	1.6%	−18.1%	−19.7%	−0.1%	−19.6%	−19.5%	4.3%	−23.9%	−26.8%
With children under age 18									
2000	24,674	1,910	7.7%	19,118	726	3.8%	4,154	991	23.9%
1999	24,784	1,984	8.0	19,185	744	3.9	4,252	1,079	25.4
1998	25,109	2,282	9.1	19,327	859	4.5	4,427	1,275	28.8
1997	25,374	2,478	9.8	19,588	842	4.3	4,320	1,420	32.9
1996	25,381	2,424	9.6	19,729	884	4.5	4,357	1,351	31.0
1995	25,497	2,445	9.6	19,866	948	4.8	4,361	1,294	29.7
1994	25,734	2,733	10.6	20,276	1,101	5.4	4,386	1,471	33.5
1993	25,477	2,946	11.6	20,166	1,263	6.3	4,330	1,506	34.8
1992	25,090	2,817	11.2	19,905	1,177	5.9	4,150	1,474	35.5
1991	24,909	2,722	10.9	19,845	1,152	5.8	4,067	1,429	35.1
1990	24,764	2,522	10.2	19,957	1,085	5.4	3,929	1,317	33.5
1990–2000	−0.4%	−24.3%	−24.5%	−4.2%	−33.1%	−29.6%	5.7%	−24.8%	−28.7%

Source: Bureau of the Census, Current Population Survey, Internet site <www.census.gov/hhes/poverty/histpov/ hstpov4.html> and <http://ferret.bls.census.gov/macro/032001/pov/new16a_000.htm>; calculations by New Strategist

Poverty Status of Whites by Sex and Age, 2000

(total number of whites, and number and percent below poverty level by sex and age, 2000; people in thousands as of 2001)

	total	in poverty number	in poverty percent
Total whites	**225,997**	**21,242**	**9.4%**
Under age 18	56,412	7,283	12.9
Aged 18 to 24	21,532	2,709	12.6
Aged 25 to 34	29,867	2,738	9.2
Aged 35 to 44	36,691	2,569	7.0
Aged 45 to 54	31,964	1,661	5.2
Aged 55 to 59	11,450	854	7.5
Aged 60 to 64	8,960	828	9.2
Aged 65 or older	29,122	2,601	8.9
Aged 65 to 74	15,604	1,190	7.6
Aged 75 or older	13,518	1,412	10.4
White females	**114,700**	**12,001**	**10.5**
Under age 18	27,462	3,608	13.1
Aged 18 to 24	10,626	1,597	15.0
Aged 25 to 34	14,930	1,706	11.4
Aged 35 to 44	18,299	1,466	8.0
Aged 45 to 54	16,169	862	5.3
Aged 55 to 59	5,893	497	8.4
Aged 60 to 64	4,761	479	10.1
Aged 65 or older	16,560	1,785	10.8
Aged 65 to 74	8,369	731	8.7
Aged 75 or older	8,191	1,055	12.9
White males	**111,297**	**9,241**	**8.3**
Under age 18	28,950	3,674	12.7
Aged 18 to 24	10,906	1,111	10.2
Aged 25 to 34	14,937	1,032	6.9
Aged 35 to 44	18,392	1,103	6.0
Aged 45 to 54	15,795	800	5.1
Aged 55 to 59	5,557	357	6.4
Aged 60 to 64	4,198	348	8.3
Aged 65 or older	12,562	816	6.5
Aged 65 to 74	7,235	459	6.3
Aged 75 or older	5,326	357	6.7

Source: Bureau of the Census, Current Population Survey, Internet site <http://ferret.bls.census.gov/macro/032001/pov/new01_001.htm>; calculations by New Strategist

Poverty Status of Non-Hispanic Whites by Sex and Age, 2000

(total number of non-Hispanic whites, and number and percent below poverty level by sex and age, 2000; people in thousands as of 2001)

	total	in poverty number	in poverty percent
Total non-Hispanic whites	**193,917**	**14,532**	**7.5%**
Under age 18	45,155	4,185	9.3
Aged 18 to 24	17,534	1,862	10.6
Aged 25 to 34	24,501	1,715	7.0
Aged 35 to 44	31,925	1,838	5.8
Aged 45 to 54	28,887	1,284	4.4
Aged 55 to 59	10,440	730	7.0
Aged 60 to 64	8,168	654	8.0
Aged 65 or older	27,308	2,264	8.3
Aged 65 to 74	14,498	982	6.8
Aged 75 or older	12,810	1,282	10.0
Non-Hispanic white females	**98,711**	**8,384**	**8.5**
Under age 18	22,010	2,079	9.4
Aged 18 to 24	8,650	1,108	12.8
Aged 25 to 34	12,310	1,124	9.1
Aged 35 to 44	15,948	1,044	6.5
Aged 45 to 54	14,580	652	4.5
Aged 55 to 59	5,363	416	7.8
Aged 60 to 64	4,350	378	8.7
Aged 65 or older	15,501	1,582	10.2
Aged 65 to 74	7,746	621	8.0
Aged 75 or older	7,756	961	12.4
Non-Hispanic white males	**95,206**	**6,148**	**6.5**
Under age 18	23,146	2,106	9.1
Aged 18 to 24	8,883	754	8.5
Aged 25 to 34	12,191	591	4.8
Aged 35 to 44	15,977	795	5.0
Aged 45 to 54	14,307	632	4.4
Aged 55 to 59	5,077	314	6.2
Aged 60 to 64	3,818	275	7.2
Aged 65 or older	11,807	681	5.8
Aged 65 to 74	6,752	361	5.3
Aged 75 or older	5,054	320	6.3

Source: Bureau of the Census, Current Population Survey, Internet site <http://ferret.bls.census.gov/macro/032001/pov/new01_001.htm>; calculations by New Strategist

Thirty-One Percent of White Workers Are Employed in Managerial or Professional Specialty Occupations

Seventy-five percent of white men and 60 percent of white women were in the labor force in 2000. Because whites comprise the great majority of the population, their labor force participation rate closely matches that of the total population.

The largest share of whites (31 percent) are employed in managerial or professional specialty occupations. Another 29 percent work in technical, sales, or administrative support.

Forty-six percent of white households have two or more earners. Among white couples, the 56 percent majority are dual earners. Only 22 percent are traditional, that is, only the husband works.

Between 2000 and 2010, the number of white workers will grow 9 percent, while the number of non-Hispanic white workers will increase a smaller 6 percent. In the year 2010, non-Hispanic whites will account for just 69 percent of the labor force.

■ White households have much higher incomes than black and Hispanic households because so many are headed by dual-earner married couples. Until the dual-earner share of black and Hispanic households matches that of whites, the income gap will remain.

Most non-Hispanic white couples are dual earners

(percent distribution of non-Hispanic white married couples by labor force status of husband and wife, 2000)

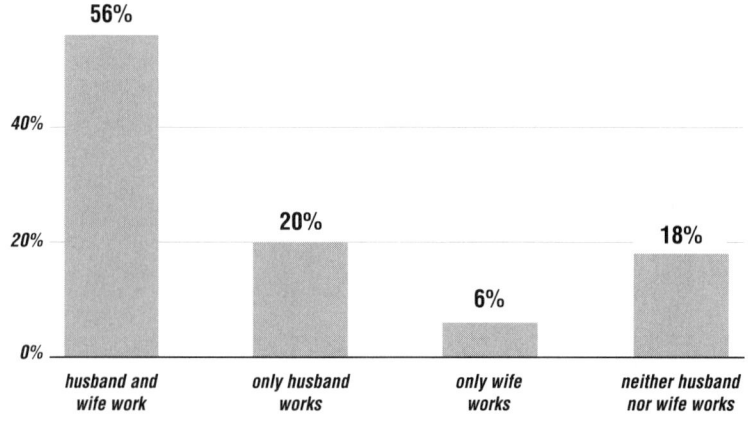

Labor Force Participation Rate of Whites by Age and Sex, 2000

(percent of whites aged 16 or older in the civilian labor force, by age and sex, 2000)

	men	*women*
Total whites	**75.4%**	**59.8%**
Aged 16 to 19	56.6	54.7
Aged 20 to 24	85.0	74.7
Aged 25 to 29	93.9	76.9
Aged 30 to 34	94.9	74.9
Aged 35 to 39	94.2	75.5
Aged 40 to 44	93.3	78.8
Aged 45 to 49	91.5	79.7
Aged 50 to 54	87.8	74.9
Aged 55 to 59	78.1	61.6
Aged 60 to 64	55.6	40.9
Aged 65 or older	17.7	9.4
Aged 65 to 69	30.9	19.7
Aged 70 to 74	18.3	10.3
Aged 75 or older	8.2	3.5

Note: The civilian labor force equals the number of employed plus the number of unemployed.
Source: Bureau of Labor Statistics, Employment and Earnings, *January 2001*

Employment Status of Whites by Sex and Age, 2000

(employment status of the civilian noninstitutionalized white population aged 16 or older, by sex and age, 2000; numbers in thousands)

	civilian labor force					not in labor force	
	total	percent of population	employed	unemployed	percent unemployed	total	percent of population
Total whites	**117,574**	**67.4%**	**113,475**	**4,099**	**3.5%**	**56,854**	**32.6%**
Aged 16 to 19	7,075	55.7	6,270	805	11.4	5,632	44.3
Aged 20 to 24	11,762	79.9	11,078	684	5.8	2,958	20.1
Aged 25 to 34	25,482	85.1	24,678	804	3.2	4,469	14.9
Aged 35 to 44	31,346	85.4	30,522	825	2.6	5,342	14.6
Aged 45 to 54	25,968	83.5	25,384	585	2.3	5,123	16.5
Aged 55 to 64	12,192	60.0	11,901	290	2.4	8,132	40.0
Aged 65 or older	3,749	13.0	3,643	106	2.8	25,198	87.0
White men	**63,861**	**75.4**	**61,696**	**2,165**	**3.4**	**20,786**	**24.6**
Aged 16 to 19	3,679	56.6	3,227	452	12.3	2,817	43.4
Aged 20 to 24	6,308	85.0	5,939	369	5.9	1,112	15.0
Aged 25 to 34	14,043	94.4	13,634	409	2.9	827	5.6
Aged 35 to 44	17,158	93.7	16,749	409	2.4	1,146	6.3
Aged 45 to 54	13,783	89.8	13,484	298	2.2	1,573	10.2
Aged 55 to 64	6,692	68.2	6,532	159	2.4	3,119	31.8
Aged 65 or older	2,198	17.7	2,130	68	3.1	10,192	82.3
White women	**53,714**	**59.8**	**51,780**	**1,934**	**3.6**	**36,068**	**40.2**
Aged 16 to 19	3,396	54.7	3,043	353	10.4	2,815	45.3
Aged 20 to 24	5,455	74.7	5,140	315	5.8	1,846	25.3
Aged 25 to 34	11,439	75.9	11,043	396	3.5	3,642	24.1
Aged 35 to 44	14,188	77.2	13,772	415	2.9	4,196	22.8
Aged 45 to 54	12,186	77.4	11,899	286	2.3	3,550	22.6
Aged 55 to 64	5,500	52.3	5,369	131	2.4	5,013	47.7
Aged 65 or older	1,550	9.4	1,512	38	2.4	15,007	90.6

Note: The civilian labor force equals the number of employed plus the number of unemployed. The civilian population equals the number in the labor force plus the number not in the labor force.
Source: Bureau of Labor Statistics, Employment and Earnings, *January 2001; calculations by New Strategist*

White Workers by Occupation, 2000

(total number of employed people aged 16 or older in the civilian labor force; number and percent distribution of employed whites, and white share of total, by occupation, 2000; numbers in thousands)

	total	white number	white percent distribution	white share of total
Total employed	**135,208**	**113,475**	**100.0%**	**83.9%**
Managerial and professional specialty	40,887	35,304	31.1	86.3
Executive, administrative, and managerial	19,774	17,372	15.3	87.9
Professional specialty	21,113	17,932	15.8	84.9
Technical, sales, and administrative support	39,442	33,146	29.2	84.0
Technicians and related support	4,385	3,611	3.2	82.3
Sales occupations	16,340	14,169	12.5	86.7
Administrative support, including clerical	18,717	15,366	13.5	82.1
Service occupations	18,278	14,066	12.4	77.0
Private household	792	631	0.6	79.7
Protective service	2,399	1,860	1.6	77.5
Service, except private household and protective	15,087	11,575	10.2	76.7
Precision production, craft, and repair	14,882	13,133	11.6	88.2
Mechanics and repairers	4,875	4,293	3.8	88.1
Construction trades	6,120	5,540	4.9	90.5
Other precision production, craft, and repair	3,887	3,300	2.9	84.9
Operators, fabricators, and laborers	18,319	14,680	12.9	80.1
Machine operators, assemblers, and inspectors	7,319	5,802	5.1	79.3
Transportation and material moving occupations	5,557	4,476	3.9	80.5
Handlers, equipment cleaners, helpers, and laborers	5,443	4,402	3.9	80.9
Construction laborers	1,015	876	0.8	86.3
Other handlers, equipment cleaners, helpers, and laborers	4,428	3,526	3.1	79.6
Farming, forestry, and fishing	3,399	3,146	2.8	92.6

Source: Bureau of Labor Statistics, Employment and Earnings, *January 2001; calculations by New Strategist*

White Workers by Industry, 2000

(total number of employed people aged 16 or older in the civilian labor force; number and percent distribution of employed whites, and white share of total, by industry, 2000; numbers in thousands)

	total	white number	white percent distribution	white share of total
Total employed	**135,208**	**113,475**	**100.0%**	**83.9%**
Agriculture	3,305	3,099	2.7	93.8
Mining	521	478	0.4	91.7
Construction	9,433	8,552	7.5	90.7
Manufacturing	19,940	16,817	14.8	84.3
Durable goods	12,168	10,318	9.1	84.8
Nondurable goods	7,772	6,498	5.7	83.6
Transportation, communications, and other public utilities	9,740	7,769	6.8	79.8
Wholesale and retail trade	27,832	23,783	21.0	85.5
Wholesale trade	5,421	4,785	4.2	88.3
Retail trade	22,411	18,998	16.7	84.8
Finance, insurance, real estate	8,727	7,408	6.5	84.9
Services	49,695	40,807	36.0	82.1
Private households	894	709	0.6	79.3
Other service industries	48,801	40,099	35.3	82.2
Professional, related services	32,784	26,978	23.8	82.3
Public administration	6,015	4,763	4.2	79.2

Source: Bureau of Labor Statistics, Employment and Earnings, *January 2001; calculations by New Strategist*

White Households by Number of Earners, 2000

(number and percent distribution of white households by number of earners, 2000; numbers in thousands)

	number	percent distribution
White households	**87,671**	**100.0%**
No earners	17,500	20.0
One earner	29,544	33.7
Two or more earners	40,627	46.3
Two earners	31,761	36.2
Three earners	6,526	7.4
Four or more earners	2,340	2.7

Source: Bureau of the Census, Current Population Survey, Internet site <http://ferret.bls.census.gov/macro/ 032000/hhinc/new01_002 .htm>; calculations by New Strategist

Non-Hispanic White Households by Number of Earners, 2000

(number and percent distribution of non-Hispanic white households by number of earners, 2000; numbers in thousands)

	number	percent distribution
Non-Hispanic white households	**78,819**	**100.0%**
No earners	16,400	20.8
One earner	26,381	33.5
Two or more earners	36,038	45.7
Two earners	28,581	36.3
Three earners	5,591	7.1
Four or more earners	1,866	2.4

Source: Bureau of the Census, Current Population Survey, Internet site <http://ferret.bls.census.gov/macro/ 032000/hhinc/new01_005 .htm>; calculations by New Strategist

Labor Force Status of White Married Couples, 2000

(number and percent distribution of white married couples by age of householder and labor force status of husband and wife, 2000; numbers in thousands)

| | *total* | husband and/or wife in labor force | | | *neither husband nor wife in labor force* |
		husband and wife	*husband only*	*wife only*	
Total white couples	**48,790**	**27,240**	**10,587**	**2,708**	**8,256**
Under age 20	76	39	38	–	–
Aged 20 to 24	1,222	771	407	28	16
Aged 25 to 29	3,293	2,332	887	39	34
Aged 30 to 34	4,835	3,307	1,389	85	54
Aged 35 to 39	6,016	4,200	1,624	131	62
Aged 40 to 44	6,255	4,558	1,430	193	74
Aged 45 to 54	11,174	7,920	2,248	618	389
Aged 55 to 64	7,269	3,374	1,594	915	1,385
Aged 65 or older	8,650	739	971	700	6,243
Total white couples	**100.0%**	**55.8%**	**21.7%**	**5.6%**	**16.9%**
Under age 20	100.0	51.3	50.0	–	–
Aged 20 to 24	100.0	63.1	33.3	2.3	1.3
Aged 25 to 29	100.0	70.8	26.9	1.2	1.0
Aged 30 to 34	100.0	68.4	28.7	1.8	1.1
Aged 35 to 39	100.0	69.8	27.0	2.2	1.0
Aged 40 to 44	100.0	72.9	22.9	3.1	1.2
Aged 45 to 54	100.0	70.9	20.1	5.5	3.5
Aged 55 to 64	100.0	46.4	21.9	12.6	19.1
Aged 65 or older	100.0	8.5	11.2	8.1	72.2

Note: (–) means sample is too small to make a reliable estimate.
Source: Bureau of the Census, Household and Family Characteristics: March 2000 (Update), *detailed tables for Current Population Report P20-537, Internet site <www.census.gov/population/socdemo/hh-fam/p20-537/ 2000/tabFG1.txt>; calculations by New Strategist*

Labor Force Status of Non-Hispanic White Married Couples, 2000

(number and percent distribution of non-Hispanic white married couples by age of householder and labor force status of husband and wife, 2000; numbers in thousands)

| | total | husband and/or wife in labor force | | | neither husband nor wife in labor force |
		husband and wife	husband only	wife only	
Total non-Hispanic white couples	**43,865**	**24,731**	**8,872**	**2,503**	**7,759**
Under age 20	48	30	18	–	–
Aged 20 to 24	944	656	257	18	13
Aged 25 to 29	2,708	2,029	625	35	19
Aged 30 to 34	4,055	2,897	1,053	67	39
Aged 35 to 39	5,183	3,670	1,338	121	53
Aged 40 to 44	5,609	4,142	1,242	175	50
Aged 45 to 54	10,293	7,386	1,991	567	348
Aged 55 to 64	6,784	3,203	1,424	852	1,304
Aged 65 or older	8,242	717	926	668	5,932
Total non-Hispanic white couples	**100.0%**	**56.4%**	**20.2%**	**5.7%**	**17.7%**
Under age 20	100.0	62.5	37.5	–	–
Aged 20 to 24	100.0	69.5	27.2	1.9	1.4
Aged 25 to 29	100.0	74.9	23.1	1.3	0.7
Aged 30 to 34	100.0	71.4	26.0	1.7	1.0
Aged 35 to 39	100.0	70.8	25.8	2.3	1.0
Aged 40 to 44	100.0	73.8	22.1	3.1	0.9
Aged 45 to 54	100.0	71.8	19.3	5.5	3.4
Aged 55 to 64	100.0	47.2	21.0	12.6	19.2
Aged 65 or older	100.0	8.7	11.2	8.1	72.0

Note: (–) means sample is too small to make a reliable estimate.
Source: Bureau of the Census, Household and Family Characteristics: March 2000 (Update), *detailed tables for Current Population Report P20-537, Internet site <www.census.gov/population/socdemo/hh-fam/p20-537/2000/tabFG1.txt>; calculations by New Strategist*

Union Membership of Whites, 2000

(number of employed white wage and salary workers aged 16 or older, number and percent represented by unions or who are union members, and median weekly earnings by union membership status; by sex, 2000; numbers in thousands)

	total	men	women
Total employed whites	**100,455**	**53,105**	**47,350**
Represented by unions	14,453	8,541	5,912
Percent of employed	14.4%	16.1%	12.5%
Members of unions	13,094	7,911	5,183
Percent of employed	13.0%	14.9%	10.9%
Median weekly earnings, total	**$591**	**$669**	**$500**
Represented by unions	711	755	627
Members of unions	716	757	631
Non-union	565	641	482

Note: Workers represented by unions are either members of a labor union or similar employee association or workers who report no union affiliation but whose jobs are covered by a union or an employee association contract. Members of unions are union members as well as members of employee associations similar to unions.
Source: Bureau of Labor Statistics, Employment and Earnings, *January 2001*

Projections of the White Labor Force by Sex, 2000 and 2010

(number of whites in the civilian labor force, labor force participation rate of whites, and white share of total labor force, by sex, 2000 and 2010; percent change in number and percentage point change in rate and share, 2000–2010; numbers in thousands)

	whites in labor force		
	2000	2010	percent change 2000–10
Total	117,574	128,043	8.9%
Men	63,861	68,159	6.7
Women	53,714	59,884	11.5

	white labor force participation rate		
	2000	2010	percentage point change 2000–10
Total	67.4%	67.6%	0.2
Men	75.4	73.8	−1.6
Women	59.8	61.6	1.8

	white share of total labor force		
	2000	2010	percentage point change 2000–10
Total	83.5%	81.2%	−2.3
Men	45.3	43.2	−2.1
Women	38.1	38.0	−0.1

Source: Bureau of Labor Statistics, Monthly Labor Review, *November 2001*

Projections of the Non-Hispanic White Labor Force by Sex, 2000 and 2010

(number of non-Hispanic whites in the civilian labor force, labor force participation rate of non-Hispanic whites and non-Hispanic white share of total labor force, by sex, 2000 and 2010; percent change in number and percentage point change in rate and share, 2000–2010; numbers in thousands)

	non-Hispanic whites in labor force		
	2000	*2010*	*percent change 2000–10*
Total	**102,963**	**109,118**	**6.0%**
Men	55,359	57,538	3.9
Women	47,604	51,580	8.4

	non-Hispanic white labor force participation rate		
	2000	*2010*	*percentage point change 2000–10*
Total	**67.2%**	**67.3%**	**0.1**
Men	74.7	72.9	−1.8
Women	60.3	62.0	1.7

	non-Hispanic white share of total labor force		
	2000	*2010*	*percentage point change 2000–10*
Total	**73.1%**	**69.2%**	**−3.9**
Men	39.3	36.5	−2.8
Women	38.1	32.7	−5.4

Source: Bureau of Labor Statistics, Monthly Labor Review, *November 2001*

Most Non-Hispanic White Households Are Headed by Married Couples

Because most Americans are white, the household composition and living arrangements of whites mirror those of the total population. Because whites—and in particular non-Hispanic whites—are older, on average, than Asians, blacks, or Hispanics, the non-Hispanic white share of households is much greater among older householders than young adults. Fewer than 70 percent of householders under age 35 are non-Hispanic white, for example, versus 85 percent of householders aged 65 or older.

Fifty-six percent of non-Hispanic white households are married couples, and 23 percent are nuclear families—defined as a husband, wife, and children under age 18 at home. These figures are about the same as for households in the nation as a whole. Families headed by women account for 9 percent of non-Hispanic white households, smaller than their 12 percent share of all households. People who live alone account for 27 percent of non-Hispanic white households.

Seventy-seven percent of non-Hispanic white children live with both parents, and 16 percent live with their mother only. Fifty-one percent of non-Hispanic white men aged 20 to 24 still live with their parents. For their female counterparts, the figure is 44 percent.

Fifty-nine percent of non-Hispanic white men aged 15 or older are currently married. The proportion is somewhat smaller 56 percent among non-Hispanic white women. The majority of non-Hispanic white men aged 30 or older are married, as are most non-Hispanic white women between the ages of 25 and 74.

■ The composition of non-Hispanic white households—fewer single-parent families and more people living alone—reflects the older age of the non-Hispanic white population.

Many non-Hispanic whites live alone

(percent distribution of households headed by non-Hispanic whites by household type, 2000)

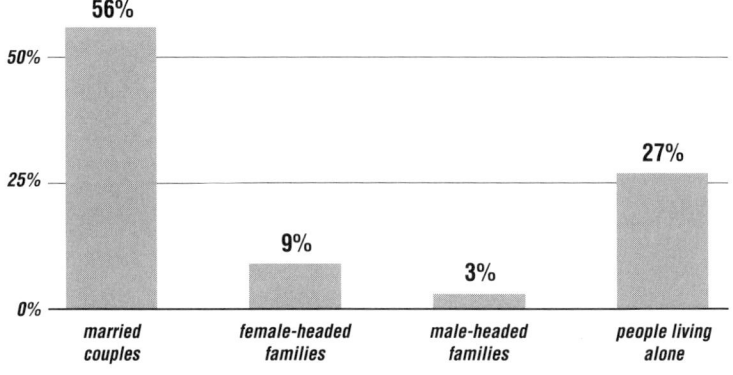

White Households by Age of Householder, 2000

(number of total households, number and percent distribution of white households, and white share of total, by age of householder, 2000, numbers in thousands)

		white households		
	total	*number*	*percent distribution*	*share of total*
Total households	**104,705**	**87,671**	**100.0%**	**83.7%**
Under age 20	914	661	0.8	72.3
Aged 20 to 24	4,946	3,880	4.4	78.4
Aged 25 to 29	8,520	6,744	7.7	79.2
Aged 30 to 34	10,107	8,127	9.3	80.4
Aged 35 to 39	11,728	9,724	11.1	82.9
Aged 40 to 44	12,227	10,084	11.5	82.5
Aged 45 to 54	20,927	17,475	19.9	83.5
Aged 55 to 64	13,592	11,599	13.2	85.3
Aged 65 or older	21,744	19,376	22.1	89.1
Aged 65 to 74	11,325	9,883	11.3	87.3
Aged 75 or older	10,419	9,493	10.8	91.1

Source: Bureau of the Census, America's Families and Living Arrangements: March 2000, *detailed tables from Current Population Report P20-537, Internet site <www.census.gov/population/www/socdemo/hh-fam/p20-537_00.html>; calculations by New Strategist*

Non-Hispanic White Households by Age of Householder, 2000

(number of total households, number and percent distribution of non-Hispanic white households, and non-Hispanic white share of total, by age of householder, 2000, numbers in thousands)

| | total | non-Hispanic white households | | |
		number	percent distribution	share of total
Total households	**104,705**	**78,819**	**100.0%**	**75.3%**
Under age 20	914	520	0.7	56.9
Aged 20 to 24	4,946	3,201	4.1	64.7
Aged 25 to 29	8,520	5,678	7.2	66.6
Aged 30 to 34	10,107	6,855	8.7	67.8
Aged 35 to 39	11,728	8,409	10.7	71.7
Aged 40 to 44	12,227	9,031	11.5	73.9
Aged 45 to 54	20,927	16,008	20.3	76.5
Aged 55 to 64	13,592	10,704	13.6	78.8
Aged 65 or older	21,744	18,412	23.4	84.7
Aged 65 to 74	11,325	9,273	11.8	81.9
Aged 75 or older	10,419	9,139	11.6	87.7

Source: Bureau of the Census, America's Families and Living Arrangements: March 2000, *detailed tables from Current Population Report P20-537, Internet site <www.census.gov/population/www/socdemo/hh-fam/p20-537_00.html>; calculations by New Strategist*

White Households by Household Type, 2000

(number of total households, number and percent distribution of white households, and white share of total, by type, 2000; numbers in thousands)

		white households		
	total	number	percent distribution	share of total
Total households	**104,705**	**87,671**	**100.0%**	**83.7%**
Family households	**72,025**	**60,251**	**68.7**	**83.7**
Married couples	55,311	48,790	55.7	88.2
With children under age 18	25,248	21,809	24.9	86.4
Without children under age 18	30,062	26,981	30.8	89.8
Female householder, no spouse present	12,687	8,380	9.6	66.1
With children under age 18	7,571	4,869	5.6	64.3
Without children under age 18	5,116	3,511	4.0	68.6
Male householder, no spouse present	4,028	3,081	3.5	76.5
With children under age 18	1,786	1,429	1.6	80.0
Without children under age 18	2,242	1,652	1.9	73.7
Nonfamily households	**32,680**	**27,420**	**31.3**	**83.9**
Female householder	18,039	15,215	17.4	84.3
Living alone	15,543	13,109	15.0	84.3
Male householder	14,641	12,204	13.9	83.4
Living alone	11,181	9,198	10.5	82.3

Source: Bureau of the Census, America's Families and Living Arrangements: March 2000, *detailed tables from Current Population Report P20-537, Internet site <www.census.gov/population/www/socdemo/hh-fam/p20-537_00.html>; calculations by New Strategist*

Non-Hispanic White Households by Household Type, 2000

(number of total households, number and percent distribution of non-Hispanic white households, and non-Hispanic white share of total, by type, 2000; numbers in thousands)

		non-Hispanic white households		
	total	*number*	*percent distribution*	*share of total*
Total households	**104,705**	**78,819**	**100.0%**	**75.3%**
Family households	**72,025**	**53,066**	**67.3**	**73.7**
Married couples	55,311	43,865	55.7	79.3
With children under age 18	25,248	18,516	23.5	73.3
Without children under age 18	30,062	25,349	32.2	84.3
Female householder, no spouse present	12,687	6,732	8.5	53.1
With children under age 18	7,571	3,815	4.8	50.4
Without children under age 18	5,116	2,917	3.7	57.0
Male householder, no spouse present	4,028	2,468	3.1	61.3
With children under age 18	1,786	1,202	1.5	67.3
Without children under age 18	2,242	1,267	1.6	56.5
Nonfamily households	**32,680**	**25,753**	**32.7**	**78.8**
Female householder	18,039	14,475	18.4	80.2
Living alone	15,543	12,508	15.9	80.5
Male householder	14,641	11,278	14.3	77.0
Living alone	11,181	8,562	10.9	76.6

Source: Bureau of the Census, America's Families and Living Arrangements: March 2000, *detailed tables from Current Population Report P20-537, Internet site <www.census.gov/population/www/socdemo/hh-fam/p20-537_00.html>; calculations by New Strategist*

White Households by Household Type, 2000 Census

(number of total households, number and percent distribution of white households, and white share of total, by type, 2000)

	total	white households number	white households percent distribution	white households share of total
Total households	**105,480,101**	**85,223,091**	**100.0%**	**80.8%**
Family households	**71,787,347**	**57,202,648**	**67.1**	**79.7**
Married couples	54,493,232	46,212,090	54.2	84.8
With children under age 18	24,835,505	20,002,369	23.5	80.5
Without children under age 18	29,657,727	26,209,721	30.8	88.4
Female householder, no spouse present	12,900,103	7,901,635	9.3	61.3
With children under age 18	7,561,874	4,417,574	5.2	58.4
Without children under age 18	5,338,229	3,484,061	4.1	65.3
Male householder, no spouse present	4,394,012	3,088,923	3.6	70.3
With children under age 18	2,190,989	1,566,556	1.8	71.5
Without children under age 18	2,203,023	1,522,367	1.8	69.1
Nonfamily households	**33,692,754**	**28,020,443**	**32.9**	**83.2**
Living alone	27,230,075	22,701,823	26.6	83.4
Living with nonrelatives	6,462,679	5,318,620	6.2	82.3

Note: Number of white households includes householders who identified themselves as white alone and in combination with other races.
Source: Bureau of the Census, Census 2000 PHC-T-15, Table 1, General Demographic Characteristics for the White Population; calculations by New Strategist

White Households by Size, 2000

(number of total households, number and percent distribution of white households, and white share of total, by size, 2000; numbers in thousands)

		white households		
	total	number	percent distribution	share of total
Total households	**104,705**	**87,671**	**100.0%**	**83.7%**
One person	26,724	22,307	25.4	83.5
Two people	34,666	30,142	34.4	86.9
Three people	17,152	13,837	15.8	80.7
Four people	15,309	12,798	14.6	83.6
Five people	6,981	5,682	6.5	81.4
Six people	2,445	1,837	2.1	75.1
Seven or more people	1,428	1,066	1.2	74.6

Source: Bureau of the Census, America's Families and Living Arrangements: March 2000, *detailed tables from Current Population Report P20-537, Internet site <www.census.gov/population/www/socdemo/hh-fam/p20-537_00.html>; calculations by New Strategist*

Non-Hispanic White Households by Size, 2000

(number of total households, number and percent distribution of non-Hispanic white households, and non-Hispanic white share of total, by size, 2000; numbers in thousands)

		non-Hispanic white households		
	total	number	percent distribution	share of total
Total households	**104,705**	**78,819**	**100.0%**	**75.3%**
One person	26,724	21,070	26.7	78.8
Two people	34,666	28,314	35.9	81.7
Three people	17,152	12,144	15.4	70.8
Four people	15,309	10,962	13.9	71.6
Five people	6,981	4,476	5.7	64.1
Six people	2,445	1,299	1.6	53.1
Seven or more people	1,428	555	0.7	38.9

Source: Bureau of the Census, America's Families and Living Arrangements: March 2000, *detailed tables from Current Population Report P20-537, Internet site <www.census.gov/population/www/socdemo/hh-fam/p20-537_00.html>; calculations by New Strategist*

White Households by Age of Householder and Household Type, 2000

(number and percent distribution of white households by age of householder and household type, 2000; numbers in thousands)

	total	family households total	married couples	female hh, no spouse present	male hh, no spouse present	nonfamily households female house-holder	male house-holder
White households	**87,671**	**60,251**	**48,790**	**8,380**	**3,081**	**15,215**	**12,204**
Under age 20	661	369	76	181	112	135	156
Aged 20 to 24	3,880	2,100	1,222	589	289	838	942
Aged 25 to 29	6,744	4,349	3,293	733	323	971	1,424
Aged 30 to 34	8,127	6,027	4,835	853	339	729	1,371
Aged 35 to 39	9,724	7,592	6,016	1,174	402	772	1,361
Aged 40 to 44	10,084	7,976	6,255	1,281	440	786	1,322
Aged 45 to 54	17,475	13,301	11,174	1,555	573	2,048	2,126
Aged 55 to 64	11,599	8,237	7,269	701	268	2,071	1,291
Aged 65 or older	19,376	10,299	8,650	1,313	336	6,866	2,211
Aged 65 to 74	9,883	6,171	5,380	632	159	2,670	1,042
Aged 75 to 84	9,493	4,128	3,270	681	177	4,196	1,169
White households	**100.0%**	**68.7%**	**55.7%**	**9.6%**	**3.5%**	**17.4%**	**13.9%**
Under age 20	100.0	55.8	11.5	27.4	16.9	20.4	23.6
Aged 20 to 24	100.0	54.1	31.5	15.2	7.4	21.6	24.3
Aged 25 to 29	100.0	64.5	48.8	10.9	4.8	14.4	21.1
Aged 30 to 34	100.0	74.2	59.5	10.5	4.2	9.0	16.9
Aged 35 to 39	100.0	78.1	61.9	12.1	4.1	7.9	14.0
Aged 40 to 44	100.0	79.1	62.0	12.7	4.4	7.8	13.1
Aged 45 to 54	100.0	76.1	63.9	8.9	3.3	11.7	12.2
Aged 55 to 64	100.0	71.0	62.7	6.0	2.3	17.9	11.1
Aged 65 or older	100.0	53.2	44.6	6.8	1.7	35.4	11.4
Aged 65 to 74	100.0	62.4	54.4	6.4	1.6	27.0	10.5
Aged 75 to 84	100.0	43.5	34.4	7.2	1.9	44.2	12.3

Source: Bureau of the Census, America's Families and Living Arrangements: March 2000, *detailed tables from Current Population Report P20-537, Internet site <www.census.gov/population/www/socdemo/hh-fam/p20-537_00.html>; calculations by New Strategist*

Non-Hispanic White Households by Age of Householder and Household Type, 2000

(number and percent distribution of non-Hispanic white households by age of householder and household type, 2000; numbers in thousands)

	total	family households				nonfamily households	
		total	married couples	female hh, no spouse present	male hh, no spouse present	female house-holder	male house-holder
Non-Hispanic white households	**78,819**	**53,066**	**43,865**	**6,732**	**2,468**	**14,475**	**11,278**
Under age 20	520	260	48	129	83	122	138
Aged 20 to 24	3,201	1,584	944	458	181	775	842
Aged 25 to 29	5,678	3,481	2,708	550	223	907	1,290
Aged 30 to 34	6,855	4,942	4,055	635	253	686	1,226
Aged 35 to 39	8,409	6,433	5,183	918	333	729	1,247
Aged 40 to 44	9,031	7,044	5,609	1,050	386	751	1,235
Aged 45 to 54	16,008	12,077	10,293	1,277	508	1,938	1,994
Aged 55 to 64	10,704	7,544	6,784	548	213	1,961	1,199
Aged 65 or older	18,412	9,699	8,242	1,169	288	6,606	2,106
Aged 65 to 74	9,273	5,769	5,104	532	133	2,531	973
Aged 75 to 84	9,139	3,930	3,138	637	155	4,075	1,133
Non-Hispanic white households	**100.0%**	**67.3%**	**55.7%**	**8.5%**	**3.1%**	**18.4%**	**14.3%**
Under age 20	100.0	50.0	9.2	24.8	16.0	23.5	26.5
Aged 20 to 24	100.0	49.5	29.5	14.3	5.7	24.2	26.3
Aged 25 to 29	100.0	61.3	47.7	9.7	3.9	16.0	22.7
Aged 30 to 34	100.0	72.1	59.2	9.3	3.7	10.0	17.9
Aged 35 to 39	100.0	76.5	61.6	10.9	4.0	8.7	14.8
Aged 40 to 44	100.0	78.0	62.1	11.6	4.3	8.3	13.7
Aged 45 to 54	100.0	75.4	64.3	8.0	3.2	12.1	12.5
Aged 55 to 64	100.0	70.5	63.4	5.1	2.0	18.3	11.2
Aged 65 or older	100.0	52.7	44.8	6.3	1.6	35.9	11.4
Aged 65 to 74	100.0	62.2	55.0	5.7	1.4	27.3	10.5
Aged 75 to 84	100.0	43.0	34.3	7.0	1.7	44.6	12.4

Source: Bureau of the Census, America's Families and Living Arrangements: March 2000, *detailed tables from Current Population Report P20-537, Internet site <www.census.gov/population/www/socdemo/hh-fam/p20-537_00.html>; calculations by New Strategist*

White Married Couples by Age of Children and Age of Householder, 2000

(number and percent distribution of white married couples by presence and age of own children at home and age of householder, 2000; numbers in thousands)

	total					age of householder					
		<age 20	20–24	25–29	30–34	35–39	40–44	45–54	55–64	65–74	75+
White married couples	**48,790**	**76**	**1,222**	**3,293**	**4,835**	**6,016**	**6,255**	**11,174**	**7,269**	**5,380**	**3,270**
With children of any age	**26,798**	**49**	**704**	**2,147**	**3,771**	**5,149**	**5,249**	**6,825**	**1,938**	**703**	**262**
With children under age 18	21,809	49	704	2,145	3,763	5,064	4,871	4,576	552	67	17
Aged 12 to 17	9,839	2	9	113	574	2,034	3,068	3,547	435	48	8
Aged 6 to 11	10,736	1	86	834	1,898	3,239	2,810	1,682	153	22	10
Under age 6	9,942	48	689	1,858	2,902	2,615	1,254	514	53	6	2
Under age 1	2,001	14	227	495	662	405	143	48	7	–	–
White married couples	**100.0%**	**100.0%**	**100.0%**	**100.0%**	**100.0%**	**100.0%**	**100.0%**	**100.0%**	**100.0%**	**100.0%**	**100.0%**
With children of any age	**54.9**	**64.5**	**57.6**	**65.2**	**78.0**	**85.6**	**83.9**	**61.1**	**26.7**	**13.1**	**8.0**
With children under age 18	44.7	64.5	57.6	65.1	77.8	84.2	77.9	41.0	7.6	1.2	0.5
Aged 12 to 17	20.2	2.6	0.7	3.4	11.9	33.8	49.0	31.7	6.0	0.9	0.2
Aged 6 to 11	22.0	1.3	7.0	25.3	39.3	53.8	44.9	15.1	2.1	0.4	0.3
Under age 6	20.4	63.2	56.4	56.4	60.0	43.5	20.0	4.6	0.7	0.1	0.1
Under age 1	4.1	18.4	18.6	15.0	13.7	6.7	2.3	0.4	0.1	0.1	–

Note: Numbers will not add to total because households may have children in more than one age group; (–) means sample is too small to make a reliable estimate.
Source: Bureau of the Census, America's Families and Living Arrangements: March 2000, detailed tables from Current Population Report P20-537, Internet site <www.census.gov/population/www/socdemo/hh-fam/p20-537_00.html>; calculations by New Strategist

Non-Hispanic White Married Couples by Age of Children and Age of Householder, 2000

(number and percent distribution of non-Hispanic white married couples by presence and age of own children at home and age of householder, 2000; numbers in thousands)

	total					age of householder					
		< age 20	20–24	25–29	30–34	35–39	40–44	45–54	55–64	65–74	75+
Non-Hispanic white married couples	**43,865**	**48**	**944**	**2,708**	**4,055**	**5,183**	**5,609**	**10,293**	**6,784**	**5,104**	**3,138**
With children of any age	**22,979**	**24**	**482**	**1,661**	**3,078**	**4,394**	**4,654**	**6,150**	**1,683**	**625**	**228**
With children under age 18	18,516	24	482	1,661	3,070	4,324	4,316	4,107	464	55	13
Aged 12 to 17	8,429	–	9	83	399	1,650	2,691	3,188	364	41	4
Aged 6 to 11	8,997	–	50	615	1,457	2,750	2,472	1,502	124	17	9
Under age 6	8,148	24	473	1,429	2,408	2,242	1,088	436	40	6	2
Under age 1	1,686	6	165	410	580	351	123	44	6	–	–
Non-Hispanic white married couples	**100.0%**	**100.0%**	**100.0%**	**100.0%**	**100.0%**	**100.0%**	**100.0%**	**100.0%**	**100.0%**	**100.0%**	**100.0%**
With children of any age	**52.4**	**50.0**	**51.1**	**61.3**	**75.9**	**84.8**	**83.0**	**59.7**	**24.8**	**12.2**	**7.3**
With children under age 18	42.2	50.0	51.1	61.3	75.7	83.4	76.9	39.9	6.8	1.1	0.4
Aged 12 to 17	19.2	–	1.0	3.1	9.8	31.8	48.0	31.0	5.4	0.8	0.1
Aged 6 to 11	20.5	–	5.3	22.7	35.9	53.1	44.1	14.6	1.8	0.3	0.3
Under age 6	18.6	50.0	50.1	52.8	59.4	43.3	19.4	4.2	0.6	0.1	0.1
Under age 1	3.8	12.5	17.5	15.1	14.3	6.8	2.2	0.4	0.1	–	–

Note: Numbers will not add to total because households may have children in more than one age group; (–) means sample is too small to make a reliable estimate.
Source: Bureau of the Census, America's Families and Living Arrangements: March 2000, detailed tables from Current Population Report P20-537, Internet site <www.census.gov/population/www/socdemo/hh-fam/p20-537_00.html>; calculations by New Strategist

White Female-Headed Families by Age of Children and Age of Householder, 2000

(number and percent distribution of white female-headed families by presence and age of own children at home and age of householder, 2000; numbers in thousands)

	total						age of householder				
		< age 20	20-24	25-29	30-34	35-39	40-44	45-54	55-64	65-74	75+
White female-headed families	8,380	181	589	733	853	1,174	1,281	1,555	701	632	681
With children of any age	7,405	82	490	672	791	1,140	1,238	1,372	556	500	564
With children under age 18	4,869	79	482	669	780	1,081	1,055	650	69	2	2
Aged 12 to 17	2,306	4	4	25	276	661	747	532	54	2	2
Aged 6 to 11	2,294	–	63	409	542	624	472	173	10	1	–
Under age 6	1,730	79	450	461	354	224	123	31	7	–	–
Under age 1	300	38	123	67	34	32	5	–	–	–	–
White female-headed families	100.0%	100.0%	100.0%	100.0%	100.0%	100.0%	100.0%	100.0%	100.0%	100.0%	100.0%
With children of any age	88.4	45.3	83.2	91.7	92.7	97.1	96.6	88.2	79.3	79.1	82.8
With children under age 18	58.1	43.6	81.8	91.3	91.4	92.1	82.4	41.8	9.8	0.3	0.3
Aged 12 to 17	27.5	2.2	0.7	3.4	32.4	56.3	58.3	34.2	7.7	0.3	0.3
Aged 6 to 11	27.4	–	10.7	55.8	63.5	53.2	36.8	11.1	1.4	0.2	–
Under age 6	20.6	43.6	76.4	62.9	41.5	19.1	9.6	2.0	1.0	–	–
Under age 1	3.6	21.0	20.9	9.1	4.0	2.7	0.4	–	–	–	–

Note: Numbers will not add to total because households may have children in more than one age group; (–) means sample is too small to make a reliable estimate.
Source: Bureau of the Census, America's Families and Living Arrangements: March 2000, detailed tables from Current Population Report P20-537, Internet site <www.census.gov/population/www/socdemo/hh-fam/p20-537_00.html>; calculations by New Strategist

Non-Hispanic White Female-Headed Families by Age of Children and Age of Householder, 2000

(number and percent distribution of non-Hispanic white female-headed families by presence and age of own children at home and age of householder, 2000; numbers in thousands)

	total	< age 20	20–24	25–29	30–34	35–39	40–44	45–54	55–64	65–74	75+
						age of householder					
Non-Hispanic white female-headed families	6,732	129	458	550	635	918	1,050	1,277	548	532	637
With children of any age	5,970	59	385	512	594	899	1,019	1,121	435	412	536
With children under age 18	3,815	56	380	508	586	852	871	516	42	2	2
Aged 12 to 17	1,796	4	2	16	190	502	620	422	36	2	2
Aged 6 to 11	1,751	–	43	302	390	500	377	136	3	1	–
Under age 6	1,312	56	356	346	265	157	102	27	3	–	–
Under age 1	228	27	97	50	20	28	5	–	–	–	–
Non-Hispanic white female-headed families	100.0%	100.0%	100.0%	100.0%	100.0%	100.0%	100.0%	100.0%	100.0%	100.0%	100.0%
With children of any age	88.7	45.7	84.1	93.1	93.5	97.9	97.0	87.8	79.4	77.4	84.1
With children under age 18	56.7	43.4	83.0	92.4	92.3	92.8	83.0	40.4	7.7	0.4	0.3
Aged 12 to 17	26.7	3.1	0.4	2.9	29.9	54.7	59.0	33.0	6.6	0.4	0.3
Aged 6 to 11	26.0	–	9.4	54.9	61.4	54.5	35.9	10.6	0.5	0.2	–
Under age 6	19.5	43.4	77.7	62.9	41.7	17.1	9.7	2.1	0.5	–	–
Under age 1	3.4	20.9	21.2	9.1	3.1	3.1	0.5	–	–	–	–

Note: Numbers will not add to total because households may have children in more than one age group; (–) means sample is too small to make a reliable estimate.
Source: Bureau of the Census, America's Families and Living Arrangements: March 2000, detailed tables from Current Population Report P20-\-537, Internet site <www.census.gov/population/www/socdemo/hh-fam/p20-537_00.html>; calculations by New Strategist

White Single-Person Households by Age of Householder, 2000

(total number of white households, number and percent distribution of white single-person households, and single-person household share of total, by age of householder, 2000; numbers in thousands)

	total	single-person households		
		number	percent distribution	share of total
White households	**87,671**	**22,307**	**100.0%**	**25.4%**
Under age 20	661	91	0.4	13.8
Under age 25	3,880	770	3.5	19.8
Aged 25 to 29	6,744	1,442	6.5	21.4
Aged 30 to 34	8,127	1,517	6.8	18.7
Aged 35 to 39	9,724	1,580	7.1	16.2
Aged 40 to 44	10,084	1,711	7.7	17.0
Aged 45 to 54	17,475	3,500	15.7	20.0
Aged 55 to 64	11,599	2,942	13.2	25.4
Aged 65 to 74	9,883	3,542	15.9	35.8
Aged 75 or older	9,493	5,212	23.4	54.9

Source: Bureau of the Census, America's Families and Living Arrangements: March 2000, *detailed tables from Current Population Report P20-537, Internet site <www.census.gov/population/www/socdemo/hh-fam/p20-537_00.html>; calculations by New Strategist*

Non-Hispanic White Single-Person Households by Age of Householder, 2000

(total number of non-Hispanic white households, number and percent distribution of non-Hispanic white single-person households, and single-person household share of total, by age of householder, 2000; numbers in thousands)

| | | single-person households | | |
	total	number	percent distribution	share of total
Non-Hispanic white households	**78,819**	**21,070**	**100.0%**	**26.7%**
Under age 20	520	80	0.4	15.4
Under age 25	3,201	703	3.3	22.0
Aged 25 to 29	5,678	1,331	6.3	23.4
Aged 30 to 34	6,855	1,394	6.6	20.3
Aged 35 to 39	8,409	1,467	7.0	17.4
Aged 40 to 44	9,031	1,623	7.7	18.0
Aged 45 to 54	16,008	3,303	15.7	20.6
Aged 55 to 64	10,704	2,761	13.1	25.8
Aged 65 to 74	9,273	3,345	15.9	36.1
Aged 75 or older	9,139	5,065	24.0	55.4

Source: Bureau of the Census, America's Families and Living Arrangements: March 2000, *detailed tables from Current Population Report P20-537, Internet site <www.census.gov/population/www/socdemo/hh-fam/p20-537_00.html>; calculations by New Strategist*

White Children by Living Arrangement and Age, 2000

(number and percent distribution of white children under age 18 by living arrangement, 2000; numbers in thousands)

	number	percent distribution
Total white children	**56,455**	**100.0%**
Living with both parents	42,497	75.3
Living with mother only	9,765	17.3
Living with father only	2,427	4.3
Living with neither parent	1,752	3.1
In group quarters	14	0.0
Living with both parents	**42,497**	**100.0**
Child of householder	41,795	98.3
Grandchild of householder	404	1.0
Other relative of householder	281	0.7
Nonrelative of householder	16	0.0
Living with mother only	**9,765**	**100.0**
Child of householder	7,964	81.6
Grandchild of householder	991	10.1
Other relative of householder	271	2.8
Nonrelative of householder	539	5.5
Living with father only	**2,427**	**100.0**
Child of householder	2,138	88.1
Grandchild of householder	163	6.7
Other relative of householder	61	2.5
Nonrelative of householder	65	2.7
Living with neither parent	**1,752**	**100.0**
Grandchild of householder	676	38.6
Other relative of householder	456	26.0
Foster child	140	8.0
Other nonrelative of householder	480	27.4
In group quarters	14	0.0

Source: Bureau of the Census, America's Families and Living Arrangements: March 2000, *detailed tables from Current Population Report P20-537, Internet site <www.census.gov/population/www/socdemo/hh-fam/p20-537_00.html>; calculations by New Strategist*

Non-Hispanic White Children by Living Arrangement and Age, 2000

(number and percent distribution of non-Hispanic white children under age 18 by living arrangement, 2000; numbers in thousands)

	number	percent distribution
Total non-Hispanic white children	**45,407**	**100.0%**
Living with both parents	35,188	77.5
Living with mother only	7,095	15.6
Living with father only	1,951	4.3
Living with neither parent	1,161	2.6
In group quarters	12	0.0
Living with both parents	**35,188**	**100.0**
Child of householder	34,798	98.9
Grandchild of householder	271	0.8
Other relative of householder	111	0.3
Nonrelative of householder	8	0.0
Living with mother only	**7095**	**100.0**
Child of householder	5,906	83.2
Grandchild of householder	666	9.4
Other relative of householder	101	1.4
Nonrelative of householder	422	5.9
Living with father only	**1951**	**100.0**
Child of householder	1,759	90.2
Grandchild of householder	119	6.1
Other relative of householder	20	1.0
Nonrelative of householder	52	2.7
Living with neither parent	**1161**	**100.0**
Grandchild of householder	509	43.8
Other relative of householder	222	19.1
Foster child	96	8.3
Other nonrelative of householder	334	28.8
In group quarters	12	0.0

Source: Bureau of the Census, America's Families and Living Arrangements: March 2000, *detailed tables from Current Population Report P20-537, Internet site <www.census.gov/population/www/socdemo/hh-fam/p20-537_00.html>; calculations by New Strategist*

White Men by Living Arrangement and Age, 2000

(number and percent distribution of white men aged 15 or older by living arrangement and age, 2000; numbers in thousands)

	total	15-19	20-24	25-29	30-34	35-39	40-44	45-54	55-64	65-74	75+
White men	86,442	8,119	7,425	7,273	7,869	9,189	9,305	15,204	9,724	7,093	5,242
Householder	64,018	315	2,226	4,812	6,462	7,693	8,038	13,869	8,977	6,732	4,895
Married couple hh or spouse	47,786	47	995	3,065	4,751	5,930	6,276	11,170	7,417	5,531	3,549
Male family householder	4,028	112	289	323	339	402	440	573	268	159	177
Living alone	9,198	50	390	813	954	1,009	1,087	1,760	1,062	957	1,117
Living with nonrelatives	3,006	106	552	611	418	352	235	366	230	85	52
Not a householder	22,424	7,804	5,199	2,461	1,407	1,496	1,267	1,335	747	361	374
Child of householder	14,034	6,951	3,554	1,166	519	642	539	462	175	27	27
In family, other relative of hh	3,342	480	540	380	277	245	214	409	333	207	257
Not in family	5,048	373	1,105	915	611	609	514	464	239	127	90
White men	100.0%	100.0%	100.0%	100.0%	100.0%	100.0%	100.0%	100.0%	100.0%	100.0%	100.0%
Householder	74.1	3.9	30.0	66.2	82.1	83.7	86.4	91.2	92.3	94.9	93.4
Married couple hh or spouse	55.3	0.6	13.4	42.1	60.4	64.5	67.4	73.5	76.3	78.0	67.7
Male family householder	4.7	1.4	3.9	4.4	4.3	4.4	4.7	3.8	2.8	2.2	3.4
Living alone	10.6	0.6	5.3	11.2	12.1	11.0	11.7	11.6	10.9	13.5	21.3
Living with nonrelatives	3.5	1.3	7.4	8.4	5.3	3.8	2.5	2.4	2.4	1.2	1.0
Not a householder	25.9	96.1	70.0	33.8	17.9	16.3	13.6	8.8	7.7	5.1	7.1
Child of householder	16.2	85.6	47.9	16.0	6.6	7.0	5.8	3.0	1.8	0.4	0.5
In family, other relative of hh	3.9	5.9	7.3	5.2	3.5	2.7	2.3	2.7	3.4	2.9	4.9
Not in family	5.8	4.6	14.9	12.6	7.8	6.6	5.5	3.1	2.5	1.8	1.7

Source: Bureau of the Census, America's Families and Living Arrangements: March 2000, detailed tables from Current Population Report P20-537, Internet site <www.census.gov/population/www/socdemo/hh-fam/p20-537_00.html>; calculations by New Strategist

Non-Hispanic White Men by Living Arrangement and Age, 2000

(number and percent distribution of non-Hispanic white men aged 15 or older by living arrangement and age, 2000; numbers in thousands)

	total	15–19	20–24	25–29	30–34	35–39	40–44	45–54	55–64	65–74	75+
Non-Hispanic white men	75,692	6,686	6,030	5,940	6,513	7,846	8,313	13,783	8,936	6,645	4,997
Householder	**57,536**	**257**	**1,801**	**3,991**	**5,469**	**6,667**	**7,236**	**12,743**	**8,333**	**6,350**	**4,690**
Married couple hh or spouse	43,790	35	777	2,477	3,990	5,087	5,614	10,242	6,921	5,244	3,402
Male family householder	2,468	83	181	223	253	333	386	508	213	133	155
Living alone	8,562	44	356	734	866	933	1,021	1,651	978	893	1,087
Living with nonrelatives	2,716	95	487	557	360	314	215	342	221	80	46
Not a householder	**18,156**	**6,429**	**4,229**	**1,949**	**1,044**	**1,179**	**1,077**	**1,040**	**603**	**295**	**307**
Child of householder	11,984	5,874	3,060	992	419	560	493	398	159	27	–
In family, other relative of hh	1,990	284	278	184	134	124	136	249	232	150	217
Not in family	4,182	271	891	773	491	495	448	393	212	118	90
Non-Hispanic white men	**100.0%**	**100.0%**	**100.0%**	**100.0%**	**100.0%**	**100.0%**	**100.0%**	**100.0%**	**100.0%**	**100.0%**	**100.0%**
Householder	**76.0**	**3.8**	**29.9**	**67.2**	**84.0**	**85.0**	**87.0**	**92.5**	**93.3**	**95.6**	**93.9**
Married couple hh or spouse	57.9	0.5	12.9	41.7	61.3	64.8	67.5	74.3	77.5	78.9	68.1
Male family householder	3.3	1.2	3.0	3.8	3.9	4.2	4.6	3.7	2.4	2.0	3.1
Living alone	11.3	0.7	5.9	12.4	13.3	11.9	12.3	12.0	10.9	13.4	21.8
Living with nonrelatives	3.6	1.4	8.1	9.4	5.5	4.0	2.6	2.5	2.5	1.2	0.9
Not a householder	**24.0**	**96.2**	**70.1**	**32.8**	**16.0**	**15.0**	**13.0**	**7.5**	**6.7**	**4.4**	**6.1**
Child of householder	15.8	87.9	50.7	16.7	6.4	7.1	5.9	2.9	1.8	0.4	–
In family, other relative of hh	2.6	4.2	4.6	3.1	2.1	1.6	1.6	1.8	2.6	2.3	4.3
Not in family	5.5	4.1	14.8	13.0	7.5	6.3	5.4	2.9	2.4	1.8	1.8

Note: (–) means sample is too small to make a reliable estimate.
Source: Bureau of the Census, America's Families and Living Arrangements: March 2000, detailed tables from Current Population Report P20-537, Internet site <www.census.gov/population/www/socdemo/hh-fam/p20-537_00.html>; calculations by New Strategist

White Women by Living Arrangement and Age, 2000

(number and percent distribution of white women aged 15 or older by living arrangement and age, 2000; numbers in thousands)

	total	15–19	20–24	25–29	30–34	35–39	40–44	45–54	55–64	65–74	75+
White women	91,138	7,725	7,248	7,283	7,894	9,136	9,287	15,587	10,439	8,436	8,109
Householder	72,244	501	3,186	5,572	6,891	8,252	8,508	14,375	9,764	7,916	7,280
Married couple hh or spouse	48,649	185	1,759	3,868	5,309	6,307	6,441	10,772	6,992	4,613	2,403
Female family householder	8,380	181	589	733	853	1,174	1,281	1,555	701	632	681
Living alone	13,109	41	380	629	563	571	624	1,740	1,881	2,585	4,095
Living with nonrelatives	2,106	94	458	342	166	200	162	308	190	86	101
Not a householder	18,894	7,224	4,062	1,711	1,003	884	779	1,212	675	520	829
Child of householder	11,103	6,305	2,648	741	394	287	276	323	112	15	2
In family, other relative of hh	3,537	463	321	257	159	148	211	445	376	419	740
Not in family	4,254	456	1,093	713	450	449	292	444	187	86	87
White women	100.0%	100.0%	100.0%	100.0%	100.0%	100.0%	100.0%	100.0%	100.0%	100.0%	100.0%
Householder	79.3	6.5	44.0	76.5	87.3	90.3	91.6	92.2	93.5	93.8	89.8
Married couple hh or spouse	53.4	2.4	24.3	53.1	67.3	69.0	69.4	69.1	67.0	54.7	29.6
Female family householder	9.2	2.3	8.1	10.1	10.8	12.9	13.8	10.0	6.7	7.5	8.4
Living alone	14.4	0.5	5.2	8.6	7.1	6.3	6.7	11.2	18.0	30.6	50.5
Living with nonrelatives	2.3	1.2	6.3	4.7	2.1	2.2	1.7	2.0	1.8	1.0	1.2
Not a householder	20.7	93.5	56.0	23.5	12.7	9.7	8.4	7.8	6.5	6.2	10.2
Child of householder	12.2	81.6	36.5	10.2	5.0	3.1	3.0	2.1	1.1	0.2	0.0
In family, other relative of hh	3.9	6.0	4.4	3.5	2.0	1.6	2.3	2.9	3.6	5.0	9.1
Not in family	4.7	5.9	15.1	9.8	5.7	4.9	3.1	2.8	1.8	1.0	1.1

Source: Bureau of the Census, America's Families and Living Arrangements: March 2000, detailed tables from Current Population Report P20-537, Internet site <www.census.gov/population/www/socdemo/hh-fam/p20-537_00.html>; calculations by New Strategist

Non-Hispanic White Women by Living Arrangement and Age, 2000

(number and percent distribution of non-Hispanic white women aged 15 or older by living arrangement and age, 2000; numbers in thousands)

	total	15–19	20–24	25–29	30–34	35–39	40–44	45–54	55–64	65–74	75+
Non-Hispanic white women	80,227	6,411	6,009	5,949	6,576	7,801	8,233	14,157	9,546	7,796	7,747
Householder	64,781	390	2,580	4,644	5,788	7,096	7,615	13,182	9,042	7,426	7,017
Married couple hh or spouse	43,574	139	1,347	3,187	4,467	5,449	5,814	9,967	6,533	4,363	2,305
Female family householder	6,732	129	458	550	635	918	1,050	1,277	548	532	637
Living alone	12,508	36	347	597	527	534	602	1,652	1,782	2,452	3,978
Living with nonrelatives	1,967	86	428	310	159	195	149	286	179	79	97
Not a householder	15,446	6,021	3,429	1,305	788	705	618	975	504	370	730
Child of householder	9,463	5,373	2,286	588	329	237	237	296	100	15	2
In family, other relative of hh	2,335	283	182	130	76	88	135	279	234	284	644
Not in family	3,648	365	961	587	383	380	246	400	170	71	84
Non-Hispanic white women	100.0%	100.0%	100.0%	100.0%	100.0%	100.0%	100.0%	100.0%	100.0%	100.0%	100.0%
Householder	80.7	6.1	42.9	78.1	88.0	91.0	92.5	93.1	94.7	95.3	90.6
Married couple hh or spouse	54.3	2.2	22.4	53.6	67.9	69.9	70.6	70.4	68.4	56.0	29.8
Female family householder	8.4	2.0	7.6	9.2	9.7	11.8	12.8	9.0	5.7	6.8	8.2
Living alone	15.6	0.6	5.8	10.0	8.0	6.8	7.3	11.7	18.7	31.5	51.3
Living with nonrelatives	2.5	1.3	7.1	5.2	2.4	2.5	1.8	2.0	1.9	1.0	1.3
Not a householder	19.3	93.9	57.1	21.9	12.0	9.0	7.5	6.9	5.3	4.7	9.4
Child of householder	11.8	83.8	38.0	9.9	5.0	3.0	2.9	2.1	1.0	0.2	0.0
In family, other relative of hh	2.9	4.4	3.0	2.2	1.2	1.1	1.6	2.0	2.5	3.6	8.3
Not in family	4.5	5.7	16.0	9.9	5.8	4.9	3.0	2.8	1.8	0.9	1.1

Source: Bureau of the Census, America's Families and Living Arrangements: March 2000, detailed tables from Current Population Report P20-537, Internet site <www.census.gov/population/www/socdemo/hh-fam/p20-537_00.html>; calculations by New Strategist

White Men by Marital Status and Age, 2000

(number and percent distribution of white men aged 15 or older by age and marital status, 2000; numbers in thousands)

	total	never married	married	divorced	widowed
White men	**86,443**	**25,113**	**50,651**	**8,483**	**2,196**
Under age 20	8,118	7,986	71	58	3
Aged 20 to 24	7,424	6,119	1,166	139	–
Aged 25 to 29	7,274	3,556	3,299	410	9
Aged 30 to 34	7,870	2,188	4,965	703	13
Aged 35 to 39	9,189	1,693	6,174	1,291	31
Aged 40 to 44	9,305	1,330	6,476	1,455	45
Aged 45 to 49	8,172	865	5,968	1,299	40
Aged 50 to 54	7,032	402	5,583	964	83
Aged 55 to 59	5,309	287	4,093	803	125
Aged 60 to 64	4,415	214	3,547	518	135
Aged 65 or older	12,335	471	9,308	843	1,714
Aged 65 to 69	3,818	175	3,040	357	246
Aged 70 to 74	3,275	98	2,600	262	315
Aged 75 or older	5,242	198	3,668	224	1,153
White men	**100.0%**	**29.1%**	**58.6%**	**9.8%**	**2.5%**
Under age 20	100.0	98.4	0.9	0.7	0.0
Aged 20 to 24	100.0	82.4	15.7	1.9	–
Aged 25 to 29	100.0	48.9	45.4	5.6	0.1
Aged 30 to 34	100.0	27.8	63.1	8.9	0.2
Aged 35 to 39	100.0	18.4	67.2	14.0	0.3
Aged 40 to 44	100.0	14.3	69.6	15.6	0.5
Aged 45 to 49	100.0	10.6	73.0	15.9	0.5
Aged 50 to 54	100.0	5.7	79.4	13.7	1.2
Aged 55 to 59	100.0	5.4	77.1	15.1	2.4
Aged 60 to 64	100.0	4.8	80.3	11.7	3.1
Aged 65 or older	100.0	3.8	75.5	6.8	13.9
Aged 65 to 69	100.0	4.6	79.6	9.4	6.4
Aged 70 to 74	100.0	3.0	79.4	8.0	9.6
Aged 75 or older	100.0	3.8	70.0	4.3	22.0

Note: (–) means sample is too small to make a reliable estimate.
Source: Bureau of the Census, Marital Status and Living Arrangements: March 2000 (Update), *detailed tables for Current Population Report P20-537, 2001; Internet site <www.census.gov/population/socdemo/hh-fam/p20-537/2000/tabA1.txt>*

Non-Hispanic White Men by Marital Status and Age, 2000

(number and percent distribution of non-Hispanic white men aged 15 or older by age and marital status, 2000; numbers in thousands)

	total	never married	married	divorced	widowed
Non-Hispanic white men	**75,692**	**21,109**	**44,957**	**7,596**	**2,030**
Under age 20	6,685	6,583	49	49	3
Aged 20 to 24	6,030	5,057	858	115	–
Aged 25 to 29	5,940	3,010	2,586	335	9
Aged 30 to 34	6,514	1,799	4,091	615	9
Aged 35 to 39	7,847	1,432	5,227	1,164	24
Aged 40 to 44	8,313	1,203	5,732	1,336	42
Aged 45 to 49	7,400	763	5,413	1,188	36
Aged 50 to 54	6,384	363	5,094	850	78
Aged 55 to 59	4,868	260	3,786	718	104
Aged 60 to 64	4,069	193	3,298	460	119
Aged 65 or older	11,643	445	8,824	767	1,608
Aged 65 to 69	3,559	165	2,852	318	225
Aged 70 to 74	3,086	89	2,470	236	291
Aged 75 or older	4,998	191	3,502	213	1,092
Non-Hispanic white men	**100.0%**	**27.9%**	**59.4%**	**10.0%**	**2.7%**
Under age 20	100.0	98.5	0.7	0.7	0.0
Aged 20 to 24	100.0	83.9	14.2	1.9	–
Aged 25 to 29	100.0	50.7	43.5	5.6	0.2
Aged 30 to 34	100.0	27.6	62.8	9.4	0.1
Aged 35 to 39	100.0	18.2	66.6	14.8	0.3
Aged 40 to 44	100.0	14.5	69.0	16.1	0.5
Aged 45 to 49	100.0	10.3	73.1	16.1	0.5
Aged 50 to 54	100.0	5.7	79.8	13.3	1.2
Aged 55 to 59	100.0	5.3	77.8	14.7	2.1
Aged 60 to 64	100.0	4.7	81.1	11.3	2.9
Aged 65 or older	100.0	3.8	75.8	6.6	13.8
Aged 65 to 69	100.0	4.6	80.1	8.9	6.3
Aged 70 to 74	100.0	2.9	80.0	7.6	9.4
Aged 75 or older	100.0	3.8	70.1	4.3	21.8

Note: (–) means sample is too small to make a reliable estimate.
Source: Bureau of the Census, Marital Status and Living Arrangements: March 2000 (Update), *detailed tables for Current Population Report P20-537, 2001; Internet site <www.census.gov/population/socdemo/hh-fam/p20-537/2000/tabA1.txt>*

White Women by Marital Status and Age, 2000

(number and percent distribution of white women aged 15 or older by age and marital status, 2000; numbers in thousands)

	total	never married	married	divorced	widowed
White women	**91,138**	**20,184**	**50,578**	**11,040**	**9,336**
Under age 20	7,724	7,378	276	68	3
Aged 20 to 24	7,247	5,016	1,938	288	5
Aged 25 to 29	7,282	2,460	4,115	699	9
Aged 30 to 34	7,894	1,408	5,487	951	48
Aged 35 to 39	9,135	1,031	6,528	1,470	106
Aged 40 to 44	9,286	833	6,652	1,663	139
Aged 45 to 49	8,303	634	5,984	1,462	224
Aged 50 to 54	7,282	425	5,083	1,462	313
Aged 55 to 59	5,770	261	4,005	1,043	460
Aged 60 to 64	4,670	167	3,182	637	683
Aged 65 or older	16,544	572	7,328	1,298	7,347
Aged 65 to 69	4,282	130	2,645	474	1,033
Aged 70 to 74	4,153	155	2,138	378	1,482
Aged 75 or older	8,109	287	2,545	446	4,832
White women	**100.0%**	**22.1%**	**55.5%**	**12.1%**	**10.2%**
Under age 20	100.0	95.5	3.6	0.9	0.0
Aged 20 to 24	100.0	69.2	26.7	4.0	0.1
Aged 25 to 29	100.0	33.8	56.5	9.6	0.1
Aged 30 to 34	100.0	17.8	69.5	12.0	0.6
Aged 35 to 39	100.0	11.3	71.5	16.1	1.2
Aged 40 to 44	100.0	9.0	71.6	17.9	1.5
Aged 45 to 49	100.0	7.6	72.1	17.6	2.7
Aged 50 to 54	100.0	5.8	69.8	20.1	4.3
Aged 55 to 59	100.0	4.5	69.4	18.1	8.0
Aged 60 to 64	100.0	3.6	68.1	13.6	14.6
Aged 65 or older	100.0	3.5	44.3	7.8	44.4
Aged 65 to 69	100.0	3.0	61.8	11.1	24.1
Aged 70 to 74	100.0	3.7	51.5	9.1	35.7
Aged 75 or older	100.0	3.5	31.4	5.5	59.6

Source: Bureau of the Census, Marital Status and Living Arrangements: March 2000 (Update), *detailed tables for Current Population Report P20-537, 2001; Internet site <www.census.gov/population/socdemo/hh-fam/p20-537/2000/tabA1.txt>*

Non-Hispanic White Women by Marital Status and Age, 2000

(number and percent distribution of non-Hispanic white women aged 15 or older by age and marital status, 2000; numbers in thousands)

	total	never married	married	divorced	widowed
Non-Hispanic white women	**80,228**	**17,070**	**44,899**	**9,611**	**8,647**
Under age 20	6,412	6,177	186	49	–
Aged 20 to 24	6,009	4,330	1,441	234	5
Aged 25 to 29	5,950	2,022	3,329	596	3
Aged 30 to 34	6,576	1,173	4,580	785	36
Aged 35 to 39	7,801	855	5,610	1,251	84
Aged 40 to 44	8,234	719	5,972	1,432	111
Aged 45 to 49	7,579	558	5,537	1,301	183
Aged 50 to 54	6,578	354	4,646	1,308	269
Aged 55 to 59	5,259	218	3,705	936	401
Aged 60 to 64	4,286	148	2,968	559	610
Aged 65 or older	15,543	514	6,924	1,159	6,945
Aged 65 to 69	3,922	114	2,474	411	922
Aged 70 to 74	3,873	130	2,018	335	1,389
Aged 75 or older	7,748	270	2,432	413	4,634
Non-Hispanic white women	**100.0%**	**21.3%**	**56.0%**	**12.0%**	**10.8%**
Under age 20	100.0	96.3	2.9	0.8	–
Aged 20 to 24	100.0	72.1	24.0	3.9	0.1
Aged 25 to 29	100.0	34.0	55.9	10.0	0.1
Aged 30 to 34	100.0	17.8	69.6	11.9	0.5
Aged 35 to 39	100.0	11.0	71.9	16.0	1.1
Aged 40 to 44	100.0	8.7	72.5	17.4	1.3
Aged 45 to 49	100.0	7.4	73.1	17.2	2.4
Aged 50 to 54	100.0	5.4	70.6	19.9	4.1
Aged 55 to 59	100.0	4.1	70.5	17.8	7.6
Aged 60 to 64	100.0	3.5	69.2	13.0	14.2
Aged 65 or older	100.0	3.3	44.5	7.5	44.7
Aged 65 to 69	100.0	2.9	63.1	10.5	23.5
Aged 70 to 74	100.0	3.4	52.1	8.6	35.9
Aged 75 or older	100.0	3.5	31.4	5.3	59.8

Note: (–) means sample is too small to make a reliable estimate.
Source: Bureau of the Census, Marital Status and Living Arrangewoments: March 2000 (Update), *detailed tables for Current Population Report P20-537, 2001; Internet site <www.census.gov/population/socdemo/hh-fam/p20-537/2000/tabA1.txt>*

The Non-Hispanic White Population Grew Little between 1990 and 2000

Non-Hispanic whites accounted for 69 percent of the total population in 2000, down from 76 percent in 1990. The white population as a whole grew faster than the non-Hispanic white population during the decade, increasing 6 or 9 percent depending on whether the 2000 count of whites used is that of those identifying themselves as white alone or that of those identifying themselves as white alone or in combination with other races. Nine percent of whites are Hispanic, who may be of any race.

Non-Hispanic whites account for a smaller share of children and young adults than of older Americans because Hispanics are a growing proportion of the younger age groups. Just 58 percent of children under age 5 are non-Hispanic white, versus 87 percent of people aged 85 or older.

The number of non-Hispanic whites grew slowly in most regions during the 1990s. In the Northeast, the number of non-Hispanic whites declined 3 percent. Non-Hispanic whites account for the largest share of the population in the Midwest's West North Central division (87 percent) and for the smallest share of the population in the Pacific division of the West (53 percent).

The number of non-Hispanic whites declined in 12 states during the 1990s. In 2000, non-Hispanic whites accounted for only 47 percent of California's population and 52 percent of the population of Texas. Non-Hispanic whites account for just 36 percent of the Miami metropolitan population, 39 percent of the Los Angeles population, and 48 percent of Houston's population.

■ In a growing number of states and metropolitan areas, non-Hispanic whites are no longer in the majority, changing America's social fabric.

The number of non-Hispanic whites grew only 3 percent during the 1990s

(number of non-Hispanic whites, 1990 and 2000; numbers in millions)

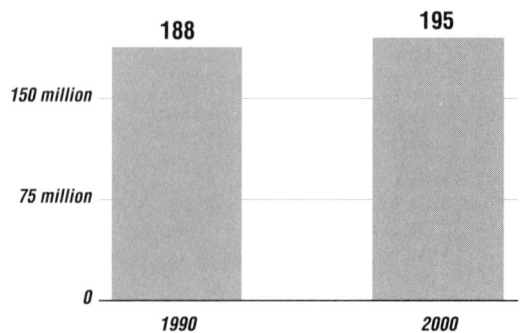

Whites, 1990 and 2000 Censuses

(number of whites 1990 and 2000; percent change 1990–2000)

		2000		percent change 1990–2000	
	1990	*white alone*	*white, alone or in combination*	*white alone*	*white, alone or in combination*
Total whites	199,686,070	211,460,626	216,930,975	5.9%	8.6%

Source: Bureau of the Census, The White Population: 2000, *Census 2000 Brief, C2KBR/01-4, 2001; calculations by New Strategist*

Non-Hispanic Whites, 1990 and 2000 Censuses

(number of total people, number of non-Hispanic whites, and non-Hispanic white share of total, 1990 and 2000; percent change in non-Hispanic whites, 1990–2000)

	1990			2000			percent change in non-Hispanic whites 1990–2000
		non-Hispanic white			non-Hispanic white		
	total	*number*	*share of total*	*total*	*number*	*share of total*	
Total people	248,709,873	188,315,298	75.7%	281,421,906	194,552,774	69.1%	3.3%

Note: The 2000 figures for non-Hispanic whites include only those who identified themselves as white alone and non-Hispanic.
Source: Bureau of the Census, The White Population: 2000, *Census 2000 Brief, C2KBR/01-4, 2001; and Internet site <http://eire.census.gov/popest/archives/state/srh/srhmars.txt>; calculations by New Strategist*

Whites by Racial Combination, 2000 Census

(number of total people, number of whites by racial identification, and white share of total; number and percent distribution of whites by racial combination, 2000)

	number	percent
Total people	**281,421,906**	**100.0%**
White, alone or in combination with one or more other races	**216,930,975**	**77.1**
White alone	211,460,626	75.1
White in combination	5,470,349	1.9
White, alone or in combination with one or more other races	**216,930,975**	**100.0**
White alone	211,460,626	97.5
White in combination	5,470,349	2.5
White and other race	2,206,251	1.0
White and American Indian	1,082,683	0.5
White and Asian	868,395	0.4
White and black	784,764	0.4
White and Native Hawaiian	112,964	0.1
All other combinations	2,621,543	1.2

Note: American Indians include Alaska Natives. Native Hawaiians include other Pacific Islanders.
Source: Bureau of the Census, Overview of Race and Hispanic Origin, *Census 2000 Brief, CENBR/01-1, 2001;*
and The White Population: 2000, *Census 2000 Brief, C2KBR/01-4, 2001*

Whites by Hispanic Origin, 2000 Census

(number and percent distribution of whites by Hispanic origin and racial combination, 2000)

	white, alone or in combination		white alone		white in combination	
	number	percent distribution	number	percent distribution	number	percent distribution
Total whites	**216,930,975**	**100.0%**	**211,460,626**	**100.0%**	**5,470,349**	**100.0%**
Hispanic	18,753,075	8.6	16,907,852	8.0	1,845,223	33.7
Mexican	10,685,890	4.9	9,789,599	4.6	896,291	16.4
Puerto Rican	1,798,213	0.8	1,612,113	0.8	186,100	3.4
Cuban	1,086,288	0.5	1,048,321	0.5	37,967	0.7
Other Hispanic	5,182,684	2.4	4,457,819	2.1	724,865	13.3
Non-Hispanic	198,177,900	91.4	194,552,774	92.0	3,625,126	66.3

Source: Bureau of the Census, Census 2000 PHC-T-15, Table 1, General Demographic Characteristics for the White Population; calculations by New Strategist

Whites by Age, 2000 Census

(number of people identifying themselves as white alone or in combination, white alone, and white in combination, and percent of white alone or in combination identifying themselves as white in combination, by age, 2000)

	white, alone or in combination	white alone	white in combination number	white in combination percent of white, alone or in combination
Total whites	**216,930,975**	**211,460,626**	**5,470,349**	**2.5%**
Under age 5	13,656,252	12,859,892	796,360	5.8
Aged 5 to 9	14,632,897	13,944,882	688,015	4.7
Aged 10 to 14	14,899,672	14,322,638	577,034	3.9
Aged 15 to 19	14,666,888	14,167,148	499,740	3.4
Aged 20 to 24	13,497,559	13,064,891	432,668	3.2
Aged 25 to 29	13,901,171	13,501,773	399,398	2.9
Aged 30 to 34	15,194,805	14,818,786	376,019	2.5
Aged 35 to 39	17,395,108	17,031,493	363,615	2.1
Aged 40 to 44	17,588,919	17,265,995	322,924	1.8
Aged 45 to 49	16,070,375	15,810,626	259,749	1.6
Aged 50 to 54	14,423,239	14,213,875	209,364	1.5
Aged 55 to 59	11,256,685	11,107,247	149,438	1.3
Aged 60 to 64	9,059,558	8,945,842	113,716	1.3
Aged 65 to 69	8,130,453	8,040,225	90,228	1.1
Aged 70 to 74	7,722,044	7,648,193	73,851	1.0
Aged 75 to 79	6,585,517	6,530,019	55,498	0.8
Aged 80 to 84	4,442,647	4,408,597	34,050	0.8
Aged 85 or older	3,807,186	3,778,504	28,682	0.8
Aged 18 to 24	19,389,359	18,761,162	628,197	3.2
Aged 18 or older	164,967,066	161,862,337	3,104,729	1.9
Aged 65 or older	30,687,847	30,405,538	282,309	0.9

Source: U.S. Census Bureau, Census 2000 Summary File 1; calculations by New Strategist

Non-Hispanic Whites by Age, 2000 Census

(number of people identifying themselves as white alone, number of white alone who identify themselves as non-Hispanic, and non-Hispanic share of white alone population, by age, 2000)

| | | non-Hispanic | |
	total	*number*	*percent*
Total white alone	**211,460,626**	**194,552,774**	**92.0%**
Under age 5	12,859,892	11,194,346	87.0
Aged 5 to 9	13,944,882	12,303,903	88.2
Aged 10 to 14	14,322,638	12,882,540	89.9
Aged 15 to 19	14,167,148	12,759,934	90.1
Aged 20 to 24	13,064,891	11,594,742	88.7
Aged 25 to 29	13,501,773	11,990,863	88.8
Aged 30 to 34	14,818,786	13,365,410	90.2
Aged 35 to 39	17,031,493	15,665,973	92.0
Aged 40 to 44	17,265,995	16,135,362	93.5
Aged 45 to 49	15,810,626	14,908,211	94.3
Aged 50 to 54	14,213,875	13,478,949	94.8
Aged 55 to 59	11,107,247	10,545,669	94.9
Aged 60 to 64	8,945,842	8,482,012	94.8
Aged 65 to 69	8,040,225	7,650,827	95.2
Aged 70 to 74	7,648,193	7,327,622	95.8
Aged 75 to 79	6,530,019	6,307,373	96.6
Aged 80 to 84	4,408,597	4,284,906	97.2
Aged 85 or older	3,778,504	3,674,132	97.2
Aged 18 to 24	18,761,162	16,708,378	89.1
Aged 18 or older	161,862,337	150,525,687	93.0
Aged 65 or older	30,405,538	29,244,860	96.2

Source: U.S. Census Bureau, Census 2000 Summary File 1; calculations by New Strategist

White Share of Total Population by Age, 2000 Census

(number of total people, number and percent distribution of those identifying themselves as white alone or in combination, and white alone or in combination share of total, by age, 2000)

| | | white, alone or in combination | | |
	total	number	percent distribution	share of total
Total people	**281,421,906**	**216,930,975**	**100.0%**	**77.1%**
Under age 5	19,175,798	13,656,252	6.3	71.2
Aged 5 to 9	20,549,505	14,632,897	6.7	71.2
Aged 10 to 14	20,528,072	14,899,672	6.9	72.6
Aged 15 to 19	20,219,890	14,666,888	6.8	72.5
Aged 20 to 24	18,964,001	13,497,559	6.2	71.2
Aged 25 to 29	19,381,336	13,901,171	6.4	71.7
Aged 30 to 34	20,510,388	15,194,805	7.0	74.1
Aged 35 to 39	22,706,664	17,395,108	8.0	76.6
Aged 40 to 44	22,441,863	17,588,919	8.1	78.4
Aged 45 to 49	20,092,404	16,070,375	7.4	80.0
Aged 50 to 54	17,585,548	14,423,239	6.6	82.0
Aged 55 to 59	13,469,237	11,256,685	5.2	83.6
Aged 60 to 64	10,805,447	9,059,558	4.2	83.8
Aged 65 to 69	9,533,545	8,130,453	3.7	85.3
Aged 70 to 74	8,857,441	7,722,044	3.6	87.2
Aged 75 to 79	7,415,813	6,585,517	3.0	88.8
Aged 80 to 84	4,945,367	4,442,647	2.0	89.8
Aged 85 or older	4,239,587	3,807,186	1.8	89.8
Aged 18 to 24	27,143,454	19,389,359	8.9	71.4
Aged 18 or older	209,128,094	164,967,066	76.0	78.9
Aged 65 or older	34,991,753	30,687,847	14.1	87.7

Source: U.S. Census Bureau, Census 2000 Summary File 1; calculations by New Strategist

Non-Hispanic White Share of Total Population by Age, 2000 Census

(number of total people, number and percent distribution of those identifying themselves as non-Hispanic white, and non-Hispanic white share of total, by age, 2000)

	total	non-Hispanic white number	percent distribution	share of total
Total people	281,421,906	194,552,774	100.0%	69.1%
Under age 5	19,175,798	11,194,346	5.8	58.4
Aged 5 to 9	20,549,505	12,303,903	6.3	59.9
Aged 10 to 14	20,528,072	12,882,540	6.6	62.8
Aged 15 to 19	20,219,890	12,759,934	6.6	63.1
Aged 20 to 24	18,964,001	11,594,742	6.0	61.1
Aged 25 to 29	19,381,336	11,990,863	6.2	61.9
Aged 30 to 34	20,510,388	13,365,410	6.9	65.2
Aged 35 to 39	22,706,664	15,665,973	8.1	69.0
Aged 40 to 44	22,441,863	16,135,362	8.3	71.9
Aged 45 to 49	20,092,404	14,908,211	7.7	74.2
Aged 50 to 54	17,585,548	13,478,949	6.9	76.6
Aged 55 to 59	13,469,237	10,545,669	5.4	78.3
Aged 60 to 64	10,805,447	8,482,012	4.4	78.5
Aged 65 to 69	9,533,545	7,650,827	3.9	80.3
Aged 70 to 74	8,857,441	7,327,622	3.8	82.7
Aged 75 to 79	7,415,813	6,307,373	3.2	85.1
Aged 80 to 84	4,945,367	4,284,906	2.2	86.6
Aged 85 or older	4,239,587	3,674,132	1.9	86.7
Aged 18 to 24	27,143,454	16,708,378	8.6	61.6
Aged 18 or older	209,128,094	150,525,687	77.4	72.0
Aged 65 or older	34,991,753	29,244,860	15.0	83.6

Note: Non-Hispanic whites include only those who identified themselves as white alone and non-Hispanic.
Source: U.S. Census Bureau, Census 2000 Summary File 1; calculations by New Strategist

Whites by Age and Sex, 2000 Census

(number of whites by age and sex, and sex ratio by age, 2000)

	total	females	males	sex ratio
Total whites	**216,930,975**	**110,409,779**	**106,521,196**	**96**
Under age 5	13,656,252	6,653,324	7,002,928	105
Aged 5 to 9	14,632,897	7,123,510	7,509,387	105
Aged 10 to 14	14,899,672	7,245,608	7,654,064	106
Aged 15 to 19	14,666,888	7,124,819	7,542,069	106
Aged 20 to 24	13,497,559	6,600,130	6,897,429	105
Aged 25 to 29	13,901,171	6,851,167	7,050,004	103
Aged 30 to 34	15,194,805	7,511,240	7,683,565	102
Aged 35 to 39	17,395,108	8,664,810	8,730,298	101
Aged 40 to 44	17,588,919	8,793,700	8,795,219	100
Aged 45 to 49	16,070,375	8,084,799	7,985,576	99
Aged 50 to 54	14,423,239	7,297,158	7,126,081	98
Aged 55 to 59	11,256,685	5,768,508	5,488,177	95
Aged 60 to 64	9,059,558	4,712,551	4,347,007	92
Aged 65 to 69	8,130,453	4,334,890	3,795,563	88
Aged 70 to 74	7,722,044	4,282,017	3,440,027	80
Aged 75 to 79	6,585,517	3,866,218	2,719,299	70
Aged 80 to 84	4,442,647	2,785,988	1,656,659	59
Aged 85 or older	3,807,186	2,709,342	1,097,844	41
Aged 18 to 24	19,389,359	9,477,340	9,912,019	105
Aged 18 or older	164,967,066	85,139,728	79,827,338	94
Aged 65 or older	30,687,847	17,978,455	12,709,392	71

Note: Whites include those who identified themselves as white alone and those who identified themselves as white in combination with one or more other races; the sex ratio is the number of males per 100 females.
Source: U.S. Census Bureau, Census 2000 Summary File 1; calculations by New Strategist

Non-Hispanic Whites by Age and Sex, 2000 Census

(number of non-Hispanic whites by age and sex, and sex ratio by age, 2000)

	total	females	males	sex ratio
Total non-Hispanic whites	**194,552,774**	**99,395,043**	**95,157,731**	**96**
Under age 5	11,194,346	5,446,604	5,747,742	106
Aged 5 to 9	12,303,903	5,982,208	6,321,695	106
Aged 10 to 14	12,882,540	6,259,312	6,623,228	106
Aged 15 to 19	12,759,934	6,228,997	6,530,937	105
Aged 20 to 24	11,594,742	5,729,667	5,865,075	102
Aged 25 to 29	11,990,863	5,952,235	6,038,628	101
Aged 30 to 34	13,365,410	6,642,233	6,723,177	101
Aged 35 to 39	15,665,973	7,829,977	7,835,996	100
Aged 40 to 44	16,135,362	8,077,349	8,058,013	100
Aged 45 to 49	14,908,211	7,497,327	7,410,884	99
Aged 50 to 54	13,478,949	6,809,448	6,669,501	98
Aged 55 to 59	10,545,669	5,393,811	5,151,858	96
Aged 60 to 64	8,482,012	4,402,685	4,079,327	93
Aged 65 to 69	7,650,827	4,072,035	3,578,792	88
Aged 70 to 74	7,327,622	4,060,120	3,267,502	80
Aged 75 to 79	6,307,373	3,703,906	2,603,467	70
Aged 80 to 84	4,284,906	2,687,860	1,597,046	59
Aged 85 or older	3,674,132	2,619,269	1,054,863	40
Aged 18 to 24	16,708,378	8,247,549	8,460,829	103
Aged 18 or older	150,525,687	77,995,804	72,529,883	93
Aged 65 or older	29,244,860	17,143,190	12,101,670	71

Note: Non-Hispanic whites include only those who identified themselves as white alone and non-Hispanic; the sex ratio is the number of males per 100 females.
Source: U.S. Census Bureau, Census 2000 Summary File 1; calculations by New Strategist

Whites by Region, 1990 and 2000 Censuses

(number of whites by region, 1990 and 2000; percent change in number identifying themselves as white alone and as white alone or in combination, 1990–2000)

		2000		percent change 1990–2000	
	1990	**white alone**	**white, alone or in combination**	**white alone**	**white, alone or in combination**
Total whites	**199,686,070**	**211,460,626**	**216,930,975**	**5.9%**	**8.6%**
Northeast	42,068,904	41,533,502	42,395,625	–1.3	0.8
Midwest	52,017,957	53,833,651	54,709,407	3.5	5.2
South	65,582,199	72,819,399	74,303,744	11.0	13.3
West	40,017,010	43,274,074	45,522,199	8.1	13.8

Source: Bureau of the Census, The White Population: 2000, *Census 2000 Brief, C2KBR/01-4, 2001; calculations by New Strategist*

Non-Hispanic Whites by Region, 1990 and 2000 Censuses

(number of non-Hispanic whites by region, 1990 and 2000; percent change 1990–2000)

	1990	**2000**	**percent change 1990–2000**
Total non-Hispanic whites	**188,315,298**	**194,552,774**	**3.3%**
Northeast	40,421,900	39,327,262	–2.7
Midwest	51,201,563	52,386,131	2.3
South	61,402,817	65,927,794	7.4
West	35,289,018	36,911,587	4.6

Note: The 2000 figures for non-Hispanic whites include only those who identified themselves as white alone and non-Hispanic.
Source: Bureau of the Census, Profiles of General Demographic Characteristics, *2000 Census of Population and Housing, 2001; and 1990 census figures from Internet site <http://eire.census.gov/popest/archives/state/srh/srhmars.txt>; calculations by New Strategist*

Whites by Region and Division, 2000 Census

(number of total people, number and percent distribution of whites, and white share of total, by region and division, 2000)

	total	*white*		
		number	*percent distribution*	*share of total*
Total population	**281,421,906**	**216,930,975**	**100.0%**	**77.1%**
Northeast	**53,594,378**	**42,395,625**	**19.5**	**79.1**
New England	13,922,517	12,262,195	5.7	88.1
Middle Atlantic	39,671,861	30,133,430	13.9	76.0
Midwest	**64,392,776**	**54,709,407**	**25.2**	**85.0**
East North Central	45,155,037	37,450,314	17.3	82.9
West North Central	19,237,739	17,259,093	8.0	89.7
South	**100,236,820**	**74,303,744**	**34.3**	**74.1**
South Atlantic	51,769,160	37,969,901	17.5	73.3
East South Central	17,022,810	13,257,904	6.1	77.9
West South Central	31,444,850	23,075,939	10.6	73.4
West	**63,197,932**	**45,522,199**	**21.0**	**72.0**
Mountain	18,172,295	15,032,215	6.9	82.7
Pacific	45,025,637	30,489,984	14.1	67.7

Note: Whites include those who identified themselves as white alone, and those who identified themselves as white in combination with one or more other races.
Source: Bureau of the Census, Profiles of General Demographic Characteristics, *2000 Census of Population and Housing, 2001; calculations by New Strategist*

Non-Hispanic Whites by Region and Division, 2000 Census

(number of total people, number and percent distribution of non-Hispanic whites, and non-Hispanic white share of total, by region and division, 2000)

| | | non-Hispanic white | | |
	total	*number*	*percent distribution*	*share of total*
Total population	**281,421,906**	**194,552,774**	**100.0%**	**69.1%**
Northeast	**53,594,378**	**39,327,262**	**20.2**	**73.4**
New England	13,922,517	11,686,617	6.0	83.9
Middle Atlantic	39,671,861	27,640,645	14.2	69.7
Midwest	**64,392,776**	**52,386,131**	**26.9**	**81.4**
East North Central	45,155,037	35,669,945	18.3	79.0
West North Central	19,237,739	16,716,186	8.6	86.9
South	**100,236,820**	**65,927,794**	**33.9**	**65.8**
South Atlantic	51,769,160	34,575,917	17.8	66.8
East South Central	17,022,810	12,967,670	6.7	76.2
West South Central	31,444,850	18,384,207	9.4	58.5
West	**63,197,932**	**36,911,587**	**19.0**	**58.4**
Mountain	18,172,295	12,883,812	6.6	70.9
Pacific	45,025,637	24,027,775	12.4	53.4

Note: Non-Hispanic whites include only those who identified themselves as white alone and non-Hispanic.
Source: Bureau of the Census, Profiles of General Demographic Characteristics, *2000 Census of Population and Housing, 2001; calculations by New Strategist*

Whites by State, 1990 and 2000 Censuses

(number of whites by state, 1990 and 2000; percent change in number identifying themselves as white alone and identifying themselves as white alone or in combination, 1990–2000)

		2000		percent change 1990–2000	
	1990	*white alone*	*white, alone or in combination*	*white alone*	*white, alone or in combination*
Total whites	**199,686,070**	**211,460,626**	**216,930,975**	**5.9%**	**8.6%**
Alabama	2,975,797	3,162,808	3,199,953	6.3	7.5
Alaska	415,492	434,534	463,999	4.6	11.7
Arizona	2,963,186	3,873,611	3,998,154	30.7	34.9
Arkansas	1,944,744	2,138,598	2,170,534	10.0	11.6
California	20,524,327	20,170,059	21,490,973	–1.7	4.7
Colorado	2,905,474	3,560,005	3,665,638	22.5	26.2
Connecticut	2,859,353	2,780,355	2,835,974	–2.8	–0.8
Delaware	535,094	584,773	594,425	9.3	11.1
District of Columbia	179,667	176,101	184,309	–2.0	2.6
Florida	10,749,285	12,465,029	12,734,292	16.0	18.5
Georgia	4,600,148	5,327,281	5,412,371	15.8	17.7
Hawaii	369,616	294,102	476,162	–20.4	28.8
Idaho	950,451	1,177,304	1,201,113	23.9	26.4
Illinois	8,952,978	9,125,471	9,322,831	1.9	4.1
Indiana	5,020,700	5,320,022	5,387,174	6.0	7.3
Iowa	2,683,090	2,748,640	2,777,183	2.4	3.5
Kansas	2,231,986	2,313,944	2,363,412	3.7	5.9
Kentucky	3,391,832	3,640,889	3,678,740	7.3	8.5
Louisiana	2,839,138	2,856,161	2,894,983	0.6	2.0
Maine	1,208,360	1,236,014	1,247,776	2.3	3.3
Maryland	3,393,964	3,391,308	3,465,697	–0.1	2.1
Massachusetts	5,405,374	5,367,286	5,472,809	–0.7	1.2
Michigan	7,756,086	7,966,053	8,133,283	2.7	4.9
Minnesota	4,130,395	4,400,282	4,466,325	6.5	8.1
Mississippi	1,633,461	1,746,099	1,761,658	6.9	7.8
Missouri	4,486,228	4,748,083	4,819,487	5.8	7.4
Montana	741,111	817,229	831,978	10.3	12.3
Nebraska	1,480,558	1,533,261	1,554,164	3.6	5.0
Nevada	1,012,695	1,501,886	1,565,866	48.3	54.6
New Hampshire	1,087,433	1,186,851	1,198,927	9.1	10.3
New Jersey	6,130,465	6,104,705	6,261,187	–0.4	2.1

(continued)

(continued from previous page)

	1990	2000 white alone	2000 white, alone or in combination	percent change 1990–2000 white alone	percent change 1990–2000 white, alone or in combination
New Mexico	1,146,028	1,214,253	1,272,116	6.0%	11.0%
New York	13,385,255	12,893,689	13,275,834	–3.7	–0.8
North Carolina	5,008,491	5,804,656	5,884,608	15.9	17.5
North Dakota	604,142	593,181	599,918	–1.8	–0.7
Ohio	9,521,756	9,645,453	9,779,512	1.3	2.7
Oklahoma	2,583,512	2,628,434	2,770,035	1.7	7.2
Oregon	2,636,787	2,961,623	3,055,670	12.3	15.9
Pennsylvania	10,520,201	10,484,203	10,596,409	–0.3	0.7
Rhode Island	917,375	891,191	910,630	–2.9	–0.7
South Carolina	2,406,974	2,695,560	2,727,208	12.0	13.3
South Dakota	637,515	669,404	678,604	5.0	6.4
Tennessee	4,048,068	4,563,310	4,617,553	12.7	14.1
Texas	12,774,762	14,799,505	15,240,387	15.8	19.3
Utah	1,615,845	1,992,975	2,034,448	23.3	25.9
Vermont	555,088	589,208	596,079	6.1	7.4
Virginia	4,791,739	5,120,110	5,233,601	6.9	9.2
Washington	4,308,937	4,821,823	5,003,180	11.9	16.1
West Virginia	1,725,523	1,718,777	1,733,390	–0.4	0.5
Wisconsin	4,512,523	4,769,857	4,827,514	5.7	7.0
Wyoming	427,061	454,670	462,902	6.5	8.4

Source: Bureau of the Census, The White Population: 2000, *Census 2000 Brief, C2KBR/01-4, 2001; calculations by New Strategist*

Non-Hispanic Whites by State, 1990 and 2000 Censuses

(number of non-Hispanic whites by state, 1990 and 2000; percent change 1990–2000)

	1990	2000	percent change 1990–2000
Total non-Hispanic whites	**188,315,298**	**194,552,774**	**3.3%**
Alabama	2,960,447	3,125,819	5.6
Alaska	407,029	423,788	4.1
Arizona	2,629,757	3,274,258	24.5
Arkansas	1,933,328	2,100,135	8.6
California	17,072,047	15,816,790	–7.4
Colorado	2,662,659	3,202,880	20.3
Connecticut	2,756,868	2,638,845	–4.3
Delaware	528,388	567,973	7.5
District of Columbia	166,460	159,178	–4.4
Florida	9,481,641	10,458,509	10.3
Georgia	4,545,136	5,128,661	12.8
Hawaii	348,585	277,091	–20.5
Idaho	929,107	1,139,291	22.6
Illinois	8,556,289	8,424,140	–1.5
Indiana	4,967,443	5,219,373	5.1
Iowa	2,664,883	2,710,344	1.7
Kansas	2,191,755	2,233,997	1.9
Kentucky	3,380,117	3,608,013	6.7
Louisiana	2,778,241	2,794,391	0.6
Maine	1,203,754	1,230,297	2.2
Maryland	3,328,086	3,286,547	–1.2
Massachusetts	5,297,982	5,198,359	–1.9
Michigan	7,653,892	7,806,691	2.0
Minnesota	4,103,816	4,337,143	5.7
Mississippi	1,624,900	1,727,908	6.3
Missouri	4,450,147	4,686,474	5.3
Montana	734,036	807,823	10.1
Nebraska	1,460,829	1,494,494	2.3
Nevada	947,181	1,303,001	37.6
New Hampshire	1,079,913	1,175,252	8.8
New Jersey	5,726,089	5,557,209	–2.9
New Mexico	767,056	813,495	6.1
New York	12,475,496	11,760,981	–5.7

(continued)

(continued from previous page)

	1990	2000	percent change 1990–2000
North Carolina	4,975,409	5,647,155	13.5%
North Dakota	601,731	589,149	–2.1
Ohio	9,449,624	9,538,111	0.9
Oklahoma	2,548,670	2,556,368	0.3
Oregon	2,581,271	2,857,616	10.7
Pennsylvania	10,428,351	10,322,455	–1.0
Rhode Island	901,034	858,433	–4.7
South Carolina	2,390,246	2,652,291	11.0
South Dakota	634,900	664,585	4.7
Tennessee	4,028,558	4,505,930	11.8
Texas	10,308,331	10,933,313	6.1
Utah	1,572,078	1,904,265	21.1
Vermont	552,413	585,431	6.0
Virginia	4,705,525	4,965,637	5.5
Washington	4,225,295	4,652,490	10.1
West Virginia	1,719,334	1,709,966	–0.5
Wisconsin	4,466,254	4,681,630	4.8
Wyoming	412,917	438,799	6.3

Note: Non-Hispanic whites include only those who identified themselves as white alone and non-Hispanic.
Source: Bureau of the Census, Profiles of General Demographic Characteristics, *2000 Census of Population and Housing, 2001; and Internet site <http://eire.census.gov/popest/archives/state/srh/srhmars.txt>; calculations by New Strategist*

White Share of Total Population by State, 2000 Census

(number of total people, number and percent distribution of whites, and white share of total, by state, 2000)

	total	white number	white percent distribution	white share of total
Total population	**281,421,906**	**216,930,975**	**100.0%**	**77.1%**
Alabama	4,447,100	3,199,953	1.5	72.0
Alaska	626,932	463,999	0.2	74.0
Arizona	5,130,632	3,998,154	1.8	77.9
Arkansas	2,673,400	2,170,534	1.0	81.2
California	33,871,648	21,490,973	9.9	63.4
Colorado	4,301,261	3,665,638	1.7	85.2
Connecticut	3,405,565	2,835,974	1.3	83.3
Delaware	783,600	594,425	0.3	75.9
District of Columbia	572,059	184,309	0.1	32.2
Florida	15,982,378	12,734,292	5.9	79.7
Georgia	8,186,453	5,412,371	2.5	66.1
Hawaii	1,211,537	476,162	0.2	39.3
Idaho	1,293,953	1,201,113	0.6	92.8
Illinois	12,419,293	9,322,831	4.3	75.1
Indiana	6,080,485	5,387,174	2.5	88.6
Iowa	2,926,324	2,777,183	1.3	94.9
Kansas	2,688,418	2,363,412	1.1	87.9
Kentucky	4,041,769	3,678,740	1.7	91.0
Louisiana	4,468,976	2,894,983	1.3	64.8
Maine	1,274,923	1,247,776	0.6	97.9
Maryland	5,296,486	3,465,697	1.6	65.4
Massachusetts	6,349,097	5,472,809	2.5	86.2
Michigan	9,938,444	8,133,283	3.7	81.8
Minnesota	4,919,479	4,466,325	2.1	90.8
Mississippi	2,844,658	1,761,658	0.8	61.9
Missouri	5,595,211	4,819,487	2.2	86.1
Montana	902,195	831,978	0.4	92.2
Nebraska	1,711,263	1,554,164	0.7	90.8
Nevada	1,998,257	1,565,866	0.7	78.4
New Hampshire	1,235,786	1,198,927	0.6	97.0
New Jersey	8,414,350	6,261,187	2.9	74.4

(continued)

(continued from previous page)

	total	white		
		number	percent distribution	share of total
New Mexico	1,819,046	1,272,116	0.6%	69.9%
New York	18,976,457	13,275,834	6.1	70.0
North Carolina	8,049,313	5,884,608	2.7	73.1
North Dakota	642,200	599,918	0.3	93.4
Ohio	11,353,140	9,779,512	4.5	86.1
Oklahoma	3,450,654	2,770,035	1.3	80.3
Oregon	3,421,399	3,055,670	1.4	89.3
Pennsylvania	12,281,054	10,596,409	4.9	86.3
Rhode Island	1,048,319	910,630	0.4	86.9
South Carolina	4,012,012	2,727,208	1.3	68.0
South Dakota	754,844	678,604	0.3	89.9
Tennessee	5,689,283	4,617,553	2.1	81.2
Texas	20,851,820	15,240,387	7.0	73.1
Utah	2,233,169	2,034,448	0.9	91.1
Vermont	608,827	596,079	0.3	97.9
Virginia	7,078,515	5,233,601	2.4	73.9
Washington	5,894,121	5,003,180	2.3	84.9
West Virginia	1,808,344	1,733,390	0.8	95.9
Wisconsin	5,363,675	4,827,514	2.2	90.0
Wyoming	493,782	462,902	0.2	93.7

Note: Whites include those who identified themselves as white alone and those who identified themselves as white in combination with one or more other races.
Source: Bureau of the Census, Profiles of General Demographic Characteristics, *2000 Census of Population and Housing, 2001; calculations by New Strategist*

Non-Hispanic White Share of Total Population by State, 2000 Census

(number of total people, and number and percent distribution of non-Hispanic whites, and non-Hispanic white share of total, by state, 2000)

| | | non-Hispanic white | | |
	total	number	percent distribution	share of total
Total population	**281,421,906**	**194,552,774**	**100.0%**	**69.1%**
Alabama	4,447,100	3,125,819	1.6	70.3
Alaska	626,932	423,788	0.2	67.6
Arizona	5,130,632	3,274,258	1.7	63.8
Arkansas	2,673,400	2,100,135	1.1	78.6
California	33,871,648	15,816,790	8.1	46.7
Colorado	4,301,261	3,202,880	1.6	74.5
Connecticut	3,405,565	2,638,845	1.4	77.5
Delaware	783,600	567,973	0.3	72.5
District of Columbia	572,059	159,178	0.1	27.8
Florida	15,982,378	10,458,509	5.4	65.4
Georgia	8,186,453	5,128,661	2.6	62.6
Hawaii	1,211,537	277,091	0.1	22.9
Idaho	1,293,953	1,139,291	0.6	88.0
Illinois	12,419,293	8,424,140	4.3	67.8
Indiana	6,080,485	5,219,373	2.7	85.8
Iowa	2,926,324	2,710,344	1.4	92.6
Kansas	2,688,418	2,233,997	1.1	83.1
Kentucky	4,041,769	3,608,013	1.9	89.3
Louisiana	4,468,976	2,794,391	1.4	62.5
Maine	1,274,923	1,230,297	0.6	96.5
Maryland	5,296,486	3,286,547	1.7	62.1
Massachusetts	6,349,097	5,198,359	2.7	81.9
Michigan	9,938,444	7,806,691	4.0	78.6
Minnesota	4,919,479	4,337,143	2.2	88.2
Mississippi	2,844,658	1,727,908	0.9	60.7
Missouri	5,595,211	4,686,474	2.4	83.8
Montana	902,195	807,823	0.4	89.5
Nebraska	1,711,263	1,494,494	0.8	87.3
Nevada	1,998,257	1,303,001	0.7	65.2
New Hampshire	1,235,786	1,175,252	0.6	95.1
New Jersey	8,414,350	5,557,209	2.9	66.0

(continued from previous page)

	total	non-Hispanic white		
		number	percent distribution	share of total
New Mexico	1,819,046	813,495	0.4%	44.7%
New York	18,976,457	11,760,981	6.0	62.0
North Carolina	8,049,313	5,647,155	2.9	70.2
North Dakota	642,200	589,149	0.3	91.7
Ohio	11,353,140	9,538,111	4.9	84.0
Oklahoma	3,450,654	2,556,368	1.3	74.1
Oregon	3,421,399	2,857,616	1.5	83.5
Pennsylvania	12,281,054	10,322,455	5.3	84.1
Rhode Island	1,048,319	858,433	0.4	81.9
South Carolina	4,012,012	2,652,291	1.4	66.1
South Dakota	754,844	664,585	0.3	88.0
Tennessee	5,689,283	4,505,930	2.3	79.2
Texas	20,851,820	10,933,313	5.6	52.4
Utah	2,233,169	1,904,265	1.0	85.3
Vermont	608,827	585,431	0.3	96.2
Virginia	7,078,515	4,965,637	2.6	70.2
Washington	5,894,121	4,652,490	2.4	78.9
West Virginia	1,808,344	1,709,966	0.9	94.6
Wisconsin	5,363,675	4,681,630	2.4	87.3
Wyoming	493,782	438,799	0.2	88.9

Note: Non-Hispanic whites include only those who identified themselves as white alone and non-Hispanic.
Source: Bureau of the Census, Profiles of General Demographic Characteristics, *2000 Census of Population and Housing, 2001; calculations by New Strategist*

Whites in Combination by State, 2000 Census

(number of whites identifying themselves as white alone or in combination, number identifying themselves as white in combination, and white alone or in combination share of white alone or in combination, by state, 2000)

		white in combination	
	white, alone or in combination	*number*	*percent of white, alone or in combination*
Total whites	**216,930,975**	**5,470,349**	**2.5%**
Alabama	3,199,953	37,145	1.2
Alaska	463,999	29,465	6.4
Arizona	3,998,154	124,543	3.1
Arkansas	2,170,534	31,936	1.5
California	21,490,973	1,320,914	6.1
Colorado	3,665,638	105,633	2.9
Connecticut	2,835,974	55,619	2.0
Delaware	594,425	9,652	1.6
District of Columbia	184,309	8,208	4.5
Florida	12,734,292	269,263	2.1
Georgia	5,412,371	85,090	1.6
Hawaii	476,162	182,060	38.2
Idaho	1,201,113	23,809	2.0
Illinois	9,322,831	197,360	2.1
Indiana	5,387,174	67,152	1.2
Iowa	2,777,183	28,543	1.0
Kansas	2,363,412	49,468	2.1
Kentucky	3,678,740	37,851	1.0
Louisiana	2,894,983	38,822	1.3
Maine	1,247,776	11,762	0.9
Maryland	3,465,697	74,389	2.1
Massachusetts	5,472,809	105,523	1.9
Michigan	8,133,283	167,230	2.1
Minnesota	4,466,325	66,043	1.5
Mississippi	1,761,658	15,559	0.9
Missouri	4,819,487	71,404	1.5
Montana	831,978	14,749	1.8
Nebraska	1,554,164	20,903	1.3
Nevada	1,565,866	63,980	4.1

(continued)

(continued from previous page)

	white, alone or in combination	white in combination	
		number	*percent of white, alone or in combination*
New Hampshire	1,198,927	12,076	1.0%
New Jersey	6,261,187	156,482	2.5
New Mexico	1,272,116	57,863	4.5
New York	13,275,834	382,145	2.9
North Carolina	5,884,608	79,952	1.4
North Dakota	599,918	6,737	1.1
Ohio	9,779,512	134,059	1.4
Oklahoma	2,770,035	141,601	5.1
Oregon	3,055,670	94,047	3.1
Pennsylvania	10,596,409	112,206	1.1
Rhode Island	910,630	19,439	2.1
South Carolina	2,727,208	31,648	1.2
South Dakota	678,604	9,200	1.4
Tennessee	4,617,553	54,243	1.2
Texas	15,240,387	440,882	2.9
Utah	2,034,448	41,473	2.0
Vermont	596,079	6,871	1.2
Virginia	5,233,601	113,491	2.2
Washington	5,003,180	181,357	3.6
West Virginia	1,733,390	14,613	0.8
Wisconsin	4,827,514	57,657	1.2
Wyoming	462,902	8,232	1.8

Source: Bureau of the Census, The White Population: 2000, *Census 2000 Brief, C2KBR/01-4, 2001; calculations by New Strategist*

Whites by Metropolitan Area, 2000 Census

(number of total people, number of whites, and white share of total in the 100 largest metropolitan areas, 2000)

	total population	white number	white share of total
1. New York–Northern New Jersey–Long Island, NY–NJ–CT–PA CMSA	21,199,865	14,058,565	66.3%
• Bergen–Passaic, NJ PMSA	1,373,167	1,028,630	74.9
• Bridgeport, CT PMSA	459,479	366,935	79.9
• Danbury, CT PMSA	217,980	196,834	90.3
• Dutchess County, NY PMSA	280,150	238,527	85.1
• Jersey City, NJ PMSA	608,975	364,673	59.9
• Middlesex–Somerset–Hunterdon, NJ PMSA	1,169,641	883,491	75.5
• Monmouth–Ocean, NJ PMSA	1,126,217	1,008,184	89.5
• Nassau–Suffolk, NY PMSA	2,753,913	2,300,082	83.5
• New Haven–Meriden, CT PMSA	542,149	428,133	79.0
• New York, NY PMSA	9,314,235	4,801,743	51.6
• Newark, NJ PMSA	2,032,989	1,376,033	67.7
• Newburgh, NY–PA PMSA	387,669	335,456	86.5
• Stamford–Norwalk, CT PMSA	353,556	292,135	82.6
• Trenton, NJ PMSA	350,761	245,471	70.0
• Waterbury, CT PMSA	228,984	192,238	84.0
2. Los Angeles–Riverside–Orange County, CA CMSA	16,373,645	9,668,664	59.1
• Los Angeles–Long Beach, CA PMSA	9,519,338	5,022,646	52.8
• Orange County, CA PMSA	2,846,289	1,945,080	68.3
• Riverside–San Bernardino, CA PMSA	3,254,821	2,148,514	66.0
• Ventura, CA PMSA	753,197	552,424	73.3
3. Chicago–Gary–Kenosha, IL–IN–WI CMSA	9,157,540	6,288,946	68.7
• Chicago, IL PMSA	8,272,768	5,597,506	67.7
• Gary, IN PMSA	631,362	472,498	74.8
• Kankakee, IL PMSA	103,833	84,205	81.1
• Kenosha, WI PMSA	149,577	134,737	90.1
4. Washington–Baltimore, DC–MD–VA–WV CMSA	7,608,070	4,932,663	64.8
• Baltimore, MD PMSA	2,552,994	1,748,440	68.5
• Hagerstown, MD PMSA	131,923	119,601	90.7
• Washington, DC–MD–VA–WV PMSA	4,923,153	3,064,622	62.2
5. San Francisco–Oakland–San Jose, CA CMSA	7,039,362	4,410,454	62.7
• Oakland, CA PMSA	2,392,557	1,427,773	59.7
• San Francisco, CA PMSA	1,731,183	1,075,787	62.1
• San Jose, CA PMSA	1,682,585	969,182	57.6
• Santa Cruz–Watsonville, CA PMSA	255,602	201,777	78.9
• Santa Rosa, CA PMSA	458,614	390,660	85.2
• Vallejo–Fairfield–Napa, CA PMSA	518,821	345,275	66.5

(continued)

(continued from previous page)

	total population	white number	white share of total
6. Philadelphia–Wilmington–Atlantic City, PA–NJ–DE–MD CMSA	6,188,463	4,562,328	73.7%
• Atlantic–Cape May, NJ PMSA	354,878	271,854	76.6
• Philadelphia, PA–NJ PMSA	5,100,931	3,738,044	73.3
• Vineland–Millville–Bridgeton, NJ PMSA	146,438	99,382	67.9
• Wilmington–Newark, DE–MD PMSA	586,216	453,048	77.3
7. Boston–Worcester–Lawrence, MA–NH–ME–CT CMSA	5,819,100	5,043,145	86.7
• Boston, MA–NH PMSA	3,406,829	2,867,860	84.2
• Brockton, MA PMSA	255,459	214,636	84.0
• Fitchburg–Leominster, MA PMSA	142,284	129,569	91.1
• Lawrence, MA–NH PMSA	396,230	346,285	87.4
• Lowell, MA–NH PMSA	301,686	263,646	87.4
• Manchester, NH PMSA	198,378	189,484	95.5
• Nashua, NH PMSA	190,949	180,400	94.5
• New Bedford, MA PMSA	175,198	155,241	88.6
• Portsmouth–Rochester, NH–ME PMSA	240,698	234,539	97.4
• Worcester, MA–CT PMSA	511,389	461,485	90.2
8. Detroit–Ann Arbor–Flint, MI CMSA	5,456,428	4,083,156	74.8
• Ann Arbor, MI PMSA	578,736	503,871	87.1
• Detroit, MI PMSA	4,441,551	3,242,897	73.0
• Flint, MI PMSA	436,141	336,388	77.1
9. Dallas–Fort Worth, TX CMSA	5,221,801	3,735,092	71.5
• Dallas, TX PMSA	3,519,176	2,435,594	69.2
• Fort Worth–Arlington, TX PMSA	1,702,625	1,299,498	76.3
10. Houston–Galveston–Brazoria, TX CMSA	4,669,571	3,027,709	64.8
• Brazoria, TX PMSA	241,767	191,169	79.1
• Galveston–Texas City, TX PMSA	250,158	186,294	74.5
• Houston, TX PMSA	4,177,646	2,650,246	63.4
11. Atlanta, GA MSA	4,112,198	2,638,924	64.2
12. Miami–Fort Lauderdale, FL CMSA	3,876,380	2,805,633	72.4
• Fort Lauderdale, FL PMSA	1,623,018	1,175,608	72.4
• Miami, FL PMSA	2,253,362	1,630,025	72.3
13. Seattle–Tacoma–Bremerton, WA CMSA	3,554,760	2,941,228	82.7
• Bremerton, WA PMSA	231,969	204,804	88.3
• Olympia, WA PMSA	207,355	184,578	89.0
• Seattle–Bellevue–Everett, WA PMSA	2,414,616	1,972,612	81.7
• Tacoma, WA PMSA	700,820	579,234	82.7
14. Phoenix–Mesa, AZ MSA	3,251,876	2,582,573	79.4
15. Minneapolis–St. Paul, MN–WI MSA	2,968,806	2,604,861	87.7
16. Cleveland–Akron, OH CMSA	2,945,831	2,365,731	80.3
• Akron, OH PMSA	694,960	604,956	87.0
• Cleveland–Lorain–Elyria, OH PMSA	2,250,871	1,760,775	78.2

(continued)

(continued from previous page)

	total population	white number	white share of total
17. San Diego, CA MSA	2,813,833	1,979,176	70.3%
18. St. Louis, MO–IL MSA	2,603,607	2,064,275	79.3
19. Denver–Boulder–Greeley, CO CMSA	2,581,506	2,143,608	83.0
• Boulder–Longmont, CO PMSA	291,288	263,618	90.5
• Denver, CO PMSA	2,109,282	1,727,853	81.9
• Greeley, CO PMSA	180,936	152,137	84.1
20. Tampa–St. Petersburg–Clearwater, FL MSA	2,395,997	2,024,565	84.5
21. Pittsburgh, PA MSA	2,358,695	2,129,448	90.3
22. Portland–Salem, OR–WA CMSA	2,265,223	1,974,348	87.2
• Portland–Vancouver, OR–WA PMSA	1,918,009	1,676,073	87.4
• Salem, OR PMSA	347,214	298,275	85.9
23. Cincinnati–Hamilton, OH–KY–IN CMSA	1,979,202	1,707,135	86.3
• Cincinnati, OH–KY–IN PMSA	1,646,395	1,400,253	85.0
• Hamilton–Middletown, OH PMSA	332,807	306,882	92.2
24. Sacramento–Yolo, CA CMSA	1,796,857	1,331,302	74.1
• Sacramento, CA PMSA	1,628,197	1,209,823	74.3
• Yolo, CA PMSA	168,660	121,479	72.0
25. Kansas City, MO–KS MSA	1,776,062	1,464,703	82.5
26. Milwaukee–Racine, WI CMSA	1,689,572	1,337,201	79.1
• Milwaukee–Waukesha, WI PMSA	1,500,741	1,177,619	78.5
• Racine, WI PMSA	188,831	159,582	84.5
27. Orlando, FL MSA	1,644,561	1,266,975	77.0
28. Indianapolis, IN MSA	1,607,486	1,336,237	83.1
29. San Antonio, TX MSA	1,592,383	1,172,557	73.6
30. Norfolk–Virginia Beach–Newport News, VA–NC MSA	1,569,541	1,006,441	64.1
31. Las Vegas, NV–AZ MSA	1,563,282	1,204,986	77.1
32. Columbus, OH MSA	1,540,157	1,273,752	82.7
33. Charlotte–Gastonia–Rock Hill, NC–SC MSA	1,499,293	1,118,150	74.6
34. New Orleans, LA MSA	1,337,726	781,334	58.4
35. Salt Lake City–Ogden, UT MSA	1,333,914	1,196,260	89.7
36. Greensboro–Winston-Salem–High Point, NC MSA	1,251,509	943,061	75.4
37. Austin–San Marcos, TX MSA	1,249,763	933,922	74.7
38. Nashville, TN MSA	1,231,311	992,546	80.6
39. Providence–Fall River–Warwick, RI–MA MSA	1,188,613	1,046,453	88.0
40. Raleigh–Durham–Chapel Hill, NC MSA	1,187,941	838,266	70.6
41. Hartford, CT MSA	1,183,110	973,121	82.3
42. Buffalo–Niagara Falls, NY MSA	1,170,111	992,820	84.8
43. Memphis, TN–AR–MS MSA	1,135,614	609,218	53.6
44. West Palm Beach–Boca Raton, FL MSA	1,131,184	909,541	80.4
45. Jacksonville, FL MSA	1,100,491	815,347	74.1
46. Rochester, NY MSA	1,098,201	937,049	85.3
47. Grand Rapids–Muskegon–Holland, MI MSA	1,088,514	950,650	87.3
48. Oklahoma City, OK MSA	1,083,346	856,243	79.0

(continued)

(continued from previous page)

	total population	white	
		number	share of total
49. Louisville, KY–IN MSA	1,025,598	860,896	83.9%
50. Richmond–Petersburg, VA MSA	996,512	656,880	65.9
51. Greenville–Spartanburg–Anderson, SC MSA	962,441	768,645	79.9
52. Dayton–Springfield, OH MSA	950,558	794,451	83.6
53. Fresno, CA MSA	922,516	545,795	59.2
54. Birmingham, AL MSA	921,106	626,126	68.0
55. Honolulu, HI MSA	876,156	308,838	35.2
56. Albany–Schenectady–Troy, NY MSA	875,583	793,577	90.6
57. Tucson, AZ MSA	843,746	656,275	77.8
58. Tulsa, OK MSA	803,235	645,863	80.4
59. Syracuse, NY MSA	732,117	660,982	90.3
60. Omaha, NE–IA MSA	716,998	621,318	86.7
61. Albuquerque, NM MSA	712,738	521,986	73.2
62. Knoxville, TN MSA	687,249	634,563	92.3
63. El Paso, TX MSA	679,622	521,892	76.8
64. Bakersfield, CA MSA	661,645	430,745	65.1
65. Allentown–Bethlehem–Easton, PA MSA	637,958	581,106	91.1
66. Harrisburg–Lebanon–Carlisle, PA MSA	629,401	559,358	88.9
67. Scranton–Wilkes-Barre–Hazleton, PA MSA	624,776	608,221	97.4
68. Toledo, OH MSA	618,203	517,891	83.8
69. Baton Rouge, LA MSA	602,894	395,547	65.6
70. Youngstown–Warren, OH MSA	594,746	525,722	88.4
71. Springfield, MA MSA	591,932	493,185	83.3
72. Sarasota–Bradenton, FL MSA	589,959	535,904	90.8
73. Little Rock–North Little Rock, AR MSA	583,845	441,304	75.6
74. McAllen–Edinburg–Mission, TX MSA	569,463	453,753	79.7
75. Stockton–Lodi, CA MSA	563,598	353,443	62.7
76. Charleston–North Charleston, SC MSA	549,033	363,183	66.1
77. Wichita, KS MSA	545,220	458,264	84.1
78. Mobile, AL MSA	540,258	379,224	70.2
79. Columbia, SC MSA	536,691	347,980	64.8
80. Colorado Springs, CO MSA	516,929	436,548	84.5
81. Fort Wayne, IN MSA	502,141	448,841	89.4
82. Daytona Beach, FL MSA	493,175	431,202	87.4
83. Lakeland–Winter Haven, FL MSA	483,924	391,312	80.9
84. Johnson City–Kingsport–Bristol, TN–VA MSA	480,091	465,280	96.9
85. Lexington, KY MSA	479,198	419,871	87.6
86. Augusta–Aiken, GA–SC MSA	477,441	298,733	62.6
87. Melbourne–Titusville–Palm Bay, FL MSA	476,230	420,406	88.3
88. Lancaster, PA MSA	470,658	435,385	92.5
89. Chattanooga, TN–GA MSA	465,161	389,192	83.7
90. Des Moines, IA MSA	456,022	415,327	91.1
91. Kalamazoo–Battle Creek, MI MSA	452,851	393,243	86.8

(continued)

(continued from previous page)

	total population	white number	share of total
92. Lansing–East Lansing, MI MSA	447,728	387,285	86.5%
93. Modesto, CA MSA	446,997	330,141	73.9
94. Fort Myers–Cape Coral, FL MSA	440,888	391,840	88.9
95. Jackson, MS MSA	440,801	234,029	53.1
96. Boise City, ID MSA	432,345	398,088	92.1
97. Madison, WI MSA	426,526	386,155	90.5
98. Spokane, WA MSA	417,939	392,527	93.9
99. Pensacola, FL MSA	412,153	327,221	79.4
100. Canton–Massillon, OH MSA	406,934	374,730	92.1

Note: Whites include those who identified themselves as white alone and those who identified themselves as white in combination with one or more other races. For definitions of CMSA, PMSA, and MSA, see glossary.
Source: Bureau of the Census, Profiles of General Demographic Characteristics, *2000 Census of Population and Housing, May 2001; calculations by New Strategist*

Non-Hispanic Whites by Metropolitan Area, 2000 Census

(number of total people, number of non-Hispanic whites, and non-Hispanic white share of total in the 100 largest metropolitan areas, 2000)

	total population	non-Hispanic white number	non-Hispanic white share of total
1. New York–Northern New Jersey–Long Island, NY–NJ–CT–PA CMSA	21,199,865	11,953,732	56.4%
• Bergen–Passaic, NJ PMSA	1,373,167	890,640	64.9
• Bridgeport, CT PMSA	459,479	331,048	72.0
• Danbury, CT PMSA	217,980	184,661	84.7
• Dutchess County, NY PMSA	280,150	224,913	80.3
• Jersey City, NJ PMSA	608,975	215,216	35.3
• Middlesex–Somerset–Hunterdon, NJ PMSA	1,169,641	797,594	68.2
• Monmouth–Ocean, NJ PMSA	1,126,217	955,076	84.8
• Nassau–Suffolk, NY PMSA	2,753,913	2,105,352	76.4
• New Haven–Meriden, CT PMSA	542,149	395,573	73.0
• New York, NY PMSA	9,314,235	3,684,669	39.6
• Newark, NJ PMSA	2,032,989	1,196,664	58.9
• Newburgh, NY–PA PMSA	387,669	306,329	79.0
• Stamford–Norwalk, CT PMSA	353,556	263,926	74.6
• Trenton, NJ PMSA	350,761	225,284	64.2
• Waterbury, CT PMSA	228,984	176,787	77.2
2. Los Angeles–Riverside–Orange County, CA CMSA	16,373,645	6,387,094	39.0
• Los Angeles–Long Beach, CA PMSA	9,519,338	2,959,614	31.1
• Orange County, CA PMSA	2,846,289	1,458,978	51.3
• Riverside–San Bernardino, CA PMSA	3,254,821	1,541,053	47.3
• Ventura, CA PMSA	753,197	427,449	56.8
3. Chicago–Gary–Kenosha, IL–IN–WI CMSA	9,157,540	5,435,440	59.4
• Chicago, IL PMSA	8,272,768	4,798,533	58.0
• Gary, IN PMSA	631,362	428,791	67.9
• Kankakee, IL PMSA	103,833	80,829	77.8
• Kenosha, WI PMSA	149,577	127,287	85.1
4. Washington–Baltimore, DC–MD–VA–WV CMSA	7,608,070	4,572,610	60.1
• Baltimore, MD PMSA	2,552,994	1,692,851	66.3
• Hagerstown, MD PMSA	131,923	117,518	89.1
• Washington, DC–MD–VA–WV PMSA	4,923,153	2,762,241	56.1
5. San Francisco–Oakland–San Jose, CA CMSA	7,039,362	3,559,668	50.6
• Oakland, CA PMSA	2,392,557	1,140,504	47.7
• San Francisco, CA PMSA	1,731,183	885,518	51.2
• San Jose, CA PMSA	1,682,585	744,282	44.2
• Santa Cruz–Watsonville, CA PMSA	255,602	167,464	65.5
• Santa Rosa, CA PMSA	458,614	341,686	74.5
• Vallejo–Fairfield–Napa, CA PMSA	518,821	280,214	54.0

(continued)

(continued from previous page)

	total population	non-Hispanic white number	non-Hispanic white share of total
6. Philadelphia–Wilmington–Atlantic City, PA–NJ–DE–MD CMSA	6,188,463	4,355,529	70.4%
• Atlantic–Cape May, NJ PMSA	354,878	253,623	71.5
• Philadelphia, PA–NJ PMSA	5,100,931	3,583,090	70.2
• Vineland–Millville–Bridgeton, NJ PMSA	146,438	85,510	58.4
• Wilmington–Newark, DE–MD PMSA	586,216	433,306	73.9
7. Boston–Worcester–Lawrence, MA–NH–ME–CT CMSA	5,819,100	4,802,519	82.5
• Boston, MA–NH PMSA	3,406,829	2,726,018	80.0
• Brockton, MA PMSA	255,459	206,421	80.8
• Fitchburg–Leominster, MA PMSA	142,284	121,562	85.4
• Lawrence, MA–NH PMSA	396,230	323,521	81.6
• Lowell, MA–NH PMSA	301,686	251,027	83.2
• Manchester, NH PMSA	198,378	183,925	92.7
• Nashua, NH PMSA	190,949	175,222	91.8
• New Bedford, MA PMSA	175,198	146,723	83.7
• Portsmouth–Rochester, NH–ME PMSA	240,698	230,770	95.9
• Worcester, MA–CT PMSA	511,389	437,330	85.5
8. Detroit–Ann Arbor–Flint, MI CMSA	5,456,428	3,904,427	71.6
• Ann Arbor, MI PMSA	578,736	484,391	83.7
• Detroit, MI PMSA	4,441,551	3,096,900	69.7
• Flint, MI PMSA	436,141	323,136	74.1
9. Dallas–Fort Worth, TX CMSA	5,221,801	3,096,104	59.3
• Dallas, TX PMSA	3,519,176	1,979,218	56.2
• Fort Worth–Arlington, TX PMSA	1,702,625	1,116,886	65.6
10. Houston–Galveston–Brazoria, TX CMSA	4,669,571	2,239,893	48.0
• Brazoria, TX PMSA	241,767	158,052	65.4
• Galveston–Texas City, TX PMSA	250,158	157,851	63.1
• Houston, TX PMSA	4,177,646	1,923,990	46.1
11. Atlanta, GA MSA	4,112,198	2,460,740	59.8
12. Miami–Fort Lauderdale, FL CMSA	3,876,380	1,407,446	36.3
• Fort Lauderdale, FL PMSA	1,623,018	941,674	58.0
• Miami, FL PMSA	2,253,362	465,772	20.7
13. Seattle–Tacoma–Bremerton, WA CMSA	3,554,760	2,737,902	77.0
• Bremerton, WA PMSA	231,969	190,751	82.2
• Olympia, WA PMSA	207,355	172,963	83.4
• Seattle–Bellevue–Everett, WA PMSA	2,414,616	1,841,254	76.3
• Tacoma, WA PMSA	700,820	532,934	76.0
14. Phoenix–Mesa, AZ MSA	3,251,876	2,140,171	65.8
15. Minneapolis–St. Paul, MN–WI MSA	2,968,806	2,514,494	84.7
16. Cleveland–Akron, OH CMSA	2,945,831	2,291,105	77.8
• Akron, OH PMSA	694,960	593,445	85.4
• Cleveland–Lorain–Elyria, OH PMSA	2,250,871	1,697,660	75.4

(continued)

(continued from previous page)

	total population	non-Hispanic white	
		number	share of total
17. San Diego, CA MSA	2,813,833	1,548,833	55.0%
18. St. Louis, MO–IL MSA	2,603,607	2,014,776	77.4
19. Denver–Boulder–Greeley, CO CMSA	2,581,506	1,854,428	71.8
• Boulder–Longmont, CO PMSA	291,288	243,512	83.6
• Denver, CO PMSA	2,109,282	1,484,343	70.4
• Greeley, CO PMSA	180,936	126,573	70.0
20. Tampa–St. Petersburg–Clearwater, FL MSA	2,395,997	1,821,955	76.0
21. Pittsburgh, PA MSA	2,358,695	2,100,501	89.1
22. Portland–Salem, OR–WA CMSA	2,265,223	1,835,959	81.0
• Portland–Vancouver, OR–WA PMSA	1,918,009	1,564,685	81.6
• Salem, OR PMSA	347,214	271,274	78.1
23. Cincinnati–Hamilton, OH–KY–IN CMSA	1,979,202	1,676,345	84.7
• Cincinnati, OH–KY–IN PMSA	1,646,395	1,375,267	83.5
• Hamilton–Middletown, OH PMSA	332,807	301,078	90.5
24. Sacramento–Yolo, CA CMSA	1,796,857	1,144,558	63.7
• Sacramento, CA PMSA	1,628,197	1,046,616	64.3
• Yolo, CA PMSA	168,660	97,942	58.1
25. Kansas City, MO–KS MSA	1,776,062	1,391,492	78.3
26. Milwaukee–Racine, WI CMSA	1,689,572	1,266,388	75.0
• Milwaukee–Waukesha, WI PMSA	1,500,741	1,116,150	74.4
• Racine, WI PMSA	188,831	150,238	79.6
27. Orlando, FL MSA	1,644,561	1,070,460	65.1
28. Indianapolis, IN MSA	1,607,486	1,299,311	80.8
29. San Antonio, TX MSA	1,592,383	627,176	39.4
30. Norfolk–Virginia Beach–Newport News, VA–NC MSA	1,569,541	959,404	61.1
31. Las Vegas, NV–AZ MSA	1,563,282	986,463	63.1
32. Columbus, OH MSA	1,540,157	1,238,296	80.4
33. Charlotte–Gastonia–Rock Hill, NC–SC MSA	1,499,293	1,067,594	71.2
34. New Orleans, LA MSA	1,337,726	731,514	54.7
35. Salt Lake City–Ogden, UT MSA	1,333,914	1,104,467	82.8
36. Greensboro–Winston-Salem–High Point, NC MSA	1,251,509	905,018	72.3
37. Austin–San Marcos, TX MSA	1,249,763	758,302	60.7
38. Nashville, TN MSA	1,231,311	960,118	78.0
39. Providence–Fall River–Warwick, RI–MA MSA	1,188,613	990,722	83.4
40. Raleigh–Durham–Chapel Hill, NC MSA	1,187,941	793,714	66.8
41. Hartford, CT MSA	1,183,110	915,287	77.4
42. Buffalo–Niagara Falls, NY MSA	1,170,111	965,233	82.5
43. Memphis, TN–AR–MS MSA	1,135,614	588,808	51.8
44. West Palm Beach–Boca Raton, FL MSA	1,131,184	798,484	70.6
45. Jacksonville, FL MSA	1,100,491	775,279	70.4
46. Rochester, NY MSA	1,098,201	902,811	82.2
47. Grand Rapids–Muskegon–Holland, MI MSA	1,088,514	903,766	83.0

(continued)

(continued from previous page)

	total population	non-Hispanic white number	share of total
48. Oklahoma City, OK MSA	1,083,346	789,780	72.9%
49. Louisville, KY–IN MSA	1,025,598	840,677	82.0
50. Richmond–Petersburg, VA MSA	996,512	637,800	64.0
51. Greenville–Spartanburg–Anderson, SC MSA	962,441	747,540	77.7
52. Dayton–Springfield, OH MSA	950,558	776,050	81.6
53. Fresno, CA MSA	922,516	374,913	40.6
54. Birmingham, AL MSA	921,106	611,574	66.4
55. Honolulu, HI MSA	876,156	175,633	20.0
56. Albany–Schenectady–Troy, NY MSA	875,583	771,049	88.1
57. Tucson, AZ MSA	843,746	518,720	61.5
58. Tulsa, OK MSA	803,235	593,498	73.9
59. Syracuse, NY MSA	732,117	644,035	88.0
60. Omaha, NE–IA MSA	716,998	593,902	82.8
61. Albuquerque, NM MSA	712,738	340,286	47.7
62. Knoxville, TN MSA	687,249	623,048	90.7
63. El Paso, TX MSA	679,622	115,535	17.0
64. Bakersfield, CA MSA	661,645	327,190	49.5
65. Allentown–Bethlehem–Easton, PA MSA	637,958	552,429	86.6
66. Harrisburg–Lebanon–Carlisle, PA MSA	629,401	544,078	86.4
67. Scranton–Wilkes–Barre-Hazleton, PA MSA	624,776	600,830	96.2
68. Toledo, OH MSA	618,203	495,070	80.1
69. Baton Rouge, LA MSA	602,894	385,099	63.9
70. Youngstown–Warren, OH MSA	594,746	513,967	86.4
71. Springfield, MA MSA	591,932	459,511	77.6
72. Sarasota–Bradenton, FL MSA	589,959	505,267	85.6
73. Little Rock–North Little Rock, AR MSA	583,845	429,131	73.5
74. McAllen–Edinburg–Mission, TX MSA	569,463	59,423	10.4
75. Stockton–Lodi, CA MSA	563,598	267,002	47.4
76. Charleston–North Charleston, SC MSA	549,033	351,434	64.0
77. Wichita, KS MSA	545,220	430,553	79.0
78. Mobile, AL MSA	540,258	370,631	68.6
79. Columbia, SC MSA	536,691	337,574	62.9
80. Colorado Springs, CO MSA	516,929	393,819	76.2
81. Fort Wayne, IN MSA	502,141	435,024	86.6
82. Daytona Beach, FL MSA	493,175	404,681	82.1
83. Lakeland–Winter Haven, FL MSA	483,924	361,366	74.7
84. Johnson City–Kingsport–Bristol, TN–VA MSA	480,091	459,120	95.6
85. Lexington, KY MSA	479,198	407,486	85.0
86. Augusta–Aiken, GA–SC MSA	477,441	287,867	60.3
87. Melbourne–Titusville–Palm Bay, FL MSA	476,230	398,695	83.7
88. Lancaster, PA MSA	470,658	420,366	89.3
89. Chattanooga, TN–GA MSA	465,161	381,598	82.0

(continued)

(continued from previous page)

	total population	non-Hispanic white	
		number	share of total
90. Des Moines, IA MSA	456,022	401,078	88.0%
91. Kalamazoo–Battle Creek, MI MSA	452,851	377,369	83.3
92. Lansing–East Lansing, MI MSA	447,728	367,996	82.2
93. Modesto, CA MSA	446,997	256,001	57.3
94. Fort Myers–Cape Coral, FL MSA	440,888	361,439	82.0
95. Jackson, MS MSA	440,801	229,969	52.2
96. Boise City, ID MSA	432,345	374,997	86.7
97. Madison, WI MSA	426,526	372,597	87.4
98. Spokane, WA MSA	417,939	375,427	89.8
99. Pensacola, FL MSA	412,153	313,597	76.1
100. Canton–Massillon, OH MSA	406,934	367,203	90.2

Note: Non-Hispanic whites include only those who identified themselves as white alone and non-Hispanic. For definitions of CMSA, PMSA, and MSA, see glossary.
Source: Bureau of the Census, Profiles of General Demographic Characteristics, *2000 Census of Population and Housing, May 2001; calculations by New Strategist*

Whites: Spending

The Spending of Non-Hispanic Whites Is Close to the Average on Most Items

The nation's 88 million non-Hispanic white households (called consumer units by the Bureau of Labor Statistics) spent an average of $39,991 in 2000, according to the Consumer Expenditure Survey—5 percent more than the average consumer unit. The income of non-Hispanic whites is 6 percent above average.

Because most households are non-Hispanic white, non-Hispanic white spending is necessarily close to the average on most items. On a handful of categories, non-Hispanic whites spend significantly less than the average consumer unit. These include flour, rice, sugar, rented dwellings, coin-operated laundries, children's clothes, intracity mass transit fares, taxi fares, tape recorders, and wigs.

Non-Hispanic whites spend significantly more than the average consumer unit on items such as vacation homes, adult day care centers, housekeeping and lawn care services, stationery supplies and giftwrap, ship and airline fares, hearing aids, fees and admissions to entertainment events, recreational vehicles, and contributions to political organizations.

■ Non-Hispanic whites are older, on average, than blacks or Hispanics. The higher spending of non-Hispanic whites on such items as adult day care centers, hearing aids, and contributions to political organizations reflects their older age.

Non-Hispanic whites spend 5 percent more than average

(average annual spending of total and non-Hispanic white consumer units, 2000)

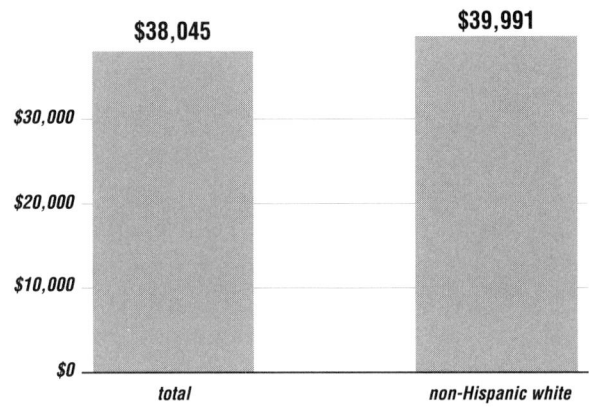

Average and Indexed Spending of Non-Hispanic White Households, 2000

(average annual expenditures of total and non-Hispanic white consumer units, and indexed expenditures of non-Hispanic white consumer units, 2000)

	average spending of total consumer units	non-Hispanic white consumer units average spending	non-Hispanic white consumer units indexed spending*
Number of consumer units (in 000s)	109,367	88,112	–
Average before-tax income of consumer unit	$44,649.00	$47,357.00	106
Average spending of consumer unit, total	38,044.67	39,991.48	105
FOOD	**$5,157.88**	**$5,279.28**	**102**
FOOD AT HOME	**3,021.00**	**3,018.48**	**100**
Cereals and bakery products	**453.33**	**458.22**	**101**
Cereals and cereal products	156.40	152.23	97
Flour	7.98	6.78	85
Prepared flour mixes	13.35	13.57	102
Ready-to-eat and cooked cereals	86.88	86.76	100
Rice	19.55	17.36	89
Pasta, cornmeal, and other cereal products	28.64	27.77	97
Bakery products	296.93	305.99	103
Bread	84.04	84.49	101
White bread	36.62	36.02	98
Bread, other than white	47.42	48.47	102
Crackers and cookies	71.03	74.73	105
Cookies	47.71	49.81	104
Crackers	23.32	24.92	107
Frozen and refrigerated bakery products	24.53	25.85	105
Other bakery products	117.33	120.92	103
Biscuits and rolls	38.53	41.94	109
Cakes and cupcakes	38.42	37.93	99
Bread and cracker products	4.41	4.73	107
Sweetrolls, coffee cakes, doughnuts	22.68	22.87	101
Pies, tarts, turnovers	13.28	13.46	101
Meats, poultry, fish, and eggs	**795.43**	**754.70**	**95**
Beef	238.19	229.58	96
Ground beef	87.76	84.48	96
Roast	39.84	39.60	99
Chuck roast	13.33	12.71	95
Round roast	11.46	11.73	102
Other roast	15.05	15.16	101
Steak	94.52	90.10	95
Round steak	15.31	13.62	89
Sirloin steak	29.86	28.63	96
Other steak	49.35	47.85	97
Other beef	16.08	15.40	96

(continued)

(continued from previous page)

	average spending of total consumer units	non-Hispanic white consumer units	
		average spending	indexed spending
Pork	$166.94	$156.99	94
Bacon	26.05	24.93	96
Pork chops	40.57	36.45	90
Ham	36.26	34.96	96
Ham, not canned	34.52	33.19	96
Canned ham	1.74	1.77	102
Sausage	25.24	24.00	95
Other pork	38.82	36.66	94
Other meats	100.54	97.70	97
Frankfurters	20.68	19.92	96
Lunch meats (cold cuts)	67.99	68.81	101
Bologna, liverwurst, salami	23.73	22.72	96
Other lunch meats	44.26	46.09	104
Lamb, organ meats, and others	11.87	8.97	76
Lamb and organ meats	9.71	7.86	81
Mutton, goat, and game	2.16	1.11	51
Poultry	145.16	135.24	93
Fresh and frozen chicken	114.43	105.42	92
Fresh and frozen whole chicken	31.25	26.81	86
Fresh and frozen chicken parts	83.18	78.61	95
Other poultry	30.73	29.82	97
Fish and seafood	110.14	104.07	94
Canned fish and seafood	15.67	15.86	101
Fresh fish and shellfish	66.82	60.55	91
Frozen fish and shellfish	27.65	27.67	100
Eggs	34.46	31.13	90
Dairy products	**324.63**	**332.64**	**102**
Fresh milk and cream	131.22	131.71	100
Fresh milk, all types	119.61	119.47	100
Cream	11.61	12.24	105
Other dairy products	193.41	200.93	104
Butter	17.00	17.70	104
Cheese	95.96	99.73	104
Ice cream and related products	56.56	58.54	104
Miscellaneous dairy products	23.89	24.96	104
Fruits and vegetables	**520.83**	**515.37**	**99**
Fresh fruits	163.17	160.93	99
Apples	29.49	29.20	99
Bananas	31.70	30.14	95
Oranges	18.93	18.02	95
Citrus fruits, excl. oranges	14.31	13.62	95
Other fresh fruits	68.74	69.95	102

(continued)

(continued from previous page)

	average spending of total consumer units	non-Hispanic white consumer units	
		average spending	indexed spending
Fresh vegetables	$158.72	$156.08	98
Potatoes	28.07	27.79	99
Lettuce	20.75	20.65	100
Tomatoes	29.53	27.58	93
Other fresh vegetables	80.38	80.06	100
Processed fruits	115.01	113.81	99
Frozen fruits and fruit juices	14.37	15.14	105
Frozen orange juice	6.90	7.21	104
Frozen fruits	3.62	3.99	110
Frozen fruit juices	3.84	3.94	103
Canned fruits	15.48	16.03	104
Dried fruits	5.50	5.83	106
Fresh fruit juice	23.44	23.29	99
Canned and bottled fruit juice	56.21	53.52	95
Processed vegetables	83.94	84.54	101
Frozen vegetables	26.42	27.65	105
Canned and dried vegetables and juices	57.52	56.89	99
Canned beans	12.67	12.71	100
Canned corn	6.80	6.38	94
Canned miscellaneous vegetables	17.95	18.81	105
Dried peas	0.34	0.34	100
Dried beans	2.53	1.90	75
Dried miscellaneous vegetables	7.22	6.83	95
Dried processed vegetables	0.41	0.30	73
Frozen vegetable juices	0.29	0.27	93
Fresh and canned vegetable juices	9.30	9.34	100
Other food at home	**926.77**	**957.55**	**103**
Sugar and other sweets	117.14	121.42	104
Candy and chewing gum	76.30	82.35	108
Sugar	16.80	14.82	88
Artificial sweeteners	4.19	3.98	95
Jams, preserves, other sweets	19.86	20.28	102
Fats and oils	83.09	81.47	98
Margarine	11.61	11.66	100
Fats and oils	23.35	20.76	89
Salad dressings	27.18	27.24	100
Nondairy cream and imitation milk	9.15	9.69	106
Peanut butter	11.81	12.13	103
Miscellaneous foods	437.02	457.15	105
Frozen prepared foods	90.20	96.25	107
Frozen meals	28.50	30.35	106
Other frozen prepared foods	61.70	65.90	107
Canned and packaged soups	35.54	36.59	103

(continued)

(continued from previous page)

	average spending of total consumer units	non-Hispanic white consumer units	
		average spending	indexed spending
Potato chips, nuts, and other snacks	$92.50	$100.00	108
Potato chips and other snacks	71.67	77.42	108
Nuts	20.83	22.59	108
Condiments and seasonings	84.61	87.87	104
Salt, spices, and other seasonings	20.65	19.82	96
Olives, pickles, relishes	9.77	10.41	107
Sauces and gravies	37.23	39.20	105
Baking needs and misc. products	16.96	18.44	109
Other canned/packaged prepared foods	134.17	136.43	102
Prepared salads	18.55	19.74	106
Prepared desserts	9.31	9.67	104
Baby food	32.26	32.40	100
Miscellaneous prepared foods	73.91	74.47	101
Vitamin supplements	0.14	0.16	114
Nonalcoholic beverages	249.58	253.58	102
Cola	86.99	87.43	101
Other carbonated drinks	47.39	48.91	103
Coffee	41.85	43.94	105
Roasted coffee	27.50	28.96	105
Instant and freeze-dried coffee	14.35	14.97	104
Noncarbonated fruit-flavored drinks, incl. nonfrozen lemonade	19.42	18.31	94
Tea	15.68	16.04	102
Nonalcoholic beer	0.27	0.34	126
Other nonalcoholic beverages and ice	37.99	38.62	102
Food prepared by CU on out-of-town trips	39.94	43.92	110
FOOD AWAY FROM HOME	**2,136.88**	**2,260.79**	**106**
Meals at restaurants, carry-outs, other	**1,750.33**	**1,831.26**	**105**
Lunch	662.90	677.53	102
At fast food, take-out, delivery, concession stands, buffet, cafeteria (other than employer, school cafeteria)	368.00	365.69	99
At full-service restaurants	208.12	229.04	110
At vending machines, mobile vendors	6.52	5.21	80
At employer and school cafeterias	80.26	77.58	97
Dinner	697.99	753.97	108
At fast food, take-out, delivery, concession stands, buffet, cafeteria (other than employer and school cafeteria)	206.92	206.48	100
At full-service restaurants	487.70	544.45	112
At vending machines, mobile vendors	1.02	0.79	77
At employer and school cafeterias	2.35	2.25	96
Snacks and nonalcoholic beverages	227.71	234.01	103
At fast food, take-out, delivery, concession stands, buffet, cafeteria (other than employer and school cafeteria)	158.55	164.62	104

(continued)

(continued from previous page)

	average spending of total consumer units	non-Hispanic white consumer units	
		average spending	indexed spending
At full-service restaurants	$20.15	$20.85	103
At vending machines, mobile vendors	38.52	38.25	99
At employer and school cafeterias	10.49	10.28	98
Breakfast and brunch	161.73	165.75	102
At fast food, take-out, delivery, concession stands, buffet, cafeteria (other than employer and school cafeteria)	77.12	74.50	97
At full-service restaurants	79.64	86.96	109
At vending machines, mobile vendors	1.35	1.09	81
At employer and school cafeterias	3.62	3.20	88
Board (including at school)	**39.03**	**41.76**	**107**
Catered affairs	**54.02**	**62.89**	**116**
Food on trips	**216.06**	**244.28**	**113**
School lunches	**58.46**	**61.21**	**105**
Meals as pay	**18.97**	**19.39**	**102**
ALCOHOLIC BEVERAGES	**$371.81**	**$401.28**	**108**
At home	**226.64**	**242.05**	**107**
Beer and ale	112.01	112.82	101
Whiskey	13.49	14.17	105
Wine	80.04	92.15	115
Other alcoholic beverages	21.10	22.90	109
Away from home	**145.17**	**159.23**	**110**
Beer and ale	62.46	66.73	107
At fast food, take-out, delivery, concession stands, buffet, and cafeteria	13.37	14.32	107
At full-service restaurants	45.05	51.24	114
At vending machines, mobile vendors	0.40	0.42	105
At catered affairs	3.64	0.75	21
Wine	17.79	19.89	112
At fast food, take-out, delivery, concession stands, buffet and cafeteria	1.23	1.28	104
At full-service restaurants	16.16	18.53	115
At catered affairs	0.39	0.08	21
Other alcoholic beverages	64.92	72.62	112
At fast food, take-out, delivery, concession stands, buffet, and cafeteria	3.04	3.29	108
At full-service restaurants	25.74	29.40	114
At machines and mobile vendors	0.29	0.24	83
At catered affairs	1.60	0.33	21
Alcoholic beverages purchased on trips	34.24	39.36	115
HOUSING	**$12,318.51**	**$12,823.62**	**104**
SHELTER	**7,114.26**	**7,402.10**	**104**
Owned dwellings**	**4,602.32**	**5,047.15**	**110**

(continued)

(continued from previous page)

	average spending of total consumer units	non-Hispanic white consumer units	
		average spending	indexed spending
Mortgage interest and charges	$2,638.81	$2,879.12	109
Mortgage interest	2,460.48	2,679.67	109
Interest paid, home equity loan	98.22	106.72	109
Interest paid, home equity line of credit	79.76	92.46	116
Prepayment penalty charges	0.34	0.27	79
Property taxes	1,138.55	1,253.85	110
Maintenance, repairs, insurance, other expenses	824.96	914.18	111
Homeowner's and related insurance	234.84	256.43	109
Homeowner's insurance	234.84	256.43	109
Ground rent	38.67	43.24	112
Maintenance and repair services	438.92	491.90	112
Painting and papering	49.93	56.20	113
Plumbing and water heating	41.62	45.55	109
Heat, air conditioning, electrical work	79.19	91.07	115
Roofing and gutters	75.27	83.28	111
Other repair and maintenance services	157.99	176.16	112
Repair, replacement of hard-surface flooring	33.61	38.11	113
Repair of built-in appliances	1.31	1.53	117
Maintenance and repair materials	78.08	85.38	109
Paints, wallpaper, and supplies	16.03	17.52	109
Tools, equipment for painting, wallpapering	1.72	1.88	109
Plumbing supplies and equipment	6.13	6.66	109
Electrical supplies, heating and cooling equipment	4.35	4.86	112
Hard-surface flooring, repair and replacement	6.98	7.64	109
Roofing and gutters	6.41	6.81	106
Plaster, paneling, siding, windows, doors, screens, awnings	12.14	13.10	108
Patio, walk, fence, driveway, masonry, brick, and stucco materials	0.60	0.65	108
Landscape maintenance	2.92	3.36	115
Miscellaneous supplies and equipment	20.80	22.89	110
Insulation, other maintenance, repair	13.45	14.41	107
Finish basement, remodel rooms, build patios, walks, etc.	7.35	8.49	116
Property management and security	30.99	33.48	108
Property management	21.49	22.85	106
Management and upkeep services for security	9.50	10.62	112
Parking	3.45	3.75	109
Rented dwellings	**2,034.11**	**1,809.14**	**89**
Rent	1,977.33	1,759.75	89
Rent as pay	29.24	20.35	70
Maintenance, insurance, and other expenses	27.54	29.04	105
Tenant's insurance	8.86	10.08	114

(continued)

(continued from previous page)

	average spending of total consumer units	non-Hispanic white consumer units	
		average spending	indexed spending
Maintenance and repair services	$11.13	$12.24	110
Repair and maintenance services	9.98	10.84	109
Repair and replacement of hard-surface flooring	1.08	1.32	122
Repair of built-in appliances	0.07	0.07	100
Maintenance and repair materials	7.55	6.72	89
Paint, wallpaper, and supplies	1.54	1.42	92
Painting and wallpapering tools	0.17	0.15	88
Plastering, paneling, roofing, gutters, etc.	0.48	0.50	104
Patio, walk, fence, driveway, masonry, brick, and stucco materials	0.03	–	–
Plumbing supplies and equipment	0.39	0.29	74
Electrical supplies, heating and cooling equipment	0.25	0.30	120
Miscellaneous supplies and equipment	3.60	3.02	84
Insulation, other maintenance and repair	0.92	1.01	110
Materials for additions, finishing basements, remodeling rooms	2.67	2.00	75
Construction materials for jobs not started	0.01	0.02	200
Hard-surface flooring	0.49	0.28	57
Landscape maintenance	0.60	0.75	125
Other lodging	**477.84**	**545.82**	**114**
Owned vacation homes	147.91	170.76	115
Mortgage interest and charges	63.65	73.37	115
Mortgage interest	61.19	70.34	115
Interest paid, home equity loan	1.35	1.65	122
Interest paid, home equity line of credit	1.11	1.38	124
Property taxes	51.97	59.86	115
Maintenance, insurance and other expenses	32.29	37.53	116
Homeowner's and related insurance	10.74	11.61	108
Homeowner's insurance	10.74	11.61	108
Ground rent	2.97	3.45	116
Maintenance and repair services	13.56	16.65	123
Maintenance and repair materials	0.48	0.59	123
Property management and security	3.89	4.45	114
Property management	2.56	2.97	116
Management and upkeep services for security	1.33	1.48	111
Parking	0.65	0.78	120
Housing while attending school	78.31	87.39	112
Lodging on out-of-town trips	251.62	287.67	114
UTILITIES, FUELS, PUBLIC SERVICES	**2,488.90**	**2,511.61**	**101**
Natural gas	**307.35**	**309.56**	**101**
Natural gas (renter)	60.47	49.83	82

(continued)

(continued from previous page)

	average spending of total consumer units	non-Hispanic white consumer units	
		average spending	indexed spending
Natural gas (owner)	$244.63	$257.11	105
Natural gas (vacation)	2.25	2.54	113
Electricity	**911.44**	**923.20**	**101**
Electricity (renter)	213.85	178.35	83
Electricity (owner)	690.09	736.10	107
Electricity (vacation)	7.50	8.76	117
Fuel oil and other fuels	**96.94**	**111.45**	**115**
Fuel oil	55.08	64.04	116
Fuel oil (renter)	6.54	7.40	113
Fuel oil (owner)	47.74	55.68	117
Fuel oil (vacation)	0.81	0.97	120
Coal	0.58	0.72	124
Coal (renter)	0.14	0.17	121
Coal (owner)	0.44	0.55	125
Bottled/tank gas	35.26	40.00	113
Gas (renter)	4.76	5.40	113
Gas (owner)	28.79	32.56	113
Gas (vacation)	1.71	2.05	120
Wood and other fuels	6.02	6.69	111
Wood and other fuels (renter)	1.09	1.27	117
Wood and other fuels (owner)	4.88	5.38	110
Wood and other fuels (vacation)	0.05	0.04	80
Telephone services	**876.75**	**863.35**	**98**
Telephone services in home city, excl. mobile phones	757.26	738.99	98
Telephone services for mobile phones	119.49	124.36	104
Water and other public services	**296.42**	**304.04**	**103**
Water and sewerage maintenance	212.72	215.53	101
Water and sewerage maintenance (renter)	29.99	24.90	83
Water and sewerage maintenance (owner)	181.10	188.76	104
Water and sewerage maintenance (vacation)	1.63	1.88	115
Trash and garbage collection	81.74	86.21	105
Trash and garbage collection (renter)	8.30	6.98	84
Trash and garbage collection (owner)	71.34	76.78	108
Trash and garbage collection (vacation)	2.10	2.45	117
Septic tank cleaning	1.96	2.30	117
Septic tank cleaning (renter)	0.04	0.03	75
Septic tank cleaning (owner)	1.92	2.27	118
HOUSEHOLD SERVICES	**684.38**	**738.83**	**108**
Personal services	**326.20**	**339.82**	**104**
Babysitting and child care in own home	32.21	32.84	102
Babysitting and child care in someone else's home	32.59	28.62	88
Care for elderly, invalids, handicapped, etc.	50.38	60.18	119

(continued)

	average spending of total consumer units	non-Hispanic white consumer units	
		average spending	indexed spending
Adult day care centers	$2.60	$3.08	118
Day care centers, nurseries, and preschools	208.42	215.10	103
Other household services	**358.18**	**399.01**	**111**
Housekeeping services	88.15	101.79	115
Gardening, lawn care service	78.26	88.67	113
Water softening service	3.11	3.60	116
Nonclothing laundry and dry cleaning, sent out	1.48	1.47	99
Nonclothing laundry and dry cleaning, coin-operated	4.64	3.44	74
Termite/pest control services	9.57	10.87	114
Home security system service fee	18.67	18.32	98
Other home services	14.28	16.18	113
Termite/pest control products	0.49	0.56	114
Moving, storage, and freight express	32.43	35.94	111
Appliance repair, including service center	12.58	13.86	110
Reupholstering and furniture repair	9.26	10.99	119
Repairs/rentals of lawn/garden equipment, hand/power tools, etc.	4.96	5.65	114
Appliance rental	3.77	3.56	94
Rental of office equipment for nonbusiness use	0.53	0.59	111
Repair of misc. household equipment and furnishings	11.73	11.96	102
Repair of computer systems for nonbusiness use	2.75	2.87	104
Computer information services	61.36	68.53	112
Rental, installation of dishwashers, range hoods, and garbage disposals	0.15	0.17	113
HOUSEKEEPING SUPPLIES	**482.32**	**506.45**	**105**
Laundry and cleaning supplies	**130.76**	**126.77**	**97**
Soaps and detergents	69.27	65.42	94
Other laundry cleaning products	61.49	61.35	100
Other household products	**225.90**	**239.10**	**106**
Cleansing and toilet tissue, paper towels, and napkins	68.45	67.38	98
Miscellaneous household products	90.48	97.36	108
Lawn and garden supplies	66.97	74.37	111
Postage and stationery	**125.66**	**140.58**	**112**
Stationery, stationery supplies, giftwrap	63.65	72.39	114
Postage	60.60	66.71	110
Delivery services	1.41	1.49	106
HOUSEHOLD FURNISHINGS, EQUIPMENT	**1,548.63**	**1,664.62**	**107**
Household textiles	**106.49**	**114.58**	**108**
Bathroom linens	17.55	17.58	100
Bedroom linens	44.52	47.41	106
Kitchen and dining room linens	9.31	9.97	107
Curtains and draperies	21.06	23.37	111

(continued)

(continued from previous page)

	average spending of total consumer units	non-Hispanic white consumer units	
		average spending	indexed spending
Slipcovers and decorative pillows	$2.75	$3.20	116
Sewing materials for household items	9.75	11.42	117
Other linens	1.53	1.62	106
Furniture	**390.63**	**399.71**	**102**
Mattresses and springs	52.89	51.35	97
Other bedroom furniture	69.11	65.44	95
Sofas	89.15	91.80	103
Living room chairs	43.84	48.43	110
Living room tables	17.19	18.02	105
Kitchen and dining room furniture	46.46	47.01	101
Infants' furniture	6.22	5.91	95
Outdoor furniture	15.16	17.66	116
Wall units, cabinets, and other furniture	50.61	54.10	107
Floor coverings	**44.38**	**48.53**	**109**
Wall-to-wall carpet (renter)	1.38	1.33	96
Wall-to-wall carpet (replacement) (owner)	27.78	29.94	108
Room-size rugs and other floor coverings, nonpermanent	15.22	17.26	113
Major appliances	**188.96**	**202.94**	**107**
Dishwashers (built-in), garbage disposals, range hoods (renter)	0.87	0.96	110
Dishwashers (built-in), garbage disposals, range hoods (owner)	14.10	16.72	119
Refrigerators and freezers (renter)	7.35	6.96	95
Refrigerators and freezers (owner)	44.34	49.54	112
Washing machines (renter)	4.79	4.33	90
Washing machines (owner)	18.53	19.47	105
Clothes dryers (renter)	3.36	3.42	102
Clothes dryers (owner)	12.02	12.88	107
Cooking stoves, ovens (renter)	2.80	2.55	91
Cooking stoves, ovens (owner)	23.95	26.08	109
Microwave ovens (renter)	2.38	2.12	89
Microwave ovens (owner)	7.36	8.25	112
Portable dishwashers (renter)	0.16	0.20	125
Portable dishwashers (owner)	0.76	0.90	118
Window air conditioners (renter)	1.85	1.50	81
Window air conditioners (owner)	4.82	4.83	100
Electric floor-cleaning equipment	25.98	28.02	108
Sewing machines	4.78	4.72	99
Miscellaneous household appliances	8.77	9.49	108
Small appliances and miscellaneous housewares	**87.37**	**96.85**	**111**
Housewares	64.87	72.62	112
Plastic dinnerware	1.45	1.53	106
China and other dinnerware	11.43	13.22	116

(continued)

(continued from previous page)

	average spending of total consumer units	non-Hispanic white consumer units average spending	indexed spending
Flatware	$3.61	$4.03	112
Glassware	8.02	9.14	114
Silver serving pieces	2.35	2.74	117
Other serving pieces	1.43	1.55	108
Nonelectric cookware	16.67	17.20	103
Tableware, nonelectric kitchenware	19.90	23.21	117
Small appliances	22.51	24.23	108
Small electric kitchen appliances	17.04	18.39	108
Portable heating and cooling equipment	5.47	5.84	107
Miscellaneous household equipment	**730.81**	**802.02**	**110**
Window coverings	13.02	14.62	112
Infants' equipment	8.01	8.64	108
Laundry and cleaning equipment	10.08	10.45	104
Outdoor equipment	18.39	21.12	115
Clocks	13.91	15.93	115
Lamps and lighting fixtures	10.80	11.95	111
Other household decorative items	177.30	194.68	110
Telephones and accessories	29.19	30.51	105
Lawn and garden equipment	46.82	54.77	117
Power tools	21.32	21.87	103
Office furniture for home use	13.67	15.03	110
Hand tools	7.26	8.23	113
Indoor plants and fresh flowers	57.01	65.48	115
Closet and storage items	8.03	8.83	110
Rental of furniture	3.12	2.55	82
Luggage	8.32	9.36	113
Computers and computer hardware, nonbusiness use	187.83	203.22	108
Computer software and accessories, nonbusiness use	17.49	19.22	110
Telephone answering devices	1.97	2.14	109
Calculators	1.64	1.70	104
Business equipment for home use	1.83	1.83	100
Other hardware	24.09	27.80	115
Smoke alarms (owner)	0.56	0.58	104
Smoke alarms (renter)	0.16	0.17	106
Other household appliances (owner)	7.59	8.11	107
Other household appliances (renter)	1.22	0.90	74
Miscellaneous household equipment and parts	40.18	42.31	105
APPAREL AND SERVICES	**$1,856.16**	**$1,852.66**	**100**
Men, aged 16 or older	**344.29**	**355.74**	**103**
Suits	33.23	34.34	103
Sport coats and tailored jackets	11.31	12.63	112
Coats and jackets	34.76	35.84	103

(continued)

(continued from previous page)

	average spending of total consumer units	non-Hispanic white consumer units	
		average spending	indexed spending
Underwear	$17.45	$17.69	101
Hosiery	11.50	11.33	99
Nightwear	3.34	3.63	109
Accessories	23.29	23.87	102
Sweaters and vests	15.96	17.22	108
Active sportswear	16.11	17.37	108
Shirts	85.47	89.78	105
Pants	68.65	67.40	98
Shorts and shorts sets	13.64	14.74	108
Uniforms	5.52	5.63	102
Costumes	4.06	4.26	105
Boys, aged 2 to 15	**95.76**	**85.54**	**89**
Coats and jackets	7.84	6.77	86
Sweaters	3.56	3.36	94
Shirts	20.84	17.72	85
Underwear	5.09	4.23	83
Nightwear	2.95	2.70	92
Hosiery	4.30	3.85	90
Accessories	4.40	4.55	103
Suits, sport coats, and vests	3.64	3.29	90
Pants	23.39	20.56	88
Shorts and shorts sets	8.95	8.28	93
Uniforms	3.66	3.68	101
Active sportswear	3.81	3.13	82
Costumes	3.33	3.42	103
Women, aged 16 or older	**607.11**	**745.08**	**123**
Coats and jackets	43.26	44.13	102
Dresses	86.74	85.90	99
Sport coats and tailored jackets	8.33	9.37	112
Sweaters and vests	49.27	54.27	110
Shirts, blouses, and tops	99.26	103.43	104
Skirts	12.76	13.59	107
Pants	85.55	87.69	103
Shorts and shorts sets	20.40	21.85	107
Active sportswear	27.78	30.52	110
Nightwear	32.21	34.80	108
Undergarments	32.20	30.86	96
Hosiery	20.95	21.13	101
Suits	33.80	34.75	103
Accessories	39.29	43.78	111
Uniforms	8.69	9.10	105
Costumes	6.63	7.32	110

(continued)

(continued from previous page)

	average spending of total consumer units	non-Hispanic white consumer units	
		average spending	indexed spending
Girls, aged 2 to 15	**$118.09**	**$112.59**	**95**
Coats and jackets	6.95	5.98	86
Dresses and suits	18.19	17.64	97
Shirts, blouses, and sweaters	28.79	28.29	98
Skirts and pants	21.75	19.88	91
Shorts and shorts sets	8.35	7.71	92
Active sportswear	8.97	8.95	100
Underwear and nightwear	7.40	7.02	95
Hosiery	4.92	4.54	92
Accessories	4.98	5.31	107
Uniforms	3.90	3.01	77
Costumes	3.87	4.25	110
Children under age 2	**81.92**	**75.52**	**92**
Coats, jackets, and snowsuits	2.70	2.65	98
Outerwear including dresses	22.97	21.88	95
Underwear	44.65	40.90	92
Nightwear and loungewear	3.99	3.83	96
Accessories	7.61	6.26	82
Footwear	**343.09**	**320.68**	**93**
Men's	117.55	109.77	93
Boys'	37.26	31.82	85
Women's	155.95	151.09	97
Girls'	32.33	28.00	87
Other apparel products and services	**265.90**	**270.09**	**102**
Material for making clothes	4.75	5.69	120
Sewing patterns and notions	4.69	5.35	114
Watches	22.63	21.99	97
Jewelry	107.32	120.00	112
Shoe repair and other shoe services	1.83	2.02	110
Coin-operated apparel laundry and dry cleaning	37.93	27.11	71
Apparel alteration, repair, and tailoring services	5.70	6.33	111
Clothing rental	3.37	3.79	112
Watch and jewelry repair	4.74	4.93	104
Professional laundry, dry cleaning	72.40	72.21	100
Clothing storage	0.55	0.65	118
TRANSPORTATION	**$7,417.36**	**$7,806.04**	**105**
VEHICLE PURCHASES	**3,418.27**	**3,614.05**	**106**
Cars and trucks, new	**1,604.95**	**1,757.00**	**109**
New cars	917.02	1,002.25	109
New trucks	687.94	754.75	110
Cars and trucks, used	**1,769.85**	**1,804.42**	**102**
Used cars	1,011.25	996.87	99
Used trucks	758.60	807.55	106

(continued)

(continued from previous page)

	average spending of total consumer units	non-Hispanic white consumer units	
		average spending	indexed spending
Other vehicles	**$43.46**	**$52.63**	**121**
New motorcycles	18.45	22.18	120
Used motorcycles	17.38	20.98	121
GASOLINE AND MOTOR OIL	**1,291.25**	**1,340.94**	**104**
Gasoline	1,175.50	1,213.82	103
Diesel fuel	12.98	13.59	105
Gasoline on trips	91.79	102.19	111
Motor oil	10.05	10.32	103
Motor oil on trips	0.93	1.03	111
OTHER VEHICLE EXPENSES	**2,281.28**	**2,394.95**	**105**
Vehicle finance charges	**328.24**	**338.01**	**103**
Automobile finance charges	169.25	167.64	99
Truck finance charges	138.62	145.32	105
Motorcycle and plane finance charges	1.58	1.94	123
Other vehicle finance charges	18.79	23.11	123
Maintenance and repairs	**623.76**	**656.83**	**105**
Coolant, additives, brake and transmission fluids	4.47	4.55	102
Tires	87.23	92.02	105
Parts, equipment, and accessories	48.46	51.05	105
Vehicle audio equipment	2.41	2.46	102
Vehicle products	4.10	4.45	109
Miscellaneous auto repair, servicing	26.74	29.39	110
Body work and painting	26.35	29.30	111
Clutch, transmission repair	42.61	43.23	101
Drive shaft and rear-end repair	3.66	3.82	104
Brake work	54.04	57.69	107
Repair to steering or front-end	18.02	18.57	103
Repair to engine cooling system	20.55	21.34	104
Motor tune-up	44.41	45.77	103
Lube, oil change, and oil filters	58.75	62.33	106
Front-end alignment, wheel balance, rotation	10.79	11.40	106
Shock absorber replacement	4.25	4.48	105
Gas tank repair, replacement	3.55	3.22	91
Tire repair and other repair work	29.75	31.78	107
Vehicle air conditioning repair	19.80	21.19	107
Exhaust system repair	13.34	14.59	109
Electrical system repair	30.31	31.96	105
Motor repair, replacement	64.46	65.61	102
Auto repair service policy	5.71	6.61	116
Vehicle insurance	**778.13**	**807.33**	**104**
Vehicle rental, leases, licenses, other charges	**551.15**	**592.78**	**108**
Leased and rented vehicles	392.88	421.73	107

(continued)

(continued from previous page)

	average spending of total consumer units	non-Hispanic white consumer units	
		average spending	*indexed spending*
Rented vehicles	$44.95	$48.97	109
Auto rental	7.21	7.45	103
Auto rental, out-of-town trips	29.62	33.13	112
Truck rental	3.21	3.30	103
Truck rental, out-of-town trips	4.71	4.88	104
Leased vehicles	347.93	372.77	107
Car lease payments	174.84	191.18	109
Cash down payment (car lease)	13.99	14.47	103
Termination fee (car lease)	1.81	0.70	39
Truck lease payments	148.45	157.18	106
Cash down payment (truck lease)	7.72	8.25	107
Termination fee (truck lease)	1.11	0.99	89
State and local registration	85.19	92.41	108
Driver's license	6.85	7.31	107
Vehicle inspection	9.41	9.60	102
Parking fees	29.38	32.10	109
Parking fees in home city, excluding residence	25.33	27.58	109
Parking fees, out-of-town trips	4.05	4.52	112
Tolls	10.90	11.34	104
Tolls on out-of-town trips	3.51	3.90	111
Towing charges	4.68	4.90	105
Automobile service clubs	8.35	9.49	114
PUBLIC TRANSPORTATION	**426.56**	**456.10**	**107**
Airline fares	274.02	305.61	112
Intercity bus fares	16.10	16.70	104
Intracity mass transit fares	47.41	36.72	77
Local transportation on out-of-town trips	10.66	11.95	112
Taxi fares and limousine service on trips	6.26	7.02	112
Taxi fares and limousine service	12.15	10.27	85
Intercity train fares	21.12	24.04	114
Ship fares	36.58	41.88	114
School bus	2.26	1.90	84
HEALTH CARE	**$2,065.67**	**$2,282.60**	**111**
HEALTH INSURANCE	**982.65**	**1,069.44**	**109**
Commercial health insurance	**194.39**	**220.47**	**113**
Traditional fee-for-service health plan (not BCBS)	77.07	87.14	113
Preferred-provider health plan (not BCBS)	117.32	133.34	114
Blue Cross, Blue Shield	**232.50**	**259.48**	**112**
Traditional fee-for-service health plan	49.89	56.51	113
Preferred-provider health plan	60.94	67.98	112
Health maintenance organization	73.18	77.77	106

(continued)

(continued from previous page)

	average spending of total consumer units	non-Hispanic white consumer units	
		average spending	indexed spending
Commercial Medicare supplement	$43.77	$52.12	119
Other BCBS health insurance	4.71	5.09	108
Health maintenance plans (HMOs)	**254.81**	**260.14**	**102**
Medicare payments	**164.04**	**174.85**	**107**
Commercial Medicare supplements/ other health insurance	**136.91**	**154.50**	**113**
Commercial Medicare supplement (not BCBS)	88.22	99.42	113
Other health insurance (not BCBS)	48.69	55.08	113
MEDICAL SERVICES	**567.85**	**641.06**	**113**
Physician's services	134.41	149.19	111
Dental services	220.79	252.46	114
Eye care services	35.05	38.50	110
Service by professionals other than physician	36.87	43.23	117
Lab tests, X-rays	20.12	22.43	111
Hospital room	35.95	39.80	111
Hospital services other than room	41.13	43.76	106
Care in convalescent or nursing home	32.35	39.49	122
Repair of medical equipment	0.61	0.05	8
Other medical services	10.56	12.14	115
DRUGS	**416.45**	**462.17**	**111**
Nonprescription drugs	65.09	69.90	107
Nonprescription vitamins	46.19	52.45	114
Prescription drugs	305.17	339.82	111
MEDICAL SUPPLIES	**98.73**	**109.94**	**111**
Eyeglasses and contact lenses	58.43	64.49	110
Hearing aids	11.78	14.45	123
Topicals and dressings	20.99	22.29	106
Medical equipment for general use	2.04	2.28	112
Supportive, convalescent medical equipment	3.18	3.66	115
Rental of medical equipment	0.85	1.00	118
Rental of supportive, convalescent medical equipment	1.46	1.76	121
ENTERTAINMENT	**$1,863.50**	**$2,053.80**	**110**
FEES AND ADMISSIONS	**514.85**	**587.45**	**114**
Recreation expenses on trips	25.49	28.50	112
Social, recreation, civic club membership	98.18	114.84	117
Fees for participant sports	71.49	82.52	115
Participant sports on trips	35.05	40.89	117
Movie, theater, opera, ballet	89.16	96.96	109
Movie, other admissions on trips	44.94	50.91	113
Admission to sports events	35.33	41.08	116
Admission to sports events on trips	14.98	16.97	113

(continued)

(continued from previous page)

	average spending of total consumer units	non-Hispanic white consumer units	
		average spending	indexed spending
Fees for recreational lessons	$74.74	$86.27	115
Other entertainment services on trips	25.49	28.50	112
TELEVISION, RADIO, SOUND EQUIPMENT	**621.82**	**637.66**	**103**
Television	**453.53**	**459.57**	**101**
Community antenna and cable service	321.18	325.52	101
Black-and-white TV sets	0.77	0.72	94
Color TV, console	30.19	30.49	101
Color TV, portable, table model	34.35	33.36	97
VCRs and video disc players	23.80	23.99	101
Video cassettes, tapes, and discs	20.80	22.16	107
Video game hardware and software	18.72	19.63	105
Repair of TV, radio, and sound equipment	3.23	3.38	105
Rental of television sets	0.49	0.32	65
Radio and sound equipment	**168.29**	**178.09**	**106**
Radios	10.44	11.08	106
Tape recorders and players	4.39	3.64	83
Sound components and component systems	23.16	23.08	100
Miscellaneous sound equipment	0.42	0.51	121
Sound equipment accessories	4.04	4.38	108
Satellite dishes	2.70	2.53	94
Compact disc, tape, record, video mail order clubs	8.52	9.10	107
Records, CDs, audio tapes, needles	39.46	41.15	104
Rental of VCR, radio, sound equipment	0.54	0.55	102
Musical instruments and accessories	31.70	37.23	117
Rental and repair of musical instruments	1.34	1.48	110
Rental of video cassettes, tapes, discs, films	41.56	43.36	104
PETS, TOYS, PLAYGROUND EQUIPMENT	**333.71**	**369.44**	**111**
Pets	**209.43**	**236.74**	**113**
Pet food	85.97	95.25	111
Pet purchase, supplies, and medicines	38.10	41.61	109
Pet services	19.36	22.75	118
Veterinarian services	66.00	77.13	117
Toys, games, hobbies, and tricycles	**120.96**	**129.09**	**107**
Playground equipment	**3.32**	**3.61**	**109**
OTHER ENTERTAINMENT SUPPLIES, EQUIPMENT, SERVICES	**393.12**	**459.25**	**117**
Unmotored recreational vehicles	**48.06**	**59.40**	**124**
Boat without motor and boat trailers	15.87	19.45	123
Trailer and other attachable campers	32.19	39.95	124
Motorized recreational vehicles	**81.96**	**101.22**	**123**
Motorized camper	21.35	26.50	124
Other vehicle	21.74	26.97	124

(continued)

(continued from previous page)

	average spending of total consumer units	non-Hispanic white consumer units	
		average spending	indexed spending
Motorboats	$38.87	$47.75	123
Rental of recreational vehicles	**2.79**	**3.22**	**115**
Boat and trailer rental on trips	0.59	0.67	114
Rental of campers on trips	0.61	0.73	120
Rental of other vehicles on trips	1.40	1.60	114
Rental of other RVs	0.03	0.04	133
Outboard motors	**3.58**	**4.44**	**124**
Docking and landing fees	**8.17**	**9.71**	**119**
Sports, recreation, exercise equipment	143.58	162.86	113
Athletic gear, game tables, exercise equipment	58.64	66.17	113
Bicycles	11.73	11.98	102
Camping equipment	17.02	19.51	115
Hunting and fishing equipment	25.85	29.84	115
Winter sports equipment	5.84	7.09	121
Water sports equipment	8.24	10.01	121
Other sports equipment	14.25	15.94	112
Rental and repair of miscellaneous sports equipment	2.02	2.33	115
Photographic equipment and supplies	**94.91**	**107.09**	**113**
Film	21.40	23.67	111
Other photographic supplies	1.44	1.49	103
Film processing	31.43	35.67	113
Repair and rental of photographic equipment	0.27	0.29	107
Photographic equipment	20.21	23.11	114
Photographer fees	20.17	22.86	113
Fireworks	**1.18**	**1.33**	**113**
Souvenirs	**2.00**	**2.44**	**122**
Visual goods	**1.09**	**1.35**	**124**
Pinball, electronic video games	**5.80**	**6.19**	**107**
PERSONAL CARE PRODUCTS AND SERVICES	**$563.62**	**$554.61**	**98**
Personal care products	**256.30**	**255.91**	**100**
Hair care products	51.46	49.79	97
Hair accessories	6.59	6.75	102
Wigs and hairpieces	1.17	0.57	49
Oral hygiene products	25.78	25.64	99
Shaving products	13.19	13.95	106
Cosmetics, perfume, and bath products	119.91	119.84	100
Deodorants, feminine hygiene, miscellaneous products	29.21	29.51	101
Electric personal care appliances	8.99	9.86	110
Personal care services	**307.31**	**298.70**	**97**
READING	**$146.47**	**$165.87**	**113**
Newspaper subscriptions	47.43	54.28	114

(continued)

(continued from previous page)

	average spending of total consumer units	non-Hispanic white consumer units	
		average spending	indexed spending
Newspapers, nonsubscriptions	$12.26	$12.51	102
Magazine subscriptions	19.10	21.84	114
Magazines, nonsubscriptions	9.50	10.54	111
Books purchased through book clubs	8.03	9.02	112
Books not purchased through book clubs	49.52	56.93	115
Encyclopedia and other reference book sets	0.51	0.58	114
EDUCATION	**$631.93**	**$699.95**	**111**
College tuition	363.29	412.30	113
Elementary and high school tuition	101.42	111.26	110
Other school tuition	24.42	25.91	106
Other school expenses including rentals	24.00	25.70	107
Books, supplies for college	52.66	57.86	110
Books, supplies for elementary, high school	13.92	13.91	100
Books, supplies for day care, nursery school	3.09	3.16	102
Miscellaneous school expenses and supplies	49.13	49.86	101
TOBACCO PRODUCTS AND SMOKING SUPPLIES	**$318.62**	**$343.66**	**108**
Cigarettes	293.90	315.34	107
Other tobacco products	22.52	25.91	115
Smoking accessories	2.03	2.20	108
FINANCIAL PRODUCTS AND SERVICES	**$775.78**	**$823.65**	**106**
Miscellaneous fees, gambling losses	41.60	45.85	110
Legal fees	103.96	120.86	116
Funeral expenses	70.69	70.87	100
Safe deposit box rental	4.58	5.36	117
Checking accounts, other bank service charges	19.89	20.48	103
Cemetery lots, vaults, and maintenance fees	13.47	14.08	105
Accounting fees	55.18	61.74	112
Miscellaneous personal services	31.39	32.94	105
Finance charges, except mortgage and vehicles	253.37	252.21	100
Occupational expenses	96.24	103.32	107
Expenses for other properties	79.73	89.69	112
Interest paid, home equity line of credit (other property)	0.98	1.21	123
Credit card memberships	4.71	5.04	107
CASH CONTRIBUTIONS	**$1,192.44**	**$1,319.39**	**111**
Cash contributions to non-household members, including students, alimony, child support	296.07	323.66	109
Gifts of cash, stocks, bonds to non-household members	267.48	316.72	118
Contributions to charities	139.87	164.56	118
Contributions to religious organizations	445.63	463.75	104

(continued)

(continued from previous page)

	average spending of total consumer units	non-Hispanic white consumer units	
		average spending	indexed spending
Contributions to educational organizations	$19.96	$23.02	115
Political contributions	6.65	8.01	120
Other contributions	16.80	19.67	117
PERSONAL INSURANCE, PENSIONS	**$3,364.92**	**$3,585.08**	**107**
Life and other personal insurance	**398.61**	**425.87**	**107**
Life, endowment, annuity, other personal insurance	387.97	414.11	107
Other nonhealth insurance	10.64	11.76	111
Pensions and Social Security	**2,966.31**	**3,159.21**	**107**
Deductions for government retirement	70.32	73.13	104
Deductions for railroad retirement	3.29	3.08	94
Deductions for private pensions	362.64	400.47	110
Nonpayroll deposit to retirement plans	389.65	450.57	116
Deductions for Social Security	2,140.41	2,231.96	104
PERSONAL TAXES	**$3,117.45**	**$3,497.96**	**112**
Federal income taxes	2,409.33	2,700.85	112
State and local income taxes	561.80	626.41	112
Other taxes	146.32	170.71	117
GIFTS*	**$1,083.14**	**$1,180.11**	**109**
FOOD	**70.09**	**78.49**	**112**
Fresh fruits	4.58	5.00	109
Candy and chewing gum	12.50	14.62	117
Board (including at school)	20.21	20.58	102
Catered affairs	15.59	18.92	121
ALCOHOLIC BEVERAGES	**14.49**	**15.35**	**106**
Beer and ale	3.64	3.68	101
Wine	6.76	7.22	107
Whiskey and other alcoholic beverages	3.73	4.06	109
HOUSING	**291.10**	**320.43**	**110**
Housekeeping supplies	**39.10**	**42.72**	**109**
Miscellaneous household products	7.32	8.09	111
Lawn and garden supplies	3.08	3.22	105
Postage and stationery	24.95	27.86	112
Stationery, stationery supplies, giftwraps	20.28	23.29	115
Postage	4.57	4.45	97
Household textiles	**13.20**	**14.61**	**111**
Bathroom linens	2.79	3.03	109
Bedroom linens	6.85	7.46	109
Appliances and miscellaneous housewares	**28.14**	**32.73**	**116**
Major appliances	7.61	8.21	108
Electric floor-cleaning equipment	3.01	3.08	102

(continued)

	average spending of total consumer units	non-Hispanic white consumer units	
		average spending	indexed spending
Small appliances and miscellaneous housewares	$20.53	$24.52	119
Glassware	3.60	4.31	120
Nonelectric cookware	3.66	4.45	122
Tableware, nonelectric kitchenware	4.34	5.22	120
Small electric kitchen appliances	2.68	2.99	112
Miscellaneous household equipment	70.31	80.57	115
Infants' equipment	2.72	2.85	105
Outdoor equipment	2.86	3.53	123
Household decorative items	27.33	30.86	113
Indoor plants, fresh flowers	16.04	18.56	116
Computers and computer hardware, nonbusiness use	8.97	10.87	121
Miscellaneous household equipment and parts	2.53	3.00	119
Other housing	**140.36**	**149.80**	**107**
Repair or maintenance services	3.74	4.33	116
Housing while attending school	42.32	46.69	110
Natural gas (renter)	3.11	2.92	94
Electricity (renter)	13.28	13.10	99
Telephone services in home city, excl. mobile phones	13.64	13.16	96
Water, sewerage maintenance (renter)	2.67	2.57	96
Care for elderly, invalids, handicapped	2.10	2.22	106
Day-care centers, nurseries, and preschools	21.46	22.31	104
Housekeeping services	3.44	4.03	117
Gardening, lawn care service	3.14	3.62	115
Repair of misc. household equipment and furnishings	7.78	9.60	123
Bedroom furniture except mattresses and springs	2.06	2.35	114
APPAREL AND SERVICES	**244.25**	**247.21**	**101**
Men and boys, aged 2 or older	**67.55**	**72.23**	**107**
Men's coats and jackets	3.30	2.53	77
Men's underwear	2.10	2.14	102
Men's accessories	3.40	4.02	118
Men's sweaters and vests	2.72	3.17	117
Men's active sportswear	4.35	5.10	117
Men's shirts	20.77	23.04	111
Men's pants	7.11	7.84	110
Boys' shirts	5.56	5.62	101
Boys' pants	2.84	2.66	94
Women and girls, aged 2 or older	**85.28**	**84.69**	**99**
Women's coats and jackets	3.57	3.28	92
Women's dresses	10.62	9.88	93
Women's vests and sweaters	8.86	9.74	110
Women's shirts, tops, blouses	10.59	10.28	97
Women's pants	5.94	5.31	89

(continued)

(continued from previous page)

	average spending of total consumer units	non-Hispanic white consumer units	
		average spending	indexed spending
Women's active sportswear	$3.47	$3.75	108
Women's sleepwear	6.15	6.10	99
Women's undergarments	2.69	2.31	86
Women's accessories	4.17	4.66	112
Girls' dresses and suits	4.03	3.62	90
Girls' shirts, blouses, sweaters	6.18	6.39	103
Girls' skirts and pants	2.78	2.80	101
Girls' active sportswear	2.10	1.89	90
Girls' accessories	2.18	2.50	115
Children under age 2	**40.71**	**39.56**	**97**
Infant dresses, outerwear	14.51	14.85	102
Infant underwear	18.27	17.10	94
Infant nightwear, loungewear	2.46	2.51	102
Infant accessories	4.02	3.61	90
Other apparel products and services	**50.71**	**50.73**	**100**
Watches	3.43	3.68	107
Jewelry	16.85	19.21	114
Men's footwear	8.66	8.02	93
Boys' footwear	4.70	4.61	98
Women's footwear	10.06	8.58	85
Girls' footwear	5.21	4.49	86
TRANSPORTATION	**70.27**	**81.77**	**116**
New cars	6.08	7.55	124
New trucks	14.04	17.42	124
Used cars	12.52	15.50	124
Used trucks	2.82	3.50	124
Gasoline on trips	12.55	14.30	114
Airline fares	8.51	9.09	107
Local transportation on trips	2.13	2.40	113
Intercity train fares	2.23	2.38	107
Ship fares	2.98	3.10	104
HEALTH CARE	**38.08**	**45.24**	**119**
Physician's services	2.66	3.01	113
Dental services	3.49	4.14	119
Hospital room	2.73	3.39	124
Care in convalescent or nursing home	18.42	22.86	124
Nonprescription drugs	2.15	2.22	103
ENTERTAINMENT	**93.76**	**103.10**	**110**
Toys, games, hobbies, and tricycles	29.58	32.16	109
Movie, other admissions on trips	9.17	10.30	112
Admission to sports events on trips	3.06	3.43	112
Fees for recreational lessons	6.30	7.02	111

(continued)

(continued from previous page)

	average spending of total consumer units	non-Hispanic white consumer units	
		average spending	indexed spending
Cable service and community antenna	$4.65	$4.30	92
Color TV, portable, table model	2.10	2.43	116
Musical instruments and accessories	2.32	2.66	115
Athletic gear, game tables, and exercise equipment	9.47	9.79	103
PERSONAL CARE PRODUCTS AND SERVICES	**19.20**	**19.17**	**100**
Hair care products	2.14	1.49	70
Cosmetics, perfume, bath preparation	13.00	13.00	100
Deodorants, feminine hygiene, misc. personal care	2.00	2.00	100
READING	**2.00**	**2.00**	**100**
EDUCATION	**151.00**	**175.00**	**116**
College tuition	114.00	133.00	117
Elementary and high school tuition	11.00	13.00	118
Other school tuition	3.00	4.00	133
Other school expenses including rentals	5.00	6.00	120
College books and supplies	10.00	12.00	120
Miscellaneous school supplies	5.00	6.00	120
ALL OTHER GIFTS	**89.00**	**92.00**	**103**
Gifts of trip expenses	49.00	56.00	114
Miscellaneous fees, gambling losses	2.00	2.00	100
Legal fees	4.00	4.00	100
Funeral expenses	28.00	23.00	82
Cemetery lots, vaults, maintenance fees	3.00	3.00	100
Accounting fees	2.00	2.00	100

* The index compares the spending of the average non-Hispanic white consumer unit with the spending of the average consumer unit by dividing non-Hispanic white spending by average spending in each category and multiplying by 100. An index of 100 means non-Hispanic white spending in the category equals average spending. An index of 125 means non-Hispanic white spending is 25 percent above average, while an index of 75 means non-Hispanic white spending is 25 percent below average.
** This figure does not include the amount paid for mortgage principal, which is considered an asset.
*** Expenditures on gifts are also included in the preceding product and service categories. Food spending, for example, includes the amount spent on gifts of food. Only gift expenditures exceeding $2.00 for the average consumer unit are shown.
Note: Non-Hispanic whites are defined here as non-Hispanic, non-African American consumer units and they include a small number of Asian and American Indian consumer units. The Bureau of Labor Statistics uses consumer unit rather than household as the sampling unit in the Consumer Expenditure Survey. For the definition of consumer unit, see glossary. Expenditures for gifts may not add to the category total because the listings are incomplete.
(–) means not applicable or sample is too small to make a reliable estimate.
Source: Bureau of Labor Statistics, unpublished data from the 2000 Consumer Expenditure Survey; calculations by New Strategist

Non-Hispanic Whites Are the Only Population Segment with Significant Wealth

The median net worth (assets minus debts) of non-Hispanic white households stood at $94,900 in 1998, far above the $71,600 net worth of the average American household. The net worth of non-Hispanic white householders is above average because the group is much more likely to own a home than are other segments of the population. Home equity accounts for the largest share of Americans' net worth. Fully 66 percent of non-Hispanic white house-holders owned their home in 1998. Their homes were worth a median of $100,000.

Non-Hispanic white householders had $29,900 in financial assets in 1998, with trans-action accounts (such as checking accounts) owned by the largest share (95 percent). Twenty-two percent owned stock in 1998, worth a median of $20,000. Nineteen percent owned mutual funds, worth a larger $29,000. The 54 percent majority owned retirement accounts, worth a median of $26,000. Three out of four non-Hispanic white households had debts in 1998. Mortgages accounted for the largest share of debt.

Nearly half of employed non-Hispanic white men and 43 percent of employed non-Hispanic white women are covered by an employer's pension plan. Older professionals working for large corporations are most likely to have pension coverage.

■ The net worth of non-Hispanic white householders will continue to rise because baby boomers are entering the ages of serious home buying.

The net worth of non-Hispanic whites is well above average

(median net worth of total and non-Hispanic white households, 1998)

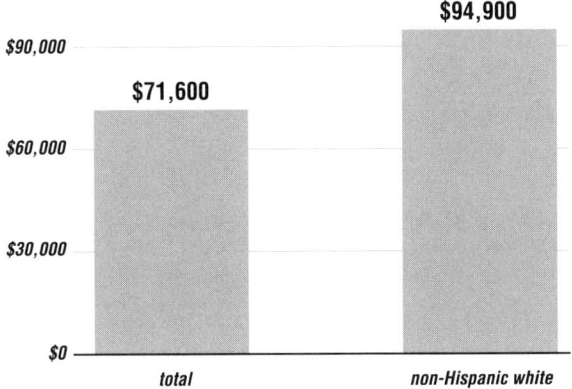

Net Worth, Assets, and Debt of Non-Hispanic White Households, 1998

(median net worth, median value of assets for owners, and median amount of debt for debtors, for total and non-Hispanic white households, and index of non-Hispanic white to total, 1998)

	total	non-Hispanic white	index of non-Hispanic white to total
Median net worth	**$71,600**	**$94,900**	**133**
Median value of financial assets	22,400	29,900	133
Median value of nonfinancial assets	97,800	107,600	110
Median amount of debt	33,300	40,000	120

Note: The index is calculated by dividing the non-Hispanic white figure by the total figure and multiplying by 100.
Source: Federal Reserve Board, Family Finances in the U.S.: Recent Evidence from the 1998 Survey of Consumer Finances, *Federal Reserve Bulletin, January 2000; calculations by New Strategist*

Financial Assets of Non-Hispanic White Households, 1998

(percent of non-Hispanic white households owning financial assets, and median value of assets for owners, 1998)

	percent owning asset	median value
Any financial asset	**96.3%**	**$29,900**
Transaction accounts	94.7	3,700
Certificates of deposit	17.9	17,000
Savings bonds	22.2	1,000
Bonds	3.7	46,000
Stocks	22.1	20,000
Mutual funds	18.8	29,000
Retirement accounts	53.7	26,000
Life insurance	32.1	7,500
Other managed assets	7.1	32,000
Other financial assets	9.7	4,000

Source: Federal Reserve Board, Family Finances in the U.S.: Recent Evidence from the 1998 Survey of Consumer Finances, *Federal Reserve Bulletin, January 2000; calculations by New Strategist*

Nonfinancial Assets of Non-Hispanic White Households, 1998

(percent of non-Hispanic white households owning nonfinancial assets, and median value of assets for owners, 1998)

	percent owning asset	median value
Any nonfinancial asset	**93.8%**	**$107,600**
Vehicles	87.3	11,800
Primary residence	71.8	100,000
Other residential property	14.1	67,000
Nonresidential property	9.4	42,500
Business	13.2	67,600
Other nonfinancial asset	10.0	10,000

Source: Federal Reserve Board, Family Finances in the U.S.: Recent Evidence from the 1998 Survey of Consumer Finances, *Federal Reserve Bulletin, January 2000; calculations by New Strategist*

Debt of Non-Hispanic White Households, 1998

(percent of non-Hispanic white households with debt, and median amount of debt for those with debts, 1998)

	percent with debt	median amount
Any debt	**74.9%**	**$40,000**
Home-secured	46.7	62,000
Other residential property	5.4	42,600
Installment	44.3	9,000
Other lines of credit	2.4	2,800
Credit card	44.4	2,000
Other debt	8.8	3,300

Source: Federal Reserve Board, Family Finances in the U.S.: Recent Evidence from the 1998 Survey of Consumer Finances, *Federal Reserve Bulletin, January 2000; calculations by New Strategist*

Pension Coverage of White Men, 2000

(total number of employed white men aged 15 or older, number and percent with an employer-offered pension plan, and number and percent included in pension plan by selected characteristics, 2000; numbers in thousands)

| | | with employer-offered pension plan at work | | | |
| | | | | included in plan | |
	total	number	percent	number	percent
Employed white men	**67,100**	**38,653**	**57.6%**	**31,539**	**47.0%**
Age					
Under age 65	64,169	37,509	58.5	30,750	47.9
Aged 15 to 24	11,001	4,255	38.7	1,640	14.9
Aged 25 to 44	31,556	19,034	60.3	16,082	51.0
Aged 45 to 64	21,612	14,220	65.8	13,028	60.3
Aged 65 or older	2,931	1,144	39.0	790	26.9
Worked					
Full-time	58,410	35,734	61.2	30,599	52.4
50 weeks or more	49,976	31,931	63.9	28,266	56.6
27 to 49 weeks	5,131	2,576	50.2	1,795	35.0
26 weeks or less	3,303	1,227	37.2	538	16.3
Part-time	8,690	2,919	33.6	940	10.8
50 weeks or more	3,928	1,413	36.0	612	15.6
27 to 49 weeks	1,717	647	37.7	156	9.1
26 weeks or less	3,045	859	28.2	172	5.6
Size of employer					
Under 25 employees	21,147	5,164	24.4	4,203	19.9
25 to 99 employees	9,237	5,027	54.4	3,934	42.6
100 to 499 employees	9,076	6,348	69.9	5,191	57.2
500 to 999 employees	3,097	2,343	75.7	1,874	60.5
1,000 or more employees	24,542	19,772	80.6	16,337	66.6

(continued)

(continued from previous page)

	total	with employer-offered pension plan at work		included in plan	
		number	percent	number	percent
Occupation					
Executive, administrative, and managerial	10,156	6,952	68.5%	6,263	61.7%
Professional specialty	8,790	6,489	73.8	5,678	64.6
Technical, related support	1,892	1,427	75.4	1,195	63.2
Sales workers	7,759	4,160	53.6	3,210	41.4
Administrative support, including clerical	3,493	2,393	68.5	1,769	50.6
Precision production, craft, and repair	12,898	6,690	51.9	5,823	45.1
Machine operators, assemblers, inspectors	4,004	2,442	61.0	1,994	49.8
Transportation, material moving occupations	4,396	2,443	55.6	1,910	43.5
Handlers, equip. cleaners, helpers, and laborers	4,126	1,847	44.8	1,000	24.2
Service workers	6,187	2,913	47.1	2,047	33.1
Private household	32	2	6.2	2	6.2
Service workers except private household	6,155	2,911	47.3	2,045	33.2
Farming, forestry, fishing	2,902	519	17.9	318	11.0
Armed forces	496	378	76.2	333	67.1
Earnings					
Under $15,000	14,950	4,502	30.1	1,483	9.9
$15,000 to $24,999	10,913	4,770	43.7	3,217	29.5
$25,000 to $49,999	22,203	14,803	66.7	12,986	58.5
$50,000 to $74,999	10,633	8,178	76.9	7,764	73.0
$75,000 to $99,999	3,998	3,151	78.8	2,996	74.9
$100,000 or more	4,324	3,240	74.9	3,093	71.5

Source: Bureau of the Census, Current Population Survey, Internet site <http://ferret.bls.census.gov/macro/032001/noncash/nc8_005 .htm>; calculations by New Strategist

Pension Coverage of Non-Hispanic White Men, 2000

(total number of employed non-Hispanic white men aged 15 or older, number and percent with an employer-offered pension plan, and number and percent included in pension plan by selected characteristics, 2000; numbers in thousands)

| | | with employer-offered pension plan at work | | | |
| | | | | included in plan | |
	total	number	percent	number	percent
Employed non-Hispanic white men	**58,423**	**35,344**	**60.5%**	**29,137**	**49.9%**
Age					
Under age 65	55,649	34,245	61.5	28,378	51.0
Aged 15 to 24	9,199	3,781	41.1	1,460	15.9
Aged 25 to 44	26,728	17,164	64.2	14,662	54.9
Aged 45 to 64	19,723	13,300	67.4	12,255	62.1
Aged 65 or older	2,774	1,099	39.6	759	27.4
Worked					
Full-time	50,605	32,660	64.5	28,261	55.8
50 weeks or more	43,516	29,254	67.2	26,149	60.1
27 to 49 weeks	4,319	2,309	53.5	1,624	37.6
26 weeks or less	2,770	1,097	39.6	488	17.6
Part-time	7,818	2,684	34.3	876	11.2
50 weeks or more	3,498	1,297	37.1	559	16.0
27 to 49 weeks	1,569	589	37.6	150	9.5
26 weeks or less	2,750	798	29.0	167	6.1
Size of employer					
Under 25 employees	18,128	4,803	26.5	3,940	21.7
25 to 99 employees	7,690	4,563	59.3	3,606	46.9
100 to 499 employees	7,954	5,821	73.2	4,819	60.6
500 to 999 employees	2,719	2,111	77.6	1,698	62.4
1,000 or more employees	21,931	18,047	82.3	15,074	68.7

(continued)

(continued from previous page)

| | | with employer-offered pension plan at work | | | |
| | | | | included in plan | |
Occupation	total	number	percent	number	percent
Executive, administrative, and managerial	9,642	6,669	69.2%	6,024	62.5%
Professional specialty	8,401	6,232	74.2	5,464	65.0
Technical, related support	1,747	1,322	75.7	1,107	63.3
Sales workers	7,118	3,907	54.9	3,055	42.9
Administrative support, including clerical	3,053	2,156	70.6	1,595	52.2
Precision production, craft, and repair	11,002	6,028	54.8	5,312	48.3
Machine operators, assemblers, inspectors	3,098	2,066	66.7	1,697	54.8
Transportation, material moving occupations	3,763	2,174	57.8	1,723	45.8
Handlers, equip. cleaners, helpers, and laborers	3,148	1,535	48.8	825	26.2
Service workers	4,808	2,482	51.6	1,762	36.6
Private household	14	2	13.7	2	13.7
Service workers except private household	4,793	2,480	51.7	1,760	36.7
Farming, forestry, fishing	2,179	422	19.4	265	12.1
Armed forces	463	353	76.2	309	66.8
Earnings					
Under $15,000	12,228	3,991	32.6	1,332	10.9
$15,000 to $24,999	8,401	3,999	47.6	2,710	32.3
$25,000 to $49,000	19,680	13,411	68.1	11,824	60.1
$50,000 to $74,999	9,994	7,739	77.4	7,363	73.7
$75,000 to $99,999	3,854	3,036	78.8	2,895	75.1
$100,000 or more	4,192	3,158	75.3	3,010	71.8

Source: Bureau of the Census, Current Population Survey, Internet site <http://ferret.bls.census.gov/macro/ 032001/noncash/nc8_014 .htm>; calculations by New Strategist

Pension Coverage of White Women, 2000

(total number of employed white women aged 15 or older, number and percent with an employer-offered pension plan, and number and percent included in pension plan by selected characteristics, 2000; numbers in thousands)

| | | with employer-offered pension plan at work | | | |
| | | | | included in plan | |
Employed white women	total	number	percent	number	percent
Employed white women	**58,131**	**33,172**	**57.1%**	**25,047**	**43.1%**
Age					
Under age 65	56,082	32,355	57.7	24,570	43.8
Aged 15 to 24	10,101	3,841	38.0	1,364	13.5
Aged 25 to 44	26,777	16,352	61.1	12,791	47.8
Aged 45 to 64	19,204	12,162	63.3	10,415	54.2
Aged 65 or older	2,049	817	39.9	478	23.3
Worked					
Full-time	41,376	26,685	64.5	22,041	53.3
50 weeks or more	33,161	22,458	67.7	19,275	58.1
27 to 49 weeks	4,954	3,003	60.6	2,162	43.6
26 weeks or less	3,261	1,224	37.5	603	18.5
Part-time	16,755	6,487	38.7	3,007	17.9
50 weeks or more	8,377	3,537	42.2	2,005	23.9
27 to 49 weeks	3,725	1,543	41.4	689	18.5
26 weeks or less	4,653	1,407	30.2	312	6.7
Size of employer					
Under 25 employees	16,589	3,891	23.5	2,706	16.3
25 to 99 employees	6,992	3,586	51.3	2,594	37.1
100 to 499 employees	7,623	5,218	68.4	4,035	52.9
500 to 999 employees	3,385	2,494	73.7	1,962	57.9
1,000 or more employees	23,541	17,983	76.4	13,752	58.4

(continued)

(continued from previous page)

| | | with employer-offered pension plan at work | | | |
| | | | | included in plan | |
	total	number	percent	number	percent
Occupation					
Executive, administrative, and managerial	8,446	5,764	68.2%	4,900	58.0%
Professional specialty	10,356	7,575	73.1	6,405	61.9
Technical, related support	2,134	1,528	71.6	1,154	54.1
Sales workers	7,780	3,740	48.1	2,278	29.3
Administrative support, including clerical	13,601	8,668	63.7	6,531	48.0
Precision production, craft, and repair	1,111	589	53.1	486	43.8
Machine operators, assemblers, inspectors	2,297	1,231	53.6	878	38.3
Transportation, material moving occupations	562	308	54.8	246	43.7
Handlers, equip. cleaners, helpers, and laborers	998	498	49.9	267	26.8
Service workers	10,056	3,095	30.8	1,778	17.7
Private household	736	30	4.1	21	2.8
Service workers except private household	9,320	3,065	32.9	1,757	18.8
Farming, forestry, fishing	740	131	17.7	81	11.0
Armed forces	51	44	86.6	42	82.7
Earnings					
Under $15,000	22,330	7,659	34.3	3,174	14.2
$15,000 to $24,999	12,153	7,317	60.2	5,543	45.6
$25,000 to $49,999	17,373	13,181	75.9	11,698	67.3
$50,000 to $74,999	4,472	3,663	81.9	3,404	76.1
$75,000 to $99,999	910	755	83.0	702	77.1
$100,000 or more	790	586	74.2	526	66.6

Source: Bureau of the Census, Current Population Survey, Internet site <http://ferret.bls.census.gov/macro/ 032001/noncash/nc8_006 .htm>; calculations by New Strategist

Pension Coverage of Non-Hispanic White Women, 2000

(total number of employed non-Hispanic white women aged 15 or older, number and percent with an employer-offered pension plan, and number and percent included in pension plan by selected characteristics, 2000; numbers in thousands)

| | | with employer-offered pension plan at work | | | |
| | | | | included in plan | |
	total	number	percent	number	percent
Employed non-Hispanic white women	**51,476**	**30,395**	**59.0%**	**23,127**	**44.9%**
Age					
Under age 65	49,514	29,609	59.8	22,671	45.8
Aged 15 to 24	8,647	3,385	39.2	1,205	13.9
Aged 25 to 44	23,256	14,803	63.7	11,660	50.1
Aged 45 to 64	17,612	11,421	64.8	9,806	55.7
Aged 65 or older	1,962	785	40.0	456	23.3
Worked					
Full-time	36,256	24,359	67.2	20,293	56.0
50 weeks or more	29,291	20,550	70.2	17,764	60.6
27 to 49 weeks	4,331	2,719	62.8	1,989	45.9
26 weeks or less	2,634	1,090	41.4	540	20.5
Part-time	15,221	6,036	39.7	2,834	18.6
50 weeks or more	7,636	3,303	43.2	1,900	24.9
27 to 49 weeks	3,408	1,432	42.0	651	19.1
26 weeks or less	4,177	1,301	31.1	283	6.8
Size of employer					
Under 25 employees	14,712	3,672	25.0	2,553	17.4
25 to 99 employees	6,082	3,276	53.9	2,406	39.6
100 to 499 employees	6,802	4,846	71.2	3,768	55.4
500 to 999 employees	3,038	2,292	75.5	1,822	60.0
1,000 or more employees	20,843	16,309	78.2	12,579	60.3

(continued)

(continued from previous page)

	total	with employer-offered pension plan at work		included in plan	
		number	percent	number	percent
Occupation					
Executive, administrative, and managerial	7,842	5,412	69.0%	4,621	58.9%
Professional specialty	9,796	7,197	73.5	6,086	62.1
Technical, related support	1,953	1,415	72.4	1,068	54.7
Sales workers	6,965	3,444	49.5	2,126	30.5
Administrative support, including clerical	12,213	7,910	64.8	5,993	49.1
Precision production, craft, and repair	920	502	54.6	430	46.7
Machine operators, assemblers, inspectors	1,658	1,004	60.6	734	44.3
Transportation, material moving occupations	509	283	55.5	227	44.7
Handlers, equip. cleaners, helpers, and laborers	756	415	54.9	220	29.1
Service workers	8,266	2,668	32.3	1,521	18.4
Private household	492	25	5.1	21	4.2
Service workers except private household	7,775	2,643	34.0	1,500	19.3
Farming, forestry, fishing	557	111	19.9	70	12.5
Armed forces	40	33	83.6	31	78.7
Earnings					
Under $15,000	18,947	6,846	36.1	2,839	15.0
$15,000 to $24,999	10,509	6,469	61.6	4,931	46.9
$25,000 to $49,999	16,053	12,275	76.5	10,920	68.0
$50,000 to $74,999	4,252	3,499	82.3	3,249	76.4
$75,000 to $99,999	857	715	83.4	664	77.5
$100,000 or more	765	580	75.8	522	68.2

Source: Bureau of the Census, Current Population Survey, Internet site <http://ferret.bls.census.gov/macro/ 032001/noncash/nc8_015 .htm>; calculations by New Strategist

7

Total Population

■ Between 1990 and 2000, the U.S. population grew 13 percent, to 281 million. The non-Hispanic white share of the population fell from 76 to 69 percent during those years.

■ Eighty-four percent of Americans had a high school diploma in 2000, and 26 percent had a college degree. Among the 15 million Americans enrolled in college, 14 percent are black, 9 percent Hispanic, and 7 percent Asian.

■ Among the 4 million babies born in 2000, only 58 percent were born to non-Hispanic white women. Twenty percent were born to Hispanics and 15 percent to blacks.

■ A 47 percent minority of the nation's 31 million poor in 2000 were non-Hispanic white. Twenty-five percent of the poor were black and 23 percent were Hispanic.

■ Only 61 percent of workers entering the labor force between 2000 and 2010 will be non-Hispanic white. Eighteen percent will be Hispanic, 14 percent black, and 8 percent Asian.

■ Non-Hispanic whites head 84 percent of married couples without children at home, 73 percent of couples with children at home, and only 50 percent of female-headed single-parent families.

■ The United States received more than 849,000 immigrants in fiscal year 2000. Thirty-one percent of immigrants were from Asia and 45 percent were from Mexico, Central or South America, or the Caribbean.

More than 30 percent of Americans are minorities

(percent distribution of people by race and Hispanic origin, 2000)

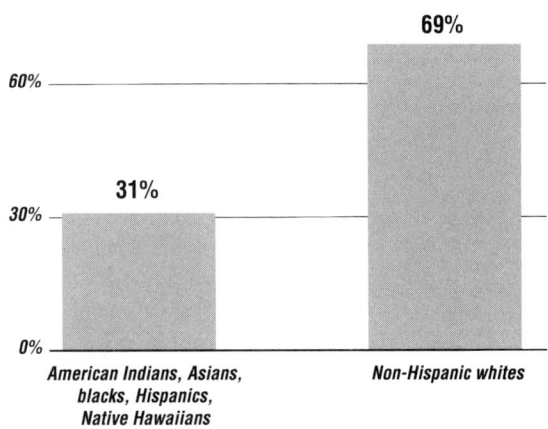

Minorities Own Fifteen Percent of U.S. Businesses

Minorities own 3 million of the nation's 21 million businesses, according to the Survey of Minority-Owned Business Enterprises, a part of the 1997 Economic Censuses. The survey counts as minority-owned any firm in which the majority of owners is black, Alaska Native, American Indian, Asian, Native Hawaiian, other Pacific Islander, or Hispanic. Minority ownership is determined by the demographic make-up of firms in their entirety rather than at individual locations.

Hispanics (who may be of any race) own the largest share of minority-owned businesses, at 39 percent. Asians are second to Hispanics, owning 30 percent. Blacks own 27 percent of minority businesses. Minorities own 28 percent of food stores, 24 percent of eating and drinking places, and 20 percent of hotels and motels. They own fully 45 percent of local and interurban passenger transportation businesses. Eighty-two percent of minority-owned firms are individual proprietorships.

Twenty-four percent of minority-owned firms are in California, where they account for 29 percent of businesses in the state. Among the nation's ten largest metropolitan areas, minorities own the largest share of firms in Los Angeles—37 percent in 1997.

Most minority-owned firms have receipts below $25,000

(percent distribution of receipts for firms owned by minorities, 1997)

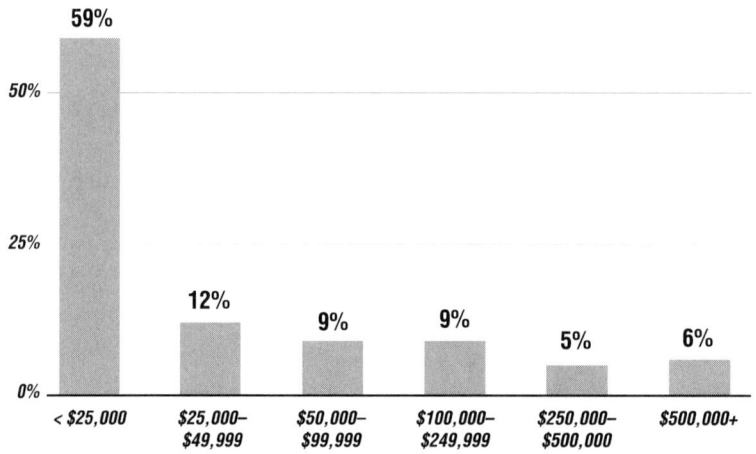

Number and Percent Distribution of Total and Minority-Owned Businesses by Industry, 1997

(number and percent distribution of total and minority-owned firms by industry, and minority-owned firms as a share of total firms, 1997)

SIC code		total firms	percent distribution	minority-owned total	percent distribution	percent of total
	All industries	**20,821,935**	**100.0%**	**3,039,033**	**100.0%**	**14.6%**
	Agricultural services, forestry, fishing	**496,164**	**2.4**	**71,921**	**2.4**	**14.5**
07	Agricultural services	412,852	2.0	58,982	1.9	14.3
08	Forestry	14,051	0.1	789	0.0	5.6
09	Fishing, hunting, and trapping	69,271	0.3	12,150	0.4	17.5
	Mineral industries	**126,809**	**0.6**	**3,578**	**0.1**	**2.8**
10	Metal mining	1,819	0.0	102	0.0	5.6
12	Coal mining	2,242	0.0	27	0.0	1.2
13	Oil and gas extraction	115,953	0.6	3,338	0.1	2.9
14	Nonmetallic minerals, except fuels	6,862	0.0	111	0.0	1.6
	Construction industries, subdividers, developers	**2,333,424**	**11.2**	**255,251**	**8.4**	**10.9**
15	Building construction, general contractors and operative builders	472,111	2.3	32,222	1.1	6.8
16	Heavy construction contractors other than buildings	64,314	0.3	5,317	0.2	8.3
17	Special trade contractors	1,739,060	8.4	215,561	7.1	12.4
6552	Subdividers and developers not elsewhere classified (excl. cemeteries)	58,362	0.3	2,158	0.1	3.7
	Manufacturing	**688,782**	**3.3**	**63,640**	**2.1**	**9.2**
20	Food and kindred products	30,256	0.1	4,626	0.2	15.3
21	Tobacco products	133	0.0	–	–	–
22	Textile mill products	8,213	0.0	1,028	0.0	12.5
23	Apparel and other textile products	54,889	0.3	13,784	0.5	25.1
24	Lumber and wood products	106,569	0.5	5,967	0.2	5.6
25	Furniture and fixtures	28,712	0.1	2,373	0.1	8.3
26	Paper and allied products	7,186	0.0	619	0.0	8.6
27	Printing and publishing	119,936	0.6	10,359	0.3	8.6
28	Chemicals and allied products	10,941	0.1	673	0.0	6.2
29	Petroleum and coal products	1,434	0.0	41	0.0	2.9
30	Rubber and miscellaneous plastics	16,296	0.1	801	0.0	4.9
31	Leather and leather products	5,251	0.0	949	0.0	18.1
32	Stone, clay, and glass products	29,262	0.1	1,714	0.1	5.9
33	Primary metal industries	7,703	0.0	526	0.0	6.8

(continued)

(continued from previous page)

SIC code		total firms	percent distribution	minority-owned total	minority-owned percent distribution	minority-owned percent of total
34	Fabricated metal products	63,141	0.3%	4,547	0.1%	7.2%
35	Industrial machinery and equipment	85,401	0.4	5,150	0.2	6.0
36	Electronic and other electric equipment	28,324	0.1	3,127	0.1	11.0
37	Transportation equipment	13,673	0.1	536	0.0	3.9
38	Instruments and related products	12,423	0.1	638	0.0	5.1
39	Miscellaneous manufacturing industries	65,185	0.3	6,212	0.2	9.5
	Transportation, communications, utilities	**919,570**	**4.4**	**190,564**	**6.3**	**20.7**
41	Local and interurban passenger transportation	116,993	0.6	52,144	1.7	44.6
42	Motor freight transportation, warehousing	544,523	2.6	101,707	3.3	18.7
44	Water transportation	15,788	0.1	650	0.0	4.1
45	Transportation by air	20,706	0.1	1,411	0.0	6.8
46	Pipelines, except natural gas	136	0.0	6	0.0	4.4
47	Transportation services	129,652	0.6	24,544	0.8	18.9
48	Communications	61,180	0.3	8,187	0.3	13.4
49	Electric, gas, and sanitary services	31,345	0.2	1,946	0.1	6.2
	Wholesale trade	**797,856**	**3.8**	**92,727**	**3.1**	**11.6**
50	Durable goods	489,308	2.3	52,953	1.7	10.8
51	Nondurable goods	309,731	1.5	39,781	1.3	12.8
	Retail trade	**2,889,041**	**13.9**	**439,450**	**14.5**	**15.2**
52	Building materials, hardware, garden supply, and mobile home dealers	85,060	0.4	5,305	0.2	6.2
53	General merchandise stores	35,027	0.2	6,371	0.2	18.2
54	Food stores	216,067	1.0	59,914	2.0	27.7
55	Automotive dealers and gasoline service stations	255,259	1.2	23,426	0.8	9.2
56	Apparel and accessory stores	127,848	0.6	28,596	0.9	22.4
57	Home furniture, furnishings, and equipment stores	153,248	0.7	15,066	0.5	9.8
58	Eating and drinking places	493,313	2.4	117,366	3.9	23.8
59	Miscellaneous retail	1,528,857	7.3	183,589	6.0	12.0
	Finance, insurance, real estate (excl. subdividers and developers)	**2,237,675**	**10.7**	**164,043**	**5.4**	**7.3**
60	Depository institutions	24,616	0.1	872	0.0	3.5
61	Nondepository credit institutions	45,905	0.2	4,375	0.1	9.5
62	Security and commodity brokers, dealers, exchanges, and services	91,446	0.4	6,841	0.2	7.5
63	Insurance carriers	9,108	0.0	303	0.0	3.3
64	Insurance agents, brokers, and services	411,902	2.0	33,553	1.1	8.1

(continued)

(continued from previous page)

SIC code		total firms	percent distribution	minority-owned		
				total	percent distribution	percent of total
65pt	Real estate (excl. subdividers and developers)	1,503,438	7.2%	111,806	3.7%	7.4%
67	Holding and other investment offices, except trusts	157,652	0.8	6,353	0.2	4.0
	Service industries (excl. membership organizations, private household)	**8,891,024**	**42.7**	**1,339,486**	**44.1**	**15.1**
70	Hotels, rooming houses, camps, and other lodging places	93,380	0.4	18,539	0.6	19.9
72	Personal services	1,348,554	6.5	299,074	9.8	22.2
73	Business services	2,221,047	10.7	353,082	11.6	15.9
75	Automotive repair, services, and parking	448,584	2.2	64,259	2.1	14.3
76	Miscellaneous repair services	231,371	1.1	23,418	0.8	10.1
78	Motion pictures	87,700	0.4	10,654	0.4	12.1
79	Amusement and recreation services	603,896	2.9	66,324	2.2	11.0
80	Health services	1,004,672	4.8	169,470	5.6	16.9
81	Legal services	353,147	1.7	24,509	0.8	6.9
82	Educational services	270,648	1.3	25,552	0.8	9.4
83	Social services	665,067	3.2	122,819	4.0	18.5
84	Museums, art galleries, botanical and zoological gardens	5,205	0.0	21	0.0	0.4
87	Engineering, accounting, research, management and related services	1,446,195	6.9	152,937	5.0	10.6
89	Services not elsewhere classified	119,931	0.6	9,084	0.3	7.6
	Industries not classified	**1,480,003**	**7.1**	**419,522**	**13.8**	**28.3**

Source: Bureau of the Census, Minority- and Women-Owned Businesses, *1997 Economic Census, Internet site <www.census.gov/csd/mwb/>; calculations by New Strategist*

Characteristics of Total Businesses by Industry, 1997

(total number of firms by industry and selected characteristics of firm, 1997)

SIC code		total		firms with paid employees			
		number	sales, receipts (in 000s)	number	sales, receipts (in 000s)	employees	payroll (in 000s)
	Total firms	20,821,935	$18,553,243,047	5,295,152	$17,907,940,321	103,359,815	$2,936,492,940
	Agricultural services, forestry, fishing	**496,164**	**64,032,640**	**114,587**	**50,775,178**	**725,410**	**14,923,855**
07	Agricultural services	412,852	57,086,633	109,721	46,387,756	687,332	13,853,993
08	Forestry	14,051	2,817,356	2,434	2,346,506	25,526	660,824
09	Fishing, hunting, and trapping	69,271	4,128,651	2,442	2,040,916	12,552	409,038
	Mineral industries	**126,809**	**176,609,179**	**20,917**	**171,107,096**	**616,232**	**27,397,247**
10	Metal mining	1,819	12,068,979	600	12,022,441	54,291	2,497,161
12	Coal mining	2,242	24,288,482	1,422	24,170,302	99,403	4,561,564
13	Oil and gas extraction	115,953	122,848,428	15,210	117,695,150	353,276	16,204,547
14	Nonmetallic minerals, except fuels	6,862	17,403,290	3,752	17,219,203	109,262	4,133,975
	Construction industries, subdividers, developers	**2,333,424**	**944,154,542**	**675,160**	**863,945,192**	**5,678,306**	**176,476,246**
15	Building construction, general contractors and operative builders	472,111	389,134,702	197,147	363,751,353	1,304,365	40,998,809
16	Heavy construction contractors other than buildings	64,314	130,870,724	37,019	129,420,619	842,230	30,247,697
17	Special trade contractors	1,739,060	398,976,380	430,259	351,814,374	3,477,921	103,427,193
6552	Subdividers and developers not elsewhere classified (excl. cemeteries)	58,362	25,172,736	11,158	18,958,846	53,790	1,802,547

(continued)

(continued from previous page)

SIC code		total		firms with paid employees			
		number	sales, receipts (in 000s)	number	sales, receipts (in 000s)	employees	payroll (in 000s)
	Manufacturing	**688,782**	**$4,021,515,429**	**334,084**	**$4,005,607,057**	**18,968,167**	**$685,313,617**
20	Food and kindred products	30,256	490,130,601	16,737	489,187,047	1,702,489	51,117,934
21	Tobacco products	133	36,645,733	88	36,641,662	43,567	2,399,430
22	Textile mill products	8,213	84,021,370	5,178	83,887,889	600,144	15,209,210
23	Apparel and other textile products	54,889	83,380,324	22,646	82,432,510	876,897	17,120,728
24	Lumber and wood products	106,569	115,219,866	34,713	111,907,874	776,944	19,626,459
25	Furniture and fixtures	28,712	62,551,208	11,470	61,900,220	537,731	14,019,789
26	Paper and allied products	7,186	161,211,853	4,373	161,071,165	676,510	26,870,903
27	Printing and publishing	119,936	216,211,945	57,891	213,862,501	1,645,771	55,216,424
28	Chemicals and allied products	10,941	409,994,222	8,871	409,320,937	1,044,085	54,469,556
29	Petroleum and coal products	1,434	176,788,852	1,193	176,756,460	137,388	7,821,475
30	Rubber and miscellaneous plastics	16,296	162,732,650	13,975	162,495,829	1,081,225	32,657,397
31	Leather and leather products	5,251	10,275,926	1,733	10,173,915	82,881	1,893,820
32	Stone, clay, and glass products	29,262	88,090,813	12,135	87,638,425	533,650	18,025,290
33	Primary metal industries	7,703	191,711,591	5,294	191,540,047	720,972	28,543,314
34	Fabricated metal products	63,141	235,330,354	35,141	234,014,337	1,600,272	53,819,427
35	Industrial machinery and equipment	85,401	411,881,461	53,821	410,326,739	2,110,272	83,490,307
36	Electronic and other electric equipment	28,324	355,193,235	15,200	354,444,237	1,778,698	73,112,444
37	Transportation equipment	13,673	518,958,599	11,158	518,680,590	1,712,407	77,941,602
38	Instruments and related products	12,423	157,672,122	10,647	157,507,128	892,135	40,414,901
39	Miscellaneous manufacturing industries	65,185	53,512,704	17,966	51,817,545	414,129	11,543,207

(continued)

(continued from previous page)

SIC code		total		firms with paid employees			
		number	sales, receipts (in 000s)	number	sales, receipts (in 000s)	employees	payroll (in 000s)
	Transportation, communications, utilities	**919,570**	**$1,183,669,281**	**218,834**	**$1,151,582,436**	**5,883,270**	**$207,281,648**
41	Local and interurban passenger transportation	116,993	21,713,557	17,319	19,114,727	467,046	8,004,735
42	Motor freight transportation and warehousing	544,523	221,521,560	117,306	198,846,704	2,014,484	57,852,063
44	Water transportation	15,788	36,039,949	8,227	35,477,732	187,575	6,765,391
45	Transportation by air	20,706	48,149,574	6,542	47,511,569	395,263	11,938,856
46	Pipelines, except natural gas	136	7,347,288	92	7,338,906	13,903	807,394
47	Transportation services	129,652	44,873,144	41,338	41,523,634	458,324	13,647,643
48	Communications	61,180	354,151,879	17,597	352,588,611	1,494,770	65,781,116
49	Electric, gas, and sanitary services	31,345	449,872,330	11,166	449,180,553	851,905	42,484,450
	Wholesale trade	**797,856**	**4,270,041,314**	**415,833**	**4,237,594,031**	**6,877,507**	**252,891,380**
50	Durable goods	489,308	2,317,534,951	267,480	2,298,657,857	4,100,254	158,602,734
51	Nondurable goods	309,731	1,952,506,363	149,536	1,938,936,174	2,777,253	94,288,646
	Retail trade	**2,889,041**	**2,649,085,229**	**1,096,856**	**2,577,370,639**	**22,268,978**	**324,734,467**
52	Building materials, hardware, garden supply, and mobile home dealers	85,060	149,891,611	52,017	147,572,959	868,645	17,911,810
53	General merchandise stores	35,027	329,908,211	9,740	328,700,392	2,713,459	37,775,544
54	Food stores	216,067	428,384,106	124,962	420,580,053	3,328,123	49,793,387
55	Automotive dealers, gasoline service stations	255,259	807,900,003	140,686	792,042,625	2,345,611	57,564,224
56	Apparel and accessory stores	127,848	121,293,150	53,890	118,323,373	1,229,852	17,316,674
57	Home furniture, furnishings, equipment stores	153,248	141,376,667	83,946	137,258,560	931,008	18,362,057
58	Eating and drinking places	493,313	256,489,798	363,179	250,616,760	7,866,488	74,619,242
59	Miscellaneous retail	1,528,857	413,841,683	274,074	382,275,917	2,985,792	51,391,529

(continued)

(continued from previous page)

SIC code	total		firms with paid employees			
	number	sales, receipts (in 000s)	number	sales, receipts (in 000s)	employees	payroll (in 000s)
Finance, insurance, real estate (excl. subdividers and developers)	**2,237,675**	**$2,567,560,021**	**449,713**	**$2,420,115,913**	**7,430,891**	**$314,464,560**
60 Depository institutions	24,616	573,212,932	23,498	572,965,319	2,159,506	74,998,700
61 Nondepository credit institutions	45,905	196,564,220	24,540	194,815,280	618,811	25,624,676
62 Security and commodity brokers, dealers, exchanges, and services	91,446	268,894,838	30,086	259,286,735	676,013	71,055,775
63 Insurance carriers	9,108	1,003,355,294	6,677	1,000,358,615	1,620,543	67,004,231
64 Insurance agents, brokers, and services	411,902	91,960,902	121,540	77,460,848	731,461	26,846,764
65pt Real estate (excl. subdividers and developers)	1,503,438	269,580,890	222,727	168,794,615	1,336,389	33,451,364
67 Holding and other investment offices, except trusts	157,652	163,990,945	27,037	146,434,501	288,168	15,483,050
Service industries (excl. membership organizations and private household)	**8,891,024**	**2,614,964,642**	**1,976,745**	**2,427,078,076**	**34,884,760**	**932,349,593**
70 Hotels, rooming houses, camps, and other lodging places	93,380	102,590,165	49,842	99,639,330	1,768,242	28,634,509
72 Personal services	1,348,554	75,580,916	177,583	53,815,269	1,333,183	18,593,604
73 Business services	2,221,047	585,990,807	348,229	538,045,410	8,858,136	222,439,658
75 Automotive repair, services, and parking	448,584	115,321,750	167,975	104,399,866	1,147,865	24,305,080
76 Miscellaneous repair services	231,371	42,959,645	63,803	37,802,866	428,378	11,647,760
78 Motion pictures	87,700	70,467,490	32,461	68,215,128	587,125	14,535,748
79 Amusement and recreation services	603,896	106,375,756	91,954	94,732,397	1,555,454	30,570,262
80 Health services	1,004,672	755,681,519	425,337	726,846,432	10,416,489	313,352,409

(continued)

(continued from previous page)

SIC code		total		firms with paid employees			
		number	sales, receipts (in 000s)	number	sales, receipts (in 000s)	employees	payroll (in 000s)
81	Legal services	353,147	$133,560,231	164,110	$124,517,693	985,331	$48,394,192
82	Educational services	270,648	139,395,624	43,896	135,892,563	2,191,548	47,366,748
83	Social services	665,067	101,319,229	121,636	93,509,763	2,272,674	34,729,175
84	Museums, art galleries, botanical and zoological gardens	5,205	6,763,777	4,987	6,614,268	89,776	1,807,256
87	Engineering, accounting, research, management and related services	1,446,195	356,417,568	276,601	322,154,868	3,143,751	130,511,362
89	Services not elsewhere classified	119,931	22,540,165	16,704	20,892,223	106,808	5,461,830
	Industries not classified	**1,480,003**	**61,610,770**	**30,836**	**2,764,703**	**26,294**	**660,327**

Source: Bureau of the Census, Minority- and Women-Owned Businesses, 1997 Economic Census, Internet site <www.census.gov/csd/mwb/>

Minority-Owned Businesses by Race and Hispanic Origin of Owners, 1997

(number of minority-owned firms by industry and race and Hispanic origin of owners, 1997)

SIC code		total	American Indians	Asians	blacks	Hispanics
	Total minority-owned firms	**3,039,033**	**197,300**	**912,960**	**823,499**	**1,199,896**
	Agricultural services, forestry, fishing	**71,921**	**8,942**	**12,988**	**12,464**	**40,040**
07	Agricultural services	58,982	4,637	7,965	11,742	36,872
08	Forestry	789	209	62	223	334
09	Fishing, hunting, and trapping	12,150	4,096	4,961	500	2,835
	Mineral industries	**3,578**	**947**	**660**	**231**	**1,909**
10	Metal mining	102	28	16	13	45
12	Coal mining	27	—	5	6	9
13	Oil and gas extraction	3,338	862	620	202	1,801
14	Nonmetallic minerals, except fuels	111	37	18	9	55
	Construction industries, subdividers, developers	**255,251**	**27,435**	**27,711**	**56,508**	**152,573**
15	Building construction, general contractors and operative builders	32,222	3,129	5,707	8,159	16,345
16	Heavy construction contractors other than buildings	5,317	1,095	415	1,305	2,643
17	Special trade contractors	215,561	23,100	20,621	46,819	132,656
6552	Subdividers and developers not elsewhere classified (excl. cemeteries)	2,158	115	970	225	930
	Manufacturing	**63,640**	**6,717**	**23,242**	**10,447**	**25,552**
20	Food and kindred products	4,626	216	1,732	783	2,207
21	Tobacco products	–	1	0	1	23
22	Textile mill products	1,028	71	522	57	409
23	Apparel and other textile products	13,784	474	8,406	1,115	4,157
24	Lumber and wood products	5,967	1,640	384	2,498	1,715
25	Furniture and fixtures	2,373	242	429	337	1,503
26	Paper and allied products	619	49	204	202	206
27	Printing and publishing	10,359	598	3,409	2,763	3,736
28	Chemicals and allied products	673	41	383	112	160
29	Petroleum and coal products	41	–	23	5	12
30	Rubber and miscellaneous plastics	801	25	359	51	372
31	Leather and leather products	949	88	437	58	397
32	Stone, clay, and glass products	1,714	339	436	268	746
33	Primary metal industries	526	53	127	94	276
34	Fabricated metal products	4,547	851	897	464	2,504
35	Industrial machinery and equipment	5,150	675	1,381	497	2,830
36	Electronic and other electric equipment	3,127	165	1,676	388	977

(continued)

(continued from previous page)

SIC code		total	American Indians	Asians	blacks	Hispanics
37	Transportation equipment	536	63	191	60	289
38	Instruments and related products	638	21	397	38	183
39	Miscellaneous manufacturing industries	6,212	1,112	1,885	662	2,858
	Transportation, communications, utilities	**190,564**	**6,291**	**37,501**	**71,586**	**84,554**
41	Local/interurban passenger transportation	52,144	736	17,544	24,086	14,063
42	Motor freight transportation, warehousing	101,707	3,644	9,170	37,429	54,981
44	Water transportation	650	102	146	124	308
45	Transportation by air	1,411	142	303	210	856
46	Pipelines, except natural gas	6	4	0	1	–
47	Transportation services	24,544	848	8,280	5,720	10,649
48	Communications	8,187	411	1,887	3,307	2,935
49	Electric, gas, and sanitary services	1,946	419	176	711	766
	Wholesale trade	**92,727**	**4,365**	**50,400**	**8,120**	**31,480**
50	Durable goods	52,953	2,980	28,444	4,013	18,231
51	Nondurable goods	39,781	1,385	21,962	4,107	13,251
	Retail trade	**439,450**	**14,768**	**195,691**	**87,568**	**155,061**
52	Building materials, hardware, garden supply, and mobile home dealers	5,305	564	1,221	944	2,793
53	General merchandise stores	6,371	459	3,274	993	1,867
54	Food stores	59,914	1,403	35,796	8,255	18,063
55	Automotive dealers and gasoline service stations	23,426	1,853	7,314	4,073	10,950
56	Apparel and accessory stores	28,596	788	12,777	6,646	9,585
57	Home furniture, furnishings, and equipment stores	15,066	1,104	5,061	2,823	6,577
58	Eating and drinking places	117,366	1,724	69,903	13,111	34,862
59	Miscellaneous retail	183,589	6,885	60,444	50,754	70,413
	Finance, insurance, real estate (excl. subdividers and developers)	**164,043**	**4,616**	**68,765**	**37,934**	**56,629**
60	Depository institutions	872	39	269	347	252
61	Nondepository credit institutions	4,375	202	1,307	982	1,960
62	Security and commodity brokers, dealers, exchanges, and services	6,841	438	2,821	1,749	2,057
63	Insurance carriers	303	29	81	111	97
64	Insurance agents, brokers, and services	33,553	1,016	9,985	11,373	11,915
65pt	Real estate (excl. subdividers, developers)	111,806	2,573	50,783	22,118	39,060
67	Holding and other investment offices, except trusts	6,353	323	3,549	1,263	1,304

(continued)

(continued from previous page)

SIC code		total	American Indians	Asians	blacks	Hispanics
	Service industries (excl. membership organizations and private household)	**1,339,486**	**34,144**	**406,010**	**437,646**	**500,449**
70	Hotels, rooming houses, camps, and other lodging places	18,539	589	15,153	1,222	1,795
72	Personal services	299,074	5,534	99,829	103,865	99,389
73	Business services	353,082	8,267	92,061	104,939	157,907
75	Automotive repair, services, and parking	64,259	2,575	10,744	15,922	37,357
76	Miscellaneous repair services	23,418	1,500	4,935	5,049	12,655
78	Motion pictures	10,654	503	4,338	2,297	3,958
79	Amusement and recreation services	66,324	2,180	11,920	29,343	24,622
80	Health services	169,470	2,167	74,471	51,732	44,806
81	Legal services	24,509	815	5,634	8,799	9,903
82	Educational services	25,552	817	9,026	8,249	8,170
83	Social services	122,819	3,427	13,158	66,530	44,993
84	Museums, art galleries, botanical and zoological gardens	21	1	11	6	3
87	Engineering, accounting, research, management and related services	152,937	5,076	61,767	37,505	51,740
89	Services not elsewhere classified	9,084	745	3,024	2,279	3,203
	Industries not classified	**419,522**	**89,243**	**90,509**	**101,128**	**151,931**

Note: Numbers will not add to total because Hispanics may be of any race; American Indians include Alaska Natives; Asians include Native Hawaiians and other Pacific Islanders; (–) means data not available or suppressed for purposes of confidentiality.
Source: Bureau of the Census, Minority- and Women-Owned Businesses*, 1997 Economic Census, Internet site* <www.census.gov/csd/mwb/>

Distribution of Minority-Owned Businesses by Race and Hispanic Origin of Owners, 1997

(percent distribution of minority-owned firms by industry and race and Hispanic origin of owners, by industry, 1997)

SIC code		total	American Indians	Asians	blacks	Hispanics
	Total minority-owned firms	**100.0%**	**6.5%**	**30.0%**	**27.1%**	**39.5%**
	Agricultural services, forestry, fishing	**100.0**	**12.4**	**18.1**	**17.3**	**55.7**
07	Agricultural services	100.0	7.9	13.5	19.9	62.5
08	Forestry	100.0	26.5	7.9	28.3	42.3
09	Fishing, hunting, and trapping	100.0	33.7	40.8	4.1	23.3
	Mineral industries	**100.0**	**26.5**	**18.4**	**6.5**	**53.4**
10	Metal mining	100.0	27.5	15.7	12.7	44.1
12	Coal mining	100.0	–	18.5	22.2	33.3
13	Oil and gas extraction	100.0	25.8	18.6	6.1	54.0
14	Nonmetallic minerals, except fuels	100.0	33.3	16.2	8.1	49.5
	Construction industries, subdividers, developers	**100.0**	**10.7**	**10.9**	**22.1**	**59.8**
15	Building construction, general contractors and operative builders	100.0	9.7	17.7	25.3	50.7
16	Heavy construction contractors other than buildings	100.0	20.6	7.8	24.5	49.7
17	Special trade contractors	100.0	10.7	9.6	21.7	61.5
6552	Subdividers and developers not elsewhere classified (excl. cemeteries)	100.0	5.3	44.9	10.4	43.1
	Manufacturing	**100.0**	**10.6**	**36.5**	**16.4**	**40.2**
20	Food and kindred products	100.0	4.7	37.4	16.9	47.7
21	Tobacco products	–	–	–	–	–
22	Textile mill products	100.0	6.9	50.8	5.5	39.8
23	Apparel and other textile products	100.0	3.4	61.0	8.1	30.2
24	Lumber and wood products	100.0	27.5	6.4	41.9	28.7
25	Furniture and fixtures	100.0	10.2	18.1	14.2	63.3
26	Paper and allied products	100.0	7.9	33.0	32.6	33.3
27	Printing and publishing	100.0	5.8	32.9	26.7	36.1
28	Chemicals and allied products	100.0	6.1	56.9	16.6	23.8
29	Petroleum and coal products	100.0	–	56.1	12.2	29.3
30	Rubber and miscellaneous plastics	100.0	3.1	44.8	6.4	46.4
31	Leather and leather products	100.0	9.3	46.0	6.1	41.8
32	Stone, clay, and glass products	100.0	19.8	25.4	15.6	43.5
33	Primary metal industries	100.0	10.1	24.1	17.9	52.5
34	Fabricated metal products	100.0	18.7	19.7	10.2	55.1
35	Industrial machinery and equipment	100.0	13.1	26.8	9.7	55.0
36	Electronic and other electric equipment	100.0	5.3	53.6	12.4	31.2

(continued)

(continued from previous page)

SIC code		total	American Indians	Asians	blacks	Hispanics
37	Transportation equipment	100.0%	11.8%	35.6%	11.2%	53.9%
38	Instruments and related products	100.0	3.3	62.2	6.0	28.7
39	Miscellaneous manufacturing industries	100.0	17.9	30.3	10.7	46.0
	Transportation, communications, utilities	**100.0**	**3.3**	**19.7**	**37.6**	**44.4**
41	Local/interurban passenger transportation	100.0	1.4	33.6	46.2	27.0
42	Motor freight transportation, warehousing	100.0	3.6	9.0	36.8	54.1
44	Water transportation	100.0	15.7	22.5	19.1	47.4
45	Transportation by air	100.0	10.1	21.5	14.9	60.7
46	Pipelines, except natural gas	100.0	66.7	0.0	16.7	–
47	Transportation services	100.0	3.5	33.7	23.3	43.4
48	Communications	100.0	5.0	23.0	40.4	35.8
49	Electric, gas, and sanitary services	100.0	21.5	9.0	36.5	39.4
	Wholesale trade	**100.0**	**4.7**	**54.4**	**8.8**	**33.9**
50	Durable goods	100.0	5.6	53.7	7.6	34.4
51	Nondurable goods	100.0	3.5	55.2	10.3	33.3
	Retail trade	**100.0**	**3.4**	**44.5**	**19.9**	**35.3**
52	Building materials, hardware, garden supply, and mobile home dealers	100.0	10.6	23.0	17.8	52.6
53	General merchandise stores	100.0	7.2	51.4	15.6	29.3
54	Food stores	100.0	2.3	59.7	13.8	30.1
55	Automotive dealers, gasoline service stations	100.0	7.9	31.2	17.4	46.7
56	Apparel and accessory stores	100.0	2.8	44.7	23.2	33.5
57	Home furniture, furnishings, and equipment stores	100.0	7.3	33.6	18.7	43.7
58	Eating and drinking places	100.0	1.5	59.6	11.2	29.7
59	Miscellaneous retail	100.0	3.8	32.9	27.6	38.4
	Finance, insurance, real estate (excl. subdividers and developers)	**100.0**	**2.8**	**41.9**	**23.1**	**34.5**
60	Depository institutions	100.0	4.5	30.8	39.8	28.9
61	Nondepository credit institutions	100.0	4.6	29.9	22.4	44.8
62	Security and commodity brokers, dealers, exchanges, and services	100.0	6.4	41.2	25.6	30.1
63	Insurance carriers	100.0	9.6	26.7	36.6	32.0
64	Insurance agents, brokers, and services	100.0	3.0	29.8	33.9	35.5
65pt	Real estate (excl. subdividers, developers)	100.0	2.3	45.4	19.8	34.9
67	Holding and other investment offices, except trusts	100.0	5.1	55.9	19.9	20.5

(continued)

(continued from previous page)

SIC code		total	American Indians	Asians	blacks	Hispanics
	Service industries (excl. membership organizations and private household)	**100.0%**	**2.5%**	**30.3%**	**32.7%**	**37.4%**
70	Hotels, rooming houses, camps, and other lodging places	100.0	3.2	81.7	6.6	9.7
72	Personal services	100.0	1.9	33.4	34.7	33.2
73	Business services	100.0	2.3	26.1	29.7	44.7
75	Automotive repair, services, and parking	100.0	4.0	16.7	24.8	58.1
76	Miscellaneous repair services	100.0	6.4	21.1	21.6	54.0
78	Motion pictures	100.0	4.7	40.7	21.6	37.2
79	Amusement and recreation services	100.0	3.3	18.0	44.2	37.1
80	Health services	100.0	1.3	43.9	30.5	26.4
81	Legal services	100.0	3.3	23.0	35.9	40.4
82	Educational services	100.0	3.2	35.3	32.3	32.0
83	Social services	100.0	2.8	10.7	54.2	36.6
84	Museums, art galleries, botanical and zoological gardens	100.0	4.8	52.4	28.6	14.3
87	Engineering, accounting, research, management and related services	100.0	3.3	40.4	24.5	33.8
89	Services not elsewhere classified	100.0	8.2	33.3	25.1	35.3
	Industries not classified	**100.0**	**21.3**	**21.6**	**24.1**	**36.2**

Note: Numbers will not add to total because Hispanics may be of any race; American Indians include Alaska Natives; Asians include Native Hawaiians and other Pacific Islanders; (–) means data not available or suppressed for purposes of confidentiality.
Source: Bureau of the Census, Minority- and Women-Owned Businesses, *1997 Economic Census, Internet site <www.census.gov/csd/mwb/>; calculations by New Strategist*

Total and Minority-Owned Businesses by Legal Form of Organization, Receipt Size, and Employees, 1997

(number and percent distribution of total and minority-owned firms by legal form of organization, size of receipts, and number of employees, 1997)

			minority-owned firms		
	total	percent distribution	number	percent distribution	percent of total
Total firms	**20,821,934**	**100.0%**	**3,039,033**	**100.0%**	**14.6%**
Legal form of organization					
C corporations	2,390,478	11.5	252,935	8.3	10.6
Subchapter S corporations	1,979,425	9.5	194,386	6.4	9.8
Individual proprietorships	15,122,882	72.6	2,501,802	82.3	16.5
Partnerships	1,226,455	5.9	84,770	2.8	6.9
Other	102,694	0.5	5,139	0.2	5.0
Size of receipts					
Under $5,000	4,625,337	22.2	692,861	22.8	15.0
$5,000 to $9,999	2,760,243	13.3	487,107	16.0	17.6
$10,000 to $24,999	3,619,150	17.4	627,591	20.7	17.3
$25,000 to $49,999	2,396,802	11.5	360,260	11.9	15.0
$50,000 to $99,999	2,106,310	10.1	288,635	9.5	13.7
$100,000 to $249,999	2,213,767	10.6	269,855	8.9	12.2
$250,000 to $499,999	1,221,990	5.9	143,164	4.7	11.7
$500,000 to $999,999	827,956	4.0	85,293	2.8	10.3
$1,000,000 or more	1,050,379	5.0	84,267	2.8	8.0
Number of employees					
Firms with employees	5,295,151	100.0	615,222	100.0	11.6
No employees*	619,990	11.7	90,171	14.7	14.5
1 to 3 employees	2,569,184	48.5	316,449	51.4	12.3
5 to 9 employees	966,871	18.3	110,481	18.0	11.4
10 to 19 employees	570,401	10.8	54,701	8.9	9.6
20 to 49 employees	359,358	6.8	30,595	5.0	8.5
50 to 99 employees	113,693	2.1	8,394	1.4	7.4
100 to 499 employees	79,688	1.5	4,114	0.7	5.2
500 employees or more	15,966	0.3	318	0.1	2.0

* Firms that reported annual payroll but no employees on the payroll during the specified period in 1997.
Source: Bureau of the Census, Summary, *1997 Economic Census, Survey of Minority-Owned Business Enterprises, Company Statistics Series, EC97CS-7, 2001; calculations by New Strategist*

Total and Minority-Owned Businesses by State, 1997

(number and percent distribution of minority-owned firms and minority share of total firms, by state 1997)

	total	minority-owned firms number	minority-owned firms percent distribution	minority-owned firms percent of total
Total firms	**20,821,900**	**3,039,000**	**100.0%**	**14.6%**
Alabama	285,200	28,300	0.9	9.9
Alaska	64,100	10,700	0.4	16.7
Arizona	329,000	43,300	1.4	13.2
Arkansas	193,400	13,000	0.4	6.7
California	2,565,700	738,000	24.3	28.8
Colorado	410,200	37,000	1.2	9.0
Connecticut	284,000	20,400	0.7	7.2
Delaware	56,600	5,300	0.2	9.4
District of Columbia	45,300	15,200	0.5	33.6
Florida	1,301,900	286,900	9.4	22.0
Georgia	568,600	88,700	2.9	15.6
Hawaii	94,000	54,300	1.8	57.8
Idaho	109,800	5,200	0.2	4.7
Illinois	882,100	110,300	3.6	12.5
Indiana	413,400	22,800	0.8	5.5
Iowa	227,600	5,300	0.2	2.3
Kansas	213,400	11,700	0.4	5.5
Kentucky	281,600	12,700	0.4	4.5
Louisiana	295,700	41,700	1.4	14.1
Maine	127,500	2,800	0.1	2.2
Maryland	400,200	82,600	2.7	20.6
Massachusetts	537,200	39,000	1.3	7.3
Michigan	677,500	51,800	1.7	7.6
Minnesota	410,600	15,300	0.5	3.7
Mississippi	167,900	22,000	0.7	13.1
Missouri	411,400	26,600	0.9	6.5
Montana	93,700	3,400	0.1	3.6
Nebraska	138,800	4,600	0.2	3.3
Nevada	129,800	15,200	0.5	11.7
New Hampshire	115,700	3,200	0.1	2.8
New Jersey	654,200	102,300	3.4	15.6
New Mexico	131,700	37,500	1.2	28.5
New York	1,509,800	296,500	9.8	19.6
North Carolina	570,500	61,600	2.0	10.8
North Dakota	55,300	1,500	0.0	2.7

(continued)

(continued from previous page)

	total	minority-owned firms		
		number	percent distribution	percent of total
Ohio	781,300	49,400	1.6%	6.3%
Oklahoma	280,700	28,500	0.9	10.2
Oregon	291,600	18,200	0.6	6.2
Pennsylvania	837,800	49,500	1.6	5.9
Rhode Island	80,900	4,800	0.2	5.9
South Carolina	260,300	30,800	1.0	11.8
South Dakota	65,800	1,700	0.1	2.6
Tennessee	415,900	32,500	1.1	7.8
Texas	1,526,000	365,500	12.0	24.0
Utah	169,200	8,600	0.3	5.1
Vermont	67,500	2,100	0.1	3.1
Virginia	480,100	71,700	2.4	14.9
Washington	447,400	42,900	1.4	9.6
West Virginia	111,700	4,300	0.1	3.8
Wisconsin	366,400	13,700	0.5	3.7
Wyoming	49,400	2,100	0.1	4.3

Note: Numbers will not add to total because a firm may be counted in more than one state.
Source: Bureau of the Census, Minority-Owned Firms Grow Four Times Faster than National Average, *Census Bureau Reports, U.S. Dept. of Commerce News, July 12, 2001*

Total and Minority-Owned Firms in the Ten Largest Metropolitan Areas, 1997

(number and percent distribution of firms and receipts in the ten largest metropolitan areas by race and Hispanic origin of owner, 1997)

	firms	percent distribution	receipts (in 000s)	percent distribution
1. Los Angeles–Long Beach CA, PMSA				
Total firms	**778,577**	**100.0%**	**$666,791,111**	**100.0%**
Total minority-owned firms	**289,293**	**37.2**	**76,372,804**	**11.5**
American Indian	8,541	1.1	2,890,042	0.4
Asian	114,462	14.7	55,113,170	8.3
Black	38,277	4.9	3,321,671	0.5
Hispanic	136,678	17.6	16,245,931	2.4
2. New York, NY PMSA				
Total firms	**784,876**	**100.0**	**944,904,775**	**100.0**
Total minority-owned firms	**236,809**	**30.2**	**37,324,160**	**4.0**
American Indian	2,801	0.4	890,806	0.1
Asian	101,814	13.0	25,500,359	2.7
Black	69,410	8.8	4,003,193	0.4
Hispanic	84,880	10.8	8,053,667	0.9
3. Chicago, IL PMSA				
Total firms	**598,175**	**100.0**	**747,227,967**	**100.0**
Total minority-owned firms	**95,685**	**16.0**	**21,437,261**	**2.9**
American Indian	2,161	0.4	370,927	0.0
Asian	32,733	5.5	13,244,106	1.8
Black	35,569	5.9	3,374,570	0.5
Hispanic	27,482	4.6	4,554,316	0.6
4. Philadelphia, PA–NJ PMSA				
Total firms	**353,657**	**100.0**	**388,727,494**	**100.0**
Total minority-owned firms	**37,699**	**10.7**	**6,122,019**	**1.6**
American Indian	1,603	0.5	115,923	0.0
Asian	13,399	3.8	3,444,576	0.9
Black	17,863	5.1	1,659,837	0.4
Hispanic	5,558	1.6	933,247	0.2
5. Washington, DC–MD–VA–WV PMSA				
Total firms	**394,576**	**100.0**	**319,761,981**	**100.0**
Total minority-owned firms	**99,393**	**25.2**	**16,053,881**	**5.0**
American Indian	1,639	0.4	381,498	0.1
Asian	30,784	7.9	7,462,080	2.3
Black	48,709	12.3	5,410,464	1.7
Hispanic	19,392	4.9	3,019,391	0.9

(continued)

(continued from previous page)

	firms	*percent distribution*	*receipts (in 000s)*	*percent distribution*
6. Detroit, MI PMSA				
Total firms	**289,080**	**100.0%**	**$409,094,596**	**100.0%**
Total minority-owned firms	**31,023**	**10.7**	**9,086,078**	**2.2**
American Indian	1,862	0.6	331,317	0.1
Asian	7,473	2.6	3,901,437	1.0
Black	17,692	6.1	3,507,051	0.9
Hispanic	4,377	1.5	1,377,932	0.3
7. Houston, TX PMSA				
Total firms	**326,513**	**100.0**	**424,116,351**	**100.0**
Total minority-owned firms	**92,423**	**28.3**	**23,440,561**	**5.5**
American Indian	3,128	1.0	476,984	0.1
Asian	25,576	7.9	8,813,730	2.1
Black	24,286	7.4	1,845,644	0.4
Hispanic	41,769	12.8	12,415,381	2.9
8. Atlanta, GA MSA				
Total firms	**327,053**	**100.0**	**387,465,384**	**100.0**
Total minority-owned firms	**58,776**	**18.0**	**9,887,454**	**2.6**
American Indian	2,227	0.7	244,756	0.1
Asian	14,337	4.4	5,206,147	1.3
Black	34,592	10.6	2,959,189	0.8
Hispanic	8,543	2.6	1,504,077	0.4
9. Dallas, TX MSA				
Total firms	**288,728**	**100.0**	**341,313,795**	**100.0**
Total minority-owned firms	**52,852**	**18.3**	**9,807,980**	**2.9**
American Indian	2,510	0.9	728,673	0.2
Asian	13,230	4.7	4,180,041	1.2
Black	14,021	4.9	2,217,466	0.6
Hispanic	24,573	8.5	2,753,256	0.8
10. Boston, MA-NH PMSA				
Total firms	**313,437**	**100.0**	**353,972,020**	**100.0**
Total minority-owned firms	**25,015**	**8.0**	**4,703,323**	**1.3**
American Indian	1,376	0.4	130,838	0.0
Asian	9,124	2.9	2,970,338	0.8
Black	8,043	2.6	681,280	0.2
Hispanic	7,325	2.3	964,320	0.3

Note: Numbers will not add to total because Hispanics may be of any race. American Indians include Alaska Natives. Asian Americans include Native Hawaiians and other Pacific Islanders. For definition of PMSA and MSA, see glossary.
Source: Bureau of the Census, 1997 Economic Census, Minority- and Women-Owned Businesses, *Internet site <www.census.gov/epcd/mwb97/us/us.html>; calculations by New Strategist*

The Educational Attainment of Americans Soared over the Past Few decades

Overall, 84 percent of Americans had a high school diploma in 2000, up from 69 percent in 1980. The proportion of Americans with a high school diploma did not top 50 percent until the late 1960s, then rose rapidly as the well-educated baby-boom generation entered adulthood.

Twenty-six percent of Americans have a college degree, including 28 percent of men and 24 percent of women. Fully 34 percent of men aged 50 to 54 have a college degree, making the age group the most educated. Among women, those aged 25 to 29 are most likely to have a college degree, at 30 percent.

Among families with children aged 18 to 24, 47 percent have a child in college full-time. The proportion of families with a child in college rises steadily with income, to 64 percent among families with incomes of $75,000 or more.

More than 1.2 million bachelor's degrees were awarded in 1999–2000, as well as 457,000 master's degrees and nearly 45,000 doctorates. The number of people earning first-professional degrees, 80,259, is far greater than the number earning doctorates. Nonresident aliens earned one in four doctorates awarded in the United States in 1999-00.

■ The educational attainment of Americans will continue to rise as well-educated younger adults replace less educated older people.

Big gains in educational attainment

(percent of people aged 25 or older who are high school or college graduates, 1980 and 2000)

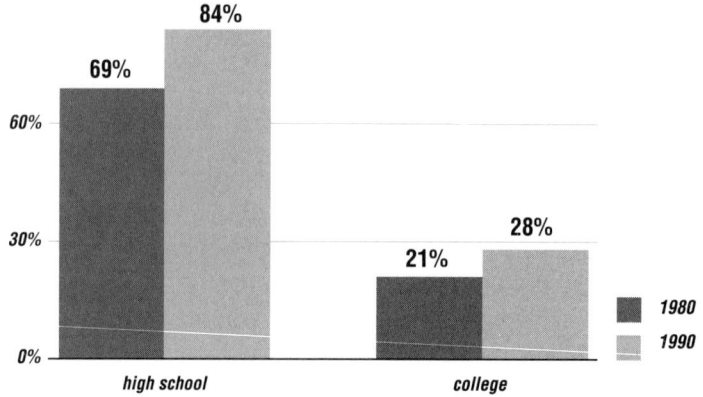

Educational Attainment of Total People by Sex, 2000

(number and percent distribution of total people aged 25 or older by educational attainment and sex, 2000; numbers in thousands)

	total		men		women	
	number	*percent*	*number*	*percent*	*number*	*percent*
Total people	**175,230**	**100.0%**	**83,611**	**100.0%**	**91,620**	**100.0%**
Not a high school graduate	27,854	15.9	13,216	15.8	14,639	16.0
High school graduate or more	147,376	84.1	70,396	84.2	76,982	84.0
High school graduate only	58,086	33.1	26,651	31.9	31,435	34.3
Some college or associate's degree	44,445	25.4	20,493	24.5	23,953	26.1
Bachelor's degree or more	44,845	25.6	23,252	27.8	21,594	23.6
Bachelor's degree only	29,840	17.0	14,909	17.8	14,931	16.3
Master's degree	10,396	5.9	5,166	6.2	5,230	5.7
Professional degree	2,586	1.5	1,752	2.1	834	0.9
Doctoral degree	2,023	1.2	1,425	1.7	599	0.7

Source: Bureau of the Census, Educational Attainment in the United States: March 2000 (Update), *detailed tables for Current Population Report P20-536, 2000; Internet site <www.census.gov/population/socdemo/education/p20-536/tab01.txt>; calculations by New Strategist*

Educational Attainment of Total Men by Age, 2000

(number and percent distribution of men aged 25 or older by age and educational attainment, 2000; numbers in thousands)

	total	not a high school graduate	total	high school graduate only	some college	associate's degree	high school graduate or more — total	bachelor's degree or more — total	bachelor's degree only	master's degree	professional degree	doctoral degree
Total men	83,611	13,216	70,396	26,651	14,540	5,953	23,252	14,909	14,909	5,166	1,752	1,425
Aged 25 to 29	8,942	1,186	7,756	2,831	1,770	657	2,498	2,079	2,079	287	96	36
Aged 30 to 34	9,621	1,199	8,421	3,158	1,713	730	2,820	2,055	2,055	514	145	106
Aged 35 to 39	11,032	1,306	9,726	3,861	1,978	872	3,015	2,018	2,018	654	185	158
Aged 40 to 44	11,103	1,316	9,789	3,785	1,956	992	3,056	1,959	1,959	707	204	186
Aged 45 to 49	9,654	1,030	8,624	3,002	1,832	828	2,962	1,802	1,802	754	237	169
Aged 50 to 54	8,235	960	7,276	2,197	1,584	674	2,821	1,657	1,657	741	230	193
Aged 55 to 59	6,105	913	5,191	1,982	1,015	369	1,825	965	965	495	195	170
Aged 60 to 64	5,032	1,083	3,948	1,609	745	311	1,283	694	694	359	136	94
Aged 65 or older	13,886	4,223	9,662	4,225	1,947	519	2,971	1,679	1,679	655	324	313
Aged 65 to 69	4,376	1,075	3,300	1,413	665	198	1,024	559	559	239	94	132
Aged 70 to 74	3,673	1,099	2,576	1,098	507	150	821	454	454	197	82	88
Aged 75 or older	5,837	2,049	3,787	1,714	775	171	1,127	667	667	219	147	94

(continued)

(continued from previous page)

	total	not a high school graduate	high school graduate or more				bachelor's degree or more				
			total	high school graduate only	some college	associate's degree	total	bachelor's degree only	master's degree	professional degree	doctoral degree
Total men	**100.0%**	**15.8%**	**84.2%**	**31.9%**	**17.4%**	**7.1%**	**27.8%**	**17.8%**	**6.2%**	**2.1%**	**1.7%**
Aged 25 to 29	100.0	13.3	86.7	31.7	19.8	7.3	27.9	23.2	3.2	1.1	0.4
Aged 30 to 34	100.0	12.5	87.5	32.8	17.8	7.6	29.3	21.4	5.3	1.5	1.1
Aged 35 to 39	100.0	11.8	88.2	35.0	17.9	7.9	27.3	18.3	5.9	1.7	1.4
Aged 40 to 44	100.0	11.9	88.2	34.1	17.6	8.9	27.5	17.6	6.4	1.8	1.7
Aged 45 to 49	100.0	10.7	89.3	31.1	19.0	8.6	30.7	18.7	7.8	2.5	1.8
Aged 50 to 54	100.0	11.7	88.4	26.7	19.2	8.2	34.3	20.1	9.0	2.8	2.3
Aged 55 to 59	100.0	15.0	85.0	32.5	16.6	6.0	29.9	15.8	8.1	3.2	2.8
Aged 60 to 64	100.0	21.5	78.5	32.0	14.8	6.2	25.5	13.8	7.1	2.7	1.9
Aged 65 or older	100.0	30.4	69.6	30.4	14.0	3.7	21.4	12.1	4.7	2.3	2.3
Aged 65 to 69	100.0	24.6	75.4	32.3	15.2	4.5	23.4	12.8	5.5	2.1	3.0
Aged 70 to 74	100.0	29.9	70.1	29.9	13.8	4.1	22.4	12.4	5.4	2.2	2.4
Aged 75 or older	100.0	35.1	64.9	29.4	13.3	2.9	19.3	11.4	3.8	2.5	1.6

Source: Bureau of the Census, Educational Attainment in the United States: March 2000 (Update), detailed tables for Current Population Report P20-536, 2000; Internet site <www.census.gov/population/socdemo/education/p20-536/tab01.txt>; calculations by New Strategist

Educational Attainment of Total Women by Age, 2000

(number and percent distribution of women aged 25 or older by age and educational attainment, 2000; numbers in thousands)

| | total | not a high school graduate | high school graduate or more | | | | | bachelor's degree or more | | | |
			total	high school graduate only	some college	associate's degree	total	bachelor's degree only	master's degree	professional degree	doctoral degree
Total women	**91,620**	**14,639**	**76,982**	**31,435**	**16,213**	**7,740**	**21,594**	**14,931**	**5,230**	**834**	**599**
Aged 25 to 29	9,326	988	8,339	2,604	1,992	932	2,811	2,234	449	89	39
Aged 30 to 34	9,896	1,099	8,799	2,953	1,901	1,006	2,939	2,194	529	149	67
Aged 35 to 39	11,288	1,270	10,019	3,661	2,119	1,144	3,095	2,226	666	134	69
Aged 40 to 44	11,382	1,207	10,176	3,805	2,179	1,246	2,946	2,040	680	116	110
Aged 45 to 49	10,094	1,047	9,048	3,151	1,862	1,022	3,013	1,984	841	98	90
Aged 50 to 54	8,647	1,021	7,627	3,018	1,574	759	2,276	1,400	695	95	86
Aged 55 to 59	6,763	1,142	5,622	2,566	1,210	448	1,398	791	492	54	61
Aged 60 to 64	5,487	1,143	4,343	2,201	842	313	987	608	320	32	27
Aged 65 or older	18,735	5,722	13,013	7,476	2,534	871	2,132	1,454	558	69	51
Aged 65 to 69	4,976	1,223	3,753	2,162	689	194	708	442	228	19	19
Aged 70 to 74	4,771	1,300	3,471	1,975	667	265	564	395	123	30	16
Aged 75 or older	8,988	3,199	5,788	3,339	1,178	412	859	617	207	20	15

(continued)

(continued from previous page)

	total	not a high school graduate	high school graduate or more				bachelor's degree or more				
			total	high school graduate only	some college	associate's degree	total	bachelor's degree only	master's degree	professional degree	doctoral degree
Total women	**100.0%**	**16.0%**	**84.0%**	**34.3%**	**17.7%**	**8.4%**	**23.6%**	**16.3%**	**5.7%**	**0.9%**	**0.7%**
Aged 25 to 29	100.0	10.6	89.4	27.9	21.4	10.0	30.1	24.0	4.8	1.0	0.4
Aged 30 to 34	100.0	11.1	88.9	29.8	19.2	10.2	29.7	22.2	5.3	1.5	0.7
Aged 35 to 39	100.0	11.3	88.8	32.4	18.8	10.1	27.4	19.7	5.9	1.2	0.6
Aged 40 to 44	100.0	10.6	89.4	33.4	19.1	10.9	25.9	17.9	6.0	1.0	1.0
Aged 45 to 49	100.0	10.4	89.6	31.2	18.4	10.1	29.8	19.7	8.3	1.0	0.9
Aged 50 to 54	100.0	11.8	88.2	34.9	18.2	8.8	26.3	16.2	8.0	1.1	1.0
Aged 55 to 59	100.0	16.9	83.1	37.9	17.9	6.6	20.7	11.7	7.3	0.8	0.9
Aged 60 to 64	100.0	20.8	79.2	40.1	15.3	5.7	18.0	11.1	5.8	0.6	0.5
Aged 65 or older	100.0	30.5	69.5	39.9	13.5	4.6	11.4	7.8	3.0	0.4	0.3
Aged 65 to 69	100.0	24.6	75.4	43.4	13.8	3.9	14.2	8.9	4.6	0.4	0.4
Aged 70 to 74	100.0	27.2	72.8	41.4	14.0	5.6	11.8	8.3	2.6	0.6	0.3
Aged 75 or older	100.0	35.6	64.4	37.1	13.1	4.6	9.6	6.9	2.3	0.2	0.2

Source: Bureau of the Census, Educational Attainment in the United States: March 2000 (Update), detailed tables for Current Population Report P20-536, 2000; Internet site <www.census.gov/population/socdemo/education/p20-536/tab01.txt>; calculations by New Strategist

Total High School and College Graduates by Age and Sex, 2000

(percent of people aged 25 or older who are high school or college graduates by age and sex, 2000)

	total	men	women
High school graduates			
Total people	**84.1%**	**84.2%**	**84.0%**
Aged 25 to 29	88.1	86.7	89.4
Aged 30 to 34	88.2	87.5	88.9
Aged 35 to 39	88.5	88.2	88.8
Aged 40 to 44	88.8	88.2	89.4
Aged 45 to 49	89.5	89.3	89.6
Aged 50 to 54	88.3	88.4	88.2
Aged 55 to 59	84.0	85.0	83.1
Aged 60 to 64	78.8	78.5	79.2
Aged 65 or older	69.5	69.6	69.5
Aged 65 to 69	75.4	75.4	75.4
Aged 70 to 74	71.6	70.1	72.8
Aged 75 or older	64.6	64.9	64.4
College graduates			
Total people	**25.6**	**27.8**	**23.6**
Aged 25 to 29	29.1	27.9	30.1
Aged 30 to 34	29.5	29.3	29.7
Aged 35 to 39	27.4	27.3	27.4
Aged 40 to 44	26.7	27.5	25.9
Aged 45 to 49	30.3	30.7	29.8
Aged 50 to 54	30.2	34.2	26.3
Aged 55 to 59	25.0	29.9	20.7
Aged 60 to 64	21.6	25.5	18.0
Aged 65 or older	15.6	21.4	11.4
Aged 65 to 69	18.5	23.4	14.2
Aged 70 to 74	16.4	22.3	11.8
Aged 75 or older	13.4	19.3	9.6

Source: Bureau of the Census, Educational Attainment in the United States: March 2000 (Update), *detailed tables for Current Population Report P20-536, 2000; Internet site <www.census.gov/population/socdemo/education/p20-536/tab01a.txt>*

Total High School and College Graduates by Age and Region, 2000

(percent of people aged 25 or older who are high school or college graduates, by age and region, 2000)

	Northeast	Midwest	South	West
High school graduates				
Total people	**85.0%**	**86.9%**	**81.7%**	**84.3%**
Aged 25 to 34	90.2	91.4	88.0	83.8
Aged 35 to 44	91.3	90.7	87.3	86.1
Aged 45 to 54	90.1	92.8	86.1	88.3
Aged 55 to 64	82.8	86.1	76.5	85.0
Aged 65 or older	68.1	69.9	66.3	76.6
College graduates				
Total people	**28.4**	**24.8**	**23.6**	**27.2**
Aged 25 to 34	35.1	30.6	26.7	27.5
Aged 35 to 44	29.4	26.1	25.3	28.6
Aged 45 to 54	33.5	28.7	28.1	32.3
Aged 55 to 64	27.7	22.7	19.8	26.8
Aged 65 or older	15.8	13.2	15.7	18.3

Source: Bureau of the Census, Educational Attainment in the United States: March 2000 (Update), *Detailed tables for Current Population Report P20-536, 2000; Internet site <www.census.gov/population/socdemo/ education/p20-536/tab12.txt>; calculations by New Strategist*

Total High School and College Graduates by State, 2000

(percent of people aged 25 or older who are high school or college graduates, for the 25 largest states, 2000)

	high school graduate or more	college graduate
Total people	**84.1%**	**25.6%**
Alabama	77.5	20.4
Arizona	85.1	24.6
California	81.2	27.5
Colorado	89.7	34.6
Florida	84.0	22.8
Georgia	82.6	23.1
Illinois	85.5	27.1
Indiana	84.6	17.1
Kentucky	78.7	20.5
Louisiana	80.8	22.5
Maryland	85.7	32.3
Massachusetts	85.1	32.7
Michigan	86.2	23.0
Minnesota	90.8	31.2
Missouri	86.6	26.2
New Jersey	87.3	30.1
New York	82.5	28.7
North Carolina	79.2	23.2
Ohio	87.0	24.6
Pennsylvania	85.7	24.3
Tennessee	79.9	22.0
Texas	79.2	23.9
Virginia	86.6	31.9
Washington	91.8	28.6
Wisconsin	86.7	23.8

Source: Bureau of the Census, Educational Attainment in the United States: March 2000 (Update), *Detailed tables for Current Population Report P20-536, 2000; Internet site <www.census.gov/population/socdemo/education/p20-536/tab14.txt>*

Total School Enrollment by Age and Sex, 2000

(number and percent of people aged 3 or older enrolled in school, by age and sex, October 2000; numbers in thousands)

	total		men		women	
	number	*percent*	*number*	*percent*	*number*	*percent*
Total people	**72,214**	**27.5%**	**35,838**	**28.0%**	**36,376**	**26.9%**
Aged 3 to 4	4,097	52.1	2,035	50.8	2,062	53.4
Aged 5 to 6	7,648	95.6	3,903	95.1	3,745	96.1
Aged 7 to 9	12,083	98.1	6,177	98.0	5,906	98.2
Aged 10 to 13	16,213	98.3	8,308	98.3	7,905	98.3
Aged 14 to 15	7,885	98.7	4,050	98.7	3,836	98.6
Aged 16 to 17	7,341	92.8	3,767	92.7	3,575	92.9
Aged 18 to 19	4,926	61.2	2,353	58.3	2,573	64.2
Aged 20 to 21	3,314	44.1	1,548	41.0	1,766	47.3
Aged 22 to 24	2,731	24.6	1,320	23.9	1,411	25.3
Aged 25 to 29	2,030	11.4	860	10.0	1,170	12.7
Aged 30 to 34	1,292	6.7	536	5.6	757	7.7
Aged 35 to 44	1,632	3.7	651	3.0	980	4.3
Aged 45 to 54	810	2.2	250	1.4	560	2.9
Aged 55 or older	211	0.4	80	0.3	131	0.4

Source: Bureau of the Census, Current Population Reports, Internet site <www.census.gov/population/ socdemo/school/ppl-148/tab01.txt>

School Enrollment by Age, Race, and Hispanic Origin, 2000

(number and percent distribution of people aged 3 or older enrolled in school, by age, race, and Hispanic origin, October 2000; numbers in thousands)

	total	Asian	black	Hispanic	white total	white non-Hispanic
Total people	**72,214**	**3,442**	**11,503**	**10,163**	**56,344**	**46,660**
Aged 3 to 4	4,097	224	725	518	3,091	2,607
Aged 5 to 6	7,648	366	1,219	1,390	5,959	4,639
Aged 7 to 9	12,083	484	1,975	1,936	9,441	7,576
Aged 10 to 13	16,213	638	2,700	2,437	12,620	10,305
Aged 14 to 15	7,885	335	1,260	1,093	6,176	5,135
Aged 16 to 17	7,341	292	1,106	959	5,845	4,933
Aged 18 to 19	4,926	257	716	617	3,924	3,337
Aged 20 to 21	3,314	206	416	311	2,688	2,388
Aged 22 to 24	2,731	229	393	309	2,101	1,809
Aged 25 to 29	2,030	188	353	198	1,473	1,286
Aged 30 to 34	1,292	86	252	160	939	785
Aged 35 to 44	1,632	98	249	173	1,256	1,092
Aged 45 to 54	810	29	97	48	670	622
Aged 55 or older	211	8	41	14	161	147

Percent distribution by race and Hispanic origin

	total	Asian	black	Hispanic	white total	white non-Hispanic
Total people	**100.0%**	**4.8%**	**15.9%**	**14.1%**	**78.0%**	**64.6%**
Aged 3 to 4	100.0	5.5	17.7	12.6	75.4	63.6
Aged 5 to 6	100.0	4.8	15.9	18.2	77.9	60.7
Aged 7 to 9	100.0	4.0	16.3	16.0	78.1	62.7
Aged 10 to 13	100.0	3.9	16.7	15.0	77.8	63.6
Aged 14 to 15	100.0	4.2	16.0	13.9	78.3	65.1
Aged 16 to 17	100.0	4.0	15.1	13.1	79.6	67.2
Aged 18 to 19	100.0	5.2	14.5	12.5	79.7	67.7
Aged 20 to 21	100.0	6.2	12.6	9.4	81.1	72.1
Aged 22 to 24	100.0	8.4	14.4	11.3	76.9	66.2
Aged 25 to 29	100.0	9.3	17.4	9.8	72.6	63.3
Aged 30 to 34	100.0	6.7	19.5	12.4	72.7	60.8
Aged 35 to 44	100.0	6.0	15.3	10.6	77.0	66.9
Aged 45 to 54	100.0	3.6	12.0	5.9	82.7	76.8
Aged 55 or older	100.0	3.8	19.4	6.6	76.3	69.7

Note: Numbers will not add to total because Hispanics may be of any race.
Source: Bureau of the Census, Current Population Reports, Internet site <www.census.gov/population/socdemo/school/ppl-148/tab01.txt>; calculations by New Strategist

Total Families with Children in College, 2000

(number of families, number with children aged 18 to 24, and number and percent with children aged 18 to 24 attending college full-time as of October 2000, by household income in 1999; numbers in thousands)

	total	with children aged 18–24	with one or more children attending college full-time		
			number	percent of total families	percent of families with children 18–24
Total families	**73,075**	**10,684**	**5,048**	**6.9%**	**47.2%**
Under $20,000	10,971	1,498	344	3.1	23.0
$20,000 to $29,999	8,536	1,069	414	4.9	38.7
$30,000 to $39,999	8,093	1,044	426	5.3	40.8
$40,000 to $49,999	6,252	856	398	6.4	46.5
$50,000 to $74,999	12,679	1,923	1,062	8.4	55.2
$75,000 or more	14,970	2,748	1,758	11.7	64.0

Note: Numbers will not add to total because "not reported" is not shown.
Source: Bureau of the Census, Current Population Reports, Internet site <www.census.gov/population/socdemo/school/ppl-148/tab15.txt>

College Enrollment of Total People by Age, 2000

(number and percent distribution of people aged 15 or older enrolled in college by age and type of school, October 2000; numbers in thousands)

	total	undergraduate total	two-year	four-year	graduate
Total people enrolled	**15,313**	**12,401**	**3,882**	**8,519**	**2,912**
Aged 15 to 17	149	144	63	81	5
Aged 18 to 19	3,599	3,566	1,169	2,397	33
Aged 20 to 21	3,171	3,094	711	2,383	77
Aged 22 to 24	2,683	2,113	526	1,587	570
Aged 25 to 29	1,963	1,246	416	830	717
Aged 30 to 34	1,244	742	257	485	502
Aged 35 to 39	877	583	291	292	294
Aged 40 to 44	685	430	198	232	255
Aged 45 to 49	476	272	140	132	204
Aged 50 to 54	289	124	68	56	165
Aged 55 or older	174	85	42	43	89
Percent distribution by age					
Total people enrolled	**100.0%**	**100.0%**	**100.0%**	**100.0%**	**100.0%**
Aged 15 to 17	1.0	1.2	1.6	1.0	0.2
Aged 18 to 19	23.5	28.8	30.1	28.1	1.1
Aged 20 to 21	20.7	24.9	18.3	28.0	2.6
Aged 22 to 24	17.5	17.0	13.5	18.6	19.6
Aged 25 to 29	12.8	10.0	10.7	9.7	24.6
Aged 30 to 34	8.1	6.0	6.6	5.7	17.2
Aged 35 to 39	5.7	4.7	7.5	3.4	10.1
Aged 40 to 44	4.5	3.5	5.1	2.7	8.8
Aged 45 to 49	3.1	2.2	3.6	1.5	7.0
Aged 50 to 54	1.9	1.0	1.8	0.7	5.7
Aged 55 or older	1.1	0.7	1.1	0.5	3.1

(continued)

(continued from previous page)

| Percent distribution by type of school | total | undergraduate | | | graduate |
		total	two-year	four-year	
Total people enrolled	**100.0%**	**81.0%**	**25.4%**	**55.6%**	**19.0%**
Aged 15 to 17	100.0	96.6	42.3	54.4	3.4
Aged 18 to 19	100.0	99.1	32.5	66.6	0.9
Aged 20 to 21	100.0	97.6	22.4	75.1	2.4
Aged 22 to 24	100.0	78.8	19.6	59.2	21.2
Aged 25 to 29	100.0	63.5	21.2	42.3	36.5
Aged 30 to 34	100.0	59.6	20.7	39.0	40.4
Aged 35 to 39	100.0	66.5	33.2	33.3	33.5
Aged 40 to 44	100.0	62.8	28.9	33.9	37.2
Aged 45 to 49	100.0	57.1	29.4	27.7	42.9
Aged 50 to 54	100.0	42.9	23.5	19.4	57.1
Aged 55 or older	100.0	48.9	24.1	24.7	51.1

Source: Bureau of the Census, Current Population Reports, Internet site <www.census.gov/population/ socdemo/school/ppl-148/tab09.txt>; calculations by New Strategist

College Enrollment by Age, Race, and Hispanic Origin, 2000

(number and percent distribution of people aged 15 or older enrolled in college by age, race, and Hispanic origin, October 2000; numbers in thousands)

	total	Asian	black	Hispanic	white total	white non-Hispanic
Total people enrolled	**15,313**	**1,048**	**2,165**	**1,426**	**12,002**	**10,637**
Aged 15 to 17	149	12	19	24	117	91
Aged 18 to 19	3,599	212	455	348	2,915	2,580
Aged 20 to 21	3,171	201	375	268	2,590	2,333
Aged 22 to 24	2,683	227	386	281	2,063	1,794
Aged 25 to 29	1,963	188	325	167	1,432	1,275
Aged 30 to 34	1,244	81	242	141	908	770
Aged 35 to 39	877	54	134	99	677	585
Aged 40 to 44	685	43	109	48	521	473
Aged 45 to 49	476	11	58	21	399	378
Aged 50 to 54	289	14	33	21	241	220
Aged 55 or older	117	8	27	2	89	87

Percent distribution by race and Hispanic origin

	total	Asian	black	Hispanic	white total	white non-Hispanic
Total people enrolled	**100.0%**	**6.8%**	**14.1%**	**9.3%**	**78.4%**	**69.5%**
Aged 15 to 17	100.0	8.1	12.8	16.1	78.5	61.1
Aged 18 to 19	100.0	5.9	12.6	9.7	81.0	71.7
Aged 20 to 21	100.0	6.3	11.8	8.5	81.7	73.6
Aged 22 to 24	100.0	8.5	14.4	10.5	76.9	66.9
Aged 25 to 29	100.0	9.6	16.6	8.5	72.9	65.0
Aged 30 to 34	100.0	6.5	19.5	11.3	73.0	61.9
Aged 35 to 39	100.0	6.2	15.3	11.3	77.2	66.7
Aged 40 to 44	100.0	6.3	15.9	7.0	76.1	69.1
Aged 45 to 49	100.0	2.3	12.2	4.4	83.8	79.4
Aged 50 to 54	100.0	4.8	11.4	7.3	83.4	76.1
Aged 55 or older	100.0	6.8	23.1	1.7	76.1	74.4

Note: Numbers will not add to total because Hispanics may be of any race.
Source: Bureau of the Census, Current Population Reports, Internet site <www.census.gov/population/socdemo/school/ppl-148/tab09.txt>; calculations by New Strategist

As Asian, Black, and Hispanic Populations Grow, a Smaller Share of Newborns Are Non-Hispanic White

More than 4 million babies were born to American women in 2000, most born to women in their twenties. One-third of births are to unmarried women. Only 58 percent of newborns in 2000 were non-Hispanic white, while 20 percent were Hispanic and 15 percent were black.

Sixty-four percent of Americans have employment-based health insurance, while 14 percent are without health insurance coverage. Overall, Americans visit a doctor an average of 2.8 times a year, with those aged 75 or older seeing a doctor nearly 7 times a year.

Heart disease and cancer are the leading causes of death among Americans, accounting for 53 percent of all deaths in 1999. At birth, the average American male can expect to live 74.1 years, while the average female can expect to live 79.5 years. At age 65, people have an average of 17.9 more years of life.

■ Because of the aging of the population, the proportion of Americans with disabilities is certain to rise.

Many newborns are black or Hispanic

(percent distribution of births by race and Hispanic origin of mother, 2000)

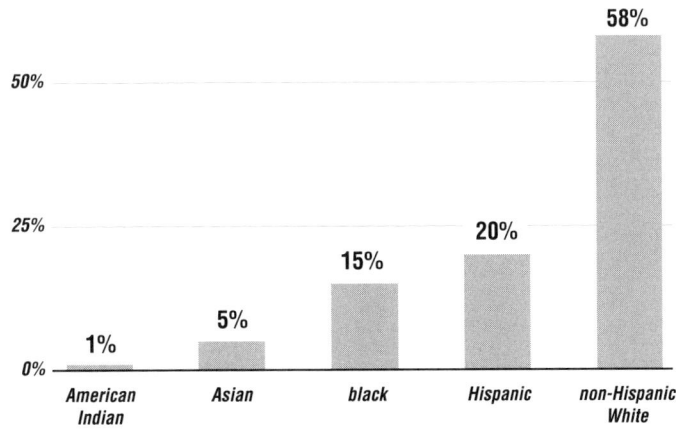

Births to Total Women by Age, 2000

(number and percent distribution of births to total women, by age, 2000)

	number	percent distribution
Total births	**4,058,814**	**100.0%**
Under age 15	8,519	0.2
Aged 15 to 19	468,990	11.6
Aged 20 to 24	1,017,806	25.1
Aged 25 to 29	1,087,547	26.8
Aged 30 to 34	929,278	22.9
Aged 35 to 39	452,057	11.1
Aged 40 to 44	90,013	2.2
Aged 45 or older	4,604	0.1

Source: National Center for Health Statistics, Births: Final Data for 2000, *National Vital Statistics Report, Vol. 50, No. 5, 2002; calculations by New Strategist*

Births to Women by Age, Race, and Hispanic Origin, 2000

(number and percent distribution of births to women by age, race, and Hispanic origin, 2000)

	total	American Indian	Asian	black	Hispanic	white total	white non-Hispanic
Total births	**4,058,814**	**41,668**	**200,543**	**622,598**	**815,868**	**3,194,005**	**2,362,968**
Under age 15	8,519	160	112	3,808	2,638	4,439	1,840
Aged 15 to 19	468,990	8,055	8,968	118,954	129,469	333,013	204,056
Aged 20 to 24	1,017,806	13,633	28,766	202,596	247,552	772,811	523,971
Aged 25 to 29	1,087,547	10,053	61,346	141,968	218,167	874,180	651,445
Aged 30 to 34	929,278	6,097	63,665	94,808	141,493	764,708	617,371
Aged 35 to 39	452,057	2,983	31,068	49,295	62,993	368,711	302,576
Aged 40 to 44	90,013	658	6,242	10,699	12,987	72,414	58,631
Aged 45 or older	4,604	29	376	470	569	3,729	3,078

Percent distribution by race and Hispanic origin

	total	American Indian	Asian	black	Hispanic	white total	white non-Hispanic
Total births	**100.0%**	**1.0%**	**4.9%**	**15.3%**	**20.1%**	**78.7%**	**58.2%**
Under age 15	100.0	1.9	1.3	44.7	31.0	52.1	21.6
Aged 15 to 19	100.0	1.7	1.9	25.4	27.6	71.0	43.5
Aged 20 to 24	100.0	1.3	2.8	19.9	24.3	75.9	51.5
Aged 25 to 29	100.0	0.9	5.6	13.1	20.1	80.4	59.9
Aged 30 to 34	100.0	0.7	6.9	10.2	15.2	82.3	66.4
Aged 35 to 39	100.0	0.7	6.9	10.9	13.9	81.6	66.9
Aged 40 to 44	100.0	0.7	6.9	11.9	14.4	80.4	65.1
Aged 45 or older	100.0	0.6	8.2	10.2	12.4	81.0	66.9

Note: Numbers will not add to total because Hispanics may be of any race. American Indians include Aleuts and Eskimos; Asians include Pacific Islanders.
Source: National Center for Health Statistics, Births: Final Data for 2000, *National Vital Statistics Report, Vol. 50, No. 5, 2002; calculations by New Strategist*

Births to Total Women by Birth Order, 2000

(number and percent distribution of births to total women, by birth order, 2000)

	number	percent distribution
Total births	**4,058,814**	**100.0%**
First child	1,622,404	40.0
Second child	1,312,687	32.3
Third child	676,597	16.7
Fourth or later child	429,555	10.6

Note: Numbers will not add to total because not stated is not shown.
Source: National Center for Health Statistics, Births: Final Data for 2000, *National Vital Statistics Report, Vol. 50, No. 5, 2002; calculations by New Strategist*

Births to Total Unmarried Women by Age, 2000

(number of total births, and number and percent to unmarried women, by age, 2000)

	total	unmarried women	
		number	percent
Total births	**4,058,814**	**1,347,043**	**33.2%**
Under age 15	8,519	8,219	96.5
Aged 15 to 19	468,990	369,456	78.8
Aged 20 to 24	1,017,806	503,602	49.5
Aged 25 to 29	1,087,547	255,092	23.5
Aged 30 to 34	929,278	130,213	14.0
Aged 35 to 39	452,057	64,523	14.3
Aged 40 or older	94,617	15,938	16.8

Source: National Center for Health Statistics, Births: Final Data for 2000, *National Vital Statistics Report, Vol. 50, No. 5, 2002*

Births to Women by State, Race, and Hispanic Origin, 2000

(total number of births and percent distribution by race and Hispanic origin of mother, by state, 2000)

	total number	percent	American Indian	Asian	black	white total	white non-Hispanic	Hispanic
Total births	**4,058,814**	**100.0%**	**1.0%**	**4.9%**	**15.3%**	**78.7%**	**58.2%**	**20.1%**
Alabama	63,299	100.0	0.3	0.9	32.4	66.4	63.4	3.0
Alaska	9,974	100.0	25.2	6.4	4.6	63.8	57.9	6.0
Arizona	85,273	100.0	6.7	2.4	3.3	87.7	46.8	40.7
Arkansas	37,783	100.0	0.6	1.3	21.1	76.9	70.6	6.2
California	531,959	100.0	0.6	12.1	6.6	80.8	32.2	48.5
Colorado	65,438	100.0	1.0	3.2	4.6	91.2	63.9	27.9
Connecticut	43,026	100.0	0.3	4.2	12.3	83.2	66.9	15.0
Delaware	11,051	100.0	0.4	3.3	23.8	72.5	63.3	9.2
District of Columbia	7,666	100.0	0.1	2.3	67.3	30.3	19.1	11.4
Florida	204,125	100.0	0.6	2.5	23.2	73.8	52.0	22.5
Georgia	132,644	100.0	0.2	2.7	33.3	63.8	53.2	10.1
Hawaii	17,551	100.0	1.1	73.3	2.7	22.9	18.7	13.1
Idaho	20,366	100.0	1.4	1.5	0.4	96.8	83.6	12.8
Illinois	185,036	100.0	0.1	4.4	18.5	77.0	55.8	21.2
Indiana	87,699	100.0	0.2	1.4	10.9	87.6	81.2	6.2
Iowa	38,266	100.0	0.6	2.4	3.2	93.8	87.8	5.6
Kansas	39,666	100.0	1.1	2.7	7.2	89.0	76.1	12.0
Kentucky	56,029	100.0	0.1	1.1	9.2	89.6	87.7	1.9
Louisiana	67,898	100.0	0.6	1.5	41.8	56.2	53.9	2.3
Maine	13,603	100.0	0.9	1.4	0.8	96.9	95.7	1.0
Maryland	74,316	100.0	0.3	4.9	33.5	61.3	55.2	6.5
Massachusetts	81,614	100.0	0.2	5.9	9.9	84.0	74.0	11.4
Michigan	136,171	100.0	0.5	2.8	17.9	78.8	68.0	5.1
Minnesota	67,604	100.0	1.8	5.2	6.6	86.4	77.1	5.8
Mississippi	44,075	100.0	0.6	0.9	45.1	53.4	51.9	1.4
Missouri	76,463	100.0	0.4	1.9	15.0	82.6	79.1	3.5
Montana	10,957	100.0	12.1	1.0	0.4	86.4	80.6	3.0
Nebraska	24,646	100.0	1.7	2.3	5.6	90.3	77.9	10.5
Nevada	30,829	100.0	1.4	6.5	7.7	84.4	51.0	33.1
New Hampshire	14,609	100.0	0.2	2.3	1.2	96.3	89.9	2.6
New Jersey	115,632	100.0	0.2	8.2	18.3	73.4	55.4	19.4

(continued)

(continued from previous page)

	total number	percent	American Indian	Asian	black	white total	non-Hispanic	Hispanic
New Mexico	27,223	100.0%	12.6%	1.5%	1.8%	84.1%	33.3%	51.2%
New York	258,737	100.0	0.3	7.5	21.2	71.0	48.5	20.8
North Carolina	120,311	100.0	1.4	2.3	24.4	71.8	61.5	10.4
North Dakota	7,676	100.0	10.3	1.3	1.1	87.4	83.3	1.7
Ohio	155,472	100.0	0.2	1.9	15.3	82.7	80.0	2.7
Oklahoma	49,782	100.0	10.5	2.0	9.6	77.9	68.5	8.8
Oregon	45,804	100.0	1.6	5.1	2.2	91.1	74.9	16.2
Pennsylvania	146,281	100.0	0.3	2.7	14.1	82.9	77.6	5.2
Rhode Island	12,505	100.0	1.2	3.5	9.0	86.3	62.6	16.8
South Carolina	56,114	100.0	0.3	1.5	35.2	63.0	59.1	4.0
South Dakota	10,345	100.0	16.3	1.3	1.0	81.4	79.5	2.2
Tennessee	79,611	100.0	0.2	1.7	21.2	76.9	72.9	4.0
Texas	363,414	100.0	0.2	3.2	11.4	85.2	39.1	45.9
Utah	47,353	100.0	1.5	3.0	0.7	94.8	82.0	12.5
Vermont	6,500	100.0	0.3	1.3	0.5	98.0	95.0	0.5
Virginia	98,938	100.0	0.1	5.2	22.8	72.0	64.2	7.8
Washington	81,036	100.0	2.4	8.5	4.3	84.7	68.8	14.0
West Virginia	20,865	100.0	0.1	0.5	3.7	95.7	95.2	0.2
Wisconsin	69,326	100.0	1.4	3.0	9.4	86.2	79.9	6.5
Wyoming	6,253	100.0	4.3	0.9	0.9	93.9	84.9	9.1

Note: Numbers will not add to total because Hispanics may be of any race. American Indians include Aleuts and Eskimos; Asians include Pacific Islanders
Source: National Center for Health Statistics, Births: Final Data for 2000, National Vital Statistics Report, Vol. 50, No. 5, 2002; calculations by New Strategist

Health Insurance Coverage of Total People by Age, 2000

(number and percent distribution of total people by age and health insurance coverage status, 2000; numbers in thousands)

		covered by private or government health insurance							
		private health insurance			government health insurance				
	total	total	total	employ-ment based	total	Medicaid	Medicare	Military	not covered
Total people	**276,540**	**237,857**	**200,249**	**177,286**	**66,935**	**28,613**	**37,028**	**8,334**	**38,683**
Under 18	72,553	64,148	51,193	48,082	16,916	14,739	517	2,133	8,405
Aged 18–24	26,965	19,615	17,472	14,404	3,198	2,344	161	777	7,350
Aged 25–34	37,440	29,514	27,009	25,497	3,367	2,355	424	822	7,926
Aged 35–44	44,780	37,842	35,212	33,254	3,885	2,399	815	1,167	6,938
Aged 45–54	38,040	33,469	31,050	29,009	3,775	1,869	1,319	1,142	4,571
Aged 55–64	23,784	20,536	18,022	15,881	3,947	1,615	2,058	898	3,248
Aged 65+	32,978	32,733	20,292	11,160	31,847	3,293	31,733	1,395	245
Total people	**100.0%**	**86.0%**	**72.4%**	**64.1%**	**24.2%**	**10.3%**	**13.4%**	**3.0%**	**14.0%**
Under 18	100.0	88.4	70.6	66.3	23.3	20.3	0.7	2.9	11.6
Aged 18–24	100.0	72.7	64.8	53.4	11.9	8.7	0.6	2.9	27.3
Aged 25–34	100.0	78.8	72.1	68.1	9.0	6.3	1.1	2.2	21.2
Aged 35–44	100.0	84.5	78.6	74.3	8.7	5.4	1.8	2.6	15.5
Aged 45–54	100.0	88.0	81.6	76.3	9.9	4.9	3.5	3.0	12.0
Aged 55–64	100.0	86.3	75.8	66.8	16.6	6.8	8.7	3.8	13.7
Aged 65+	100.0	99.3	61.5	33.8	96.6	10.0	96.2	4.2	0.7

Note: Numbers will not add to total because some people have more than one type of health insurance.
Source: Bureau of the Census, Current Population Reports, Internet site <http://ferret.bls.census.gov/macro/032001/health/h01_001.htm>

Physician Office Visits by Total People, 1999

(total number and percent distribution of physician office visits and number of visits per person per year, by age, 1999)

	number of visits (in 000s)	percent distribution	per person per year
Total visits	**756,734**	**100.0%**	**2.8**
Under age 15	116,904	15.4	1.9
Aged 15 to 24	59,706	7.9	1.6
Aged 25 to 44	186,022	24.6	2.3
Aged 45 to 64	201,911	26.7	3.4
Aged 65 to 74	92,642	12.2	5.2
Aged 75 or older	99,548	13.2	6.8

Source: National Center for Health Statistics, National Ambulatory Medical Care Survey: 1999 Summary, *Advance Data, No. 322, 2001; calculations by New Strategist*

Total People with Disabilities by Age, 1997

(total number of people and number and percent with disabilities, by age and severity of disability, 1997; numbers in thousands)

| | | with a disability | | | | | |
| | | total | | severe | | needs assistance | |
	total	number	percent	number	percent	number	percent
Total people	**267,665**	**52,596**	**19.7%**	**32,970**	**12.3%**	**10,076**	**3.8%**
Under age 15	59,606	4,661	7.8	2,256	3.8	224	0.4
Aged 15 to 24	36,897	3,961	10.7	1,942	5.3	372	1.0
Aged 25 to 44	83,887	11,200	13.4	6,793	8.1	1,635	1.9
Aged 45 to 54	33,620	7,585	22.6	4,674	13.9	1,225	3.6
Aged 55 to 64	21,591	7,708	35.7	5,233	24.2	1,280	5.9
Aged 65 or older	32,064	17,480	54.5	12,073	37.7	5,339	16.7
Total females	**136,680**	**28,265**	**20.7**	**18,216**	**13.3**	**5,927**	**4.3**
Under age 15	29,112	1,646	5.7	754	2.6	95	0.3
Aged 15 to 24	18,235	1,795	9.8	935	5.1	156	0.9
Aged 25 to 44	42,316	5,797	13.7	3,470	8.2	789	1.9
Aged 45 to 54	17,202	4,158	24.2	2,536	14.7	690	4.0
Aged 55 to 64	11,250	4,190	37.2	2,869	25.5	695	6.2
Aged 65 or older	18,565	10,679	57.5	7,652	41.2	3,502	18.9
Total males	**130,985**	**24,331**	**18.6**	**14,754**	**11.3**	**4,149**	**3.2**
Under age 15	30,494	3,015	9.9	1,502	4.9	130	0.4
Aged 15 to 24	18,663	2,166	11.6	1,007	5.4	216	1.2
Aged 25 to 44	41,571	5,403	13.0	3,323	8.0	846	2.0
Aged 45 to 54	16,418	3,427	20.9	2,138	13.0	535	3.3
Aged 55 to 64	10,342	3,518	34.0	2,364	22.9	584	5.7
Aged 65 or older	13,498	6,801	50.4	4,421	32.8	1,838	13.6

Note: For the definition of disability, see the glossary.
Source: Bureau of the Census, Americans with Disabilities: 1997, *detailed tables from Current Population Reports P70-73, 2001*

Total People with Disabilities by Employment Status and Earnings, 1997

(number of total people aged 21 to 64, number and percent employed, median earnings, and index of earnings to total, by disability status, 1997)

| | total (in 000s) | employed | | | index of earnings by disability status to total earnings |
		number (in 000s)	percent	median earnings	
Total people	**152,886**	**119,616**	**78.2%**	**$22,941**	**100**
Not disabled	**125,165**	**105,694**	**84.4**	**23,645**	**103**
Disabled	**27,721**	**13,922**	**50.2**	**17,667**	**77**
Not severely	10,403	8,529	82.0	20,469	89
Severely	17,318	5,393	31.1	13,234	58

Note: For the definition of disability, see the glossary.
Source: Bureau of the Census, Americans with Disabilities: 1997, *detailed tables from Current Population Reports P70-73, 2001; calculations by New Strategist*

Leading Causes of Death among Total People, 1999

(total number of deaths, and number and percent of deaths accounted for by the ten leading causes of death, 1999)

		number	percent
Total deaths		**2,391,399**	**100.0%**
1.	Diseases of heart	725,192	30.3
2.	Malignant neoplasms	549,838	23.0
3.	Cerebrovascular diseases	167,366	7.0
4.	Chronic lower respiratory diseases	124,181	5.2
5.	Accidents	97,860	4.1
6.	Diabetes mellitus	68,399	2.9
7.	Pneumonia and influenza	63,730	2.7
8.	Alzheimer's disease	44,536	1.9
9.	Nephritis, nephrotic syndrom, nephrosis	35,525	1.5
10.	Septicemia	30,680	1.3
	All other causes	484,092	20.2

Source: National Center for Health Statistics, Deaths: Final Data for 1999, *National Vital Statistics Reports, Vol. 49, No. 8, 2001; calculations by New Strategist*

Life Expectancy of Total People at Birth and Age 65 by Sex, 1990 and 2000

(number of years of life remaining at birth and age 65, by sex, 1990 to 2000; change in years, 1990–2000)

	total	female	male
Birth			
2000	76.9	79.5	74.1
1990	75.4	78.8	71.8
Change, 1990–2000	1.5	0.7	2.3
Age 65			
2000	17.9	19.2	16.3
1990	17.2	18.9	15.1
Change, 1990–2000	0.7	0.3	1.2

Source: National Center for Health Statistics, Health, United States, 2001*; and* Deaths: Preliminary Data for 2000, *National Vital Statistics Report, Vol. 49, No. 12, 2001; calculations by New Strategist*

Homeownership Is at a Record High in the U.S.

Homeownership stood at a record high in 1999, when 67 percent of American households owned their home. Homeownership is greatest in the Midwest, at 72 percent. It is lowest in the West, where just 61 percent of householders are homeowners.

Among married couples, 82 percent are homeowners. The homeownership rate peaks at 93 percent for couples aged 65 to 74. The 58 percent majority of male-headed families own their home, but only 47 percent of female-headed families are homeowners.

Sixty-three percent of all occupied housing units in the U.S. are single-family detached structures. Most American homes have five or more rooms, and the 58 percent majority have more than one bathroom. Most homes have dishwashers; washing machines; clothes dryers; a porch, deck, balcony, or patio; a telephone; and a garage or carport. Most also have central air conditioning. More than 90 percent of householders own a car or truck.

Sixty-eight percent of householders rate their home at least an eight on a scale of one to ten. This includes 75 percent of homeowners and 54 percent of renters. Fourteen percent of householders think crime is a problem in their area, including 11 percent of homeowners and 20 percent of renters. But only 2 percent of owners and 6 percent of renters are so bothered by crime that they want to move. Homeowners paid a median of $61,244 for their home, which is currently valued at a median of $108,300.

Sixteen percent of Americans moved between March 1999 and March 2000. Mobility rates are highest for those aged 20 to 24, more than one-third of whom moved during those 12 months.

■ Homeownership will continue to increase as boomers age into their fifties and sixties.

Homeownership is highest in the Midwest

(percent of households that own their home, by region, 1999)

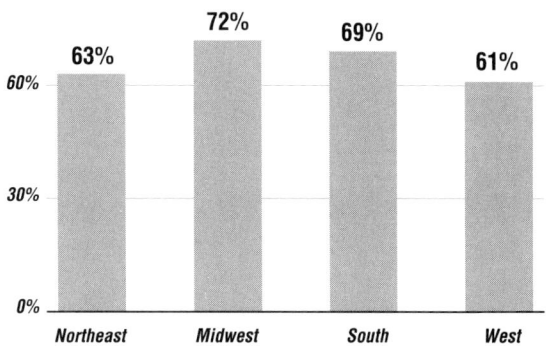

Region of Residence and Metropolitan Status of Total Housing Units, 1999

(number, percent distribution, and percent of total occupied housing units by regional, metropolitan, and homeownership status, 1999; numbers in thousands)

	total		owner			renter		
	number	percent distribution	number	percent distribution	share of total	number	percent distribution	share of total
Total occupied housing units	**102,803**	**100.0%**	**68,796**	**100.0%**	**66.9%**	**34,007**	**100.0%**	**33.1%**
Northeast	19,958	19.4	12,644	18.4	63.4	7,314	21.5	36.6
Midwest	24,360	23.7	17,568	25.5	72.1	6,791	20.0	27.9
South	36,389	35.4	25,180	36.6	69.2	11,209	33.0	30.8
West	22,096	21.5	13,403	19.5	60.7	8,692	25.6	39.3
In metropolitan areas	79,911	77.7	51,527	74.9	64.5	28,385	83.5	35.5
In central cities	31,131	30.3	15,512	22.5	49.8	15,619	45.9	50.2
In suburbs	48,780	47.4	36,015	52.4	73.8	12,766	37.5	26.2
Outside metro areas	22,891	22.3	17,269	25.1	75.4	5,622	16.5	24.6

Source: Bureau of the Census, American Housing Survey for the United States: 1999, *Current Housing Reports, H150/99, 2000; calculations by New Strategist*

Total Homeowners by Family Type and Age of Householder, 2000

(number of total families, and number and percent of families owning a home, by family type and age of householder, 2000; numbers in thousands)

	total	homeowners number	percent
Total married couples	**55,311**	**45,382**	**82.0%**
Under age 25	1450	538	37.1
Aged 25 to 29	3,775	2,072	54.9
Aged 30 to 34	5,615	3,964	70.6
Aged 35 to 39	6,886	5,377	78.1
Aged 40 to 44	7,218	6,077	84.2
Aged 45 to 54	12,792	11,301	88.3
Aged 55 to 64	8,138	7,330	90.1
Aged 65 to 74	5,929	5,525	93.2
Aged 75 or older	3,508	3,197	91.1
Total female-headed families	**12,687**	**6,015**	**47.4**
Under age 25	1342	214	15.9
Aged 25 to 29	1,289	261	20.2
Aged 30 to 34	1,443	417	28.9
Aged 35 to 39	1,676	738	44.0
Aged 40 to 44	1,823	919	50.4
Aged 45 to 54	2,299	1,318	57.3
Aged 55 to 64	1,080	739	68.4
Aged 65 to 74	894	699	78.2
Aged 75 or older	841	710	84.4
Total male-headed families	**4,028**	**2,319**	**57.6**
Under age 25	560	219	39.1
Aged 25 to 29	426	143	33.6
Aged 30 to 34	460	239	52.0
Aged 35 to 39	537	263	49.0
Aged 40 to 44	565	352	62.3
Aged 45 to 54	713	491	68.9
Aged 55 to 64	351	260	74.1
Aged 65 to 74	203	165	81.3
Aged 75 or older	213	186	87.3

Source: Bureau of the Census, America's Families and Living Arrangements: March 2000, detailed tables from Current Population P20–537, Internet site <www.census.gov/population/www/socdemo/hh-fam/p20-537_00.html>; calculations by New Strategist

Characteristics of Total Occupied Housing Units, 1999

(number and percent distribution of total occupied housing units by selected housing characteristics and homeownership status, 1999; numbers in thousands)

	total		owner-occupied		renter-occupied	
	number	*percent distribution*	*number*	*percent distribution*	*number*	*percent distribution*
Total occupied housing units	**102,803**	**100.0%**	**68,796**	**100.0%**	**34,007**	**100.0%**
Units in structure						
One, detached	64,536	62.8	56,471	82.1	8,065	23.7
One, attached	6,963	6.8	3,499	5.1	3,465	10.2
Two to four	8,572	8.3	1,466	2.1	7,105	20.9
Five to nine	4,847	4.7	469	0.7	4,378	12.9
10 to 19	4,416	4.3	357	0.5	4,059	11.9
20 to 49	3,343	3.3	341	0.5	3,002	8.8
50 or more	3,341	3.2	544	0.8	2,797	8.2
Mobile home or trailer	6,785	6.6	5,649	8.2	1,136	3.3
Median square footage of unit	1,730	–	1,795	–	1,293	–
Number of rooms in unit						
One room	407	0.4	5	0.0	401	1.2
Two rooms	1,014	1.0	70	0.1	943	2.8
Three rooms	8,973	8.7	996	1.4	7,977	23.5
Four rooms	19,390	18.9	7,322	10.6	12,068	35.5
Five rooms	23,733	23.1	16,395	23.8	7,338	21.6
Six rooms	21,662	21.1	18,174	26.4	3,488	10.3
Seven rooms	13,457	13.1	12,314	17.9	1,143	3.4
Eight rooms	7,985	7.8	7,583	11.0	401	1.2
Nine rooms	3,565	3.5	3,427	5.0	137	0.4
Ten or more rooms	2,618	2.5	2,508	3.6	110	0.3
Complete bathrooms						
None	676	0.7	263	0.4	413	1.2
One	42,838	41.7	18,650	27.1	24,188	71.1
One and one-half	16,189	15.7	12,743	18.5	3,446	10.1
Two or more	43,100	41.9	37,140	54.0	5,960	17.5

(continued)

(continued from previous page)

	total		owner-occupied		renter-occupied	
	number	percent distribution	number	percent distribution	number	percent distribution
Heating fuel						
Housing units with heating fuel	102,259	100.0%	68,590	100.0%	33,669	100.0%
Electricity	31,142	30.5	17,770	25.9	13,372	39.7
Piped gas	52,366	51.2	37,031	54.0	15,335	45.5
Bottled gas	5,905	5.8	4,954	7.2	951	2.8
Fuel oil	10,026	9.8	6,665	9.7	3,361	10.0
Kerosene or other liquid fuel	724	0.7	509	0.7	216	0.6
Coal or coke	168	0.2	147	0.2	21	0.1
Wood	1,703	1.7	1,433	2.1	270	0.8
Solar energy	19	0.0	11	0.0	8	0.0
Other	205	0.2	68	0.1	136	0.4
Selected equipment						
Dishwasher	57,703	56.1	44,904	65.3	12,799	37.6
Washing machine	80,543	78.3	65,140	94.7	15,403	45.3
Clothes dryer	78,454	76.3	62,738	91.2	13,716	40.3
Disposal in kitchen sink	45,345	44.1	31,659	46.0	13,685	40.2
Central air conditioning	54,878	53.4	41,167	59.8	13,711	40.3
Porch, deck, balcony, or patio	83,498	81.2	61,556	89.5	21,942	64.5
Telephone	98,449	95.8	66,658	96.9	31,791	93.5
Usable fireplace	33,269	32.4	29,243	42.5	4,026	11.8
Garage or carport	60,553	58.9	49,941	72.6	10,612	31.2
No cars, trucks, or vans	9,542	9.3	2,674	3.9	6,867	20.2
Overall opinion of housing unit						
1 (worst)	561	0.5	168	0.2	392	1.2
2	363	0.4	121	0.2	241	0.7
3	737	0.7	228	0.3	509	1.5
4	1,302	1.3	395	0.6	907	2.7
5	6,376	6.2	2,743	4.0	3,633	10.7
6	5,564	5.4	2,746	4.0	2,817	8.3
7	13,902	13.5	8,044	11.7	5,858	17.2
8	28,184	27.4	19,376	28.2	8,807	25.9
9	14,516	14.1	10,978	16.0	3,539	10.4
10 (best)	27,147	26.4	21,207	30.8	5,940	17.5

Note: Numbers may not add to total because not reported is not shown and more than one category may apply; (–) means not applicable or sample is too small to make a reliable estimate.
Source: Bureau of the Census, American Housing Survey for the United States: 1999, *Current Housing Reports, H150/99, 2000; calculations by New Strategist*

Neighborhood Characteristics of Total Occupied Housing Units, 1999

(number and percent distribution of total occupied housing units by selected neighborhood characteristics and homeownership status, 1999; numbers in thousands)

	total		owner-occupied		renter-occupied	
	number	*percent distribution*	*number*	*percent distribution*	*number*	*percent distribution*
Total occupied housing units	**102,803**	**100.0%**	**68,796**	**100.0%**	**34,007**	**100.0%**
Overall opinion of neighborhood						
1 (worst)	885	0.9	354	0.5	531	1.6
2	657	0.6	248	0.4	409	1.2
3	1,151	1.1	459	0.7	692	2.0
4	1,621	1.6	650	0.9	971	2.9
5	7,051	6.9	3,617	5.3	3,434	10.1
6	5,974	5.8	3,172	4.6	2,802	8.2
7	13,313	13.0	8,266	12.0	5,047	14.8
8	26,599	25.9	18,421	26.8	8,179	24.1
9	15,707	15.3	11,655	16.9	4,052	11.9
10 (best)	25,215	24.5	18,838	27.4	6,377	18.8
Neighborhood problems						
Street noise or traffic present	28,991	28.2	16,561	24.1	12,430	36.6
Condition not bothersome	17,311	16.8	9,907	14.4	7,404	21.8
Condition bothersome	11,624	11.3	6,632	9.6	4,992	14.7
So bothered they want to move	4,486	4.4	2,150	3.1	2,336	6.9
Neighborhood crime present	14,429	14.0	7,566	11.0	6,863	20.2
Condition not bothersome	6,011	5.8	3,123	4.5	2,888	8.5
Condition bothersome	8,384	8.2	4,435	6.4	3,949	11.6
So bothered they want to move	3,653	3.6	1,483	2.2	2,170	6.4
Odors present	6,343	6.2	3,649	5.3	2,695	7.9
Condition not bothersome	2,356	2.3	1,396	2.0	960	2.8
Condition bothersome	3,983	3.9	2,250	3.3	1,733	5.1
So bothered they want to move	1,546	1.5	661	1.0	885	2.6
No other problems	85,719	83.4	57,506	83.6	28,213	83.0
With other problems	15,470	15.0	10,235	14.9	5,234	15.4
Noise	2,659	2.6	1,502	2.2	1,157	3.4
Litter or housing deterioration	1,821	1.8	1,159	1.7	662	1.9
Poor city or county services	847	0.8	532	0.8	316	0.9
Undesirable commercial, institutional, industrial	759	0.7	485	0.7	275	0.8
People	4,494	4.4	2,736	4.0	1,758	5.2
Other	7,855	7.6	5,327	7.7	2,527	7.4

(continued)

(continued from previous page)

	total		owner-occupied		renter-occupied	
	number	percent distribution	number	percent distribution	number	percent distribution
Neighborhood conditions						
With public transportation	55,565	54.0%	31,813	46.2%	23,752	69.8%
Satisfactory public elementary school*	23,740	77.1	16,046	79.3	7,694	72.8
Satisfactory neighborhood shopping	83,927	81.6	54,613	79.4	29,314	86.2
Satisfactory police protection	91,245	88.8	61,312	89.1	29,933	88.0
Description of area within 300 feet						
Single-family detached homes	80,921	78.7	58,082	84.4	22,840	67.2
Single-family attached homes	12,933	12.6	6,279	9.1	6,654	19.6
Apartment buildings	31,985	31.1	8,812	12.8	23,172	68.1
Mobile homes	11,530	11.2	9,011	13.1	2,518	7.4
Commercial, institutional	26,614	25.9	11,329	16.5	15,285	44.9
Industrial	3,996	3.9	1,775	2.6	2,222	6.5
Body of water	16,406	16.0	11,987	17.4	4,419	13.0
Open space, park, woods, farm, or ranch	39,742	38.7	28,217	41.0	11,525	33.9
Four-or-more lane highway, railroad, airport	13,859	13.5	6,712	9.8	7,147	21.0

* Percentage based only on households with children aged 0 to 13.
Note: Numbers may not add to total because more than one problem could be cited and not reported is not shown;
Source: Bureau of the Census, American Housing Survey for the United States: 1999, *Current Housing Reports, H150/99, 2000; calculations by New Strategist*

Housing Value and Purchase Price for Total Homeowners, 1999

(number and percent distribution of total homeowners, by value of home, purchase price, and major source of down payment, 1999; numbers in thousands)

	number	percent distribution
Total homeowners	**68,796**	**100.0%**
Value of home		
Under $50,000	10,665	15.5
$50,000 to $79,999	11,909	17.3
$80,000 to $99,999	9,085	13.2
$100,000 to $149,999	15,217	22.1
$150,000 to $199,999	9,129	13.3
$200,000 to $299,999	7,391	10.7
$300,000 or more	5,399	7.8
Median value	$108,300	–
Purchase price*		
Home purchased or built	65,334	95.0
Under $50,000	25,748	37.4
$50,000 to $79,999	11,102	16.1
$80,000 to $99,999	5,801	8.4
$100,000 to $149,999	8,150	11.8
$150,000 to $199,999	4,471	6.5
$200,000 to $299,999	3,082	4.5
$300,000 or more	1,836	2.7
Received as inheritance or gift	2,414	3.5
Median purchase price	$61,244	–
Major source of down payment		
Home purchased or built	65,334	95.0
Sale of previous home	20,622	30.0
Savings or cash on hand	31,552	45.9
Sale of other investment	603	0.9
Borrowing, other than mortgage on this property	2,279	3.3
Inheritance or gift	1,508	2.2
Land where built used for financing	523	0.8
Other	2,361	3.4
No down payment	4,318	6.3

Note: Numbers may not add to total because not reported is not shown; (–) means not applicable.
Source: Bureau of the Census, American Housing Survey for the United States: 1999, Current Housing Reports, H150/99, 2000; calculations by New Strategist

Geographical Mobility of the Total Population by Age, 1999–2000

(total number of people aged 1 or older and number and percent who moved between March 1999 and March 2000, by age of person and type of move; numbers in thousands)

	total	same house (non-movers)	total movers in U.S.	same county	different county, same state	different state, same division	different division, same region	different region	moved from abroad
Total aged 1 or older	270,219	226,831	43,388	24,399	8,814	4,062	1,261	3,105	1,746
Aged 1–4	15,740	12,075	3,665	2,220	685	263	122	243	131
Aged 5–9	20,379	16,685	3,694	2,233	650	315	101	253	141
Aged 10–14	20,328	17,487	2,841	1,588	544	309	57	220	123
Aged 15–17	12,011	10,461	1,550	865	284	158	52	126	65
Aged 18–19	8,091	6,278	1,813	1,026	368	207	31	103	78
Aged 20–24	18,441	11,942	6,499	3,756	1,311	540	189	413	291
Aged 25–29	18,268	12,358	5,910	3,280	1,305	446	193	452	234
Aged 30–34	19,518	15,216	4,302	2,411	890	370	135	281	215
Aged 35–39	22,320	18,606	3,714	2,087	759	368	67	280	154
Aged 40–44	22,485	19,573	2,912	1,622	572	364	73	188	93
Aged 45–49	19,748	17,772	1,976	1,029	466	228	58	115	79
Aged 50–54	16,882	15,438	1,444	772	313	168	51	85	56
Aged 55–59	12,868	11,851	1,017	521	218	125	32	93	27
Aged 60–61	4,383	4,091	292	123	71	48	14	29	8
Aged 62–64	6,136	5,802	334	148	72	49	12	40	14
Aged 65–69	9,352	8,919	433	247	75	28	26	48	10
Aged 70–74	8,444	8,054	390	196	75	27	22	51	20
Aged 75–79	7,192	6,932	260	114	66	14	23	39	4
Aged 80–84	4,493	4,301	192	86	51	28	1	25	1
Aged 85+	3,140	2,992	148	74	39	9	3	20	2

(continued)

(continued from previous page)

	total	same house (non-movers)	total movers in U.S.	same county	different county, same state	different state, same division	different division, same region	different region	moved from abroad
Total aged 1 or older	**100.0%**	**83.9%**	**16.1%**	**9.0%**	**3.3%**	**1.5%**	**0.5%**	**1.1%**	**0.6%**
Aged 1–4	100.0	76.7	23.3	14.1	4.4	1.7	0.8	1.5	0.8
Aged 5–9	100.0	81.9	18.1	11.0	3.2	1.5	0.5	1.2	0.7
Aged 10–14	100.0	86.0	14.0	7.8	2.7	1.5	0.3	1.1	0.6
Aged 15–17	100.0	87.1	12.9	7.2	2.4	1.3	0.4	1.0	0.5
Aged 18–19	100.0	77.6	22.4	12.7	4.5	2.6	0.4	1.3	1.0
Aged 20–24	100.0	64.8	35.2	20.4	7.1	2.9	1.0	2.2	1.6
Aged 25–29	100.0	67.6	32.4	18.0	7.1	2.4	1.1	2.5	1.3
Aged 30–34	100.0	78.0	22.0	12.4	4.6	1.9	0.7	1.4	1.1
Aged 35–39	100.0	83.4	16.6	9.4	3.4	1.6	0.3	1.3	0.7
Aged 40–44	100.0	87.0	13.0	7.2	2.5	1.6	0.3	0.8	0.4
Aged 45–49	100.0	90.0	10.0	5.2	2.4	1.2	0.3	0.6	0.4
Aged 50–54	100.0	91.4	8.6	4.6	1.9	1.0	0.3	0.5	0.3
Aged 55–59	100.0	92.1	7.9	4.0	1.7	1.0	0.2	0.7	0.2
Aged 60–61	100.0	93.3	6.7	2.8	1.6	1.1	0.3	0.7	0.2
Aged 62–64	100.0	94.6	5.4	2.4	1.2	0.8	0.2	0.7	0.2
Aged 65–69	100.0	95.4	4.6	2.6	0.8	0.3	0.3	0.5	0.1
Aged 70–74	100.0	95.4	4.6	2.3	0.9	0.3	0.3	0.6	0.2
Aged 75–79	100.0	96.4	3.6	1.6	0.9	0.2	0.3	0.5	0.1
Aged 80–84	100.0	95.7	4.3	1.9	1.1	0.6	0.0	0.6	0.0
Aged 85+	100.0	95.3	4.7	2.4	1.2	0.3	0.1	0.6	0.1

Source: Bureau of the Census, Geographical Mobility: March 1999 to March 2000, *Current Population Reports, P20-538, 2001; Internet site <www.census.gov/population/www/socdemo/migrate/p20-538.html>; calculations by New Strategist*

Reasons for Moving among Total Households by Homeownership Status, 1999

(number and percent distribution of total households moving in the past 12 months by main reason for move and for choosing new neighborhood and house, and by comparison with previous home and neighborhood, by homeownership status, 1999; numbers in thousands)

	total		owner-occupied		renter-occupied	
	number	percent distribution	number	percent distribution	number	percent distribution
Total movers	**17,825**	**100.0%**	**5,788**	**100.0%**	**12,037**	**100.0%**
Main reason for leaving previous housing unit						
Private displacement	210	1.2	17	0.3	193	1.6
Government displacement	50	0.3	12	0.2	38	0.3
Disaster loss (fire, flood, etc.)	100	0.6	33	0.6	67	0.6
New job or job transfer	2,011	11.3	507	8.8	1,504	12.5
To be closer to work/school/other	1,611	9.0	237	4.1	1,374	11.4
Other financial/employment	553	3.1	110	1.9	443	3.7
To establish own household	2,095	11.8	709	12.2	1,386	11.5
Needed larger house or apartment	1,814	10.2	708	12.2	1,106	9.2
Married, widowed, divorced, separated	1,033	5.8	327	5.6	706	5.9
Other family/personal	1,350	7.6	388	6.7	961	8.0
Wanted better home	1,337	7.5	515	8.9	823	6.8
Change from owner to renter/ renter to owner	914	5.1	791	13.7	123	1.0
Wanted lower rent or maintenance	648	3.6	116	2.0	532	4.4
Other housing related reasons	835	4.7	246	4.3	589	4.9
Other	1,952	11.0	647	11.2	1,305	10.8
All reported reasons equal	424	2.4	146	2.5	279	2.3
Main reason for choosing present neighborhood						
Convenient to job	3,277	18.4	623	10.8	2,654	22.0
Convenient to friends or relatives	2,246	12.6	685	11.8	1,560	13.0
Convenient to leisure activities	312	1.8	117	2.0	195	1.6
Convenient to public transportation	189	1.1	18	0.3	171	1.4
Good schools	1,137	6.4	358	6.2	779	6.5
Other public services	177	1.0	28	0.5	149	1.2
Looks/design of neighborhood	2,612	14.7	1,239	21.4	1,372	11.4
House most important consideration	2,491	14.0	1,091	18.8	1,400	11.6
Other	2,771	15.5	750	13.0	2,021	16.8
All reported reasons equal	636	3.6	251	4.3	385	3.2
Neighborhood search						
Looked at just this neighborhood	7,881	44.2	2,276	39.3	5,605	46.6
Looked at other neighborhood(s)	9,332	52.4	3,305	57.1	6,027	50.1

(continued)

(continued from previous page)

Main reason for choosing present home	total		owner-occupied		renter-occupied	
	number	percent distribution	number	percent distribution	number	percent distribution
Financial reasons	4,954	27.8%	1,355	23.4%	3,599	29.9%
Room layout/design	2,961	16.6	1,340	23.2	1,621	13.5
Kitchen	90	0.5	41	0.7	49	0.4
Size	2,093	11.7	612	10.6	1,481	12.3
Exterior appearance	589	3.3	297	5.1	293	2.4
Yard/trees/view	625	3.5	262	4.5	363	3.0
Quality of construction	499	2.8	309	5.3	190	1.6
Only one available	1,244	7.0	125	2.2	1,120	9.3
Other	2,141	12.0	542	9.4	1,598	13.3
All reported reasons equal	847	4.8	355	6.1	492	4.1
Comparison to previous home						
Better home	9,420	52.8	3,850	66.5	5,570	46.3
Worse home	2,963	16.6	522	9.0	2,441	20.3
About the same	4,751	26.7	1,184	20.5	3,568	29.6
Comparison to previous neighborhood						
Better neighborhood	7,257	40.7	2,980	51.5	4,277	35.5
Worse neighborhood	2,317	13.0	372	6.4	1,945	16.2
About the same	6,777	38.0	1,961	33.9	4,816	40.0
Same neighborhood	750	4.2	223	3.9	527	4.4

Note: Numbers may not add to total because more than one category may apply and unreported reasons are not shown.
Source: Bureau of the Census, American Housing Survey for the United States: 1999, *Current Housing Reports, H150/99, 2000; calculations by New Strategist*

Total Population: Income

The Affluence of Americans Reached an All-Time High in the Late 1990s

The median income of American households rose 10 percent between 1990 and 2000, to $42,151 after adjusting for inflation. More than one in ten households have incomes of $100,000 or more.

Household income peaks among householders aged 45 to 54, standing at a median of $58,217 in 2000. Among household types, incomes are greatest for married couples, with a median of $59,343. Twenty-one percent of married couples had incomes of $100,000 or more in 2000. For men who work full-time, median income stood at $39,020 in 2000. For their female counterparts, the figure was $28,820.

Between 1990 and 2000, the median earnings of men who work full-time rose 5 percent, after adjusting for inflation. Women's median earnings grew 7 percent. Consequently, the median earnings of women grew from 72 to 73 percent of the median earnings of men between 1990 and 2000.

Nine percent of American families were poor in 2000, a slightly smaller proportion than in 1990. The nation's children have the highest poverty rate by age. Sixteen percent of people under age 18 are poor versus 11 percent of the population as a whole.

■ When the baby-boom generation begins to retire, the proportion of American households with affluent incomes will fall.

Household income peaks in the 45-to-54 age group

(median income of households by age of householder, 2000)

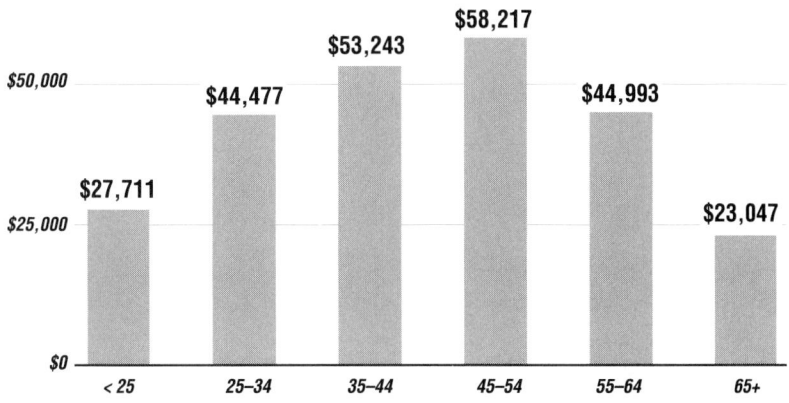

Median Income of Total Households, 1990 to 2000

(median income of total households, 1990 to 2000; percent change in income, 1990–2000; in 2000 dollars)

	median income
2000	$42,151
1999	42,187
1998	41,032
1997	39,594
1996	38,798
1995	38,262
1994	37,136
1993	36,746
1992	36,965
1991	37,314
1990	38,446

Percent change

1990–2000	9.6%

Source: Bureau of the Census, Current Population Survey, Internet site <www.census.gov/hhes/income/histinc/h05.html>; calculations by New Strategist

High-Income Total Households, 2000

(number, percent distribution, and average income of total households with incomes of $100,000 or more, 2000; households in thousands as of 2001)

	total	percent	average income
Total households	**106,417**	**100.0%**	**$57,045**
$100,000 to $149,999	9,283	8.7	118,737
$150,000 to $199,999	2,622	2.5	169,364
$200,000 to $249,999	1,051	1.0	218,912
$250,000 or more	1,305	1.2	464,461

Source: Bureau of the Census, Current Population Survey, Internet site <http://ferret.bls.census.gov/macro/ 032001/hhinc/new07_000 .htm>; calculations by New Strategist

Income Distribution of Total Households by Age of Householder, 2000

(number and percent distribution of total households by income and age of householder, 2000; households in thousands as of 2001)

	total	< 25	25–34	35–44	45–54	55–64	65+
Total households	**106,418**	**6,393**	**18,554**	**23,904**	**21,797**	**13,944**	**21,827**
Under $10,000	9,540	922	1,223	1,221	1,257	1,416	3,499
$10,000 to $19,999	14,525	1,246	1,918	2,030	1,710	1,585	6,037
$20,000 to $29,999	14,053	1,283	2,605	2,474	1,919	1,684	4,088
$30,000 to $39,999	12,428	947	2,556	2,695	2,145	1,499	2,587
$40,000 to $49,999	10,461	598	2,114	2,611	2,142	1,426	1,572
$50,000 to $59,999	9,051	447	2,028	2,392	1,977	1,173	1,032
$60,000 to $69,999	7,783	344	1,617	2,189	1,883	1,000	748
$70,000 to $79,999	6,184	165	1,163	1,878	1,607	866	503
$80,000 to $89,999	4,659	124	779	1,428	1,355	617	354
$90,000 to $99,999	3,473	68	609	1,024	1,072	450	251
$100,000 or more	14,262	248	1,940	3,962	4,730	2,227	1,156
Median income	$42,151	$27,711	$44,477	$53,243	$58,217	$44,993	$23,047
Total households	**100.0%**	**100.0%**	**100.0%**	**100.0%**	**100.0%**	**100.0%**	**100.0%**
Under $10,000	9.0	14.4	6.6	5.1	5.8	10.2	16.0
$10,000 to $19,999	13.6	19.5	10.3	8.5	7.8	11.4	27.7
$20,000 to $29,999	13.2	20.1	14.0	10.3	8.8	12.1	18.7
$30,000 to $39,999	11.7	14.8	13.8	11.3	9.8	10.8	11.9
$40,000 to $49,999	9.8	9.4	11.4	10.9	9.8	10.2	7.2
$50,000 to $59,999	8.5	7.0	10.9	10.0	9.1	8.4	4.7
$60,000 to $69,999	7.3	5.4	8.7	9.2	8.6	7.2	3.4
$70,000 to $79,999	5.8	2.6	6.3	7.9	7.4	6.2	2.3
$80,000 to $89,999	4.4	1.9	4.2	6.0	6.2	4.4	1.6
$90,000 to $99,999	3.3	1.1	3.3	4.3	4.9	3.2	1.1
$100,000 or more	13.4	3.9	10.5	16.6	21.7	16.0	5.3

Source: Bureau of the Census, Current Population Survey, Internet site <http://ferret.bls.census.gov/macro/032001/hhinc/new02_001 .htm>; calculations by New Strategist

Income Distribution of Total Households by Household Type, 2000

(number and percent distribution of total households by income and household type, 2000; households in thousands as of 2001)

		family households				nonfamily households				
							female householder		male householder	
	total	total	married couples	female hh, no spouse present	male hh, no spouse present	total	total	living alone	total	living alone
Total households	106,418	72,380	55,603	12,525	4,252	34,039	18,821	16,283	15,218	11,536
Under $10,000	9,540	3,257	1,326	1,665	267	6,282	4,209	4,107	2,073	1,896
$10,000 to $19,999	14,525	7,009	3,902	2,643	461	7,517	4,832	4,624	2,684	2,402
$20,000 to $29,999	14,053	8,507	5,511	2,352	646	5,544	3,058	2,728	2,485	2,019
$30,000 to $39,999	12,428	8,285	5,952	1,741	593	4,144	2,114	1,814	2,030	1,606
$40,000 to $49,999	10,461	7,644	5,827	1,299	519	2,816	1,348	1,044	1,471	1,052
$50,000 to $59,999	9,051	6,849	5,590	840	420	2,201	948	636	1,254	816
$60,000 to $69,999	7,783	6,284	5,243	635	406	1,498	648	412	850	515
$70,000 to $79,999	6,184	5,094	4,469	390	234	1,090	467	299	624	373
$80,000 to $89,999	4,659	3,969	3,526	270	174	689	297	169	393	218
$90,000 to $99,999	3,473	2,981	2,669	189	122	493	168	73	325	167
$100,000 or more	14,262	12,499	11,586	503	410	1,763	734	377	1,029	473
Median income	$42,151	$51,751	$59,343	$28,126	$42,143	$25,439	$20,929	$18,163	$31,269	$26,723

(continued)

(continued from previous page)

Total households	total	family households				nonfamily households				
		total	married couples	female hh, no spouse present	male hh, no spouse present	total	female householder		male householder	
							total	living alone	total	living alone
	100.0%	100.0%	100.0%	100.0%	100.0%	100.0%	100.0%	100.0%	100.0%	100.0%
Under $10,000	9.0	4.5	2.4	13.3	6.3	18.5	22.4	25.2	13.6	16.4
$10,000 to $19,999	13.6	9.7	7.0	21.1	10.8	22.1	25.7	28.4	17.6	20.8
$20,000 to $29,999	13.2	11.8	9.9	18.8	15.2	16.3	16.2	16.8	16.3	17.5
$30,000 to $39,999	11.7	11.4	10.7	13.9	13.9	12.2	11.2	11.1	13.3	13.9
$40,000 to $49,999	9.8	10.6	10.5	10.4	12.2	8.3	7.2	6.4	9.7	9.1
$50,000 to $59,999	8.5	9.5	10.1	6.7	9.9	6.5	5.0	3.9	8.2	7.1
$60,000 to $69,999	7.3	8.7	9.4	5.1	9.5	4.4	3.4	2.5	5.6	4.5
$70,000 to $79,999	5.8	7.0	8.0	3.1	5.5	3.2	2.5	1.8	4.1	3.2
$80,000 to $89,999	4.4	5.5	6.3	2.2	4.1	2.0	1.6	1.0	2.6	1.9
$90,000 to $99,999	3.3	4.1	4.8	1.5	2.9	1.4	0.9	0.4	2.1	1.4
$100,000 or more	13.4	17.3	20.8	4.0	9.6	5.2	3.9	2.3	6.8	4.1

Source: Bureau of the Census, Current Population Survey, Current Population Survey, Internet site <http://ferret.bls.census.gov/macro/032001/hhinc/new01_001.htm>; calculations by New Strategist

Income Distribution of Total Men by Age, 2000

(number and percent distribution of total men aged 15 or older by income and age, median income of men with income, percent working full-time, and median income of full-time workers, 2000; men in thousands as of 2001)

	total	< 25	25–34	35–44	45–54	55–64	65+
Total men	**104,273**	**19,636**	**18,451**	**22,177**	**18,578**	**11,253**	**14,179**
Without income	7,290	5,152	629	493	423	353	242
With income	96,983	14,484	17,822	21,684	18,155	10,900	13,937
Under $10,000	15,994	7,434	1,500	1,669	1,528	1,263	2,600
$10,000 to $19,999	18,217	3,629	3,279	2,704	2,080	1,824	4,698
$20,000 to $29,999	16,113	1,970	3,791	3,703	2,310	1,597	2,740
$30,000 to $39,999	13,276	851	3,426	3,462	2,744	1,465	1,329
$40,000 to $49,999	9,223	254	2,062	2,648	2,361	1,093	805
$50,000 to $74,999	13,347	254	2,450	4,255	3,683	1,815	889
$75,000 to $99,999	5,140	68	697	1,578	1,625	800	371
$100,000 or more	5,674	20	615	1,666	1,826	1,042	505
Median income of men with income	$28,269	$9,548	$30,633	$37,088	$41,072	$34,414	$19,167
Percent working full-time	56.4%	23.9%	76.4%	80.7%	77.3%	56.6%	9.5%
Median income of men working full-time	$39,020	$20,824	$34,213	$41,560	$46,672	$46,753	$47,964
Total men	**100.0%**	**100.0%**	**100.0%**	**100.0%**	**100.0%**	**100.0%**	**100.0%**
Without income	7.0	26.2	3.4	2.2	2.3	3.1	1.7
With income	93.0	73.8	96.6	97.8	97.7	96.9	98.3
Under $10,000	15.3	37.9	8.1	7.5	8.2	11.2	18.3
$10,000 to $19,999	17.5	18.5	17.8	12.2	11.2	16.2	33.1
$20,000 to $29,999	15.5	10.0	20.5	16.7	12.4	14.2	19.3
$30,000 to $39,999	12.7	4.3	18.6	15.6	14.8	13.0	9.4
$40,000 to $49,999	8.8	1.3	11.2	11.9	12.7	9.7	5.7
$50,000 to $74,999	12.8	1.3	13.3	19.2	19.8	16.1	6.3
$75,000 to $99,999	4.9	0.3	3.8	7.1	8.7	7.1	2.6
$100,000 or more	5.4	0.1	3.3	7.5	9.8	9.3	3.6

Source: Bureau of the Census, Current Population Survey, Internet sites <http://ferret.bls.census.gov/macro/032001/perinc/new01_006 .htm> and <http://ferret.bls.census.gov/macro/032001/perinc/new01_022.htm>; calculations by New Strategist

Income Distribution of Total Women by Age, 2000

(number and percent distribution of total women aged 15 or older by income and age, median income of women with income, percent working full-time, and median income of full-time workers, 2000; women in thousands as of 2001)

	total	< 25	25–34	35–44	45–54	55–64	65+
Total women	**111,735**	**19,349**	**18,989**	**22,603**	**19,462**	**12,532**	**18,799**
Without income	11,761	5,323	1,849	1,631	1,345	1,132	479
With income	99,974	14,026	17,140	20,972	18,117	11,400	18,320
Under $10,000	33,646	8,070	4,171	5,153	3,967	3,948	8,337
$10,000 to $19,999	24,001	3,475	3,948	4,342	3,641	2,483	6,112
$20,000 to $29,999	16,505	1,611	3,698	4,085	3,366	1,806	1,939
$30,000 to $39,999	10,554	526	2,588	2,847	2,557	1,210	823
$40,000 to $49,999	5,905	190	1,138	1,741	1,720	718	397
$50,000 to $74,999	6,494	107	1,101	1,927	2,067	849	445
$75,000 to $99,999	1,590	24	298	459	432	238	141
$100,000 or more	1,278	23	198	419	366	148	124
Median income of women with income	$16,188	$7,742	$20,940	$21,861	$24,193	$16,468	$10,898
Percent working full-time	37.2%	19.8%	51.5%	53.3%	55.5%	35.8%	3.5%
Median income of women working full-time	$28,820	$18,950	$27,954	$30,471	$31,983	$30,282	$34,171
Total women	**100.0%**	**100.0%**	**100.0%**	**100.0%**	**100.0%**	**100.0%**	**100.0%**
Without income	10.5	27.5	9.7	7.2	6.9	9.0	2.5
With income	89.5	72.5	90.3	92.8	93.1	91.0	97.5
Under $10,000	30.1	41.7	22.0	22.8	20.4	31.5	44.3
$10,000 to $19,999	21.5	18.0	20.8	19.2	18.7	19.8	32.5
$20,000 to $29,999	14.8	8.3	19.5	18.1	17.3	14.4	10.3
$30,000 to $39,999	9.4	2.7	13.6	12.6	13.1	9.7	4.4
$40,000 to $49,999	5.3	1.0	6.0	7.7	8.8	5.7	2.1
$50,000 to $74,999	5.8	0.6	5.8	8.5	10.6	6.8	2.4
$75,000 to $99,999	1.4	0.1	1.6	2.0	2.2	1.9	0.8
$100,000 or more	1.1	0.1	1.0	1.9	1.9	1.2	0.7

Source: Bureau of the Census, Current Population Survey, Internet sites <http://ferret.bls.census.gov/macro/ 032001/perinc/new01_011 .htm> and <http://ferret.bls.census.gov/macro/032001/perinc/new01_026.htm>; calculations by New Strategist

Median Earnings of Total People Working Full-Time by Sex, 1990 to 2000

(median earnings of total people working full-time, year-round by sex; and women's earnings as a percent of men's earnings, 1990 to 2000; percent change, 1990–2000; in 2000 dollars)

	men's earnings	women's earnings	women's earnings as a percent of men's earnings
2000	$37,339	$27,355	73.3%
1999	37,701	27,208	72.2
1998	37,296	27,290	73.2
1997	36,030	26,720	74.2
1996	35,138	25,919	73.8
1995	35,365	25,260	71.4
1994	35,513	25,558	72.0
1993	35,765	25,579	71.5
1992	36,436	25,791	70.8
1991	36,440	25,457	69.9
1990	35,538	25,451	71.6

Percent change

1990–2000	5.1%	7.5%	2.3%

Source: Bureau of the Census, Current Population Survey, Internet site <www.census.gov/hhes/income/histinc/ p38.html>; calculations by New Strategist

Median Earnings of Total People Working Full-Time by Education and Sex, 2000

(median earnings of total people aged 25 or older working full-time, year-round by educational attainment and sex, and women's earnings as a percent of men's earnings, 2000)

	men	women	women's earnings as a percent of men's earnings
Total people	**$40,181**	**$28,977**	**72.1%**
Less than 9th grade	20,447	15,399	75.3
9th to 12th grade, no diploma	24,439	17,210	70.4
High school graduate	32,494	23,721	73.0
Some college, no degree	38,650	27,190	70.3
Associate's degree	41,072	30,180	73.5
Bachelor's degree or more	60,449	41,131	68.0
Bachelor's degree	53,508	38,213	71.4
Master's degree	65,058	47,052	72.3
Professional degree	91,318	56,089	61.4
Doctoral degree	75,630	55,631	73.6

Source: Bureau of the Census, Current Population Survey, Internet sites <http://ferret.bls.census.gov/macro/032001/perinc/new03_076 .htm> and <http://ferret.bls.census.gov/macro/032001/perinc/new03_146.htm>; calculations by New Strategist

Poverty Status of Total Families, 1990 to 2000

(total number of families, and number and percent below poverty level by type of family and presence of children under age 18 at home, 1990 to 2000; percent change in numbers and rates, 1990–2000; families in thousands as of March the following year)

| | total families | | | married couples | | | female hh, no spouse present | | |
| | | in poverty | | | in poverty | | | in poverty | |
	total	number	percent	total	number	percent	total	number	percent
With and without children < age 18									
2000	72,388	6,222	8.6%	55,611	2,638	4.7%	12,525	3,096	24.7%
1999	72,031	6,676	9.3	55,315	2,673	4.8	12,687	3,531	27.8
1998	71,551	7,186	10.0	54,778	2,879	5.3	12,796	3,831	29.9
1997	70,884	7,324	10.3	54,321	2,821	5.2	12,652	3,995	31.6
1996	70,241	7,708	11.0	53,604	3,010	5.6	12,790	4,167	32.6
1995	69,597	7,532	10.8	53,570	2,982	5.6	12,514	4,057	32.4
1994	69,313	8,053	11.6	53,885	3,272	6.1	12,220	4,232	34.6
1993	68,506	8,393	12.3	53,181	3,481	6.5	12,411	4,424	35.6
1992	68,216	8,144	11.9	53,090	3,385	6.4	12,061	4,275	35.4
1991	67,173	7,712	11.5	52,457	3,158	6.0	11,692	4,161	35.6
1990	66,322	7,098	10.7	52,147	2,961	5.7	11,268	3,768	33.4
Percent change									
1990–2000	9.1%	−12.3%	−19.6%	6.6%	−10.9%	−17.5%	11.2%	−17.8%	−26.0%
With children under age 18									
2000	37,327	4,730	12.7%	26,563	1,604	6.0%	8,510	2,763	32.5%
1999	37,277	5,129	13.8	26,373	1,662	6.3	8,736	3,116	35.7
1998	37,268	5,628	15.1	26,226	1,822	6.9	8,934	3,456	38.7
1997	37,427	5,884	15.7	26,430	1,863	7.1	8,822	3,614	41.0
1996	37,204	6,131	16.5	26,184	1,964	7.5	8,957	3,755	41.9
1995	36,719	5,976	16.3	26,034	1,961	7.5	8,751	3,634	41.5
1994	36,782	6,406	17.4	26,367	2,197	8.3	8,665	3,816	44.0
1993	36,456	6,751	18.5	26,121	2,363	9.0	8,758	4,034	46.1
1992	35,851	6,457	18.0	25,907	2,237	8.6	8,375	3,887	46.2
1991	34,862	6,170	17.7	25,357	2,106	8.3	7,992	3,767	47.1
1990	34,503	5,676	16.4	25,410	1,990	7.8	7,707	3,426	44.5
Percent change									
1990–2000	8.2%	−16.7%	−22.6%	4.5%	−19.4%	−23.1%	10.4%	−19.4%	−27.0%

Source: Bureau of the Census, Current Population Survey, Internet sites <www.census.gov/hhes/poverty/histpov/hstpov4.html> and <http://ferret.bls.census.gov/macro/032001/pov/new16a_000.htm>; calculations by New Strategist

Poverty Status of Total People by Sex and Age, 2000

(total number of people, and number and percent below poverty level by sex and age, 2000; people in thousands as of 2001)

		in poverty	
	total	*number*	*percent*
Total people	**275,924**	**31,054**	**11.3%**
Under age 18	71,936	11,553	16.1
Aged 18 to 24	26,965	3,890	14.4
Aged 25 to 34	37,440	3,892	10.4
Aged 35 to 44	44,780	3,678	8.2
Aged 45 to 54	38,040	2,441	6.4
Aged 55 to 59	13,338	1,175	8.8
Aged 60 to 64	10,447	1,066	10.2
Aged 65 or older	32,978	3,359	10.2
Aged 65 to 74	17,878	1,592	8.9
Aged 75 or older	15,100	1,767	11.7
Total females	**140,981**	**17,637**	**12.5**
Under age 18	35,107	5,717	16.3
Aged 18 to 24	13,489	2,323	17.2
Aged 25 to 34	18,989	2,472	13.0
Aged 35 to 44	22,603	2,158	9.5
Aged 45 to 54	19,462	1,319	6.8
Aged 55 to 59	6,932	698	10.1
Aged 60 to 64	5,600	655	11.7
Aged 65 or older	18,799	2,296	12.2
Aged 65 to 74	9,691	1,017	10.5
Aged 75 or older	9,108	1,279	14.0
Total males	**134,943**	**13,417**	**9.9**
Under age 18	36,830	5,836	15.8
Aged 18 to 24	13,476	1,568	11.6
Aged 25 to 34	18,451	1,421	7.7
Aged 35 to 44	22,177	1,520	6.9
Aged 45 to 54	18,578	1,122	6.0
Aged 55 to 59	6,406	477	7.4
Aged 60 to 64	4,847	411	8.5
Aged 65 or older	14,179	1,063	7.5
Aged 65 to 74	8,187	575	7.0
Aged 75 or older	5,992	488	8.2

Source: Bureau of the Census, Current Population Survey, Internet site <http://ferret.bls.census.gov/macro/032001/pov/new01_001.htm>; calculations by New Strategist

Poverty Status of People by Age, Race, and Hispanic Origin, 2000

(number and percent distribution of total people below poverty level by age, race, and Hispanic origin, 2000; people in thousands as of 2001)

	total	black	Hispanic	white total	white non-Hispanic white
Total people	**31,054**	**7,862**	**7,153**	**21,242**	**14,532**
Under age 18	11,553	3,487	3,328	7,283	4,185
Aged 18 to 24	3,890	941	896	2,709	1,862
Aged 25 to 34	3,892	882	1,080	2,738	1,715
Aged 35 to 44	3,678	896	782	2,569	1,838
Aged 45 to 54	2,441	582	395	1,661	1,284
Aged 55 to 59	1,175	253	134	854	730
Aged 60 to 64	1,066	197	184	828	654
Aged 65 or older	3,359	623	353	2,601	2,264
Aged 65 to 74	1,592	317	218	1,190	982
Aged 75 or older	1,767	306	135	1,412	1,282
Percent distribution by race and Hispanic origin					
Total people	**100.0%**	**25.3%**	**23.0%**	**68.4%**	**46.8%**
Under age 18	100.0	30.2	28.8	63.0	36.2
Aged 18 to 24	100.0	24.2	23.0	69.6	47.9
Aged 25 to 34	100.0	22.7	27.7	70.3	44.1
Aged 35 to 44	100.0	24.4	21.3	69.8	50.0
Aged 45 to 54	100.0	23.8	16.2	68.0	52.6
Aged 55 to 59	100.0	21.5	11.4	72.7	62.1
Aged 60 to 64	100.0	18.5	17.3	77.7	61.4
Aged 65 or older	100.0	18.5	10.5	77.4	67.4
Aged 65 to 74	100.0	19.9	13.7	74.7	61.7
Aged 75 or older	100.0	17.3	7.6	79.9	72.6

Source: Bureau of the Census, Current Population Survey, Internet site <http://ferret.bls.census.gov/macro/032001/pov/new01_001.htm>; calculations by New Strategist

Thirty Percent of American Workers Are Managers or Professionals

Sixty-seven percent of Americans aged 16 or older are in the labor force, including 75 percent of men and 60 percent of women. The labor force participation rate peaks among men aged 30 to 34 at 94 percent. Among women, participation peaks at 79 percent among those aged 40 to 49.

The largest share of workers is employed in managerial or professional specialty occupations (30 percent). Another 29 percent hold technical, sales, or administrative support jobs. Farming, forestry, and fishing employ fewer than 3 percent of American workers.

Among all married couples, 56 percent are dual earners. Just 21 percent are traditional, that is, only the husband works. For 6 percent of couples, the wife is the only worker, while for another 16 percent neither husband nor wife is in the labor force. Forty-five percent of all households have two or more earners, while 20 percent have no earners—most of them the retired elderly.

It takes the average worker a median of 21 minutes to get to work each day. The median distance from home to work is 10 miles. Fully 78 percent of workers drive in their car by themselves to work. Only 5 percent use mass transit.

Between 2000 and 2010, the number of Americans in the labor force will grow 12 percent. The labor force participation rate of women is projected to rise to 62 percent, while that of men should fall to 73 percent. The non-Hispanic white share of workers will decline during the decade from 73 to 69 percent.

■ As the American population becomes more diverse, business and government leaders will also become more diverse.

Most men and women work

(percent of people aged 16 or older in the civilian labor force, by sex, 2000)

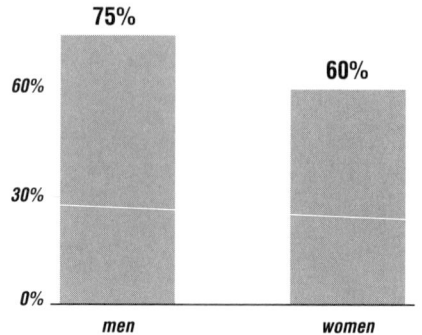

Labor Force Participation Rate of Total People by Age and Sex, 2000

(percent of total people aged 16 or older in the civilian labor force, by age and sex, 2000)

	men	*women*
Total people	**74.7%**	**60.2%**
Aged 16 to 19	53.0	51.3
Aged 20 to 24	82.6	73.3
Aged 25 to 29	92.4	77.1
Aged 30 to 34	94.2	75.6
Aged 35 to 39	93.2	75.8
Aged 40 to 44	92.1	78.7
Aged 45 to 49	90.1	79.1
Aged 50 to 54	86.8	74.1
Aged 55 to 59	77.1	61.2
Aged 60 to 64	54.8	40.1
Aged 65 or older	17.5	9.4
Aged 65 to 69	30.1	19.4
Aged 70 to 74	17.9	9.9
Aged 75 or older	8.0	3.5

Note: The civilian labor force equals the number of employed plus the number of unemployed.
Source: Bureau of Labor Statistics, Employment and Earnings, *January 2001*

Employment Status of Total People by Sex and Age, 2000

(employment status of the civilian noninstitutionalized population aged 16 or older, by sex and age, 2000; numbers in thousands)

		civilian labor force				not in labor force	
	total	percent of population	employed	unemployed	percent unemployed	total	percent of population
Total people	**140,863**	**67.2%**	**135,208**	**5,655**	**4.0%**	**68,836**	**32.8%**
Aged 16 to 19	8,369	52.2	7,276	1,093	13.1	7,673	47.8
Aged 20 to 24	14,346	77.9	13,321	1,025	7.1	4,065	22.1
Aged 25 to 34	31,669	84.6	30,501	1,168	3.7	5,748	15.4
Aged 35 to 44	37,838	84.8	36,697	1,141	3.0	6,767	15.2
Aged 45 to 54	30,467	82.6	29,717	749	2.5	6,438	17.4
Aged 55 to 64	13,974	59.2	13,627	347	2.5	9,641	40.8
Aged 65 or older	4,200	12.8	4,070	131	3.1	28,505	87.2
Total men	**75,247**	**74.7**	**72,293**	**2,954**	**3.9**	**25,484**	**25.3**
Aged 16 to 19	4,317	53.0	3,713	604	14.0	3,834	47.0
Aged 20 to 24	7,558	82.6	7,009	549	7.3	1,596	17.4
Aged 25 to 34	17,073	93.4	16,494	579	3.4	1,216	6.6
Aged 35 to 44	20,334	92.6	19,770	564	2.8	1,617	7.4
Aged 45 to 54	15,951	88.6	15,561	391	2.4	2,052	11.4
Aged 55 to 64	7,574	67.3	7,389	185	2.4	3,683	32.7
Aged 65 or older	2,439	17.5	2,357	82	3.4	11,487	82.5
Total women	**65,616**	**60.2**	**62,915**	**2,701**	**4.1**	**43,352**	**39.8**
Aged 16 to 19	4,051	51.3	3,563	489	12.1	3,839	48.7
Aged 20 to 24	6,788	73.3	6,312	476	7.0	2,469	26.7
Aged 25 to 34	14,596	76.3	14,006	590	4.0	4,532	23.7
Aged 35 to 44	17,504	77.3	16,927	577	3.3	5,150	22.7
Aged 45 to 54	14,515	76.8	14,156	359	2.5	4,386	23.2
Aged 55 to 64	6,400	51.8	6,238	162	2.5	5,958	48.2
Aged 65 or older	1,762	9.4	1,713	49	2.8	17,018	90.6

Note: The civilian labor force equals the number of employed plus the number of unemployed. The civilian population equals the number in the labor force plus the number not in the labor force.
Source: Bureau of Labor Statistics, Employment and Earnings, *January 2001; calculations by New Strategist*

Total Workers by Occupation, 2000

(number and percent distribution of employed people aged 16 or older in the civilian labor force by occupation, 2000; numbers in thousands)

	number	percent distribution
Total employed	**135,208**	**100.0%**
Managerial and professional specialty	40,887	30.2
Executive, administrative, and managerial	19,774	14.6
Professional specialty	21,113	15.6
Technical, sales, and administrative support	39,442	29.2
Technicians and related support	4,385	3.2
Sales occupations	16,340	12.1
Administrative support, including clerical	18,717	13.8
Service occupations	18,278	13.5
Private household	792	0.6
Protective service	2,399	1.8
Service, except private household and protective	15,087	11.2
Precision production, craft, and repair	14,882	11.0
Mechanics and repairers	4,875	3.6
Construction trades	6,120	4.5
Other precision production, craft, and repair	3,887	2.9
Operators, fabricators, and laborers	18,319	13.5
Machine operators, assemblers, and inspectors	7,319	5.4
Transportation and material moving occupations	5,557	4.1
Handlers, equipment cleaners, helpers, and laborers	5,443	4.0
Construction laborers	1,015	0.8
Other handlers, equipment cleaners, helpers, and laborers	4,428	3.3
Farming, forestry, and fishing	3,399	2.5

Source: Bureau of Labor Statistics, Employment and Earnings, *January 2001; calculations by New Strategist*

Total Workers by Industry, 2000

(number and percent distribution of employed people aged 16 or older in the civilian labor force by industry, 2000; numbers in thousands)

	number	percent distribution
Total employed	**135,208**	**100.0%**
Agriculture	3,305	2.4
Mining	521	0.4
Construction	9,433	7.0
Manufacturing	19,940	14.7
Durable goods	12,168	9.0
Nondurable goods	7,772	5.7
Transportation, communications, and other public utilities	9,740	7.2
Wholesale and retail trade	27,832	20.6
Wholesale trade	5,421	4.0
Retail trade	22,411	16.6
Finance, insurance, and real estate	8,727	6.5
Services	49,695	36.8
Private households	894	0.7
Other service industries	48,801	36.1
Professional and related services	32,784	24.2
Public administration	6,015	4.4

Source: Bureau of Labor Statistics, Employment and Earnings, *January 2001; calculations by New Strategist*

Total Households by Number of Earners, 2000

(number and percent distribution of total households by number of earners, 2000; numbers in thousands)

	number	percent
Total households	**104,705**	**100.0%**
No earners	20,521	19.6
One earner	36,689	35.0
Two or more earners	47,495	45.4
Two earners	37,070	35.4
Three earners	7,687	7.3
Four or more earners	2,738	2.6

Source: Bureau of the Census, Current Population Survey, Internet site <http://ferret.bls.census.gov/macro/032000/hhinc/new01_001 .htm>; calculations by New Strategist

Labor Force Status of Total Married Couples, 2000

(number and percent distribution of total married couples by age of householder and labor force status of husband and wife, 2000; numbers in thousands)

	total	*husband and/or wife in labor force*			*neither husband nor wife in labor force*
		husband and wife	*husband only*	*wife only*	
Total couples	**55,311**	**31,095**	**11,815**	**3,301**	**9,098**
Under age 20	96	49	47	–	–
Aged 20 to 24	1,354	848	448	39	21
Aged 25 to 29	3,775	2,656	1,021	55	44
Aged 30 to 34	5,615	3,876	1,556	119	64
Aged 35 to 39	6,886	4,850	1,802	162	72
Aged 40 to 44	7,218	5,241	1,612	255	110
Aged 45 to 54	12,792	9,046	2,499	772	475
Aged 55 to 64	8,138	3,739	1,782	1,086	1,530
Aged 65 or older	9,437	790	1,049	814	6,783
Total couples	**100.0%**	**56.2%**	**21.4%**	**6.0%**	**16.4%**
Under age 20	100.0	51.0	49.0	–	–
Aged 20 to 24	100.0	62.6	33.1	2.9	1.6
Aged 25 to 29	100.0	70.4	27.0	1.5	1.2
Aged 30 to 34	100.0	69.0	27.7	2.1	1.1
Aged 35 to 39	100.0	70.4	26.2	2.4	1.0
Aged 40 to 44	100.0	72.6	22.3	3.5	1.5
Aged 45 to 54	100.0	70.7	19.5	6.0	3.7
Aged 55 to 64	100.0	45.9	21.9	13.3	18.8
Aged 65 or older	100.0	8.4	11.1	8.6	71.9

Note: (–) means sample is too small to make a reliable estimate.
Source: Bureau of the Census, Household and Family Characteristics: March 2000 (Update), *detailed tables for Current Population Report P20-537, Internet site <www.census.gov/population/socdemo/hh-fam/p20-537/2000/tabFG1.txt>; calculations by New Strategist*

Union Membership of Total Employed Workers, 2000

(total number of employed wage and salary workers aged 16 or older, number and percent represented by unions or who are union members, and median weekly earnings by union membership status; by sex, 2000; numbers in thousands)

	total	men	women
Total employed	**120,786**	**62,853**	**57,933**
Represented by unions	17,944	10,355	7,590
Percent of employed	14.9%	16.5%	13.1%
Members of unions	16,258	9,578	6,680
Percent of employed	13.5%	15.2%	11.5%
Median weekly earnings, total	**$576**	**$646**	**$491**
Represented by unions	691	737	613
Members of unions	696	739	616
Non-union	542	620	472

Note: Workers represented by unions are either members of a labor union or similar employee association or workers who report no union affiliation but whose jobs are covered by a union or an employee association contract. Members of unions are union members as well as members of employee associations similar to unions.
Source: Bureau of Labor Statistics, Employment and Earnings, *January 2001*

Journey to Work for Total Workers, 1999

(number and percent distribution of total workers aged 16 or older by principal means of transportation to work, travel time from home to work, distance from home to work, and departure time to work, 1999; numbers in thousands)

	number	percent
Total workers	**118,041**	**100.0%**
Principal means of transportation to work		
Drives self	92,363	78.2
Car pool	11,103	9.4
Mass transportation	5,779	4.9
Taxicab	144	0.1
Bicycle or motorcycle	749	0.6
Walks only	3,627	3.1
Other means	987	0.8
Works at home	3,288	2.8
Travel time from home to work		
Less than 15 minutes	38,311	32.5
15 to 29 minutes	38,138	32.3
30 to 44 minutes	16,605	14.1
45 to 59 minutes	6,366	5.4
1 hour or more	5,356	4.5
Works at home	3,288	2.8
No fixed place of work	9,976	8.5
Median travel time (minutes)	21	–
Distance from home to work		
Less than 1 mile	4,863	4.1
1 to 4 miles	24,507	20.8
5 to 9 miles	23,568	20.0
10 to 19 miles	29,286	24.8
20 to 29 miles	12,611	10.7
30 miles or more	9,942	8.4
Works at home	3,288	2.8
No fixed place of work	9,976	8.5
Median distance (miles)	10	–
Departure time to work		
12:00 a.m. to 2:59 a.m.	729	0.6%
3:00 a.m. to 5:59 a.m.	11,355	9.6
6:00 a.m. to 6:59 a.m.	20,737	17.6
7:00 a.m. to 7:29 a.m.	16,604	14.1
7:30 a.m. to 7:59 a.m.	15,328	13.0
8:00 a.m. to 8:29 a.m.	12,622	10.7
8:30 a.m. to 8:59 a.m.	5,790	4.9
9:00 a.m. to 9:59 a.m.	5,646	4.8
10:00 a.m. to 3:59 p.m.	10,777	9.1
4:00 p.m. to 11:59 p.m.	7,050	6.0

Note: Numbers may not add to total because not reported is not shown; (–) means not applicable.
Source: Bureau of the Census, American Housing Survey for the United States: 1999, *Current Housing Reports, H150/99, 2000; calculations by New Strategist*

Workers Entering and Leaving the Labor Force, 2000 to 2010

(number and percent distribution of people aged 16 or older in the civilian labor force by race and Hispanic origin, 2000 and 2010; projected entrants, leavers, and stayers, 2000–2010; numbers in thousands)

	total labor force, 2000	2000–10			total labor force, 2010
		entrants	leavers	stayers	
Total people	**140,864**	**41,048**	**24,191**	**116,673**	**157,721**
Asian and other, non-Hispanic	6,404	3,218	879	5,526	8,743
Black, non-Hispanic	16,129	5,627	2,843	13,286	18,913
Hispanic	15,368	7,331	1,752	13,617	20,947
White, non-Hispanic	102,962	24,873	18,717	84,245	109,118
Total people	**100.0%**	**100.0%**	**100.0%**	**100.0%**	**100.0%**
Asian and other, non-Hispanic	4.5	7.8	3.6	4.7	5.5
Black, non-Hispanic	11.5	13.7	11.8	11.4	12.0
Hispanic	10.9	17.9	7.2	11.7	13.3
White, non-Hispanic	73.1	60.6	77.4	72.2	69.2

Source: Bureau of Labor Statistics, Monthly Labor Review, *November 2001*

Labor Force Projections of the Total Population by Sex, 2000 and 2010

(number of people in the civilian labor force, and labor force participation rate, by sex, 2000 and 2010; percent change in number and percentage point change in rate, 2000–2010; numbers in thousands)

	number in labor force		
	2000	*2010*	*percent change 2000–10*
Total	**140,863**	**157,721**	**12.0%**
Men	75,247	82,221	9.3
Women	65,616	75,500	15.1

	labor force participation rate		
	2000	*2010*	*percentage point change 2000–10*
Total	**67.2%**	**67.5%**	**0.3**
Men	74.7	73.2	−1.5
Women	60.2	62.2	2.0

Source: Bureau of Labor Statistics, Monthly Labor Review, *November 2001*

Total Population: Living Arrangements

Asians, Blacks, and Hispanics Account for a Large Share of Households

Because the Asian, black, and Hispanic populations are younger, on average, than the non-Hispanic white population, these groups account for a relatively large share of young-adult householders. More than 30 percent of householders under age 35 are Asian, black, or Hispanic. Among households headed by people aged 65 or older, minorities head a much smaller 15 percent share.

The minority share of households varies greatly by household type. Asians, blacks, Hispanics, and other minorities head half of female-headed families with children. But they head only 16 percent of married couples without children at home. Because many minority households include children, their household size is above average. Asians, blacks, and Hispanics head the majority of the nation's households with seven or more people. They head only 18 percent of two-person households.

Sixty-nine percent of American children live with both parents, while 22 percent live with their mother only. Among children living with their mother only, 35 percent are black and 18 percent are Hispanic. Most children living with neither parent are black or Hispanic.

■ With immigration adding substantially to U.S. population growth each year, the minority share of households will grow rapidly.

The minority share of households is much greater among young adults

(percent of households headed by Asians, blacks, and Hispanics, by age, 2000)

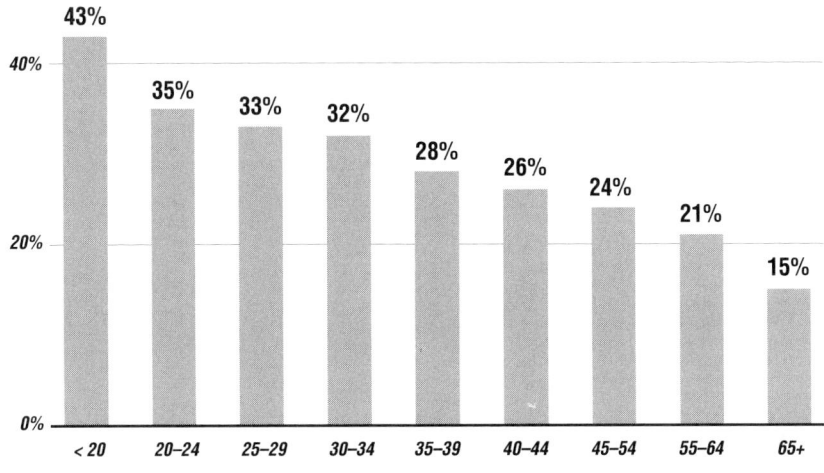

Total Households by Age of Householder, 2000

(number and percent distribution of total households by age of householder, 2000, numbers in thousands)

	number	percent distribution
Total households	**104,705**	**100.0%**
Under age 20	914	0.9
Aged 20 to 24	4,946	4.7
Aged 25 to 29	8,520	8.1
Aged 30 to 34	10,107	9.7
Aged 35 to 39	11,728	11.2
Aged 40 to 44	12,227	11.7
Aged 45 to 54	20,927	20.0
Aged 55 to 64	13,592	13.0
Aged 65 or older	21,744	20.8
Aged 65 to 74	11,325	10.8
Aged 75 or older	10,419	10.0

Source: Bureau of the Census, America's Families and Living Arrangements: March 2000, *detailed tables from Current Population Report P20-537, Internet site <www.census.gov/population/www/socdemo/hh-fam/p20-537_00.html>; calculations by New Strategist*

Households by Age, Race, and Hispanic Origin of Householder, 2000

(number of total households and percent distribution by race and Hispanic origin of householder, by age of householder, 2000; numbers in thousands)

| | total | | race and Hispanic origin | | | white | |
| | | | | | | | non- |
	number	percent	Asian	black	Hispanic	total	Hispanic
Total households	**104,705**	**100.0%**	**3.2%**	**12.3%**	**8.9%**	**83.7%**	**75.3%**
Under age 20	914	100.0	5.6	20.6	17.1	72.3	56.9
Aged 20 to 24	4,946	100.0	3.8	16.5	14.5	78.4	64.7
Aged 25 to 29	8,520	100.0	4.7	15.2	13.3	79.2	66.6
Aged 30 to 34	10,107	100.0	4.4	14.2	13.3	80.4	67.8
Aged 35 to 39	11,728	100.0	3.4	12.9	11.7	82.9	71.7
Aged 40 to 44	12,227	100.0	3.5	13.4	9.2	82.5	73.9
Aged 45 to 54	20,927	100.0	3.5	12.3	7.4	83.5	76.5
Aged 55 to 64	13,592	100.0	2.5	11.2	6.8	85.3	78.8
Aged 65 or older	21,744	100.0	1.7	8.7	4.6	89.1	84.7
Aged 65 to 74	11,325	100.0	2.2	9.8	5.7	87.3	81.9
Aged 75 or older	10,419	100.0	1.1	7.4	3.4	91.1	87.7

Note: Percentages will not sum to 100 because Hispanics may be of any race and not all races are shown.
Source: Bureau of the Census, America's Families and Living Arrangements: March 2000, detailed tables from Current Population Report P20-537, Internet site <www.census.gov/population/www/socdemo/hh-fam/p20-537_00.html>; calculations by New Strategist

Total Households by Household Type, 2000

(number and percent distribution of total households by type, 2000; numbers in thousands)

	number	percent distribution
Total households	**104,705**	**100.0%**
Family households	**72,025**	**68.8**
Married couples	55,311	52.8
With children under age 18	25,248	24.1
Without children under age 18	30,062	28.7
Female householder, no spouse present	12,687	12.1
With children under age 18	7,571	7.2
Without children under age 18	5,116	4.9
Male householder, no spouse present	4,028	3.8
With children under age 18	1,786	1.7
Without children under age 18	2,242	2.1
Nonfamily households	**32,680**	**31.2**
Female householder	18,039	17.2
Living alone	15,543	14.8
Male householder	14,641	14.0
Living alone	11,181	10.7

Source: Bureau of the Census, America's Families and Living Arrangements: March 2000, *detailed tables from Current Population Report P20-537, Internet site <www.census.gov/population/www/socdemo/hh-fam/p20-537_00.html>; calculations by New Strategist*

Households by Type, Race, and Hispanic Origin of Householder, 2000

(number of total households and percent distribution by race and Hispanic origin of householder, by household type, 2000)

	total		race and Hispanic origin			white	
	number	percent	Asian	black	Hispanic	total	non-Hispanic
Total households	**104,705**	**100.0%**	**3.2%**	**12.3%**	**8.9%**	**83.7%**	**75.3%**
Family households	**72,025**	**100.0**	**3.5**	**12.0**	**10.5**	**83.7**	**73.7**
Married couples	55,311	100.0	3.6	7.5	9.3	88.2	79.3
With children under age 18	25,248	100.0	4.5	8.3	13.6	86.4	73.3
Without children under age 18	30,062	100.0	2.8	6.8	5.7	89.8	84.3
Female householder, no spouse present	12,687	100.0	2.6	30.1	13.9	66.1	53.1
With children under age 18	7,571	100.0	2.2	31.8	15.1	64.3	50.4
Without children under age 18	5,116	100.0	3.2	27.5	12.2	68.6	57.0
Male householder, no spouse present	4,028	100.0	4.4	17.5	16.3	76.5	61.3
With children under age 18	1,786	100.0	2.2	15.7	13.8	80.0	67.3
Without children under age 18	2,242	100.0	6.2	19.0	18.4	73.7	56.5
Nonfamily households	**32,680**	**100.0**	**2.5**	**12.8**	**5.4**	**83.9**	**78.8**
Female householder	18,039	100.0	2.2	12.8	4.3	84.3	80.2
Living alone	15,543	100.0	2.0	13.0	4.1	84.3	80.5
Male householder	14,641	100.0	3.0	12.8	6.7	83.4	77.0
Living alone	11,181	100.0	2.8	14.1	6.0	82.3	76.6

Note: Percentages will not sum to 100 because Hispanics may be of any race and not all races are shown.
Source: Bureau of the Census, America's Families and Living Arrangements: March 2000, *detailed tables from Current Population Report P20-537, Internet site <www.census.gov/population/www/socdemo/hh-fam/p20-537_00.html>; calculations by New Strategist*

Total Households by Household Type, 2000 Census

(number and percent distribution of total households by household type, 2000)

	number	percent distribution
Total households	**105,480,101**	**100.0%**
Family households	**71,787,347**	**68.1**
Married couples	54,493,232	51.7
With children under age 18	24,835,505	23.5
Without children under age 18	29,657,727	28.1
Female householder, no spouse present	12,900,103	12.2
With children under age 18	7,561,874	7.2
Without children under age 18	5,338,229	5.1
Male householder, no spouse present	4,394,012	4.2
With children under age 18	2,190,989	2.1
Without children under age 18	2,203,023	2.1
Nonfamily households	**33,692,754**	**31.9**
Living alone	27,230,075	25.8
Living with nonrelatives	6,462,679	6.1

Source: Bureau of the Census, Census 2000, Table DP-1, Profile of General Demographic Characteristics for the United States: 2000; *and Census 2000 PHC-T-15, Tables 1–5,* General Demographic Characteristics by Race for the United Sates: 2000; *calculations by New Strategist*

Households by Type and Race of Householder, 2000 Census

(number and percent distribution of total households by household type and race of householder, 2000)

	total		race				
	number	percent	American Indian	Asian	black	Native Hawaiian	white
Total households	105,480,101	100.0%	1.3%	3.3%	11.8%	0.2%	80.8%
Family households	71,787,347	100.0	1.3	3.6	11.8	0.2	79.7
Married couples	54,493,232	100.0	1.1	3.8	7.2	0.2	84.8
With children <18	24,835,505	100.0	1.2	4.8	8.1	0.3	80.5
Without children <18	29,657,727	100.0	0.9	3.0	6.4	0.2	88.4
Female householder, no spouse present	12,900,103	100.0	2.0	2.6	29.6	0.3	61.3
With children <18	7,561,874	100.0	2.2	2.2	31.7	0.3	58.4
Without children <18	5,338,229	100.0	1.8	3.2	26.6	0.3	65.3
Male householder, no spouse present	4,394,012	100.0	2.1	3.9	16.5	0.4	70.3
With children <18	2,190,989	100.0	2.4	2.5	16.4	0.4	71.5
Without children <18	2,203,023	100.0	1.8	5.4	16.6	0.4	69.1
Nonfamily households	33,692,754	100.0	1.2	2.7	11.9	0.2	83.2
Living alone	27,230,075	100.0	1.2	2.4	12.3	0.1	83.4
Living with nonrelatives	6,462,679	100.0	1.4	3.9	9.9	0.3	82.3

Note: Percentages will not sum to 100 because some householders identified themselves as belonging to more than one race, and because not all races are shown.
Source: Bureau of the Census, Census 2000, Table DP-1, Profile of General Demographic Characteristics for the United States: 2000; and Census 2000 PHC-T-15, Tables 1–5, General Demographic Characteristics by Race for the United Sates: 2000; calculations by New Strategist

Total Households by Size, 2000

(number and percent distribution of total households by size, 2000; numbers in thousands)

	number	percent distribution
Total households	**104,705**	**100.0%**
One person	26,724	25.5
Two people	34,666	33.1
Three people	17,152	16.4
Four people	15,309	14.6
Five people	6,981	6.7
Six people	2,445	2.3
Seven or more people	1,428	1.4

Source: Bureau of the Census, America's Families and Living Arrangements: March 2000, *detailed tables from Current Population Report P20-537, Internet site <www.census.gov/population/www/socdemo/hh-fam/p20-537_00.html>; calculations by New Strategist*

Households by Size, Race, and Hispanic Origin of Householder, 2000

(number of total households and percent distribution by race and Hispanic origin of householder, by size, 2000; numbers in thousands)

	total		race and Hispanic origin			white	
	number	percent	Asian	black	Hispanic	total	non-Hispanic
Total households	**104,705**	**100.0%**	**3.2%**	**12.3%**	**8.9%**	**83.7%**	**75.3 %**
One person	26,724	100.0	2.3	13.5	4.8	83.5	78.8
Two people	34,666	100.0	2.5	9.9	5.6	86.9	81.7
Three people	17,152	100.0	3.7	14.7	10.4	80.7	70.8
Four people	15,309	100.0	4.2	11.4	12.7	83.6	71.6
Five people	6,981	100.0	4.1	12.9	18.1	81.4	64.1
Six people	2,445	100.0	6.8	17.1	22.8	75.1	53.1
Seven or more people	1,428	100.0	7.4	16.0	37.0	74.6	38.9

Note: Percentages will not sum to 100 because Hispanics may be of any race and not all races are shown.
Source: Bureau of the Census, America's Families and Living Arrangements: March 2000, *detailed tables from Current Population Report P20-537, Internet site <www.census.gov/population/www/socdemo/hh-fam/p20-537_00.html>; calculations by New Strategist*

Total Households by Age of Householder and Household Type, 2000

(number and percent distribution of total households by age of householder and household type, 2000; numbers in thousands)

	total	family households total	married couples	female hh, no spouse present	male hh, no spouse present	nonfamily households female house-holder	male house-holder
Total households	**104,705**	**72,025**	**55,311**	**12,687**	**4,028**	**18,039**	**14,641**
Under age 20	914	553	96	295	162	183	178
Aged 20 to 24	4,946	2,800	1,354	1,047	398	1,038	1,108
Aged 25 to 29	8,520	5,489	3,775	1,289	426	1,249	1,782
Aged 30 to 34	10,107	7,518	5,615	1,443	460	923	1,666
Aged 35 to 39	11,728	9,100	6,886	1,676	537	974	1,655
Aged 40 to 44	12,227	9,606	7,218	1,823	565	1,015	1,606
Aged 45 to 54	20,927	15,803	12,792	2,299	713	2,541	2,583
Aged 55 to 64	13,592	9,569	8,138	1,080	351	2,490	1,533
Aged 65 or older	21,744	11,587	9,437	1,735	416	7,626	2,530
Aged 65 to 74	11,325	7,025	5,929	894	203	3,079	1,221
Aged 75 to 84	10,419	4,562	3,508	841	213	4,547	1,309
Total households	**100.0%**	**68.8%**	**52.8%**	**12.1%**	**3.8%**	**17.2%**	**14.0%**
Under age 20	100.0	60.5	10.5	32.3	17.7	20.0	19.5
Aged 20 to 24	100.0	56.6	27.4	21.2	8.0	21.0	22.4
Aged 25 to 29	100.0	64.4	44.3	15.1	5.0	14.7	20.9
Aged 30 to 34	100.0	74.4	55.6	14.3	4.6	9.1	16.5
Aged 35 to 39	100.0	77.6	58.7	14.3	4.6	8.3	14.1
Aged 40 to 44	100.0	78.6	59.0	14.9	4.6	8.3	13.1
Aged 45 to 54	100.0	75.5	61.1	11.0	3.4	12.1	12.3
Aged 55 to 64	100.0	70.4	59.9	7.9	2.6	18.3	11.3
Aged 65 or older	100.0	53.3	43.4	8.0	1.9	35.1	11.6
Aged 65 to 74	100.0	62.0	52.4	7.9	1.8	27.2	10.8
Aged 75 to 84	100.0	43.8	33.7	8.1	2.0	43.6	12.6

Source: Bureau of the Census, America's Families and Living Arrangements: March 2000, *detailed tables from Current Population Report P20-537, Internet site <www.census.gov/population/www/socdemo/hh-fam/p20-537_00.html>; calculations by New Strategist*

Total Married Couples by Age of Children and Age of Householder, 2000

(number and percent distribution of total married couples by presence and age of own children at home and age of householder, 2000; numbers in thousands)

	total	< age 20	20–24	25–29	30–34	35–39	40–44	45–54	55–64	65–74	75+
							age of householder				
Total married couples	55,311	96	1,354	3,775	5,615	6,886	7,218	12,792	8,138	5,929	3,508
With children of any age	**31,065**	**59**	**779**	**2,441**	**4,399**	**5,887**	**6,076**	**7,969**	**2,300**	**843**	**312**
With children under age 18	25,248	55	779	2,439	4,391	5,796	5,609	5,401	671	88	19
Aged 12 to 17	11,567	5	9	133	721	2,366	3,532	4,192	534	66	8
Aged 6 to 11	12,501	1	100	974	2,234	3,674	3,254	2,029	198	25	12
Under age 6	11,393	52	754	2,113	3,355	2,964	1,463	612	70	6	5
Under age 1	2,264	14	244	573	744	450	175	56	7	–	–
Total married couples	100.0%	100.0%	100.0%	100.0%	100.0%	100.0%	100.0%	100.0%	100.0%	100.0%	100.0%
With children of any age	**56.2**	**61.5**	**57.5**	**64.7**	**78.3**	**85.5**	**84.2**	**62.3**	**28.3**	**14.2**	**8.9**
With children under age 18	45.6	57.3	57.5	64.6	78.2	84.2	77.7	42.2	8.2	1.5	0.5
Aged 12 to 17	20.9	5.2	0.7	3.5	12.8	34.4	48.9	32.8	6.6	1.1	0.2
Aged 6 to 11	22.6	1.0	7.4	25.8	39.8	53.4	45.1	15.9	2.4	0.4	0.3
Under age 6	20.6	54.2	55.7	56.0	59.8	43.0	20.3	4.8	0.9	0.1	0.1
Under age 1	4.1	14.6	18.0	15.2	13.3	6.5	2.4	0.4	0.1	–	–

Note: Numbers will not add to total because households may have children in more than one age group; (–) means sample is too small to make a reliable estimate.
Source: Bureau of the Census, America's Families and Living Arrangements: March 2000, detailed tables from Current Population Report P20-537, Internet site <www.census.gov/population/www/socdemo/hh-fam/p20-537_00.html>; calculations by New Strategist

Total Female-Headed Families by Age of Children and Age of Householder, 2000

(number and percent distribution of total female-headed families by presence and age of own children at home and age of householder, 2000; numbers in thousands)

	total		age of householder								
		<age 20	20–24	25–29	30–34	35–39	40–44	45–54	55–64	65–74	75+
Total female-headed families	12,687	295	1,047	1,289	1,443	1,676	1,823	2,299	1,080	894	841
With children of any age	**11,131**	**161**	**899**	**1,173**	**1,368**	**1,618**	**1,726**	**1,996**	**839**	**672**	**680**
With children under age 18	7,571	151	891	1,169	1,356	1,529	1,433	911	119	5	6
Aged 12 to 17	3,463	9	7	67	542	983	1,015	733	101	4	3
Aged 6 to 11	3,775	7	153	797	987	893	663	256	18	1	–
Under age 6	2,887	144	828	779	573	319	191	45	7	–	2
Under age 1	501	63	219	116	56	36	11	–	–	–	–
Total female-headed families	100.0%	100.0%	100.0%	100.0%	100.0%	100.0%	100.0%	100.0%	100.0%	100.0%	100.0%
With children of any age	**87.7**	**54.6**	**85.9**	**91.0**	**94.8**	**96.5**	**94.7**	**86.8**	**77.7**	**75.2**	**80.9**
With children under age 18	59.7	51.2	85.1	90.7	94.0	91.2	78.6	39.6	11.0	0.6	0.7
Aged 12 to 17	27.3	3.1	0.7	5.2	37.6	58.7	55.7	31.9	9.4	0.4	0.4
Aged 6 to 11	29.8	2.4	14.6	61.8	68.4	53.3	36.4	11.1	1.7	0.1	–
Under age 6	22.8	48.8	79.1	60.4	39.7	19.0	10.5	2.0	0.6	–	0.2
Under age 1	3.9	21.4	20.9	9.0	3.9	2.1	0.6	–	–	–	–

Note: Numbers will not add to total because households may have children in more than one age group; (–) means sample is too small to make a reliable estimate. Source: Bureau of the Census, America's Families and Living Arrangements: March 2000, detailed tables from Current Population Report P20-537, Internet site <www.census.gov/population/www/socdemo/hh-fam/p20-537_00.html>; calculations by New Strategist

Total Single-Person Households by Age of Householder, 2000

(number of total households, number and percent distribution of single-person households, and single-person households as a share of total, by age of householder, 2000; numbers in thousands)

		single-person households		
	total	number	percent distribution	share of total
Total households	**104,705**	**26,724**	**100.0%**	**25.5%**
Under age 20	914	127	0.5	13.9
Under age 25	4,946	1,016	3.8	20.5
Aged 25 to 29	8,520	1,927	7.2	22.6
Aged 30 to 34	10,107	1,921	7.2	19.0
Aged 35 to 39	11,728	1,976	7.4	16.8
Aged 40 to 44	12,227	2,133	8.0	17.4
Aged 45 to 54	20,927	4,304	16.1	20.6
Aged 55 to 64	13,592	3,538	13.2	26.0
Aged 65 to 74	11,325	4,091	15.3	36.1
Aged 75 or older	10,419	5,692	21.3	54.6

Source: Bureau of the Census, America's Families and Living Arrangements: March 2000, *detailed tables from Current Population Report P20-537, Internet site <www.census.gov/population/www/socdemo/hh-fam/p20-537_00.html>; calculations by New Strategist*

Total Children by Living Arrangement and Age, 2000

(number and percent distribution of total children under age 18 by living arrangement, 2000; numbers in thousands)

	number	percent distribution
Total children	**72,012**	**100.0%**
Living with both parents	49,795	69.1
Living with mother only	16,162	22.4
Living with father only	3,058	4.2
Living with neither parent	2,981	4.1
In group quarters	15	0.0
Living with both parents	**49,795**	**100.0**
Child of householder	48,921	98.2
Grandchild of householder	531	1.1
Other relative of householder	328	0.7
Nonrelative of householder	16	0.0
Living with mother only	**16,162**	**100.0**
Child of householder	13,283	82.2
Grandchild of householder	1,732	10.7
Other relative of householder	420	2.6
Nonrelative of householder	727	4.5
Living with father only	**3,058**	**100.0**
Child of householder	2,670	87.3
Grandchild of householder	220	7.2
Other relative of householder	92	3.0
Nonrelative of householder	77	2.5
Living with neither parent	**2,981**	**100.0**
Grandchild of householder	1,359	45.6
Other relative of householder	799	26.8
Foster child	219	7.3
Other nonrelative of householder	603	20.2
In group quarters	15	0.0

Source: Bureau of the Census, America's Families and Living Arrangements: March 2000, detailed tables from Current Population Report P20-537, Internet site <www.census.gov/population/www/socdemo/hh-fam/p20-537_00.html>; calculations by New Strategist

Children by Living Arrangement, Race, and Hispanic Origin, 2000

(number and percent distribution of total children under age 18 by living arrangement, race, and Hispanic origin, 2000; numbers in thousands)

| | | | | | race and Hispanic origin | |
| | | | | | white | |
	total	Asian	black	Hispanic	total	non-Hispanic
Total children	**72,012**	**3,047**	**11,412**	**11,613**	**56,455**	**45,407**
Living with both parents	49,795	2,454	4,286	7,561	42,497	35,188
Living with mother only	16,162	428	5,596	2,919	9,765	7,095
Living with father only	3,058	76	484	506	2,427	1,951
Living with neither parent	2,981	88	1,046	626	1,752	1,161
In group quarters	15	–	1	2	14	12
Total children	**100.0%**	**4.2%**	**15.8%**	**16.1%**	**78.4%**	**63.1%**
Living with both parents	100.0	4.9	8.6	15.2	85.3	70.7
Living with mother only	100.0	2.6	34.6	18.1	60.4	43.9
Living with father only	100.0	2.5	15.8	16.5	79.4	63.8
Living with neither parent	100.0	3.0	35.1	21.0	58.8	38.9
In group quarters	100.0	–	6.7	13.3	93.3	80.0

Note: Numbers will not add to total because Hispanics may be of any race and not all races are shown; (–) means sample is too small to make a reliable estimate.
Source: Bureau of the Census, America's Families and Living Arrangements: March 2000, *detailed tables from Current Population Report P20-537, Internet site <www.census.gov/population/www/socdemo/hh-fam/p20-537_00.html>; calculations by New Strategist*

Total Men by Living Arrangement and Age, 2000

(number and percent distribution of total men aged 15 or older by living arrangement and age, 2000; numbers in thousands)

	total	15–19	20–24	25–29	30–34	35–39	40–44	45–54	55–64	65–74	75+
Total men	**103,114**	**10,296**	**9,208**	**8,940**	**9,620**	**11,031**	**11,104**	**17,889**	**11,138**	**8,048**	**5,836**
Householder	**73,980**	**388**	**2,627**	**5,701**	**7,601**	**9,020**	**9,417**	**16,110**	**10,222**	**7,520**	**5,372**
Married couple hh or spouse	55,311	47	1,121	3,493	5,476	6,828	7,246	12,815	8,338	6,096	3,850
Male family householder	4,028	162	398	426	460	537	565	713	351	203	213
Living alone	11,181	62	494	1,079	1,200	1,240	1,329	2,146	1,276	1,108	1,247
Living with nonrelatives	3,460	117	614	703	465	415	277	436	257	113	62
Not a householder	**29,134**	**9,908**	**6,581**	**3,239**	**2,019**	**2,011**	**1,687**	**1,779**	**916**	**528**	**464**
Child of householder	18,026	8,746	4,446	1,566	819	901	689	604	206	49	–
In family, other relative of hh	4,792	744	787	525	406	355	349	546	423	296	361
Not in family	6,316	418	1,348	1,148	794	755	649	629	287	183	103
Total men	**100.0%**	**100.0%**	**100.0%**	**100.0%**	**100.0%**	**100.0%**	**100.0%**	**100.0%**	**100.0%**	**100.0%**	**100.0%**
Householder	**71.7**	**3.8**	**28.5**	**63.8**	**79.0**	**81.8**	**84.8**	**90.1**	**91.8**	**93.4**	**92.0**
Married couple hh or spouse	53.6	0.5	12.2	39.1	56.9	61.9	65.3	71.6	74.9	75.7	66.0
Male family householder	3.9	1.6	4.3	4.8	4.8	4.9	5.1	4.0	3.2	2.5	3.6
Living alone	10.8	0.6	5.4	12.1	12.5	11.2	12.0	12.0	11.5	13.8	21.4
Living with nonrelatives	3.4	1.1	6.7	7.9	4.8	3.8	2.5	2.4	2.3	1.4	1.1
Not a householder	**28.3**	**96.2**	**71.5**	**36.2**	**21.0**	**18.2**	**15.2**	**9.9**	**8.2**	**6.6**	**8.0**
Child of householder	17.5	84.9	48.3	17.5	8.5	8.2	6.2	3.4	1.8	0.6	–
In family, other relative of hh	4.6	7.2	8.5	5.9	4.2	3.2	3.1	3.1	3.8	3.7	6.2
Not in family	6.1	4.1	14.6	12.8	8.3	6.8	5.8	3.5	2.6	2.3	1.8

Note: (–) means sample is too small to make a reliable estimate.
Source: Bureau of the Census, America's Families and Living Arrangements: March 2000, detailed tables from Current Population Report P20-537, Internet site <www.census.gov/population/www/socdemo/hh-fam/p20-537_00.html>; calculations by New Strategist

Total Women by Living Arrangement and Age, 2000

(number and percent distribution of total women aged 15 or older by living arrangement and age, 2000; numbers in thousands)

	total	15–19	20–24	25–29	30–34	35–39	40–44	45–54	55–64	65–74	75+
Total women	110,660	9,809	9,233	9,327	9,896	11,289	11,382	18,742	12,250	9,748	8,987
Householder	86,036	693	4,050	7,020	8,521	9,994	10,279	17,107	11,386	9,042	7,945
Married couple hh or spouse	55,310	214	1,965	4,483	6,155	7,344	7,441	12,267	7,815	5,069	2,557
Female family householder	12,687	295	1,047	1,289	1,443	1,676	1,823	2,299	1,080	894	841
Living alone	15,543	66	522	848	720	736	804	2,158	2,262	2,983	4,444
Living with nonrelatives	2,496	118	516	400	203	238	211	383	229	96	103
Not a householder	24,624	9,116	5,183	2,307	1,375	1,295	1,103	1,635	864	706	1,042
Child of householder	14,335	7,847	3,451	1,039	564	448	398	431	134	20	4
In family, other relative of hh	5,119	731	468	406	254	246	319	657	513	584	940
Not in family	5,170	538	1,264	862	557	601	386	547	217	102	98
Total women	100.0%	100.0%	100.0%	100.0%	100.0%	100.0%	100.0%	100.0%	100.0%	100.0%	100.0%
Householder	77.7	7.1	43.9	75.3	86.1	88.5	90.3	91.3	92.9	92.8	88.4
Married couple hh or spouse	50.0	2.2	21.3	48.1	62.2	65.1	65.4	65.5	63.8	52.0	28.5
Female family householder	11.5	3.0	11.3	13.8	14.6	14.8	16.0	12.3	8.8	9.2	9.4
Living alone	14.0	0.7	5.7	9.1	7.3	6.5	7.1	11.5	18.5	30.6	49.4
Living with nonrelatives	2.3	1.2	5.6	4.3	2.1	2.1	1.9	2.0	1.9	1.0	1.1
Not a householder	22.3	92.9	56.1	24.7	13.9	11.5	9.7	8.7	7.1	7.2	11.6
Child of householder	13.0	80.0	37.4	11.1	5.7	4.0	3.5	2.3	1.1	0.2	0.0
In family, other relative of hh	4.6	7.5	5.1	4.4	2.6	2.2	2.8	3.5	4.2	6.0	10.5
Not in family	4.7	5.5	13.7	9.2	5.6	5.3	3.4	2.9	1.8	1.0	1.1

Source: Bureau of the Census, America's Families and Living Arrangements: March 2000, detailed tables from Current Population Report P20-537, Internet site <www.census.gov/population/www/socdemo/hh-fam/p20-537_00.html>; calculations by New Strategist

Total People by Living Arrangement, 2000 Census

(number and percent distribution of total people by living arrangement, 2000)

	number	*percent*
Total people	**281,421,906**	**100.0%**
In households	**273,643,273**	**97.2**
Householder	105,480,101	37.5
Spouse	54,493,232	19.4
Child	83,393,392	29.6
Own child under age 18	64,494,637	22.9
Other relative	15,684,318	5.6
Under age 18	6,042,435	2.1
Nonrelatives	14,592,230	5.2
Unmarried partner	5,475,768	1.9
In group quarters	**7,778,633**	**2.8**
Institutionalized population	4,059,039	1.4
Noninstitutionalized population	3,719,594	1.3

Source: Bureau of the Census, Table DP-1, Profile of General Demographic Characteristics for the United States: 2000*; calculations by New Strategist*

Total Men by Marital Status and Age, 2000

(number and percent distribution of total men aged 15 or older by age and marital status, 2000; numbers in thousands)

	total	never married	married	divorced	widowed
Total men	**103,114**	**32,253**	**57,866**	**10,390**	**2,604**
Under age 20	10,295	10,140	72	80	3
Aged 20 to 24	9,208	7,710	1,327	171	–
Aged 25 to 29	8,942	4,625	3,797	512	9
Aged 30 to 34	9,621	2,899	5,791	917	15
Aged 35 to 39	11,032	2,241	7,171	1,577	42
Aged 40 to 44	11,103	1,740	7,526	1,783	54
Aged 45 to 49	9,654	1,156	6,836	1,611	53
Aged 50 to 54	8,235	541	6,446	1,144	104
Aged 55 to 59	6,105	347	4,652	948	158
Aged 60 to 64	5,032	265	3,969	627	171
Aged 65 or older	13,886	590	10,283	1,022	1,994
Aged 65 to 69	4,376	227	3,412	453	285
Aged 70 to 74	3,673	121	2,860	311	382
Aged 75 or older	5,837	242	4,011	258	1,327
Total men	**100.0%**	**31.3%**	**56.1%**	**10.1%**	**2.5%**
Under age 20	100.0	98.5	0.7	0.8	0.0
Aged 20 to 24	100.0	83.7	14.4	1.9	–
Aged 25 to 29	100.0	51.7	42.5	5.7	0.1
Aged 30 to 34	100.0	30.1	60.2	9.5	0.2
Aged 35 to 39	100.0	20.3	65.0	14.3	0.4
Aged 40 to 44	100.0	15.7	67.8	16.1	0.5
Aged 45 to 49	100.0	12.0	70.8	16.7	0.5
Aged 50 to 54	100.0	6.6	78.3	13.9	1.3
Aged 55 to 59	100.0	5.7	76.2	15.5	2.6
Aged 60 to 64	100.0	5.3	78.9	12.5	3.4
Aged 65 or older	100.0	4.2	74.1	7.4	14.4
Aged 65 to 69	100.0	5.2	78.0	10.4	6.5
Aged 70 to 74	100.0	3.3	77.9	8.5	10.4
Aged 75 or older	100.0	4.1	68.7	4.4	22.7

Note: (–) means sample is too small to make a reliable estimate.
Source: Bureau of the Census, Marital Status and Living Arrangements: March 2000 (Update), *detailed tables for Current Population Report P20-537, 2001; Internet site <www.census.gov/population/socdemo/hh-fam/p20-537/2000/tabA1.txt>*

Total Women by Marital Status and Age, 2000

(number and percent distribution of women aged 15 or older by age and marital status, 2000; numbers in thousands)

	total	never married	married	divorced	widowed
Total women	**110,660**	**27,763**	**57,866**	**13,970**	**11,061**
Under age 20	9,807	9,401	309	87	10
Aged 20 to 24	9,233	6,720	2,169	332	11
Aged 25 to 29	9,326	3,627	4,817	864	18
Aged 30 to 34	9,896	2,172	6,417	1,245	63
Aged 35 to 39	11,288	1,610	7,632	1,915	131
Aged 40 to 44	11,382	1,341	7,741	2,128	172
Aged 45 to 49	10,094	1,008	6,883	1,895	309
Aged 50 to 54	8,647	598	5,787	1,846	416
Aged 55 to 59	6,763	377	4,527	1,281	578
Aged 60 to 64	5,487	229	3,553	843	863
Aged 65 or older	18,735	680	8,032	1,535	8,490
Aged 65 to 69	4,976	175	2,945	579	1,277
Aged 70 to 74	4,771	188	2,360	446	1,778
Aged 75 or older	8,988	317	2,727	510	5,435
Total women	**100.0%**	**25.1%**	**52.3%**	**12.6%**	**10.0%**
Under age 20	100.0	95.9	3.2	0.9	0.1
Aged 20 to 24	100.0	72.8	23.5	3.6	0.1
Aged 25 to 29	100.0	38.9	51.7	9.3	0.2
Aged 30 to 34	100.0	21.9	64.8	12.6	0.6
Aged 35 to 39	100.0	14.3	67.6	17.0	1.2
Aged 40 to 44	100.0	11.8	68.0	18.7	1.5
Aged 45 to 49	100.0	10.0	68.2	18.8	3.1
Aged 50 to 54	100.0	6.9	66.9	21.3	4.8
Aged 55 to 59	100.0	5.6	66.9	18.9	8.5
Aged 60 to 64	100.0	4.2	64.8	15.4	15.7
Aged 65 or older	100.0	3.6	42.9	8.2	45.3
Aged 65 to 69	100.0	3.5	59.2	11.6	25.7
Aged 70 to 74	100.0	3.9	49.5	9.3	37.3
Aged 75 or older	100.0	3.5	30.3	5.7	60.5

Source: Bureau of the Census, Marital Status and Living Arrangements: March 2000 (Update), *detailed tables for Current Population Report P20-537, 2001; Internet site <www.census.gov/population/socdemo/hh-fam/p20-537/2000/tabA1.txt>*

Married Couples by Race of Husband and Wife, 2000

(number and percent distribution of married-couple family groups by race of husband and wife, 2000; numbers in thousands)

	number	percent distribution
Total married couples	**56,497**	**100.0%**
Both white	48,917	86.6
Both black	3,989	7.1
Both American Indian	209	0.4
Both Asian	1,914	3.4
Husband white, wife black	95	0.2
Husband white, wife American Indian	203	0.4
Husband white, wife Asian	452	0.8
Husband black, wife white	268	0.5
Husband black, wife American Indian	12	0.0
Husband black, wife Asian	25	0.0
Husband American Indian, wife white	193	0.3
Husband American Indian, wife black	13	0.0
Husband American Indian, wife Asian	2	0.0
Husband Asian, wife white	203	0.4
Husband Asian, wife American Indian	2	0.0

Note: Figures include Hispanics, who may be of any race.
Source: Bureau of the Census, America's Families and Living Arrangements: March 2000, *detailed tables from Current Population Report P20-537, Internet site <www.census.gov/population/www/socdemo/hh-fam/p20-537_00.html>; calculations by New Strategist*

Married Couples by Race and Hispanic Origin of Husband and Wife, 2000

(number and percent distribution of married-couple family groups by race and Hispanic origin of husband and wife, 2000; numbers in thousands)

	number	percent distribution
Total married couples	**56,497**	**100.0%**
Both non-Hispanic white	42,845	75.8
Both non-Hispanic black	3,809	6.7
Both Hispanic	4,739	8.4
Both non-Hispanic other race	2,059	3.6
Husband non-Hispanic white, wife non-Hispanic black	80	0.1
Husband non-Hispanic white, wife Hispanic	824	1.5
Husband non-Hispanic white, wife non-Hispanic other	600	1.1
Husband non-Hispanic black, wife non-Hispanic white	227	0.4
Husband non-Hispanic black, wife Hispanic	72	0.1
Husband non-Hispanic black, wife non-Hispanic other	35	0.1
Husband Hispanic, wife non-Hispanic white	723	1.3
Husband Hispanic, wife non-Hispanic black	41	0.1
Husband Hispanic, wife non-Hispanic other	47	0.1
Husband non-Hispanic other, wife non-Hispanic white	348	0.6
Husband non-Hispanic other, wife non-Hispanic black	11	0.0
Husband non-Hispanic other, wife Hispanic	35	0.1

Source: Bureau of the Census, America's Families and Living Arrangements: March 2000, *detailed tables from Current Population Report P20-537, Internet site <www.census.gov/population/www/socdemo/hh-fam/p20-537_00.html>; calculations by New Strategist*

The United States Is Rapidly Becoming More Diverse

The U.S. population grew from 249 million in 1990 to 281 million in 2000, an increase of 13 percent. The non-Hispanic white share of the population fell from 76 to 69 percent during those years as minority populations grew.

The 2000 census was the first to allow Americans to identify themselves as multiracial. Nearly 7 million people (2 percent) did so, the largest share identifying themselves as white and "other" race. Most of those identifying themselves as "other" race are Hispanic. (See the Hispanic population chapter for more about the "other" race population.) The multiracial population is much younger than the single-race population. Forty-two percent of the multiracial population is under age 18 versus just 25 percent of the single-race population.

The United States is becoming more diverse because of immigration. Between 1991 and 2000, more than 9 million immigrants came to the United States, an all-time high. More than 28 million Americans are foreign-born, or 10 percent of the total population. Fully 20 percent are of foreign stock—meaning foreign-born or of foreign-born parents.

The largest share of the foreign born live in the West, which accounts for that region's rapid growth. During the 1990s, the West grew 20 percent, faster than any other region. The West is also the most diverse region, with non-Hispanic whites accounting for only 58 percent of its population.

■ The nation's growing diversity provides economic opportunity for immigrants and entrepreneurs alike, but it strains the political and social fabric of communities struggling to adapt to rapidly changing populations.

Minorities account for more than 30 percent of Americans

(percent distribution of the total population by race and Hispanic origin, 2000)

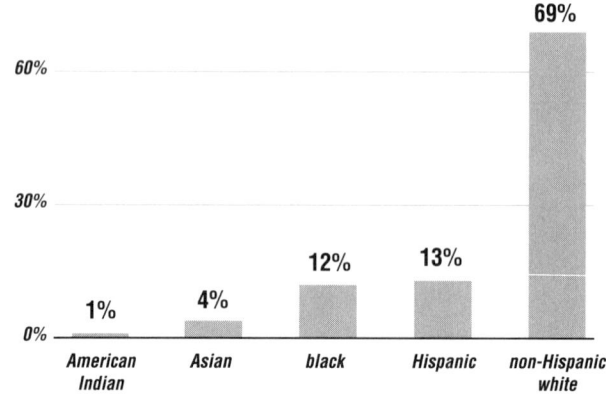

Total Population by Race and Hispanic Origin, 1990 and 2000 Censuses

(number of people by race and Hispanic origin, 1990 and 2000; percent change in number identifying themselves as race alone and identifying themselves as race alone or in combination, 1990–2000)

		2000		percent change, 1990–2000	
	1990	*race alone*	*race, alone or in combination*	*race alone*	*race, alone or in combination*
Race					
Total population	**248,709,873**	**281,421,906**	**281,421,906**	**13.2%**	**13.2%**
American Indian	1,959,234	2,475,956	4,119,301	26.4	110.3
Asian	6,908,638	10,242,998	11,898,828	48.3	72.2
Black	29,986,060	34,658,190	36,419,434	15.6	21.5
Native Hawaiian	365,024	398,835	874,414	9.3	139.5
White	199,686,070	211,460,626	216,930,975	5.9	8.6
Other	9,804,847	15,359,073	18,521,486	56.6	88.9
Hispanic origin					
Total population	**248,709,873**	**281,421,906**	**281,421,906**	**13.2**	**13.2**
Hispanic	22,354,059	35,305,818	35,305,818	57.9	57.9
Non-Hispanic	226,355,814	246,116,088	246,116,088	8.7	8.7
American Indian	1,793,773	2,068,883	3,444,700	15.3	92.0
Asian	6,642,481	10,123,169	11,579,494	52.4	74.3
Black	29,216,293	33,947,837	35,383,751	16.2	21.1
Native Hawaiian	325,878	353,509	748,149	8.5	129.6
White	188,128,296	194,552,774	198,177,900	3.4	5.3
Other	249,093	467,770	1,770,645	87.8	610.8

Note: Race alone numbers will not add to total because they do not include the multiracial population. Race alone or in combination numbers will not add to total because they count the multiracial population more than once. Hispanics may be of any race. American Indians include Alaska Natives. Native Hawaiians include other Pacific Islanders.
Source: Bureau of the Census, Census 2000 Redistricting Data, P.L. 94-171

Total Population by Race Alone and Race in Combination, 2000 Censuses

(number and percent distribution of people by race alone, race in combination, and race alone or in combination, by race and Hispanic origin, 2000)

	race, alone or in combination		race alone		race in combination	
	number	percent	number	percent	number	percent
Race						
Total population	**281,421,906**	**100.0%**	**281,421,906**	**100.0%**	**281,421,906**	**100.0%**
American Indian	4,119,301	1.5	2,475,956	0.9	1,643,345	0.6
Asian	11,898,828	4.2	10,242,998	3.6	1,655,830	0.6
Black	36,419,434	12.9	34,658,190	12.3	1,761,244	0.6
Native Hawaiian	874,414	0.3	398,835	0.1	475,579	0.2
White	216,930,975	77.1	211,460,626	75.1	5,470,349	1.9
Other	18,521,486	6.6	15,359,073	5.5	3,162,413	1.1
Hispanic origin						
Total population	**281,421,906**	**100.0**	**281,421,906**	**100.0**	**281,421,906**	**100.0**
Hispanic	35,305,818	12.5	35,305,818	12.5	35,305,818	12.5
Non-Hispanic	246,116,088	87.5	246,116,088	87.5	246,116,088	87.5
American Indian	3,444,700	1.2	2,068,883	0.7	1,375,817	0.5
Asian	11,579,494	4.1	10,123,169	3.6	1,456,325	0.5
Black	35,383,751	12.6	33,947,837	12.1	1,435,914	0.5
Native Hawaiian	748,149	0.3	353,509	0.1	394,640	0.1
White	198,177,900	70.4	194,552,774	69.1	3,625,126	1.3
Other	1,770,645	0.6	467,770	0.2	1,302,875	0.5

Note: Race alone numbers will not add to total because they do not include the multiracial population. Race alone or in combination numbers will not add to total because they count the multiracial population more than once. Hispanics may be of any race. American Indians include Alaska Natives. Native Hawaiians include other Pacific Islanders.
Source: Bureau of the Census, Census 2000 Redistricting Data, P.L. 94-171

Total Population by Racial Identification, 2000 Census

(number and percent distribution of people by racial identification, 2000)

	number	percent distribution
Total population	**281,421,906**	**100.0%**
One race	274,595,678	97.6
Two or more races	6,826,228	2.4
Two races	6,368,075	2.3
Three races	410,285	0.1
Four races	38,408	0.0
Five races	8,637	0.0
Six races	823	0.0

Source: Bureau of the Census, Census 2000 Redistricting Data, P.L. 94-171; and The Two or More Races
Population: 2000, *Census 2000 Brief, C2KBR/01-6, 2001*

Multiracial Population by Racial Combination, 2000 Census

(number and percent distribution of people by racial combination, 2000)

	number	percent distribution
Total population	**281,421,906**	**100.0%**
One race	**274,595,678**	**100.0**
White	211,460,626	77.0
Black	34,658,190	12.6
Other	15,359,073	5.6
Asian	10,242,998	3.7
American Indian	2,475,956	0.9
Native Hawaiian	398,835	0.1
Two races	**6,368,075**	**100.0**
White and other	2,206,251	34.6
White and American Indian	1,082,683	17.0
White and Asian	868,395	13.6
White and black	784,764	12.3
Black and other	417,249	6.6
Asian and other	249,108	3.9
Black and American Indian	182,494	2.9
Asian and Native Hawaiian	138,802	2.2
White and Native Hawaiian	112,964	1.8
Black and Asian	106,782	1.7
American Indian and other	93,842	1.5
American Indian and Asian	52,429	0.8
Native Hawaiian and other	35,108	0.6
Black and Native Hawaiian	29,876	0.5
American Indian and Native Hawaiian	7,328	0.1
Three races	**410,285**	**100.0**
White, black, and American Indian	112,207	27.3
White, Asian, and Native Hawaiian	89,611	21.8
White, black, and other	43,172	10.5
White, Asian, and other	34,962	8.5
White, American Indian, and other	29,095	7.1
White, American Indian, and Asian	23,766	5.8
White, black, and Asian	21,166	5.2
White, Native Hawaiian, and other	8,364	2.0
Black, Asian, and other	8,069	2.0
Black, American Indian, and other	7,023	1.7
Black, American Indian, and Asian	5,798	1.4
Black, Asian, and Native Hawaiian	5,309	1.3
White, American Indian, and Native Hawaiian	4,843	1.2

(continued)

(continued from previous page)

	number	percent distribution
Asian, Native Hawaiian, and other	4,604	1.1%
American Indian, Asian, and Native Hawaiian	3,063	0.7
White, black, and Native Hawaiian	2,938	0.7
American Indian, Asian, and other	2,544	0.6
Black, Native Hawaiian, and other	2,167	0.5
Black, American Indian, and Native Hawaiian	998	0.2
American Indian, Native Hawaiian, and other	586	0.1
Four races	**38,408**	**100.0**
White, black, American Indian, and Asian	10,672	27.8
White, Asian, Native Hawaiian, and other	7,932	20.7
White, American Indian, Asian, and Native Hawaiian	6,450	16.8
White, black, American Indian, and other	4,645	12.1
White, black, Asian, and Native Hawaiian	2,128	5.5
White, black, Asian, and other	1,376	3.6
White, American Indian, Asian, and other	1,099	2.9
Black, Asian, Native Hawaiian, and other	1,082	2.8
White, black, American Indian, Native Hawaiian	988	2.6
Black, American Indian, Asian, Native Hawaiian	750	2.0
Black, American Indian, Asian, and other	334	0.9
White, black, Native Hawaiian, and other	325	0.8
White, American Indian, Native Hawaiian, other	309	0.8
American Indian, Asian, Native Hawaiian, other	207	0.5
Black, American Indian, Native Hawaiian, other	111	0.3
Five races	**8,637**	**100.0**
White, black, American Indian, Asian, and Native Hawaiian	6,611	76.5
White, black, American Indian, Asian, and other	724	8.4
White, American Indian, Asian, Native Hawaiian, and other	639	7.4
White, black, Asian, Native Hawaiian, and other	379	4.4
Black, American Indian, Asian, Native Hawaiian, and other	216	2.5
White, black, American Indian, Native Hawaiian, and other	68	0.8
Six races: white, black, American Indian, Asian, Native Hawaiian, and other	**823**	**100.0**

Note: American Indians include Alaska Natives. Native Hawaiians include other Pacific Islanders.
Source: Bureau of the Census, Census 2000 Redistricting Data, P.L. 94-171; and The Two or More Races
Population: 2000, *Census 2000 Brief, C2KBR/01-6, 2001*

Total Population by Age, 1990 and 2000 Censuses

(number of total people by age, 1990 and 2000; percent change 1990–2000)

	1990	2000	percent change 1990–2000
Total population	**248,709,873**	**281,421,906**	**13.2%**
Under age 5	18,354,443	19,175,798	4.5
Aged 5 to 9	18,099,179	20,549,505	13.5
Aged 10 to 14	17,114,249	20,528,072	19.9
Aged 15 to 19	17,754,015	20,219,890	13.9
Aged 20 to 24	19,020,312	18,964,001	–0.3
Aged 25 to 29	21,313,045	19,381,336	–9.1
Aged 30 to 34	21,862,887	20,510,388	–6.2
Aged 35 to 39	19,963,117	22,706,664	13.7
Aged 40 to 44	17,615,786	22,441,863	27.4
Aged 45 to 49	13,872,573	20,092,404	44.8
Aged 50 to 54	11,350,513	17,585,548	54.9
Aged 55 to 59	10,531,756	13,469,237	27.9
Aged 60 to 64	10,616,167	10,805,447	1.8
Aged 65 to 69	10,111,735	9,533,545	–5.7
Aged 70 to 74	7,994,823	8,857,441	10.8
Aged 75 to 79	6,121,369	7,415,813	21.1
Aged 80 to 84	3,933,739	4,945,367	25.7
Aged 85 or older	3,080,165	4,239,587	37.6
Aged 18 to 24	26,737,766	27,143,454	1.5
Aged 18 or older	185,105,441	209,128,094	13.0
Aged 65 or older	31,241,831	34,991,753	12.0

Source: U.S. Census Bureau, Census 2000 Summary File 1; and 1990 Census of Population and Housing, Summary Tape File 1; calculations by New Strategist

Single Race Population by Age, 2000 Census

(number and percent distribution of total people, number and percent distribution of those identifying themselves as of one race, and one-race share of total, by age, 2000)

	total population		one race		
	number	percent distribution	number	percent distribution	share of total
Total population	**281,421,906**	**100.0%**	**274,595,678**	**100.0%**	**97.6%**
Under age 5	19,175,798	6.8	18,227,583	6.6	95.1
Aged 5 to 9	20,549,505	7.3	19,719,732	7.2	96.0
Aged 10 to 14	20,528,072	7.3	19,824,608	7.2	96.6
Aged 15 to 19	20,219,890	7.2	19,597,998	7.1	96.9
Aged 20 to 24	18,964,001	6.7	18,411,917	6.7	97.1
Aged 25 to 29	19,381,336	6.9	18,868,887	6.9	97.4
Aged 30 to 34	20,510,388	7.3	20,026,210	7.3	97.6
Aged 35 to 39	22,706,664	8.1	22,235,945	8.1	97.9
Aged 40 to 44	22,441,863	8.0	22,021,176	8.0	98.1
Aged 45 to 49	20,092,404	7.1	19,754,156	7.2	98.3
Aged 50 to 54	17,585,548	6.2	17,316,932	6.3	98.5
Aged 55 to 59	13,469,237	4.8	13,280,566	4.8	98.6
Aged 60 to 64	10,805,447	3.8	10,662,421	3.9	98.7
Aged 65 to 69	9,533,545	3.4	9,421,591	3.4	98.8
Aged 70 to 74	8,857,441	3.1	8,766,843	3.2	99.0
Aged 75 to 79	7,415,813	2.6	7,348,823	2.7	99.1
Aged 80 to 84	4,945,367	1.8	4,904,714	1.8	99.2
Aged 85 or older	4,239,587	1.5	4,205,576	1.5	99.2
Aged 18 to 24	27,143,454	9.6	26,344,912	9.6	97.1
Aged 18 or older	209,128,094	74.3	205,158,752	74.7	98.1
Aged 65 or older	34,991,753	12.4	34,647,547	12.6	99.0

Source: U.S. Census Bureau, Census 2000 Summary File 1; calculations by New Strategist

Multiracial Population by Age, 2000 Census

(number of total people, number and percent distribution of those identifying themselves as of two or more races, and multiracial share of total, by age, 2000)

	total population		two or more races		
	number	percent distribution	number	percent distribution	share of total
Total population	281,421,906	100.0%	6,826,228	100.0%	2.4%
Under age 5	19,175,798	6.8	948,215	13.9	4.9
Aged 5 to 9	20,549,505	7.3	829,773	12.2	4.0
Aged 10 to 14	20,528,072	7.3	703,464	10.3	3.4
Aged 15 to 19	20,219,890	7.2	621,892	9.1	3.1
Aged 20 to 24	18,964,001	6.7	552,084	8.1	2.9
Aged 25 to 29	19,381,336	6.9	512,449	7.5	2.6
Aged 30 to 34	20,510,388	7.3	484,178	7.1	2.4
Aged 35 to 39	22,706,664	8.1	470,719	6.9	2.1
Aged 40 to 44	22,441,863	8.0	420,687	6.2	1.9
Aged 45 to 49	20,092,404	7.1	338,248	5.0	1.7
Aged 50 to 54	17,585,548	6.2	268,616	3.9	1.5
Aged 55 to 59	13,469,237	4.8	188,671	2.8	1.4
Aged 60 to 64	10,805,447	3.8	143,026	2.1	1.3
Aged 65 to 69	9,533,545	3.4	111,954	1.6	1.2
Aged 70 to 74	8,857,441	3.1	90,598	1.3	1.0
Aged 75 to 79	7,415,813	2.6	66,990	1.0	0.9
Aged 80 to 84	4,945,367	1.8	40,653	0.6	0.8
Aged 85 or older	4,239,587	1.5	34,011	0.5	0.8
Aged 18 to 24	27,143,454	9.6	798,542	11.7	2.9
Aged 18 or older	209,128,094	74.3	3,969,342	58.1	1.9
Aged 65 or older	34,991,753	12.4	344,206	5.0	1.0

Source: U.S. Census Bureau, Census 2000 Summary File 1; calculations by New Strategist

Total Population by Age, Race, and Hispanic Origin, 2000 Census

(number of total people and percent distribution by race and Hispanic origin, by age, 2000)

	total	American Indian	Asian	black	Native Hawaiian	white total	white non-Hispanic	other race	Hispanic
Total population	**281,421,906**	**1.5%**	**4.2%**	**12.9%**	**0.3%**	**77.1%**	**69.1%**	**6.6%**	**12.5%**
Under age 5	19,175,798	1.9	4.8	16.5	0.5	71.2	58.4	10.5	19.4
Aged 5 to 9	20,549,505	1.9	4.4	17.0	0.4	71.2	59.9	9.5	17.6
Aged 10 to 14	20,528,072	2.0	4.3	16.2	0.4	72.6	62.8	8.3	15.4
Aged 15 to 19	20,219,890	1.9	4.5	15.3	0.4	72.5	63.1	8.6	15.7
Aged 20 to 24	18,964,001	1.7	5.1	14.6	0.4	71.2	61.1	10.2	18.0
Aged 25 to 29	19,381,336	1.5	5.8	13.7	0.4	71.7	61.9	9.7	17.5
Aged 30 to 34	20,510,388	1.4	5.2	13.2	0.3	74.1	65.2	8.2	15.2
Aged 35 to 39	22,706,664	1.4	4.5	12.8	0.3	76.6	69.0	6.5	12.4
Aged 40 to 44	22,441,863	1.4	4.2	12.4	0.3	78.4	71.9	5.4	10.3
Aged 45 to 49	20,092,404	1.4	4.1	11.6	0.2	80.0	74.2	4.5	8.8
Aged 50 to 54	17,585,548	1.3	3.9	10.5	0.2	82.0	76.6	3.7	7.7
Aged 55 to 59	13,469,237	1.2	3.5	9.9	0.2	83.6	78.3	3.1	7.1
Aged 60 to 64	10,805,447	1.1	3.4	10.1	0.2	83.8	78.5	2.8	6.9
Aged 65 to 69	9,533,545	0.9	3.1	9.4	0.2	85.3	80.3	2.3	6.3
Aged 70 to 74	8,857,441	0.8	2.7	8.4	0.1	87.2	82.7	1.9	5.4
Aged 75 to 79	7,415,813	0.7	2.3	7.6	0.1	88.8	85.1	1.6	4.4

(continued)

(continued from previous page)

	total	American Indian	Asian	black	Native Hawaiian	white total	white non-Hispanic	other race	Hispanic
Aged 80 to 84	4,945,367	0.6%	1.9%	7.1%	0.1%	89.8%	86.6%	1.3%	3.6%
Aged 85 or older	4,239,587	0.6	1.6	7.5	0.1	89.8	86.7	1.3	3.6
Aged 18 to 24	27,143,454	1.7	5.0	14.7	0.4	71.4	61.6	9.9	17.5
Aged 18 or older	209,128,094	1.3	4.1	11.8	0.3	78.9	72.0	5.7	11.0
Aged 65 or older	34,991,753	0.7	2.5	8.2	0.1	87.7	83.6	1.8	5.0

Note: Numbers will not add to total because each racial category includes those who identified themselves as of the race alone and those who identified themselves as of the race in combination with one or more other races, and because Hispanics may be of any race. Non-Hispanic whites include only those who identified themselves as white alone and non-Hispanic.

Source: U.S. Census Bureau, Census 2000 Summary File 1; calculations by New Strategist

Total Population by Age and Sex, 2000 Census

(number of total people by age and sex, and sex ratio by age, 2000)

	total	females	males	sex ratio
Total population	281,421,906	143,368,343	138,053,563	96
Under age 5	19,175,798	9,365,065	9,810,733	105
Aged 5 to 9	20,549,505	10,026,228	10,523,277	105
Aged 10 to 14	20,528,072	10,007,875	10,520,197	105
Aged 15 to 19	20,219,890	9,828,886	10,391,004	106
Aged 20 to 24	18,964,001	9,276,187	9,687,814	104
Aged 25 to 29	19,381,336	9,582,576	9,798,760	102
Aged 30 to 34	20,510,388	10,188,619	10,321,769	101
Aged 35 to 39	22,706,664	11,387,968	11,318,696	99
Aged 40 to 44	22,441,863	11,312,761	11,129,102	98
Aged 45 to 49	20,092,404	10,202,898	9,889,506	97
Aged 50 to 54	17,585,548	8,977,824	8,607,724	96
Aged 55 to 59	13,469,237	6,960,508	6,508,729	94
Aged 60 to 64	10,805,447	5,668,820	5,136,627	91
Aged 65 to 69	9,533,545	5,133,183	4,400,362	86
Aged 70 to 74	8,857,441	4,954,529	3,902,912	79
Aged 75 to 79	7,415,813	4,371,357	3,044,456	70
Aged 80 to 84	4,945,367	3,110,470	1,834,897	59
Aged 85 or older	4,239,587	3,012,589	1,226,998	41
Aged 18 to 24	27,143,454	13,269,625	13,873,829	105
Aged 18 or older	209,128,094	108,133,727	100,994,367	93
Aged 65 or older	34,991,753	20,582,128	14,409,625	70

Note: The sex ratio is the number of males per 100 females.
Source: U.S. Census Bureau, Census 2000 Summary File 1; calculations by New Strategist

Language Spoken at Home, 2000

(number and percent distribution of total people aged 5 or older by language spoken at home and ability to speak English, 2000)

	number	percent
Total people aged 5 or older	**254,762,734**	**100.0%**
English only	209,817,282	82.4
Language other than English	44,945,452	17.6
Speak English less than very well	19,526,233	7.7
Spanish	26,771,035	10.5
Speak English less than very well	12,479,051	4.9
Other Indo-European languages	9,493,791	3.7
Speak English less than very well	3,109,639	1.2
Asian and Pacific Islander languages	6,884,637	2.7
Speak English less than very well	3,407,880	1.3
Other languages	1,795,989	0.7
Speak English less than very well	529,663	0.2

Note: The Census 2000 Supplementary Survey is limited to people living in households and excludes people living in institutions, college dormitories, and other group quarters.
Source: Bureau of the Census, Profile of Selected Social Characteristics: 2000, *Census 2000 Supplementary Survey Summary Tables, Internet site <http://factfinder.census.gov/home/en/c2ss.html>*

Ancestry of the Total Population, 2000

(number and percent distribution of total people by ancestry, ranked by size of ancestry group, 2000)

	number	percent
Total people	**273,643,269**	**100.0%**
German	46,452,074	17.0
Irish	33,026,795	12.1
English	28,255,308	10.3
United States or American	19,643,045	7.2
Italian	15,903,962	5.8
French (except Basque)	9,768,319	3.6
Polish	9,050,122	3.3
Scottish	5,418,746	2.0
Scotch-Irish	5,223,468	1.9
Dutch	5,219,074	1.9
Norwegian	4,547,291	1.7
Swedish	4,332,226	1.6
Russian	2,987,143	1.1
French Canadian	2,201,977	0.8
West Indian (excluding Hispanics)	1,928,658	0.7
Welsh	1,899,196	0.7
Hungarian	1,516,645	0.6
Subsaharan African	1,504,985	0.5
Danish	1,499,804	0.5
Czech	1,395,867	0.5
Portuguese	1,311,008	0.5
Arab	1,249,160	0.5
Greek	1,179,737	0.4
Swiss	996,671	0.4
Ukrainian	862,416	0.3
Slovak	820,711	0.3
Lithuanian	714,729	0.3

Note: The Census 2000 Supplementary Survey is limited to people living in households and excludes people living in institutions, college dormitories, and other group quarters.
Source: Bureau of the Census, Profile of Selected Social Characteristics: 2000, *Census 2000 Supplementary Survey Summary Tables, Internet site <http://factfinder.census.gov/home/en/c2ss.html>; calculations by New Strategist*

Total Immigrants by Country of Birth, 2000

(number and percent distribution of immigrants to the U.S. by world region and country of birth, 2000; for countries sending at least 1,000 immigrants to the U.S., ranked by number of immigrants within regions)

	number	percent
Total immigrants	**849,807**	**100.0%**
Africa	44,731	5.3
Nigeria	7,853	0.9
Egypt	4,461	0.5
Ghana	4,344	0.5
Ethiopia	4,061	0.5
Morocco	3,626	0.4
South Africa	2,833	0.3
Somalia	2,465	0.3
Kenya	2,210	0.3
Sierra Leone	1,590	0.2
Liberia	1,575	0.2
Sudan	1,538	0.2
Cape Verde	1,083	0.1
Asia	265,400	31.2
China, People's Republic	45,652	5.4
Philippines	42,474	5.0
India	42,046	4.9
Vietnam	26,747	3.1
Korea	15,830	1.9
Pakistan	14,535	1.7
Taiwan	9,040	1.1
Iran	8,519	1.0
Bangladesh	7,215	0.8
Japan	7,094	0.8
Hong Kong	5,419	0.6
Iraq	5,134	0.6
Jordan	3,909	0.5
Thailand	3,785	0.4
Lebanon	3,674	0.4
Israel	2,806	0.3
Turkey	2,613	0.3
Syria	2,374	0.3
Cambodia	2,142	0.3
Yemen	1,789	0.2
Indonesia	1,774	0.2
Malaysia	1,556	0.2

(continued)

(continued from previous page)

	number	percent
Laos	1,380	0.2%
Burma	1,201	0.1
Sri Lanka	1,123	0.1
Saudi Arabia	1,063	0.1
Kuwait	1,018	0.1
Afghanistan	1,012	0.1
Caribbean	88,198	10.4
Haiti	22,364	2.6
Cuba	20,831	2.5
Dominican Republic	17,536	2.1
Jamaica	16,000	1.9
Trinidad and Tobago	6,660	0.8
Central America	66,443	7.8
Nicaragua	24,029	2.8
El Salvador	22,578	2.7
Guatemala	9,970	1.2
Honduras	5,939	0.7
Panama	1,843	0.2
Costa Rica	1,324	0.2
Europe	132,480	15.6
Russia	17,110	2.0
Ukraine	15,810	1.9
United Kingdom	13,385	1.6
Bosnia-Herzegovina	11,828	1.4
Poland	10,114	1.2
Germany	7,638	0.9
Romania	6,879	0.8
Bulgaria	4,925	0.6
Albania	4,756	0.6
France	3,465	0.4
Soviet Union*	3,332	0.4
Yugoslavia**	2,774	0.3
Italy	2,489	0.3
Belarus	2,207	0.3
Uzbekistan	1,659	0.2
Kazakhstan	1,509	0.2
Portugal	1,372	0.2
Lithuania	1,354	0.2
Netherlands	1,351	0.2
Ireland	1,315	0.2
Moldova	1,273	0.1
Sweden	1,269	0.1
Spain	1,264	0.1

(continued)

(continued from previous page)

	number	percent
Armenia	1,259	0.1%
Croatia	1,078	0.1
Azerbaijan	1,054	0.1
Switzerland	1,039	0.1
Hungary	1,025	0.1
North America	344,805	40.6
Mexico	173,919	20.5
Canada	16,210	1.9
Oceania	5,136	0.6
Australia	2,059	0.2
Fiji	1,487	0.2
South America	56,074	6.6
Colombia	14,498	1.7
Peru	9,613	1.1
Ecuador	7,685	0.9
Brazil	6,959	0.8
Guyana	5,746	0.7
Venezuela	4,716	0.6
Argentina	2,331	0.3
Bolivia	1,772	0.2
Chile	1,712	0.2
Unknown or not reported	1,181	0.1

* From former Soviet Union, unknown republic.
** From former Yugoslavia, unknown republic.
Note: Numbers will not add to regional totals because not all countries are shown.
Source: U.S. Immigration and Naturalization Service, 2000 Statistical Yearbook of the Immigration and Naturalization Service, *Internet site <www.ins.usdoj.gov/graphics/aboutins/statistics/IMM00yrbk/ IMM2000list.htm>; calculations by New Strategist*

Foreign-Born by Citizenship Status, Year of Entry, and Place of Birth, 2000

(number of total people by foreign-born status, number and percent distribution of the foreign-born by citizenship status, year of entry into the U.S., and world region of birth, 2000; numbers in thousands)

	number	percent
Total population	**274,087**	**100.0%**
Native born	245,708	89.6
Foreign-born	28,379	10.4
Foreign-born by naturalization status		
Total foreign-born	28,379	100.0
Naturalized citizen	10,622	37.4
Not a citizen	17,758	62.6
Foreign-born by year of entry		
Total foreign-born	28,379	100.0
Entered 1990 to 2000	11,206	39.5
Entered 1980 to 1989	8,022	28.3
Entered 1970 to 1979	4,605	16.2
Entered before 1970	4,547	16.0
Foreign-born by world region of birth		
Total foreign-born	28,379	100.0
Asia	7,246	25.5
Europe	4,355	15.3
Latin America	14,477	51.0
Other	2,301	8.1

Source: Bureau of the Census, detailed tables for The Foreign-born Population in the United States: March 2000, Current Population Report P20-534; Internet site <www.census.gov/population/www/socdemo/foreign/p20-534.html>; calculations by New Strategist

Total Foreign-Born by Age, 2000

(number and percent distribution of total and foreign-born populations by age, and foreign born share of total, 2000; numbers in thousands)

	total		foreign-born		
	number	percent distribution	number	percent distribution	share of total
Total population	**274,087**	**100.0%**	**28,379**	**100.0%**	**10.4%**
Under age 18	72,325	26.4	2,837	10.0	3.9
Aged 18 to 24	26,532	9.7	3,148	11.1	11.9
Aged 25 to 34	37,786	13.8	6,135	21.6	16.2
Aged 35 to 44	44,805	16.3	6,235	22.0	13.9
Aged 45 to 54	36,631	13.4	4,289	15.1	11.7
Aged 55 to 64	23,387	8.5	2,621	9.2	11.2
Aged 65 or older	32,621	11.9	3,115	11.0	9.5

Source: Bureau of the Census, detailed tables for The Foreign Born Population in the United States: March 2000, Current Population Report P20-534; Internet site <www.census.gov/population/www/socdemo/foreign/ p20-534.html>; calculations by New Strategist

Foreign-Born by Region of Residence and Place of Birth, 2000

(number and percent distribution of the total and foreign-born populations by region of residence and world region of birth, 2000; numbers in thousands)

	total	foreign-born total	Asia	Europe	Latin America	other
Total population	274,087	28,379	7,246	4,355	14,477	2,301
Northeast	52,038	6,420	1,398	1,712	2,652	658
Midwest	63,595	3,036	930	729	1,012	365
South	95,928	7,596	1,457	857	4,718	564
West	62,526	11,327	3,461	1,057	6,096	714

Percent distribution by region of residence

Total foreign-born	100.0%	100.0%	100.0%	100.0%	100.0%	100.0%
Northeast	19.0	22.6	19.3	39.3	18.3	28.6
Midwest	23.2	10.7	12.8	16.7	7.0	15.9
South	35.0	26.8	20.1	19.7	32.6	24.5
West	22.8	39.9	47.8	24.3	42.1	31.0

Percent distribution by world region of birth

Total foreign-born	100.0%	10.4%	2.6%	1.6%	5.3%	0.8%
Northeast	100.0	12.3	2.7	3.3	5.1	1.3
Midwest	100.0	4.8	1.5	1.1	1.6	0.6
South	100.0	7.9	1.5	0.9	4.9	0.6
West	100.0	18.1	5.5	1.7	9.7	1.1

Source: Bureau of the Census, detailed tables for The Foreign Born Population in the United States: March 2000, *Current Population Report P20-534; Internet site <www.census.gov/population/www/socdemo/foreign/p20-534.html>; calculations by New Strategist*

Total Foreign-Born by Sex, Race, Hispanic Origin, Income, and Education, 2000

(number and percent distribution of the foreign-born population by sex, race, Hispanic origin, income, poverty status, and education, 2000; numbers in thousands)

	number	percent
Total foreign-born	**28,379**	**100.0%**
Male	14,200	50.0
Female	14,179	50.0
Race	**28,379**	**100.0**
American Indian	191	0.7
Asian	6,706	23.6
Black	2,221	7.8
White	19,261	67.9
Hispanic origin	**28,379**	**100.0**
Hispanic	12,841	45.2
Non-Hispanic white	7,045	24.8
Household income in 1999		
Total households	**11,643**	**100.0**
Under $5,000	483	4.1
$5,000 to $9,999	727	6.2
$10,000 to $14,999	992	8.5
$15,000 to $24,999	1,817	15.6
$25,000 to $34,999	1,635	14.0
$35,000 to $49,999	1,779	15.3
$50,000 to $74,999	1,807	15.5
$75,000 to $99,999	1,008	8.7
$100,000 and over	1,396	12.0
Median income	$36,048	–
Poverty rate	16.8%	–
Median earnings of full-time year-round workers aged 16+		
Men	$27,239	–
Women	22,139	–
Education		
Total people aged 25 or older	**22,394**	**100.0**
Not a high school graduate	7,397	33.0
High school graduate or more	14,997	67.0
Bachelors degree or more	5,778	25.8
Graduate/professional degree	2,162	9.7

Note: (–) means not applicable.
Source: Bureau of the Census, detailed tables for The Foreign Born Population in the United States: March 2000, Current Population Report P20-534; Internet site <www.census.gov/population/www/socdemo/foreign/p20-534.html>; calculations by New Strategist

Total Population by Region, 1990 and 2000 Censuses

(number of total people by region, 1990 and 2000; percent change in number, 1990–2000)

	1990	*2000*	*percent change 1990–2000*
Total population	**248,709,873**	**281,421,906**	**13.2%**
Northeast	50,809,229	53,594,378	5.5
Midwest	59,668,632	64,392,776	7.9
South	85,445,930	100,236,820	17.3
West	52,786,082	63,197,932	19.7

Source: Bureau of the Census, Population Change and Distribution, 1990 to 2000, *Census 2000 Brief, C2KBR/01-2*

Total Population by Region, Division, Race, and Hispanic Origin, 2000 Census

(number and percent distribution of total people by region, division, race, and Hispanic origin, 2000)

	total	American Indian	Asian	black	Native Hawaiian	white total	white non-Hispanic	other race	Hispanic
Total population	281,421,906	4,119,301	11,898,828	36,419,434	874,414	216,930,975	194,552,774	18,521,486	35,305,818
Northeast	53,594,378	374,035	2,368,297	6,556,909	63,907	42,395,625	39,327,262	3,138,918	5,254,087
New England	13,922,517	100,700	426,140	821,871	16,440	12,262,195	11,686,617	594,992	875,225
Middle Atlantic	39,671,861	273,335	1,942,157	5,735,038	47,467	30,133,430	27,640,645	2,543,926	4,378,862
Midwest	64,392,776	714,792	1,392,938	6,838,669	55,364	54,709,407	52,386,131	1,769,970	3,124,532
East North Central	45,155,037	382,297	1,017,361	5,649,306	34,785	37,450,314	35,669,945	1,396,012	2,478,719
West North Central	19,237,739	332,495	375,577	1,189,363	20,579	17,259,093	16,716,186	373,958	645,813
South	100,236,820	1,259,230	2,267,094	19,528,231	117,947	74,303,744	65,927,794	4,719,249	11,586,696
South Atlantic	51,769,160	444,058	1,305,708	11,379,006	64,545	37,969,901	34,575,917	1,592,466	4,243,946
East South Central	17,022,810	127,744	168,719	3,475,933	12,819	13,257,904	12,967,670	161,570	299,176
West South Central	31,444,850	687,428	792,667	4,673,292	40,583	23,075,939	18,384,207	2,965,213	7,043,574
West	63,197,932	1,771,244	5,870,499	3,495,625	637,196	45,522,199	36,911,587	8,893,349	15,340,503
Mountain	18,172,295	754,952	455,816	611,049	68,776	15,032,215	12,883,812	1,790,704	3,543,573
Pacific	45,025,637	1,016,292	5,414,683	2,884,576	568,420	30,489,984	24,027,775	7,102,645	11,796,930

(continued)

(continued from previous page)

Percent distribution by race and Hispanic origin	total	American Indian	Asian	black	Native Hawaiian	white total	white non-Hispanic	other race	Hispanic
Total population	**100.0%**	**1.5%**	**4.2%**	**12.9%**	**0.3%**	**77.1%**	**69.1%**	**6.6%**	**12.5%**
Northeast	**100.0**	**0.7**	**4.4**	**12.2**	**0.1**	**79.1**	**73.4**	**5.9**	**9.8**
New England	100.0	0.7	3.1	5.9	0.1	88.1	83.9	4.3	6.3
Middle Atlantic	100.0	0.7	4.9	14.5	0.1	76.0	69.7	6.4	11.0
Midwest	**100.0**	**1.1**	**2.2**	**10.6**	**0.1**	**85.0**	**81.4**	**2.7**	**4.9**
East North Central	100.0	0.8	2.3	12.5	0.1	82.9	79.0	3.1	5.5
West North Central	100.0	1.7	2.0	6.2	0.1	89.7	86.9	1.9	3.4
South	**100.0**	**1.3**	**2.3**	**19.5**	**0.1**	**74.1**	**65.8**	**4.7**	**11.6**
South Atlantic	100.0	0.9	2.5	22.0	0.1	73.3	66.8	3.1	8.2
East South Central	100.0	0.8	1.0	20.4	0.1	77.9	76.2	0.9	1.8
West South Central	100.0	2.2	2.5	14.9	0.1	73.4	58.5	9.4	22.4
West	**100.0**	**2.8**	**9.3**	**5.5**	**1.0**	**72.0**	**58.4**	**14.1**	**24.3**
Mountain	100.0	4.2	2.5	3.4	0.4	82.7	70.9	9.9	19.5
Pacific	100.0	2.3	12.0	6.4	1.3	67.7	53.4	15.8	26.2

(continued)

(continued from previous page)

Percent distribution by region/division

	total	American Indian	Asian	black	Native Hawaiian	white total	white non-Hispanic	other race	Hispanic
Total population	100.0%	100.0%	100.0%	100.0%	100.0%	100.0%	100.0%	100.0%	100.0%
Northeast	**19.0**	**9.1**	**19.9**	**18.0**	**7.3**	**19.5**	**20.2**	**16.9**	**14.9**
New England	4.9	2.4	3.6	2.3	1.9	5.7	6.0	3.2	2.5
Middle Atlantic	14.1	6.6	16.3	15.7	5.4	13.9	14.2	13.7	12.4
Midwest	**22.9**	**17.4**	**11.7**	**18.8**	**6.3**	**25.2**	**26.9**	**9.6**	**8.8**
East North Central	16.0	9.3	8.6	15.5	4.0	17.3	18.3	7.5	7.0
West North Central	6.8	8.1	3.2	3.3	2.4	8.0	8.6	2.0	1.8
South	**35.6**	**30.6**	**19.1**	**53.6**	**13.5**	**34.3**	**33.9**	**25.5**	**32.8**
South Atlantic	18.4	10.8	11.0	31.2	7.4	17.5	17.8	8.6	12.0
East South Central	6.0	3.1	1.4	9.5	1.5	6.1	6.7	0.9	0.8
West South Central	11.2	16.7	6.7	12.8	4.6	10.6	9.4	16.0	20.0
West	**22.5**	**43.0**	**49.3**	**9.6**	**72.9**	**21.0**	**19.0**	**48.0**	**43.5**
Mountain	6.5	18.3	3.8	1.7	7.9	6.9	6.6	9.7	10.0
Pacific	16.0	24.7	45.5	7.9	65.0	14.1	12.4	38.3	33.4

Note: Numbers will not add to total because each race includes those who identified themselves as of the race alone and those who identified themselves as of the race in combination with one or more other races, and because Hispanics may be of any race. Non-Hispanic whites include only those who identified themselves as white alone and non-Hispanic. American Indians include Alaska Natives. Native Hawaiians include other Pacific Islanders.

Source: Bureau of the Census, Profiles of General Demographic Characteristics, 2000 Census of Population and Housing, 2001; calculations by New Strategist

Multiracial Population by Region, 2000 Census

(number and percent distribution of total people, number and percent distribution of those identifying themselves as of two or more races, and two-or-more race share of total, by region, 2000)

			two or more races		
	total	percent distribution	number	percent distribution	share of total
Total population	**281,421,906**	**100.0%**	**6,826,228**	**100.0%**	**2.4%**
Northeast	53,594,378	19.0	1,228,461	18.0	2.3
Midwest	64,392,776	22.9	1,022,468	15.0	1.6
South	100,236,820	35.6	1,847,015	27.1	1.8
West	63,197,932	22.5	2,728,284	40.0	4.3

Source: Bureau of the Census, The Two or More Races Population: 2000, *Census 2000 Brief, C2KBR/01-6, 2001*

Total Population by State, 1990 and 2000 Censuses

(number of total people by state, 1990 and 2000; percent change, 1990–2000)

	1990	2000	percent change 1990–2000
Total population	**248,709,873**	**281,421,906**	**13.2%**
Alabama	4,040,587	4,447,100	10.1
Alaska	550,043	626,932	14.0
Arizona	3,665,228	5,130,632	40.0
Arkansas	2,350,725	2,673,400	13.7
California	29,760,021	33,871,648	13.8
Colorado	3,294,394	4,301,261	30.6
Connecticut	3,287,116	3,405,565	3.6
Delaware	666,168	783,600	17.6
District of Columbia	606,900	572,059	-5.7
Florida	12,937,926	15,982,378	23.5
Georgia	6,478,216	8,186,453	26.4
Hawaii	1,108,229	1,211,537	9.3
Idaho	1,006,749	1,293,953	28.5
Illinois	11,430,602	12,419,293	8.6
Indiana	5,544,159	6,080,485	9.7
Iowa	2,776,755	2,926,324	5.4
Kansas	2,477,574	2,688,418	8.5
Kentucky	3,685,296	4,041,769	9.7
Louisiana	4,219,973	4,468,976	5.9
Maine	1,227,928	1,274,923	3.8
Maryland	4,781,468	5,296,486	10.8
Massachusetts	6,016,425	6,349,097	5.5
Michigan	9,295,297	9,938,444	6.9
Minnesota	4,375,099	4,919,479	12.4
Mississippi	2,573,216	2,844,658	10.5
Missouri	5,117,073	5,595,211	9.3
Montana	799,065	902,195	12.9
Nebraska	1,578,385	1,711,263	8.4
Nevada	1,201,833	1,998,257	66.3
New Hampshire	1,109,252	1,235,786	11.4
New Jersey	7,730,188	8,414,350	8.9
New Mexico	1,515,069	1,819,046	20.1
New York	17,990,455	18,976,457	5.5

(continued)

(continued from previous page)

	1990	2000	percent change 1990–2000
North Carolina	6,628,637	8,049,313	21.4%
North Dakota	638,800	642,200	0.5
Ohio	10,847,115	11,353,140	4.7
Oklahoma	3,145,585	3,450,654	9.7
Oregon	2,842,321	3,421,399	20.4
Pennsylvania	11,881,643	12,281,054	3.4
Rhode Island	1,003,464	1,048,319	4.5
South Carolina	3,486,703	4,012,012	15.1
South Dakota	696,004	754,844	8.5
Tennessee	4,877,185	5,689,283	16.7
Texas	16,986,510	20,851,820	22.8
Utah	1,722,850	2,233,169	29.6
Vermont	562,758	608,827	8.2
Virginia	6,187,358	7,078,515	14.4
Washington	4,866,692	5,894,121	21.1
West Virginia	1,793,477	1,808,344	0.8
Wisconsin	4,891,769	5,363,675	9.6
Wyoming	453,588	493,782	8.9

Source: Bureau of the Census, 1990 and 2000 censuses, Internet site <www.census.gov/population/cen2000/phc-t2/tab01.xls>

Distribution of Population by State, Race, and Hispanic Origin, 2000 Census

(number of total people by state and percent distribution by race and Hispanic origin, 2000)

	total	American Indian	Asian	black	Native Hawaiian	white total	white non-Hispanic	other	Hispanic
Total population	**281,421,906**	**1.5%**	**4.2%**	**12.9%**	**0.3%**	**77.1%**	**69.1%**	**6.6%**	**12.5%**
Alabama	4,447,100	1.0	0.9	26.3	0.1	72.0	70.3	0.9	1.7
Alaska	626,932	19.0	5.2	4.3	0.9	74.0	67.6	2.4	4.1
Arizona	5,130,632	5.7	2.3	3.6	0.3	77.9	63.8	13.2	25.3
Arkansas	2,673,400	1.4	1.0	16.0	0.1	81.2	78.6	1.8	3.2
California	33,871,648	1.9	12.3	7.4	0.7	63.4	46.7	19.4	32.4
Colorado	4,301,261	1.9	2.8	4.4	0.2	85.2	74.5	8.5	17.1
Connecticut	3,405,565	0.7	2.8	10.0	0.1	83.3	77.5	5.5	9.4
Delaware	783,600	0.8	2.4	20.1	0.1	75.9	72.5	2.6	4.8
District of Columbia	572,059	0.8	3.1	61.3	0.1	32.2	27.8	5.0	7.9
Florida	15,982,378	0.7	2.1	15.5	0.2	79.7	65.4	4.4	16.8
Georgia	8,186,453	0.6	2.4	29.2	0.1	66.1	62.6	2.9	5.3
Hawaii	1,211,537	2.1	58.0	2.8	23.3	39.3	22.9	3.9	7.2
Idaho	1,293,953	2.1	1.3	0.6	0.2	92.8	88.0	5.0	7.9
Illinois	12,419,293	0.6	3.8	15.6	0.1	75.1	67.8	6.8	12.3
Indiana	6,080,485	0.6	1.2	8.8	0.1	88.6	85.8	2.0	3.5
Iowa	2,926,324	0.6	1.5	2.5	0.1	94.9	92.6	1.6	2.8
Kansas	2,688,418	1.8	2.1	6.3	0.1	87.9	83.1	4.0	7.0
Kentucky	4,041,769	0.6	0.9	7.7	0.1	91.0	89.3	0.8	1.5
Louisiana	4,468,976	1.0	1.4	32.9	0.1	64.8	62.5	1.1	2.4
Maine	1,274,923	1.0	0.9	0.7	0.1	97.9	96.5	0.4	0.7
Maryland	5,296,486	0.7	4.5	28.8	0.1	65.4	62.1	2.5	4.3
Massachusetts	6,349,097	0.6	4.2	6.3	0.1	86.2	81.9	5.1	6.8
Michigan	9,938,444	1.3	2.1	14.8	0.1	81.8	78.6	2.0	3.3
Minnesota	4,919,479	1.6	3.3	4.1	0.1	90.8	88.2	1.8	2.9
Mississippi	2,844,658	0.7	0.8	36.6	0.1	61.9	60.7	0.7	1.4
Missouri	5,595,211	1.1	1.4	11.7	0.1	86.1	83.8	1.2	2.1
Montana	902,195	7.4	0.8	0.5	0.1	92.2	89.5	0.9	2.0
Nebraska	1,711,263	1.3	1.6	4.4	0.1	90.8	87.3	3.3	5.5
Nevada	1,998,257	2.1	5.6	7.5	0.8	78.4	65.2	9.7	19.7
New Hampshire	1,235,786	0.6	1.6	1.0	0.1	97.0	95.1	0.9	1.7

(continued)

(continued from previous page)

	total	American Indian	Asian	black	Native Hawaiian	white total	white non-Hispanic	other	Hispanic
New Jersey	8,414,350	0.6%	6.2%	14.4%	0.1%	74.4%	66.0%	6.9%	13.3%
New Mexico	1,819,046	10.5	1.5	2.3	0.2	69.9	44.7	19.4	42.1
New York	18,976,457	0.9	6.2	17.0	0.2	70.0	62.0	9.1	15.1
North Carolina	8,049,313	1.6	1.7	22.1	0.1	73.1	70.2	2.8	4.7
North Dakota	642,200	5.5	0.8	0.8	0.1	93.4	91.7	0.6	1.2
Ohio	11,353,140	0.7	1.4	12.1	0.1	86.1	84.0	1.1	1.9
Oklahoma	3,450,654	11.4	1.7	8.3	0.1	80.3	74.1	3.0	5.2
Oregon	3,421,399	2.5	3.7	2.1	0.5	89.3	83.5	5.2	8.0
Pennsylvania	12,281,054	0.4	2.0	10.5	0.1	86.3	84.1	1.9	3.2
Rhode Island	1,048,319	1.0	2.7	5.5	0.2	86.9	81.9	6.6	8.7
South Carolina	4,012,012	0.7	1.1	29.9	0.1	68.0	66.1	1.3	2.4
South Dakota	754,844	9.0	0.8	0.9	0.1	89.9	88.0	0.7	1.4
Tennessee	5,689,283	0.7	1.2	16.8	0.1	81.2	79.2	1.3	2.2
Texas	20,851,820	1.0	3.1	12.0	0.1	73.1	52.4	13.3	32.0
Utah	2,233,169	1.8	2.2	1.1	1.0	91.1	85.3	5.1	9.0
Vermont	608,827	1.1	1.1	0.7	0.1	97.9	96.2	0.4	0.9
Virginia	7,078,515	0.7	4.3	20.4	0.1	73.9	70.2	2.7	4.7
Washington	5,894,121	2.7	6.7	4.0	0.7	84.9	78.9	4.9	7.5
West Virginia	1,808,344	0.6	0.7	3.5	0.0	95.9	94.6	0.3	0.7
Wisconsin	5,363,675	1.3	1.9	6.1	0.1	90.0	87.3	2.0	3.6
Wyoming	493,782	3.0	0.8	1.0	0.1	93.7	88.9	3.2	6.4

Note: Percentages will not add to 100 because each race includes those who identified themselves as of the race alone and those who identified themselves as of the race in combination with one or more other races, and because Hispanics may be of any race. Non-Hispanic whites include only those who identified themselves as white alone and non-Hispanic. American Indians include Alaska Natives. Native Hawaiians include other Pacific Islanders. Source: Bureau of the Census, Census 2000 Redistricting Data, P.L. 94-171

Multiracial Population by State, 2000 Census

(number and percent distribution of total people, number and percent distribution of people who identified themselves as of two or more races, and multiracial share of total, by state, 2000)

| | total population | | two or more races | | |
	number	percent distribution	number	percent distribution	share of total
Total population	**281,421,906**	**100.0%**	**6,826,228**	**100.0%**	**2.4%**
Alabama	4,447,100	1.6	44,179	0.6	1.0
Alaska	626,932	0.2	34,146	0.5	5.4
Arizona	5,130,632	1.8	146,526	2.1	2.9
Arkansas	2,673,400	0.9	35,744	0.5	1.3
California	33,871,648	12.0	1,607,646	23.6	4.7
Colorado	4,301,261	1.5	122,187	1.8	2.8
Connecticut	3,405,565	1.2	74,848	1.1	2.2
Delaware	783,600	0.3	13,033	0.2	1.7
District of Columbia	572,059	0.2	13,446	0.2	2.4
Florida	15,982,378	5.7	376,315	5.5	2.4
Georgia	8,186,453	2.9	114,188	1.7	1.4
Hawaii	1,211,537	0.4	259,343	3.8	21.4
Idaho	1,293,953	0.5	25,609	0.4	2.0
Illinois	12,419,293	4.4	235,016	3.4	1.9
Indiana	6,080,485	2.2	75,672	1.1	1.2
Iowa	2,926,324	1.0	31,778	0.5	1.1
Kansas	2,688,418	1.0	56,496	0.8	2.1
Kentucky	4,041,769	1.4	42,443	0.6	1.1
Louisiana	4,468,976	1.6	48,265	0.7	1.1
Maine	1,274,923	0.5	12,647	0.2	1.0
Maryland	5,296,486	1.9	103,587	1.5	2.0
Massachusetts	6,349,097	2.3	146,005	2.1	2.3
Michigan	9,938,444	3.5	192,416	2.8	1.9
Minnesota	4,919,479	1.7	82,742	1.2	1.7
Mississippi	2,844,658	1.0	20,021	0.3	0.7
Missouri	5,595,211	2.0	82,061	1.2	1.5
Montana	902,195	0.3	15,730	0.2	1.7
Nebraska	1,711,263	0.6	23,953	0.4	1.4
Nevada	1,998,257	0.7	76,428	1.1	3.8
New Hampshire	1,235,786	0.4	13,214	0.2	1.1
New Jersey	8,414,350	3.0	213,755	3.1	2.5

(continued)

(continued from previous page)

	total population		two or more races		
	number	percent distribution	number	percent distribution	share of total
New Mexico	1,819,046	0.6%	66,327	1.0%	3.6%
New York	18,976,457	6.7	590,182	8.6	3.1
North Carolina	8,049,313	2.9	103,260	1.5	1.3
North Dakota	642,200	0.2	7,398	0.1	1.2
Ohio	11,353,140	4.0	157,885	2.3	1.4
Oklahoma	3,450,654	1.2	155,985	2.3	4.5
Oregon	3,421,399	1.2	104,745	1.5	3.1
Pennsylvania	12,281,054	4.4	142,224	2.1	1.2
Rhode Island	1,048,319	0.4	28,251	0.4	2.7
South Carolina	4,012,012	1.4	39,950	0.6	1.0
South Dakota	754,844	0.3	10,156	0.1	1.3
Tennessee	5,689,283	2.0	63,109	0.9	1.1
Texas	20,851,820	7.4	514,633	7.5	2.5
Utah	2,233,169	0.8	47,195	0.7	2.1
Vermont	608,827	0.2	7,335	0.1	1.2
Virginia	7,078,515	2.5	143,069	2.1	2.0
Washington	5,894,121	2.1	213,519	3.1	3.6
West Virginia	1,808,344	0.6	15,788	0.2	0.9
Wisconsin	5,363,675	1.9	66,895	1.0	1.2
Wyoming	493,782	0.2	8,883	0.1	1.8

Source: Bureau of the Census, The Two or More Races Population: 2000, *Census 2000 Brief, C2KBR/01-6, 2001*

Population by State, Age, Race, and Hispanic Origin, 2000 Census

(total number of people by state and percent distribution by age, race, and Hispanic origin, 2000)

	total	American Indian	Asian	black	Native Hawaiian	white total	white non-Hispanic	other	Hispanic
Alabama, total	**4,447,100**	**1.0%**	**0.9%**	**26.3%**	**0.1%**	**72.0%**	**70.3%**	**0.9%**	**1.7%**
Under age 5	295,992	0.9	1.1	32.2	0.1	66.1	63.0	1.7	2.9
Aged 5–9	315,345	1.0	0.9	33.4	0.1	65.0	62.7	1.2	2.2
Aged 10–14	320,252	1.1	0.9	32.6	0.1	65.7	63.9	0.9	1.7
Aged 15–19	324,580	1.2	1.0	32.8	0.1	65.0	63.1	1.1	2.2
Aged 20–24	306,865	1.0	1.3	31.0	0.1	66.0	63.7	1.8	3.2
Aged 25–29	301,196	0.9	1.4	27.5	0.1	69.4	67.3	1.6	3.0
Aged 30–34	301,819	1.0	1.2	25.7	0.1	71.8	70.0	1.2	2.3
Aged 35–39	340,300	1.1	1.0	25.3	0.1	72.6	71.1	0.8	1.7
Aged 40–44	345,212	1.2	0.9	25.8	0.1	72.4	71.0	0.6	1.3
Aged 45–49	315,173	1.1	0.8	24.9	0.1	73.5	72.2	0.4	1.0
Aged 50–54	285,036	1.1	0.8	21.3	0.1	77.3	76.1	0.3	0.8
Aged 55–59	225,450	1.1	0.6	18.6	0.0	80.2	79.1	0.3	0.8
Aged 60–64	190,082	0.8	0.5	18.8	0.0	80.3	79.3	0.2	0.7
Aged 65–69	167,968	0.7	0.5	18.7	0.0	80.6	79.6	0.2	0.6
Aged 70–74	148,780	0.6	0.3	18.6	0.0	80.9	80.0	0.2	0.5
Aged 75–79	118,108	0.6	0.2	18.2	0.0	81.4	80.6	0.1	0.5
Aged 80–84	77,641	0.5	0.2	18.6	0.0	81.1	80.3	0.2	0.5
Aged 85 or older	67,301	0.4	0.2	22.3	0.1	77.5	76.8	0.2	0.5
Alaska, total	**626,932**	**19.0**	**5.2**	**4.3**	**0.9**	**74.0**	**67.6**	**2.4**	**4.1**
Under age 5	47,591	25.5	6.4	7.4	1.5	68.8	56.1	3.5	6.7
Aged 5–9	53,771	25.8	5.6	6.0	1.3	68.8	58.2	3.0	5.6
Aged 10–14	56,661	25.8	5.5	5.1	1.2	69.0	59.7	2.5	4.6
Aged 15–19	50,094	24.0	5.5	4.6	1.2	70.2	61.8	2.5	4.6
Aged 20–24	39,892	20.7	5.5	5.8	1.2	69.6	62.5	3.4	5.8
Aged 25–29	42,987	17.7	5.2	5.1	0.9	72.9	66.9	3.1	5.2
Aged 30–34	46,486	17.4	5.2	4.4	0.9	73.4	68.1	2.8	4.6
Aged 35–39	55,723	16.4	4.9	4.1	0.7	75.4	70.5	2.3	3.9
Aged 40–44	58,326	14.4	4.8	3.4	0.6	78.2	73.9	2.1	3.3
Aged 45–49	53,515	13.0	4.6	2.9	0.5	80.2	76.6	1.8	2.6
Aged 50–54	41,437	12.4	4.6	2.3	0.5	81.3	77.9	1.7	2.4
Aged 55–59	27,423	14.0	4.5	2.2	0.4	80.3	76.9	1.4	2.1
Aged 60–64	17,327	16.0	5.0	2.6	0.3	77.4	73.9	1.4	2.3
Aged 65–69	12,626	18.8	5.2	2.3	0.5	75.1	71.8	1.1	1.8
Aged 70–74	9,881	17.7	5.6	2.1	0.4	76.1	72.9	1.0	1.5
Aged 75–79	6,863	16.6	5.5	1.9	0.2	77.2	74.5	1.1	1.2
Aged 80–84	3,695	16.1	5.0	2.3	0.3	77.5	75.1	1.2	1.2
Aged 85 or older	2,634	19.2	3.8	2.0	0.1	75.9	73.7	1.0	1.2

(continued)

(continued from previous page)

	total	American Indian	Asian	black	Native Hawaiian	white total	white non-Hispanic	other	Hispanic
Arizona, total	**5,130,632**	**5.7%**	**2.3%**	**3.6%**	**0.3%**	**77.9%**	**63.8%**	**13.2%**	**25.3%**
Under age 5	382,386	7.7	2.7	5.3	0.4	69.1	46.1	21.2	40.1
Aged 5–9	389,869	8.5	2.5	5.1	0.4	69.6	48.6	19.4	36.9
Aged 10–14	378,211	9.0	2.3	4.8	0.3	70.7	52.2	17.5	33.1
Aged 15–19	367,722	8.1	2.5	4.4	0.4	70.8	53.2	17.9	33.1
Aged 20–24	362,860	6.4	2.8	4.1	0.4	70.0	52.2	19.9	35.3
Aged 25–29	374,106	5.7	3.4	3.9	0.3	71.4	54.6	18.5	33.1
Aged 30–34	368,559	5.5	3.0	3.9	0.3	74.1	58.8	15.9	29.2
Aged 35–39	392,687	5.5	2.6	3.8	0.2	77.0	63.9	13.2	24.6
Aged 40–44	376,117	5.1	2.4	3.7	0.2	79.9	68.6	10.9	20.7
Aged 45–49	331,903	4.7	2.2	3.2	0.2	82.4	72.0	9.2	18.1
Aged 50–54	296,001	4.2	2.0	2.6	0.2	85.3	76.0	7.4	15.3
Aged 55–59	238,675	3.8	1.7	2.3	0.2	87.9	79.0	5.6	13.3
Aged 60–64	203,697	3.6	1.6	2.2	0.1	89.1	80.7	4.8	12.0
Aged 65–69	189,007	3.0	1.4	1.9	0.1	90.9	83.4	3.8	10.3
Aged 70–74	174,834	2.4	1.1	1.5	0.1	92.8	86.1	3.2	8.9
Aged 75–79	144,201	2.0	0.8	1.3	0.1	94.2	88.7	2.5	7.2
Aged 80–84	91,272	1.8	0.6	1.2	0.1	94.7	89.9	2.3	6.4
Aged 85 or older	68,525	2.3	0.6	1.5	0.1	93.9	89.2	2.3	6.2
Arkansas, total	**2,673,400**	**1.4**	**1.0**	**16.0**	**0.1**	**81.2**	**78.6**	**1.8**	**3.2**
Under age 5	181,585	1.4	1.2	21.7	0.2	74.8	69.7	3.5	6.2
Aged 5–9	187,224	1.6	1.0	21.9	0.1	74.9	70.9	2.7	4.8
Aged 10–14	192,935	1.7	1.0	21.2	0.1	75.8	72.6	2.1	3.8
Aged 15–19	198,765	1.6	1.1	20.9	0.2	75.5	72.4	2.4	4.2
Aged 20–24	181,598	1.3	1.4	19.5	0.2	75.7	72.1	3.4	5.8
Aged 25–29	176,674	1.3	1.5	16.8	0.2	78.3	74.8	3.3	5.7
Aged 30–34	176,171	1.4	1.3	15.7	0.1	80.1	77.1	2.6	4.6
Aged 35–39	200,340	1.5	1.0	15.4	0.1	81.4	79.0	1.7	3.2
Aged 40–44	197,787	1.5	1.0	15.7	0.1	81.6	79.4	1.3	2.5
Aged 45–49	181,913	1.5	0.9	14.9	0.1	82.7	80.9	1.0	1.9
Aged 50–54	167,606	1.6	0.8	11.9	0.1	86.1	84.4	0.8	1.5
Aged 55–59	139,393	1.4	0.6	9.9	0.1	88.6	87.0	0.6	1.2
Aged 60–64	117,390	1.2	0.5	9.8	0.0	89.0	87.5	0.4	1.0
Aged 65–69	105,175	1.0	0.5	9.5	0.1	89.5	88.3	0.3	0.8
Aged 70–74	93,159	0.9	0.4	9.6	0.1	89.6	88.5	0.3	0.6
Aged 75–79	76,517	0.8	0.3	9.4	0.0	90.1	89.1	0.2	0.5
Aged 80–84	52,676	0.8	0.2	10.1	0.0	89.4	88.4	0.2	0.5
Aged 85 or older	46,492	0.7	0.2	12.7	0.1	86.9	86.1	0.2	0.4

(continued)

(continued from previous page)

	total	American Indian	Asian	black	Native Hawaiian	white total	white non-Hispanic	other	Hispanic
California, total	**33,871,648**	**1.9%**	**12.3%**	**7.4%**	**0.7%**	**63.4%**	**46.7%**	**19.4%**	**32.4%**
Under age 5	2,486,981	2.1	11.8	8.8	0.9	57.0	31.7	28.5	47.8
Aged 5–9	2,725,880	2.2	11.4	9.2	0.9	57.3	33.7	27.1	45.4
Aged 10–14	2,570,822	2.3	11.9	9.2	0.8	58.3	37.4	24.6	40.6
Aged 15–19	2,450,888	2.3	13.0	8.2	0.9	56.7	37.3	25.4	40.4
Aged 20–24	2,381,288	2.0	13.1	7.4	0.8	54.9	35.4	27.5	42.9
Aged 25–29	2,543,541	1.8	13.8	6.9	0.7	56.1	37.0	25.8	41.0
Aged 30–34	2,685,521	1.8	12.9	7.3	0.7	59.6	41.5	22.5	37.0
Aged 35–39	2,814,743	1.8	12.4	7.6	0.6	63.1	47.3	18.8	31.1
Aged 40–44	2,670,598	1.9	12.6	7.4	0.6	65.5	51.8	16.1	26.5
Aged 45–49	2,331,792	1.8	12.9	6.9	0.5	67.7	55.5	13.7	22.9
Aged 50–54	1,999,843	1.8	12.4	6.4	0.5	70.9	59.9	11.2	19.5
Aged 55–59	1,467,252	1.7	11.6	6.4	0.5	73.2	62.0	9.7	18.3
Aged 60–64	1,146,841	1.6	12.3	6.8	0.4	73.0	61.4	8.9	17.8
Aged 65–69	984,535	1.3	12.3	6.2	0.4	74.8	63.4	7.7	16.6
Aged 70–74	903,288	1.1	11.4	5.3	0.3	77.9	67.3	6.5	14.7
Aged 75–79	779,347	0.9	9.7	4.8	0.2	81.3	72.8	5.1	11.6
Aged 80–84	502,831	0.8	8.5	4.6	0.2	83.5	76.4	4.3	9.5
Aged 85 or older	425,657	0.7	7.0	4.6	0.2	84.9	78.2	4.3	9.1
Colorado, total	**4,301,261**	**1.9**	**2.8**	**4.4**	**0.2**	**85.2**	**74.5**	**8.5**	**17.1**
Under age 5	297,505	2.3	3.8	6.5	0.4	79.8	62.0	13.9	27.2
Aged 5–9	308,428	2.3	3.1	6.4	0.3	81.0	65.6	12.4	24.0
Aged 10–14	311,497	2.3	3.0	5.7	0.3	82.5	69.0	10.7	21.0
Aged 15–19	307,238	2.4	3.3	5.1	0.3	82.1	68.7	11.1	21.7
Aged 20–24	306,238	2.2	3.5	4.7	0.4	80.1	66.2	12.9	24.2
Aged 25–29	331,795	1.9	3.9	4.5	0.3	80.8	68.4	11.6	21.8
Aged 30–34	332,232	1.9	3.4	4.6	0.3	82.9	72.0	9.7	18.7
Aged 35–39	366,092	1.8	2.8	4.5	0.2	85.1	75.9	7.8	15.4
Aged 40–44	370,731	1.8	2.4	4.1	0.2	87.1	79.4	6.4	12.7
Aged 45–49	334,855	1.7	2.2	3.6	0.2	88.8	81.7	5.3	11.2
Aged 50–54	279,270	1.6	2.0	3.1	0.2	90.1	83.0	4.7	10.6
Aged 55–59	194,722	1.5	1.9	3.1	0.1	90.9	83.5	4.0	10.2
Aged 60–64	144,585	1.3	2.0	3.3	0.1	91.1	83.1	3.7	10.6
Aged 65–69	121,222	1.1	2.0	3.3	0.1	91.6	83.9	3.3	10.0
Aged 70–74	105,088	1.0	1.8	2.6	0.1	92.9	85.8	2.8	9.0
Aged 75–79	85,922	0.7	1.6	2.1	0.1	94.1	88.0	2.4	7.6
Aged 80–84	55,625	0.7	1.2	1.9	0.1	95.0	89.8	2.0	6.4
Aged 85 or older	48,216	0.6	0.7	1.9	0.1	95.7	90.8	1.9	6.0

(continued)

(continued from previous page)

	total	American Indian	Asian	black	Native Hawaiian	white total	white non-Hispanic	other	Hispanic
Connecticut, total	**3,405,565**	**0.7%**	**2.8%**	**10.0%**	**0.1%**	**83.3%**	**77.5%**	**5.5%**	**9.4%**
Under age 5	223,344	0.9	4.0	14.2	0.2	77.0	67.2	8.7	15.1
Aged 5–9	244,144	0.9	3.1	13.8	0.1	78.0	69.5	8.0	13.8
Aged 10–14	241,587	0.9	2.8	13.2	0.1	78.7	71.1	7.5	12.9
Aged 15–19	216,627	1.0	3.2	13.2	0.2	77.6	69.9	8.1	13.5
Aged 20–24	187,571	1.0	4.2	13.5	0.3	74.7	65.8	9.9	16.0
Aged 25–29	201,467	0.8	5.1	12.2	0.2	75.7	67.6	9.0	14.7
Aged 30–34	250,173	0.8	4.0	10.9	0.1	79.5	72.9	7.0	11.7
Aged 35–39	290,866	0.7	3.1	9.7	0.1	82.9	77.4	5.4	9.2
Aged 40–44	290,183	0.7	2.5	8.6	0.1	85.6	80.9	4.2	7.4
Aged 45–49	252,754	0.7	2.4	7.8	0.1	87.2	83.0	3.4	6.2
Aged 50–54	228,053	0.6	2.1	7.6	0.1	88.0	84.2	3.0	5.6
Aged 55–59	176,961	0.5	1.9	7.3	0.1	88.9	85.3	2.6	5.0
Aged 60–64	131,652	0.5	1.8	7.9	0.1	88.5	84.9	2.5	4.8
Aged 65–69	117,556	0.4	1.4	6.6	0.1	90.7	87.7	1.9	3.8
Aged 70–74	114,009	0.4	1.0	5.3	0.0	92.8	90.7	1.3	2.6
Aged 75–79	101,096	0.3	0.7	4.4	0.0	94.2	92.5	1.1	2.0
Aged 80–84	73,249	0.3	0.5	3.3	0.0	95.6	94.0	1.0	1.7
Aged 85 or older	64,273	0.3	0.4	3.4	0.0	95.8	94.2	0.8	1.6
Delaware, total	**783,600**	**0.8**	**2.4**	**20.1**	**0.1**	**75.9**	**72.5**	**2.6**	**4.8**
Under age 5	51,531	0.9	3.2	26.6	0.1	69.2	61.7	4.9	8.8
Aged 5–9	55,813	0.9	2.6	26.6	0.1	69.3	63.8	4.0	7.1
Aged 10–14	55,274	0.9	2.4	26.0	0.1	70.1	65.8	3.3	5.7
Aged 15–19	55,632	1.0	2.3	24.7	0.1	70.9	66.5	3.4	6.3
Aged 20–24	51,665	0.9	2.7	22.5	0.1	71.4	66.3	4.4	8.2
Aged 25–29	51,219	0.8	4.0	21.2	0.1	71.1	66.3	4.7	8.4
Aged 30–34	57,621	0.8	3.3	21.7	0.1	72.2	68.5	3.5	6.2
Aged 35–39	64,654	0.8	2.8	20.5	0.1	74.8	71.9	2.3	4.4
Aged 40–44	62,947	0.8	2.3	19.5	0.1	76.7	74.4	1.8	3.2
Aged 45–49	54,775	0.8	2.2	18.5	0.1	78.0	76.0	1.5	2.8
Aged 50–54	49,224	0.8	2.2	16.5	0.1	80.3	78.4	1.3	2.4
Aged 55–59	39,320	0.6	1.9	14.7	0.1	82.5	80.9	1.0	2.0
Aged 60–64	32,199	0.6	2.0	14.2	0.0	83.0	81.6	0.8	1.7
Aged 65–69	29,952	0.6	1.3	12.7	0.0	85.4	84.1	0.6	1.4
Aged 70–74	26,463	0.5	0.9	10.7	0.0	88.0	86.9	0.5	1.2
Aged 75–79	21,248	0.4	0.7	10.7	0.0	88.2	87.4	0.3	0.9
Aged 80–84	13,514	0.5	0.5	9.7	0.1	89.4	88.7	0.4	0.7
Aged 85 or older	10,549	0.5	0.5	10.9	0.1	88.3	87.2	0.4	1.0

(continued)

(continued from previous page)

	total	American Indian	Asian	black	Native Hawaiian	white total	white non-Hispanic	other	Hispanic
District of Columbia, total	**572,059**	**0.8%**	**3.1%**	**61.3%**	**0.1%**	**32.2%**	**27.8%**	**5.0%**	**7.9%**
Under age 5	32,536	0.9	2.9	71.1	0.2	21.1	14.9	7.9	11.8
Aged 5–9	35,385	0.7	1.9	79.2	0.1	14.7	10.1	6.2	9.5
Aged 10–14	30,018	0.8	1.9	79.0	0.1	15.0	11.1	5.8	8.7
Aged 15–19	37,867	0.7	3.2	62.0	0.2	30.1	25.8	6.0	9.0
Aged 20–24	51,823	0.8	5.3	46.4	0.3	43.2	37.5	7.2	10.6
Aged 25–29	52,849	0.7	5.7	44.6	0.2	45.1	38.9	7.0	10.8
Aged 30–34	48,913	0.8	4.3	48.8	0.1	42.7	36.5	6.4	10.4
Aged 35–39	45,949	0.9	3.0	58.5	0.1	34.5	29.3	5.8	9.1
Aged 40–44	41,728	0.9	2.6	64.5	0.1	29.8	25.8	4.7	7.2
Aged 45–49	39,397	1.1	2.7	64.3	0.1	30.4	26.8	3.8	6.2
Aged 50–54	35,913	1.1	2.6	60.2	0.1	35.3	32.1	3.0	5.1
Aged 55–59	27,803	0.9	2.2	59.6	0.1	36.6	33.7	2.5	4.5
Aged 60–64	21,980	0.8	2.2	66.5	0.1	30.0	27.1	2.1	4.2
Aged 65–69	18,525	0.7	2.1	71.4	0.1	25.7	23.2	1.5	3.4
Aged 70–74	17,394	0.8	1.7	72.3	0.1	25.2	23.2	1.5	2.8
Aged 75–79	14,976	0.8	1.5	70.2	0.0	27.6	25.7	1.3	2.5
Aged 80–84	10,028	0.8	1.4	67.5	0.0	30.6	28.8	1.1	2.2
Aged 85 or older	8,975	0.9	1.4	62.1	0.1	36.1	34.4	1.0	1.9
Florida, total	**15,982,378**	**0.7**	**2.1**	**15.5**	**0.2**	**79.7**	**65.4**	**4.4**	**16.8**
Under age 5	945,823	0.8	2.6	22.9	0.2	71.4	54.1	6.7	20.5
Aged 5–9	1,031,718	0.8	2.3	23.2	0.2	71.2	55.2	6.1	19.1
Aged 10–14	1,057,024	0.9	2.3	22.7	0.2	71.6	56.4	5.7	18.4
Aged 15–19	1,014,067	0.9	2.5	22.3	0.2	70.8	55.3	6.5	19.6
Aged 20–24	928,310	0.9	2.8	20.6	0.3	71.0	53.6	7.8	22.8
Aged 25–29	995,358	0.8	3.1	18.3	0.2	73.8	55.8	6.8	22.7
Aged 30–34	1,088,742	0.8	2.8	16.6	0.2	76.6	59.1	5.8	21.3
Aged 35–39	1,261,040	0.8	2.3	15.7	0.2	78.7	62.4	4.8	19.3
Aged 40–44	1,224,207	0.9	2.3	15.4	0.2	79.5	65.7	4.1	16.3
Aged 45–49	1,085,400	0.9	2.3	14.2	0.1	81.1	68.1	3.5	15.0
Aged 50–54	984,079	0.8	2.1	12.0	0.1	84.1	71.9	2.8	13.7
Aged 55–59	821,517	0.7	1.7	10.5	0.1	86.4	74.0	2.3	13.4
Aged 60–64	737,496	0.6	1.5	9.9	0.1	87.5	74.9	1.9	13.6
Aged 65–69	727,495	0.4	1.1	8.2	0.1	89.9	78.5	1.5	12.1
Aged 70–74	724,681	0.4	0.8	6.5	0.0	92.1	82.2	1.1	10.4
Aged 75–79	616,693	0.3	0.5	5.3	0.0	93.7	85.3	0.9	8.7
Aged 80–84	407,441	0.3	0.4	5.1	0.0	94.1	86.2	0.8	8.1
Aged 85 or older	331,287	0.3	0.4	5.5	0.1	93.7	85.1	0.8	8.8

(continued)

(continued from previous page)

	total	American Indian	Asian	black	Native Hawaiian	white total	white non-Hispanic	other	Hispanic
Georgia, total	**8,186,453**	**0.6%**	**2.4%**	**29.2%**	**0.1%**	**66.1%**	**62.6%**	**2.9%**	**5.3%**
Under age 5	595,150	0.6	2.8	34.6	0.2	60.2	54.3	4.8	8.2
Aged 5–9	615,584	0.6	2.5	36.5	0.1	59.0	54.5	3.6	6.2
Aged 10–14	607,759	0.7	2.3	35.9	0.1	60.2	56.8	2.7	4.7
Aged 15–19	596,277	0.7	2.6	34.3	0.2	60.0	55.8	4.0	7.0
Aged 20–24	592,196	0.7	2.9	32.0	0.2	59.8	53.9	6.2	11.0
Aged 25–29	641,750	0.7	3.5	30.1	0.2	62.0	56.7	5.3	9.4
Aged 30–34	657,506	0.7	3.1	29.7	0.1	63.9	59.7	3.9	7.1
Aged 35–39	698,735	0.7	2.6	29.4	0.1	65.7	62.5	2.7	5.0
Aged 40–44	654,773	0.7	2.5	28.6	0.1	67.3	64.8	2.0	3.7
Aged 45–49	573,017	0.7	2.3	27.2	0.1	69.2	67.1	1.4	2.8
Aged 50–54	506,975	0.7	2.1	23.5	0.1	73.5	71.8	1.0	2.1
Aged 55–59	375,651	0.6	1.9	21.2	0.1	76.2	74.6	0.8	1.8
Aged 60–64	285,805	0.6	1.8	21.1	0.1	76.5	75.0	0.7	1.7
Aged 65–69	236,634	0.5	1.5	20.3	0.1	77.9	76.5	0.5	1.3
Aged 70–74	199,061	0.5	1.1	19.2	0.1	79.4	78.2	0.4	1.1
Aged 75–79	157,569	0.4	0.8	18.3	0.0	80.7	79.7	0.4	0.9
Aged 80–84	104,154	0.4	0.6	19.2	0.1	80.1	79.1	0.3	0.8
Aged 85 or older	87,857	0.4	0.5	21.8	0.1	77.6	76.7	0.3	0.9
Hawaii, total	**1,211,537**	**2.1**	**58.0**	**2.8**	**23.3**	**39.3**	**22.9**	**3.9**	**7.2**
Under age 5	78,163	3.5	58.6	5.6	37.8	47.0	15.8	6.5	14.0
Aged 5–9	84,980	3.2	60.0	4.5	37.3	44.4	15.0	5.7	12.0
Aged 10–14	83,106	3.1	60.6	3.4	36.5	43.2	15.0	5.0	10.7
Aged 15–19	81,002	2.9	60.2	3.2	34.5	41.0	15.7	5.0	10.4
Aged 20–24	83,409	2.5	50.5	4.7	26.5	43.7	24.8	5.5	10.3
Aged 25–29	84,000	2.2	52.7	4.4	24.3	41.3	24.1	5.0	8.8
Aged 30–34	87,159	2.1	54.7	3.6	22.8	39.8	24.2	4.2	7.5
Aged 35–39	95,935	2.0	54.7	2.9	21.4	39.6	25.6	3.8	6.6
Aged 40–44	95,242	1.9	56.3	2.1	19.3	38.7	26.2	3.4	5.8
Aged 45–49	90,404	1.8	55.4	1.5	17.5	40.0	28.9	2.9	4.6
Aged 50–54	80,575	1.6	54.8	1.2	15.7	40.6	30.7	2.6	3.9
Aged 55–59	60,561	1.2	57.0	0.9	16.5	38.1	28.8	2.4	3.5
Aged 60–64	46,400	1.0	60.7	0.8	15.6	33.6	25.5	2.4	3.3
Aged 65–69	42,847	0.8	65.5	0.6	13.5	29.5	22.2	2.1	3.2
Aged 70–74	42,415	0.6	69.1	0.5	10.6	27.0	21.0	1.9	2.5
Aged 75–79	35,386	0.5	69.5	0.5	8.4	27.6	22.4	1.6	2.0
Aged 80–84	22,389	0.5	69.9	0.4	7.7	27.2	22.7	1.4	1.8
Aged 85 or older	17,564	0.4	71.4	0.4	6.8	25.8	21.6	1.6	1.9

(continued)

(continued from previous page)

	total	American Indian	Asian	black	Native Hawaiian	white total	white non-Hispanic	other	Hispanic
Idaho, total	**1,293,953**	**2.1%**	**1.3%**	**0.6%**	**0.2%**	**92.8%**	**88.0%**	**5.0%**	**7.9%**
Under age 5	97,643	2.7	1.8	1.4	0.3	89.6	80.7	8.6	13.8
Aged 5–9	100,756	2.7	1.5	1.1	0.3	90.4	82.4	7.7	12.5
Aged 10–14	104,608	2.7	1.4	0.8	0.3	91.6	85.2	6.3	10.0
Aged 15–19	110,858	2.3	1.4	0.7	0.3	91.5	86.0	6.2	9.6
Aged 20–24	93,994	2.2	1.6	1.0	0.4	89.9	84.0	7.3	11.1
Aged 25–29	85,128	2.3	2.0	0.7	0.3	89.6	83.8	7.3	11.2
Aged 30–34	84,305	2.3	1.8	0.6	0.3	90.7	85.4	6.3	9.9
Aged 35–39	94,913	2.3	1.4	0.6	0.2	92.2	88.0	5.0	7.7
Aged 40–44	98,055	2.0	1.2	0.4	0.2	94.0	90.3	3.8	5.9
Aged 45–49	92,172	2.0	1.2	0.4	0.1	94.7	91.7	3.1	4.7
Aged 50–54	78,076	1.9	1.0	0.3	0.1	95.6	92.9	2.4	3.9
Aged 55–59	60,024	1.8	0.9	0.2	0.1	96.3	93.7	2.0	3.3
Aged 60–64	47,505	1.6	0.7	0.2	0.1	96.9	94.5	1.6	2.8
Aged 65–69	40,169	1.4	0.8	0.2	0.1	97.1	95.1	1.4	2.4
Aged 70–74	35,801	1.1	0.8	0.1	0.1	97.6	96.0	1.1	1.8
Aged 75–79	30,443	0.8	0.8	0.1	0.0	98.1	96.8	0.8	1.4
Aged 80–84	21,446	0.7	0.6	0.1	0.1	98.4	97.3	0.6	1.0
Aged 85 or older	18,057	0.6	0.4	0.2	0.1	98.7	97.5	0.6	1.0
Illinois, total	**12,419,293**	**0.6**	**3.8**	**15.6**	**0.1**	**75.1**	**67.8**	**6.8**	**12.3**
Under age 5	876,549	0.7	4.3	19.6	0.1	68.6	55.9	10.9	20.1
Aged 5–9	929,858	0.7	3.5	20.9	0.1	68.6	58.0	9.5	17.4
Aged 10–14	905,097	0.7	3.5	19.7	0.1	70.4	61.7	8.3	14.8
Aged 15–19	894,002	0.7	3.9	18.3	0.1	70.3	61.5	9.1	15.8
Aged 20–24	850,843	0.7	4.8	16.7	0.2	69.0	58.7	11.1	19.4
Aged 25–29	891,759	0.6	5.7	15.8	0.1	69.5	59.5	10.5	18.6
Aged 30–34	919,915	0.6	4.9	14.9	0.1	72.9	64.3	8.4	15.3
Aged 35–39	996,886	0.6	3.9	14.8	0.1	75.8	69.1	6.4	11.8
Aged 40–44	986,984	0.6	3.6	14.6	0.1	77.2	71.7	5.3	9.6
Aged 45–49	873,812	0.6	3.7	13.9	0.1	78.5	73.7	4.6	8.1
Aged 50–54	752,930	0.6	3.8	13.1	0.1	79.8	75.5	3.9	7.0
Aged 55–59	577,747	0.5	3.6	12.9	0.1	80.8	76.8	3.2	6.1
Aged 60–64	462,886	0.4	3.3	13.6	0.1	80.8	76.9	2.9	5.6
Aged 65–69	397,443	0.4	2.6	13.0	0.0	82.6	79.0	2.3	4.9
Aged 70–74	374,804	0.3	2.0	11.4	0.0	85.3	82.5	1.7	3.7
Aged 75–79	316,948	0.3	1.7	9.7	0.0	87.7	85.5	1.3	2.7
Aged 80–84	218,799	0.2	1.4	8.3	0.0	89.6	88.0	1.0	1.8
Aged 85 or older	192,031	0.2	1.0	8.1	0.0	90.3	88.9	0.9	1.7

(continued)

(continued from previous page)

	total	American Indian	Asian	black	Native Hawaiian	white total	white non-Hispanic	other	Hispanic
Indiana, total	**6,080,485**	**0.6%**	**1.2%**	**8.8%**	**0.1%**	**88.6%**	**85.8%**	**2.0%**	**3.5%**
Under age 5	423,215	0.7	1.6	12.6	0.1	84.9	79.1	3.7	6.2
Aged 5–9	443,273	0.7	1.2	12.2	0.1	85.6	81.1	2.8	4.9
Aged 10–14	443,416	0.7	1.2	11.1	0.1	86.7	83.1	2.2	3.9
Aged 15–19	453,482	0.7	1.4	10.1	0.1	86.8	83.4	2.5	4.4
Aged 20–24	425,731	0.7	1.9	9.9	0.1	85.3	81.4	3.7	6.3
Aged 25–29	409,035	0.7	2.0	9.7	0.1	85.4	81.9	3.4	5.8
Aged 30–34	422,090	0.7	1.8	8.8	0.1	87.2	84.5	2.5	4.4
Aged 35–39	478,207	0.7	1.3	8.3	0.1	88.8	86.6	1.8	3.2
Aged 40–44	482,496	0.7	1.0	8.2	0.1	89.4	87.4	1.4	2.6
Aged 45–49	437,122	0.7	0.9	7.6	0.1	90.3	88.6	1.1	2.2
Aged 50–54	379,743	0.7	0.9	6.8	0.0	91.4	89.7	0.9	1.9
Aged 55–59	294,169	0.6	0.8	6.5	0.0	92.1	90.5	0.7	1.5
Aged 60–64	235,675	0.5	0.7	6.6	0.0	92.1	90.7	0.6	1.4
Aged 65–69	203,737	0.4	0.6	6.7	0.0	92.3	91.0	0.5	1.3
Aged 70–74	191,656	0.4	0.4	6.1	0.0	93.1	91.9	0.5	1.2
Aged 75–79	159,833	0.3	0.3	5.4	0.0	94.1	93.0	0.4	0.9
Aged 80–84	106,047	0.3	0.2	4.9	0.0	94.7	93.9	0.3	0.7
Aged 85 or older	91,558	0.3	0.2	5.0	0.0	94.6	93.8	0.3	0.6
Iowa, total	**2,926,324**	**0.6**	**1.5**	**2.5**	**0.1**	**94.9**	**92.6**	**1.6**	**2.8**
Under age 5	188,413	0.9	2.3	5.1	0.1	91.7	85.8	3.5	6.0
Aged 5–9	202,603	0.9	1.8	4.5	0.1	92.7	88.2	2.7	4.7
Aged 10–14	210,547	0.9	1.7	3.5	0.1	93.7	90.4	2.0	3.6
Aged 15–19	226,420	0.8	1.8	3.0	0.1	93.8	91.0	2.0	3.5
Aged 20–24	203,663	0.7	2.4	3.3	0.2	92.0	89.0	2.8	4.6
Aged 25–29	177,259	0.7	2.9	3.1	0.1	91.5	88.4	2.9	4.9
Aged 30–34	185,801	0.7	2.3	2.6	0.1	93.0	90.4	2.3	3.9
Aged 35–39	217,897	0.6	1.5	2.2	0.1	94.8	92.9	1.6	2.7
Aged 40–44	227,302	0.6	1.1	1.9	0.1	95.9	94.4	1.1	2.0
Aged 45–49	212,663	0.5	1.0	1.7	0.0	96.4	95.2	0.8	1.5
Aged 50–54	180,131	0.5	1.0	1.5	0.0	96.8	95.7	0.7	1.3
Aged 55–59	139,052	0.4	0.9	1.3	0.0	97.2	96.3	0.5	1.1
Aged 60–64	118,360	0.4	0.8	1.2	0.0	97.6	96.7	0.4	0.9
Aged 65–69	107,373	0.3	0.6	1.1	0.0	98.0	97.2	0.3	0.7
Aged 70–74	104,562	0.2	0.4	1.0	0.0	98.4	97.7	0.2	0.6
Aged 75–79	91,505	0.2	0.2	0.8	0.1	98.8	98.2	0.2	0.5
Aged 80–84	67,655	0.2	0.2	0.6	0.0	99.0	98.6	0.2	0.4
Aged 85 or older	65,118	0.2	0.2	0.6	0.0	99.2	98.7	0.2	0.3

(continued)

(continued from previous page)

	total	American Indian	Asian	black	Native Hawaiian	white total	white non-Hispanic	other	Hispanic
Kansas, total	**2,688,418**	**1.8%**	**2.1%**	**6.3%**	**0.1%**	**87.9%**	**83.1%**	**4.0%**	**7.0%**
Under age 5	188,708	2.2	2.8	9.5	0.2	83.4	73.2	7.5	13.1
Aged 5–9	195,574	2.2	2.3	9.2	0.2	84.3	76.1	6.2	10.8
Aged 10–14	204,018	2.3	2.1	8.1	0.1	85.7	79.3	5.1	8.7
Aged 15–19	210,118	2.2	2.3	7.4	0.2	85.8	79.9	5.0	8.6
Aged 20–24	190,167	2.1	3.0	7.4	0.2	83.4	77.2	6.4	10.7
Aged 25–29	172,975	2.0	3.8	7.0	0.2	82.8	76.6	6.5	11.1
Aged 30–34	175,878	1.9	2.9	6.5	0.1	84.9	79.6	5.5	9.4
Aged 35–39	207,549	1.7	2.2	6.4	0.1	87.4	83.4	3.8	6.5
Aged 40–44	212,802	1.7	1.8	6.0	0.1	89.0	85.7	2.9	5.0
Aged 45–49	192,679	1.6	1.7	5.0	0.1	90.5	87.7	2.3	4.0
Aged 50–54	161,468	1.6	1.7	4.6	0.1	91.4	88.7	1.9	3.5
Aged 55–59	121,645	1.5	1.5	4.3	0.1	92.3	89.7	1.5	3.0
Aged 60–64	98,608	1.4	1.3	4.4	0.1	92.7	90.2	1.3	2.7
Aged 65–69	90,085	1.1	1.0	4.2	0.0	93.5	91.3	1.1	2.4
Aged 70–74	85,831	0.9	0.7	3.6	0.0	94.7	92.8	0.9	2.1
Aged 75–79	75,125	0.7	0.5	3.1	0.0	95.5	93.8	0.8	1.8
Aged 80–84	53,418	0.6	0.4	2.9	0.0	96.1	94.9	0.5	1.2
Aged 85 or older	51,770	0.5	0.3	2.8	0.0	96.3	95.4	0.5	1.0
Kentucky, total	**4,041,769**	**0.6**	**0.9**	**7.7**	**0.1**	**91.0**	**89.3**	**0.8**	**1.5**
Under age 5	265,901	0.5	1.2	10.9	0.1	88.5	84.6	1.7	2.5
Aged 5–9	279,258	0.6	1.0	10.5	0.1	88.8	86.0	1.2	1.9
Aged 10–14	279,481	0.6	1.0	9.6	0.1	89.5	87.3	0.9	1.5
Aged 15–19	289,004	0.7	0.9	9.3	0.1	89.3	87.2	1.0	1.9
Aged 20–24	283,032	0.6	1.2	9.2	0.1	88.4	86.1	1.6	3.0
Aged 25–29	281,134	0.6	1.5	8.3	0.1	89.1	87.1	1.4	2.6
Aged 30–34	286,974	0.6	1.4	7.5	0.1	90.2	88.5	1.0	2.0
Aged 35–39	321,931	0.6	1.1	7.5	0.1	90.8	89.4	0.7	1.5
Aged 40–44	320,734	0.7	0.8	7.5	0.1	91.2	90.0	0.5	1.1
Aged 45–49	293,976	0.7	0.7	6.8	0.1	92.1	90.9	0.4	0.9
Aged 50–54	262,956	0.7	0.7	5.8	0.0	93.2	92.1	0.3	0.7
Aged 55–59	204,483	0.6	0.6	5.1	0.0	94.0	93.0	0.2	0.6
Aged 60–64	168,112	0.6	0.6	5.2	0.0	94.0	93.1	0.2	0.6
Aged 65–69	144,671	0.6	0.5	5.3	0.0	94.1	93.1	0.2	0.5
Aged 70–74	129,272	0.6	0.3	5.1	0.0	94.4	93.5	0.2	0.5
Aged 75–79	104,760	0.5	0.2	5.0	0.0	94.7	93.8	0.1	0.4
Aged 80–84	67,829	0.6	0.2	4.9	0.0	94.9	94.0	0.1	0.4
Aged 85 or older	58,261	0.5	0.2	5.8	0.0	94.0	93.2	0.1	0.4

(continued)

(continued from previous page)

	total	American Indian	Asian	black	Native Hawaiian	white total	non-Hispanic	other	Hispanic
Louisiana, total	**4,468,976**	**1.0%**	**1.4%**	**32.9%**	**0.1%**	**64.8%**	**62.5%**	**1.1%**	**2.4%**
Under age 5	317,392	1.1	1.6	40.7	0.1	57.3	54.1	1.4	2.8
Aged 5–9	336,780	1.1	1.5	41.7	0.1	56.1	53.5	1.2	2.5
Aged 10–14	347,912	1.1	1.5	40.3	0.1	57.4	55.1	1.0	2.3
Aged 15–19	365,945	1.1	1.6	38.9	0.1	58.4	56.2	1.1	2.5
Aged 20–24	325,571	1.0	1.9	37.0	0.1	59.7	57.1	1.6	3.2
Aged 25–29	296,161	0.9	2.1	33.3	0.1	63.2	60.7	1.6	3.1
Aged 30–34	305,001	1.0	1.8	32.2	0.1	64.7	62.3	1.3	2.8
Aged 35–39	343,128	1.0	1.5	31.3	0.1	66.0	63.8	1.1	2.6
Aged 40–44	348,838	0.9	1.4	30.7	0.1	66.8	64.8	1.0	2.3
Aged 45–49	315,768	0.9	1.4	30.1	0.1	67.6	65.6	0.8	2.1
Aged 50–54	270,503	1.0	1.3	27.4	0.1	70.4	68.5	0.8	2.0
Aged 55–59	208,761	0.9	1.1	25.5	0.1	72.6	70.6	0.7	2.0
Aged 60–64	170,287	0.8	1.0	25.5	0.1	72.8	70.7	0.7	2.0
Aged 65–69	148,004	0.7	0.9	24.1	0.1	74.5	72.5	0.6	1.9
Aged 70–74	134,921	0.7	0.7	22.7	0.0	76.1	74.3	0.5	1.7
Aged 75–79	106,823	0.5	0.5	21.4	0.0	77.8	76.1	0.5	1.5
Aged 80–84	68,505	0.6	0.4	21.7	0.0	77.6	76.0	0.5	1.3
Aged 85 or older	58,676	0.5	0.4	24.5	0.1	74.9	73.3	0.5	1.3
Maine, total	**1,274,923**	**1.0**	**0.9**	**0.7**	**0.1**	**97.9**	**96.5**	**0.4**	**0.7**
Under age 5	70,726	1.5	1.7	1.9	0.1	96.6	93.5	0.8	1.4
Aged 5–9	83,022	1.4	1.4	1.6	0.1	97.0	94.5	0.6	1.2
Aged 10–14	92,252	1.4	1.2	1.3	0.1	97.1	95.1	0.6	1.1
Aged 15–19	89,485	1.4	1.4	1.2	0.1	96.8	94.9	0.7	1.1
Aged 20–24	69,656	1.4	1.5	1.3	0.1	96.5	94.6	0.7	1.2
Aged 25–29	71,951	1.2	1.4	0.9	0.1	97.0	95.5	0.6	1.0
Aged 30–34	85,666	1.1	1.2	0.8	0.1	97.3	96.0	0.5	0.9
Aged 35–39	104,149	1.1	0.9	0.6	0.1	97.8	96.7	0.4	0.7
Aged 40–44	108,831	1.1	0.8	0.5	0.1	98.1	97.0	0.3	0.6
Aged 45–49	101,921	0.9	0.7	0.4	0.1	98.4	97.5	0.3	0.5
Aged 50–54	90,675	0.8	0.6	0.3	0.1	98.6	97.7	0.2	0.4
Aged 55–59	68,490	0.8	0.5	0.3	0.1	98.9	98.1	0.2	0.3
Aged 60–64	54,697	0.7	0.5	0.2	0.0	98.9	98.1	0.2	0.3
Aged 65–69	50,100	0.6	0.4	0.2	0.0	99.1	98.4	0.2	0.3
Aged 70–74	46,096	0.4	0.3	0.2	0.0	99.4	98.8	0.1	0.2
Aged 75–79	38,098	0.4	0.2	0.2	0.0	99.5	98.9	0.1	0.3
Aged 80–84	25,792	0.3	0.2	0.2	0.0	99.6	99.0	0.2	0.2
Aged 85 or older	23,316	0.4	0.1	0.1	0.0	99.7	99.1	0.2	0.2

(continued)

(continued from previous page)

	total	American Indian	Asian	black	Native Hawaiian	white total	non-Hispanic	other	Hispanic
Maryland, total	**5,296,486**	**0.7%**	**4.5%**	**28.8%**	**0.1%**	**65.4%**	**62.1%**	**2.5%**	**4.3%**
Under age 5	353,393	0.8	5.1	34.2	0.1	60.4	54.1	4.0	6.5
Aged 5–9	391,318	0.8	4.4	34.8	0.1	60.1	55.2	3.2	5.4
Aged 10–14	392,135	0.9	4.3	33.6	0.1	61.2	57.2	2.8	4.6
Aged 15–19	356,119	0.9	4.8	33.0	0.2	60.7	56.7	3.2	5.3
Aged 20–24	314,129	0.9	5.8	32.5	0.2	58.8	54.1	4.5	7.4
Aged 25–29	342,870	0.8	6.1	31.6	0.2	59.4	54.9	4.2	7.0
Aged 30–34	405,651	0.8	5.3	31.0	0.1	61.4	57.6	3.5	5.8
Aged 35–39	464,788	0.8	4.7	29.6	0.1	64.0	60.8	2.6	4.5
Aged 40–44	451,368	0.8	4.4	28.2	0.1	66.0	63.3	2.1	3.7
Aged 45–49	399,390	0.8	4.3	26.7	0.1	67.8	65.5	1.8	3.0
Aged 50–54	355,642	0.8	4.1	25.2	0.1	69.9	67.8	1.3	2.4
Aged 55–59	268,647	0.7	4.1	23.5	0.1	71.7	69.7	1.1	2.2
Aged 60–64	201,729	0.6	4.3	23.7	0.1	71.4	69.5	1.0	2.1
Aged 65–69	168,242	0.5	3.5	22.1	0.1	73.9	72.2	0.8	1.8
Aged 70–74	153,043	0.4	2.7	18.9	0.1	78.1	76.5	0.7	1.6
Aged 75–79	128,491	0.4	2.1	16.4	0.1	81.3	80.0	0.6	1.2
Aged 80–84	82,629	0.3	1.7	15.3	0.1	82.8	81.6	0.5	1.1
Aged 85 or older	66,902	0.4	1.4	15.8	0.1	82.5	81.3	0.5	1.1
Massachusetts, total	**6,349,097**	**0.6**	**4.2**	**6.3**	**0.1**	**86.2**	**81.9**	**5.1**	**6.8**
Under age 5	397,268	0.7	5.4	8.9	0.2	81.5	73.8	8.0	11.3
Aged 5–9	430,861	0.8	4.6	9.2	0.2	81.5	74.6	7.7	10.9
Aged 10–14	431,247	0.8	4.3	8.7	0.2	82.3	76.3	7.1	9.9
Aged 15–19	415,737	0.8	5.4	8.1	0.2	81.2	75.3	7.7	9.8
Aged 20–24	404,279	0.7	6.8	7.9	0.2	79.5	73.1	8.3	10.6
Aged 25–29	434,024	0.6	7.2	7.1	0.2	80.9	75.2	6.9	9.4
Aged 30–34	492,764	0.6	5.5	6.7	0.1	83.6	78.7	6.0	8.1
Aged 35–39	540,593	0.6	4.2	6.2	0.1	86.0	82.0	4.9	6.6
Aged 40–44	522,402	0.6	3.6	5.7	0.1	87.8	84.5	4.0	5.2
Aged 45–49	461,945	0.6	3.3	5.1	0.1	89.1	86.3	3.3	4.4
Aged 50–54	411,408	0.5	2.8	4.6	0.1	90.5	87.9	2.8	3.8
Aged 55–59	310,002	0.5	2.6	4.5	0.1	91.3	88.8	2.4	3.3
Aged 60–64	236,405	0.4	2.6	4.5	0.1	91.2	88.9	2.4	3.1
Aged 65–69	216,498	0.4	2.3	3.8	0.1	92.6	90.7	1.9	2.4
Aged 70–74	211,332	0.3	1.8	3.2	0.1	94.2	92.6	1.5	1.7
Aged 75–79	184,941	0.3	1.4	2.6	0.1	95.3	93.9	1.2	1.3
Aged 80–84	130,699	0.3	1.0	2.3	0.1	96.1	94.8	1.1	1.1
Aged 85 or older	116,692	0.3	0.9	2.1	0.1	96.5	95.3	1.0	1.0

(continued)

(continued from previous page)

	total	American Indian	Asian	black	Native Hawaiian	white total	white non-Hispanic	other	Hispanic
Michigan, total	**9,938,444**	**1.3%**	**2.1%**	**14.8%**	**0.1%**	**81.8%**	**78.6%**	**2.0%**	**3.3%**
Under age 5	672,005	1.6	3.0	19.4	0.1	77.2	70.3	3.6	5.9
Aged 5–9	745,181	1.6	2.3	20.8	0.1	76.2	70.7	2.9	4.8
Aged 10–14	747,012	1.6	2.1	18.3	0.1	78.5	74.0	2.4	4.1
Aged 15–19	719,867	1.6	2.3	16.1	0.1	80.0	75.7	2.6	4.3
Aged 20–24	643,839	1.4	2.9	16.5	0.1	78.3	73.9	3.3	5.2
Aged 25–29	654,629	1.3	3.7	17.4	0.1	76.6	72.7	3.1	4.8
Aged 30–34	707,542	1.3	3.1	15.3	0.1	79.6	76.4	2.4	3.8
Aged 35–39	787,367	1.3	2.3	13.4	0.1	82.7	80.0	1.8	2.9
Aged 40–44	811,006	1.2	1.7	13.3	0.1	83.6	81.4	1.4	2.4
Aged 45–49	734,905	1.2	1.6	13.1	0.1	84.1	82.1	1.3	2.1
Aged 50–54	633,034	1.1	1.6	12.6	0.0	84.8	82.9	1.1	1.8
Aged 55–59	485,895	1.0	1.5	11.4	0.0	86.3	84.5	0.9	1.6
Aged 60–64	377,144	0.9	1.4	10.9	0.0	87.0	85.2	0.8	1.5
Aged 65–69	328,835	0.8	1.0	11.2	0.0	87.2	85.5	0.7	1.4
Aged 70–74	314,045	0.6	0.7	10.3	0.0	88.4	87.0	0.6	1.2
Aged 75–79	260,144	0.5	0.6	9.6	0.0	89.4	88.2	0.6	1.0
Aged 80–84	173,534	0.5	0.4	8.7	0.0	90.6	89.6	0.5	0.7
Aged 85 or older	142,460	0.4	0.4	8.7	0.0	90.7	89.8	0.4	0.7
Minnesota, total	**4,919,479**	**1.6**	**3.3**	**4.1**	**0.1**	**90.8**	**88.2**	**1.8**	**2.9**
Under age 5	329,594	2.6	5.4	7.8	0.2	85.4	79.0	3.7	5.9
Aged 5–9	355,894	2.5	5.1	7.1	0.2	86.2	81.3	2.7	4.5
Aged 10–14	374,995	2.5	5.0	5.9	0.2	87.3	83.6	2.1	3.4
Aged 15–19	374,362	2.2	4.6	4.9	0.2	88.3	84.9	2.3	3.6
Aged 20–24	322,483	2.0	4.5	5.5	0.2	86.7	82.9	3.4	5.3
Aged 25–29	319,826	1.8	5.3	5.6	0.2	85.7	82.3	3.4	5.2
Aged 30–34	353,312	1.6	4.0	4.9	0.1	88.5	85.8	2.3	3.7
Aged 35–39	412,490	1.5	2.8	3.9	0.1	91.3	89.3	1.6	2.6
Aged 40–44	411,692	1.4	2.1	3.3	0.1	92.8	91.2	1.1	1.9
Aged 45–49	364,247	1.3	2.0	2.7	0.1	93.8	92.5	0.9	1.5
Aged 50–54	301,449	1.2	1.9	2.1	0.1	94.8	93.6	0.7	1.2
Aged 55–59	226,857	1.1	1.7	1.7	0.1	95.5	94.5	0.6	1.0
Aged 60–64	178,012	1.0	1.6	1.6	0.1	95.9	94.9	0.5	0.9
Aged 65–69	153,169	0.8	1.4	1.4	0.0	96.5	95.7	0.4	0.7
Aged 70–74	142,656	0.6	1.0	1.1	0.0	97.3	96.7	0.3	0.5
Aged 75–79	122,677	0.5	0.9	0.9	0.0	97.9	97.3	0.3	0.5
Aged 80–84	90,163	0.4	0.6	0.7	0.0	98.4	97.9	0.2	0.4
Aged 85 or older	85,601	0.3	0.5	0.6	0.0	98.6	98.1	0.2	0.4

(continued)

(continued from previous page)

	total	American Indian	Asian	black	Native Hawaiian	white total	white non-Hispanic	other	Hispanic
Mississippi, total	**2,844,658**	**0.7%**	**0.8%**	**36.6%**	**0.1%**	**61.9%**	**60.7%**	**0.7%**	**1.4%**
Under age 5	204,364	0.8	1.0	45.2	0.1	53.5	51.5	1.0	1.9
Aged 5–9	216,920	0.7	0.9	46.6	0.1	52.1	50.6	0.7	1.5
Aged 10–14	218,742	0.8	0.9	45.0	0.1	53.6	52.4	0.6	1.3
Aged 15–19	233,188	0.8	0.9	44.6	0.1	53.7	52.5	0.8	1.6
Aged 20–24	212,947	0.7	1.0	42.1	0.1	55.7	54.2	1.2	2.2
Aged 25–29	192,526	0.7	1.1	38.2	0.1	59.4	58.0	1.2	2.2
Aged 30–34	189,272	0.7	1.2	36.4	0.1	61.4	60.1	0.9	1.9
Aged 35–39	212,309	0.7	0.9	35.3	0.1	63.0	61.8	0.7	1.5
Aged 40–44	213,063	0.7	0.8	35.5	0.1	63.0	61.9	0.5	1.2
Aged 45–49	192,111	0.7	0.8	33.8	0.1	64.9	63.9	0.4	1.1
Aged 50–54	169,870	0.7	0.7	28.8	0.1	70.0	69.1	0.3	0.9
Aged 55–59	132,202	0.6	0.6	25.7	0.0	73.3	72.4	0.3	0.8
Aged 60–64	113,621	0.6	0.5	25.5	0.0	73.6	72.7	0.2	0.7
Aged 65–69	98,179	0.5	0.5	24.6	0.0	74.8	74.0	0.2	0.7
Aged 70–74	87,531	0.5	0.4	24.2	0.1	75.3	74.6	0.2	0.5
Aged 75–79	68,558	0.4	0.3	24.1	0.0	75.5	74.8	0.2	0.5
Aged 80–84	46,364	0.4	0.3	25.2	0.0	74.5	73.9	0.1	0.5
Aged 85 or older	42,891	0.5	0.2	29.7	0.1	70.0	69.3	0.1	0.5
Missouri, total	**5,595,211**	**1.1**	**1.4**	**11.7**	**0.1**	**86.1**	**83.8**	**1.2**	**2.1**
Under age 5	369,898	1.1	1.8	15.7	0.2	82.6	77.8	2.2	3.7
Aged 5–9	398,898	1.2	1.4	16.7	0.1	81.6	77.8	1.7	3.0
Aged 10–14	412,080	1.2	1.3	15.2	0.1	83.0	79.9	1.4	2.6
Aged 15–19	413,296	1.3	1.5	13.7	0.2	83.8	80.9	1.5	2.7
Aged 20–24	369,498	1.1	2.0	13.1	0.2	83.2	80.2	2.1	3.5
Aged 25–29	362,305	1.1	2.5	13.0	0.2	82.9	80.2	1.9	3.2
Aged 30–34	376,428	1.1	2.0	12.4	0.1	84.2	81.9	1.5	2.7
Aged 35–39	443,250	1.1	1.4	11.4	0.1	86.1	84.1	1.1	2.0
Aged 40–44	444,319	1.2	1.2	11.1	0.1	86.7	84.9	0.9	1.7
Aged 45–49	395,616	1.2	1.1	10.2	0.1	87.8	86.1	0.7	1.4
Aged 50–54	346,846	1.1	1.1	9.2	0.1	88.9	87.4	0.5	1.2
Aged 55–59	279,073	1.1	1.0	8.5	0.1	89.9	88.4	0.4	1.0
Aged 60–64	228,325	1.0	0.9	8.5	0.0	90.1	88.7	0.4	1.0
Aged 65–69	205,372	0.8	0.7	8.2	0.0	90.8	89.5	0.3	0.8
Aged 70–74	187,854	0.7	0.6	7.5	0.0	91.6	90.4	0.3	0.8
Aged 75–79	157,207	0.6	0.4	6.7	0.0	92.7	91.6	0.3	0.6
Aged 80–84	106,375	0.5	0.3	6.2	0.0	93.3	92.4	0.3	0.5
Aged 85 or older	98,571	0.5	0.2	6.4	0.0	93.3	92.4	0.2	0.5

(continued)

(continued from previous page)

	total	American Indian	Asian	black	Native Hawaiian	white total	white non-Hispanic	other	Hispanic
Montana, total	**902,195**	**7.4%**	**0.8%**	**0.5%**	**0.1%**	**92.2%**	**89.5%**	**0.9%**	**2.0%**
Under age 5	54,869	12.3	1.2	1.3	0.2	87.5	82.1	1.5	3.9
Aged 5–9	61,963	11.8	1.1	1.0	0.2	88.2	83.6	1.2	3.2
Aged 10–14	69,298	11.2	1.1	0.7	0.1	88.6	84.6	1.1	2.9
Aged 15–19	71,310	10.0	1.0	0.7	0.2	89.7	86.0	1.1	2.8
Aged 20–24	58,379	8.4	1.3	0.8	0.2	90.0	86.8	1.3	2.8
Aged 25–29	51,104	8.2	1.2	0.6	0.1	90.4	87.6	1.2	2.5
Aged 30–34	52,175	8.0	0.9	0.5	0.1	91.1	88.5	1.0	2.2
Aged 35–39	66,580	7.5	0.7	0.4	0.1	91.9	89.5	0.9	1.9
Aged 40–44	75,361	6.4	0.6	0.3	0.1	93.2	91.1	0.8	1.6
Aged 45–49	73,398	5.3	0.6	0.2	0.1	94.3	92.6	0.6	1.3
Aged 50–54	61,690	4.9	0.5	0.2	0.1	94.8	93.2	0.6	1.2
Aged 55–59	47,174	4.8	0.5	0.2	0.1	95.2	93.5	0.5	1.0
Aged 60–64	37,945	4.7	0.4	0.2	0.1	95.2	93.6	0.4	1.0
Aged 65–69	32,541	3.9	0.5	0.2	0.1	95.9	94.5	0.4	0.9
Aged 70–74	29,978	2.9	0.3	0.1	0.0	97.0	95.8	0.4	0.8
Aged 75–79	24,703	2.2	0.2	0.1	0.1	97.7	96.6	0.3	0.7
Aged 80–84	18,390	1.7	0.2	0.1	0.0	98.2	97.2	0.3	0.5
Aged 85 or older	15,337	1.8	0.1	0.1	0.1	98.2	97.3	0.3	0.4
Nebraska, total	**1,711,263**	**1.3**	**1.6**	**4.4**	**0.1**	**90.8**	**87.3**	**3.3**	**5.5**
Under age 5	117,048	2.1	2.3	7.2	0.1	85.9	78.0	6.5	11.0
Aged 5–9	123,445	2.1	1.8	7.0	0.1	87.0	80.7	5.1	8.9
Aged 10–14	128,934	1.9	1.6	6.1	0.1	88.8	84.1	3.9	6.5
Aged 15–19	134,909	1.7	1.7	5.3	0.2	89.1	84.9	3.9	6.5
Aged 20–24	120,331	1.5	2.4	5.1	0.2	87.3	82.7	5.3	8.5
Aged 25–29	112,049	1.4	3.1	4.9	0.2	86.3	81.6	5.7	9.1
Aged 30–34	111,224	1.5	2.4	4.7	0.1	87.9	83.8	4.8	7.8
Aged 35–39	130,027	1.2	1.5	4.3	0.1	90.7	87.9	3.1	5.2
Aged 40–44	133,807	1.1	1.2	3.9	0.1	92.2	89.8	2.4	4.0
Aged 45–49	122,714	1.0	1.1	3.4	0.1	93.3	91.4	1.8	3.1
Aged 50–54	103,040	0.9	1.2	3.1	0.1	93.9	92.1	1.4	2.6
Aged 55–59	77,584	0.8	1.0	2.9	0.1	94.6	93.1	1.2	2.2
Aged 60–64	63,956	0.8	0.9	2.9	0.0	95.0	93.5	0.9	1.9
Aged 65–69	59,391	0.6	0.6	2.5	0.0	95.9	94.6	0.7	1.6
Aged 70–74	56,308	0.4	0.5	2.2	0.0	96.7	95.6	0.6	1.3
Aged 75–79	47,991	0.4	0.4	1.6	0.0	97.4	96.5	0.5	1.0
Aged 80–84	34,552	0.3	0.3	1.4	0.0	97.9	97.3	0.3	0.7
Aged 85 or older	33,953	0.3	0.2	1.5	0.0	98.1	97.4	0.3	0.6

(continued)

(continued from previous page)

	total	American Indian	Asian	black	Native Hawaiian	white total	white non-Hispanic	other	Hispanic
Nevada, total	**1,998,257**	**2.1%**	**5.6%**	**7.5%**	**0.8%**	**78.4%**	**65.2%**	**9.7%**	**19.7%**
Under age 5	145,817	2.5	6.0	10.1	1.2	72.9	49.7	15.9	33.2
Aged 5–9	149,322	2.5	5.6	10.6	1.1	72.9	52.8	14.4	29.6
Aged 10–14	139,193	2.8	5.6	10.1	1.0	74.2	57.4	12.6	24.9
Aged 15–19	127,169	2.7	6.0	9.0	1.1	73.5	57.0	13.2	25.8
Aged 20–24	130,006	2.3	6.6	8.0	1.2	71.1	52.7	15.7	30.5
Aged 25–29	148,726	2.1	6.3	7.6	1.0	73.1	55.8	14.2	28.3
Aged 30–34	157,885	2.1	6.1	7.6	0.9	74.9	59.9	12.2	24.4
Aged 35–39	165,910	2.2	5.8	7.6	0.8	77.4	65.2	9.6	19.2
Aged 40–44	156,051	2.1	5.9	7.2	0.7	79.4	69.5	7.7	15.1
Aged 45–49	140,214	2.0	6.1	6.5	0.6	81.3	72.8	6.2	12.4
Aged 50–54	128,836	1.9	5.8	5.6	0.6	84.0	76.7	4.6	9.8
Aged 55–59	105,057	1.8	4.9	5.4	0.5	85.8	78.9	3.8	8.7
Aged 60–64	85,142	1.6	5.0	5.8	0.5	86.0	79.4	3.2	7.9
Aged 65–69	71,387	1.4	5.0	5.3	0.4	87.2	81.2	2.6	6.8
Aged 70–74	60,388	1.1	4.0	4.5	0.3	89.5	84.3	2.1	5.8
Aged 75–79	44,851	1.1	2.8	3.8	0.2	91.7	87.3	1.7	4.6
Aged 80–84	25,314	1.0	2.5	3.6	0.2	92.4	88.4	1.7	4.1
Aged 85 or older	16,989	1.1	2.1	4.1	0.2	92.2	88.0	1.7	4.5
New Hampshire, total	**1,235,786**	**0.6**	**1.6**	**1.0**	**0.1**	**97.0**	**95.1**	**0.9**	**1.7**
Under age 5	75,685	0.7	2.5	2.0	0.1	95.7	91.7	1.6	3.1
Aged 5–9	88,537	0.7	1.7	1.5	0.1	96.6	93.5	1.3	2.6
Aged 10–14	93,255	0.7	1.5	1.3	0.1	96.9	94.2	1.1	2.1
Aged 15–19	86,688	0.8	1.7	1.3	0.1	96.3	93.8	1.2	2.3
Aged 20–24	68,766	0.8	2.5	1.5	0.1	95.2	92.4	1.5	2.7
Aged 25–29	71,355	0.6	3.1	1.3	0.1	94.7	92.3	1.4	2.6
Aged 30–34	88,706	0.6	2.2	1.1	0.1	95.8	93.9	1.2	2.1
Aged 35–39	109,654	0.7	1.6	1.0	0.1	96.8	95.1	0.8	1.6
Aged 40–44	111,525	0.7	1.3	0.7	0.1	97.5	96.1	0.6	1.2
Aged 45–49	98,117	0.7	1.2	0.6	0.1	97.6	96.3	0.5	1.1
Aged 50–54	85,869	0.7	1.0	0.5	0.0	98.0	96.8	0.5	0.8
Aged 55–59	62,664	0.6	0.9	0.5	0.0	98.2	97.1	0.4	0.7
Aged 60–64	46,995	0.4	0.8	0.5	0.0	98.4	97.4	0.4	0.8
Aged 65–69	41,143	0.4	0.8	0.4	0.0	98.6	97.7	0.3	0.5
Aged 70–74	37,184	0.4	0.5	0.3	0.0	99.0	98.3	0.2	0.4
Aged 75–79	30,593	0.3	0.4	0.2	0.0	99.3	98.6	0.2	0.3
Aged 80–84	20,819	0.3	0.4	0.1	0.0	99.5	98.8	0.2	0.3
Aged 85 or older	18,231	0.3	0.2	0.2	0.0	99.5	98.9	0.1	0.3

(continued from previous page)

	total	American Indian	Asian	black	Native Hawaiian	white total	white non-Hispanic	other	Hispanic
New Jersey, total	**8,414,350**	**0.6%**	**6.2%**	**14.4%**	**0.1%**	**74.4%**	**66.0%**	**6.9%**	**13.3%**
Under age 5	563,785	0.7	7.7	17.6	0.1	69.2	57.6	9.4	17.6
Aged 5–9	604,529	0.7	6.7	18.3	0.1	69.5	59.3	8.5	16.1
Aged 10–14	590,577	0.7	6.3	17.8	0.1	70.3	60.9	8.2	15.2
Aged 15–19	525,216	0.7	6.5	17.9	0.2	68.4	58.4	9.7	17.3
Aged 20–24	480,079	0.8	7.2	17.8	0.2	65.6	53.7	12.0	21.5
Aged 25–29	544,917	0.7	9.1	16.3	0.2	66.3	55.1	10.8	19.5
Aged 30–34	644,123	0.6	8.0	15.3	0.1	69.9	60.0	8.9	16.6
Aged 35–39	727,924	0.6	7.0	14.3	0.1	73.3	64.5	7.3	14.0
Aged 40–44	707,182	0.6	6.6	13.2	0.1	75.7	68.2	6.2	11.7
Aged 45–49	611,357	0.6	6.2	12.4	0.1	77.5	70.8	5.4	10.4
Aged 50–54	547,541	0.5	5.7	11.9	0.1	79.0	72.7	4.6	9.4
Aged 55–59	423,338	0.5	5.2	12.1	0.1	79.9	73.6	3.9	8.8
Aged 60–64	330,646	0.4	4.9	12.8	0.1	79.7	73.2	3.7	8.9
Aged 65–69	293,196	0.4	3.7	11.3	0.1	83.1	77.3	2.8	7.4
Aged 70–74	281,473	0.3	2.6	9.2	0.0	86.8	82.4	2.1	5.5
Aged 75–79	240,131	0.3	2.0	7.7	0.0	89.3	85.9	1.6	4.1
Aged 80–84	162,337	0.3	1.6	6.7	0.0	90.9	87.9	1.3	3.4
Aged 85 or older	135,999	0.3	1.2	7.0	0.0	91.1	88.1	1.3	3.3
New Mexico, total	**1,819,046**	**10.5**	**1.5**	**2.3**	**0.2**	**69.9**	**44.7**	**19.4**	**42.1**
Under age 5	130,628	13.8	1.9	3.7	0.3	61.2	29.6	26.4	54.1
Aged 5–9	141,171	14.9	1.5	3.1	0.2	61.7	31.7	24.6	51.3
Aged 10–14	147,309	14.5	1.5	2.8	0.2	62.6	34.1	23.7	49.0
Aged 15–19	145,751	13.1	1.5	2.7	0.2	63.4	35.3	23.7	48.9
Aged 20–24	121,291	12.4	1.8	2.9	0.2	61.5	35.1	25.3	49.0
Aged 25–29	115,387	11.8	2.1	2.5	0.2	63.3	37.4	24.0	47.3
Aged 30–34	118,704	11.1	1.9	2.4	0.2	65.5	40.1	22.3	45.4
Aged 35–39	140,378	10.4	1.6	2.3	0.2	68.0	43.8	20.7	42.7
Aged 40–44	141,631	9.4	1.4	2.1	0.2	71.4	49.1	18.6	38.8
Aged 45–49	131,000	8.2	1.4	2.0	0.2	75.0	53.7	16.0	35.2
Aged 50–54	114,819	7.6	1.3	1.6	0.1	78.1	56.6	14.1	33.4
Aged 55–59	87,140	7.3	1.1	1.5	0.1	80.6	58.7	11.9	31.6
Aged 60–64	71,612	7.2	1.0	1.5	0.1	81.5	58.0	11.2	32.7
Aged 65–69	63,227	6.1	0.9	1.7	0.1	83.5	60.1	9.9	31.5
Aged 70–74	54,518	5.2	0.8	1.4	0.1	85.5	62.9	9.2	29.9
Aged 75–79	43,729	4.6	0.6	1.3	0.1	87.4	66.6	8.0	27.1
Aged 80–84	27,445	4.7	0.4	1.2	0.1	87.9	69.4	7.5	24.5
Aged 85 or older	23,306	5.5	0.4	1.4	0.1	86.7	67.3	7.6	25.5

(continued)

(continued from previous page)

	total	American Indian	Asian	black	Native Hawaiian	white total	white non-Hispanic	other	Hispanic
New York, total	**18,976,457**	**0.9%**	**6.2%**	**17.0%**	**0.2%**	**70.0%**	**62.0%**	**9.1%**	**15.1%**
Under age 5	1,239,417	1.2	6.5	21.0	0.2	64.0	52.9	12.6	20.5
Aged 5–9	1,351,857	1.2	5.8	21.6	0.2	63.9	53.9	11.8	19.5
Aged 10–14	1,332,433	1.1	5.7	21.0	0.2	65.2	56.1	10.8	17.8
Aged 15–19	1,287,544	1.1	6.3	20.2	0.2	64.7	55.7	11.4	18.4
Aged 20–24	1,244,309	1.1	7.9	18.9	0.2	62.8	53.0	13.1	20.7
Aged 25–29	1,304,725	1.0	8.8	17.7	0.2	63.8	54.0	12.4	19.8
Aged 30–34	1,452,599	0.9	7.6	17.4	0.2	66.3	57.3	11.1	17.8
Aged 35–39	1,566,083	0.9	6.9	17.3	0.2	68.5	60.4	9.5	15.6
Aged 40–44	1,508,215	0.9	6.7	16.3	0.1	70.8	63.7	8.2	13.5
Aged 45–49	1,341,138	0.9	6.3	15.2	0.1	72.8	66.3	7.4	12.2
Aged 50–54	1,211,798	0.8	5.9	14.4	0.1	74.8	68.4	6.5	11.3
Aged 55–59	932,008	0.7	5.1	15.1	0.1	75.5	69.0	5.8	10.9
Aged 60–64	755,979	0.7	5.2	15.3	0.1	75.5	68.8	5.6	10.8
Aged 65–69	657,600	0.6	4.4	13.5	0.1	78.9	72.9	4.5	9.3
Aged 70–74	618,446	0.5	3.4	11.6	0.1	82.6	77.7	3.5	7.3
Aged 75–79	514,132	0.4	2.8	10.3	0.1	85.0	80.9	2.8	5.8
Aged 80–84	346,686	0.4	2.3	9.2	0.1	86.9	83.3	2.4	5.0
Aged 85 or older	311,488	0.4	1.9	8.8	0.1	87.9	84.4	2.2	4.5
North Carolina, total	**8,049,313**	**1.6**	**1.7**	**22.1**	**0.1**	**73.1**	**70.2**	**2.8**	**4.7**
Under age 5	539,509	2.1	2.4	26.6	0.2	67.2	61.0	5.1	8.5
Aged 5–9	562,553	2.0	2.1	28.4	0.1	66.3	62.0	3.6	5.9
Aged 10–14	551,367	2.0	1.9	28.0	0.1	67.1	63.9	2.7	4.4
Aged 15–19	539,931	2.0	2.1	26.5	0.2	67.0	63.2	4.0	6.6
Aged 20–24	577,508	1.9	2.2	23.7	0.2	67.4	61.9	6.4	10.8
Aged 25–29	601,522	1.8	2.4	22.1	0.1	69.7	65.0	5.4	9.1
Aged 30–34	611,893	1.6	2.2	21.8	0.1	71.7	68.2	3.8	6.5
Aged 35–39	655,440	1.6	1.8	21.8	0.1	73.2	70.6	2.5	4.4
Aged 40–44	631,680	1.6	1.6	21.7	0.1	74.2	72.2	1.8	3.1
Aged 45–49	570,411	1.6	1.4	21.2	0.1	75.3	73.7	1.2	2.1
Aged 50–54	514,739	1.5	1.2	18.6	0.1	78.5	77.2	0.9	1.6
Aged 55–59	400,207	1.4	1.1	16.7	0.1	80.8	79.7	0.6	1.2
Aged 60–64	323,505	1.3	0.9	16.7	0.1	81.2	80.2	0.5	1.0
Aged 65–69	282,836	1.0	0.8	16.2	0.0	82.1	81.3	0.4	0.8
Aged 70–74	250,941	0.9	0.5	15.9	0.0	82.8	82.1	0.3	0.6
Aged 75–79	201,444	0.9	0.4	15.3	0.0	83.6	82.9	0.2	0.5
Aged 80–84	128,366	0.9	0.3	15.6	0.0	83.4	82.8	0.2	0.5
Aged 85 or older	105,461	0.8	0.3	17.0	0.0	82.1	81.5	0.2	0.5

(continued)

(continued from previous page)

	total	American Indian	Asian	black	Native Hawaiian	white total	white non-Hispanic	other	Hispanic
North Dakota, total	642,200	5.5%	0.8%	0.8%	0.1%	93.4%	91.7%	0.6%	1.2%
Under age 5	39,400	10.0	1.3	2.3	0.1	88.7	84.3	1.3	2.7
Aged 5–9	42,982	9.9	1.1	1.5	0.1	89.0	85.9	1.0	2.1
Aged 10–14	47,464	9.0	0.9	1.1	0.1	90.2	87.5	0.8	1.6
Aged 15–19	53,618	7.2	0.7	1.1	0.1	91.6	89.5	0.8	1.6
Aged 20–24	50,503	5.9	1.0	1.6	0.1	91.5	89.5	1.1	2.0
Aged 25–29	38,792	6.3	1.5	1.2	0.1	91.2	89.3	1.0	1.8
Aged 30–34	38,095	6.3	1.3	0.9	0.1	91.8	90.1	0.7	1.4
Aged 35–39	46,991	5.6	0.9	0.7	0.1	93.0	91.7	0.5	1.1
Aged 40–44	51,013	4.3	0.5	0.6	0.1	94.7	93.7	0.4	0.8
Aged 45–49	47,436	3.6	0.5	0.4	0.1	95.7	94.8	0.4	0.6
Aged 50–54	37,995	3.5	0.7	0.2	0.0	95.8	94.9	0.4	0.7
Aged 55–59	28,926	3.3	0.5	0.2	0.0	96.1	95.3	0.3	0.5
Aged 60–64	24,507	3.0	0.4	0.2	0.0	96.6	95.8	0.2	0.5
Aged 65–69	23,142	2.3	0.3	0.1	0.0	97.5	96.8	0.2	0.4
Aged 70–74	22,759	1.8	0.3	0.1	0.0	98.1	97.5	0.2	0.3
Aged 75–79	19,085	1.4	0.1	0.0	0.0	98.6	98.1	0.2	0.3
Aged 80–84	14,766	1.2	0.1	0.1	0.0	98.8	98.3	0.1	0.3
Aged 85 or older	14,726	0.8	0.1	0.1	0.0	99.2	98.7	0.2	0.2
Ohio, total	**11,353,140**	**0.7**	**1.4**	**12.1**	**0.1**	**86.1**	**84.0**	**1.1**	**1.9**
Under age 5	754,930	0.7	1.9	16.8	0.1	82.3	77.5	2.2	3.3
Aged 5–9	816,346	0.7	1.5	16.9	0.1	81.9	78.2	1.8	2.8
Aged 10–14	827,811	0.8	1.3	15.3	0.1	83.3	80.3	1.5	2.4
Aged 15–19	816,868	0.8	1.4	13.8	0.1	84.3	81.6	1.5	2.5
Aged 20–24	728,928	0.8	2.1	13.3	0.1	83.7	81.1	1.8	2.9
Aged 25–29	735,582	0.7	2.5	13.1	0.1	83.4	81.1	1.7	2.7
Aged 30–34	784,312	0.7	2.0	12.0	0.1	85.1	83.1	1.3	2.2
Aged 35–39	883,771	0.7	1.5	11.5	0.1	86.2	84.5	1.0	1.8
Aged 40–44	921,545	0.7	1.2	11.2	0.1	86.9	85.4	0.9	1.5
Aged 45–49	834,831	0.7	1.2	10.5	0.0	87.7	86.3	0.7	1.3
Aged 50–54	731,553	0.7	1.2	9.5	0.0	88.9	87.6	0.6	1.1
Aged 55–59	553,174	0.6	1.1	9.1	0.0	89.5	88.2	0.5	1.0
Aged 60–64	455,732	0.5	1.0	9.5	0.0	89.3	88.1	0.4	0.9
Aged 65–69	402,668	0.5	0.7	9.7	0.0	89.4	88.3	0.4	0.9
Aged 70–74	387,584	0.4	0.5	8.8	0.0	90.6	89.6	0.3	0.7
Aged 75–79	325,468	0.3	0.4	7.6	0.0	91.9	91.0	0.3	0.6
Aged 80–84	215,241	0.3	0.3	6.9	0.0	92.7	91.9	0.3	0.5
Aged 85 or older	176,796	0.3	0.3	7.1	0.0	92.5	91.8	0.3	0.4

(continued)

(continued from previous page)

	total	American Indian	Asian	black	Native Hawaiian	white total	white non-Hispanic	other	Hispanic
Oklahoma, total	**3,450,654**	**11.4%**	**1.7%**	**8.3%**	**0.1%**	**80.3%**	**74.1%**	**3.0%**	**5.2%**
Under age 5	236,353	16.1	2.1	12.0	0.3	73.1	62.0	5.4	9.7
Aged 5–9	244,525	16.1	1.8	11.8	0.2	73.4	63.9	4.4	7.9
Aged 10–14	252,029	15.8	1.7	10.6	0.2	74.8	66.2	3.7	6.8
Aged 15–19	269,373	14.7	1.9	10.0	0.2	75.3	67.2	4.0	7.0
Aged 20–24	247,165	11.9	2.8	10.0	0.2	74.8	67.5	5.1	8.4
Aged 25–29	229,026	11.5	2.9	9.2	0.2	75.9	69.1	4.7	7.8
Aged 30–34	222,621	11.0	2.3	8.5	0.2	78.0	71.8	4.0	6.7
Aged 35–39	259,131	10.7	1.8	8.3	0.1	80.0	74.6	2.9	5.0
Aged 40–44	264,391	10.2	1.5	7.9	0.1	81.7	76.8	2.3	3.9
Aged 45–49	240,805	9.8	1.5	7.0	0.1	83.4	78.9	1.8	3.1
Aged 50–54	212,956	9.5	1.4	6.0	0.1	85.0	80.8	1.4	2.5
Aged 55–59	173,199	9.0	1.1	5.3	0.1	86.8	82.7	1.1	2.1
Aged 60–64	143,130	8.4	1.0	5.2	0.1	87.7	83.8	0.9	1.8
Aged 65–69	128,756	7.5	0.8	4.8	0.1	89.0	85.5	0.8	1.5
Aged 70–74	113,743	6.6	0.7	4.4	0.1	90.4	87.1	0.7	1.3
Aged 75–79	94,068	6.1	0.4	4.1	0.0	91.2	88.3	0.6	1.0
Aged 80–84	62,208	5.4	0.3	4.1	0.0	92.0	89.4	0.4	0.7
Aged 85 or older	57,175	4.9	0.3	4.7	0.1	91.8	89.4	0.4	0.7
Oregon, total	**3,421,399**	**2.5**	**3.7**	**2.1**	**0.5**	**89.3**	**83.5**	**5.2**	**8.0**
Under age 5	223,005	3.2	5.2	3.9	0.8	84.0	71.6	10.2	16.6
Aged 5–9	234,474	3.3	4.5	3.5	0.7	85.6	75.5	8.4	13.5
Aged 10–14	242,098	3.6	4.1	3.0	0.7	87.6	79.3	6.5	10.2
Aged 15–19	244,427	3.2	4.4	2.6	0.7	86.7	79.1	7.0	10.7
Aged 20–24	230,406	2.8	5.0	2.6	0.8	83.6	75.5	9.4	14.0
Aged 25–29	233,850	2.7	5.5	2.3	0.6	83.4	75.9	8.8	13.5
Aged 30–34	236,845	2.5	4.8	2.3	0.6	85.8	79.5	7.0	10.8
Aged 35–39	255,751	2.6	4.1	2.0	0.4	88.5	83.5	5.0	7.6
Aged 40–44	270,823	2.5	3.4	1.9	0.4	90.6	86.5	3.6	5.5
Aged 45–49	271,315	2.3	3.0	1.6	0.3	92.4	89.0	2.6	4.0
Aged 50–54	235,840	2.2	2.6	1.4	0.3	93.5	90.4	2.0	3.2
Aged 55–59	173,008	2.1	2.4	1.2	0.2	94.3	91.6	1.6	2.6
Aged 60–64	131,380	1.9	2.4	1.2	0.2	94.5	91.8	1.4	2.3
Aged 65–69	112,614	1.6	2.3	1.1	0.2	95.2	92.8	1.1	1.9
Aged 70–74	106,728	1.2	2.0	0.9	0.1	96.1	94.2	0.9	1.5
Aged 75–79	95,059	1.0	1.5	0.8	0.1	96.8	95.2	0.8	1.2
Aged 80–84	66,345	0.8	1.3	0.7	0.1	97.4	96.1	0.6	0.9
Aged 85 or older	57,431	0.7	0.9	0.7	0.1	97.8	96.6	0.6	0.8

(continued)

(continued from previous page)

	total	American Indian	Asian	black	Native Hawaiian	white total	white non-Hispanic	other	Hispanic
Pennsylvania, total	**12,281,054**	**0.4%**	**2.0%**	**10.5%**	**0.1%**	**86.3%**	**84.1%**	**1.9%**	**3.2%**
Under age 5	727,804	0.5	2.8	15.0	0.1	81.3	76.3	3.7	5.9
Aged 5–9	827,945	0.5	2.2	15.1	0.1	81.3	77.4	3.3	5.2
Aged 10–14	863,849	0.5	2.1	14.0	0.1	82.4	79.2	2.8	4.6
Aged 15–19	850,986	0.5	2.6	12.3	0.1	83.4	80.5	2.7	4.5
Aged 20–24	746,086	0.5	3.3	12.3	0.1	82.2	79.1	3.2	5.1
Aged 25–29	732,701	0.5	3.6	11.9	0.1	82.3	79.5	3.0	4.8
Aged 30–34	827,785	0.4	2.8	11.1	0.1	84.2	81.8	2.5	4.0
Aged 35–39	951,400	0.4	2.1	10.4	0.1	86.0	84.0	1.9	3.2
Aged 40–44	996,676	0.4	1.8	9.6	0.1	87.4	85.8	1.5	2.5
Aged 45–49	908,650	0.4	1.7	8.9	0.1	88.4	86.9	1.2	2.1
Aged 50–54	796,382	0.4	1.7	8.3	0.1	89.1	87.8	1.1	1.9
Aged 55–59	619,969	0.4	1.5	8.0	0.0	89.8	88.5	0.9	1.7
Aged 60–64	511,656	0.3	1.4	8.1	0.0	90.0	88.8	0.8	1.5
Aged 65–69	480,656	0.3	1.0	7.8	0.0	90.8	89.8	0.6	1.2
Aged 70–74	488,616	0.2	0.7	6.7	0.0	92.3	91.5	0.4	0.8
Aged 75–79	422,311	0.2	0.5	6.1	0.0	93.2	92.5	0.4	0.7
Aged 80–84	290,015	0.2	0.4	5.4	0.0	94.1	93.4	0.3	0.6
Aged 85 or older	237,567	0.2	0.4	5.5	0.0	94.0	93.3	0.3	0.5
Rhode Island, total	**1,048,319**	**1.0**	**2.7**	**5.5**	**0.2**	**86.9**	**81.9**	**6.6**	**8.7**
Under age 5	63,896	1.6	3.7	9.0	0.3	79.9	69.9	11.6	16.3
Aged 5–9	71,905	1.6	3.5	8.7	0.2	80.6	71.7	10.5	14.9
Aged 10–14	71,370	1.5	3.4	8.2	0.2	81.5	74.4	9.6	12.7
Aged 15–19	75,445	1.4	4.4	7.5	0.2	81.4	75.3	8.9	11.5
Aged 20–24	71,813	1.1	4.7	7.5	0.3	80.6	74.0	9.5	12.5
Aged 25–29	64,732	1.0	4.0	6.6	0.2	82.0	75.4	9.4	12.7
Aged 30–34	75,594	0.9	3.1	5.8	0.2	84.7	79.1	8.0	10.9
Aged 35–39	85,364	0.9	2.5	5.1	0.2	87.3	82.7	6.4	8.6
Aged 40–44	84,946	0.9	2.3	4.8	0.1	88.8	85.1	5.2	6.6
Aged 45–49	75,429	0.9	2.1	4.5	0.1	90.0	86.7	4.4	5.6
Aged 50–54	66,434	0.8	1.7	3.5	0.1	92.1	89.2	3.5	4.6
Aged 55–59	49,982	0.7	1.6	3.1	0.1	92.8	90.2	3.3	4.0
Aged 60–64	39,007	0.8	1.7	3.5	0.1	92.3	89.6	3.3	3.7
Aged 65–69	36,023	0.7	1.3	3.2	0.1	93.3	91.1	2.9	3.0
Aged 70–74	37,661	0.5	0.9	2.5	0.1	95.1	93.4	2.1	2.1
Aged 75–79	34,076	0.4	0.7	2.0	0.1	96.3	94.8	1.6	1.5
Aged 80–84	23,745	0.4	0.5	1.5	0.1	97.0	95.6	1.6	1.4
Aged 85 or older	20,897	0.5	0.4	1.1	0.1	97.7	96.3	1.1	1.1

(continued)

(continued from previous page)

	total	American Indian	Asian	black	Native Hawaiian	white total	white non-Hispanic	other	Hispanic
South Carolina, total	**4,012,012**	**0.7%**	**1.1%**	**29.9%**	**0.1%**	**68.0%**	**66.1%**	**1.3%**	**2.4%**
Under age 5	264,679	0.8	1.4	35.8	0.1	62.4	58.7	2.1	3.6
Aged 5–9	285,243	0.7	1.2	38.2	0.1	60.2	57.6	1.5	2.7
Aged 10–14	290,479	0.8	1.1	38.3	0.1	60.0	58.0	1.2	2.2
Aged 15–19	295,377	0.8	1.3	36.5	0.1	60.8	58.5	1.8	3.3
Aged 20–24	281,714	0.8	1.5	32.6	0.2	63.3	60.3	3.0	5.2
Aged 25–29	276,855	0.7	1.6	29.7	0.1	66.5	63.8	2.4	4.4
Aged 30–34	283,976	0.7	1.5	29.4	0.1	67.4	65.3	1.8	3.3
Aged 35–39	314,558	0.7	1.2	29.1	0.1	68.4	66.7	1.2	2.4
Aged 40–44	310,566	0.8	1.1	29.4	0.1	68.6	67.1	0.9	1.8
Aged 45–49	287,778	0.7	1.1	28.8	0.1	69.4	68.3	0.7	1.3
Aged 50–54	262,543	0.7	1.0	25.5	0.1	73.0	72.0	0.5	1.1
Aged 55–59	206,762	0.6	0.8	22.6	0.1	76.1	75.1	0.4	0.9
Aged 60–64	166,149	0.5	0.8	22.2	0.1	76.7	75.8	0.3	0.8
Aged 65–69	145,599	0.5	0.6	21.5	0.0	77.7	76.9	0.2	0.7
Aged 70–74	124,449	0.4	0.5	21.1	0.0	78.3	77.6	0.2	0.6
Aged 75–79	101,445	0.4	0.3	20.4	0.1	79.1	78.5	0.2	0.5
Aged 80–84	63,571	0.3	0.3	22.1	0.0	77.6	77.0	0.2	0.5
Aged 85 or older	50,269	0.3	0.2	24.3	0.1	75.4	74.8	0.2	0.4
South Dakota, total	**754,844**	**9.0**	**0.8**	**0.9**	**0.1**	**89.9**	**88.0**	**0.7**	**1.4**
Under age 5	51,069	16.0	1.3	2.2	0.2	82.8	78.4	1.4	2.9
Aged 5–9	54,486	15.9	1.1	1.6	0.1	83.3	79.7	1.0	2.3
Aged 10–14	59,463	15.0	1.0	1.2	0.1	84.4	81.5	0.8	1.9
Aged 15–19	62,463	12.4	0.8	1.1	0.1	86.7	84.4	0.7	1.7
Aged 20–24	52,802	9.9	1.3	1.3	0.1	87.8	85.6	1.1	2.1
Aged 25–29	45,084	10.3	1.4	1.4	0.1	86.9	84.9	1.3	2.2
Aged 30–34	45,929	9.5	1.0	1.2	0.1	88.2	86.5	1.1	1.9
Aged 35–39	56,587	8.1	0.8	0.8	0.1	90.4	89.0	0.7	1.4
Aged 40–44	58,799	6.9	0.7	0.6	0.1	92.2	90.9	0.5	1.1
Aged 45–49	53,865	5.8	0.6	0.4	0.0	93.4	92.4	0.4	0.8
Aged 50–54	43,817	5.8	0.5	0.3	0.1	93.7	92.7	0.3	0.7
Aged 55–59	33,611	5.2	0.5	0.3	0.0	94.3	93.4	0.3	0.6
Aged 60–64	28,738	5.2	0.4	0.2	0.0	94.6	93.6	0.2	0.6
Aged 65–69	27,126	4.1	0.3	0.2	0.0	95.6	94.9	0.2	0.5
Aged 70–74	26,003	3.0	0.2	0.1	0.0	96.9	96.2	0.2	0.4
Aged 75–79	22,520	2.4	0.1	0.1	0.0	97.5	97.0	0.2	0.3
Aged 80–84	16,396	2.0	0.1	0.1	0.0	97.9	97.4	0.1	0.3
Aged 85 or older	16,086	1.7	0.1	0.1	0.0	98.3	97.8	0.1	0.3

(continued)

(continued from previous page)

	total	American Indian	Asian	black	Native Hawaiian	white total	non-Hispanic	other	Hispanic
Tennessee, total	**5,689,283**	**0.7%**	**1.2%**	**16.8%**	**0.1%**	**81.2%**	**79.2%**	**1.3%**	**2.2%**
Under age 5	374,880	0.6	1.6	22.4	0.1	75.7	71.6	2.4	3.8
Aged 5–9	395,813	0.6	1.3	23.1	0.1	75.2	72.3	1.7	2.6
Aged 10–14	395,155	0.7	1.3	21.9	0.1	76.4	74.0	1.3	2.1
Aged 15–19	395,184	0.7	1.4	20.6	0.1	76.7	74.3	1.8	3.0
Aged 20–24	386,345	0.7	1.6	19.5	0.1	76.5	73.7	2.8	4.6
Aged 25–29	403,829	0.6	1.9	17.8	0.1	78.3	75.7	2.4	4.0
Aged 30–34	412,072	0.7	1.6	16.9	0.1	79.9	77.8	1.8	3.0
Aged 35–39	453,327	0.7	1.3	16.5	0.1	81.1	79.4	1.2	2.1
Aged 40–44	449,200	0.8	1.2	16.3	0.1	81.6	80.2	0.9	1.6
Aged 45–49	412,704	0.8	1.1	15.4	0.1	82.8	81.5	0.7	1.2
Aged 50–54	374,212	0.8	0.9	12.8	0.0	85.7	84.6	0.5	1.0
Aged 55–59	293,942	0.7	0.8	11.0	0.0	87.7	86.7	0.3	0.8
Aged 60–64	239,309	0.6	0.8	11.0	0.0	88.0	87.0	0.3	0.7
Aged 65–69	204,571	0.6	0.6	11.0	0.0	88.3	87.3	0.2	0.5
Aged 70–74	178,281	0.5	0.5	10.6	0.0	88.8	88.0	0.2	0.5
Aged 75–79	144,848	0.5	0.3	10.0	0.0	89.6	88.8	0.2	0.4
Aged 80–84	94,146	0.5	0.3	10.2	0.0	89.4	88.6	0.2	0.4
Aged 85 or older	81,465	0.4	0.2	11.8	0.0	87.9	87.2	0.1	0.4
Texas, total	**20,851,820**	**1.0**	**3.1**	**12.0**	**0.1**	**73.1**	**52.4**	**13.3**	**32.0**
Under age 5	1,624,628	1.0	3.3	13.4	0.2	67.5	39.5	19.3	44.0
Aged 5–9	1,654,184	1.0	2.9	14.0	0.2	68.1	41.6	17.5	41.3
Aged 10–14	1,631,192	1.1	2.9	13.8	0.2	69.3	45.0	16.0	38.0
Aged 15–19	1,636,232	1.1	3.0	13.2	0.2	68.9	45.0	16.5	38.4
Aged 20–24	1,539,404	1.1	3.5	12.5	0.2	67.0	43.1	18.6	40.5
Aged 25–29	1,591,522	1.0	4.2	12.2	0.2	67.5	44.4	17.5	38.6
Aged 30–34	1,570,561	1.0	4.1	12.3	0.2	69.6	47.8	15.4	35.3
Aged 35–39	1,688,883	1.1	3.4	12.4	0.1	72.3	53.0	12.9	30.5
Aged 40–44	1,633,355	1.1	3.2	12.1	0.1	74.6	57.2	10.9	26.7
Aged 45–49	1,416,178	1.1	3.2	11.5	0.1	76.6	60.2	9.4	24.2
Aged 50–54	1,194,959	1.1	3.0	10.2	0.1	79.2	63.5	8.1	22.4
Aged 55–59	896,521	1.1	2.6	9.4	0.1	81.7	66.4	6.8	20.6
Aged 60–64	701,669	1.0	2.4	9.4	0.1	82.6	67.1	6.2	20.3
Aged 65–69	610,432	0.8	2.0	9.3	0.1	83.8	68.8	5.5	19.3
Aged 70–74	532,176	0.7	1.6	8.6	0.1	85.4	71.2	5.0	18.1
Aged 75–79	424,034	0.6	1.2	7.9	0.1	87.1	74.4	4.3	15.9
Aged 80–84	267,950	0.6	1.0	7.9	0.0	88.1	77.6	3.5	13.0
Aged 85 or older	237,940	0.5	0.8	9.0	0.1	87.4	77.0	3.4	12.8

(continued)

(continued from previous page)

	total	American Indian	Asian	black	Native Hawaiian	white		other	Hispanic
						total	non-Hispanic		
Utah, total	**2,233,169**	**1.8%**	**2.2%**	**1.1%**	**1.0%**	**91.1%**	**85.3%**	**5.1%**	**9.0%**
Under age 5	209,378	2.2	2.4	1.8	1.5	89.6	80.1	7.1	12.8
Aged 5–9	193,033	2.4	2.2	1.7	1.4	89.8	81.5	6.4	11.5
Aged 10–14	192,288	2.4	2.0	1.3	1.3	90.7	83.9	5.3	9.5
Aged 15–19	216,278	2.1	2.1	1.1	1.2	90.9	84.9	5.2	9.1
Aged 20–24	225,152	1.7	2.3	1.0	1.0	90.0	83.9	6.0	10.3
Aged 25–29	178,474	1.8	2.9	1.1	1.0	88.0	81.1	7.3	12.4
Aged 30–34	148,590	1.9	2.8	1.2	0.9	88.3	81.6	6.8	11.8
Aged 35–39	150,695	2.0	2.3	1.0	0.8	89.9	84.5	5.6	9.6
Aged 40–44	148,841	1.7	2.1	1.0	0.7	91.6	87.2	4.3	7.4
Aged 45–49	131,665	1.5	2.1	0.8	0.6	92.6	89.0	3.6	6.2
Aged 50–54	106,045	1.4	2.0	0.7	0.6	93.6	90.0	2.9	5.4
Aged 55–59	80,053	1.2	1.7	0.5	0.5	94.6	91.3	2.4	4.7
Aged 60–64	62,455	1.1	1.6	0.5	0.5	95.1	91.8	2.1	4.5
Aged 65–69	53,734	0.9	1.5	0.4	0.4	95.8	92.8	1.7	3.9
Aged 70–74	47,814	0.9	1.4	0.4	0.3	96.2	93.7	1.5	3.3
Aged 75–79	39,745	0.6	1.4	0.5	0.2	96.7	94.4	1.2	2.8
Aged 80–84	27,178	0.5	1.2	0.3	0.2	97.2	95.6	1.1	2.0
Aged 85 or older	21,751	0.7	0.8	0.4	0.2	97.6	95.9	1.0	1.9
Vermont, total	**608,827**	**1.1**	**1.1**	**0.7**	**0.1**	**97.9**	**96.2**	**0.4**	**0.9**
Under age 5	33,989	1.1	2.1	1.7	0.1	96.9	93.9	0.7	1.3
Aged 5–9	41,101	1.3	1.4	1.4	0.1	97.3	94.6	0.7	1.3
Aged 10–14	45,397	1.2	1.3	1.1	0.1	97.5	95.1	0.6	1.2
Aged 15–19	45,770	1.3	1.5	1.2	0.1	97.1	94.7	0.7	1.4
Aged 20–24	37,852	1.1	1.9	1.1	0.1	96.4	94.1	0.8	1.6
Aged 25–29	34,182	1.1	2.1	0.9	0.0	96.5	94.7	0.6	1.1
Aged 30–34	40,385	1.1	1.5	0.6	0.1	97.4	95.7	0.5	0.9
Aged 35–39	49,376	1.1	0.9	0.6	0.1	98.0	96.5	0.4	0.7
Aged 40–44	52,513	1.1	0.8	0.5	0.0	98.2	96.8	0.4	0.7
Aged 45–49	50,107	1.2	0.7	0.5	0.0	98.3	96.9	0.3	0.7
Aged 50–54	43,725	1.1	0.6	0.3	0.0	98.6	97.3	0.3	0.6
Aged 55–59	32,603	1.0	0.5	0.4	0.0	98.8	97.6	0.2	0.5
Aged 60–64	24,317	0.9	0.6	0.2	0.0	98.9	97.8	0.2	0.5
Aged 65–69	21,126	0.8	0.4	0.3	0.0	99.1	98.1	0.2	0.4
Aged 70–74	19,557	0.6	0.3	0.2	0.0	99.4	98.4	0.1	0.5
Aged 75–79	15,930	0.6	0.2	0.2	0.0	99.5	98.6	0.1	0.4
Aged 80–84	10,901	0.4	0.2	0.1	0.0	99.6	98.7	0.2	0.4
Aged 85 or older	9,996	0.4	0.2	0.2	–	99.7	98.8	0.2	0.5

(continued)

(continued from previous page)

	total	American Indian	Asian	black	Native Hawaiian	white total	white non-Hispanic	other	Hispanic
Virginia, total	**7,078,515**	**0.7%**	**4.3%**	**20.4%**	**0.1%**	**73.9%**	**70.2%**	**2.7%**	**4.7%**
Under age 5	461,982	0.8	5.2	24.6	0.2	69.9	62.6	4.5	7.3
Aged 5–9	495,084	0.8	4.5	25.7	0.2	69.2	63.5	3.5	6.0
Aged 10–14	495,955	0.8	4.3	25.2	0.2	69.7	65.1	2.9	5.0
Aged 15–19	484,065	0.9	4.6	24.3	0.2	69.4	64.8	3.4	5.7
Aged 20–24	480,574	0.9	5.2	22.3	0.3	69.0	63.7	5.1	8.2
Aged 25–29	497,172	0.8	6.4	20.3	0.2	70.1	65.1	4.7	7.6
Aged 30–34	539,793	0.7	5.4	20.5	0.2	71.5	67.2	3.8	6.4
Aged 35–39	610,810	0.8	4.5	20.4	0.1	73.2	69.6	2.8	4.9
Aged 40–44	589,880	0.8	4.2	20.0	0.1	74.2	71.2	2.2	3.9
Aged 45–49	526,221	0.8	4.0	18.7	0.1	76.1	73.6	1.6	3.0
Aged 50–54	473,035	0.7	3.7	15.9	0.1	79.5	77.3	1.2	2.4
Aged 55–59	358,442	0.7	3.5	15.2	0.1	80.7	78.7	0.9	2.1
Aged 60–64	273,169	0.6	3.3	16.2	0.1	80.0	78.2	0.8	1.8
Aged 65–69	229,553	0.5	2.9	16.5	0.0	80.3	78.7	0.6	1.5
Aged 70–74	202,903	0.4	2.1	15.8	0.0	81.8	80.4	0.5	1.3
Aged 75–79	166,178	0.4	1.6	15.1	0.0	83.2	82.0	0.4	1.0
Aged 80–84	106,433	0.4	1.3	14.8	0.0	83.7	82.6	0.4	0.9
Aged 85 or older	87,266	0.4	1.0	15.2	0.1	83.6	82.5	0.4	0.9
Washington, total	**5,894,121**	**2.7**	**6.7**	**4.0**	**0.7**	**84.9**	**78.9**	**4.9**	**7.5**
Under age 5	394,306	3.7	8.2	6.8	1.2	80.4	67.5	9.3	14.7
Aged 5–9	425,909	3.6	7.4	6.2	1.1	81.5	70.9	7.8	12.3
Aged 10–14	434,836	3.7	7.2	5.4	1.0	82.6	73.9	6.4	9.9
Aged 15–19	427,968	3.5	7.9	4.9	1.1	81.7	73.7	6.6	9.9
Aged 20–24	390,185	3.1	8.4	4.8	1.1	79.4	71.3	8.1	12.1
Aged 25–29	403,652	2.8	8.8	4.5	0.9	79.5	72.3	7.4	11.3
Aged 30–34	437,478	2.6	7.7	4.4	0.8	82.0	76.1	5.8	9.0
Aged 35–39	483,950	2.6	6.8	4.1	0.7	84.3	79.5	4.4	6.7
Aged 40–44	491,137	2.5	6.3	3.7	0.6	86.1	82.0	3.4	5.2
Aged 45–49	454,223	2.4	5.9	3.1	0.5	87.7	84.3	2.7	4.0
Aged 50–54	391,749	2.2	5.5	2.6	0.4	89.1	86.1	2.1	3.3
Aged 55–59	285,505	2.1	5.0	2.3	0.4	90.1	87.3	1.8	2.9
Aged 60–64	211,075	2.1	5.5	2.2	0.3	89.9	87.2	1.7	2.7
Aged 65–69	176,225	1.7	5.2	2.0	0.3	90.8	88.5	1.4	2.2
Aged 70–74	160,941	1.3	4.7	1.8	0.2	92.1	90.1	1.1	1.8
Aged 75–79	142,708	1.0	3.6	1.6	0.1	93.8	92.2	0.8	1.3
Aged 80–84	98,189	0.8	2.9	1.4	0.1	95.0	93.6	0.8	1.0
Aged 85 or older	84,085	0.8	2.3	1.2	0.1	95.8	94.4	0.7	1.1

(continued)

(continued from previous page)

	total	American Indian	Asian	black	Native Hawaiian	white total	white non-Hispanic	other	Hispanic
West Virginia, total	**1,808,344**	**0.6%**	**0.7%**	**3.5%**	**0.0%**	**95.9%**	**94.6%**	**0.3%**	**0.7%**
Under age 5	101,805	0.5	0.9	5.4	0.1	94.9	91.9	0.7	1.1
Aged 5–9	111,150	0.5	0.7	4.8	0.1	95.1	92.8	0.6	1.0
Aged 10–14	116,182	0.6	0.7	4.2	0.1	95.3	93.5	0.4	0.9
Aged 15–19	125,578	0.7	0.7	4.3	0.1	95.0	93.3	0.4	0.9
Aged 20–24	120,109	0.5	1.2	4.5	0.1	94.1	92.8	0.5	0.9
Aged 25–29	113,577	0.5	1.0	3.6	0.1	95.1	93.9	0.4	0.9
Aged 30–34	115,517	0.6	0.8	3.3	0.0	95.6	94.5	0.3	0.8
Aged 35–39	129,816	0.6	0.7	3.3	0.0	95.8	94.8	0.2	0.6
Aged 40–44	142,433	0.7	0.5	3.3	0.0	95.9	94.9	0.2	0.6
Aged 45–49	141,229	0.7	0.5	3.3	0.0	96.0	95.0	0.2	0.5
Aged 50–54	129,237	0.7	0.6	2.6	0.0	96.6	95.7	0.2	0.4
Aged 55–59	98,916	0.7	0.6	2.2	0.0	97.0	96.0	0.1	0.5
Aged 60–64	85,900	0.6	0.5	2.2	0.0	97.1	96.2	0.1	0.5
Aged 65–69	75,863	0.5	0.3	2.2	0.0	97.3	96.5	0.1	0.4
Aged 70–74	72,600	0.4	0.3	2.7	0.0	97.0	96.2	0.1	0.4
Aged 75–79	58,802	0.5	0.2	2.6	0.0	97.2	96.2	0.1	0.4
Aged 80–84	37,851	0.5	0.2	2.7	0.0	97.0	96.2	0.1	0.3
Aged 85 or older	31,779	0.4	0.2	3.4	0.0	96.4	95.6	0.1	0.3
Wisconsin, total	**5,363,675**	**1.3**	**1.9**	**6.1**	**0.1**	**90.0**	**87.3**	**2.0**	**3.6**
Under age 5	342,340	1.9	3.3	10.6	0.1	84.0	77.6	3.9	7.2
Aged 5–9	379,484	1.9	3.2	10.4	0.1	84.2	79.4	3.1	5.6
Aged 10–14	403,074	1.9	3.1	8.9	0.1	85.8	82.0	2.4	4.5
Aged 15–19	407,195	1.7	2.8	7.6	0.1	86.9	83.3	2.6	4.8
Aged 20–24	357,292	1.5	2.7	7.2	0.1	86.5	82.6	3.6	6.2
Aged 25–29	333,913	1.5	2.8	7.5	0.1	86.1	82.3	3.5	6.1
Aged 30–34	372,255	1.4	2.2	6.3	0.1	88.6	85.7	2.5	4.5
Aged 35–39	435,255	1.3	1.6	5.4	0.1	90.8	88.7	1.7	3.1
Aged 40–44	440,267	1.2	1.2	5.0	0.1	92.0	90.2	1.3	2.5
Aged 45–49	397,693	1.1	1.1	4.6	0.0	92.8	91.3	1.0	2.0
Aged 50–54	334,613	1.0	1.0	4.1	0.1	93.6	92.3	0.9	1.7
Aged 55–59	252,742	0.9	0.9	3.6	0.0	94.4	93.1	0.7	1.4
Aged 60–64	204,999	0.8	0.8	3.5	0.0	94.7	93.5	0.5	1.3
Aged 65–69	182,119	0.7	0.7	3.2	0.0	95.4	94.3	0.5	1.1
Aged 70–74	173,188	0.5	0.6	2.7	0.0	96.2	95.4	0.4	0.9
Aged 75–79	146,675	0.4	0.5	2.0	0.0	97.1	96.5	0.3	0.7
Aged 80–84	104,946	0.4	0.4	1.5	0.0	97.8	97.2	0.3	0.5
Aged 85 or older	95,625	0.3	0.3	1.4	0.0	98.0	97.4	0.3	0.4

(continued)

(continued from previous page)

	total	American Indian	Asian	black	Native Hawaiian	white total	white non-Hispanic	other	Hispanic
Wyoming, total	**493,782**	**3.0%**	**0.8%**	**1.0%**	**0.1%**	**93.7%**	**88.9%**	**3.2%**	**6.4%**
Under age 5	30,940	4.6	1.2	2.0	0.2	90.9	81.8	5.5	11.3
Aged 5–9	34,127	4.5	1.0	1.5	0.2	91.5	84.1	4.5	9.4
Aged 10–14	38,376	4.3	0.9	1.3	0.2	92.4	85.9	3.8	8.0
Aged 15–19	41,903	3.6	0.9	1.2	0.2	92.7	86.8	3.8	7.8
Aged 20–24	33,455	3.3	1.3	1.6	0.2	91.0	85.5	4.6	8.6
Aged 25–29	30,084	3.4	1.3	1.2	0.2	91.4	86.0	4.4	8.2
Aged 30–34	29,770	3.5	1.1	1.1	0.1	92.1	87.1	3.8	7.3
Aged 35–39	36,482	3.0	0.8	0.9	0.1	93.5	89.3	3.2	6.1
Aged 40–44	42,283	2.7	0.7	0.7	0.1	94.5	90.8	2.7	5.2
Aged 45–49	40,701	2.4	0.7	0.6	0.1	95.3	91.9	2.2	4.4
Aged 50–54	33,378	2.3	0.6	0.5	0.1	95.8	92.2	2.0	4.3
Aged 55–59	24,935	2.3	0.6	0.4	0.1	96.2	93.0	1.6	3.6
Aged 60–64	19,655	2.2	0.6	0.5	0.0	96.2	92.9	1.5	3.9
Aged 65–69	16,598	1.7	0.5	0.5	0.1	96.8	93.6	1.4	3.7
Aged 70–74	14,745	1.4	0.5	0.5	0.0	97.2	94.3	1.2	3.3
Aged 75–79	11,808	1.2	0.4	0.3	0.0	97.6	94.7	1.2	3.0
Aged 80–84	7,807	1.1	0.2	0.5	0.0	98.2	95.4	1.1	2.5
Aged 85 or older	6,735	0.9	0.1	0.4	0.0	98.0	95.7	1.3	2.5

Note: Percentages will not add to 100 because each race includes those who identified themselves as the race alone and those who identified themselves as the race in combination with one or more other races, and because Hispanics may be of any race. Non-Hispanic whites include only those who identified themselves as white alone and non-Hispanic. American Indians include Alaska natives. Native Hawaiians include other Pacific Islanders. (–) represents zero.
Source: U.S. Census Bureau, Census 2000 Summary File 2; calculations by New Strategist

Metropolitan Areas by Race and Hispanic Origin, 2000 Census

(number of total people and percent distribution by race and Hispanic origin in the 100 largest metropolitan areas, 2000)

	total population	American Indian	Asian	black	Native Hawaiian	white total	white non-Hispanic	other	Hispanic
1. New York–Northern New Jersey–Long Island, NY–NJ–CT–PA CMSA	21,199,865	0.8%	7.5%	18.4%	0.2%	66.3%	56.4%	10.5%	18.2%
• Bergen–Passaic, NJ PMSA	1,373,167	0.5	8.8	8.8	0.1	74.9	64.9	9.9	17.3
• Bridgeport, CT PMSA	459,479	0.6	2.7	12.5	0.1	79.9	72.0	6.9	12.4
• Danbury, CT PMSA	217,980	0.5	3.6	3.5	0.1	90.3	84.7	4.2	7.0
• Dutchess County, NY PMSA	280,150	0.7	2.9	10.2	0.1	85.1	80.3	3.1	6.4
• Jersey City, NJ PMSA	608,975	0.8	10.3	14.7	0.2	59.9	35.3	19.9	39.8
• Middlesex–Somerset–Hunterdon, NJ PMSA	1,169,641	0.5	11.9	8.6	0.1	75.5	68.2	5.7	11.2
• Monmouth–Ocean, NJ PMSA	1,126,217	0.4	3.1	6.3	0.1	89.5	84.8	2.2	5.7
• Nassau–Suffolk, NY PMSA	2,753,913	0.5	4.0	9.2	0.1	83.5	76.4	4.9	10.3
• New Haven–Meriden, CT PMSA	542,149	0.7	3.1	14.1	0.1	79.0	73.0	5.4	9.8
• New York, NY PMSA	9,314,235	1.0	10.1	26.3	0.2	51.6	39.6	15.7	25.1
• Newark, NJ PMSA	2,032,989	0.5	4.5	23.3	0.1	67.7	58.9	6.7	13.3
• Newburgh, NY–PA PMSA	387,669	0.8	1.7	8.4	0.1	86.5	79.0	4.7	10.8
• Stamford–Norwalk, CT PMSA	353,556	0.4	4.4	9.9	0.1	82.6	74.6	4.9	10.8
• Trenton, NJ PMSA	350,761	0.5	5.5	20.7	0.2	70.0	64.2	5.4	9.7
• Waterbury, CT PMSA	228,984	0.7	1.6	9.3	0.1	84.0	77.2	6.8	11.5
2. Los Angeles–Riverside–Orange County, CA CMSA	16,373,645	1.6	11.5	8.3	0.5	59.1	39.0	24.0	40.3
• Los Angeles–Long Beach, CA PMSA	9,519,338	1.5	13.1	10.5	0.5	52.8	31.1	26.9	44.6
• Orange County, CA PMSA	2,846,289	1.3	14.9	2.1	0.6	68.3	51.3	17.1	30.8

(continued)

(continued from previous page)

	total population	American Indian	Asian	black	Native Hawaiian	white total	white non-Hispanic	other	Hispanic
• Riverside–San Bernardino, CA PMSA	3,254,821	2.1%	5.2%	8.6%	0.5%	66.0%	47.3%	22.6%	37.8%
• Ventura, CA PMSA	753,197	1.8	6.5	2.4	0.5	73.3	56.8	19.7	33.4
3. Chicago–Gary–Kenosha, IL–IN–WI CMSA	9,157,540	0.6	4.7	19.2	0.1	68.7	59.4	9.0	16.4
• Chicago, IL PMSA	8,272,768	0.6	5.1	19.4	0.1	67.7	58.0	9.5	17.1
• Gary, IN PMSA	631,362	0.7	1.1	20.1	0.1	74.8	67.9	5.0	10.5
• Kankakee, IL PMSA	103,833	0.6	0.9	16.0	0.1	81.1	77.8	2.9	4.8
• Kenosha, WI PMSA	149,577	0.9	1.2	5.8	0.1	90.1	85.1	4.0	7.2
4. Washington–Baltimore, DC–MD–VA–WV CMSA	7,608,070	0.8	6.0	27.1	0.1	64.8	60.1	3.8	6.4
• Baltimore, MD PMSA	2,552,994	0.7	3.1	28.1	0.1	68.5	66.3	1.2	2.0
• Hagerstown, MD PMSA	131,923	0.5	1.0	8.2	0.1	90.7	89.1	0.6	1.2
• Washington, DC–MD–VA–WV PMSA	4,923,153	0.8	7.6	27.1	0.2	62.2	56.1	5.2	8.8
5. San Francisco–Oakland–San Jose, CA CMSA	7,039,362	1.5	20.3	8.1	1.0	62.7	50.6	11.7	19.7
• Oakland, CA PMSA	2,392,557	1.6	18.8	13.8	1.0	59.7	47.7	11.0	18.5
• San Francisco, CA PMSA	1,731,183	1.1	24.5	6.0	1.2	62.1	51.2	9.8	16.8
• San Jose, CA PMSA	1,682,585	1.3	27.5	3.4	0.7	57.6	44.2	14.5	24.0
• Santa Cruz–Watsonville, CA PMSA	255,602	2.1	4.7	1.5	0.4	78.9	65.5	17.2	26.8
• Santa Rosa, CA PMSA	458,614	2.4	4.1	2.0	0.5	85.2	74.5	10.2	17.3
• Vallejo–Fairfield–Napa, CA PMSA	518,821	2.0	12.6	13.0	1.3	66.5	54.0	10.9	19.1
6. Philadelphia–Wilmington–Atlantic City, PA–NJ–DE–MD CMSA	6,188,463	0.6	3.6	20.3	0.1	73.7	70.4	3.4	5.6
• Atlantic City–Cape May, NJ PMSA	354,878	0.7	4.2	14.9	0.1	76.6	71.5	5.8	9.6
• Philadelphia, PA–NJ PMSA	5,100,931	0.5	3.8	20.9	0.1	73.3	70.2	3.2	5.1
• Vineland–Millville–Bridgeton, NJ PMSA	146,438	1.7	1.2	21.5	0.2	67.9	58.4	10.6	19.0
• Wilmington–Newark, DE–MD PMSA	586,216	0.6	2.6	18.5	0.1	77.3	73.9	2.5	4.7

(continued)

(continued from previous page)

	total population	American Indian	Asian	black	Native Hawaiian	white total	white non-Hispanic	other	Hispanic
7. Boston–Worcester–Lawrence, MA–NH–ME–CT CMSA	5,819,100	0.6%	4.4%	6.0%	0.1%	86.7%	82.5%	4.6%	6.2%
• Boston, MA–NH PMSA	3,406,829	0.5	5.4	7.9	0.1	84.2	80.0	4.4	5.9
• Brockton, MA PMSA	255,459	0.6	1.6	9.8	0.1	84.0	80.8	7.6	3.7
• Fitchburg–Leominster, MA PMSA	142,284	0.6	2.7	3.2	0.1	91.1	85.4	4.4	8.3
• Lawrence, MA–NH PMSA	396,230	0.6	2.4	2.4	0.1	87.4	81.6	9.4	14.0
• Lowell, MA–NH PMSA	301,686	0.5	8.2	2.3	0.1	87.4	83.2	3.5	5.7
• Manchester, NH PMSA	198,378	0.6	2.0	1.7	0.1	95.5	92.7	1.5	3.0
• Nashua, NH PMSA	190,949	0.5	2.7	1.6	0.1	94.5	91.8	1.9	3.4
• New Bedford, MA PMSA	175,198	1.0	0.9	4.2	0.2	88.6	83.7	9.2	5.9
• Portsmouth–Rochester, NH–ME PMSA	240,698	0.6	1.6	1.0	0.1	97.4	95.9	0.5	1.0
• Worcester, MA–CT PMSA	511,389	0.7	3.3	3.5	0.1	90.2	85.5	4.2	7.1
8. Detroit–Ann Arbor–Flint, MI CMSA	5,456,428	1.0	2.7	21.7	0.1	74.8	71.6	1.9	2.9
• Ann Arbor, MI PMSA	578,736	1.0	4.2	8.0	0.1	87.1	83.7	1.7	3.1
• Detroit, MI PMSA	4,441,551	0.9	2.7	23.5	0.1	73.0	69.7	2.0	2.9
• Flint, MI PMSA	436,141	1.6	1.1	21.3	0.1	77.1	74.1	1.2	2.3
9. Dallas–Fort Worth, TX CMSA	5,221,801	1.1	4.2	14.3	0.2	71.5	59.3	11.3	21.5
• Dallas, TX PMSA	3,519,176	1.1	4.5	15.5	0.1	69.2	56.2	12.1	23.0
• Fort Worth–Arlington, TX PMSA	1,702,625	1.2	3.6	11.6	0.2	76.3	65.6	9.5	18.2
10. Houston–Galveston–Brazoria, TX CMSA	4,669,571	0.8	5.4	17.4	0.1	64.8	48.0	14.3	28.9
• Brazoria, TX PMSA	241,767	1.0	2.3	8.8	0.1	79.1	65.4	11.0	22.8
• Galveston–Texas City, TX PMSA	250,158	0.9	2.5	15.8	0.1	74.5	63.1	8.4	18.0
• Houston, TX PMSA	4,177,646	0.8	5.8	17.9	0.1	63.4	46.1	14.8	29.9
11. Atlanta, GA MSA	4,112,198	0.7	3.7	29.6	0.1	64.2	59.8	3.6	6.5
12. Miami–Fort Lauderdale, FL CMSA	3,876,380	0.5	2.2	21.9	0.2	72.4	36.3	6.7	40.3

(continued)

(continued from previous page)

	total population	American Indian	Asian	black	Native Hawaiian	white total	white non-Hispanic	other	Hispanic
		0.5%	2.8%	22.2%	0.2%	72.4%	58.0%	5.4%	16.7%
• Fort Lauderdale, FL PMSA	1,623,018								
• Miami, FL PMSA	2,253,362	0.4	1.8	21.6	0.2	72.3	20.7	7.6	57.3
13. Seattle–Tacoma–Bremerton, WA CMSA	3,554,760	2.3	9.5	5.7	1.0	82.7	77.0	3.3	5.2
• Bremerton, WA PMSA	231,969	3.2	6.3	3.8	1.3	88.3	82.2	2.3	4.1
• Olympia, WA PMSA	207,355	2.8	5.8	3.1	0.9	89.0	83.4	2.5	4.5
• Seattle–Bellevue–Everett, WA PMSA	2,414,616	2.0	10.9	5.3	0.8	81.7	76.3	3.4	5.2
• Tacoma, WA PMSA	700,820	2.8	7.0	8.6	1.4	82.7	76.0	3.3	5.5
14. Phoenix–Mesa, AZ MSA	3,251,876	2.8	2.6	4.2	0.3	79.4	65.8	13.7	25.1
15. Minneapolis–St. Paul, MN–WI MSA	2,968,806	1.3	4.7	6.2	0.1	87.7	84.7	2.2	3.3
16. Cleveland–Akron, OH CMSA	2,945,831	0.6	1.6	17.4	0.1	80.3	77.8	1.6	2.7
• Akron, OH PMSA	694,960	0.7	1.5	11.6	0.1	87.0	85.4	0.5	0.8
• Cleveland–Lorain–Elyria, OH PMSA	2,250,871	0.6	1.6	19.2	0.1	78.2	75.4	2.0	3.3
17. San Diego, CA MSA	2,813,833	1.6	10.5	6.6	0.9	70.3	55.0	15.1	26.7
18. St. Louis, MO–IL MSA	2,603,607	0.6	1.7	18.8	0.1	79.3	77.4	0.8	1.5
19. Denver–Boulder–Greeley, CO CMSA	2,581,506	1.6	3.5	5.3	0.2	83.0	71.8	9.4	18.5
• Boulder–Longmont, CO PMSA	291,288	1.2	3.7	1.2	0.2	90.5	83.6	5.5	10.5
• Denver, CO PMSA	2,109,282	1.7	3.6	6.2	0.2	81.9	70.4	9.5	18.8
• Greeley, CO PMSA	180,936	1.6	1.2	0.8	0.2	84.1	70.0	14.8	27.0
20. Tampa–St. Petersburg–Clearwater, FL MSA	2,395,997	0.8	2.3	10.8	0.1	84.5	76.0	3.6	10.4
21. Pittsburgh, PA MSA	2,358,695	0.4	1.3	8.6	0.1	90.3	89.1	0.4	0.7
22. Portland–Salem, OR–WA CMSA	2,265,223	2.0	5.1	3.0	0.6	87.2	81.0	5.7	8.7
• Portland–Vancouver, OR–WA PMSA	1,918,009	1.9	5.6	3.4	0.6	87.4	81.6	4.8	7.4
• Salem, OR PMSA	347,214	2.7	2.2	1.2	0.5	85.9	78.1	10.8	15.6
23. Cincinnati–Hamilton, OH–KY–IN CMSA	1,979,202	0.6	1.5	12.1	0.1	86.3	84.7	0.7	1.1
• Cincinnati, OH–KY–IN PMSA	1,646,395	0.6	1.4	13.5	0.1	85.0	83.5	0.6	1.1

(continued)

(continued from previous page)

	total population	American Indian	Asian	black	Native Hawaiian	white total	white non-Hispanic	other	Hispanic
• Hamilton–Middletown, OH PMSA	332,807	0.6%	1.8%	5.7%	0.1%	92.2%	90.5%	0.8%	1.4%
24. Sacramento–Yolo, CA CMSA	1,796,857	2.4	10.8	8.2	0.9	74.1	63.7	9.2	15.5
• Sacramento, CA PMSA	1,628,197	2.4	10.7	8.8	0.9	74.3	64.3	8.5	14.4
• Yolo, CA PMSA	168,660	2.2	11.7	2.6	0.6	72.0	58.1	16.4	25.9
25. Kansas City, MO–KS MSA	1,776,062	1.2	2.0	13.4	0.2	82.5	78.3	2.9	5.2
26. Milwaukee–Racine, WI CMSA	1,689,572	0.9	2.2	15.8	0.1	79.1	75.0	3.6	6.5
• Milwaukee–Waukesha, WI PMSA	1,500,741	1.0	2.4	16.3	0.1	78.5	74.4	3.6	6.3
• Racine, WI PMSA	188,831	0.8	0.9	11.2	0.1	84.5	79.6	4.3	7.9
27. Orlando, FL MSA	1,644,561	0.8	3.3	14.9	0.2	77.0	65.1	6.8	16.5
28. Indianapolis, IN MSA	1,607,486	0.6	1.5	14.5	0.1	83.1	80.8	1.6	2.7
29. San Antonio, TX MSA	1,592,383	1.3	2.0	7.2	0.2	73.6	39.4	19.4	51.2
30. Norfolk–Virginia Beach–Newport News, VA–NC MSA	1,569,541	1.0	3.5	31.9	0.2	64.1	61.1	1.7	3.1
31. Las Vegas, NV–AZ MSA	1,563,282	1.7	5.9	8.9	0.9	77.1	63.1	9.9	20.6
32. Columbus, OH MSA	1,540,157	0.8	2.7	14.4	0.1	82.7	80.4	1.3	1.8
33. Charlotte–Gastonia–Rock Hill, NC–SC MSA	1,499,293	0.7	2.2	21.0	0.1	74.6	71.2	2.8	5.1
34. New Orleans, LA MSA	1,337,726	0.8	2.4	38.0	0.1	58.4	54.7	1.8	4.4
35. Salt Lake City–Ogden, UT MSA	1,333,914	1.3	2.8	1.5	1.2	89.7	82.8	6.1	10.8
36. Greensboro–Winston-Salem–High Point, NC MSA	1,251,509	0.7	1.6	20.7	0.1	75.4	72.3	2.9	5.0
37. Austin–San Marcos, TX MSA	1,249,763	1.1	4.1	8.5	0.2	74.7	60.7	14.3	26.2
38. Nashville, TN MSA	1,231,311	0.7	2.0	16.0	0.1	80.6	78.0	2.1	3.3
39. Providence–Fall River–Warwick, RI–MA MSA	1,188,613	0.9	2.6	4.9	0.2	88.0	83.4	6.0	7.9
40. Raleigh–Durham–Chapel Hill, NC MSA	1,187,941	0.8	3.3	23.3	0.1	70.6	66.8	3.7	6.1
41. Hartford, CT MSA	1,183,110	0.6	2.6	10.3	0.1	82.3	77.4	6.3	9.6

(continued)

(continued from previous page)

Total Population: Population

	total population	American Indian	Asian	black	Native Hawaiian	white total	white non-Hispanic	other	Hispanic
42. Buffalo–Niagara Falls, NY MSA	1,170,111	1.0%	1.5%	12.3%	0.1%	84.8%	82.5%	1.7%	2.9%
43. Memphis, TN–AR–MS MSA	1,135,614	0.5	1.6	43.8	0.1	53.6	51.8	1.4	2.4
44. West Palm Beach–Boca Raton, FL MSA	1,131,184	0.5	1.9	14.9	0.2	80.4	70.6	4.6	12.4
45. Jacksonville, FL MSA	1,100,491	0.8	2.9	22.2	0.2	74.1	70.4	1.8	3.8
46. Rochester, NY MSA	1,098,201	0.7	2.1	11.0	0.1	85.3	82.2	2.5	4.3
47. Grand Rapids–Muskegon–Holland, MI MSA	1,088,514	1.1	1.8	8.0	0.1	87.3	83.0	3.7	6.3
48. Oklahoma City, OK MSA	1,083,346	6.6	3.0	11.4	0.2	79.0	72.9	3.9	6.7
49. Louisville, KY–IN MSA	1,025,598	0.6	1.3	14.5	0.1	83.9	82.0	0.9	1.6
50. Richmond–Petersburg, VA MSA	996,512	0.8	2.4	30.8	0.1	65.9	64.0	1.5	2.3
51. Greenville–Spartanburg–Anderson, SC MSA	962,441	0.5	1.4	17.8	0.1	79.9	77.7	1.5	2.7
52. Dayton–Springfield, OH MSA	950,558	0.7	1.6	15.0	0.1	83.6	81.6	0.7	1.2
53. Fresno, CA MSA	922,516	2.8	8.2	5.7	0.3	59.2	40.6	28.8	44.0
54. Birmingham, AL MSA	921,106	0.6	1.0	30.3	0.1	68.0	66.4	0.9	1.8
55. Honolulu, HI MSA	876,156	1.8	61.6	3.4	21.6	35.2	20.0	3.7	6.7
56. Albany–Schenectady–Troy, NY MSA	875,583	0.6	2.1	6.8	0.1	90.6	88.1	1.4	2.7
57. Tucson, AZ MSA	843,746	4.0	2.7	3.7	0.2	77.8	61.5	15.1	29.3
58. Tulsa, OK MSA	803,235	10.7	1.6	9.5	0.1	80.4	73.9	2.7	4.8
59. Syracuse, NY MSA	732,117	1.2	1.7	7.2	0.1	90.3	88.0	1.1	2.1
60. Omaha, NE–IA MSA	716,998	1.0	1.9	8.9	0.1	86.7	82.8	3.2	5.5
61. Albuquerque, NM MSA	712,738	6.6	2.2	3.1	0.2	73.2	47.7	19.0	41.6
62. Knoxville, TN MSA	687,249	0.8	1.2	6.1	0.1	92.3	90.7	0.7	1.3
63. El Paso, TX MSA	679,622	1.1	1.3	3.5	0.2	76.8	17.0	20.4	78.2
64. Bakersfield, CA MSA	661,645	2.6	4.2	6.6	0.3	65.1	49.5	25.6	38.4
65. Allentown–Bethlehem–Easton, PA MSA	637,958	0.4	1.9	3.5	0.1	91.1	86.6	4.7	7.9

(continued)

RACIAL AND ETHNIC DIVERSITY **899**

(continued from previous page)

	total population	American Indian	Asian	black	Native Hawaiian	white total	white non-Hispanic	other	Hispanic
66. Harrisburg–Lebanon–Carlisle, PA MSA	629,401	0.4%	1.8%	8.5%	0.1%	88.9%	86.4%	1.8%	3.1%
67. Scranton–Wilkes-Barre–Hazleton, PA MSA	624,776	0.3	0.7	1.7	0.0	97.4	96.2	0.6	1.2
68. Toledo, OH MSA	618,203	0.7	1.4	13.5	0.1	83.8	80.1	2.5	4.4
69. Baton Rouge, LA MSA	602,894	0.5	1.7	32.2	0.1	65.6	63.9	0.8	1.8
70. Youngstown–Warren, OH MSA	594,746	0.6	0.6	10.8	0.0	88.4	86.4	0.8	1.8
71. Springfield, MA MSA	591,932	0.7	2.2	7.6	0.2	83.3	77.6	8.3	12.5
72. Sarasota–Bradenton, FL MSA	589,959	0.6	1.1	6.3	0.1	90.8	85.6	2.4	6.6
73. Little Rock–North Little Rock, AR MSA	583,845	1.0	1.3	22.3	0.1	75.6	73.5	1.2	2.1
74. McAllen–Edinburg–Mission, TX MSA	569,463	0.6	0.7	0.6	0.0	79.7	10.4	20.6	88.3
75. Stockton–Lodi, CA MSA	563,598	2.3	13.6	7.5	0.8	62.7	47.4	19.5	30.5
76. Charleston–North Charleston, SC MSA	549,033	0.8	1.7	31.3	0.1	66.1	64.0	1.3	2.4
77. Wichita, KS MSA	545,220	2.1	3.3	9.2	0.1	84.1	79.0	4.6	7.4
78. Mobile, AL MSA	540,258	1.1	1.3	27.7	0.1	70.2	68.6	0.7	1.4
79. Columbia, SC MSA	536,691	0.6	1.8	32.6	0.1	64.8	62.9	1.4	2.4
80. Colorado Springs, CO MSA	516,929	2.0	3.6	7.7	0.5	84.5	76.2	6.0	11.3
81. Fort Wayne, IN MSA	502,141	0.7	1.2	8.1	0.1	89.4	86.6	2.0	3.3
82. Daytona Beach, FL MSA	493,175	0.8	1.3	9.7	0.1	87.4	82.1	2.3	6.4
83. Lakeland–Winter Haven, FL MSA	483,924	0.8	1.2	14.1	0.1	80.9	74.7	4.7	9.5
84. Johnson City–Kingsport–Bristol, TN–VA MSA	480,091	0.6	0.5	2.3	0.0	96.9	95.6	0.4	0.9
85. Lexington, KY MSA	479,198	0.6	1.8	10.0	0.1	87.6	85.0	1.3	2.5
86. Augusta–Aiken, GA–SC MSA	477,441	0.8	1.9	35.0	0.2	62.6	60.3	1.2	2.4
87. Melbourne–Titusville–Palm Bay, FL MSA	476,230	0.9	2.0	9.0	0.2	88.3	83.7	1.7	4.6
88. Lancaster, PA MSA	470,658	0.4	1.6	3.3	0.1	92.5	89.3	3.4	5.7
89. Chattanooga, TN–GA MSA	465,161	0.7	1.2	14.6	0.1	83.7	82.0	0.9	1.5

(continued)

(continued from previous page)

	total population	American Indian	Asian	black	Native Hawaiian	white total	white non-Hispanic	other	Hispanic
90. Des Moines, IA MSA	456,022	0.6%	2.6%	4.6%	0.1%	91.1%	88.0%	2.6%	4.2%
91. Kalamazoo–Battle Creek, MI MSA	452,851	1.4	1.6	10.3	0.1	86.8	83.3	2.1	3.6
92. Lansing–East Lansing, MI MSA	447,728	1.2	3.0	9.1	0.1	86.5	82.2	2.6	4.7
93. Modesto, CA MSA	446,997	2.5	5.5	3.2	0.8	73.9	57.3	19.9	31.7
94. Fort Myers–Cape Coral, FL MSA	440,888	0.6	1.0	7.1	0.1	88.9	82.0	3.9	9.5
95. Jackson, MS MSA	440,801	0.3	0.9	45.9	0.1	53.1	52.2	0.4	1.0
96. Boise City, ID MSA	432,345	1.5	2.1	0.8	0.3	92.1	86.7	5.8	8.8
97. Madison, WI MSA	426,526	0.8	3.9	4.7	0.1	90.5	87.4	1.9	3.4
98. Spokane, WA MSA	417,939	2.4	2.6	2.2	0.3	93.9	89.8	1.4	2.8
99. Pensacola, FL MSA	412,153	1.8	2.6	17.0	0.2	79.4	76.1	1.2	2.6
100. Canton–Massillon, OH MSA	406,934	0.7	0.7	7.4	0.0	92.1	90.2	0.5	0.9

Note: Numbers will not add to total because each race includes those who identified themselves as of the race alone and those who identified themselves as of the race in combination with one or more other races. Non-Hispanic whites include only those who identified themselves as white alone and non-Hispanic. American Indians include Alaska natives. Native Hawaiians include other Pacific Islanders. For definitions of CMSA, PMSA, and MSA, see glossary.

Source: Bureau of the Census, Profiles of General Demographic Characteristics, 2000 Census of Population and Housing, 2001; compiled by New Strategist Publications, <www.newstrategist.com>

The Median Net Worth of Americans Stood at $71,600 in 1998

The median net worth (assets minus debts) of American households varies sharply by race and Hispanic origin of householders. The median net worth of non-Hispanic white households was a lofty $94,900 in 1998, while that of nonwhite and Hispanic households was a much smaller $16,400. The net worth of non-Hispanic white households is much higher than that of others because non-Hispanic whites are more likely to own a home. Home equity accounts for the largest share of Americans' net worth.

The average household had only $22,400 in financial assets in 1998, with transaction accounts (such as checking accounts) owned by the largest share. Nineteen percent of households owned stock, worth a median of $17,500. A slightly smaller percentage (16.5 percent) owned mutual funds, worth a median of $25,000. Forty-nine percent owned retirement accounts, and 30 percent had life insurance.

Sixty-six percent of households owned a home in 1998. The median value of the primary residence stood at $100,000.

Nearly three out of four households are in debt, owing a median of $33,300 in 1998. Mortgage debt accounts for the largest amount owed.

Forty-six percent of employed men and 43 percent of employed women were covered by an employer's pension plan in 2000. Older professionals working for large corporations are most likely to have coverage .

■ The wealth of Americans should rise substantially as the large baby-boom generation enters the ages of peak homeownership and begins to save seriously for retirement.

Net worth varies sharply by race and Hispanic origin

(median net worth of households by race and Hispanic origin of householder, 1998)

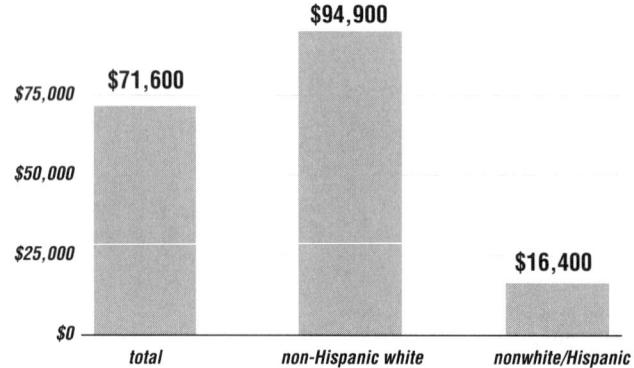

Net Worth, Assets, and Debt of Total Households by Race and Hispanic Origin, 1998

(median net worth, median value of assets for owners, and median amount of debt for debtors, by race and Hispanic origin of householder, 1998)

	total	non-Hispanic white	nonwhite and Hispanic
Median net worth	**$71,600**	**$94,900**	**$16,400**
Median value of financial assets	22,400	29,900	6,400
Median value of nonfinancial assets	97,800	107,600	52,000
Median amount of debt	33,300	40,000	15,300

Source: Federal Reserve Board, Family Finances in the U.S.: Recent Evidence from the 1998 Survey of Consumer Finances, *Federal Reserve Bulletin, January 2000; calculations by New Strategist*

Financial Assets of Total Households, 1998

(percent of total households owning financial assets, and median value of assets for owners, 1998)

	percent owning asset	median value
Any financial asset	**92.9%**	**$22,400**
Transaction accounts	90.5	3,100
Certificates of deposit	15.3	15,000
Savings bonds	19.3	1,000
Bonds	3.0	44,800
Stocks	19.2	17,500
Mutual funds	16.5	25,000
Retirement accounts	48.8	24,000
Life insurance	29.6	7,300
Other managed assets	5.9	31,500
Other financial assets	9.4	3,000

Source: Federal Reserve Board, Family Finances in the U.S.: Recent Evidence from the 1998 Survey of Consumer Finances, *Federal Reserve Bulletin, January 2000; calculations by New Strategist*

Nonfinancial Assets of Total Households, 1998

(percent of total households owning nonfinancial assets, and median value of assets for owners, 1998)

	percent owning asset	median value
Any nonfinancial asset	**89.9%**	**$97,800**
Vehicles	82.8	10,800
Primary residence	66.2	100,000
Other residential property	12.8	65,000
Nonresidential property	8.6	38,000
Business	11.5	60,000
Other nonfinancial assets	8.5	10,000

Source: Federal Reserve Board, Family Finances in the U.S.: Recent Evidence from the 1998 Survey of Consumer Finances, *Federal Reserve Bulletin, January 2000; calculations by New Strategist*

Debt of Total Households, 1998

(percent of total households with debt, and median amount of debt for those with debts, 1998)

	percent with debt	median amount
Any debt	**74.1%**	**$33,300**
Home-secured	43.1	62,000
Other residential property	5.1	40,000
Installment	43.7	8,700
Other lines of credit	2.3	2,500
Credit card	44.1	1,700
Other debt	8.8	3,000

Source: Federal Reserve Board, Family Finances in the U.S.: Recent Evidence from the 1998 Survey of Consumer Finances, *Federal Reserve Bulletin, January 2000; calculations by New Strategist*

Pension Coverage of Total Men, 2000

(total number of employed men aged 15 or older, number and percent with an employer-offered pension plan, and number and percent included in pension plan by selected characteristics, 2000; numbers in thousands)

		with employer-offered pension plan at work			
				included in plan	
	total	number	percent	number	percent
Total employed men	**79,180**	**45,200**	**57.1%**	**36,591**	**46.2%**
Age					
Under age 65	75,918	43,921	57.9	35,716	47.0
Aged 15 to 24	12,962	4,980	38.4	1,929	14.9
Aged 25 to 44	37,985	22,795	60.0	19,009	50.0
Aged 45 to 64	24,972	16,147	64.7	14,778	59.2
Aged 65 or older	3,261	1,278	39.2	875	26.8
Worked					
Full-time	68,985	41,804	60.6	35,492	51.4
50 weeks or more	58,765	37,251	63.4	32,790	55.8
27 to 49 weeks	6,106	3,008	49.3	2,043	33.5
26 weeks or less	4,114	1,545	37.6	659	16.0
Part-time	10,194	3,396	33.3	1,099	10.8
50 weeks or more	4,546	1,654	36.4	711	15.6
27 to 49 weeks	1,981	737	37.2	191	9.6
26 weeks or less	3,667	1,005	27.4	197	5.4
Size of employer					
Under 25 employees	23,924	5,693	23.8	4,622	19.3
25 to 99 employees	10,650	5,633	52.9	4,361	40.9
100 to 499 employees	10,692	7,280	68.1	5,897	55.1
500 to 999 employees	3,817	2,809	73.6	2,242	58.7
1,000 or more employees	30,096	23,784	79.0	19,469	64.7

(continued)

(continued from previous page)

	total	with employer-offered pension plan at work		included in plan	
		number	percent	number	percent
Occupation					
Executive, administrative, and managerial	11,413	7,698	67.5%	6,912	60.6%
Professional specialty	10,289	7,555	73.4	6,558	63.7
Technical, related support	2,224	1,669	75.0	1,388	62.4
Sales workers	8,815	4,628	52.5	3,518	39.9
Administrative support, including clerical	4,430	2,938	66.3	2,189	49.4
Precision production, craft, and repair	14,493	7,500	51.7	6,473	44.7
Machine operators, assemblers, inspectors	4,875	2,961	60.7	2,423	49.7
Transportation, material moving occupations	5,485	3,018	55.0	2,365	43.1
Handlers, equip. cleaners, helpers, and laborers	5,205	2,357	45.3	1,287	24.7
Service workers	8,142	3,799	46.7	2,679	32.9
Private household	50	2	4.0	2	4.0
Service workers except private household	8,092	3,797	46.9	2,677	33.1
Farming, forestry, fishing	3,180	606	19.1	389	12.2
Armed forces	630	471	74.8	409	64.8
Earnings					
Under $15,000	18,171	5,564	30.6	1,903	10.5
$15,000 to $24,999	13,268	5,896	44.4	4,022	30.3
$25,000 to $49,999	26,267	17,315	65.9	15,121	57.6
$50,000 to $74,999	12,122	9,310	76.8	8,815	72.7
$75,000 to $99,999	4,549	3,568	78.4	3,370	74.1
$100,000 or more	4,723	3,536	74.9	3,357	71.1

Source: Bureau of the Census, Current Population Survey, Internet site <http://ferret.bls.census.gov/macro/ 032001/noncash/nc8_002 .htm>; calculations by New Strategist

Pension Coverage of Total Women, 2000

(total number of employed women aged 15 or older, number and percent with an employer-offered pension plan, and number and percent included in pension plan by selected characteristics, 2000; numbers in thousands)

	total	with employer-offered pension plan at work		included in plan	
		number	percent	number	percent
Total employed women	**70,827**	**40,235**	**56.8%**	**30,224**	**42.7%**
Age					
Under age 65	68,506	39,308	57.4	29,686	43.3
Aged 15 to 24	12,277	4,727	38.5	1,699	13.8
Aged 25 to 44	33,560	20,335	60.6	15,774	47.0
Aged 45 to 64	22,669	14,246	62.8	12,212	53.9
Aged 65 or older	2,320	927	39.9	538	23.2
Worked					
Full-time	51,687	32,901	63.7	26,907	52.1
50 weeks or more	41,600	27,791	66.8	23,632	56.8
27 to 49 weeks	5,980	3,574	59.8	2,547	42.6
26 weeks or less	4,106	1,536	37.4	728	17.7
Part-time	19,140	7,334	38.3	3,316	17.3
50 weeks or more	9,419	3,926	41.7	2,174	23.1
27 to 49 weeks	4,215	1,766	41.9	781	18.5
26 weeks or less	5,506	1,642	29.8	361	6.6
Size of employer					
Under 25 employees	19,139	4,408	23.0	3,052	15.9
25 to 99 employees	8,457	4,189	49.5	2,976	35.2
100 to 499 employees	9,294	6,128	65.9	4,676	50.3
500 to 999 employees	4,172	2,996	71.8	2,334	55.9
1,000 or more employees	29,764	22,514	75.6	17,186	57.7

(continued)

(continued from previous page)

| | | with employer-offered pension plan at work | | | |
| | | | | included in plan | |
Occupation	*total*	*number*	*percent*	*number*	*percent*
Executive, administrative, and managerial	10,065	6,814	67.7%	5,809	57.7%
Professional specialty	12,158	8,830	72.6	7,452	61.3
Technical, related support	2,654	1,863	70.2	1,427	53.8
Sales workers	9,264	4,421	47.7	2,616	28.2
Administrative support, including clerical	16,371	10,488	64.1	7,889	48.2
Precision production, craft, and repair	1,380	740	53.6	594	43.1
Machine operators, assemblers, inspectors	3,055	1,643	53.8	1,147	37.6
Transportation, material moving occupations	704	398	56.5	324	46.0
Handlers, equip. cleaners, helpers, and laborers	1,254	605	48.2	323	25.7
Service workers	13,065	4,216	32.3	2,487	19.0
Private household	925	35	3.8	24	2.6
Service workers except private household	12,140	4,180	34.4	2,462	20.3
Farming, forestry, fishing	785	151	19.2	93	11.8
Armed forces	71	65	90.5	63	87.8
Earnings					
Under $15,000	26,994	9,319	34.5	3,821	14.2
$15,000 to $24,999	15,199	9,160	60.3	6,951	45.7
$25,000 to $49,999	21,212	15,885	74.9	14,033	66.2
$50,000 to $74,999	5,346	4,306	80.5	3,991	74.7
$75,000 to $99,999	1,082	896	82.8	826	76.3
$100,000 or more	886	657	74.2	595	67.2

Source: Bureau of the Census, Current Population Survey, Internet site <http://ferret.bls.census.gov/macro/ 032001/noncash/nc8_003 .htm>; calculations by New Strategist

8

Attitudes and Behavior

Relations among racial and ethnic groups in the United States are frequently difficult. Group stereotypes persist and frustrations erupt over perceived inequities. Nevertheless, Americans are surprisingly tolerant toward one another and united on many fronts.

The tables in this chapter reveal similarities and differences in the attitudes of racial and ethnic groups. Within the chapter, tables are organized into six topical areas: Perceptions of Diversity, Black Progress, Group Stereotypes, Immigration, Language, and Personal Outlook and Behavior. Most of the data presented stem from the 2000 General Social Survey, taken biennially by the University of Chicago's National Opinion Research Center. The GSS divides respondents into three racial groups—white, black, and other. The "other" racial category includes Asians, American Indians, and Hispanics who did not identify themselves as white or black. The GSS also collects attitudinal data by Hispanic origin, but only Hispanics who speak English are included in the sample. Most of the GSS questions shown in quotes are exact citations. Occasionally, however, questions were edited slightly to fit the space or style of a table.

America's tolerance of diversity will be tested in the years ahead as racial and ethnic minorities become a larger share of the population, jockeying for power as they strive for the opportunity to get ahead. Fortunately, opportunity is not in short supply. Every racial and ethnic group firmly believes the United States offers them an opportunity to improve their standard of living. Every racial and ethnic group believes their standard of living is better than that of their parents'. Every racial and ethnic group believes its children will have a higher standard of living than they themselves do today. The tolerance Americans show toward one another each day will determine whether these dreams come true.

Perceptions of Diversity

The public is almost evenly divided over whether racial and ethnic groups should maintain their distinct cultures (30 percent) or blend in (34 percent). Hispanics are most likely to favor maintaining a distinction (41 percent), while non-Hispanic whites are least likely to feel that way (28 percent).

The majority of the public views the changing racial and ethnic composition of the United States as neither good nor bad. Hispanics and people of "other" race are most likely to feel the change is good (45 percent), while non-Hispanic whites are most likely to think it is bad (21 percent).

Interestingly, most Americans think the United States is more diverse than it actually is. When asked to estimate the size of minority groups in the U.S. population, most respondents overestimate. Thirty-nine percent of the public believes that at least half the population is of mixed race, for example. According to the 2000 census, however, only 2 percent identify themselves being of as mixed race. Thirty-four percent of Hispanics estimate that their group accounts for at least half the U.S. population, but only 13 percent of Americans are Hispanic, according to the census. Similarly, 28 percent of blacks estimate that half of Americans are black. In reality, the black share is also 13 percent.

The clustering of racial and ethnic groups in neighborhoods and workplaces can be seen when respondents are asked to estimate the size of various groups in their local community and workplace. Forty-seven percent of blacks say their community is at least 50 percent black, for example. One-third of Hispanics live in a community that is at least half Hispanic. Twenty-eight percent of Hispanics say their workplace is mostly or entirely Hispanic. Nineteen percent of blacks work mostly or entirely with blacks.

Many Americans think racial/ethnic groups should blend in

(percent of people aged 18 or older who think racial/ethnic groups should blend in, by race and Hispanic origin, 2000)

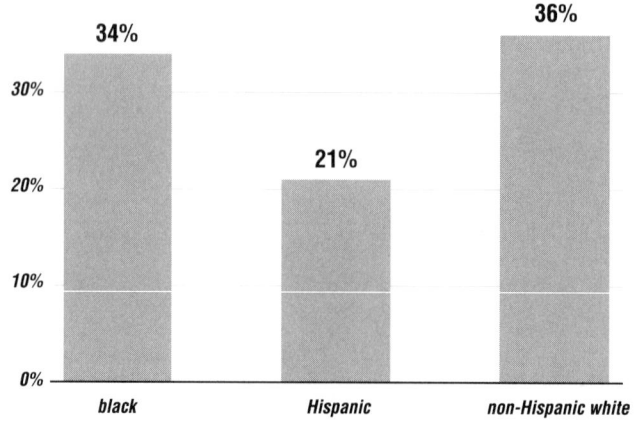

Should Racial/Ethnic Groups Maintain Distinct Cultures or Blend In? 2000

"Some people say that it is better for America if different racial and ethnic groups maintain their distinct cultures. Others say it is better if groups change so that they blend into the larger society as in the idea of a melting pot. Think of a score of 1 as meaning that racial and ethnic groups should maintain their distinct cultures, and a score of 7 as meaning that groups should change so that they blend into the larger society. What score between 1 and 7 comes closest to the way you feel?"

(percent of people aged 18 or older responding by race and Hispanic origin, 2000)

	maintain distinct cultures (1–3)	(4)	blend in (5–7)	don't know
Total	**30%**	**32%**	**34%**	**4%**
Black	35	24	34	7
White	29	33	35	3
Other	33	38	19	9
Hispanic	41	32	21	6
Non-Hispanic white	28	33	36	3

Source: 2000 General Social Survey, National Opinion Research Center, University of Chicago; calculations by New Strategist

Opinion of Future Change in Racial/Ethnic Composition of U.S., 2000

"When you think about changes in the racial and ethnic make-up of the country in the next 25 years, do you think they will be a very good thing for the country, a good thing, neither good nor bad, a bad thing, or a very bad thing?"

(percent of adults aged 18 or older responding by race and Hispanic origin, 2000)

	very good or good	neither	bad or very bad
Total	**25%**	**53%**	**18%**
Black	34	49	10
White	22	54	20
Other	43	50	3
Hispanic	45	42	10
Non-Hispanic white	21	55	21

Note: Percentages may not add to 100 because "don't know" is not shown.
Source: 2000 General Social Survey, National Opinion Research Center, University of Chicago; calculations by New Strategist

Estimated Percentage of Racial/Ethnic Group in the U.S. Population, 2000

"Just your best guess—what percentage of the United States population is made up of the following racial or ethnic groups?"

(percent of people aged 18 or older responding by race and Hispanic origin, 2000)

	total	race			Hispanic origin	
		black	white	other	Hispanic	non-Hispanic white
Mixed race						
Under 25 percent	26%	21%	27%	28%	17%	28%
25 to 49 percent	29	27	30	18	26	31
50 percent or higher	39	45	38	50	51	37
American Indians						
Under 25 percent	74	63	77	67	57	78
25 to 49 percent	11	10	11	15	22	11
50 percent or higher	6	12	5	6	10	5
Asians						
Under 25 percent	69	58	71	68	53	72
25 to 49 percent	18	17	18	17	18	18
50 percent or higher	6	12	5	9	21	4
Blacks						
Under 25 percent	37	24	39	45	35	39
25 to 49 percent	42	40	43	34	34	44
50 percent or higher	17	28	15	19	27	14
Hispanics						
Under 25 percent	54	46	56	52	32	58
25 to 49 percent	28	25	29	23	30	28
50 percent or higher	12	18	10	21	34	9
Jews						
Under 25 percent	65	50	68	61	56	69
25 to 49 percent	18	22	18	14	21	17
50 percent or higher	6	11	5	8	11	5
Whites						
Under 25 percent	2	5	1	2	3	1
25 to 49 percent	16	16	16	22	20	16
50 percent or higher	79	69	80	76	74	81

Note: Percentages may not add to 100 because "don't know" is not shown.
Source: 2000 General Social Survey, National Opinion Research Center, University of Chicago; calculations by New Strategist

Estimated Percentage of Racial/Ethnic Group in Local Community, 2000

"Just your best guess—what percentage of the people who live in your local community are made up of the following racial or ethnic groups?"

(percent of people aged 18 or older responding by race and Hispanic origin, 2000)

		race			Hispanic origin	
	total	black	white	other	Hispanic	non-Hispanic white
American Indians						
None	39%	41%	40%	42%	25%	38%
Less than 10 percent	38	23	41	36	36	41
10 to 49 percent	14	10	15	17	28	14
50 percent or higher	2	2	1	8	1	1
Asians						
None	25	40	23	16	12	24
Less than 10 percent	41	27	44	35	31	45
10 to 49 percent	26	21	26	40	44	25
50 percent or higher	2	3	1	5	6	1
Blacks						
None	7	0	9	4	5	9
Less than 10 percent	31	6	36	27	21	37
10 to 49 percent	47	42	47	61	59	47
50 percent or higher	11	47	6	7	12	5
Hispanics						
None	14	25	13	6	0	14
Less than 10 percent	33	26	35	28	13	36
10 to 49 percent	41	36	42	43	52	41
50 percent or higher	7	6	6	20	32	4
Jews						
None	28	46	25	32	22	25
Less than 10 percent	38	23	41	27	39	41
10 to 49 percent	22	17	22	25	26	22
50 percent or higher	2	3	2	3	3	3
Whites						
None	1	7	0	0	0	0
Less than 10 percent	3	18	1	5	7	0
10 to 49 percent	14	27	11	27	37	9
50 percent or higher	79	43	86	65	53	90

Note: Percentages may not add to 100 because "don't know" is not shown.
Source: 2000 General Social Survey, National Opinion Research Center, University of Chicago; calculations by New Strategist

Hispanics and Non-Hispanics in the Workplace, 2000

"How many of the people who work where you work are Hispanic?"

(percent of people aged 18 or older responding by race and Hispanic origin, 2000)

	all non-Hispanic	mostly non-Hispanic	about half and half	mostly Hispanic	all Hispanic
Total	36%	49%	8%	5%	1%
Black	32	48	9	7	1
White	37	50	8	4	0
Other	27	40	12	11	10
Hispanic	10	46	14	23	5
Non-Hispanic white	40	50	7	2	0

Note: Asked only of respondents who were currently employed. Percentages may not add to 100 because "don't know" and "works alone" are not shown.
Source: 2000 General Social Survey, National Opinion Research Center, University of Chicago; calculations by New Strategist

Blacks and Whites in the Workplace, 2000

"Are the people who work where you work all white, mostly white, about half and half, mostly black, or all black?"

(percent of people aged 18 or older responding by race and Hispanic origin, 2000)

	all white	mostly white	about half and half	mostly black	all black
Total	26%	48%	20%	4%	1%
Black	9	36	35	14	5
White	29	50	17	3	0
Other	19	44	29	4	0
Hispanic	14	50	32	2	1
Non-Hispanic white	31	50	16	3	0

Note: Asked only of respondents who were currently employed. Percentages may not add to 100 because "don't know" and "works alone" are not shown.
Source: 2000 General Social Survey, National Opinion Research Center, University of Chicago; calculations by New Strategist

Black Progress

Most Americans, regardless of race or ethnicity, believe conditions for blacks have improved over the past few years, including the 53 percent majority of blacks and fully two-thirds of non-Hispanic whites. Attitudes diverge, however, on the reasons for blacks' lower socioeconomic status in comparison to whites. The largest share of blacks blame discrimination (60 percent), while non-Hispanic whites are most likely to blame blacks' supposed lack of will or motivation (46 percent) and their lack of educational opportunity (43 percent). Hispanics are most likely to blame blacks' lack of will or motivation (51 percent). Blacks are least likely to feel this way (39 percent).

A minority of blacks, but the majority of other racial and ethnic groups, believe blacks should work their way up without special favors. Half of blacks think the government should help them. Most non-Hispanic whites disagree. Hispanics and people of "other" race are divided in their attitude toward government help for blacks.

Interestingly, majorities of all groups, including blacks, oppose affirmative action for blacks. Only 39 percent of blacks favor affirmative action, while 51 percent oppose it. The opposition to affirmative action is greatest among non-Hispanic whites (82 percent).

Most think conditions for blacks have improved

(percent of people aged 18 or older who think conditions for blacks have improved over the past few years, by race and Hispanic origin, 2000)

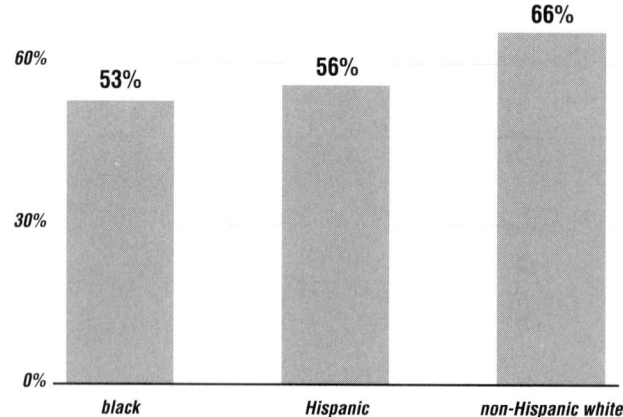

Changing Conditions for Blacks, 2000

"In the past few years, do you think conditions for black people
have improved, gotten worse, or stayed about the same?"

(percent of people aged 18 or older responding by race and Hispanic origin, 2000)

	improved	stayed the same	gotten worse
Total	**63%**	**29%**	**5%**
Black	53	39	7
White	65	27	4
Other	58	29	7
Hispanic	56	28	11
Non-Hispanic white	66	27	4

Note: Percentages may not add to 100 because "don't know" is not shown.
Source: 2000 General Social Survey, National Opinion Research Center, University of Chicago; calculations by New Strategist

Causes of Socioeconomic Differences between Blacks and Whites, 2000

"On the average, blacks have worse jobs, income, and housing than white people.
What do you think these differences are mainly due to?"

(percent of people aged 18 or older responding by race and Hispanic origin, 2000)

	discrimination		lack of chance for education		lack of will or motivation		less ability to learn	
	yes	no	yes	no	yes	no	yes	no
Total	**36%**	**58%**	**44%**	**52%**	**46%**	**48%**	**12%**	**85%**
Black	60	33	56	43	39	57	13	86
White	31	63	42	54	47	46	12	85
Other	39	57	42	54	46	48	17	82
Hispanic	38	57	36	59	51	45	14	79
Non-Hispanic white	31	64	43	54	46	46	11	86

Note: Percentages may not add to 100 because "don't know" is not shown.
Source: 2000 General Social Survey, National Opinion Research Center, University of Chicago; calculations by New Strategist

Should Blacks Work Their Way Up without Special Favors? 2000

"Do you agree strongly, agree somewhat, neither agree nor disagree, disagree somewhat, or disagree strongly with the following statement: Irish, Italians, Jewish, and many other minorities overcame prejudice and worked their way up. Blacks should do the same without special favors."

(percent of people aged 18 or older responding by race and Hispanic origin, 2000)

	agree strongly	agree somewhat	neither	disagree somewhat	disagree strongly
Total	**43%**	**28%**	**11%**	**9%**	**7%**
Black	26	20	13	14	22
White	47	29	10	8	4
Other	41	35	10	5	6
Hispanic	46	32	6	7	4
Non-Hispanic white	47	29	11	9	4

Note: Percentages may not add to 100 because "don't know" is not shown.
Source: 2000 General Social Survey, National Opinion Research Center, University of Chicago; calculations by New Strategist

Should Government Help Blacks? 2000

"Some people think that blacks have been discriminated against for so long that the government has a special obligation to help improve their living standards. Others believe that the government should not be giving special treatment to blacks. Where would you place yourself on a scale of 1 to 5, or haven't you made up your mind?"

(percent of people aged 18 or older responding by race and Hispanic origin, 2000)

	government should help (1–2)	agree with both (3)	no special treatment (4–5)
Total	**19%**	**31%**	**46%**
Black	50	32	14
White	13	30	52
Other	19	32	41
Hispanic	20	37	35
Non-Hispanic white	13	30	54

Note: Percentages may not add to 100 because "don't know" is not shown.
Source: 2000 General Social Survey, National Opinion Research Center, University of Chicago; calculations by New Strategist

Affirmative Action, 2000

"Some people say that because of past discrimination, blacks should be given preference in hiring and promotion. Others say that such preference in hiring and promotion of blacks is wrong because it discriminates against whites. What about your opinion—are you for or against preferential hiring and promotion of blacks?"

(percent of people aged 18 or older responding by race and Hispanic origin, 2000)

	strongly support	support	oppose	strongly oppose
Total	**11%**	**7%**	**25%**	**51%**
Black	29	10	21	30
White	6	7	26	55
Other	17	9	20	42
Hispanic	12	9	25	45
Non-Hispanic white	6	6	26	56

Note: Percentages may not add to 100 because "don't know" is not shown.
Source: 2000 General Social Survey, National Opinion Research Center, University of Chicago; calculations by New Strategist

Are Whites Disadvantaged by Affirmative Action? 2000

"What do you think the chances are these days that a white person won't get a job or promotion while an equally or less qualified black person gets one instead? Is this very likely, somewhat likely, or not very likely to happen these days?"

(percent of people aged 18 or older responding by race and Hispanic origin, 2000)

	very likely	somewhat likely	not very likely
Total	**20%**	**46%**	**33%**
Black	14	32	50
White	21	48	30
Other	14	46	38
Hispanic	24	45	30
Non-Hispanic white	21	48	30

Note: Percentages may not add to 100 because "don't know" is not shown.
Source: 2000 General Social Survey, National Opinion Research Center, University of Chicago; calculations by New Strategist

Group Stereotypes

A look at how racial and ethnic groups feel about one another reveals a great degree of tolerance, but lingering distrust. The 52 percent majority of Hispanics, for example, say blacks are not committed to the fair and equal treatment of all groups in society. The plurality (40 percent) of blacks say whites lack such commitment. Among non-Hispanic whites, only about one in four believe Asians, blacks, and Hispanics are committed to fairness and equal treatment.

Blacks receive particularly low marks from other groups when rated on their commitment to strong families. Only 26 percent of Hispanics and 23 percent of people of "other" race say blacks are committed to strong families. Among blacks, 49 percent say blacks are committed to strong families. Blacks are the only group in which the majority fails to give itself high marks on this measure.

Regardless of race or Hispanic origin, few say they would object to living in a neighborhood in which half the residents are of another racial or ethnic group. Nevertheless, most groups tend to favor living in neighborhoods populated by their own kind. Few say they would object to having a close relative marry into another group. But many think other groups are lacking in intelligence. Twenty-one percent of blacks think Hispanics are unintelligent. Twenty-eight percent of Hispanics think blacks are unintelligent. Twenty-two percent of non-Hispanic whites think blacks and Hispanics are unintelligent.

Many doubt whites' commitment to fair and equal treatment

(percent of people aged 18 or older who do not think whites are committed to the fair and equal treatment of all groups in society, by race and Hispanic origin, 2000)

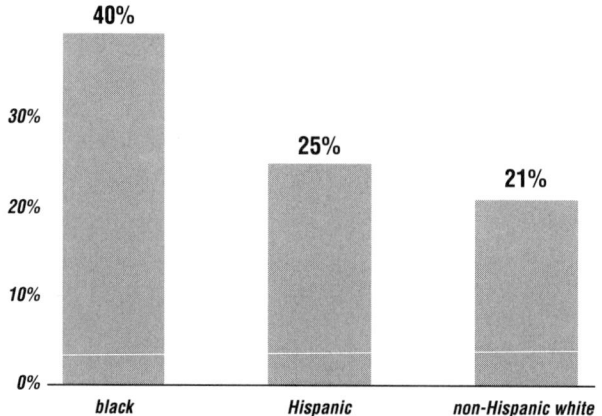

Commitment of Racial/Ethnic Group to Fair and Equal Treatment, 2000

"A score of 1 means that you think almost all of the people in the group have a commitment to the fair and equal treatment of all groups in society. A score of 7 means that you think almost everyone in the group lacks a commitment to the fair and equal treatment of all groups in society. A score of 4 means that you think that the group is not toward one end or the other, and of course you may choose any number in between that comes closest to where you think people in the group stand."

(percent of people aged 18 or older responding by race and Hispanic origin, 2000)

		race			Hispanic origin	
	total	black	white	other	Hispanic	non-Hispanic white
Asians						
Commited (1–3)	27%	22%	28%	36%	38%	27%
Neither (4)	37	28	40	26	27	40
Not commited (5–7)	21	25	20	17	23	20
Don't know	15	24	12	21	12	13
Blacks						
Commited (1–3)	25	35	24	23	19	24
Neither (4)	33	41	32	21	25	33
Not commited (5–7)	37	19	39	47	52	38
Don't know	5	5	5	9	3	5
Hispanics						
Commited (1–3)	26	25	25	33	47	24
Neither (4)	38	34	39	31	29	39
Not commited (5–7)	26	22	27	25	20	27
Don't know	10	18	9	11	3	9
Jews						
Commited (1–3)	34	30	34	39	36	35
Neither (4)	35	31	37	18	27	37
Not commited (5–7)	17	19	16	21	20	16
Don't know	14	20	12	22	17	12
Whites						
Commited (1–3)	41	27	43	47	47	43
Neither (4)	30	29	32	17	24	32
Not commited (5–7)	24	40	21	29	25	21
Don't know	4	4	4	7	4	4

Source: 2000 General Social Survey, National Opinion Research Center, University of Chicago; calculations by New Strategist

Commitment of Racial/Ethnic Group to Strong Families, 2000

"A score of 1 means that you think almost all of the people in the group have a commitment to strong families. A score of 7 means that you think almost everyone in the group lacks a commitment to strong families. A score of 4 means that you think that the group is not toward one end or the other, and of course you may choose any number in between that comes closest to where you think people in the group stand."

(percent of people aged 18 or older responding by race and Hispanic origin, 2000)

	total	black	white	other	Hispanic	non-Hispanic white
		race			Hispanic origin	
Asians						
Commited (1–3)	56%	51%	57%	61%	59%	56%
Neither (4)	25	25	25	18	13	26
Not commited (5–7)	7	6	7	6	15	7
Don't know	12	18	11	15	13	11
Blacks						
Commited (1–3)	33	49	31	23	26	31
Neither (4)	32	33	32	29	27	33
Not commited (5–7)	31	14	33	37	44	32
Don't know	5	4	4	11	3	4
Hispanics						
Commited (1–3)	53	52	53	54	70	52
Neither (4)	26	22	27	27	17	28
Not commited (5–7)	12	11	12	11	11	12
Don't know	9	15	8	9	2	8
Jews						
Commited (1–3)	59	55	60	65	61	60
Neither (4)	24	21	24	17	22	24
Not commited (5–7)	5	4	5	3	4	5
Don't know	12	19	11	15	13	10
Whites						
Commited (1–3)	52	55	52	51	55	52
Neither (4)	31	30	32	22	27	32
Not commited (5–7)	13	9	14	19	15	13
Don't know	3	6	3	8	3	3

Source: 2000 General Social Survey, National Opinion Research Center, University of Chicago; calculations by New Strategist

Opinion of Living in Neighborhood with Racial/Ethnic Group, 2000

"I'm going to ask you about different types of contact with various groups of people. In each situation would you please tell me whether you would be very much in favor of it happening, somewhat in favor, neither in favor nor opposed to it happening, somewhat opposed, or very opposed to it happening. Living in a neighborhood where half of your neighbors are:"

(percent of people aged 18 or older respondent by race and Hispanic origin, 2000)

		race			Hispanic origin	
	total	black	white	other	Hispanic	non-Hispanic white
Asian						
Somewhat or very much in favor	28%	28%	27%	38%	30%	27%
Neither favor nor oppose	50	42	51	48	51	51
Somewhat or very much opposed	18	19	18	8	14	18
Don't know	5	11	4	6	5	4
Black						
Somewhat or very much in favor	27	51	23	24	20	23
Neither favor nor oppose	45	40	46	49	51	45
Somewhat or very much opposed	26	9	30	24	27	30
Don't know	1	0	1	3	2	1
Hispanic						
Somewhat or very much in favor	27	32	26	30	46	25
Neither favor nor oppose	45	41	45	49	42	45
Somewhat or very much opposed	25	20	27	22	12	28
Don't know	3	7	3	0	0	3
Jewish						
Somewhat or very much in favor	34	32	34	28	29	35
Neither favor nor oppose	52	41	53	57	53	53
Somewhat or very much opposed	9	15	8	11	12	8
Don't know	5	12	4	4	6	4
White						
Somewhat or very much in favor	52	44	54	53	46	54
Neither favor nor oppose	40	47	39	42	51	38
Somewhat or very much opposed	7	7	7	5	2	7
Don't know	1	2	1	0	0	1

Source: 2000 General Social Survey, National Opinion Research Center, University of Chicago; calculations by New Strategist

Opinion of Close Relative Marrying Person in Racial/Ethnic Group, 2000

"What about having a close relative marry a person in the following racial or ethnic groups? Would you be very in favor of it happening, somewhat in favor, neither in favor nor opposed to it happening, somewhat opposed, or very opposed to it happening?"

(percent of people aged 18 or older responding by race and Hispanic origin, 2000)

	total	race black	white	other	Hispanic origin Hispanic	non-Hispanic white
Asian						
Somewhat or very in favor	32%	36%	31%	45%	40%	30%
Neither favor nor oppose	44	37	46	35	42	46
Somewhat or very opposed	20	18	21	13	12	22
Don't know	4	9	3	7	5	3
Black						
Somewhat or very in favor	30	64	23	37	34	23
Neither favor nor oppose	39	30	40	47	51	39
Somewhat or very opposed	30	6	36	13	13	37
Don't know	1	0	1	3	2	1
Hispanic						
Somewhat or very in favor	34	42	32	50	66	30
Neither favor nor oppose	43	37	45	36	33	46
Somewhat or very opposed	19	14	21	8	0	22
Don't know	3	7	3	6	0	2
Jew						
Somewhat or very in favor	36	37	36	34	36	36
Neither favor nor oppose	47	40	49	43	45	49
Somewhat or very opposed	12	14	12	14	10	12
Don't know	5	9	4	9	9	3
White						
Somewhat or very in favor	65	49	69	51	56	70
Neither favor nor oppose	31	40	29	37	40	28
Somewhat or very opposed	3	10	1	9	3	1
Don't know	1	1	1	3	1	1

Source: 2000 General Social Survey, National Opinion Research Center, University of Chicago; calculations by New Strategist

Work Habits of Racial/Ethnic Group, 2000

"Here are some questions about different groups in our society. I'm going to show you a seven-point scale on which characteristics of people in a group can be rated.

A score of 1 means you think almost all of the people in that group are hard working. A score of 7 means you think almost all of the people in the group are lazy. Where would you rate the following racial and ethnic groups on this scale?"

(percent of people aged 18 or older responding by race and Hispanic origin, 2000)

| | | race | | | Hispanic origin | |
	total	black	white	other	Hispanic	non-Hispanic white
Asians						
Hard working (1–3)	52%	48%	52%	62%	60%	52%
Neither (4)	28	24	30	16	19	30
Lazy (5–7)	10	9	10	6	10	9
Don't know	10	18	8	16	10	9
Blacks						
Hard working (1–3)	22	38	19	19	15	19
Neither (4)	41	41	42	27	32	43
Lazy (5–7)	33	18	35	47	47	35
Don't know	4	3	4	7	6	3
Hispanics						
Hard working (1–3)	35	43	33	49	53	32
Neither (4)	37	32	39	20	28	39
Lazy (5–7)	20	11	21	21	15	21
Don't know	8	14	7	10	4	7
Jews						
Hard working (1–3)	49	44	50	46	39	51
Neither (4)	31	28	31	29	36	31
Lazy (5–7)	7	9	7	9	8	7
Don't know	13	19	11	16	17	11
Whites						
Hard working (1–3)	45	42	45	49	48	45
Neither (4)	41	39	43	30	30	43
Lazy (5–7)	11	17	9	16	15	9
Don't know	3	3	3	5	7	2

Source: 2000 General Social Survey, National Opinion Research Center, University of Chicago; calculations by New Strategist

Intelligence of Racial/Ethnic Group, 2000

"Here are some questions about different groups in our society. I'm going to show you a seven-point scale on which characteristics of people in a group can be rated. A score of 1 means you think almost all of the people in that group are unintelligent. A score of 7 means you think almost all of the people in the group are intelligent. Where would you rate the following groups on this scale?"

(percent of people aged 18 or older responding by race and Hispanic origin, 2000)

	total	black	white	other	Hispanic origin Hispanic	non-Hispanic white
Asians						
Unintelligent (1–3)	9%	12%	9%	11%	10%	9%
Neither (4)	35	26	37	31	32	38
Intelligent (5–7)	45	45	45	39	46	45
Don't know	11	17	9	19	12	9
Blacks						
Unintelligent (1–3)	21	12	22	26	28	22
Neither (4)	46	40	47	45	35	48
Intelligent (5–7)	29	45	26	19	27	26
Don't know	5	4	5	9	9	4
Hispanics						
Unintelligent (1–3)	21	21	21	21	15	22
Neither (4)	47	34	49	41	43	50
Intelligent (5–7)	23	30	22	23	37	20
Don't know	9	15	8	14	5	8
Jews						
Unintelligent (1–3)	5	6	5	5	5	5
Neither (4)	36	29	38	31	34	38
Intelligent (5–7)	47	48	47	47	46	47
Don't know	11	17	10	17	15	10
Whites						
Unintelligent (1–3)	7	11	6	9	10	6
Neither (4)	39	35	40	33	27	41
Intelligent (5–7)	50	50	50	52	55	50
Don't know	4	4	4	6	8	3

Source: 2000 General Social Survey, National Opinion Research Center, University of Chicago; calculations by New Strategist

Immigration

The 2000 General Social Survey shows the public is about evenly divided on whether immigration to the United States should remain the same or be cut. Forty-four percent of the public want immigration levels to stay the same. A slightly smaller 42 percent share want to see immigration decreased. Only 9 percent want it to increase.

Those most in favor of increasing immigration are groups with large shares of immigrants—people of "other" race (many are Asians) and Hispanics. Only 26 percent of "others" and 29 percent of Hispanics wanted immigration levels decreased in 2000. Twenty-one percent of "others" and 25 percent of Hispanics wanted immigration increased.

"Others" and Hispanics think immigrants have a more positive effect on the U.S. than blacks or non-Hispanic whites do. People of "other" race and Hispanics are less likely to think immigration will lead to higher crime rates, that natives will lose jobs, or that immigration makes it harder to unite the country. They are more likely to say immigration leads to higher economic growth and makes the country more open minded.

The immigrant group that has contributed the most to the U.S., according to the largest share of Americans, is the English, followed by Jews, blacks, Irish, and Italians. Each racial and ethnic group tends to rate its own contribution more highly than that of other groups. Seventy-six percent of non-Hispanic whites, for example, say the English have mad important contributions to the U.S. Only 49 percent of blacks agree. Fifty-nine percent of blacks say the black contribution has been important compared to a smaller 48 percent of non-Hispanic whites who feel that way.

Many people want to see immigration decreased

(percent of people aged 18 or older who think immigration to the U.S. should be decreased, by race and Hispanic origin, 2000)

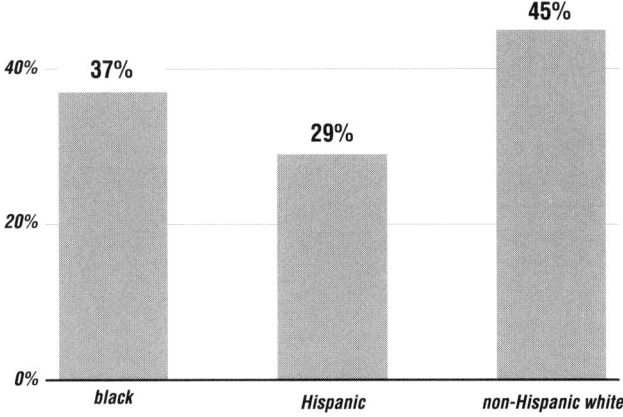

Appropriate Immigration Level, 2000

"Do you think the number of immigrants from foreign countries who are permitted to come to the United States to live should be increased a lot, increased a little, left the same as it is now, decreased a little, or decreased a lot?"

(percent of people aged 18 or older responding by race and Hispanic origin, 2000)

| | | race | | | Hispanic origin | |
	total	black	white	other	Hispanic	non-Hispanic white
Total immigrants						
Increased	9%	9%	8%	21%	25%	7%
Same as now	44	49	43	41	38	43
Decreased	42	37	44	26	29	45
Don't know	5	4	5	12	7	5
Asian immigrants						
Increased	8	7	7	28	26	6
Same as now	45	49	45	38	40	45
Decreased	40	39	41	25	27	42
Don't know	6	5	6	9	7	7
European immigrants						
Increased	9	8	8	26	25	8
Same as now	51	53	51	45	45	52
Decreased	33	35	34	20	21	35
Don't know	6	5	6	9	9	6
Latin American immigrants						
Increased	9	10	7	30	30	6
Same as now	44	49	44	39	37	44
Decreased	42	37	44	23	27	45
Don't know	5	4	5	9	6	5

Source: 2000 General Social Survey, National Opinion Research Center, University of Chicago; calculations by New Strategist

Effects of Increased Immigration, 2000

"What do you think will happen as a result of more immigrants coming to this country? Is each of these possible results very likely, somewhat likely, not too likely, or not likely at all?"

(percent of people aged 18 or older responding by race and Hispanic origin, 2000)

| | | race | | | Hispanic origin | |
| | | | | | | non-Hispanic |
	total	black	white	other	Hispanic	white
Higher crime rates						
Somewhat or very likely	70%	68%	72%	55%	59%	72%
Not too or not at all likely	25	25	25	33	31	25
Don't know	5	7	4	12	10	3
Higher economic growth						
Somewhat or very likely	48	49	46	70	74	44
Not too or not at all likely	47	43	49	20	19	51
Don't know	5	9	5	10	7	4
Make U.S. more open-minded						
Somewhat or very likely	73	73	73	79	78	73
Not too or not at all likely	23	22	24	13	16	24
Don't know	3	5	3	8	6	2
U.S. natives lose jobs						
Somewhat or very likely	57	60	59	34	40	60
Not too or not at all likely	40	34	39	59	56	38
Don't know	3	7	2	7	4	2
Harder to keep country united						
Somewhat or very likely	53	55	54	37	40	55
Not too or not at all likely	43	37	43	55	54	42
Don't know	4	8	3	8	6	2

Source: 2000 General Social Survey, National Opinion Research Center, University of Chicago; calculations by New Strategist

Contribution of Immigrant Groups to the U.S., 2000

"Since the beginning of our country, people of many different races, nationalities, and religions have come here and settled. As I name some of these groups please tell me if the group has made one of the most important positive contributions to this country, an important contribution, some contributions, or little positive contribution to this country. "

(percent of people aged 18 or older responding by race and Hispanic origin, 2000)

| | | race | | | Hispanic origin | |
	total	black	white	other	Hispanic	non-Hispanic white
Most important/important contribution						
Blacks	48%	59%	47%	36%	41%	48%
Chinese	39	32	40	35	44	39
Cubans	16	17	16	14	18	16
English	71	49	76	63	69	76
Irish	48	28	52	33	35	53
Italians	48	30	53	32	38	53
Japanese	40	32	41	46	45	41
Jews	53	39	56	43	46	56
Mexicans	28	26	28	28	37	28
Muslims	17	23	16	15	9	16
Puerto Ricans	18	18	18	20	21	18
Vietnamese	18	17	18	22	21	18
Little positive contribution						
Blacks	11	4	11	16	16	11
Chinese	12	16	11	11	14	11
Cubans	34	33	35	28	27	35
English	3	4	2	10	3	2
Irish	7	14	5	19	16	4
Italians	5	11	4	9	9	4
Japanese	14	20	13	11	14	12
Jews	5	11	4	10	10	4
Mexicans	20	22	20	14	9	20
Muslims	29	24	31	22	35	30
Puerto Ricans	26	30	26	20	22	26
Vietnamese	30	35	29	31	32	28

Note: Percentages will not add to 100 because "some contribution" and "don't know" are not shown.
Source: 2000 General Social Survey, National Opinion Research Center, University of Chicago; calculations by New Strategist

Language

More than one in four Americans speak a language other than English, according to the General Social Survey. This figure is most certainly an underestimate since the GSS only interviews English speakers. Among people of "other" race and Hispanics, fully 86 percent can speak a language other than English. More than three out of four Hispanics and people of "other" race who speak a language other than English do so on a daily basis.

Most Americans hear other languages spoken in their community (54 percent) and at work (56 percent) at least weekly. The majority of Hispanics hear a language other than English spoken in their community and in their workplace every day.

Although most Americans do not consider the use of other languages to be a threat to English, nearly three out of four favor making English the official language. Most, including the majority of Hispanics and people of "other" race, think the use of English unites Americans. Most Americans favor bilingual education and think learning a foreign language is as important as learning math and science in school. Most also think election ballots should be printed in other languages in areas where a lot of people do not speak English.

Most Hispanics speak a language other than English

(percent of people aged 18 or older who speak a language other than English, by race and Hispanic origin, 2000)

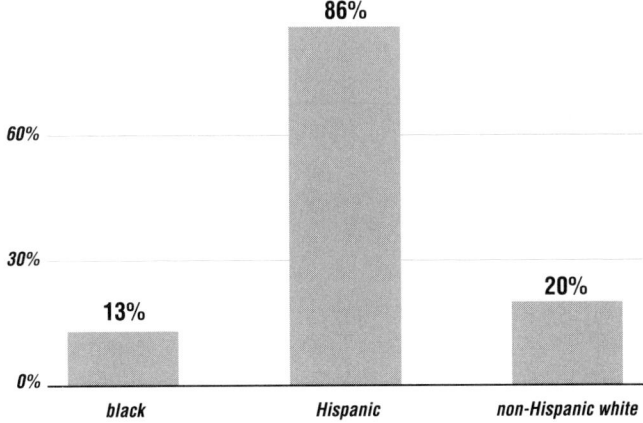

Do You Speak a Language Other than English? 2000

"Can you speak a language other than English?"

(percent of people aged 18 or older responding by race and Hispanic origin, 2000)

	yes	no
Total	**26%**	**74%**
Black	13	87
White	24	76
Other	86	14
Hispanic	86	14
Non-Hispanic white	20	80

Source: 2000 General Social Survey, National Opinion Research Center, University of Chicago; calculations by New Strategist

How Often Do You Speak Other Languages? 2000

"How often do you use a language other than English in your everyday life?"

(percent of people aged 18 or older responding by race and Hispanic origin, 2000)

	never	less than once a week	weekly	daily
Total	**21%**	**19%**	**16%**	**44%**
Black	–	–	–	–
White	25	22	16	36
Other	3	6	12	79
Hispanic	4	3	15	78
Non-Hispanic white	30	28	17	25

Note: Asked only of respondents who speak a language other than English. Answers shown are for respondents first mentioned language. (–) means sample is too small to make a reliable estimate.
Source: 2000 General Social Survey, National Opinion Research Center, University of Chicago; calculations by New Strategist

How Often Do You Hear Other Languages Spoken in Your Community? 2000

"How often do you hear languages other than English
spoken in the local community where you live?"

(percent of people aged 18 or older responding by race and Hispanic origin, 2000)

	never	less than once a week	weekly	daily
Total	27%	18%	29%	25%
Black	38	11	26	22
White	26	20	30	23
Other	11	9	22	57
Hispanic	8	7	25	59
Non-Hispanic white	27	21	31	21

Note: Percentages may not add to 100 because "don't know" is not shown.
Source: 2000 General Social Survey, National Opinion Research Center, University of Chicago; calculations by New Strategist

How Often Do You Hear Other Languages Spoken at Work? 2000

"How often do you hear languages other than English
spoken in the place where you work?"

(percent of people aged 18 or older responding by race and Hispanic origin, 2000)

	never	less than once a week	weekly	daily
Total	33%	10%	22%	34%
Black	32	5	25	38
White	35	11	20	32
Other	10	6	38	46
Hispanic	13	5	23	58
Non-Hispanic white	37	11	20	30

Note: Asked only of respondents who were currently working. Percentages may not add to 100 because "don't know" is not shown.
Source: 2000 General Social Survey, National Opinion Research Center, University of Chicago; calculations by New Strategist

English as Official Language, 2000

"Do you favor a law making English the official language of
the United States, or do you oppose such a law?"

(percent of people aged 18 or older responding by race and Hispanic origin, 2000)

	favor	oppose	don't know
Total	**73%**	**21%**	**5%**
Black	71	24	5
White	75	20	5
Other	51	38	11
Hispanic	44	47	9
Non-Hispanic white	77	18	5

Source: 2000 General Social Survey, National Opinion Research Center, University of Chicago; calculations by New Strategist

Use of Other Languages by Immigrants Threatens English, 2000

"Please tell us whether you strongly agree, agree, disagree, or strongly
disagree with each of these statements: English will be threatened if other
languages are frequently used in large immigrant communities in the U.S."

(percent of people aged 18 or older responding by race and Hispanic origin, 2000)

	strongly agree	agree	disagree	strongly disagree
Total	**9%**	**23%**	**51%**	**15%**
Black	9	22	53	13
White	9	23	50	14
Other	6	13	49	28
Hispanic	7	14	45	30
Non-Hispanic white	9	24	51	13

Note: Percentages may not add to 100 because "don't know" is not shown.
Source: 2000 General Social Survey, National Opinion Research Center, University of Chicago; calculations by New Strategist

Does Speaking English Unite Americans? 2000

"Please tell us whether you strongly agree, agree, disagree, or strongly disagree with this statement: Speaking English as the common national language is what unites all Americans."

(percent of people aged 18 or older responding by race and Hispanic origin, 2000)

	strongly agree	agree	disagree	strongly disagree
Total	**26%**	**47%**	**21%**	**3%**
Black	26	50	19	1
White	27	47	21	2
Other	21	47	18	9
Hispanic	22	38	32	4
Non-Hispanic white	27	48	21	2

Note: Percentages may not add to 100 because "don't know" is not shown.
Source: 2000 General Social Survey, National Opinion Research Center, University of Chicago; calculations by New Strategist

Should Bilingual Education Be Eliminated? 2000

"Please tell us whether you strongly agree, agree, disagree, or strongly disagree with this statement: Bilingual education programs should be eliminated in American public schools."

(percent of people aged 18 or older responding by race and Hispanic origin, 2000)

	strongly agree	agree	disagree	strongly disagree
Total	**6%**	**16%**	**47%**	**28%**
Black	4	11	55	25
White	7	17	46	27
Other	2	9	46	39
Hispanic	1	9	42	45
Non-Hispanic white	7	18	47	26

Note: Percentages may not add to 100 because "don't know" is not shown.
Source: 2000 General Social Survey, National Opinion Research Center, University of Chicago; calculations by New Strategist

Should Children Be Bilingual? 2000

"Please tell us whether you strongly agree, agree, disagree, or strongly disagree with this statement: Children in the U.S. should learn a second language fluently before they finish high school."

(percent of people aged 18 or older responding by race and Hispanic origin, 2000)

	strongly agree	agree	disagree	strongly disagree
Total	25%	48%	21%	3%
Black	25	54	18	2
White	25	47	23	3
Other	31	53	11	1
Hispanic	41	44	9	3
Non-Hispanic white	24	48	23	3

Note: Percentages may not add to 100 because "don't know" is not shown.
Source: 2000 General Social Survey, National Opinion Research Center, University of Chicago; calculations by New Strategist

Are Foreign Languages as Valuable as Math and Science? 2000

"Please tell us whether you strongly agree, agree, disagree, or strongly disagree with this statement: Learning a foreign language is as valuable as learning math and science in school."

(percent of people aged 18 or older responding by race and Hispanic origin, 2000)

	strongly agree	agree	disagree	strongly disagree
Total	21%	42%	30%	5%
Black	25	41	27	3
White	19	41	32	6
Other	32	53	10	1
Hispanic	29	52	15	3
Non-Hispanic white	18	41	33	6

Note: Percentages may not add to 100 because "don't know" is not shown.
Source: 2000 General Social Survey, National Opinion Research Center, University of Chicago; calculations by New Strategist

Should Ballots Be Printed in Other Languages? 2000

"Please tell us whether you strongly agree, agree, disagree, or strongly disagree with this statement: Election ballots should be printed in other languages in areas where lots of people don't speak English."

(percent of people aged 18 or older responding by race and Hispanic origin, 2000)

	strongly agree	agree	disagree	strongly disagree
Total	**16%**	**47%**	**22%**	**12%**
Black	18	53	15	9
White	15	46	23	13
Other	30	45	16	3
Hispanic	28	50	14	7
Non-Hispanic white	15	45	24	13

Note: Percentages may not add to 100 because "don't know" is not shown.
Source: 2000 General Social Survey, National Opinion Research Center, University of Chicago; calculations by New Strategist

Personal Outlook and Behavior

Although most Americans are "pretty" or "very happy," minority groups are more likely to be "not too happy" than non-Hispanic whites. Minorities are also less likely than non-Hispanic whites to say most people can be trusted. More than three out of four blacks say most people cannot be trusted.

Religious preferences vary sharply by race and ethnicity. Fully 76 percent of blacks are Protestant, while nearly half of Hispanics are Catholic.

Minorities are less satisfied with their financial situation than non-Hispanic whites. But everyone agrees that the U.S. offers them an opportunity to improve their standard of living. Among blacks, "others," and Hispanics, most say their job status is higher than their father's. Most think their children's future standard of living will be better than theirs.

The divergent experiences of racial and ethnic groups emerge in the political arena. The majority of blacks are Democrats (59 percent), while non-Hispanic whites are most likely to say they are Republican (31 percent). Hispanics are split between Democrat (40 percent) and independent (43 percent).

Fifty-five percent of registered voters went to the polls in the election of November 2000. Among Asians, however, only 25 percent voted. Among Hispanics, the figure was just 27 percent. Behind these low voter participation rates is the fact that many Hispanic and Asian adults are not citizens—39 percent of Hispanics and 41 percent of Asians.

Computer and Internet use varies greatly by race and Hispanic origin. Asians are most likely to have computers (71 percent) and be online (60 percent). Hispanics are least likely to have computers (49 percent) or be online (32 percent).

Blacks are less trusting

(percent of people aged 18 or older who think most people can be trusted, by race and Hispanic origin, 2000)

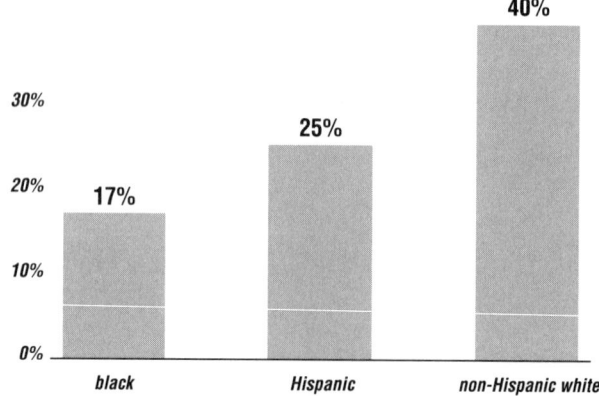

Personal Happiness, 2000

"Taken all together, how would you say things are these days—would you say that you are very happy, pretty happy, or not too happy?"

(percent of people aged 18 or older responding by race and Hispanic origin, 2000)

	very happy	pretty happy	not too happy
Total	**34%**	**56%**	**10%**
Black	26	57	17
White	36	56	8
Other	28	58	14
Hispanic	32	52	15
Non-Hispanic white	36	56	8

Source: 2000 General Social Survey, National Opinion Research Center, University of Chicago; calculations by New Strategist

Can Most People Be Trusted? 2000

"Do you think most people can be trusted?"

(percent of people aged 18 or older responding by race and Hispanic origin, 2000)

	can be trusted	cannot be trusted	depends*
Total	**35%**	**58%**	**6%**
Black	17	76	6
White	39	55	6
Other	23	65	11
Hispanic	25	66	8
Non-Hispanic white	40	54	6

Volunteered response.
Note: Percentages may not add to 100 because "don't know" is not shown.
Source: 2000 General Social Survey, National Opinion Research Center, University of Chicago; calculations by New Strategist

Religious Preference, 2000

"What is your religious preference?"

(percent of people aged 18 or older responding by race and Hispanic origin, 2000)

	Protestant	Catholic	Jewish	none	other
Total	**53%**	**25%**	**2%**	**14%**	**6%**
Black	76	7	1	12	5
White	51	27	3	14	4
Other	17	47	0	16	21
Hispanic	14	71	0	11	4
Non-Hispanic white	54	24	3	15	5

Note: Percentages may not add to 100 because "don't know" is not shown.
Source: 2000 General Social Survey, National Opinion Research Center, University of Chicago; calculations by New Strategist

Satisfaction with Financial Situation, 2000

"So far as you and your family are concerned, would you say that
you are pretty well satisfied with your present financial situation,
more or less satisfied, or not satisfied at all?"

(percent of people aged 18 or older by race and Hispanic origin, 2000)

	pretty well satisfied	more or less satisfied	not at all satisfied
Total	**31%**	**45%**	**24%**
Black	15	45	39
White	34	45	21
Other	21	51	28
Hispanic	17	58	25
Non-Hispanic white	35	44	21

Source: 2000 General Social Survey, National Opinion Research Center, University of Chicago; calculations by New Strategist

The U.S. Provides Opportunity to Improve Standard of Living, 2000

"The way things are in America, people like me and my family have a good chance of improving our standard of living—do you agree or disagree?"

(percent of people aged 18 or older responding by race and Hispanic origin, 2000)

	strongly agree	agree	neither	disagree	strongly disagree
Total	**24%**	**53%**	**9%**	**11%**	**2%**
Black	20	56	10	11	2
White	24	52	9	12	2
Other	26	58	8	4	2
Hispanic	27	58	8	5	1
Non-Hispanic white	24	52	9	12	2

Note: Percentages may not add to 100 because "can't choose" is not shown
Source: 2000 General Social Survey, National Opinion Research Center, University of Chicago; calculations by New Strategist

Job Status Compared to Father's, 2000

"Please think about your present job (or your last one if you don't have one now). If you compare this job with the job your father had when you were 16, would you say that the level or status of your job is (or was) much higher than your father's, higher, about equal, lower, or much lower?"

(percent of people aged 18 or older responding by race and Hispanic origin, 2000)

	much higher or higher	about equal	lower or much lower
Total	**48%**	**26%**	**26%**
Black	53	21	26
White	47	27	26
Other	60	24	15
Hispanic	56	22	22
Non-Hispanic white	47	27	26

Note: Excludes respondents who never had a job or whose father never had a job.
Source: 2000 General Social Survey, National Opinion Research Center, University of Chicago; calculations by New Strategist

Standard of Living Relative to Parents', 2000

"Compared to your parents when they were the age you are now, do you think your own standard of living now is much better, somewhat better, about the same, somewhat worse, or much worse than theirs was?"

(percent of people aged 18 or older responding by race and Hispanic origin, 2000)

	much better	somewhat better	about the same	somewhat worse	much worse
Total	35%	31%	21%	9%	3%
Black	36	27	23	8	3
White	34	32	21	9	3
Other	46	25	13	10	5
Hispanic	36	33	16	8	4
Non-Hispanic white	34	32	21	9	3

Note: Percentages may not add to 100 because "don't know" is not shown.
Source: 2000 General Social Survey, National Opinion Research Center, University of Chicago; calculations by New Strategist

Children's Future Standard of Living, 2000

"When your children are at the age you are now, do you think their standard of living will be much better, somewhat better, about the same, somewhat worse, or much worse than yours is now?"

(percent of people aged 18 or older responding by race and Hispanic origin, 2000)

	much better	somewhat better	about the same	somewhat worse	much worse
Total	32%	34%	18%	8%	4%
Black	47	29	9	8	3
White	28	34	21	9	4
Other	42	43	5	3	3
Hispanic	50	32	11	2	2
Non-Hispanic white	26	35	22	9	4

Note: Percentages may not add to 100 because "don't know" is not shown.
Source: 2000 General Social Survey, National Opinion Research Center, University of Chicago; calculations by New Strategist

Political Party Identification, 2000

"Generally speaking, do you usually think of yourself as a
Republican, Democrat, independent, or what?"

(percent of people aged 18 or older responding by race and Hispanic origin, 2000)

	Democrat	independent	Republican
Total	**32%**	**41%**	**25%**
Black	59	34	6
White	26	42	30
Other	37	47	15
Hispanic	40	43	15
Non-Hispanic white	26	42	31

Note: Percentages may not add to 100 because "don't know" and "other party" are not shown.
Source: 2000 General Social Survey, National Opinion Research Center, University of Chicago; calculations by New Strategist

Voting by Race, Hispanic Origin, and Age, November 2000

(total number of people aged 18 or older, number and percent distribution of those voting in the election of November 2000, and voter share of total, by race, Hispanic origin, and age; numbers in thousands)

		voters		
	total	*number*	*percent distribution*	*share of total*
Total people	**202,609**	**110,826**	**100.0%**	**54.7%**
Aged 18 to 24	26,712	8,635	7.8	32.3
Aged 25 to 44	81,780	40,738	36.8	49.8
Aged 45 to 64	61,352	39,301	35.5	64.1
Aged 65 to 74	17,819	12,450	11.2	69.9
Aged 75 or older	14,945	9,702	8.8	64.9
Asians	**8,041**	**2,045**	**100.0**	**25.4**
Aged 18 to 24	1,237	196	9.6	15.9
Aged 25 to 44	3,818	846	41.4	22.2
Aged 45 to 64	2,187	700	34.2	32.0
Aged 65 to 74	472	191	9.3	40.4
Aged 75 or older	327	112	5.5	34.4
Blacks	**24,132**	**12,917**	**100.0**	**53.5**
Aged 18 to 24	3,944	1,335	10.3	33.9
Aged 25 to 44	10,816	5,641	43.7	52.1
Aged 45 to 64	6,585	4,140	32.1	62.9
Aged 65 to 74	1,754	1,194	9.2	68.1
Aged 75 or older	1,033	608	4.7	58.8
Hispanics	**21,598**	**5,934**	**100.0**	**27.5**
Aged 18 to 24	4,169	644	10.9	15.4
Aged 25 to 44	10,640	2,474	41.7	23.2
Aged 45 to 64	4,962	1,902	32.1	38.3
Aged 65 to 74	1,110	565	9.5	50.9
Aged 75 or older	718	349	5.9	48.7
Whites	**168,733**	**95,098**	**100.0**	**56.4**
Aged 18 to 24	21,295	7,032	7.4	33.0
Aged 25 to 44	66,378	33,953	35.7	51.2
Aged 45 to 64	52,038	34,150	35.9	65.6
Aged 65 to 74	15,493	11,009	11.6	71.1
Aged 75 or older	13,529	8,954	9.4	66.2
Non-Hispanic whites	**148,035**	**89,469**	**100.0**	**60.4**
Aged 18 to 24	17,293	6,425	7.2	37.2
Aged 25 to 44	56,222	31,637	35.4	56.3
Aged 45 to 64	47,290	32,345	36.2	68.4
Aged 65 to 74	14,407	10,457	11.7	72.6
Aged 75 or older	12,823	8,604	9.6	67.1

Source: Bureau of the Census, Voting and Registration in the Election of November 2000, *detailed tables from Current Population Report P20-542, 2002; Internet site <www.census.gov/population/www/socdemo/voting/p20-542.html>; calculations by New Strategist*

Percent Distribution of Voters by Race and Hispanic Origin, November 2000

(total number of people aged 18 or older, number and percent distribution of those voting in the election of November 2000, and voter share of total, by race, Hispanic origin, and age; numbers in thousands)

	total	Asian	black	Hispanic	white total	white non-Hispanic
Total voters	**110,826**	**2,045**	**12,917**	**5,934**	**95,098**	**89,469**
Aged 18 to 24	8,635	196	1,335	644	7,032	6,425
Aged 25 to 44	40,738	846	5,641	2,474	33,953	31,637
Aged 45 to 64	39,301	700	4,140	1,902	34,150	32,345
Aged 65 to 74	12,450	191	1,194	565	11,009	10,457
Aged 75 or older	9,702	112	608	349	8,954	8,604
Total voters	**100.0%**	**1.8%**	**11.7%**	**5.4%**	**85.8%**	**80.7%**
Aged 18 to 24	100.0	2.3	15.5	7.5	81.4	74.4
Aged 25 to 44	100.0	2.1	13.8	6.1	83.3	77.7
Aged 45 to 64	100.0	1.8	10.5	4.8	86.9	82.3
Aged 65 to 74	100.0	1.5	9.6	4.5	88.4	84.0
Aged 75 or older	100.0	1.2	6.3	3.6	92.3	88.7

Source: Bureau of the Census, Voting and Registration in the Election of November 2000, *detailed tables from Current Population Report P20-542, 2002; Internet site <www.census.gov/population/www/socdemo/voting/p20-542.html>; calculations by New Strategist*

Computer and Internet Use by Race and Hispanic Origin, 2001

(number and percent of people aged 3 or older who use computers or go online, by race and Hispanic origin, 2001; numbers in thousands)

	computer users		Internet users	
	number	percent	number	percent
Total people	**174,051**	**65.6%**	**142,823**	**53.9%**
Asian	7,600	71.2	6,452	60.4
Black	18,544	55.7	13,237	39.8
Hispanic	15,690	48.8	10,141	31.6
White	130,848	70.0	111,942	59.9

Note: Numbers will not add to total because Hispanics may be of any race and not all races are shown.
Source: National Telecommunications and Information Administration, A Nation Online: How Americans Are Expanding Their Use of the Internet, *2002*

For More Information

The federal government is a rich source of data on almost every aspect of American life. Below are the Internet addresses of federal and other agencies that collect the demographic data analyzed in this book. Also shown are phone numbers of the agencies and of the subject specialists at the Census Bureau and the Bureau of Labor Statistics, organized alphabetically by name of agency or specialty topic. A list of State Data Centers and Small Business Development Centers is also included to help you track down demographic and economic information for your state or local area. E-mail addresses are shown when available.

Internet addresses

- Bureau of the Census; www.census.gov
- Bureau of Labor Statistics; www.bls.gov
- Current Population Survey; www.bls.census.gov/cps
- Immigration and Naturalization Service; www.ins.usdoj.gov/graphics/aboutins/statistics/index.htm
- National Center for Education Statistics; http://nces.ed.gov
- National Center for Health Statistics; www.cdc.gov/nchs
- National Opinion Research Center; www.norc.uchicago.edu
- National Telecommunications and Information Administration; www.ntia.doc.gov
- Federal Reserve Board, Survey of Consumer Finances; www.federalreserve.gov/pubs/OSS/oss2/scfindex.html

Subject specialists

Absences from work, Staff 202-691-6378
Aging population, Staff 301-457-2422
American Community Survey/C2SS Results, Larry McGinn 301-457-8050
Ancestry, Staff 301-457-2403
Apportionment, Edwin Byerly 301-457-2381
Apportionment and redistricting, Cathy McCully 301-457-4039
Business expenditures, Sheldon Ziman 301-457-3315
Business investment, Charles Funk 301-457-3324

Census 2000
- Aging population, Staff 301-457-2378
- American Community Survey, Larry McGinn 301-457-8050
- American Factfinder, Staff 301-763-INFO (4636)
- Annexations/boundary changes, Joe Marinucci 301-457-1099
- Apportionment, Edwin Byerly 301-457-2381
- Briefs, Staff 301-457-2437
- Census 2010, Paulette Lichtman-Panzer 301-457-4027
- Census history, Dave Pemberton 301-457-1167
- Citizenship, Staff 301-457-2403
- Commuting and place of work, Clara Reschovsky/Celia Boertlein 301-457-2454
- Confidentiality and privacy, Jerry Gates 301-457-2515
- Count question resolution, Staff 866-546-0527
- Count review, Paul Campbell 301-457-2390
- Data dissemination, Staff 301-763-INFO(4636)
- Disability, Sharon Stern 301-457-3213
- Education, Staff 301-457-2464
- Employment/unemployment, Staff 301-457-3242
- Foreign born, Staff 301-457-2403
- Geographic entities, Staff 301-457-1099
- Grandparents as caregivers, Staff 301-457-2465
- Group quarters population, Denise Smith 301-457-2378
- Hispanic origin, ethnicity, ancestry, Staff 301-457-2403
- Homeless, Edison Gore/Fay Nash 301-457-3998
- Housing, Staff 301-457-3237
- Immigration/emigration, Dianne Schmidley 301-457-2403
- Income, Staff 301-457-3242
- Island areas, Idabelle Hovland 301-457-8443
- Labor force status/work experience, Staff 301-457-3220
- Language spoken in home, Staff 301-457-2464
- Living arrangements, Staff 301-457-2465
- Marital status, Staff 301-457-2465
- Metropolitan areas, concepts and standards, Michael Ratcliffe 301-457-2419
- Microdata files, Amanda Shields 301-457-1326
- Migration, Jason Schachter/Carol Faber 301-457-2454

- Occupation/industry, Staff 301-457-3210
- Place of birth/native born, Carol Faber/Bonny Berkner 301-457-2454
- Population (general information), Staff 301-457-2422
- Poverty, Alemayehu Bishaw 301-457-3213
- Race, Staff 301-457-2402
- Redistricting, Cathy McCully 301-457-4039
- Residence rules, Karen Mills 301-457-2390
- Small area income and poverty estimates, David Waddington 301-457-3195
- Special populations, Staff 301-457-2378
- Undercount, Rajendra Singh 301-457-4199
  Demographic analysis, Greg Robinson 301-457-2103
- Unmarried partners, Staff 301-457-2465
- Urban/rural, Ryan Short 301-457-1099
- U.S. citizens abroad, Staff 301-457-2422
- Veteran status, Staff 301-457-3228
- Voting districts, John Byle 301-457-1099
- Women, Staff 301-457-2378
- ZIP codes, Staff 301-457-2422

Census Bureau customer service, Staff 301-763-INFO (4636)

Characteristics of business owners, Valerie Strang 301-457-3316

Child care, Martin O'Connell/Kristin Smith 301-457-2465

Children, Staff 301-457-2465

Citizenship, Staff 301-457-2403

Communications and Utilities
- Current programs, Ruth Bramblett 301-457-2766
- Economic census, Jim Barron 301-457-2786

Commuting and place of work, Phil Salopek/Celia Boertlein 301-457-2454

Construction
- Building permits, Staff 301-457-1321
- Census, Pat Horning 301-457-4680
- Housing starts and completions, Staff 301-457-1321
- Residential characteristics, price index and sales, Staff 301-457-1321
- Residential improvements and repairs, Joe Huesman 301-457-4822
- Value of new construction, Mike Davis 301-457-1605

Consumer Expenditure Survey, Staff 202-691-6900; cexinfo@bls.gov

Contingent workers, Staff 202-691-6378

County Business Patterns, Paul Hanczaryk 301-457-2580

County populations, Staff 301-457-2422

Crime, Marilyn Monahan 301-457-3925

Current Population Survey, general information, Staff, 301-457-3806

Demographic surveys, demographic statistics, Staff 301-457-2422

Disability, Sharon Stern 301-457-3213

Discouraged workers, Staff 202-691-6378

Displaced workers, Staff 202-691-6378

Economic Census 1997
- Accommodations and food services, Fay Dorsett 301-457-2687
- Construction, Pat Horning 301-457-4680
- Finance and insurance, Faye Jacobs 301-457-2824
- General information, Robert Marske 301-457-2547
- Internet dissemination, Paul Zeisset 301-457-4151
- Manufacturing
  - Consumer goods industries, Robert Reinard
  - 301-457-4810
  - Investment goods industries, Kenneth Hansen 301-457-4755
  - Primary goods industries, Nat Shelton 301-457-6614
- Mining, Pat Horning 301-457-4680
- Minority/women-owned businesses, Valerie Strang 301-457-3316
- North American Industry Class. System, Wanda Dougherty 301-457-2772
- Puerto Rico and the Insular Areas, Irma Harahush 301-457-3314
- Real estate and rental/leasing, Pam Palmer 301-457-2811
- Retail trade, Fay Dorsett 301-457-2687
- Services, Jack Moody 301-457-2689
- Transportation and Utilities
  - Commodity Flow Survey, John Fowler 301-457-2108
  - Establishments, James Barron 301-457-2786
  - Vehicle Inventory and Use Survey, Kim Moore 301-457-2797
- Wholesale Trade, Donna Hambric 301-457-2725

Economic studies, Arnold Reznek 301-457-1856

Education surveys, Steve Tourkin 301-457-3791

Educational attainment, Staff 301-457-2464

Emigration, Staff 301-457-2403

Employee Benefits Survey, Staff 202-691-6199

Employment and Earnings Periodical, John Stinson 202-691-6373

Employment and unemployment trends, Staff
  202-691-6378
Employment projections, Staff 202-691-5745
Enterprise statistics, Trey Cole 301-457-3321
Equal employment opportunity data, Staff
  301-457-3242
Fertility, Barbara Downs 301-457-2449
Finance, insurance and real estate, Economic
  Census, Faye Jacobs 301-457-2824
Flexitime and shift work, Staff 202-691-6378
Foreign-Born
• Current Population Survey, Staff 301-457-2403
• Decennial census, Kevin Deardorff 301-457-2403
Geographic concepts
• American Indian areas, Vince Osier 301-457-1099
• Annexations and boundary changes, Dorothy
  Stroz 301-457-1099
• Census blocks, Valerie Pfeiffer 301-457-1099
• Census county divisions, Pat Ream 301-457-1099
• Census designated places, Pat Ream 301-457-1099
• Census geographic concepts, Staff 301-457-1099
• Census tracts, Dan Flynn 301-457-1099
• Centers of population, Staff 301-457-1128
• Congressional districts, boundaries, Donna Zorn
  301-457-1099
• Island areas, Jim Davis 301-457-1099
• Metropolitan areas, Rodger Johnson 301-457-2419
• Postal geography, Dan Sweeney 301-457-1106
• School districts, Dave Aultman 301-457-1106
• Traffic analysis zones, Carrie Saunders
  301-457-1099
• Urban/rural concepts, Ryan Short 301-457-1099
• Urbanized areas, Ryan Short 301-457-1099
• Voting districts, John Byle 301-457-1099
• Zip code tabulation areas, Andy Flora
  301-457-1100
• Zip codes, demographic data, Staff
  301-763-INFO(4636)
• Zip codes, economic data, Andy Hait 301-457-8125
• Zip codes, geography, Andy Flora 301-457-1100
Governments
• Census of governments, Stephen Poyta
  301-457-1486
• Criminal justice, Charlene Sebold 301-457-1591
• Education and library statistics, Johnny Monaco
  301-457-2584
• Education, elementary-secondary, Larry
  MacDonald 301-457-1563
• Employment, Ellen Thompson 301-457-1531

• Federal expenditure data, Gerard Keffer
  301-457-1522
• Finance, Stephen Owens 301-457-1485
• Government information, Staff 301-457-1580
• Governmental organization, Robert McArthur
  301-457-1582
• Public retirement systems, Sandra Reading
  301-457-1517
Group quarters population, Denise Smith
  301-457-2378
Health insurance statistics, Staff 301-457-3242
Health surveys, Adrienne Oneto 301-457-3879
Hispanic statistics, Staff 301-457-2403
Home-based work, Staff 202-691-6378
Homeless, Fay Nash 301-457-3998
Households and families, Staff 301-457-2465
Household wealth, Staff 301-457-3242
Housing
• American Housing Survey, Jane Kneessi/Barbara
  Williams 301-457-3235
• Census, Staff 301-457-3237
• Homeownership, vacancy data, Linda
  Cavanaugh/Robert Callis 301-457-3199
• Housing affordability, Howard Savage
  301-457-3199
• Market absorption, Alan Friedman/Mary
  Schwartz 301-457-3199
• New York City Housing and Vacancy Survey,
  Alan Friedman/Robert Callis 301-457-3199
• Residential finance, Howard Savage 301-457-3199
Illegal immigration, Staff 301-457-2403
Immigration, general information, Staff
  301-457-2422
Income statistics, Staff 301-457-3242
Industry and commodity classification, James
  Kristoff 301-457-4631
International Statistics
• Africa, Asia, Latin Am., North Am., and Oceania,
  Patricia Rowe 301-457-1358
• Aging population, Victoria Velkoff 301-457-1371
• China, People's Republic, Loraine West
  301-457-1363
• Europe, former Soviet Union, Marc Rubin
  301-457-1362
• Health, Karen Stanecki 301-457-1406
• International data base, Pat Dickerson/Peter
  Johnson 301-457-1403
• Technical assistance and training, Diana Lopez-
  Meisel 301-457-1444

- Women in development, Victoria Velkoff
  301-457-1371
Job tenure, Staff 202-691-6378
Journey to work, Phil Salopek/Celia Boertlein
  301-457-2454
Labor force concepts, Staff 202-691-6378
Language, Staff 301-457-2464
Longitudinal data/gross flows, Staff 202-691-6345
Longitudinal surveys, Ron Dopkowski 301-457-3801
Manufacturing and Mining
- Concentration, Patrick Duck 301-457-4699
- Exports from manufacturing establishments, John
  Gates 301-457-4589
- Financial statistics (Quarterly Financial Report),
  Ronald Horton 301-457-3343
- Foreign direct investment, Ron Taylor
  301-457-1313
- Fuels, electric energy consumed and prod. index,
  Pat Horning 301-457-4680
- General information and data request, Nishea
  Quash 301-457-4673
- Industries
  - Electrical and trans. equip., instruments, misc.,
    Milbren Thomas 301-457-4821
  - Food, textiles, and apparel, Robert Reinard
    301-457-4810
  - Furniture, printing, Robert Reinard 301-457-4810
  - Metals and industrial machinery, Kenneth
    Hansen 301-457-4757
  - Wood, paper, chem., pet. prod., rubber, plastics,
    Nat Shelton 301-457-6614
- Mining, Pat Horning 301-457-4680
- Monthly shipments, inventories, and orders, Lee
  Wentela 301-457-4832
- Technology, research and development, and
  capacity use, Ron Taylor 301-457-4683
Marital and family characteristics of workers, Staff
  202-691-6378
Metropolitan areas, Staff 301-457-2422
Metropolitan standards, Rodger Johnson
  301-457-2419
Migration, Jason Schachter/Carol Faber
  301-457-2454
Mineral industries, Pat Horning 301-457-4680
Minimum wage data, Steven Haugen 202-691-6378
Minority/women-owned businesses, Valerie Strang
  301-457-3316
Minority workers, Staff 202-691-6378
Multiple jobholders, Staff 202-691-6373

National Center for Education Statistics, Staff
  202-502-7300
National Center for Health Statistics, Staff
  301-458-4636,
National Opinion Research Center, Staff
  773-256-6000; norcinfo@norcmail.uchicago.edu
National Telecommunications and Information
  Administration, Staff 202-482-7002
North Am. Industry Class. System (NAICS), Wanda
  Dougherty 301-457-2772
Occupational and industrial statistics, Staff
  301-457-3242
Occupational data, Staff 202-691-6378
Occupational employment statistics, Staff
  202-691-6569; oesinfo@bls.gov
Older workers, Staff 202-691-6378
Outlying areas, population, Michael Levin
  301-457-1444
Part-time workers, Staff 202-691-6378
Place of birth, Bonnie Berkner/Carol Faber
  301-457-2454
Population estimates and projections, Staff
  301-457-2422
Population information, Staff 301-457-2422
Poverty statistics, Staff 301-457-3242
Prisoner surveys, Marilyn Monahan 301-457-3925
Puerto Rico, Idabelle Hovland 301-457-8443
Quarterly Financial Report, Ronald Horton
  301-457-3343
Race, concepts and interpretation, Staff 301-457-2402
Race statistics, Staff 301-457-2422
Retail Trade
- Advance monthly, Scott Scheleur 301-457-2713;
  svsd@census.gov
- Annual retail, Scott Scheleur 301-457-2713;
  svsd@census.gov
- Economic census, Fay Dorsett 301-457-2687;
  rcb@census.gov
- Monthly sales and inventory, Nancy Piesto
  301-457-2706; retail.trade@census.gov
- Quarterly Financial Report, Ronald Horton
  301-457-3343; cad@census.gov
School enrollment, Staff 301-457-2464
Seasonal adjustment methodology, Robert McIntire
  202-691-6345
Services
- Current Reports, Ruth Bramblett 301-457-2766
- Economic census, Jack Moody 301-457-2689
- General information, Staff 1-800-541-8345

Small-area income and poverty estimates, David
 Waddington 301-457-3195
Special censuses, Josephine Ruffin 301-457-3577
Special surveys, Ron Dopkowski 301-457-3801
Special tabulations, Marie Pees 301-457-2447
State population estimates, Staff 301-457-2422
Statistics of U.S. businesses, Trey Cole 301-457-3321
Survey of Income and Program Participation (SIPP),
 Staff 301-457-3242
Transportation
- Commodity Flow Survey, John Fowler
 301-457-2108; svsd@census.gov
- Economic census, James Barron 301-457-2811;
 ucb@census.gov
- Vehicle inventory and use, Kim Moore
 301-457-2797; vius@census.gov
- Warehousing and trucking, Ruth Bramblett
 301-457-2766; svsd@census.gov
Undercount, demographic analysis, Gregg Robinson
 301-457-2103
Union membership, Staff 202-691-6378
Urban/rural population, Michael Ratcliff/Rodger
 Johnson 301-457-2419
Veterans in labor force, Staff 202-691-6378
Veterans' status, Staff 301-457-3242
Voters, characteristics, Staff 301-457-2445
Voting age population, Jennifer Day 301-457-2464
Weekly earnings, Staff 202-691-6378
Wholesale Trade
- Annual wholesale, Scott Scheleur 301-457-2713;
 svsd@census.gov
- Current sales and inventories, Scott Scheleur 301-
 457-2713; svsd@census.gov
- Economic census, Donna Hambric 301-457-2725;
 wcb@census.gov
- Quarterly Financial Report, Ronald Horton
 301-457-3343; csd@census.gov
Women, Staff 301-457-2378
Women in the labor force, Staff 202-691-6378
Work experience, Staff 202-691-6378
Working poor, Staff 202-691-6378
Youth, students, and dropouts in labor force, Staff
 202-691-6378

Census Regional Offices

Information specialists in the Census Bureau's
12 regional offices answer thousands of questions each year. If you have questions about the
Census Bureau's products and services, you can

contact the regional office serving your state.
The states served by each regional office are
listed in parentheses.

- Atlanta (AL, FL, GA) 404-730-3833;
 www.census.gov/atlanta
- Boston, MA (CT, MA, ME, NH, NY, RI, VT)
 617-424-0510; www.census.gov/boston
- Charlotte (KY, NC, SC, TN, VA) 704-344-6144;
 www.census.gov/charlotte
- Chicago (IL, IN, WI) 708-562-1350;
 www.census.gov/chicago
- Dallas (LA, MS, TX) 214-253-4481;
 www.census.gov/dallas
- Denver (AZ, CO, MT, NE, ND, NM, NV, SD, UT,
 WY) 303-969-7750; www.census.gov/denver
- Detroit (MI, OH, WV) 313-259-1875;
 www.census.gov/detroit
- Kansas City (AR, IA, KS, MN, MO, OK)
 913-551-6711; www.census.gov/kansascity
- Los Angeles (southern CA, HI) 818-904-6339;
 www.census.gov/losangeles
- New York (NY, NJ—selected counties)
 212-264-4730; www.census.gov/newyork
- Philadelphia (DE, DC, MD, NJ—selected
 counties, PA) 215-656-7578;
 www.census.gov/philadelphia
- Seattle (northern CA, AK, ID, OR, WA)
 206-553-5835; www.census.gov/seattle
- Puerto Rico and the U.S. Virgin Islands are
 serviced by the Boston regional office. All other
 outlying areas are serviced by the Los Angeles
 regional office.

State Data Centers and Business and
Industry Data Centers

For demographic and economic information
about states and local areas, contact your State
Data Center (SDC) or Business and Industry
Data Center (BIDC). Every state has a State Data
Center. Below are listed the leading centers for
each state—usually a state government agency,
university, or library that heads a network of
affiliate centers. Asterisks (*) identify states that
also have BIDCs. In some states, one agency
serves as the lead for both the SDC and the BIDC.
The BIDC is listed separately if a separate agency
serves as the lead.

- Alabama, Annette Watters, University of Alabama 205-348-6191; awatters@cba.ua.edu
- Alaska, Kathryn Lizik, Department of Labor 907-465-2437; kathryn_lizik@labor.state.ak.us
- American Samoa, Vaitoelav Filiga, Department of Commerce 684-633-5155; vfiliga@doc.asg.as
- Arizona,* Betty Jeffries, Department of Economic Security 602-542-5984; popstats@de.state.az.us
- Arkansas, Sarah Breshears, Univ. of Arkansas/ Little Rock 501-569-8530; sgbreshears@ualr.edu
- California, Julie Hoang, Department of Finance 916-323-4086; fijhoang@dof.ca.gov
- Colorado, Rebecca Picaso, Dept. of Local Affairs 303-866-2156; rebecca.picaso@state.co.us
- Connecticut, Bill Kraynak, Office of Policy and Management 860-418-6230; william.kraynak@po.state.ct.us
- Delaware,* O'Shell Howell, Economic Development Office 302-739-4271; oshowell@state.de.us
- District of Columbia, Herb Bixhorn, Mayor's Office of Planning 202-442-7603; herb.bixhorn@dc.gov
- Florida,* Pam Schenker, Dept. of Labor and Employment Security 850-488-1048; pamela.schenker@awi.state.fl.us
- Georgia, Robert Giacomini, Office of Planning and Budget 404-463-1115; robert.giacomini@sdrc.gadata.org
- Guam, Isabel Lujan, Department of Commerce 671-475-0321; idlujan@mail.gov.gu
- Hawaii, Jan Nakamoto, Dept. of Business, Econ. Dev., and Tourism 808-586-2493; jnakamot@dbedt.hawaii.gov
- Idaho, Alan Porter, Department of Commerce 208-334-2470; aporter@idoc.state.id.us
- Illinois, Suzanne Ebetsch, Bureau of the Budget 217-782-1381; sebetsch@commerce.state.il.us
- Indiana,* Roberta Brooker, State Library 317-232-3733; rbooker@statelib.lib.in.us
- Indiana BIDC, Carol Rogers, Business Research Center 317-274-2205; rogersc@iupui.edu
- Iowa, Beth Henning, State Library 515-281-4350; beth.henning@lib.state.ia.us
- Kansas, Marc Galbraith, State Library 785-296-3296; ksstl3lb@ink.org
- Kentucky,* Ron Crouch, University of Louisville 502-852-7990; rtcrou01gwise@louisville.edu
- Louisiana, Karen Paterson, Office of Planning and Budget 225-219-4025; webmaster@doa.state.la.us
- Maine,* Eric Vonmagnus, State Planning Office 207-287-2989; eric.vonmagnus@state.me.us
- Maryland,* Jane Traynham, Office of Planning 410-767-4450; jtraynham@mdp.state.md.us
- Massachusetts,* John Gaviglio, Institute for Social and Econ. Research 413-545-3460; miser@miser.umass.edu
- Michigan, Carolyn Lauer, Dept. of Management and Budget 517-373-7910; Lauerc@state.mi.us
- Minnesota,* David Birkholz, State Demographer's Office 651-296-2557; david.birkholz@mnplan.state.mn.us
- Minnesota BIDC, Barbara Ronningen, State Demographer's Office 651-296-2557; barbara.ronningen@mnplan.state.mn.us
- Mississippi,* Rachel McNeely, University of Mississippi 662-915-7288; rmcneely@olemiss.edu
- Mississippi BIDC, Deloise Tate, Dept. of Econ. and Comm. Dev. 601-359-3593; dtate@mississippi.org
- Missouri,* Debra Pitts, State Library 573-526-7648; pittsd@sosmail.state.mo.us
- Missouri BIDC, Fred Goss, Small Business Development Center 573-341-4559; fredgoss@umr.edu
- Montana,* Pam Harris, Department of Commerce 406-444-4302; paharris@state.mt.us
- Nebraska, Jerome Deichert, University of Nebraska at Omaha 402-554-2134; jerome_deichert@unomaha.edu
- Nevada, Ramona Reno, State Library and Archives 775-684-3326; rlreno@clan.lib.nv.us
- New Hampshire, Thomas Duffy, Office of State Planning 603-271-2155; t_duffy@osp.state.nh.us
- New Jersey,* David Joye, Department of Labor 609-984-2595; djoye@dol.state.nj.us
- New Mexico,* Kevin Kargacin, University of New Mexico 505-277-6626; kargacin@unm.edu
- New Mexico BIDC, Beth Davis, Economic Development Dept. 505-827-0264; edavis@yucca.edd.state.nm.us
- New York,* Staff, Department of Economic Development 518-292-5300; rscardamalia@empire.state.ny.us
- North Carolina,* Staff, State Library 919-733-3270; francine@ospl.state.nc.us
- North Dakota, Richard Rathge, State University 701-231-8621; Richard.rathge@ndsu.nodak.edu

- Northern Mariana Islands, Diego A. Sasamoto, Dept. of Commerce 670-664-3034; csd@itecnmi.com
- Ohio,* Barry Bennett, Department of Development 614-466-2115; bbennett@odod.state.oh.us
- Oklahoma,* Jeff Wallace, Dept. of Commerce 405-815-5184; jeff_wallace@odoc.state.ok.us
- Oregon, George Hough, Portland State University. 503-725-5159; houghg@mail.pdx.edu
- Pennsylvania,* Sue Copella, Pennsylvania State Univ./Harrisburg 717-948-6336; sdc3@psu.edu
- Puerto Rico, Lillian Torres Aguirre, Planning Bd. 787-728-4430; torres_l@jp.prstar.net
- Rhode Island, Mark Brown, Department of Administration 401-222-6183; mbrown@planning.state.ri.us
- South Carolina, Mike MacFarlane, Budget and Control Board 803-734-3780; mmacfarl@drss.state.sc.us
- South Dakota, Nancy Nelson, Univ. of South Dakota 605-677-5287; nnelson@usd.edu
- Tennessee, Betty Vickers, University of Tennessee 423-974-6080; bvickers@utk.edu
- Texas,* Steve Murdock, Texas A&M University 409-845-5115/5332; smurdock@rsocsun.tamu.edu
- Texas BIDC, Michael West, Dept. of Econ. Dev. 512-936-0292; mwest@ded.state.tx.us
- Utah,* Lisa Hillman, Office of Planning and Budget 801-537-9013; lhillman@gov.state.ut.us
- Vermont, Sharon Whitaker, University of Vermont 802-656-3021; sharon.whitaker@uvm.edu
- Virgin Islands, Frank Mills, University of the Virgin Islands 340-693-1027; fmills@uvi.edu
- Virginia,* Don Lillywhite, Virginia Employment Comm. 804-786-7496; dlillywhite@vec.state.va.us
- Washington,* Yi Zhao, Office of Financial Management 360-902-0599; yi.zhao@ofm.wa.gov
- West Virginia,* Delphine Coffey, Office of Comm. and Ind. Dev. 304-558-4010; dcoffey@wvdo.org
- West Virginia BIDC, Randy Childs, Center for Economic Research 304-293-6524; childs@be.wvu.edu
- Wisconsin,* Robert Naylor, Depart of Admin. 608-266-1927; bob.naylor@doa.state.wi.us
- Wisconsin BIDC, Dan Veroff, Univ. of Wisc. 608-265-9545; dlveroff@facstaff.wisc.edu
- Wyoming, Wenlin Liu, Dept. of Admin. and Information 307-766-2925; wliu@state.wy.us

Glossary

adjusted for inflation Income or a change in income that has been adjusted for the rise in the cost of living, or the consumer price index (CPI-U-XI).

age Classification by age is based on the age of the person at his/her last birthday.

American Indians and Alaska Natives American Indians and Alaska Natives (Eskimos and Aleuts) are people who reported their race as American Indian and/or entered the name of an American Indian tribe on the 2000 census form. Tribal data are based on written entries on the 2000 census questionnaire. American Indians could name more than one tribal group, just as they could name more than one race. In 2000 census data, the term "American Indian" includes those who identified themselves as American Indian and no other race (called "American Indian alone") and those who identified themselves as American Indian and some other race (called "American Indian in combination"). The combination of the two groups is termed "American Indian, alone or in combination."

ancestry Information on ancestry is based on written responses to the ancestry question on the Census 2000 Supplementary Survey.

Asian The term "Asian" is defined differently depending on whether census or survey data are shown. In 2000 census data, Asians do not include Pacific Islanders. The term "Asian" includes those who identified themselves as Asian and no other race (called "Asian alone") and those who identified themselves as Asian and some other race (called "Asian in combination"). The combination of the two groups is termed "Asian, alone or in combination." Census data further break down the Asian population by ethnic origin, such as Chinese and Vietnamese. Asian estimates in survey data differ from 2000 census counts in part because the multiracial option was not yet included in surveys and other data collection efforts in 2000. Also, in surveys and other data collections, Asian figures include Pacific Islanders. The Immigration and Naturalization Service includes Middle Eastern nations-such as Israel, Jordan, Egypt, Iran, and so on-in its Asian world region. Immigrants from the Middle East are included as Asians in the immigration tables.

baby boom Americans born between 1946 and 1964. Baby boomers were aged 36 to 54 in 2000.

baby bust Americans born between 1965 and 1976, also known as Generation X. In 2000, baby busters were aged 24 to 35.

black The black racial category includes those who identified themselves as "black or African American." The term "black" is defined differently depending on whether census or survey data are shown. In 2000 census data, the term "black" includes those who identified themselves as black and no other race (called "black alone") and those who identified themselves as black and some other race (called "black in combination"). The combination of the two groups is termed "black, alone or in combination." Because the multiracial option was not yet included in surveys and other data collection efforts in 2000, black estimates from survey data will be different from 2000 census counts.

Census 2000 Supplementary Survey The Census 2000 Supplementary Survey was an operational test conducted as part of Census 2000. The survey collected demographic, social, economic, and housing data from a national sample, testing the feasibility of converting from the census long form to the new American Community Survey. The American Community Survey is planned to be a continuous demographic survey conducted by the Census Bureau to provide accurate and up-to-date annual profiles of America's communities. The survey will provide data for the nation, states, and most cities and counties with 250,000 or more population.

central cities The largest city in a metropolitan area is called the central city. The balance of the metropolitan area outside the central city is regarded as the "suburbs."

Consolidated Metropolitan Statistical Area (CMSA) A geographic entity defined by the federal Office of Management and Budget for use by federal statistical agencies. An area becomes a CMSA if it qualifies as a metropolitan statistical area, has a population of 1,000,000 or more, if component parts are recognized as Primary Metropolitan Statistical Areas, and if local opinion favors the designation.

Consumer Expenditure Survey The Consumer Expenditure Survey (CEX) is an ongoing survey of the day-to-day spending of American households administered by the Bureau of Labor Statistics. Results are used to update prices for the Consumer Price Index. The CEX includes an interview survey and a diary survey. The average spending figures shown in this book are the integrated data from both the diary and interview components of the survey. Two separate, nationally representative samples are used for the interview and diary surveys. For the interview survey, about 7,500 consumer units are interviewed on a rotating panel basis each quarter for five consecutive quarters. For the diary survey, 7,500 consumer units keep weekly diaries of spending for two consecutive weeks.

consumer unit For convenience, the terms consumer unit and household are used interchangeably in the spending tables of this book, although consumer units are somewhat different from the Census Bureau's households. Consumer units are all related members of a household, or financially independent members of a household. A household may include more than one consumer unit.

Current Population Survey A nationally representative survey of the civilian noninstitutional population aged 15 or older. It is taken monthly by the Census Bureau, collecting information from 50,000 households on employment and unemployment. In March of each year, the survey includes a demographic supplement which is the source of most national data on the characteristics of Americans, such as their educational attainment, living arrangements, and incomes. The survey has been conducted for more than 50 years.

disability People were considered to have a disability if they met any of the following criteria: 1) used a wheelchair, cane, crutches, or walker; 2) had difficulty performing one or more functional activities (seeing, hearing, speaking, lifting, carrying, using stairs, walking, or grasping small objects); 3) had difficulty with one or more activities of daily living (the ADLs include getting around inside the home, getting in or out of a bed or chair, bathing, dressing, eating, and toileting); 4) had difficulty with one or more instrumental activities of daily living (the IADLs include going outside the home, keeping track of money and bills, preparing meals, doing light housework, taking prescription medicines in the right amount at the right time, and using the telephone); 5) had one or more conditions (learning disability, mental retardation, Alzheimer's disease, or some other type of mental or emotional condition); 6) had any other mental or emotional condition that seriously interfered with everyday activities (frequently depressed or anxious, trouble getting along with others, trouble concentrating, trouble coping with day-to-day stress); 7) had a condition that limited the ability to work around the house; 8) if age 16 to 67, had a condition that made it difficult to work at a job or business; 9) received federal benefits based on an inability to work. Individuals were considered to have a severe disability if they met criteria 1, 6, or 9; or had Alzheimer's disease, mental retardation, or another developmental disability; or were unable to perform or needed help to perform one or more of the activities in criteria 2, 3, 4, 7, or 8.

dual-earner couple A married couple in which both husband and wife are in the labor force.

earnings A type of income, earnings is the amount of money a person receives from his or her job. See also Income.

economic census Collective name for the censuses of construction, manufactures, minerals, minority- and women-owned businesses, retail trade, service industries, transportation, and wholesale trade. The economic censuses are conducted by the Census Bureau every five years, in years ending in 2 and 7.

employed All civilians who did any work as a paid employee or farmer/self-employed worker, or who worked 15 hours or more as an unpaid farm worker or in a family-owned business, during the reference period. All those who have jobs but who are temporarily absent from their jobs due to illness, bad weather, vacation, labor management dispute, or personal reasons are considered employed.

expenditure The transaction cost including excise and sales taxes of goods and services acquired during the survey period. The full cost of each purchase is recorded even though full payment may not have been made at the date of purchase. Average expenditure figures may be artificially low for infrequently purchased items such as cars because figures are calculated using all consumer units within a demographic segment rather than just purchasers. Expenditure estimates include money spent on gifts.

family A group of two or more people (one of whom is the householder) related by birth, marriage, or adoption and living in the same household.

family household A household maintained by a householder who lives with one or more people related to him or her by blood, marriage, or adoption.

female/male householder A woman or man who maintains a household without a spouse present. May head family or nonfamily households.

firm In the business tables, a firm is a business consisting of one or more domestic establishments specified by the reporting firm as under its ownership or control at the end of 1997. If a company owned or controlled other companies, all establishments of the subsidiaries are included as part of the owning or controlling company.

foreign-born population People who are not U.S. citizens at birth.

full-time employment Full-time is 35 or more hours of work per week during a majority of the weeks worked during the preceding calendar year.

full-time, year-round Indicates 50 or more weeks of full-time employment during the previous calendar year.

General Social Survey The General Social Survey (GSS) is a biennial survey of the attitudes of Americans taken by the University of Chicago's National Opinion Research Center (NORC). NORC conducts the GSS through face-to-face interviews with an independently drawn, representative sample of 1,500 to 3,000 noninstitutionalized English-speaking people aged 18 or older who live in the United States.

generation X Americans born between 1965 and 1976, also known as the baby-bust generation. Generation Xers were aged 24 to 35 in 2000.

geographic regions The four major regions and nine census divisions of the United States are the state groupings as shown below:

Northeast:
—New England: Connecticut, Maine, Massachusetts, New Hampshire, Rhode Island, and Vermont
—Middle Atlantic: New Jersey, New York, and Pennsylvania

Midwest:
—East North Central: Illinois, Indiana, Michigan, Ohio, and Wisconsin
—West North Central: Iowa, Kansas, Minnesota, Missouri, Nebraska, North Dakota, and South Dakota

South:
—South Atlantic: Delaware, District of Columbia, Florida, Georgia, Maryland, North Carolina, South Carolina, Virginia, and West Virginia
—East South Central: Alabama, Kentucky, Mississippi, and Tennessee
—West South Central: Arkansas, Louisiana, Oklahoma, and Texas

West:
—Mountain: Arizona, Colorado, Idaho, Montana, Nevada, New Mexico, Utah, and Wyoming
—Pacific: Alaska, California, Hawaii, Oregon, and Washington

group quarters The Census Bureau classifies all people not living in households as living in group quarters. There are two types of group quarters: institutional

(for example, correctional facilities, nursing homes, and mental hospitals), and noninstitutional (for example, college dormitories, military barracks, group homes, missions, and shelters).

group quarters population People living in group quarters as of the date on which a particular survey was conducted. The Census Bureau recognizes two categories of people in group quarters: 1) the institutionalized population, and 2) the noninstitutionalized population. The institutionalized population includes people under formally authorized supervised care or custody in institutions at the time of enumeration. Such people are classified as "patients or inmates" of an institution regardless of the availability of nursing or medical care, the length of stay, or the number of people in the institution. Generally, the institutionalized population is restricted to the institutional buildings and grounds (or must have passes or escorts to leave) and thus have limited interaction with the surrounding community. Also, they are generally under the care of trained staff who have responsibility for their safekeeping and supervision. The noninstitutionalized population includes people who live in group quarters other than institutions.

Hispanic Hispanic origin is self-reported in a question separate from race. Because Hispanic is an ethnic origin rather than a race, Hispanics may be of any race. While most Hispanics are white, there are black, Asian, American Indian, and even Native Hawaiian Hispanics. The Hispanic population is broken down into individual ethnic groups, principally Mexican, Puerto Rican, Cuban, and other Spanish/Hispanic origin. "Other" Hispanic origin includes people from Spain, Central and South America, and the Dominican Republic. On the 2000 census, many Hispanics identified their race as "other" rather than white, black, and so on. In fact, 90 percent of people identifying their race as "other" also identified themselves as Hispanic. Therefore, tables showing the "other race" population are included in the Hispanic population chapter. The 2000 census count of Hispanics differs from estimates in the Current Population Survey and other data collections in part due to methodological differences. Numbers from the 2000 census are more accurate than survey data.

household All the people who occupy a housing unit. A household includes the related family members and all the unrelated people, if any, such as lodgers, foster children, wards, or employees who share the housing unit. A person living alone is counted as a household. A group of unrelated people who share a housing unit as roommates or unmarried partners also counts as a household. Households do not include group quarters such as college dormitories, prisons, or nursing homes.

household, race/ethnicity of Households are categorized according to the race or ethnicity of the householder only.

householder The householder is the person (or one of the persons) in whose name the housing unit is owned or rented or, if there is no such person, any adult member. With married couples, the householder may be either the husband or wife. The householder is the reference person for the household.

householder, age of The age of the householder is used to categorize households into age groups such as those used in this book. Married couples, for example, are classified according to the age of either the husband or wife, depending on which one identified him or herself as the householder.

housing unit A housing unit is a house, an apartment, a group of rooms, or a single room occupied or intended for occupancy as separate living quarters. Separate living quarters are those in which the occupants do not live and eat with any other persons in the structure and that have direct access from the outside of the building or through a common hall that is used or intended for use by the occupants of another unit or by the general public. The occupants may be a single family, one person living alone, two or more families living together, or any other group of related or unrelated persons who share living arrangements.

immigrants Aliens admitted for legal permanent residence in the United States.

income Money received in the preceding calendar year by each person aged 15 or older from each of the following sources: (1) earnings from longest job (or self-employment); (2) earnings from jobs other than longest job; (3) unemployment compensation; (4) workers' compensation; (5) Social Security; (6) Supplemental Security income; (7) public assistance; (8) veterans' payments; (9) survivor benefits; (10) disability benefits; (11) retirement pensions; (12) interest; (13) dividends; (14) rents and royalties or estates and trusts; (15) educational assistance; (16) alimony; (17) child support; (18) financial assistance from outside the household, and other periodic income. Income is reported in several ways in this book. Household income is the combined income of all household members. Income of persons is all income accruing to a person from all sources. Earnings is the amount of money a person receives from his or her job.

industry The kind of business conducted by a worker's employing organization. For those who work at two or more jobs, the data refer to the job at which the person worked the greatest number of hours.

institutionalized population People under formally authorized, supervised care or custody in institutions at the time of enumeration. Generally, they are restricted to the institution, under the care or supervision of trained staff, and classified as "patients" or "inmates."

labor force The labor force tables in this book show the civilian labor force only. The labor force includes both the employed and the unemployed (people who are looking for work). People are counted as in the labor force if they were working or looking for work during the reference week in which the Census Bureau fields the Current Population Survey.

labor force participation rate The percent of people in the labor force, which includes both the employed and unemployed. Labor force participation rates may be shown for sex-age groups or other special populations such as mothers of children of a given age.

legal form of organization In the business tables, there are five legal forms of organization: 1) C corporation, any legally incorporated business, except subchapter S, under state laws; 2) Subchapter S corporations, legally incorporated businesses under state laws. A subchapter S corporation is a special IRS designation for legally incorporated businesses with 75 or fewer shareholders who, because of tax advantages, elect to be taxed as individual shareholders rather than as a corporation; 3) individual proprietorships, unincorporated businesses owned by individuals. Also included in this category are self-employed persons. The business may be the only occupation of an individual or the secondary activity of an individual who works full-time for someone else; 4) partnerships, unincorporated businesses owned by two or more people; and 5) other, includes cooperatives, estates, receiverships, and businesses classified as unknown legal forms of organization.

married-couple family group Married couples who may or may not be householders. Those who are householders are "married-couple households." Those who are not householders are married couples living in a household headed by someone else, such as a parent. Because married-couple family groups include married-couple households, the number of married-couple family group will always outnumber married-couple households.

married couples with or without children under age 18 Refers to married couples with or without children under age 18 living in the same household. Couples without children under age 18 may be parents of grown children who live elsewhere, or they could be childless couples.

median The median is the amount that divides the population or households into two equal portions: one below and one above the median. Medians can be calculated for income, age, and many other characteristics.

median income The amount that divides the income distribution into two equal groups, half having incomes above the median, half having incomes below the median. The medians for households or families are based on all households or families. The median for people is based on all people aged 15 or older with income.

Metropolitan Statistical Area (MSA) A geographic entity defined by the federal Office of Management and Budget for use by federal statistical agencies, based on the concept of a core area with a large population nucleus, plus adjacent communities having a high degree of economic and social integration with that core. Qualification as an MSA requires the presence of a city with 50,000 or more inhabitants, or the presence of an Urbanized Area (UA) and a total population of at least 100,000 (75,000 in New England). The county or counties containing the largest city and surrounding densely settled territory are central counties of the MSA. Additional outlying counties qualify to be included in the MSA by meeting certain other criteria of metropolitan character, such as a specified minimum population density or percentage of the population that is urban. MSAs in New England are defined in terms of minor civil divisions, following rules concerning commuting and population density.

millennial generation Americans born between 1977 and 1994. Millennials were aged 6 to 23 in 2000.

mobility status People are classified according to their mobility status on the basis of a comparison between their place of residence at the time of the March Current Population Survey and their place of residence in March of the previous year. Nonmovers are people living in the same house at the end of the period as at the beginning of the period. Movers are people living in a different house at the end of the period than at the beginning of the period. Movers from abroad are either citizens or aliens whose place of residence is outside the United States at the beginning of the period, that is, in an outlying area under the jurisdiction of the United States or in a foreign country. The mobility status for children is fully allocated

from the mother if she is in the household; otherwise it is allocated from the householder.

Native Hawaiian and other Pacific Islander The 2000 census, for the first time, identified this group as a separate racial category from Asians. The term "Native Hawaiian and other Pacific Islander" includes those who identified themselves as Native Hawaiian and other Pacific Islander and no other race (called "Native Hawaiian and other Pacific Islander alone") and those who identified themselves as Native Hawaiian and other Pacific Islander and some other race (called "Native Hawaiian and other Pacific Islander in combination"). The combination of the two groups is termed "Native Hawaiian and other Pacific Islander, alone or in combination." Native Hawaiians and other Pacific Islanders are further subdivided in census data by their ethnic origin, such as Tongan, Fijian, and the individual ethnic category of Native Hawaiian. Native Hawaiians and other Pacific Islanders could identify themselves as belonging to more than one Pacific Islander ethnic group, just as they could identify themselves as more than one race.

nonfamily household A household maintained by a householder who lives alone or who lives with people to whom he or she is not related.

nonfamily householder A householder who lives alone or with nonrelatives.

non-Hispanic white The 2000 census classified people as non-Hispanic white if they identified their race as "white alone" and did not indicate their ethnicity as Hispanic. This definition is close to the one used in the Current Population Survey and other government data collection efforts. Tables on the non-Hispanic white population are found in the white chapters.

noninstitutionalized population People who live in group quarters other than institutions, such as college dormitories, rooming houses, religious group homes, communes, and halfway houses.

nonmetropolitan area Counties that are not classified as metropolitan areas.

occupation Occupational classification is based on the kind of work a person did at his or her job during the previous calendar year. If a person changed jobs during the year, the data refer to the occupation of the job held the longest during the year.

occupied housing units A housing unit is classified as occupied if a person or group of people is living in it or if the occupants are only temporarily absent-on vacation, example. By definition, the count of occupied housing units is the same as the count of households.

other race The 2000 census included "other race" as a sixth racial category. The category was meant to capture the few Americans, such as Creoles, who may not consider themselves as belonging to the other five racial groups. In fact, more than 18 million Americans identified themselves as "other race," including 42 percent of the nation's Hispanics. Among the 18 million people who claim to be of "other" race, 90 percent also identified themselves as Hispanic. The government considers Hispanic to be an ethnic identification rather than a race since there are white, black, American Indian, and Asian Hispanics. But many Hispanics consider their ethnicity to be a separate race. Because most people of "other" race are also Hispanic, tables showing the other race population are included in the Hispanic population chapter. In 2000 census tables, the term "Other race" includes those who identified themselves as "other alone" and those who identified themselves as "other in combination" with white, black, or another of the racial categories. The combination of the two groups is termed "other, alone or in combination."

outside central city The portion of a metropolitan county or counties that falls outside of the central city or cities; generally regarded as the suburbs.

own children A child under age 18 who is a son or daughter by birth, marriage (stepchild), or adoption. For 100 percent tabulations, own children are all sons/daughters of householders who are under age 18. In sample data, own children are sons/daughters of householders who are under age 18 and who have never been married. Therefore, numbers of own children will differ depending on how the data were collected.

owner occupied A housing unit is "owner occupied" if the owner lives in the unit, even if it is mortgaged or not fully paid for. A cooperative or condominium unit is "owner occupied" only if the owner lives in it. All other occupied units are classified as "renter occupied."

part-time employment Part-time employment is less than 35 hours of work per week in a majority of the weeks worked during the year.

payroll In the business tables, payroll is the combined amount of wages, tips, and other compensation including salaries, vacation allowances, bonuses, commissions, sick-leave pay, and the value of payments-in-kind paid to all employees during the calendar year

before deductions for Social Security, income tax, insurance, union dues, etc.

pension plan Pension plan participation is collected by the March Current Population Survey. The CPS asks respondents whether pension plan coverage is available to them through an employer or union and if they are included in the plan. This information was collected for people aged 15 or older who worked during the previous calendar year.

percent change The change (either positive or negative) in a measure that is expressed as a proportion of the starting measure. When median income changes from $20,000 to $25,000, for example, this is a 25 percent increase.

percentage point change The change (either positive or negative) in a value which is already expressed as a percentage. When a labor force participation rate changes from 70 percent of 75 percent, for example, this is a 5 percentage point increase.

poverty level The official income threshold below which families and persons are classified as living in poverty. The threshold rises each year with inflation and varies depending on family size and age of householder.

Primary Metropolitan Statistical Area (PMSA) A geographic entity defined by the federal Office of Management and Budget for use by federal statistical agencies. PMSAs are the components of Consolidated Metropolitan Statistical Areas. If an area meets the requirements to qualify as a metropolitan statistical area and has a population of 1,000,000 or more, two or more PMSAs may be defined within it if statistical criteria are met and local opinion favors the designation.

proportion or share The value of a part expressed as a percentage of the whole. If there are 4 million people aged 25 and 3 million of them are white, then the white proportion is 75 percent.

purchase price The purchase price refers to the price of the house or apartment and lot at the time the property was purchased. Closing costs are excluded from the purchase price.

race Race is self-reported and is defined differently depending on the data source. On the 2000 census form, respondents were asked to identify themselves as belonging to one or more of six racial groups: American Indians and Alaska Natives, Asians, blacks, Native Hawaiians and other Pacific Islanders, whites, and other. In publishing the results, the Census Bureau created three new terms to distinguish one group from another. The "race alone" population is people who identified themselves as only one race. The "race in combination" population is people who identified themselves as more than one race, such as white and black. The "race, alone or in combination" population includes both those who identified themselves as one race and those who identified themselves as more than one race. Other government data collection efforts must offer the multiracial option by 2003, but they did not do so in 2000. Therefore, tables based on government surveys—such as the Current Population Survey—show different counts for racial groups than does the census. In general, census counts of the "race alone" population will be smaller than survey estimates. Census counts of the "race, alone or in combination" population will be larger than survey estimates.

renter occupied *See* Owner occupied.

rounding Percentages are rounded to the nearest tenth of a percent; therefore, the percentages in a distribution do not always add exactly to 100.0 percent. The totals, however, are always shown as 100.0. Moreover, individual figures are rounded to the nearest thousand without being adjusted to group totals, which are independently rounded; percentages are based on the unrounded numbers.

sales and receipts In the business tables, sales and receipts are defined as the receipts for goods produced or distribution or services provided. Excluded from sales are nonoperating receipts, returns on investments, and interest.

sex ratio The number of men per 100 women.

suburbs The portion of a metropolitan area that is outside the central city.

Survey of Consumer Finances The Survey of Consumer Finances is a triennial survey taken by the Federal Reserve Board. It collects data on the assets, debts, and net worth of American households. For the 1998 survey, the Federal Reserve Board interviewed a random sample of 2,813 households and a supplemental sample of 1,496 wealthy households based on tax-return data.

Survey of Minority-Owned Business Enterprises The survey is part of the economic censuses. The economic censuses are required by law and taken by the Census Bureau every five years in years ending in 2 and 7. The survey counts as minority-owned any firm in which a majority of owners is black, Alaska Native, American Indian, Asian, Native Hawaiian, Pacific Islander, or Hispanic. Minority ownership is determined by firms in their entirety rather than at individual locations.

tribe The 2000 census asked people of American Indian descent to identify the tribe or tribes to which they belong.

unemployed Those who, during the survey period, had no employment but were available and looking for work. Those who were laid off from their jobs and were waiting to be recalled are also classified as unemployed.

value, of housing unit The respondent's estimate of how much his or her house and lot would sell for if it were for sale.

white The term "white" is defined differently depending on whether census or survey data are shown. In 2000 census data, the term "white" includes those who identified themselves as white and no other race (called "white alone") and those who identified themselves as white and some other race (called "white in combination"). The combination of the two groups is termed "white, alone or in combination." Because the multiracial option was not yet included in surveys and other data collection efforts in 2000, the white totals in survey data will be different from 2000 census counts. In the immigration tables in the Total Population chapter, people from the Middle East-such as Israel, Egypt, Jordan, Iran, and so on-are identified by the Immigration and Naturalization Service as immigrants from the Asian world region, although the Census Bureau would classify them as white.

Bibliography

Bureau of the Census

—*American Housing Survey for the United States in 1999*, H150/99, http://www.census.gov/hhes/www/housing/ahs/ahs99/ahs99.html

—*The American Indian and Alaska Native Population: 2000*, Census 2000 Brief, C2KBR/01-15, 2002

—*Americans with Disabilities, 1997*, detailed tables for Current Population Report P70-73, 2001, http://www.census.gov/hhes/www/disable/sipp/disable97.html

¤ *America's Families and Living Arrangements: March 2000*, detailed tables for Current Population Report P20-537, http://www.census.gov/population/www/socdemo/hh-fam/p20-537_00.html

—*The Asian and Pacific Islander Population in the United States: March 2000 (Update)*, PPL-146, http://www.census.gov/population/www/socdemo/race/ppl-146.html1999

—*The Asian Population: 2000*, Census 2000 Brief, C2KBR/01-16, 2002

—*The Black Population: 2000*, Census 2000 Brief, C2KBR/01-5, 2001

—Census 2000, http://www.census.gov/main/www/cen2000.html

—Census 2000 Supplementary Survey, http://www.census.gov/c2ss/www/

—Current Population Survey, Annual Demographic Survey: March Supplement, http://www.bls.census.gov/cps/ads/2001/sdata.htm

—Current Population Survey, Historical Income Tables, http://www.census.gov/hhes/income/histinc/histinctb.html

—Current Population Survey, Historical Poverty Tables, http://www.census.gov/hhes/income/histinc/histpovtb.html

—*Educational Attainment in the United States: March 2000*, detailed tables for Current Population Report P20-536, http://www.census.gov/population/www/socdemo/education/p20-536.html

—*The Foreign-Born Population in the United States: March 2000*, detailed tables for Current Population Report P20-534, PPL-135, http://www.census.gov/population/www/socdemo/foreign/p20-534.html

—*The Foreign-Born Population in the United States: March 2000*, detailed tables for Current Population Report P23-206, PPL-145, http://www.census.gov/population/www/socdemo/foreign/ppl-145.html

—*Geographic Mobility: March 1999 to March 2000*, detailed tables for Current Population Report P20-538, http://www.census.gov/population/www/socdemo/migrate/p20-538.html

—*The Hispanic Population: 2000*, Census 2000 Brief, C2KBR/01-3, 2001

—*The Hispanic Population in the United States: March 2000*, detailed tables for Current Population Report P20-535, http://www.census.gov/population/www/socdemo/hispanic/ho00dtabs.html

—*Money Income in the United States: 2000*, Current Population Reports, P60-213, 2001

—*The Native Hawaiian and Other Pacific Islander Population: 2000*, Census 2000 Brief, C2KBR/01-14, 2001

—*Population Change and Distribution, 1990 to 2000*, Census 2000 Brief, C2KBR/01-2, 2001

—*Poverty in the United States: 2000*, Current Population Reports, P60-214, 2001

—*School Enrollment—Social and Economic Characteristics of Students: October 2000*, PPL-148, http://www.census.gov/population/www/socdemo/school/ppl-148.html

—Surveys of Minority- and Women-Owned Business Enterprises, 1997 Economic Census, http://www.census.gov/csd/mwb/

—*The Two or More Races Population: 2000*, Census 2000 Brief, C2KBR/01-6, 2001

—*Voting and Registration in the Election of November 2000*, detailed tables for Current Population Report P20-542, 2002, http://www.census.gov/population/www/socdemo/voting/p20-542.html

—*The White Population: 2000*, Census 2000 Brief, C2KBR/01-4, 2001

Bureau of Labor Statistics

—2000 Consumer Expenditure Survey, unpublished data

—*Employment and Earnings*, January 2001

—*Monthly Labor Review*, November 2001

Federal Reserve Board

—*Recent Changes in U.S. Family Finances: Results from the 1998 Survey of Consumer Finances*, Federal Reserve Bulletin, January 2000

Immigration and Naturalization Service

—*2000 Statistical Yearbook of the Immigration and Naturalization Service*, 2002, http://www.ins.usdoj.gov/graphics/aboutins/statistics/IMM00yrbk/IMM2000list.htm

National Center for Education Statistics

—*Digest of Education Statistics* 2001

—Projections of Education Statistics to 2011

National Center for Health Statistics

—*Births and Deaths: Preliminary Data for 1998*, National Vital Statistics Report, Vol. 47, No. 25, 1999

—*Births: Final Data for 2000*, National Vital Statistics Report, Vol. 50, No. 5, 2002

—*Current Estimates from the National Health Interview Survey, 1996*, Series 10, No. 200, 1999

—*Deaths: Final Data for 1999*, National Vital Statistics Report, Vol. 49, No. 8, 2001

—*Deaths: Preliminary Data for 2000*, National Vital Statistics Report, Vol. 49, No. 12, 2001

—*Health, United States, 2001*

—*Healthy People 2000 Final Review*, 2001

—National Ambulatory Medical Care Survey: 1999 Summary, Advance Data, No. 322, 2001

National Opinion Research Center

—2000 General Social Survey, unpublished data

National Telecommunications and Information Administration

—*A Nation Online: How Americans Are Expanding Their Use of the Internet*, 2002

Index